INTERNATIONAL ENCYCLOPEDIA OF LINGUISTICS

Editorial Advisers

INTERNATIONAL ENCYCLOPEDIA
OF
LINGUISTICS

WILLIAM BRIGHT
Editor in Chief

Volume 1

New York Oxford
OXFORD UNIVERSITY PRESS
1992

OXFORD UNIVERSITY PRESS

Oxford New York Toronto
Delhi Bombay Calcutta Madras Karachi
Petaling Jaya Singapore Hong Kong Tokyo
Nairobi Dar es Salaam Cape Town
Melbourne Auckland

and associated companies in
Berlin Ibadan

Published by Oxford University Press, Inc.,
200 Madison Avenue, New York, NY 10016

Library of Congress Cataloging-in-Publication Data

International encyclopedia of linguistics / William Bright, editor-in-chief
p. cm.
Includes bibliographical references and index.
1. Linguistics—Encyclopedias. I. Bright, William, 1928–
P29.I58 1992 410'.3—dc20 91-7349 CIP
ISBN 0-19-505196-3 (set)

Project Editor: JEFFREY P. EDELSTEIN
Copyeditor and Indexer: JANE MCGARY
Bibliographic Research and Illustrations Editor: PHILOMENA MARIANI
Proofreader: KATHLEEN M. FENTON
Production Coordinator: DONNA NG
Manufacturing Controller: BENJAMIN LEE
Book Design: JOAN GREENFIELD
Cartography and Line Illustrations: VANTAGE ART

Special acknowledgment is made to Stephen Austin and Sons, Ltd., for providing characters used in tables of writing systems for Burmese, Georgian, Kannada, Khmer, Malayalam, and Tibetan.

9 8 7 6 5 4 3 2 1

Printed in the United States of America
on acid-free paper

CONTENTS

TOPIC EDITORS

KEITH ALLAN
Editor for Semantics
Senior Lecturer in Linguistics, Monash University

WALLACE L. CHAFE
Editor for Discourse and Text
Professor of Linguistics, University of California, Santa Barbara

EVE CLARK
Editor for Psycholinguistics
Professor of Linguistics, Stanford University

BERNARD COMRIE
Editor for Languages and Language Families
Professor of Linguistics, University of Southern California

DAVID CRYSTAL
Editor for Terminology
Professor of Linguistics, University College of North Wales

WOLFGANG DRESSLER
Editor for Morphology
Professor of Linguistics, Institut für Sprachwissenschaft, Universität Wien

WILLIAM FRAWLEY
Editor for Language and Literature
Professor of Linguistics, University of Delaware

GERALD GAZDAR
Editor for Computational Linguistics
Professor of Computational Linguistics, School of Cognitive and Computing Sciences, University of Sussex

BARBARA F. GRIMES
Co-editor for Language Identification
Ethnologue Editor, Summer Institute of Linguistics, Dallas

JOSEPH E. GRIMES
Co-editor for Language Identification
Professor Emeritus of Linguistics, Cornell University

JANE H. HILL
Editor for Anthropological Linguistics
Professor of Anthropology, University of Arizona

HENRY HOENIGSWALD
Co-editor for Historical Linguistics
Professor of Linguistics, University of Pennsylvania

ROBERT B. KAPLAN
Co-editor for Applied Linguistics
Professor of Applied Linguistics and Director, American Language Institute, University of Southern California

SARA E. KIMBALL
Co-editor for Historical Linguistics
Assistant Professor of English, University of Texas, Austin

PETER LADEFOGED
Editor for Phonetics
Professor of Linguistics, University of California, Los Angeles

DAVID LIGHTFOOT
Editor for Formal Grammar
Professor of Linguistics, University of Maryland, College Park

JOHN MCCARTHY
Editor for Phonology
Professor of Linguistics, University of Massachusetts, Amherst

LISE MENN
Editor for Neurolinguistics
Associate Professor of Linguistics, University of Colorado, Boulder

GEOFFREY K. PULLUM
Editor for Mathematical Linguistics
Professor of Linguistics, Cowell College, University of California, Santa Cruz

R. H. ROBINS
Editor for History of Linguistics
Professor Emeritus of Linguistics, School of Oriental and African Studies, University of London

SCOTT SOAMES
Editor for Philosophy of Language
Professor of Philosophy, Princeton University

DEBORAH TANNEN
Editor for Written Language
Professor of Linguistics, Georgetown University

SANDRA THOMPSON
Editor for Functional and Typological Grammar
Professor of Linguistics, University of California, Santa Barbara

PETER TRUDGILL
Editor for Sociolinguistics
Professor of Linguistics, University of Essex

HENRY G. WIDDOWSON
Co-editor for Applied Linguistics
Professor of Linguistics, Institute of Education, University of London

INTRODUCTION

The intention of the *International Encyclopedia of Linguistics (IEL)* is to provide a comprehensive source of up-to-date information on all branches of linguistics, aimed primarily at an audience of students and professional scholars in linguistics and adjacent fields. The publisher, Oxford University Press, has given me the fullest support in my effort to produce a reference work oriented toward the broadest possible view of linguistics, toward the importance of interdisciplinary studies, and toward open-minded attitudes toward theoretical controversies.

This work is designed to embrace the full range of linguistics, including descriptive, historical, comparative, typological, functionalist, and formalist specialties. Special attention is given to interrelations within branches of linguistics—with articles on the interface of, e.g., syntax and semantics—and to relations of linguistics with other disciplines. Areas of intersection with the social and behavioral sciences (such as ethnolinguistics, sociolinguistics, and psycholinguistics) receive major coverage, as does interdiscplinary work in language and literature, language and philosophy, mathematical linguistics, computational linguistics, and applied linguistics, in particular as concerned with language education.

The work is alphabetically, rather than topically, ordered. We have nevertheless attempted to preserve topical cohesion through three devices: (a) extensive cross-references between related articles; (b) a detailed index, including topical labels, technical terms, personal names, and geographical names; and (c) the organization of some articles in terms of composite entries—e.g. entries with subentries, as in 'Acquisition of Language', which is discussed with reference to first-language development under the headings (a) 'Meanings and Forms' and (b) 'Phonology', and then with reference to (c) 'Second-language Acquisition'. Note that such subentries are ordered alphabetically except under 'History of Linguistics', where they are arranged chronologically.

The longer articles consist of signed essays of up to five thousand words in length, surveying large fields of study—e.g. phonetics, formal grammar, or anthropological linguistics. Shorter essays (also signed) deal with more specific topics within those fields; or with particular languages and language families which have been topics of extensive linguistic research; or with important scholars in the history of linguistics. A category of unsigned articles provides information on less-studied language families. Appended to both types of article on language families are 'language lists', which as a group give specific information on all the living languages of the world. The work concludes with a glossary and an extensive index.

The primary audience is seen as academic and professional, but interdisciplinary; thus articles are designed to be intelligible and useful to people in related disciplines, including teachers and advanced students in computer science, mathematics, philosophy, the social and behavioral sciences, and literary studies. It is hoped that readers will find the *IEL* to be unique in its comprehensive and authoritative coverage of all significant topics and viewpoints in linguistics, with attention both to 'accumulated wisdom' and to current research findings, at the professional academic level.

Some articles in this encyclopedia contain new research findings, not yet published elsewhere in comparable form. Most of them, however, are intended as research tools, serving to bring together timely information on the diverse subject matter and interdisciplinary connections which characterize the study of human language and languages. Because of the rapid development of linguistics, few individuals can control the current scholarly literature in all branches of the field; the goal of the *IEL,* then, is to give summaries of research, with detailed cross-references and bibliographies, to provide convenient access to the broadest possible spectrum of specialties.

Details on various aspects of the *IEL*'s background, policies, and practices are given in the following paragraphs.

Models and motivations. In many ways, a model for the present work was provided by the *International Encyclopedia of the Social Sciences* (ed. by David L. Sills, 1968). That work featured important coverage of linguistic topics, in particular as related to cultural anthropology. I was a contributor to it, and I have frequently consulted it for my research in anthropological linguistics and sociolinguistics. Some twenty years later, it seemed to me that linguistics had arrived at a stage of maturity and complexity to justify an encyclopedic reference work of its own, incorporating many features of the *IESS.*

Another factor in the planning of this encyclopedia has been my personal experience as an editor in the linguistic field. From 1966 to 1988, I served as editor of *Language,* the journal of the Linguistic Society of America; before and during that period, I also edited several books. In my editorial capacity, I dealt with scholars from all over the world, working in every subfield and school of linguistics, and I exercised the responsibility of holding their work to high standards of validity, originality, and clarity. As an officer of a major international scholarly organization, I also took pains to avoid partisanship, and I strove to give full consideration to quality research of all theoretical orientations. Finally, as a linguist having strong links with the social and behavioral sciences, I maintained a broad interdisciplinary outlook as to what could properly be considered as 'linguistics'. With this background, my goals for the *IEL* have been to maintain the same academic standards and interdisciplinary breadth, while nevertheless focusing the work toward the needs of reference users.

Until recently, no publication of encyclopedic scope has existed for the field of linguistics. However, such works clearly constitute 'an idea whose time has come'. During the period that the *IEL* has been in preparation, two such publications have appeared—and the scholars responsible for both are, in fact, also valued contributors to the *IEL!* One is *The Cambridge Encyclopedia of Language,* a one-volume work written by a single author (David Crystal, 1987) and aimed at a general audience; the other is *Linguistics: The Cambridge Survey* (ed. by F. J. Newmeyer, 1987), a four-volume collection of 'state of the art' papers, written for professionals and emphasizing formal approaches to language. Still other publications have been announced: another one-volume, topically arranged work (but aimed at a more specialized audience than Crystal's); a work focusing primarily on language teaching; and a very ambitious, multivolume compendium on an advanced scholarly level.

It is clear that a rich choice will be available to the reading public. Nevertheless, I believe that the *IEL* makes a contribution not duplicated by any other work. Shorter encyclopedias are less expensive, and are easy to handle, but are limited not only in their subject coverage but in their diversity of viewpoint. Larger works overcome those defects; however, apart from their bulk and expense, the greater period required for their preparation increases the risk that their contents will become outdated during that time—especially in a field which changes as rapidly as modern linguistics. A work which is organized topically, rather than alphabetically, can give a more unified view of individual subfields; nevertheless, the *IEL*'s use of composite entries and extensive cross-references allows readers to integrate subfields, and at the same time preserves the convenience of alphabetical reference. More specialized works of reference will serve specialist audiences; however, I believe that the distinctive qualities of the *IEL* will meet the needs of a large core of students and scholars, in linguistics and adjacent disciplines, who are interested in the diversity of subfields and approaches which characterize the present-day study of language.

Goals. The aim of the *IEL,* and of individual articles within it, is not to say everything about any topic, but rather to give readers an appropriate orientation. For this reason, cross-references are used extensively, to avoid excessive repetition between articles. In addition, authors were asked to provide key bibliographical references for their articles, which will enable readers to pursue topics of interest as far as they desire.

It has been considered important that articles should be open to alternative viewpoints, and that they should avoid dogmatism. We have thought it especially desirable to maintain an even-handed approach in the *IEL*—considering the diverse intended readership, and considering too how rapidly orthodoxies can change in linguistics. Authors and topic editors (and indeed, the editor in chief) all have very definite opinions on particular matters of theory and methodology; but we have taken seriously our responsibility to let readers know what major viewpoints exist, and what the values of each may be. When topics involve a history of dispute, our desideratum has been that the relevant articles should reflect current consensus or its lack, whichever the case may be. We have felt that an encyclopedia is a place to explain unresolved issues, not to debate them.

How well have the *IEL*'s goals been achieved? What might have been done differently? As we go to press, I feel satisfied that we have met the goals of being wide-ranging, of representing a fair diversity of opinions, and of being as up-to-date as publication schedules will allow. My main autocriticism is that, although our articles on particular languages or language families contain abundant examples, I wish I had asked the authors of the other articles to put more emphasis on concrete exemplification. But reviewers and readers will have their own opinions; I hope they will let me know about them, in as much detail as possible.

Personnel and procedures. The board of editorial advisers, broad-based and international in scope, has provided top-level counsel both to the publisher and to myself as editor in chief. Its members have worked closely with me to determine the contents of the *IEL,* and to determine what individuals should serve as topic editors and as authors of articles. A number of these scholars have also agreed to serve as topic editors.

The topic editors, twenty-five in number, were appointed by me; each one has taken responsibility for a major subject area. I consulted them in order to determine the articles to be commissioned, the projected length of each, and the scholars who should be requested to write them. The topic editors then provided editorial supervision of the articles as they were written, and approved the manuscripts before sending them to me for final coordination and copyediting; I also continued to rely on their advice with regard to problems which arose during copyediting and proofreading. In some cases, topic editors nominated themselves to write specific articles in their areas of responsibility.

The authors, over four hundred in number, were chosen from around the world, on the basis of their reputation and expertise as known both to the topic editors and to me. Efforts were made to recruit authors who were not only recognized authorities on their subjects but who could also be relied on for clarity and definitiveness of statement.

After all bibliographical references were checked, copyediting of the articles was carried out by me and my assistants. Clarifications were sought, as necessary, through correspondence with authors—during the copyediting process, into the stage of reading galley proofs, and in some cases even beyond, to the stage of revised proofs.

Entry terms. Keeping in mind that the *IEL* will be consulted by readers who have some sophistication in linguistics but who nevertheless come from varying backgrounds, we have made an effort to choose entry terms (article titles) based on specific but relatively established concepts, and the articles themselves are organized with consideration for those concepts. We avoid entry terms beginning with the word 'Language' or 'Linguistics'; rather, we use terms such as 'Law and Language' (instead of 'Language of the Law'). Access to topics not chosen as entry terms is, of course, made possible through the index.

Spelling and alphabets. For consistency, American standard spellings have been used (e.g. *color, recognize*). Phonetic transcriptions follow either the International Phonetic Alphabet or conventional 'American usage', following authors' preference (see Pullum & Ladusaw 1986). Material from languages written in non-Latin alphabets is, in general, transliterated in the systems most used by international scholars of those languages; e.g., Cyrillic is transcribed with *š ž č j,* rather than *sh zh ch y.* Greek is also transliterated. Mandarin Chinese is written in pinyin spellings with tone marks.

Illustrative material. Care has been taken to make the content of articles as useful as possible through the inclusion of two types of illustrative material. One type consists of linguistic examples: words, phrases, and sentences in a wide range of natural languages. We follow the general practice of scholarly literature in linguistics by setting these off from the main text, for improved readability, and by numbering them for cross-reference. In complex examples, we give interlinear glosses for each morpheme or word, in addition to a freer translation.

The second type of illustrative material consists of graphic aids of several kinds, including hierarchical outlines, paradigmatic tables, graphs, sound spectrograms, and charts of writing systems, as well as maps to show the geographical distributions of dialects, languages, or language families. In complex illustrations, especially in the maps, the basic material was provided by authors in the form of informal sketches; these have then been reworked by professional graphic artists and cartographers, and checked by the authors and editors.

Biographies. Short biographical articles are included for a limited number of major linguists now deceased. The scholars for whom such articles have been written are ones who made contributions 'across the board' in linguistics, e.g. Edward Sapir and Roman Jakobson. Information on the work of other scholars, past and present, can be found in entries relating to their specialties or their schools of thought; e.g., contributions made to the field by J. R. Firth and by Noam Chomsky, respectively, are discussed under 'History of Linguistics' (in the article on 'The London School') and under 'Generative Grammar'.

Bibliography. Since an encyclopedia article cannot possibly say everything that is relevant about a topic, an important function of each essay is to direct readers to sources. All essays therefore end with a bibliographical listing of works cited, alphabetically arranged; typically, these include not only citations relevant to particular points but also works useful for general reference on a topic. Preference is given (other things being equal) to books rather than articles; to works in western European languages, especially English, rather than others; and to easily available rather than hard-to-find works such as unpublished dissertations. It is realized that linguistic research has progressed so rapidly in recent years that authors must often make reference to work which was not scheduled for publication at the time the articles were written; in such cases, however, acknowledgment is made by in-text reference, rather than by bibliographical citation of unpublished research.

In cases where publications are more accessible in reprinted form, we give information on the original publication first, because of its historical relevance, and then data on later and more available versions.

Language lists. Appended to the articles on language families are 'language lists' which represent an attempt to provide geographical, statistical, nomenclatural, and sociolinguistic information, to the extent that data are available for all living languages of the world, as well as for a selection of extinct languages. (Language names not used as headwords in these lists can be accessed through the index.) These lists have been prepared by Joseph and Barbara Grimes, based on the computerized files of the Summer Institute of Linguistics, with the permission of that organization (see also Grimes 1988). Additional information and corrections have been obtained from the authors of articles and from other reference sources, but the final form of the lists is my own responsibility. Readers should appreciate that the nomenclature and classification of languages are often controversial, and that data from different sources vary greatly in reliability; suggestions for further improvements will be welcome.

Glossary. A list of technical linguistic terms, prepared by David Crystal, is found at the end of this work. It is based both on definitions of technical terms given by *IEL* authors, in their respective articles, and on the files prepared by Crystal for his 1985 *Dictionary of Linguistics and Phonetics*.

Acknowledgments. Thanks for essential help of many kinds go to the Department of Linguistics at the University of California, Los Angeles; to the Department of Linguistics and the Institute of Cognitive Science at the University of Colorado, Boulder; to Professor Akio Kamio and the Department of English, Dokkyo University, Soka City, Japan, who provided me with an academic home during two periods in that country; to the members of the editorial board; to the topic editors; to all the authors; to Lise Menn, for constant supportiveness as both wife and colleague; to Claude Conyers and Jeffrey Edelstein at Oxford University Press, New York, who saw the project through to the end; to my indispensable editorial associate, Jane McGary; and to Gale Arce, David Attwooll, Melissa Axelrod, Kathleen M. Fenton, Daniel Hack, Philomena Mariani, William Mitchell, Susan Remkus, and Kenneth Wright.

WILLIAM BRIGHT, *Editor in Chief*

BIBLIOGRAPHY

CRYSTAL, DAVID. 1985. *A dictionary of linguistics and phonetics*. 2nd edition. Oxford: Blackwell.

CRYSTAL, DAVID. 1987. *The Cambridge encyclopedia of language*. Cambridge & New York: Cambridge University Press.

GRIMES, BARBARA (ed.) 1988. *Ethnologue: Languages of the world*. 11th edition. Dallas: Summer Institute of Linguistics.

NEWMEYER, FREDERICK J. (ed.) 1987. *Linguistics: The Cambridge survey*. 4 vols. Cambridge & New York: Cambridge University Press.

PULLUM, GEOFFREY K., & WILLIAM A. LADUSAW. 1986. *Phonetic symbol guide*. Chicago: University of Chicago Press.

SILLS, DAVID L. (ed.) 1968. *International encyclopedia of the social sciences*. 17 vols. New York: Macmillan & Free Press.

ABBREVIATIONS AND SYMBOLS

A adjective; agent; argument
A any syntactic category (in A-binding, A-over-A Principle)
AA Afro-Asiatic; Austro-Asiatic
abbr. abbreviation
abl. ablative
abs. absolutive
acc. accusative
ACH Association for Computers and the Humanities
ACL Association for Computational Linguistics
act. active; actor
AD Alzheimer's dementia
adess. adessive
adj. adjective
ADJP adjective phrase
adv. adverb(ial)
ADVP adverbial phrase
AE Achaemenid Elamite
AGR agreement
agt. agent(ive)
AI Artificial Intelligence
ALLC Association for Literary and Linguistic Computing
AM Ancient Mongolian
AMR Allomorphic Morphological Rule
AN Austronesian
an. animate
aor. aorist
AP adjective phrase
APG Arc Pair Grammar
API Association Phonétique Internationale
A-position argument position
AR Arumanian
Ar. Arabic
Arm. Armenian
ART article
ASL American Sign Language
ASP aspect
ASR Automatic Speech Recognition
ATN Augmented Transition Network
ATR advanced tongue root
AUX auxiliary
Av. Avestan
BCE Before Common Era (= B.C.)
BEAM Brain Electrical Activity Mapping
BI Bahasa Indonesia
BM Bahasa Melayu; Bokmål
BP bound pronoun; Brazilian Portuguese
BS Balto-Slavic
BVC bound verb complement
C complement; complementizer; consonant
c. century
CA Classical Arabic; Componential Analysis; Contrastive Analysis; Conversational Analysis
ca. *circa,* approximately
CAP Control Agreement Principle
CAT Computerized Axial Tomography
caus. causative
c-command constituent command
CD Communicative Dynamism; Conceptual Dependency
CE Common Era (= A.D.)
CED Condition on Extraction Domain
CF Context-Free
CFG Context-Free Grammar
CFL Context-Free Language
Ch.Sl. Church Slavic
CHO chômeur (in Relational Grammar)
CL Classical Latin; compensatory lengthening
clf. classifier
col. column
COMP complementizer
comp. comparative; complement
conj. conjunction; conjunctive
cont. continuative
cop. copula
CP Complementizer Phrase; Cooperative Principle
CR Comparative Reconstruction
CS Context-Sensitive
CSR Contemporary Standard Russian
c-structure constituent structure
CV cardinal vowel; consonant-vowel (syllable structure)
D dative; derivational; determiner; diacritic feature; dictionary
d. died
Da. Danish
DA Discourse Analysis
DAF delayed auditory feedback
dat. dative
dat.-acc. dative-accusative
DCG Definite-Clause Grammar
DD developmental dysphasia
decl. declension
def. definite
dem. demonstrative
deriv. derivative
desid. desiderative
DET determiner
dim. diminutive
dir. direction(al)
DM discourse marker
DO direct object
DP Determiner Phrase
DR Daco-Rumanian; discourse representation
DRS Discourse Representation Structure
DS marking Different Subject marking
D-structure an alternative conception to 'deep structure'
DTC Derivational Theory of Complexity
DTW Dynamic Time Warping
du. dual
DV dynamic verb
e empty category
E externalized
EA Eskimo-Aleut
ECP Empty Category Principle
emph. emphatic

encl. enclitic
Eng. English
ENHG Early New High German
EP European Portuguese
EQUI Equi-NP Deletion
erg. ergative
EST Extended Standard Theory
ex. example
exx. examples
F fall; formant
f. feminine; and following
F-R fall-rise
f-structure functional structure
F_0 fundamental frequency
Fa. Faliscan
fact. factive
FCR Feature Cooccurrence Restriction
fem. feminine
ff. and following (plural)
fig. figure
fl. *floruit,* flourished, lived
FLRP Fixed Language Recognition Problem
FN first name
foc. focus
Fr. French
FSD Feature Specification Default
FSP Functional Sentence Perspective
fut. future
G gender; glide
Gael. Gaelic
GB Government/Binding
G/D genitive/dative
gen. genitive
Ger. German
ger. gerund
Gk. Greek
Gmc. Germanic
Go. Gothic
GPC grapheme-phoneme conversion
GPSG Generalized Phrase-Structure Grammar
GR Grammatical Relation
GS Generative Semantics
Guj. Gujarati
H hearer; high; hold (ASL)
habit. habitual
Hitt. Hittite
HM Hmong-Mien
hon. honorific
HPSG Head-driven Phrase-Structure Grammar
HR high rise
Hz Hertz (cycles per second)
I inflection; internalized
IA Indo-Aryan; Item-and-Arrangement
IC Immediate Constituent; Inherent Complement
ICA Initial Consonant Alternation
ICM Idealized Cognitive Model
ID Immediate Dominance
IE Indo-European
iff if and only if
IG intonation group
II Indo-Iranian
IL Intensional Logic
ill. illative
imper. imperative
impers. impersonal
impf. imperfect(ive)
inan. inanimate
incl. including, inclusive
ind. independent
indef. indefinite
indic. indicative
inf. infinitive
INFL inflection
inst. instrumental
interj. interjection
intrans. intransitive
invol. involuntary
IO indirect object
IP Inflection Phrase; Item-and-Process
IPA International Phonetic Association or Alphabet
IR Internal Reconstruction
Ir. Iranian
irreg. irregular
IS Interactional Sociolinguistics
Ital. Italian
KA Krama Andhap (= Middle Javanese)
KI Krama Inggil (= High Javanese)
L language; location (ASL); low
L1 first language
L2 second language
LA Latin America; linguistic area
La. Latin; Latvian
LAD Language Acquisition Device
LBH Late Biblical Hebrew
LF Lexical Function; Logical Form
LFG Lexical-Functional Grammar
LH left hemisphere
Lh. Lhasa
Li. Lithuanian
LIC lower incisor cavity
LIPOC language-independent preferred order of constituents
lit. literally
Lith. Lithuanian
LM Literary Mongolian
l-marking marking a lexical category
LN last name
loc. locative
LP Language Planning; Linear Precedence
LPC Linear Prediction Coefficient
LR low rise
LSA Linguistic Society of America
LSP Language for Specific Purposes
LU lexical unit
Lyc. Lycian
M mid; movement (in ASL); modal; mot (in Metrical Phonology)
m. masculine
MA Meso-American
masc. masculine
m-command maximal command
MCS Mildly Context-Sensitive
MDP Minimal Distance Principle
ME Middle English
MG Montague Grammar
MH Middle/Mishnaic Hebrew
MHG Middle High German
MIA Middle Indo-Aryan
mid. middle
MIT Massachusetts Institute of Technology
MK Mon-Khmer
MLU mean length of utterance
MM Middle Mongolian
Mod. modern
Mod.E. Modern English
MOP Maximal Onset Principle
MP Malayo-Polynesian; Middle Persian
MPR Mongolian People's Republic; morphophonological rule
ms millisecond
ms. manuscript
MSA Modern Standard Arabic
MSC Morpheme Structure Constraint
MSK Modern Standard Khmer
mss. manuscripts
MST Modern Standard Telugu
MT Machine Translation
N noun; number
n. note
NA North America; Northern Athabaskan
N/A nominative/accusative
NC Niger-Congo
NCC North Central Caucasian
n.d. no date
NE New English (= Modern English)
neg. negative
neut. neuter
Ng. Ngoko (= colloquial Javanese)
NGP Natural Generative Phonology
NHG New High German
NIA New Indo-Aryan
NL natural language
NLI Natural Language Interface
NLP Natural Language Processing
NM Natural Morphology
NN Nynorsk
No. Norwegian
nom. nominative

NOM nominal(ization)
nonfin. non-finite
NP New Persian; noun phrase
NS Nilo-Saharan
n.s. new series
NWC Northwest Caucasian
O object
obj. object
obl. oblique
obs. obsolete
OCS Old Church Slavic
OE Old English
OG Old Georgian
OHG Old High German
OI Old Iranian
OIA Old Indo-Aryan
OK Old Khmer
OM object marker
ON Old Norse
OP Old Persian; Old Portuguese; Old Prussian
OP null operator
OPer. Old Persian
opt. optative
ORuss. Old Russian
Os. Oscan
o.s. old series
P person; patient; phrase; predicator; preposition; position (in ASL)
PA Proto-Australian
PAE Proto-Athabaskan-Eyak
PAN Proto-Austronesian
PAn. Proto-Anatolian
PAS Preferred Argument Structure
pass. passive
pat. patient
PC pronominal clitic
PCA Pacific Coast Athabaskan
PCF Phonetically Consistent Form
pcl. particle
pcpl. participle
PCU Preferred Clause Unit
PD Proto-Dravidian
PDP Parallel Distributed Processing
Per. Persian
perf. perfect(ive)
pers. person
PET Positron Emission Tomography
PF Phonetic Form
pf. perfect(ive)
PGmc. Proto-Germanic
Phryg. Phrygian
PIE Proto-Indo-European
Pkt. Prakrit
pl. plural
PLD Primary Linguistic Data
PLu. Proto-Luvian
plupf. pluperfect
PM phrase-marker; Proto-Mayan
PN predicate nominal
PNC Proto-Niger-Congo
PNI Proto-Northern Iroquoian
POc. Proto-Oceanic
Pol. Polish
pol. polite
poss. possessive
postpos. postposition
PP prepositional phrase
PR Phonological Representation; Phonological Rule
PRED predicate
pref. prefix
prep. preposition
pres. present
prev. preverb
PRO pronoun, pronominal
prog. progressive
pron. pronoun
prt. particle
P-rule phonological rule
PS Phrase Structure; Preference Semantics
PSG Phrase-Structure Grammar
PST Proto-Sino-Tibetan
PT patient-trigger; Proto-Tai
PTB Proto-Tibeto-Burman
Q quantifier; question
QH Qumranic Hebrew
q.v. *quod vide,* which see
qq.v. *quae vide,* which see (plural)
R root
RC relative clause
RE Recursively Enumerable
real. realis
redup. reduplication
refl. reflexive
rel. relative
rem. remote
repr. reprinted
REST Revised Extended Standard Theory
rev. revised
R-expression referring expression
RG Relational Grammar
RH right hemisphere
RN Relational Network
RP Recognition Problem; Received Pronunciation; referential pronoun
RR Readjustment Rule
R-rule Redundancy Rule
RT reading tradition
RTN Recursive Transition Network
Ru. Russian
S sentence; speaker; subject
SA stem augment
SAAD simple active affirmative declarative (sentence)
SBH Standard Biblical Hebrew
SC small clause; South Caucasian; Structural Change
Sc. Scandinavian
SCC Strict Cycle Condition
SD South Dravidian; Structural Description
SEA Southeast Asia(n)
sec. secondary; section
ser. series
SFH Semantic Feature Hypothesis
SG Stratificational Grammar; Standard Gujarati
sg. singular
SGML Standard Generalized Markup Language
SH Standard Hausa
SHWNG South Halmahera—West New Guinea
Skt. Sanskrit
Sl. Slavic
SM series marker
soc. sociative
SP Semantic Parsing; subject pronoun
Sp. Spanish
SPE *The Sound Pattern of English*
SS marking Same Subject marking
S-structure shallow structure
ST Sino-Tibetan
stat. stative
sub. subordinator
SUBCAT subcategorization
subj. subject
subjunc. subjunctive
subord. subordinate, subordinative
subst. substantive
superess. superessive
SUR Speech Understanding Research
SV stative verb
Sw. Swedish
SWITCH switch reference
syn. synonym, synonymous
Syr. Syriac
t trace
T title; *tu* (familiar address)
TAP tense-aspect pronoun (Hausa)
TB Tibeto-Burman
TBU Tone-Bearing Unit
TG Transformational Grammar; Tupí-Guaraní
Tib. Tibetan
TK Tai-Kadai
Toch. Tocharian
TOP topic
tr. transitive
trans. transitive
trig. trigger
T-rule transformational rule
TV transitive verb
U utterance

UA Uto-Aztecan
UC ultimate constituent
UG Universal Grammar
Ukr. Ukrainian
Um. Umbrian
URP Universal Recognition Problem
V verb; vowel; *vous* (polite address)
Ved. Vedic (Sanskrit)
ver. version
VH vowel harmony
VL Vulgar Latin
voc. vocative
vol. volume
VOT voice-onset time
VP verb phrase
W word
WFR Word-Formation Rule
WH Western Hausa
WH-word question-word (*what,* etc.)
W* language non-configurational language
WMP Western Malayo-Polynesian
WP Word-and-Paradigm
WT Western Tibetan
X any syntactic category (in X-Bar Theory)
∅ zero (covert element)
1 first person; subject (Relational Grammar)
2 second person; direct object (Relational Grammar)
3 third person; indirect object (Relational Grammar)
* non-attested form (hypothetical or reconstructed); Kleene star
$<$ comes from
$>$ becomes
$\rightarrow$ is rewritten as (phrase structure rule)
$\Rightarrow$ is transformed into
α alpha, a variable
Δ delta, a dummy element in syntax
θ theta, thematic (role)
σ sentence; syllable
Σ sentence; stress

INTERNATIONAL ENCYCLOPEDIA OF LINGUISTICS

A

ABBREVIATION, as a morphological process, is based in some cases on orthography: INITIALISMS such as *TV* or *teevee,* ACRONYMS like *scuba,* and CLIPPED FORMS like *prof.* Other cases are phonological, e.g. *natch* from *naturally.* (For general reference, see Marchand 1969:391–395, 441–454; Adams 1973:135–160; Algeo 1975, 1977, 1978, 1980; Kreidler 1979; Bauer 1983:230–240; and Cannon 1987:99–155.)

A word may be clipped to one of its morphemes, which then assumes the semantic range of the original word, as *parachute* is clipped in *paradoctor, paraglider,* and *paratrooper.* Similarly, a compound may be clipped to one of its words, which then becomes semantically equivalent to the original compound, e.g. *jet* from *jet plane.*

Shortening by the omission of a supposed derivational affix, as in *burgle* from *burglar,* is BACK FORMATION. This process may also reanalyze the constituent structure of existing morphemes, as *typewrite* was formed from *typewriter,* historically *type + writer,* but understood as *typewrite + -er.*

BLENDS are either syntagmatic or paradigmatic. Syntagmatic parts of a compound may be combined by back-clipping, e.g. *sitcom* from *situation comedy*; or by contraction (combined back- and fore-clipping), e.g. *motel* from *motor hotel.* Paradigmatic blends may derive from synonyms, as *bonk* from *bong + conk,* or from words otherwise associated, as *workaholic* from *work + alcoholic.* Some forms involve both syntagmatic and paradigmatic blending; thus the computer term *bit* is from *binary digit,* but the word *bit* 'small piece' doubtless influenced its making.

JOHN ALGEO

BIBLIOGRAPHY

ADAMS, VALERIE. 1973. *An introduction to Modern English word-formation.* London: Longman.

ALGEO, JOHN. 1975. The acronym and its congeners. In *The First LACUS Forum, 1974,* edited by Adam Makkai & Valerie B. Makkai, pp. 217–234. Columbia, S.C.: Hornbeam.

ALGEO, JOHN. 1977. Blends: A structural and systemic view. *American Speech* 52.47–64.

ALGEO, JOHN. 1978. The taxonomy of word making. *Word* 29.122–131.

ALGEO, JOHN. 1980. Where do all the new words come from? *American Speech* 55.264–277.

BAUER, LAURIE. 1983. *English word-formation.* Cambridge & New York: Cambridge University Press.

CANNON, GARLAND. 1987. *Historical change and English word-formation: Recent vocabulary.* New York: Peter Lang.

KREIDLER, CHARLES W. 1979. Creating new words by shortening. *Journal of English Linguistics* 13.24–36.

MARCHAND, HANS. 1969. *The categories and types of present-day English word-formation: A synchronic-diachronic approach.* 2d ed. Munich: Beck.

ACCENT. *See* Stress; Tone.

ACOUSTIC PHONETICS is the study of the sound waves which form the physical link between speaker and hearer. Central to the field are the concepts and techniques of acoustic physics; but acoustic phonetic research also integrates knowledge about how speech signals are produced by a speaker, how they are perceived by a hearer, and how they are structured by the phonology of languages. From the linguist's point of view, acoustic phonetics provides quantitative information on the realization of the sound system of a language, supplementing the data available from auditory phonetics.

Acoustic phonetics is a relative newcomer to the discipline of phonetics. Developments in the 19th century in the field of acoustics laid its theoretical foundations; but it was given its real impetus in the 20th century, by techniques for recording sound and analyzing it electronically. The availability of computers for digital processing of signals gave it further momentum. Acoustic phonetics has become arguably the most successful branch of phonetics. Its primary data are easy to obtain (unlike, e.g., data on muscle activity in speech production); and advances in acoustic phonetics are often stimulated by the prospect of practical applications in such areas as telecommunications—and, increasingly, human/computer interaction through speech.

This article will offer an introduction to some background concepts in acoustic phonetics, a summary of the acoustic properties of major classes of speech sounds, and a review of some of the roles of acoustic phonetics. For general references, see Fant 1960, Flanagan 1972, Fry 1979, and Lieberman & Blumstein 1988.

1. Background concepts. Sound consists of vibrations to which the ear is sensitive. Usually the ear is responding to tiny, fast oscillations of air molecules, which originate at a sound source. A tuning fork provides a familiar illustration: as an arm of the fork swings in one direction, it shunts adjacent molecules nearer to subsequent ones, causing a brief local increase in air pressure. The shunting effect spreads outward through further molecules; a wave of high pressure is radiating from the arm. Meanwhile, the arm swings back to, and overshoots, its rest position—as do the adjacent molecules. Their momentary increased separation from subsequent molecules means a reduction in pressure ('rarefaction'). A wave of low pressure now radiates in the wake of the wave of high pressure. As the oscillation of the fork continues, a regular succession of pressure highs and lows spreads outward.

At a point in the path of the radiating pressure changes, we could plot pressure against time as they sweep by. Figure 1 does this for a tone produced by an 'ideal' tuning fork. Notice three properties of this waveform. First, the peaks and troughs have a particular AMPLITUDE; increasing the amplitude would cause the tone to sound louder. Second, the cycle of pressure variation takes a given time to repeat itself; this is the PERIOD of the wave. The shorter the period, the more repetitions or cycles of the wave there will be per second: i.e., its FREQUENCY will be higher. The wave shown has a period of .01 s (second); its frequency is 1/.01 = 100 Hz (Hertz, meaning cycles per second). Increasing the tone's frequency would cause it to sound higher in pitch. Third,

FIGURE 1. *Changes in Air Pressure through Time Associated with a Pure Tone.* The form is that of a sine wave.

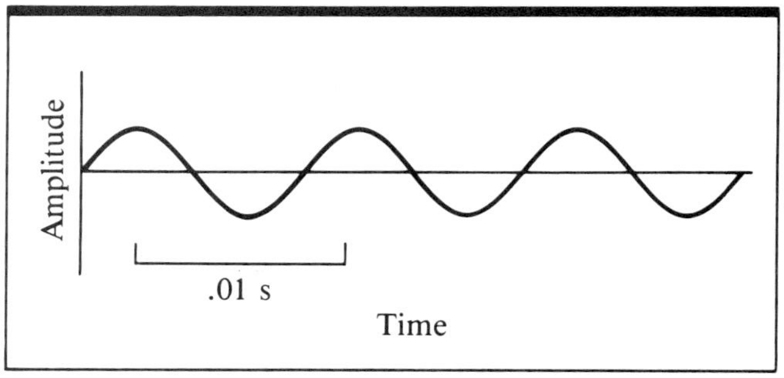

the particular wave in Fig. 1 shows a simple pattern of rising and falling pressure, called a SINE WAVE.

The wave at the top of Figure 2 is more complex. Crucially, however, a complex wave can be analyzed as being made up of a number of sine waves of different frequencies—for this wave, three, as shown below it. If we add together the amplitudes of the component sine waves, or HARMONICS, at each point in time, we can recreate the complex wave. Such analysis of a complex wave is known as FOURIER ANALYSIS; it is now commonly carried out by computer.

The graph at the right in Fig. 2 is another way of showing the essential information from this type of analysis. It plots each harmonic at its frequency by a line which shows the harmonic's relative amplitude. This kind of representation, called an AMPLITUDE SPECTRUM, is of central importance in acoustic phonetics, as is the information it contains about the distribution of acoustic energy at different frequencies.

The harmonics in Fig. 2 are at 100, 300, and 400 Hz. The highest common factor of these values is 100 Hz; this is the frequency of repetition of the complex wave, which is called its FUNDAMENTAL FREQUENCY, and which determines our perception of the pitch of this sound.

A repetitive or PERIODIC wave will thus have energy in discrete harmonics at some (but not necessarily all) of the frequencies which are whole-number multiples of its fundamental frequency. In many occurring waves, however, it is not possible to discern a repeating cycle. In such APERIODIC waves, there is no fundamental frequency; energy is present throughout the frequency range, rather than being banded into discrete harmonics.

2. Acoustics of speech. Figure 3 shows brief extracts from the waveforms of two rather different sounds taken from the word *speech*: the vowel [i] above, and the

FIGURE 2. *Analysis of a Complex Periodic Wave into Harmonics.* The frequencies and relative amplitudes of the harmonics are represented in the spectrum at right.

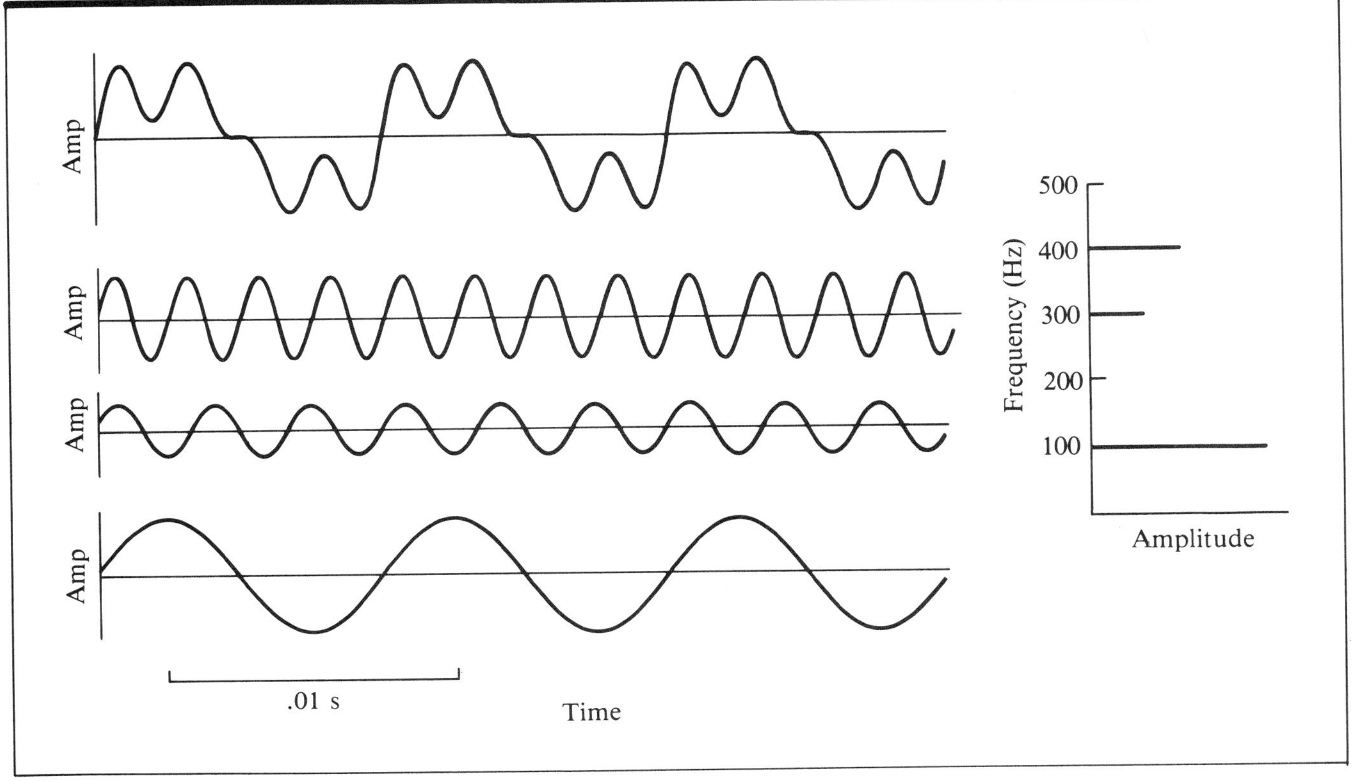

consonant [s] below. The vowel's waveform is roughly periodic, though more complex than that in Fig. 2. The second waveform, from [s], consists of aperiodic noise. In general, voiced speech sounds (for which the vocal cords are vibrating) will have periodic waveforms. The rate of repetition of the wave, i.e. its fundamental frequency, directly reflects the rate of vibration of the vocal cords, and it cues the hearer's perception of pitch.

The schematic amplitude spectrum of the magnified fragment of [i] shows that it is rich in harmonics. Their amplitude is greater at certain frequencies, and this 'shaping' of the spectrum determines the perception of a particular sound. The spectrum for the aperiodic [s] shows energy that is not banded into harmonics, but is present continuously over a range of frequencies. Again, the shape of the spectrum characterizes the sound.

Figure 4 illustrates the production of two different vowels, [ɑ] as in *palm* and [i] as in *heed.* At the bottom of the figure is the spectrum of the waveform produced by the vibrating larynx. This laryngeal SOURCE wave would sound like a buzz, if we could isolate it from the vocal tract. Its spectrum is rich in harmonics, whose amplitude gradually decreases with increasing frequency.

Above that can be seen alternative vocal tract shapes: on the left, that for [ɑ], and on the right that for [i]. The vocal tract is, in effect, a tube; and like any tube, e.g. a wind instrument, it has a number of RESONANT FREQUENCIES, at which the air in the tube is especially liable to vibrate in sympathy with another sound. The spectrum next to each vocal tract in Fig. 4 shows how well the tract resonates at any frequency: in each case, three resonance peaks, or FORMANTS, can be seen. In practice, further formants exist at higher frequencies; but the first three are most important in determining vowel quality. Note that [ɑ] has a relatively high first formant (F_1) and a low second formant (F_2); for [i], F_1 is low and F_2 is high. The frequency of the formants is dependent on the shape of the vocal tract, and hence on the positioning of the tongue and lips.

The vocal tract acts on the laryngeal source as a FILTER, which enhances some harmonics relative to others. Thus, in the spectrum of the speech waveform as it emerges at the lips, each harmonic of the laryngeal

FIGURE 3. *Waveforms of* [i] *and* [s]. Waveforms from (top) the vowel [i] and (bottom) the voiceless fricative [s], together with their schematic spectra.

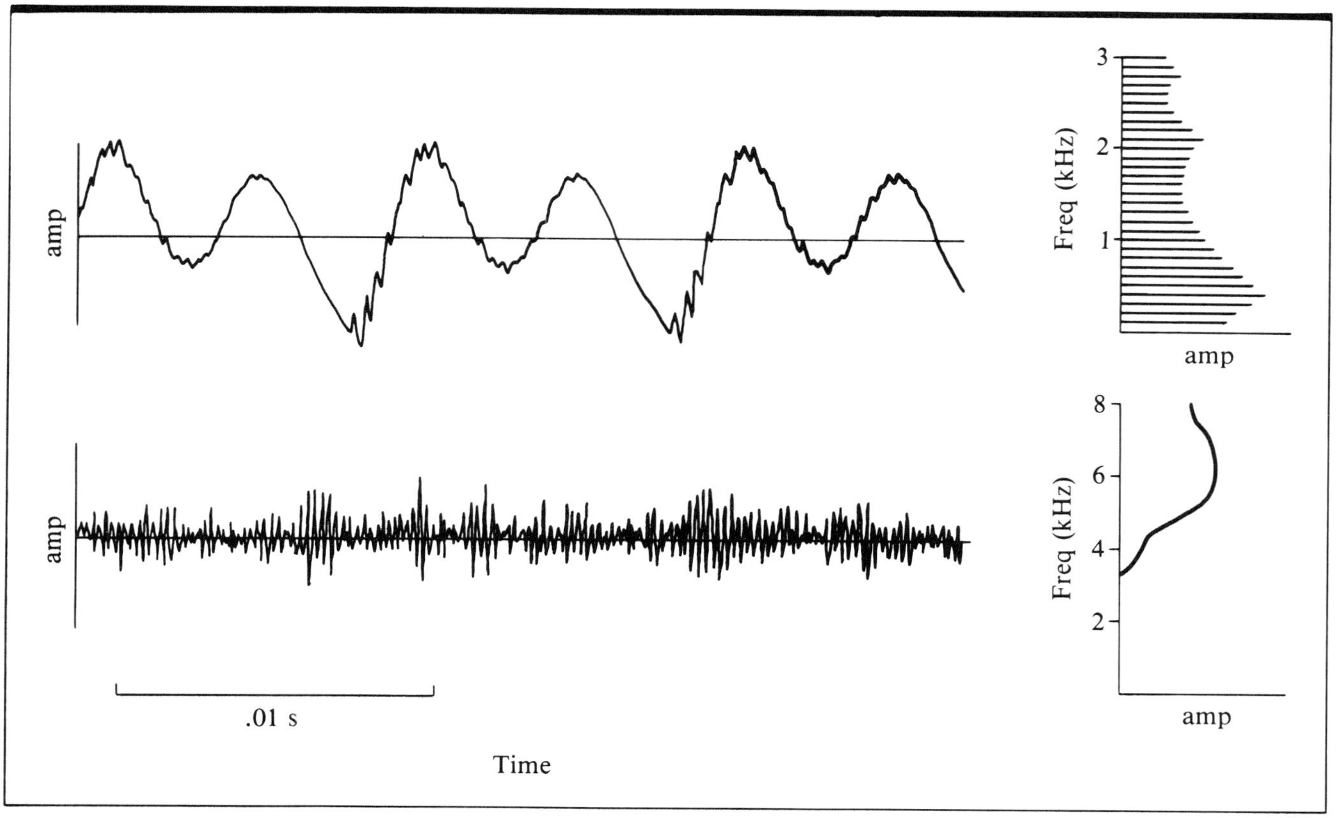

source has an amplitude which is modified according to how near it is in frequency to a formant—as shown schematically in the two spectra at the top of Fig. 4. Some details have been omitted for simplicity; however, this general conception of vowel production as the combination of a sound source at the larynx and the spectral shaping function of the vocal tract, known as the SOURCE-FILTER MODEL, has been highly influential in acoustic phonetics.

Vowels have been discussed so far as though they were characterized by a steady-state vocal tract posture and corresponding spectrum. In fact, speech sounds rarely involve steady states: the vocal tract is in almost constant motion, and hence the spectrum of the speech wave is constantly changing. It would be possible to represent this as a series of spectra, and this is sometimes done; but another kind of display is more common in acoustic phonetics. This is illustrated schematically at the top of Fig. 4. Assume that the vocal tract is moving continuously from the [ɑ] configuration to the [i] configuration. This would produce a diphthong sounding something like the word *eye*. In the new display, time runs from left to right; frequency, as before, is shown on the vertical axis. In effect, there is a third dimension: high-amplitude parts of the spectrum are shown as black. Thus it is possible to trace the changing formant frequencies as movements in the black bands. Note how, at the start and end of the diphthong, the bands coincide with the peaks in the spectra of the individual words.

This general kind of display is called a SPECTROGRAM. Real, as opposed to schematic, spectrograms have a range of shades of gray which indicate increasing amplitude; they allow much of the detail of the spectrum at a particular point to be inferred. From the 1940s onward, use was made of the SOUND SPECTROGRAPH, a machine that uses analog electronics to produce spectrograms and other spectral displays; since the 1970s, digital computers have increasingly shared this function.

Figure 5 shows a real spectrogram of the rhyming phrases *a bye, a dye, a guy*. The movement of the first two formants in each word is similar to that shown in Fig. 4; like *eye,* these words have a diphthong that moves from an open vowel something like [ɑ] toward a close front vowel something like [i]. The consonants appear as almost blank on the spectrogram, because little sound radiates from the vocal tract when it is closed. Adjacent to them, the detailed trajectory of the formants, particularly F_2 and F_3, differs according to the consonant; thus, for the velar [g], these two formants appear rather close together. Such differing FORMANT TRANSITIONS are vital cues to our perception of consonants. They occur because, as the vocal tract closes for a consonant and as it opens again, its resonances change (as always when a tube changes shape). The way in which they change depends on where, along its length, the tract is closing—i.e. on the PLACE OF ARTICULATION of the consonant.

Part of the acoustic character of a consonant, then, seems to be explicable like that of a vowel: as changes in the resonances of the vocal tract tube. But consonants are considerably more complex acoustically than vowels. Many consonants have a source of acoustic energy other than the vibrating larynx; e.g., in an [s] (see Fig. 3), aperiodic noise is produced when air is forced through a narrow gap at the alveolar ridge, and the flow becomes turbulent.

All fricatives involve the production of such noise at some point in the vocal tract. Voiceless fricatives like [s] have only this kind of source of acoustic energy; in voiced fricatives, like [z], noise is superimposed on energy from the vibrating vocal cords. The spectrum of the noise depends on the kind of turbulence which produces it, and on the way in which it is shaped by the resonances of the vocal tract. An [h] will have a formant structure rather like that of a vowel, because the aperi-

FIGURE 4. *The Source-Filter Model of Speech Production.* The two vowel spectra (top) reflect the spectrum of the laryngeal source-wave, modified by the resonances (formants) of the vocal tract for [ɑ] (left) and [i] (right). At the top it is assumed that the vocal tract is moving between the two vowels, and the schematic spectrogram shows the changes through time of the first three spectral peaks.

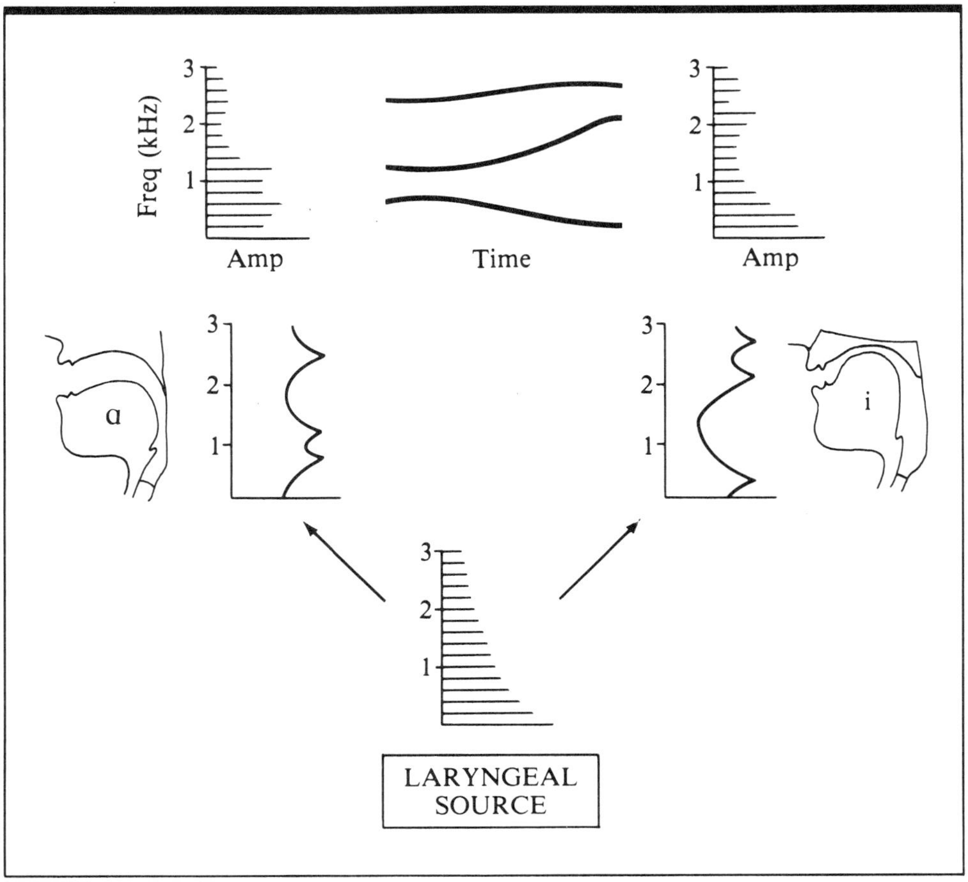

FIGURE 5. *Spectrogram of 'a bye, a dye, a guy.'* The frequencies of the first three formants at the start of the transitions from the stops are indicated in the stop portions.

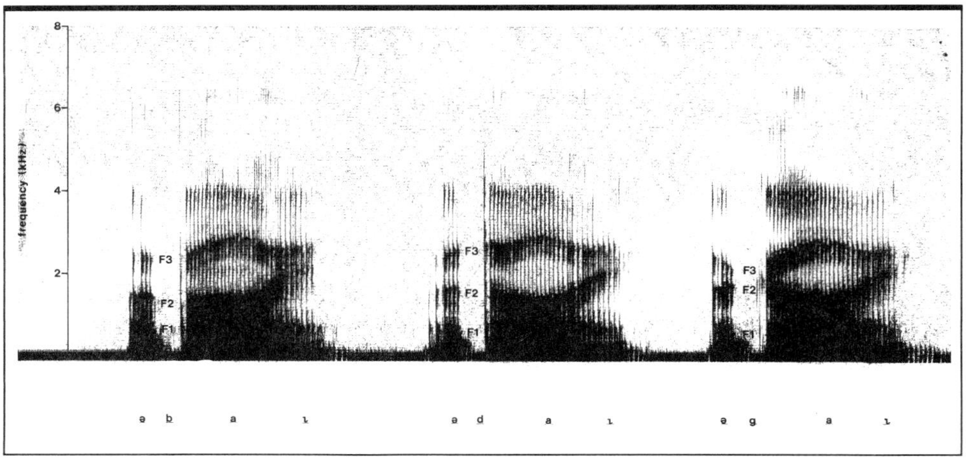

odic noise source (like the periodic voicing of a vowel) is at the end of the vocal tract. An [s], by contrast, will have a spectral shaping quite unlike that of a vowel.

Figure 6 is a spectrogram of *hazy sunshine*. The [h] has a formant pattern somewhat like that of the vowel following it. The [z] shows two cues to the voicing which differentiates it from [s]: low-frequency energy at the bottom of the pattern, and a continuity of the vertical striations (each of which, as in vowels, indicates a cycle of vocal-cord vibration). By contrast, [s] and [z] share a similar high-frequency noise spectrum, because they are both alveolars; the spectrum of the palato-alveolar [š] is rather different.

While fricatives result from turbulence in a steady airflow, the release of a stop brings a short burst of aperiodic acoustic energy at the moment when the air pressure, built up behind the closure, is released. The spectral distribution of energy in the burst varies according to the place of articulation of the stop; this supplements the formant transition cues discussed above.

Nasals are like vowels in that energy produced at the larynx is spectrally shaped by the resonance of a tube; here, however, the tube extends from the larynx through the nasal cavities. The acoustic complexity is increased because there is interaction with the resonances of the mouth cavity behind the oral closure. Nasalized vowels, as in French [ɔ̃] *on,* are similar to oral vowels, except that their spectrum is made more complex by the interaction of the resonances of the nasal cavity.

This treatment of the acoustics of speech has been far from complete. Not all types of segments have been considered, and little has been said about the prosodic or suprasegmental properties of speech. More generally, it has not explored the quantitative mathematical models

FIGURE 6. *Spectrogram of 'hazy sunshine'*

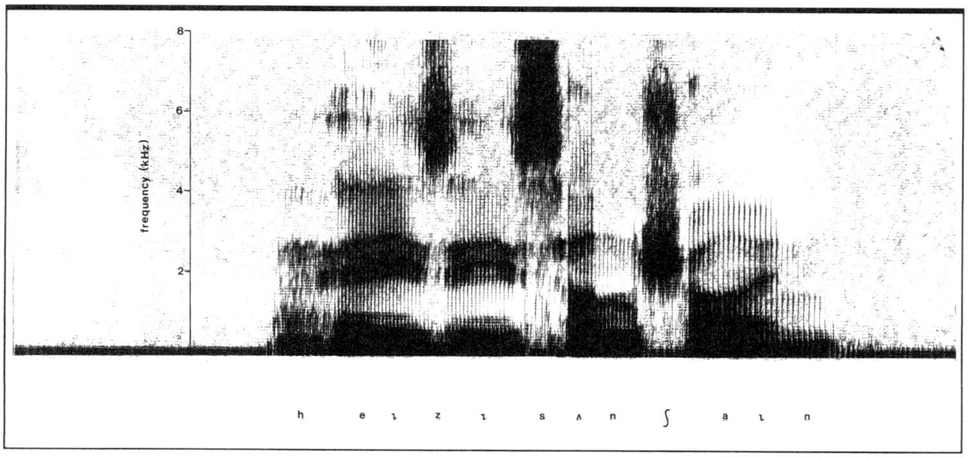

which underlie the analysis of speech. It is this quantitative ACOUSTIC THEORY OF SPEECH which gives acoustic phonetics the power to manipulate and replicate speech signals, and which opens the way to many of the applications discussed below.

3. The roles of acoustic phonetics. As an adjunct to phonology, acoustic phonetics can supplement the information on phonetic realization which is provided by auditory phonetics. The exact nature of a fine auditory distinction often is not clear from skilled listening alone; acoustic analysis can show objectively the contribution of spectral, durational, and other acoustic dimensions to the realization of a phonological contrast. Beyond this, acoustic phonetics can suggest appropriate PHONOLOGICAL FEATURES [*q.v.*] for descriptive use. For example, there is little motivation in articulatory terms for the sound change by which the Germanic velar fricative at the end of the word *laugh* became labio-dental in modern English; but acoustic analysis suggests a similarity in terms of spectral shape. Both fricatives have a weighting of their energy toward the lower end of the spectrum; in terms of phonological features, they share the value [+grave].

Acoustic phonetics has an important role in the branch of cognitive psychology which deals with the perception of speech. In particular, the analyses of acoustic phonetics provide techniques for manipulating real speech signals, and for creating speech signals artificially by SPEECH SYNTHESIS [*q.v.*]. Thus experimental stimuli can be created whose acoustic properties are clearly known, and which can be varied in controlled ways. It is then possible to discover precisely which properties of a sound are crucial for its perception by a hearer. For instance, it can be shown that, in identifying an English stop as voiceless rather than voiced (e.g., as a realization of /p/ rather than /b/), hearers are mainly sensitive to the delay in the onset of voicing after the release of the stop; but they also integrate information such as the strength of the stop burst and the trajectory of F_1 at the start of the vowel.

The study of how humans produce speech, too, benefits from a well worked-out acoustic theory of speech. It is now possible to implement, on electrical analogs or on digital computers, mathematically explicit models of how certain aspects of the speech signal are created in the vocal tract. Perhaps the most advanced are analogs of the vocal tract tube as it acts as a filter on the glottal source. Given such a model, it is possible to predict formant values for any variation in the shape of the tube. Working back from the observed acoustic pattern of a speech sound, the articulatory events underlying the sound can be inferred. Quantitative models also exist for the creation of acoustic energy in the vocal tract, either by a purely aerodynamic process (as with fricative energy), or—in the case of the vocal cords—a process involving complex interactions of aerodynamics and properties of the vocal-cord tissues. To the extent that such models yield realistic acoustic signals, they confirm progress in understanding SPEECH PRODUCTION.

Acoustic phonetic knowledge is crucial in speech technology, including automatic SPEECH RECOGNITION [*q.v.*], and speech output by computers. Much work in this area is motivated by the goal of allowing humans to interact with machines by using natural language. Part of the challenge is to find explicit and computationally tractable ways to represent existing acoustic phonetic knowledge. One particularly successful technique is LINEAR PREDICTION, which in some ways can be seen as an approximation to the source-filter model; it is applicable in speech synthesis and recognition. However, there are areas where existing knowledge is itself incomplete; this is particularly so in connection with the acoustic variation in a sound which occurs because of differences among individuals' vocal tracts, and which causes difficulties in designing systems of speech recognition that can cope with a variety of speakers.

Acoustic phonetics is not an isolated discipline with sharply defined borders. Its central object of study is the acoustic speech signal; but a purely physics-based study of the signal—ignoring how the signal is produced and perceived, and how it is structured linguistically—would contribute relatively little to our understanding of spoken communication. Acoustic phonetics thus proceeds in symbiosis with the study of speech production, speech perception, and linguistics generally. [*See also* Articulatory Phonetics; Organs of Speech.]

FRANCIS NOLAN

BIBLIOGRAPHY

FANT, GUNNAR. 1960. *Acoustic theory of speech production.* The Hague: Mouton.

FLANAGAN, JAMES L. 1972. *Speech analysis: Synthesis and perception.* 2d ed. New York: Springer.

FRY, DENNIS B. 1979. *The physics of speech.* Cambridge & New York: Cambridge University Press.

LIEBERMAN, PHILIP, & SHEILA E. BLUMSTEIN. 1988. *Speech physiology, speech perception, and acoustic phonetics.* Cambridge & New York: Cambridge University Press.

ACQUISITION OF LANGUAGE. [*This entry is concerned with children's learning of their native language, as well as with the learning of a second language by children or adults. It comprises three articles:*

Meanings and Forms
Phonology
Second-Language Acquisition

For related topics, see also Psycholinguistics, *overview article, and* Bilingualism.]

Meanings and Forms

Language in children first emerges at around one year of age, when they begin to understand and produce their first words. Their meanings for words and phrases, like their early pronunciations, often diverge from those of adults. Working out which meanings go with which forms is a lengthy task; the acquisition of meaning is intimately linked to the acquisition of morphological and syntactic forms as well. The major problem children face is how to assign to each form the meaning it conventionally carries in the speech community. They have to test their hypotheses about meanings and revise them when necessary. Research has focused on where children's hypotheses about meanings come from, and on the stages they go through as they move closer to the adult meanings.

Children also make errors in the forms of their first language. They over-regularize inflectional and derivational endings; they over-extend syntactic patterns; and they impose regularity in the shape of paradigms, where the language around them is irregular. Here research has focused on two problems: first, how children master conventional but irregular forms of the language, and second, how children get rid of regularized forms which they themselves have constructed. The first problem has received more attention than the second, and the kinds of over-regularization that children come up with are well-documented for a variety of languages. Less is known about how and why children get rid of early regularizations.

In acquisition, meaning and form must be taken together; one cannot be acquired without the other. But researchers have sometimes focused on a single aspect, without considering the necessary coordination between the two. Data from a variety of languages (Slobin 1985) suggest that all children start their acquisition of meaning and form in much the same way. Whether they continue on the same route, as they learn more complex meanings and forms, depends on how similar languages are—and on how many possible routes children may find, as they move toward an adult-like mastery of a language.

1. Lexical meanings. Children's earliest lexical meanings emerge with their first words, and often diverge from adult's meanings for the same words (Clark 1983). Children may OVER-EXTEND a word beyond its adult meaning, e.g. using *dog* for horses and sheep as well as dogs; or they may UNDER-EXTEND a word, e.g. using *shoe* only for laced shoes being worn on the feet, but not for shoes of other types or in other places. They may use a word so that its meaning OVERLAPS with, but does not coincide with, the adult's meaning—as when *horse* is used for riding horses and is extended to donkeys and zebras, but is not used for cart-horses. Finally, children's earliest meanings may be complete MISMATCHES, and fail to overlap at all with adult meanings.

However, production does not necessarily match comprehension. Children who produce *dog* for four-legged mammals other than dogs typically understand that *dog*, when heard from others, denotes only dogs and not other kinds of animals. Over-extensions in production, therefore, probably reflect a communicative strategy for talking about things, prior to mastery of the relevant labels. As children learn to produce their first hundred words, they may over-extend up to 40 percent of them. Under-extensions and overlaps are harder to document; however, they may be even more pervasive in children's meanings, during a longer period, than over-extensions. The latter become rare by the age of 2;0 (i.e., 2 years, 0 months) to 2;6. Most observations about early meanings have come from diary studies of language production; however, researchers have also examined some sources of children's hypotheses about word-meanings by looking systematically at how children understand words, as well as when they produce them.

The stages in children's acquisition of word-meanings, in specific semantic domains, have been studied in some detail. Children's earliest hypotheses about word-meanings are often based on general conceptual knowledge about relevant domains. Thus, in the acquisition of locative terms, children appear to rely on two general (non-linguistic) strategies for interpreting instructions with words like *in, on,* and *under*. The first, 'Put X inside', applies to any locations that are containers; the second, 'Put X on top', to places that are not containers. Children's attention to containers and supporting surfaces, in other words, provides their first hypotheses about the locative relations that words encode. Later, these interpretations become more specific, as they work out the contrasts in meaning of *in* and *on,* or *on* and *above* or *under*.

The routes which children follow as they do this have been traced for a variety of locative terms; for kinship terms; for verbs of possession (e.g. *give, take, trade, buy, sell*); for verbs of speaking (e.g. *ask, tell*); for verbs of motion; and for deictic terms (e.g. *I, here, that, go, bring*). There has also been some research on how children build up taxonomies of terms in a hierarchy, for such domains as animals (e.g. *animal, dog, collie*); here we find little consistency in whether a superordinate like *animal* appears before or after a subordinate like *collie,* although terms at the generic or basic level (e.g. *dog*) typically enter first. Otherwise, the level of the earliest terms acquired appears to depend on their immediate usefulness to the young child. For instance, the lower-level *apple* and *orange* will be more useful than *fruit*; but higher-level *bug* will be more useful than *stag-beetle* or *aphid,* and *tree* more useful than *oak* or *elm*.

2. Word combinations. In their earliest word combinations, children talk about ROLES (e.g. agent, location, recipient) and ACTIONS in events; but they give little evidence of marking such grammatical relations as 'subject of' or 'direct object of'. The kinds of two-word combinations observable in children acquiring different languages appear very similar in meaning; however, not all children try the same kinds of combinations prior to acquisition of morphological marking or of word order to signal grammatical relations (Brown 1973). A number of studies suggest that the earliest uses of word order in production are actually to signal new information, as opposed to information already given in the conversation or the non-linguistic context. Only later, in languages where word order has a grammatical function, do children learn that too. Meanings attributable to structures emerge in production somewhat later than those attached to individual words within such structural units as noun phrases, verb phrases, or prepositional phrases.

As their word combinations become longer, children fill out more of their phrases—adding articles, quantifiers, adjectives, prepositions, and other indicators of grammatical functions. They also begin to produce relative clauses, adverbial phrases and clauses, and complements; all these may require use of both word order and grammatical morphemes to mark structural relations among linguistic units (Maratsos 1983, Wanner & Gleitman 1982).

3. Grammatical morphemes. The affixes or free morphemes that mark grammatical relations among words begin to emerge during the first year of speech. In English, the first morphemes produced by children include aspectual *-ing,* plural *-s,* and past tense *-ed.* Later acquisitions are the articles *a* and *the,* the copula verb *be,* prepositions, and complementizers (e.g. *to, for, that*). In languages with case-marking, children begin using case for such grammatical relations as 'subject of' and 'object of' quite early; however, the complexity and regularity of the case-markers affects the rate at which such elements are acquired. Regular systems with few exceptions are mastered faster than systems with numerous small paradigms, or with several genders marked by different affixes. It also takes time to master the affixes needed for agreement in gender and number for noun and article, noun and adjective, or noun and verb combinations.

When children acquire inflections—whether for case, number, gender, person, tense, or aspect—they regularize the system. They typically choose the paradigm with the largest number of members (types, not tokens), and use it as the model for other nouns or verbs. Thus, in English, children regularize the past tense forms of irregular verbs like *see, buy, go* to produce *seed, buyed, goed.* In French, children often regularize irregular verbs in *-ir* or *-re* to the *-er* paradigm, as in the regularized past participles *couré* (for *couru* 'ran' < *courir* 'to run'), *metté* (for *mis* < *mettre* 'to put'), or *mordé* (for *mordu* < *mordre* 'to bite'). In fact, where children have to choose among several different affixes which, for instance, all mark the same case but are used with nouns of different gender, they often choose a single form and apply it in all contexts that call for that meaning. Thus, in Russian, children at this stage produce *-om* for the instrumental on all nouns—masculine, feminine, and neuter.

The overall pattern of acquisition which children display in their production of grammatical morphemes can be characterized as falling into four stages. After an initial period of no use, one may find sporadic use of irregular forms, followed by the earliest uses of regular forms; then comes a flood of regularizations which are gradually replaced by appropriate irregular forms. A major theoretical question here is how and under what circumstances children come to replace *bringed,* say, by *brought,* or *foots* by *feet.* The same question applies to children's over-regularizations of syntactic patterns, as in such forms as *Don't say me that* (for *Don't say that to me*), or *Can I fill some salt into the bear?* (for *fill the bear with salt*) (MacWhinney 1987).

4. Word formation. The same question arises again in the domain of word formation. Here too, children regularize irregular forms to fit their paradigms. They construct nouns for agents (e.g. *cooker* for *a cook*), for instruments (*driller* for *a drill*) and for states (*longness* for *length*). They often construct compound nouns; but in the early stage, they fail to do so appropriately (*open-man, open-door,* or *opener-door,* all for *door-opener*). And they also coin verbs—from nouns (e.g *to broom* for *to sweep*), from adjectives (*to dark* for *to darken*), and from prepositions (*to up* for *to raise*). In each case, some formations are pre-empted by existing words, and children have to learn that those meanings are conventionally expressed by other established forms.

5. Errors and principles. Children make consistent errors as they acquire different parts of their first language. These errors provide important clues to the meanings which children have identified, and the forms with which they have associated them. Consistency in the errors children make also offers crucial information about general strategies of acquisition: how children analyze the speech stream they hear into smaller units of form and meaning for comprehension, and how they combine units of different sizes for production. Similarities in types of errors across languages suggest that children may begin with certain universal OPERATING PRINCIPLES for comprehension and for production; but these strategies are then modified by the typology of the specific language being acquired. [*See* Psycholinguistics, *overview article.*] Research on the general process of acquisition—on what is universal, and what is shaped by the structure of specific languages—contributes essential information to the puzzle of what should be counted as universal across languages. The study of language acquisition also offers insight into the learning of complex systems, and raises new questions about the kinds of models that will account adequately for both what and how children learn as they acquire a first language.

EVE V. CLARK

BIBLIOGRAPHY

BROWN, ROGER. 1973. *A first language: The early stages.* Cambridge, Mass.: Harvard University Press.

CLARK, EVE V. 1983. Meanings and concepts. In Flavell & Markman 1983, pp. 787–840.

FLAVELL, JOHN H., & ELLEN M. MARKMAN, eds. 1983. *Handbook of child psychology,* vol. 3, *Cognitive development.* New York: Wiley.

MACWHINNEY, BRIAN, ed. 1987. *Mechanisms of language acquisition.* Hillsdale, N.J.: Erlbaum.

MARATSOS, MICHAEL. 1983. Some current issues in the study of the acquisition of grammar. In Flavell & Markman 1983, pp. 707–786.

SLOBIN, DAN I., ed. 1985. *The cross-linguistic study of language acquisition.* 2 vols. Hillsdale, N.J.: Erlbaum.

WANNER, ERIC, & LILA R. GLEITMAN, eds. 1982. *Language acquisition: The state of the art.* Cambridge & New York: Cambridge University Press.

Phonology

The acquisition of phonology in a child's native language is generally taken to include mastery of the phonetic targets, phonemic contrasts, and morphophonemic alternations in recognition and production. Most of the published data deal with English, but materials on many other European languages, Chinese, Japanese, Thai, and Quiché Mayan have also become available.

1. Pre-speech phonetic development. Experimental studies have shown that the young infant, and probably the neonate, discriminates and responds categorically to sounds with respect to voice onset time and many of the other acoustic parameters that mark phonemic boundaries, and that they do so regardless of whether those parameters are phonemic in the ambient language (Jusczyk 1984); e.g., Japanese infants discriminate [r] from [l] in the same way that American infants do. Very young infants also associate the visual appearance of degree of mouth opening with the corresponding vowel sound (Kuhl & Meltzoff 1984). It is not clear whether this cross-modal link is 'hard-wired' into the brain (i.e. innate), or learned very early.

Infant sound production develops steadily, starting with a first period of reflexive cries and involuntary sounds, and continuing through four further, generally recognized stages (ages are approximate): 8–20 weeks, social and comfortable cooing ([u]-like sounds, sometimes preceded by [k]- or [g]-like consonants) and laughter; 16–30 weeks, transitional single-syllable vocal play; 25–50 weeks, reduplicated solo or social babbling of strings of identical or near-identical consonant-vowel syllables; 40 weeks to 18 months, non-reduplicated babbling (solo and social), also referred to as EXPRESSIVE JARGON. The last stage derives its name from the fact that a string of syllables is no longer constrained to reiteration of a single CV pattern, but may contain several different consonants and vowels. Longitudinal single-child studies (e.g. Halliday 1975) have shown that different communicative intentions—as judged by the child's concurrent or subsequent actions—can be correlated with differential use of pitch and intonation contour during this stage; however, the contours used vary from child to child, and may not completely match the use of pitch and intonation contour in the ambient language.

Recent work has shown that, contrary to long-held opinion, the repertory of sounds used in babbling by any given child is rather small, and tends to consist of a subset of the phones of the ambient language (Oller 1980). The period of non-reduplicated babbling generally overlaps considerably with the early production of recognizable words; sounds preferred by a given child in non-reduplicated babbling tend also to be used in these words (Vihman et al. 1985). In tone languages, correct lexical tones are generally found on the earliest words used.

2. Characteristics of early words. The earliest systematic sound/meaning correspondences that a child uses may or may not have adult models; they may also differ from adult lexical items in being phonetically less well controlled. (Their semantic properties may also be somewhat anomalous; they may be social or action-accompanying rather than referential.) For these reasons, terms such as PROTO-WORD, P[HONETICALLY] C[ONSISTENT] F[ORM], and VOCABLE have been used instead of 'word' for the first recognizably recurrent, meaningful units that a child produces.

Some 'earliest' words (termed 'progressive phonological idioms') are quite accurate renditions of their adult models; however, a beginning speaker apparently cannot maintain much accuracy or contrast. Typically, each child develops a more-or-less systematic way of rendering adult words within his/her limited output repertoire of sound-sequences. The inaccuracies in these renditions appear to result, with a few exceptions, from motor programming problems, rather than from misperceptions of the adult sound pattern; children can usually discriminate between two words which they render identically, except sometimes in the case of a few very similar phones like [f] and [θ].

If the mapping from the adult model to the child's form is highly systematic, it can be captured by writing phonological rules; but this is not the case for all children. For example, some children map entire multi-word phrases onto loosely articulated sequences (e.g. *I don't want it* rendered [ãõã:]) (Peters 1977); others re-order the sounds of adult words to fit into their own restricted output templates (Macken 1979). Output templates for words may include patterns like 'First vowel higher than second vowel,' or 'Medial consonant = glottal stop,' or 'First consonant labial, second alveolar.'

The rules used by children who do have somewhat systematic mapping patterns include a number of natural processes (Stampe 1969). [*See* Natural Phonology.] Examples are devoicing of final stops ([bɪp] for *bib*); substitution of stops for fricatives ([ti] for *see*); reduction of consonant clusters to singletons ([pat], less commonly [fat], for *spot*); deletion of initial [h]; and deletion of unstressed syllables ([næ], [nǽnæ] for *banana*). However, it has been noted that a child may fail to use such processes with his/her earliest words, and then start to use them somewhat later; this has led many researchers to regard these processes as natural failure modes, rather than as innate rules which must be unlearned by the child (Kiparsky & Menn 1977). Other common rules for English-acquiring children which are not prominent (or in some cases, even attested) in adult language include voicing of initial stop consonants—as well as various assimilation rules that ensure whole-word consonant harmonies, especially place assimilation and nasal assimilation. For English, it has been observed that an unstressed syllable in a word may be replaced by a 'dummy syllable' (either a stereotyped near-constant shape or a copy of the stressed syllable) instead of being deleted. Consonant cluster simplification, usually accomplished by preservation of the most obstruent element, may instead be done by combining features from the several segments (e.g. /s/ + nasal rendered as voiceless nasal, /sk/ rendered as [x]), even when the adult language does not possess the resulting feature combination.

In ascribing rules or processes to a child, the investigator must take into account the surface forms of the words that the child is being exposed to by family and peers. Dialect variants are not 'errors' for the child, regardless of their social valuation. In addition, it should be noted that the normal assimilations and reductions of fluent speech (e.g. English [hǽftə] for *have to*) are not incorrect forms or outputs of phonological processes for the child who is too young to be aware of the underlying forms.

3. Strategy variations and metalinguistic awareness. Individual children vary in the extent to which they prefer to avoid adult words which they cannot yet render accurately. Children as young as fifteen months have been shown in diary studies to avoid attempting words outside their existing production repertory, indicating an unexpected degree of metalinguistic ability. Experimental work (Schwartz & Leonard 1982) suggests that such avoidance is especially likely to be found in children who have acquired fewer than twenty-five to seventy-five words of output vocabulary. There is much other evidence (e.g. repeated attempts at self-correction) to indicate that very young children are often aware of inadequacies in their renditions of adult words.

However, children certainly are not always aware of how accurate their attempts are. With respect to any given adult target which a child does attempt to match, there appears generally to be a progression. First, there may be an initial stage at which the child seems unable to become aware that his/her rendition is not the same as the adult's—perhaps in spite of strenuous efforts by the adult to get the child to attend to the disparity. Numerous studies have reported interchanges in which a child mispronounces a word (e.g. [fɩs] for *fish*); then an adult requests the child to say [fɩš] (emphasizing the final [š]); and finally the child responds *I did say* [fɩs] (with similar emphasis). Given the experimental evidence that infants can, in general, make such discriminations between stimuli (Gottlieb & Krasnegor 1985), a possible explanation for such responses is that the child is attending only to the meaning of the word that the adult is repeating and its emphatic quality, but not to its articulatory details.

Later, the child attends to the difference but cannot manage any change in production—and at this point may be able to comment on his/her inability. Afterwards, correction can be approximated in imitation but not maintained in spontaneous speech. Still later, a more correct form and the earlier form appear variably in production; and finally, the more correct form is maintained. Progress through these phases may be slow or rapid; a child may be at an advanced stage with respect to an early-acquired sound or sequence, yet still at a beginning stage with respect to a more difficult target.

4. Order of acquisition for phones and contrasts. The order of mastery of phones and of phonemic contrasts and the age of mastery are variable across children. The order of contrast acquisition proposed by Jakobson 1941 on the basis of general markedness is quite a good fit probabilistically, but many exceptions have been reported in the literature; thus his description in terms of 'laws of irreversible solidarity' can no longer be considered appropriate. It does seem that phones which are dependent on precise relative timing of glottal and supra-laryngeal events (e.g. aspirated or glottalized stops) are generally acquired later than those which are not so dependent, other things being equal. Furthermore, phones which seem to require more precise positioning without tactile feedback (fricatives and liquids, as opposed to stops) are acquired relatively late. The relatively early acquisition of glides has not yet been fully rationalized.

Phonotactic considerations play a great role in acquisition. The 'order of acquisition' question is often unanswerable in any simple form, even for an individual child: thus production of a particular phoneme might be generally correct for its intervocalic allophone, fully correct word-initially, absent in particular clusters, and incorrect in word-final position—all this apart from the possible interference of consonant assimilation in certain words. Although new consonant phones often are first mastered as initial singletons, there is much individual variation within and across children; for English-speaking children, it is not uncommon for some or all of the fricatives to first appear word-finally, while stops first appear word-initially.

There is yet no general theory able to account for both the degree of observed variation and the degree of observed commonality of acquisition of phones and of phonemic contrasts across children. However, Lindblom et al. 1983 have attempted a promising model of early phonemic development in terms of self-organizing systems.

5. Perception versus production. Investigating the relation of perception to production during the period of the acquisition of the sound system has required devising different experimental techniques appropriate to the rapidly changing cognitive and motor abilities of the infant and young child; there is still a gap in our knowledge of the development of perceptual abilities from about twelve to eighteen months. As stated above, infants have phonetic perceptual and categorization abilities similar to, or indeed better than, those of adults. On the other hand, children as old as two often confuse minimal pairs; they have a heavy bias to respond to the less familiar member of such a pair of stimulus words as though it were the more familiar one (e.g. pointing to a 'coat' instead of a 'goat' after the word *goat* has been especially taught to test the *k/g* discrimination; Barton 1980). Consequently, it has been suggested that very different mechanisms are involved in recognizing and discriminating meaningless sounds, as opposed to words. For example, differential response to words invokes long-term memory for the sound-meaning correspondence, even if the experimental paradigm does not actually require this, while the discrimination paradigms used with infants do not.

6. Later phonological development. Well before children finish mastering the phonetic details of the ambient language, they have begun to acquire its morphology and morphophonemics. [*See* Processing.] Phonological rules with a heavy natural component (e.g. voicing assimilation) appear to be acquired early, with the correct output form always present; but forms in which an ending happens to be very similar to the final stem syllable or consonant which precedes (e.g. the English [əz] plural) tend to be acquired late. Many factors interact in the acquisition of rules which apply to particular classes of morphemes (MacWhinney 1978, Slobin 1973); these factors include the frequency and the transparency and reliability of semantic and/or phonological conditioning factors. Rote application of a rule to a few frequent words precedes general application of a rule. In this area as elsewhere, overgeneralization of a rule to cases where it should not apply is taken as the hallmark of actual rule learning; this interacts with the learning of subregularities conditioned by phonological factors, or by membership in gender classes and conjugational or declensional classes. Some non-productive but well attested morphophonological rules, such as the stem-final palatalizations in the Romance stratum of English *(correct/correction, invade/invasion)* apparently are not learned until mid or late adolescence.

Little is known about the acquisition of segmental rules or of tonal sandhi rules, which apply across word boundaries, or about rules that apply in rapid speech, in spite of their evident productivity. The ability to understand and produce many aspects of English stress and intonation patterns is developed gradually during the elementary school years (Cruttenden 1974).

LISE MENN

BIBLIOGRAPHY

BARTON, DAVID. 1980. Phonemic perception in children. In *Child phonology,* vol. 2, *Perception,* edited by Grace H. Yeni-Komshian et al., pp. 97–116. New York: Academic Press.

CRUTTENDEN, ALAN. 1974. An experiment involving comprehension of intonation in children from 7 to 10. *Journal of Child Language* 1.221–231.

GOTTLIEB, GILBERT, & NORMAN A. KRASNEGOR, eds. 1985. *Measurement of audition and vision in the first year of postnatal life: A methodological overview.* Norwood, N.J.: Ablex.

HALLIDAY, MICHAEL A. K. 1975. *Learning how to mean: Explorations in the development of language.* London: Arnold.

JAKOBSON, ROMAN. 1941. *Kindersprache, Aphasie, und allgemeine Lautgesetze.* Uppsala: Almqvist & Wiksell. Translated as *Child language, aphasia, and phonological universals* (The Hague: Mouton, 1968).

JUSCZYK, PETER W. 1984. On characterizing the development of speech perception. In *Neonate cognition: Beyond the blooming, buzzing confusion,* edited by Jacques Mehler & Robin Fox, pp. 199–229. Hillsdale, N.J.: Erlbaum.

KIPARSKY, PAUL, & LISE MENN. 1977. On the acquisition of phonology. In *Language learning and thought,* edited by John Macnamara, pp. 47–78. New York: Academic Press.

KUHL, PATRICIA K., & ANDREW N. MELTZOFF. 1984. Intermodal representation of speech in infants. *Infant Behavior and Development* 7.361–381.

LINDBLOM, BJÖRN; PETER MACNEILAGE; & MICHAEL STUDDERT-KENNEDY. 1983. Self-organizing processes and the explanation of phonological universals. In *Explanation of language universals* (Linguistics, vol. 21), edited by Brian Butterworth et al., pp. 181–203. The Hague: Mouton.

MACKEN, MARLYS A. 1979. Developmental reorganization of phonology: A hierarchy of basic units of acquisition. *Lingua* 49.11–49.

MACWHINNEY, BRIAN. 1978. *The acquisition of morphophonology.* (Monographs of the Society for Research in Child Development, 43:1/2). Chicago: University of Chicago Press.

OLLER, D. KIMBROUGH. 1980. The emergence of the sounds of speech in infancy. In *Child phonology,* vol. 1, *Production,* edited by Grace H. Yeni-Komshian et al., pp. 93–112. New York: Academic Press.

PETERS, ANN. 1977. Language learning strategies. *Language* 53.560–573.

SCHWARTZ, RICHARD, & LAURENCE B. LEONARD. 1982. Do children pick and choose? An examination of phonological selection and avoidance in early lexical acquisition. *Journal of Child Language* 9.319–336.

SLOBIN, DAN I. 1973. Cognitive prerequisites for the development of grammar. In *Studies of child language development,* edited by Charles A. Ferguson & Dan I. Slobin, pp. 175–211. New York: Holt, Rinehart & Winston.

STAMPE, DAVID. 1969. The acquisition of phonetic representation. *Chicago Linguistic Society* 5.433–444.

VIHMAN, MARILYN M. et al. 1985. From babbling to speech. *Language* 61.397–445.

Second-Language Acquisition

The study of S[econd]-L[anguage] A[cquisition] is a broad, interdisciplinary field of inquiry which aims to describe and explain the development and non-development of languages and language varieties beyond the first language. SLA researchers study children and adults learning naturalistically or with the aid of formal instruction, as individuals or in groups, and in foreign- and second-language settings. The research draws upon and contributes to knowledge and procedures in a variety of disciplines, including theoretical linguistics, neurolinguistics, psycholinguistics, sociolinguistics, historical linguistics, pidgin/creole studies, applied linguistics, psychology, sociology, anthropology, and education. SLA research findings are used to test hypotheses and build theories in those areas, as well as for a variety of practical purposes such as the improvement of language teaching, language testing, teacher education, and the design of instructional programs delivered through the medium of a second language or dialect (Larsen-Freeman & Long 1990).

The conditions producing SLA are diverse. It can result, for example, from simultaneous or sequential bilingual or multilingual exposure in infancy—as in the case of children born to parents with different first languages (L1s) who use them in the home and who may also live in a country where a third language is spoken. It is sometimes the product of either forced or voluntary educational experience, including submersion, immersion, bilingual education, foreign-language teaching, and other school, university, or vocational programs in which a second language (L2) is the medium or object of instruction. It can follow informal exposure to languages later in life, as with millions of migrant workers, refugees, and tourists. Finally, it is a routine experience for a substantial part of the world's population who live in multilingual societies.

While the SLA phenomenon is widespread, many aspects of the process itself remain something of a mystery. Only severely subnormal children fail to develop a high degree of proficiency in their native language; but relatively few people, however intelligent and motivated, reach such high standards in a second or third language, especially if they are first exposed to the additional language as adults. Is it that unsuccessful older learners simply do not learn as much as cognitively less developed children? Or is it that they cannot learn as much, or in the same way? Part of their INTERLANGUAGE [*q.v.*] often appears to stabilize, or cease to develop, far short of a communicatively adequate and/or socially acceptable level. Sometimes, it is claimed, the stabilization is permanent, in which case it is referred to as FOSSILIZATION.

Various explanations have been proposed for the heterogeneous achievement of SL learners, for both success and failure (McLaughlin 1987). Some researchers believe that development of both L1 and L2 is maturationally constrained, and that biological (usually neurophysiological) changes progressively diminish the older learner's capacity to learn—i.e., that there are one or more sensitive periods for SLA (Scovel 1988). Others hold that psychological and social factors, such as attitude, motivation, and social distance—or, collectively, the degree to which someone acculturates to the target language group—determine success and failure (Schumann 1978, Andersen 1983). Still others claim that learning depends on the degree of access to input and/or conversational opportunities, particularly access to comprehensible L2 samples from which the grammatical rules of the L2 can be induced (Hatch 1983, Krashen 1985). While all these variables may be relevant in some cases, counter-evidence exists to each as a single-factor explanation, and no one theory enjoys wide acceptance.

While unresolved issues abound, a good deal has been discovered about SLA through a relatively recent but steady empirical tradition. To begin with, learner language is quite variable. Part of the variability is systematic, i.e. rule-governed, such that a learner may use alternate forms according to linguistic environment, situation, task, degree of planning, attention to speech, etc. For example, reflecting variation in linguistic context, learners initially tend to use the English regular past tense marker *-ed* and plural *-s* only on certain verbs and nouns, and to omit the forms elsewhere. They do so in a fairly predictable manner. However, part of the variability is non-systematic, or free. Thus learners may temporarily alternate between two verb forms or two negators (e.g. *No have* and *Don't have*) in an apparently arbitrary fashion, before gradually assigning different functions to the two items; at that point the variability begins to become systematic (Ellis 1986, Huebner 1983).

As in other kinds of language change, variation in

INTERLANGUAGE (IL) at one point in time often reflects developmental change over time. [*See* Interlanguage.] This is one reason why the documented variability of ILs is not inconsistent with another of their well established qualities, namely systematicity. Some of the early research demonstrating this was inspired by work on L1 development. Thus, in longitudinal and cross-sectional studies, L1 researchers in the early 1970s discovered a common order of appearance for a set of grammatical morphemes 90 percent accurately supplied, in the speech of children learning English as L1, in obligatory contexts (linguistic environments where omission of the morphemes would result in ungrammaticality). The finding was quickly replicated for E[NGLISH AS A] S[ECOND] L[ANGUAGE]—where, although not invariant, a common accuracy order (slightly different from the L1 order) was established for the elicited and spontaneous speech of children and adults, with or without formal instruction, and most interestingly, from a variety of L1 backgrounds. The following nine items, for example, were repeatedly found to reach 80 or 90 percent accurate suppliance in ESL in approximately this order: *-ing,* plural, copula, auxiliary, article, irregular past, regular past, 3sg. *-s,* and possessive *-'s.* Small but clear effects were observed for L1 differences, such as the later development of accuracy in articles by Japanese learners (with no articles in their L1); however, these were too rare to alter the sequence to any statistically significant degree.

Explanations for the L1 and L2 orders were elusive. Researchers found no consistent relationship to the syntactic and/or semantic complexity of the grammatical items concerned, their markedness, their perceptual saliency or, in the L2 case, their position in an instructional sequence. A combination of factors was probably at work. Accuracy orders did often correlate significantly with input frequency; however, input alone clearly could not account for the data—given that, among other problems, articles were always the most frequent item in English input, but reached criterion (in the sense of accurate suppliance) relatively late in the learner output.

While the morpheme studies were criticized methodologically, and the orders themselves remain in need of explanation, both L1 and L2 findings were usually accepted as demonstrating a role for powerful internal factors in the acquisition process—or, as was sometimes said, of an internal learner syllabus. This was an interpretation consistent with nativist theories in linguistics. Noam Chomsky's claims about acquisition, for example, would predict that an order would exist, although not the specific orders observed. As critics pointed out, the L1 and L2 findings pertained to a theoretically unmotivated miscellany of linguistically unrelated items, which, because language-specific, also revealed little about SLA in general.

While the accuracy orders were perhaps marginal with respect to nativist claims, providing only language-specific evidence, they certainly posed problems for neo-behaviorist models of language learning, and in SLA also for the C[ONTRASTIVE] A[NALYSIS] H[YPOTHESIS]. [*See* Contrastive Analysis.] This had claimed that differences between L1 and L2 led to difficulty in SLA, and governed the course of acquisition. Coupled with neo-behaviorist learning theory, the CAH had motivated the audio-lingual method of language teaching and its many variants, whose practitioners set out to eradicate L1 language 'habits' and to inculcate new ones in learners through intensive drill work in areas of contrast between the L1 and the L2.

Strong independent evidence against the CAH, for systematicity in IL, and for a major learner contribution to SLA, was provided by work on so-called DEVELOPMENTAL SEQUENCES in IL, such as those for ESL negation and interrogatives, ESL and Swedish SL relative clauses, and German word order. Developmental sequences are fixed series of overlapping stages, each identified by the relative frequency and/or order of emergence of an interim IL structure, which learners must traverse in the acquisition of a target construction or rule system. Numerous studies have shown, for example, that ESL negation has a four-stage sequence, as shown in Table 1.

If only, say, Spanish speakers (whose L1 has preverbal negation) produced pre-verbally negated constructions at stages (1) and (2), then L1 transfer could explain that aspect of the sequence. But in fact, all SL learners, whether naturalistic or instructed, initially produce pre-

TABLE 1. *Emergence of Negation*

Stage	Sample	Utterances
(1)	*No* + X	*No is cheap.* *No you give him.*
(2)	*no/not/don't* + V	*He not living here.* *They don't have.*
(3)	AUX + NEG	*I can't sing.* *You mustn't go.*
(4)	analyzed *don't*	*I didn't tell him.* *She doesn't play.*

verbal negation—including Japanese speakers, whose L1 system is post-verbal. Turkish speakers begin Swedish SL negation that way, too, even though both L1 and L2 are post-verbal.

Why developmental sequences look the way they do is still unclear. It is difficult to untangle the effects of several forces which often converge on the same construction. In the early stages of many sequences, when the learner's linguistic resources in the L2 are limited, processing constraints are presumably at least partially responsible (Clahsen et al. 1982). The need to reduce redundancy and discontinuity for ease of production and comprehension favors one simple, fixed word order, rather than more complex, variable orders (e.g. with the verb phrase interrupted by the negator). Language universals and typological markedness also seem to be at work (Rutherford 1984), since pre-verbal position is the most preferred (least marked) for negators in natural languages—including early child language, pidgins, creoles, ungrammatical foreigner talk (*No drink water!*), and highly conventionalized formulas (*No can do, Long time no see*).

There is clearly a danger of circularity in attempting to explain developmental IL constructions and sequences by appeals to universals and markedness, while simultaneously using the IL data to establish the universals and markedness relationships. Further, cognitive factors like processing constraints may themselves be causal where universals are concerned, in that some linguistic universals may be a function of universal processing constraints. However, the fact that several studies have found six stages in the development of Swedish SL and ESL relative clauses, corresponding to those predictable from Keenan & Comrie's (1977) noun phrase accessibility hierarchy, suggests that ILs tend to develop in ways consistent with typological universals, whatever gives rise to the universals in the first place. Some studies even find learners accepting and producing pronominal copies on grammaticality judgment and elicited production tasks (e.g. *Number seven is the woman who she is holding the child*), when neither their L1 nor the L2 (e.g. Italian and English) permit copies in any kind of relative clause. Results like these not only support the idea that ILs are responsive to language universals, but also that they are to some degree autonomous linguistic systems, not simply relexified versions of the L1 or poor approximations to the L2 (Davies et al. 1984).

Despite the striking commonality of the stages in developmental sequences, as with morpheme accuracy orders, local effects for L1 can be seen (Gass & Selinker 1983, Kellerman & Sharwood Smith 1986). Studies show that, while the order of basic stages in sequences appears to be immutable, L1 differences sometimes result in additional sub-stages, and also in swifter or slower passage through stages. L1 influence seems most likely at points in a sequence when an IL form is similar to an L1 structure. German learners of ESL, for example, sometimes follow their L1 pattern in producing utterances with the negator after the main verb (**David plays not soccer very good*), when they correctly begin to place it after the auxiliary. Likewise, speakers of languages like Spanish with pre-verbal negation in their L1 are slower to relinquish this as an IL strategy than speakers of languages like Japanese which do not have pre-verbal systems—presumably they perceive a similarity between their L1 systems and the pre-verbal negation of IL stages (1) and (2).

As indicated by these findings, the role of the L1 in SLA is far more complex than originally believed. To begin with, not just differences but also similarities between languages can cause learners difficulty. However, structural identity between L1 and L2 idioms, lexis, and syntax (but probably not phonology) does not necessarily result in transfer, as shown for example by adult Dutch learners' reluctance to transfer correct Dutch uses of the verb *break* into English (e.g. *His voice broke* and *She broke the world record*) if their L1 usages seem to them to be too idiomatic to be likely to occur in the L2. When the structure of the L1 does influence SLA, it generally operates in harmony with what appear to be natural developmental processes—as revealed by the findings on developmental sequences, which show them to be modified but not fundamentally altered by transfer. L1 influences also appear to be constrained by various kinds of linguistic markedness. In general, typologically unmarked L1 forms are more likely to be transferred than marked ones, unless the corresponding L2 form is also marked; however, beginners seem more willing to transfer both marked and unmarked forms. There is some evidence that learning difficulty arises only from L1/L2 differences involving greater L2 markedness, with degree of difficulty reflecting degree of markedness.

Many of the findings described briefly here suggest a more important role for classroom language learners than they have traditionally been accorded (Hyltenstam & Pienemann 1985, Chaudron 1988). Errors are largely beyond the teacher's control; they are inevitable and often a sign of progress, indicating formation of interim

IL rules. They also show, if evidence were still needed, that SLA is not simply a process of habit formation. Acquisition sequences do not reflect instructional sequences; learning difficulty is a function of several factors, not just L1/L2 differences, some of them as yet rather poorly understood by researchers and teachers. Finally, learners do not pass from zero to full knowledge of a target construction in one step, although many syllabuses, textbooks, and teachers (and some SLA researchers) implicitly assume that they do—presenting one native-speaker structure at a time and practicing it, followed by another, in building-block fashion.

Formal instruction is still very valuable, however. Other SLA research is beginning to suggest that, while developmental sequences are unaffected, at least a periodic focus on language as object, or form, does have important benefits. It increases the rate of development. It appears to sensitize learners to communicatively redundant language forms—as evidenced by instructed learners' initial over-use of certain grammatical morphology, compared with naturalistic acquirers' greater tendency to delete those items. Finally, it may also raise the level of ultimate attainment where marked, low-frequency, or perceptually non-salient L2 structures are concerned. These are three of the areas otherwise particularly susceptible to premature stabilization.

MICHAEL H. LONG

BIBLIOGRAPHY

ANDERSEN, ROGER W., ed. 1983. *Pidginization and creolization as language acquisition.* Rowley, Mass.: Newbury House.

CHAUDRON, CRAIG. 1988. *Second language classrooms: Research on teaching and learning.* Cambridge & New York: Cambridge University Press.

CLAHSEN, HARALD; JÜRGEN M. MEISEL; & MANFRED PIENEMANN. 1982. *Deutsch als Zweitsprache: Der Spracherwerb ausländischer Arbeiter.* Tübingen: Narr.

DAVIES, ALAN, et al., eds. 1984 *Interlanguage.* Edinburgh: Edinburgh University Press.

ELLIS, ROD. 1986. *Understanding second language acquisition.* Oxford & New York: Oxford University Press.

GASS, SUSAN, & LARRY SELINKER, eds. 1983. *Language transfer in language learning.* Rowley, Mass.: Newbury House.

HATCH, EVELYN MARCUSSEN. 1983. *Psycholinguistics: A second language perspective.* Rowley, Mass.: Newbury House.

HUEBNER, THOM. 1983. *A longitudinal analysis of the acquisition of English.* Ann Arbor: Karoma.

HYLTENSTAM, KENNETH, & MANFRED PIENEMANN, eds. 1985. *Modelling and assessing second language acquisition.* Clevedon, Avon, England: Multilingual Matters. San Diego, Calif.: College-Hill.

KEENAN, EDWARD L., & BERNARD COMRIE. 1977. Noun phrase accessibility and universal grammar. *Linguistic Inquiry* 8.63–99.

KELLERMAN, ERIC, & MICHAEL SHARWOOD SMITH, eds. 1986. *Crosslinguistic influence in second language acquisition.* Oxford: Pergamon.

KRASHEN, STEPHEN D. 1985. *The input hypothesis.* London: Longman.

LARSEN-FREEMAN, DIANE, & MICHAEL H. LONG. 1990. *An introduction to second language acquisition research.* London: Longman.

MCLAUGHLIN, BARRY. 1987. *Theories of second-language learning.* London: Arnold.

RUTHERFORD, WILLIAM E., ed. 1984. *Language universals and second language acquisition.* (Typological studies in language, 5.) Amsterdam: Benjamins.

SCHUMANN, JOHN H. 1978. *The pidginization process: A model for second language acquisition.* Rowley, Mass.: Newbury House.

SCOVEL, THOMAS. 1988. *A time to speak: A psycholinguistic inquiry into the critical period for human speech.* New York: Newbury House.

ADAMAWA LANGUAGES are spoken in eastern Nigeria, northern Cameroon, and southern Chad, with some extension into the Central African Republic. They form one of the two branches of the Adamawa-Ubangi subgroup of the Niger-Congo languages [*qq.v.*]. The internal classification of the Adamawa languages given in Figure 1 is based on Raymond Boyd, 'Adamawa-Ubangi', in *The Niger-Congo languages,* ed. by John Bendor-Samuel (Lanham, Md.: University Press of America, 1989), pp. 178–215.

LANGUAGE LIST

Awak: spoken in Kaltungo District, Gombe Division, Gongola State, Nigeria. Also called Awok.

Bali: 1,000 speakers reported by 1973, in Batta District, Numan Division, Gongola State, Nigeria. Also called Ndagam or Boli.

Bambuka: 10,000 speakers reported in 1973, in Wurkum District, Muri Division, Gongola State, Nigeria.

Bangwinji: spoken in Dadiya District, Gombe Division, Bauchi State, Nigeria. Also called Bangunji.

Besme: spoken in Chad. Also called Huner. Apparently distinct from Besme of the Central African Republic, which is Chadic. May be mutually intelligible with Mambai.

Bolgo: spoken in south central Chad. Also called Bolgo Durag.

FIGURE 1. *Subgrouping of Adamawa Languages*

- Fali
- Gueve
- Kam
- Kwa
- La'bi
- **Leko-Nimbari**
  - **Duru**
    - **Dii**
      - Dii (proper), Duupa, Pape, Saa
    - Duli
    - **Voko-Dowayo**
      - Kutin (Peere)
      - **Vere-Dowayo**
        - Dowayo
        - **Vere-Gimme**
          - **Gimme**
            - Gimme (proper), Gimnime
          - **Vere**
            - Koma, Vere (proper)
      - Voko (Longto)
  - **Leko**
    - Chamba Leko, Dong, Kolbila, Mumbake, Wom
  - **Mumuye-Yandang**
    - **Mumuye**
      - Gengle, Gongla, Kumba, Mumuye (proper), Teme, Waka
    - **Yandang**
      - Bali, Kugama, Passam, Yandang (proper)
  - Nimbari
- **Mbum-Day**
  - **Bua**
    - **Fanya**
      - Fanya (proper), Mana
    - **Unclassified Bua**
      - Bolgo, Bua (proper), Buso, Gula, Koke, Nielim, Tunya
  - Day

Mbum-Day (continued)

  - Kim
  - **Mbum**
    - **Central Mbum**
      - **Karang**
        - Karang (proper), Kari, Pana
      - **Koh-Sakpu**
        - Kuo, Sakpu
    - **Northern Mbum**
      - **Dama-Galke**
        - Dama, Mono, Ndai
      - **Tupuri-Mambai**
        - Mambai, Mundang, Tupuri
    - **(Southern) Mbum**
    - **Unclassified Mbum**
      - Besme, Dek, Lakka, Pam, To
- **Waja-Jen**
  - **Jen**
    - Bambuka, Burak, Gwomu, Janjo, Lelau, Lo, Munga, Panyam
  - Longuda
  - **Waja**
    - **Awak**
      - Awak (proper), Kamo
    - **Cham-Mona**
      - Cham-Mwana, Lotsu-Piri
    - Dadiya
    - **Tula**
      - Bangwinji, Tula (proper), Waja (proper)
  - **Yungur**
    - Libo
    - Mboi
    - **Yungur-Roba**
      - Yungur (proper), Roba
- **Unclassified Adamawa**
  - Budugum, Oblo

Bua: 20,000 speakers reported in 1972, in Chad. Also called Boa or Bwa. Different from Bua (Bwa) of Zaïre, which is Benue-Congo. Most men are bilingual in Arabic.

Budugum: 10,000 speakers reported in 1972, in Chad. Also called Bugudum.

Burak: 2,000 speakers reported in 1976, in Kaltungo District, Gombe Division, Bauchi State, Nigeria.

Buso: 40 to 50 speakers reported in 1971, in Chad. Also called Busso.

Cham-Mwana: spoken in Cham and Dadiya Districts, Gombe Division, Bauchi State, Nigeria. Also called Cham-Mwona or Cham-Mona. Cham and Mwana may be separate languages.

Chamba Leko: spoken by around 42,000 people west of Poli and south of Beka District, Cameroon, in Faro Division, North Province, along the Nigerian border; also in Ndop Subdivision and Bamenda Subdivision, Mezam Division, North West Province. Also in Leko District, Ganye Division, and Suntai District, Wukari Division, Gongola State, Nigeria. Also called Samba Leeko. Distinct from Chamba Daka.

Dadiya: 2,300 speakers reported in 1973, in Dadiya District, Gombe Division, Bauchi State, Nigeria. Also called Dadianci, Nda Dia, Dadia, or Boleri.

Dama: spoken primarily in Chad and in North Province, Cameroon. May be a dialect of Mono.

Day: 1,600 speakers reported in 1971, in Chad and the Central African Republic. Also called Dai.

Dek: spoken in North Province, Cameroon.

Dii: 47,000 speakers reported in 1982, on the plains of Benoue, Benoue Division, and in Tchollire District, Mayo-Rey Division, North Province, Cameroon; also north and east of Ngaoundere, Vina Division, Adamawa Province. Also called Duru, Dourou, Durru, Nyag Dii, Dui, or Zaa. Speakers refer to themselves as Yag Dii. Goom is a related variety.

Dong: spoken in Binyeri District, Adamawa Division, Gongola State, Nigeria. Also called Donga. Different from Dongo (Donga) of Zaïre, which is Ubangi.

Dowayo: 18,000 speakers reported in 1985, in northern Poli Subdivision and around Poli, Benoue Division, North Province, Cameroon. Also called Doohyaayo, Dowayayo, Dooyaayo, Doyayo, Doyau, Donyanyo, Doayo, Tunga, Tuuno, Tungbo, or Nomai. Namshi is a derogatory name sometimes used. The people are called Doowaayo. Perhaps 20 percent of the men are fairly bilingual in Bilkire Fulani for trading and everyday conversation, and 5 percent are bilingual in French.

Duli: spoken near Pitoa, Benoue Division, North Province, Cameroon. Also called Dui. May be the same as Dii.

Duupa: spoken by some 2,000 people east of Poli in Faro and Benoue Divisions, North Province, Cameroon. Also called Nduupa or Dupa.

Fali, North: 16,000 speakers reported in 1982, around Dourbeye and Mayo-Oulo in Mayo-Oulo Subdivision, Mayo-Louti Division, North Province, Cameroon. Speakers are rapidly shifting to Fulfulde.

Fali, South: 20,000 speakers reported in 1982, around Hossere Bapara, Tsolaram, Hossere Toro, and Ndoudja in Pitoa District, Benoue Division, North Province, Cameroon. Different from North Fali and from Fali (Bana) of Nigeria and Cameroon, which is Chadic.

Fanya: 1,500 speakers reported in 1971, in southeast Chad near Singako, between Lake Boli and Lake Iro. Also called Fagnia, Fanyan, or Fana.

Gengle: spoken in Mayo Belwa District, Adamawa Division, Gongola State, Nigeria. Also called Wegele. Possibly the same as Gongla.

Gimme: 3,000 speakers reported in 1982, west of Poli along the Nigerian border in the Atlantika Mountains and on Saptou Plain, Faro Division, North Province, Cameroon. Also called Kompara, Koma Kompana, Panbe, or Gimma. Distinct from Koma Ndera or Gimnime. Speakers call their language Gimma.

Gimnime: 3,000 speakers reported in 1982, northwest of Poli along the Nigerian border and around Wangay in the Atlantika Mountains, Faro Division, North Province, Cameroon. Also called Kadam, Komlama, Gimbe, Koma Kadam, Laame, or Yotubo. Distinct from Kadam (Pokoot) of Uganda and Kenya, and from Koma Ndera and Gimme of Cameroon, but close to Gimme.

Gongla: spoken in Jereng District, Adamawa Division, Gongola State, Nigeria. Also called Bomla, Bajama, or Jareng. Possibly the same as Gengle.

Gueve: now extinct, formerly spoken east of Pitoa in Benoue Division, North Province, Cameroon. Also called Gey or Gewe. The people are ethnically still somewhat distinct, but now speak Fulani.

Gula: spoken by 2,500 or more people in Chad. Different from Gula of Chad and Sudan, which is Nilo-Saharan. Speakers use Sar as a lingua franca.

Gwomu: spoken in Wurkum District, Muri Division, Gongola State, Nigeria. Also called Gwomo. Possibly a dialect of Janjo.

Janjo: 6,100 speakers reported in 1952, in Wurkum District, Muri Division, Gongola State, Nigeria. Also called Jenjo, Jen, Dza, Gwomo, Karenjo, or Njeng.

Kam: spoken in Bakundi District, Muri Division, Gongola State, Nigeria.

Kamo: spoken by around 3,000 people in Kaltungo and West Tangale Districts, Gombe Division, Bauchi State, Nigeria. Also called Kamu.

Karang: 10,000 or more speakers reported in 1982, between Tchollire and Touboro in the Mayo-Rey Division, North Province, Cameroon; also some speakers in Chad. Also called Laka, Lakka, or Kareng. Different from Laka (Kabba Laka) of the Central African Republic and Chad.

Kari: spoken by around 40,000 people, primarily in Chad; also spoken in the northwest Central African Republic and in Adamawa and North Provinces, Cameroon. Also called Karre or Kali. Mutually intelligible with Mbum. Different from Kari of the Central African Republic and Zaïre, which is Bantu.

Kim: spoken in Chad.

Koke: 1,000 speakers reported in 1971, in south central Chad north of Sarh. Also called Khoke. May be mutually intelligible with other languages in the Bua group.

Kolbila: 2,500 speakers reported in 1985, south of Poli in Faro Division, North Province, Cameroon. Also called Kolbilari, Kolena, Kolbili, or Zoono.

Koma: 35,000 speakers reported in 1989, including 32,000 in Koma Vomni District, Ganye Division, Gongola State, Nigeria, and 3,000 in Faro Division, North Province, Cameroon. Also called Kuma. Different from Koma of Ethiopia and Sudan.

Kugama: spoken in Wafanga District, Adamawa Division, Gongola State, Nigeria. Also called Kugamma or Wegam. Possibly a Yandang dialect.

Kumba: spoken in Mayo Belwa District, Adamawa Division, Gongola State, Nigeria. Also called Sate or Yofo.

Kuo: 10,000 speakers reported in 1985, primarily in Chad. Also between Sorombeo and the Chad border, and around Garoua in North Province, Cameroon. Also called Ko or Koh.

Kwa: 1,000 speakers reported in 1973, in Bachama District, Numan Division, Gongola State, Nigeria. Different from Kwa' of Cameroon in the Bamileke group, and from the Kwa family.

La'bi: spoken in Touboro Subdivision, Mayo-Rey Division, North Province, Cameroon. The language of initiation rites practiced by the Gbaya, Mbum, and some Sara-Laka.

Lakka: 500 speakers reported in 1973, in Yola District, Adamawa Division, and in Lau District, Muri Division, Gongola State, Nigeria; may also be spoken in Cameroon. Also called Lau or Lao Habe. Different from Laka (Kabba Laka) of the Central African Republic and Chad.

Lelau: spoken in Wurkum District, Muri Division, Gongola State, Nigeria.

Libo: spoken in Shellem and Mbula Districts, Numan Division, Gongola State, Nigeria. Also called Libbo.

Lo: 2,000 speakers reported in 1973, in Wurkum District, Muri Division, Gongola State, Nigeria.

Longto: 2,400 speakers reported in 1982 around Voko, southwest of Poli to Faro Reserve, North Province, Cameroon. Possibly also spoken in Nigeria. Also called Woko, Boko, Lonto, Longbo, Longa, or Gobeyo.

Longuda: 32,000 speakers reported in 1973, in Longuda District, Numan Division, Gongola State, Nigeria; also in Waja and Cham Districts, Gombe Division, Bauchi State. Also called Nunguda, Nunguraba, Nungura, or Languda.

Lotsu-Piri: 2,000 speakers reported in 1952, in Bachama District, Numan Division, Gongola State, Nigeria. Also called Kitta.

Mambai: 2,500 speakers reported in 1982, along the Mayo-Kebi River in extreme northern Bibemi District, Benoue Division, North Province, Cameroon; also spoken in the adjacent area of Chad. Also called Mangbei, Manbai, Mamgbay, or Mongbay. Speakers are reported to be bilingual in Mundang.

Mana: spoken in Chad.

Mboi: 3,200 speakers reported in 1973, in Song District, Adamawa Division, Gongola State, Nigeria. Also called Mboire or Mboyi.

Mbum: 38,600 speakers reported in 1982, in isolated groups—one south and southwest of Ngaoundere in Vina and Djerem Divisions, Adamawa Province, Cameroon; another northwest of Ngaoundere in Faro Division, North Province; and a third in Belabo Subdivision, Lom and Djerem Division, East Province. 10,000 speakers reported in Chad in 1990. Also called Mboum, Mboumtiba, Wuna, Buna, Nzak Mbay, or Mbai. Speakers are rapidly becoming bilingual in Fulani. Distinct from Mbai, which is Nilo-Saharan.

Mono: 1,100 speakers reported in 1982, north of Rey-Bouba, around Kongrong, along the Mayo-Godi River in Mayo-Rey Division, North Province, Cameroon. Also called Mon-Non. Different from Mono in Zaïre, of the Banda group.

Mumbake: spoken by some 10,000 people in Yelwa and Sugu Districts, Zing Division, Gongola State, Nigeria, and possibly north of Ngoundere in North Province, Cameroon. Also called Mubako or Nyongnepa.

Mumuye: 400,000 speakers reported in 1980, in Mumuye, Lau, Kwajji, Jalingo, and Zing Districts, Muri Division, Gongola State, Nigeria. Also possibly spoken in Cameroon.

Mundang: 100,000 speakers reported in 1982, including 44,700 north and west of Kaele, Far North Province, and south of Mayo-Kebi in Benoue Division, North Province, Cameroon; also spoken in adjacent areas of Chad. Also called Moundan, Kaele, Nda, Marhay, or Musemban. The Gelama variety may be a separate language.

Munga: spoken in Wurkum District, Muri Division, Gongola State, Nigeria.

Ndai: only a few speakers left, in Tchollire, Mayo-Rey Division, North Province, Cameroon. Also called Galke.

Nielim: 2,000 speakers reported in 1971, in south central Chad around Nielim. Also called Mjillem or Nyilem. May be mutually intelligible with Bwa, Tounia, Fanian, Koke, or Day.

Nimbari: 120 or more speakers in Gashaka District, Mambilla Division, Gongola State, Nigeria. Also in North Province, Cameroon, and possibly in Chad. Also called Nyamnyam, Niamniam, Bari, or Nimbari-Kebi.

Oblo: spoken near Tchollire in Mayo-Rey Division, North Province, Cameroon.

Pam: spoken near Tchollire in Mayo-Rey Division, North Province, Cameroon.

Pana: 40,000 speakers reported in 1986, in the northwest Central African Republic; also spoken in Chad, in North Province, Cameroon, and in urban areas of Cameroon and Nigeria. Also called Pani.

Panyam: spoken in Wurkum District, Numan Division, Gongola State, Nigeria.

Pape: 3,000 speakers reported in 1982, southeast of Poli, Faro Division, North Province, Cameroon. Also called Pa'non or Dugun. Has 80 percent lexical similarity with Dii. Speakers refer to themselves as Dugun.

Passam: spoken in Batta District, Numan Division, Gongola State, Nigeria. Also called Nyisam.

Peere: 20,000 speakers reported in 1987, between Tignere and the Nigerian border in Faro and Deo Division, and northeast of Banyo in Mayo-Banyo Division, Adamawa Province, Cameroon; also in Adamawa and Ganye Divisions, Gongola State, Nigeria. Also called Pere, Koutin, Kutine, Kutinn, Kotopo, Kotofo, Kotpojo, Potopo, Potopore, or Patapori. Peer is the name the people use for themselves.

Roba: 30,000 speakers reported in 1973, in Shellem District, Numan Division, and in Ga'anda, Song, and Yungur Districts, Adamawa Division, Gongola State, Nigeria. Also called Lalla, Lala, Robba, or Gworam.

Saa: 3,500 speakers reported in 1982, in the middle of a massif southeast of Poli, Faro Division, North Province, Cameroon. Also called Sari, Saapa, or Yinga.

Sakpu: 7,000 speakers reported in 1982, in Pandjama and Touboro in Mayo-Rey Division, North Province, Cameroon. Also called Pandama.

Teme: spoken in Mayo Belwa District, Adamawa Division, Gongola State, Nigeria. Also called Tema.

To: spoken in Touboro Subdivision, Mayo-Rey Division, North Province, Cameroon; also spoken in the Central African Republic. Said to be a secret male initiation language of the Gbaya, with vocabulary and syntax similar to that of the Mbum languages.

Tula: 19,000 speakers reported in 1973, in Kaltungo District, Gombe Division, Bauchi State, Nigeria. Also called Ture, Kotule, or Kutele.

Tunya: 800 speakers reported in 1971, in the Central African Republic and Chad. Also called Tounia.

Tupuri: 180,000 speakers reported in 1989, with 90,000 on southeastern Moulvouday plain east of Kaele, and in Kar-Hay Subdivision, Mayo-Danay Division, Far North Province, Cameroon, as well as 90,000 in southwest Chad around Fianga. Also called Toubouri, Ndore, Ndoore, Wina, Tongoyna, Honya, Dema, or Mata.

Vere: 20,000 speakers reported in 1982, with 16,000 in Verre District, Adamawa Division, Gongola State, Nigeria, and 4,000 in Cameroon. Also called Verre or Were.

Waja: 30,000 speakers reported in 1973, in Waja District, Gombe Division, Bauchi State, Nigeria. Also called Wagga or Wuya.

Waka: spoken in Lau District, Muri Division, Gongola State, Nigeria.

Wom: 23,000 speakers reported in 1982, with 13,000 southwest of Garoua, North Province, Cameroon, and 10,000 in Adamawa Division, Gongola State, Nigeria. Also called Pereba or Zagai.

Yandang: 10,000 speakers reported in 1973, in Jereng and Kwajji Districts, Adamawa Division, and in Jalingo and Lau Districts, Muri Division, Gongola State, Nigeria. Also called Yendam, Yendang, Nyandang, or Yundum.

Yungur: 44,300 speakers reported in 1963, in Song and Yungur Districts, Adamawa Division, Gongola State, Nigeria. Also called Binna, Ebina, Ebuna, or Buna.

ADAMAWA-UBANGI LANGUAGES (formerly known as Adamawa-Eastern) form one of the major branches of the Niger-Congo family [*q.v.*]. Adamawa-Ubangi languages are spoken in an area from eastern Nigeria through eastern Cameroon, southern Chad, the Central African Republic, and northern Zaïre, and into southwestern Sudan. The family falls into two subgroups, Adamawa and Ubangi. [*For detailed lists of Adamawa-Ubangi languages, see* Adamawa Languages, Ubangi Languages.]

ADDRESS. Forms of address are one of the linguistic means by which speakers mark their psycho-social orientation to their addressees. Forms such as pronouns, names, and terms of endearment encode both status and solidarity relationships between speaker and addressee. (For reference, see R. Brown & Gilman 1960, R. Brown & Ford 1961, Ervin-Tripp 1969, P. Brown & Levinson 1987.)

It appears to be a world-wide phenomenon that PLURAL pronouns can be used to SINGULAR addressees to show respect. In languages where this occurs, speakers have the choice of two forms when addressing someone; they choose between a singular, FAMILIAR form and a plural, POLITE form. These forms are conventionally referred to as T AND V forms; cf. French *tu* and *vous,* from Latin *tū* and *vōs*. (In some languages—e.g. modern German, Italian, and Spanish—third person forms are also used for politeness.)

When people interact, three patterns of pronoun usage are possible: mutual T, mutual V, and asymmetrical usage. Mutual T indicates that the interactants consider themselves to be socially INTIMATE (intimacy is defined in terms of both shared values—kinship, sex, nationality, occupation, etc.—and frequency of contact). Mutual V, conversely, signals that the interactants do not consider themselves to be socially intimate. In symmetrical encounters, then, T forms are seen as encoding INTIMACY and social CLOSENESS, and V forms as encoding RESPECT and social DISTANCE.

Asymmetrical T/V usage is found in interactions where there is a power imbalance: the more powerful speaker has the right to say T and to receive V. In different societies and at different times, the following relationships have been viewed as unequal, and have accordingly been characterized by asymmetrical pronoun usage: master/servant, parent/child, husband/wife, officer/soldier, employer/employee, or customer/waiter.

The use of names mirrors the use of pronouns. Speakers can choose between symmetrical or asymmetrical naming, and symmetrical naming can mark intimacy or distance. In American and British English, for example, the three-way opposition consists of mutual F[irst] N[ame] *(Jane),* mutual T[itle +] L[ast] N[ame] *(Mrs. Jones),* or asymmetrical naming.

Asymmetrical usage encodes relationships of POWER or STATUS, while symmetrical usage encodes SOLIDARITY. The co-existence of these two dimensions means that T forms and FN express both CONDESCENSION and intimacy, while V forms and TLN express both DEFERENCE and distance.

It has been argued that the use of particular address forms to encode deference is one aspect of Negative Politeness; i.e., by using V or TLN, or by saying *Sir/*

Madam, the speaker respects the hearer's 'negative face'. Conversely, the reciprocal use of T forms or FN, or of endearments and terms like *mate* and *buddy,* signals in-group solidarity, and is thus an aspect of Positive Politeness (the speaker pays attention to the hearer's 'positive face'; see P. Brown & Levinson 1987).

Terms of endearment (e.g. *dear, honey*) are unmarked when used symmetrically between people who perceive their relationship as intimate. But these terms are also used asymmetrically in service encounters, where the relationship between server and customer is not one of intimacy. Age and sex seem to be salient categories here: younger customers can be called *dear* by older service personnel, and female customers by male personnel (Wolfson & Manes 1980). Such asymmetrical usage signals condescension; it is interesting to note that the only other context in which asymmetrical use of intimate forms is found is in the family, between parents and children.

Historically, there has been a shift from the STATUS semantic to the SOLIDARITY semantic. This has been well documented for pronouns of address in European languages; symmetrical pronoun usage has become the norm in more and more contexts, and the use of mutual T is slowly growing. The same is true of other address forms: reciprocal FN is expanding at the expense of both reciprocal TLN and asymmetrical naming. This shift seems to reflect the development of more egalitarian societies; in language communities which retain more rigid social stratification, the power semantic continues to prevail linguistically (e.g. Afrikaans). [*See also* Power and Language.]

JENNIFER COATES

BIBLIOGRAPHY

BROWN, PENELOPE, & STEPHEN LEVINSON. 1987. *Politeness: Some universals in language usage.* (Studies in interactional sociolinguistics, 4.) Cambridge & New York: Cambridge University Press.

BROWN, ROGER, & MARGUERITE FORD. 1961. Address in American English. *Journal of Abnormal and Social Psychology* 62.375–385.

BROWN, ROGER, & ALBERT GILMAN. 1960. The pronouns of power and solidarity. In *Style in language,* edited by Thomas A. Sebeok, pp. 253–276. Cambridge, Mass.: MIT Press.

ERVIN-TRIPP, SUSAN M. 1969. Sociolinguistics. In *Advances in experimental social psychology,* edited by Leonard Berkowitz, vol. 4, pp. 93–107. New York: Academic Press.

WOLFSON, NESSA, & JOAN MANES. 1980. Don't 'dear' me! In *Women and language in literature and society,* edited by Sally McConnell-Ginet et al., pp. 79–92. New York: Praeger.

ADELBERT RANGE LANGUAGES

ADELBERT RANGE LANGUAGES are spoken in northern Papua New Guinea. Stephen A. Wurm, *Papuan languages of Oceania* (Tübingen: Narr, 1982), pp. 170–171, combines the Adelbert Range superstock with the Madang superstock to form the Madang–Adelbert Range phylum, a top-level constituent of his controversial Trans–New Guinea phylum [*q.v.*]. He subgroups the Adelbert Range group into constituent families as shown in Figure 1.

LANGUAGE LIST

Abasakur: 760 speakers reported in 1981, in Madang Province.

Amaimon: 370 speakers reported in 1981, in Madang Province.

Apal: 745 speakers reported in 1981, in Angguna village, upper Ramu River area, Madang Province. Also called Emerum.

Atemble: 65 speakers reported in 1981, in Madang Province. Also called Atemple-Apris or Atemple.

Bargam: 3,500 to 4,000 speakers reported in 1987, on the north coast just opposite Karkar Island, Madang Province. Also called Mugil, Bunu, or Saker.

Bepour: 60 speakers reported in 1981, in Madang Province.

Bilakura: 35 speakers reported in 1981, in Madang Province.

Biyom: 380 speakers reported in 1981, southeast of Gende, Madang Province. Also called Sasime.

Bunabun: 500 speakers reported in 1975, in Madang Province. Also called Bunubun or Bububun.

Dimir: 1,700 speakers reported in 1986, in Madang Province. Also called Boskien or Bosiken.

Faita: 60 speakers reported in 1981, in Madang Province.

Hinihon: 1,100 speakers reported in 1981, in Madang Province.

Ikundun: around 1,050 speakers reported in 1981, in Madang Province. Also called Mindivi.

Isabi: 280 speakers reported in 1981, in Madang Province. Also called Maruhia.

Katiati: around 3,300 speakers reported in 1981, in Madang Province.

Koguman: 945 speakers reported in 1981, in Madang Province.

Korak: 205 speakers reported in 1981, in Madang Province.

Kowaki: 30 speakers reported in 1981, in Madang Province.

Maia: 2,500 speakers reported in 1987, on the mainland south of Manam Island, Madang Province. Also called Saki, Turutap, Yakiba, or Maya.

Maiani: around 2,500 speakers reported in 1981, in Madang

FIGURE 1. *Subgrouping of Adelbert Range Languages*

Brahman
  Biyom, Faita, Isabi, Tauya
Josephstaal-Wanang
  Josephstaal
    Osum
    Pomoikan
      Ikundun, Moresada, Pondoma
    Sikan
      Katiati, Sileibi
    Wadaginam
  Wanang
    Atan
      Atemble, Nent
    Emuan
      Apal, Musak
    Paynamar
Mugil-Isumrud-Pihom
  Isumrud
    Dimir
    Kowan
      Korak, Waskia
    Mabuan
      Bunabun, Malas
  Mugil (Bargam)
  Pihom
    Amaimon
    Kaukombaran
      Maia, Maiani, Mala, Miani
    Kumilan
      Bepour, Mauwake, Moere
    Numagenan
      Bilakura, Parawen, Ukuriguma, Usan, Yaben, Yarawata
    Omosan
      Abasakur, Koguman
    Tiboran
      Hinihon, Kowaki, Mawak, Musar, Wanambre
    Wasembo

Province. Also called Tani, Banara, Wagimuda, or Miami. Different from Mala (Banara).

Mala: 770 speakers reported in 1981, east of Bogia, Madang Province. Also called Pay, Banara, Dagoi, Hatzfeldhafen, Malala, Pai, or Dagui. Different from Maiani (Banara), and from Pei (Pai) in the Walio group.

Malas: 220 speakers reported in 1981, near Tokain, Madang Province.

Mauwake: 2,000 speakers reported in 1987, west of Tokain, Madang Province. Also called Ulingan or Mawake.

Mawak: 31 speakers reported in 1981, southwest of Mauwake, Madang Province.

Miani: 1,500 speakers reported in 1987, southeast of Bogia, inland Madang Province. Also called Pila, Bonaputa-Mopu, or Suaru.

Moere: 60 speakers reported in 1981, in Madang Province.

Moresada: 200 speakers reported in 1981, in Madang Province. Also called Murisapa or Murusapa-Sarewa.

Musak: 355 speakers reported in 1981, east of Astrolabe Bay on the Ramu River, Madang Province.

Musar: 685 speakers reported in 1981, inland west of Tokain, Madang Province. Also called Aregerek.

Nent: around 1,770 speakers reported in 1981, in Pasinkap village, central Madang Province. Also called Angaua.

Osum: 580 speakers reported in 1981, in Madang Province.

Parawen: 430 speakers reported in 1981, in Madang Province. Also called Para.

Paynamar: 150 speakers reported in 1975, in Madang Province.

Pondoma: 600 speakers reported in 1981, in Madang Province.

Sileibi: 260 speakers reported in 1981, in Madang Province.

Tauya: 350 speakers reported in 1981, in Madang Province. Also called Inafosa.

Ukuriguma: 135 speakers reported in 1981, in Madang Province.

Usan: 1,300 speakers reported in 1987, in Madang Subprovince, Madang Province. Also called Wanuma.

Wadaginam: 545 speakers reported in 1981, in Madang Province. Also called Wadaginamb.

Wanambre: 490 speakers reported in 1981, in Madang Province. Also called Vanambere.

Wasembo: 590 speakers reported in 1980, west of Ufim, Morobe Province. Also called Gusap, Yankowan, or Biapim.

Waskia: 12,000 speakers reported in 1987, in Karkar Island, Madang Subprovince, Madang Province. Also called Woskia or Vaskia.

Yaben: 700 speakers reported in 1981, in Madang Province.

Yarawata: 100 speakers reported in 1981, in Madang Province.

ADJACENCY.

Word-internal conditioning, of whatever kind, is commonly observed to be LOCAL rather than REMOTE. In rules of derivation and compounding which are conditional on word-class categorizations, it tends to be the category of the immediate base, rather than of forms from which the base may itself be derived, which prohibits or encourages the rules' application. In the case of allomorphy and similar adjustments (such as additions, eliminations, or re-arrangements of formatives), alternations likewise tend to be conditioned by neighboring rather than distant elements. (For general reference, see Harris 1942, Siegel 1978, Williams 1981, Plank 1985, and Carstairs 1987.)

The notion of distance admits of two interpretations: operational and linear. What seems to count in rules of word formation is the preceding category-determining operation, regardless of the location of its exponent. For example, the derivation of Eng. patient nouns in *-ee* is subject to a categorial restriction to verbs; thus it makes no difference whether these verbal bases are formed by suffixation (e.g. $[[magnet]_N\text{-}ize]_V\text{-}ee$) or prefixation (e.g. $[de\text{-}[throne]_N]_V\text{-}ee$). The *-ee* is not syntagmatically contiguous with the verb-forming prefix *de-*, the exponent of the operation upon which the application of *-ee* suffixation is conditional. By contrast, in INFLECTIONAL morphology, there is generally less reason to assign hierarchical constituent structure, corresponding to sequences of operations, to complex words; thus distance is perhaps more appropriately defined linearly, over strings of formatives.

Observations of instances of local word-internal conditioning, in English and elsewhere, have inspired the postulate of a general ADJACENCY CONSTRAINT. Its several versions, accommodated in various theoretical frameworks, differ somewhat in formulation and substance. Their restrictive force is difficult to gauge as long as no principled constraints are imposed on the passing-on of morphological properties throughout subsequent derivational stages or along strings of neighboring formatives, enabling these 'inherited' properties to make their influence felt at a distance. [*See* Inheritance.]

FRANS PLANK

BIBLIOGRAPHY

CARSTAIRS, ANDREW. 1987. *Allomorphy in inflexion.* London: Croom Helm.

HARRIS, ZELLIG S. 1942. Morpheme alternants in linguistic analysis. *Language* 18.169–180.

PLANK, FRANS. 1985. How disgrace-ful. *Acta Linguistica Hafniensia* 19:2.64–80.

SIEGEL, DOROTHY. 1978. The Adjacency Constraint and the theory of morphology. *Northeastern Linguistic Society* 8.189–197. Amherst: University of Massachusetts.

WILLIAMS, EDWIN. 1981. On the notions 'lexically related' and 'head of a word'. *Linguistic Inquiry* 12.245–274.

ADJECTIVES. Although this word class is now considered a major part of speech, it was long held to be a special type of noun ('noun adjective'), and did not achieve autonomous word class status until the late 17th century. Recent references include Ljung 1970, Meys 1975, Levi 1978, Aarts & Calbert 1979, Bartning 1980, Beard 1981, Dixon 1982, Warren 1984, Riegel 1985, and Rusiecki 1985.

The distinguishing feature of the adjective is the fact that it modifies a noun. Accordingly, adjectives function syntactically as pre- or post-modifiers of nouns, or as complements of nouns or nominal clauses. In many languages, adjectives are inflected in agreement with their nominal heads. [*See* Heads.]

Another distinctive feature of adjectives is their ability to suggest characterizing qualities. Indeed, some linguists do not award full adjectival status to those premodifiers which have purely restrictive functions (e.g. *tidal* in *tidal wave,* or *previous* in *the previous chapter*), or to complements which simply denote states (e.g. *be asleep*).

Characterizing and state-denoting adjectives frequently refer to features which are perceived as variable in degree. If so, the adjective becomes gradable. A gradable adjective can be modified by adverbs of degree, and can occur in comparative *(sweeter)* and superlative *(sweetest)* forms. [*See* Gradation.]

Adjectives may also be modified by prefixes (e.g. *unkind, hyperactive*), by nouns *(grass-green),* and by other adjectives *(red hot).* In the latter two cases, they normally form compound adjectives. By means of derivational suffixes, including so-called zero-suffixation, adjectives can be converted into nouns, verbs, and almost regularly into adverbs. [*See* Derivational Morphology.] In many languages, it is also possible to use adjectives as heads of noun phrases without the addition of an affix *(the poor and the rich).*

BEATRICE WARREN

BIBLIOGRAPHY

AARTS, JAN M. G., & JOSEPH P. CALBERT. 1979. *Metaphor and non-metaphor: The semantics of adjective-noun combinations.* (Linguistische Arbeiten, 74.) Tübingen: Niemeyer.

BARTNING, INGE. 1980. *Remarques sur la syntaxe et la sémantique de pseudo-adjectifs dénominaux en français.* 2d ed. Stockholm: Almqvist & Wiksell.

BEARD, ROBERT. 1981. *The Indo-European lexicon: A full synchronic theory.* (North-Holland linguistic series, 44.) Amsterdam: North-Holland.

DIXON, ROBERT M. W. 1982. *Where have all the adjectives gone? and other essays in semantics and syntax.* (Janua linguarum, Series minor, 107.) Berlin: Mouton.

LEVI, JUDITH N. 1978. *The syntax and semantics of complex nominals.* New York: Academic Press.

LJUNG, MAGNUS. 1970. *English denominal adjectives.* Göteborg: Acta Universitatis Gothoburgensis.

MEYS, W. J. 1975. *Compound adjectives in English and the ideal speaker-listener: A study of compounds in a transfor-*

mational-generative framework. (North-Holland linguistic series, 18.) Amsterdam: North-Holland.

RIEGEL, MARTIN. 1985. *L'adjectif attribut.* Paris: Presses Universitaires de France.

RUSIECKI, JAN. 1985. *Adjectives and comparison in English: A semantic study.* London: Longman.

WARREN, BEATRICE. 1984. *Classifying adjectives.* (Gothenburg studies in English, 56.) Göteborg: Acta Universitatis Gothoburgensis.

ADJUNCTION. In the theory of generative grammar, TRANSFORMATIONS [*q.v.*] are said to map phrase markers into other phrase markers. Transformational operations are composed of elementary operations of permutation, deletion, copying, etc. (cf. Chomsky 1955:339–340). Transformations of permutation, or movement, are of two types: adjunction and substitution.

SUBSTITUTION transformations (formally defined in Chomsky 1955:350) replace one terminal element with another without effecting any change in the structure produced by the phrase structure rules. The moved category is thus placed in a structural position which is generated independently of the transformational operation. An example is Raising to Subject (**e** is the identity element):

(1a) **e** *appears* [$_S$ *Harry to like music*].
(1b) *Harry appears* [$_S$ *to like music*].

Raising to Subject is a substitution operation which replaces **e** in the matrix subject position of ex. 1a with the moved N[oun] P[hrase] *Harry,* deriving 1b.

ADJUNCTION transformations differ from substitution transformations in that further structure is created at the LANDING SITE of movement (Baltin 1978). Three kinds of adjunction have been discussed in the generative literature—SISTER ADJUNCTION, CHOMSKY ADJUNCTION, and DAUGHTER ADJUNCTION. These operations are illustrated schematically in Figure 1a-c. All types of adjunction can place material to the right or to the left of the node adjoined to; here the various types of adjunction to the right are illustrated.

These operations can be exemplified with rules proposed by Ross 1967. That work formulates EXTRAPOSITION as a rule which sister-adjoins a S[entence] to either a containing V[erb] P[hrase] or a containing S (Ross, p. 110). The operation of the rule is shown in Figure 2. Here S is sister-adjoined either to VP or to S (Ross does

FIGURE 1. *Types of Adjunction.* (a) Sister adjunction of X to VP; (b) Chomsky adjunction of X to S; (c) Daughter adjunction of X to VP.

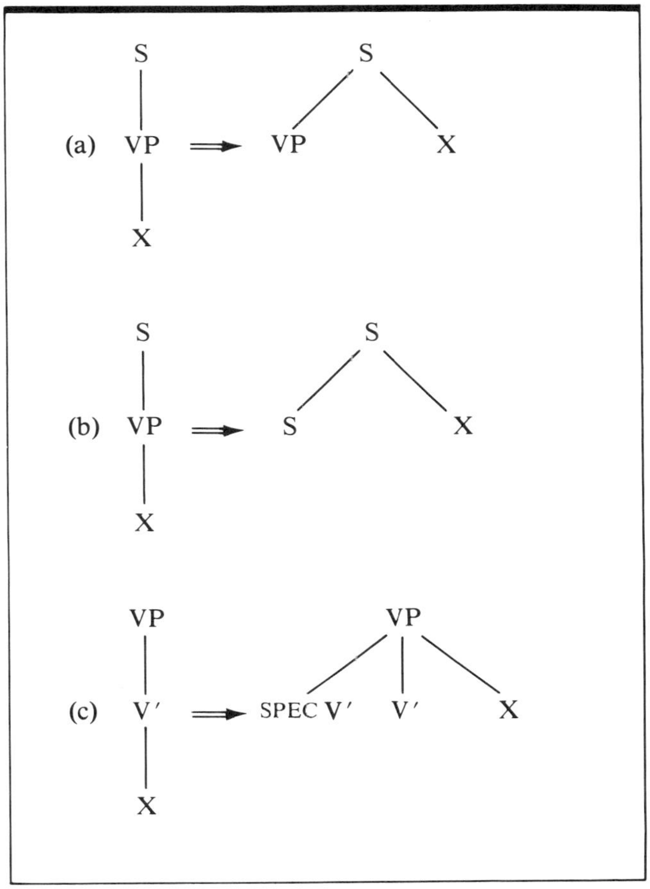

not take a position on which possibility is correct). A later rule deletes *it*—resulting in an instance of 'vacuous extraposition', as no reordering takes place.

Relative Clause Formation is formulated as a Chomsky adjunction (Ross, p. 113). The operation of this rule is illustrated in Figure 3. The second occurrence of *the boy* is here Chomsky-adjoined to the S which contains it. A later rule presumably changes the second occurrence of *the boy* into a relative pronoun.

It-Replacement, a precursor of the rule of raising in ex. 1, is illustrated by Figure 4a–b (Ross, p. 158; cf. also Rosenbaum 1967). The subject of the S contained in the subject NP of Fig. 4a is substituted for *it* (this is an alternative formulation of the substitution operation discussed above); the remnant of that S, *for to like music,* is daughter-adjoined to the matrix VP. In this way, Fig. 4b is derived from Fig. 4a. *For* is deleted by a later rule, giving the correct surface structure.

FIGURE 2. *Extraposition*

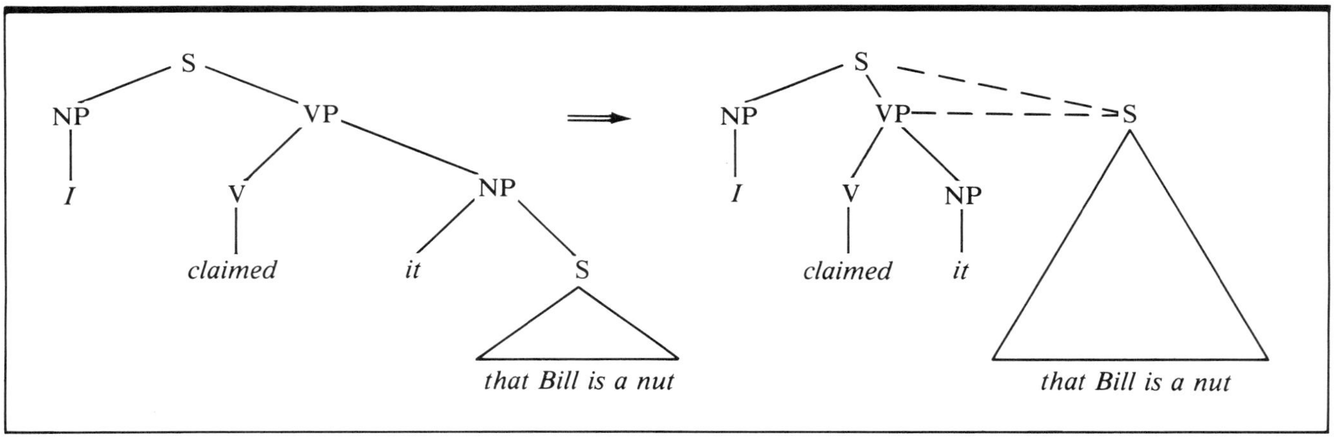

FIGURE 3. *Relative Clause Formation*

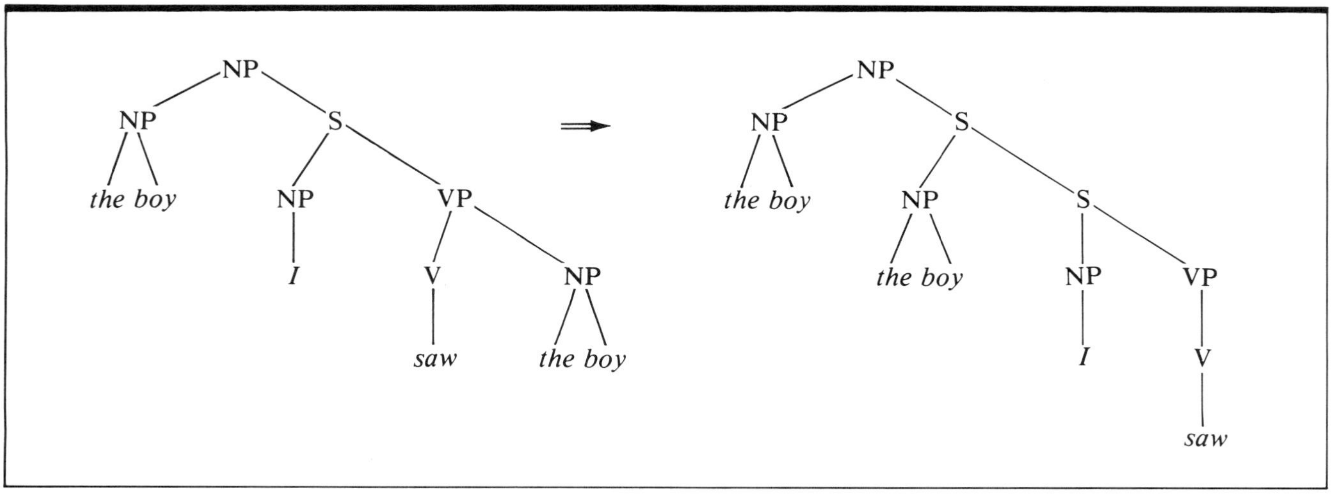

FIGURE 4. It-*Replacement*

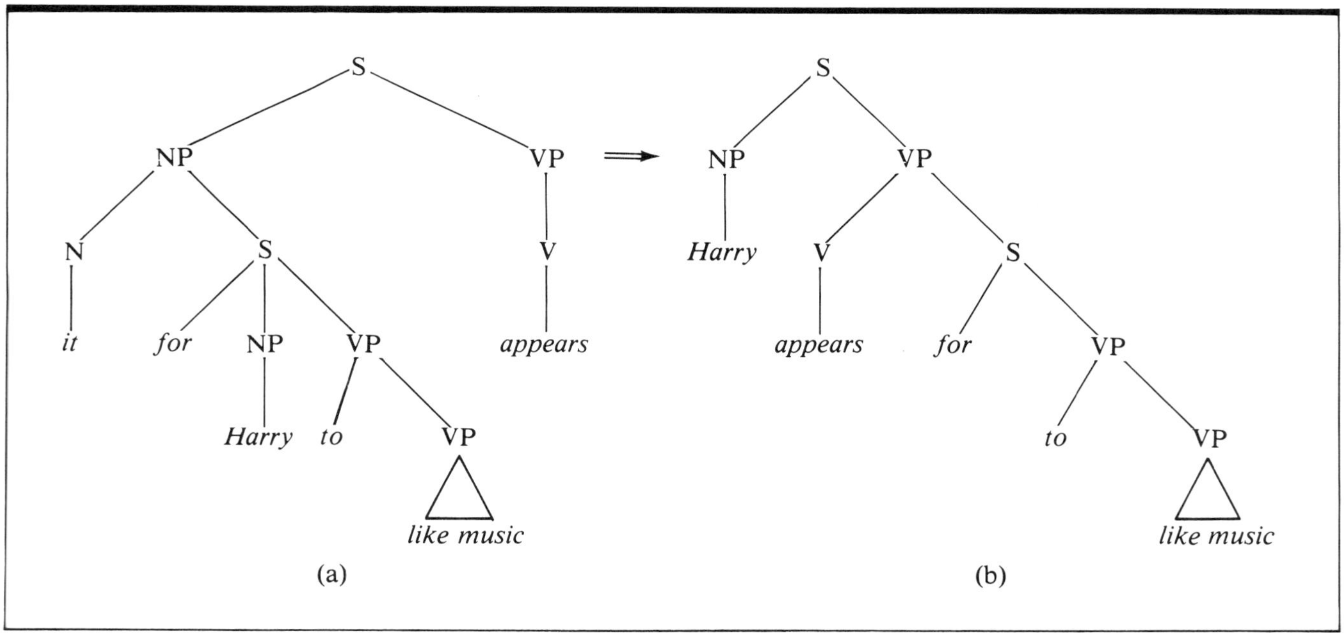

An emphasis on restricting the power of transformations, characteristic of later versions of generative grammar, led to the proposal that only Chomsky adjunction was possible. This operation, unlike the other two, preserves intact the internal structure of the category adjoined to (cf. Chomsky 1981:141, fn. 39; and Riemsdijk's Principle of External Adjunction, 1978:284). May 1985 and Chomsky 1986 develop a rich theory of adjunction which has given rise to much discussion.

IAN G. ROBERTS

BIBLIOGRAPHY

BALTIN, MARK R. 1978. *Toward a theory of movement rules.* MIT dissertation. Published, New York: Garland, 1985.

CHOMSKY, NOAM. 1955. *The logical structure of linguistic theory.* Published, New York: Plenum, 1975. Reprinted, Chicago: University of Chicago Press, 1985.

CHOMSKY, NOAM. 1981. *Lectures on government and binding.* (Studies in generative grammar, 9.) Dordrecht: Foris.

CHOMSKY, NOAM. 1986. *Barriers.* (Linguistic Inquiry monographs, 13.) Cambridge, Mass.: MIT Press.

MAY, ROBERT. 1985. *Logical Form: Its structure and derivation.* (Linguistic Inquiry monographs, 12.) Cambridge, Mass.: MIT Press.

RIEMSDIJK, HENK C. VAN. 1978. *A case study in syntactic markedness: The binding nature of prepositional phrases.* Lisse, Netherlands: de Ridder.

ROSENBAUM, PETER S. 1967. *The grammar of English predicate complement constructions.* Cambridge, Mass.: MIT Press.

ROSS, JOHN ROBERT. 1967. *Constraints on variables in syntax.* MIT dissertation. Published as *Infinite syntax* (Norwood, N.J.: Ablex, 1986).

ADMIRALTY ISLANDS LANGUAGES

ADMIRALTY ISLANDS LANGUAGES are spoken in Papua New Guinea, on the Admiralty Islands (to the north of the island of New Guinea); they constitute a top-level component of Oceanic [*q.v.*]. The subgrouping of the Admiralty Islands languages given in Figure 1 is based on Merritt Ruhlen, *A guide to the world's languages,* vol. 1, *Classification* (Stanford, Calif.: Stanford University Press, 1987).

FIGURE 1. *Subgrouping of Admiralty Islands Languages*

Eastern Admiralty Islands
- **Manus**
  - **Northwest Islands**
    - Andra-Hus, Bipi, Hermit, Leipon, Loniu, Ponam, Sori-Harengan
  - **West Manus**
    - Bohuai, Levei-Ndrehet, Likum, Lindrou, Mondropolon
  - **East Manus**
    - Elu, Ere, Kele, Koro, Kurti, Lele, Mokerang, Nali, Okro, Papitalai, Titan
- **Southeast Islands**
  - Baluan-Pam, Lenkau, Lou, Nauna, Pak-Tong, Penchal

Western Admiralty Islands
- **Ninigo**
  - Kaniet, Seimat
- Wuvulu (Wuvulu-Aua)

LANGUAGE LIST

Andra-Hus: 810 speakers reported in 1977, in Andra and Hus islands, Manus Province. Also called Ahus or Ha'us. Speakers are bilingual in Kurti.

Baluan-Pam: 1,000 speakers reported in 1982, in Baluan and Pam islands, Manus Province. Speakers are moderately bilingual in Lou or Titan.

Bipi: 530 speakers reported in 1977, in Maso, Matahei, and Salapai villages, Bipi and Sisi islands, west coast of Manus Province. Also called Sisi-Bipi.

Bohuai: 1,400 speakers reported in 1982, in Manus Province. Also called Pahavai, Pelipowai, Bowai, Pohuai, or Tulu-Bohuai. Speakers are bilingual in Kurti, Titan, or Ere.

Elu: 215 speakers reported in 1983, on the north coast of Manus Island, Manus Province. Most speakers are bilingual in Kurti.

Ere: 800 speakers reported in 1982, in Drabitou, Lohe, Londru, Metawari, Pau, Piterait, Taui-Undrau, Hatwara, and Loi villages, south coast of Manus Province. Some speakers are bilingual in Kele.

Hermit: 20 elderly speakers reported in 1977, on Luf and Maron islands, Western Manus Province. Also called Agomes, Luf, or Maron.

Kaniet: extinct since 1950, formerly spoken on the western Anchorite and Kaniet islands, Manus Province.

Kele: 600 speakers reported in 1982, in Buyang, Droia, Kawaliap, Koruniat, and Tingau, on the south coast and inland in Manus Province. Also called Gele'. Speakers are bilingual in Kurti and Ere.

Koro: 400 speakers reported in 1983, in Manus Province.

Kurti: some 2,300 speakers reported in 1982, on the north central coast, Manus Province. Also called Kuruti or Kuruti-Pare.

Leipon: 650 speakers reported in 1977, in Lolo village, Hauwai, Ndrilo, and Pityilu islands, Manus Province. Also called Pitilu or Pityilu. Speakers are highly bilingual in Lele.

Lele: some 1,300 speakers reported in 1982, in Manus Island. Also called Hai, Usiai, Moanus, Manus, or Elu-Kara.

Lenkau: 250 speakers reported in 1982, in one village on southwest Rambutyo Island, Manus Province. Speakers are bilingual in Titan or Penchal.

Levei-Ndrehet: 1,160 speakers reported in 1981, in Manus Province. Also called Levei, Lebei, or Lebej.

Likum: 100 speakers reported in 1977, in Manus Province. Speakers are all bilingual in Lindrou.

Lindrou: 3,000 speakers reported in 1985, in Manus Province. Also called Nyindrou, Lindau, Salien, or Nyada. Speakers are bilingual in Kurti.

Loniu: 460 speakers reported in 1977, in Lolak and Loniu villages, on the south coast of Los Negros Island, Manus Province. Also called Lonio or Ndroku. Speakers are moderately bilingual in Lele or Papitalai.

Lou: 600 speakers reported in 1982, on Lou Island, Manus Province. Speakers are highly bilingual in Baluan-Pam or Titan. Distinct from Torricelli (Lou) in East Sepik Province or Tate (Lou) in Gulf Province.

Mokerang: 200 speakers reported in 1981, on north Los Negros Island and Ndrilo Island, Manus Province. Also called Mokareng or Mokoreng.

Mondropolon: 300 speakers reported in 1981, on the north central coast of Manus Island, Manus Province. Most speakers are bilingual in Kurti.

Nali: some 1,800 speakers reported in 1982, on southeast Manus Island, Manus Province. Also called Yiru. Speakers are moderately bilingual in Lele.

Nauna: 130 speakers reported in 1977, on Nauna Island, Manus Province. Also called Naune. Speakers are bilingual in Titan.

Okro: 200 speakers reported in 1981, on the south central coast northwest of Titan, Manus Province.

Pak-Tong: 970 speakers reported in 1977, on Pak and Tong Islands, Manus Province. Also called Tong-Pak.

Papitalai: 520 speakers reported in 1977, in Naringel and Papitalai, Los Negros Island, Manus Province. Speakers are moderately bilingual in Loniu.

Penchal: 550 speakers reported in 1982, on Rambutyo Island, Manus Province. Speakers are moderately bilingual in Titan.

Ponam: 420 speakers reported in 1977, on Ponam Island, Manus Province. Speakers are moderately bilingual in Kurti.

Seimat: 600 speakers reported in 1982, on the Ninigo Islands and the Anchorite Islands, western Manus Province. Also called Ninigo.

Sori-Harengan: 570 speakers reported in 1977, on the northwest coast of Manus Island and on the Sori and Harengan islands off its coast, Manus Province. Speakers are moderately bilingual in Lindrou.

Titan: around 3,000 speakers reported in 1987, on M'buke, Mouk, and Rambutyo islands, Manus Province. Also called Manus, Moanus, Tito, or M'bunai.

Wuvulu-Aua: 1,000 speakers reported in 1982, on Aua, Durour, Maty, and Wuvulu islands, western Manus Province. Also called Aua-Viwulu or Viwulu-Aua.

AFFIXATION is the technique of concatenating affixes—morphological (not lexical) elements which are non-words—either directly to roots, or to affixes in the case of affix cumulation, e.g. *conven-tion-al-iz-ation.* This 'concatenative morphology' is generally more common than other techniques (conversion, ablaut, umlaut—or subtraction, as in dialectal German *hond* 'dog', *hon* 'dog-s', cf. Dressler et al. 1987).

Affixes which follow roots are SUFFIXES, e.g. *dark-en(-ed)*; affixes which precede roots are PREFIXES, e.g. *(re-)en-list.* Suffixes are in general more common than prefixes (Cutler et al. 1985), and both are more common than other types of affix. The combination of a prefix and a suffix (e.g. *en-light-en*) is classified by some as a CIRCUMFIX or AMBIFIX, but only when the prefix and suffix parts are not themselves autonomous (cf. *en-* and *-en* in *en-light-en,* cf. *en-list, dark-en*), but rather are divided parts of an autonomous affix.

An INFIX is an affix which divides the root by being inserted into it, e.g. the Latin *n-* infix in *vi/n/c-ō* 'I win' vs. *vīc-ī* 'I won' (cf. Moravcsik 1977). An INTERFIX is a meaningless affix inserted between words (e.g. Spanish *-i-* in *pel-i-rrojo* 'red-haired' from *pelo* 'hair' and *rojo* 'red'), or between root and suffix (e.g. Spanish *-eg-* in *pedr-eg-oso* 'rocky', adjective from *piedra* 'rock', similar to *pel-oso* 'hairy' from *pelo*; cf. Dressler and Merlini 1990). The existence of TRANSFIXES (infixed circumfixes, Mel'čuk 1982) is dubious; see Kilani-Schoch & Dressler 1984.

WOLFGANG U. DRESSLER

BIBLIOGRAPHY

CUTLER, ANNE; JOHN A. HAWKINS; & GARY GILLIGAN. 1985. The suffixing preference: A processing explanation. *Linguistics* 23.723–758.

DRESSLER, WOLFGANG U., et al. 1987. *Leitmotifs in Natural Morphology.* (Studies in Language, Companion series, 10.) Amsterdam: Benjamins.

DRESSLER, WOLFGANG U., & LAVINIA MERLINI. 1990. How to fix interfixes? *Acta Linguistica Hungarica,* to appear.

KILANI-SCHOCH, MARIANNE, & WOLFGANG U. DRESSLER. 1984. Natural morphology and classical vs. Tunisian Arabic. *Wiener Linguistische Gazette* 33/34.51–68. Also in *Studia Gramatyczne* 7.27–47, 1985.

MEL'ČUK, IGOR A. 1982. *Towards a language of linguistics:*

A system of formal notions for theoretical morphology. Munich: Fink.

MORAVCSIK, EDITH A. 1977. *On rules of infixing.* Bloomington: Indiana University Linguistics Club.

AFRICAN LANGUAGES. The African continent forms one of the most complex linguistic areas of the world; estimates of the number of languages spoken there range from seven hundred to three thousand. Barely more than one hundred have developed into standard languages. The majority of the languages are still unrecorded; for many, little but the name is known. Although early descriptions of African languages date back to the 17th century, African linguistics as a research field developed only during the 19th century.

1. Genetic classification. Until the 1950s, work on the linguistic classification of African languages was dominated by a threefold division into 'Hamitic', 'Sudanic', and 'Bantu' languages (Meinhof 1936, Westermann 1935). This classification was based on a mixture of genetic/diachronic and typological/synchronic criteria; it was also used to develop a theory of the typological evolution of languages from an isolating structure (Sudanic) via an agglutinating stage (Bantu) to an inflectional (Hamitic) type.

The work of Greenberg 1955 marks a milestone in the history of language classification in Africa. It proposed a genetic classification of African languages into sixteen families; Greenberg 1963 presented a revised classification which reduced the number to four—Niger-Congo, Afro-Asiatic, Khoisan, and Nilo-Saharan (see Map 1). This work differs from that of various European scholars mainly in that it relies entirely on material relevant to

MAP 1. *Distribution of African Language Families*

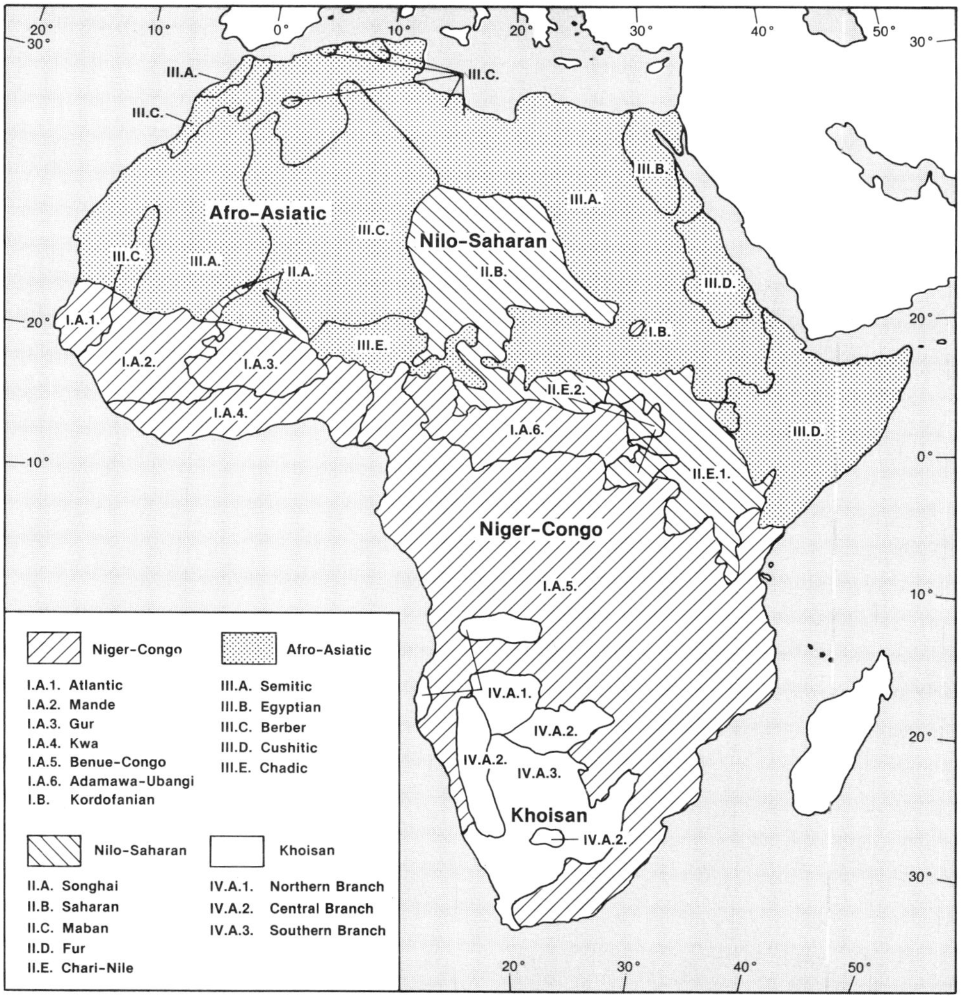

genetic classification, as opposed to typological, areal, or other kinds of organization. Greenberg's methodological principles are: (i) the sole relevance of forms; (ii) mass comparison, as against isolated comparisons between pairs of languages; and (iii) the exclusive use of linguistic evidence (Greenberg 1963:1). The last principle might seem redundant, but the history of language classification in Africa provides a number of cases where non-linguistic data have been adduced in order to define linguistic relationships.

The NIGER-CONGO family [*q.v.*], in its current revision, contains by far the largest number of languages. It includes Kordofanian, a group of languages spoken in the western part of the Republic of the Sudan as well as most of the languages of western, central, and southern Africa, belonging to such groups as Atlantic, Mande, Gur, Kwa, Benue-Congo, and Adamawa-Ubangi [*qq.v.*]. The Benue-Congo branch includes more than three hundred Bantu languages, which in earlier classifications had been treated as a separate family. Some of the most important African languages belong to Niger-Congo, e.g. Swahili [*q.v.*], Zulu, Kikongo, Yoruba [*q.v.*], Igbo, Twi, Manding (Bambara, Malinke, Dyula), Fula, and Wolof.

The AFRO-ASIATIC family [*q.v.*], also called Erythraic or 'Hamito-Semitic', is distributed throughout northern and eastern Africa. It includes the following sub-families: Semitic, Berber, Cushitic, Chadic, and extinct Egyptian [*qq.v.*]. With the exception of Semitic, all Afro-Asiatic languages are spoken exclusively on the African continent. While a number of Semitic languages are now spoken in Africa, they all originated in the Arabian peninsula. The Afro-Asiatic family includes such major African languages as Arabic [*q.v.*], Hausa [*q.v.*], Amharic [*q.v.*], Oromo (Galla), and Somali [*q.v.*].

Most of the NILO-SAHARAN languages [*q.v.*] are found in the area of the Congo-Nile divide. This family includes the following branches: Songhai, Saharan, Maban, Fur, Chari-Nile, and Komuz. With the exception of Saharan and Chari-Nile, these branches consist essentially of one language each. Among the better known Nilo-Saharan languages are Nubian and Maasai (both of the Chari-Nile branch), and Kanuri, a Saharan language spoken to the west of Lake Chad.

KHOISAN [*q.v.*], referred to in Greenberg's earlier writings as the 'Click family', includes the languages of the San ('Bushmen') and Khoekhoe ('Hottentots') of southern and southwestern Africa—as well as two East African 'click languages', Sandawe and Hadza, both spoken in central Tanzania.

The overall framework of genetic classification proposed by Greenberg 1963 has remained largely unchanged since that date. However, a number of revisions have been proposed, and some have been accepted by the majority of Africanists. One issue concerns the relationship between two of the four language families. According to Gregersen 1972, Niger-Kordofanian and Nilo-Saharan belong to a single macro-family, which he proposes to call 'Kongo-Saharan'. Another topic of research has been the position of the Mande languages; Greenberg placed them in Niger-Congo, but other authors claim that they are not even part of Niger-Kordofanian (Mukarovsky 1966, Köhler 1975:240–45).

Khoisan, as a genetic unit, is accepted by the majority of scholars, with one exception: Hadza, the language of a few hundred traditional hunter-gatherers in the Lake Eyasi basin of northern Tanzania, shows relationships with Cushitic. The implications for the relationship between Khoisan and Afro-Asiatic, which includes Cushitic, remain to be investigated.

Although Greenberg's work represents considerable progress over that of previous writers, it leaves a number of questions open. His approach is largely inadequate for the PROOF of genetic relationship; it can do little more than offer initial hypotheses, to be substantiated by more reliable techniques like the comparative method. In a number of instances, languages or language groups have been placed in a given family solely on the basis of a handful of 'look-alikes', i.e. morphemes of similar sound shape and meaning. The Nilo-Saharan family, in particular, must be regarded as a tentative grouping, the genetic unity of which remains to be established.

Observations like these have led some scholars to reject macro-level classifications, and to concentrate on small-scale comparisons which involve only a limited number of closely related languages. This was the policy adopted by the International African Institute in its monograph series 'Handbook of African Languages', published between 1948 and 1967. Other scholars have proposed 'practical', referential classifications, based on arbitrary criteria; these provide convenient reference systems, but are of limited scientific use. The best known of these classifications is that of Guthrie 1948 for Bantu; another has been proposed by Dalby 1970 for the entire continent. [*For data on individual African languages, see the Language Lists following the articles on the language families listed above as well as the list of unclassified languages at the end of this article.*]

2. Typological and areal characteristics. Language comparison in Africa has overwhelmingly been confined to diachronic studies, especially to the reconstruction of patterns of genetic relationship. Interest in other kinds of linguistic classification has been limited. Until the 1950s, studies on the typology of African languages were based largely on a framework going back to Schlegel (cf. Doke 1950). However, the work of Houis 1970, 1971 marks a departure from 19th century typology. He correlates phonological and morphological features with word order, and distinguishes two main types in Africa. The first type has head + attribute word order, with noun + adjective and preposition + noun constructions—as well as both closed and open syllables, complex word structure, and rich morphology; this type lacks a phonemic contrast between oral and nasal vowels. Examples include West Atlantic languages like Fula, Temne, Diola, and Wolof as well as Hausa, the Bantu languages, and Nilotic languages like Acholi or Kalenjin. The second type has *rectum-regens* order (e.g. noun + postposition), open syllables only, simple word structure, and limited morphology; but there is a productive pattern of nominal compounding as well as distinct nasal vowels. Examples are the languages of the Voltaic, Mande, and Kwa groups of the Niger-Congo family.

Based on work on the order of meaningful elements (Greenberg 1966), a word-order typology of more than three hundred African languages has been presented by Heine 1975, 1976, and by Heine & Vossen (1981:422–436). Their taxonomy distinguishes eight discrete types, based on word order and on the presence vs. absence of a noun class system, of nominal case inflection, and of derivative verbal extension.

Like typology, areal linguistics is still a greatly underdeveloped field in Africa, although areal considerations have usually played a role in works on language classification. For instance, ten of the fourteen criteria listed by Westermann 1935 in defining the 'Sudanic' family—a grouping of several hundred languages, spoken in a broad belt from the extreme west to the extreme east of Africa—are suggestive of an areal relationship. Although systematic research is still lacking, it seems that the structures of African languages can be correlated with combinations of genetic and areal factors. The Ethiopian Highlands can be defined as a kind of *Sprachbund* or LANGUAGE AREA. Of the six branches of the Afro-Asiatic family found there, three—Cushitic, Omotic, and Ethiopian Semitic—show a number of features which are virtually absent from Afro-Asiatic languages outside the area, but which are shared by non-Afro-Asiatic languages within it, e.g. the presence of ejective consonants and of Subject-Object-Verb syntax.

3. Features characteristic of African languages. None of the attempts made in the past has succeeded in proving that the African languages form a historical and/or typological unit. However, there are some features which are found only in Africa, or which are widespread there. Thus click consonants occur in three of the four African language families; but while they are found throughout the Khoisan family, they occur in only one Afro-Asiatic language, Dahalo; and of the Niger-Congo languages, they are found only in those spoken in the vicinity of Khoisan, i.e. the Bantu languages of southern Africa.

Other noteworthy phonological characteristics of African languages include the widespread occurrence of complex tone systems, of vowel harmony, and of implosive or labiovelar consonants (*kp, gb*). African consonant systems have rightly been described as 'simple' (Greenberg 1959:23); however, the language with the largest number of consonants in the world is thought to be !Xóõ (/Hua-Owani), a Khoisan language of Botswana and Namibia, which has 117 consonant phonemes (Traill 1985).

The majority of African languages have a system of noun classes, or genders. For one language, Zande, a Niger-Congo language of the Adamawa-Ubangi branch, the origin of a gender system has been described in detail (Claudi 1985). By contrast, there is a conspicuous lack of ergative languages in Africa. So far, only two have been reported: Loma, a Mande language, and Anuak, a Western Nilotic language of the Nilo-Saharan family.

Semantic features which are characteristic of many African languages include the following: comparison is expressed by means of the verb 'defeat' ('X is big, defeats Y' = 'X is bigger than Y'); feeling and understanding by the verb 'see' or 'hear' ('I don't see/hear you' = 'I don't understand you'); conquering or having sexual intercourse, by the verb 'eat'; and smoking by the verb 'drink' ('Do you drink cigarettes?' = 'Do you smoke?').

The expression of spatial organization in terms of body parts is very common, with typical metaphorical equations such as these (Heine 1986:4):

(1)	'head'	'above, upon, in front'
	'eye'	'before, in front'
	'face'	'in front'
	'back'	'behind'
	'buttock'	'under, behind'
	'belly'	'inside'

'heart' 'in the middle'
'foot/leg' 'under, below'

In many African languages, though not all, spatial orientation is structured differently than in European languages (cf. Hill 1974). In English, for instance, objects which do not have an inherent front-back orientation, like mountains or trees, are conceived as facing the speaker or deictic center. Thus *The tree is in front of the mountain* means that the tree is located between the mountain and the speaker, since the mountain is assumed to face the speaker. In many African languages, by contrast, such objects are conceived as facing in the SAME direction as the speaker or deictic center. Thus, in the example, the mountain is 'looking' in the same direction as the speaker, and therefore turns its 'back' to him/her. A tree between mountain and speaker is 'behind' rather than 'in front of' the mountain.

4. Lingua francas. The majority of African nations use European languages for official purposes—in most cases, English or French (in Cameroon, both of these). A few African languages have been recognized as national official media, e.g. Swahili in Tanzania, Amharic in Ethiopia, and Somali in Somalia. National and international communication in Africa is determined to some extent by the distribution of indigenous lingua francas, i.e. languages which are used habitually between people whose mother tongues are different (see Map 2). Some

MAP 2. *Lingua Francas of Africa*

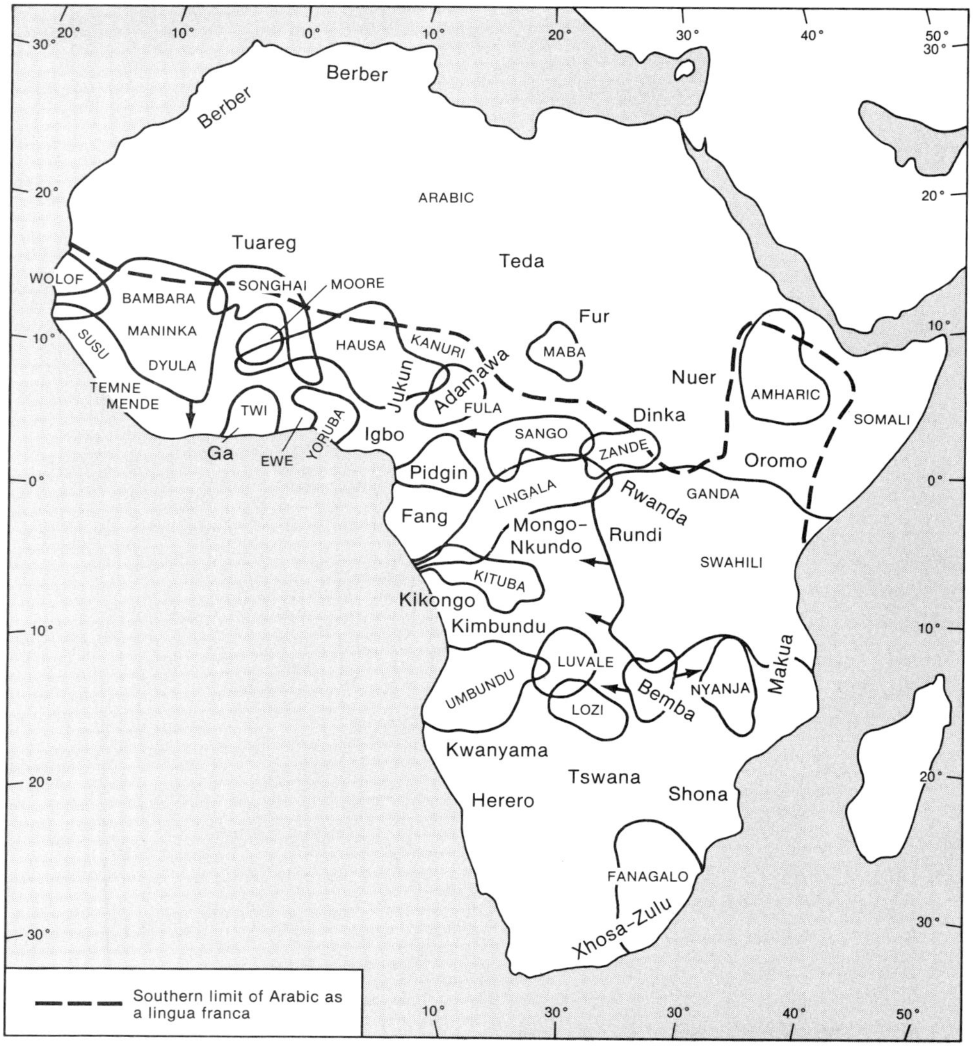

of these, like Swahili in East Africa or Maninka in West Africa, have spread over areas almost as large as Europe (see Heine 1970). Some have assumed the role of de facto national languages, e.g. Swahili in Kenya, Sango in Central Africa, Bambara (a variety of Maninka) in Mali, and Wolof in Senegal.

BERND HEINE

BIBLIOGRAPHY

CLAUDI, ULRIKE. 1985. *Zur Entstehung von Genussystemen: Überlegungen zu einigen theoretischen Aspekten, verbunden mit einer Fallstudie des Zande.* Hamburg: Buske.

DALBY, DAVID. 1970. Reflections on the classification of African languages, with special reference to the work of Sigismund Wilhelm Koelle and Malcolm Guthrie. *African Language Studies* 11.147–171.

DOKE, CLEMENT M. 1950. Bantu languages, inflexional with a tendency towards agglutination. *African Studies* 9.1–19.

GREENBERG, JOSEPH H. 1955. *Studies in African linguistic classification.* New Haven, Conn.: Compass.

GREENBERG, JOSEPH H. 1959. Africa as a linguistic area. In *Continuity and change in African cultures,* edited by William R. Bascom & Melville J. Herskovits, pp. 15–27. Chicago: University of Chicago Press.

GREENBERG, JOSEPH H. 1963. *The languages of Africa.* (Indiana University Research Center in Anthropology, Folklore, and Linguistics, Publication 25; International Journal of American Linguistics, 29:1, part 2.) Bloomington.

GREENBERG, JOSEPH H. 1966. Some universals of grammar with particular reference to the order of meaningful elements. In *Universals of language,* 2d ed., edited by Joseph H. Greenberg, pp. 73–113. Cambridge, Mass.: MIT Press.

GREGERSEN, EDGAR A. 1972. Kongo-Saharan. *Journal of African Languages* 11.69–89.

GUTHRIE, MALCOLM. 1948. *The classification of Bantu languages.* London & New York: Oxford University Press.

HEINE, BERND. 1970. *Status and use of African lingua francas.* (Afrika-Studien, 49.) Munich: Weltforum.

HEINE, BERND. 1975. Language typology and convergence areas in Africa. *Linguistics* 144.27–47.

HEINE, BERND. 1976. *A typology of African languages, based on the order of meaningful elements.* (Kölner Beiträge zur Afrikanistik, 4.) Berlin: Reimer.

HEINE, BERND. 1986. *The rise of grammatical categories: Cognition and language change in Africa.* (Sixteenth Annual Hans Wolff Memorial Lecture.) Bloomington: African Studies Program, Indiana University.

HEINE, BERND, & RAINER VOSSEN. 1981. Sprachtypologie. In *Die Sprachen Afrikas,* edited by Bernd Heine et al., pp. 407–444. Hamburg: Buske.

HILL, CLIFFORD ALDEN. 1974. Spatial perception and linguistic encoding: A case study in Hausa and English. *Studies in African Linguistics,* Suppl. 5, pp. 135–148. Los Angeles: UCLA.

HOUIS, MAURICE. 1970. Réflexion sur une double corrélation typologique. *Journal of West African Linguistics* 7:2.59–68.

HOUIS, MAURICE. 1971. *Anthropologie linguistique de l'Afrique Noire.* (Le linguiste, 11.) Paris: Presses Universitaires de France.

KÖHLER, OSWIN. 1975. Geschichte und Probleme der Gliederung der Sprachen Afrikas. In *Die Völker Afrikas und ihre traditionellen Kulturen,* vol. 1, *Allgemeiner Teil und südliches Afrika* (Studien zur Kulturkunde, 34), edited by Hermann Baumann, pp. 141–373. Wiesbaden: Steiner.

MEINHOF, CARL. 1936. *Die Entstehung flektierender Sprachen.* Berlin: Reimer.

MUKAROVSKY, HANS. 1976–77. *A study of Western Nigritic.* 2 vols. (Beiträge zur Afrikanistik, 1–2.) Vienna: Institut für Ägyptologie und Afrikanistik der Universität Wien.

TRAILL, ANTHONY. 1985. *Phonetic and phonological studies of !Xóõ Bushman.* (Quellen zur Khoisan-Forschung, 1.) Hamburg: Buske.

WESTERMANN, DIEDRICH. 1935. Charakter und Einteilung der Sudansprachen. *Africa* 8.129–149.

LANGUAGE LIST

[*For data on individual languages, see the Language Lists after the articles on the African language families named above. In addition, the following data pertain to African languages which have been reported, but not clearly assigned to any of the families named.*]

Anlo: around 2,020 speakers reported in 1981, in Togo. Also called Ahonlan. May be the same as Igo.

Bete: spoken in Bete town, Ayikiben District, Wukari Division, Gongola State, Nigeria. The language is dying out.

Birale: spoken on Lake Weyto north of the Tsamai, Ethiopia. Also called Shanqilla. Some local people say the Birale are Tsamai or Hamer.

Bomou: 15,000 speakers reported in 1967, in northern Chad.

Ekpari: 10,000 speakers reported in 1982, in Nigeria.

Hwla: some 31,700 speakers reported in 1983, in Togo. May be the same as Hwe in Togo or Xwla-Gbe in Benin.

Kalamse: 2,560 speakers reported in 1987, in Sourou Province, Tougan Subdistrict, Burkina Faso. Also called Samoma.

Kokola: some 74,500 speakers reported in 1966, in Malawi.

Koroboré: spoken in two or three villages northwest of Barsalogo, Sanmatenga Province, Burkina Faso. May be the same as Koroboro, an alternate name for Songhai. Apparently not the same as Karaboro.

Lufu: now extinct, formerly spoken in Wukari and Lufu Divisions, Gongola State, Nigeria.

Maransé: 2,400 speakers reported in 1987, in Sanmatenga, Bam, and Yatenga Provinces, Burkina Faso. Also called Kaadkiine.

Noumou: spoken in Sindou Subdistrict, Comoé Province, Burkina Faso. Also called Numukan, Tutume, or Cugurde. Possibly the language of the Numu caste of blacksmiths who speak Ligbi in Ghana and Ivory Coast; but Noumou is not called a variety of Ligbi.

Rer Bare: spoken in the Webi Shebelle River area around Gode in the eastern Ogaden area of Harar Province, Ethiopia, near the Somali border, and along the Ganale and Dawa rivers. Sometimes called Rerebere or Adona. Speakers use Somali as well as their own language. They may be the same as the Nara.

Sininkere: some 300 speakers reported in 1987, in Sanmatenga Province near Pensa, Burkina Faso. Also called Silinkere or Silanke. Speakers are bilingual in Moore.

Weyto: now extinct, formerly spoken in Ethiopia. The ethnic group now speaks an Amharic-based language.

Yana: 14,500 speakers reported in 1987, in Pama, Comin-Yanga, and Diabo Subdistricts, Gourma Province, Burkina Faso. Also called Jaan.

Yauma: spoken in the Kwando River area in the southeast corner of Angola. Also in Zambia.

Zaoré: 23,500 speakers reported in 1987, in Boulgou and Gourma Provinces, Diabo Subdistrict, Burkina Faso. Also called Joore.

AFRO-ASIATIC LANGUAGES include the Semitic, Berber, Cushitic, Egyptian, and Chadic branches [*qq.v.*]. Altogether, about 250 members of the family are known, most of them belonging to Chadic (120–150 languages) and Cushitic (about 50). A[fro-]A[siatic] languages today dominate the Middle East and North Africa. For a survey, see D. Cohen 1968.

For the past forty years, scholars have rejected a twofold division into Semitic and 'Hamitic'; the latter was formerly conceived as comprising Berber, Cushitic, Egyptian, and part of Chadic—and sometimes other languages of Africa (now considered non-AA) which have a masculine/feminine gender opposition. The term 'Hamitic' is no longer used, though the whole family is still sometimes referred to as 'Hamito-Semitic' (or rarely, 'Semito-Hamitic'). New names for the whole family have gained little acceptance: Afrasian, Erythraic, and Lisramic. A hypothesis based on lexicostatistics, claiming that the Omotic languages of southwestern Ethiopia may constitute another major AA branch, now appears incorrect; these languages are again classified as the most innovating section of West Cushitic. Also unaccepted are attempts to classify North Cushitic Beja, spoken mainly in Sudan, as another major independent branch of AA. The Berber branch is sometimes called 'Libyco-Berber' or 'Berber-Libyan', but this usage does not appear justified. The language of the so-called Libyan inscriptions seems to be Berber, but is poorly attested—like the extinct Guanche of the Canary Islands, which shows at least partial connections to Berber.

There is broad consensus that the five major branches of AA are parallel and equal; but it is probable that the Semitic branch is closer to Berber, both of them being related to a somewhat more distant Cushitic. The resulting group is in turn close to Egyptian. Chadic, which has so far been explored only in part, can be considered provisionally as the most distant branch of AA. [*For data on individual languages, see the Language Lists following the articles on the families named above.*]

There is as yet no comparative grammar of AA—or even of Berber, Cushitic, or Chadic. The most important general sketch is still Diakonoff 1965. The first comprehensive dictionary, apart from the pioneering work of M. Cohen 1947, has been compiled by Diakonoff and his collaborators, but in late 1988 was still to appear. It now seems that the Semitic languages, especially Akkadian and (Classical) Arabic [*qq.v.*], are the most archaic, i.e. closest to the Proto-AA stage. Within Berber, Tuareg is considered most archaic; and within Cushitic, Beja and Afar-Saho. Egyptian has many archaisms, but its verbal system has been radically restructured (though this interpretation is not universally accepted). The Chadic languages that we know at present seem to be innovative.

The main morphological elements common to AA are the personal pronouns: the independent forms; the suffixed forms, used for direct object or as possessive; and the verbal formant forms, prefixed and suffixed. These pronouns, which are remarkably uniform, have been considered proof of the existence of the AA family since about 1850; see Table 1.

TABLE 1. *Afro-Asiatic Pronominal Elements*

	'I'	'we'	'your' (masc.)	'your' (fem.)
Akkadian	*anāku*		*-ka*	*-ki*
Arabic		*naħnu*		
Berber	*nəkk*	*nəkunn*	*-k*	
Beja		*hanan*	*-ka*	*-ki*
Egyptian	*ˀi-n-k*	*ˀi-n-n*	*-k*	*-č*
Hausa			*-ka*	*-ki*

The feminine suffix *-at,* also used for abstracts and singulatives, is also Proto-AA. Shared case morphemes include at least *-u* nominative, *-i* genitive, and *-a* absolute. Other common nominal elements are plural *-ū*/-V*w*, *-ān*, *-āt*; internal plural with ablaut, e.g. *-a-*; a nominal prefix *m*V-; and an adjectival suffix *-ī*/-V*y*. The verbal system has a basic morphological opposition between the so-called 'suffixal' conjugation (with suffixed pronominal morphemes)—which is mainly stative—and the 'prefixal' conjugation, which is used with different ablaut patterns and/or endings to mark various tense/aspect functions. Thus, in the suffixal conjugation, we have 1sg. Akkadian *-āku,* Berber -V*g*, Egyptian *-k-w-y*; in the prefixal conjugation, we have Proto-AA 1sg. **'a-*, 2sg. **t*V- (with *-i* for feminine), 3sg. masc. **y*V-, 3sg. fem. **t*V-; 1pl. **n*V-, 2pl. **t*V-, 3pl. **y*V-, with special plural and feminine suffixes in the 2nd and 3rd persons plural. With different ablaut patterns, we have, e.g., Akkadian *i-prus* 'he split', *i-parras* 'he splits'; Somali *ya-qaan* 'he knows', *yi-qiin* 'he knew'. The verbal derivational affixes of Proto-AA include causative *s-*, reflexive and medial *t-*, passive *n-*, and reduplication for intensive.

From a typological viewpoint, an extremely widespread use of internal flection (ablaut) is the most characteristic trait of all the archaic and middle-stage AA languages, along with mainly consonantal (usually tri- or bi-consonantal) roots. On the phonological level, a typical feature is the set of so-called emphatic consonants (realized phonetically as pharyngealized, velarized, glottalized, etc.), as well as the occurrence of several laryngeal and pharyngeal phonemes. The vowel system was probably limited to three vowels *i a u,* with distinctive length.

Attempts to prove a relationship between AA and other languages or language families, such as Nubian or Meroitic, have been unsuccessful. The only hypotheses of broader relationship which currently merit attention are that of association with 'Nostratic' (including Indo-European), and that of possible genetic links with Nilo-Saharan (e.g. Teda).

ANDRZEJ ZABORSKI

BIBLIOGRAPHY

COHEN, DAVID. 1968. Les langues chamito-semitiques. In *Le langage,* edited by André Martinet, pp. 1288–1330. Paris: Gallimard.

COHEN, MARCEL. 1947. *Essai comparatif sur le vocabulaire et la phonétique du chamito-sémitique.* Paris: Champion.

DIAKONOFF, IGOR M. 1965. *Semito-Hamitic languages: An essay in classification.* Moscow: Nauka.

AGRAMMATISM classically refers to a pathological verbal behavior sometimes observed in Broca's aphasia following a left prerolandic cerebral lesion. [*See* Aphasia.] Generally occurring after a period of evolution (Alajouanine 1968), such behavior is basically characterized, at the surface level, by the production of lacunary, 'telegraphic' syntactic structures which prototypically lack grammatical morphemes:

(1) *Ah yes! Strikes, uh, strikes, uh, red flags. Uh, uh, bludgeons, finally bludgeons, universities. Uh, ah yes! Ten per cent, uh, wages. Uh, oof! That's all.* (Lecours et al. 1983:52)

(2) *My uh mother died . . . uh . . . me . . . uh fi'teen. Uh, oh, I guess six month . . . my mother pass away. An'uh . . . an'en . . . uh . . . ah . . . seventeen . . . seventeen . . . go . . . uh high school. An uh . . . Christmas . . . well, uh, I uh . . . Pitt'burgh.* (Goodglass 1976:239)

According to Pitres 1898, J. P. F. J. Deleuze was the first clinician (in 1819) to report on an aphasic patient whose verbal output was deprived of pronouns, and was made up of infinitive verbs. The term 'agrammatism' was introduced to the aphasiological literature by Kussmaul 1877.

The more specific surface manifestations of such a syndrome are easily identified in clinical terms:

(a) The rate of speech is slowed.
(b) Grammatical morphemes are deleted in most, if not all, tasks of sentence and discourse production.
(c) Verbal inflections are lost, with preferential use of the infinitive (e.g. in French) or the gerund (e.g. in English) instead of finite verb forms.
(d) The number and complexity of syntactic structures are reduced.
(e) The patient produces shortened ('telegraphic') utterances which show a preference for juxtaposition over embedding of sentence constituents (Goodglass 1976, Lecours et al. 1983).

Such symptoms are often accompanied by a comprehension deficit, which disrupts processing of the same grammatical constituents and structures which are affected in production (Zurif et al. 1972). However, there are counter-examples to such a 'parallelistic' account of agrammatism; in these, 'pure agrammatism of speech' is presented in the absence of any comprehension disorder (Miceli et al. 1983, Nespoulous et al. 1988).

Neuropsychologists, linguists, and psycholinguists have proposed many interpretative models of agrammatism; all attempt to link the pathological surface manifestations of the deficit with underlying, functional causes. They aim at determining whether the underlying deficit is an amodal structural deficit which affects one or several sub-components of the grammar of a natural language in all production and comprehension tasks—or a processing deficit, which disrupts the computations responsible for the active, dynamic, 'on-line' processing of linguistic structures in production and/or comprehension. The frequent observation of cross-modal (or across-task) variability, in agrammatic patients as well as in other clinical types of aphasics, seems to support the latter hypothesis; however, the question is open to debate.

On the basis of the parallel presence of similar impairments in both production and comprehension, Zurif et al. 1972 thus claim that agrammatism is indeed a central grammatical deficit, crucially affecting syntax. However, Miceli et al. 1983 and Nespoulous et al. 1988, lacking such a parallel in their patients' symptomatology, conclude that agrammatism can disrupt the (syntactic?) processes necessary for sentence production without affecting language comprehension.

Psycholinguistic models of speech production (e.g. Garrett 1980) all require, in order to process information from meaning to sound, the existence of different levels of linguistic representation, and of processes transcoding each representation into the next. Neurolinguists employ these models in attempts to determine the levels at which the causal deficit of agrammatic symptoms is located. Whether they state so explicitly or not, most consider the deficit to be a syntactic one, which thus disrupts both the building up and the parsing of syntactic structures. Other researchers report clearcut cases of pathological dissociation between morphological and syntactic processes (Tissot et al. 1973, Miceli et al. 1983, Nespoulous et al. 1988). For still others, the deficit is phonological: it leads to the deletion of grammatical markers in both production and comprehension, because these items are 'clitic', unstressed morphemes, rather than 'phonological words' (Kean 1979). Finally, some believe that agrammatism is the outcome of a specific processing deficit which reduces the availability of 'closed-class' morphemes (Bradley et al. 1979).

Neurolinguists more involved in the interpretation of 'agrammatic comprehension' have put forward different strategies that are supposedly used by agrammatics to compensate for their syntactic parsing deficit. Thus they identify 'heuristic' procedures which rely on semantic plausibility (Caramazza & Zurif 1976, Deloche & Seron 1981), animacy (Schwartz et al. 1980), or the linear order of nouns (Caplan 1983); agrammatic patients are said to resort to these strategies in an attempt to overcome the impaired 'algorithmic' syntactic processes that normally assign thematic roles to sentence constituents.

In aphasic symptomatology in general, and in agrammatic symptomatology in particular, many researchers identify more than the mere negative manifestation of some underlying deficit. This dictates that, together with the direct effects of the impairment resulting from a cerebral lesion, its indirect effects—arising from potential adaptive strategies—must be carefully appraised (Marshall 1977, Kolk & van Grunsven 1985, Nespoulous et al. 1988).

Aphasia, and thus agrammatism, are almost never 'all-or-none' phenomena; thus variability in performance must be accounted for, and its causal factors must be apprehended, be they temporal, mnestic or attentional (Kolk & van Grunsven 1985).

Classical teaching on aphasia tended to distinguish agrammatism, characterized mainly by omissions of grammatical morphemes, from PARAGRAMMATISM [*q.v.*], characterized by replacements of items. Late 20th century neurolinguists have become uncomfortable with such a dichotomy (Heeschen 1985), especially considering the following facts:

(i) Both omissions and substitutions may be observed in a single agrammatic patient, and may systematically involve the same grammatical morphemes.
(ii) Language-specific structural constraints sometimes force the patient to produce substitutions rather than omissions, e.g. in Hebrew.

The study of agrammatism, at the end of the 20th century, is a prototypical example of multidisciplinary interaction among linguists, psycholinguists, and neuropsychologists; it clearly stresses the need for future research 'to combine principled linguistic descriptions and careful on-line examinations' of actual linguistic behaviors following brain lesions (Grodzinsky et al. 1985).

JEAN-LUC NESPOULOUS

BIBLIOGRAPHY

ALAJOUANINE, THÉOPHILE. 1968. *L'aphasie et le langage pathologique.* Paris: Baillière.

BRADLEY, DIANNE C., et al. 1979. Syntactic deficits in Broca's aphasia. In *Biological studies of mental processes,* edited by David Caplan, pp. 269–286. Cambridge, Mass.: MIT Press.

CAPLAN, DAVID. 1983. A note on the 'word order' problem in agrammatism. *Brain & Language* 10.155–165.

CARAMAZZA, ALFONSO, & EDGAR B. ZURIF. 1976. Dissociation of algorithmic and heuristic processes in language comprehension: Evidence from aphasia. *Brain & Language* 3.572–582.

DELOCHE, GÉRARD, & XAVIER SERON. 1981. Sentence understanding and knowledge of the world: Evidence from a sentence-picture matching task performed by aphasic patients. *Brain & Language* 14.57–69.

GARRETT, MERRILL F. 1980. Levels of processing in sentence production. In *Language production,* vol. 1, *Speech and talk,* edited by Brian Butterworth, pp. 177–220. London: Academic Press.

GOODGLASS, HAROLD. 1976. Agrammatism. In *Studies in neurolinguistics,* vol. 1, edited by Haiganoosh Whitaker & Harry A. Whitaker, pp. 237–260. New York: Academic Press.

GRODZINSKY, YOSEF, et al. 1985. Agrammatism: Structural deficits and antecedent processing disruptions. In Kean 1985, pp. 65–81.

HEESCHEN, CLAUS. 1985. Agrammatism versus paragrammatism: A fictitious opposition. In Kean 1985, pp. 207–248.

KEAN, MARY-LOUISE. 1979. Agrammatism: A phonological deficit? *Cognition* 7.69–83.

KEAN, MARY-LOUISE, ed. 1985. *Agrammatism.* Orlando, Fla.: Academic Press.

KOLK, HERMAN H. J., & MARIANNE J. F. VAN GRUNSVEN. 1985. Agrammatism as a variable phenomenon. *Cognitive Neuropsychology* 2.347–384.

KUSSMAUL, ADOLF. 1877. *Die Störungen der Sprache.* Leipzig: Vogel. 5th ed., 1885.

LECOURS, ANDRÉ ROCH, et al. 1983. *Aphasiology.* London: Baillière/Tindall.

MARSHALL, JOHN C. 1977. Disorders in the expression of language. In *Psycholinguistics: Developmental and pathological,* edited by John Morton & John C. Marshall, pp. 125–160. Ithaca, N.Y.: Cornell University Press.

MICELI, GABRIELE, et al. 1983. Contrasting cases of Italian agrammatic aphasia without comprehension disorder. *Brain & Language* 19.65–97.

NESPOULOUS, JEAN-LUC, et al. 1988. Agrammatism in sentence production without comprehension deficits: Reduced availability of syntactic structures and/or of grammatical morphemes? *Brain & Language* 33.273–295.

PITRES, A. 1898. *L'aphasie amnésique et ses variétés cliniques.* Paris: Aljean.

SCHWARTZ, MYRNA, et al. 1980. The word order problem in agrammatism: Comprehension. *Brain & Language* 10.249–262.

TISSOT, RENÉ, et al. 1973. *L'agrammatisme: Études neuropsycholinguistiques.* Brussels: Dessart.

ZURIF, EDGAR B., et al. 1972. Grammatical judgments of agrammatic aphasics. *Neuropsychologia* 10.405–418.

AKKADIAN is a Semitic language which was spoken from the early 3rd to the middle of the 1st millennium BCE, in the area corresponding to modern Iraq and Syria and some neighboring regions. [*See* Semitic Languages.] The term subsumes two major dialects, BABYLONIAN and ASSYRIAN. These underwent three broad stages of development, labeled Old (ca. 2000–1500 BCE), Middle (1500–1000), and Neo- (1000–500); their forerunner is known as Old Akkadian (2500–2000 BCE). Some scholars consider Eblaite as a form of Old Akkadian, with which it is contemporary.

1. History. Old Babylonian is generally viewed as the classical stage of the language, because of a convergence of cultural and diachronic factors: it is the earliest stage of the language for which we have a large, differentiated, and culturally significant body of written documents. That Old Babylonian had a certain normative value is suggested by the fact that later cultural manifestations of the language were consciously modeled on it—especially Standard Babylonian, a literary 'dialect' used in the mid-1st millennium BCE, when Akkadian as a spoken language had begun to disappear.

During the second half of the 2nd millennium, Akkadian came to be used as a lingua franca over all of southwestern Asia. Through its use as a shared medium of expression by speakers of different languages, it developed into a scribal lingo rather divorced from the natural linguistic development which it underwent separately in the core area of Babylonia and Assyria.

External influences are important in the study of Akkadian. Because of its cultural primacy, Sumerian [*q.v.*] seems clearly to have played a significant role in shaping linguistic development. Apart from its strong influence on the lexicon, characteristics that are frequently adduced are the fact that the configuration of Akkadian phonology is typologically highly advanced vis-à-vis later Semitic languages; and the Subject Object Verb character of its syntax. Other significant lexical influences came from Hurrian and Aramaic [*qq.v.*].

2. Sources. For sources on Akkadian, see Soden 1952, Gelb 1961, Hecker 1968, Groneberg 1987, and Huehnergard 1988. For historical connections, see Castellino 1962, Gelb 1969; for the writing system, Soden & Röllig 1967; and for dictionaries, Gelb et al. 1956, Soden 1965–81. The work of Reiner 1966 is a major reference.

The nature of the available sources places some significant limits on our understanding of Akkadian as a linguistic reality. First, there is the obvious fact that Akkadian is an extinct language. Exactly when it died is not apparent from the record: it is conceivable that, by the end of the Assyrian empire (7th c. BCE), Aramaic had already replaced Akkadian as the common spoken language in Mesopotamia.

Second, the textual evidence on which our knowledge of the language is based—while massive in size, and relatively varied in the nature and range of its repertory—does not provide a transparent record of the spoken language. Except for letters, the bulk of the evidence comes to us through a pervasive scribal filter. Especially noticeable in formulaic, technical texts (whether pertaining to administration, law, cult, or scholarly practice), standardization is also to be reckoned with in the literary tradition, from myths and epics to hymns and wisdom texts. Finally, the extant evidence pertains primarily to urban elites; Amorite can be understood as the rural counterpart of urban Akkadian/Eblaite (though this is not the usual interpretation of Amorite).

3. Writing system. Graphemic analysis is of particular importance for a proper linguistic understanding of Akkadian—not only because our documentation is exclusively written, but also because of the complexities of the writing system. [*See also* Decipherment.] The philological tradition of Assyriology was intuitively responsive to the needs of graphemic analysis long before the concept was articulated theoretically; witness the modern repertories of both syllabic and logographic values, which are based on rigorous applications of a coherently perceived system of graphemic rules. The signs of the CUNEIFORM script [*q.v.*] number in the hundreds, and corresponding values in the thousands (allowing for multiple values for each sign, or 'polyphony'); however, it appears that the operative sign inventory within any given text genre ranges between two hundred and three hundred, and that multiple values are restricted in usage by rules of correlation. The incidence and significance of graphemics is such that independent linguistic work on the textual data must be based on knowledge of their graphemic embodiment. The fact that the writing system includes full vocalic notation (in contrast to the writing systems used for other Semitic languages) is deceptively simple in this respect.

We can claim only an approximate knowledge of phonetic realizations, gathered mostly from the comparative evidence of living Semitic languages; however, Akkadian phonemics is well understood. Uncertainties that still remain pertain primarily to distributional arrangements, rather than specific inventory items. Among the latter is the possibility of an extra sibilant in Old Akkadian; among the former, the questions of (i) whether vowels were allowed in word-initial position (alternatively, glottal stop would be required), and of (ii) the nature and position of stress.

Diachronically, Akkadian phonology is much more innovative than that of much later Semitic languages, as shown by the loss (already in Old Akkadian) of most laryngeals and pharyngeals, only partly offset by a vocalic change of *a* to *e*. An interesting phenomenon is Old Assyrian vowel harmony, whereby short unstressed vowels in pre-final position are assimilated in quality to the vowel that follows.

4. Morphology. Two major systems are operative, as in other Semitic languages. One, 'internal' inflection, is built on the obligatory and exclusive interrelationship of two morphemes, called 'root' and 'pattern'; the other, 'external' inflection, is based on the cumulative clustering of affixes before or after the nucleus—which in turn may or may not be derived through internal inflection. (In standard Akkadian grammars, internal inflection is understood as a process of word formation.) In contrast with other Semitic languages, where internal inflection is freely superimposed on loanwords, Akkadian avoids such new formations: this means that, since all verbal forms are based on internal inflection, the language has no clear examples of borrowed verbs. This is all the more striking in light of the heavy dependence of Akkadian on Sumerian in its nominal lexicon.

The nominal system makes full use of case endings. Three major cases are operative in the singular, roughly correlated with specific syntactic functions: the nominative (in *-um*) identifies the subject; the accusative (in *-am*), the object; and the genitive (in *-im*), the second component of a nominalized construct (e.g. *bīt awīlim* 'house of the man'). In the plural, a single oblique case (in *-ī*) subsumes the functions of both accusative and genitive, and *-ū* marks the case of the nominative. Partly retained in the script, case endings seem to have been lost by the early 1st millennium BCE.

An important characteristic of the verbal system is the absence of an aspect category. Instead, there are two other fundamental dimensions of verbal inflection. First, there are true tenses which locate the process in a temporal relationship to the speaker; besides the 'present' (for present/future) and the preterit, there is a form distinctive of Akkadian, the 'perfect'—this form, with infixed *t,* expresses (at least in Old Babylonian) anteriority in the future or posteriority in the past (*iktašad* 'he will have then reached' or 'he then had reached'). Second, inflection denotes either action or condition; the former is expressed by finite forms (the tenses and the imperative), and the latter by a form peculiar to Akkadian, the 'permansive.' This is traditionally viewed as a separate component of the verbal paradigm; however, it may be structurally more appropriate to view it as an inflectional variation of the noun, including adjectives which can be derived from verbal roots.

Important morphophonemic rules have been identified in Akkadian, with alternations conditioned by both internal and external inflection. A characteristic rule states that a sequence which contains (i) three syllables, of which the last two are short, and (ii) a certain type of morpheme boundary, is realized as two syllables; e.g., morphemic {damiq-um} is realized phonemically as /damqum/.

An interesting diachronic change is represented by the trend to abandon inflectional in favor of periphrastic forms. Thus for instance the separative form of the verb (with infixed *t,* e.g. *ittalak* 'he went away from, he left') or the allative (with suffixed *-am,* etc., e.g. *illikam* 'he went to, he came') may be understood (in the early periods) as synthetically referential to adjuncts of motion, even when such an adjunct is absent from the discourse; in later dialects, the referential value of the affixed forms is at best vestigial, and an analytical adjunct is required.

5. Syntax and semantics. These fields have been generally neglected, even though there has been a burgeoning interest in lexical matters. For semantics, this has meant that words have been studied for their denotational value in regard to specific realia; for syntax, phrases and sentences have been studied with attention to morphemic keywords.

Several syntactic traits are distinctive of Akkadian among Semitic languages. The following may be mentioned:

(a) The use of 'virtual subordination' (where sentences are conjoined by the enclitic *-ma*) all but replaces normal subordination, in spite of the existence of a rich but underutilized inventory of conjunctions.
(b) Restrictive relative clauses occur without the use of a relative pronoun; instead, the noun occurs in a shortened form (the 'construct state')—e.g. *awīl illiku* 'the man who came', vs. a non-restrictive clause with the relative pronoun, *awīlum ša illiku* 'the man, who came . . .'.
(c) Three nominal forms which are morphologically part of the inflectional structure of the verbal system (infinitive, verbal adjective, and participle) may govern the accusative, e.g. *bītam ina amārim* 'in seeing the house'.

GIORGIO BUCCELLATI

BIBLIOGRAPHY

CASTELLINO, GIORGIO R. 1962. *The Akkadian personal pronouns and verbal system in the light of Semitic and Hamitic.* Leiden: Brill.

GELB, IGNACE J. 1961. *Old Akkadian writing and grammar.* (Materials for the Assyrian dictionary, 2.) 2d ed. Chicago: University of Chicago Press.

GELB, IGNACE J. 1969. *Sequential reconstruction of Proto-Akkadian.* (Assyrological studies, 18.) Chicago: University of Chicago Press.

GELB, IGNACE J., et al. 1956–. *The Assyrian dictionary of the Oriental Institute of the University of Chicago.* 16 vols. Glückstadt, Germany: Augustin.

GRONEBERG, BRIGITTE R. M. 1987. *Syntax, Morphologie und Stil der jungbabylonischen 'hymnischen' Literatur:* Teil 1, *Grammatik;* Teil 2, *Belegsammlung und Textkatalog.* (Freiburger altorientalische Studien, 14.) Wiesbaden: Steiner.

HECKER, KARL. 1968. *Grammatik der Kültepe-Texte.* (Analecta orientalia, 44.) Rome: Pontificium Institutum Biblicum.

HUEHNERGARD, JOHN. 1988. *The Akkadian of Ugarit.* (Harvard Semitic studies, 34.) Cambridge, Mass.: Harvard University Press.

REINER, ERICA. 1966. *A linguistic analysis of Akkadian.* (Janua linguarum, Series practica, 21.) The Hague: Mouton.

SODEN, WOLFRAM VON. 1952. *Grundriss der akkadischen*

Grammatik. (Analecta orientalia, 33.) Rome: Pontificium Institutum Biblicum.

SODEN, WOLFRAM VON. 1965–81. *Akkadisches Handwörterbuch*. 3 vols. Wiesbaden: Harrassowitz.

SODEN, WOLFRAM VON, & WOLFGANG RÖLLIG. 1967. *Das akkadische Syllabar*. (Analecta orientalia, 42.) 2d ed. Rome: Pontificium Institutum Biblicum.

ALACALUFAN LANGUAGES constitute an isolated group native to southernmost Chile and the adjacent part of Argentina; see Čestmír Loukotka, *Classification of South American Indian languages* (Los Angeles: Latin American Center, University of California, Los Angeles, 1968), pp. 44–45.

LANGUAGE LIST

Kakauhua: now extinct, formerly spoken in Chile. Also called Kaukaue.

Kawesqar: 47 speakers reported in 1982 off the south Chilean coast, around Puerto Edén. Also called Kawaskar, Qawasqar, Qawashqar, Alacaluf, or Halakwalip. Speakers are monolingual.

ALBANIAN constitutes a branch of the Indo-European family, spoken predominantly in Albania and in the Kosovo province of Yugoslavia. The two main varieties are Tosk (the basis of the standard language) and Gheg. Arvanitika is the name given to the variety of Tosk spoken in Greece.

LANGUAGE LIST

Arvanitika: around 140,000 speakers reported in 1977, in Greece. Also known as Arvanitic. Partial mutual intelligibility with Tosk. Spoken by older people.

Gheg: around 2,000,000 speakers reported in 1980, in northern Albania. Later reports list 1,700,000 in Yugoslavia, 17,400 in the United States, and others in Bulgaria. Sometimes known as Geg or Shqipni.

Tosk: around 4,000,000 speakers reported in 1986, with 2,850,000 in south Albania (the figure does not distinguish Tosk from Gheg), 82,000 from an ethnic population of 260,000 in Italy, 15,000 from an ethnic population of 61,000 in Turkey, 4,000 in the USSR, and others in Egypt, Canada, and the United States. Sometimes known as Arber, Arbresh, Arnaut, Shqip, Skchip, Shqiperi, or Zhgabe. Tosk has been the official variety for Standard Albanian since 1945.

ALEXIA (sometimes called 'acquired dyslexia') is the disturbance of reading subsequent to brain injury in a previously literate adult. Deficits may take the form of difficulty in reading comprehension and/or in oral reading. (For reference, see Hinshelwood 1900, Coltheart 1981, Newcombe & Marshall 1981, Patterson 1981, Friedman & Albert 1985, Patterson et al. 1985, Friedman 1988.)

Earlier classifications of the alexias were formulated by neurologists, primarily on the basis of accompanying neurological symptoms or anatomical loci. The most common distinction made was between alexia without AGRAPHIA (also called 'pure alexia'), and alexia with agraphia. A distinction was also made between 'literal alexia', the inability to name letters, and 'verbal alexia', the inability to read words; the distinction has turned out to be of little use, and is no longer in vogue. Current classification schemes still include the syndrome of pure alexia, but 'alexia without agraphia' has been found to include many different disorders.

1. Types of paralexia. The characterization of alexic disorders now centers around specific symptoms which are said to reflect disturbances in different underlying functional mechanisms. Attention is focused on the types of PARALEXIAS or reading errors that are produced, and on the properties of words that affect word-reading.

There are three main types of paralexias: SEMANTIC, DERIVATIONAL, and ORTHOGRAPHIC. Semantic paralexias are related to the target word semantically, but not orthographically (e.g. *forest* → 'trees'). They may be synonyms of the target word, or they may be antonyms, subordinates, superordinates, or associates. Derivational paralexias are derived from the target word by adding, deleting, or substituting an affix (*building* → 'builder'). Orthographic paralexias share many letters with the target word (*sleep* → 'step'). These errors are sometimes called 'visual paralexias'; however, often they do not share even such gross visual features as over-all shape or length (*appraise* → 'arise').

Several properties of words have been shown to affect reading ability in alexic patients. Some patients have particular trouble in reading long words. Some are sensitive to form class, and have particular difficulty with function words. The degree of abstractness of a word may affect alexic patients' reading performance. Some have particular trouble with pseudo-words like *jup*; others read pseudo-words quite well, but get stuck on orthographically irregular words like *yacht*. The tendency of some of these alexic symptoms to occur together, but dissociated from other symptoms, has led to the description of the major varieties of alexia shown in Table 1.

TABLE 1. *Characteristic Features of the Alexias*

Type	Pure	Surface	Phonological	Deep
Orthographic regularity	−	+	−	−
Length	+	+	−	−
Form class	−	−	+/−	+
Word vs. pseudo-word	−	−	+	+
Concreteness	−	−	−	+
Paralexias				
Semantic	−	−	−	+
Derivational	−	−	+	+
Orthographic	+	+	+	+
'Regularizations'	−	+	−	−

2. Pure alexia, also called 'letter-by-letter reading', is characterized by an effect of word length on reading ability. The more letters in a word, the longer pure alexic patients will take to read the word, and the more likely it is that they will misread it. Words spelled aloud to the patient can be identified; writing remains intact; and speech and language are normal, with the exception of occasional mild ANOMIA [*q.v.*], particularly for colors. Reading often appears to be accomplished in a left-to-right, letter-by-letter fashion.

Anatomically, pure alexia is thought to reflect a 'disconnection' of visual input to the left angular gyrus, caused by lesions in the left primary visual cortex and the splenium of the corpus callosum. Three functional explanations have been put forth. One postulates damage to the mechanism that recognizes 'visual word forms'. A second proposes that the mechanism that analyzes 'letter forms' is disconnected from the visual word-form system. A third explanation sees the problem as a deficit of automatic identification of visual input—which includes, but is not limited to, the letter/form analysis system.

3. Surface alexia is primarily characterized by difficulty in reading 'irregular' words, as compared with regular words. (An irregular word is one whose pronunciation does not conform to the spelling-to-sound correspondence rules of the language, e.g. Eng. *pint*; a regular word is completely predictable on the basis of such rules, e.g. *mint*.) Two types of surface-alexic patients have been described. One group produces many paralexias that appear to result from attempts to apply spelling-to-sound conversion rules in incorrect ways (e.g. *unite* → 'unit'; *guest* → 'just'). This has led to the characterization of surface alexia as a 'failure' or 'misapplication' of grapheme/phoneme conversion rules. Another group of surface-alexic patients is said to produce primarily 'regularization' errors when they attempt to read irregular words. These paralexias are pronounced just as would be expected on the basis of grapheme/phoneme conversion rules, but the answer is incorrect because the word is irregular (e.g. *come* → 'comb').

Patients with surface alexia read pseudo-words well. When they read real words, their comprehension is based on the pronunciation they give to the word. For example, if the word *come* were read as 'comb', the meaning attached to the word would be related to grooming hair, not to the act of moving toward something.

The writing of patients with surface alexia tends to mirror the reading deficit, in that regular words are more likely to be written correctly than irregular words. These patients are almost always aphasic; their aphasias differ, but all are fluent. Most have left temporal or temporal-parietal lesions.

4. Phonological alexia characterizes a group of patients whose primary deficit is a relative inability to read pseudo-words, as compared with real words. These patients usually also experience difficulty reading function words and words with affixes. They typically have aphasia, but the type is not consistent; some are fluent, others are not. Agraphia is always present, but the type of agraphia is not consistent. Lesion site varies within the left hemisphere; and some patients with phonological alexia have strictly right-hemisphere lesions.

5. Deep alexia applies to a particular group of patients who have difficulty in reading pseudo-words: the distinguishing feature of these patients is that they produce semantic paralexias during oral reading. In addition, their success in reading real words is affected by the part of speech and by the concreteness of the word. They also produce derivational and orthographic paralexias. Their lesions are large, and include the left frontal lobe, with extension posterior to the central sulcus. Proposed explanations of deep alexia are numerous (see Coltheart et al. 1987). [*See also* Dyslexia.]

RHONDA FRIEDMAN

BIBLIOGRAPHY

COLTHEART, MAX. 1981. Disorders of reading and their implications for models of normal reading. *Visible Language* 15.245–286.

COLTHEART, MAX, et al., eds. 1987. *Deep dyslexia.* 2d ed. London: Routledge & Kegan Paul.

FRIEDMAN, RHONDA B. 1988. Acquired alexia. In *Handbook of neuropsychology,* edited by François Boller & Jordan Grafman, pp. 377–391. Amsterdam: Elsevier.

FRIEDMAN, RHONDA B., & MARTIN L. ALBERT. 1985. Alexia. In *Clinical neuropsychology,* 2d ed., edited by Kenneth M. Heilman & Edward Valenstein, pp. 49–73. Oxford & New York: Oxford University Press.

HINSHELWOOD, JAMES. 1900. *Letter-, word-, and mind-blindness.* London: H. K. Lewis.

NEWCOMBE, FREDA, & JOHN C. MARSHALL. 1981. On psycholinguistic classifications of the acquired dyslexias. *Bulletin of the Orton Society* 31.29–46.

PATTERSON, KARALYN E. 1981. Neuropsychological approaches to the study of reading. *British Journal of Psychology* 72.151–174.

PATTERSON, KARALYN E., et al., eds. 1985. *Surface dyslexia: Neuropsychological and cognitive studies of phonological meaning.* London: Erlbaum.

ALGIC LANGUAGES constitute a family of North America, comprising the Algonkian languages [*q.v.*] as well as two languages of northwestern California, Wiyot and Yurok. The term Ritwan is sometimes used as a cover term for Wiyot and Yurok, but it is not clear that these languages are more closely related to each other than to the Algonkian group.

LANGUAGE LIST

Wiyot: now extinct, formerly spoken in northwestern California. The last speaker died in 1962; in 1977 there were 120 in the ethnic group.

Yurok: 10 or fewer speakers reported in 1982 from a population of 3,000 to 4,500 in northwestern California.

ALGONKIAN LANGUAGES (often spelled Algonquian by specialists) constitute a family of twenty-five or more languages, spoken ca. 1600 in northeastern and central North America—and, by the late 1980s, in parts of its original territory and at additional locations to the west and south. Proto-Algonkian has been reconstructed in considerable detail, and the internal history of the family is generally well understood. Algonkian is related to Wiyot and Yurok, two neighboring though quite dissimilar languages of northern California, which some specialists group together as the Ritwan family; the larger grouping is referred to as Algonkian-Wiyot-Yurok, Algonkian-Ritwan, or Algic. Proposed more distant relationships are extremely controversial. Useful references on the family include the descriptive and historical/comparative study of Bloomfield 1946; the grammars of Bloomfield 1962, Voorhis 1974, and Wolfart & Carroll 1981; the descriptive papers of Dahlstrom 1987 and Goddard 1990; and the bibliography of Pentland & Wolfart 1982.

The Algonkian languages are conventionally divided into three geographical groupings: EASTERN, CENTRAL, and PLAINS (see Map 1). The Eastern languages were, from north to south, Micmac and Maliseet-Passamaquoddy in the Maritime provinces and eastern Maine; Eastern Abenaki and Western Abenaki in the rest of northern New England; a diverse continuum of dialects and languages in southern New England and on eastern Long Island, including Massachusett and Narragansett; Mahican on the upper Hudson River; the Delaware languages Munsee and Unami in the lower Hudson valley, the Delaware River valley, and the area between; and the poorly known languages of the coastal plain south to northeastern North Carolina—those with some documentation are Nanticoke, Piscataway (Conoy), Powhatan or Virginia Algonkian, and Carolina Algonkian. In the 1980s, there were Micmac and Maliseet-Passamaquoddy speech communities in their original territories, and a few speakers each of the Abenaki and Delaware languages; all the other Eastern languages were extinct.

The Central languages are Cree-Montagnais—a continuum of dialects diverse enough to be counted as two or perhaps more languages—spoken from the lower north shore of the Gulf of St. Lawrence to the Rocky Mountains; Ojibwa-Algonkin, a less diverse and less extensive dialect continuum centering on the upper Great Lakes; Menominee, in Wisconsin; and several languages whose speakers have moved south and west from the upper Great Lakes in the historical period, namely Potawatomi, Fox-Kickapoo, Shawnee, and Miami-Illinois. The Plains languages are Blackfoot, in Alberta and Montana; Arapaho-Atsina, in Wyoming, Montana, and Oklahoma; and Cheyenne, in Montana and Oklahoma. In the 1980s, all the Central and Plains languages except Miami-Illinois were still spoken. [*For data on individual Algonkian languages, see the Language List at the end of this article.*]

The Eastern languages form a genetic subgroup, though a diverse one. (Less plausibly, the innovations they share have been explained as resulting from massive diffusion.) The similarities of the Central languages are considered to be the result of some diffusion and, in general, of the conservatism of these languages. The Plains languages are the most divergent; all have undergone radical sound changes, and Blackfoot in particular has many features that are poorly understood historically.

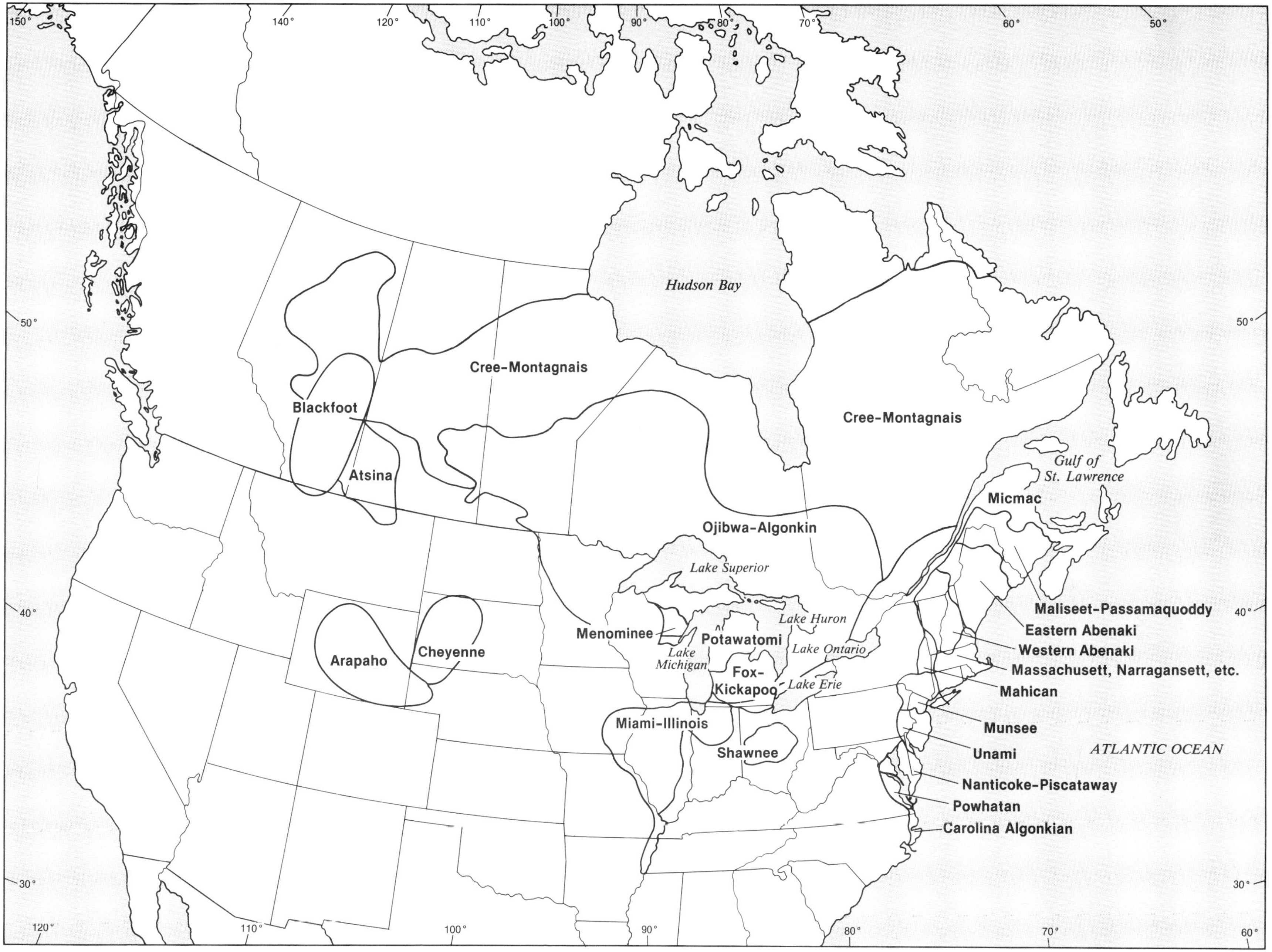

Map 1. *Distribution of Algonkian Languages*. The map shows the approximate locations of the speakers of the principal Algonkian languages at the times of their earliest documentation, ranging from 1584 (Carolina Algonkian) to 1805 (Arapaho and Cheyenne).

The Algonkian languages generally have small phoneme inventories and simple phonologies; they have extensive head-marking inflectional morphology, and complex derivational morphology. Their syntax is predominantly non-configurational: grammatical functions are expressed morphologically, and discourse features are encoded by word order and sentence particles. Discontinuous syntactic constituents are common.

Proto-Algonkian had a single series of stops */p t č k/ and fricatives */s š h/, two phonetically indeterminate continuants */l θ/, the nasals */m n/, and the semivowels */w y/. There were four short and four long vowels, */i e a o/ and */i: e: a: o:/. Clusters, with a limited number of partly indeterminate first members, occurred only medially; there were no vowel sequences. The modern languages all lose some contrasts among the clusters and obstruents; they have from three to twelve vowels. Some have developed two series of stops and fricatives, and several have developed contrastive stress or pitch accent. Cheyenne has developed four contrastive tones from the interaction of length and tonal contrasts. In several languages, rhythmically determined vowel weakening and strengthening have given rise to divergent surface alternates for many morphemes.

Nouns are of animate or inanimate gender; many names for non-animate entities are grammatically animate. Nouns are inflected for number, possessor, and locative. Verbs appear in derivationally related pairs: intransitives are differentiated for the gender of the subject, and transitives for that of the object. Verbs are inflected for subject and (primary) object, and in some languages for secondary object; they may also bear a lexically specified valence for any of several oblique categories (location, oblique goal, manner, extent, etc.). Typically, there are many modes, divided into formally distinct orders; and most languages mark negation on the verb. The inflections for possessor, subject, and object function pronominally—or, with a coreferential noun phrase, as agreement. Pronominal inflection for possessor, and for some verbal arguments in the independent order, uses a set of prefixes; initial change, a modification in the first stem vowel, marks certain modes of the conjunct order; and all other inflection is by suffixes. Several patterns of stem-initial reduplication are found. Animate nouns, and some pronominal inflections on verbs, may mark a secondary 3rd person, the obviative, in the context of a primary animate 3rd person. The languages differ in the details, but basically the use of the obviative differentiates 3rd person animate arguments and tracks coreference or non-coreference. In addition, the assignment and shifting of obviative status can indicate focus, point of view, etc.

Stems normally are internally complex, except for some primary nouns and intransitive verbs. The verb-stem template includes an initial, an optional medial, and a final; each of the three components may be internally complex or derived from a stem. Primary initials ('roots') generally denote manner, state, condition, relation, or configuration, either inherent or resulting from an action; medials are incorporated nominals, sometimes functioning locatively or as classifiers; finals determine the category of the verb. Concrete finals denote the basic verbal notion—including, for transitives, the instrumentality of causation. A typical verb form is Fox *ka:hkihkinameške:nawote* 'if an arrow scratches him on the skin': a stem consisting of initial *ka:hkihk-* 'scratched' + medial *-inameške:-* 'skin' + final *-(e)naw* 'hit (animate) by missile (causing . . .)', inflected with *-et* (3rd person passive, conjunct order, > *-ot* after *w*) + *-e* (subjunctive mode of conjunct order). Secondary derivation makes, e.g., (from nouns) verbs of being and possession, and (from verbs) agent, instrument, and abstract nouns—as well as transitivized and detransitivized verbs of several types, including reciprocals, middle reflexives, and derived passives.

IVES GODDARD

BIBLIOGRAPHY

BLOOMFIELD, LEONARD. 1946. Algonquian. In *Linguistic structures of Native America* (Viking Fund publications in anthropology, 6), by Harry Hoijer et al., pp. 85–129. New York.

BLOOMFIELD, LEONARD. 1962. *The Menomini language*. Edited by Charles F. Hockett. New Haven: Yale University Press.

DAHLSTROM, AMY. 1987. Discontinuous constituents in Fox. In *Native American languages and grammatical typology*, edited by Paul D. Kroeber & Robert E. Moore, pp. 53–73. Bloomington: Indiana University Linguistics Club.

GODDARD, IVES. 1990. Aspects of the topic structure of Fox narratives: Proximate shifts and the use of overt and inflectional NPs. *International Journal of American Linguistics* 56.317–340.

PENTLAND, DAVID H., & H. CHRISTOPH WOLFART. 1982. *A bibliography of Algonquian linguistics*. Winnipeg: University of Manitoba Press.

VOORHIS, PAUL H. 1974. *Introduction to the Kickapoo language.* (Language science monographs, 13.) Bloomington: Indiana University Research Center for the Language Sciences.

WOLFART, H. CHRISTOPH, & JANET F. CARROLL. 1981. *Meet Cree: A guide to the Cree language.* 2d ed. Edmonton: University of Alberta Press.

LANGUAGE LIST

Abenaki, Eastern: one speaker of the Penobscot dialect reported in 1990, in Maine, USA.

Abenaki, Western: fewer than 20 elderly speakers reported in 1982 in Quebec, Canada. Also called Abnaki.

Algonkin: around 3,000 speakers reported in 1987 in southwestern Quebec and in adjacent areas of Ontario, Canada. Also spelled Algonquin. In the west children and young adults prefer the national language, although some may speak Algonkin; most adults speak Algonkin. Elsewhere Algonkin is the principal means of communication for all ages.

Arapaho: around 1,500 speakers reported in 1977 from a population of 5,000, in Wyoming, USA, and associated with the Cheyenne in western Oklahoma. Also spelled Arapahoe. Most speakers are middle-aged or older.

Atikamek: around 3,230 speakers reported in 1986 on reservations in Quebec, Canada. Also known as Tête de Boule, Atihkamekw, or Atikamekw. Closely related to Cree. Language use is vigorous.

Atsina: 10 or fewer speakers reported in 1977 from a population of 1,200, in north central Montana, USA. Also known as Gros Ventre.

Blackfoot: around 9,000 speakers reported in 1977 from a population of 15,000, on the Blackfoot, Peigan, and Blood Reserves in southern Alberta, Canada, and on the Blackfeet Reservation in Montana, USA. In some Canadian locations, Blackfoot remains the principal means of communication for older adults, though children and young adults tend to prefer English.

Carolina Algonkian: an extinct language formerly spoken in northeastern North Carolina, USA.

Cheyenne: around 2,000 speakers reported in 1987 from a population of 5,000, in southeastern Montana, USA, and with the Arapaho in western Oklahoma. In Montana most adults speak the language, but many younger people prefer English. In Oklahoma most speakers are middle-aged or older.

Cree, Central: around 4,500 speakers reported in 1982 from a population of 5,000, from James Bay in Ontario northwestward into northeastern Manitoba, Canada. Includes the major varieties Western Swampy Cree, Eastern Swampy Cree, and Moose Cree. Language use is vigorous. All Cree mother-tongue speakers in Canada total 67,495 according to the 1981 census.

Cree, Coastal Eastern: around 5,000 speakers reported in 1987 from a population of 5,800, in Quebec, Canada. Also known as East Cree and Eastern James Bay Cree. Language use is vigorous.

Cree, Inland Eastern: around 2,200 speakers reported in 1987 in Quebec, Canada. Also known as Mistassini. Language use is vigorous.

Cree, Western: around 35,000 speakers reported in 1982 from a population of 53,000 or more, in north central Manitoba, Canada, westward across Saskatchewan and Alberta, and in Montana, USA. Includes the major varieties Plains Cree and Woods Cree. Vigorous language use by all ages in the north; in the south, speakers are mainly middle-aged or older.

Fox: 800 speakers reported in 1977 from a population of 2,500, including the Mesquakie at Tama, Iowa, USA, and the Sac and Fox on the eastern Kansas-Nebraska border and in central Oklahoma. Also known as Sauk-Fox. Language use is vigorous in Iowa; elsewhere most speakers are middle-aged or older.

Kickapoo: around 1,200 total speakers reported in 1977 from a population of 1,500, including 500 in Coahuila, Mexico; the rest are in northeastern Kansas and central Oklahoma, USA. Sometimes spelled Kikapu. Speakers are partially bilingual in English in the USA, and in Spanish in Mexico.

Mahican: an extinct language formerly spoken on the upper Hudson River.

Maliseet-Passamaquoddy: around 1,500 speakers reported in 1982 in New Brunswick, Canada, and Maine, USA, from a population of 3,000. Maliseet (also spelled Malecite) is spoken mainly in Canada, Passamaquoddy in Maine. Most speakers are older; in some communities younger people may speak the language, though English is preferred by most younger people.

Massachusett: an extinct language of southeastern Massachusetts, USA. Also known as Natick or Wampanoag. Probably extinct.

Menominee: 50 elderly speakers reported in 1977 from a population of 3,500, in northeastern Wisconsin, USA.

Miami-Illinois: now extinct, formerly spoken in Illinois and north central Indiana and by displaced populations in northeast Oklahoma, USA.

Micmac: around 8,100 speakers reported in 1977 from a population of 11,000, with 6,000 in parts of Nova Scotia, Prince Edward Island, New Brunswick, and Quebec, Canada. Most adults speak Micmac. Younger people may prefer English in some communities. The Restigouche Quebec dialect is not fully mutually intelligible with other dialects.

Montagnais: around 7,000 speakers reported in 1987 from a population of 9,000, along the north shore of the Gulf of St. Lawrence and the St. Lawrence River, Quebec, Canada, and on the Labrador coast. Language use is vigorous except in the southwest.

Munsee: fewer than 15 speakers estimated in 1990 from a population of 400 on the Moraviantown Reserve, Ontario, Canada. Formerly spoken in the lower Hudson and upper Delaware valleys, USA. Locally called Delaware.

Nanticoke: now extinct, formerly spoken in southern Delaware, USA.

Narragansett: an extinct language formerly spoken in New England. Very similar to Massachusett.

Naskapi: 400 speakers reported in 1987 from a population of 765, on the Labrador coast, Canada. Closely related to Montagnais, but distinct. Language use is vigorous.

Ojibwa, Eastern: around 8,000 speakers reported in 1977 from a population of 25,000, around Lake Huron and southeastern Ontario, Canada; also spoken by the Chippewa and Ottawa of Michigan, USA, and by the Algonkin of eastern Ontario and Maniwaki, Quebec. The language is dying out in many areas, but is still spoken by most adults and some younger people of the large Indian population on Manitoulin Island in Lake Huron, where it is sometimes called Odawa.

Ojibwa, Northern: around 8,000 speakers reported in 1977, in Manitoba and northern Ontario, Canada. Also known as Cree-Saulteaux, Cree, or Severn Ojibwa. Language use is vigorous.

Ojibwa, Western: around 35,000 speakers reported in 1977 from a population of 60,000. Spoken in southern Canada from Lake Superior westward and northwestward into Saskatchewan, with outlying groups as far west as British Columbia. Also from Lake Superior to North Dakota and Montana in the USA. Sometimes known as Saulteaux, Chippewa, or Southern Ojibway. Ojibwa is the major means of communication of most in Canada, although in some areas young people and children may prefer English. In the USA, most speakers are middle-aged or older.

Piscataway: an extinct language formerly spoken on the Atlantic coast of the southern USA. Also called Conoy.

Potawatomi: 500 speakers reported in 1977 from a population of 7,500, in Michigan, Wisconsin, Kansas, and Oklahoma, USA, and Ontario, Canada. Most speakers are middle-aged or older.

Powhatan: now extinct, formerly spoken in eastern Virginia, USA. Also called Virginia Algonkian.

Shawnee: 200 speakers reported in 1977 from a population of 2,000, in central and northeastern Oklahoma, USA. Most speakers are middle-aged or older.

Unami: fewer than 10 speakers estimated in 1990 from a population of 2,000 in Oklahoma, USA. Formerly spoken in the lower Delaware Valley and New Jersey. Also called Delaware and Lenape.

ALTAIC LANGUAGES constitute a widely, though not universally, accepted linguistic stock uniting the Turkic, Mongolian, and Tungusic families [*qq.v.*]. (For reference, see Poppe 1965, Clauson 1956). Proposals have been made for classifying other languages or language families within the stock: the inclusion of Korean and Japanese (Miller 1971), and to a lesser extent, Ainu (Patrie 1982), is widely promoted at present; but the suggestion of a particularly close genetic relationship with Uralic is now out of favor.

The MONGOLIAN family of languages (Poppe 1955) are spoken primarily in the Mongolian People's Republic and adjacent parts of China (Inner Mongolia) and the USSR, with the majority of speakers in China; there is also an outlier, Mogholi, in Afghanistan, and Kalmyk is spoken northwest of the Caspian Sea. The most divergent members of the family—Mogholi, Bonan, Dagur, Tu or Monguor, and Dongxiang or Santa (the last four spoken in China)—are clearly distinct languages. Other varieties are sufficiently close to be viewed as dialects of a single Mongolian language, and are usually so considered in China. In the USSR, Buryat and Kalmyk (the latter properly a subvariety of Oirat) have the status of distinct languages, and are written in the Cyrillic alphabet—as is Mongolian in the Mongolian People's Republic. The Mongolian language itself is a typical member of the family. 'Classical Mongolian' refers to the written language of the Mongols, attested from the 13th century; it is written in the vertical Uighur script which still serves as the writing system for Mongolian in China.

The TUNGUSIC languages are spoken in eastern Siberia (Benzing 1955). The family has two branches, Northern and Southern. The Northern branch consists of Evenki (Tungus, also perhaps including the varieties referred to as Ewenki and Oroqen in China—although in China these two are considered distinct languages), Even (Lamut), and Negidal. The Southern branch in turn divides into Southwestern and Southeastern. The Southwestern branch includes the extinct Juchen (Jurchen, Nuzhen) and the virtually extinct Manchu, the language of the dynasty that ruled China from 1644 to 1911; one aberrant variety of Manchu, Xibo, is considered a distinct language in China. The Southeastern branch consists of two subgroups: the Nanai subgroup includes Nanai (Gold), Ulcha, and Orok (Ulta), while the Udehe subgroup includes Udehe and Oroch. The language referred to as Hezhe in China, and often called Nanai by Soviet scholars, seems to be closer to the Udehe subgroup. For the locations of Mongolian and Tungusic languages in China and Mongolia, see Map 1; for Kalmyk, see Map 2. [*For locations in the USSR, see also* Siberian Languages.]

Manchu has a traditional writing system, using a derivative of the Uighur vertical script. Evenki, Even, and Nanai are written languages in the USSR, and use the Cyrillic alphabet.

Typologically, the Altaic languages are very similar, though this is of course no indication of genetic relatedness. Vowel harmony is found in all three branches; but in Turkic and Mongolian it is based on the front/back opposition, while in Tungusic it is based on a higher/lower vowel opposition (perhaps originally reflecting advanced/retracted tongue root harmony; see Ard 1980). The latter type is also found in some other languages of the area (Chukotko-Kamchatkan, Gilyak, and Middle Korean). Phoneme inventories are relatively simple, other than as required by the exigencies of vowel harmony (e.g. front rounded and non-low back unrounded vowels). Morphology is predominantly agglutinating and almost exclusively suffixing. Word order is of the head-final type, with the verb normally clause-final; adjectives, genitives, relative clauses etc. precede their head nouns, and postpositions are used. The combination of clauses into complex sentences is primarily by means of non-finite constructions, such as participles

MAP 1. *Distribution of Mongolian and Tungusic Languages of China and Mongolia*

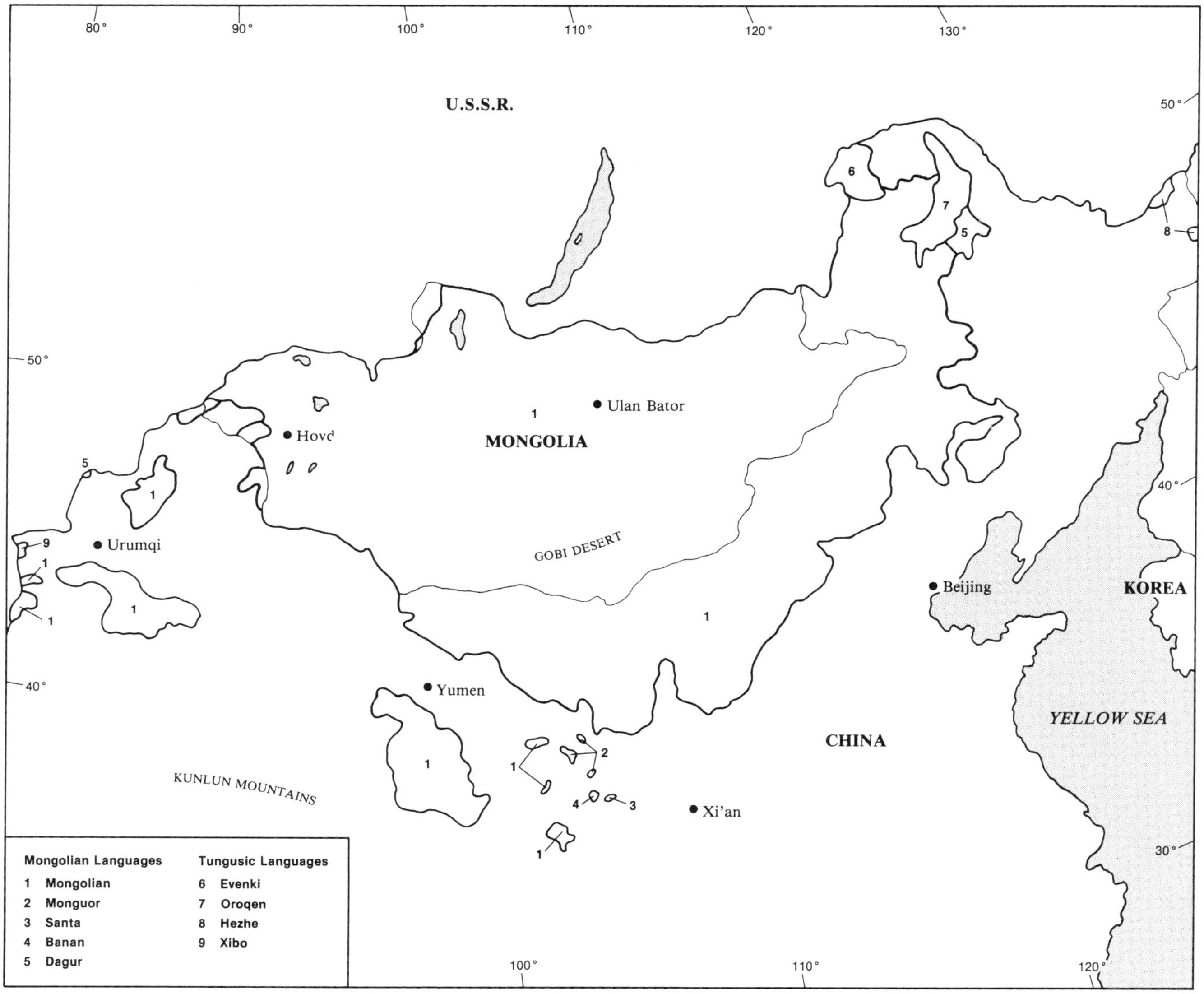

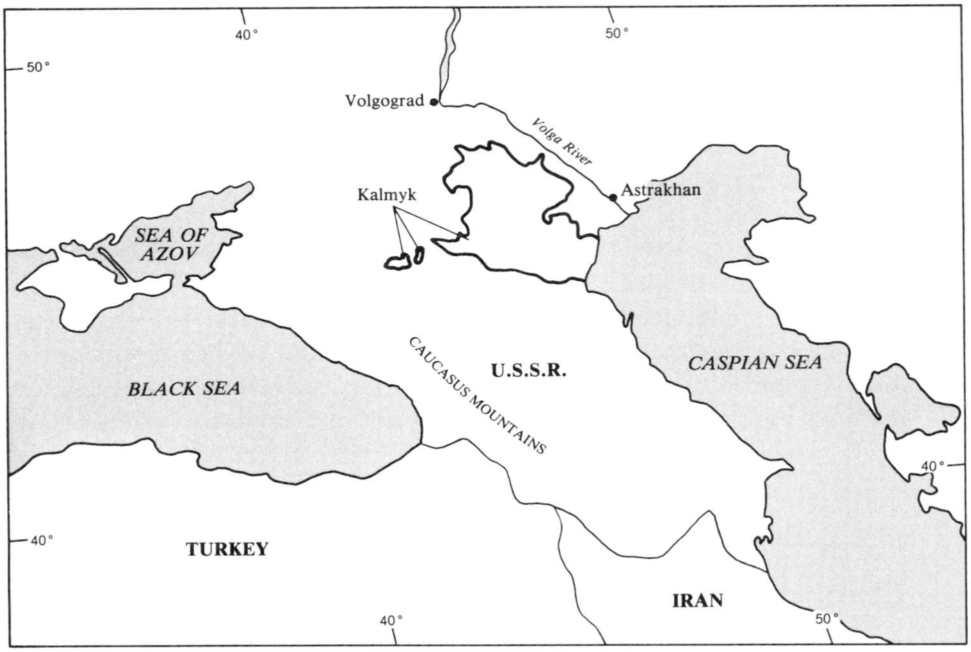

MAP 2. *Location of Kalmyk*

(verbal adjectives) and nominalizations—which are not always clearly distinguished from one another—and 'gerunds' (verbal adverbs). Turkish and Mongolian are typical Altaic languages in these respects.

It is clear that the Turkic, Mongolian, and Tungusic languages share much vocabulary; however, controversy surrounds the issue of whether this reflects a shared inheritance from a common ancestor, or widespread borrowing as a result of contacts among the languages. The controversy increases when more distant members of the stock, such as Korean, are proposed. One problem is that few lexical items are shared by all of Turkic, Mongolian, and Tungusic: usually one finds Turkic/Mongolian or Mongolian/Tungusic parallels in the absence of Turkic/Tungusic parallels, and this reflects the pattern of cultural contacts. The shared material includes bound affixes; but the usually transparently agglutinating nature of Altaic morphology makes it not improbable that even such affixes spread by diffusion. For instance, the agentive suffixes Turkic *-či* and Mongolian *-če* are clearly cognate; but precisely this suffix has been borrowed from the Turkic language Uzbek into the Iranian (Indo-European) language Tajik—which attests to its ease of diffusion. Striking similarities exist among the pronominal systems of the three branches of Altaic; but since similar forms are also found in Indo-European, Uralic, Yukaghir, and Chukotko-Kamchatkan, they are probably indicative of a deeper-level genetic relationship (Nostratic, Eurasiatic), rather than of particularly close links among Turkic, Mongolian, and Tungusic. The pattern involves a labial in the 1st person and a dental in the 2nd, as shown in Table 1.

BERNARD COMRIE

TABLE 1. *Pronoun Forms in Altaic and Some Other Languages*

	'I'	'you' (sg.)	'we'	'you' (pl.)
Turkish	*ben*	*sen*	*biz*	*siz*
Mongolian	*bi*	*či* (< **ti*)	*bid*	*ta*
Manchu	*bi*	*si*	*be*	*suwe*
Finnish	*mina*	*sina* (< **tina*)	*me*	*te*
Yukagir	*met*	*tet*	*mit*	*tit*
Chukchi	*gəm*	*gət*	*muri*	*turi*
Latin (acc.)	*me*	*te*	(*nōs*)	(*vōs*)

BIBLIOGRAPHY

ARD, JOSH. 1980. A sketch of vowel harmony in the Tungus languages. In *Studies in the languages of the USSR* (International Review of Slavic Linguistics, 5), edited by Bernard Comrie, pp. 23–43. Edmonton: Linguistic Research.

BENZING, JOHANNES. 1955. *Die tungusischen Sprachen: Versuch einer vergleichenden Grammatik.* Wiesbaden: Steiner.

CLAUSON, GERARD. 1956. The case against the Altaic theory. *Central Asiatic Journal* 2.181–187.

MILLER, ROY ANDREW. 1971. *Japanese and the other Altaic languages.* Chicago: University of Chicago Press.

PATRIE, JAMES. 1982. *The genetic relationship of the Ainu language.* Honolulu: University Press of Hawaii.

POPPE, NICHOLAS. 1955. *Introduction to Mongolian comparative studies.* (Mémoires de la Société Finno-Ougrienne, 110.) Helsinki: Suomalais-Ugrilainen Seura.

POPPE, NICHOLAS. 1965. *Introduction to Altaic linguistics.* (Ural-Altaische Bibliothek, 14.) Wiesbaden: Harrassowitz.

AMERICAN INDIAN LANGUAGES. *See* Anthropological Linguistics, *article on* Early History in North America; *see also* Central American Languages; Meso-American Languages; North American Languages; South American Languages.

AMHARIC is the official language of Ethiopia, according to the constitution adopted in 1987. It is the language of instruction through grade 6, and will be extended to grades 7–12 and possibly to the university level. A 1984 census of Addis Ababa, the capital and dominant urban center, shows that about half its 1,412,000 people claim Amharic as their first language. Nationally, an estimate is difficult; but a study of distribution and population density done in 1968–69 (Bender et al. 1976:10 ff.) shows that about one-third of the Ethiopian population is likely to speak Amharic as first language. This would imply about 14 million out of a total population of over 42 million in 1985. The number of other users of Amharic might bring the total to two-thirds or about 28 million—plus several hundred thousand outside Ethiopia, especially in Sudan. Thus, in number of speakers, Amharic is second only to Arabic among living Semitic languages [*q.v.*], and behind only Swahili and Hausa among indigenous African languages.

For the most recent general background on Ethiopian languages, as of the early 1970s, see Bender et al. 1976; in addition to sociolinguistics and language in education, the volume includes a general overview, descriptions of Ethio-Semitic, the Ethiopian language area, Amharic (including regional variation), Tigrinya, Gi'iz, the Ethiopian writing system, and descriptions of other languages. For Amharic and the Amhara people, see Messing 1985. Among grammars of Amharic, Cohen 1936 is the classic. Dawkins 1960 is a good reference grammar. Pedagogically, Leslau 1967 and Obolensky et al. 1964–65 are outstanding. Leslau 1973 is a monumental English-Amharic dictionary; a concise edition was issued in 1976. No recent, accessible Amharic-English dictionary is available. For classification, see Hetzron 1972. Leslau 1965 is indispensable for literature on Ethio-Semitic up to 1965.

1. Classification. Amharic belongs to a branch of the Semitic family which also includes the extinct Epigraphic South Arabian and the Modern South Arabian languages. The Ethio-Semitic languages are divided into two branches: Northern, which consists of the extinct liturgical Gi'iz [gɨʕɨz] plus modern Tigré and Tigrinya; and Southern, a much larger and more complex group consisting of Amharic, Argobba, Gafat (extinct), Harari, and a geographical cluster of about fifteen 'Gurage' languages. Ethio-Semitic is surrounded and interpenetrated by two distantly related Afro-Asiatic families, Cushitic and Omotic; it has little direct contact with scattered languages of the Nilo-Saharan phylum along the northern, western, and southwestern periphery of Ethiopia. Other than Amharic, the most important languages of Ethiopia and the adjoining 'African horn' area are Tigrinya to the north, Oromo (formerly known as 'Galla', a pejorative term) mainly to the south, and Somali to the east.

The major linguistic influence on Amharic and other Ethio-Semitic languages has been from Cushitic, especially the Agew (Central Cushitic) and H[ighland] E[ast] C[ushitic] branches (Sidamo and relatives).

2. Lexicon. The basic lexicon of Amharic is about 75 percent Semitic, including such items as *dʌm* 'blood', *ɨsat* 'fire', *ras* 'head', *motʌ* 'die', *bʌlla* 'eat', *hullu* 'all', and *nʌcc'* 'white'. It also has such intrusions as *wɨšša* 'dog' (< HEC, cf. Sem. *kʌlb*); *sɨga* 'meat' (< Agew; cf. Sem. *bsr*); and *wɨha* 'water' (< Agew or HEC, cf. Sem. *may*).

Classical Gi'iz is a source of religious terms, and more recently of technical terminology. Greek also contributed religious terms, starting with the origins of Ethiopian Orthodox Christianity in the 4th century. Other languages have also had their periods and domains of influence, including Arabic, Portuguese, Italian, French, and English: e.g. *bunna* 'coffee' (Ar.); *fabrika* 'factory' (It.); *bosta* 'post (office)', *bolis* 'police' (Fr.); and *tayp* 'typewriter' (Eng.)

In the 1970s and 1980s, much word-coinage was underway as the Marxist-Leninist government attempted to develop political lexicon for use in education and literacy. Direct loans were to be used only where internal sources, such as previously unused derived forms, were not available.

3. Variation. Part of the reason for the dearth of systematic studies of Amharic dialectology may be the relative uniformity of the language over its core area. Phonologically, the present and former dominant urban centers of Addis Ababa and Gonder (the latter up to the end of the 18th century) form one group; but syntactically, Addis Ababa groups with Shewa and Wello provinces.

There are lexical differences between town and countryside, some phonological and semantic shifts, and some genuine lexical doublets—e.g., 'knife' is *billawa* in Addis Ababa, *karra* in some other areas. There are interesting secret languages or argots, especially those reported on by Leslau 1964; they include varieties used by merchants, minstrels, and persons 'possessed by a *zar* spirit'. In Addis Ababa around 1980, the basic formula of one variety transposed *gɨn* 'but' into *gaynʌn*, and *bunna bet* 'coffee house, bar' into *bwaynʌn baytʌt* (cf. Teshome & Bender 1983).

4. History. The self-name of Amharic is *am(h)arɨñña,* in which *-ñña* denotes 'language of' (similarly Tigrinya, Orominya, etc.). The term 'Amhara' is folk-etymologized as being from a root *amr* 'be beautiful, peaceful, lovable, seductive'. Certainly there is a region named Amhara on the northern side of the Blue Nile near the Bashilo confluence, in what is today Begemidir and Wello provinces; from there the language presumably spread over the past eight centuries. Early Amharic documents are relatively scarce; Gi'iz was used for most literary purposes.

Hetzron 1972 argues that Gi'iz was not the ancestor of the present-day Ethio-Semitic languages, but was instead a sister to Tigré and Tigrinya in the Northern group. Even before the fall of the early Christian Ethiopian state at Aksum in the late 10th century, we find the beginnings of Amhara in a region whose autochthons were probably Agews. It is quite possible that by the 17th century, the recruitment of military forces from diverse ethnicities in and around Amhara may have resulted in a triglossic situation—with the rulers speaking a Gi'iz-like language, the soldiers speaking a Gi'iz-based creole in addition to their own tongues, and the peasantry using both the creole and Agew. As with the Romance languages, the modern language is a descendant not of the literary standard, but of a vernacular—in this case, creolized.

Attempts at standardizing Amharic are mainly 20th-century developments. The establishment of an Ethiopian Language Academy began with an imperial proclamation of 1943; an Amharic Language Academy was implemented in 1972, and expansion to multilingual status occurred under the provisional military government in 1976. Among the tasks of the new Academy have been the preparation of an Amharic dictionary, the coining of terms in technical areas such as physics and biology, and the preparation of dictionaries and literacy programs in several languages.

5. Phonology. Compared to 'classical' Semitic languages, Amharic can be characterized as having ejective ('glottalized') consonants instead of pharyngealized ('emphatic') ones; a near lack of laryngeals and pharyngeals; a new palatal series; and an unusually rich vowel inventory of seven qualities, making up for loss of vowel length.

The consonantal phonemes are shown in Table 1 (cf. Cohen 1936:30); those which do not occur in all dialects, or are marginal where they occur, are enclosed in parentheses.

TABLE 1. *Amharic Consonant Phonemes*

	Labial	Apical	Palatal	Velar	Labio-velar	Laryngeal
Occlusives						
Plain	(p)	t	c	k	(k^w)	(ʔ)
Voiced	b	d	j	g	(g^w)	
Ejective	(p')	t'	c'	k'	(k'^w)	
Fricatives						
Plain	f	s	š		(h^w)	(h)
Voiced		z	ž			
Ejective		(s')				
Nasals	m	n	ñ			
Lateral		l				
Vibrant		r				
Semivowels	w		y			

Articulation of consonants is not subject to much variation. Note the following:

(a) Labials: *b* → [β] between vowels, e.g. *addis abʌba* → [addis aβʌβa] → [addis aββa]. Labial *p p'* are rare (an Ethiopian and Middle Eastern areal characteristic): *p* is mainly in French loans (e.g. *posta*, usually pronounced *bosta* by the unsophisticated).
(b) Alveolars: Ejective *s'* (sometimes pronounced [ts']) yields to *t'* in Shewa Province (e.g. *s'ʌhay* 'sun' > *t'ʌhay*).
(c) Palatals: *j* > *ž*, e.g. *jɨb* > *žɨb* 'hyena'. Even though palatals historically arose from apicals or velars, the process is not automatic today; e.g., in verbs, the fem. sg. imperative shows palatalization (*hid-i* 'go!' → *hij-i, hij*), but cf. *bet-e* 'my house', *anat'i* 'carpenter'.
(d) Velars and labiovelars: a common change is illustrated by *gondʌr* (a placename) > *gwʌndʌr*. Labials may also be rounded to [bʷ mʷ fʷ]. Contrasts like *gʌddʌlʌ* 'kill' vs. *gwʌddʌlʌ* 'lack' are rare. In Shewa, medial *k'* varies with ʔ, e.g. *bʌk'lo* 'mule' > *bʌʔlo*.
(e) Laryngeals: *h* is retained in common words like *wɨha* 'water', *c'ohʌ* 'shout'; but elsewhere, *h*~*k*~Ø, e.g. *(h)amsa*~*kamsa* 'fifty', *(h)agʌr* 'country', *am(h)ara* 'Amhara'. The glottal stop is often lost in words like *sʌʔat* 'hour, watch' and *sɨʔɨl* 'picture'.

The vowel phonemes consist of *i u e o a* plus higher central *ɨ* and lower centralized *ʌ* (sometimes transcribed *ä* or ɛ). The quality of the latter ranges from more fronted to lower and more back. It is the most frequent vowel in the language; e.g., it is the usual vowel in basic verb forms such as *sʌbbʌrʌ* 'he broke'.

The higher central *ɨ* corresponds to the neutral shwa (usually indicated by *ə*) elsewhere in Semitic. Although *ɨ* is largely predictable from phonotactics, it is distinctive—as seen by pairs like *sɨm* 'name' vs. *sʌm* 'wax', *gɨm* 'putrid' vs. *gum* 'fog', *t'ɨm* 'thirst' vs. *t'im* 'beard'.

Dialectally, *e* often has a palatal on-glide, e.g. [bʸet] 'house'. In words which once had laryngeals or pharyngeals, *ʌ* is often replaced by *a*. Vowels in sequence obey a hierarchy of strength; *a* absorbs others at one end, while *ɨ* is absorbed by others at the other end, and identical vowels generally coalesce. In some cases, however, glides are inserted (*o*+*o* → [oʷo], *i*+*a* → [iʸa]).

There are no long vowels, but geminate consonants abound, both lexically and morphologically. Initial clusters must have *l r* as a second member; finals are less restricted; and medials of more than two are broken up by epenthesis of *ɨ*.

6. Writing system. Amharic has an 'alpha-syllabic' script; i.e., basic characters for consonants are obligatory, modified for seven 'orders' of vowels, as shown in Table 2. The sixth order corresponds to both *ɨ* and zero, because of the often epenthetic nature of *ɨ*.

The script is a continuation of the one found in northern Ethiopia and coastal Arabia, used in ancient times for Epigraphic South Arabian languages and for Gi'iz. It is related to the other consonantal scripts of Middle Eastern antiquity. The innovation of a modification for vowels, beginning about 350 CE, may be a result of stimulus diffusion from India. Complications are introduced by the retention of two (consonantal!) symbols for *a* (representing ancient ʔ ʕ), three symbols for *h* (ancient *h ḥ x*), and two for *s'*. The system does not mark gemination; the sixth order is ambiguous; several distinctions are today only etymological; and there is a fair degree of irregularity. For these reasons, a revised, governmentally approved system has recently been announced, after many decades of struggle with conservative clergy and literati.

In Table 2, note the set of special symbols for labialized consonants, the punctuation marks, and the numeration symbols (some said to be derived from Greek letters). The latter are almost never used, except in dates, since their lack of zero makes arithmetic difficult.

7. Grammar. All modern Ethio-Semitic languages belong to a Northeast African convergence area, which also includes Cushitic, Omotic, and Nilo-Saharan languages. The basis of this convergence is S[ubject] O[bject] V[erb] syntax in the normal independent clause order. Semitic probably had VSO order in ancient times; Gi'iz shows VSO with much variation—perhaps an effect of written transmission by non-native speakers.

Amharic marks number and gender in nouns, pronouns, and verbs, but the Semitic dual is absent. With nouns, number is often unmarked (e.g. *wʌmbʌr amt'a* 'bring a chair (or chairs)!' When necessary, *-oc* (from older *-at*) is used, e.g. *wʌndɨmmoc* 'brothers'. A few examples of archaic Semitic plural formations are preserved; and 'brother' and 'sister' have reciprocal plurals, *wʌndɨmmamac* 'brothers (to each other)' and *ɨhitɨmmamac* 'sisters (to each other)'.

Gender distinctions consist of masculine (unmarked) and feminine (marked by suffix *-t* or concord in verb form). The latter is used for female beings, in diminu-

TABLE 2. *The Amharic Script.* (From Bender et al. 1976: 121–22.)

Basic Character	Order							Labialized					
	1st ʌ	2nd u	3rd i	4th a	5th e	6th ɨ	7th o	-wʌ	-wi	-wa	-we	-wɨ	-ya
h	ሀ	ሁ	ሂ	ሃ	ሄ	ህ	ሆ						
l	ለ	ሉ	ሊ	ላ	ሌ	ል	ሎ			ሏ			
h	ሐ	ሑ	ሒ	ሓ	ሔ	ሕ	ሖ			ሗ			
m	መ	ሙ	ሚ	ማ	ሜ	ም	ሞ			ᎀ ሟ			
s	ሠ	ሡ	ሢ	ሣ	ሤ	ሥ	ሦ			ሧ			
r	ረ	ሩ	ሪ	ራ	ሬ	ር	ሮ			ሯ ሯ			ፘ
s	ሰ	ሱ	ሲ	ሳ	ሴ	ስ	ሶ			ሷ			
š	ሸ	ሹ	ሺ	ሻ	ሼ	ሽ	ሾ			ሿ			
k'	ቀ	ቁ	ቂ	ቃ	ቄ	ቅ	ቆ	ቈ	ቊ	ቋ	ቌ	ቍ	
b	በ	ቡ	ቢ	ባ	ቤ	ብ	ቦ			ቧ			
t	ተ	ቱ	ቲ	ታ	ቴ	ት	ቶ			ቷ			
c	ቸ	ቹ	ቺ	ቻ	ቼ	ች	ቾ			ቿ			
h	ኀ	ኁ	ኂ	ኃ	ኄ	ኅ	ኆ	ኈ	ኊ	ኋ	ኌ	ኍ	
n	ነ	ኑ	ኒ	ና	ኔ	ን	ኖ			ኗ			
ñ	ኘ	ኙ	ኚ	ኛ	ኜ	ኝ	ኞ			ኟ			
(a)	አ	ኡ	ኢ	ኣ	ኤ	እ	ኦ						
k	ከ	ኩ	ኪ	ካ	ኬ	ክ	ኮ	ኰ	ኲ	ኳ	ኴ	ኵ	
h	ኸ	ኹ	ኺ	ኻ	ኼ	ኽ	ኾ			ዃ			
w	ወ	ዉ	ዊ	ዋ	ዌ	ው	ዎ						
(a)	ዐ	ዑ	ዒ	ዓ	ዔ	ዕ	ዖ						
z	ዘ	ዙ	ዚ	ዛ	ዜ	ዝ	ዞ			ዟ			
ž	ዠ	ዡ	ዢ	ዣ	ዤ	ዥ	ዦ			ዧ			
y	የ	ዩ	ዪ	ያ	ዬ	ይ	ዮ						
d	ደ	ዱ	ዲ	ዳ	ዴ	ድ	ዶ			ዷ			
j	ጀ	ጁ	ጂ	ጃ	ጄ	ጅ	ጆ			ጇ			
g	ገ	ጉ	ጊ	ጋ	ጌ	ግ	ጎ	ጐ	ጒ	ጓ	ጔ	ጕ	
t'	ጠ	ጡ	ጢ	ጣ	ጤ	ጥ	ጦ			ጧ			
c'	ጨ	ጩ	ጪ	ጫ	ጬ	ጭ	ጮ			ጯ			
p'	ጰ	ጱ	ጲ	ጳ	ጴ	ጵ	ጶ						
s'	ጸ	ጹ	ጺ	ጻ	ጼ	ጽ	ጾ			ጿ			
s'	ፀ	ፁ	ፂ	ፃ	ፄ	ፅ	ፆ						
f	ፈ	ፉ	ፊ	ፋ	ፌ	ፍ	ፎ			ፏ ፚ			
p	ፐ	ፑ	ፒ	ፓ	ፔ	ፕ	ፖ						

tives, and for endearment or solidarity; thus a small boy or girl may be addressed as feminine, and *ayt'* 'mouse' is usually feminine.

N[oun] P[hrase]s are marked as definite by use of a demonstrative, possessive, or definite article (masc. *-u*, fem. *-wa, -itu, -itwa*). Definite NPs as objects are marked as accusative by *-n*. Nominative is unmarked; other case-marking is by prepositions and postpositions. Possessed nouns take two forms, e.g. *bet-e* 'house-my' or *yʌ-ne bet* 'of-me house'.

Pronouns mark gender in the 2/3sg.; deference is expressed by the use of variants of plural forms for 2nd and 3rd persons. The persons of verb subjects follow the Semitic pattern, with some idiosyncrasies, as shown in Table 3.

Amharic maintains the Semitic characteristic of consonantal skeletons carrying semantic values, with vocalic inserts for tense, aspect, etc. Verbs fall into two main lexical classes: (i) those with geminated medial consonant in the Imperfective (e.g. *yɨ-fʌllɨg-al* 'he wants'); and (ii) those without (*yɨ-sʌbr-al* 'he breaks'). The Semitic gemination for transitives, with non-gemination

TABLE 3. *Amharic Subject Pronouns*

Singular		Plural
1sg.	Ø	1pl. *n*
2sg.masc.	*t* or *k* > *h*	2pl. *t* + pl. *-u*
2sg.fem.	*t, š*	
3sg.masc.	*y*, Ø	3pl. *y* + pl. *-u*
3sg.fem.	*t, c*	

for intransitives, seems to have been transferred into aspects (on the contrary; i.e., gemination for Imperfect occurs in North Ethio-Semitic).

Verbs show the Semitic major division into Perfective (complete) vs. Imperfective (incomplete) action; the former has pronominal suffixes, while the latter has both prefixes and suffixes. There are five tenses:

(1)	Non-past:	*yɨ-sʌbr-al(l)*	'he breaks, is breaking, will break'
	Past:	*sʌbbʌr-ʌ*	'he broke'
	Past Continuous:	*yɨsʌbɨr nʌbbʌr*	'he was breaking'
	Perfect:	*sʌbro-al(l)*	'he has broken'
	Past Perfect:	*sʌbro nʌbbʌr*	'he had broken'

The past and perfect fall together in the negative. In subordinate clauses, normally only Non-past and Past are distinguished.

Morphological derivation is very active in Amharic. Most verbs have an intransitive (passive) *tʌ-* form (e.g. *tʌ-bʌlla* 'it was eaten'); many have forms with transitive (causative) *a-* or factitive (indirect causative) *as-* (*a-mʌtt'a* 'he brought', *as-bʌlla* 'he caused someone to eat'). Other derivative verbs include the reciprocal, repetitive, and conative. Nouns and other form classes are also derived; e.g.,

(2) *s'af-i* 'writer' < *s'af-ʌ* 'he wrote'
s'ɨt'ota 'gift' < *s'ʌtt'-ʌ* 'he gave'

Amharic is not a 'rigid' SOV language. It has some features which can be seen as transitional from the older Semitic VSO type. Thus Amharic retains Semitic prepositions like *lʌ-* 'for', *bʌ-* 'by', but it also has postpositions like *-wɨst'* 'in(side)', *-lay* 'on'. More common are 'parapositions' having both components:

(3) *ɨ-bet-wɨst'* 'at-house-in'
kʌ-bet-hwala 'from-house-back'

Among typical SOV features are the preposing of subordinate clauses (e.g. *yʌ-hedʌ sʌw* 'of-went person', i.e. 'a person who went'), and the extensive use of a subordinate form known as the 'converb' (less accurately, gerund):

(4) *dabbo bʌl-t-ʌn wʌtʌt t'ʌtt'-ɨt-ʌn t'ʌgb-ʌn tʌgwaznʌ.*
bread eaten milk drunk satisfied we.set.out
'Having eaten bread and drunk milk, we set out satisfied.'

An interesting Ethiopian areal feature is the use of the verb 'say' as an auxiliary, both in many idiomatic expressions (ex. 5) and in subordinate constructions (ex. 6):

(5) *zɨmm bʌl* 'say *zɨmm*', i.e. 'be quiet!'
k'ucc' bʌl 'say *k'ucc'*', i.e. 'sit!'

(6) *gʌrʌdwa yʌne nʌw bɨla wʌssʌdʌccɨw.*
'The maid took it, saying, "It is mine"', i.e. '. . . thinking it was hers'.

There are two basic conjugated copular forms, both also used as verbal auxiliaries: (3sg. masc.) *nʌw* 'be', *allʌ* 'exist'. These are used only in the present; their shared past is *nʌbbʌr*. For the future, etc., *honʌ* 'become' and *norʌ* 'dwell', respectively, are used. Negatives are *aydʌllʌm* and *yʌllʌm,* respectively.

M. LIONEL BENDER

BIBLIOGRAPHY

BENDER, MARVIN LIONEL, et al., eds. 1976. *Language in Ethiopia.* London & New York: Oxford University Press.

COHEN, MARCEL. 1936. *Traité de langue amharique (Abyssinie).* Paris: Institut d'Ethnologie. Reprinted, New York: Altai Press, 1970.

DAWKINS, C. H. 1960. *The fundamentals of Amharic.* Addis Ababa: Sudan Interior Mission. Reprinted, 1969.

HETZRON, ROBERT. 1972. *Ethiopian Semitic: Studies in classification.* (Journal of Semitic Studies, Monograph 2.) Manchester, England: Manchester University Press.

LESLAU, WOLF. 1964. *Ethiopian argots.* (Janua linguarum, Series practica, 17.) The Hague: Mouton.

LESLAU, WOLF. 1965. *An annotated bibliography of the Semitic languages of Ethiopia.* The Hague: Mouton.

LESLAU, WOLF. 1967. *Amharic textbook.* Wiesbaden: Harrassowitz.

LESLAU, WOLF. 1973. *English-Amharic context dictionary.* Wiesbaden: Harrassowitz. Concise edition, 1976.

Messing, Simon D. 1985. *The Highland Plateau Amhara of Ethiopia*. Edited by M. Lionel Bender. New Haven: Human Relations Area Files.

Obolensky, Serge, et al. 1964–65. *Amharic, basic course.* 2 vols. Washington, D.C.: Foreign Service Institute, U.S. Department of State. (With tapes.)

Teshome Demissie & Marvin Lionel Bender. 1983. An argot of Addis Ababa unattached girls. *Language in Society* 12.339–347.

AMTO-MUSAN LANGUAGES constitute a family comprising the two languages Amto and Musan, spoken to the south of the Upper Sepik River in Papua New Guinea, not far from the border with Irian Jaya (Indonesia). No higher-level genetic grouping of this family has been generally accepted.

LANGUAGE LIST

Amto: 230 speakers reported in 1981, toward the headwaters of the Left May River on the Samaia River, south of the upper Sepik River, Amanab District, West Sepik Province, Papua New Guinea. Also called Ki.

Musan: 75 speakers reported in 1981, in a village east of Amto, West Sepik Province, Papua New Guinea. Also known as Musian or Musa. Has 29 percent lexical similarity with Amto.

ANALOGY. Analogical change, or simply analogy, is a historical process which projects a generalization from one set of expressions to another. The term 'analogy' has been used also in reference to the acquisition of grammatical regularities by child or adult learners, and to the use (production or comprehension) of novel utterances. The latter was traditionally attributed wholly to analogy; today, analogy is sometimes postulated as a supplementary mechanism of derivative generation accounting for the use of utterances that are not directly generatable by the grammar.

Since the Neogrammarians, analogy has been ranked with regular phonological change [*q.v.*] and BORROWING [*q.v.*] as one of the three basic kinds of linguistic change. It is the most heterogeneous and problematic of them; indeed, we are still not sure what the various processes considered 'analogical' have in common, what causes them, or how they are constrained.

1. The traditional view distinguishes two types of analogy, PROPORTIONAL and NON-PROPORTIONAL. Proportional analogy is represented as the solving of equations of the form A:B = C:X, where the terms are related by 'associative links', e.g. *nose* : *noses* = *eye* : X, where X = *eyes* (replacing the older plural *eyne*). But many putatively proportional changes cannot be represented as proportions, and many proportions do not correspond to plausible analogical changes; moreover, the 'associative links' are ill-defined, and in any case insufficient (Morpurgo Davies 1978). Non-proportional analogy, for its part, subsumes an assortment of phenomena without unified analysis or principled relationship to proportional analogy. (The 'Connectionist' morphology of Rumelhart & McClelland 1986 is similarly unconstrained; see Pinker & Prince 1988.)

Kuryłowicz 1964, 1977 sought to resolve the problems with proportional analogy by two means, as follows. First, Kuryłowicz proposed to enrich proportions, letting their terms be made more abstract by (i) stripping words of 'redundant' morphemes, (ii) undoing the effects of automatic phonological rules, and (iii) allowing terms to be categories instead of particular words. Related proposals are that proportions can operate on distinctive feature representations (Garey 1959), and that several proportions can operate simultaneously in a single analogical change (Leed 1970).

Two examples can be cited from Kuryłowicz. First, Latin *-a* stems replace gen. sg. *-ās* with *-ī* from *-o* stems: fem. *bonās* > **bonaī* (> *bonae*), after masc. *bonī*. The proportion '*bonus* : *bonī* = *bona* : X' fails. Stripping the 'redundant' masc. nom. sg. *-us* gives the correct *bon-* : *bon + ī* = *bona* : **bonaī*. Second, in Classical Greek, *-nū*-stem verbs acquired subjunctives with long *-ō-/-ē-* by analogy with the subjunctives of the thematic verbs, e.g. 3sg. middle subjunc. *rhēgnuḗtai* from indic. *rhḗgnutai*, after subjunc. *lūḗtai* from indic. *lū́etai*. The proportion '*lū́etai* : *lūḗtai* = *rhḗgnutai* : X' yields only **rhēgnū́tai*. If we suppose that thematic subjunctives were reanalyzed as containing the theme vowel *e*, contracted with a subjunctive morpheme *ē* (i.e. *lūḗtai* = /lū + e + ḗ + tai/), then we get *rhēgnuḗtai* by building the proportion from the UNDERLYING forms: *lū́ + e + tai* : *lū + e + ḗ + tai* = *rhḗg + nu + tai* : *rhēg + nu + ḗ + tai*.

Second, Kuryłowicz proposed to constrain proportions by six 'Laws of Analogy'. The second of these says: 'Analogy proceeds from basic forms to subordinated forms.' The basic form, predicted to spread by analogy, is defined as one of the following:

(a) The most widely distributed form—i.e. unmarked morphological categories such as 3rd person, singular, present, indicative, nominative, masculine
(b) The structurally most differentiated form, from which

the others are most simply predictable (the basic allomorph of a morpheme)

These principles eliminate the worst weakness of proportions: their reversibility. For example, '*bona* : *bonās* = *bonus* : X' is impossible because masculine gender is unmarked.

Kuryłowicz's theory explicitly relates analogy to grammatical structure, replacing the 'associative links' of the Neogrammarians by the morphological categories and relations of the language, and the morphological analysis of the terms of proportions. This is important because, as in our Greek example, analogical proportions may presuppose a covert REANALYSIS, which may be syntagmatic or paradigmatic. All such reanalyses determine the possible course of analogy.

SYNTAGMATIC REANALYSIS, or resegmentation, may reassign segments or features of a stem to its affixes, or vice versa. It may reduce allomorphy, spawn new affixes ('secretion'), relocate a contrast (paradigmatic displacement'), or amalgamate affixes. An example is Eng. *-ist+ic*, in words like *cannibalistic*; here *-ist* is itself an amalgam in Greek of *-iz* (Eng. *-ize*) with the agent suffix *-tēs*, and both of these are in turn composites. Affix merger is often triggered by loss or semantic isolation of the intermediate stem (Kuryłowicz 1977:19).

PARADIGMATIC REANALYSIS includes several types. First, in MORPHOLOGIZATION, phonological variants become morphologically conditioned, typically when the rules relating them become opaque. Second, in LEXICALIZATION, phrases coalesce into compound words, and derived words into simple words. Third, in GRAMMATICALIZATION [*q.v.*], morphemes lose some or all of their lexical content. Thus lexical categories such as nouns, verbs, adjectives, and adverbs become non-lexical categories: auxiliaries, complementizers, pronouns, articles, pre- and post-positions, and other clitics (Givón 1971, Anderson 1980, 1988, Bybee 1985, Disterheft 1987). Similarly, heads of compounds and clitics become affixes; e.g., La. *cantāre habeō*, lit. 'to-sing I-have', becomes French *chanterai* 'I will sing'. Semantic case becomes grammatical case, and derivation becomes inflection. The reverse direction of change occurs, but is rare. Finally, in RECATEGORIZATION, a stem is assigned to a different morphological category. Thus deverbal analysis of originally denominal words like Eng. *doubtful, hateful* led to unambiguously deverbal *resentful, forgetful*.

2. Analogy as optimization. Going a step further, we can eliminate the proportions altogether, and treat analogy as a process of optimization of grammatical structure. We can take the acquisition process as the causal mechanism: if learners' successive grammars increase in coverage and complexity, then analogical change is 'imperfect learning', occurring when rules of intermediate grammars (or forms generated by them) are retained and become part of the linguistic norm. This approach has several advantages, as listed below.

The discontinuity of language transmission explains the possibility of radical reanalysis. Since learners try to match the speech of the community without having access to others' internalized grammars, they may construct very different grammars—as long as these generate nearly the same language. Even unique patterns may come to be apprehended as linguistic regularities, and may spread by analogy. For example, the suffix *-ess* is ultimately from the unique Gk. *basílissa* 'queen'. Again, in Old English (Anglian), the suppletive paradigm of 'to be'—1sg. *eam,* 2sg. *earþ,* 3sg. *is,* pl. *sind*—gave rise to a unique 1sg. suffix *-m,* which was generalized first to the synonymous verb *bēon* (1sg. *bīo* > *bīo+m*), and from there to other 'contracted' verbs, e.g. 1sg. *flēo* > *flēo+m* 'I flee' (Hogg 1980).

The optimization approach predicts that analogical change can be channeled by the structure of the language as a whole. For example, obeying the rule of English that all prefixes are derivational, analogy has 'secreted' new inflectional suffixes, such as the plural *-en* in *ox+en*—or the *-n* of predicative possessive pronouns, dialectally extended from *my, mine* to *your, yourn,* and *his, hisn.* But it has produced no inflectional prefixes. Thus the pattern *I, my* is not analyzed as prefixation of a genitive *m-*; analogical *you, *myou* or *it, *mit* are unthinkable. This analysis would also violate the English-specific constraint that prefixes are syllabic.

The optimization approach also brings many 'nonproportional' analogical changes out of their theoretical limbo, as with the following processes.

First, ADAPTATION—'a type of linguistic change which resembles analogic change, but goes on without model sets' (Bloomfield 1933:420)—arises from the composition of grammatical regularities. Thus the Eng. coinages *sclerosed, cirrhosed* combine regular suffixation of *-ed* (cf. *jaundic+ed*) with regular 'truncation' of suffixal *-is* (cf. *synthes+ize*).

Second, CONTAMINATION and BLENDING are illuminated by prosodic morphology (McCarthy & Prince 1990). Thus a productive derivational pattern in English is superimposition of the phonemic melody of one word upon the first foot of another, on the universal 'Procrustean' principle that long melodies are chopped off *(choco-holic, tele-thon),* while short melodies are extended to fit the template *(worka-holic, walka-thon).*

Third, LEVELING, which is 'non-proportional' because it does not require a non-alternating model paradigm, is the loss of listed allomorphs, or the simplification of the structural change of a rule. This includes partial leveling, which is especially recalcitrant to proportional treatment: in Sanskrit, the weak grade of laryngeal roots in *-am* changed from *-ā* to *-ām* (past pple. **krā + ta > krān + ta*); the rule 'Lengthen *a* and delete *n*' was simplified to 'Lengthen *a*.'

Fourth, PHONOLOGICAL ANALOGY, the generalization of purely phonotactic distributional regularities (with no associative links or morphological relationships on which to build a proportion) is the generalization of phonological rules. For example, the voiceless aspirated palatal /ch/ of Sanskrit happened to occur, when medial, mostly as a geminate [cch]; the few simple occurrences were later geminated, generalizing the rule 'Aspirated palatals, when medial, are geminated.'

The optimization approach explains the above-mentioned properties of proportions. Why is it that proportions (i) relate basic and subordinate forms, (ii) can interact, (iii) are applicable to feature representations, and (iv) presuppose a morphological analysis of words? It is because grammatical rules do these things. 'Basic forms' win out (Kuryłowicz's second law) because they correspond to the 'elsewhere' forms which appear wherever they are not pre-empted by other forms or rules—the least specified (maximally 'unmarked') morpheme of a paradigmatic set, the least contextually restricted allomorph of a morpheme, or the underlying form among phonologically conditioned alternants. When the least specified form is indeterminate, so is the direction of leveling. For example, the allomorphy of the Sanskrit gerund, *-tvā* after simple roots and *-(t)ya* after compounds, is leveled in both directions in Middle Indic. (On bidirectional leveling, see Tiersma 1978, Hock 1986—though some of their cases arguably involve predictable, contextually dependent directionality.)

Moreover, BACK-FORMATION—which requires 'backward' proportions such as *relation* : *relate* = *emotion* : X (where X = *emote*), and is against Kuryłowicz's second law—is explainable as actualization of a latent base form, eliminating the obligatory subcategorization of the base.

Optimization theories differ on the criteria that they assume. For early generative theory, the grammar attained by learners (under the idealizations of instantaneous acquisition and homogeneous data) was the simplest grammar for the primary linguistic data on which it was based, given a canonical descriptive format. From this perspective, optimization is just grammar SIMPLIFICATION. This is attractive because it is precisely defined, and because much of analogical change clearly does eliminate arbitrary complexity from the grammar—e.g. loss or simplification of rules, or of grammatical formatives. But it is too unconstrained, and fails to account for some systematic structural preferences.

Current theory envisages a set of structural PARAMETERS, each with a fixed number of settings, one of which is unmarked. The learner determines the values of those parameters, choosing the unmarked settings unless there is evidence to the contrary. Acquisition depends only on positive evidence, with linguistic data serving as a 'triggering experience' rather than as a basis for hypothesis-formation. Analogy should then tend towards unmarked parameter settings. (Bickerton 1981 suggests that creole languages have the unmarked parameter settings because they pass through a stage where the input is impoverished.) Suppose, e.g., that affix position is a morphological parameter, with suffixation unmarked. Then prefixing languages should be receptive to innovations introducing suffixes, while suffixing languages should not be receptive to innovations introducing prefixes. (Like many putative parameters, the crosslinguistic preference for suffixation invites processing explanations; see Cutler et al. 1985.) A similar phenomenon is the preference for head-marking, e.g. agreement, over dependent-marking, e.g. case (Nichols 1986:88, Van Valin 1987:393).

Formal optimization fails for analogy because it precludes non-structural factors like function and frequency, as well as local optimization—word-by-word rule generalization or parameter unmarking, which need not simplify the grammar until completed. There have been attempts to sustain the view of analogy as simplification by requiring more 'concrete' grammars, e.g. the Alternation Condition (Kiparsky 1973) and Natural Generative Grammar (Vennemann 1974, Hooper 1976): if the lexical entry of a morpheme lists all its allomorphs, even when these are fully predictable from general rules, then sporadic leveling will count as simplification because it reduces the lexicon. This approach proved inadequate for both synchrony and change, and has been largely abandoned.

NATURALNESS THEORIES attempt to capture features of

both synchrony and change by 'substantive' conditions which designate certain structures as preferred—e.g. unmarked feature specifications (Chomsky & Halle 1968, chap. 9); unmarked rule order (Kiparsky 1968); natural processes (characterized by 'metarules' in Chen 1973 and Ralph 1975); transparent rules (Kiparsky 1971, 1973); or paradigmatic uniformity and distinctness (Kiparsky 1972).

In Natural Morphology [*q.v.*], such preference conditions are not just supplements to formal simplicity; they are supposed to do the entire job. This theory posits five parameters of optimization, weighted as follows:

(a) System congruity: words should conform to the organizing principles of the language's morphology
(b) Uniformity of inflection classes
(c) Uniformity of encoding: allomorphy should be avoided
(d) Transparency: morphology should be compositional and unambiguous
(e) Constructional iconicity (diagrammaticity): formal marking (e.g. by an affix) should coincide with morphological markedness

Parameters (a)-(b) are defined on the grammatical system of each language; the others are grammar-independent semiotic criteria. Thus Natural Morphology builds 'functional' considerations directly into the definition of optimality; and it allows local checking of each condition, so that gradual changes driven by them optimize the system at each step. For details, see Mayerthaler 1981—where (e) is ranked above (c)-(d)—as well as Vennemann 1983, Wurzel 1984, 1985, 1987, Mayerthaler 1987, and Dressler 1987a.

Points (c)-(d) together constitute the 'one-form/one-meaning' principle, alias 'Humboldt's Universal' (Vennemann 1972) or 'unifunctionality' (Slobin 1973, 1985). Avoidance of polysemy and blocking effects are also related (Aronoff 1976, Kiparsky 1983, Anderson 1988, Markman 1986, Clark 1987).

3. Interactionist theories. A problem for all optimization theories is that no single ranking is possible, because different kinds of 'optimality' conflict. Thus parameter (c) of Natural Morphology, that allomorphy tends to be minimized, contradicts Kuryłowicz's first law, by which allomorphy tends to spread. This reflects conflicting functional pressures: allomorphy complicates the speaker's and learner's tasks; but it facilitates the hearer's, by increasing redundancy (see Shapiro 1974, Anttila 1975, Robinson 1980, Werner 1987). In addition, the role of frequency and saliency in determining the course of change remains unexplained, since they have no general structural correlate (although frequency for morphological categories partly corresponds to unmarked status).

Interactionist theories instead attempt to derive functional and frequency effects from the real-time acquisition and use of language, interacting with linguistic competence (Bever & Langendoen 1972, Vincent 1974, Kiparsky 1978). They see the constraints on analogical change as jointly determined by the source of innovated forms (imperfect learning, and perhaps lapses), and by their selective adoption into the linguistic system, the latter accounting for local analogy.

Specifically, let us assume that the likelihood of an innovation being adopted at a given point of the system is locally proportional to its functional value, and to the productivity (frequency and compositionality) of the process that derives it—but inversely proportional to its saliency, as measured by its distance from the old form, and to the old form's entrenchment, measured primarily by frequency. Hence the first innovations may penetrate, on the one hand, in productive morphological categories, and on the other hand, in infrequent lexemes (or uses of lexemes). The same factors appear to account also for selective actuation of other kinds of change (Naro 1981, Guy 1990).

As an illustration, consider phenomena of lexical split. An example of preferential regularization in productive categories is Eng. *elder* > *older* in the comparative; the old form is retained as an extraparadigmatic derivative, with the specialized meaning 'senior'. An example of preferential regularization in less entrenched uses of a lexeme is *wove* > *weaved* in the specialized meaning 'moved irregularly': here there is a single morphological category, which is regularized in a specialized meaning of the lexeme. Thus, in lexical split, the 'secondary function' is sometimes reserved for the old form *(elder)*, and sometimes for the new *(weaved)*—a fact for which structural optimization theories offer no account. One proposal is that, in the *elder* type, the functional distinction arises after the regularization; but in the *wove* type, it predates it (Hock 1986:226, following Kuryłowicz's fourth law of analogy: 'When a form is differentiated after a morphological change, the new form corresponds to its primary function, and the old form is restricted to its secondary function'). But this is not explanatory, and in any case contradicts the actual chronology. In fact, in the *elder* type, the rise of the secondary meaning typically predates the regularization; the secondary meanings of *elder, tithe,* and *straight* are attested well before the appearance of regularized *older, tenth* and *stretched.* In the *weaved* type, the meaning shift need not predate the regularization; e.g., the motion-verb use of *weave* is attested long after its first weak forms. Another proposal is that *elder* is first lexicalized in a specialized function, escaping the morphological regularization which affects its non-lexicalized homonym; but in *weaved/wove,* the semantic shift yields a new lexeme unburdened with the morphological irregularity of its source (Kiparsky 1974, Anderson 1988:359). This motivates the distinction between the two types, and fits the chronology; but the assumption of lexicalization is unwarranted. It is preferable to recognize degrees of productivity, with lexicalization as only the limiting case of unproductivity.

Interactionist theories thus see analogy as driven mainly by the acquisition of language, but shaped mainly by its use. This reconciles the apparent conflict between (i) the system-governed, global properties of analogy, explained by optimization theories, and (ii) its piecemeal spread through the system, in patterns explainable through the real-time production and comprehension of speech.

PAUL KIPARSKY

BIBLIOGRAPHY

ANDERSON, JOHN M., & CHARLES JONES, eds. 1974. *Historical linguistics: Proceedings of the First International Conference on Historical Linguistics,* vol. 2, *Theory and description in phonology.* Amsterdam: North-Holland.

ANDERSON, STEPHEN R. 1980. On the development of morphology from syntax. In *Historical morphology* (Trends in linguistics, Studies and monographs, 17), edited by Jacek Fisiak, pp. 51–69. The Hague: Mouton.

ANDERSON, STEPHEN R. 1988. Morphological change. In *Linguistics: The Cambridge survey,* vol. 1, *Linguistic theory: Foundations,* edited by Frederick J. Newmeyer, pp. 324–362. Cambridge & New York: Cambridge University Press.

ANTTILA, RAIMO. 1975. *The indexical element in morphology.* (Innsbrucker Beiträge zur Sprachwissenschaft, 12.) Innsbruck: Institut für Sprachwissenschaft der Universität.

ARONOFF, MARK. 1976. *Word formation in generative grammar.* (Linguistic Inquiry monographs, 1.) Cambridge, Mass.: MIT Press.

BEVER, THOMAS G., & D. TERENCE LANGENDOEN. 1972. The interaction of speech perception and grammatical structure in the evolution of language. In *Linguistic change and generative theory,* edited by Robert P. Stockwell & Ronald K. S. Macaulay, pp. 32–95. Bloomington: Indiana University Press.

BICKERTON, DEREK. 1981. *Roots of language.* Ann Arbor: Karoma.

BLOOMFIELD, LEONARD. 1933. *Language.* New York: Holt.

BYBEE, JOAN L. 1985. *Morphology: A study of the relation between meaning and form.* (Typological studies in language, 9.) Amsterdam: Benjamins.

CHEN, MATTHEW. 1973. On the formal expression of natural rules in phonology. *Journal of Linguistics* 9.223–249.

CHOMSKY, NOAM, & MORRIS HALLE. 1968. *The sound pattern of English.* New York: Harper & Row.

CLARK, EVE V. 1987. The principle of contrast. In *Mechanisms of language acquisition,* edited by Brian MacWhinney, pp. 2–10. Hillsdale, N.J.: Erlbaum.

CUTLER, ANNE; JOHN A. HAWKINS; & GARY GILLIGAN. 1985. The suffixing preference: A processing explanation. *Linguistics* 23.723–758.

DISTERHEFT, DOROTHY. 1987. The diachronic relationship of morphology and syntax. In Ramat et al. 1987, pp. 211–220.

DRESSLER, WOLFGANG U. 1987a. Word formation as part of natural morphology. In Dressler 1987b, pp. 99–126.

DRESSLER, WOLFGANG U., ed. 1987b. *Leitmotifs in Natural Morphology.* (Studies in language, Companion series, 10.) Amsterdam: Benjamins.

GAREY, HOWARD. 1959. *Verte, grande* and *longue*: Three types of analogy in Old French. *Language* 35.605–611.

GIVÓN, TALMY. 1971. Historical syntax and synchronic morphology: An archaeologist's field trip. *Chicago Linguistic Society* 7.394–415.

GUY, GREGORY. 1990. Saliency and the direction of syntactic change. To appear in *Language.*

HOCK, HANS HENRICH. 1986. *Principles of historical linguistics.* (Trends in linguistics, studies and monographs, 34.) Berlin: Mouton de Gruyter.

HOGG, RICHARD M. 1980. Analogy as a source of morphological complexity. *Folia Linguistica Historica* 1:2.277–284.

HOOPER, JOAN B. 1976. *An introduction to natural generative phonology.* New York: Academic Press.

KIPARSKY, PAUL. 1968. Linguistic universals and linguistic change. In *Universals in linguistic theory,* edited by Emmon Bach & Robert T. Harms, pp. 171–204. New York: Holt, Rinehart & Winston.

KIPARSKY, PAUL. 1971. Historical linguistics. In *A survey of linguistic science,* edited by William O. Dingwall, pp. 577–642. College Park: University of Maryland Linguistics Program.

KIPARSKY, PAUL. 1972. Explanation in phonology. In *Goals of linguistic theory,* edited by Stanley Peters, pp. 189–227. New York: Prentice-Hall.

KIPARSKY, PAUL. 1973. Phonological representations. In *Three dimensions of linguistic theory,* edited by Osamu Fujimura, pp. 1–136. Tokyo: TEC.

KIPARSKY, PAUL. 1974. Remarks on analogical change. In Anderson & Jones 1974, pp. 257–275.

KIPARSKY, PAUL. 1978. Analogical change as a problem for linguistic theory. In *Linguistics in the seventies: Directions and prospects* (Studies in the linguistic sciences, 8), edited by Braj B. Kachru, pp. 79–96. Urbana: University of Illinois.

KIPARSKY, PAUL. 1983. Word-formation and the lexicon. In *1982 Mid-America Linguistics Conference papers,* edited by Frances Ingemann, pp. 3–29. Lawrence: Department of Linguistics, University of Kansas.

KURYŁOWICZ, JERZY. 1964. *The inflectional categories of Indo-European.* Heidelberg: Winter.

KURYŁOWICZ, JERZY. 1977. Problèmes morphologiques généraux. In his *Problèmes de linguistique indo-européenne,* pp. 7–52. Warsaw: Wydawnictwo Polskiej Akademii Nauk.

LEED, RICHARD L. 1970. Distinctive features and analogy. *Lingua* 26.1–24.

MARKMAN, ELLEN M. 1986. How children constrain the possible meanings of words. In *The ecology and intellectual basis of categorization,* edited by Ulric Neisser. Cambridge & New York: Cambridge University Press.

MAYERTHALER, WILLI. 1981. *Morphologische Natürlichkeit.* (Linguistische Forschungen, 28.) Wiesbaden: Athenaion.

MAYERTHALER, WILLI. 1987. System-independent morphological naturalness. In Dressler 1987b, pp. 25–58.

MCCARTHY, JOHN, & ALAN PRINCE. 1990. *Prosodic morphology.* Cambridge, Mass.: MIT Press.

MORPURGO DAVIES, ANNA. 1978. Analogy, segmentation and the early Neogrammarians. *Transactions of the Philological Society* (London) 1978:36–60.

NARO, ANTHONY. 1981. The social and structural dimensions of a syntactic change. *Language* 57.62–98.

NICHOLS, JOHANNA. 1986. Head-marking and dependent-marking grammar. *Language* 62.56–119.

PINKER, STEVEN, & ALAN PRINCE. 1988. On language and connectionism: Analysis of a parallel distributed processing model of language acquisition. *Cognition* 28.73–194.

RALPH, BO. 1975. *Phonological differentiation: Studies in Nordic language history.* Göteborg: Acta Universitatis Gothoburgiensis.

RAMAT, ANNA GIACOLONE, et al., eds. 1987. *Papers from the Seventh International Conference on Historical Linguistics.* (Current issues in linguistic theory, 48.) Amsterdam: Benjamins.

ROBINSON, ORRIN WARNER. 1980. An exception to Old High German umlaut. In *American Indian and Indo-European studies: Papers in honor of Madison S. Beeler* (Trends in linguistics, Studies and monographs, 16), edited by Kathryn Klar et al., pp. 449–460. The Hague: Mouton.

RUMELHART, DAVID E., & JAMES L. MCCLELLAND. 1986. On learning the past tenses of English verbs. In *Parallel distributed processing: Explorations in the microstructure of cognition,* vol. 2, *Psychological and biological models,* edited by David E. Rumelhart et al., pp. 216–271. Cambridge, Mass.: MIT Press.

SHAPIRO, MICHAEL. 1974. Morphophonemics as semiotic. *Anthropological Linguistics* 15.29–49.

SLOBIN, DAN I. 1973. Cognitive prerequisites for the development of grammar. In *Studies of child language development,* edited by Charles A. Ferguson & Dan I. Slobin, pp. 175–211. New York: Holt, Rinehart & Winston.

SLOBIN, DAN I. 1985. Crosslinguistic evidence for the language-making capacity. In *The crosslinguistic study of language acquisition,* vol. 2, *Theoretical issues,* edited by Dan I. Slobin, pp. 1157–1256. Hillsdale, N.J.: Erlbaum.

TIERSMA, PETER. 1978. Bidirectional leveling as evidence for relational rules. *Lingua* 45.65–77.

VAN VALIN, ROBERT D., JR. 1987. The role of government in the grammar of head-marking languages. *International Journal of American Linguistics* 53.371–397.

VENNEMANN, THEO. 1972. Phonetic analogy and conceptual analogy. In *Schuchardt, the Neogrammarians, and the transformational theory of phonological change,* edited by Theo Vennemann & Terence H. Wilbur, pp. 181–204. Frankfurt: Athenäum.

VENNEMANN, THEO. 1974. Restructuring. *Lingua* 33.137–156.

VENNEMANN, THEO. 1983. Causality in language change: Theories of linguistic preferences as a basis for linguistic explanations. *Folia Linguistica Historica* 4.5–26.

VINCENT, NIGEL. 1974. Analogy reconsidered. In Anderson & Jones 1974, pp. 427–445.

WERNER, OTMAR. 1987. The aim of morphological change is a good mixture—not a uniform language type. In Ramat et al. 1987, pp. 591–606.

WURZEL, WOLFGANG U. 1984. On morphological naturalness. *Nordic Journal of Linguistics* 7.165–183.

WURZEL, WOLFGANG U. 1985. Morphologische Natürlichkeit und morphologischer Wandel: Zur Vorhersagbarkeit von Sprachveränderungen. In *Papers from the Sixth International Conference on Historical Linguistics,* edited by Jacek Fisiak, pp. 587–599. Amsterdam: Benjamins.

WURZEL, WOLFGANG U. 1987. System-dependent morphological naturalness in inflection. In Dressler 1987b, pp. 59–96.

ANAPHORA, as a term, is used in two ways in the linguistic literature:

(a) As a general description of coreferential processes, where one element refers back to another.

(b) In the restrictive and 'technical' sense of anaphoric

binding (cf. Chomsky 1981), where the term 'anaphor' is restricted to necessarily referentially dependent N[oun] P[hrase]s, e.g. *himself, each other*. [*See* Binding; Traces.]

The term is used in its first sense, for example, in the work of Hankamer & Sag 1976, who contrast what they call 'deep' and 'surface' anaphora. An instance of DEEP ANAPHORA would be that in ex. 1a, where it refers back to a clause of earlier D-STRUCTURE [*q.v.*]. SURFACE ANAPHORA is displayed in ex. 1b, where the null VP after *do* refers back to the V[erb] P[hrase] in the first clause:

(1a) *Mary said that John seems* TO BE *a fool, but I don't believe* IT.

(1b) *John* LIKES MARY, *and Bill does* __ *too*.

The latter type of anaphora requires that the element referred back to must form a constituent at S-STRUCTURE [*q.v.*] (Hankamer & Sag 1976, Sag 1979).

In recent literature, particularly that in the G[OVERNMENT/]B[INDING] framework [*q.v.*], 'anaphora' takes a more restrictive sense, referring to the relation to its antecedent of a necessarily dependent NP such as *himself* or *each other*. The examples in 2 show ANAPHORIC BINDING in this sense, marking the dependence relation with COINDEXING:

(2a) *John*$_i$ *likes himself*$_i$ *too well*.

(2b) *The boys*$_i$ *thought that pictures of each other*$_i$ *were on sale*.

The description of anaphoric binding in this sense requires a specification of the LOCALITY domain that surrounds the anaphor, within which the anaphor must find an antecedent in order for the sentence to be grammatical. This is shown below, where the anaphor with the near antecedent (3a) is grammatical, but that with a 'far-away' potential antecedent (3b) is not:

(3a) *John thinks that Bill*$_i$ *likes himself*$_i$.

(3b) **John*$_i$ *thinks that Bill likes himself*$_i$.

Anaphoric binding in this sense is assumed in the GB literature to fall under a set of Binding Conditions, which contain the restrictions as stated below on coreference and disjoint reference. ('Bound', here, means coindexed with an element under C-COMMAND [*q.v.*].)

(4) Binding Theory:
A. Anaphors must be bound in their governing category.
B. Pronouns must be free (i.e. may not be bound) in their governing category.
C. Names must be free.

Given this form of the theory, two questions arise for the linguist (or language learner): (i) What counts as an anaphor in a given language? and (ii) What is the relevant locality domain in which it must be bound—i.e., what counts as the governing category for anaphors?

The locality domain varies to some degree from language to language; hence the conclusion that the governing domain must be 'parameterized', i.e. individually specified from language to language. In addition, some languages, especially in the Germanic family, employ more than one anaphor (e.g. in German, *sich, sich selbst*); hence, the binding domain parameter must be specified by lexical item, rather than for the language as a whole.

The simplicity of the formulation in 4 hides a number of important and vexed questions. For example, why should a language choose one locality domain rather than another? Is this simply to be taken as a primitive specification, or does it depend on other structural and lexical factors in the language? Second, given more than one anaphor in a language, what is the relation between them (Koster 1985, Everaert 1986)? More technically, the FEATURE definition of Chomsky 1981 [*see* Syntactic Features] leads one to expect only one instance of the feature set [+anaphor, −pronominal] per language, and raises the question of how a pair of anaphors would be defined. A third question bears on indexing as a proper notation for anaphoric dependence: as Higginbotham 1983 has noted, an asymmetrical notation, like bidirectional arrows, might be more appropriate for recording this sort of dependence. Fourth, given that the grammar has several levels, where in the grammar does the Binding theory apply, and why is it earmarked for that particular level? Questions like these guarantee that the treatment of anaphora, and in general the treatment of necessarily dependent elements, will be an exciting and exacting research area through the 1990s.

DAVID LEBEAUX

BIBLIOGRAPHY

CHOMSKY, NOAM. 1981. *Lectures on government and binding*. (Studies in generative grammar, 9.) Dordrecht: Foris.

EVERAERT, MARTIN. 1986. *The syntax of reflexivization.* (Publications in language sciences, 22.) Dordrecht: Foris.

HANKAMER, JORGE, & IVAN A. SAG. 1976. Deep and surface anaphora. *Linguistic Inquiry* 7.391–426.

HIGGINBOTHAM, JAMES. 1983. Logical Form, binding, and nominals. *Linguistic Inquiry* 14.395–420.

KOSTER, JAN. 1985. Reflexives in Dutch. In *Grammatical representations*, vol. 2 (Studies in generative grammar, 22), edited by Jacqueline Guéron et al., pp. 141–167. Dordrecht: Foris.

SAG, IVAN A. 1979. The non-unity of anaphora. *Linguistic Inquiry* 10.152–164.

ANATOLIAN LANGUAGES constitute an extinct branch of the Indo-European family [*q.v.*], spoken in ancient Asia Minor.

LANGUAGE LIST

Hittite: attested from extensive cuneiform inscriptions on clay tablets discovered at Boğazköy, Turkey. Used between 1700 and 1200 BCE.

Luvian: attested in fragmentary cuneiform remains associated with Hittite inscriptions, and in a native hieroglyphic script; used over much of southern and western Anatolia and northern Syria. Also called Luwian.

Lycian: attested from alphabetic inscriptions in southwestern Anatolia, dating from the 5th-4th centuries BCE. Evidently descended from a variety of Luvian.

Lydian: attested in alphabetic inscriptions from Sardis in western Anatolia, dating from the 6th-4th centuries BCE.

Palaic: attested in fragmentary materials associated with Hittite inscriptions.

ANCIENT HISTORY. *See* History of Linguistics, *articles on* Ancient India *and* Ancient Greece and Rome.

ANDAMANESE LANGUAGES constitute a family which comprises the indigenous languages of the Andaman Islands (India). No higher-level genetic connection has been generally accepted. The languages are divided into the subgroups shown in Figure 1 by Stephen A. Wurm and Shirô Hattori, eds., *Language atlas of the Pacific area* (Canberra: Australian Academy of the Humanities, 1981).

LANGUAGE LIST

Aka-Bea: now extinct. Also called Bea, Beada, Biada, Aka-Beada, Bojigniji, or Bogijiab.

FIGURE 1. *Subgrouping of Andamanese Languages*

Great Andamanese
  Central Andamanese
    Aka-Bea, Aka-Kede, Aka-Kol, Akar-Bale, A-Pucikwar, Oko-Juwoi
  Northern Andamanese
    Aka-Bo, Aka-Cari, Aka-Jeru, Aka-Kora
South Andamanese
  Jarawa, Önge, Sentinel

Aka-Bo: now extinct. Also called Bo or Ba.

Aka-Cari: now extinct. Also called Cari or Chariar.

Aka-Jeru: now extinct. Also called Jeru or Yerawa.

Aka-Kede: now extinct. Also called Kede.

Aka-Kol: now extinct. Also called Kol.

Aka-Kora: now extinct. Also called Kora.

Akar-Bale: now extinct. Also called Bale or Balwa.

A-Pucikwar: 24 speakers reported in 1981. Also called Pucikwar or Puchikwar.

Jarawa: 250 speakers reported in 1981. Distinct from Önge and Sentinel.

Oko-Juwoi: now extinct. Also called Juwoi or Junoi.

Önge: 106 speakers reported in 1981, in the southern Andaman Islands. Also called Ong.

Sentinel: 50 speakers reported in 1981, in the southeastern Andaman Islands. Similar to Önge, but a distinct language.

ANGAN LANGUAGES are spoken in southeastern Papua New Guinea. Stephen A. Wurm, *Papuan languages of Oceania* (Tübingen: Narr, 1982), pp. 140–142, regards the Angan languages as a stock within the Central and Western part of the main section of his controversial Trans–New Guinea phylum [*q.v.*]. The subgrouping is shown in Figure 1.

LANGUAGE LIST

Ampeeli-Wojokeso: around 2,390 speakers reported in 1980, in Kaiapit, Mumeng, and Menyamya Subprovinces, Morobe Province. Also called Ampale, Ampele, Ambari, or Safeyoka. The second languages used are Tok Pisin and Yabim.

Angaatiha: around 1,000 speakers reported in 1982, in Menyamya District, Morobe Province. Also called Langimar, Angataha, or Angaatiya.

FIGURE 1. *Subgrouping of Angan Languages*

Angaatiha
Angan (proper)
  Ampeeli-Wojokeso, Angoya, Ankave, Baruya, Hamtai, Ivori, Kamasa, Kawacha, Menya, Simbari, Yagwoia

Angoya: 850 speakers reported in 1977, in the valleys between the Nabo Range and the Albert Mountains, on the Lohiki River, Gulf Province. Also called Akoyi, Lohiki, Obi, Mai-Hea-Ri, or Maihiri.

Ankave: 1,600 speakers reported in 1987, in the valleys of the Mbwei and Swanson rivers, Gulf Province. Also called Angave.

Baruya: 6,000 speakers reported in 1975, in Marawaka Subprovince, Eastern Highlands Province. Also called Barua.

Hamtai: 40,000 speakers reported in 1986, along the Tauri River inland east to the Ladedamu River, in Kukipi and Kerema Subprovinces, Gulf Province, and in the Kodama Range into the Bulolo-Watut divide, across to Mt. Grosse and north to Mt. Taylor, Lae and Menyama Subprovinces, Morobe Province. Also called Hamde, Hamday, Kapau, or Watut. Speakers dislike the name Kukukuku. The name Kamea is used in Gulf Province.

Ivori: 800 speakers reported in 1987, in the villages of Pio, Famba, and Paiguna, Gulf Province. Also called Tainae.

Kamasa: 20 speakers reported in 1978, in part of the Katsiong census unit, Morobe Province.

Kawacha: 30 speakers reported in 1978, east of Ampale, in part of the Katsiong census unit, Morobe Province. Also called Kawatsa. Speakers are bilingual in Yagwoia.

Menya: 13,000 speakers reported in 1987, from the Papua border north along the Tauri River and tributaries, Menyamya Subprovince, Morobe Province. Also called Menye or Menyama.

Simbari: 3,000 speakers reported in 1982, in Marawaka Subprovince, Eastern Highlands Province. Also called Chimbari.

Yagwoia: around 9,000 speakers reported in 1987, in Morobe Province, extending into Gulf Province; and in one section west of Tauri River, the other north of Menye, Eastern Highlands Province. Also called Kokwaiyakwa or Yeghuye.

ANOMIA refers to mild or severe impairments of naming or word-finding following focal brain damage. Testing for anomia typically includes requesting the subject to name pictures of objects, or requesting the correct response to a verbal description. Except when they also suffer obvious object agnosia, aphasic patients usually have little trouble recognizing the objects they cannot name; they can typically mime the object's use, select it from among others when its name is spoken, or give the correct name when they are supplied with its initial sound.

Within the generality that common names are easier to retrieve than rare ones (Newcombe et al. 1971), anomia can be modality-specific (tactile, visual, or auditory); there are also reports of category-specific anomias, such as color anomia—i.e. an inability to name colors in the absence of known impairment in visual color-sensitivity. Especially intriguing are occasional reports of naming deficits limited to specific semantic categories, such as the patient reported by Hart et al. 1985 who had a naming deficit primarily confined to the names of fruits and vegetables. By contrast, some semantic categories can be relatively spared in patients with otherwise severe naming deficits (Goodglass et al. 1986).

Anomic errors can take the form of semantic or phonological paraphasias. Semantic (verbal) paraphasias are incorrect responses that are related in meaning or in category to the desired name, e.g. producing the word *soldier* for 'policeman'. This could reflect either (i) a looseness in category specification, or (ii) parallel activation of related responses, without inhibition of those which are not the best fit. Phonological (literal) paraphasias are responses in which phonemic elements are absent, distorted, or misplaced within an otherwise recognizable word. Such paraphasias can appear as complete neologisms.

While some degree of anomia is common in all forms of aphasia, anomia can appear as the primary form of language deficit. This is called 'anomic aphasia' (also 'nominal' or 'amnesic' aphasia). Its clinical picture is that of a patient whose speech output is fluent and grammatical, but lacks essential content words. In the place of the substantive nouns and verbs, for example, the patient might produce numerous empty circumlocutions, using *that* and *do* in a variety of noun and verb positions, as in this example from Goodglass (1980:647), in which an anomic aphasic describes his son's career:

(1) *Well he was two years away, away down for nothing. He didn't do it and got out and said I want to go over there and . . . how to do things, what he's doing now.*

As distinct from Wernicke's aphasia [*see* Aphasia], anomic aphasics show relatively good auditory comprehension.

Although often associated with temporal-parietal injury, anomia has proven difficult to localize, since it can follow damage to a variety of cortical areas. Attempts to distinguish naming deficits by qualitative analyses of patients' errors (e.g. the relative proportion of semantic vs. phonological paraphasias) has met with only mixed success. (See Kohn 1984 for an illustration of how such error analyses can be conducted.)

Anomia can also appear as an early symptom of

Alzheimer's dementia, and is often observable earlier than other language deficits associated with that disorder. [*See* Dementia and Language.]

ARTHUR WINGFIELD

BIBLIOGRAPHY

GOODGLASS, HAROLD. 1980. Disorders of naming following brain injury. *American Scientist* 68.647–655.

GOODGLASS, HAROLD, et al. 1986. Category-specific dissociations in naming and recognition by aphasic patients. *Cortex* 22.87–102.

HART, J., et al. 1985. Category-specific naming deficit following cerebral infarction. *Nature* 316.439–440.

KOHN, SUSAN E. 1984. The nature of the phonological disorder in conduction aphasia. *Brain & Language* 23.97–115.

NEWCOMBE, FREDA, et al. 1971. Recognition and naming of object drawings by men with focal brain wounds. *Journal of Neurology, Neurosurgery and Psychiatry* 34.329–340.

ANTHROPOLOGICAL LINGUISTICS. [*This entry is concerned with the study of language within the framework of cultural anthropology; the field frequently deals with the languages of preliterate societies. The entry comprises two articles:*

An Overview

Early History in North America

For related topics, see also Ethnosemantics; Fieldwork and Linguistic Theory; Text and Discourse in Anthropological Linguistics; Semiotics, *article on* Semiotics and Anthropological Linguistics; *and* World View and Language.]

An Overview

The field of anthropological linguistics—or, as some prefer, 'linguistic anthropology'—is dominated in the 1980s by North American scholars; they are heirs to a tradition of the 'four-field' study of human beings, including physical anthropology, archeology, socio-cultural anthropology, and linguistic anthropology. Many senior linguistic anthropologists trained with students of Edward Sapir [*q.v.*]; and linguistic anthropologists usually claim Sapir's teacher Franz Boas, Sapir himself, and his student Benjamin Whorf [*q.v.*] as the founders of their discipline. Yet the intellectual ancestry of this diverse field is complex, with roots in Prague School functionalism, 'Neo-Bloomfieldian' American structuralism, dialectology, and social psychology (see Murray 1983). Outside the United States and Canada, recent attention in British social anthropology to the place of language in society claims descent from Malinowski's work on the functions of 'primitive' languages (cf. Ardener 1971); Parkin 1982 labels this development 'semantic anthropology.' Other influential British work includes that of Bloch 1975 on political oratory in traditional societies, and Goody's cross-cultural studies of the impact of literacy (e.g. 1977). In France, the work of Claude Lévi-Strauss on the structural analysis of myth is especially significant; also to be noted are the studies of language among the Dogon of West Africa by Calame-Griaule 1965, and the cognitive anthropology of Sperber 1985. In addition, French scholarship in general social theory has influenced linguistic anthropology internationally—e.g. Pierre Bourdieu's proposal that the forms of language can constitute a type of 'symbolic capital,' or Michel Foucault's concept of limits on expression constituted through a historical formation called the 'order of discourse'.

In North America, the term 'anthropological linguistics' denotes a tradition of the description of non-Western languages, especially those of the Americas. [*See* North American Languages.] Among those who might be called anthropological linguists, many are not academics (especially those affiliated with missionary organizations such as the Summer Institute of Linguistics); however, this designation was especially appropriate when linguistics was housed mainly within language departments. Thus students of non-Western languages, especially those not associated with Orientalist scholarship, were likely to affiliate with departments of anthropology. This association weakened with the founding of many new departments of linguistics between 1950 and 1980—and with an increasing tendency for linguists who were not anthropologists to see the structure of language as a cognitive, rather than social, phenomenon. However, anthropological linguistics continues as a strong empiricist strand in linguistics. In addition to work on the structure of individual languages, recent scholarship in the field has emphasized areal studies and language contact phenomena. The study of language typology and universals, following especially on seminal proposals by Joseph Greenberg, has also been important.

In the past thirty years, a new 'linguistic anthropology', which explores the place of language in the life of human communities, has developed within anthropology, alongside 'anthropological linguistics'. The two sub-specialties have a combined influence out of proportion to the small number of their scholars. This influence is partly a product of the honor accorded to the Boasian 'four-field' tradition in American anthropology; in the 1984 reorganization of the American Anthropological Association, a permanent position on the governing board of the Association was reserved for the president of the Society for Linguistic Anthropology, regardless of the size of that body's membership. But it also arises from the centrality of the intellectual concerns of linguistic anthropology for the larger field, as well as from a tradition of theoretical influence from linguistics on anthropology. The latter is apparent in Lévi-Strauss's use of Jakobson's concept of 'opposition' in structural anthropology; in the borrowing by Ward Goodenough, from the structuralist definition of grammar (especially from George Trager, cf. Murray 1983), of the idea that a culture consists of a set of rules which generate appropriate behavior; and in the continuing importance of the distinction of two types of ethnographic analysis, 'emic' (insiders' categories) vs. 'etic' (outsiders' categories), borrowed from the work of Kenneth Pike.

The recognition that human beings are biologically far more closely related to the great apes than had been imagined, and the identification of 'protocultural' phenomena such as tool-making among chimpanzees, has given new importance to the study of language, both verbal and gestural, in the traditional anthropological task of defining human nature. [*See* Origins of Language.] Elsewhere, the methods of historical linguistics are important for the study of prehistory in archaeology. [*See* Culture History and Historical Linguistics.] However, linguistic anthropology in the 1980s is most closely linked to the many sub-specialties of socio-cultural anthropology—especially to those which explore the realm of symbols, ideas, and knowledge.

Cognitive anthropology, which studies the organization of the kinds of knowledge possessed by human beings as members of specific cultures and communities, is a modern development of an important strand of the Boasian tradition: the proposal that the patterns of language may reveal the structure of what Boas called 'the fundamental ethnic ideas'. One form of this proposal is the Sapir-Whorf Hypothesis. [*See* World View and Language.] This strand can be traced through the work of ethnosemanticists such as Ward Goodenough, Floyd Lounsbury, and Charles Frake; they argued that ethnography could be given a rigorous methodological foundation through the structural analysis of carefully defined domains of language patterning, such as kinship and disease terminologies, using a distinctive-feature approach ('componential analysis'). Such analysis would provide evidence for the 'rules of culture', i.e. the abstract knowledge that underlay cultural behavior. While some current cognitive anthropology deals with non-linguistic phenomena, most scholars in the field find their fundamental material in language observed in natural contexts, in relatively unstructured interviews, and in experimentation. Their concern is what 'ways of speaking', thus observed, can reveal about the representation of cultural knowledge in a wide variety of domains: how such representations are organized, how they are deployed and reproduced, and what might be the limits on their diversity. Perhaps the most important contribution to the last question is the work on color terminology universals initiated by Brent Berlin and Paul Kay. [*See* Ethnosemantics.] The idea of the structure of knowledge as a checklist of distinctive features has been largely replaced by new conceptualizations, such as prototype theory and fuzzy logic; and by theories of radial and metaphorical categories, developed in cognitive linguistics (cf. Lakoff 1987). Sophisticated quantitative methods, such as factor analysis and multidimensional scaling, are used in the cognitive-anthropological analysis of language data; Dougherty 1985 and Holland & Quinn 1987 are good introductions to this field.

A second important strand in linguistic anthropology is the ETHNOGRAPHY OF SPEAKING [*q.v.*], pioneered by Dell Hymes, John Gumperz, and their students. It develops the Prague School insight that language need not have the same functions in every social group; Hymes 1974 and Bauman & Sherzer 1974 are good introductions to this field. The ethnography of speaking views speech (and other forms of communication, such as writing or sign languages) as social institutions, of which the 'structure' of phonology, morphology, and syntax is only one component. These institutions can be investigated with ethnographic techniques, especially by participant observation of naturally occurring discourse in its cultural context. Ethnographers of speaking emphasize language use—since they see the skills manifested in use ('communicative competence'), rather than abstract knowledge of grammar, as most important in the construction of the social order through language. Usage is organized through higher-level patterning of a system of 'speech events', i.e. communicative exchanges made meaningful by culturally specific structures of participants, codes and genres, affective tones, and other context-constructing elements.

The repertory of communicative events and their organization differ among speech communities. These are not defined and differentiated by their dominant codes, e.g. 'English', since many speech communities are multilingual. Instead, ethnographers of speaking endorse the view of Joshua Fishman that multilingualism is just one type of a more general phenomenon of code variation, which includes the register and dialect differentiation observed in relatively 'monolingual' communities. Speech communities are differentiated by characteristic 'discourse strategies' (Gumperz 1982), and by understandings about the purposes of communicative events of the type called 'metapragmatic,' discussed below.

Mismatches in speech-event structures, and differences in discourse strategies and metapragmatic norms, complicate communication across cultural boundaries, even where codes are shared. In complex pluralistic societies, they may cause 'miscommunication', i.e. misunderstandings that result from differences in ways of using language, and may lead to negative evaluations of speakers. These, in turn, influence the unequal distribution of resources in society. Thus the distribution of discourse strategies in communities is an important focus for linguistic anthropologists; they share with variationist sociolinguists (e.g. Labov 1972) an interest in the social stratification of language variation, and in the organization of communicative networks.

The importance of discourse strategies in access to resources has led to increasing emphasis on the analysis of certain types of speech events which may be critical to such access. Thus linguistic anthropologists, sociologists, and others have taken techniques developed in the analysis of such events as greetings and curing rituals in traditional societies, and turned them to the investigation of communicative events in complex societies. The latter include political meetings, courtroom procedures, classroom discourse, and medical interviews, analyzed in order to understand how the allocation of power and resources is organized and reproduced through speaking; an example is the work of Philips 1983, who explores the communicative roots of educational failure among American Indian children.

Interest in the reproduction of social order through language use has also led to work on 'language socialization', i.e. the development in children of characteristic patterns of usage (cf. Schieffelin & Ochs 1986). The conceptual apparatus for the analysis of speech events has been considerably refined; examples are the work of Philips 1972 on participant structures, Irvine 1979 on formality, and Brenneis 1987 on indirection. Such work also reveals an interest in cross-cultural regularities in the relationship between language form and language function—in the last work mentioned, common patterns in the use of indirection during the constitution of political arenas in 'embedded egalitarian' speech communities.

Linguistic anthropologists emphasize language use. Thus the concept of 'speech act', as used in pragmatics, has drawn their close attention, since it seems to offer a basic unit for the analysis of speaking. [*See* Pragmatics, Implicature, and Presupposition; Speech Acts.] But problems in applying the concept cross-culturally to natural discourse have also led to empirical critiques of theories of speech acts and inference in pragmatics; these included a challenge to the universality of Grice's conversational postulates (Ochs Keenan 1976), and a critique of speech act theory (Rosaldo 1982).

The work of Silverstein (cf. 1976, 1979), influenced by the SEMIOTICS of Charles Peirce, is an important anthropological critique of pragmatics. [*See* Semiotics, *article on* Semiotics and Anthropological Linguistics.] Silverstein sees the patterning of goals and purposes in language use—'metapragmatics'—as variable across cultures. Metapragmatic patterning is expressed not only in usage, but also in 'linguistic ideologies.' These are beliefs about language structure and use which derive their supposedly self-evident nature from the important 'indexical' function of language. Silverstein argues that the Western semantic and pragmatic tradition (including the work of Austin, Searle, and Grice), which emphasizes the referential functions of language and neglects indexicality, is an example of such a 'linguistic ideology.' Friedrich 1986 has also criticized the exclusive attention to referential function; his work emphasizes poetic imagination as an important source of patterning in language.

The findings of linguistic anthropology have yielded an important critique of field method. The linguistic-anthropological emphasis on observation of naturally occurring discourse derives partly from a suspicion that social-science interviewing and the techniques of linguistic elicitation may be metapragmatically biased (Briggs 1986). [*See* Fieldwork and Linguistic Theory.] Hence linguistic anthropology continues to rely on 'texts', i.e. recordings of discourse which is situated as naturally as possible. This has led to important developments in the analysis of patterning in texts across cultures. [*See* Text and Discourse in Anthropological Linguistics.] Linguistic anthropologists have also criticized the use of spoken words as 'raw data' by other cultural anthropologists; they see discourse not as a transparent window through which norms and knowledge may be viewed, but as the very threads from which these are woven.

Linguistic anthropologists increasingly emphasize that language is locally constituted action and practice, rather than a manifestation of underlying 'structure' (Duranti 1988). [*See* Social Structure and Language.] This is a natural theoretical development, given the emphasis on language use; but it also derives from CONVERSATION ANALYSIS [*q.v.*], as carried out by ethnomethodologists in sociology, and from the increasing emphasis on action and practice in socio-cultural anthropology. Thus linguistic anthropologists tend to find grammatical theories such as those of Noam Chomsky—who sees the structure of language as entirely autonomous of its communicative use—to be somewhat irrelevant to their concerns. While linguistic anthropologists acknowledge the probability that there are biological constraints on the forms of language, many are critical of 'biologism' as the privileged theoretical account of language universals; they argue that the search for explanations of language universals must include attention to the processes of interaction.

Linguistic anthropology is a diverse and eclectic field, and not all scholars who have connections with it would necessarily endorse all the positions noted above. Linguistic anthropologists are, however, united by common emphases on the study of naturally occurring talk, and on recognition of the importance of cross-cultural diversity in the functions of language. They are also united by an insistence that language is closely embedded in human culture and society, and to a great degree constitutive of them. Thus they see the study of language structure and use as a logical project for anthropology.

JANE H. HILL

BIBLIOGRAPHY

ARDENER, EDWIN, ed. 1971. *Social anthropology and language.* London: Tavistock.

BAUMAN, RICHARD, & JOEL SHERZER, eds. 1974. *Explorations in the ethnography of speaking.* London & New York: Cambridge University Press.

BLOCH, MAURICE, ed. 1975. *Political language and oratory in traditional society.* New York: Academic Press.

BRENNEIS, DONALD. 1987. Talk and transformation. *Man* 22.499–510.

BRIGGS, CHARLES L. 1986. *Learning how to ask.* Cambridge & New York: Cambridge University Press.

CALAME-GRIAULE, GENEVIÈVE. 1965. *Ethnologie et langage.* Paris: Gallimard.

DOUGHERTY, JANET W. D., ed. 1985. *New directions in cognitive anthropology.* Urbana: University of Illinois Press.

DURANTI, ALESSANDRO. 1988. Ethnography of speaking: Towards a linguistics of the praxis. In *Linguistics: The Cambridge survey,* vol. 4, *Language: The socio-cultural context,* edited by Frederick J. Newmeyer, pp. 210–228. Cambridge & New York: Cambridge University Press.

FRIEDRICH, PAUL. 1986. *The language parallax: Linguistic parallelism and poetic indeterminacy.* Austin: University of Texas Press.

GOODY, JACK. 1977. *The domestication of the savage mind.* Cambridge & New York: Cambridge University Press.

GUMPERZ, JOHN J. 1982. *Discourse strategies.* (Studies in interactional sociolinguistics, 1.) Cambridge & New York: Cambridge University Press.

HOLLAND, DOROTHY, & NAOMI QUINN, eds. 1987. *Cultural models in language and thought.* Cambridge & New York: Cambridge University Press.

HYMES, DELL. 1974. *Foundations in sociolinguistics: An ethnographic approach.* Philadelphia: University of Pennsylvania Press.

IRVINE, JUDITH T. 1979. Formality and informality in communicative events. *American Anthropologist* 81.773–790.

LABOV, WILLIAM. 1972. *Language in the inner city: Studies in the Black English vernacular.* Philadelphia: University of Pennsylvania Press.

LAKOFF, GEORGE. 1987. *Women, fire, and dangerous things: What categories reveal about the mind.* Chicago: University of Chicago Press.

MURRAY, STEPHEN O. 1983. *Group formation in social science.* Edmonton, Alta.: Linguistic Research.

OCHS KEENAN, ELINOR. 1976. On the universality of conversational postulates. *Language in Society* 5.67–80.

PARKIN, DAVID, ed. 1982. *Semantic anthropology.* London: Academic Press.

PHILIPS, SUSAN U. 1972. Participant structures and communicative competence: Warm Springs children in community and classroom. In *Functions of language in the classroom,* edited by Courtney B. Cazden et al., pp. 370–394. New York: Teacher's College Press.

PHILIPS, SUSAN U. 1983. *The invisible culture: Communication in classroom and community on the Warm Springs Indian Reservation.* New York: Longman.

ROSALDO, MICHELLE Z. 1982. The things we do with words: Ilongot speech acts and speech act theory in philosophy. *Language in Society* 11.203–237.

SCHIEFFELIN, BAMBI B., & ELINOR OCHS, eds. 1986. *Language socialization across cultures.* (Studies in the social and cultural foundations of language, 3.) Cambridge & New York: Cambridge University Press.

SILVERSTEIN, MICHAEL. 1976. Shifters, linguistic categories, and cultural description. In *Meaning in anthropology,* edited by Keith H. Basso & Henry A. Selby, pp. 11–55. Albuquerque: University of New Mexico Press.

SILVERSTEIN, MICHAEL. 1979. Language structure and linguistic ideology. In *The elements: A parasession on linguistic units and levels,* edited by Paul R. Clyne et al., pp. 191–247. Chicago: Chicago Linguistic Society.

SPERBER, DAN. 1985. *On anthropological knowledge.* (Cambridge studies in social anthropology, 54.) Cambridge & New York: Cambridge University Press.

Early History in North America

The history of anthropological linguistics in North America is parallel with the history of the description and classification of native American languages, and is also closely related to the development and institutionalization of American anthropology. Hallowell (1960:23) notes: 'Perhaps the underlying unity implied in the study of the inhabitants of a single great continent, despite their great diversity in many respects, accounts, in part, for the traditional emphasis later given in the United States to anthropology as the unified study of man.' Language was the most effective means of categorizing the diverse Indian cultures.

The earliest students were amateurs in contact with native peoples. Cleric John Eliot (1604–1690) translated the Bible into an Algonkian language. His 1666 work, *The Indian grammar begun: An essay to bring the Indian language into rules,* assumed that all Indian languages were essentially the same, as did Roger Williams's *Key into the language of America* in 1643.

European philosophers eagerly incorporated such initial descriptions into their picture of human history. The discovery by William Jones [*q.v.*] that Sanskrit was related to Greek and Latin precipitated interest in collecting vocabularies from all of the world's languages. Catherine the Great of Russia collected masses of data in the late 18th century; both Benjamin Franklin and George Washington were consulted for the second edition of her work, revised by J. S. Pallas. This project culminated in *Mithridates,* edited by J. C. Adelung and J. S. Vater between 1806 and 1817; over eight hundred pages were devoted to New World languages (Hallowell 1960:23–24).

Many American intellectuals and statesmen studied Indian languages as an avocation. This interest centered in the American Philosophical Society, founded in Philadelphia by Benjamin Franklin in 1769. Early members included Benjamin Smith Barton (1766–1815), Peter Stephen Duponceau (1760–1844), John Pickering (1777–1846), Jonathan Edwards (1745–1801), David Zeisberger (1721–1808), John Heckewelder (1743–1823), Thomas Jefferson (1743–1826), Albert Gallatin (1761–1849), Henry Rowe Schoolcraft (1793–1864), and later John Wesley Powell (1834–1902), founder of the Bureau of American Ethnology.

The most distinguished amateur linguist was Thomas Jefferson, who devoted considerable energy to collecting Indian vocabularies in the years before his presidency. His *Notes on the State of Virginia,* not published until 1861, proposed collecting universal words for basic objects, to permit comparison with languages of the Old World; he believed that preservation of such materials was crucial, to allow study for all time. He also recognized the value of grammar in categorizing 'the affinities of nations' (Hallowell 1960:25, 31–32). His plan to compare more than fifty Indian languages was sidetracked by the loss of his linguistic manuscripts in 1809, and by his political responsibilities. Jefferson's intellectual prestige did much to ensure that American scholars would take seriously their responsibility to describe and classify Indian languages.

During Jefferson's presidency, the Louisiana Purchase of 1803 led to the Lewis and Clark Expedition of 1804. Jefferson wrote a scientific questionnaire for the Expedition; this was broadly ethnological, and vocabulary collection was emphasized. However, complete descriptions were not obtained for any tribe. The Literary and Historical Committee of the American Philosophical Society, which Jefferson headed until 1815, produced a late 18th century circular on the scope of ethnology, giving considerable attention to linguistics (Hallowell 1960:26).

Benjamin S. Barton, a professor of natural history and botany at the University of Pennsylvania, collected comparative vocabularies, mostly American Indian, and hoped to link North American languages to those of Asia. His work was dedicated to Jefferson.

John Pickering, a classical scholar and the first president of the American Oriental Society, edited the works of Williams and Eliot, making them more widely available, and collaborated on the *Mithridates* project. His 1820 'Essay on a uniform orthography for the Indian languages of North America' was widely used by missionaries to introduce an element of standardization and to permit comparison of diverse Indian languages.

Stephen Duponceau translated the works of Zeisberger and Heckewelder for the American Philosophical Society, identified Osage as a Siouan language, and attempted to link American and Siberian languages. His essay on American grammatical systems, then still seen as essentially uniform, received a prestigious prize in France in 1838. Duponceau coined the term 'polysynthetic', first used in print in 1819, to refer to the peculiar grammatical structure of American languages (Hallowell 1960:28).

Henry Rowe Schoolcraft married an Ojibwa woman and learned that language. He coined the terms 'inclusive' and 'exclusive' in 1834, to refer to the first person plural distinction in Amerindian languages. Schoolcraft was also influential in collecting Indian narratives and folklore (Murray 1983:32).

Albert Gallatin, Jefferson's Secretary of the Treasury and later ambassador to France and England, persuaded the Secretary of War (under whose jurisdiction Indian affairs fell), to circulate an extensive questionnaire. The results appeared in 1836 in Gallatin's *Synopsis of the Indians within the United States east of the Rocky Mountains and in the British and Russian possessions in North America*. This massive work included a map of tribal and linguistic groups.

Gallatin was the first president of the American Ethnological Society, founded in 1842, whose founders attempted to classify the Indians of the continent linguistically (Murray 1983:33). Gallatin established the comparative method in Amerindian linguistics, and set the boundaries of many linguistic families. His summary, recognizing 32 distinct families, was published by the Society in 1848 as an introduction to Horatio Hale's *Indians of North West America*.

The trend toward systematization of Indian linguistic and cultural boundaries continued through the work of George Gibbs for the Smithsonian Institution, founded in 1846. Gibbs's 1863 *Instructions for research relative to the ethnology and philology of America* adapted Pickering's phonetic alphabet, and proposed a 211-word vocabulary based primarily on Gallatin. This questionnaire was widely circulated; its results added substantially to the Smithsonian archives.

Joseph Henry (1797–1878), Secretary of the Smithsonian, considered anthropology crucial to reconstructing the past history of mankind. He encouraged John Wesley Powell, head of the Geological Survey of the Rocky Mountain Region, to concentrate on fieldwork, to distinguish his survey from the other three existing at the time. Powell's fieldwork with the Ute and Shoshone in the Southwest emphasized language, although he had no formal linguistic training.

In 1876, Powell received permission to use the 670 vocabularies then in the possession of the Smithsonian. A year later, he revised the Gibbs questionnaire in his *Introduction to the study of Indian languages* (issued in 1880 with slight revisions). Powell's linguistic questionnaire was used by many investigators, contributing further data to Smithsonian collections.

In 1879, Powell became head of the Bureau of (American) Ethnology, under the auspices of the Smithsonian—the first professional institution for anthropology in North America. Linguistics was crucial to Powell's mandate of mapping the diversity of native languages and cultures. With a small permanent staff, and many amateur collaborators in direct contact with Indians, Powell produced in 1891 the first complete classification of American Indian languages into fifty-five independent stocks, later revised to fifty-eight (Darnell 1971a). Minimal attention was paid to grammar, because Powell believed that American Indian grammars reflected stages of cultural evolution of the Indians, rather than historical diversity among them. Moreover, little systematic information about grammar was available to Powell and his staff. The taxonomic portion of the classification was largely the work of William Henshaw, a biologist. Albert Gatschet (the only staff member with any training in Indo-European linguistics) and John Owen Dorsey, a former missionary to the Sioux, were most directly responsible for the fieldwork; this was intended to fill gaps in basic knowledge, rather than to provide full descriptions of particular languages.

The classification was based—necessarily, given the skills of the Bureau staff—on surface inspection of vocabularies for cognates, rather than on the comparative method used in Indo-European studies. Powell was, in any case, more interested in grouping closely related tribes for practical purposes than in larger groupings which might reflect the culture history of the continent. Much of his linguistic classificatory work was supported by the United States Census, and was intended to aid in settling compatible groups together on reservations. The Bureau was supported by Congressional appropriation, and had to show practical relevance as well as scientific quality.

Powell presented no evidence for the connections he recognized; but he discussed each family, and indicated connections that might justify further study. In spite of his experience with Ute and Shoshone, Powell failed to accept the validity of the Uto-Aztecan stock, which links these languages to Nahuatl, the language of the Aztecs.

An alternative classification was proposed, also in 1891, by Daniel Garrison Brinton (1837–1899), a medical doctor associated with the American Philosophical Society (Darnell 1988). Brinton lacked the resources of Powell's Bureau for fieldwork and manuscript access; in fact, he declined to consult Smithsonian manuscripts, wanting to maintain the independence of his classification. Brinton proposed thirteen linguistic families for the continent; many of his categories are geographical units, unsupported by specific linguistic evidence. He presented very limited evidence for his classification, which was included in a larger ethnological study of the American Indian. He relied more extensively on grammar than did Powell, and correctly recognized the Uto-Aztecan stock. His effort was entirely eclipsed by the much more systematic efforts of Powell and his staff, which reflected the professionalization of American linguistics and anthropology, and left Brinton an anachronism in his own lifetime.

Brinton is best remembered for his *Library of Aboriginal American literature*—eight volumes published privately between 1882 and 1890, and largely devoted to his own library-based work with Mexican languages. Brinton's presentation of consecutive texts in addition to vocabulary and grammar was an important (although largely unacknowledged) precedent for the next, professional, generation of linguists and anthropologists.

Powell was explicit that his classification was a preliminary one, intended to provide a baseline for further work by the Bureau and others. But the prestige and funding of the Bureau declined after Powell's death in 1902. In practice, moreover, the classification was perceived by American Indian linguists and anthropologists as an integrated unit. It remains the conservative baseline for Amerindian linguistics; however, the fieldwork of the next generation of anthropologists, largely trained by Franz Boas at Columbia University, resulted in a very different kind of classification of only six 'superstocks' by Edward Sapir (1888–1939), published in 1921 and revised slightly in 1929 (see Darnell 1971b). Sapir's classification was directed toward reconstructing culture history, and explicitly applied the historical/comparative methods of Indo-European philology. It dominated American linguistics until the 1960s, when a more conservative standard for evidence of genetic relationship became widely held. Sapir's work on language varieties (according to, e.g., gender or social context) foreshadowed today's emphasis on these themes. [*See* Sapir, Edward.]

Powell was convinced of the importance of descriptions of particular Indian languages. The Bureau, along with the British Association for the Advancement of Science, supported the Northwest Coast fieldwork of Franz Boas (1858–1942) in the late 1880s and 1890s. Boas was appointed 'Honorary Philologist' of the Bureau, and was assigned the task of preparing a *Handbook of North American Indian languages*. This turned out to be a long-range project, with three volumes of grammatical sketches appearing in 1911, 1922, and 1938. Boas depended not on the self-trained staff of the Bureau, but on his own first generation of students (Stocking 1974). The focus of American linguistics had shifted, largely due to Boas's efforts, toward the publication of texts, grammars, and dictionaries for each language as a prelude to serious classificatory effort. This continues in the modern tradition of American Indian linguistics. [*See* North American Languages.]

REGNA DARNELL

BIBLIOGRAPHY

DARNELL, REGNA. 1971a. The Powell classification of American Indian languages. *Papers in Linguistics* 4.70–110.

DARNELL, REGNA. 1971b. The revision of the Powell classification. *Papers in Linguistics* 4.233–257.

DARNELL, REGNA. 1988. *Daniel Garrison Brinton: The 'fearless critic' of Philadelphia.* Philadelphia: Department of Anthropology, University of Pennsylvania.

HALLOWELL, A. IRVING. 1960. The beginnings of anthropology in America. In *Selected papers from The American Anthropologist, 1888–1920,* edited by Frederica de Laguna, pp. 1–90. New York: Harper & Row.

MURRAY, STEPHEN O. 1983. *Group formation in social science.* Edmonton: Linguistic Research.

STOCKING, GEORGE W., JR. 1974. The Boas plan for the study of American Indian languages. In *Studies in the history of linguistics: Traditions and paradigms,* edited by Dell Hymes, pp. 454–484. Bloomington: Indiana University Press.

APHASIA is a disruption or loss of the language faculty, caused by focal damage to the brain of a previously normal language user. Language functions are asymmetrically represented in the brain; virtually all right-handed persons, and a majority of left-handers, are believed to have language lateralized to the left cerebral hemisphere. [*See* Lateralization of Language.] Thus most aphasias result from damage to the left hemisphere. The primary cause of aphasia in contemporary society is the interruption of the cerebral blood flow by stroke; however, aphasia can result from any abrupt disruption of neural functioning in the left hemisphere. Aphasia is not a particularly rare event; it is estimated that approximately one million Americans have some form of permanent aphasia.

1. Neuro-anatomical approaches: the 'classical' model. In 1874, Carl Wernicke, a young German neurologist, published a paper which described a type of aphasic language disturbance—and a related neuro-anatomical site of damage—that differed from the type of aphasia, and site of lesion, that had been described previously by the French neurologist Paul Broca. The type subsequently called WERNICKE'S APHASIA is characterized by well-articulated, fluent speech which lacks content, and which is often marked by PARAPHASIAS, i.e. obviously incorrect selection or execution of words. Wernicke noted that patients with these kinds of production difficulties also suffered from a disruption of the ability to comprehend speech. The lesion responsible for this set of symptoms is said to be situated in a section of the posterior superior temporal lobe ('Wernicke's area'), immediately adjacent to the primary auditory receiving area, which is not affected. [*See* Neural Structures.]

The type of aphasia that had been described previous to Wernicke's publication presents quite a different pattern (Broca 1865). The set of symptoms that came to be called BROCA'S APHASIA is characterized by slow and labored articulation of speech, with poor production of structural sentence elements. Comprehension of the speech of others is spared, relative to the severity of the production deficit; and it is less disturbed than in Wernicke's aphasia. The lesion site responsible for this pattern of symptoms was said to be an area in the left inferior frontal lobe ('Broca's area'), adjacent to the area of the motor cortex that controls the movement of the lips, jaw, tongue, and vocal folds.

Wernicke argued that damage to different brain regions caused different patterns of aphasic disturbance; this implied that complex language functions, such as 'comprehension', could be strictly localized to particular neural tissue. Perhaps more importantly, Wernicke's descriptions were accompanied by the outline of a formal model of the neuro-anatomical organization of language. This model, as developed in later papers by Wernicke and his followers, has dominated thinking about language/brain relationships into the 1980s.

2. The 'disconnection' model. In 1965, Wernicke's model was formally modernized and extended by the American neurologist Norman Geschwind, to account for a variety of disturbances to higher cortical function. This DISCONNECTION approach defined the specific brain regions that are responsible for the execution of functions such as the auditory analysis of speech, or the programming of the motor speech system. Geschwind argued that these regions are connected in very specific ways—so that information is transmitted, often in only one direction, between centers. Perhaps the best-known example of a neuro-anatomical connection between centers within Geschwind's model is the ARCUATE FASCICULUS, a bundle of fibers which connect the center for the auditory analysis of speech sounds (Wernicke's area) to the center for motor speech programming (Broca's area). According to the model, when these connections are damaged, the resulting pattern of language symptoms is one in which speech is fluent (Broca's area intact), and comprehension is normal (Wernicke's area intact), but patients have difficulty repeating words that are spoken to them. This pattern of symptoms was called CONDUCTION APHASIA, to express the view that it represents a failure of transmission or 'conduction' from Wernicke's area, where incoming speech sounds are interpreted, to Broca's area, where the motor programs required for production are prepared.

Other symptom patterns, i.e. the transcortical aphasias, have been described in which these 'transmission' areas are intact, and patients are able to repeat utterances despite difficulty in comprehension and/or production (see Berndt 1988). There have been numerous challenges to the disconnection analysis of conduction aphasia and the transcortical aphasias, and more generally to the 'classical' model of language localization. Nonetheless, these ideas continue to dominate neurologists' views of the cortical language representations that give rise to the aphasias.

3. Linguistic and psycholinguistic approaches to aphasia. Historically, neurologists have used the structure/function relationships represented by aphasic disorders to address basic neurological questions; similarly, linguists and psycholinguists have attempted to use performance data from aphasic patients to assess theories of language representation and processing. [*See* Psycholinguistics, *article on* Approaches to Neurolinguistics.] Much of this work has been carried out since the middle of the 20th century, perhaps stimulated by the assertion of Jakobson 1956 that linguistics was the proper discipline in which to study aphasia—since it is, after all, a disorder of language. Subsequent linguistically oriented investigations of aphasia were motivated by the belief that the forms that aphasia can take are constrained by the functional organization of the normal language system. Thus the various patterns of language impairment that occur in aphasia should be explainable within the framework of existing linguistic theories. A corollary to this notion was later made explicit, in the form of an argument that the development of linguistic theories and psycholinguistic processing models could themselves be informed and constrained by the existence of particular forms of aphasic disorders (cf. the chapters on phonological and syntactic aspects of aphasia in Sarno 1981).

4. The syndrome approach. Linguistic and psycholinguistic investigations of aphasia since Jakobson's day have focused on the apparently contrasting language disorders represented by Broca's and Wernicke's aphasias. Two major and related influences have shaped these investigations. The first is methodological: studies of aphasia, which historically were dominated by the case-study methods of neurology, have increasingly adopted the experimental approach of the emerging field of psycholinguistics. In contrast to the purely descriptive study of the types of language impairments that can occur, special tests have been designed as explicit assessments of the integrity of different language functions; testing is carried out on groups of patients thought to be homogeneous (i.e. Broca's vs. Wernicke's aphasics); and results are subjected to statistical analysis. These methods, pioneered by Harold Goodglass and his colleagues at the Boston University Aphasia Research Center, have dominated the field of aphasia research, in the United States and in much of Europe, for several decades (see Goodglass & Blumstein 1973).

The second major influence on linguistic and psycholinguistic investigations of aphasia is the development and specification of the theory of generative transformational grammar (Chomsky 1957). There have been a few attempts to explain particular aphasic deficits by reference to specific aspects of the theory, but the major influence of Chomsky's theory on aphasia research has been more general. Examinations of aphasic deficits have been motivated by the view that language is organized as a set of mental processes that can be investigated experimentally. The approach adopted is that language involves a set of independent components (e.g. phonology, syntax, and semantics) which interact in the performance of language tasks, such as comprehending and producing sentences. The field of psycholinguistics generally has been dominated by attempts to test these notions; psycholinguistic investigations of aphasia have been similarly influenced (see Lesser 1978 for review).

Various studies published since 1960 have argued that the symptom complexes of Broca's and Wernicke's aphasias arise from impairments to specific aspects of the language system. For example, the empty speech and disturbed comprehension of Wernicke's aphasia have been attributed to a specific disorder of the semantic component of the system. The speech characteristics that support this analysis [*see* Paragrammatism] are illustrated by the relatively sparse content and incorrect word usage in the following transcription of a Wernicke's aphasic patient telling the story of Cinderella:

(1) *The girl the ladies wh the girl and two little girls and they have on the hair and all that jazz uh she two the two girls she said uh she dressing their hair dress their hair I think and dress your hair and beautiful dress . . . nose and big mouth not you know but she is very pretty.* (Time: 110 seconds.)

This production pattern is often accompanied (as in this patient's case) by serious difficulty in understanding the meanings of single words, especially if semantically similar items are included as distractors.

Some Wernicke's aphasics produce more distorted word forms, i.e. phonemic PARAPHASIC errors, than are evident in this sample. Experimental study of the disordered productions of these patients has suggested that they have a deficit at the level of selecting phonemic sequences for output, rather than in achieving a correct phonetic execution. It has also been argued that at least some Wernicke's aphasics have central phonological problems which underlie both the comprehension deficit and the phonemic distortions that sometimes occur in their speech.

Despite these attempts to characterize linguistically the disorders found in Wernicke's aphasia, most research attention within this framework has been on Broca's aphasia. It has long been noted that the effortful speech of Broca's aphasics often results in utterances that are not structurally complete. [*See* Agrammatism.] As suggested by the following transcription of a Broca's aphasic patient telling the Cinderella story, the major content of the patient's speech may be apparent, but the syntactic elements that provide sentence structure (the grammatical morphemes) are often missing:

(2) *One time* (8 sec) *the girl* (13 sec) *workin' workin'* (20 sec) *two two two three two* (4 sec) *two mother and two sister* (6 sec) *ok* (21 sec) *the man uh the prince prince* (Time: 136 seconds).

This pattern of production was accompanied in these patients by a sentence comprehension disorder, manifested only when content words were not sufficient to support correct interpretation—e.g. in semantically reversible active and passive sentences like *The boy is kissed by the girl.* This apparent congruence of symptoms that involved syntactic elements in both comprehension and production has led to the hypothesis that the symptoms found in Broca's aphasia represent a disruption of syntactic representations that affect performance in all modalities.

5. Criticisms of the 'syndrome approach'. All these explanatory accounts of aphasia types have suffered from several kinds of problems. First, it is not always possible to assign an aphasic patient to one of the classical syndromes; by some estimates, only about half of all aphasic patients can be classified. Thus many types of language deficits cannot be addressed using this approach. Second and more important, the elements of the symptom patterns that support the explanations given for a particular syndrome—e.g. problems with sentence structural elements in all modalities—do not always occur together. Careful study of individual patients has revealed many dissociations among symptoms that had been argued to arise from a single cause (see contributions in Kean 1985 for a review of this evidence).

Not only do these dissociations undermine attempts to attribute the major aphasic syndromes to a common, linguistically specifiable deficit; they also present a major challenge to the dominant psychometric methodology of contrasting the performance of clinically defined groups of patients on experimental tests. In the mid-1980s, a lively debate developed on the topic of the proper methodology for aphasia research. One argument held that studies of clinically defined groups of aphasic patients could not be expected to yield any interpretable results with regard to language functions. Others argued that the study of groups of aphasic patients has yielded many insights into language/brain relationships, as well as into the organization of language itself, and should continue to do so. It is unlikely that this debate will be definitively resolved. However, recent publications exhibit one effect of the demonstration of heterogeneity within clinical groups: a tendency to provide more descriptive information about the individuals constituting the groups. That is, an overt demonstration of the presence of particular symptoms is supplanting the assumption that they are present simply because the patients fall into a particular clinical group.

6. The single case-study approach. Another change evident in recent studies of aphasia, which is both a cause and an effect of the heterogeneity debate, is the increasing prevalence of single case studies. Linguistically and psychologically sophisticated studies of individual aphasic patients, until recently rather rare among American researchers, have long been a mainstay of the methodological arsenal of aphasia researchers in Europe (see contributions in Coltheart et al. 1987). In fact, the demonstrations of symptom dissociations that undermined the syntactic account of Broca's aphasia came, in large part, from studies of individual Italian- and Dutch-speaking patients.

In addition to providing a means for investigating the extent to which the 'classical' aphasia types constitute homogeneous groups, single case-study methods in aphasia have uncovered numerous phenomena with linguistic and psycholinguistic relevance. For example, Elizabeth Warrington and her colleagues at the National Hospital in London have published a series of case reports documenting the occurrence of remarkably selective disruption or loss of semantic information (e.g. Warrington & Shallice 1984). Individual patients have been described in whom brain damage has very selectively affected the ability to comprehend or to produce words from specific semantic categories. The occurrence of such deficits suggests that distinctions such as 'concrete vs. abstract', 'animate vs. inanimate', and 'naturally occurring vs. human-made' (or even finer distinctions) are honored in the cerebral organization of semantic information.

Warrington and her colleagues also inaugurated a series of case studies, followed up over the years by numerous other investigators, on the occurrence of deficits to 'short-term memory' following brain damage (see Vallar & Shallice 1990). Such patients, trying to repeat what they hear, have difficulty disproportionate to their relatively well-preserved fluency and comprehension. Although they are frequently classified as 'conduction aphasics,' the functional account of their repetition disorder, as a consequence of memory impairment, is quite different from that proposed by Wernicke and elaborated by Geschwind.

Patients with selective deficit to short-term memory have provided a means of studying the relationship between memory and language processes. Although little evidence has been garnered that identifies a role for short-term memory in sentence production, it has frequently been noted that patients with such impairment have difficulty in understanding syntactically complex sentences. This association of symptoms is consonant with contemporary views of auditory language comprehension, which assume that segments of at least clause-length must be stored, available for reinterpretation, as comprehension proceeds. The processing details of the putative relationship between short-term memory and sentence comprehension are far from clear. Nonetheless, data from aphasic patients can be expected to contribute to the eventual specification of such a relationship, if it exists.

7. Therapeutic approaches to aphasia. During the twenty-five years or so that these linguistically and psycholinguistically motivated investigations of aphasia have been carried out, the development of therapies directed at improving language functions in aphasic patients has proceeded largely independently. Approaches to treatment have not usually adopted a componential view of language; and psycholinguistic researchers have not, in general, considered the rich source of information provided by patients' responses to particular interventions.

Methods of treating aphasia have been motivated largely by the theoretical view, set forth most compellingly by Schuell 1965, that different types of aphasia represent different levels of severity of impairment to a unitary language system. The apparent differences among patients are attributed to deficits of processes (e.g. sensorimotor and visual) which are judged to be peripheral to the central, unitary language faculty. The 'stimulation' approach to aphasia therapy, engendered by this view, has taken a variety of forms; but its basic view of language as a relatively undifferentiated system is in direct contrast to the componential view assumed by proponents of the psycholinguistic approach. This essential difference of opinion about the nature of language, and hence about the nature of aphasia, is probably responsible for the fact that aphasia research motivated by linguistic and psycholinguistic considerations has, until recently, had little impact on the development of aphasia therapies, and vice versa.

This situation has changed in recent years with the development of language-oriented therapies, and of systems focused on specific language components such as syntax (see Howard & Hatfield 1987). Moreover, researchers interested in aphasia and related disorders have begun systematically testing hypotheses about the nature of patients' deficits by introducing training focused on carefully circumscribed functions. This trend has been most evident among 'cognitive neuropsychologists' in Great Britain, who rely on detailed models of cognitive/linguistic function to provide a basis for clinical diagnosis and treatment. This model-oriented approach serves a dual purpose: the components of the model provide a basis for predicting the response to a specific intervention; and the response to intervention yields empirical evidence regarding the functional role of the target component in the model. This methodology is an emerging technique that can be used to relate the behavior of aphasic patients in more detail to models of normal language processing.

Rita Sloan Berndt

BIBLIOGRAPHY

Berndt, Rita Sloan. 1988. Repetition in aphasia. In *Handbook of neuropsychology,* vol. 1, edited by François Boller & Jordan Grafman, pp. 329–348. Amsterdam: Elsevier.

Broca, Paul. 1865. Sur la siège de la faculté du langage articulé. *Bulletin de la Société d'Anthropologie de Paris* 6.377–393.

Chomsky, Noam. 1957. *Syntactic structures.* (Janua linguarum, Series minor, 4.) The Hague: Mouton.

Coltheart, Max, et al., eds. 1987. *The cognitive neuropsychology of language.* London: Erlbaum.

Geschwind, Norman. 1965. Disconnexion syndromes in animals and man. *Brain* 88.237–294, 585–644.

Goodglass, Harold, & Sheila Blumstein, eds. 1973. *Psycholinguistics and aphasia.* Baltimore, Md.: Johns Hopkins University Press.

Howard, David, & Frances M. Hatfield. 1987. *Aphasia therapy: Historical and contemporary issues.* London: Erlbaum.

Jakobson, Roman. 1956. Two aspects of language and two types of aphasic disturbances. In Roman Jakobson & Morris Halle, *Fundamentals of language* (Janua linguarum, Series minor, 1), pp. 69–96. The Hague: Mouton.

Kean, Mary-Louise, ed. 1985. *Agrammatism.* Orlando: Academic Press.

Lesser, Ruth. 1978. *Linguistic investigations of aphasia.* New York: Elsevier.

SARNO, MARTHA TAYLOR, ed. 1981. *Acquired aphasia.* New York: Academic Press.

SCHUELL, HILDRED. 1965. *Differential diagnosis of aphasia with the Minnesota Test.* Minneapolis: University of Minnesota Press.

VALLAR, GIUSEPPE, & TIM SHALLICE. 1990. *Neuropsychological impairments of short-term memory.* Cambridge & New York: Cambridge University Press.

WARRINGTON, ELIZABETH K., & TIM SHALLICE. 1984. Category-specific semantic impairments. *Brain* 107.829–854.

WERNICKE, CARL. 1874. *Der aphasische Symptomcomplex: Eine psychologische Studie auf anatomischer Basis.* Breslau: Cohn & Weigert. Translated in Carl Wernicke, *Works on aphasia: A sourcebook and review* (Janua linguarum, Series minor, 28), pp. 91–145. The Hague: Mouton, 1977.

APO DUAT LANGUAGES are spoken in the northeastern part of the island of Borneo. They form a top-level constituent of the Borneo subgroup of West Malayo-Polynesian [*qq.v.*].

LANGUAGE LIST

Kelabit: 1,650 speakers reported in 1981, in northern Sarawak, Malaysia, in the mountains. Also spoken in Kalimantan, Indonesia. Also called Kalabit or Kerabit.

Lengilu: 10 speakers reported in 1981, in northeast Kalimantan, Indonesia, between Sa'ban and Lundayeh.

Lundayeh: 15,700 speakers reported in 1981, from Brunei Bay to the headwaters of the Padas, Baram, and Sesayap rivers at the meeting of Sabah and Sarawak (Malaysia) and Kalimantan (Indonesia). Also called Southern Murut (though it is not a Murutic language) or Lun Bawang. Most speakers live in Indonesia.

Putoh: 6,000 speakers reported in 1981, in northeast Kalimantan, Indonesia, around the Mentarang River.

Sa'ban: 1,000 speakers reported in 1981, in northeast Kalimantan, Indonesia, on the border with Sarawak, south of Lundayeh. Also spoken in Sarawak, Malaysia.

APPLIED LINGUISTICS. [*This entry is concerned with the practical use of linguistics in such fields as language education, lexicography, translation, and the use of language in the professions. It comprises four articles:*

An Overview
History of the Field
Language Planning
Minorities and Applied Linguistics

For related topics, see Applied Pragmatics; Assessment; Bilingualism; Classroom-Oriented Research; Computer-Assisted Instruction; Contrastive Rhetoric; Critical Linguistics; Institutional Linguistics; Language-in-Education Planning; Lexicography; Literacy; Pathology of Language; Pedagogical Linguistics; Reading Research; Scientific Nomenclature; Style; Translation and Interpretation; *and* Writing Research.]

An Overview

The application of linguistic knowledge to real-world problems is a process that has been going on through recorded history, and probably before that. Whenever knowledge about language is used to solve a basic language-related problem, one may say that A[pplied] L[inguistics] is being practiced. AL is a technology which makes abstract ideas and research findings accessible and relevant to the real world; it mediates between theory and practice. The quest for knowledge characteristic of established academic disciplines is vitally important, in part because all furtherance of our understanding of the world we live in is worthwhile in itself; but it is also crucial that the understanding gained in the quest for 'pure' knowledge be somehow related to everyday human experience. Scholarship has obligations to the non-scholarly world, and it is this need that AL intends to meet. Its starting point lies in the language-related problems of practical life, and it adduces insights from disciplinary areas of language study to the extent that such insights are relevant to the clarification and solution of these problems. But it is not confined to these areas; it can derive insights from any field of inquiry, whether based in language study or not; the essential principle is that of relevance. (For general reference, see Lado 1964, Mackey 1965, Corder 1973, Wardhaugh 1974, Crystal 1981, Stern 1983, and Widdowson 1979–84.)

1. Scope. If we accept a definition of the field like that offered above, two questions follow from it. First, what kind of real-world problems does AL typically address? Second, which areas of theoretical inquiry have provided relevant insights?

A general answer to the first question is provided by the cumulative indices of the journal *Applied Linguistics*, of the *Annual Review of Applied Linguistics*, of the descriptors in the dictionary used to access the ERIC educational resources system, and of the list of the

Scientific Commissions of the International Association for Applied Linguistics (AILA). A review of the ERIC system over the past twenty years, for example, shows some 209 entries, of which approximately 45 percent are in some way concerned with language teaching; the remainder are scattered over inquiries into reading, coherence, contrastive analysis, psycholinguistics, literacy, language policy, sociolinguistics, translation, bilingualism (including language varieties), language and culture, computational linguistics, pragmatics, lexicography, discourse analysis, and artificial languages, in descending order of occurrence. In addition, some headings suggest the existence of metaconcerns such as teacher training, research design, and the possibility of careers in the field. An analysis of the cumulative index of *Applied Linguistics* over the first eight years of its existence shows a significant overlap in topics—e.g. second language acquisition, pragmatics, discourse analysis, cross-cultural issues, teaching/learning issues, lexicography, communicative competence, and special-purposes teaching account for two-thirds of the nearly two hundred entries. The AILA Scientific Commissions reflect a similar set of concerns: computational linguistics, child language, contrastive/error analysis, discourse analysis, educational technology, interpreting and translating, language planning, language testing, lexicography, psycholinguistics, rhetoric and stylistics, second-language acquisition, sociolinguistics, and terminology. (None of the lists are exhaustive; they are intended only to demonstrate significant overlap.) These lists identify a number of main areas of interest, as follows.

(a) Speech therapy: the treatment of linguistic disorders, whether physiological or psychological
(b) Communicative interactions—essentially, the relationship of POWER AND LANGUAGE [*q.v.*]; the uses of language to assert authority and to maintain institutional control (as demonstrated in studies of language in the professions); the uses of language to further ideological influence, to cajole, and to persuade; the uses of language to make meaning more accessible to those (e.g. the aged) who might otherwise be deprived of rights; the problems of sociological disadvantage
(c) Language planning and language policy
(d) Language in education—including issues of bilingualism, multilingualism, bidialectalism, and multiculturalism
(e) Language teaching and learning, where major developments in AL to date can most clearly be seen

2. Main areas. Each of the five major areas listed above requires reference to different aspects of language study and, perhaps more significantly, to an interdisciplinary combining of insights from different domains. It is not merely a matter of applying linguistics in a narrow sense. The very problems that the field approaches require the application of knowledge derived from linguistic theory, but also and importantly from anthropology, learning theory, psychology, sociology, and a variety of other disciplines, depending on the sort of problem being solved—and including economics, as one attempts to solve problems in a cost-effective manner. Kaplan 1980 takes the view that AL is the stage upon which all of the human (social) sciences coalesce in the solution of human problems based in language. Each of the five main areas needs to be examined in some depth to determine which areas of language study are relevant, and the ways in which various areas intersect.

2.1. ***Speech therapy.*** Microlinguistic investigations in phonetics and in syntax provide the means for diagnosis of pathological disorders. Once diagnosis has been achieved, treatment needs to take account of various psycholinguistic and sociolinguistic factors, the attitudes of the patient, and the views of the larger society with reference to the condition and the patient. There is some significant similarity here to the conditions which apply in any instance of linguistic nonconformity, e.g. in the case of the second-language learner or the speaker of a nonstandard variety. [*See* Pathology of Language.]

2.2. ***Communicative interactions.*** Applied linguists have turned their attention to the social environment in which language is used, and to the ways in which it is used by various constituencies. Careful investigations have been undertaken of the interactions between segments of the population, interactions between physicians and their patients, between teachers and their students, interactions in the courts of law, and uses of language by advertisers, governments, and politicians. [*See* Institutional Linguistics.] These studies go well beyond providing lists of special terms used in the contexts described; rather, they examine the syntactic and rhetorical structure of different discourse types and the interaction strategies employed, particularly when the relative roles of the participants are unequal. Such studies call for reference to discourse analysis and pragmatics, to the description of rhetorical regularities which characterize various types of use, to genre analysis, and to the notion of schema in artificial intelligence studies (which attempt to design computer programs to simulate the process of language use). This area of AL can be seen as the development of conventional textual study in rhetoric and literary criticism. It makes reference, however, to a wider range of disciplinary inquiry, and focuses specifically on the language of everyday life and its role in the exercise of power and maintenance of civil liberties.

2.3. ***Language planning and language policy.*** Another complex set of concerns stems from the reality of bilingualism and multilingualism in the 20th century. [*See* Bilingualism.] Political events have caused vast dislocations of populations during this century, called by some 'the age of the refugee'; great redistributions of population, particularly in urban centers, have thrown together speakers of different languages and varieties. This, coupled with the emergence of new political states out of former colonial empires, has created a need for language planning and language policy. [*See article on* Language Planning *below.*] Planning has essentially separated into two major subcategories: CORPUS PLANNING and STATUS PLANNING. Corpus planning deals with norm selection and codification; that is, when a government chooses a previously unwritten variety as a national language or an official language, it is necessary to identify an orthography for the new language, to describe its grammar and lexicon, to develop means by which that language may be taught to the citizens of the new polity who do not know it, to provide literacy programs in that language, etc. Corpus planning results in the writing of dictionaries and grammars, in the standardization of spelling and pronunciation, and in the preparation of literacy materials. Status planning, on the other hand, is concerned with the initial choice of language. It studies attitudes toward particular languages, functions of particular varieties within a society, and the social and political implications of various language choices. The issue of modernization is necessarily subsumed; as new nations emerge, they have concerns for the economic capacity of the polity to provide for its citizens. Modernization implies the availability of scientific and technical information, and a concern with appropriate technology and its transfer. These matters are constrained by the fact that English has become a world language of science and technology. A polity which has chosen an indigenous language as a national language for purposes of unity and identity remains faced with the need for a language of wider communication, in order to develop contacts beyond its own borders and to move toward modernization. This area, then, draws upon studies in language choice, language change, language standardization, language politics (glottopolitics), geolinguistics, language teaching, and literacy.

2.4. ***Language in education*** is centrally concerned with the institutional role of language; it involves consideration of the relationship between the languages and varieties used as media for formal instruction, and those of the home and of other contexts of social interaction (the religious sector, the marketplace, etc.). Such matters have a bearing both on general educational policy and on the particular attitudes and practices of everyone concerned with the educational process. They raise fundamental issues about norms of language behavior, the definition of competence, and the means for assessing proficiency in language. These issues need to be referred to inquiries in the sociology of education, the sociology of language, discourse analysis, the sociology of knowledge, microlinguistics (in order to provide the categories of description needed to characterize different competencies), and the whole area of language measurement. [*See* Language-in-Education Planning.]

2.5. ***Language teaching and learning.*** Because AL has been, for most of its current incarnation, associated with language teaching, this is the area of greatest development. Indeed, the term AL probably first occurred in the United States in the 1940s—as Mackey 1965 suggests, inspired by a desire among language teachers to be perceived as scientists rather than as humanists, and to distinguish themselves from teachers of literature. Language teachers have looked to disciplinary domains of language study for guidance in answering two basic questions:

(a) How should language be defined/constrained so that it will be possible to determine what to teach?
(b) How may language learning itself be characterized?

Developments in language teaching may be divided historically into a series of phases which can be characterized in terms of the relationship between these two questions. In the early 20th century, language teaching was focused on the definition of what was to be taught, without regard to the actual process of learning. It was based on a grammar/translation approach. This was grounded in philology and in a comparative methodology which took Latin as the basic norm of reference for all other languages. The model for such an approach derived from the teaching of classical languages, where the available corpus was closed and limited largely to literary texts. Since there were no living native speakers of these languages, the ways in which native speakers acquired and used languages could not be adduced as relevant to the pedagogic process. The approach, therefore, was concerned exclusively with transmitting the formal properties of language defined in reference to classical categories, and learning was seen as the reflex of teaching. The purpose of the approach was not to induce spoken communicative abilities, but to provide access to the thought and art expressed through the language.

The advent of structuralism in linguistics coincided with the development of behaviorist psychology. With structuralism, the formal properties of language were independently described in internal distributional terms, not in reference to an external classical norm. Such an approach to linguistic description defined units for teaching as structures or sentence patterns which were specific to particular languages. Behaviorist psychology, in its turn, provided a model of learning as stimulus/response habit formation. So pedagogy now had authority from linguistics for a description of units to be taught, and authority from psychology for a definition of the learning process. Answers to the two questions converged on an approach which provided repetitive practice of structures so that the forms of language would become habitual.

This convergence of influence from the two disciplines was disturbed by the appearance of Noam Chomsky. On the one hand, he challenged the behaviorist account of learning; on the other hand, he proposed a theory of language structure which was more abstract than the immediate appearance of surface forms. Chomsky's cognitive theory of language essentially denied the primacy of overt behavior and the grammatical structures which corresponded to it, characterizing them as superficial effects of deep-seated cognitive causes which were a function of an innate pre-programmed language faculty, a L[anguage] A[cquisition] D[evice]. With Chomsky, then, the nature of language was necessarily bound up with the nature of language acquisition. In respect to language pedagogy, this had the effect of focusing attention on the second question, that of the process of language learning; and it stimulated the extensive activity in AL concerned with S[ECOND] L[ANGUAGE] A[CQUISITION]. The starting point of this inquiry was the redefinition of nonconformist 'deviant' learner utterances as evidence not of error or failure to learn, but of underlying cognitive and creative processes necessary to the learning activity and informed by its developmental logic. Overt behavior was simply superficial evidence of something more cognitively significant going on in the deeper recesses of the mind.

SLA research had the general effect of shifting the emphasis in pedagogy from teaching to learning. It was recognized that forcing learners into conformity to a fixed pattern of behavior, determined by the teacher, could inhibit language acquisition; that teacher input was not at all the same as learner intake; and that errors called not for summary correction, but for more careful appraisal as positive signs of achievement. Such views found independent support in humanistic approaches to pedagogy, some of which tended to excess in suggesting that all teaching was an interference in the natural process of learning.

The next major phase of development focused attention not on the question of the learning process, but on the question of how the language to be learned should itself be defined. This was inspired by ideas in sociolinguistics, with Dell Hymes and the notion of COMMUNICATIVE COMPETENCE [*q.v.*]; by coincident development in philosophy with SPEECH ACT theory [*see* Speech Acts]; and by the British tradition of contextual linguistics, as realized particularly in the work of Michael A. K. Halliday (*see* Halliday et al. 1964). [*See also* Systemic Grammar.] What pedagogy derived from these sources of influence was a definition of the language to be taught in communicative rather than formal terms. This resulted in the design of curricula based on notions and functions rather than on grammatical structures, most notably in the THRESHOLD LEVEL specifications of the Council of Europe. Subsequently, it was realized that communication cannot be characterized in terms of isolates; under the influence of DISCOURSE ANALYSIS and CONVERSATION ANALYSIS, there was a shift of emphasis from curriculum design to methodology. [*See* Conversation Analysis; Discourse.] Communicative abilities, it was suggested, could best be developed by the devising of activities in the classroom which engaged learners in the negotiation of meaning by problem-solving.

Here again consideration of the two questions converges. In SLA, research has come latterly to a recognition that the learning process is not simply a matter of determination by innate cognitive forces, but is a function of strategies which learners employ in the negotiation of meaning. The process of acquisition and use would appear to be activated by the same sort of pragmatic factors of communicative interaction. Different disciplinary influences all currently seem to suggest an approach to teaching which sees what to teach and how to learn as, in effect, aspects of the same question. [*See also* Acquisition of Language; Pedagogical Linguistics.]

3. Goals. Five broad areas have been identified to characterize the kinds of real-world problems that AL is able to deal with appropriately; the areas of language study which have provided relevant insights have also been identified. Two points need to be clarified: first, virtually all areas of language study contribute to AL; and second, linguistics as the central area of such study has itself evolved and moved though a number of different paradigms in a relatively short time. More importantly, AL is in a sense a misnomer, because it is not specifically the application of linguistics to anything; rather, it is an independent area of inquiry with its own conditions of adequacy, drawing upon linguistics and other disciplinary areas, but not determined by them. Unlike general linguistics—which studies language in dissociation from its context in order to devise formal models accounting for all and only the possible structures of a language, to unearth language universals, and to investigate the relationship between language and mind—AL restores language to its context of social actuality. It concerns itself with how real people in real situations achieve communicative objectives, and why they do so. It seeks to establish the relationship between what is said and the social roles of the sayers, so that the manipulations and motivations of language users may be more clearly understood. It concerns itself with what can reasonably be taught; the circumstances under which it can be taught; the activities through which it can be taught; the political, social, and economic structures that will permit the teaching and learning to occur; and the real costs and benefits of the entire enterprise. It has been suggested that, granted that AL is a misnomer, the term 'educational linguistics' might be more appropriate; it should be clear from the discussion here that educational linguistics is indeed a part of AL. But AL is much more broadly based.

This is not to claim that applied linguists should take on the roles of sociolinguists or psycholinguists or grammarians; rather, the claim is that applied linguists, in the pursuit of relevant insights, draw upon knowledge from all of these areas and many others. It is necessarily interdisciplinary, because the real-world problems which AL has to tackle are not idealized so as to fit the specialist and partial interests of particular disciplines. The interdisciplinary nature of AL is an inevitable consequence of its mediating role between theory and practice, and its adherence to the principle of relevance. It should be noted, however, that as an area of inquiry which is accountable to this principle, AL is also itself capable of opening up avenues of theoretical study. As is evident from such activities as ethnographic description conducted without fixed preconceptions, the quest for understanding of real-life problems itself raises issues of theoretical significance which, in its current state, theory might not envision. There is nothing so practical as a good theory, as long as its relevance can be established. Equally, there is nothing so theoretical, in implication, as a practical problem. It is no doubt for this reason that AL is both intellectually satisfying and practically accountable, that there are significant numbers of scholars who happily accept the designation 'applied linguist', and that AL is now internationally established as an independent field of inquiry of great and growing importance.

ROBERT B. KAPLAN & HENRY G. WIDDOWSON

BIBLIOGRAPHY

CORDER, S. PIT. 1973. *Introducing applied linguistics.* Harmondsworth: Penguin.

CRYSTAL, DAVID. 1981. *Directions in applied linguistics.* London: Academic Press.

HALLIDAY, MICHAEL A. K., et al. 1964. *The linguistic sciences and language teaching.* London: Longman.

KAPLAN, ROBERT B., ed. 1980. *On the scope of applied linguistics.* Rowley, Mass.: Newbury House.

LADO, ROBERT. 1964. *Language teaching.* New York: McGraw-Hill.

MACKEY, WILLIAM F. 1965. *Language teaching analysis.* London: Longman. Bloomington: Indiana University Press.

STERN, H. H. 1983. *Fundamental concepts of language teaching.* Oxford & New York: Oxford University Press.

WARDHAUGH, RONALD. 1974. *Topics in applied linguistics.* Rowley, Mass.: Newbury House.

WIDDOWSON, HENRY G. 1979–84. *Explorations in applied linguistics.* 2 vols. Oxford & New York: Oxford University Press.

History of the Field

Since its emergence as a multi-disciplinary field of studies, focusing mainly on systematic ways of improving the learning and teaching of English as a foreign language in developing countries, A[pplied] L[inguistics] has become established in numerous academic institutions worldwide. The relevance of AL now extends to all languages, not only English; increasingly, it is evoked for the solution of language-based problems other than [F]oreign [L]anguage [T]eaching—e.g. national language policy planning; aspects of communications research; 'language engineering' for special circumstances, such as SEASPEAK for maritime VHF radio communications; improved systems for translation and interpreting; and aspects of artificial intelligence research. AL is neither 'linguistics applied' nor 'applications of linguistic theory', since some other activity determines the focus; furthermore, it makes use not only of linguistics, but also of other disciplines. Nevertheless, the majority of work in AL has been directly concerned with language teaching and learning.

In the years following World War II, scholars asked what lessons might be learned from wartime experience for the future improvement of FLT. Between 1939 and 1945, specialists in linguistics were engaged in many countries, notably by the military in the United States and Britain, in order quickly to produce large numbers of personnel having competence in one or more foreign languages, including many previously regarded as 'exotic', e.g. Arabic, Burmese, and Japanese.

From 1956, the concept that linguists could usefully contribute to the principled study of language learning and teaching gave rise to two pioneering institutions with the term 'applied linguistics' in their title: the S[chool of] A[pplied] L[inguistics] at Edinburgh University, and the C[enter for] A[pplied] L[inguistics] in Washington, D.C. The Edinburgh SAL was initially funded by the British Council, the quasi-governmental body whose mandate includes the promotion of the English language abroad. SAL was set up as a department providing courses for experienced teachers and teacher trainers from Britain and overseas countries. The initiative in establishing SAL came from David Abercrombie and Angus McIntosh on the university side, and from H. Harvey Wood and A. H. King of the British Council. Under its pioneering first director, J. C. Catford, and his successor S. Pit Corder, SAL became a seminal force in spreading the concepts of applied linguistics worldwide, both through its many hundreds of students and through the publication of the *Edinburgh Course in Applied Linguistics* (Allen & Corder 1973–77, 4 vols.).

CAL was established a few months later, in 1957, by the Ford Foundation, whose concern to assist the rapid expansion of education in developing countries had led it to propose a series of language surveys in former British or French colonies of Africa that were approaching political independence. Out of these surveys, it was envisaged that large-scale projects would be set up to devise new curricula for the teaching of English, together with new classroom textbooks and teaching materials, and associated teacher-training programs. Within the Ford Foundation, the main impetus for establishing CAL was supplied by Melvin J. Fox—encouraged by J Milton Cowan, who had been associated with the establishment of the very first Language Center, at Cornell University. The first director of CAL was Charles Ferguson of Stanford University, under whose leadership the Center achieved international renown as the base for the language surveys mentioned and for many other projects in applied linguistics.

Both SAL and CAL reflect certain philosophical tenets concerning the educational and socio-political needs of developing countries:

(a) Such societies require rapid access by a substantial part of their population to a language of wider communication like English.
(b) The change from colonial status to independence must lead to a rapid change in the provision of access to English, from schooling only for a small elite towards universal education.
(c) Conventional language-teaching methods are incapable of providing what is needed sufficiently quickly.
(d) A broad AL approach is more likely to succeed.

This optimism has been largely vindicated; virtually all schemes for the extension and improvement of national language-teaching systems today make use of applied linguists at some stage in the process.

As for French, the campaign to revitalize the teaching of the language led to two government-backed AL projects. First, research into vocabulary frequency in spoken French was aimed at producing *Le français fondamental*, a definitive list of the twelve hundred most frequent words, to be used as the basis of coursebooks for foreign learners of French. Second, the use of audiovisual technology in language-teaching led to the structuro-global method and the pioneering audio-visual course, *Voix et images de France*, in which a coursebook closely controlled in its vocabulary and grammar was integrated with slide-projection, tape recordings, language laboratory work, and a strongly oral classroom style. Many of France's leading linguists were involved in these early AL projects.

The Council of Europe, backed by the ministries of education of all European countries (and influenced by SAL, CAL, and the French work), set up a Languages Project under the leadership of John L. Trim, then head of the Linguistics Department at Cambridge University. Trim's group, which included scholars from most European countries, set out to establish what were the practical language needs, in work and leisure, of particular groups of language learners within Europe, and how those needs could be met. They were required to provide, for use by designers of language-teaching courses, basic information about what each category of learners would need to do in the foreign language, and about how to express such communicative activity in each of the languages concerned. They pioneered techniques for needs-analysis and language description in the domain of language communication, invoking David Wilkins's concepts of NOTIONS (of time, place, motion, quantity, intellectual and emotional attitudes, etc.) and FUNCTIONS (describing, narrating, apologizing, questioning, etc.). For each language of Europe, they postulated an equivalent language-learning/teaching load to reach a given minimum standard of achievement—a THRESHOLD. The work took over a decade to complete, and resulted in the publication of T[HRESHOLD] L[EVEL]s for most European languages. The first of these, *Threshold Level English* (Van Ek 1975), incorporates not only Wilkins's work on notions and functions, but also an appendix by Louis Alexander on methodological implications of the threshold concepts. TLs are not themselves coursebooks, but they are used widely as sources for the design of curricula and courses.

These projects are typical of AL in that they apply the principles of rigorous linguistic study to provide the intellectual basis for the development and improvement of FLT. Such a tradition goes back at least to John Comenius in the 17th century, Bernard Miège in the 18th, and François Gouin in the 19th: these scholars predate the existence of modern linguistics, but exemplify the historical development of the philosophical study of FLT. Increasingly since ca. 1900, this development has been associated with the linguistic sciences (see Halliday et al. 1964): first with phonetics (Henry Sweet and Paul Passy), and eventually with a more general conception of linguistics in the work of such scholars as Otto Jespersen, Harold E. Palmer, C. C. Fries, Kenneth Pike, and Robert Lado (for an overview, see Howatt 1984).

The first international conference on applied linguistics was held in Nancy, France, in 1964. The participants were representative of most schools of thought in linguistics at that time. From it emerged l'Association Internationale de Linguistique Appliquée (AILA), an association of national AL associations, which publishes the *International Review of Applied Linguistics (IRAL)*. Among the national affiliates of AILA are the American Association for Applied Linguistics (AAAL) and the British Association of Applied Linguistics (BAAL), which jointly sponsor the journal *Applied Linguistics*.

AL can take different paths because of differing theoretical perspectives; different paradigms in linguistics have already contributed in different ways to its evolution. From Bloomfieldian linguistics, particularly through the work of Robert Lado, who had popularized the term 'applied linguistics', came three important ideas.

(a) The concept of CONTRASTIVE ANALYSIS [*q.v.*], in which the comparison of the learner's language and the target language was believed to enable teachers to anticipate areas of learning difficulty
(b) A belief that Bloomfield's linguistic theory, allied to B. F. Skinner's operant-conditioning psychological theory, should determine the content and method of language teaching
(c) The elaboration of discrete-item techniques for testing based on the same set of assumptions

With the rise of Chomsky's cognitive view of language and learning, a gradual shift in linguistic paradigm took place. This had an indirect effect on US language teaching in the development of various cognitive approaches, although Chomsky's model of linguistic description had itself virtually no direct influence on language pedagogy, at least in part because Chomsky and his followers denied the applicability of the description to language teaching. Chomsky maintained that the explanation of the child's ability to acquire its mother tongue is the central task of linguistic theory; an important line of research then developed within psycholinguistics into first-language acquisition. This work in turn gave rise to S[ECOND] L[ANGUAGE] A[CQUISITION] research. [*See* Acquisition of Language, *article on* Second-Language Acquisition.] The early research by S. Pit Corder and Larry Selinker into INTERLANGUAGE [*q.v.*], the work of Marina Burt, Heidi Dulay, and Stephen Krashen, and notably Krashen's Monitor Theory, all developed under the influence of Chomsky's ideas. Within the spectrum of AL—between language teaching with minimal input from linguistics, and linguistics with little input from pedagogy—SLA is close to the latter.

Whereas work under the influence of Chomsky aligns

linguistics with psychology, another and concurrent development which AL has drawn upon aligns linguistics with sociology and the study of language in use. In the United States, Dell Hymes, in the tradition of anthropological linguistics, asserted the significance of social context in the study of language and proposed the concept of COMMUNICATIVE COMPETENCE [*q.v.*]. This concept, together with the work of the ethnomethodologists on CONVERSATION ANALYSIS [*q.v.*], the speech act theory of the philosophers Austin and Searle [*see* Speech Acts], M. A. K. Halliday's social semiotic model of language [*see* Systemic Grammar], and extensive work on discourse analysis [*see* Discourse] have all been influential in the formulation of communicative approaches to language teaching. These approaches have been evident in the threshold level specification referred to earlier, and particularly effective in the design of programs of L[ANGUAGE FOR] S[PECIFIC] P[URPOSES] [*q.v.*], where teaching is directed to particular communicative needs associated with academic and occupational goals. (For a comprehensive treatment of the 'communicative' aspects of AL, the contributions from philosophy and anthropology, and the development of LSP, see especially Widdowson 1979–84.) At the same time, the emphasis on context and communication in the learning process has led to recognizing the importance of engaging learners as interactive participants in experiential learning, whereby their interests and personal concerns are involved in the negotiation of meaning significant to themselves [*see* Classroom-Oriented Research].

The first thirty years of AL in language teaching created two distinct approaches. One of these starts from the standpoint of practical language teaching and applies intellectual rigor and classroom research to improving language learning through the deliberate, principled redesign of teaching, which thereby extends our understanding of the underlying theory. The other approach starts from SLA theory, and devises empirical research whose validated results justify the use of particular techniques and methods in classroom teaching. The first of these approaches concentrates on using AL in order to differentiate the concepts and mechanisms at work when teachers teach and learners learn, and to create effective organizing principles for the design and use of teaching materials. Out of this 'teaching/learning-oriented AL' has come, e.g., the implementation of concepts such as 'approach, curriculum/syllabus, methodology, materials design, assessment (tests and examinations), teacher training'; the principled and appropriate use of educational technology, especially audio and video recording and replay; the use of computers and of interactive videodisc; LSP; and the Council of Europe work mentioned above, etc. (See especially Stern 1983 for a comprehensive discussion of these and other fundamental concepts in AL.) Demand for the services of AL specialists has also led to the establishment of a number of institutions of AL teaching and research.

The second SLA approach has concentrated on studying, from a theoretical perspective, the characteristics of the learner of language, in both classroom and non-classroom conditions, while seeing the teacher more as a 'promoter of acquisition'. Classroom research, which can be either observer- or participant-oriented, goes some way toward linking the two main approaches, by encouraging and enabling classroom teachers without theoretical leanings nevertheless to understand the concepts used in both paradigms, and within their own circumstances to contribute to further progress within the profession.

Four main functional developments in AL since 1956 should be mentioned. First, centers offering courses in applied linguistics are now found in many countries, and the numbers of specialists they train have greatly increased. Second, many universities have set up language centers in which intensive tuition in the practical command of foreign languages is provided as an end in itself, outside the conventional degree frameworks. These serve to keep applied linguistics accountable to criteria of relevance in the practical domain. Third, AL increasingly contributes to the rising level of professionalism among foreign-language teachers by relating practical problems to a broader theoretical framework, and by showing how the systematic study of language is educationally and pedagogically relevant. (For a number of papers discussing professionalism in LT, see Alatis et al. 1983.) Fourth, although the relation with language teaching remains predominant, AL is increasingly found to be of practical value in other fields also.

Centers of AL teaching and research are now many, and not confined to the United States and Europe. Some—e.g. in the Philippines, Latin America, Egypt, China, Southeast Asia, and elsewhere—arose as a result of large-scale educational aid programs in which American universities (e.g. UCLA, Columbia Teachers' College, Pittsburgh, Georgetown, etc.) sent teams to develop teaching systems and teacher education courses for English; others were the consequence of schemes assisted by the British Council, USIA, and USAID, such as the Regional English Language Centre in Singapore and the Central Institute for English in Hyderabad, India. Still others reflect the rise of Canada, Australia, and other nations as 'resource countries' for AL.

These projects, coupled with the fact that training in AL has been given by the main British and American centers to many thousands of specialists from most countries in the world who now work in their own countries, have led to AL becoming established worldwide as an essential element in the systematic improvement of the effectiveness of language learning and teaching.

PETER STREVENS

BIBLIOGRAPHY

ALATIS, JAMES E.; H. H. STERN; & PETER STREVENS, eds. 1983. *Applied linguistics and the preparation of second language teachers: Towards a rationale.* (Georgetown University Round Table on Languages and Linguistics, 1983.) Washington, D.C.: Georgetown University Press.

ALLEN, J. P. B., & S. PIT CORDER, eds. 1973–77. *The Edinburgh course in applied linguistics.* Vol. 1 (1973); Vol. 2, *Papers in applied linguistics* (1975); vol. 3, *Techniques in applied linguistics* (1974); vol. 4 (edited by J. P. B. Allen and A. Davies), *Testing and experimental methods* (1977). London: Oxford University Press.

HALLIDAY, MICHAEL A. K.; ANGUS MCINTOSH; & PETER STREVENS. 1964. *The linguistic sciences and language teaching.* London: Longman.

HOWATT, A. P. R. 1984. *A history of English language teaching.* Oxford & New York: Oxford University Press.

STERN, H. H. 1983. *Fundamental concepts of language teaching.* Oxford & New York: Oxford University Press.

VAN EK, J. A. 1975. *Threshold level English in a European unit/credit system for modern language learning by adults.* Oxford: Pergamon Press. 2d ed., 1980.

WIDDOWSON, HENRY G. 1979–84. *Explorations in applied linguistics.* 2 vols. Oxford & New York: Oxford University Press.

Language Planning

The term L[anguage] P[lanning] generally denotes a deliberate response to language problems—systematic, future-oriented, and based on a theoretical framework. The use of the term by Haugen 1966, still widely accepted, included virtually all societal attention to language problems. Neustupný 1983 offers a scheme in which CORRECTION or MANAGEMENT of language is the widest frame of reference; language TREATMENT covers organized societal attention to language problems, and language PLANNING refers to certain contemporary varieties of language treatment which aim at being highly systematic and theoretical. [*See also* Sociolinguistics, *article on* Language Planning.]

Some examples of issues with which LP has dealt are the creation of new alphabets, the codification of morphology, standardization, the development of 'plain language', spelling reform, language maintenance, and the elimination of gender discrimination in language. Kloss 1969a distinguishes STATUS PLANNING, concerned with the standing of one language in relation to others, from CORPUS PLANNING, where the shape of a language is changed by proposing new technical terms, spelling reforms, a new script, or even changes to morphology (e.g. gender endings). A similar framework was introduced by Neustupný 1978, who claimed that some societies concentrate on policy, others on cultivation. The two types of planning may take place together or separately.

Status planning is generally aimed at (a) developing a marker of national identity (NATIONISM, cf. Fishman 1968); (b) spreading a language, nationally or internationally; and/or (c) giving rights to minority groups (PLURALISM). Corpus planning is intended (i) to give its language a terminology for scientific and technical purposes; (ii) to resolve normative/structural questions of correctness, efficiency, and stylistic levels; and/or (iii) to support an ideological cause by eliminating sexist, racist, or militaristic elements in the language. Corpus and status planning have gone hand in hand in the revival of Hebrew, and the development of its functions and vocabulary—as well as in the avoidance of 'foreign' words by the use of neologisms of 'native' origin in German (1933–1945), Icelandic, and Estonian. Several steps in LP are discussed by Haugen 1966: SELECTION of form, CODIFICATION, IMPLEMENTATION, and ELABORATION (including cultivation). Rubin 1973 has added the step of EVALUATION.

1. Issues in LP include alphabetization, standardization, codification, modernization, multilingualism, and spread. These are discussed in turn below.

1.1. *Alphabetization.* The creation of a writing system enables a language to develop non-traditional functions (e.g. public administration and trade). The adoption of a different script often later facilitates the acceptance of linguistic autonomy, as in the case of Hindi/Urdu and Croatian/Serbian. In some languages (e.g. Indonesian and Turkish), the adoption of roman script has been part of a modernization process.

1.2. *Standardization.* The process of Ausbau or elaboration (Kloss 1978) has allowed the creation of new standard languages out of nonstandard varieties. Thus

Bahasa Indonesia was formed out of Bazaar Malay; Norwegian Landsmål (later developed into Nynorsk) was created out of conservative western dialects at the time of Norwegian independence; Moldavian was formed from a Rumanian dialect in the Soviet Union. Afrikaans developed out of Dutch in South Africa, with features from other languages, and probably underwent creolization. Similarly, national varieties of PLURICENTRIC (supranational) languages—e.g. American English, Austrian German, Brazilian Portuguese—have been codified as standard.

1.3. ***Codification.*** The Prague school concept of 'language culture' refers to the literate users of a language. For such users, norms of the standard language can be supported and codified by corpus planning to ensure clarity, economy, aesthetic appeal, and functional differentiation and adequacy (Havránek 1938). This relates to the language system, to its use, and to special literary applications.

1.4. ***Modernization.*** If a language is to function for science, technology, commerce, politics, and scholarship, then new lexical items must be introduced. This has occurred in decolonization situations, among others. Alternatives include borrowed terms (in Papua New Guinea, Tok Pisin *dimokretik*), loan-translation (Afrikaans *draadloos* < Eng. *wireless*), formations based on existing words (Tok Pisin *wok dokta* 'health service'), and semantic extensions (Icelandic *sima* 'rope' > 'telephone'). As corpus treatment systems become established, the ideology of indigenization as a driving force becomes less motivated (Jernudd 1983).

During much of the 20th century, even in Western societies, attempts have been made to standardize terminology, including definitions and abbreviations in specialized fields such as electrical engineering and navigation. [*See* Scientific Nomenclature.] This has only been partly achieved. Terminological planning has occurred at three levels: national, supranational (within one language), and international (across languages).

1.5. ***Multilingualism.*** As a result of status planning, a language may be recognized as the sole official standard (e.g. French in France); as one of two or more co-dominant languages (English and French in Canada, English and Afrikaans in South Africa); or as having regional official status (Igbo, Yoruba, and Hausa in Nigeria; German in Belgium). Minority languages may be promoted, or merely tolerated—i.e. accepted insofar as they do not challenge the supremacy of the national language (Kloss 1969b). Since the 1970s, Canada and Australia have changed their policies on minority languages as part of a shift from assimilation to multiculturalism. In the United States, however, some pluralist measures (bilingual ballots, bilingual education) have recently been modified, and there is a movement toward declaring English the official language of the United States.

1.6. ***Spread.*** LP takes place at both the international and national levels. The former includes language spread as well as the coordination of planning of pluricentric languages. As part of their foreign and economic policy, certain nations have sponsored the international use and learning of their languages—which have, in turn, influenced the lexicon and grammar of other languages. In the present era, this has been the case especially with English, with its dominant role in NATO; its position is particularly strong as the language used for the transfer of technology from developed countries to developing ones, and between western developed countries. Computer data banks and retrieval networks are largely in English, and this will reinforce its continuing international dominance. Another language benefiting from international technology transfer, but much less, has been German, which has been used for the exchange of information between Eastern and Western Europe.

2. Domains of LP include, in particular, public administration, education, and the communications media. Others are religion, work, the armed forces, and libraries. Many new nations have maintained the languages of their former colonizers as the media of secondary education, e.g. English in Kenya and in Papua New Guinea, or French in Zaïre. Others have developed one or more of the indigenous languages into an official language and medium of education, e.g. Vietnamese. Religious denominations determine whether to hold services in the national language, in one or more minority languages, or both—or bilingually, or in an ancient form of speech.

3. Agents of planning. Corpus planning is carried out by linguists, on their own behalf or under commission, and by academies—as well as by special interest groups, such as feminists and pacifists. Without official or popular support, LP by some groups may lead only to specific varieties or registers. Status planning, however, is usually the work of politicians and bureaucrats.

LP sometimes takes place through legislation, e.g. the Quebec law that all government notices be in French. However, since the 16th century, some countries have set up academies for corpus planning (e.g. the Accademia della Crusca, Florence, 1512, and the influential Académie Française, 1635). Others, such as Britain, have rejected this course. New academies have been established recently, as in Indonesia/Malaysia.

The mass media have also been involved in LP. Newspapers have been instrumental in introducing or propagating particular words, constructions, or spellings. In some countries, such as Australia, the national broadcasting network has appointed a committee to determine appropriate forms.

Other agents of planning include dictionaries—to which users refer for acceptable words, appropriate meanings, standard pronunciations, and spellings—as well as journals on 'correct usage', and language advice bureaus. The relative importance of codification by dictionaries and grammars varies among language communities. There are also committees on national and international terminology and standards, such as the Engineering Standards Committee in Britain, the International Electrotechnical Commission, and the International Standardization Organization. The latter has developed guidelines for the preparation of classified vocabularies.

Some pluricentric languages have coordinating organizations, such as La Francophonie (French) and De Taalunie (Dutch). Language spread may be propagated by the cultural wing of the foreign office (e.g. the British Council), by private international bodies of enthusiasts (such as the Alliance Francaise), or by multinational companies with their own policies on language and language training.

4. Piecemeal or coordinated policies. Some policies are ad hoc; others (such as Australia's National Policy on Languages) are intended as coordinated planning—transcending all spheres of activity, all languages used in the community, and all aspects of language. Many countries have 'language in education' policies, or policies on indigenous or immigrant languages; but these are not always part of a more comprehensive national language policy. [*See* Language-in-Education Planning.]

5. The discipline. LP has been a concern principally for pre- and post-structural linguists—since structuralists showed a strong negative reaction to LP (cf. Hall 1950). However, the Prague school incorporated their interest in solving language problems into their structural framework. By the late 1960s, scholars were developing LP as a subdiscipline. According to Jernudd & Neustupný 1987, this discipline has not yet analyzed the differential interests which are served by planning. There is, however, a vast literature, including discussions of LP efforts (Haugen 1966, 1987; Kloss 1969b, 1978; Fishman et al. 1968); basic principles (Rubin & Jernudd 1971); and 'state of the art' volumes (Tauli 1968, Fishman 1974, Cobarrubias & Fishman 1983). An annotated bibliography exists (Rubin & Jernudd 1979), but there is a shortage of appropriate introductory textbooks. Two periodicals, *Language Problems and Language Planning* and the *Language Planning Newsletter,* are devoted to the field; in addition, the *INFOTERM Newsletter* covers new terminology. Contributions can also be found in other journals, notably in the *International Journal of the Sociology of Language.*

MICHAEL CLYNE

BIBLIOGRAPHY

COBARRUBIAS, JUAN, & JOSHUA A. FISHMAN, eds. 1983. *Progress in language planning: International perspectives.* (Contributions to the sociology of language, 31.) Berlin: Mouton.

FISHMAN, JOSHUA A. 1968. Nationality/nationalism and nation/nationism. In Fishman et al. 1968, pp. 39–52.

FISHMAN, JOSHUA A., ed. 1974. *Advances in language planning.* The Hague: Mouton.

FISHMAN, JOSHUA A.; CHARLES A. FERGUSON; & JYOTIRINDRA DAS GUPTA. 1968. *Language problems of developing nations.* New York: Wiley.

HALL, ROBERT A., JR. 1950. *Leave your language alone!* Ithaca, N.Y.: Linguistica.

HAUGEN, EINAR. 1966. *Language conflict and language planning.* Cambridge, Mass.: Harvard University Press.

HAUGEN, EINAR. 1987. *The blessings of Babel: Bilingualism and language planning.* (Contributions to the sociology of language, 46.) Berlin: Mouton de Gruyter.

HAVRÁNEK, BOHUSLAV. 1938. Zum Problem der Norm in der heutigen Sprachwissenschaft und Sprachkultur. *Actes du Quatrième Congrès International des Linguistes, Copenhague, 1936,* edited by Kaj Barr et al., pp. 151–156. Copenhagen: Munksgaard.

JERNUDD, BJÖRN H. 1983. Evaluation of language planning: What has the last decade accomplished? In Cobarrubias & Fishman 1983, pp. 345–378.

JERNUDD, BJÖRN H., & JIŘÍ V. NEUSTUPNÝ. 1987. Language planning for whom? In *Proceedings of the International Colloquium on Language Planning,* edited by Lorne Laforge, pp. 69–84. Québec: Les Presses de l'Université Laval.

KLOSS, HEINZ. 1969a. *Research possibilities on group bilingualism: A report.* Québec: International Center for Research on Bilingualism.

KLOSS, HEINZ. 1969b. *Grundfragen der Ethnopolitik im 20. Jahrhundert.* Vienna: Braumüller.

KLOSS, HEINZ. 1978. *Die Entwicklung neuer germanischer Kultursprachen seit 1850.* 2d ed. Düsseldorf: Schwann.

NEUSTUPNÝ, JIŘÍ V. 1978. *Post-structural approaches to language: Language theory in a Japanese context.* Tokyo: University of Tokyo Press.

NEUSTUPNÝ, JIŘÍ V. 1983. Towards a paradigm for language planning. *Language Planning Newsletter* 9.6.

RUBIN, JOAN. 1973. Language planning: Discussion of some current issues. In *Language planning: Current issues and research,* edited by Joan Rubin & Roger Shuy, pp. 1–10. Washington, D.C.: Georgetown University Press.

RUBIN, JOAN, & BJÖRN H. JERNUDD, eds. 1971. *Can language be planned? Sociolinguistic theory and practice for developing nations.* Honolulu: University of Hawaii Press.

RUBIN, JOAN, & BJÖRN H. JERNUDD. 1979. *References for students of language planning.* Honolulu: University Press of Hawaii.

TAULI, VALTER. 1968. *Introduction to a theory of language planning.* Uppsala: University of Uppsala Press.

Minorities and Applied Linguistics

The term 'linguistic minorities' designates, within a wider ethnolinguistic framework, subgroups which define their distinctive social identity in terms of language. As a result of large-scale migrations associated with such diverse factors as colonialism, trade, economic pressures, political strife, or natural calamities, the presence of linguistic minorities is a world-wide phenomenon, one which has been noted since earliest recorded history. (For general reference, see Fishman 1978, Megarry et al. 1981, Cobarrubias & Fishman 1983, Glazer & Young 1983, Linguistic Minorities Project 1983, Kennedy 1984, Edwards 1984, 1985, McKay & Wong 1988.) [*See also* Bilingualism.]

The characteristics of linguistic minorities vary greatly from one setting to another. In Third World regions, contemporary political boundaries cut across genetic or tribal boundaries and other territorial distinctions (see Kaplan 1982, 1985). In Western societies, Churchill 1986 notes three main types of language minority:

(a) INDIGENOUS PEOPLES, long established in their native contemporary industrial societies, e.g. Australian aboriginal people, or the native American peoples of the United States

(b) ESTABLISHED MINORITIES, long established in their native countries, whose lifestyle has tended to evolve with that of the mainstream, though sometimes at a slower rate, e.g. Catalans in Spain, Bretons in France, or Canadian francophones

(c) 'NEW' MINORITIES, more recent immigrant or refugee groups, e.g. Indian and Pakistani migrants in the United Kingdom, or Vietnamese refugees in the United States

All three of the above definitions, however, could be applied to the American Hispanic group.

While language policy decisions have accompanied the transition to independence in most Third World countries, increasing pressure for the recognition of cultural pluralism in many industrialized societies is creating the need for LANGUAGE PLANNING in these settings. [*See article on* Language Planning *above.*] Schools are often the first social institutions to be affected by minority group pressures. Policies devised to allow the use of minority languages in the development of initial literacy are generally first conceived as remedial measures, designed to combat educational disadvantage while the child makes the transition to the mainstream language. However, pressures from groups seeking to maintain their languages give rise to the need for policies regulating the teaching of minority languages as school subjects, and the eventual use of such languages as media of instruction. Not surprisingly, some minority languages previously used exclusively in the private domain (home, church, and cultural activities) eventually become candidates for use in the wider public domain (media, schools, courts, and social services). Given the close link between language and social identity, policies regulating the relative status and function of national and minority group languages in the public domain are usually controversial; their enactment is frequently accompanied by social tension.

The recognition of linguistic pluralism and the emergence of new social functions for minority group languages presents interesting challenges to the field of linguistics. Issues which must be dealt with by multilingual societies include the development of orthographies for the introduction of literacy to minorities from preliterate cultures; the description and measurement of linguistic proficiency in various domains and across languages; the modernization or standardization of orthography or terminology; and the development and evaluation of language policy, to mention only a few. To address such issues adequately, linguists must be prepared to view minority languages from a broad social perspective, drawing on knowledge from such adjacent disciplines as psychology, sociology, demography, ethnography, and law.

ALISON D'ANGLEJAN

BIBLIOGRAPHY

Churchill, Stacy. 1986. *The education of linguistic and cultural minorities in the OECD countries.* Clevedon, Avon, England: Multilingual Matters. San Diego, Calif.: College-Hill.

Cobarrubias, Juan, & Joshua A. Fishman, eds. 1983. *Progress in language planning: International perspectives.* (Contributions to the sociology of language, 31.) Berlin: Mouton.

Edwards, John, ed. 1984. *Linguistic minorities, policies and pluralism.* London: Academic Press.

Edwards, John. 1985. *Language, society, and identity.* Oxford: Blackwell.

Fishman, Joshua A., ed. 1978. *Advances in the study of societal multilingualism.* (Contributions to the sociology of language, 9.) The Hague: Mouton.

Glazer, Nathan, & Ken Young, eds. 1983. *Ethnic pluralism and public policy.* London: Heinemann.

Kaplan, Robert B., ed. 1982. *Linguistics and written discourse.* (Annual review of applied linguistics, 3.) Rowley, Mass.: Newbury House.

Kaplan, Robert B., ed. 1985. *Multilingualism.* (Annual review of applied linguistics, 6.) Cambridge & New York: Cambridge University Press.

Kennedy, Chris, ed. 1984. *Language planning and language education.* London: Allen & Unwin.

Linguistic Minorities Project. 1983. *Linguistic minorities in England.* London: Institute of Education.

McKay, Sandra Lee, & Sau-Ling Cynthia Wong, eds. 1988. *Language diversity: Problem or resource?* New York: Newbury House.

Megarry, Jacquetta., et al., eds. 1981. *World yearbook of education, 1981: Education of minorities.* London: Kogan Page.

APPLIED PRAGMATICS. Since the early 1970s, theories about the pragmatics of communication, as formulated in the philosophy of language, linguistics, and psychology, have had a strong impact on 'gate-keeping' domains where verbal interaction is of crucial importance, e.g. counseling, doctor/patient interaction, judicial court sessions, and all forms of institutionalized instruction. Most pervasively, the influence of pragmatic theories has made itself felt in second-language or F[oreign] L[anguage] T[eaching], which will therefore be the concern of this article. [*See also* Institutional Linguistics; Pragmatics, Implicature, and Presupposition.]

The specific interest which FLT theoreticians and practitioners take in pragmatics results from the well established fact that learners who have been taught according to grammatical syllabi and methods frequently fail to communicate successfully in a FL. In order to develop alternative, communicative approaches to FLT, a variety of pragmatic theories have been invoked: the SEMIOTICS [*q.v.*] of Charles S. Peirce and Charles Morris; SPEECH ACT theory [*q.v.*] as formulated by John L. Austin, John R. Searle, and Dieter Wunderlich; British contextualism in the tradition of John R. Firth and M. A. K. Halliday [*see* Systemic Grammar]; the functional linguistics and stylistics of the Prague School [*see* History of Linguistics, *article on* The Prague School]; and theories of COMMUNICATIVE COMPETENCE [*q.v.*] as proposed in the anthropological model of Dell Hymes—and, from a socio-philosophical perspective, by Jürgen Habermas. The common denominator of these otherwise different theories is their concept of language as an essentially social phenomenon, rather than as a system of rules, as cognitive structure, or as a 'mental organ'.

In addition to theoretical approaches to language as communication, empirical studies of discourse and speech act performance provide significant input to communicative FLT. These include descriptive accounts of target language use, cross-linguistic and cross-cultural analyses, and interlanguage pragmatics (cf. Blum-Kulka et al. 1988).

Pragmatic theory and empirical studies inform the different stages of the communicative approach to FLT: curriculum design and its implementation in syllabus specifications, classroom interaction and teaching methodology, and language testing (cf. Widdowson 1978).

According to Canale & Swain 1980, the components of communicative competence, as a learning objective, include grammatical, pragmatic (in their terminology, 'sociolinguistic'), and strategic (i.e. problem-solving) competence. Breen & Candlin 1980 propose a communicative curriculum that defines language-learning as a convention-creating and convention-following activity; it enhances the development of communicative knowledge in the context of personal and social development. The socializing aspects of communicative FLT have also been emphasized in Piepho's suggestion (1974) of communicative competence as the overall learning objective, which is explicitly based on Habermas's notion of the term. Especially in West Germany and Scandinavia, Habermas's concept of communicative competence has had a deep impact not only on FLT, but also on curriculum design and educational theory generally.

Based on analyses of learners' needs for FL use, communicative syllabi specify the functional and formal linguistic knowledge requisite for learners to interact successfully in relevant contexts (see Yalden 1983 for a detailed list of syllabus components). Various types of communicative syllabi have been suggested; they range from STRUCTURAL/FUNCTIONAL syllabi, where the functional component is merely added to the specifications of linguistic forms, to fully COMMUNICATIVE syllabi, which are essentially learner-directed and negotiable, rather than based on a pre-established program. The most explicitly formulated types of communicative syllabus are the NOTIONAL syllabus advanced by Wilkins 1976, and the T[HRESHOLD-]LEVEL model developed by Van Ek 1975. Under the direction of the Council of Europe, the latter has served as a framework to establish communicative syllabi for a variety of European languages.

The original T-level for English provides catalogs of situations, language activities, language functions, concepts, and linguistic forms. Both the T-level and the notional syllabus have been criticized for merely listing isolated categories of functions and linguistic means, rather than indicating how discourse is cooperatively produced. Even though the fundamental issue of this criticism cannot be met by any detailed pre-planned syllabus, considerable improvements of the original T-level model have been achieved in the T-levels for French (Coste et al. 1976) and German (Baldegger et al. 1980); these versions include aspects of discourse organization (e.g. cohesion, the structure of discourse types and phases) and discourse management (e.g. turn-taking). [*See also* Conversation Analysis.]

The interactional structure of the traditional language classroom has proved to be unsuitable for achieving the objectives specified in communicative syllabi. Teacher-fronted interaction based on the 'pedagogical exchange' (teacher initiation—learner response—teacher feedback) leaves little room for students to take initiative in discourse, to practice turn-taking and other discourse strategies, or to carry out a variety of communicative acts in accordance with contextual requirements. In order to perform such functions, communicative classroom methodology has developed a number of activity types, the main characteristic of which is that teacher control is relaxed to favor direct student-to-student interaction. Communicative exercise typologies (e.g. Candlin 1981, Littlewood 1981) include tasks where increasing control is delegated to students (cf. Littlewood's distinction between 'pre-communicative' and 'communicative' exercises); they also feature activities where different aspects of language use are in focus. Thus problem-solving tasks, such as instructions, typically aim at developing students' ability to perform referential functions in representative and directive speech acts, whereas role-plays and simulations are also suitable for training in communicative acts which require that relational aspects be linguistically marked, e.g. by choosing appropriate politeness strategies.

Testing the outcome of communicative FLT programs presents a major difficulty for test construction; communicative ability manifested in discourse performance does not lend itself well to assessment by traditional discrete point tests. Furthermore, test procedures with a high validity in assessing oral communicative performance (e.g. role plays, oral interviews, and group discussions) resist objective measurement; the typical evaluative instrument is the (holistic or analytic) rating scale. However, it has been demonstrated that satisfactory inter-rater reliability can be obtained by training judges in assessing samples of communicative performance (Carroll 1980, Shohamy 1985, Underhill 1987). [*See* Assessment.]

GABRIELE KASPER

BIBLIOGRAPHY

BALDEGGER, MARKUS; MARTIN MÜLLER; & GÜNTHER SCHNEIDER. 1980. *Kontaktschwelle*. Strasbourg: Council of Europe.

BLUM-KULKA, SHOSHANA; JULIANE HOUSE; & GABRIELE KASPER, eds. 1988. *Cross-cultural pragmatics: Requests and apologies*. Norwood, N.J.: Ablex.

BREEN, MICHAEL P., & CHRISTOPHER N. CANDLIN. 1980. The essentials of a communicative curriculum in language teaching. *Applied Linguistics* 1.89–112.

CANALE, MICHAEL, & MERRILL SWAIN. 1980. Theoretical bases of communicative approaches to second language teaching and testing. *Applied Linguistics* 1.1–47.

CANDLIN, CHRISTOPHER N., ed. 1981. *The communicative teaching of English: Principles and an exercise typology*. Harlow: Longman.

CARROLL, BRENDAN J. 1980. *Testing communicative performance*. Oxford: Pergamon.

COSTE, DANIEL, et al. 1976. *Un niveau seuil: Systèmes d'apprentissage des langues vivantes par les adultes*. Strasbourg: Council of Europe.

LITTLEWOOD, WILLIAM. 1981. *Communicative language teaching*. Cambridge & New York: Cambridge University Press.

PIEPHO, HANS-EBERHARD. 1974. *Kommunikative Kompetenz als übergeordnetes Lernziel im Englischunterricht*. Dornburg-Frickenhofen: Frankonius.

SHOHAMY, ELANA. 1985. *A practical handbook in language testing for the second language teacher*. Raanana, Israel: Shohamy.

UNDERHILL, NIC. 1987. *Testing spoken language: A handbook of oral testing techniques.* Cambridge & New York: Cambridge University Press.

VAN EK, JAN A. 1975. *The threshold level in a European unit/credit system for modern language learning by adults.* Strasbourg: Council of Europe.

WIDDOWSON, HENRY G. 1978. *Teaching language as communication.* Oxford & New York: Oxford University Press.

WILKINS, DAVID A. 1976. *Notional syllabuses: A taxonomy and its relevance to foreign language curriculum development.* London: Oxford University Press.

YALDEN, JANICE. 1983. *The communicative syllabus: Evolution, design and implementation.* Oxford: Pergamon.

APRAXIA. In the neurological literature, the term 'apraxia' defines the inability shown by some patients with left-brain damage to carry out correctly purposeful actions, although there are no elementary motor, sensory, or coordination deficits. In the majority of cases, the impairment is not contingent on the type of movement—symbolic, expressive, describing the use of objects, etc.—or on the way it is elicited, e.g. by verbal command or imitation. What appears to be critical is the artificial condition in which the movement is produced: it is not prompted by environmental cues or internal urges, but by an examiner's request. Thus the patient may fail to wave goodbye on command, but does so when he leaves the room. (For reference, see Roy 1985, Miller 1989.)

Since apraxia is predominantly associated with left-hemisphere disease, the great majority of apraxic patients also have APHASIA [*q.v.*]. Therefore it is important to make sure that patients' failure to execute the examiner's command does not result from a deficit of verbal comprehension. In some cases, the resemblance of the executed movement to the correct action (e.g., they put the palm of their hand on their forehead, when requested to salute) provides evidence that the message has been decoded. If doubt remains, one can test the imitation of movements made by the examiner, or one can present objects for the patient to demonstrate their use.

Different forms of apraxia have been distinguished, with reference to the stage at which the action program is disrupted and to the body part involved. In IDEATIONAL apraxia, it is the idea of the movement that patients cannot evoke (De Renzi & Lucchelli 1988). Requested to demonstrate the use of objects, they hesitate, or use them in a wrong way, in wrong places, or in the wrong order. In IDEOMOTOR apraxia, the difficulty affects not the conceptual stage of the motor program, but its transfer to the executive areas, where it must be translated in appropriate commands to the muscles. Consequently, patients also fail when they are simply required to imitate movements, whether meaningful or meaningless, carried out by the examiner. They know what to do, but cannot select the appropriate innervation pattern.

Apraxia affects mainly the musculature of the limbs and mouth. The finding that limb and oral apraxia may occur independently suggests that they are related to discrete anatomical/functional structure. The planning of limb movements is organized by the left parietal lobe, which monitors the activity of motor areas through ipsilateral connections with the left premotor cortex, and through trans-callosal connections with the right premotor cortex. Accordingly, a left parietal lesion results in apraxia of both limbs, while a callosal lesion is associated with left-limb apraxia alone. Oral movements are organized more anteriorly in the left frontal premotor area, concerned with facial muscles. It apparently does not need the cooperation of the corresponding right cortical region to guide the activity of the brain-stem motor centers for cranial nerves. Oral apraxia has been implicated in the mechanism underlying the distorted speech of Broca's aphasics. The patient is unable to carry out on command, or to imitate, non-linguistic movements with the muscles of the mouth, lips, tongue, and throat (e.g. to whistle, to kiss, or to stick out the tongue). However, the same actions are performed correctly when carried out spontaneously. Some authors have endorsed the view that the lack of motor control on non-verbal movements, exhibited by Broca's aphasics, is also responsible for their laborious, effortful articulation and their distorted phonetic production. The term APRAXIA OF SPEECH has become popular to indicate the motor, rather than linguistic, nature of this speech disorder. It is not altogether clear, however, whether oral apraxia and apraxia of speech express disruption of the same mechanism. The finding that a few patients show oral apraxia without phonological articulatory impairment, and that the severity of the two disorders is not closely correlated, warns against their complete assimilation.

ENNIO DE RENZI

BIBLIOGRAPHY

DE RENZI, ENNIO, & F. LUCCHELLI. 1988. Ideational apraxia. *Brain* 111.1173–1185.

MILLER, NIKLAS. 1989. *Dyspraxia and its management.* London: Croom Helm. Rockville, Md.: Aspen.

ROY, ERIC A., ed. 1985. *Neuropsychological studies of apraxia and related disorders.* Amsterdam: North-Holland.

ARABIC. Before the Arab expansion as a result of the Muslim conquests in the 7th and 8th centuries CE, Arabic was the language of the nomadic tribes of northwestern and central Arabia; thus it is sometimes called 'North Arabian', in contrast to Ancient or Epigraphic South Arabian, once spoken in Yemen and Hadhramaut. Along with Ancient South Arabian, Modern South Arabian, and the Semitic languages of Ethiopia, Arabic is often classified as South Semitic; it shares with these languages its very conservative phonology and the trait of 'broken plurals' (see below). [*See* Semitic Languages.] A new classification of the Semitic languages, proposed by Hetzron 1974, attaches more importance to features which Arabic shares with Canaanite (Ugaritic, Phoenician, and Hebrew), such as the 1st/2nd person markers in the perfect (*-t-*, against *-k-* in South Arabian and Ethiopian), the internal passive, and the definite article *ha-* (with gemination of the following consonant, Arabic **ha-*, **han-* > *ʔal-*). Arabic is thus linked to Canaanite and Aramaic within the central branch of West Semitic.

The most detailed grammar of C[lassical] A[rabic] is Wright 1896. For a modern discussion of morphological and syntactic structures, see Fleisch 1968; for a dictionary, see Wehr 1979.

1. History. Arabic is first attested in epigraphic material found in central and northwestern Arabia, possibly dating back to between the 5th century BCE and the 3rd century CE. These Ancient North Arabian inscriptions are written in an alphabet derived from the South Arabian script, but the language is clearly different from Epigraphic South Arabian. Dialectal features and geographical distribution make it possible to distinguish Thamudic, Lihyanite, Safaitic, and Hasaitic (see Fischer 1982:17–29).

CA occurs in some inscriptions from the 2nd century CE onward. In its fully developed form, however, it appears first in pre-Islamic poetry, and then in the Qur'ān, during the first half of the 7th century (see Fück 1955, Fischer 1982:30–49). After the expansion of Islam, CA became the literary language of Islamic civilization, used by all educated people, whatever their native tongue. The commonly accepted form of CA was described by Arab grammarians during the 8th and 9th centuries. They standardized it at the same time; even so, they transmitted some information on dialectal variation. As a language of poetry and literature, CA has survived to the present. In the 19th and 20th centuries, it went through a process of revival, and developed into a linguistic medium appropriate for all areas of modern life. M[odern] S[tandard] A[rabic] is the official language of all Arab countries—and, alongside Hebrew, of Israel. MSA differs from CA only in vocabulary and stylistic features; the morphology and the basic syntactic norms have remained unchanged (see Beeston 1970, Stetkevych 1970).

Arabic was also adopted as a literary language by non-Muslims. When writing Arabic, the non-Muslims (and even some Muslims) did not always observe the norms laid down by the grammarians; thus they wrote Arabic with interference from their vernaculars. As a result, special sociolects, called Middle Arabic, arose—most importantly, Christian and Jewish Arabic. From the linguistic point of view, the texts of Middle Arabic give information about the dialects of their time; they prove that diglossia, typical of the Arabic-speaking world today, emerged during the expansion of Islam, and perhaps even earlier (see Blau 1965, 1988).

As the language of Islamic education, Arabic deeply influenced the languages of all peoples who embraced Islam: first Persian, and then other Iranian languages, Turkish languages, Urdu, Bengali, Malay, etc., as well as African languages like Hausa and Swahili. Speakers of these languages adopted an enormous number of Arabic loanwords and expressions, especially in the field of Islamic religion and civilization. Muslims made use of the Arabic script to write their own native languages; some, like Persian and Urdu, are still written in Arabic letters. Just as Latin and Greek supply the European language community with scientific terms and an educated vocabulary, Arabic performs that function within the Islamic world; thus lexical items like *jāmiʕ* 'mosque', *madrasa* 'school', *qāʕida* 'rule' exist in nearly all languages of Muslim peoples.

Loanwords from Arabic entered European languages through language contact, mostly in Spain and Sicily, but also during the Crusades in Syria and Palestine. Words of Arabic origin, e.g. *algebra, alcohol* (both with the definite article *ʔal-*) *cotton, gazelle,* and *tariff*, are found in all European languages. The names of stars, e.g. *Algol, Altair, Fomalhaut,* and *Rigel*, owe their existence to scholarly language contacts at the end of the Middle Ages.

Arabic as a spoken language is widespread over an area from West Africa to the Persian Gulf; it is also spoken by more or less important minorities in non-Arab countries, including Nigeria, Chad, Turkey, and Iran. Small Arabic-speaking communities are found in Soviet Central Asia and Afghanistan; their dialects are greatly influenced by Iranian languages. In the Sudan, between Nigeria and Uganda, a pidginized variety of Arabic is used for communication among speakers of different African languages.

The Modern Arabic or Neo-Arabic colloquial language is structurally different from CA, and splits into numerous dialects (see Fischer & Jastrow 1980). In countries where MSA is the official language—used in writing, education, literature, and formal settings—a situation of diglossia exists. Native speakers acquire a Neo-Arabic dialect first, then learn MSA as a second language, according to the level of their education. Dialects of regions which are separated by great distances are not mutually intelligible, or only barely so; and speakers of such dialects communicate in a prestige dialect, such as the colloquial Arabic of Cairo, which has gained a high degree of acceptance because of its use in films. A spoken variety of MSA, commonly called Intermediate Arabic, lacks case markers and other specific features of CA, and shows interference from the dialects; it is increasingly used by educated people when they have to speak extemporaneously in interviews, debates, and similar semiformal settings.

Neo-Arabic dialects sometimes occur in a written standardized variety, e.g. in private letters, stage-plays, and songs; however, only Maltese Arabic has reached the status of an independent literary language. Maltese is mixed with numerous elements from Sicilian and Italian, especially in its lexicon, but also in syntactic structures. It is the native tongue of the Christian population of Malta, and is written in Latin characters.

Linguistic minorities live in great numbers in the Arab countries; the most important are the Berber-speaking populations in North Africa; the Kurdish-speaking tribes and the Neo-Aramaic-speaking groups in Syria and Iraq; and the speakers of Modern South Arabian languages in southern Yemen and Dhofar (Oman). The majority of people who belong to these minorities are bilingual. Another kind of bilingualism exists in Morocco, Algeria, and Tunisia, where educated people are generally familiar with French.

2. Phonology. The vowel inventory of CA consists of *a i u*, short and long. The consonants are shown in Table 1. The phoneme inventory of CA has preserved that of Proto-Semitic (PS) almost completely, with a few exceptions: PS **p* > CA *f*, PS **g* > CA *j*, PS **ś* (perhaps a lateral) > CA *š*; by contrast, PS **š* > CA *s*. Hence CA has lost only one phoneme, PS **ś*.

This description of the phonemes reflects the standard of the Qur'ān readers, but regional allophonic variations exist. The glottal stop ʔ has phonemic status in every position: *ʔamara* 'he ordered', *yaʔmuru* 'he orders'; *saʔala* 'he asked', *yasʔalu* 'he asks'. The so-called 'emphatics' are now pronounced as velarized, or sometimes as pharyngealized consonants. All consonants

TABLE 1. *Arabic Consonants*

	Labial	Interdental	Alveolar	Palatal	Velar	Uvular	Pharyngeal	Glottal
Occlusives								
Voiceless								
Plain			t		k	q		ʔ
Emphatic			ṭ					
Voiced								
Plain	b		d	j	g			
Emphatic			ḍ					
Fricatives								
Voiceless								
Plain	f	θ	s	š	x		ḥ	h
Emphatic		θ̣	ṣ					
Voiced								
Plain		ð	z		γ		ʕ	
Emphatic		ð̣	(ẓ)					
Nasals	m		n					
Lateral			l					
Vibrant			r					
Semivowels	w			y				

may be geminated; they are then pronounced as long consonants: *ra[ḥ]ala* 'he departed', *ra[ḥ:]ala* 'he transferred'.

Word stress is not distinctive, but is bound to syllabic structure: it falls upon the heavy syllable (CVC or CV̄) nearest the end of the word, except for the last syllable. However, it does not move beyond the third syllable from the end: *yastáʕmilu* 'he employs', *kitā́bun* 'a book', but *madrásatun* 'a school', *kátaba* 'he wrote'.

Vowels cannot be combined; however, there are combinations vowel + semivowel, e.g. *aw ay*. One may also interpret *ī* as *iy*, and *ū* as *uw*. The combinations **iw *uy* produced by derivational rules become *iy uw*, respectively: **raʔā* + masc. pl. *ū* → *raʔaw* 'they saw', **miwlādun* 'birthday' (root morpheme *w-l-d*) → *mīlādun*, **buyḍun* 'white' (pl.) (root morpheme *b-y-ḍ*) → *bīḍun*.

Three-consonant clusters and syllables of the form CV̄C are not permitted. Where they would otherwise occur, an auxiliary vowel (usually *i*, seldom *u*) prevents their realization, or V̄C is shortened to VC. These rules influence the morphology: word forms beginning with CC must add an initial ʔV when they come at the beginning of an utterance, but not when internal: *šrab* 'drink!' → *#ʔišrab*, *ktub* 'write!' → *#ʔuktub*, but *#ʔuktub θumma šrab* 'Write, then drink!' The *ʔa* of the definite article *ʔal-* is also omitted within an utterance, and after a consonant it is replaced by an auxiliary vowel: *lam ʔaktub* 'I did not write' + *ʔal-kitāba* 'the book' → *lam ʔaktub-i l-kitāba*.

Shortening of V̄C takes place in the last syllable of the inflectional base: *qūmū* 'stand up! (masc. pl.)', but *qumna* 'stand up! (fem. pl.)'; *ʔal-qāḍī* 'the judge', but **qāḍī-n* → *qāḍin* 'a judge'.

Before a pause, one or more of the final segments of the word are dropped. Readers of the Qur'ān observe the following rules: long vowels are shortened; short vowels are dropped; *-n* is dropped if it is the marker of the indefinite, except that *-a-n* 'indefinite accusative' becomes *-ā*; and feminine nouns ending in *-at-u(n), -at-i(n), -at-a(n)* have the pausal form *-ah*. Examples are *rabbī* 'my lord' → *rabbi#* and even *rabb#*; *yuʕīdu* 'he brings back' → *yuʕīd#*; *ḥakīmun* 'wise' -> *ḥakīm#*; *ʕajaban* 'a wonder' → *ʕajabā#*; *raqabatin, raqabatun, raqabatan* 'a neck' → *raqabah#*.

3. Writing system. Arabic was first written in the Aramaic alphabet of the Nabateans. Around 500 CE, the Nabatean characters became the Arabic script. The Aramaic alphabet consisted of twenty-two graphemes, some of which had assumed the same shape; these graphemes had to be differentiated by diacritical dots above or below the letters in order to provide one grapheme for each of the twenty-eight consonantal phonemes of Arabic (see Fischer 1982:165–97). The present-day system is shown in Table 2. The graphemes represent consonantal phonemes. Gemination is indicated not by doubling the grapheme, but by the optional use of the sign ّ (*tašdīd*).

The graphemes *ʔalif, wāw, yāʔ* are ambiguous; in addition to their consonantal values, they indicate the long vowels—*ʔalif* = *ā*, *wāw* = *ū*, *yāʔ* = *ī*; and in connection with the supplementary sign ء (*hamza*) they represent the glottal stop. The *ʔalif* indicates ʔ only in word-initial position, or when followed by *a*. In other cases, *wāw, yāʔ*, or Ø is written in positions where ʔ is to be read. Therefore *hamza* has been invented as a supplementary grapheme. The reason for this orthographic feature is that the writing system was originally established for the Hejaz dialect of CA, in which ʔ was preserved only in initial position, and otherwise was replaced by *y, w*, or Ø.

Special signs have been introduced to mark the short vowels: َ (*fatḥa*) = *a*, ِ (*kasra*) = *i*, ُ (*ḍamma*) = *u*. The sign ْ (*sukūn*) indicates that a consonant is not followed by a vowel. However, these signs are used only rarely, e.g. in the Qur'ān and in poetry, or sometimes to avoid misinterpretation.

The writing system does not represent speech in its textual phonemic form, since every unit is spelled as if spoken in isolation; i.e., every word appears in its pausal form. Initial auxiliary vowels are represented by ʔ, and the feminine endings *-at-u(n), -at-i(n), -at-a(n)* are written with *hāʔ* (with two additional dots indicating the reading *t*). Thus the phrase *ʔinnī štaraytu baytan qabla sanatin* '(Verily) I bought a house one year ago' is written ⟨ʔinnī ʔištarayt baytā qabl sanah⟩. As a result of this and other orthographic rules, a written Arabic text is not a direct representation of its phonemic equivalent.

4. Derivational morphology. Like other Semitic languages, Arabic has root morphemes which consist solely of consonants. More than 90 percent of these have three consonants, and the rest have four or five. In addition to derivational prefixes and suffixes, discontinuous base morphemes combine with the roots. Thus the perfect base of the verb *katab-* 'wrote' contains the root morpheme *ktb* and the base morpheme $C_1aC_2aC_3$-. Combinations of morphemes establish nominal and verbal pat-

TABLE 2. *The Arabic Script*

Phonemic Value	Final	Medial	Initial	Alone	Numerical Value	Name
ʔ	ـا			ا	1	ʔalif
b	ـب	ـبـ	بـ	ب	2	bāʔ
t	ـت	ـتـ	تـ	ت	400	tāʔ
θ	ـث	ـثـ	ثـ	ث	500	θāʔ
j	ـج	ـجـ	جـ	ج	3	jīm
ḥ	ـح	ـحـ	حـ	ح	8	ḥāʔ
x	ـخ	ـخـ	خـ	خ	600	xāʔ
d	ـد			د	4	dāl
ð	ـذ			ذ	700	ðāl
r	ـر			ر	200	rāʔ
z	ـز			ز	7	zāy
s	ـس	ـسـ	سـ	س	60	sīn
š	ـش	ـشـ	شـ	ش	300	šīn
ṣ	ـص	ـصـ	صـ	ص	90	ṣād
ḍ	ـض	ـضـ	ضـ	ض	800	ḍād
ṭ	ـط	ـطـ	طـ	ط	9	ṭāʔ
ð̣	ـظ	ـظـ	ظـ	ظ	900	ð̣āʔ
ʕ	ـع	ـعـ	عـ	ع	70	ʕayn
ɣ	ـغ	ـغـ	غـ	غ	1000	ɣayn
f	ـف	ـفـ	فـ	ف	80	fāʔ
q	ـق	ـقـ	قـ	ق	100	qāf
k	ـك	ـكـ	كـ	ك	20	kāf
l	ـل	ـلـ	لـ	ل	30	lām
m	ـم	ـمـ	مـ	م	40	mīm
n	ـن	ـنـ	نـ	ن	50	nūn
h	ـه	ـهـ	هـ	ه	5	hāʔ
w	ـو			و	6	wāw
y	ـى	ـيـ	يـ	ى	10	yāʔ

terns, which are often related to a certain semantic class; the following are examples:

(a) $C_1aC_2iC_3$- to the active participle, e.g. *kātibun* 'writing' to *ktb*
(b) $C_1aCC_2\bar{a}C_3$- to nouns denoting habitual occupations, e.g. *ṣarrāfun* 'cashier' to *ṣrf, xabbāzun* 'baker' to *xbz*
(c) $C_1uC_2ayC_3$- to diminutives, e.g. *kulaybun* 'little dog' to *klb*
(d) *ʔa*-$C_1C_2aC_3$- to nouns denoting colors or defects, e.g. *ʔabyaḍu* 'white' to *byḍ, ʔaṭrašu* 'deaf' to *ṭrš*
(e) *ma*-$C_1C_2aC_3$- to nouns of place, e.g. *mašrabun* 'drinking place' to *šrb*

Root morphemes with a semivowel are called 'weak' roots; the instability of the semivowel in most patterns results in a long vowel, as in *qām*- 'stood up' = $C_1aC_2aC_3$- from *qwm*.

5. Noun inflection. The morphologically marked categories are gender (masculine and feminine), number (singular, dual, and plural), case (nominative, genitive, and accusative), and definiteness/indefiniteness. The masculine is unmarked. The feminine markers are *-at, -ā, -āʔ*; however, some feminine nouns lack the feminine marker, especially (but not exclusively) those which denote female beings, e.g. *ḥāmilun* 'a pregnant (woman)', *rijlun* 'foot'. However, when nouns marked with *-at* denote male beings, they are masculine, e.g. *xalīf-at-un* 'caliph'. The case-markers of the singular are nom. *-u*, gen. *-i*, acc. *-a*; the plural has a single marker for genitive and accusative. Definiteness is marked by the article *ʔal-* (with assimilation to the following consonant, if interdental, alveolar, or *š*). Indefiniteness is marked by *-n* in the singular and in the feminine plural. Sample paradigms are shown in Table 3.

The genitive attribute follows its head noun immedi-

TABLE 3. *Arabic Noun Paradigms*

	Indefinite	Definite
Masculine		
Singular		
Nom.	*muʕallimun* 'a teacher'	*ʔal-muʕallimu* 'the teacher'
Gen.	*muʕallimin*	*ʔal-muʕallimi*
Acc.	*muʕalliman*	*ʔal-muʕallima*
Dual		
Nom.	*muʕallimāni*	*ʔal-muʕallimāni*
Gen.-Acc.	*muʕallimayni*	*ʔal-muʕallimayni*
Plural		
Nom.	*muʕallimūna*	*ʔal-muʕallimūna*
Gen.-Acc.	*muʕallimīna*	*ʔal-muʕallimīna*
Feminine		
Singular		
Nom.	*muʕallimatun* 'a female teacher'	*ʔal-muʕallimatu* 'the female teacher'
Gen.	*muʕallimatin*	*ʔal-muʕallimati*
Acc.	*muʕallimatan*	*ʔal-muʕallimata*
Dual		
Nom.	*muʕallimatāni*	*ʔal-muʕallimatāni*
Gen.-Acc.	*muʕallimatayni*	*ʔal-muʕallimatayni*
Plural		
Nom.	*muʕallimātun*	*ʔal-muʕallimātu*
Gen.-Acc.	*muʕallimātin*	*ʔal-muʕallimāti*

ately. Indefiniteness vs. definiteness is then indicated only on the second entity, the genitive:

(1) *muʕallimu madrasati-n* 'a teacher of a school'
muʕallimu l-madrasati 'the teacher of the school'

Plural forms marked by suffixes, the so-called 'sound' plurals, seldom occur. Most nouns take 'broken' plurals, i.e. lexically fixed plurals in a variety of patterns. The plural pattern relating to a given singular is not predictable, as the following examples suggest:

(2) $C_1iC_2\bar{a}C_3$-*un*: *rajulun* 'man', pl. *rijālun*.
(3) $C_1uC_2uC_3$-*un*: *kitābun* 'book', pl. *kutubun*; *safīnatun* 'ship', pl. *sufunun*.
(4) $ʔaC_1C_2\bar{a}C_3$-*un*: *qalamun* 'pencil', pl. *ʔaqlāmun*.
(5) $C_1aC_2\bar{a}C_3iC_4$-*u*: *madrasatun* 'school', pl. *madārisu*.

All these plural forms are inflected like singular nouns.

6. Personal pronouns. There are two sets of personal pronouns: independent ones, and bound forms suffixed to nouns, particles, and verbs. The suffixed pronouns, shown in Table 4 (except *-nī* 1sg.), have a possessive function when combined with nouns.

TABLE 4. *Arabic Pronominal Forms*

	Independent Forms	Suffixal Forms
1sg.	*ʔanā*	*-ī/-nī*
1pl.	*naḥnu*	*-nā*
2sg.		
m.	*ʔanta*	*-ka*
f.	*ʔanti*	*-ki*
2du.	*ʔantumā*	*-kumā*
2pl.		
m.	*ʔantum*	*-kum*
f.	*ʔantunna*	*-kunna*
3sg.		
m.	*huwa*	*-hū/-hī*
f.	*hiya*	*-hā*
3du.	*humā*	*-humā/-himā*
3pl.		
m.	*hum(ū)*	*-hum/-him*
f.	*hunna*	*-hunna/-hinna*

7. Verb inflection. The verb is given in dictionaries in the 3sg. masc. form of the perfect. Each verb yields two inflectional bases: one for conjugation with suffixed person markers, i.e. the perfect; and one for conjugation with prefixed person markers, i.e. the imperfect, sub-

TABLE 5. *Arabic Verb Paradigms*

	Perfect	Imperfect
1sg.	*katab-tu*	*ʔa-ktub-u*
1pl.	*katab-na*	*na-ktub-u*
2sg.		
m.	*katab-ta*	*ta-ktub-u*
f.	*katab-ti*	*ta-ktub-ī-na*
2du.	*katab-tumā*	*ta-ktub-ā-ni*
2pl.		
m.	*katab-tum*	*ta-ktub-ū-na*
f.	*katab-na*	*ta-ktub-na*
3sg.		
m.	*katab-a*	*ya-ktub-u*
f.	*katab-at*	*ta-ktub-u*
3du.		
m.	*katab-ā*	*ya-ktub-ā-ni*
f.	*katab-at-ā*	*ta-ktub-ā-ni*
3pl.		
m.	*katab-ū*	*ya-ktub-ū-na*
f.	*katab-na*	*ya-ktub-na*

junctive, and jussive (or apocopate). In most cases, these bases are differentiated by ablaut, e.g. suffixal *katab-*, prefixal *-ktub* 'write', as shown in Table 5.

The prefixal conjugation contains three moods: the imperfect indicative, marked by *-u* and *-na*/*-ni* in plural and dual forms, as well as in the 2sg. fem; the subjunctive, marked by *-a* and the absence of *-na*/*-ni* (*yaktub-a, yaktub-ū, yaktub-ā*); and the jussive or 'apocopate' (shortened form), marked by Ø and absence of *-na*/*-ni* (*yaktub, yaktub-ū, yaktub-ā*). The suffixal conjugation refers to the perfective aspect and past time; the imperfect, to the imperfect aspect and to present/future time. However, the CA system of aspect and tense is very complex in its textual realization. The subjunctive and apocopate forms appear in specific syntactic environments: the apocopate is jussive, and is a reflex of the Proto-Semitic past tense. In CA, it is restricted to negative (*lam yaktub* 'he did not write') and conditional clauses. The imperative has no prefix: sg. masc. *ktub* (→ *ʔuktub*), *ktubī* (→ *ʔuktubī*), pl. masc. *ktubū* (→ *ʔuktubū*), fem. *ktubna* (→ *ʔuktubna*), du. *ktubā* (→ *ʔuktubā*).

The bulk of the verbs can be classified into ten patterns or stems. To demonstrate the verbal patterns, we use here the method of the Arab grammarians, who take *fʕl* from the verb *faʕala* 'to act'; see Table 6. The nominal pattern of Stem IX is reserved for colors and physical defects.

TABLE 6. *Arabic Verb Stems*

		Perfect	Imperfect
Basic	I.	*faʕala*	*yafʕalu*
		faʕila	*yafʕilu*
		faʕula	*yafʕulu*
Transitive/Causative	II.	*faʕʕala*	*yufaʕʕilu*
(*a:i*)	III.	*fāʕala*	*yufāʕilu*
	IV.	*ʔafʕala*	*yufʕilu*
Intransitive/Reflexive	V.	*tafaʕʕala*	*tafāʕala*
(no ablaut)	VI.	*tafāʕala*	*yatafāʕalu*
Passive	VII.	*ʔinfaʕala*	*yanfaʕilu*
Reflexive	VIII.	*ʔiftaʕala*	*yaftaʕilu*
Nominal	IX.	*ʔifʕalla*	*yafʕallu*
Causative + Reflexive	X.	*ʔistafʕala*	*yastafʕilu*

Besides these stems, an internal passive is marked by the perfect morpheme C*u*C*i*C- and the imperfect morpheme C(*a*)C*a*C, in combination with *u* as vowel of the person-markers:

(6) *qatala* 'he killed', *qutila* 'he was killed'
(7) *yaqtulu* 'he kills', *yuqtalu* 'he is killed'
(8) *ʔistaʕmala* (*yastaʕmilu*) 'he employed (employs)', *ʔustuʕmila* (*yustaʕmalu*) 'he was (is) employed'

8. Syntax. The attribute follows its head noun. It agrees in gender, number, case, and definiteness with the nouns it qualifies:

(9) *ʔumm-u-n qaliq-at-u-n* 'an uneasy mother'
(10) *fī bayt-i-hī l-qadīm-i* 'in his old house' (the personal pronoun makes the noun definite)
(11) *ʔal-rajul-āni l-ṣāliḥ-āni* 'the two good men'

In plurals, the adjective agrees with nouns denoting human beings only. In other cases, it takes the feminine singular:

(12) *jijāl-u-n ṣāliḥ-ūna* 'good men'
(13) *ban-āt-u-n ṣāliḥ-āt-u-n* 'good girls'
but *ʔaʕmāl-u-n ṣāliḥ-at-u-n* 'good actions'

Demonstratives precede the noun, which takes the definite article:

(14) *hāðā l-bayt-u* 'this house'
hāʔulāʔi l-rijāl-u 'these men'

The construction of the numerals is very complex. The cardinal numerals from three to ten have forms with and without the feminine marker *-at*; the quantified noun follows in the genitive plural. The numerals are marked with *-at* if the quantified noun is masculine, but are not marked in connection with feminine nouns. Compare the following:

(15) *θalāθ-at-u muʕallim-īna* 'three teachers'
θalāθ-u muʕallim-āt-i-n 'three female teachers'

With numerals from eleven to nineteen and with the tens, the quantified noun appears in the accusative singular:

(16) *θalāθūna muʕallim-a-n* 'thirty teachers'

After the hundreds and thousands, the noun comes in the genitive singular:

(17) *θalāθ-u miʔ-at-i muʕallim-i-n* 'three hundred teachers'

The accusative is the case of the object, but it assumes other (mainly adverbial) functions:

(18) *ʕamaltu ʕamal-an ṣāliḥ-an* 'I did a good doing.'
(19) *γādartu l-bayta mašy-an* 'I left the house by walking.'

Thus the accusative ending *-a(n)* has become a marker for adverbial lexical units:

(20) *γād-an* 'tomorrow'
al-batt-at-a 'definitely (not)'

The nominal sentence has no copula. Word order is subject + predicate:

(21) *ʔal-ʔumm-u qaliq-at-u-n* 'The mother is uneasy.'
(22) *bayt-u-hū qadīm-u-n* 'His house is old.'

In the verbal sentence, the verb precedes the subject and agrees with it in gender, but not in number:

(23) *jāʔ-a l-muʕallim-ūna* 'The teachers came.'
(24) *jāʔ-at i-l-muʕallim-āt-u* 'The female teachers came.'

However, if the verb refers to a noun subject mentioned before, it must agree fully:

(25) *hāʔulāʔi muʕallim-ūna jāʔ-ū ʔamsi.*
'These are teachers (who) came yesterday.'

A nominal sentence may be transferred to the past by the verb *kāna* 'he was'. It then becomes a verbal sentence, and the predicate must be put in the accusative:

(26) *kānat i-l-ʔumm-u qaliq-at-a-n.*
'The mother was uneasy.'

There is a special type of clause expressing coincidence. It is coordinated by *wa-* 'and', and its word order is subject-predicate:

(27) *jāʔa l-muʕallimu wa-huwa yabtasimu/mubtasimun.*
'The teacher came, and he is smiling', i.e. 'The teacher came smiling.'

9. Modern dialects. MSA differs from CA in its loss of case endings, as well as of the markers of indicative and subjunctive. (On the whole, the CA pausal forms continue in modern dialects.) However, this loss of inflection had consequences for the linguistic structure. Neo-Arabic dialects have developed new markers for the genitive relationship, e.g. Egyptian Arabic *il-bēt bitāʕ-ī* 'the house of mine', with *bitāʕ* as an independent genitive morpheme. In many dialects, the system of personal pronouns has lost the contrast between masculine and feminine in the plural. In the verbal morphology, new markers of the indicative imperfect have developed, like Egyptian Arabic *bi-yiktib* 'he is writing' vs. *yiktib* (subjunctive). In all dialects except some in Yemen, the CA phonemes *ḍ* and *ð̣* have merged to *ð̣*. Moreover, the interdental fricatives *ð ð̣ θ* have become alveolar stops (*d ḍ t*) in most urban dialects; there too, CA *q* is usually pronounced as [ʔ]. These and many other phonological and morphological changes give each dialect its specific characteristics.

WOLFDIETRICH FISCHER

BIBLIOGRAPHY

BEESTON, ALFRED F. L. 1970. *The Arabic language today.* London: Hutchinson.

BLAU, JOSHUA. 1965. *The emergence and linguistic background of Judaeo-Arabic: A study of the origins of Middle Arabic.* (Scripta judaica, 5.) Oxford: Oxford University Press. 2d ed., Jerusalem: Ben-Zvi Institute, 1981.

BLAU, JOSHUA. 1988. *Studies in Middle Arabic and its Judaeo-Arabic variety.* Jerusalem.

Fischer, Wolfdietrich, ed. 1982. *Grundriss der arabischen Philologie,* vol. 1, *Sprachwissenschaft.* Wiesbaden: Reichert.

Fischer, Wolfdietrich, & Otto Jastrow, eds. 1980. *Handbuch der Arabischen Dialekte.* (Porta linguarum orientalium, n.s., 16.) Wiesbaden: Harrassowitz.

Fleisch, Henri. 1968. *L'Arabe classique: Esquisse d'une structure linguistique.* 2d ed. Beirut: Dar el-Machreq.

Fück, Johann. 1955. *Arabiya: Recherches sur l'histoire de la langue et du style arabe.* Paris: Didier.

Hetzron, Robert. 1974. La division des langues sémitiques. *Actes du Premier Congrès International de Linguistique Sémitique et Chamito-Sémitique* (Janua linguarum, Series practica, 159), edited by André Caquet & David Cohen, pp. 181–194. The Hague: Mouton.

Stetkevych, Jaroslav. 1970. *The modern Arabic literary language: Lexical and stylistic developments.* Chicago: University of Chicago Press.

Wehr, Hans. 1979. *A dictionary of Modern Written Arabic.* Edited by J Milton Cowan. 4th ed. Wiesbaden: Harrassowitz.

Wright, William, ed. 1896. *A grammar of the Arabic language.* 3d ed. 2 vols. Cambridge: Cambridge University Press. Reprinted, 1951.

ARAMAIC is a branch of the Semitic language family [*q.v.*]; it comprises languages of inscriptions and documents dating from the 10th century BCE onward, several literary languages, and diverse dialects spoken to this day. It was a medium of international communication in the Near East for well over a thousand years, and is the language of important Christian and Jewish literatures; now, however, it has only about 200,000 speakers. The usual classification divides Aramaic languages into five periods: Old, Imperial, Middle, Late, and Modern. Geographical variation is evident in all these periods. (For reference, see Nöldeke 1904, Rosenthal 1961, 1967, Kutscher 1970, 1971, Kaufman 1974, Segert 1975, Fitzmyer 1979, Krotkoff 1982, and Beyer 1986.)

Old Aramaic is attested in inscriptions from the 10th to the 7th centuries BCE, found in Syria and Turkey. Of the two attested dialects, Samalian (sometimes referred to as Yaudic) disappeared early, and only Common Old Aramaic is closely related to later varieties of the language. For locations, see Map 1.

Imperial (or Official) Aramaic was widely used in the Assyrian, Babylonian, and Persian empires from about 700 to 200 BCE. It is attested in inscriptions and documents from Egypt to Pakistan, and in the Biblical books of Daniel and Ezra. An important reason for the widespread official adoption of Aramaic, besides the movement of Arameans into Mesopotamia, may have been the simplicity of the Aramaic alphabet, as compared with the cuneiform syllabic/logographic writing system of Akkadian [*q.v.*]. Many pan-Aramaic phonological features emerged only after the Old Aramaic period and probably spread as characteristics of Imperial Aramaic. These include the shift of the proto-Semitic interdentals to stops; the shift of the proto-Semitic emphatic lateral consonant to ʕ; the reduction of unstressed short vowels in open syllables; and spirantization (see below).

Middle Aramaic comprises a diverse set of forms written from about 200 BCE to about 200 CE. All were approximations to Imperial Aramaic at a time when the spoken languages were more like Late Aramaic. Some of the Dead Sea Scrolls are written in Middle Aramaic, and a spoken form of the language was the native tongue of Jesus.

Late Aramaic includes six literary languages, the only surviving records of a dialect continuum which stretched from Palestine through Mesopotamia. In the west were Jewish Palestinian Aramaic and Samaritan, as well as Christian Palestinian Aramaic. In the east were Mandaic and Jewish Babylonian Aramaic; the latter is the language of the Babylonian Talmud, the core of traditional Jewish education to this day. Syriac, the literary and liturgical language of Christians throughout the Middle East, is geographically and linguistically intermediate between the Palestinian and Babylonian varieties. Aramaic gradually receded in most areas after the spread of Islam and Arabic, beginning in the 7th century.

Modern Aramaic includes four languages spoken today: (i) the Maʻlūla group, in Syria; (ii) Ṭūrōyo, in southeastern Turkey; (iii) Northeastern Aramaic, in a region straddling northern Iraq and adjacent parts of Iran and Turkey; and (iv) modern Mandaic, in Khuzistan, Iran. For locations, see Map 2. The great majority of modern Aramaic speakers speak Northeastern Aramaic; they are the Christian and Jewish minorities of a region in which the Muslim majority speaks Kurdish and Azerbaijani Turkish. Northeastern Aramaic exhibits an astonishing amount of dialect variation; however, the ethnic self-designations 'Assyrian' and 'Chaldean' correlate mainly with Christian denomination, not with dialect; the term 'Modern Syriac' is justified only by the script used by Christian speakers.

Throughout its history, Aramaic has both influenced and been influenced by many neighboring languages in vocabulary and in grammatical structure. The most im-

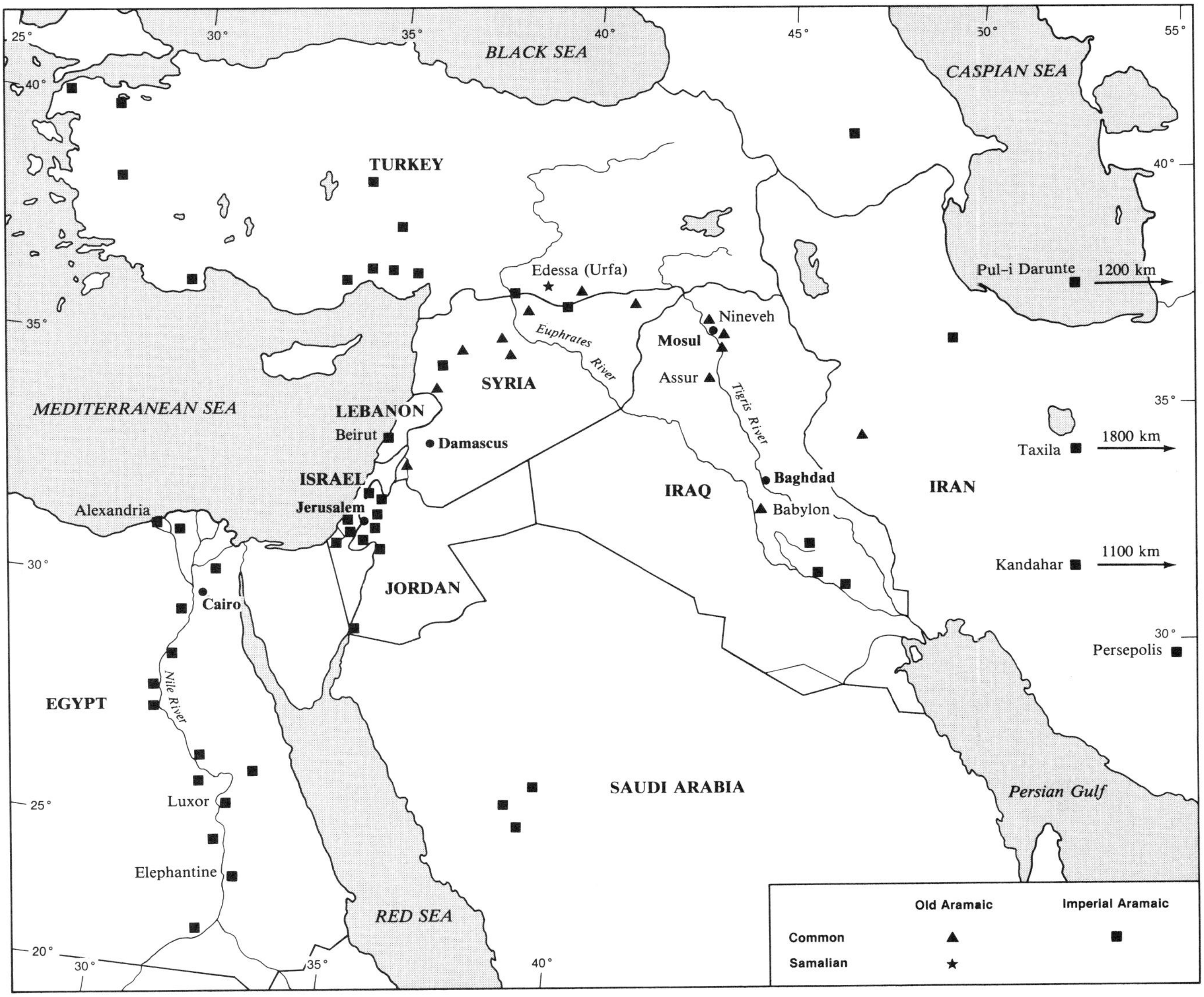

Map 1. *Sites of Early Aramaic Inscriptions*

portant were Akkadian, Persian, Greek, and Hebrew—in varying degrees, according to time, place, and religious/cultural affiliation. Modern Aramaic has much vocabulary from Arabic, Kurdish, and Turkish as well as grammatical features. Yet even in the modern language, the great majority of the vocabulary can be traced to the native Aramaic lexicon.

Classical Syriac is the most extensively and precisely documented Aramaic language; its consonantal phonemes are shown in Table 1.

Labial, dental, and velar fricatives are phonemic at the surface level; but at a more abstract level, *p̄ ḇ ṯ ḏ ḵ ḡ* are variants of the corresponding stops *p b t d k g*. In an earlier stage of the language, the stops other than *t* and *q*, when postvocalic and not geminate, became fricatives by a rule of spirantization. However, in attested Syriac, this rule became much less transparent—partly through the deletion of vowels after spirantization, and partly through the creation of morphological and lexical exceptions.

We can reconstruct the following vowels for early Syriac: long *ī ẹ̄ ē ā ō ū*, short *e a u* (*ẹ̄*, higher than *ē*, is relatively rare). Short vowels are generally elided (not merely reduced) in open syllables. There is no known significant accent in Syriac, although both earlier and later Aramaic (Biblical and Modern) have phonemic stress.

Syriac was written from right to left in three related

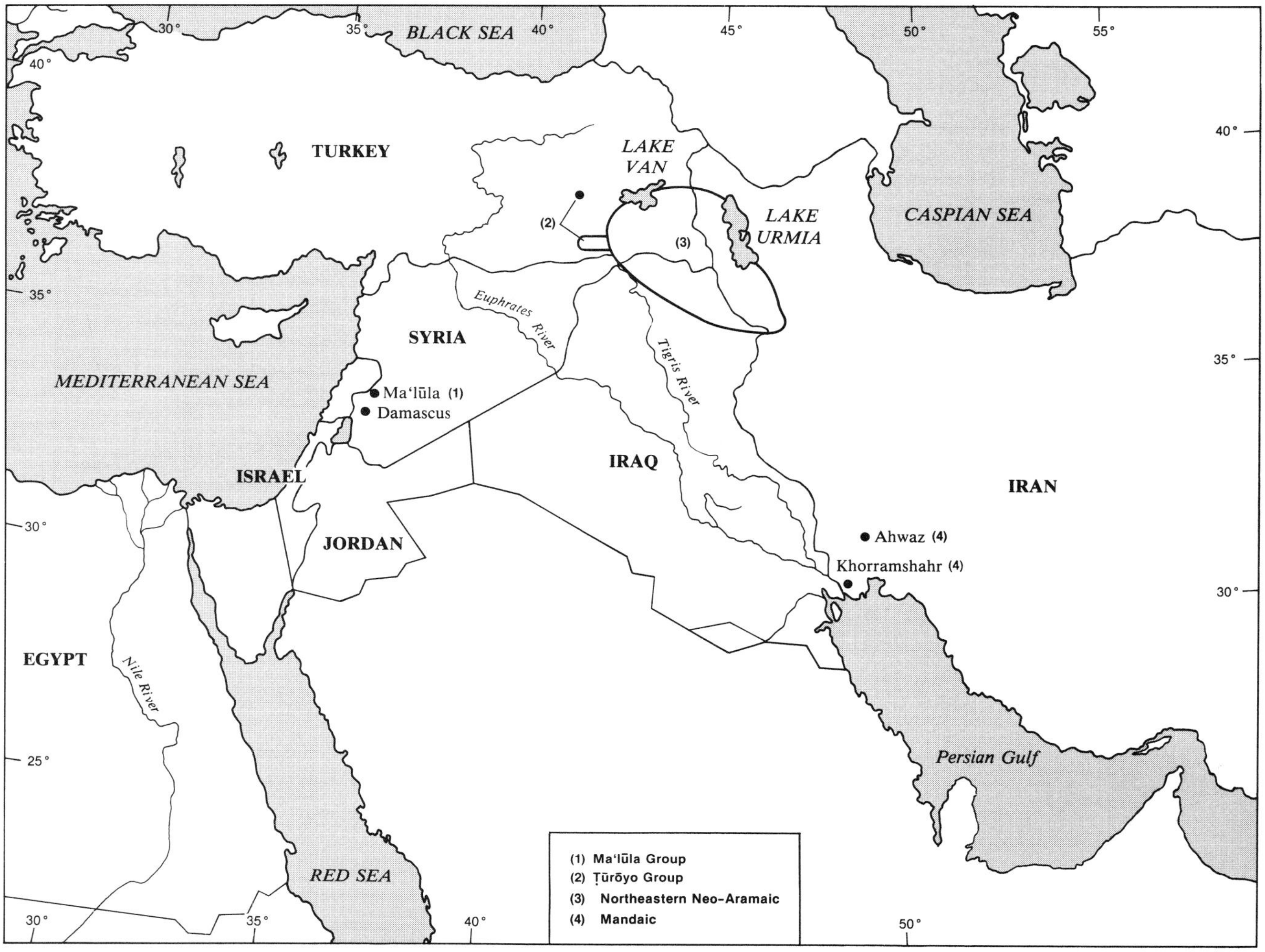

MAP 2. *Locations Where Aramaic Is Spoken*

TABLE 1. *Syriac Consonants*

	Labial	Dental	Alveolar	Palatal	Velar	Uvular	Pharyngeal	Glottal
Stops								
Voiced	b	d			g			
Voiceless	p	t			k			(ʾ)
Emphatic		ṭ				q		
Fricatives								
Voiced	b̲	d̲	z		ḡ		ʕ	
Voiceless	p̄	t̲	s	š	k̲		ḥ	
Emphatic			ṣ					
Nasals	m	n						
Vibrant		r						
Lateral		l						
Glide	w			y				h

scripts, as shown in Tables 2a–b. Distinctive vowel qualities were indicated by optional diacritics, as in Hebrew and Arabic script.

Syriac has typical Semitic morphology, with prefixes and suffixes as well as discontinuous consonantal roots and vocalic stem morphemes. Nominal and verbal derivation involves both affixes and discontinuous morphology, as does verbal inflection; but nominal inflection is almost entirely affixal. As a consequence, borrowed nouns may retain their original vowels and syllabic shapes, but borrowed verbs are restructured to fit into Syriac canonical patterns.

The inflectional categories of the Syriac noun are gender (masculine/feminine), number (singular/plural), and 'state'. The last includes the categories Determinate, which is functionally unmarked; Absolute, found chiefly in predicate adjectives and in quantified nouns; and Construct, bound to a following possessor or specifying noun. (In earlier Aramaic, the unmarked state was the Absolute; while the Determinate state, formed with the suffix *-ā,* was semantically similar to English *the.*) An attributive adjective agrees with its noun in gender, number, and state.

Verbal derivation has three basic canonical patterns: an unmarked pattern; an 'intensive' pattern, marked by the gemination of the middle root consonant; and a causative pattern with the prefix *a-*. For each of the three, a corresponding passive/reflexive is formed with the prefix *et(t)-* and a change of the stem vowels.

A Syriac verb has the following inflectional forms: Perfect (a past tense), Imperfect (future and modal), Active Participle (serving as the present tense), Passive Participle (perfect), Imperative, and Infinitive. The Perfect and Imperfect are inflected for the gender, number, and person of the subject; the Participles and Imperative are marked for gender and number only. The Passive Participle appears frequently in a syntactically active construction with present perfect meaning; the agent (the syntactic subject) is then marked with the preposition *l-,* which otherwise marks direct or indirect objects or possessors, but not agents of passives. In this construction, the so-called Passive Participle can be formed even from intransitive verbs: *šmīʕ l-ī* 'I have heard', *azīl l-ī* 'I have gone'.

The order of verb, subject, and object in a sentence varies freely, but other features of word order follow Verb + Object typology; thus adjectives follow nouns, and prepositions precede their objects. Syriac sentences meaning 'A is B' contain no verb; instead, they have either (i) an enclitic pronoun representing the subject, but following the first word of the predicate, or (ii) the particle *ʔīṯ* 'there is', with a pronominal suffix representing the subject.

ROBERT D. HOBERMAN

TABLE 2a. *Traditional Order of Consonants in Syriac Scripts.* Variant forms used at the ends of words appear to the left in the table. Some of the sounds occur only in certain periods or dialects.

Serto	Estrangelo	Nestorian	Transcription
ܐ	ܐ	ܐ	ʔ, zero
ܒ	ܒ	ܒ	b, ḇ
ܓ	ܓ	ܓ	g, ḡ
ܕ	ܕ	ܕ	d, ḏ
ܗ	ܗ	ܗ	h
ܘ	ܘ	ܘ	w
ܙ	ܙ	ܙ	z
ܚ	ܚ	ܚ	ḥ
ܛ ܛ	ܛ	ܛ	ṭ
ܝ	ܝ	ܝ	y
ܟ ܟ	ܟ ܟ	ܟ ܟ	k, ḵ
ܠ ܠ	ܠ	ܠ	l
ܡ ܡ	ܡ ܡ	ܡ ܡ	m
ܢ ܢ	ܢ ܢ	ܢ ܢ	n
ܣ	ܣ	ܣ	s
ܥ ܥ	ܥ	ܥ	ʕ
ܦ	ܦ	ܦ	p, p̄
ܨ	ܨ	ܨ	ṣ
ܩ	ܩ	ܩ	q
ܪ	ܪ	ܪ	r
ܫ	ܫ	ܫ	š
ܬ ܬ	ܬ	ܬ	t, ṯ

TABLE 2b. *Syriac Vowel Diacritics.* Jacobite symbols are written either above or below consonants; placement of Nestorian symbols is shown by the dash.

Jacobite (Western)		Nestorian (Eastern)	
◌ܺ	i	—ܝܻ	ī
◌ܶ	e	—݂◌ܹ	ē
◌ܰ	a	◌ܸ	e
◌ܳ	o (< ā)	◌ܲ	a
◌ܽ	u	◌ܵ	ā
		ܘܿ—	o, ō
		ܘܼ—	u, ū

BIBLIOGRAPHY

BEYER, KLAUS. 1986. *The Aramaic language: Its distribution and subdivisions.* Göttingen: Vandenhoeck & Ruprecht.

FITZMYER, JOSEPH A. 1979. The phases of the Aramaic language. In Joseph A. Fitzmyer, *A wandering Aramean: Collected Aramaic essays* (Society of Biblical Literature, Monograph series, 25), pp. 57–84. Chico, Calif.: Scholars Press.

KAUFMAN, STEPHEN A. 1974. *The Akkadian influences on Aramaic.* (Assyriological studies, 19.) Chicago: University of Chicago Press.

KROTKOFF, GEORG. 1982. *A Neo-Aramaic dialect of Kurdistan: Texts, grammar, and vocabulary.* (American Oriental series, 64.) New Haven: American Oriental Society.

KUTSCHER, EDUARD YECHEZKEL. 1970. Aramaic. In *Current trends in linguistics,* edited by Thomas A. Sebeok, vol. 6, *Linguistics in South West Asia and North Africa,* pp. 347–412. The Hague: Mouton. Reprinted in E. Y. Kutscher, *Hebrew and Aramaic studies* (Jerusalem: Magnes, 1977), pp. 90–155.

KUTSCHER, EDUARD YECHEZKEL. 1971. Aramaic. *Encyclopaedia Judaica* 3.259–287. Jerusalem: Keter.

NÖLDEKE, THEODOR. 1904. *Compendious Syriac grammar.* London: Williams & Norgate.

ROSENTHAL, FRANZ. 1961. *A grammar of Biblical Aramaic.* (Porta linguarum Orientalium, n.s., 5.) Wiesbaden: Harrassowitz.

ROSENTHAL, FRANZ, ed. 1967. *An Aramaic handbook.* (Porta linguarum Orientalium, n.s., 10.) Wiesbaden: Harrassowitz.

SEGERT, STANISLAV. 1975. *Altaramäische Grammatik mit Bibliographie, Chrestomathie und Glossar.* Leipzig: VEB Verlag Enzyklopädie.

ARANDIC LANGUAGES are a group spoken in the Northern Territory, Australia; they form a branch of the Pama-Nyungan family of Australian languages [*qq.v.*]. Their subgrouping is shown in Figure 1.

LANGUAGE LIST

Alyawarra: 500 or more speakers reported in 1983, in the Lake Nash area, Ali Curung, Northern Territory. Also called Iliaura. The people are somewhat bilingual in English.

Andegerebinha: 10 speakers reported in 1981, on the Hay River, in the Pituri Creek area, east of Alyawarra, Northern Territory.

Anmatjirra: 800 speakers reported in 1983, in the Stuart Bluff Range, around Aileron, Northern Territory.

Aranda, Eastern: 1,000 speakers reported in 1981, in the Alice Springs area, Northern Territory. Also called Eastern Arrernte.

Aranda, Western: some 1,000 speakers reported in 1981, in the Alice Springs area, Northern Territory.

Gaididj: 200 speakers reported in 1983, north of Alice Springs, Northern Territory. Also called Kaititj. The people generally speak Kriol.

FIGURE 1. *Subgrouping of Arandic Languages*

Artuya (Gaididj)
Urtwa
  Alyawarra, Andegerebinha, Anmatjirra, Eastern Aranda, Western Aranda

ARAUCANIAN LANGUAGES are spoken in southern Chile and in adjacent areas of Argentina. No higher-level affiliation has been generally accepted. The surviving languages are listed below.

LANGUAGE LIST

Huilliche: spoken in Chile south of Mapudungun. Also called Veliche. Related to Mapudungun, but barely mutually intelligible with it.

Mapudungun: 440,000 speakers reported in 1982, with around 400,000 in Chile between the Itata and Toltén rivers, and 40,000 or more in Argentina. Also called Mapudungu, Araucano, or Mapuche. The language is called Mapudungun, the people Mapuche. Population includes 8 percent nearly monolingual, 80 percent with routine ability, and 12 percent with nearly native ability in Spanish.

ARAWAKAN LANGUAGES. The Arawakan family has the greatest geographical spread of any language family in Central and South America, extending south from Belize to Paraguay, and east from the Andes to the mouth of the Amazon. [*See* South American Languages.] Voegelin & Voegelin 1977 list 119 languages in the family, showing sixteen as extinct. Grimes 1988, a generally more reliable and up-to-date source, identifies fewer than fifty extant Arawakan languages. According to her estimates, the total number of Arawakan speakers could be as high as 350,000, of whom nearly 80 percent belong to three groups: Goajiro (127,000), Black Carib (100,000), and Campa (49,000). For reference, see Noble 1965, Matteson et al. 1972, Derbyshire & Pullum 1986.

Figure 1 shows an internal classification of Maipuran, which has long been recognized as the core of the Arawakan family; see Map 1. It is based on Payne 1990, which uses a larger and more accurate set of data than

FIGURE 1. *Subgrouping of Maipuran*

Central
Mehinácu, Parecís, Waurá, Yawalapití
Eastern (Palikúr)
Northern
Caribbean
Black Carib, Guajiro, Island Carib, Lokono (Arawak), Paraujano, Taino
Inland
Achagua, Baniwa, Baré, Cabiyarí, Curripaco, Guarequena, Piapoco, Resígaro, Tariano, Yavitero, Yucuna
Wapishana
Southern
Bolivia-Paraná
Baure, Guana, Ignaciano, Terêna, Trinitario
Campa
Asháninca, Ashéninca, Caquinte, Machiguenga, Nomatsiguenga, Pajonal
Purus
Apurinã, Piro
Western
Amuesha, Chamicuro

any earlier classification. Voegelin & Voegelin depended on those earlier studies, and included a number of other languages in the Arawakan family, most of which belong to subgroups postulated as coordinate with Maipuran. At the present stage of research, it is impossible to say whether all, or any, of these (or other) languages will eventually be established as having a relationship with Maipuran that is close enough for them to be regarded as Arawakan. Figure 2 (from Payne 1990) tentatively suggests the languages that are more likely to belong to such a larger Arawakan family. [*For statistical data on Arawakan languages, see the Language List at the end of this article. Note that some languages listed there have not been definitely assigned to a particular Arawakan subgroup.*]

With regard to the still higher-level relationship of Arawakan to other families and stocks, the best known (though disputed) classification is that of Greenberg 1987, who sees Arawakan as most closely related to the Katembri, Otomaco, and Tinigua families in the Macro-Arawakan division of the Equatorial section of the Andean-Equatorial phylum (as well as to Guahibo, which here is included in Figure 2). He also places Tupian in the Equatorial section; but Rodrigues (1974:56), on the basis of more detailed comparative studies, affirms that Tupian is much more closely related to Cariban (shown by Greenberg in the Gê-Pano-Carib phylum) than it is to Arawakan.

The basic core of segmental phonological units in Maipuran languages consists of occlusives *p t tʃ k,* fricatives *s h,* nasals *m n,* liquids *ł r,* semivowels *w y,* high vowels *i ɨ u,* and non-high vowels *e a o.* Phonemic length of consonants and vowels is common. Most languages have five vowels, though Amuesha has only three, and Goajiro has six. Some languages have modifications such as vowel nasalization, voicing of plosives and fricatives, and consonantal pre-aspiration, pre-nasalization, labialization, palatalization, or glottalization. The basic syllable pattern throughout the family is CV (and V word-initially); sequences of two vowels occur in many languages, but syllable-final consonants are uncommon. The most frequently occurring morphophonemic processes are vowel loss and vowel harmony. There is no evidence of lexical or grammatical tone.

Morphologically, Maipuran languages are polysynthetic, mainly agglutinative. The verbal morphology is

FIGURE 2. *Tentative Proto-Arawakan Proposal*

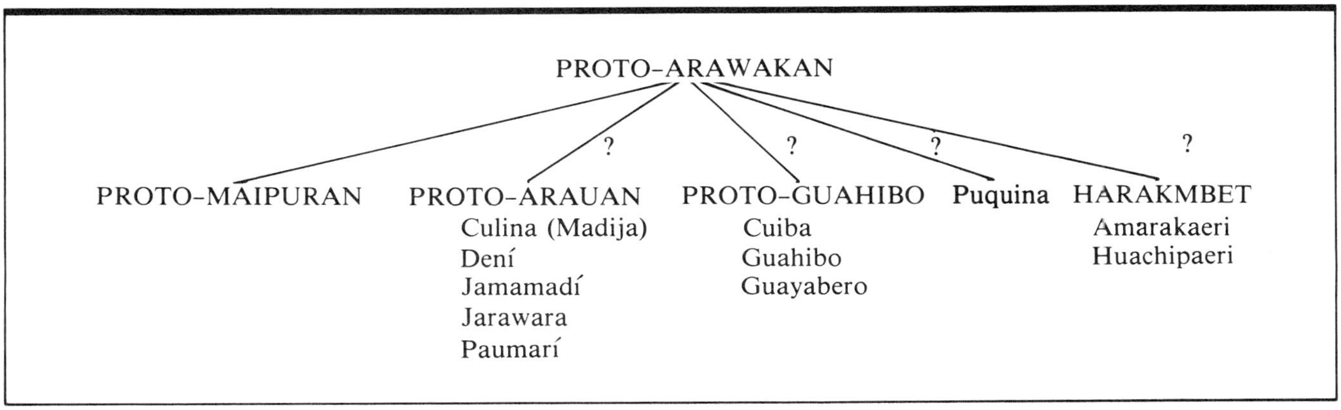

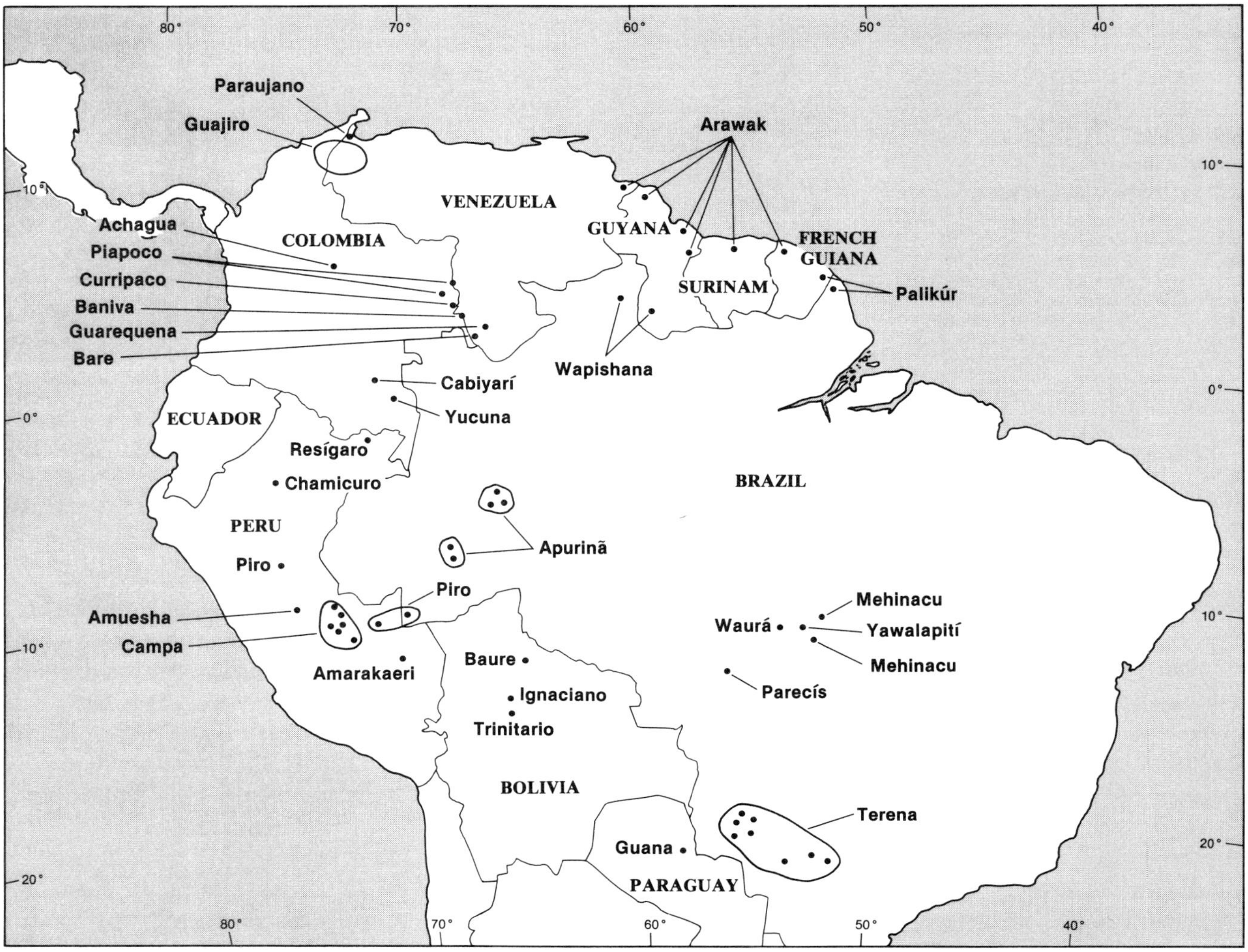

MAP 1. *Distribution of Maipuran (Arawakan) Language Groups*

relatively complex. Verb roots do not normally occur as free forms. The following categories of derivational and inflectional morphemes regularly occur (the specific forms in parentheses, or their variants, occur in several languages):

(a) Subject person-marking prefixes (1st person *n*V- and, in some Caribbean languages, *ta-/da-*; 2nd person *p*V-).
(b) Object person-marking suffixes (3rd person -*r*V).
(c) Number, either as part of the person marker or as a separate affix.
(d) Incorporated noun classifiers—see (o) below.
(e) Category-changing and valence-changing affixes, including transitivizers, detransitivizers, e.g. reflexives, reciprocals, and passives (*-oa* and *-k*V), causatives (*ka-* or *-ka*), and verbalizers (*ka-* 'attributive', *ma-* 'privative', *-ta* 'general verbalizer').
(f) Locational, positional, directional (-V*p* 'arriving, approaching'), and other suffixes of semantically adverbial type.
(g) Negation (*ma*).
(h) Verification/evidential markers which express the speaker's perspective or degree of responsibility concerning the utterance.
(i) Aspectual distinctions: perfective, completive, progressive, durative, and habitual. Sometimes a component of tense is included in the aspect marker; but tense, as a distinct category, is notably absent from most Arawakan languages.

(j) Root-final affix, empty of semantic content, of the form (V)*t*(*a*).
(k) Subordinating and nominalizing suffixes (-*n*V, -*r*V, -*t*V).
(l) Copulas and auxiliary verbs (*ni*).
(m) Nominal inflection for possession, with person-marking possessor prefix—the same forms as the subject-marking verb prefixes of (a) above—and possession suffix (-*r*V).
(n) Gender agreement systems (lacking in Amuesha and Terêna, and minor in a few other southern languages). Nouns themselves are often not marked, but have inherent gender, usually masculine or feminine (occasionally a third distinction is made for non-human or inanimate). The system governs formal marking with free and bound pronouns—and often also with demonstratives, nominalizing suffixes, adjectives, and (less often) with certain verbal categories.
(o) Noun classifier systems (not reported for some northern languages); classifier affixes, based on shape and other characteristics of their associated nouns, are attached to constituents of noun phrases or are incorporated into the verb.

Much of what would be sentence syntax in other languages is expressed in the verb in Maipuran languages. This accounts for one major syntactic characteristic: most sentences in natural discourse do not have more than two constituents. S[ubject] and O[bject] noun phrases are especially infrequent; their referents often are signaled only by person, number, and gender markers in the verb. Basic order varies, when S and O noun phrases do occur: SVO is most representative for the family, but is frequently accompanied by VS for non-active intransitive verbs. VSO occurs in Amuesha, the Campa languages, and possibly Black Carib; VOS in Baure and Terêna; OSV (probably) in Apurinã; and SOV in Piro. At an earlier historical stage, SOV was probably the basic order in the family. This is supported by the predominance in today's languages of the phrasal orders noun + postposition and genitive + noun—patterns which tend to correlate with OV order in the clause. The structure of subordinate clauses differs little from that of main clauses, except for the addition of subordinating affixes or particles. Relative clauses often occur without an overt head noun (when there is one, they usually follow it), and the relativizing suffixes function more like nominalizers. Coordination of phrases and clauses is mainly by juxtaposition, although most languages have a few forms which can have a conjoining function. Passive constructions are mostly of the non-agentive, medio-passive type.

Desmond C. Derbyshire

BIBLIOGRAPHY

Derbyshire, Desmond C., & Geoffrey K. Pullum, eds. 1986. *Handbook of Amazonian languages,* vol. 1. Berlin: Mouton de Gruyter.

Greenberg, Joseph H. 1987. *Language in the Americas.* Stanford, Calif.: Stanford University Press.

Grimes, Barbara F., ed. 1988. *Ethnologue: Languages of the world.* 11th ed. Dallas: Summer Institute of Linguistics.

Matteson, Esther, et al., eds. 1972. *Comparative studies in Amerindian languages.* (Janua linguarum, Series practica, 127.) The Hague: Mouton.

Noble, G. Kingsley. 1965. *Proto-Arawakan and its descendants.* (Indiana University Research Center in Anthropology, Folklore, and Linguistics, Publication 38; International Journal of American Linguistics, 31 3, part 2.) Bloomington.

Payne, David L. 1990. A classification of Maipuran (Arawakan) languages based on shared lexical retentions. In *Handbook of Amazonian languages,* vol. 3, edited by Desmond C. Derbyshire & Geoffrey K. Pullum, pp. 355–499. Berlin: Mouton de Gruyter.

Rodrigues, Aryon Dall'Igna. 1974. Linguistic groups of Amazonia. In *Native South Americans: Ethnology of the least known continent*, edited by Patricia J. Lyon, pp. 51–58. Boston: Little Brown.

Voegelin, Charles F., & Florence M. Voegelin. 1977. *Classification and index of the world's languages.* New York: Elsevier.

LANGUAGE LIST

Achagua: 100 or more speakers reported in 1976, in Colombia, also possibly in Venezuela. Also called Ajagua or Xagua. There is a fair degree of bilingualism in Spanish, but people speak Achagua in the home.

Amarakaeri: 500 speakers reported in 1987, on the Madre de Dios and Colorado rivers, Peru. Also called Amarakaire or Mashco, a derogatory term. Population includes 50 percent nearly monolingual, 45 percent with routine ability, and 5 percent with nearly native ability in Spanish.

Amuesha: 4,000 to 8,000 speakers reported in 1986, in eastern Peru. Also called Amuese, Amueixa, Amoishe, Amagues, Amaje, Omage, Amajo, Lorenzo, Amuetamo, or Yanesha. Speakers prefer to be called Yanesha. Population includes 20 percent nearly monolingual, 60 percent with routine ability, and 20 percent with nearly native ability in Spanish.

Apurinã: around 1,500 speakers reported in 1988, scattered over a thousand miles of the Purus River from Rio Branco to Manaus, Brazil. Also called Ipurinãn, Kangite, Popengare.

Arawak: 2,400 speakers reported in 1984, with 1,500 speakers from an ethnic population of 5,000 in Guyana, 700 speakers from an ethnic population of 2,000 in Surinam, 150 to 200 speakers in French Guiana, and a few in Venezuela. Also called Lokono, Arowak, or True Arawak. In one village in Surinam, all ages use the language; in other villages, younger speakers use Sranan.

Ashéninca Campa: 15,000 to 18,000 speakers reported in 1981, on the Apurímac, Ene, Perene, and Tambo rivers and their tributaries, in Peru.

Ashéninca Campa: 12,000 to 15,000 speakers reported in 1986 on tributaries of the Ucayali River, Peru, and 212 to 235 in Brazil. Population includes 65 percent nearly monolingual, 30 percent with routine ability, and 5 percent with nearly native ability in Spanish.

Banawá: 65 speakers reported in 1988 in Amazonas State, Brazil, upriver quite a distance from the Jamamadí. Half live on the Banawá River, others on small creeks and in scattered locations. Also called Kitiya or Jafi. Some bilingualism exists in Jamamadí, and a little in Portuguese, but the people prefer their own language. Kitiya is their name for themselves.

Baniva: now extinct, near the Colombian border in Venezuela. Also called Avani, Ayane, or Abane. Distinct from Baniwa, spoken in the Río Negro region.

Baniwa: spoken by around 5,900 people on the middle Içana River, Amazonas State, Brazil, and in Colombia and Venezuela. Also called Baniua do Içana, Maniba, or Issana. Kohoroxitari may be another name for Baniwa.

Baré: 265 members of an ethnic group reported in 1975, of whom perhaps half speak the language, with 240 in southwestern Venezuela near the Colombian border, and 25 in Brazil. Also called Barawana, Barauna, or Barauana. Bilingualism exists in Spanish. The name Baré is also a cover term for Mandahuaca, Guarekena, Baniwa, and Piapoko.

Baure: a few speakers from a reported ethnic population of over 300, in El Beni Department, Bolivia. Bilingualism exists in Spanish. Children and most adults were not using Baure in 1965.

Cabiyarí: 50 speakers reported in 1976, on a tributary of the Vaupés River, Colombia. Also called Cabiuarí, Cauyarí, Cuyare, or Kawillary. There is a high degree of intermarriage with Barasana, but the Cabiyarí continue to speak their language.

Caquinte: 200 to 300 speakers reported in 1981, on the Poyeni, Mayapo, and Picha rivers, Peru. Also called Caquinte Campa or Poyenisati; Cachomashiri is a derogatory name, and the Caquinte do not like to be called Campa. Population includes 90 percent nearly monolingual, and 10 percent with routine ability in Machiguenga. Almost none can converse in Spanish; some know Asháninca.

Carib, Black: possibly 100,000 speakers reported in 1982, including around 14,700 in Guatemala, 13,000 to 15,000 in Belize, perhaps 70,000 in Honduras, and 1,500 in Nicaragua. Also called Caribe, Central American Carib, or Garífuna. The language developed from Island Carib with borrowings from Spanish, English, and French.

Carib, Island: extinct since about 1920, in Dominica, West Indies. Also called Iñeri. Formerly also widely used in the Lesser Antilles excluding Trinidad. Island Carib was not mutually intelligible with Black Carib. Note that Black Carib and Island Carib belong to the Arawakan family, not the Cariban family.

Carútana: 250 speakers reported in 1977 in northwest Amazonas State, near Curripaco, Brazil.

Chamicuro: 5 speakers from an ethnic population of 100 to 150 reported in 1987, on a tributary of the Huallaga River, Peru. Also called Chamicura or Chamicolos. Said to be the same as the extinct Aguano, but Chamicuro speakers say they were different.

Cuiba: 2,000 speakers reported in 1979 in Colombia, with a few in Venezuela.

Cujareño: 20 to 100 speakers reported in 1976, in the Manu Park, Madre de Dios Department, Peru. Has about 60 percent mutual intelligibility with Piro.

Culina: 780 to 1,265 speakers reported in 1986, in Amazonas and Acre States, Brazil, including 150 to 400 in Peru. Also called Kulyna, Corina, Madija, or Madihá.

Cumeral: now extinct, formerly spoken in Colombia.

Curripaco: 2,550 to 4,210 speakers reported in 1977, with 2,000 to 2,500 in Colombia, 340 to 1,500 in Brazil, and 210 in Venezuela. Also called Curipaco or Koripako.

Dení: 600 speakers reported in 1986 in Amazonas State, Brazil. Also called Dani. Also called Jamamadí, but that is a separate language.

Guahibo: 20,000 speakers reported in 1982, with around 15,000 in Colombia and 5,000 in Venezuela. Also called Goahibo, Sicuani, Guaigua, Guayba, Wahibo, or Goahiva. The name Sicuani is strongly pejorative, and is disliked by most Guahibo. Speakers range from good bilinguals in Spanish to complete monolinguals.

Guajiro: 127,000 speakers reported in 1982, on the Guajira Peninsula on the Caribbean coast: around 82,000 in Colombia and 45,000 in Venezuela. Also called Goajiro or Guajira.

Guana: now extinct, formerly spoken in southern Mato Grosso State, Brazil, near the Terêna. Also called Chuala, Chana, East Paraná, Kinikinão, Kinihinão, or Equinao.

Guarequena: 700 speakers reported in 1983, with 370 in Venezuela and 330 in Brazil. Also called Arekena, Urequema, or Uerequema. All in Venezuela are bilingual in

Spanish; only older people speak the language. Some in Brazil speak Nhengatu, but most use Guarequena by preference.

Guayabero: 800 speakers reported in 1982, on the upper Guaviare River, Colombia. Also called Jiw, Mitua, or Cunimía. Population includes 83 percent nearly monolingual, and 17 percent with routine ability in Spanish.

Huachipaeri: 128 to 215 speakers reported in 1981, on the upper Madre de Dios and Keros rivers, Peru. Also called Huachipaire or Wacipaire; Mashco is a derogatory name. Some bilingualism in Spanish.

Ignaciano: around 4,000 speakers reported in 1982, in south central El Beni, Bolivia. Also called Moxo, Moxos, Mojos. Population includes 45 percent nearly monolingual, 53 percent with routine ability, and 2 percent with nearly native ability in Spanish.

Iñapari: now extinct, formerly spoken in Bolivia.

Ipeka-Tapuia: 135 speakers reported in 1976 in Içana, Amazonas State, Brazil. Also called Pato-Tapuya, Cumata, Ipeca, Pacu, Paku-Tapuya, Payuliene, Payualiene, Palioariene. The speakers may be bilingual in Tucano. Sometimes treated as a dialect of Siuci (Baniwa).

Irántxe: 150 to 194 speakers reported in 1986 in Mato Grosso State, Brazil. Also called Mundu, a self-designation. Some are bilingual in Portuguese.

Jamamadí: 460 speakers reported in 1986, in Amazonas State, Brazil, scattered over 200,000 square miles. Other groups called Jamamadí are closer to Culina or Dení. Tukurina may be a separate language.

Jarawara: 150 speakers reported in 1988 in Amazonas State, Brazil, in 6 villages near the Jamamadí. Formerly considered a dialect of Jamamadí.

Kanamanti: 130 speakers reported in 1986 in Mato Grosso State, Brazil. Appears to be different from Jamamadí.

Macaguán: 130 or more speakers reported in 1981, scattered between the Lipa, Ele, and Cuiloto Rivers and Caño Colorado, Colombia. Also called Macaguane or Agualinda Guahibo. Most are monolingual.

Machiguenga: 6,000 to 8,000 speakers reported in 1981, on the Urubamba River and tributaries, Peru. Also called Matsiganga, Matsigenka, Mañaries. Population includes 85 percent nearly monolingual, 12 percent with routine ability, and 1 percent with nearly native ability in Spanish.

Mandahuaca: around 3,030 speakers reported in 1975, with 3,000 in extreme southwestern Venezuela, on the Colombian border, and 25 in Brazil. The name Baré is also used for them.

Mehinácu: 95 to 130 speakers reported in 1986 in the Xingú Park, Mato Grosso State, Brazil. Also called Mehinaco, Mahinaku, or Minaco. Some mutual intelligibility with Waura.

Nomatsiguenga: 2,500 to 4,000 speakers reported in 1976, in south central Junín Department, Peru. Also called Nomatsiguenga Campa or Atiri. Population includes 20 percent nearly monolingual, 55 percent with routine ability, and 25 percent with nearly native ability in Spanish or Asháninca Campa.

Omejes: now extinct, formerly spoken in Colombia.

Pajonal Campa: 2,000 to 4,000 speakers reported in 1986, in the central Gran Pajonal area of Peru. Also called Atsiri. Population includes 94 percent nearly monolingual and 5 percent with routine ability in Spanish.

Palikúr: spoken by around 1,200 people including 800 in northern coastal Amapá, Brazil, and 400 in French Guiana. Also called Palijur. Some bilingualism in Portuguese.

Paraujano: 20 or fewer speakers from an ethnic population of 4,300 reported in 1975, on Lake Maracaibo, Venezuela. Also called Parahujano. Most speakers are women. All are bilingual.

Parecís: 800 speakers reported in 1988 in twenty villages in Mato Grosso State, Brazil. Also called Paressí or Haliti. Some bilingualism in Portuguese.

Paumarí: 600 speakers reported in 1988 in four villages in Amazonas State, Brazil. Also called Purupurú. Fair bilingualism in Portuguese.

Piapoco: 3,100 speakers reported in 1982, with 3,000 in Colombia and 100 in Venezuela, on the Vichada, Metá, and Guaviare Rivers. Population includes 80 percent nearly monolingual, and 20 percent with routine ability in Spanish.

Piro: 1,700 to 2,500 speakers reported in 1986, most of them in the east central Urubamba River area, Peru, and 265 to 530 in Brazil. Also called Pirro, Pira, Simirinche, Simiranch, or Contaquiro. Manitenére and Machinére in Brazil may be distinct.

Playero: 150 to 160 speakers reported in 1983, in the Arauca River region of Colombia along the Venezuelan border. Also called Rio Arauca Guahibo. Some bilingualism for trading purposes. Low mutual intelligibility with other Guahibo varieties.

Ponares: now extinct, formerly spoken in Colombia. May have been a Piapoco or Achagua subgroup.

Resígaro: 14 speakers reported in 1976, living in Bora and Ocaina villages in northeastern Peru. Also called Resígero. Bilingualism in Ocaina, Bora, Murui Huitoto, and Spanish.

Saraveca: now extinct, formerly spoken in eastern Bolivia.

Taino: now extinct, formerly spoken widely in the West Indies.

Tariano: spoken in two villages among an ethnic group of 1,600, reported in 1986 on the middle Vaupés River in Amazonas State, Brazil. Also called Tariâna or Taliáseri. No one has been located who speaks Tariano in Colombia, but the tribal identity is still maintained there. The first or second language is Tucano, and some people can speak other Tucanoan languages or Portuguese.

Terêna: around 20,000 speakers reported in 1988 in twenty villages (also living in two cities) in southern Mato Grosso State, Brazil. Also called Tereno or Etelena. Some bilingualism in Portuguese.

Tomedes: now extinct, formerly spoken in Colombia. Also called Tamudes.

Trinitario: 5,000 speakers reported, in south central El Beni Department, Bolivia. Also called Moxos or Mojos.

Tubarão: 90 speakers reported in 1986 in Rondônia Territory, Brazil. Also called Aikaná, Wari, Corumbiara, or Kolumbiara.

Wapishana: 5,500 speakers reported in 1986, with around 4,000 in Guyana and 1,500 in Brazil. Also called Wapitxana, Wapisiana, or Vapidiana. The second language is Rupununi Guyanese.

Waurá: 120 speakers reported in 1988 in the Xingú Park, Mato Grosso State, Brazil. Also called Aura. Partial mutual intelligibility with Mehinácu.

Xiriâna: on the tributaries of the Demeni and Negro rivers, Amazonas State, Brazil, near the Venezuela border. Distinct from Ninam (Xirianá), a Yanomam language.

Yabaâna: now extinct, formerly spoken in Amazonas State, Brazil, on tributaries of the Rio Negro. Also called Yabarana. Distinct from Yabarana of Venezuela. The ethnic group, with 90 persons reported in 1986, is monolingual in Portuguese.

Yavitero: now extinct, formerly spoken in Venezuela. Also called Paraene. The last known speaker died in 1984.

Yawalapití: 153 speakers reported in 1986 in the Xingú Park, Mato Grosso State, Brazil. Also called Jaulapiti. Related to but not mutually intelligible with Waurá and Mehinácu. Many understand another language of the Xingú because they have lived in other villages.

Yucuna: 800 speakers reported in 1982, in Amazonas region, Colombia. Also called Matapi. Population includes 25 percent nearly monolingual, 71 percent with routine ability, and 4 percent with nearly native ability in Spanish.

Zuruahá: 130 speakers reported in 1986 in Amazonas State, Brazil. Also called Índios do Coxodoá. The name may refer to a Jurua-Purús group of Pre-Andine Maipuran.

ARC PAIR GRAMMAR. *See* Relational Grammar and Arc Pair Grammar.

AREAL LINGUISTICS is a convenient term for the study of resemblances among languages based on geographic rather than genetic relationships. It may refer particularly to the study of linguistic areas—or, more broadly, to the study of the geographic distributions of linguistic phenomena generally, and often also to the history of those distributions.

For the synchronic study of distributions, 'linguistic geography' would be a convenient term; but that has come in many quarters to mean 'dialect geography', the detailed mapping of (mainly phonetic and lexical) variables within a single language community. The study of linguistic areas is concerned rather with phenomena that straddle language boundaries, and especially genetic boundaries. Note Emeneau's widely quoted definition of a 'linguistic area' (1980:124) as 'an area which includes languages belonging to more than one family but showing traits in common which are found not to belong to the other members of (at least) one of the families.'

Emeneau would have liked to use the term 'areal linguistics' for such studies; but he felt he could not, because the term had been pre-empted by the 'Neolinguistic' school—then of considerable influence in Romance linguistics—in a peculiar sense. As an equivalent of the Italian *linguistica spaziale,* it referred to a determinedly anti-structural kind of study of the distribution and history of individual words—pursued, to be sure, across language boundaries ('Every word has its own history, and its own area')—which set its face against both phonemic theory and the principle of the regularity of PHONOLOGICAL CHANGE [*q.v.*], and saw itself as applying Crocean idealism to the understanding of linguistic phenomena. However, after two or three decades, this was no longer a major consideration; geographical, structural, and historical linguistics had meanwhile reached an understanding of sorts, and 'areal linguistics' was freely used in other senses. Particularly in European linguistic circles, it has been used mainly in a broader sense, to cover both dialect geography and linguistic area studies, along with much in between. Although terminology is still not completely standardized, a sample of prevalent definitions follows.

Goossens (1973:319) defines the German term 'Areallinguistik' as 'that subdiscipline in which the agreements and differences among spatially contrastive linguistic systems or among geographically differentiated linguistic subsystems, and the distribution of these agreements, are interpreted with the help of cartographic representations.' He divides it into three varieties:

(a) The SUBSYSTEMIC type studies geographic differences in usage within a single 'language', e.g. standard English or standard German.

(b) The DIASYSTEMIC type is concerned with 'dialect geography' proper, and studies the distribution of features that differentiate the systems (dialects) constitutive of a geographically differentiated system-complex called 'language' in another sense—a complex loosely definable as one in which the similarities remain more fundamental than the differences.
(c) The INTERSYSTEMIC type studies agreements that cross language boundaries.

Goossens notes that type (b) is the 'most developed', having the great European linguistic atlases to its credit; and that the boundary between the first type and the second is not always clear. Here it might be remarked that dialect geography is not identical with DIALECTOLOGY. [*See* Dialectology.] As Weinreich 1954 pointed out, it is possible to have a purely 'structural' dialectology, comparing sytems as such, without reference to geography, history, or culture. It is also possible, as Goossens notes, for the interpretation of dialect-geographical data to be informed by structural, i.e. intrasystemic considerations, as well as by the extra-linguistic considerations that prevailed in the earlier decades of the 20th century.

In Soviet linguistics, where there has been considerable interest in cross-linguistic comparisons, Desnitskaja 1977 nevertheless sees such studies as only one aspect of areal linguistics *(areal'naja lingvistika)*. She proposes the following definition of the subject matter of the latter: (i) the processes of diffusion and integration of dialectal phenomena within a language; (ii) the results of language contact of both related and unrelated languages under conditions of geographic contiguity; (iii) the reflection of old contact situations in contemporary languages and toponymy ('areal reconstruction'); and (iv) the formation of new linguistic areas under the broadened conditions of linguistic and cultural contact in the present-day world, and the socio-historic typology of such areas.

Noting that 'the factor of space is always connected with the factor of time', she would include the process of differentiation of a language family in its areal aspects—with the proviso that, the further removed from ascertainable contemporary areal distributions, the more hypothetical and uncertain the results become. Extralinguistic factors (sociocultural, economic) are still of great interest in the interpretation of all these distributional facts. Desnitskaja rejects the proposal of Èdel'man (1968:3) to restrict the meaning of 'areal linguistics' to the reconstruction of ancient areas, and to redefine 'linguistic geography' as the study of contemporary distributions.

It should be clear from the foregoing that 'areal linguistics' is too widely used in a broader sense to be restrictable to the study of 'linguistic areas' as Emeneau defined them. For that subfield, the term 'contact linguistics' is sometimes used. However, that is not quite the same thing, since it takes as its focus the dynamics of what happens when two languages are in contact—whether in a geographically definable area or otherwise, e.g. a colonial or an immigrant situation—rather than the integrated results in terms of mappability.

A suitable term is still needed. Goossens noted a key difference between his sub- and dia-systemic areal linguistics, on the one hand, and his intersystemic areal linguistics on the other: the first two are concerned with features that differentiate a single underlying system, but the third is concerned with features which unite systems that are basically separate. Genetic linguistics in general may be described as concerned with divergence from a common source, and with reconstructing that source from the areally scattered products of that divergence; however, the study of linguistic areas is concerned with the convergence of originally disparate elements on a geographical basis. The two subdisciplines address opposite ends of the process of linguistic change: where languages are coming from vs. where they are going. Thus 'convergence linguistics' might be an appropriate term for that sub-field of areal linguistics concerned with linguistic areas.

Even this does not quite do justice to the complexity of the phenomenon of the linguistic area. In addition to the convergence (mutual influence) of viable neighboring languages in contact, termed ADSTRATA, the formation of such an area may also involve the action of common SUBSTRATA or SUPERSTRATA, which introduce further complications. This should be distinguished from the situation where such a substratum or superstratum uniquely affects a single language—contributing to its differentiation from its genetic kin, but not forging a hidden link between it and other languages. To oversimplify slightly, a substratum is the subordinated language of a conquered or otherwise oppressed population, while a superstratum is the superimposed language of a conquering or otherwise dominating group. The eventual disappearance of such 'strata', leaving effects on the surviving language of an area—sometimes via the route of pidginization and creolization—is part of their definition, according to some authorities. [*See* Pidgins and Creoles.] (For others, a subordinated living language affecting the dominant language of an area is also a substratum.) An example of a substratum is Gaulish in France; of a superstratum, Norman French in England. However, a superstratum should be distinguished from a SUPERIMPOSED language—i.e. a colonial, administrative, or 'national' language, which exerts influence but does not disappear, such as Russian in the non-Russian parts of the Soviet Union, or English (and Hindi) in India. It differs also from an ARCHISTRATUM, a Kultursprache from which peoples in a certain civilization draw their abstract and cultured vocabulary, such as Arabic in the Islamic world or Sanskrit in India. Such situations may change, of course—cf. the earlier position of Greek in the Balkans, or of Persian in India. This leads to a range of intermediate situations and questions; e.g., is a formerly superimposed language a 'superstratum'? [*See* Bilingualism.]

Although it is now widely used, the term 'linguistic area' itself has certain drawbacks, as Emeneau himself recognized. It was intended as an equivalent for the German *Sprachbund*; but (like 'areal linguistics'), it is susceptible of a wider interpretation, and its literal equivalents in other languages in fact often have such meanings. Weinreich (1954:378–379) suggested 'convergence area', pointing out that 'Sprachbund' is unsatisfactory because 'it implies a unit, as if a language either were or were not a member of a given Sprachbund.' Moreover, the term has not always been used with care, especially outside of its original Praguean ambiance. Becker 1948, amid much valuable discussion (praised by Weinreich), appears to confuse it at times with the spheres of influence of the great archistratal languages of civilization: Latin, Arabic, Sanskrit, and Chinese. The last three of these have only a superficial lexical basis, i.e. no structural basis.

Emeneau's definition also needs some modification, mainly with regard to the proviso that the languages involved must belong to different families. This requirement happens to fit the South Asian area with which Emeneau was mainly concerned; but it does not fit the classic case of the Balkans or that of Western Europe, where all the languages (or those primarily involved) are Indo-European, albeit of different branches. This is no doubt what Emeneau meant, and we may replace 'different families' with 'different genetic stocks'. He perhaps wished to avoid confusion with the problems of dialect distribution, language differentiation, and mutual influence within the same genetic stock that so complicate the notion of 'areal linguistics' in Europe.

The languages involved in an areal convergence may or may not ultimately be genetically related in some way; but the point is that the similarities in question, for which European scholars prefer the term 'affinities', are independent of any such relationships. For example, German and Hungarian, which are quite unrelated genetically, both have separable verbal prefixes, a feature not found in the Uralic relatives of Hungarian. Similarly, Czech and most Central and Western Slovak dialects share with neighboring Hungarian an initial word stress, a pattern alien to other Slavic languages (Alexander 1983). Equally 'areal', however, are a number of affinities between French and German, on opposite sides of the Romano-Germanic line but both Indo-European: front rounded vowels, the uvular *r,* colloquial substitution of the perfect for the preterit, the impersonal pronoun *on/man,* etc.

Despite efforts to define some constraints, it has been shown (see Thomason & Kaufman 1988, chap. 2) that languages in contact can affect one another at every level—phonetic, phonological, syntactic, semantic, idiomatic, and even morphological. The established 'areas' afford many examples of all of these. [*See* Balkan Languages; Meso-American Languages; South Asian Languages; Southeast Asian Languages.] The agency for this process is a population of bilinguals, significant either in proportionate numbers or in prestige and influence.

The real locus of language 'contact' is the mind of the bilingual individual. One theory holds that, depending on the frequency and other conditions of use and consequent pressures, the bilingual's mind may try to adjust to the demands placed upon it by constructing what is in effect a supergrammar, in which economies are effected by bringing the rules of languages concerned more closely into alignment with one another. Less speculatively, bilinguals may simply carry over some of the habits of their first language; or they may try to accommodate non-native interlocutors by adjusting their own speech in the direction of the others' imperfect version of their language—and then carry some of these habits back into their normal speech. In either situation, the resultant altered language may be imitated further by non-bilinguals.

In extreme cases, all that remains to identify the

languages concerned are some of their words; their underlying phonology, syntax, grammatical categories, etc. become identical. More frequently, perhaps, only contiguous dialects in close contact are affected to such a degree; and only certain features spread from these to the larger speech communities beyond. Often a single trait appears to diffuse over a wide area, without other features necessarily being affected.

While such single-trait distributions which cross genetic lines also create 'linguistic areas' in a minimal sense, the term is usually reserved for areas where there are many such convergences—also called areas of 'intense' convergence. Sometimes the features involved are said to constitute an 'areal type'.

When an attempt is made to map the features alleged to characterize an area, the resulting isoglosses will be found, as in dialect geography, not to coincide, but (if the area is real) to 'bundle' sufficiently to outline roughly the boundaries of the area—which may turn out to be different than previously assumed. (For one such attempt, see Masica 1976.) In the periphery, languages will turn out to be included by one isogloss and excluded by another. (Recall Weinreich's stricture against the Sprachbund concept above.) Some isoglosses will turn out not to define the area in question at all, but rather to link it (or parts of it) with other areas. In regions with a complex history of contacts in different directions, such overlap of areal affinity patterns is to be expected. Rumanian, for example, is in most respects—syntactic, semantic, and morphological—a 'Balkan' language; but at the same time it is a peripheral participant in the 'Eurasian' phonological area of Jakobson 1938.

Such mapping of features, tracing their actual distributions to their limits in surrounding languages, is essential—not only in defining the boundaries of a convergence area, but in determining whether the features are areal at all or due to random coincidence. Hook 1987 added an important tool to this line of inquiry by experimentally establishing that, when certain typological alternatives are traced on the ground, using native speakers at a series of points, they line up in a statistical progression correlated with distance, thus ruling out chance.

Not every feature characterizing an area will show such a distribution, however—or can even be plotted with isoglosses at all. In particular, the effects of substrata and superstrata may well not. They may instead show up merely as non-random distributions, e.g. as significant clustering or densities; but other techniques need to be developed to supplement the cartographic data (cf. Masica 1976, Appendix B.) It is not strictly necessary that languages sharing features be actually contiguous, but only that they be in 'proximity': recent intrusions (e.g. Turkish in Asia Minor) may have interrupted their contiguity, although its effects remain. Certain very 'broken' distributions may be the relics of former linguistic areas.

Much more work, employing more refined techniques of dialect geography—and going beyond them, since dialect geographers have rarely dealt with syntax—needs to be done on linguistic areas. Much previous research has consisted of identifying instances of convergence without pursuing distributions. A major area such as South Asia or the Balkans is likely to show complex patterns consonant with multiple origins, rather than a simple pattern of diffusion from a single center.

A precondition of the study of areal convergence is the clear identification, through sound correspondences, of the genetic relationships of the languages involved. In its absence, typological similarities among areally convergent languages have often been allowed to confuse the genetic picture, as short-cut indicators of genetic relationship. (Against taking them as such is the fact, brought to light in both areal and creole studies, that languages can drastically change their type.) Such questions have plagued the Amerindian and 'Ural-Altaic' fields in particular. Trubetzkoy 1928 attempted to sort out the two types of 'relationship': he proposed that *Sprachbünde* consist of languages which show great similarity in syntax and morphological structure, a good number of common culture-words, and sometimes also an 'external' similarity in phonology—but without any systematic sound-correspondences, or agreement in phonetic content of morphological elements, or common basic words—and which are or have been in areal contact. Languages which share a common stock of basic words, agreements in the phonetic expression of morphological categories, and 'above all' regular sound correspondences, constitute *Sprachfamilien*.

Areal factors may complicate the picture, even when genetic relationships are known—especially when closely related languages remain in contact and continue to influence one another, even while diverging from their common parent. This is the case in parts of Europe, and is particularly true of the Indo-Aryan group, where mutual borrowing and the spread of innovations across language boundaries has been so extensive as to make it difficult in some instances to identify the inherited regular element. It should be noted that linguistic areas may be characterized by common preservations, as well as by diffusion of innovations.

General typology is another subdiscipline which must be sorted out from areal linguistics. [*See* Historical Linguistics, *article on* Typology and Universals.] It turns out that a number of features such as word order and associated features of syntax, commonly studied from this viewpoint, have very skewed distributions geographically; moreover, the features that are typologically associated, from a universal statistical standpoint, may be dissociated in non-random patterns when viewed areally. By virtue of these facts, they also become grist for the areal mill, and demand explanation even though none is obvious.

COLIN P. MASICA

BIBLIOGRAPHY

ALEXANDER, RONELLE. 1983. On the definition of Sprachbund boundaries: The place of Balkan Slavic. In *Ziele und Wege der Balkanlinguistik* (Balkanologische Öffentlichungen, 5), edited by Norbert Reiter, pp. 13–26. Wiesbaden: Harrassowitz.

BECKER, HENRIK. 1948. *Der Sprachbund.* Leipzig: Humboldt.

DESNITSKAJA, AGNIJA VASIL'EVNA. 1977. K voprosu o predmete i metodax areal'noj lingvistiki. In *Areal'nye issledovanie v jazykoznanii i etnografii,* edited by M. A. Borodina, pp. 22–29. Leningrad: Nauka.

ÈDEL'MAN, DŽOJ JOSIFOVNA. 1968. *Osnovnye voprosy lingvističeskoi geografii.* Moscow: Nauka.

EMENEAU, MURRAY B. 1980. *Language and linguistic area.* Stanford, Calif.: Stanford University Press.

GOOSSENS, JAN. 1973. Areallinguistik. In *Lexikon der germanistischen Linguistik,* edited by Hans Peter Althaus et al., pp. 445–453. Tübingen: Niemeyer.

HOOK, PETER E. 1987. Linguistic areas: Getting at the grain of history. In *Festschrift for Henry M. Hoenigswald on the occasion of his seventieth birthday* (Ars linguistica, 15), edited by George Cardona & Norman H. Zide, pp. 155–168. Tübingen: Narr.

JAKOBSON, ROMAN. 1938. Sur la théorie des affinités phonologiques entre les langues. In *Actes du Quatrième Congrès International de Linguistes,* pp. 48–59. Copenhagen: Munksgaard. Reprinted, with revisions, as Appendix IV to *Principes de phonologie,* by Nikolai S. Trubetzkoy (Paris: Klincksieck, 1949), pp. 351–365; and in *Selected writings,* vol. 1, *Phonological studies,* by Roman Jakobson (The Hague: Mouton, 1962), pp. 234–246.

MASICA, COLIN P. 1976. *Defining a linguistic area: South Asia.* Chicago: University of Chicago Press.

THOMASON, SARAH GREY, & TERRENCE KAUFMAN. 1988. *Language contact, creolization, and genetic linguistics.* Berkeley: University of California Press.

TRUBETZKOY, NIKOLAI S. 1928. Proposition 16. *Acts of the First International Congress of Linguists, Leiden,* pp. 17–18.

WEINREICH, URIEL. 1954. Is a structural dialectology possible? *Word* 10.388–400.

ARGUMENT CODING. *See* Transitivity and Argument Coding.

ARMENIAN, a language known from texts written after 405 CE, is an independent branch of the I[ndo]-E[uropean] family [*q.v.*]; but it is closest to Greek, Iranian (by diffusion), and perhaps Phrygian. There is one good bilingual dictionary for the classical language (Bedrossian 1875–79); for the modern Western dialect, one may consult Kouyoumdjian 1950, 1961. A partial etymological dictionary exists in Hübschmann 1897; but the multivolume work of H. Adjarian, in Armenian (1926–35), is surely the most complete ever prepared for any language. A modern etymological dictionary to the IE components is now appearing in fascicles (Greppin 1983).

A primer to the classical language was prepared by Thomson 1975, and a primer to the modern Western dialect by Bardakjian & Thomson 1977. Minassian 1980 is a grammar of the Eastern dialect, and Gharibian 1944 is a satisfactory primer for Russophones; no suitable textbook exists in a Western language.

Armenian is distinct from the other IE languages in some notable phonological characteristics; among the most significant is a shift which resembles Grimm's Law (IE **t *d *dh* > Arm. *t' t d*), yet has satem characteristics—thus IE **k̂ *ĝ *ĝh* > Arm. *s c* ([ts]) *j* ([dz]). Further, Armenian maintains reflexes of the laryngeals in initial position—though it is not clear if the reflex is threefold, or simply initial *a-* (Polomé 1980, Olsen 1985). Armenian seems to offer no significant evidence for an IE voiceless aspirate series, and it lacks any threefold reflex of the interconsonantal laryngeal (see Hamp 1970). For the alphabet, see Table 1.

In morphology, Armenian provides limited testimony of original IE structures: with the movement of the accent to the penultimate position, Proto-Armenian lost its word-final syllables, and thus much of the nominal and verbal patterns of inflection. The aorist has the vestige of an *e-* augment, which finds parallels in Greek, Indo-Iranian, and Phrygian; however, this appears only

TABLE 1. *The Armenian Alphabet*

Upper Case	Lower Case	Transliteration	Numerical Value
Ա	ա	*a*	1
Բ	բ	*b*	2
Գ	գ	*g*	3
Դ	դ	*d*	4
Ե	ե	*e*	5
Զ	զ	*z*	6
Է	է	*ē*	7
Ը	ը	*ə*	8
Թ	թ	*tʿ*	9
Ժ	ժ	*ž*	10
Ի	ի	*i*	20
Լ	լ	*l*	30
Խ	խ	*x*	40
Ծ	ծ	*c*	50
Կ	կ	*k*	60
Հ	հ	*h*	70
Ձ	ձ	*j*	80
Ղ	ղ	*ł*	90
Ճ	ճ	*č*	100
Մ	մ	*m*	200
Յ	յ	*y*	300
Ն	ն	*n*	400
Շ	շ	*š*	500
Ո	ո	*o*	600
Չ	չ	*čʿ*	700
Պ	պ	*p*	800
Ջ	ջ	*ǰ*	900
Ռ	ռ	*ṙ*	1000
Ս	ս	*s*	2000
Վ	վ	*v*	3000
Տ	տ	*t*	4000
Ր	ր	*r*	5000
Ց	ց	*cʿ*	6000
Ւ	ւ	*w*	7000
Փ	փ	*pʿ*	8000
Ք	ք	*kʿ*	9000
Օ	օ	*ō*	——
Ֆ	ֆ	*f*	——

with monosyllabic stems—cf. Arm. *edi* 'I put', Skt. *ádhām*; Arm. *elikʿ* 'he left', Gk. *élipe*. The present active indicative reflects the IE patterns fairly closely, but the root aorist is less faithful; see Table 2.

The present active infinitive in *-l* (*berel*) corresponds to the Slavic *-l* preterit, actually an old participle (Russ. *ja byl* 'I was'), and to the Tocharian gerundive (*kenäl* 'calling'). The IE infix **-sk̂e-*, of obscure lexical value, appears as *-cʿ-* in the Armenian subjunctive (*berecʿim*

TABLE 2. *Armenian Verb Forms*

	Singular	Plural
Present Tense		
1.	*berem* 'I bear'	*beremkʿ*
2.	*beres*	*berēkʿ* (< **ber-e-y*, < **ber-e-tV-*, + *-kʿ* plural)
3.	*berē* (< **ber-e-y* < **ber-e-ti*)	*beren*
Aorist Tense		
1.	*beri* 'I bore'	*berakʿ*
2.	*berer*	*berikʿ*
3.	*eber*	*berin*

'may I bear'), as well as in the *s*-aorist (*gorc-eacʿ* 'he worked' < IE **worĝ-is-ā-sk̂-*). Full discussions of the phonology and morphology are found in Meillet 1936 and Schmitt 1981.

Armenian retains all seven IE noun cases—nominative, accusative, genitive, dative, locative, ablative, and instrumental. It has a unique plural in *-kʿ*, the same as used in verb patterns; numerous etymologies for this have been suggested, none persuasively.

Only a minority of the lexical items of Armenian descend directly from IE; a great many actively used roots are Iranian loans. At the earliest level, these were taken from Parthian (Arm. *bžišk* < Avestan *baešaza-* 'remedy'); but the traffic continued, and loans from the Islamic period are also abundant (Arm. *dirt* 'dregs' < Mod. Persian *durd*). Words came too from Greek and Syriac; but these, on the whole, were literary or religious terms, and infrequently part of the vernacular language (Arm. *xarb* 'sword' < Syr. *xarbā*; Arm. *selin* 'seat' < Gk. *sellíon*). From the 9th century, Arabic loans became common; but it often is difficult to tell which of them came directly from Arabic, and which secondarily through Persian (Arm. *mambar* 'pulpit', Ar. *minbar*, Per. *mimbar*). These various levels of borrowing are best described by Hübschmann 1897; the *Revue des études arméniennes* and the *Annual of Armenian Linguistics* have published many of the more recent contributions.

More controversial is the existence of ancient Anatolian vocabulary in Armenian. Hittite (probably actually Luwian), as well as non-IE Hurrian and Urartian, have been designated. For the former, one notes Hitt. *purut-* 'clay', Arm. *brut* 'potter'; Luwian *apparanti-* 'future', Arm. *apaṙni* 'id.' (Greppin 1982). From non-IE Anatolian, a few dozen examples are cited by Diakonoff 1971, e.g. Hurrian *hinzuri* 'apple', Arm. *xnjor*, and Urartian *ultʾu* 'camel', Arm. *ułt*.

By the 10th century, there was abundant literary evidence for two major Armenian dialects (Karst 1901). One, which continued Classical phonology, is called Eastern Armenian, and is now spoken largely in Iran and the Soviet Union. The other is called the Western dialect; it is currently spoken in Istanbul (though formerly in most of Turkey) and in the Levant, and is the most common dialect of emigrant Armenians. The situation is actually more complicated than this. Adjarian 1909 suggested that three separate dialect groups could be distinguished on the basis of morphology, rather than phonology, depending on how they formed their present tense: *sirum em* 'I love' (which essentially corresponds to the morphology of the Eastern dialects) vs. *kè sirem* and *sirel em* (in the morphology of the Western dialects). During World War II, and especially in the years following, A. S. Gharibian proposed a fourfold classification more dependent on phonology; this eventually grew to seven groups. It is well summarized by Pisowicz 1976. Finally, a more sensitive system, based on a multi-featured diagnosis which included one hundred phonological and morphological features, has been proposed by G. B. Djahukian; this system divides the Armenian dialects into eleven separate groups (a summary is found in Greppin & Khachaturian 1986).

JOHN A. C. GREPPIN

BIBLIOGRAPHY

ADJARIAN, HRATCHIA. 1909. *Classification des dialectes arméniens.* Paris: Champion.

BARDAKJIAN, KEVORK B., & ROBERT W. THOMSON. 1977. *A textbook of Modern Western Armenian.* Delmar, N.Y.: Caravan.

BEDROSSIAN, MATTHIAS. 1875–79. *New dictionary, Armenian-English.* Venice: St. Lazarus Armenian Academy. Reprinted, Beirut: Librairie du Liban, 1974.

DIAKONOFF, IGOR M. 1971. *Hurrisch und Urartäisch.* (Münchener Studien zur Sprachwissenschaft, Beiheft, n.F., 6.) Munich: Kitzinger.

GHARIBIAN, ARARAT S. 1944. *Kratkij kurs armjanskogo jazyka.* Yerevan: Izdatel'stvo Lujs.

GREPPIN, JOHN A. C. 1982. The Anatolian substrata in Armenian: An interim report. *Annual of Armenian Linguistics* 3.65–72.

GREPPIN, JOHN A. C. 1983. An etymological dictionary of the Indo-European components of Armenian. *Bazmavēp* 141.235–323.

GREPPIN, JOHN A. C., & AMALYA A. KHACHATURIAN. 1986. *A handbook of Armenian dialectology.* Delmar, N.Y.: Caravan.

HAMP, ERIC P. 1970. Sanskrit *duhitā́*, Armenian *dustr*, and IE internal schwa. *Journal of the American Oriental Society* 90.228–231.

HÜBSCHMANN, HEINRICH. 1897. *Armenische Grammatik,* vol. 1, *Armenische Etymologie.* (Bibliothek indogermanischen Grammatiken, 6.) Leipzig: Breitkopf & Härtel. Reprinted, Hildesheim: Olms, 1962.

KARST, JOSEF. 1901. *Historische Grammatik des Kilikisch-Armenischen.* Strassburg: Trübner.

KOUYOUMDJIAN, MESROB G. 1950. *A comprehensive dictionary, Armenian-English.* Cairo: Sahag-Mesrob.

KOUYOUMDJIAN, MESROB G. 1961. *A comprehensive dictionary, English-Armenian.* Cairo: Sahag-Mesrob.

MEILLET, ANTOINE. 1936. *Esquisse d'une grammaire compareé de l'arménien classique.* 2d ed. Vienna: Imprimerie des PP. Mékhitharistes.

MINASSIAN, MARTIROS. 1980. *Grammaire d'arménien oriental.* Delmar, N.Y.: Caravan.

OLSEN, BIRGIT A. 1985. On the development of Indo-European prothetic vowels in Classical Armenian. *Revue des Études Arméniennes* 19.5–9.

PISOWICZ, ANDRZEJ. 1976. *Le développement du consonantisme arménien.* Kraków: Polska Akademia Nauk.

POLOMÉ, EDGAR C. 1980. Armenian and the Proto-Indo-European laryngeals. In *Proceedings of the First International Conference on Armenian Linguistics,* edited by John A. C. Greppin, pp. 17–34. Delmar, N.Y.: Caravan.

SCHMITT, RUDIGER. 1981. *Grammatik des Klassisch-Armenischen, mit sprachvergleichenden Erläuterungen.* (Innsbrucker Beiträge zur Sprachwissenschaft, 32.) Innsbruck: Institut für Sprachwissenschaft der Universität Innsbruck.

THOMSON, ROBERT W. 1975. *An introduction to Classical Armenian.* Delmar, N.Y.: Caravan.

ARTICULATORY PHONETICS is the description of the sounds of the world's languages in terms of the postures and movements of the ORGANS OF SPEECH [*q.v.*]. A necessary tool for this description is a notation system for sound classification. The International Phonetic Alphabet [*q.v.*] is most commonly used, and will be employed here. [*See also* Phonetics, *article on* Phonetic Transcription.] (For general reference, see Ladefoged 1982, Ladefoged & Maddieson 1986.)

SPEECH PRODUCTION involves the coordinated activity of three subsystems; the RESPIRATORY system, the PHONATORY system, and the ARTICULATORY system. During speech, the respiratory system is used to expel air from the lungs under relatively constant pressure, except for episodic increases accompanying heavily stressed syllables. This PULMONIC EGRESSIVE AIRSTREAM is modulated by the action of the other two subsystems to produce the sounds of speech.

The phonatory system consists of the cartilages and muscles of the larynx—in particular, the vocal folds or vocal cords. When the space between the open folds (the glottis) is reduced by bringing them close together, the folds vibrate in response to the pulmonic egressive airstream, producing VOICING. Variation in the rate at which the folds vibrate gives rise to perceived variation of the PITCH of the voice. During speech, there is an alternation between a voiced state (typical of vowels), and a voiceless state (used for some consonants—and occasionally for vowels, as in some contexts in Japanese). In addition to normal voicing, two other phonatory states are used to distinguish certain vowels and consonants from otherwise identical ones in some languages. In BREATHY VOICE or MURMUR, the vocal folds are held somewhat apart, and voicing takes on an *h*-like quality. In CREAKY VOICE or LARYNGEALIZATION, the folds are somewhat forced together, producing a sound like that of frying, hence the alternate term 'vocal fry'.

The articulatory system contains a number of movable structures: the tongue, mandible (lower jaw), lips, and soft palate. These are brought into juxtaposition with immovable structures—the upper teeth, hard palate, and rear wall of the pharynx—and in some cases with each other, to form the great majority of speech sounds. During the voiced state of the larynx, this system acts to produce a set of variable resonating cavities in the vocal tract, i.e. the airway from the larynx to the mouth. These resonators selectively amplify portions of the acoustic energy of the voice source at frequencies which depend on their sizes and shapes. [*See* Acoustic Phonetics.] In addition, the articulatory system may produce a frictional sound source by forming a narrow constriction through which the egressive air flows in a turbulent fashion.

During speech, the articulators tend to alternate between relatively open and relatively constricted (or totally closed) configurations of the vocal tract. The open states are VOWELS; the closed or relatively closed states are CONSONANTS; and both forms are termed SEGMENTS [*q.v.*]. The above outline describes the possibilities for consonant and vowel production in the world's languages. However, some sound characteristics are present at the level of entire syllables, or larger stretches of speech: these 'suprasegmental' events are described in terms of STRESS, TONE, and INTONATION [*qq.v.*].

1. Consonants. Within traditional articulatory phonetics, consonants are classified in terms of three main attributes: PLACE of articulation, MANNER of articulation, and VOICING.

1.1. ***Place of articulation*** refers to the location of the point of maximum constriction in the vocal tract. The following is a summary of the main places of articulation, which are illustrated in Figure 1.

(a) BILABIAL: made with the two lips (e.g. Eng. [p] in *apple*).
(b) LABIODENTAL: lower lip with upper incisors (e.g. Eng. [f] in *fat*).
(c) DENTAL: tongue tip or blade with upper incisors (e.g. Eng. [θ] as in [θɩk] *thick*). (Sounds made with the tongue tip are called APICAL, and sounds made with the tongue blade are called LAMINAL.)
(d) ALVEOLAR: tongue tip or blade with the alveolar ridge (e.g. Eng. [t] as in *pat*).
(e) RETROFLEX: tongue tip with the back of the alveolar ridge (e.g. Malayalam [ʈ] as in [muʈʈu] 'knee').
(f) PALATO-ALVEOLAR: tongue blade with the back of the alveolar ridge (e.g. [ʃ] as in *she*).
(g) PALATAL: front of the tongue with the hard palate (e.g. German [χ] as in *ich*).
(h) VELAR: back of the tongue with the soft palate (e.g. Eng. [k] as in [tɩk] *tick*).

FIGURE 1. *Places of Articulation.* Key: a = bilabial, b = labiodental, c = dental, d = alveolar, e = retroflex, f = palato-alveolar, g = palatal, h = velar, i = uvular, j = pharyngeal.

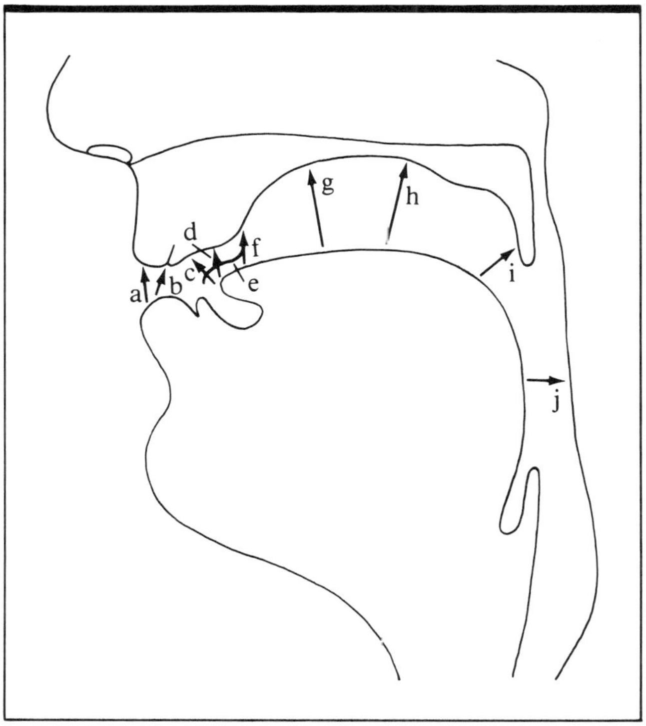

(i) UVULAR: back of the tongue with the back of the soft palate (e.g. French [ɣ] in [ɣoz] *rose*).
(j) PHARYNGEAL: root of the tongue with the pharynx wall (e.g. Arabic [ʕ] in [ʕamm] 'uncle').

Some sounds involve the simultaneous use of two places of articulation. For example, Eng. [w] as in *wet* involves simultaneous constrictions at the lips and the velum. Some West African languages have labiovelar stops and nasals (e.g. [gb] in Yoruba).

1.2. ***Manner of articulation*** refers to the degree of constriction of the vocal tract, and to the way in which the constriction is made. A main subdivision distinguishes OBSTRUENTS, in which the vocal tract is sufficiently constricted to interfere with free air flow, from APPROXIMANTS, which involve a lesser constriction more similar to that of vowels. Within the class of obstruents, three main variants can be distinguished:

(a) FRICATIVES involve sufficient constriction to produce frictional effects resulting in turbulent air flow.
(b) STOPS involve complete closure of the oral tract at some point.
(c) NASALS are a subdivision of stops; they involve complete oral tract closure, but an opening of the pathway between the soft palate and the pharynx wall—the pathway normally used for breathing through the nose.

Fricatives are made at all places of articulation, but pharyngeal nasals and labiodental stops do not occur.

LATERAL sounds are those in which the airstream is obstructed in the medial region of the vocal tract, with incomplete closure of one or both sides of the tongue. Laterals are most commonly approximants (e.g. Eng. [l] in *leaf*), but they can also be fricatives (e.g. Welsh [ɬan] 'church'). In addition, stops can be released laterally. Two minor variants in manner of articulation are TRILLS and FLAPS. In trills, the articulators being constricted are set into vibration at a rate of about 30 Hertz (e.g. the Spanish alveolar trill in *perro* 'dog'). Trills can be made at a number of places of articulation. In flaps, an articulator strikes another a glancing blow with a very short (30–40 ms) contact duration (e.g. American Eng. [ɾ] in [læɾər] *ladder*). Most flaps involve the tongue tip.

1.3. ***Voicing*** refers to the extent of vocal fold vibration during a consonant. Most consonants are either voiced or voiceless during the entire period of maximal constriction. Voiceless stop consonants are additionally distinguished in terms of the time lag between the release of the articulation and the onset of voicing. If this lag is short (less than about 40 ms), stops are described as 'voiceless unaspirated'. If the lag is longer, the open glottis during the lag period gives rise to an interval of *h*-like noise called ASPIRATION; consequently, these stops are described as 'voiceless aspirated' stops. Three varieties—voiced, voiceless unaspirated, and voiceless aspirated stops—are distinctive in many languages (e.g. Thai).

A number of consonants consist of a sequence of two distinct and usually brief articulatory postures. Best known to English speakers are AFFRICATES (e.g. the voiced palato-alveolar affricate [dʒ] bounding *judge,* or the voiceless palato-alveolar affricate [tʃ] bounding *church*). An affricate consists of a stop followed by a homorganic fricative.

1.4. ***Additional airstream mechanisms.*** Although all complete utterances in all languages are produced on a pulmonic egressive airstream, there are two additional ways in which the airstream can be actively manipulated within the vocal tract during the production of individual obstruents. In both cases, air is temporarily impounded within the tract by making an occlusion posterior to the place of articulation of an obstruent.

In the case of the GLOTTALIC airstream mechanism, the vocal folds are brought together, impounding the air in the entire vocal tract. One of two different maneuvers follows. In EJECTIVES, the closed glottis is then elevated, increasing air pressure within the vocal tract; this results in a characteristic popping sound, which is produced by the egressive airstream when the stop consonant is released. This maneuver can also be used during affricates and fricatives. The vocal folds remain tightly together during the phase of upper vocal tract obstruction. In IMPLOSIVES, following glottal closure, the glottis is lowered, reducing air pressure in the vocal tract below atmospheric levels. Consequently, on release of the obstruent, there is a tendency for an ingressive airstream to develop. These sounds are typically voiced. In the case of the VELARIC airstream mechanism, the vocal tract is occluded by tongue contact with the velum during an obstruent with a more anterior place of articulation. The body of the tongue between the two obstructions is then lowered, reducing the pressure of the impounded air. Consequently, when the anterior occlusion is released, there is an ingressive flow of air. The resultant sounds are called CLICKS; they are common in many South African languages.

2. Vowels. Traditionally vowels are classified in terms of the position of either the body, or (for some authors) the highest point of the tongue, in a hypothetical two-dimensional space within the mouth. The two dimensions are the FRONT-BACK position and the HIGH-LOW or OPEN-CLOSE dimension. The latter dimension is usually strongly related to another variable, the close-open continuum of the lower jaw or mandible. A third parameter is LIP ROUNDING, which also involves lip protrusion. The two-dimensional space for tongue position is hypothetical in the sense that it is usually inferred from auditory qualities of vowels, rather than directly observed; however, auditory qualities are not determined solely by the position of the high point of the tongue. In addition, cinefluorograms (X-ray movies) have shown that the high point of the tongue does not always coincide with the position which it is accorded in the traditional classification. Most notably, the high point for higher back vowels is lower than that for the corresponding front vowels in the traditional classification. Nevertheless, because of custom, taxonomic utility, and absence of a straightforward alternative, the traditional classification has remained popular.

In principle, the high point of the tongue for a vowel can be at any point in the mouth, within the limits prescribed by two boundary conditions. The first is that, if the vocal tract is sufficiently narrowed in a high or back vowel, an obstruent will be produced. The second is that the incompressibility of the tongue mass restricts it at the low and front extremes of the two-dimensional space.

The precise classification of a vowel phoneme in a particular language is often difficult to establish; the auditory quality of vowels varies with consonantal context, and to some extent with the idiolects of individual speakers. The most straightforward classification procedure is either to describe vowels in relation to a standard set—the Cardinal Vowels of Daniel Jones—or, more commonly, to describe particular vowels of one language in relation to another language for which there is some agreement as to vowel quality. The International Phonetic Alphabet includes categories for four levels of vowel height: close, half close, half open, and open. It also includes three categories in the front-back axis: front, central, and back. Most rounded vowels in the world's languages are back vowels, since rounded back vowels have more auditory contrast with neighboring vowels than do rounded front vowels. Like consonants, most vowels are produced by a movement of the articulators toward a single point in the vocal tract; the time taken for the movements toward and away from this point tends to be similar, if averaged across contexts. These vowels are called MONOPHTHONGS; they give rise to a single perceived auditory quality. Other vowels depart from this more or less symmetrical movement pattern, and may thus give rise to a changing auditory impression; these are called DIPHTHONGS. In some cases, they give rise to a distinctly double auditory impression, as their name implies.

Three less common properties of vowels should also be noted. In NASALIZED vowels, the soft palate is lowered as in nasal consonants. Vowels are typically nasalized in the immediate environment of nasal consonants. This is often simply a matter of COARTICULATION, and is not distinctive in a language. [*See* Coarticulation and Timing.] However, many languages have contrasts between nasalized and non-nasalized vowels in non-nasal environments (e.g. French [mɛ̃] *main* 'hand' vs. [mɛ] *mets* 'dish'). In RHOTACIZED vowels (e.g. [ɚ] as in Eng. *bird*), the tongue is elevated in the palatal region and retracted in the lower pharyngeal region; this causes a particular acoustic effect, specifically lowering of the third formant frequency. Some languages (e.g. Akan, of West Africa) have a distinction in pharynx width between pairs of vowels with the same tongue height; greater pharynx width is achieved without increase in tongue height by lowering the larynx. These are called WIDE and NARROW vowels.

A SECONDARY ARTICULATION is a vowel-like articulation with a lesser degree of closure, which occurs concurrently with a (primary) consonantal articulation. There are four types of these. PALATALIZATION, which is common in Slavic languages, is the addition of a high front tongue position (e.g. Russian [bratʲ] 'to take'). VELARIZATION involves raising the back of the tongue (e.g. Eng. syllable-final [ɫ] as in [fɛɫ] *fell*). PHARYNGEALIZATION is a narrowing of the pharynx, and is found in some Arabic 'emphatic' consonants. LABIALIZATION is the addition of lip rounding; it can be combined with any of the other three secondary articulations.

The traditional views of articulatory phonetics given above can be presented in a slightly different way that is more in accord with theories of PHONOLOGICAL FEATURES [*q.v.*]. This alternative view regards consonants and vowels as specifiable in terms of additive components within a single phonetic framework, which classifies sounds by means of a hierarchical arrangement of binary features as shown in Figure 2. At the highest level, there are four hyper-features which cover (i) the place, or articulatory gesture, (ii) the type of stricture, (iii) the oro-nasal process, and (iv) the laryngeal activity. ARTICULATORY GESTURES are divided into four types: Labial (involving the lips), Coronal (the tip or blade of

FIGURE 2. *Phonological Features*

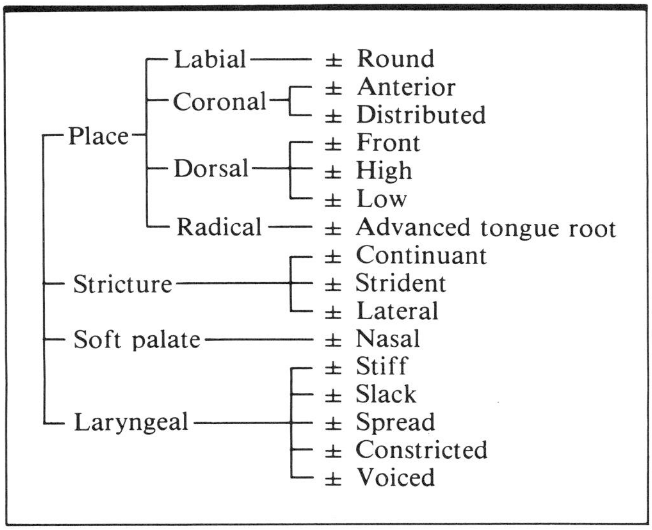

the tongue), Dorsal (the back of the tongue), and Radical (the root of the tongue).

Within the Coronal group, further distinctions are made by distinguishing [+Anterior] sounds, made in front of the center of the alveolar ridge, from [−Anterior] sounds, made further back. Further distinctions among Coronal sounds involve [+distributed] and [−distributed] sounds; the former employ a greater length along the blade of the tongue (i.e. laminal), and the latter a shorter length (i.e. apical). Dorsal gestures include not only velars and uvulars (which are distinguished by being [+high] or [−high]), but also all the tongue positions of vowels discussed above. Vowels may also be [+Labial] (if they are rounded), and may include a Radical component if there is an Advanced Tongue Root gesture (as in the Akan wide-pharynx vowels mentioned above). Radical gestures involving pharyngeal consonants also occur in Arabic and other Semitic languages.

The possible stricture types are in some dispute, but they clearly include articulatory features such as Continuant, with no oral obstruction; Strident, with a constriction that produces a turbulent airstream formed by an edge; and Lateral, with a central occlusion. There is also agreement on the necessity of an articulatory feature which specifies whether a sound is [+Nasal] or [−Nasal]. Laryngeal activity is specified in terms of articulatory features such as Stiff (vocal cords), Slack (vocal cords), Spread (glottis), and Constricted (glottis)—and also (for some linguists) by an articulatory feature Voice, which indicates whether the vocal cords are vibrating.

Articulatory phonetic descriptions made in these terms may be more appropriate than those in the more traditional phonetic terms, in that they stress the gestural nature of articulatory processes, rather than using the more passive notion of the place of articulation—which does not, in itself, specify which of the vocal organs are active.

PETER F. MACNEILAGE

BIBLIOGRAPHY

LADEFOGED, PETER. 1982. *A course in phonetics.* 2d ed. New York: Harcourt Brace Jovanovich.

LADEFOGED, PETER, & IAN MADDIESON. 1986. *Some of the sounds of the world's languages.* (UCLA working papers in phonetics, 64.) Los Angeles: Dept. of Linguistics, University of California.

ARUTANI-SAPÉ LANGUAGES constitute a group spoken on the eastern part of the Brazil-Venezuela border. No higher-level genetic affiliation has been generally accepted.

LANGUAGE LIST

Arutani: 22 speakers reported in 1986, in Roraima, Brazil, and in Venezuela below the Sapé of the Karum River area. Sometimes known as Auaké, Aoaqui, Oewaku, Uruak, or Urutani. The remaining speakers are bilingual in Ninam.

Sapé: 5 speakers from a population of fewer than 25 reported in 1977, on the Paragua and Karuna rivers, Venezuela; another report gives 60 to 100 speakers, including some in Brazil. Sometimes known as Kariana, Kaliána, or Chirichano.

ASLIAN LANGUAGES are spoken primarily in Western Malaysia. They belong to the Austro-Asiatic family [*q.v.*], probably as a top-level constituent of Mon-Khmer. The internal subgrouping of Aslian is given in Figure 1.

FIGURE 1. *Subgrouping of Aslian Languages*

Jah Hut
North Aslian
  Chewong
  Eastern branch
    Batek, Jehai, Minriq, Mintil
  Tonga
  Western branch
    Kensiu, Kintaq, Orang Benua
Senoic
  Lanoh, Sabüm, Semai, Semnam, Temiar
South Aslian
  Besisi, Semaq Beri, Semelai, Temoq

LANGUAGE LIST

Batek: 700 speakers reported in 1981, in northern Pahang, Kelantan, and Trengganu, Peninsular Malaysia. Also called Bateq, Bateg, Batok, Ķleb, Tomo, or Nong. Deq and Nong may be separate languages.

Besisi: around 1,360 speakers reported in 1981, on the Selangor coast, Malacca, Peninsular Malaysia. Also called Mah Meri or Cellate.

Chewong: 270 speakers reported in 1975, just south of Semai and Pahang, Peninsular Malaysia. Also called Cheq Wong, Che'wong, Siwang, Beri, or Chuba.

Jah Hut: around 2,450 speakers reported in 1981, in Pahang, Peninsular Malaysia. Also called Jah Het.

Jehai: 1,250 speakers reported in 1981, in northeastern Perak and western Kelantan, Peninsular Malaysia. Also called Jahai or Pangan. May be mutually intelligible with Minriq.

Kensiu: 3,300 speakers reported in 1984 in northeast Kedah, Peninsular Malaysia, and 300 in southern Yala Province, Thailand. Also called Kenseu, Kensieu, Kensiw, Semang, Moniq, Monik, Mendi, Negrito, Ngok Pa, Orang Bukit, or Orang Liar. Semang means 'debt slave' in Khmer, and is used to differentiate western groups from eastern ones, called Pangan.

Kintaq: 100 speakers reported in 1975, in the Kedah-Perak border area of Peninsular Malaysia, and across the border in southern Yala Province of Thailand. Also called Kenta, Kintak, Kintaq Bong, or Bong.

Lanoh: 260 speakers reported in 1975, in north central Perak, Peninsular Malaysia. Also called Jengjeng.

Minriq: 125 speakers reported in 1981, in southeast Kelantan, Peninsular Malaysia. Also called Menriq, Menrik, Mendriq, or Menraq. May be mutually intelligible with Jehai.

Mintil: 40 speakers reported in 1975, on the Tamun River, Pahang, Peninsular Malaysia. Also called Mitil. May be mutually intelligible with Batek.

Orang Benua: 10,000 speakers reported in 1989, on Bintan Island, Sumatra, Indonesia (in the Riau Islands southeast of Singapore). Also called Lowland Semang or Sakai.

Sabüm: spoken in north central Perak, Peninsular Malaysia.

Semai: around 18,300 speakers reported in 1981, in the central mountain area of Peninsular Malaysia. Also called Central Sakai, Senoi, or Sengoi. Sakai means 'slave' in Khmer.

Semaq Beri: 2,080 speakers reported in 1981, in Pahang, Trengganu, and Kelantan, Peninsular Malaysia. Also called Semaq Bri or Semoq Beri.

Semelai: some 2,680 speakers reported in 1981, between Segamat (Johore) and the Pahang River, Peninsular Malaysia. Two dialects became extinct in the early 20th century. May be mutually intelligible with Temoq.

Semnam: spoken in north central Perak, Peninsular Malaysia.

Temiar: around 11,600 speakers reported in 1981, mostly in Perak and Kelantan, Peninsular Malaysia, and also in Pahang. Also called Temer, Northern Sakai, Seroq, or Pie.

Temoq: 350 speakers reported in 1981, on the Jeram River in southeast Pahang, Peninsular Malaysia. May be mutually intelligible with Semelai.

Tonga: 300 speakers reported in 1981, in two areas in the south of Thailand and in Peninsular Malaysia. Also called Mos.

ASPECT. *See* Tense, *article on* Tense, Aspect, and Mood.

ASSESSMENT. In a very general sense, assessment is concerned with determining the amount of something, or with estimating its value. The things that linguists assess range from the usefulness of a particular language policy for fostering social values, to the effectiveness of a language curriculum in achieving its objectives, to a person's ability to use language in an academic setting. The procedures used in assessment are similarly varied, including such techniques as ethnographic descriptions, the ranking of students, and language tests. Rather than attempting to discuss the entire range of these activities, this article will focus on the measurement of individuals' language abilities. (For general reference, see Oller 1979, 1983; Hughes & Porter 1983; Bachman & Clark 1987; Linn 1988; and Bachman 1990.)

1. Usefulness of measures. The primary consideration in measuring language ability is the measure's intended use; thus the linguist's concern in language testing is to develop the best test possible for a given purpose. This involves the following:

(a) Defining the language ability or abilities to be measured
(b) Determining what kind of language performance adequately reflects these abilities, and how such performance can be elicited
(c) Examining the relationship between the score obtained and the language ability it is intended to reflect, or the use for which the test is intended

In addressing these concerns, language testers draw both on linguistics and on psychometrics, or measurement theory. Definitions of language abilities and the procedures followed in eliciting language performance must be consistent with the descriptions of language and language use that are developed in linguistics. Psychometrics provides the means for examining the relationship between the test score and the ability it is meant to reflect; these include both theoretical definitions and statistical analyses. Fundamental to many current linguistic theories, and also to psychometrics, is the distinction between COMPETENCE and PERFORMANCE, or between an ability and its behavioral manifestation. For language testing, this implies that the abilities to be measured cannot be observed directly, but must be inferred from test performance. An additional problem, unique to language testing, is that language ability is at once the object and the instrument of measurement.

To be useful, measures must possess two qualities: VALIDITY and RELIABILITY. Performance on tests can be influenced by a number of factors—e.g. fatigue, differences in testing conditions, and inconsistencies among different parts of a test—which constitute sources of error in measurement. A reliable score is one that is relatively free from such errors of measurement. Reliability is thus a function of the consistency of measures across differences in variable factors that are unrelated to the abilities to be measured. Validity, on the other hand, concerns the extent to which the interpretations or decisions that are made on the basis of test scores are meaningful, appropriate, and useful. To be a meaningful indicator of a particular ability, a test score must measure that ability and very little else. Thus a score that is not reliable cannot be a valid indicator of ability, since it will be affected largely by measurement error, rather than by the ability that is of interest. Moreover, a score interpretation that is appropriate for one group may not be appropriate—and hence not valid—for another. For example, scores that are valid indicators of reading comprehension in children might not be valid measures of this ability for adults. Finally, scores that are useful for one purpose may not be useful, or valid, for other purposes. Thus the fact that a score on a vocabulary test is useful for PREDICTING some future performance, such as academic achievement, does not necessarily mean that this score is a valid MEASURE of academic achievement.

2. Characteristics of tests. Language tests can be classified in terms of five characteristics, as follows:

(a) Tests can be distinguished according to their intended use, such as selection, entrance, readiness, placement, diagnosis, progress, attainment, and mastery.

(b) Tests can differ in content; ACHIEVEMENT tests are based on a syllabus, while PROFICIENCY tests derive from a theory of language ability.

(c) Different frames of reference can provide the basis for test development and score interpretation. NORM-REFERENCED tests are developed to maximize differences among individual test takers, and a test score is interpreted in relation to the scores of other test takers. CRITERION-REFERENCED tests, by contrast, are developed to represent a criterion level of ability or content domain, and individual scores are interpreted with reference to that criterion level or domain.

(d) Tests can be classified according to the scoring procedure: objective tests require no judgment on the part of the scorer; but in subjective tests, the scorer must judge the correctness of the test-taker's response.

(e) Tests may employ different testing methods, such as dictation, cloze, multiple-choice, completion, composition, and oral interview.

The above characteristics are neither mutually exclusive nor independent of one another. A particular test may be useful for more than one purpose, such as entrance and placement; and either an achievement or a proficiency test might be used for placement, depending on the specific situation. Similarly, it is possible to develop norm-referenced interpretations for scores from a test that was developed to be criterion-referenced.

3. Defining language ability. The development and use of any language test must be based on a definition of language ability. A once influential approach to defining language ability was that exemplified by models proposed by John Carroll and Robert Lado (see Carroll 1961). This approach described language ability in terms of an inventory of 'skills' (listening, speaking, reading, and writing), and 'components' (phonology, morphology, syntax, and vocabulary); it led to the development of so-called DISCRETE STRUCTURE-POINT tests, which were designed to measure specific items from the inventory of skills and components. Such tests were compatible not only with the contemporary views of American structuralist linguistics, but also with classical measurement theory.

Carroll 1961 pointed out the need to complement discrete-point testing techniques with 'integrative techniques' in order to test the 'total communicative effect of an utterance'. This sparked substantial empirical research with integrative tests such as the cloze, dictation, and oral interview. As a result of this research, and in response to developments in sociolinguistics and pragmatics, language testers in the 1970s began to take a broader view of language ability. [*See* Applied Pragmatics.] One such view is Oller's notion (1979) of 'pragmatic expectancy grammar'—i.e. the ability involved in relating aspects of discourse to elements of the extralinguistic contexts in which language use takes place. Other researchers, e.g. Canale & Swain 1980, incorporated Michael Halliday's description of language functions and J. L. Austin's theory of speech acts into Dell Hymes's notion of communicative competence, to develop a description of language ability that consists of several distinct competencies. [*See* Communicative Competence.]

These broadened views stimulated both controversy and empirical research into the nature of language ability in the late 1970s. This type of research can be generally regarded as CONSTRUCT VALIDATION: the process of gathering evidence that supports a particular interpretation or use of a test score. Evidence for construct validity can come from examining test content, from predictive studies, and from research specifically designed to investigate the relationship between test scores and the abilities they are meant to measure.

Oller's view of language led him to formulate the 'unitary trait hypothesis', according to which language ability consists of a single trait; he investigated this hypothesis through the factor analysis of a wide variety of language test scores. Other researchers, who viewed language ability as a set of distinct but interrelated abilities, also conducted construct validation studies that ultimately resulted in the rejection of the unitary trait hypothesis. Since the mid-1980s, there has been a general consensus among language testers that language ability is multi-faceted. However, there is still considerable debate over the exact nature of the various components of language ability; a clearer understanding of its nature is most likely to be found through continued construct validation research.

4. Authenticity of language tests. Language testers have also come to scrutinize more carefully the methods that are used in language tests. Research conducted in the late 1970s and early 1980s clearly demonstrated that performance on language tests can be influenced as much by the method of testing as by an individual's language ability. This research—along with the view that communicative language use involves a dynamic interaction among the language user, the context, and the discourse—has led to concern with the extent to which the methods used in language tests capture or recreate the essence of communicative language use, i.e. the extent to which they are authentic.

Since both test takers and testers are always aware that the primary purpose of the test is to demonstrate knowledge, rather than to communicate, some scholars have argued that language tests are by their very nature inauthentic. The dominant view, however, appears to be that language tests do not necessarily have to be inauthentic. Within this view, two distinct approaches to characterizing the authenticity of language tests have evolved.

4.1. The elicitation procedures used to measure language ability will themselves generally involve language use; thus the characterization of authenticity is inevitably related to the way language ability is defined. One approach, typified by the ACTFL/ILR Oral Proficiency Interview (ACTFL 1986), defines language proficiency in terms of 'real-life' language performance; designing a language test involves taking an adequate sample of tasks from an appropriate domain of real-life language use. Since proficiency is defined in terms of performance, authenticity can be characterized by the extent to which test performance replicates performance in the specified real-life (non-test) language-use domain (Clark 1975).

4.2. The other approach, articulated by Bachman 1990, defines communicative language ability in terms of several competencies: grammatical, textual, illocutionary, sociolinguistic, and strategic. Authenticity is characterized in terms of what is considered the distinguishing feature of communicative language use—namely the interaction among the language user, the context, and the discourse. Designing a language test in this approach involves both defining the abilities to be measured, and utilizing testing methods that will maximize the potential for communicative interaction among the test-taker, the testing context, and the discourse presented in the test.

5. Conclusion. The problem of defining language ability and test authenticity is the most complex and persistent issue facing language testers; it has taken them in two distinct directions, each with its advantages and problems. The advantages of the real-life approach lie in its intuitive surface appeal to test users, and in its usefulness for practical test development in situations where the criterion domain of language use can be easily specified. Its major limitation is that it does not distinguish ability from performance; thus test scores cannot appropriately be interpreted as measures of language ability. The primary problem in using this approach is that it is often difficult to determine whether the set of tasks included in the test is representative of the real-life domain. The advantage of the 'interactional/ability' approach is that it can provide a basis for making inferences about language abilities. A potential problem with this approach is that it is more demanding, since tests developed from it must be based on the specification both of the language abilities to be measured and of the tasks that are to be used in the test.

These two approaches do not necessarily lead to different types of language tests: they have developed quite similar oral interview tests. The primary difference between the two approaches is the way in which the results of language tests can be interpreted and used; and they can be seen as complementary in their applications. Thus, if the test is to be used for prediction, the real-life approach may be appropriate; if a measure of ability is required, the interactional/ability approach should be followed. In either case, it is the responsibility of the test developer to demonstrate that the scores obtained are appropriate for the intended use.

LYLE F. BACHMAN

BIBLIOGRAPHY

ACTFL. 1986. *Proficiency guidelines.* New York: American Council on the Teaching of Foreign Languages.

BACHMAN, LYLE F. 1990. *Fundamental considerations in language testing.* Oxford & New York: Oxford University Press.

BACHMAN, LYLE F., & JOHN L. D. CLARK. 1987. The measurement of foreign/second language proficiency. In *Foreign language instruction: A national agenda* (Annals of the American Academy of Political and Social Science, 490), edited by Richard D. Lambert, pp. 20–33. Newbury Park, Calif.: Sage.

CANALE, MICHAEL, & MERRILL SWAIN. 1980. Theoretical bases of communicative approaches to second language teaching and testing. *Applied Linguistics* 1:1.1–47.

CARROLL, JOHN B. 1961. Fundamental considerations in testing for English language proficiency of foreign students. In *Testing the English proficiency of foreign students,* pp. 30–40. Washington, D.C.: Center for Applied Linguistics. Reprinted in *Teaching English as a second language,* edited by Harold B. Allen & Russell N. Campbell (New York: McGraw-Hill, 1972), pp. 364–372.

CLARK, JOHN L. D. 1975. Theoretical and technical considerations in oral proficiency testing. In *Testing language proficiency,* edited by Randall L. Jones & Bernard Spolsky, pp. 10–24. Arlington, Va.: Center for Applied Linguistics.

HUGHES, ARTHUR, & DON PORTER. 1983. *Current developments in language testing.* London: Academic Press.

LINN, ROBERT L., ed. 1988. *Educational measurement.* 3rd ed. Washington, D.C.: American Council on Education.

OLLER, JOHN W. 1979. *Language tests at school: A pragmatic approach.* London: Longman.

OLLER, JOHN W., ed. 1983. *Issues in language testing research.* Rowley, Mass.: Newbury House.

ATHABASKAN LANGUAGES, with a population of 200,000 speakers (three-quarters of whom speak Navajo), constitute the most populous Amerindian language family of North America. It is widely distributed, from Alaska to the American Southwest. (The spelling 'Athapaskan' is also common.) Li 1946, on Chipewyan, is a concise grammatical sketch; see Cook 1984, on Sarcee, for a more comprehensive grammar. Young & Morgan 1987, on Navajo, offer rich descriptive, comparative, and lexical material. For details of historical/comparative studies, see Krauss 1973, Krauss & Golla 1981, and Krauss & Leer 1981 (reviewed in Cook 1981). [*For names of Athabaskan languages, see the Language List at the end of this article.*]

1. History. The interior of Alaska and the Yukon, where the most diverse and conservative languages are found, is believed to have been the American homeland of the Athabaskans; this is further substantiated by Sapir 1936, on the linguistic evidence for the northern origin of the Navajo. Krauss & Golla 1981 list twenty-three N[orthern] A[thabaskan] languages spoken in Alaska and northwestern Canada (including the extinct Tsetsaut), as shown in Map 1. They recognize only eight P[acific] C[oast] A[thabaskan] languages—many fewer than the earlier classification shown in Map 2, and eliminating the language boundaries indicated there by dotted lines. Most PCA languages of Oregon and California have become extinct—e.g. Kwalhioqua-Tlatskanai, which is known to have existed near the mouth of the Columbia River. Apachean, the southernmost group, consists of eight languages as shown in Map 3, including Navajo and the extinct Toboso. Speculating that PCA is an earlier offshoot than Apachean, Krauss 1973 proposed that much of Athabaskan is a dialect continuum with few abrupt boundaries; thus its internal relationships may be better described in terms of a wave model rather than a family-tree model.

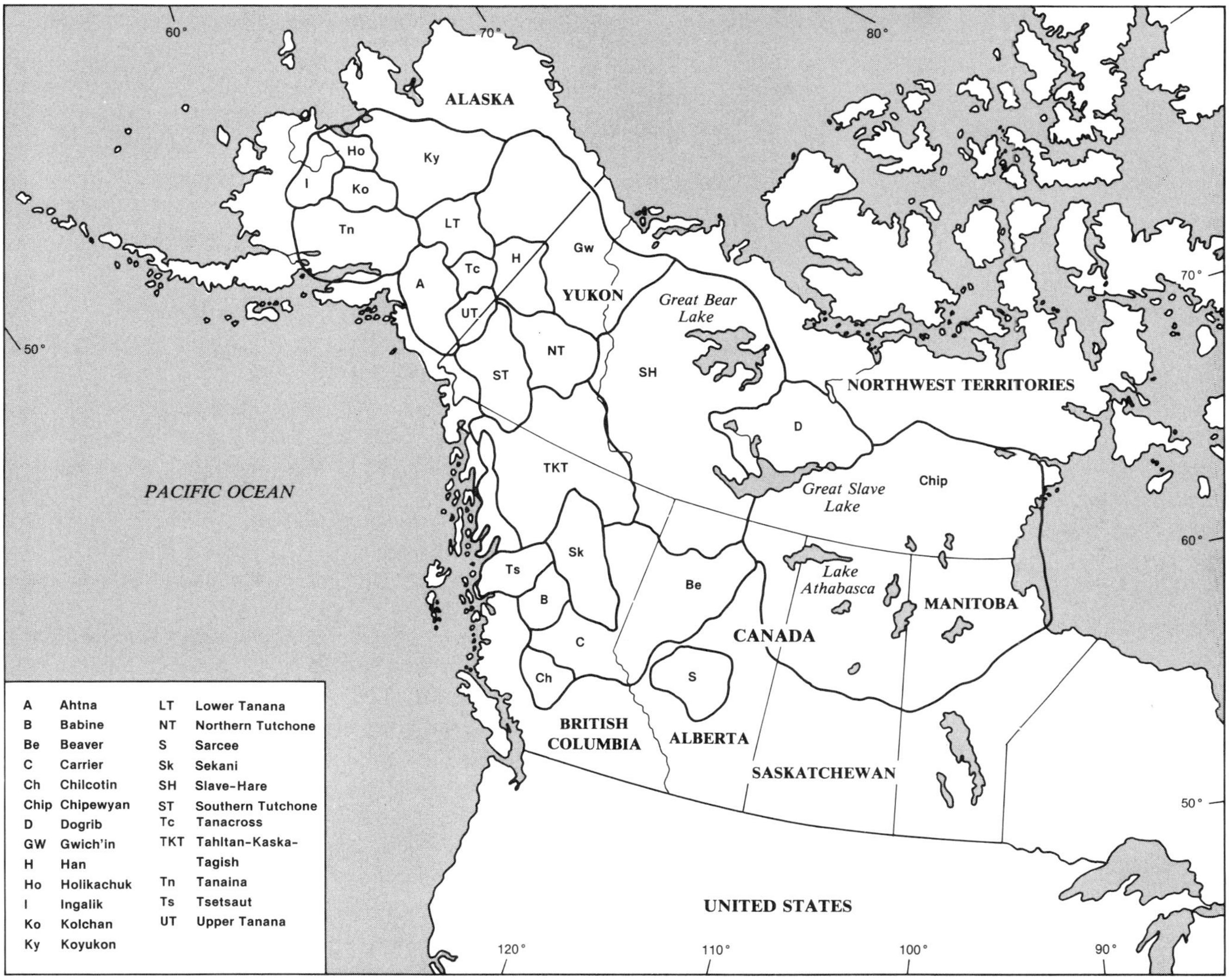

MAP 1. *Distribution of Northern Athabaskan Languages*

Athabaskan and the virtually extinct Eyak descend from P[roto-]A[thabaskan]-E[yak], itself a branch of the controversial Na-Dené phylum (Sapir 1915); see Figure 1. The phonemic inventory of PAE (along with that of P[roto-]A[thabaskan]) has been reconstructed by Krauss & Leer 1981, who also offer what might be cognate stems for PAE-Tlingit.

2. Phonology. The salient aspects of Athabaskan phonology can best be shown with reference to the PA phonemic inventory, based on work by Krauss & Leer 1981, as shown in Table 1.

Of the seven core sets of obstruents, the dental and

FIGURE 1. *The Na-Dené Phylum*

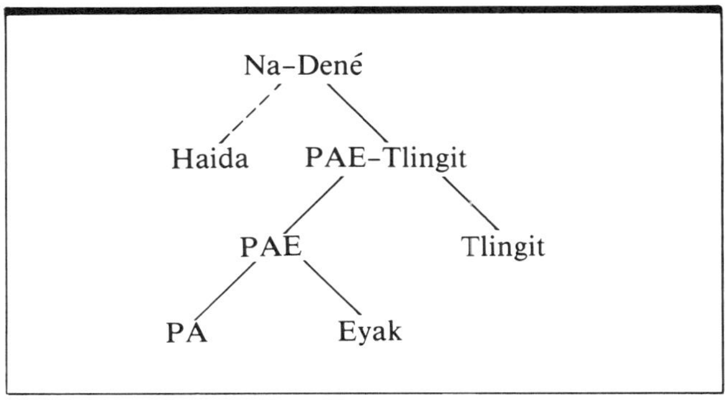

TABLE 1. *Proto-Athabaskan Phoneme Inventory*

	Dental	Lateral	Alveolar	Palatal	Labio-palatal	Front Velar	Back Velar	Glottal
Occlusives								
Plain	d	dl	dz	dž	džʷ	ĝ	G	ʔ
Aspirated	t	tł	ts	tš	tšʷ	k̂	q	
Glottalized	t'	tł'	ts'	tš'	tš'ʷ	k̂'	q'	
Fricatives								
Voiceless		ł	s	š	šʷ	χ	χ̣	h
Voiced		l	z	ž	žʷ	γ	γ̇	
			Front			Back		
Sonorants								
Oral			y			w		
Nasal			ỹ		n	w̃		
		Front			Mid		Back	
Vowels								
Full		i	e			a	u	
Reduced					ə	α	υ	

lateral sets are well preserved in daughter languages; however, the remaining sets have either shifted forward, or have merged into fewer sets. Patterns of forward shift (e.g. *q > k, *k̂ > tš, *ts > tθ*) and of mergers (e.g. *q *k̂ > k, *tš *tšʷ > tš*) in stem-initial position, and loss of consonants in stem-final position, have been the most conspicuous diachronic processes; however, these have not affected the three-way contrasts between the plain, aspirated, and glottalized series. The development of labials from the alveolar set in some Slavey dialects, Dogrib, and Tsetsaut is exceptional.

The PA(E) sonorant system is less well understood. Particularly unclear is the phonemic status of nasals and of a stem-final (or syllable-final) laryngeal feature, which eventually developed to high tone in some languages (e.g. Slavey, Chipewyan), and to low tone in others (Dogrib, Navajo), but was lost without a trace in still others (PCA). As a parallel development, syllable-final *n* either gave rise to nasal vowels (e.g. Sekani, Chilcotin), or was dropped (Sarcee, Carrier). Other major processes include sibilant harmony; the 'D-effect', by which a stem-initial consonant coalesces with a preceding *d*, e.g. *d + y → dž, d + ʔ → t'*; and gamma vocalization, i.e. C*ə* + *γə*/*γʷə* → C*a*/C*u*, which applies only across a conjunct boundary (see below).

3. Grammar. Verbs, nouns, postpositions, and particles are well defined categories. A set of pronominal prefixes denotes both the possessors of nouns and the objects of postpositions; these show person and number, as in the Chipewyan paradigms in Table 2.

The verbal morphology is notable for its complexity: e.g., ten prefix positions were established for Chipewyan

TABLE 2. *Person and Number Categories of Chipewyan in Nouns and Postpositions*

Categories	Noun Paradigm	Postposition Paradigm
1sg.	*se-lá* 'my hand'	*se-ts'ə́n* 'toward me'
2sg.	*ne-lá* 'your hand'	*ne-ts'ə́n* 'toward you'
3sg.	*be-lá* 'his/her hand'	*be-ts'ə́n* 'toward him/her'
4sg.	*ye-lá* 'the other's hand'	*ye-ts'ə́n* 'toward the other'
1/2pl.	*nuhe-lá* 'our hand'	*nuhe-ts'ə́n* 'toward us'
3pl.	*hube-lá* 'their hand'	*hube-ts'ə́n* 'toward them'
Indefinite/Areal	*ʔe-lá* 'someone's hand'	*ho-ts'ə́n* 'toward there/then'
Reflexive	*ʔede-lá* 'one's own hand'	*ʔede-ts'ə́n* 'toward oneself'
Reciprocal	*ʔeɫe-lá* 'each other's hand'	*ʔeɫe-ts'ə́n* 'toward each other'

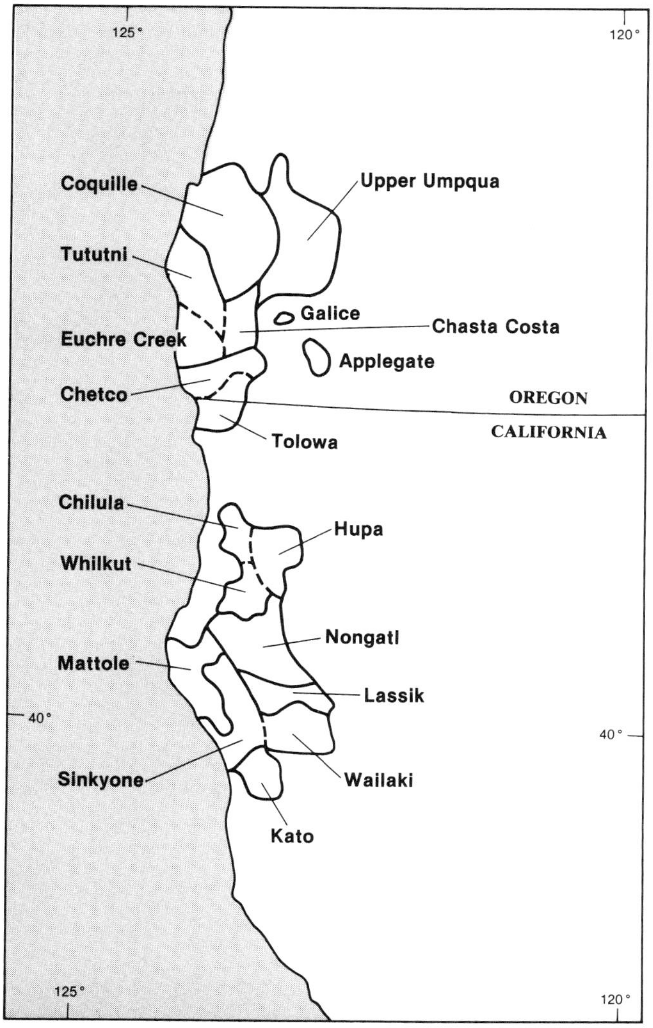

MAP 2. *Distribution of Pacific Coast Athabaskan Languages*

by Li 1946, and twenty-three for Ahtna by Kari 1979. The verb stem occurs in the rightmost position (except, in some languages, for a few suffixes and enclitics). The prefixes are divided into 'conjunct' and 'disjunct'. The former are more tightly bound morphophonologically to the stem, and include such paradigmatic elements as subject and object (marking the same person and number categories as for nouns), and aspect/mode. The disjunct prefixes include adverbials, incorporates, iterative/distributive elements, and other categories. Chipewyan prefix positions (based on Li) are shown in Table 3.

The verb stem consists historically of a root and a mode/aspect suffix; this combines with thematic elements to give a verb theme, i.e. the lexical representation of the verb. Essential characteristics of Athapaskan verbal morphology include:

(a) The derivation of aspect paradigms, determined to some extent by 'theme category'
(b) The selection of roots for certain theme categories, including 'classificatory' themes

Kari 1979 has established ten theme categories for Ahtna, which may represent the PA system. For example, the Ahtna root *de·tl'* occurs with four different sets of thematic elements, representing four different themes: 'pl. walk', 'pl. fly', 'handle pl. object quickly', and 'eat pl. object'. The first, which belongs to the 'motion' category, may be conjugated in five aspect paradigms—momentaneous, perambulative, reversative, continuative, and progressive. Table 4 shows two aspectual paradigms for Ahtna 'eat'.

Characteristic of Athabaskan is a system of classificatory verbs: these verb stems, with meanings such as 'be in position', are chosen to agree with the class of the subject (if intransitive) or object (if transitive). The selection of stems in classificatory themes is illustrated by one of four sets recorded for Navajo by Davidson et

TABLE 3. *Chipewyan Verb Prefix Positions*

10	Incorporated postposition	Disjunct
9	Adverb	
8	Iterative	
7	Incorporated stem	
6	Deictic/3rd person subject	Conjunct
5	Object	
4	Mode	
3	Aspect	
2	1/2 person Subject	
1	Classifier	
0	Stem	

TABLE 4. *The Ahtna Verb 'eat' in Two Aspect Paradigms, Inflected for Four 'Modes'.* The final element in each form, set off by a hyphen, is the stem.

Mode	Durative	Momentaneous
Imperfective	*ʔes-ya·n* 'I'm eating it'	*q'eyi-di·s* 'he's finishing eating it'
Perfective	*γas-ya·n* 'I ate it'	*q'eyi-da·n'* 'he's finished eating it'
Future	*txas-yi·ł* 'I'll eat it'	*q'eyta-di·ł* 'he'll finish eating it'
Optative	*γos-ya·n'* 'I should eat it'	*q'eyu-da·n'* 'he should finish eating it'

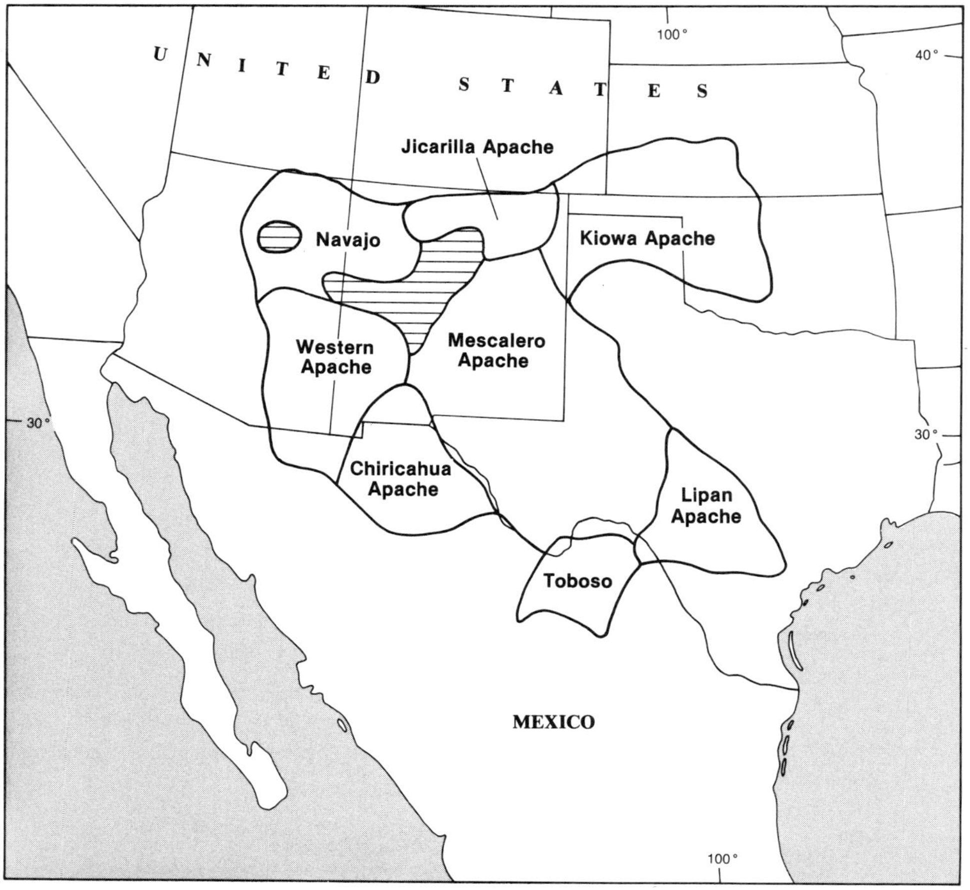

MAP 3. *Distribution of Apachean Languages*

al. 1963. Each set consists of twelve alternating stems; Set A, given in Table 5, means 'X is in a position of rest.'

Athabaskan has basic S[ubject] O[bject] V[erb] word

TABLE 5. *Navajo Classificatory Verb Stems, Set A*

Class of Subject/Object	Verb Stem
a single round solid object (e.g. a rock)	*-ʔą́*
a long slender rigid object (e.g. a stick)	*-tą́*
an animate being	*-tį́*
an aggregate of small objects (e.g. coins)	*-nìl*
a rigid container with content (e.g. a plateful)	*-ką́*
a fabric-like object (e.g. a blanket)	*-tsòòz*
a bulky object (e.g. a crate)	*-žóód*
a set of parallel long, rigid objects (e.g. logs)	*-žòòž*
a mass or collectivity (e.g. hay)	*-džààʔ*
a (ball-shaped?) wool-like mass	*-džòòl*
a rope-like object	*-lá*
a mud-like mass	*-tłééʔ*

order. However, any NP, including a direct object, may occur in the topic position before the verb (hence the controversial S/O inversion); or an overt NP may be deleted. Another familiar syntactic phenomenon is rightward movement of a P[repositional] P[hrase], whereby a PP is moved from preverbal position to follow the main verb.

EUNG-DO COOK

BIBLIOGRAPHY

COOK, EUNG-DO. 1981. Athapaskan linguistics: Proto-Athapaskan phonology. *Annual Review of Anthropology* 10.253–273.

COOK, EUNG-DO. 1984. *A Sarcee grammar.* Vancouver: University of British Columbia Press.

DAVIDSON, WILLIAM; L.W. ELFORD; & HARRY HOIJER. 1963. Athapaskan classificatory verbs. In *Studies in the Athapaskan languages* (University of California publications in linguistics, 29), by Harry Hoijer et al., pp. 30–41. Berkeley: University of California Press.

KARI, JAMES. 1979. *Athabaskan verb theme categories: Ahtna.*

(Alaska Native Language Center, Research papers, 2.) Fairbanks: University of Alaska.

KRAUSS, MICHAEL E. 1973. Na-Dene. In *Current trends in linguistics,* vol. 10, *Linguistics in North America,* edited by Thomas A. Sebeok, pp. 903–978. The Hague: Mouton.

KRAUSS, MICHAEL E., & VICTOR K. GOLLA. 1981. Northern Athapaskan languages. In *Handbook of North American Indians,* vol. 6, *Subarctic,* edited by June Helm, pp. 67–85. Washington, D.C.: Smithsonian Institution.

KRAUSS, MICHAEL E., & JEFF LEER. 1981. *Athabaskan, Eyak, and Tlingit sonorants.* (Alaska Native Language Center, Research papers, 5.) Fairbanks: University of Alaska.

LI, FANG-KUEI. 1946. Chipewyan. In *Linguistic structures of Native America* (Viking Fund publications in anthropology, 6), by Harry Hoijer et al., pp. 398–423. New York.

SAPIR, EDWARD. 1915. The Na-dene languages: A preliminary report. *American Anthropologist* 17.534–558.

SAPIR, EDWARD. 1936. Internal evidence suggestive of the northern origin of the Navaho. *American Anthropologist* 38.224–235. Reprinted in Edward Sapir, *Selected writings in language, culture, and personality* (Berkeley: University of California Press, 1949), pp. 213–224.

YOUNG, ROBERT W., & WILLIAM MORGAN, SR. 1987. *The Navajo language: A grammar and colloquial dictionary.* 2d ed. Albuquerque: University of New Mexico Press.

LANGUAGE LIST

Ahtna: 200 speakers reported in 1977 from a population of 600, in south central Alaska, USA. Also called Atna, Ahtena, or Copper River. Most speakers are middle-aged or older.

Apache, Jicarilla: around 1,500 speakers reported in 1977 from a population of 2,000, in northern New Mexico, USA. Most adults speak the language, but many young adults prefer English.

Apache, Kiowa: 10 speakers or fewer reported in 1977 from a population of 1,000, in western Oklahoma, USA. Also called Kiowa-Apache.

Apache, Lipan: 10 speakers or fewer reported in 1977 from a population of 100, among the Mescalero Apache in New Mexico, USA.

Apache, Mescalero-Chiricahua: around 1,800 speakers reported in 1977 from a population of 2,000, in New Mexico, USA, plus a small number of Chiricahua at Ft. Sill, Oklahoma. Language use is vigorous in New Mexico, but in Oklahoma most speakers are middle-aged or older.

Apache, Western: around 11,000 speakers reported in 1977 from a population of 12,000, in east central Arizona, USA. Also called Coyotero. Language use is vigorous.

Applegate: now extinct, formerly spoken in southwestern Oregon, USA.

Babine: around 1,600 speakers reported in 1982 from a population of 2,200, in west central British Columbia, Canada. Also called Babine Carrier or Northern Carrier. Babine is still the principal means of communication among adults who are middle-aged and older. Children and young adults may speak Babine, but prefer English.

Beaver: 500 speakers reported in 1987 in the Peace River area of eastern British Columbia and northwestern Alberta, Canada. Language use is vigorous.

Carrier, Central: around 1,500 speakers reported in 1987 from a population of 2,100, in central British Columbia, Canada. Also called Carrier. In some communities language use is vigorous among adults, but most children and young adults prefer English.

Carrier, Southern: 500 speakers reported in 1987 in central British Columbia, Canada. Has 90 percent lexical similarity with Central Carrier. Language use is vigorous.

Chasta Costa: now extinct, formerly spoken in southwestern Oregon, USA.

Chetco: 5 or fewer speakers reported in 1962 from a possible population of 100, on the southern coast of Oregon, USA.

Chilcotin: around 1,200 speakers reported in 1982 from a population of 1,800, in south central British Columbia, Canada. Language use is vigorous among adults, but many children prefer English.

Chilula: now extinct, formerly spoken in northwestern California, USA.

Chipewyan: around 8,000 speakers reported in 1982, in the Northwest Territories, Saskatchewan, Alberta, and Manitoba, Canada.

Coquille: now extinct, formerly spoken on the upper Coquille River in southwestern Oregon, USA. Also called Upper Coquille or Mishikhwutmetunee.

Dogrib: 2,300 to 2,400 speakers reported in 1987 between Great Slave Lake and Great Bear Lake, Northwest Territories, Canada.

Euchre Creek: now extinct, formerly spoken in southwestern Oregon, USA.

Galice: now extinct, formerly spoken in southwestern Oregon, USA.

Gwich'in: around 1,500 speakers reported in 1977 from a population of 2,600, in northeastern Alaska on the Yukon River and its tributaries, and in the Old Crow and MacKenzie River areas in Canada. Sometimes called Kutchin (called Loucheux or Takudh in Canada). Language use is vigorous in isolated communities. Many young people prefer English and many children do not speak the language.

Han: 50 or fewer speakers reported in 1977 from a population of 250, on the Yukon River in the area of the Alaska-Canada border, in both countries. Also called Han-Kutchin, Moosehide, or Dawson. Most speakers are more than 50 years old.

Holikachuk: 25 speakers reported in 1977 from a population of 160 on the lower Yukon River, Alaska, USA. Also called Innoko. All speakers are middle-aged or older.

Hupa: 50 or fewer elderly speakers reported in 1977 from a population of 1,100, in northwestern California, USA. Also called Hoopa.

Ingalik: 100 speakers reported in 1977 from a population of 300, in the lower Yukon River area of Alaska, USA. The name 'Ingalik' is pejorative; speakers call themselves and the language Deg Xit'an. All speakers are middle-aged or older.

Kaska: possibly 500 speakers from a population of 750 reported in 1977, in southeastern Yukon territory and British Columbia, Canada. Also called Eastern Nahane or Nahani. Most adults speak the language; many younger ones prefer English, and some may not speak Kaska.

Kato: 10 speakers or fewer, all over 50 years old, reported in 1962 from a population of 92, in northwestern California, USA. Also called Cahto.

Kolchan: 140 speakers reported in 1977 from a population of 150, on the upper Kuskokwim River, central Alaska, USA. Also called McGrath Ingalik or Upper Kuskokwim. At one time the people were regarded as an Ingalik band. Note that 'Kuskokwim' is a name for a Central Yupik Eskimo dialect.

Koyukon: 700 speakers reported in 1977 from a population of 2,200, in Alaska, USA. Also called Tena or Ten'a. Most speakers are middle-aged or older.

Kwalhioqua-Tlatskanai: now extinct, formerly spoken on both sides of the lower Columbia River, Washington and Oregon, USA. Also called Clatskanie.

Lassik: now extinct, formerly spoken in northwestern California, USA.

Mattole: now extinct, formerly spoken in northwestern California, USA.

Navajo: around 130,000 speakers reported in 1977 from a population of 175,000, in Arizona, Utah, and New Mexico, USA. Also spelled Navaho. Language use is vigorous.

Nongatl: now extinct, formerly spoken in northwestern California, USA.

Sarcee: 75 speakers reported in 1977 from a population or 600 near Calgary, Canada. Also spelled Sarsi. Most speakers are middle-aged or older.

Sekani: 150 speakers reported in 1982 from a population of 600, in north central British Columbia, Canada. The majority are bilingual in English. Most speakers are middle-aged or older.

Sinkyone: now extinct, formerly spoken in northwestern California, USA.

Slavey: around 4,000 speakers reported in 1982 from a population of 5,000, in northwestern Canada. Also spelled Slavi or Slave. Language use is vigorous. Hare is a related variety.

Tagish: 5 or fewer elderly speakers reported in 1982 from a possible population of 100, in southern Yukon, Canada. 'Tagish' has also been applied to Inland Tlingit.

Tahltan: 100 speakers reported in 1977 from a population of 750, in northwest British Columbia and other scattered locations in Canada. The language was being used little; few if any children spoke it.

Tanacross: 120 speakers reported in 1980 out of a population of 160, in central Alaska, USA. Also called Transitional Tanana. Partial mutual intelligibility with both Upper and Lower Tanana. Most speakers are middle-aged or older, with a few younger speakers at Tanacross village.

Tanaina: 250 speakers reported in 1977 from a population of 900, around Cook Inlet, south central Alaska, USA. Also called Dena'ina. Most speakers are middle-aged or older.

Tanana, Lower: 100 speakers reported in 1977 from a population of 360, in central Alaska, USA. Also called Minto Tanana. Most speakers are middle-aged or older.

Tanana, Upper: 370 speakers reported in 1977 from a population of 460, in east central Alaska, USA. Also a few in Canada. Sometimes called Nabesna. Partial mutual intelligibility with Tanacross. Most adults speak the language, but many younger people prefer English.

Toboso: now extinct, formerly spoken in northern Mexico.

Tolowa: 5 or fewer speakers reported in 1977, in northwestern California, USA. Also called Smith River.

Tsetsaut: now extinct, formerly spoken in northwestern British Columbia, Canada.

Tutchone: 450 speakers reported in 1982 from a population of 1,500 in central and southwestern Yukon, Canada. Also called Selkirk. Most speakers are middle-aged or older. Northern and Southern Tutchone are sometimes considered distinct languages.

Tututni: 10 or fewer speakers, all over 50 years old, reported in 1962, in southwestern Oregon, USA.

Umpqua, Upper: now extinct, formerly spoken in southwestern Oregon, USA. Note that Lower Umpqua was a Penutian language.

Wailaki: now extinct, formerly spoken in northwestern California, USA.

Whilkut: now extinct, formerly spoken in northwestern California, USA.

ATLANTIC LANGUAGES, also called West Atlantic, constitute one of the main branches of the Niger-Congo family [*q.v.*]. Atlantic languages are spoken primarily on the western coast of Africa from the Senegal River (i.e. the boundary of Mauritania and Senegal) to western Liberia; however, Fula [*q.v.*], the Atlantic language with by far the largest number of speakers, has a substantial inland population as far east as Sudan. The classification of Atlantic languages shown in Figure 1 is based on W. A. A. Wilson, 'Atlantic', in *The Niger-*

FIGURE 1. *Subgrouping of Atlantic Languages*

- Bijago (Bidyogo)
- **Northern Atlantic**
  - **Bak**
    - **Balanta-Ganja**
      - Balanta, Ganja
    - **Diola**
      - Bayot
      - **Diola branch**
        - **Diola-Gusilay**
          - Diola (proper), Gusilay, Kasa
        - Karon
        - Kwatay
    - **Manjaku-Papel**
      - Mandyak, Mankanya, Papel
  - **Cangin**
    - Lehar, Ndut, Non, Palor, Safen
  - **Eastern Senegal-Guinea**
    - **Biafada**
      - Badyara, Biafada (proper)
    - **Nun**
      - Banyum, Kasanga, Kobiana
    - **Tenda**
      - Basari, Budik, Konyagi
  - **Mbulungish-Nalu**
    - Baga Mboteni, Mbulungish, Nalu
  - **Senegambian**
    - Fula (Fulani, Fulacunda, Fulbe, Fulfulde, Fuuta Jalon, Toucouleur), Serer (Serer-Sine), Wolof
- **Southern Atlantic**
  - Limba
  - Mansoanka (Sua)
  - **Mel**
    - **Bullom-Kissi**
      - **Bullom**
        - **Northern Bullom**
          - Bom, Northern Bullom (proper)
        - **Southern Bullom**
          - Krim, Sherbro
      - Kissi
    - Gola
    - **Temne**
      - **Baga**
        - Baga Binari, Baga Koga, Baga Maduri, Baga Sitemu, Baga Sobane, Landoma
      - **Temne-Banta**
        - Banta, Themne

Congo languages, edited by John Bendor-Samuel (Lanham, Md.: University Press of America, 1989), pp. 81–104.

LANGUAGE LIST

Badyara: 5,000 to 12,000 speakers reported in 1980, in the northeast corner of Guinea Bissau. Also spoken in south central Senegal and in Guinea. Also called Badian, Badyaranke, Pajade, Pajadinca, Gola, or Bigola. Biafada is the closest language, with 52 percent lexical similarity.

Baga Binari: spoken on the coast east of the Nunez River in Cercle Boké, Guinea. Also called Barka, Binari, or Kalum.

Baga Koga: spoken on the coast between the Pongo and Konkouré rivers, extending to the Île de Kito, Guinea. Also called Barka or Koga. May be mutually intelligible with other Baga languages.

Baga Maduri: spoken on islands in the Nunez River delta, Guinea. Also called Barka, Mandari, or Maduri.

Baga Mboteni: spoken in Guinea. May be mutually intelligible with Nalu and Mbulungish.

Baga Sitemu: spoken on the southern bank of the Nunez River in the Cercles Boké and Boffa, Guinea. Also called Barka or Sitemu.

Baga Sobané: spoken between the Kapatchez and Pongo rivers, Guinea. Also called Barka or Sobané. May be mutually intelligible with other Baga languages.

Balanta: around 304,000 speakers reported in 1986, including 254,400 in north-central Guinea Bissau, 49,200 in southwest Senegal between the Casamance and Geba rivers, and some in the Cape Verde Islands. Also called Balant, Balanda, Belante, Bulanda, Brassa, Alante, or Frase. The Naga, Mane, and Kantohe varieties may be separate languages. Not mutually intelligible with Mansoanka.

Banta: reported as spoken in Sierra Leone.

Banyum: 20,000 speakers reported in 1980, with 15,000 to 17,000 in the southwest corner of Senegal between the Casamance and Cacheo rivers, north of Ziguinchor, and 3,000 to 5,000 in northwest Guinea Bissau. Also called Banyun, Bainuk, Banyuk, Banyung, Elomay, or Elunay.

Basari: 14,000 or more speakers reported in 1987, including 8,000 in Guinea, 6,000 in Senegal, and some in The Gambia. Also called Onian, Ayan, Biyan, Wo, or Tenda Basari.

Bayot: 5,000 speakers reported in 1980, in the southwest corner of Senegal, south of Ziguinchor; also spoken in The Gambia and Guinea Bissau. Also called Baiote, Baiot, or Bayotte. A separate language from Diola.

Biafada: 18,000 speakers reported in 1980, in south-central Guinea Bissau, north of the Nalu. Also called Beafada, Biafar, Bidyola, Bedfola, Dfola, or Fada. Has 52 percent lexical similarity with Badyara.

Bidyogo: 16,000 speakers reported in 1980, in the Roxa and Bijago Islands, Guinea Bissau. Also called Bijogo, Bijougot, Budjago, Bugago, or Bijuga.

Bom: spoken along the Bome River, Sierra Leone. Also called Bome, Bum, or Bomo.

Budik: 5,000 speakers reported in 1989, in southeastern Senegal. Also called Bedik, Tandanke, Tendanke, Tenda, Bande, or Basari du Bandemba. Reported to be a creole with elements from Basari, Peul, and other languages.

Bullom, Northern: spoken along the coast of Sierra Leone from the Guinea border to the Sierra Leone River. Also called Bolom, Bulem, Bullun, Bullin, Mnani, or Mandingi. Some speakers are bilingual in Temne or Susu.

Diola: 390,000 speakers reported in 1987, mainly in coastal areas of Casamance, Senegal, with 15,000 in Guinea Bissau, and some in Gambia. Also called Dyola, Dyamate, Jola, Kujamatak, Kudamata, or Yola. Recognized by the government as one of six national languages. A different language from Dioula (Dyoula, Dyula, Jula) of Mali, Burkina Faso, and Ivory Coast.

Fulacunda: around 1,440,000 speakers reported in 1986, with 1,170,000 in the upper Casamance region of Senegal, from Dianamarale north to River Gambia, and northeast to Tambacounda; 94,120 in The Gambia; some in a few communities near Sareboido in northern Guinea; and some in Guinea Bissau. Also called Fulkunda or Peul. One of six national languages of Senegal.

Fulbe Jeeri: spoken in northern Senegal.

Fulfulde, Adamawa: 759,000 or more speakers reported in 1986, including 668,700 spread all over the Far North, North, and Adamawa Provinces, Cameroon. Also spoken by some in Gongola State, eastern Nigeria, and by 90,000 in Maiurno and Kordofan, northern Sudan. Also called Adamawa Fulani, Peul, Peulh, Ful, Fula, Fulbe, Boulbe, Eastern Fulani, Foulfoulde, Pullo, Gapelta, Pelta Hay, Domona, Pladina, Palata, Paldida, Dzemay, Zaakosa, Pule, Taareyo, Sanyo, or Biira. Fulfulde is the language, Fulbe the people.

Fulfulde, Bagirmi: 52,000 speakers reported in 1979, including 28,000 in the Central African Republic and 24,000 in the Bagirmi region of Chad.

Fulfulde, Barani: spoken around Barani, Burkina Faso. Also called Barain.

Fulfulde, Benin-Togo: around 91,000 speakers reported in 1981, including 37,000 in north Togo and 54,000 in Atakora and Borgou Provinces, Benin. Also called Peulh or Peul.

Fulfulde, Gourmantche: spoken in the area from Matialoali, Burkina Faso, to Sebba, Bogandé, Koupela, and Ourgaye, east to the national park, up to Say on the Niger border, and across possibly as far as Niamey. Heavily influenced by Gourmantche. Not mutually intelligible with other Fulani varieties.

Fulfulde, Jelgooji: 250,000 speakers reported in 1982, in northeast Burkina Faso, bordering the Sahara. Also called Jelgooji, Djibo, Peul, Peuhl, Pular, Ful, or Silimiga.

Fulfulde, Kano-Katsina-Bororro: spoken from Katsina to the Jos Plateau and Bauchi, and around Maiduguri in Bornu State, Nigeria. Also spoken in Niger on the bend of the Niger River, and in northern Cameroon.

Fulfulde, Liptaako: spoken in the Dori area of Burkina Faso. Also called Liptaako or Dori. Liptaako is the official Fulfulde language in Burkina Faso.

Fulfulde, Macina: 610,000 speakers reported in 1979, with 600,000 in central Mali, 5,500 in Ghana, and 760 in Ivory Coast. Also called Peul or Maasina.

Fulfulde, Sokoto: spoken in Sokoto State, Nigeria, and in Niger on the left bank of the bend of the Niger River. One of the major Fulbe geo-political units. The language is distinct from the other Fulfulde dialects in Nigeria.

Fuuta Jalon: 2,580,000 or more speakers reported in 1986, including 2,440,000 in the Fouta Djallon area, northwest Guinea; 136,000 throughout Sierra Leone, especially in the north; and some in Senegal. Also called Fulbe, Fullo Fuuta, Futa Fula, or Foula Fouta. There are many monolinguals.

Ganja: spoken in southwest Senegal, on the north side of the river across from Balanta. Also called Ganja Blip or Bandal. The speakers are fairly bilingual in Mandinka.

Gola: some 87,500 speakers reported in 1984, including 83,100 in western Liberia between the Moa and St. Paul rivers, and 6,400 in Sierra Leone for a few miles inside the border. Also called Gula. Different from Gola of Nigeria, and from Gola (Badyara) of Guinea and Guinea Bissau.

Gusilay: spoken only in Tionk Essil, a village between Tendouck and Mlomp, north of the Casamance River, Senegal. Related to but distinct from Diola.

Karon: spoken in southwest Senegal, near the Gambia border and the coast. A separate language from Diola.

Kasa: spoken near Diola, Senegal. Also called Casa or Joola-Casa. Related to but distinct from Diola.

Kasanga: 400 speakers reported in 1980, near Felupe, northwest Guinea Bissau, in a sparsely populated border area. Also spoken in Senegal. Also called Kassanga, I-Hadja, or Haal.

Kissi, Northern: 281,000 speakers reported in 1989, with 266,000 in south central Guinea around Kissidoubou, and 15,000 in Sierra Leone. Also called Gizi, Kisi, Kissien, or Kisie. Southern Kissi of Liberia and Sierra Leone is different.

Kissi, Southern: 160,000 speakers reported in 1984, including some 84,700 in Lofa County in the extreme northwest corner of Liberia, and 75,000 in Sierra Leone. Also called Gizi, Kisi, or Kissien. Different from Northern Kissi of Guinea.

Kobiana: 300 speakers reported in 1977, near the Banyun, in Guinea Bissau and Senegal. Also called Uboi or Buy. Speakers are bilingual in Mandyak.

Konyagi: 10,000 speakers reported in 1980, in Guinea and southeast Senegal. Also called Tenda, Duka, or Conhague.

Krim: 12,800 speakers reported in 1981, along the Krim River, Sierra Leone. Also called Kim, Kittim, Kirim, or Kimi. Speakers are bilingual in Sherbro or Mende.

Kwatay: spoken in Diembering and several other villages along the coast just south of the mouth of the Casamance River, Senegal. Also called Kuwataay. Related to but distinct from Diola.

Landoma: 8,000 to 10,000 speakers reported in 1971, between the upper Rio Nunez and the upper Rio Pongas, Guinea. Also called Landouman, Landuma, or Tyapi.

Lehar: 2,500 speakers reported in 1977, north of Thies in west central Senegal, around the towns of Panbal, Mbaraglov, and Dougnan. The speakers refer to themselves as Lala. Population includes 5 percent nearly monolingual, 75 percent with routine ability, and 20 percent with nearly native ability in Wolof. Some are also bilingual in Non, Ndut, or French. Has 84 percent lexical similarity with Non, 74 percent with Safen.

Limba, East: spoken in Guinea. Different from West Limba of Sierra Leone.

Limba, West: around 269,000 speakers reported in 1981, in the north central area north of Makeni, Sierra Leone. Also called Yimbe. Different from East Limba.

Mandyak: 163,000 speakers reported in 1986, including 119,000 west and northwest of Bissao in Guinea Bissau, and 44,200 in southwestern Senegal east of Ziguinchor. Also spoken in The Gambia and the Cape Verde Islands. Also called Manjaca, Manjaco, Manjiak, Manjaku, Manjack, Ndyak, Mendyako, or Kanyop.

Mankanya: 40,000 speakers reported in 1980, including 25,000 northwest of Bissau, Guinea Bissau, and 15,000 scattered in Senegal. Also called Brame, Bola, Mancagne, or Mancang.

Mansoanka: 9,000 or more speakers reported in 1980, in north central Guinea Bissau. Also spoken in the Gambia. Also called Maswanka, Sua, Kunant, or Kunante. Not mutually intelligible with Balanta or Mandinka, although it is sometimes called 'Mandinkanized Balanta'.

Mbulungish: spoken in Guinea. Also called Baga Foré, Baga Monson, or Black Baga. May be mutually intelligible with Nalu and Baga Mboteni.

Nalu: 10,000 speakers reported in 1980, mainly in Guinea, with 5,000 or fewer in southern Guinea Bissau near the coast. May be mutually intelligible with Mbulungish or Baga Mboteni.

Ndut: 15,000 speakers reported in 1977, in west central Senegal northwest of Thies. Also called Ndoute. Population includes 5 percent nearly monolingual, 75 percent with routine ability, and 20 percent with nearly native ability in Wolof. Some are also bilingual in Lehar, Safen, or French. Has 84 percent lexical similarity with Palor, 68 percent with Safen, Non, and Lehar, and 32 percent mutual intelligibility with Palor. Speakers call themselves Ndut.

Non: 15,000 speakers reported in 1977, surrounding Thies and on the coast, Senegal. Also called Serere-Non, Serer, Dyoba, None, or Noon; speakers call themselves Non. Population includes 5 percent nearly monolingual, 75 percent with routine ability, and 20 percent with nearly native ability in Wolof. Some speakers are also bilingual in Lehar and French. Non is very different from Serere-Sine; it has 84 percent lexical similarity with Lehar, 74 percent with Safen, 68 percent with Ndut and Palor, and 22 percent with Serere-Sine.

Palor: 5,000 speakers reported in 1977, in west central Senegal, west southwest of Thies. Also called Falor, Sili, or Sili-Sili; speakers call themselves Waro. Population includes 5 percent nearly monolingual, 75 percent with routine ability, and 20 percent with nearly native ability in Wolof. Some are also bilingual in Safen or French. Has 84 percent lexical similarity with Ndut, 74 percent with Safen.

Papel: around 59,400 or more speakers reported in 1986, on Bissao Island, Guinea Bissau. Also spoken in Guinea. Also called Pepel, Papei, Moium, or Oium.

Safen: 25,000 speakers reported in 1977, to the southwest of Thies, Senegal. Also called Serer-Safen, Serere-Safen, or Saafi; speakers call themselves Safi, and their language Safi-Safi. Population includes 5 percent nearly monolingual, 75 percent with routine ability, and 20 percent with nearly native ability in Wolof. Some are bilingual in Ndut or French. Has 74 percent lexical similarity with Non, Lehar, and Palor, 68 percent with Ndut, and 22 percent with Serere-Sine.

Serer-Sine: around 650,000 speakers reported in 1972, with 420,000 in western Senegal in the Saloum Valley around Joal, and the rest in the Gambia. Also called Serrer, Seereer, Serer-Sin, Sine-Saloum, Seex, or Sine-Sine; speakers call themselves Sereer. One of six national languages of Senegal.

Sherbro: 175,000 speakers reported in 1986, in Southern Province adjoining the Western Area, and in York District on the western peninsula, Sierra Leone. Also called Southern Bullom, Shiba, Amampa, Mampa, or Mampwa. Not mutually intelligible with Krim or Northern Bullom.

Themne: 960,000 speakers estimated in 1981, in Northern Province, west of the Sewa River to Little Scarcie, Sierra Leone. Also called Temne, Timne, Timene, Timmannee, or Temen. Used as a second language by 240,000 speakers of neighboring languages. It is the predominant language of central Sierra Leone.

Toucouleur: 1,680,000 speakers reported in 1986, with 603,000 in the Senegal River Valley, 150,000 in Mauritania, and 50,000 in the Gambia. Also spoken in Guinea near Dinguiray, western Mali, Burkina Faso, and Nigeria. Also called Tukulor, Tokolor, Pulaar, or Haalpulaar. Officially recognized in Senegal.

Wolof, Gambian: around 86,900 speakers reported in 1986, in west and central Gambia. Different from Wolof of Senegal.

Wolof, Senegalese: 2,000,000 to 3,000,000 first-language speakers reported in 1989, in western and central Senegal, on the left bank of the Senegal River to Cape Vert. Also spoken in Mauritania and France. Also called Yallof, Walaf, Volof, or Waro-Waro; speakers call themselves Wolof. It is the main African language of Senegal, and the second language of at least 500,000 people, predominantly urban. Different from Wolof of Gambia, although related.

ATTITUDES TO LANGUAGE. In initial interactions, our views of others—including their supposed beliefs, capabilities, and social attributes—can be determined in part by inferences derived from our perception of their speech characteristics and language varieties. Indeed, our overt responses and communications to speakers, as well as important social decisions regarding their prospects and welfare, can be mediated by our so-called 'language attitudes'. These, in turn, can influence our own self-presentations, as we attempt to shape others' reactions to us, and their attributions of us; thus these attitudes contribute to our usage of different speech styles, dialects, creoles, and second languages in various contexts and phases of our lives. Not surprisingly, the role of language attitudes has been integral to the sociolinguistic description of many speech communities; and it is often a contributing factor in LANGUAGE PLANNING and policies. [*See* Sociolinguistics, *article on* Language Planning.] For reference, see Shuy & Fasold 1973, Cooper 1974–75, Giles & Powesland 1975, Williams 1976, Edwards 1979, Giles & Edwards 1983.

Following largely from Wallace Lambert's and William Labov's pioneering work in this domain in the 1960s, there have been an array of integrative overviews, recently that of Giles et al. 1987. Although different methods have been employed (e.g. surveys or media analyses), most examine how listeners react to supposedly different speakers reading the same neutral passage of prose. Attitudes toward speakers are tapped by means of ratings scales, which usually involve the evaluative dimensions of competence, solidarity, and dynamism. A favored method in this instance (given its advantage of experimental control) is the MATCHED GUISE technique: this utilizes 'stimulus' speakers who can assume authentic versions of the dialects, languages, or speech variables under study, while keeping other extraneous variables constant (for discussions of its methodological and empirical limitations, see Ryan & Giles 1982, chap. 13). Other types of studies, e.g. investigations of attitudes toward children's voices, adopt the procedure of using different representatives of the targeted language varieties.

A consistent, global finding is that standard-dialect or prestige varieties (and code-switches or shifts to them) confer advantages on speakers: they are stereotyped as relatively more competent and confident than their less prestigious-sounding counterparts; and their messages are perceived as having more qualitative substance and memorizability. It is interesting to note that listener/judges have often been prepared to record their language attitudes after hearing only about fifteen seconds of the stimulus. Such findings appear to be socialized in complex ways early in childhood, and to persist into later life; they have been elicited just as easily when visual cues of the speakers are available via video recordings. Moreover, the more different the 'accented' variety is from the prestige form—listeners have been shown to discriminate nine points along such a continuum—the lower, usually, are the evaluations on competence traits. However, non-prestige speakers can also have 'covert prestige'; they may then, although less consistently, be upgraded in terms of integrity and social attractiveness. [*See* Social Dialects.] Indeed, this phenomenon can be transformed into evaluative pride when the non-standard dialect is, for certain users, a valued symbol of membership in a social group (e.g. a class, ethnic group, or religion).

Other investigators have been interested in attitudes toward the code-mixing of languages common to their locale, the social meanings of which (in terms of positive values) vary cross-culturally. Standard varieties, such as R[eceived] P[ronunciation] English, appear to transcend national boundaries, and assume status across the Anglophone world (for Francophone and Hispanic settings, see Ryan & Giles 1982, chaps. 3–4); naturally enough, different non-standard varieties within any culture can themselves be hierarchically organized. Numerous studies have investigated individual and socio-demographic differences (e.g. ethnocentrism, cognitive complexity, age, gender, or cultural group membership) among listener/judges; they have demonstrated that the latters' cognitive schemata can mediate the effects thus far outlined. For example, Americans downgrade Hispanic speakers in direct proportion to the narrowness and restrictiveness of the formers' speech norms. And although important contextual caveats abound (e.g. relating to socio-physical setting, language of investigator, or timing of evaluations), the above profile has, for the most part, remained ubiquitous. It is when significant changes in socio-political history or message content are evident that radical modifications to the general evaluative pattern emerge.

When we focus on vocal features other than strictly

dialectal ones, CONTEXT has compelling effects. For instance, a positive linear relationship has repeatedly been found between speech rate and perceived competence; but this effect can be obliterated when the rating task is taken out of its 'social vacuum'. Therefore, when listeners were allowed access to information that a male speaker was taped while helping a naive audience comprehend an unfamiliar topic, they evaluated him as just as intelligent and competent when he talked slowly, as when he said the same thing much faster (in a typical monolog condition). Strictly non-dialectal characteristics such as lexical diversity, pausing, self-disclosure, pitch, or language intensity (which all have their own social meanings) are manipulated orthogonally and with other social attributes of speakers, e.g. socio-economic status; the findings of recent, more ambitious experiments suggest that the differing cues may then act together in an evaluatively cumulative fashion (Bradac 1990). Thus the least favorable judgments have been rendered against a combination of non-standard accent, low lexical diversity, and a working-class background; the opposite pattern emerged for speakers characterized by higher status rankings on these factors. Interestingly, accent can invoke less potent evaluations than either lexical diversity or speech rate.

Many processes are implicated in a shift of emphasis from expressed attitudes to actual language behaviors; nevertheless, the social consequences of language attitudes are considerable when it comes to applied domains. For instance, Australian listeners were presented with audiotapes of speakers with different accents who were accused of various crimes, and were heard protesting their innocence to one crime. RP speakers were seen as more guilty when the offence was embezzlement (a white-collar crime), whereas Australian-accented speakers were more severely judged when the crime was physical assault. Moving to Canada, reported judgments of job suitability for four foreign-accented speakers were elicited; for high-status employment, the descending order was English, German, South Asian, and West Indian, but this was reversed for low-status work. Interestingly, voice cues have been shown to predominate over physical appearance and actual schoolwork in assessments of school children's abilities by Canadian and Australian trainee teachers. Despite this, studies that examine supposed 'incongruities' between spoken language varieties and associated visual cues or other background information (e.g. middle-class-looking individual with non-standard speech) suggest that these relationships are highly complex and cue-specific—and as such, do not yet yield generalizable patterns.

Important empirical studies (usually not on-going ones) continue to be reported from different parts of the world (e.g. Nigeria, People's Republic of China); they are usually published as journal articles (see, in particular, the *Journal of Language and Social Psychology*). However, there is evidence of a movement away from the traditional research paradigm, and toward more concern for both theory development and precise linguistic specifications of the speech stimuli utilized. Such shifts are manifest in explorations of such topics as the following:

(a) The social functions of language attitudes, and the attributions which both underlie and are a consequence of them
(b) The fluctuating macro-societal backdrop to language attitudes, and the mediating role of listener/judges' social identities
(c) A focus upon beliefs about talk in general, as well as particular modes of it (e.g. marital)

Other more provocative prospects are now in view. Although not directed toward the area of language attitudes per se, Billig 1987 and Potter & Wetherell 1987 have, independently, begun to challenge (if not deconstruct) the very notion of 'attitude', as currently measured and conceptualized in social psychology. Indeed, this is the very bedrock upon which language attitude studies have been based. The latter scholars not only point to the variability inherent in people's social attitudes as expressed in talk (even within the same conversation); they also question whether attitudes can be abstracted in the minds of individuals, away from the objects to which they are assumed to be targeted in the 'outside' world. Independently yet relatedly, research has shown that our judgments about how people actually sound and speak can itself be a constantly redefining process of social construction and can be dependent on, e.g., cognitive biases. Hence 'language varieties' and 'attitudes' are symbiotically related in a subjective sense, and are not dichotomous entities. Billig also considers attitudes in a wider historical context, as positions in an argument, which are embedded in particular social controversies. An attitude in this sense is not only an explicit appraisal, for or against a position, but also includes an implicit stance against counter-positions. Moreover, justifications and criticism are viewed as part and parcel of attitudes, not as epiphenomena derived from them; they should become sharpened and modified as the argumentative context changes. Further development of these two approaches should eludicate how we negotiate our language attitudes rhetorically and interactively (Giles & Coupland 1991); it may well lead to more discourse-based and observational studies to complement traditional methods in the future.

HOWARD GILES

BIBLIOGRAPHY

BILLIG, MICHAEL. 1987. *Arguing and thinking: A rhetorical approach to social psychology.* Cambridge & New York: Cambridge University Press.

BRADAC, JAMES J. 1990. Language attitudes and impression formation. In *Handbook of language and social psychology,* edited by Howard Giles & W. Peter Robinson, pp. 387–412. Chichester, England: Wiley.

COOPER, ROBERT L., ed. 1974–75. *Language attitudes.* 2 vols. (International Journal of the Sociology of Language, 3, 6.) Amsterdam: Mouton.

EDWARDS, JOHN R. 1979. *Language and disadvantage.* London: Arnold. New York: Elsevier.

GILES, HOWARD, & JOHN EDWARDS, eds. 1983. *Language attitudes in multilingual settings.* (Journal of Multilingual and Multicultural Development, 4:2–3.) Clevedon, Avon, England: Multilingual Matters.

GILES, HOWARD, & NIKOLAS COUPLAND. 1991. Language attitudes: Discursive, contextual and gerontological considerations. In *Bilingualism, Multiculturalism, and second language learning: The McGill Conference in Honor of Wallace E. Lambert,* edited by Allan G. Reynolds, to appear. Hillsdale, N.J.: Erlbaum.

GILES, HOWARD, & PETER F. POWESLAND. 1975. *Speech style and social evaluation.* London: Academic Press.

GILES, HOWARD, et al. 1987. Research on language attitudes. In *Sociolinguistics: An international handbook of the science of language and society,* edited by Ulrich Ammon et al., vol. 1, pp. 585–597. Berlin: de Gruyter.

POTTER, JONATHAN, & MARGARET WETHERELL. 1987. *Discourse and social psychology.* London: Sage.

RYAN, ELLEN B., & HOWARD GILES, eds. 1982. *Attitudes towards language variation: Social and applied contexts.* London: Arnold.

SHUY, ROGER, & RALPH W. FASOLD, eds. 1973. *Language attitudes: Current trends and prospects.* Washington, D.C.: Center for Applied Linguistics.

WILLIAMS, FREDERICK. 1976. *Explorations of the linguistic attitudes of teachers.* Rowley, Mass.: Newbury House.

AUSTRALIAN LANGUAGES were spoken, before the European invasion (which began in 1788), by about six hundred Aboriginal tribes. Some contiguous tribes spoke what can be considered dialects of a single language; others spoke distinct languages. About two hundred different languages existed, with populations ranging from five hundred to ten thousand. Most are now extinct; some are still spoken, but are not being learned by children, and will become extinct within a few generations. Only about twenty can now be considered 'healthy'—still in daily use, and being learned by children.

All Australian languages have similar phonological systems (see below). An agglutinative, suffixing morphological profile (called the Pama-Nyungan type) is found over 90 percent of the continent. The remaining languages, in the central north, have a polysynthetic structure, with prefixes (which provide pronominal cross-reference of subject, object, etc.) and some suffixes. Recent comparative work suggests that all the Pama-Nyungan languages and most or all the prefixing tongues do belong to a single language family. Attempts to establish genetic links between Australian and language families elsewhere have so far yielded no firm results. For general surveys, see Dixon 1980 and Blake 1987; see also Map 1. [*For data on individual languages, see the Language List at the end of this article.*]

1. Phonology. Most Australian languages are remarkably similar, both in their inventories of consonant and vowel phonemes and in their phonotactic structures. There are generally no fricatives or sibilants, and voicing is not phonologically contrastive for stops. There can be from four to seven stops, with a nasal corresponding to each, and from one to four laterals. All languages have two semivowels, and almost all show two rhotics—an apico-alveolar trill, and an apico-postalveolar (semi-retroflex) continuant.

Comparative evidence indicates that P[roto-]A[ustralian] had a relatively small inventory of stops: labial *b,* apical *d,* laminal *j,* and dorsal *g*; there would have been a nasal corresponding to each stop. Some modern languages preserve this system; others have split apical and/or laminal and/or dorsal into phonemically contrastive series. It is likely that the PA laminal stop and nasal had lamino-palatal pronunciation (blade against hard palate) before *i,* and lamino-dental (blade against teeth) before *a* and *u.* Some modern languages preserve this allophonic distribution; but others have innovated lamino-dentals before *i,* and/or lamino-palatals before *a* and *u,* so that they now have two laminal stop and two laminal nasal phonemes. Similarly, the apical stop and nasal originally had a postalveolar (retroflex) articulation after *u,* but apico-alveolar articulation elsewhere. Some modern languages have also developed a phonemic contrast

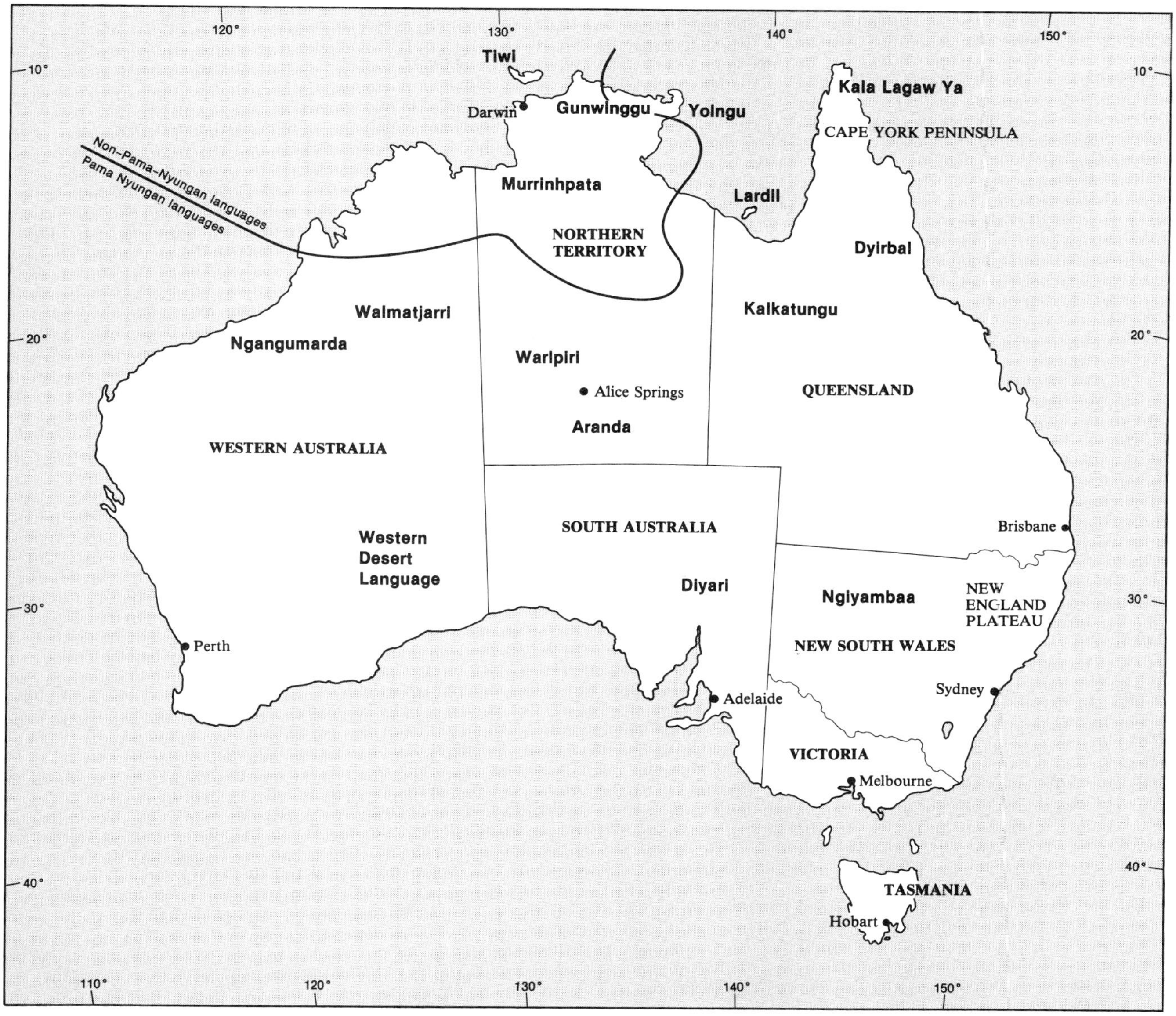

MAP 1. *Distribution of Some Languages of Australia*

between apico-alveolars and apico-postalveolars. The third split, of dorsal stop and nasal into dorso-palatal and dorso-velar series, has taken place very recently, in only two or three languages.

Languages in the western two-thirds of the continent generally have a lateral in each apical and laminal series, while those in the eastern third have a single, apico-alveolar lateral.

A system of three vowels, /a i u/, is likely for PA. This is retained in most modern languages, though five-vowel systems have developed in the northern, prefixing area. A contrast between long and short vowels applied in PA for at least the first, stressed, syllable of a word; this has been retained in some modern languages from all parts of the continent, but long and short vowels have fallen together in others.

Unusual phonological systems are found in a minority of languages from widely separated areas—the center, the New England Highlands in eastern New South Wales, and parts of Cape York Peninsula in northeast Queensland. Similar changes have applied, quite independently, in all these areas. Basically, an initial consonant has been lost, and often also the following vowel. Allophonic variants in medial consonants and vowels, conditioned by some part of the initial syllable, have become phonemically contrastive, after loss of the conditioning environment. Thus fricative phonemes, pre-stopped nasals and laterals, and more extensive vowel systems have evolved in these limited areas.

2. Morphology. Each N[oun] P[hrase] typically bears a case inflection indicating its function in the sentence (one inflection is absolutive, which in most languages has zero realization). In many languages, the case inflection appears on every word in the NP; the words from a phrase may then be scattered through the sentence (word order is remarkably free in many Australian languages). In a few languages, the case inflection can be added just to the last word in a NP.

Four nominal cases can be reconstructed for PA: ABSOLUTIVE, for intransitive subject (S) and transitive object (O) functions; ERGATIVE, for transitive subject function (the abbreviation A is used, reminiscent of 'Agent'); GENERAL LOCATIVE; and DATIVE/GENITIVE. Increments could probably be added to some of these inflections; e.g., the ablative involved a clitic on the general locative (cf. Blake 1977).

Most prefixing languages have dropped the ergative inflection, since information as to which NP is subject is coded in the verb. A few retain ergative case, but use it sparingly—only when ambiguity might otherwise result. Non-prefixing languages (i.e. Pama-Nyungan) have generally augmented the PA case system; most have six to eight nominal inflections.

In most Australian languages, pronouns have a NOMINATIVE case form for transitive subject (A) and intransitive subject (S), and an ACCUSATIVE form for transitive object (O). This is in marked contrast with the ABSOLUTIVE/ERGATIVE system of inflection on nouns and adjectives. [*See* Transitivity and Argument Coding.] Most other nominal case inflections apply rather regularly to pronouns.

The commonest system in Australia shows singular, dual, and plural distinctions for 1st and 2nd person pronouns. A few languages also have trial number; and a few others have just singular and non-singular, lacking a dual. About half the languages have an inclusive/exclusive distinction for 1st person dual and plural.

Many Pama-Nyungan languages have bound pronominal enclitics, which are attached to the verb or to the first word of the sentence. These, and bound pronominal prefixes in northern languages, are all of a nominative/accusative pattern.

Each verb in an Australian language is either strictly transitive—occurring in a sentence with NPs in A and O functions—or else strictly intransitive—occurring only with a core NP in S function. There is typically a range of derivational affixes used to form transitive stems from intransitive roots, reflexives and reciprocals (derived intransitive stems) from transitive roots, and so on.

There are typically from two to six verbal conjugations; each verbal stem takes the set of inflectional endings associated with the conjugation to which it belongs. Conjugational membership correlates with—but does not coincide with—transitivity class; 80 percent of the members of one conjugation will be transitive, 70 percent of another will be intransitive, etc. There is typically a rich set of verbal inflections, marking aspect and tense. Perhaps the most pervasive verbal inflection is purposive *-gu* (probably cognate with the nominal dative/genitive *-gu*); on a main clause verb, it indicates desire or necessity ('I SHOULD go'), while in a subordinate clause it marks a consequential activity ('I went IN ORDER TO spear wallabies.')

3. Syntax. Since syntactic function is marked by case inflections and/or by cross-referencing elements in the verb, word order can be quite free. Most Australian languages have the underlying orders A[gent] O[bject] V[erb], S[ubject] V, and noun + adjective within a NP; but there can be unlimited variation from these patterns.

Most Australian languages, especially those outside the prefixing area, have syntactic devices to indicate coreferentiality of NPs within complex sentence constructions. A number of languages in South Australia and adjacent portions of Western Australia and the Northern Territory show SWITCH-REFERENCE marking: the verb of a subordinate clause bears one inflection if it has the same subject as the main clause, but a different inflection if their subjects differ (cf. Austin 1981).

Some languages require that a NP be common to main and subordinate clauses in a complex sentence; the NP must be in S or O function in each clause. There must then be a grammatical derivation (i.e., a transformation) by which an underlying NP in A function is placed in surface S function. This is referred to as the ANTIPASSIVE derivation: deep A becomes surface S, deep O is marked by an oblique case (dative, locative, or instrumental, in different languages), and the verb bears an antipassive derivational suffix. In two small areas of the continent, the antipassive construction has been adopted as the unmarked transitive construction, and the verbal antipassive marking is dropped; this produces a grammatical system which is nominative/accusative in both morphology and syntax.

4. Speech styles. Perhaps every Australian language has a special speech style which must be used in the presence of a taboo relative (for a male, his mother-in-law). Sometimes the avoidance style involves only a few score special lexical forms; but one group of eastern tribes has a complete second vocabulary, with no lexical form common to avoidance and everyday styles (there is, in fact, a many-to-one correspondence between everyday and avoidance lexemes).

Some tribes also have 'secret languages' confined to initiated males. Initiands of the Lardil tribe learn Damin, which has a quite different phonology from their everyday speech style; it involves nasalized clicks, an ingressive lateral fricative, and glottalized ejective stops.

5. Tasmanian. At the end of the 19th century, Tasmanians were believed to be non-Australian in physical type, culture, and language. Anthropologists have now re-assessed the physical and cultural evidence; it is generally believed that the Tasmanians were a group of Australian Aborigines, isolated when their island was cut off by the rising sea level about twelve thousand years ago. Pitifully little information was gathered on Tasmanian languages before they ceased to be spoken, at the end of the 19th century; there were probably eight to twelve distinct languages. Information on Tasmanian phonology suggests that the languages were typologically similar to those of Australia. No information on grammar is available. Only a few, dubious lexical cognates can be recognized between Tasmanian and mainland languages.

R. M. W. Dixon

BIBLIOGRAPHY

Austin, Peter. 1981. Switch-reference in Australia. *Language* 57.309–334.

Blake, Barry J. 1977. *Case marking in Australian languages*. Canberra: Australian Institute of Aboriginal Studies.

Blake, Barry J. 1987. *Australian Aboriginal grammar*. London: Croom Helm.

Dixon, R. M. W. 1980. *The languages of Australia*. Cambridge & New York: Cambridge University Press.

LANGUAGE LIST

[For data on individual languages, see the Language Lists following the articles on Australian language families:

Bunaban Languages
Burarran Languages
Daly Languages
Djamindjungan Languages
Djeragan Languages
Gunwingguan Languages
Iwaidjan Languages
Laragiyan Languages
Mangerrian Languages
Maran Languages
Nyulnyulan Languages
Pama-Nyungan Languages
West Barkly Languages
Wororan Languages

In addition, data are given below on languages of isolated status or unclear classification.]

Anindilyakwa: some 1,000 speakers reported in 1983, in Groote Eylandt, Gulf of Carpintaria, Northern Territory. Also called Enindiljaugwa, Wanindilyaugwa, Ingura, or Groote Eylandt. Most young people are bilingual in English.

Gagadu: 6 speakers reported in 1981, in Oenpelli, Northern Territory, Australia. Also called Kakdjuan, Kakdju, Abdedal, or Kakakta. All speakers are bilingual in some other Aboriginal language.

Garawa: 350 speakers reported in 1985, in Borroloola, Northern Territory, and Doomadgee, Queensland. Also called Karawa or Leearrawa.

Gungaragany: 5 speakers reported in 1981, in Northern Territory, Australia, on the Finniss River, and south of Darwin around the Darwin River and Rum Jungle. Also called Gunerakan, Kangarraga, or Kungarakan.

Limilngan: 3 speakers reported in 1981, in Northern Territory, Australia, in Arnhem Land between the Mary and West Alligator Rivers, from the coast and inland. Also called Manadja or Minitji. It may be the same as Lemil (Norweilimil) or Manaidja (Manatja, Mandatja).

Ngurmbur: 1 speaker reported in 1981, in Arnhem Land, between the West and South Alligator Rivers, northeast of Umbugarla, Northern Territory, Australia. Also called Gnormbur, Gnumbu, Koarnbut, or Oormbur.

Tiwi: 1,500 speakers (including non-fluent speakers) reported in 1983, on Bathurst and Melville Islands, Nguiu, Northern Territory, Australia. All people are bilingual in English.

Umbugarla: 3 speakers reported in 1981, in Arnhem Land, southeast of Limilngan, between the Mary River and the South Alligator River, Northern Territory, Australia.

AUSTRO-ASIATIC LANGUAGES.

A[ustro-]A[siatic] is probably the most 'archaic' family in Southeast Asia and East India, in the sense that nearly all its languages are surrounded by more recent arrivals of the Austronesian, Tai-Kadai, Sino-Tibetan, and Indo-European families, or are retreating under the advance of these languages. For useful literature, see Zide 1966 and Jenner et al. 1976; see also Map 1.

1. Subclassification. The primary split of AA is between the M[on-]K[hmer] and Munda families [*qq.v.*]; the former are far more differentiated.

MK comprises well over one hundred languages. The mid-level subclassification of the family into some twelve

MAP 1. *Distribution of Austro-Asiatic Languages*

branches is clear; however, there are uncertainties in the assignment of several of these branches to certain higher-level divisions.

The Northern division of MK contains three branches: Khmuic, Palaungic, and Khasian. The Khmuic branch, found mostly in northern Laos and northern Thailand, includes the Khmu language with its many dialects, the Mal-Phrai languages, and Mlabri, spoken by hunter/gatherers nicknamed 'Spirits of the yellow leaves'.

The Palaungic branch is a very large subfamily, formerly called Palaung-Wa; it extends over northern Thailand and Laos, eastern Burma, and southwestern Yunnan. The Eastern sub-branch of Palaungic contains several Palaung languages, the Riang dialects, and Danau. The

Western sub-branch contains three language groups: Waic, Angkuic, and Lametic. The most differentiated of these is the Waic group, which includes Bulang, the many Lawa dialects, and the Wa languages, totaling over half a million speakers. The Angkuic group includes several very small and nearly unknown languages: Angku, U, Hu, Mok, Man Met, and Kiorr.

The Khasian branch is found in northeastern India in the state of Meghalaya, where Khasi is the official language. Several so-called Khasi dialects, such as Synteng, Lyng-ngam, and Amwi (also called War), are clearly distinct but related languages.

To this North MK division may be added the very small Mang language located on the border of Vietnam and China.

The Eastern division of MK contains at least three branches: Khmeric, Bahnaric, and Katuic. The Khmeric branch contains a single language, Khmer [*q.v.*], the national language of Cambodia, with Pre-Angkorian inscriptions beginning in the 6th century CE, and distinct dialects spoken in parts of Thailand and Vietnam.

The Bahnaric branch comprises about thirty-five languages located in central and southern Vietnam, southern Laos, and eastern Cambodia; it is divided into four parts. The South Bahnaric sub-branch constitutes a closely knit group of four languages—Srê, Mnong, Stieng, and Chrau, each with numerous dialects. Central Bahnaric includes Bahnar itself and several nearly unknown languages, such as Lamam and Tampuan. West Bahnaric is the least known sub-branch, including Brao, Nya-heuny, Oy, and at least six other languages of southern Laos. The North Bahnaric branch is better known, and includes Monom, Kayong, Takua, Rengao, Sedang, Hrê, Jeh, Halang, and Cua. In the ethnographic literature, these are the 'Montagnards' of the Vietnamese Highlands.

The languages of the Katuic branch are found in central Vietnam, central Laos, northeastern Thailand, and northern Cambodia. The West Katuic sub-branch includes Kuy, Bru, and Sô; the East Katuic sub-branch includes Katu, Pacoh, Ngeq, and the little known Katang, Ta-oih, Yir, Klor, and Ong.

To this East MK division might be added the languages of the Pearic branch, spoken by very small groups in western Cambodia: the Samrê, Pear, Sa-och, and Chong. These languages have been heavily influenced by Khmer.

The Viet-Muong (Vietic) branch seems to form a division by itself, though there are signs that would favor including it in the East MK division. Besides Vietnamese [*q.v.*], it comprises the Muong languages of northern Vietnam, plus two more distant sub-branches—the Cuôi languages (Uy-Lô, Hung, Pọong, Không Khêng), and the Chứt languages (Arem, Sách, Mày, Rục). To these can be added Thavứng, Pakatan, Phon Soung, and a few others spoken across the border in northern Laos. In the past, the Vietnamese language has often been classified with Chinese, or even with the Tai languages; but more recent studies show that the Muong, Cuôi, and Chứt languages, obviously related to Vietnamese but much less Sinicized, offer decisive arguments for including Vietnamese in MK, or at least in AA.

The Palyu language, called Lai in Chinese, was recently discovered on the border of Guang Xi and Gui Zhou provinces; it may be a distant offshoot of the Viet-Muong branch—or, more probably, an isolate within Mon-Khmer.

Recent work shows that the Monic branch, contrary to earlier opinion, is rather distant from the languages of the East MK division. It comprises only two languages: Mon of Burma and Thailand (with Old Mon inscriptions beginning in the 6th c. CE), and Nyahkur, spoken in eastern central Thailand (Diffloth 1984).

The Aslian branch of interior Malaysia is not a distant offshoot of AA, as previously thought; it clearly fits within MK, and may actually form (together with Monic) a southern division of the family. Aslian comprises about sixteen languages: a Senoic sub-branch (Semai, Temiar, Lanoh, Semnam, Sabum), previously known as 'Sakai'; a North Aslian sub-branch (Kintaq, Kensiw, Menriq, Jahai, Batek, Cheq Wong), previously known as 'Semang'; a South Aslian sub-branch (Mah Meri, Semelai, Semaq Beri, Temoq); and Jah Hut as a sub-branch by itself.

The languages of the Nicobar Islands, of at least four groups (Car, Nancowry, Great Nicobarese, and Chaura-Teressa), have also been considered a distant offshoot of AA. However, recent information suggests that they may form yet another branch of MK.

The Munda family is smaller, and is located in eastern India—primarily in the states of Bengal, Orissa, Bihar, and Andhra Pradesh. It is divided into North and South Munda subfamilies, which are quite different from each other. The North Munda languages are fairly closely related, in two branches: Korku, and Kherwarian (which includes Santali, Mundari, and Ho). The South Munda subfamily consists of Kharia-Juang (Central Munda) and Koraput Munda; the latter branches into Gutob-Remo-Geta' and Sora-Juray-Gorum. There are about five million speakers of Munda languages; the great majority are of the North Munda group.

It is difficult to think of more different linguistic types than those represented by Munda and MK; for this reason, some linguists have questioned their genetic relationship. Yet there are several common or reconstructed features which probably go back to Proto-AA. [*For data on individual Austro-Asiatic languages, see the Language Lists after the articles on Aslian, East Mon-Khmer, Munda, Nicobarese, North Mon-Khmer, and Viet-Muong languages. For data on the Monic and Palyu branches, see the Language List at the end of this article.*]

2. Features shared by the branches. A phonetic feature of nearly all AA languages is non-release of final stops; to be sure, this is the phonetic norm across language families in the Southeast Asian area, but it stands out as a characteristic feature of the Munda languages in the Indian linguistic area.

In phonology, both Munda and MK have complete sets of stops and nasals in root-final position in four places of articulation: velar, palatal, alveolar, and labial. In MK, but not necessarily in Munda, this position coincides with the end of the word. There is a dearth of spirants in the modern languages: typically, only *s* is found in Munda, and *s h* in MK. The canonical root forms of Proto-AA exclude final clusters, but require at least one final consonant. Many modern languages have relaxed this rule by losing final ʔ, thus allowing final open syllables. There is a great variety and frequency of consonant sequences word-initially. Attempts, notably by Schmidt 1907, to analyze complex initials as necessarily containing affixes, leaving only a single initial consonant per root, are no longer convincing: many of the purported affixes have no clearly recurrent meaning, or any other justification.

Morphologically, the nominalizing *-n-* infix is found in most AA languages, though it is much less common in Munda than in the rest of the family; the same is true of the causative labial prefix. Both these features are also old in Austronesian; this, among other things, led Schmidt to propose an Austric superstock which included AA and Austronesian.

Also common to MK and Munda is the presence of a basic lexical class of EXPRESSIVES. Adverb-like, but without predicative force, these words are similar in some ways to African ideophones. They rely primarily on iconic means to evoke sensations of all kinds, especially in the domain of visual patterns. Their rich morphology is made of iconic diagrams—e.g., partial reduplications, substitutions, infixed copying and systematic distortions—often akin to deliberate language games.

3. Distinctive Mon-Khmer features. Characteristic of all MK languages, but never of Munda, are the presence of fixed ultimate-syllable stress, and the absence of suffixation. Apparent suffixes—found in Nicobarese, some Aslian languages, and Modern Spoken Mon—seem better described as phrase-final clitics. These two features concur in making the final, 'major', syllable the richest and most stable part of the word; this is an areal feature of mainland Southeast Asian languages [*q.v.*].

The non-final, 'minor', syllables have a poor consonant inventory, as well as a vocalism which is reduced to a single possible vowel—except in Katuic and Aslian, where three or four different vowels are possible in this position. Most languages allow only one minor syllable to precede the major syllable, giving rise to a distinct language type termed 'sesquisyllabic'; this is typologically halfway between the monosyllabic languages to the north and west of MK, and the disyllabic or polysyllabic languages to the south and east.

The most notable feature of MK phonology is the large number of possible vowels in major syllables. Systems are known with five degrees of height in the front, central, and back series; and systems with four are common. Diphthongized nuclei, broken vowels, and short vowels add to the inventory, as do nasalization and phonation types. All counted, sixty-eight contrastive vocalic nuclei, probably a world record, have been claimed for one variety of Bru. Vowel systems with twenty or more units are not unusual.

Phonological contrasts in the phonation-types of vowels, termed 'voice-register' or simply REGISTER, are also characteristic of MK languages. The most common is a two-way contrast of breathy vs. clear phonation, as in Paraok, Mon, Kuy, Bru, Jeh, Halang, and certain dialects of Western Khmer. However, three-way and even four-way register contrasts, as in Chong, have been recorded. Register can be accompanied by phonetic features of diphthongization, vowel height, and pitch. Some languages, e.g. Nyah Kur, appear to be in a transitional stage from register to tone, and display both phenomena. Others, e.g. Vietnamese, are clearly tonal, but have distinct phonations which are redundantly tied to certain tones. However, the MK family has far more register languages than tone languages (the latter include U, Bulang, and Vietnamese).

Historically, the appearance of a breathy vs. clear contrast in vowels is often the result of a devoicing of initial consonants; but there are other kinds of 'registrogenesis'. It is even possible that Proto-AA had a creaky vs. clear vowel contrast, and was thus already a register language. The evolution of MK registers is intimately tied to the history of the large vowel systems, which remains mostly unknown at present.

In sharp contrast with the situation in Munda, MK morphology practically never indicates syntactic agreement. This morphology is usually derivational and non-productive—with a few exceptions, e.g. in the Aslian branch. Its typical function is to change the grammatical class or subclass of the base to which it is attached, e.g. from noun to verb, from intransitive to transitive and vice-versa, or from mass to count noun. There is a great semantic variety of causative formations and nominalizations.

The most original feature of the MK family is the presence of a great number and variety of infixes. These consist of a nasal, a liquid, or a simple vowel, inserted immediately after the first consonant of the base. It would be tempting to see here the result of an ancient process of metathesis and resyllabification, from original prefixed vocalic segments. However, there are examples of multiple infixations; and at least one non-vocalic infix, *-p-*, would be difficult to explain in this way. There are also a few languages—e.g. Lamet, Semai, Temiar, and Semelai—where practically any consonant can become an infix through a regular morphological process, which consists in copying the final consonant of the root and inserting it after the word-initial consonant: from a Semai root *cəkɔt* 'to tie' is derived *cətkɔt* 'to be tying'. This process is also found in Khmu expressives, and may have its origin in deliberate iconic sound-play.

In languages where expressives have been described—e.g. Pacoh, Khmu, Bahnar, and Semai—this word class displays a profusion of morphological patterns, including different kinds of partial or modified reduplication. Numerous substitutions of segments are possible, and convey gradations of meaning, especially with the many vowels available in such languages. It then becomes difficult to identify the root morpheme, or to describe these iconic patterns as instances of morphology. A theoretical solution to this problem would require the creation of an aesthetic component of grammar, in which iconic systems could be described.

In syntax, MK languages consistently place the object after the verb, the possessed after the possessor, the attribute after the noun, and deictics at the end of the noun phrase. This group of properties, which was identified by Schmidt 1907, forms a coherent linguistic type found all over Southeast Asia. It is diametrically opposed to that found in the Munda languages, and more generally in the Indian linguistic area.

The place of the subject with respect to the verb is not so neatly patterned. Most languages have the order S[ubject] V[erb] O[bject] when O is expressed, agreeing in this with the pattern of the dominant Tai family. But when there is no O, several languages have the verb in first position. A few languages, e.g. in the Wa group, do this for all sentence types, at least as an option. Some others have 'verb-first' as a basic order in certain constructions, but disguise it by preposing an apparent subject. Thus, in Khmer, what seems to be a SVO sentence—*khñom chɨ: kba:l* (lit. 'I sick head') 'I have a headache'—is actually an intransitive construction with the verb in first position *chɨ: kba:l* ('hurt + head'), and *khñom* 'I' preposed as an apparent subject. A closer translation would thus be 'My head hurts.' Since no neighboring language family provides a model for this pattern, there is a possibility that MK languages were originally 'verb-first', at least as an option.

4. Distinctive Munda features include an elaborate system of demonstratives, found in some of the languages, and the complex and productive morphology found in most. Certain functional properties, e.g. elaborate deixis, are common to the whole of Munda; but the systems are morphologically quite different from language to language, and are only partly cognate in terms of reconstructible morphemes and constructions.

The most elaborate demonstrative systems are found in Santali (North Munda) and Gtaˀ (South Munda). Number, gender (animate vs. inanimate), direct vs. lateral perception, sensory modality (visual vs. the rest), particularizing, emphasis, and features relating to participants in the deictic scenario can be marked in one or both of these systems. In addition, expressive features (stem vowel lengthening, reduplication, and echoing) are used in forms heavily marked for the features listed above.

The Munda verb, very different in this regard from MK, marks a variety of verbal categories of tense, aspect, and mood. In South Munda, suffixation, infixation, and prefixation are used; in North Munda, suffixation is predominant. One characteristic of the South Munda verb is the presence of two sets of tense suffixes: one for intransitives, and the other for transitives. In

Gtaʔ, two 'past' morphemes, *-ge* and *-ke*, are found; but they can mark any of a half-dozen or more different semantic features.

A negative conjugation can perhaps be reconstructed for South Munda; it contains a negative element prefixed to the positive verb form. But strangely enough, the negatives are formed not from the corresponding positives, but rather from other tense/mood forms that seem to be selected arbitrarily. Thus, in Gtaʔ, the negative of the past is formed by adding *ar-* to the 'customary' positive verb form; the negative imperative is formed from the past, and so on.

GÉRARD DIFFLOTH & NORMAN ZIDE

BIBLIOGRAPHY

DIFFLOTH, GÉRARD. 1984. *The Dvaravati Old Mon language and Nyah Kur.* Bangkok: Chulalongkorn University.

JENNER, PHILIP N., et al., eds. 1976. *Austroasiatic studies.* 2 vols. (Oceanic linguistics, Special publication, 13.) Honolulu: University of Hawaii Press.

SCHMIDT, WILHELM. 1907. *Die Mon-Khmer-Völker: Ein Bindeglied zwischen Völkern Zentralasiens und Austronesiens.* Braunschweig: Vieweg. Translated as *Les peuples mon-khmêr: Traît d'union entre les peuples de l'Asie centrale et de l'Austronésie* (Bulletin de l'École Française d'Extrême-Orient, 7–8; Hanoi, 1907).

ZIDE, NORMAN H., ed. 1966. *Studies in comparative Austroasiatic linguistics.* (Indo-Iranian monographs, 5.) The Hague: Mouton.

LANGUAGE LIST

[*For data on Aslian, East Mon-Khmer, Munda, Nicobarese, North Mon-Khmer, and Viet-Muong languages, see corresponding articles. Data on languages of the Monic and Palyu branches are given below.*]

Mon: 900,000 to 935,000 speakers reported in 1983, including some 835,000 in the eastern delta region of Burma from east of Rangoon to the Thai border, and 70,000 to 100,000 across the border in Thailand. Also called Talaing, Mun, or Peguan. The Mon are generally bilingual in Burmese; many young people use only Burmese.

Nyahkur: 300 speakers reported in 1983, in central Thailand. Also called Nyakur, Niakuol, Niakuoll, Chaobon, Chaodon, or Lawa. Speakers refer to themselves as Nyahkur. Chaobon is a Thai name and is considered derogatory.

Palyu: spoken on the border of Guangxi and Guizhou, China. Also known as Lai in Chinese.

AUSTRONESIAN LANGUAGES.

The Austronesian (AN) family (from Latin *auster* 'south', Greek *nêsos* 'island') consists of several hundred languages spoken mainly on islands extending from Southeast Asia into the central Pacific, with a western outpost in Madagascar. (The term 'Malayo-Polynesian' has also been used for this family; but see below for a more restricted usage.) Table 1 shows the geographical distribution of

MAP 1. *Major Divisions of Austronesian Languages*

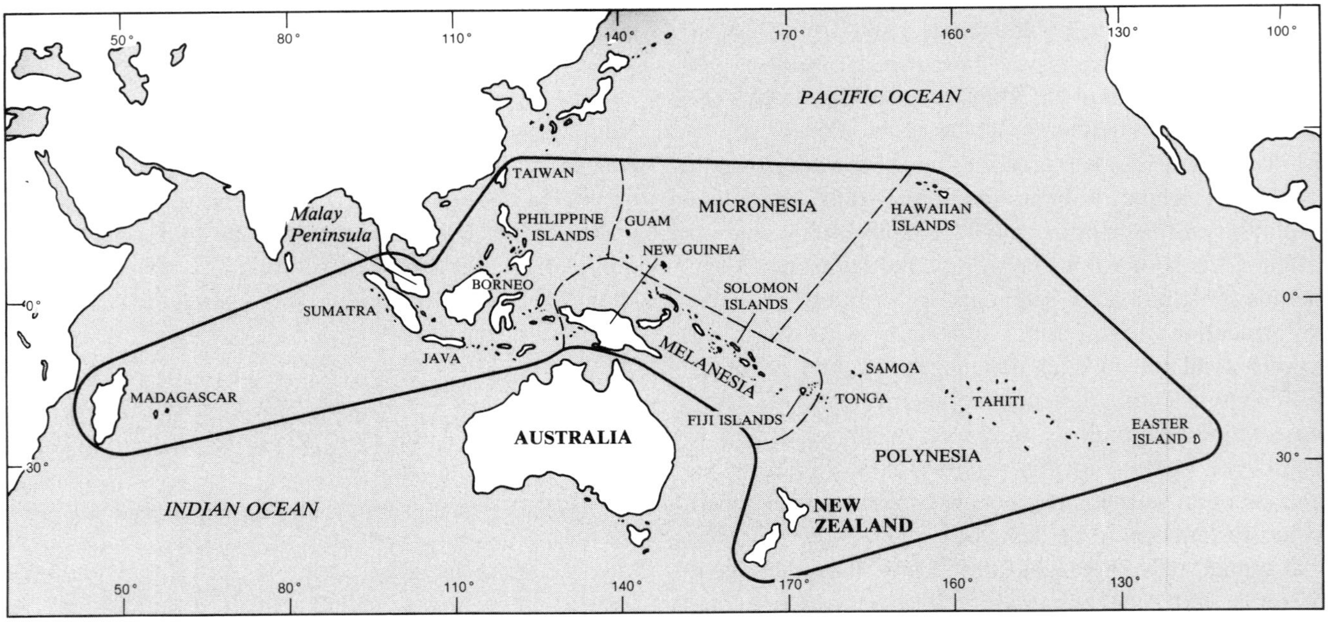

TABLE 1. *Geographical Distribution of Austronesian Languages*

Area	Number of Languages	Number of Speakers
Taiwan (Formosa)	10	200,000
Philippines	70	40,000,000
Vietnam & Cambodia[1]	7	700,000
Madagascar	1	8,000,000
Indonesia, Malaysia, Brunei[2]	300	130,000,000
Melanesia[3]	350	1,200,000
Micronesia[4]	12	200,000
Polynesia[5]	20	700,000
TOTAL	770	181,000,000

[1]Includes a small community of Cham speakers on Hainan Island, China.
[2]Includes small communities in adjoining areas of Thailand and Burma.
[3]Papua New Guinea, Solomon Islands, Vanuatu, New Caledonia, and Fiji.
[4]Belau, Guam, Northern Marianas, Federated States of Micronesia, Marshall Islands, Kiribati, and Nauru.
[5]Tuvalu, Tonga, Wallis & Futuna, Samoa, Tokelau, Niue, Hawaii, French Polynesia, Cook Islands, New Zealand, and Easter Island.

AN languages and speakers; for detailed information, see Wurm & Hattori 1981–84 (see also Map 1).

Setting aside colonial and trade languages, the Philippines, Madagascar, Micronesia, and Polynesia are entirely Austronesian-speaking. Indonesia/Malaysia and Melanesia are predominantly Austronesian, but they include two non-AN areas: the Aslian languages of the interior of the Malay peninsula, of the Austro-Asiatic family [*q.v.*], and the Papuan languages on the island of New Guinea and various smaller islands east and west of it [*see* New Guinea Languages]. The Austronesian speakers in Vietnam and Cambodia are small minority groups within a larger community whose predominant language is Vietnamese or Cambodian; likewise, the Austronesian-speaking aborigines of Taiwan are now vastly outnumbered by Chinese, who have colonized the island during the past three hundred years.

1. Comparative studies. Observations of the relatedness of various AN languages to one another go back as far as the 17th century; but systematic application of the comparative method dates from the work of Otto Dempwolff, whose major work (1934–38) remains the foundation of comparative Austronesian linguistics. Among the main contributions to comparative studies of AN as a whole since Dempwolff's time have been those of Dyen 1965, Dahl 1976, and Blust 1983–84.

Subgrouping of AN at the highest levels is still a matter of research and debate. Although lexicostatistical studies have produced some strikingly divergent results (Dyen 1965), classical comparative reasoning has led to the establishment of a number of points. The Formosan languages preserve some phonemic distinctions which have been merged in all other AN languages, and thus constitute one or more first-order subgroups. The residual, non-Formosan, group may be called M[ALAYO-] P[OLYNESIAN]. Within MP there is a major group—first postulated by Dempwolff, and now generally known as OCEANIC—which includes all the AN languages of Melanesia, Micronesia, and Polynesia, with the following exceptions: the languages of Irian Jaya from Cenderawasih Bay westward; Palauan (Belau), Chamorro (Guam and Marianas), and Yapese in western Micronesia. The Irian Jaya languages, Palauan, and Chamorro have their closest genetic connections to the west; the position of Yapese with respect to Oceanic is unclear.

A subgrouping which incorporates these and some further proposals has been proposed by Blust 1983–84. Within MP, he distinguishes three subgroups besides Oceanic. Geographically and linguistically closest to Oceanic is the South Halmahera–West New Guinea (SHWNG) group of about forty-five languages. Farther west is Central Malayo-Polynesian in the Moluccas and Lesser Sunda Islands, numbering a further fifty languages. The remaining three hundred or so languages make up the W[est] M[alayo-]P[olynesian] subgroup. The relations among these subgroups are shown in Figure 1. [*For data on individual Austronesian languages, see the Language Lists which follow the articles on the subgroups named in Fig. 1.*]

The two very large subgroups, WMP and Oceanic, thus account for about 85 percent of all AN languages. Within each, there appear to be some twenty to thirty local subgroups which would be readily accepted; but higher-level relations among these have yet to be established with certainty. Within MP, the unity of the western Indonesian/Malaysian languages with Malagasy and the Chamic group (in Vietnam/Cambodia) is generally accepted. (Despite its geographical separation, Malagasy was shown by Dahl 1951 to subgroup most closely with the Ma'anyan language of southeast Borneo.) However, the unity of the Philippine languages among themselves, and their relation to the rest of WMP, have recently been called into question (see Reid 1982, Zorc 1986.)

At the eastern limit of AN, the Polynesian languages [*q.v.*] constitute a close-knit subgroup, covering all of

FIGURE 1. *Major Subgroups of Austronesian.* (Based on Blust 1983–84.)

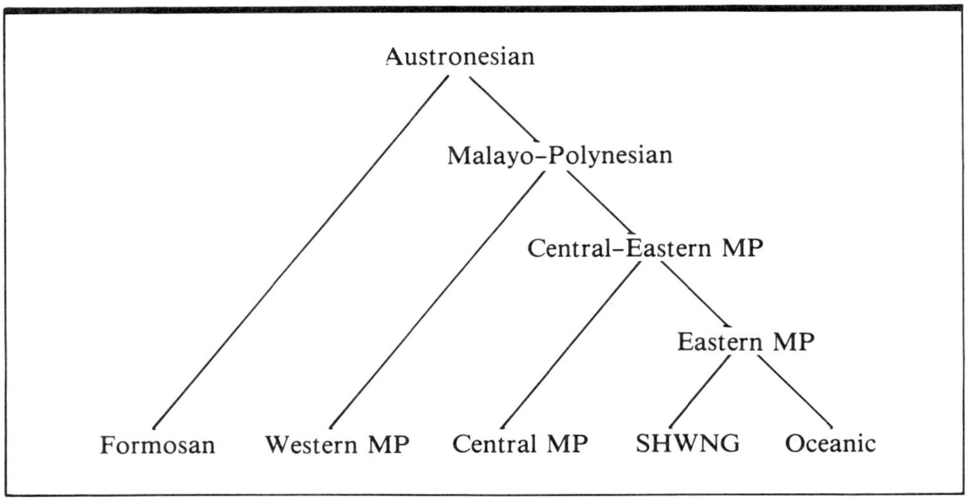

geographical Polynesia, together with about fifteen small enclaves in Melanesia and Micronesia (the 'Outliers'). Polynesian's linguistic next-of-kin are Fijian and Rotuman, forming a Central Pacific subgroup. Central Pacific in turn appears to form part of a Remote Oceanic (or 'Eastern Oceanic') group, which also includes the languages of northern and central Vanuatu, and (less clearly) the Oceanic languages of Micronesia and the southeast Solomon Islands. The AN languages of the northwestern Solomons and Papua New Guinea have been relatively poorly studied until recently; Ross 1988 has now produced a major comparative study.

The only seriously supported proposal for a wider connection of Austronesian to another language family is the 'Austro-Tai' hypothesis, which would connect AN with the Kam-Tai or Kadai family of the Southeast Asian mainland. This possibility has been explored in a number of publications, e.g. Benedict 1975, but the majority of Austronesianists remain unconvinced.

2. Structural characteristics. Austronesian phoneme inventories mainly range from medium to small on a world scale, with extreme economy being reached in Polynesia. Thus Maori, a typical Polynesian language, has ten consonants (*p t k f h m n ŋ r w*) and five vowels (*i e a o u,* with contrastive length). The east-west division is reflected in different phonological tendencies, with the reconstructed P[roto-]AN phonology more faithfully retained in the west. The PAN four-vowel system *i a u ə* became P[roto-]Oc[eanic] *i e a o u*. The PAN consonant system was simplified in Oceanic by the loss of voicing contrast in obstruents, and by the merger of several palatal consonants in POC *s*. However, Oceanic developed a new set of prenasalized consonants in opposition to the plain stops. Local developments in some areas, such as Micronesia and New Caledonia, have resulted in considerably more complex consonant and vowel systems. A favored CVCVC shape for lexical morphemes is reconstructible for PAN, with some clusters permitted medially. Many Oceanic languages, and some in the west, have categorically lost final consonants.

Prefixing, suffixing, and infixing were all productive devices in PAN morphology. Affixes marking verbs for case-orientation ('focus' or voice), transitivity, and nominalization are widespread; these have been reconstructed for PAN or other early stages. Reduplication also plays a part in most AN morphologies.

The distinction of inclusive and exclusive 1st person non-singular pronouns is a universal AN trait. Proto-Oceanic added a dual pronoun series (and possibly a trial) to the original singular/plural contrast. A distinction between proper nouns (personal pronouns and names) and common nouns is marked by articles in many languages. In PAN, pronominal suffixes marked possessors of nouns, e.g. **mata-ku* 'my eye'. Oceanic languages have elaborated this into a set of three or more contrasting categories of possession.

Two very different types of verbal syntax are found in modern AN languages. The 'focus' type, typical of Philippine and Formosan languages, marks a verb for one of (usually) four types of case-orientation. [*See* Tagalog.] The NP in the corresponding case relation is given a special marking of this privileged association with the verb, while any other NPs are marked to specify their case relation. Word order is typically verb-initial, with free order of NPs. In the 'transitive' type, typical of Oceanic languages, intransitive verbs are unmarked; transitive verbs are suffixed, sometimes with a choice of two suffixes to indicate case-orientation to the object. Word order is typically Subject Verb Object; pronominal clitics index subject and object on the verb. The historical relation between these two types has been the subject of considerable argument (see Pawley & Reid 1980).

ROSS CLARK

BIBLIOGRAPHY

BENEDICT, PAUL K. 1975. *Austro-Thai language and culture, with a glossary of roots.* New Haven: HRAF Press.

BLUST, ROBERT. 1983–84. More on the position of the languages of eastern Indonesia. *Oceanic Linguistics* 22/23.1–28.

DAHL, OTTO C. 1951. *Malgache et manjaan.* Oslo: Egede-Instituttet.

DAHL, OTTO C. 1976. *Proto-Austronesian.* 2d ed. Lund: Studentlitteratur.

DEMPWOLFF, OTTO. 1934–38. *Vergleichende Lautlehre des austronesischen Wortschatzes.* 3 vols. Berlin: Reimer.

DYEN, ISIDORE. 1965. *A lexicostatistical classification of the Austronesian languages.* (Indiana University publications in anthropology and linguistics, memoir 19; International Journal of American Linguistics, 31:1, supplement.) Baltimore.

PAWLEY, ANDREW, & LAWRENCE A. REID. 1980. The evolution of transitive constructions in Austronesian. In *Austronesian studies* (Michigan papers on South and Southeast Asia, 15), edited by Paz Buenaventura Naylor, pp. 103–130. Ann Arbor: University of Michigan.

REID, LAWRENCE A. 1982. The demise of Proto-Philippines. In *Papers from the Third International Conference on Austronesian Linguistics,* vol. 2, *Tracking the travellers* (Pacific linguistics, C-75), edited by Amran Halim et al., pp. 201–216. Canberra: Australian National University.

ROSS, MALCOLM D. 1988. *Proto Oceanic and the Austronesian languages of western Melanesia* (Pacific Linguistics, C-98.) Canberra: Australian National University.

WURM, STEPHEN A., & SHIRO HATTORI. 1981–84. *Language atlas of the Pacific area.* Canberra: Australian Academy of the Humanities.

ZORC, R. DAVID. 1986. The genetic relationships of Philippine languages. In *FOCAL: Papers from the Fourth International Conference on Austronesian Linguistics,* vol. 2 (Pacific linguistics, C-94), edited by Paul Geraghty et al., pp. 147–173. Canberra: Australia National University.

AUTOMATA THEORY. Automata are abstract mathematical models of machines that perform computations on an input by moving through a series of states or 'configurations'. If the computation of an automaton reaches an accepting configuration, it accepts that input. At each stage of the computation, a 'transition function' determines the next configuration on the basis of a finite portion of the present configuration. (For reference, see Harrison 1978, Hopcroft & Ullman 1979, Lewis & Papadimitriou 1981.)

TURING MACHINES are the most general automata. They consist of a finite set of states, and an infinite tape which contains the input and which is used to read and write symbols during the computation. Since Turing machines can leave symbols on their tape at the end of the computation, they can be viewed as computing functions, namely the partial recursive functions. Despite the simplicity of these automata, any algorithm that can be implemented on a computer can be modeled by some Turing machine.

Turing machines are used in the characterization of the complexity of a problem; this is determined by the efficiency of the best algorithm that solves it. Measures of an algorithm's efficiency are the amount of time or space that a Turing machine requires to implement the algorithm. The time of a computation is the number of configurations involved in that computation; its space corresponds to the number of positions on its tape that were used. [*See also* Recognition.]

Automata theory has close ties to formal language theory, since there is a correspondence between certain families of automata and certain classes of languages generated by grammar formalisms. A language is accepted by an automaton when it accepts all the strings in the language and no others. Thus the family of Turing machines accepts exactly the class of languages produced by Type 0 grammars. [*See* Chomsky Hierarchy.]

Linear-bounded Turing machines, whose space cannot be more than that occupied by the input, accept the class of languages generated by context-sensitive (Type 1) grammars. The most restricted family of automata are FINITE AUTOMATA, which consist of only a finite number of states and a 'read-only' tape containing the input to be read in one direction. Finite automata recognize the class of languages generated by 'regular' (finite-state or Type 3) grammars. These automata can be given a limited amount of extra power by the addition of certain forms of storage. For example, PUSHDOWN AUTOMATA involve a 'pushdown store', i.e. a sequence in which symbols can be added and removed only from one end, with the effect that the first symbols in are the last ones out. Pushdown automata accept the languages generated by context-free (Type 2) grammars.

Automata theory gave rise to the notion of deterministic computation, and hence deterministic languages. In a deterministic computation, each configuration of the machine has only one possible successor. For some families of automata, e.g. finite automata and Turing machines, deterministic and non-deterministic automata are equivalent. For others, e.g. pushdown automata, there are languages that can be accepted by a non-deterministic automaton of that family, but which cannot be accepted by any deterministic automaton.

DAVID J. WEIR

BIBLIOGRAPHY

HARRISON, MICHAEL A. 1978. *Introduction to formal language theory*. Reading, Mass.: Addison-Wesley.

HOPCROFT, JOHN E., & JEFFREY D. ULLMAN. 1979. *Introduction to automata theory, languages, and computation*. Reading, Mass.: Addison-Wesley.

LEWIS, HARRY R., & CHRISTOS H. PAPADIMITRIOU. 1981. *Elements of the theory of computation*. Englewood Cliffs, N.J.: Prentice-Hall.

AUTOSEGMENTAL PHONOLOGY, a theory of non-linear phonological representation, was developed out of research in Generative Phonology [*q.v.*] at MIT in the mid and late 1970s, as a response to certain problems in the phonological theory of that time. Most previous research in phonology had been based on the view that speech is fundamentally linear in nature—i.e., that it consists, at the phonological level, of a single sequence of phonemes (often represented as unordered sets of distinctive features), which are separated by discrete boundaries. [*See* Segments.] In the work of Roman Jakobson, Morris Halle, Noam Chomsky, and others, phonological form was represented in terms of two-dimensional feature matrices, whose columns represented sequences of phonemes and whose rows represented their features. While this account was adequate for most purposes of phonological description, it proved increasingly difficult to reconcile with evidence that speech sounds are not discrete sequential entities, but show considerable overlap.

One source of such evidence came from the accumulating descriptive literature on languages of Asia and Africa, especially those in which TONE [*q.v.*] plays a role. As such systems became described in greater detail, it was found that tone features showed patterns of distribution and alternation which suggested that they were quite loosely related to the segments that bear them, in contrast to the more 'tightly-packed' sets of features that characterize vowels and consonants. Many linguists came to believe that the theoretical implications of tone systems should be examined more systematically; indeed, the descriptivist H. A. Gleason went so far as to suggest (1961:302) that 'development of a theory better able to handle tone will result automatically in a better theory for all phonologic subsystems'. For these and other reasons—e.g. problems in the analysis of internally complex segments, long vowels and geminate consonants, and processes carrying out 'action at a distance'—an increasing number of linguists came to believe that the traditional segmental view of phonological representation was in need of substantial revision.

1. Autosegmental treatment of tone. Autosegmental phonology was initially developed in response to the challenge of developing an adequate theory of tone. Its immediate source of inspiration was the work of Williams 1971 and Leben 1973; these were the first to introduce non-linear structures into generative phonology in their treatments of tone systems in West African languages such as Margi, Igbo, and Mende. In the model proposed by these writers (termed 'suprasegmental phonology' by Leben), underlying tones were represented on separate tiers from the feature matrices representing vowels and consonants; they were subsequently MERGED with these matrices by TONE MAPPING RULES that applied in the course of derivation, creating single-tiered representations in surface structure. This model went a considerable way toward solving the descriptive problems mentioned earlier; e.g., it succeeded in showing how invariant lexical tone melodies are distributed across words of varying length.

The principal innovation of autosegmental phonology, as presented in Goldsmith 1976, was the idea that tone mapping rules do not merge tonal and segmental representations, but associate their elements by means of formal entities known as ASSOCIATION LINES. In this framework, phonological representations consist of parallel tiers of phonological segments, both tonal and segmental. A typical tonal representation might have the form shown in Figure 1, where H = high tone, L =

FIGURE 1. *Tonal Representation*

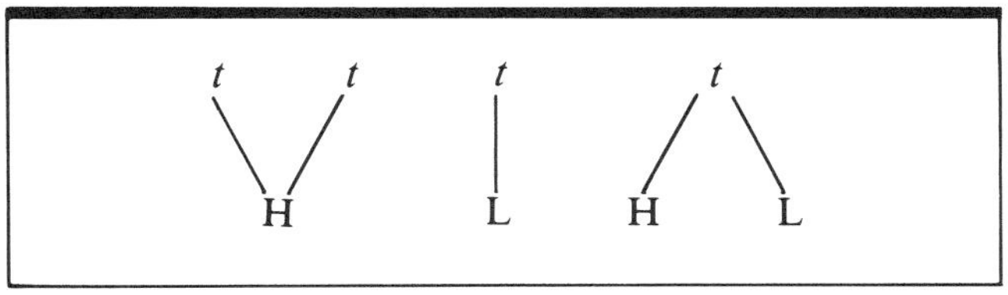

FIGURE 2. *Floating Tones and Default Tones*

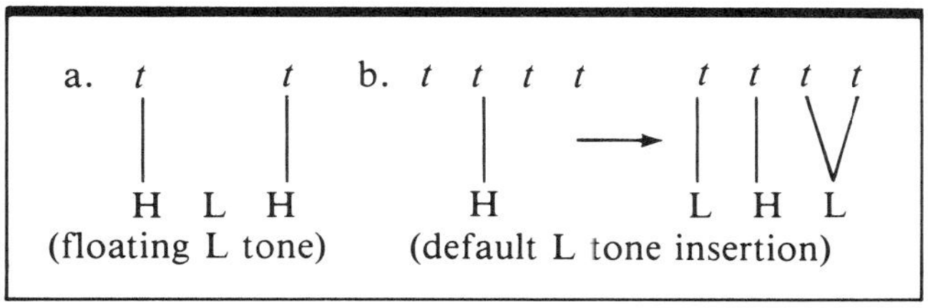

low tone, and *t* is any tone-bearing unit (e.g. vowel or syllable).

Elements of each tier, called AUTOSEGMENTS, are sequentially ordered; elements of adjacent tiers are simultaneous if and only if they are linked by association lines. As Fig. 1 shows, tones are not necessarily related to tone-bearing units in a one-to-one fashion. Rather, one tone may be linked to two or more tone-bearing units, and one tone-bearing unit may be linked to two or more tones—i.e. to a CONTOUR, such as a rising or falling tone. Phonological rules may insert or delete elements on any tier: since each tier is independent, deletion of an element on one tier does not entail deletion of the element(s) to which it is linked on another tier. In addition, phonological rules have the new function of creating and modifying the patterns of association among elements of different tiers. In this model, all tiers remain independent throughout derivations: at no point is the tonal tier merged with the segmental tier.

A further innovation of autosegmental theory is the set of universal principles termed WELL-FORMEDNESS CONDITIONS, which govern the multi-tiered structure of the representation. These principles not only define the set of theoretically possible inter-tier configurations; they also trigger the operation of a set of universal repair mechanisms, often termed ASSOCIATION CONVENTIONS, whenever configurations that violate them arise. One important condition requires that association lines may not cross. In the earliest version of the theory, further conditions required that every element be linked to at least one element on another tier at all stages of a derivation (a condition satisfied in Fig. 1). In later work, however, it was shown that certain tones could remain unlinked, accounting for the phenomenon of floating tones (Figure 2a). Further, some tone-bearing units could be toneless, accounting for the phenomenon of default tones—i.e. tones that are inserted into representations only after the initial mapping processes have been carried out, as in Fig. 2b. (For further discussion, see Clements & Goldsmith 1984, Pulleyblank 1986.)

Goldsmith's original arguments for the autosegmental analysis of tone, drawn from a survey of well attested generalizations concerning tone systems, were widely accepted; they stimulated considerable further research, not only on tonal phonology, but also on non-tonal phenomena, as we will see below.

2. Generalized autosegmental phonology. In subsequent work, autosegmental phonology underwent further development; by the mid-1980s it could be considered a fully general theory of phonological representation, radically different from the linear representational systems of more traditional approaches. The general goal of research in autosegmental phonology, much like that of concurrent work in theoretical syntax, has been to reduce the power of phonological rules by developing an enriched theory of representation. Arbitrary rule-based descriptions of languages may then be replaced, to a great extent, by constrained accounts expressed in terms of simple, recurrent phonological parameters.

The primary innovation of the generalized model has been the view that not just tone and other so-called 'prosodic' features, but ALL phonological features are arrayed on separate autosegmental tiers. In this conception, which draws upon earlier research in METRICAL PHONOLOGY and PROSODIC PHONOLOGY [*qq.v.*], phonological representations are three-dimensional structures involving numerous tiers whose feature content is linked, directly or indirectly, to a central organizational core or SKELETON which consists of a sequence of abstract TIMING UNITS. Some of these tiers have a substantive, phonetic content, providing feature information which is directly interpreted by rules of phonetic realization; others articulate the rhythmic structure characteristic of languages with stress systems; and others are purely formal and hierarchical, grouping phonetically defined features of the utterance together into higher-level structural units such as the syllable or foot. Sets of related tiers form PLANES. Rules of phonology continue to have the function of altering the content of each tier, or of readjusting the network of associations between units on related tiers. We may schematize this conception in terms of the fragment of a representation given in Figure 3; Greek letters designate structural units and Roman letters designate units with substantive content, such as features and feature classes.

This model extends the earlier tonal framework to a wide range of additional phenomena, including vowel harmony and segmental assimilation, syllable structure, phonological length, compensatory lengthening, and stress and intonation—in short, to the full domain of segmental and suprasegmental phonology. [*See* Intonation; Syllables; Vowel Harmony and Consonant Harmony.]

A central notion in this conception is the CORE or prosodic skeleton, first proposed and elaborated in work on the root-and-pattern morphology of the Semitic languages by McCarthy 1979, 1981 (see also Halle & Vergnaud 1980). In Classical Arabic, the morphological structure of a word is distributed among three types of simultaneous phonological information: the sequence of consonants which provides the lexical content, the sequence of vowels which designates the aspect/voice category, and the canonic pattern of vowels and consonants which (independently of their segmental content) indicates the derivational category, or 'measure'. Thus, in a verb stem such as *kuutib,* the consonants [k..t..b] correspond to the root meaning 'write', the vowel sequence [u..i] to the perfective passive, and the pattern CVVCVC to the 'third measure'. The descriptive problem posed by such morphological systems is to provide a principled way of accounting for the interlocking pattern of phonological information, without making use of ad-hoc constructs such as 'discontinuous morphemes'. McCarthy's solution follows from the universal postulate that the phonological content of each morpheme is represented on a separate tier, as in the lexical representation in Figure 4a. Autosegmental principles of association (identical to those assumed for tonal phonology) link the consonants and vowels to the respective C- and V-slots of the skeleton (Fig. 4b). A later process of tier conflation (McCarthy 1986) collapses all segmental features into a single phonemic or 'melody' tier, providing the surface representation (Fig. 4c).

FIGURE 3. *Autosegmental Representation*

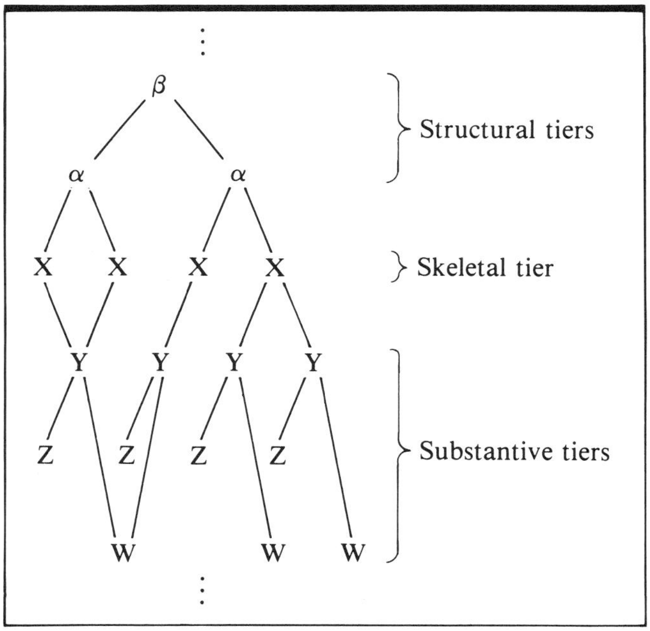

What is crucial for the present discussion is that the CV schema constitutes a separate autosegmental tier: the central core of the representation, around which vowels and consonants are articulated.

The prosodic skeleton plays not only a morphological role, but a phonological one as well. Clements & Keyser 1983 propose that the skeleton, which they term the 'CV tier', forms part of universal phonological representation, where it serves multiple roles. First, it forms the basis of syllabification rules. V-elements on the skeletal tier are syllabified as syllable peaks; thus syllabic sounds (vowels and syllabic consonants) are dominated by V, and non-syllabic sounds (glides and non-syllabic consonants) are dominated by C. Second, it forms the basis of phonological quantity. Long segments are represented as single phonemes or 'melody units', linked to two units of the CV tier; this accounts for the generalization that long segments count as one unit from the point of view of their segmental quality, but as two in regard to their quantity (see Kenstowicz 1982). Analogously, complex segments like affricates or prenasalized stops are represented as two phonemes linked to a single CV tier unit; this accounts for the fact that they count as two units from the point of view of their feature substance, but as one from that of segmental quantity. All these points can be illustrated in the autosegmental representations of *adjoin* [ədžɔyn] and *peruse* [pr̥uwz], as shown in Figure 5.

Additional evidence in favor of the phonological role of the prosodic skeleton comes from the phenomenon of COMPENSATORY LENGTHENING [*q.v.*], by which deletion of one segment is accompanied by the lengthening of another (usually adjacent) one. Under an autosegmental

FIGURE 4. *Classical Arabic Morphology*

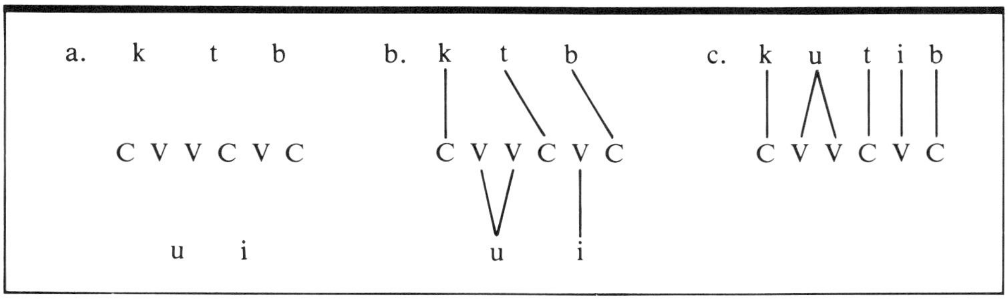

analysis, this is expressed as the spreading of a neighboring phoneme onto the skeletal position left vacant by the deleted one (Wetzels & Sezer 1986). Further, skeletal 'slots' may be totally empty of segmental content; this accounts for the synchronic traces of historically deleted consonants, such as the *h aspiré* of French or the *yumuşak g* of standard Turkish. The formal nature of the prosodic skeleton has been a matter of controversy: some investigators prefer to regard it as a sequence of undifferentiated timing points, while others suggest that it may consist of a sequence of weight units or MORAS.

The phonemic segments displayed in Figs. 4–5 are a shorthand notation for hierarchical feature complexes, arrayed on substantive tiers as suggested in Fig. 3. This analysis is motivated by extensive evidence that segmental features are themselves autosegmental in nature. For example, an autosegmental description of vowel harmony systems, in which vowel features such as lip rounding or palatality are assigned to a separate tier, provides a straightforward account of so-called 'long-distance assimilation' and related opacity effects (see Clements 1977). Furthermore, in many languages, certain subsets of features behave autonomously with respect to other subsets, as is shown by processes of partial deletion or partial assimilation; here again, we obtain a straightforward account if we assume that each such subset occupies an independent tier of its own (Thráinsson 1978). In the fully generalized model of subsegmental structure proposed in Clements 1985, all features are assigned to independent autosegmental tiers, where they form the terminal elements of feature trees. Such trees are dominated by a single node—the ROOT NODE, which takes the place of the segmental distinctive feature matrix of earlier work. Intermediate nodes, called CLASS NODES, serve a purely structural function: they group together functionally related subsets of features into subordinate hierarchical units. This model has been extended by Elizabeth Sagey, who proposes that the articulator—coronal, dorsal, labial, etc.—are not represented as terminal features of trees, but as ARTICULATOR NODES dominating terminal features. [*See* Phonological Features.]

Further developments in autosegmental phonology include the grid-based theory of stress proposed by Halle & Vergnaud 1987, and the model of intonation and prosodic structure developed by Pierrehumbert & Beckman 1988. For a more recent overview and several new proposals, see Goldsmith 1990. As remarked by Van der Hulst & Smith 1982, progress in autosegmental phonology has owed much to its 'problem-solving efficiency'—i.e., its success in finding solutions for previously unsolved representational problems, and integrating them into a consistent, over-all theoretical framework. In addition, it has had consequences in quite unexpected quarters: it has contributed to the development of the theory of non-concatenative morphology (see above); it has substantially reduced the abstractness required in earlier analyses; it has laid the basis for a substantive theory of 'natural' or widely-attested rule types; it has simplified the theory of rule application by eliminating the class of 'non-local' rules; and it has stimulated new theories of phonetic features and of articulation-based speech synthesis.

GEORGE N. CLEMENTS

FIGURE 5. *The CV Tier in English*

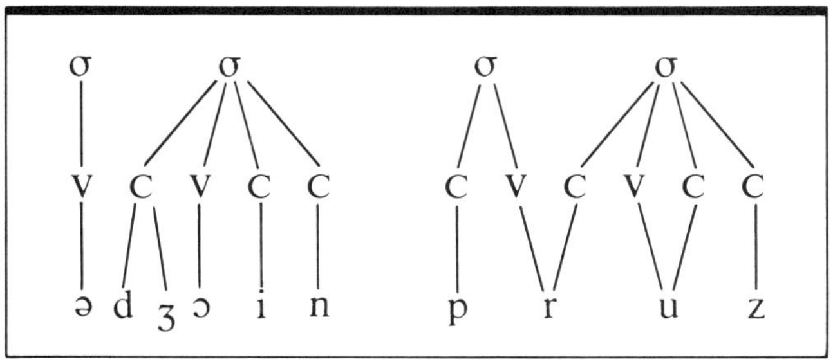

BIBLIOGRAPHY

CLEMENTS, GEORGE N. 1977. The autosegmental treatment of vowel harmony. In *Phonologica 1976* (Innsbrucker Beiträge zur Sprachwissenschaft, 19), edited by Wolfgang U. Dressler & Oskar E. Pfeiffer, pp. 111–119. Innsbruck: Institut für Sprachwissenschaft der Universität.

CLEMENTS, GEORGE N. 1985. The geometry of phonological features. *Phonology Yearbook* 2.225–252.

CLEMENTS, GEORGE N., & JOHN GOLDSMITH, eds. 1984. *Autosegmental studies in Bantu tone*. (Publications in African languages and linguistics, 3.) Dordrecht: Foris.

CLEMENTS, GEORGE N., & SAMUEL JAY KEYSER. 1983. *CV Phonology: A generative theory of the syllable*. (Linguistic Inquiry monographs, 9.) Cambridge, Mass.: MIT Press.

GLEASON, HENRY ALLAN, JR. 1961. Review of *African language studies*, vol. 1, edited by Malcolm Guthrie, and *The role of tone in Sụkų́ma*, by Irvine Richardson. *Language* 37.294–308.

GOLDSMITH, JOHN. 1976. *Autosegmental phonology*. MIT dissertation. Published, New York: Garland, 1979.

GOLDSMITH, JOHN. 1990. *Autosegmental and metrical phonology*. Oxford: Blackwell.

HALLE, MORRIS, & JEAN-ROGER VERGNAUD. 1980. Three-dimensional phonology. *Journal of Linguistic Research* 1:1.83–105.

HALLE, MORRIS, & JEAN-ROGER VERGNAUD. 1987. *An essay on stress*. (Current studies in linguistics, 15.) Cambridge, Mass.: MIT Press.

KENSTOWICZ, MICHAEL. 1982. Gemination and spirantization in Tigrinya. *Studies in the Linguistic Sciences* (University of Illinois) 12.103–122.

LEBEN, WILLIAM R. 1973. *Suprasegmental phonology*. MIT dissertation. Published, New York: Garland, 1980.

MCCARTHY, JOHN. 1979. *Formal problems in Semitic phonology and morphology*. MIT dissertation. Published, New York: Garland, 1985.

MCCARTHY, JOHN. 1981. A prosodic theory of non-concatenative morphology. *Linguistic Inquiry* 12.373–418.

MCCARTHY, JOHN. 1986. OCP effects: Gemination and antigemination. *Linguistic Inquiry* 17.207–263.

PIERREHUMBERT, JANET, & MARY BECKMAN. 1988. *Japanese tone structure*. (Linguistic Inquiry monographs, 15.) Cambridge, Mass.: MIT Press.

PULLEYBLANK, DOUGLAS. 1986. *Tone in lexical phonology*. Dordrecht: Reidel.

THRÁINSSON, HÖSKULDUR. 1978. On the phonology of Icelandic preaspiration. *Nordic Journal of Linguistics* 1.3–54.

VAN DER HULST, HARRY, & NORVAL SMITH. 1982. An overview of autosegmental and metrical phonology. In *The structure of phonological representations*, vol. 1, edited by Harry van der Hulst & Norval Smith, pp. 1–45. Dordrecht: Foris.

WETZELS, LEO, & ENGIN SEZER, eds. 1986. *Studies in compensatory lengthening*. (Publications in language sciences, 23.) Dordrecht: Foris.

WILLIAMS, EDWIN. 1971. Underlying tone in Margi and Igbo. MS. Published in *Linguistic Inquiry* 7.463–84, 1976.

AWERA LANGUAGES constitute a language family of Irian Jaya (Indonesia), recognized on the basis of a field report by Larry Jones (Summer Institute of Linguistics).

LANGUAGE LIST

Awera: 100 speakers of Awera proper reported in 1987, in the same community with 100 Ansus-speaking people, at the mouth of the Wapoga River, Waropen Bawah District. Awera is used in the home and for interaction with other Awera. Ansus and Indonesian are used widely in the community.

Rasawa: 200 or more speakers reported in 1987, near the southern coast of Waropen Bawah District.

Saponi: 10 or fewer speakers reported in 1987, in interior Waropen Bawah District.

B

BABYLONIAN GRAMMATICAL TRADITION. Linguistic analysis is at least as old as writing. The earliest writing system in the world, the CUNEIFORM system [*q.v.*], was invented in Mesopotamia, today Southern Iraq, sometime around 3100 BCE. Although not all scholars would agree, the available evidence suggests that this writing was indeed invented as a comprehensive system. It underwent many changes in its three-thousand-year history, but the basic structure was there from the beginning. (For general reference, see Edzard 1971, Jacobsen 1974, Diakonoff 1980, and Black 1984.)

A complex technology such as the cuneiform system requires systematic and effective teaching to be transmitted from generation to generation. From the very beginning of writing, there is some evidence of schooling. It must be kept in mind that Mesopotamia was always multilingual, and the written languages were often not the vernacular. SUMERIAN [*q.v.*], the language of the first texts, must have died out by the beginning of the 2nd millennium BCE, probably earlier. As a result, schooling involved instruction not only in the technology of writing, but often in a foreign language, or at least a 'high' version of the vernacular. Thus linguistic analysis, from the very beginning, undoubtedly had a practical pedagogic motivation as well as a speculative one.

One of the major components of the ancient Mesopotamian school system was a set of compositions that are now referred to as LEXICAL TEXTS or LISTS. These texts, which can be found among the earliest Mesopotamian documents (ca. 3100 BCE), are arranged either thematically, i.e. according to semantic principles, or 'phonographically', either by the shape of the signs of the cuneiform writing system or by phonological sequences. The lists are either monolingual, primarily Sumerian, or bilingual, with Sumerian terms explained by AKKADIAN translations [*q.v.*]. In the multilingual lists, the writing is arranged in parallel columns on the clay tablets. In a few texts from Western Asia, other languages such as Ugaritic, Hittite, Eblaite, or Hurrian were added. Furthermore, a few isolated vocabularies of the Kassite language and of loan words in Akkadian are explained by Akkadian translations. In the 1st millennium, new lexical texts were composed which, although ordered with the Sumerian on the left and Akkadian on the right, are actually organized on the basis of the Akkadian roots. These have been described as Akkado-Sumerian indexes to the earlier lists (Civil 1976).

Because the lexical texts formed a crucial part of writing instruction, they are found wherever the cuneiform script was used—in Iran, Syria, Anatolia, and even in Egypt and the Levant. Chronologically, the texts are attested throughout the history of cuneiform writing. Although there are important earlier texts, the first significant group of lexical texts that includes Akkadian translations is attested from the Old Babylonian period, from around 1700 BCE. The largest number of texts, however, are from the 1st millennium BCE. Sometime after the rise of the Seleucid empire, a few Greek-speaking individuals learned cuneiform; they left behind a handful of clay tablets that include Greek transliterations of the cuneiform characters.

Some of the basic lexical texts were used at an early level of instruction in the Mesopotamian schools. A good example is a series entitled, by citation of its first lines, as *á: A = nâqu*. This means that the text had three columns. The first one contained the sign *á*, a grapheme that provides a different spelling of *A*, and thus is a guide to its pronunciation (the diacritical marks and number subscripts are indicators of sign indexes and have no phonological value). The second column has *A*, the Sumerian word that is to be explained. The third column has the Akkadian translation *nâqu* 'to cry, groan'. The approximately fourteen thousand entries are arranged according to the visual appearance of the individual graphemes. An example of a different kind of list is *ur$_5$-ra* = *ḫubullu,* the Sumerian and Akkadian words for 'commercial loan'. This list, which in its 1st-millennium version contained approximately ten thousand entries on twenty-four individual cuneiform tablets, provided a virtual lexicon of Sumerian. The words, arranged thematically, cover the names of trees, reeds, pottery, animal hides, metals, domestic and wild animals, body parts, stones, plants, birds, fish, textiles, foods, and drinks, as well as geographical names and legal terminology. This list contained the Sumerian words and their translations into Akkadian. Unlike *á* : *A* = *nâqu,* it did not include a pronunciation column; as a rule, the thematic lists do not.

Related to the lexical texts are ancient COMMENTARIES. This is a relatively late genre; no known examples antedate the 1st millennium BCE. The commentaries were explanations of difficult words in literary texts, including the lists. Some simply provide synonyms or translations of individual words; others include quotations from a variety of literary sources, along with etymologies and explanations of words. Like the lexical texts, which are commented upon but are also the source of commentaries, the commentaries contain only listings of words and passages from literary texts, but do not include any metacommentary.

The above lists, which are primarily lexicographical, also contain evidence of morphological analysis. Already in the 3rd millennium, verbal paradigms of Sumerian roots are attested in a cuneiform text from Ebla (in Syria) which is undoubtedly of Mesopotamian origin. Moreover, some of the lists contain explanations of Sumerian graphemes that were used to express bound morphemes. The most developed system of morphological analysis, however, is found in lists dedicated solely to that purpose, which modern scholars call BABYLONIAN GRAMMATICAL TEXTS. These texts are, with one exception, bilingual, with Sumerian on the left and Akkadian on the right. There are three rough categories of grammatical texts: those with verbal paradigms (in the order third, second, and first person); those with pronouns and adverbs, as well as pronominal and adverbial expressions; and those that list individual morphemes. Since the cuneiform script is logographic and syllabic, the bound morphemes are listed in the form that they would acquire in writing. Hence the Sumerian 3sg. animate verbal prefix *-n-* can only be cited as *an, un,* or *in.* A simple example from the first type would be (in transcription):

idu	*illak*	'he/she is going'
idun	*allak*	'I am going'
idun	*tallak*	'you are going'

The texts list the verbs in a variety of forms, giving aspects, moods, pronominal elements, etc. In the second type of text we find examples such as:

meda	*mati*	'when?'
medakam	*matima*	'whenever'
medaš	*ana mati*	'how long?'
medata	*ištu mati*	'since when?'

One other source of information on Mesopotamian linguistics is a composition entitled 'Examination Text A' (Sjöberg 1975). This is a humorous dialog between a schoolmaster and a student. The teacher tells the student that he has learned nothing in all the years at school, and proceeds to question him on the scribal art. The text is bilingual, with each line presented in Sumerian and Akkadian. Among the questions are those pertaining to linguistic interpretation; so the student is asked if he knows lexical and bilingual texts, the various grammatical terms, and the pronominal elements and morphemes that are listed in the grammatical texts. The dialog appears to be largely structured around paradigmatic elements that were taught in the schools. The existing manuscripts of the composition are all from the 1st millennium, although it has been suggested that the original composition is much earlier. The dating is important because the 'Examination Text' includes examples of morphological analysis and Babylonian grammatical terminology. Although most scholars think that this type of analysis developed after the 2nd millennium, Black 1984 has argued that it was used earlier. The grammatical terminology consists of eighteen words that are very difficult to understand; their interpretation has been the subject of much speculation.

The evidence for grammatical theory briefly summarized above can be interpreted only within the larger framework of Mesopotamian discourse. We would look in vain for explicit statements of rules or for polemical analysis. First, the grammatical texts served only as written exercises and mnemonic devices for students; oral instruction provided the explanations and commentary. Second, these texts follow the normal Mesopotamian hermeneutic pattern in which everything is presented by means of a series of examples, often of mounting complexity, with all possible permutations of a situation given. In this way, the grammatical examples are not much different from other genres, e.g. omens in which the future is foretold on the basis of unnatural births: first an example is provided of a calf with two heads, then with three, four, etc. Similarly, mathematical exercises demonstrate that, in the 2nd millennium, the Mesopotamians were already aware of what we call the Pythagorean theory; but it was never stated, at least in writing, in the language of a theorem. We must assume that the lexical lists and grammatical paradigms are but examples of a rich linguistic tradition that flourished as early as the 2nd millennium BCE, if not earlier. It is important to stress, however, that linguistic analysis was debated and transmitted primarily through the oral tradition that accompanied the written school tradition. The lexical and grammatical texts contain only exemplary material; we shall never be able to reconstruct in detail the grammatical theories of the ancient Mesopotamians and their neighbors.

PIOTR MICHALOWSKI

BIBLIOGRAPHY

BLACK, JEREMY A. 1984. *Sumerian grammar in Babylonian theory.* (Studia Pohl, Series major 12.) Rome: Pontificio Instituto Biblico.

CIVIL, MIGUEL. 1976. Lexicography. In *Sumerological studies in honor of Thorkild Jacobsen on his seventieth birthday, June 7, 1974* (Assyriological studies, 20), edited by S. J. Lieberman, pp. 123–57. Chicago: University of Chicago Press.

DIAKONOFF, IGOR M. 1980. Babilonskaja filologija (III—I tys. do n.e.). In *Istorija lingvističeskix učenij: Drevnij mir,* edited by A. B. Desnićkaja & C. D. Kacnel'son, pp. 17–37. Leningrad: Nauka.

EDZARD, DIETZ O. 1971. Grammatik. In *Reallexikon der Assyriologie* 3.610–616. Berlin: de Gruyter.

JACOBSEN, THORKILD. 1974. Very ancient linguistics: Babylonian grammatical texts. In *Studies in the history of linguistics: Traditions and paradigms,* edited by Dell Hymes, pp. 41–62. Bloomington: University of Indiana Press.

LANDSBERGER, BENNO, ed. 1956. *Materialen zum sumerischen Lexicon,* vol. 4. Rome: Pontifical Institute Press.

SJÖBERG, ÅKE W. 1975. Der Examenstext A. *Zeitschrift für Assyriologie und Vorderasiatische Archäologie* 64.137–176.

BALI-SASAK LANGUAGES constitute a group spoken on Bali and adjacent islands of Indonesia. They form a top-level constituent of the Sundic subgroup of West Malayo-Polynesian [*q.v.*].

LANGUAGE LIST

Balinese: 3,800,000 speakers reported in 1989, on Bali, northern Nusapenida, the western Lombok Islands, and east Java, Indonesia, along with 7,000 in south Sulawesi.

Sasak: 2,100,000 speakers reported in 1989, on eastern Lombok Island in the Lesser Sunda Islands, Nusa Tenggara, Indonesia. Also called Lombok.

Sumbawa: 300,000 speakers reported in 1989, on the west end of Sumbawa Island, east of Lombok, Nusa Tenggara, Indonesia. Also called Semawa or Sumbawarese. Distinct from Sumba, a Central Malayo-Polynesian language.

BALKAN LANGUAGES. The Balkan peninsula is a rugged, mountainous land mass in southeastern Europe, bounded by the lower Danube and Sava rivers to the north (though by some accounts beginning even farther north, in the vicinity of Vienna), by the Adriatic Sea to the west, and by the Black Sea up to the mouth of the Danube river to the east; it includes all of Greece to the south. It is home to a number of languages whose interrelationships are of great interest in regard to questions of language contact, language change, AREAL LINGUISTICS [*q.v.*], and sociolinguistics. The languages in this area come from several different branches of the I[ndo-]E[uropean] family, as listed in Figure 1. [*See also* Indo-European Languages.] From the Altaic family (Turkic branch) comes Turkish [*q.v.*].

The most significant fact about these languages is that various sets of them share certain structural and lexical

FIGURE 1. *Subgrouping of Indo-European Branches of Balkan Languages*

Albanian
Geg (in the north), Tosk (in the south)
Greek
Ancient Greek, Modern Greek, Pontic, Tsakonian
Indic
Romani (Gypsy)
Balkan Romani, Carpathian Romani, Vlach Romani
Romance
Aromanian (Vlach), Daco-Rumanian, Judeo-Spanish (also known as Ladino)
South Slavic
Bulgarian, Macedonian, Serbo-Croatian (especially the southernmost dialects)

features that do not, in the case of the IE languages, derive from their being genetically related. Such features do not represent common inheritances from Proto-IE; rather, they result from linguistic convergence over a period of intense, intimate contact among the speech communities in this area. Moreover, genetic relatedness could not possibly explain the similarities between Turkish and the IE languages of the Balkans. The languages which share significant numbers of these features are often designated 'Balkan languages' (Schaller 1975), as opposed to the merely geographic designation 'languages of the Balkans'; the latter also include Slovenian, Armenian (spoken in Bulgaria), Circassian (Adygey, spoken in the Kosovo area of Yugoslavia), Ruthenian (Rusyn, spoken in the Vojvodina area of Yugoslavia), and German and Hungarian (both spoken in Rumania).

This structural and lexical convergence has led to characterization of the Balkan languages as a *Sprachbund* ('linguistic league' or 'linguistic area'). This characterization—noted as early as Miklosich 1884, and systematically elaborated in the classic work of Sandfeld 1926, 1930—is based on the belief that the convergences observable in a comparison of these languages are not chance similarities, but instead are the natural consequence of the close contact among these speech communities. The most significant such features are listed below.

1. Phonological features include the following:

(a) A stressed mid-to-high central vowel is found in Albanian, Rumanian, Bulgarian, some dialects of Macedonian and Serbo-Croatian, some Romani varieties, and Turkish.

(b) The vowel inventory contains *i e a o u*, without phonological contrasts of quantity, openness, or nasalization; this characteristic is found in Greek, Tosk Albanian, Rumanian, Macedonian, Bulgarian, Serbo-Croatian, and Romani.

2. Morphological features include the following:

(a) The nominal case system shows reduction—in particular, a falling together of the genitive and dative cases—in Greek, Albanian, Rumanian, Bulgarian, and Macedonian; the latter two have eliminated other case distinctions as well.

(b) A future tense based on a reduced, often invariant, form of the verb 'want' is found in Greek, Tosk Albanian, Rumanian, Macedonian, Bulgarian, Serbo-Croatian, and Romani.

(c) An enclitic (postposed) definite article typically occurs after the first word in the noun phrase in Albanian, Rumanian, Macedonian, Bulgarian, and southern Serbo-Croatian.

(d) The use of verbal forms to distinguish actions on the basis of the real or presumed source of information—commonly referred to as marking a witnessed/reported distinction, but also including nuances of surprise (admirative) and doubt (dubitative)—is found in Albanian, Bulgarian, Macedonian, and Turkish, and to a lesser extent in Romani, Serbo-Croatian, and Rumanian (the presumptive; see Friedman 1981).

3. Syntactic features include the following:

(a) A non-finite verbal complement (generally called an 'infinitive' in traditional grammar) is reduced in use, and is replaced by fully finite complement clauses (see Joseph 1983). This feature is found most intensively in Greek, Macedonian, Bulgarian, Serbo-Croatian (especially the Torlak dialects), and Romani; it also occurs in Albanian (especially Tosk) and Romanian.

(b) Analytic adjectival comparative structures are found in Greek, Albanian, Rumanian, Bulgarian, Macedonian, and Romani, as well as in Turkish.

(c) The pleonastic use of weak object pronominal forms in combination with full noun phrases for direct or indirect object is found in Greek, Albanian, Rumanian, Bulgarian, and Macedonian, dialectally in Serbo-Croatian, and to a limited extent in Romani.

4. Lexical parallels are found throughout the area, including shared phraseology (e.g., a phrase that is lit. 'without (an)other' means 'without doubt'), and numerous shared loanwords, many from Turkish.

5. Processes. The above features, known as 'Balkanisms', define the Balkan *Sprachbund*—even though not all are found in all the languages (see Hamp 1979). Most of these features represent synchronically valid statements about the superficial structure of these languages. However, several of them are diachronically oriented; over centuries of contact, the Balkan languages have moved away from stages in which they were typologically more different from one another, and toward their present state of structural convergence.

The causes of Balkan linguistic convergence must undoubtedly be sought in language contact, although some linguists have viewed various developments in each language as independent of those found in the others. The nature of the contact which led to convergence is a matter of some controversy. Some scholars opt for a substratum explanation which draws on facts about languages, e.g. Thracian and Illyrian, which were spoken in the Balkans in ancient times (see Katičić 1976). Others prefer an adstratum explanation, with the influence of Greek being especially important. Still others propose different models of contact, based, e.g., on bilingualism, or even on a form of pidginization. Before the matter can be fully understood, many details are still needed concerning the social situation in the medieval period, when the most significant contact occurred among these languages. (For further reference, see Schaller 1977, Solta 1980, Assenova 1983, and Feuillet 1986.)

BRIAN D. JOSEPH

BIBLIOGRAPHY

ASSENOVA, PETJA, ed. 1983. *Linguistique balkanique: Bibliographie 1966–1975.* Sofia: Académie Bulgare des Sciences.

FEUILLET, JACK. 1986. *La linguistique balkanique.* (Cahiers balkaniques, 10). Paris: INALCO.

FRIEDMAN, VICTOR A. 1981. Admirativity and confirmativity. Zeitschrift für Balkanologie 17:1.12–28.

HAMP, ERIC P. 1979. Linguistic areas or clusters? In *Quatrième Congrès International des Études du Sud-est Européen: Abrégés des communications,* pp. 282–283. Ankara: Türk Tarih Kurumu.

JOSEPH, BRIAN D. 1983. *The synchrony and diachrony of the Balkan infinitive: A study in areal, general, and historical linguistics.* (Cambridge studies in linguistics, Supplementary volume 1.) Cambridge & New York: Cambridge University Press.

KATIČIĆ, RADOSLAV. 1976. *Ancient languages of the Balkans,* vol. 1. (Trends in linguistics: State-of-the-Art reports, 4.) The Hague: Mouton.

MIKLOSICH, FRANZ. 1884. Die türkischen Elemente in den südost- und osteuropäischen Sprachen. *Denkschriften der Kaiserlichen Akademie der Wissenschaften* (Vienna), Philosophisch-historische Klasse, 34.239–338.

SANDFELD, KRISTIAN. 1926. *Balkanfilologien: En oversigt over dens resultater og problemer.* Copenhagen.

SANDFELD, KRISTIAN. 1930. *Linguistique balkanique: Problèmes et résultats.* (Collection linguistique publiée de la Société de Linguistique de Paris, 31.) Paris: Champion.

SCHALLER, HELMUT W. 1975. *Die Balkansprachen: Eine Einführung in die Balkanphilologie.* Heidelberg: Winter.

SCHALLER, HELMUT W. 1977. *Bibliographie zur Balkanphilologie.* Heidelberg: Winter.

SOLTA, GEORG R. 1980. *Einführung in die Balkanlinguistik, mit besonderer Berücksichtigung des Substrats und des Balkanlateinischen.* Darmstadt: Wissenschaftliche Buchgesellschaft.

BALTIC LANGUAGES. The Baltic family belongs to the *satem* branch of I[ndo-]E[uropean] [*q.v.*], along with Sl[avic], Indo-Iranian, and Armenian. Lithuanian, its most important member, was included in the *Comparative Grammar* of Bopp 1833; the Baltic group was recognized by George Nesselmann in 1845. For reference, see Endzelīns 1923, 1971, Trautmann 1923, Fraenkel 1950, Senn 1957, Gimbutas 1963, Stang 1966, and Schmalstieg 1974.

1. Membership. Baltic is divided into W[est] B[altic] and E[ast] B[altic]. WB is known from O[ld] P[russian], spoken formerly in East Prussia; it is attested from a 14th-century vocabulary list (Pomesan dialect) and from 16th-century catechisms (Samland dialect); it has been extinct since ca. 1700. Other Prussian ethnonyms sometimes cited, such as Pogesanian, Skalvian, and Jatvingian (Sudovian), are tribal groupings without known special linguistic features. EB includes Li[thuanian] and La[tvian], attested from the 16th century. Other EB languages sometimes mentioned—e.g. Kurish (Kuronian, Curonian), Zemgalian, and Selian—are known from names, borrowings, and substratum phenomena; none has known unique linguistic features. They are presumed to be transitional dialects, which were absorbed into either Li. or La. The East Latvian dialect area supports a separate literary language called Latgalian. Evidence also exists, from place names and other substratum phenomena, of a now-extinct Baltic language to the east, ranging as far as the territory of Moscow. [*Concerning the individual languages, see also the Language List at the end of this article.*]

2. Classification. The shared features of Baltic and Slavic have led many scholars to propose an intermediate B[alto-]Sl[avic] family within IE; however, this view has been disputed by scholars who argue for a separate, if parallel, evolution of Baltic from IE. This issue remains open. Those who argue for a BSl. unity must account for very ancient differences between Baltic and Slavic. It is not possible to reconstruct a homogeneous Common Baltic; hence it cannot be possible to reconstruct a homogeneous BSl. However, those who oppose a BSl. unity must account for many shared features, including vocabulary, accent, and the development of IE syllabic sonorants. More recently, there has been interest in the concept of a Baltic, Slavic, and Germanic community set off by an early Northern IE isogloss. Baltic can then be seen as a peripheral *satem* language, and as a transition to Germanic. There are old isoglosses which unite Baltic and Germanic, probably before 3000 BCE, and which are not shared by Sl. This suggests that

BSl. unity, if real, could not have existed later than the 4th millennium BCE. Significantly, Baltic itself is actually divided by many old isoglosses—some shared with Slavic, and some with Germanic.

In general, Baltic is closer to the classical IE languages in its structure than to modern European languages; of living languages, Li. is the closest to 'classical' reconstructed IE. Within Baltic, OPr. and Li. are conservative; but La. has developed in the analytic direction, with paradigmatic syncretism and loss. Changes in Li. have been much slower (e.g., the dual is attested and preserved in some dialects), and as much toward agglutination as analysis; the evolution of locative endings illustrates this. Modern Li. has not conserved the attested Old Li. paradigm, but neither does it follow the modern European pattern of merger and loss. Instead, there is retention of stem markers in both numbers, retention of *-s* as a plural marker, and generalization of *-e* as a mark of locative case in all declensions and numbers. By contrast, the OLi sg./pl. endings for three stem classes are *-ie/-uosu, -oj/-osu, -ej/-esu,* while their modern counterparts are *-e/-uose, -oje/-ose, -ėje/-ėse.*

3. General features. Among the typological features of Baltic are the following:

(a) Preservation and expansion of IE vowel gradation (ablaut)
(b) The tendency to insert /k/ before consonant clusters beginning with a sibilant, cf. Li. *krikštyti,* OPr. *crixtitwei* 'baptize', La. *pìrksts* 'finger'
(c) A unique verb system, including lack of number contrast in the 3rd person—cf. Li. 3rd person pres. *áuga* 'grow(s)'; a simple past formed by adding **-ā* and **-ē* themes to stems (original root aorists, *s*-aorists, perfect, and imperfect are lost); and a present tense medial suffix *-sta* where the nasal infix (limited to canonical shape CVC) cannot occur
(d) Characteristic nominal elements, including great productivity for fem. *-ē* stems (cf. OPr. *semme,* Li. *žẽmė,* La. *zeme* 'earth', O[ld] C[hurch] S[lavic] **zemia*); specifically Baltic diminutive and agentive suffixes; and personal names
(e) Characteristic Baltic vocabulary

Other features also justify a Baltic family; however, a reconstructed Common Baltic is more abstract than, e.g., Common Slavic. Most typological features that divide the Baltic languages link one or another Baltic language with Slavic, or with branches of Slavic.

4. West Baltic features include the following:

(a) Possessive adjectives cognate with Slavic, cf. OPr. *mais, twais, swais* vs. OCS *mojĭ, tvojĭ, svojĭ.* By contrast, EB uses possessive pronouns based on the pronominal declension; cf. Li. *màno, tàvo, sàvo.*
(b) The preterit of 'be', OPr. *bēi, be,* cf. OCS *běxŭ, bě.* EB has only the stems *es-, buv-.*
(c) Preservation of the neuter gender in OPr.
(d) OPr. *-o*-stem genitive in *-s*; the EB and Sl. *-o*-stem genitive is based on the IE ablative in **-ā*—cf. OPr. gen. *deiwas,* Li. *diẽvo.* The OPr. dative plural is *-mans*; cf. EB *-mus,* Sl. *-mŭ.*
(e) WB preserves an older separate pronominal declension, which has been nominalized in EB; cf. OPr. *stas,* gen. *stessei,* dat. *stesmu,* gen. pl. *steison,* dat. pl. *steimans.* Note also WB *subs* 'oneself', gen. *subsai* (EB *pats,* cf. Sanskrit *páti,* Greek *pósis* 'master'). The WB pronominal declension (like those of Sanskrit and Gothic) has a dative and locative element *-sm-,* whereas EB and Slavic have *-m-.*
(f) Present passive participle in *-man-,* whereas EB and Slavic have *-m-.* WB has a past active participle in *-uns*; cf. *iduns* 'having eaten' (EB *-usi,* Sl. *-ųš-* < **ŭsi-*).
(g) WB has some significant old lexical contrasts with EB: cf. OPr. *mentimai* 'we tell lies' (Latin *mentīre*); *seggit* 'do' vs. Li. *darýti*; *lauxnos* 'stars', Li. *žvaigždė̃*; or *emmens* 'name', Li. *var̃das.* WB *widdewu* 'widow' is absent in EB. Note also, among number terms, OPr. *ains* (Li. *víenas*), OPr. *newints* (Li. *devil̃tas*), OPr. *tīrts* (Li. *trẽčias* < **tretijas*).
(h) IE **ei* is reflected as *ei* everywhere in WB.

5. East Baltic. One can reconstruct a common EB as a fairly homogeneous language. Differences within EB have the character of a continuum, and are recent innovations (this is not true of differences between EB and WB). EB began to break up after about 600 CE, with the rapid phonological development of La.; but Li. remained conservative, or innovated differently and more slowly. The branches experienced different external influences from Germanic, Slavic, and Balto-Finnic. The phonological changes leading to La. were analogous to the changes which broke up Slavic unity during the same period (700–1100 CE), but they differ in details. These include: loss of final short vowels; shortening of long vowels; retraction and fixing of stress; iotations and palatalizations with varying structural results; and loss of tautosyllabic nasal consonants. In principle, these sound changes are spread out in continua in La. and Li. dialects. The most conservative dialects are in Li., and in the West. Li. and La. are further apart than the different Slavic languages: the two main Li. dialect groupings, Žemaitian and Aukštaitian, are as far apart as Eastern and Western Slavic.

JULES F. LEVIN

BIBLIOGRAPHY

BOPP, FRANZ. 1833. *Vergleichende Grammatik des Sanskrit, Zend, Griechischen, Lateinischen, Lithauischen, Gotischen und Deutschen,* vol. 1. Berlin: Dümmler.

ENDZELĪNS, JĀNIS. 1923. *Lettische Grammatik.* Heidelberg: Winter.

ENDZELĪNS, JĀNIS. 1971. *Comparative phonology and morphology of the Baltic languages.* The Hague: Mouton.

FRAENKEL, ERNST. 1950. *Die baltischen Sprachen.* Heidelberg: Winter.

GIMBUTAS, MARIJA. 1963. *The Balts.* London: Thames & Hudson. New York: Praeger.

SCHMALSTIEG, WILLIAM R. 1974. *An Old Prussian grammar: The phonology and morphology of the three catechisms.* University Park: Pennsylvania State University Press.

SENN, ALFRED. 1957. *Handbuch der litauischen Sprache,* vol. 1, *Grammatik.* Heidelberg: Winter.

STANG, CHRISTIAN S. 1966. *Vergleichende Grammatik der baltischen Sprachen.* Oslo: Universitetsforlaget.

TRAUTMANN, REINHOLD. 1923. *Baltisch-slavisches Wörterbuch.* Göttingen: Vandenhoeck & Ruprecht.

LANGUAGE LIST

Latvian: around 1,550,000 speakers reported in 1986, with 1,398,000 in Latvia, 29,000 in Russia, 5,000 in Lithuania, 2,600 in the Ukraine, 2,000 in Estonia, and 1,000 in Belorussia, USSR; plus 50,000 in the United States, 25,000 in Australia, and speakers in seven other countries. Also called Lettish, though speakers do not like the term. An official regional language in the Soviet Union.

Lithuanian: around 3,560,000 speakers reported in 1989, with 3,000,000 in Lithuania, plus others in North and South America, Australia, and west central Europe. An official regional language in the USSR.

Old Prussian: an extinct language spoken before 1700 in East Prussia.

BANTOID LANGUAGES constitute a group which covers most of Africa east and south of the southern part of the Nigeria-Cameroon border; they form one of the branches of the Benue-Congo group of the Niger-Congo family [*qq.v.*]. For the status and basic internal composition of Bantoid, reference may be made to John Watters, 'Bantoid overview', in *The Niger-Congo languages,* edited by John Bendor-Samuel (Lanham, Md.: University Press of America, 1989), pp. 401–420. Bantoid is here taken to comprise two subgroups, North Bantoid and South Bantoid (including Bantu), each of which is discussed in a separate article. In addition, two languages which are currently unclassified within Bantoid are listed below.

LANGUAGE LIST

Busuu: spoken west of Furu-Awa in Menchum Division, North West Province, Cameroon.

Cung: spoken northeast of Wum and west of Nkambe in Menchum Division, North West Province, Cameroon.

BANTU LANGUAGES (sometimes called 'Narrow Bantu') cover the southern half of Africa, extending from their presumed area of origin in eastern Nigeria to southern Somalia in the northeast, and southward to South Africa, including both the east and west coasts (see Map 1). Their speakers comprise slightly less than a third of Africa's total population, with more than four hundred language varieties, over twenty-five of them spoken by more than a million people each. Major languages include Bemba, Gikuyu (Kikuyu), Kamba, Kimbundu (Mbundu), Kongo, Lingala, Luba, Luganda (Ganda), Luhya (Luyia), Makua, Mongo, Nyamwezi-Sukuma, Nyanja, Nyaruanda (Rwanda), Rundi, Shona, Sotho, Swahili [*q.v.*], Thonga (Tsonga), Tswana, Xhosa, Yao, and Zulu—mostly eastern or centrally located. Although these languages are not mutually intelligible, large areas within the Bantu realm form dialect continua. Bantu speakers generally recognize the linguistic affinity of their own languages to other Bantu languages, even without mutual intelligibility—in contrast to the coterritorial non-Bantu languages found in some areas. Swahili, Lingala, and Fanagalo (a pidginized form of Zulu) serve as lingua francas for large numbers of speakers. (For reference, see Doke 1945, Guthrie 1948, 1967–71, Meussen 1967, Bryan 1959, Greenberg 1963, Welmers 1973, and Hinnebusch 1989.)

Genetically, there is consensus that Bantu is a deep member of the Niger-Congo family. It can be classified within, successively, the Atlantic-Congo, Volta-Congo, Benue-Congo, Bantoid, and South Bantoid (Broad Bantu)

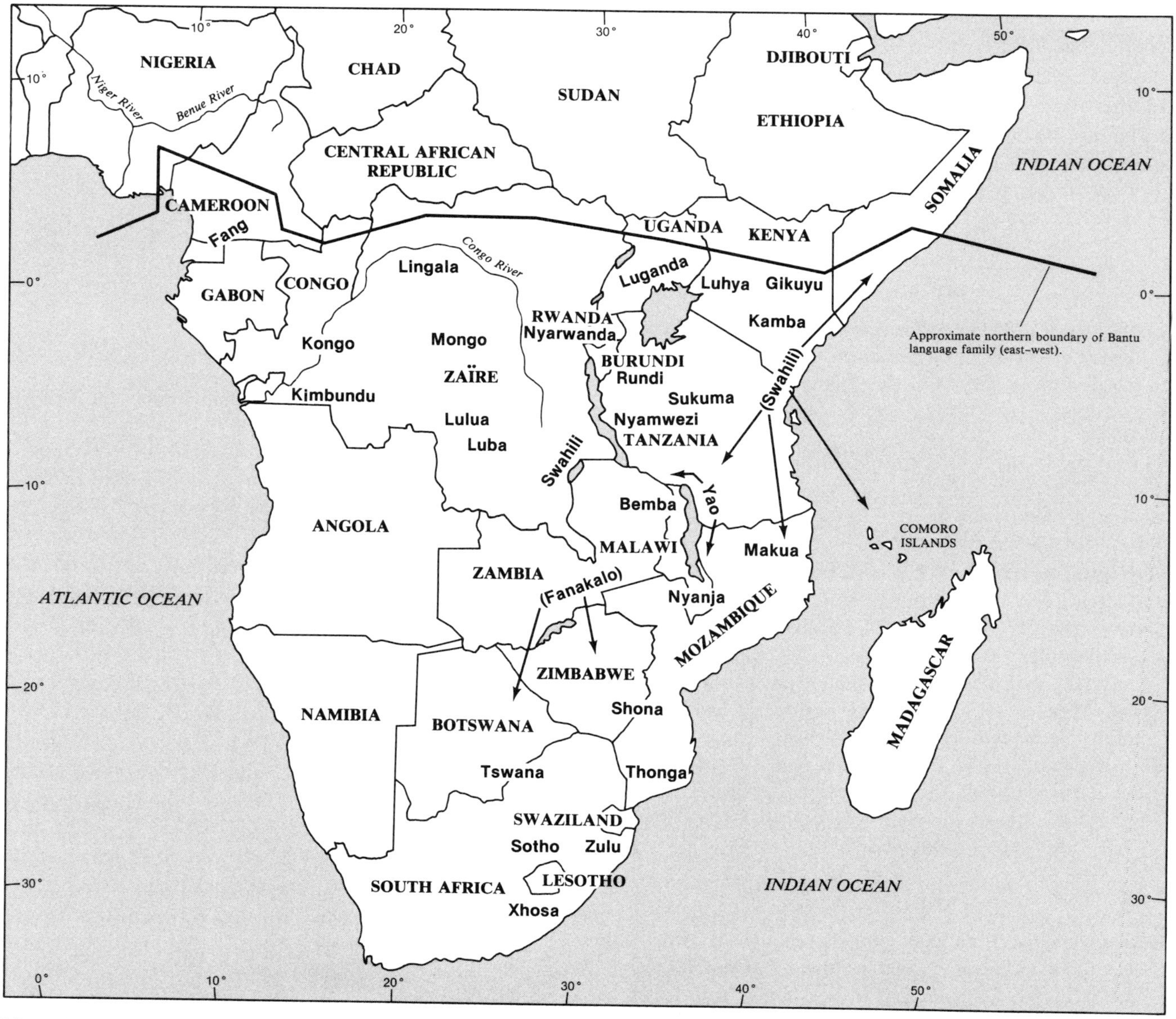

MAP 1. *Distribution of Major Bantu Languages.* Note that only languages mentioned in the text (over one million speakers) are indicated on the map. More than one hundred other Bantu languages are spoken throughout the area by smaller populations. Only central locations of languages are indicated. Most are more widely spoken (or understood). Other languages (usually Bantu) are spoken in areas indicating a major Bantu language. As a second language, Swahili is spoken throughout northeast Africa as far west as eastern Zaïre, north to southern coastal Somalia, south to northern Mozambique, and east to islands adjacent to the East African coast, including northern Madagascar.

groupings. [*See* Niger-Congo Languages; African Languages. *Narrow Bantu itself is divided into 'zones' which are labeled with the letters 'A' through 'S'; the classification used in this work is that of Bastin 1978, based on Guthrie 1967–71. For data on individual Bantu languages, see the Language Lists after articles on Narrow Bantu 'A', etc.; see also the Language List at the end of this article.*]

Historically, Bantu languages have a relatively simple phonology; words consist of open syllables, though a syllable may include prenasalized consonants like *mb* and *nd*. High and low tones are distinctive in most languages. Naturally, this reconstructed state of affairs has been somewhat complicated by changes in individual languages. Yet most languages have simplified further by merging ancient long vowels with short ones, and by reducing the seven-vowel system to five. Even tone, once apparently distinctive for each syllable, has been reduced to one distinctive tone per word in many languages.

Despite the large geographical domain, most Bantu languages display a remarkable degree of grammatical homogeneity. Most characteristic are the classification of nouns into a large number of classes, the influence of these classes on concord in a number of other grammatical categories, and the inflectional and derivational complexity of the verb. For the most part, noun and verb morphology is transparently agglutinative.

The complexity of the noun class system and the principles of class concord are the features of Bantu which were earliest recognized by linguists. All Bantu languages have a set of noun classes, usually signaled by a class prefix marking a nominal stem. Many classes come in singular/plural pairs. Thus, in Gikuyu, *mũ-* is a common class prefix for singular human nouns, with a corresponding plural *a-*, e.g., *mũ-ndũ* 'person', *a-ndũ* 'people'; another pair is *kĩ-ndũ* 'thing', *i-ndũ* 'things'. Most languages have at least six pairs of classes. A semantic basis for the classes is discernible primarily in deverbal and other forms of nominal derivation (e.g. diminutive or augmentative), but is sometimes obscure for non-derived lexical items. By patterns of class concord, a morpheme phonologically identical or similar to a noun's class prefix is extended to cross-reference grammatical categories such as subject and object markers of a verb, or noun modifiers (e.g. demonstratives, quantifiers, numerals, and adjectives).

The morphological composition of the verb suggests that the word order S[ubject] O[bject] V[erb] AUX[iliary] can be reconstructed for Bantu. Thus the typical Bantu verb has an obligatory subject marker followed by one or more tense/aspect prefixes, (optionally) one or more derivational suffixes, (possibly) one or more aspect suffixes, and an obligatory modal marker which distinguishes subjunctive from other modalities. The verb prefixes are usually monosyllabic, and those cross-referencing nouns agree with the noun in class. Syntactically, Bantu word order is overwhelmingly S AUX V O and Head + Modifier.

Pervasive in Bantu is the dynamic role played by the word in many phonological and morphological processes. Phonologically, for most of Bantu, a form of vowel harmony applies to certain derivational suffixes: a mid-vowel suffix is selected following a mid-vowel verb stem. Thus, in Gikuyu, the reversive suffix *-ũra* applied to the verb root *hing-* 'close' results in *hing-ũra* 'open'; but applied to the verb *oh-* 'tie', it results in *oh-ora* 'untie'. Similarly, but in a more limited area, some languages display a dissimilation of voiceless stops in consecutive syllables (a pattern called Dahl's Law by Bantuists). Thus, in Gikuyu, the class prefix *kĩ-* (as in *kĩ-rĩma* 'mountain') becomes *gĩ-* as in *gĩ-kũyũ* 'Gikuyu'. Morphologically, the dynamic role played by the word is illustrated by the restriction of object and tense/aspect markers in Eastern Bantu. Originally, the number of object markers and tense/aspect prefixes which could be affixed to the verb was determined solely by the respective semantics of the verb and the clause. This is still true in many languages; e.g., in Umbundu, the object markers *-u-* 'him/her' and *-n-* 'me' can be concatenatively prefixed to a verb like *-lekisa* 'show' which allows two objects, resulting in *-u-n-dekisa* 'show him/her to me'. But most Eastern coastal languages, including Swahili, allow only one object marker per verb. Similarly, concatenation of tense/aspect prefixes is common in Bantu, but some languages like Swahili have constrained the verb to a single tense/aspect prefix. Thus the concatenation of the tense/aspect prefixes *-li-* 'past' and *-ki-* 'imperfect' survives in some Northern Swahili dialects—e.g., with *-enda* 'go', forming *-li-ki-enda* 'used to go'. However, in most forms of Swahili, each tense/aspect marker must be supported by a separate verb. Thus an auxiliary verb *-ku-wa* 'be(come)' is used, resulting in the compound construction *-li-ku-wa-ki-enda*.

Semantically, Bantu languages are notable for the number of distinctions made among tenses. Two degrees of past and future, 'near' and 'more remote', are very common. Up to four degrees of past are not rare—adding 'just past', and distinguishing 'today' from other 'near'.

BENJI WALD

BIBLIOGRAPHY

BASTIN, YVONNE. 1978. Les langues bantoues. In *Inventaire des études linguistiques sur les pays d'Afrique Noire d'expression française et sur Madagascar*, edited by Daniel Barreteau, 123–186. Paris: Conseil International de la Langue Française.

Bryan, Margaret A., ed. 1959. *The Bantu languages of Africa.* London & New York: Oxford University Press.

Doke, Clement M. 1945. *Bantu: Modern grammatical, phonetical and lexicographical studies since 1860.* London: International African Institute. Reprinted, 1967.

Greenberg, Joseph H. 1963. *The languages of Africa.* (Indiana University Research Center in Anthropology, Folklore, and Linguistics, publication 25; International Journal of American Linguistics, 29:1, part 2.) Bloomington.

Guthrie, Malcolm. 1948. *The classification of Bantu languages.* London & New York: Oxford University Press. Reprinted, 1967.

Guthrie, Malcolm. 1967–71. *Comparative Bantu.* 4 vols. Farnborough, England: Gregg.

Hinnebusch, Thomas J. 1989. Bantu. In *The Niger-Congo languages,* ed. by John Bendor-Samuel & Rhonda L. Hartell, pp. 450–473. Lanham, Md.: University Press of America.

Meussen, A. E. 1967. Bantu grammatical reconstructions. *Annalen van het Koninklijk Museum voor Midden-Afrika* 61.79–121.

Welmers, William E. 1973. *African language structures.* Berkeley: University of California Press.

LANGUAGE LIST

[*For data on individual Bantu languages, see the Language Lists under Narrow Bantu. These lists distinguish sixteen traditional 'zones' or subgroups, referred to by the letters A–H, J–N, P, R, and S. In addition, the Narrow Bantu languages listed below are unclassified at present.*]

Babango: a language of Zaïre. Possibly the same as the Bango variety of Bali, or perhaps to be identified with Bwa.

Bikya: spoken west of Furu-Awa in Menchum Division, North West Province, Cameroon.

Bishuo: spoken west of Furu-Awa in Menchum Division, North West Province, Cameroon.

Borna: reported to be spoken in Zaïre. Also called Eborna. Existence unconfirmed; may be the same as Boma.

Buya: spoken in Zaïre. Also called Ibuya.

Isanzu: 32,400 speakers reported in 1987 from Tanzania. Bilingualism in Swahili exists.

Jiji: 12,000 speakers reported in 1987 from Tanzania. Bilingualism in Swahili exists.

Kichi: a language of Tanzania. Perhaps the same as Kisi.

Moingi: spoken south of the Zaïre River, opposite Basoko, Yahuma Zone, Haut-Zaïre Region, Zaïre.

Mungong: spoken northeast of Wum and west of Nkambe, Menchum Division, North West Province, Cameroon.

Ndendeule: 79,000 speakers reported in 1987 from inland Tanzania, east of the main Ngoni territory south of the 10th parallel. Also called Ndendeuli. Speakers have little understanding of other languages.

Rungi: 166,000 speakers reported in 1987 from Tanzania. Also called Irungi.

Songo: a language of Zaïre, also called Kisongo or Itsong. Perhaps the same as Nsongo of Angola.

BARIC LANGUAGES

BARIC LANGUAGES are a group spoken in northeastern India, in Burma, in southwestern China, and in adjacent areas. They constitute a subdivision of the Tibeto-Burman branch of the Sino-Tibetan languages [*qq.v.*]. They may be subgrouped as shown in Figure 1. [*For data on individual Baric languages, see the articles on Bodo-Garo, Konyak, Kuki-Chin, Mikir-Meithei, Mirish, and Naga. For data on the smaller families and language isolates—Mru, Kachinic, and Luish (Kado)—see the Language List which follows.*]

LANGUAGE LIST

Jingpho: 558,000 speakers reported in 1983, with 531,000 in Kachin State, Burma, 20,000 across the border in China, and 7,200 in adjacent parts of India. Also called Kachin, Singpo, Chingpo, Chingpaw, Jinghpaw, or Marip. Serves as a lingua franca for Atsi, Lashi, and Maru. An official nationality in China.

Kado: 229,000 or more speakers estimated in 1983, with 128,500 in Burma, 100,000 in China, and others in Laos. Also called Kadu, Katu, Kato, Kudo, Asak, Sak, Gadu, Thet, That, Mawteik, Puteik, or Woni. Distinct from Katu, a Mon-Khmer language of Vietnam, China, and Laos.

Mru: 66,500 speakers reported in 1983, with 34,100 in and near the Arakan Hills of Burma, 17,800 in Bangladesh, and 14,600 in India. Also called Mro, Murung, Niopreng, or Mrung.

Taman: 10,000 speakers reported in Burma.

Figure 1. *Subgrouping of Baric Languages*

Kachinic
  Jingpho, Taman
Konyak-Bodo-Garo
  Bodo-Garo
  Konyak
Kuki-Naga
  Kuki-Chin
  Mikir-Meithe
  Mru
  Naga
Luish (Kado)
Mirish

BARITO LANGUAGES are spoken in the southeast of the island of Borneo (Kalimantan, Indonesia), but also include Malagasy (Madagascar). They form one of the top-level constituents of the Borneo subgroup of West Malayo-Polynesian [*q.v.*]. The internal subgrouping of the Barito languages given in Figure 1 is based on Merritt Ruhlen, *A guide to the world's languages,* vol. 1, *Classification* (Stanford, Calif.: Stanford University Press, 1987).

LANGUAGE LIST

Ampanang: around 30,000 speakers reported in 1981, southeast of Tunjung, around Jambu and Lamper, east central Kalimantan.

Bakumpai: 40,000 or more speakers reported in 1981, northeast of Kualakapuas, in the Kapuas and Barito River area, Kalimantan. Also called Bara-Jida.

Dohoi: around 80,000 speakers reported in 1981, in an extensive area south of the Schwaner Range in Kalimantan. Also called Ot Danum or Uut Danum. The Dohoi and Murung 1 varieties may be separate languages.

Dusun Deyah: around 20,000 speakers reported in 1981, on the Tabalong River in southeast Kalimantan. Also called Deah or Dejah.

Dusun Malang: around 10,000 speakers reported in 1981, west of Muarainu in east central Kalimantan.

Dusun Witu: around 25,000 speakers reported in 1981 south of Muarateweh in southeast Kalimantan.

Kahayan: 45,000 speakers reported in 1981, on the Kapuas and Kahayan rivers in south central Kalimantan. Also called Kahaian or Kahajan.

Katingan: around 45,000 speakers reported in 1981, on the Katingan River in south central Kalimantan.

FIGURE 1. *Subgrouping of Barito Languages*

East Barito
- **Central-South East Barito**
  - **Central East Barito**
    - Dusun Deyah
  - **South East Barito**
    - Dusun Malang, Dusun Witu, Ma'anyan, Paku
- Malagasy
- **North East Barito**
  - Lawangan, Tawoyan

Mahakam
- Ampanang, Tunjung

West Barito
- **Northwest Barito**
  - Dohoi, Siang
- **Southwest Barito**
  - Bakumpai, Kahayan, Katingan, Ngaju

Lawangan: 100,000 speakers reported in 1981, around the Karau River in east central Kalimantan. Also called Luwangan or Northeast Barito. May be mutually intelligible with Tawoyan.

Ma'anyan: 70,000 speakers reported in 1981, around Tamianglayang in the Patai River basin in southern Kalimantan. Also called Maanyak Dayak or Siang.

Malagasy: 10,000,000 speakers reported in 1981, primarily in Madagascar, and in the Comoro Islands. Also called Malgache. Spoken by the entire population of Madagascar, for whom it is the national language. The Merina dialect is the literary variety. The most closely related language is Ma'anyan.

Ngaju: 250,000 speakers reported in 1981, on the Kapuas, Kahayan, Katingan, and Mentaya rivers in southern Kalimantan. Also called Ngaju Dayak, Biadju, or Southwest Barito.

Paku: around 20,000 speakers reported in 1981, south of Ampah in southeast Kalimantan.

Siang: around 60,000 speakers reported in 1981, east of Dohoi in central Kalimantan. Also called Ot Siang.

Tawoyan: around 20,000 speakers reported in 1981, around Palori in east central Kalimantan. Also called Tawoyan Dayak, Taboyan, Tabuyan, or Tabojan Tongka. May be inherently mutually intelligible with Lawangan.

Tunjung: around 50,000 speakers reported in 1981, in east central Kalimantan. Also called Tunjung Dayak.

BASHIIC—CENTRAL LUZON—NORTHERN MINDORO LANGUAGES constitute a group spoken on the islands of Luzon and Mindoro in the Philippines, plus Yami in southern Taiwan. They form a top-level constituent of the Northern Philippine subgroup of West Malayo-Polynesian [*q.v.*]. The subgrouping given in Figure 1 is based on Merritt Ruhlen, *A guide to the world's languages,* vol. 1, *Classification* (Stanford, Calif.: Stanford University Press, 1987).

LANGUAGE LIST

Agta, Remontado: 1,000 to 2,000 speakers reported in 1977, in Rizal and Quezon Provinces, Luzon. Also called Hatang-Kayey or Sinauna. Speakers are fairly bilingual in Tagalog. Other Philippine languages called 'Agta' belong to different groupings within Western Malayo-Polynesian.

Alangan: 4,000 speakers reported in 1987, in north central Mindoro.

Ayta, Abenlen: 6,850 speakers reported in 1985, in Tarlac Province, Luzon. Also called Abenlen, Ayta Abenlen Sambal, or Aburlin Negrito. Some speakers in remote areas are nearly monolingual.

FIGURE 1. *Subgrouping of Bashiic–Central Luzon–Northern Mindoro Languages*

Bashiic
- Yami
- **Ivatan**
  - Ibatan, Ivatan (proper)

Central Luzon
- Pampangan
- **Sambalic**
  - Abenlen Ayta, Ambala Ayta, Bataan Ayta, Mag-Anchi Ayta, Mag-Indi Ayta, Bolinao, Botolan Sambal, Tina Sambal
- Sinauna (Remontado Agta)

Northern Mindoro
- Alangan, Iraya, Tadyawan

Ayta, Ambala: around 1,660 speakers reported in 1986, in Zambales and Bataan Provinces, Luzon. Also called Ambala Agta or Ambala Sambal.

Ayta, Bataan: 570 speakers reported in 1986, in Mariveles, Bataan Province, Luzon. Also called Mariveles Ayta, Bataan Sambal, or Bataan Ayta. Speakers are fairly bilingual in Tagalog.

Ayta, Mag-Anchi: around 4,170 speakers reported in 1986, close to the Tarlac-Pampanga border and in Zambales Province, central Luzon. Also called Mag-Anchi Sambal.

Ayta, Mag-Indi: around 2,490 speakers reported in 1986, in Pampanga and Zambales Provinces, Luzon. Also called Baloga, Mag-Indi Sambal, or Indi Ayta.

Bolinao: 50,000 speakers reported in 1990, in west Pangasinan Province, Luzon. Also called Bolinao Sambal or Bolinao Zambal. Half the speakers have some bilingual proficiency in Tagalog, Ilocano, or Pangasinan.

Ibatan: 950 or more speakers reported in 1987, on Babuyan Island, north of Luzon. Also called Babuyan, Ibataan, or Ivatan. Mutual intelligibility with Ivatan of Itbayaten is only 64 percent, and that with Ivatan of Basco is 31 percent.

Iraya: 8,000 speakers reported in 1981, in northern Mindoro, Philippines. Many speak Tagalog in the home.

Ivatan: 30,000 speakers reported in 1981, in Basco, Batanes Islands, north of Luzon, including about 1,000 who have relocated on Mindanao near the boundary of Bukidnon, Lanao del Sur, and Cotabato; also some in Manila.

Pampangan: around 1,850,000 speakers reported in 1984, in Pampanga, Tarlac, and Bataan Provinces, Luzon. Also called Pampango, Pampangueño, or Kapampangan. The dominant language in Pampanga Province.

Sambal, Botolan: 31,500 speakers reported in 1975, in Zambales Province, central Luzon. Also called Aeta Negrito or Botolan Zambal. Limited bilingualism in Tagalog.

Sambal, Tina: 65,000 speakers reported in 1981, in northern Zambales Province, Luzon. Also called Tino. Moderate bilingualism in Tagalog.

Tadyawan: 2,000 speakers reported in 1982, in east central Mindoro, Philippines. Also called Pula, Tadianan, or Balaban.

Yami: 2,600 speakers reported in 1978, on Orchid and Botel Tobago (Lanyu) islands off the southeast coast of Taiwan. Also called Botel Tobago.

BASQUE is a non-Indo-European language, spoken by close to one million people in the western Pyrenees—more precisely, in a fifty-kilometer coastal strip extending from Bayonne, France, to Bilbao, Spain (see Map 1). For all the ink spent on its genetic affiliations over the past hundred years, the matter is still unclear. A few scholars hold Basque to be related to Afro-Asiatic (Hamito-Semitic); others (cf. Lafon 1972) claim genetic ties with the Kartvelian languages of the Caucasus. Most experts remain skeptical of both proposals. The once popular notion that Basque was a close relative of ancient Iberian has largely been abandoned; existing analogies seem to reflect areal phenomena rather than family resemblance. (For reference, see Tovar 1957, N'Diaye 1970, Michelena 1977, Allières 1979, Echenique 1983, Aulestia 1989, 1990, and Hualde & Ortiz de Urbina 1990.)

Of the eight Basque dialects, four have been used in literature: Guipuzcoan, Biscayan, Navarro-Labourdin, and Souletin. Adult speakers today are bilingual, their other language being that of their official nationality, French or Spanish. In the New World, to which many Basques have emigrated, Basque/English bilingualism occurs.

Numerous loan words have been integrated into Basque, mainly but not exclusively from Latin and the surrounding Romance languages: e.g. *errege* 'king', *lege* 'law', *eliza* 'church', *liburu* 'book', *zeru* 'sky', *dorre* 'tower', *katu* 'cat', *gaztelu* 'castle'. There are also a number of early loans from Celtic, e.g. *adar* 'horn', *hartz* 'bear', *maite* 'dear', *mando* 'mule', *hogei* 'twenty', *-tegi* 'hut'. The language still occasionally resorts to borrowing to cope with the novelties of modern life. However, its rich system of nominal derivation and composition generally succeeds in creating satisfactory terms to express new concepts in science and technology.

The rise of a standard language dates from 1968, when

the Basque Academy, guided by the eminent linguist Luis Michelena (1915–87), set out to create a standard dialect for written communication. This is called *Euskara Batua* 'unified Basque'. Since 1980, more than 80 percent of all Basque publications have been in this variety. With time, it may become a spoken standard as well; but given the strong attachment of most speakers to their local varieties, such a process is likely to take several generations.

1. Phonology (see Michelena 1976). The Basque vowel system is very much like that of Castilian Spanish: *a e i o u*, without distinctive length. Only the northeastern varieties of Basque have developed a sixth vowel, *ü*. There are six diphthongs, all falling: *au eu ai ei oi ui*. The consonant system is shown in Table 1.

Voiced *b d g* are subject to intervocalic spirantization and final devoicing. The nasals *m n* are neutralized in syllable-final position, where the result is dental, unless

MAP 1. *Location of the Basque Language*

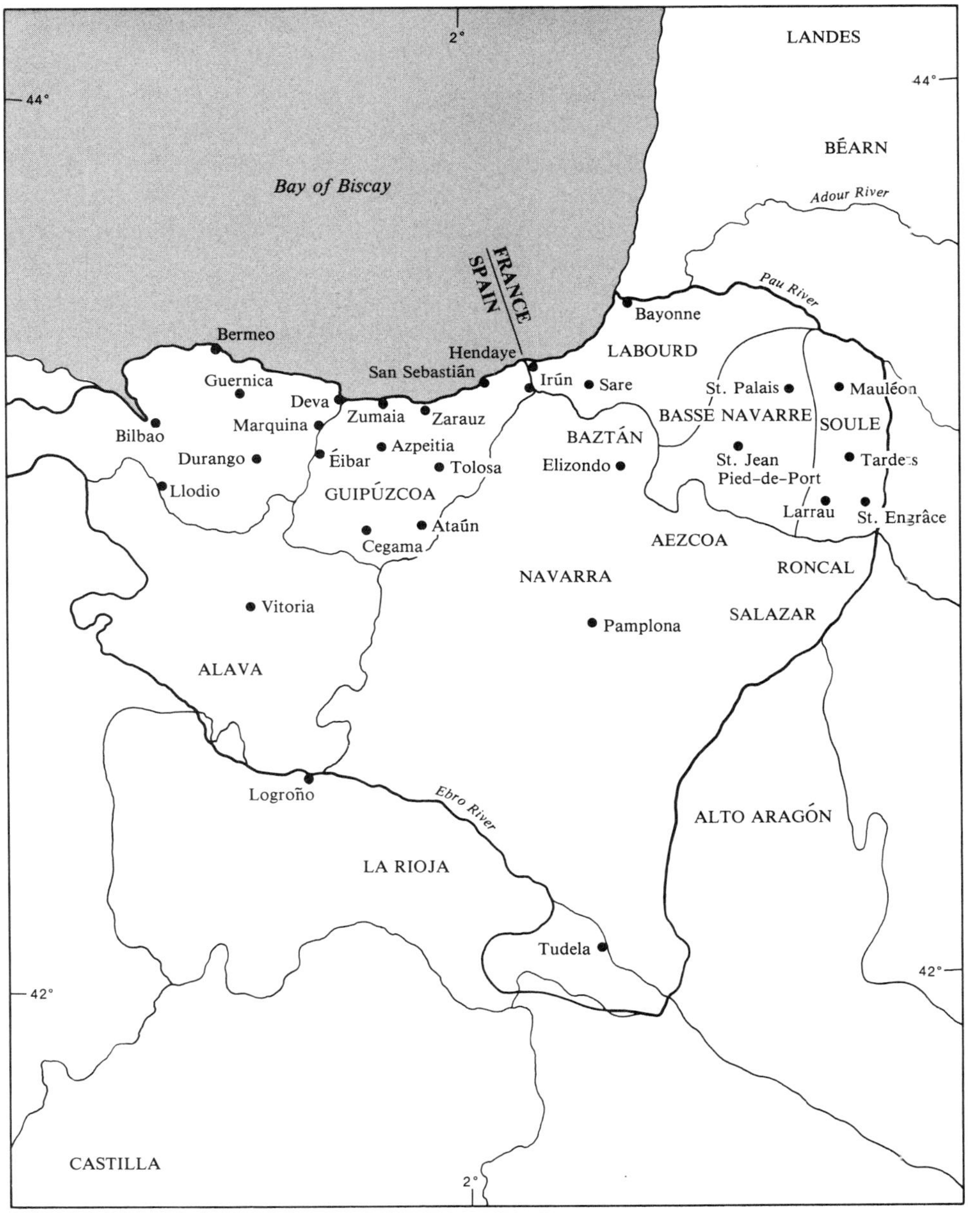

TABLE 1. *Basque Consonants in Standard Orthography*

	Labial	Dental	Dorso-alveolar	Apico-alveolar	Palatal	Velar	Glottal
Occlusives							
Voiceless	p	t	tz	ts	tx	k	
Voiced	b	d				g	
Fricatives	f		z	s	x		(h)
Nasals	m	n			(ñ)		
Vibrants							
Flap				r			
Trill				rr			
Lateral				l	(ll)		
Semivowel					j		

the following consonant determines otherwise. In most of the Basque-speaking area, an intervocalic nasal or lateral is realized as palatal after *i*. Otherwise, palatal *ñ* and *ll* occur only in place names and expressive forms.

The opposition between *rr* and *r* is quite similar to that of the corresponding phonemes in Castilian Spanish; they contrast only in intervocalic position. A noteworthy difference from Castilian is that Basque vibrants cannot begin a word (thus *Erroma* 'Rome'); this peculiarity is shared with the neighboring Romance dialects, Gascon and Aragonese.

A notable characteristic of Basque phonemics is the three-way contrast among sibilants and affricates. All sibilants and affricates are normally voiceless. The non-palatal affricates *tz ts* can be syllable-initial, but not word-initial.

The remaining consonants, *f j,* are restricted to syllable-initial position. Of the multifarious local pronunciations of *j,* two are common in the literary standard: semivocalic, like Eng. *y,* spread by Basque television; and velar, like Sp. *j,* borrowed from the Guipuzcoan dialect.

Dialects north of the French/Spanish border have a phoneme *h,* pronounced as in English; it occurs frequently, but with fairly restricted distribution. Unless word-initial, it must follow a vowel, liquid, or *n*. In the same dialects, voiceless plosives can be aspirated in certain positions, usually at the beginning of the first or second syllable. The syllable division shows that the aspirates are not to be analyzed as clusters: *a-pho* 'toad' vs. *ol-ho* 'oats'. Since the great majority of Basque speakers lack *h,* the 1968 decision of the Basque Academy to include the letter in its standard orthography stirred controversy—even though the Academy agreed to ban the writing of post-consonantal *h,* leaving it only in word-initial or intervocalic positions.

The eastern dialects have a stress system, the details of which vary considerably according to region. The sociolinguistically more important western dialects, Biscayan and Guipuzcoan, have a tonal system, remarkably uniform over the area; every phonological phrase shows either an unmarked level toneme or a marked falling one.

2. Nominal inflection (see Aulestia 1989) operates through suffixation to an invariable base. Nouns and adjectives do not distinguish gender or number; but articles and demonstratives display a singular/plural contrast. Thus, for each case inflection, there are an indefinite, a definite singular, and a definite plural form. In the non-locative cases, the indefinite marker is Ø, the definite marker is *-a,* and the plural marker is *-g* (elided with intervocalic, devoiced to *-k* in final position); the inflection of *katu* 'cat' is shown in Table 2.

Table 3 shows that, in the locative cases of inanimate nouns, the indefinite marker is *-ta-,* the definite marker Ø, and the plural marker *-eta*; however, the locative cases of animate nouns take a suffix *-gan* preceding these and affixed to the genitive, thus following the system of Table 2. (The 'terminal' case can be glossed 'up to, until', and the tendential as 'toward'.)

Finally, the partitive case ending *-(r)ik* is reserved for otherwise absolutive indefinite N[oun] P[hrase]s in negative, interrogative, or conditional contexts:

(1) *Hemen ez dago gaztelurik.*
'There is no castle here.'

(2) *Ohostu al duzu katurik?*
'Have you stolen any cat?'

Case endings in Basque do not percolate down into the constituent parts of a NP. Only the last word is inflected: *katu beltz batengatik* 'because of a black cat' (where the numeral *bat* 'one' serves as an indefinite article), *gaztelu zahar batzuetan* 'in some old castles'.

The genitive case, being adjectival, can be followed by the definite article *-a*; this serves as a pronoun whose reference is to be inferred from the context, e.g. *katuarena* 'the one of the cat'. The resulting NP may in turn take any case ending, including the genitive: *katuarenarekin* 'with the one of the cat', *katuarenarenei* 'to the ones of the one of the cat'. This kind of recursion has been misleadingly styled 'hyperdeclension'.

Spatial relationships are expressed by locative case forms of locational nouns, e.g. *aurre* 'front', *atze* 'back', and *ondo* 'proximity', constructed with the genitive: *gazteluaren aurrean* 'in front of the castle', *gaztelu baten ondoan* 'next to a castle', *katuen atzean* 'behind the cats', *katuen atzetik* 'after the cats'.

Gradable adjectives have a comparative form in *-ago,* a superlative in *-en,* and an excessive in *-egi*: *hotz* 'cold', *Bilbo baino hotzago* 'colder than Bilbao', *hotzena* 'the coldest', *hotzegi* 'too cold'.

3. Ergativity and verbal morphology. Before delving into the riches of verbal morphology—an 18th-century grammarian counted no less than 30,952 forms of a single verb—it must be noted that Basque is an ergative language. Subjects of intransitive verbs and direct objects of transitive ones are in the unmarked absolutive case; subjects of transitive verbs are in the ergative case, marked with *-(e)k*:

(3) *Jon dator* 'John is coming.'

(4) *Jonek Xixili dakar* 'John is bringing Cecily.'

The observation by Levin 1983 that all Basque intransitives with absolutive subject are 'unaccusative' (cf. Perlmutter 1978) suggests that Basque ergativity stems from the absence of a mechanism to alter the initial object case of unaccusative objects. [*See also* Relational Grammar.] Some objectless verbs which require ergative subjects (e.g. *iraun* 'to last', *irakin* 'to boil', *distiratu* 'to glitter') are then explainable as 'unergative' verbs which take the regular subject case, i.e. the ergative.

Basque ergativity is not syntactic: in embeddings, coordinate clauses, reflexives, reciprocals, etc., absolutive subjects pair with ergative subjects, not with absolutive objects. However, the ergative is not restricted to

TABLE 2. *Basque Forms of* katu *'cat'*

	Indefinite	Definite Singular	Definite Plural
Absolute	*katu*	*katua*	*katuak*
Ergative	*katuk*	*katuak*	*katuek*
Dative	*katuri*	*katuari*	*katuei*
Genitive	*katuren*	*katuaren*	*katuen*
Benefactive	*katurentzat*	*katuarentzat*	*katuentzat*
Motivational	*katurengatik*	*katuarengatik*	*katuengatik*
Sociative	*katurekin*	*katuarekin*	*katuekin*
Instrumental	*katuz*	*katuaz*	*katuez*

TABLE 3. *Basque Locative Cases of* gaztelu *'castle' and* katu *'cat'*

	Indefinite	Definite Singular	Definite Plural
Inanimate nouns			
Inessive	*gaztelutan*	*gazteluan*	*gazteluetan*
Elative	*gaztelutatik*	*gaztelutik*	*gazteluetatik*
Allative	*gaztelutara*	*gaztelura*	*gazteluetara*
Terminal	*gaztelutaraino*	*gazteluraino*	*gazteluetaraino*
Tendential	*gaztelutarantz*	*gaztelurantz*	*gazteluetarantz*
Animate nouns			
Inessive	*katurengan*	*katuarengan*	*katuengan*
Elative	*katurengandik*	*katuarengandik*	*katuengandik*
Allative	*katurengana*	*katuarengana*	*katuengana*
Terminal	*katurenganaino*	*katuarenganaino*	*katuenganaino*
Tendential	*katurenganantz*	*katuarenganantz*	*katuenganantz*

case-marking; it also governs verbal morphology. The pattern of Table 4 is typical.

The prefixed absolutive markers *n- h- g- z-* derive from the personal pronouns: *ni* 'I', *hi* 'you (familiar)', *gu* 'we', *zu* 'you (polite)'. (Third person *da-* is a tense marker.) Ergative markers are suffixes: *-t* (from *-da*), *-k* (from *-ga*), *-gu*, *-zu*. This is the only area where gender is relevant: when the 2nd person familiar is female, the suffix *-na* appears instead of the unmarked *-ga* (used even by females soliloquizing).

Pervasive in the present tense, the ergative pattern is interrupted in the past tense and in tenses based on it; this has been interpreted by Heath (1977:197) as a relic of a former antipassivization rule. Little happens as long as the direct object remains 1st or 2nd person; but when it is 3rd person, the absolutive marker drops, and the ergative subject is marked by a prefix—thus *nekarren* 'I brought him', *genekarren* 'we brought him', *zenekarren* 'you brought him', as opposed to the ergative pattern of *nindekarzun* 'you brought me'. This morphological antipassivization, however, has no clause-level effects, since it affects neither word order nor case-marking.

Multipersonal verb agreement is characteristic of Basque: any finite verb form must agree in person and number with its subject, its direct object, and (in most dialects) also its indirect object. Since non-emphatic personal pronouns serving these functions are omitted, a finite verb preceded by the affirmative particle *ba-* or the negation *ez* can constitute a complete sentence:

(5a) *Badakar* 'He is bringing it.'
(5b) *Badakarte* 'They are bringing it.'
(5c) *Badakartza* 'He is bringing them.'
(5d) *Badakartzate* 'They are bringing them.'

An indirect object may also be expressed in the verb alone:

(6a) *Badakarkio* 'He is bringing it to him.'
(6b) *Badakarkiote* 'They are bringing it to him.'
(6c) *Badakarzkio* 'He is bringing them to him.'
(6d) *Badakarzkiote* 'They are bringing them to him.'

If the indirect object is plural, *e* is substituted for *o*.

The dative markers have the same shape as the ergative ones, except for the 3rd person: dative *-o* and ergative Ø for the singular, and dative *-e* (variant *-ote*), ergative *-te* for the plural. Some verbs add the dative marker directly to the stem; others, like *ekarri* 'to bring', use an intervening segment *-ki-*. The dative marker always precedes the ergative when both are present:

(7) *Badakarkizugu* 'We're bringing it to you.'

With such verbal morphology, it is hardly surprising that Basque speakers use the dative as much as possible, e.g. preferring the 'possessive dative' *Katua hil zaigu* 'The cat has died on us' to *Gure katua hil da* 'Our cat has died.'

The verb *ekarri* 'to bring' is special in having synthetic forms. Most verbs have only a periphrastic conjugation, consisting of a non-finite verb form and a conjugated auxiliary. In Basque as commonly spoken, only about twelve verbs are 'strong', i.e. allow synthetic forms. There used to be more; but even in the 16th century, their number did not exceed fifty, as seen in Leizárraga's New Testament translation (1571) and other texts. In today's literary language, synthetic forms function as indicators of style: the loftier the style, the more synthetic forms appear, including some that are entirely innovative.

Except for one or two defective verbs, all strong verbs have periphrastic forms as well, constructed with the following non-finite verb forms:

(a) An adjectival past participle (the citation form of the verb), often characterized by a suffix *-i* or *-tu*: *ekarri* 'brought', *hartu* 'taken', *jakin* 'known', *hil* 'died'

TABLE 4. *Basque Verb Forms.* 'It' subsumes 'him' and 'her', 'he' subsumes 'she' and 'it'.

n-a-tor 'I'm coming'	*n-a-kar* 'he's bringing me'	*da-kar-t* 'I'm bringing it'
h-a-tor 'you're coming'	*h-a-kar* 'he's bringing you'	*da-kar-k* 'you're bringing it'
da-tor 'he's coming'	*da-kar* 'he's bringing it'	*da-kar* 'he's bringing it'

(b) A gerund, consisting of the verbal noun (in *-te* or *-tze*) plus an inessive ending *-n*: *ekartzen* 'bringing', *hartzen* 'taking', *jakiten* 'knowing', *hiltzen* 'dying'
(c) A future participle, consisting of the past participle plus a suffix *-ko*, or (in the eastern dialects) an indefinite genitive ending *-ren*: *ekarriko (ekarriren), hartuko (harturen), jakingo (jakinen), hilko (hilen)*
(d) A radical, consisting of the past participle minus the suffix *-i* or *-tu*: *ekar, har, jakin, hil*

To show how the periphrastic conjugation system is constructed, we break it down into five moods: indicative, conditional, subjunctive, imperative, and potential. The indicative has six major tenses:

(i) Present imperfect = gerund + present tense auxiliary: *ekartzen du* 'he brings it'
(ii) Past imperfect = gerund + past tense auxiliary: *ekartzen zuen* 'he brought it, he used to bring it'
(iii) Present perfect = past participle + present tense auxiliary: *ekarri du* 'he has brought it'
(iv) Past perfect = past participle + past tense auxiliary: *ekarri zuen* 'he brought it, he had brought it'
(v) Future = future participle + present tense auxiliary: *ekarriko du* 'he will bring it'
(vi) Past future = future participle + past tense auxiliary: *ekarriko zuen* 'he would bring it'

Strong verbs also have a simple present, e.g. *dakar* 'he is bringing it', and a simple past, *zekarren* 'he was bringing it'. Simple forms in colloquial use express momentaneous action, while the imperfect tenses express habitual action or background activity. There is also a synthetic future tense, little used except in the northeastern dialects: *dakarke* 'he will (probably) bring it'.

By adding non-finite forms of the auxiliary to the periphrastic verb forms, 'hyperperiphrastic' tenses have been created in some dialects, calqued on certain compound tense forms of Romance.

In the conditional, strong verbs have three synthetic forms: a protasis form with the conditional prefix *ba-* (*balekar* 'if he were to bring it'); an imperfect apodosis form with the irrealis suffix *-ke* (*lekarke* 'he would bring it'); and a perfect apodosis form with the past tense suffix *-en* added to *-ke* (*zekarkeen* 'he would have brought it').

Except in the northern dialects, which follow a slightly different system, conditionals have four periphrastic tense forms:

(a) Imperfect protasis = future participle + protasis form of the auxiliary: *ekarriko balu* 'if he were to bring it'
(b) Perfect protasis = past participle of main verb, optionally followed by the past participle of the auxiliary + the protasis form of the auxiliary: *ekarri (izan) balu* 'if he had brought it'
(c) Imperfect apodosis = future participle + imperfect apodosis form of the auxiliary: *ekarriko luke* 'he would bring it'
(d) Perfect apodosis = future participle + perfect apodosis form of the auxiliary: *ekarriko zukeen* 'he would have brought it'

The subjunctive has two tenses, present and past. The older language also had an irrealis, now obsolete. For most strong verbs, the subjunctive is formed from the simple indicative by adding the unmarked complementizer *-la*—or, in purpose clauses and the like, the relativizer *-n*: *dakargun* 'let us bring it', *dakarrela* 'let him bring it'. The two auxiliaries have irregular subjunctives: intransitive *izan* 'to be' has a subjunctive stem *-di-*, and transitive **edun* 'to have' has *-za-*. The periphrastic present/past subjunctive consists of a radical + present or past subjunctive auxiliary: *ekar dezan* 'that he may bring it', *ekar zezan* 'that he might bring it'.

The imperative mood has only one tense, e.g. *ekarzu* '(you) bring it!' There is also a 3rd person imperative form distinct from the subjunctive: *bekar* 'let him bring it!' The periphrastic imperative consists of a radical + imperative auxiliary: *ekar ezazu* '(you) bring it!', *ekar beza* 'let him bring it!'

The potential has three tenses: present (*dakarke* 'he can bring it'), conditional (*lekarke* 'he could bring it'), and past (*zekarkeen* 'he could have brought it'). The periphrastic potential consists of the radical + one of the auxiliary potential forms: *ekar dezake* 'he can bring it', *ekar lezake* 'he could bring it', *ekar zezakeen* 'he could have brought it'.

Within these sixteen periphrastic tenses, together with the twelve simple tenses for the strong verbs, multiple agreement operates to yield a plethora of possible verbal forms. The number is again more than doubled by a pragmatic process of addressee agreement, which gives rise to allocutive forms, a salient feature of Basque. Whenever the familiar form of address corresponding to the pronoun *hi* 'you (fam.)' is used, all non-subordinate verbs must agree with the sex of the addressee. Thus, in the central dialects, the phrase 'I know (it)' is *badakit* (unmarked), *bazekiat* (male addressee), or *bazekinat* (female addressee). In the northeastern dialects, addressee agreement also involves the *zu* (singular polite) forms.

Most (perhaps all) periphrastic transitive verb forms can be made impersonal by substituting the corresponding intransitive auxiliary for the transitive one. Thus, beside *ekartzen du* 'he brings it', we have *ekartzen da* 'it is being brought'; beside *ematen digu* 'he gives it to us', *ematen zaigu* 'it is being given to us'. These impersonals do not allow ergative subjects; they function like the agentless passives of other languages.

4. Syntax. As regards complementation, Basque verbs of communication and appearance require finite complements; verbs of perception and cognition take finite complements or gerunds; verbs of volition and command take finite subjunctive or non-finite complements; and other verbs take non-finite complements or nominalizations, as in *Badaiteke katua etortzea* 'It may be that the cat is coming.'

Basque has two finite complementizers, which are realized as suffixes to the subordinate verb: a WH-complementizer *-n,* and a regular complementizer *-la*:

(8) *Ez dakit katua nork dakarren.*
'I don't know who is bringing the cat.'

(9) *Ez dakit katua datorren* (or: *datorrenentz*).
'I don't know whether the cat is coming.'

(10) *Badakit katua ez datorrela.*
'I know that the cat is not coming.'

(11) *Katuak ez dirudi datorrela.*
'The cat does not seem to be coming' (lit. 'does not seem that he is coming').

Relativization operates by deletion of the lower NP together with its case endings. The relative clause, which must end in a finite verb bearing a relativizing suffix *-n* (homonymous with both the inessive ending and the WH-complementizer), directly precedes the antecedent in modern usage.

(12) *Sarri joaten naizen gaztelua urruti dago.*
'The castle I often go to is far.'

Finite adverbial clauses are characterized by a suffix on the subordinate verb. They are mostly derived from adjectival clauses modifying an abstract noun; the suffix is often analyzable as a relativizer followed by a case ending. Thus *gaztelura joaten naizenean* 'when I go to the castle' derives from the less common, but equally grammatical, *gaztelura joaten naizen orduan* 'at the time (*ordu*) that I go to the castle'. Likewise, *katua datorrelakoan* 'under the impression that the cat is coming' derives from *katua datorrelako ustean* 'in the belief (*uste*) that the cat is coming'.

This discussion has focused on finite clauses; however, non-finite constructions of various types involving past participles, gerunds, and verbal nouns (as well as other nominalizations) are extremely common in Basque, and occur freely in conversational speech.

Among the few monographs on Basque syntax, Rebuschi 1984 and Ortiz de Urbina 1989 deserve special mention; Lafitte 1979 and Saltarelli et al. 1988 also contain interesting observations.

5. Typology and word order. Basque is postpositional and has predominantly Subject Object Verb order, with the genitive preceding the noun and the adjective following it.

The order of constituents within a NP is: (i) relative clause; (ii) genitive; (iii) postpositional phrase followed by *-ko*; (iv) numeral; (v) head noun; (vi) adjective; (vii) determiner. All these may occur in one phrase:

(13)

gaur	*heldu*	*dire-n*	*ama-ren*	*atzerriko*
today	arrived	they.are-REL	mother-POSS	from.abroad

hiru	*adiskide*	*aberats*	*horiek*
three	friends	rich	those

'those three rich friends of mother's from abroad who arrived today'

A postpositional phrase cannot directly modify a NP (de Rijk 1988), but requires the adjectival suffix *-ko*: *gaztelurako bidea* 'the road to the castle' (in *atzerriko* 'from abroad' in 13, the ablative ending *-tik* has been deleted before *-ko*).

The underlying constituent order of Basque can be argued to be Subject + Indirect Object + Direct Object + Verb; this is also the predominant surface order. However, there is no rigid constraint on order, and all 24 possible permutations are found. Surface constituent order is largely determined by pragmatics: topic position is at the beginning of the sentence, and focus position immediately before the verb. Question words must be in focus position, but need not be sentence-initial:

(14) *Jonek zer ikusi du?*
'What has John seen?'

(15) *Jonek katu beltza ikusi du.*
'John has seen a black cat.'

Here *Jon* is topic, *katu beltza* is focus. Focus is doubly marked: by preverbal position, and by comparatively higher-pitched intonation.

The auxiliary immediately follows the main verb, except in negative sentences (and in some dialects, except in emphatic positives):

(16) *Jon Mirenekin etorri da gaur.*
'John has come today with Miren.'

(17) *Jon ez da gaur Mirenekin etorri.*
'John has not come with Miren today.'

RUDOLF P. G. DE RIJK

BIBLIOGRAPHY

ALLIÈRES, JACQUES. 1979. *Manuel pratique de basque.* (Collection 'Connaissance des langues', 13.) Paris: Picard.

AULESTIA, GORKA. 1989. *Basque–English dictionary.* Reno: University of Nevada Press.

AULESTIA, GORKA. 1990. *English–Basque dictionary.* Reno: University of Nevada Press.

DE RIJK, RUDOLF P. G. 1988. Basque syntax and universal grammar. In *Euskara Biltzarra / Conference on the Basque Language,* vol. 1, p. 69–88. Vitoria, Spain: Eusko Jaurlaritzaren Argitalpen-Zerbitzu Nagusia.

ECHENIQUE ELIZONDO, MARÍA TERESA. 1987. *Historia lingüística vasco-románica.* Revised ed. Madrid: Paraninfo.

HEATH, JEFFREY. 1977. Remarks on Basque verbal morphology. In *Anglo-American contributions to Basque studies: Essays in honor of Jon Bilbao,* edited by William A. Douglass et al., pp. 193–201. Reno, Nev.: Desert Research Institute.

HUALDE, JOSÉ IGNACIO, & JON ORTIZ DE URBINA, eds. 1990. *Generative studies in Basque linguistics.* Amsterdam: Benjamins.

LAFITTE, PIERRE. 1979. *Grammaire basque (navarro-labourdin littéraire).* Revised ed. San Sebastian: Elkar.

LAFON, RENÉ. 1972. The Basque language. In *Current trends in linguistics,* edited by Thomas A. Sebeok, vol. 9, *Linguistics in Western Europe,* pp. 1744–1792. The Hague: Mouton.

LEVIN, BETH C. 1983. Unaccusative verbs in Basque. *North Eastern Linguistic Society* 13.129–143.

MICHELENA, LUIS. 1976. *Fonética histórica vasca.* Revised ed. San Sebastián: Imprenta de la Diputación de Guipúzcoa.

MICHELENA, LUIS. 1977. Basque. *Encyclopaedia Britannica* 2.762–764.

N'DIAYE, GENEVIÈVE. 1970. *Structure du dialecte basque de Maya.* (Janua linguarum, Series practica, 86.) The Hague Mouton.

ORTIZ DE URBINA, JON. 1989. *Some parameters in the grammar of Basque.* Dordrecht: Foris.

PERLMUTTER, DAVID M. 1978. Impersonal passives and the unaccusative hypothesis. *Berkeley Linguistics Society* 4.157–189.

REBUSCHI, GEORGES. 1984. *Structure de l'énoncé en basque.* (L'Europe de tradition orale, 3.) Paris: Société d'Études Linguistiques et Anthropologiques de France.

SALTARELLI, MARIO, et al. 1988. *Basque.* London: Croom Helm.

TOVAR, ANTONIO. 1957. *The Basque language.* Philadelphia: University of Pennsylvania Press.

BEBOID LANGUAGES are spoken in western Cameroon; they form a top-level constituent of South Bantoid [*q.v.*]. The Beboid languages are subclassified as shown in Figure 1.

LANGUAGE LIST

Bebe: spoken west of Nkambe and north of Ring Road, in the west part of Ako District, Donga-Mangung Division, North West Province, Cameroon. Also called Yi Be Wu.

Bu: spoken in the villages of Bu, Za, and Ngwen, northeast of Wum, Wum Subdivision, Menchum Division, North West Province, Cameroon.

Kemezung: spoken northwest of Nkambe in the southwest corner of Ako District, Donga-Mantung Division, North West Province, Cameroon. Also called Dumbo, Dzumbo, or Kumaju.

Koskin: spoken in the villages of Koshin and Fang, Wum Subdivision, Menchum District, North West Province, Cameroon. Also called Koshin, Kosin, or Kaw.

Missong: spoken around the village of Missong, in Wum Sub-Division, Menchum Division, North West Province, Cameroon. Also called Mijong. Dzaiven Boka may be an alternate name.

Naki: spoken northeast of Wum from Mekaf south, straddling Furu-Awa District and Wum Subdivision, Menchum Division, North West Province, Cameroon. Also called Mekaf, Bunaki, Munkaf, and Nkap.

Ncane: spoken in Misaje village and south, in western Nkambe Subdivision, Donga-Mantung Division, North West Province, Cameroon. Also called Ntshanti or Cane.

FIGURE 1. *Subgrouping of Beboid Languages*

Eastern Beboid
Bebe, Kemezung, Ncane, Noone, Nsari
Western Beboid
Bu, Koskin, Missong, Naki

Noone: spoken in northwestern Kumbo Subdivision, Bui Division, North West Province, Cameroon. Also called Noni or Noori.

Nsari: spoken on both sides of Ring Road between Misaje and Nkambe, in the western part of Nkambe Subdivision, Donga-Mantung Division, North West Province, Cameroon. Also called Akweto, Pesaa, or Sali. May be mutually intelligible with other Eastern Beboid varieties.

BENGALI was reported in 1989 to have some 162 million speakers, making it a major language of the world. It is the national language of Bangladesh, where some two-thirds of its speakers reside. Most of the remainder inhabit the contiguous state of West Bengal, India. Within these boundaries, the language shows considerable dialect variation, the full extent of which is not yet adequately surveyed.

Bengali is characterized by diglossia: distinctive language styles are used in formal vs. informal social contexts. The more conservative literary or 'pundit language' (*sadhu bhasa*) prevails in formal and written discourse. However, since the early 20th century, such functions have begun to accrue to the colloquial style or 'current language' (*colit bhasa*); see Dimock 1960. The standard of colloquial spoken Bengali is identified with the speech of Calcutta, West Bengal. (For general reference, see Dimock et al. 1964, Ray et al. 1966, Čižikova & Ferguson 1969, Bender & Riccardi 1978, and Klaiman 1987.)

1. History. Bengali belongs to the Magadhan subfamily of the Indo-Aryan [*q.v.*] branch of Indo-European. The unattested ancestor of the Magadhan languages, attributed to the Middle period of Common Indo-Aryan, is called Eastern or Magadhan Apabhramsa. Bengali's closest relatives are, in order, Assamese and Oriya. Bengali has evolved in three major historical stages, designated by Chatterji (1926:130) as Old, Middle, and Modern. The sole surviving Old Bengali literary text, a collection of nearly fifty short Buddhist songs called the Caryāpada hymns, was composed sometime between 1000 and 1200 CE. The earliest surviving text of the Middle period is a much longer narrative collection of over four hundred songs composed by the poet Baṛu Caṇḍīdāsa, known as Srīkṛṣṇakīrtana. Opinions differ about its dating, but Chatterji assigns it to the late 14th century. According to him, the start of the Modern period coincides with the rise of literary interest in prose, about the beginning of the 18th century. Westerners are most likely to be acquainted with the name of Rabindranath Tagore (Ṭhākur) as a craftsman of prose and poetry in Modern Bengali, although superlative modern writers are numerous.

Over 90 percent of Modern Bengali vocabulary is Indo-Aryan, but the lexicon also shows significant foreign influences. For about six hundred years, from the beginning of the 13th century, Bengal was dominated by Islamic invaders from the northwest; they were supplanted by the British in the mid-18th century. According to Chatterji (1926:218), some 3.3 percent of Modern Bengali vocabulary consists of Persian/Arabic borrowings; about another 1 percent is from English. In addition, the influence of indigenous tribal languages—still spoken in and around the Gangetic delta—is inferable not only in Bengali vocabulary, but also in other features to be mentioned below. In light of the region's recent political history, it is noteworthy that current spoken Bengali shows minimal influences from Hindi, the national language of India, or from Urdu, the national language of Pakistan.

2. Phonology. Table 1 displays the consonant phonemes of Modern Bengali (cf. Chatterji 1921, Ferguson & Chowdhury 1960). Bengali has inherited from earlier Indo-Aryan the distinctions of aspirated vs. non-aspirated and of voiced vs. voiceless obstruents, as well as the distribution of these segments over five principal points of articulation. Modern Bengali has only one sibilant phoneme (Sanskrit had three); it is peculiar in being palatal, though realized as dental before *t th n r l*. The vowels are *i e æ a ɔ o u*. All vowels may occur with distinctive nasalization—*ĩ ẽ*, etc.

Major phonological processes involve vowels more often than consonants in Modern Bengali. One, Vowel

TABLE 1. *Consonant Phonemes of Bengali*

	Labial	Dental	Retroflex	Palatal	Velar	Glottal
Obstruents						
Voiceless						
Unaspirated	p	t	ṭ	c	k	
Aspirated	ph	th	ṭh	ch	kh	
Voiced						
Unaspirated	b	d	ḍ	j	g	
Aspirated	bh	dh	ḍh	jh	gh	
Spirants				s		h
Nasals	m	n	ṇ			
Flaps		r	ṛ			
Lateral		l				

Raising, neutralizes the close/open distinction in the mid vowels, predominantly in unstressed syllables. Since stress regularly falls on the initial syllable, the effects of vowel raising are, for the most part, observed only in non-initial position. A few illustrations appear in Table 2, Part A.

A second process, Vowel Height Assimilation, is significant for morphophonemic alternations in verbal bases. In this process, a non-high vowel other than /a/ assimilates to the height of the nearest succeeding [+high] vowel segment within the phonological word. Outside of verbal morphophonemics, the most common manifestations of the process involve neutralizations of the close/open distinction in the mid vowels before /i u/ in the following syllable. Some illustrations appear in Table 2, Part B.

3. Script. Like all other modern writing systems indigenous to the Indian subcontinent, that of Bengali is derived from the ancient Brāhmī script. The modern characters, shown in Tables 3a–b, are peculiar to Bengali and (with a few differences) Assamese. This script is read from left to right, and is 'alpha-syllabic' rather than segmental.

4. Morphology. A chart of declension for nouns appears in Table 4. It is notable that Modern Bengali lacks many of the declensional parameters of the noun which occur in earlier Indo-Aryan, such as the original system of eight cases and three genders in the noun and adjective. Modern Bengali adjectives are not declined at all. Moreover, the plural is usually marked only in nouns which have animate and/or definite reference—failing which, the singular/plural distinction tends to be neutralized.

TABLE 2. *Bengali Phonological Processes Affecting Vowel Height*

A. Vowel Raising			
mɔl	'dirt'	*ɔmol*	'pure'
sɔ	'hundred'	*ækso*	'one hundred'
æk	'one'	*ɔnek*	'many'
B. Vowel Height Assimilation			
æk	'one'	*ekṭi*	'one' (plus classifier -*ṭi*)
lɔjja	'shame'	*lojjito*	'ashamed'
nɔṭ	'actor'	*noṭi*	'actress'
æk	'one'	*ekṭu*	'a little, a bit'
tɔbe	'then'	*tobu*	'but (then)'

Verbal inflection is summarized in Table 5 (cf. Ferguson 1945, Sarkar 1976). Like the noun, the verb lacks inflectional number. However, three distinctions of status—despective, ordinary, and honorific—are made inflectionally in the 2nd and 3rd persons; the honorific inflections are derived from earlier Indo-Aryan plural terminations. The shapes of inflections in the table de-

TABLE 3a. *Traditional Order of Bengali Vowels (Initial Forms)*

Symbol	Transcription	Symbol	Transcription
অ	ɔ	ঋ	ṛ (/ri/)
আ	a	এ	e
ই	i	ঐ	oy
ঈ	ī (/i/)	ও	o
উ	u	ঔ	ow
ঊ	ū (/u/)		

TABLE 3b. *Traditional Order of Bengali Consonants (Initial Forms)*

	Occlusives								Nasals	
	Voiceless				Voiced					
	Unaspirated		Aspirated		Unaspirated		Aspirated			
Velar	ক	k	খ	kh	গ	g	ঘ	gh	ঙ	ŋ
Palatal	চ	c	ছ	ch	জ	j	ঝ	jh	ঞ	ñ
Retroflex	ট	ṭ	ঠ	ṭh	ড	ḍ	ঢ	ḍh	ণ	ṇ
Dental	ত	t	থ	th	দ	d	ধ	dh	ন	n
Labial	প	p	ফ	ph	ব	b	ভ	bh	ম	m
Resonants:	য	y (/j/)	র	r	ল	l				
Spirants:	শ	ś (/s/)	ষ	ṣ (/s/)	স	s (/s/)	হ	h		

TABLE 4. *Bengali Nominal Declension*

	Singular	Plural
Nominative	Ø	*-ra/-era; -gulo*
Objective	*-ke*	*-der(ke)/-eder(ke); -guloke*
Genitive	*-r/-er*	*-der/-eder; -gulor*
Locative/Instrumental	*-te/-e* or *-ete*	*-gulote*

pend on the shapes of the verbal stems to which they are added.

Table 6 presents a sample conjugation for the root *dækh-* 'see'. The alternation shown in the height of the vowel *æ* exemplifies the pattern of morphophonemic alternation discussed above (cf. Dimock 1957). This can be considered a conditioned phonological process, provided that the stem-forming affixes in lines 4–13 are assumed to have an underlying initial high vowel, as a required condition for Vowel Height Assimilation. In fact, a high vowel /i/ does occur initially in these stem affixes when they are added to a few monosyllabic verbal bases ending in *ɔ a*; e.g. *ga-* 'sing', *gaibe* 'will sing', *gaite* 'to sing', *gaile* 'if/when one sang'.

5. Syntax. The dominant word order in Modern Bengali sentences is Subject + Indirect Object + Direct Object + Oblique Object + Verb. Subordinate clauses which contain non-inflecting or invariant verbal forms, such as conditionals and infinitives, precede finite clauses:

(1a) *Se ele klas suru hɔbe.*
he when.comes class beginning will.be
'When he comes, class will start.'

(1b) *Se aste klas suru holo.*
he come.INF class beginning was
'On his coming, class started.'

Finite subordinate clauses are also usually initial:

(2) *Jodi se asbe (tɔbe) klas suru hɔbe.*
when he will.come then class beginning will.be
'When he comes, (then) class will start.'

TABLE 6. *Sample Verbal Conjugation of Bengali* dækh- *'see'*

1.	Verbal noun[1]	*dækha*	'seeing'
2.	Present indicative	*dækhe*	'sees'
3.	Present imperative	*dekhuk*	'let him/her/them see!'
4.	Present continuous	*dekhche*	'is seeing'
5.	Future indicative/imperative	*dekhbe*	'will see/must see!'
6.	Infinitive[1]	*dekhte*	'to see'
7.	Perfect conditional/Past habitual	*dekhto*	'would see'
8.	Imperfect conditional[1]	*dekhle*	'if/when one sees'
9.	Ordinary past	*dekhlo*	'saw'
10.	Past continuous[2]	*dekhchilo*	'was seeing'
11.	Conjunctive participle[1]	*dekhe*	'having seen'
12.	Present perfect[2]	*dekheche*	'has seen'
13.	Past perfect[2]	*dekhechilo*	'had seen'

[1] Non-inflecting verbal forms with invariant or zero termination.
[2] Stems formed with two or three successive stem-forming affixes.

However, the finite complement construction beginning with *je* 'that' is sentence-final. It often alternates with an initial construction in *bole*. Thus both these sentences mean 'I know that you will come':

(3a) *Ami jani je tumi asbe.*
I know that you will.come

(3b) *Tumi asbe bole ami jani.*
you will.come COMP I know

Conjunctive clauses also precede finite main clauses:

(4) *Bose se khabar khelo.*
sitting he food ate
'He sat and ate.'

The conjunctive form of a main verb may also appear in verbal compounds in which the succeeding finite verb aspectually modifies the main verb (such compounds are a frequent IA feature). The aspectual verbs comprise a

TABLE 5. *Bengali Verbal Inflection*

		Despective	Ordinary		Honorific
	1st Person	2nd Person	2nd Person	3rd Person	2nd/3rd Person
Present Imperative	—	Ø	*-o*	*-uk*	*-un*
Unmarked Indicative and -(*c*)*ch* stems	*-i*	*-is*	*-o*	*-e*	*-en*
-b stems	*-o*	*-i*	*-e*	*-e*	*-en*
-t and *-l* stems	*-am*	*-i*	*-e*	*-o*	*-en*

limited set, including *phæl-* (lit. 'throw'), which indicates completion of activity (e.g. *kha-* 'eat', *kheye phæl-* 'eat up'), as well as *ja-* lit. 'go', indicating motion from a point (e.g. *pa-* 'receive', *peye ja-* 'walk off with').

6. Diffusion. In some syntactic characteristics, Bengali diverges from the norms of earlier Indo-Aryan, and approaches the general types of modern South Asian languages [*q.v.*] irrespective of genetic affiliation. Thus Bengali has several dozen predicates which require subjects marked with the genitive case (rather than the more typical nominative), and which lack the otherwise usual subject/verb agreement (Klaiman 1981). Such 'indirect' subjects are typically associated with sensory, mental, emotional, corporeal, and other characteristically human experiences, e.g. thinking or recalling:

(5) *Baba-r toma-ke mon-e holo.*
of-father to-you in-mind became
'Father thought of you.'

Constructions like these are rare in earlier Indo-Aryan, although they typify modern South Asian languages (Masica 1976:169). Other non-Aryan traits in Bengali that suggest external influences include word-initial stress, absence of grammatical gender, post-verbal negatives, negative existential verbs, and a proliferation in varieties of non-finite complements and subordinate clauses.

Bengali has also apparently absorbed two non-Aryan lexical features of the greater South Asian region. It has about a dozen numeral classifiers, such as *jon* denoting human referents (e.g. *tin jon sikkhok* 'three CLF teacher', i.e. 'three teachers'), or *khana* denoting flat objects (e.g. *du khana boi* 'two CLF book', i.e. 'two books'). It also has a class of reduplicative expressives, e.g. *kickic* suggesting grittiness, *miṭmiṭ* suggesting flickering, and *ṭɔlmɔl* suggesting overflowing or a fluid state. The modern language has dozens of such expressives, in contrast to earlier Indo-Aryan, in which they were largely lacking. It seems likely that these and other features entered Bengali after its separation from the other Modern Indo-Aryan languages. They may have originated with non-Aryan languages which were gradually absorbed when Bengali became the dominant speech of the greater Gangetic delta.

M. H. KLAIMAN

BIBLIOGRAPHY

BENDER, ERNEST, & T. RICCARDI, JR. 1978. *An advanced course in Bengali.* Philadelphia: South Asia Regional Studies, University of Pennsylvania.

CHATTERJI, SUNITI KUMAR. 1921. Bengali phonetics. *Bulletin of the School of Oriental and African Studies,* University of London, 2.1–25.

CHATTERJI, SUNITI KUMAR. 1926. *The origin and development of the Bengali language.* 2 vols. London: Allen & Unwin. Reprinted with supplementary volume, 1970–72.

ČIŽIKOVA, KSENIJA L., & CHARLES A. FERGUSON. 1969. Bibliographical review of Bengali studies. In *Current trends in linguistics,* vol. 5, *Linguistics in South Asia,* edited by Thomas A. Sebeok, pp. 85–98. The Hague: Mouton.

DIMOCK, EDWARD C., JR. 1957. Notes on stem-vowel alternation in the Bengali verb. *Indian Linguistics* 17.173–177.

DIMOCK, EDWARD C., JR. 1960. Literary and colloquial Bengali in modern Bengali prose. In *Linguistic diversity in South Asia: Studies in regional, social and functional variation* (Indiana University Research Center in Anthropology, Folklore, and Linguistics, Publication 13; International Journal of American Linguistics 26:3, part 3), edited by Charles A. Ferguson & John J. Gumperz, pp. 43–63. Bloomington: Indiana University.

DIMOCK, EDWARD C., JR., et al. 1964. *Introduction to Bengali,* vol. 1. Honolulu: East-West Center Press. Reprinted, Columbia, Mo.: South Asia Books, 1976.

FERGUSON, CHARLES A. 1945. A chart of the Bengali verb. *Journal of the American Oriental Society* 65.54–55.

FERGUSON, CHARLES A., & MUNIER CHOWDHURY. 1960. The phonemes of Bengali. *Language* 36.22–59.

KLAIMAN, MIRIAM H. 1981. *Volitionality and subject in Bengali: A study of semantic parameters in grammatical processes.* Bloomington: Indiana University Linguistics Club.

KLAIMAN, MIRIAM H. 1987. Bengali. In *The world's major languages,* edited by Bernard Comrie, pp. 490–513. London: Croom Helm. New York: Oxford University Press.

MASICA, COLIN P. 1976. *Defining a linguistic area: South Asia.* Chicago: University of Chicago Press.

RAY, PUNYA SLOKA, et al. 1966. *Bengali language handbook.* Washington, D.C.: Center for Applied Linguistics.

SARKAR, PABITRA. 1976. The Bengali verb. *International Journal of Dravidian Linguistics* 5.274–297.

BENUE-CONGO LANGUAGES constitute a main branch of the Niger-Congo family. (Some languages previously assigned to the Kwa branch of Niger-Congo, namely the so-called Eastern Kwa languages, are here reassigned to Benue-Congo.) The Benue-Congo languages are spoken from the Benin-Nigeria border eastward and southward to cover most of the remainder of the continent, except the southwest corner. [*See* Niger-Congo Languages, *Map 4.*] While most of this area is occupied by the Bantu languages [*q.v.*], it should be noted that, genetically, the Bantu languages form a relatively low-level subgrouping within Benue-Congo.

The subdivisions of Benue-Congo include the following: Bantoid, Cross River (including Bendi and Delta-Cross), Defoid, Edoid, Idomoid, Igboid, Kainji, Nupoid, Platoid, and Ukaan-Akpes. [*For data on individual languages of these groups, see the Language Lists after the corresponding articles.*] The language isolate Oko is also a Benue-Congo subdivision. For more detailed discussion of this classification, see Kay Williamson, 'Benue-Congo overview', in *The Niger-Congo languages,* edited by John Bendor-Samuel (Lanham, Md.: University Press of America, 1989), pp. 248–274, especially pp. 266–269.

The Language List below provides data not given with the articles on the Benue-Congo subdivisions listed above.

LANGUAGE LIST

Beezen: spoken southwest of Furu-Awa in Menchum Division, North West Province, Cameroon. As yet unclassified within Benue-Congo.

Oko: 10,000 speakers reported in 1989, from Ogori-Magongo District, Igbirra Division, Kwara State, Nigeria. Also called Ogori-Magongo.

BERBER LANGUAGES constitute a group of closely related languages spoken in North Africa; they form a top-level component of the Afro-Asiatic family [*q.v.*]. Over most of the area where Berber is spoken, it coexists with Arabic. The most solid areas of Berber speech are in the northwest, especially in Morocco, but varieties of Berber are found as far away as Niger and western Egypt. The internal classification of the Berber languages given in Figure 1, which excludes the extinct Guanche, is based on that adopted in Merritt Ruhlen, *A guide to the world's languages,* vol. 1, *Classification* (Stanford, Calif.: Stanford University Press, 1987), pp. 93, 320—itself based on a proposal by Alexander Militarev.

LANGUAGE LIST

Awjilah: spoken in Cyrenaica, Libya. Also called Aujila, Augila, or Aoudjila.

Ghardaia: spoken in the vicinity of Ghardaia, in the Mzab region, Algeria. May be mutually intelligible with Mzab.

Ghomara: spoken in a small region near Xauen, Morocco, north and west of the Tamazight. May be mutually intelligible with Tarifit.

Gourara: spoken in an isolated area near the Mzab region, Algeria. Also called Gurara. May be mutually intelligible with Mzab, Ouargla, or Tougourt.

FIGURE 1. *Subgrouping of Berber Languages*

Eastern Berber
- **Awjila-Sokna**
  - Awjilah, Sawknah
- Siwa

Guanche

Northern Berber
- **Atlas**
  - Judeo-Berber, Tachelhit, Tamazight
- Kabyle
- **Zenati**
  - **East Zenati**
    - Jabal Nafusah, Jerba, Sened, Tamezret, Taoujjout, Tmagourt, Zawa, Zuara
  - Ghomara
  - **Mzab-Wargla**
    - Ghardaia, Gourara, Mzab, Ouargla, Tougourt
  - Riff (Tarifit)
  - Shawiya
  - Tidikelt
  - **Tuat**
    - Tit, Touat

Tamasheq
- **Northern Tamasheq**
  - Hoggar Tamahaq
- **Southern Tamasheq**
  - Air Tamajeq, Tahoua Tamajeq, Timbuktu Tamasheq

Zenaga

Guanche: extinct in the 16th century; formerly spoken in the Canary Islands.

Jabal Nafusah: spoken around Jebel Nefusa, Tripolitania, Libya. Also called Nefusi or Jebel Nefusa.

Jerba: spoken in southern Tunisia. May be mutually intelligible with Tmagourt or Sened.

Judeo-Berber: several hundred speakers reported in 1985 from Israel and Morocco. Monolingual communities may have disappeared in Morocco before 1930. The speakers also used Judeo-Arabic.

Kabyle: 2,540,000 or more speakers reported in 1987, with 2,000,000 in the Grande Kabylie Mountains of western Kabylia, Algeria, plus 537,000 in France and some in Belgium. French is used by men in trade and correspondence.

Mzab: 80,000 speakers reported in 1985, near Ghardaia in the Mzab region, and in five urban areas, Algeria. Also called Mzabi. May be mutually intelligible with Ghardaia. Some speakers are bilingual in Arabic, French, or Spanish.

Ouargla: spoken south of Constantine, Algeria. May be mutually intelligible with Mzab, Tougourt, or Gourara.

Sawknah: spoken in Tripolitania, Libya. Also called Sokna.

Sened: spoken in southern Tunisia. May be mutually intelligible with Tmagourt or Jerba.

Shawiya: 150,000 speakers reported in 1975, south and east of Grand Kabylie, Aures, Algeria. Also spelled Chaouia and Shawia. A major Berber variety.

Siwa: spoken in the northwestern desert, in several isolated villages in the western oasis, Egypt. Also called Sioua or Oasis Berber.

Tachelhit: 3,000,000 speakers reported from the Grand Atlas south to the Draa River, in southwestern Morocco, and east into Algeria at Tabelbala. Also called Tashilheet, Tachilhit, Shilha, Susiua, or Southern Shilha. Tachelhit is what speakers call their language; Shilha is the Arabic name for Moroccan Berber dialects in general. Men are bilingual in Arabic. Women do not learn Arabic.

Tamahaq, Hoggar: 25,000 speakers reported in 1987, in the south Hoggar (Ajjer) Mountain area around Tamanrasset, Algeria, south into Niger; also in southeast Algeria around Ganet, and on west Libyan oases around Ghat. Also called Tamachek, Tuareg, and Hoggar. Tuareg are the people (Targi is the singular); Tamahaq is the language.

Tamajeq, Air: 250,000 speakers reported in 1987, in the Agadez area of central Niger. Also called Tamachek or Tomacheck. The people are called Tuareg or Touareg.

Tamajeq, Tahoua: 400,000 speakers reported in 1987, with 300,000 in western Niger and 100,000 in eastern Mali. Also spoken by a few people in Nigeria. Also called Tamasheq, Tamachek, Tamashekin, Tomacheck, or Tahoua. The people are called Tuareg or Tourage.

Tamasheq, Timbuktu: around 260,000 speakers reported in 1989, with 250,000 in central and northwestern Mali around Timbuktu, and 10,000 in Oudalan Province, Burkina Faso. Also called Tomacheck, Tamashekin, or Timbuktu. The people are called Tuareg. May consist of two separate languages.

Tamazight: 3,000,000 speakers reported in 1977, with 1,800,000 in the Middle Atlas region of northern Morocco, and 1,200,000 in the Atlas Mountains and adjacent valleys in Algeria. Also called Beraber or Central Shilha. Tamazight is the name of the language, Beraber of the people.

Tamezret: reported as spoken in Tunisia.

Taoujjout: spoken in Tunisia. Also called Taujjut.

Tarifit: 1,000,000 speakers reported in northern Morocco, and along the coast of Algeria from Senhaja de Srair to near Alhucemas. Also called Riff, Rif, Rifi, Ruafa, Rifia, Northern Shilha, or Shilha. Rifia is the speakers' name for the language. Senhaja de Srair may be a separate language.

Tidikelt: spoken in the vicinity of Taourirt, Berga, Algeria.

Tit: spoken in the vicinity of Tit in southern Algeria.

Tmagourt: spoken in southern Tunisia. May be mutually intelligible with Sened and Jerba.

Touat: spoken in southern Algeria, in the vicinity of Touat.

Tougourt: spoken in the vicinity of Touggourt, Algeria. May be a dialect of Ouargla.

Zawa: spoken in Tunisia. Also called Zaoua or Zraoua.

Zenaga: 16,000 speakers reported between Mederdra and the Atlantic coast, in Mauritania. The speakers' second language is Hassaniya Arabic.

Zuara: spoken in the coastal area near Tripoli, Libya. Also called Zuwarah, Zwara, or Zuraa.

BERTA is a group of language varieties spoken in western Ethiopia and adjacent parts of Sudan. It forms a subgroup, and probably a top-level constituent, of Nilo-Saharan [*q.v.*]. Berta was assigned by Joseph H. Greenberg, *The languages of Africa* (Bloomington: Indiana University, 1963), as a subgroup of Chari-Nile within Nilo-Saharan, but the unity of Chari-Nile has been questioned in later work. Berta is conventionally considered a single language, but three language varieties are recognized in the list below.

LANGUAGE LIST

Berta: 50,000 speakers reported in 1972, including 28,000 in northwestern Wallaga Province (a corner of Ethiopia formed by the Blue Nile and the Sudan border), and in Dalati east of the Dabus River, plus 22,000 in Sudan. Also called Barta, Burta, Beni Shangul, or Wetawit.

Gamila: spoken between the Dabus and Blue Nile rivers, Ethiopia. Some bilingualism in Western Oromo.

Gobato: 1,000 speakers reported in 1975, in the Didessa Valley, Ethiopia. Also called Gebeto. Some bilingualism in Western Oromo.

BILINGUALISM. [*This entry is concerned with the use of two or more languages by individuals or communities. It comprises four articles:*

An Overview
Bilingual Education
Language Localization in Bilingualism
Multilingualism and Multiculturalism

For related topics, see also Areal Linguistics; Borrowing; Pidgins and Creoles; *and* Sociolinguistics.]

An Overview

As a term, 'bilingualism' has been applied to individuals as well as to groups and institutions. The issues raised by scholars describing individuals have been primarily psycholinguistic and social-psychological (Grosjean 1982, Baetens Beardsmore 1986). At the group level, the concept has raised sociolinguistic, educational, and political considerations (Fishman 1978). In popular usage and debate about the merits of bilingualism, considerable confusion is caused by unclear specification of whether one is referring to individuals or to social categories.

1. Definitions. A bilingual individual is someone who controls two or more languages. Beyond this simple definition, considerable fuzziness arises from the difficulty of defining what it means to control a language. Using a loose criterion, such as the ability to utter or comprehend some minimal range of sentences, the majority of the world's population would be considered bilingual. However, a strict criterion of native-like control would severely limit this number. The definitional problem is further complicated because control of language can vary as a function of the domain of language use—and because, within any domain, skill in the language can undergo development or attrition. Although there is disagreement on criteria, scholars agree on the existence of these variabilities (Haugen 1973).

Several typologies of bilingual individuals have been proposed. The best known is Weinreich's (1953) distinction between COMPOUND and COORDINATE bilingualism, referring to the lexical organization of two languages with respect to the concepts they represent. This is determined by the extent to which the languages are segregated in contexts of acquisition and usage: a compound organization integrates the languages under a single concept, whereas coordinate organization maintains separate concepts. Other distinctions refer to the age at which bilingualism is attained: thus SIMULTANEOUS vs. SEQUENTIAL bilingualism distinguishes whether the two languages are learned at the same time, or whether the second language is acquired after the primary language has been established (starting at about age three). EARLY vs. LATE bilingualism has been also used to refer to this distinction, but also serves to distinguish between sequential bilinguals who attained their second language at different ages.

Bilingualism at the group level is more complex, because it can refer to a wide range of entities—including speech communities, schools, and governments. Important here is the degree and nature of functional separation granted the two languages within these groups.

Ferguson's (1959) notion of DIGLOSSIA has been usefully applied to some settings of stable bilingualism, where more conservative and more innovative language varieties function as FORMAL and INFORMAL varieties, respectively, e.g. Classical Arabic vs. Colloquial Arabic. Many sociolinguists believe that, in the absence of diglossia, bilingualism will result in language shift. An important distinction which incorporates the notion of majority and minority languages is that between ADDITIVE and SUBTRACTIVE bilingualism—also referred to as ELITE vs. FOLK bilingualism. In additive bilingualism, as in the case of Canadian Anglophones who learn French, the majority group learns the minority language without fearing loss of the native language. Subtractive bilingualism describes the situation of language minority groups in the United States, where the second language eventually replaces the native language.

2. Developmental processes. The development of simultaneous bilingualism has been described in a number of case studies—most prominently a study by Leopold (1939–49) of his daughter, who was raised speaking German and English. Functional separation of the two linguistic systems appears early in development, although not without cross-over between languages. Some observers report delays in vocabulary development at the early stages, but with few long-term effects; however, neither observation has been substantiated against normative data. For optimal development, a one-parent/one-language method is commonly prescribed, in which each parent uses one language consistently; but practical problems are acknowledged. Long-term studies suggest that bilingualism has no harmful effects on overall linguistic or cognitive development, and possibly has beneficial effects.

Sequential bilingualism has been studied most intensively from the perspectives of phonological, morphological, and syntactic development. The driving question has been the extent to which characteristics of the FIRST or NATIVE LANGUAGE (L1) predict outcomes in acquisition of the SECOND LANGUAGE (L2); this question has been associated with CONTRASTIVE ANALYSIS [*q.v.*]. Phonological development can be described, though by no means wholly, in terms of L1 influences, particularly among adults. Morphological and syntactic aspects of L2 acquisition show far fewer effects of L1, particularly with respect to the types of errors in production. Thus L2 acquisition is governed primarily by the properties of the target language, although L1 provides the learner with a source of hypotheses about L2.

Statements about discourse factors are limited by the theoretical status of contrastive studies in this area. Theoretical approaches to L2 acquisition have tended to mimic those in L1 acquisition research, with recent interests arising in universal grammar and learnability theory. [*See* Learnability.]

3. Constraints on development. Unlike L1 acquisition, L2 acquisition is characterized by differential success, with often imperfect approximations to the target language. Selinker (1972) has introduced the term FOSSILIZATION, which has been widely accepted to refer to ARREST along the developmental continuum. A variety of factors, ranging from biological to situational variables, supposedly modulate the occurrence of this process. Many theorists have used the age of the learner as a global variable, and generally have assumed this to be equivalent to biological maturation. But the picture is considerably more complex: cognitive, social, and emotional factors also covary with age, and not all of these have wholly biological bases.

Studies have tested the truth of folk observations that, with respect to L2 acquisition, 'The younger the better.' Such observations are supported to a limited extent, particularly with respect to pronunciation, by studies of L2 learners with more than five years' opportunity to learn the L2. However, the exact shape of the declining function with age is unclear; e.g., we do not know whether it is linear, non-linear, or discontinuous. Puberty is frequently claimed to be an important breaking point, particularly by supporters of a critical period for L2 acquisition; but evidence is sparse. An advantage for older learners has also been found with respect to the rate of acquisition when exposure levels are limited.

Research which looks at individual differences in L2 acquisition within specified age groups has turned up a number of interesting factors. In addition to the variable of LANGUAGE APTITUDE (often equated with verbal intelligence), Lambert 1972 and other works have shown the importance of MOTIVATIONAL VARIABLES—such as positive attitudes toward speakers of the target language, or instrumental goals to be attained through its acquisition. While language aptitude accounts for performance on primarily academic assessments of L2 acquisition, motivational variables account for performance on listening comprehension, and on more communicatively driven tasks. Other researchers have pointed to personality variables such as field-independence, extroversion, and other learning styles as positively contributing to L2 acquisition. Another important consideration is the CULTURAL ORIENTATION of the learner, particularly in classroom situations. This complex area suggests that important interaction effects exist between predispositions of learners and the nature of the learning situation.

4. Consequences of bilingualism. Early work conducted in the psychological tradition of mental measurement gave rise to the alarming conclusion that bilingualism could have harmful effects on mental and social development. This substantial literature is notable for its flaws in subject selection, and its failure to control background variables in comparisons (see Hakuta 1986). When background factors are controlled, a large number of studies have shown a positive correlation between bilingualism and performance on a wide variety of tests of cognitive flexibility. Several studies have suggested that the direction of causality is complex; but they support the argument that bilingualism, especially when additive, fosters cognitive skills. The studies, in any event, suggest no negative effects associated with bilingualism.

5. Cognitive and neurological processes. The issue of whether compound and coordinate bilinguals show different patterns for processing information has generated a sizeable but inconclusive literature. Some researchers have avoided the problem of individual differences, and have instead focused on the organization of the mental lexicon in the two languages. Studies support the view that the two lexicons of most bilinguals are interdependent; thus, in memory experiments, they behave as though word equivalents in the two languages are repetitions in the same language. However, some experimental protocols continue to yield data for memory of the particular language of presentation—suggesting that, in certain contexts, the form of the presentation is retained in memory.

Studies of the neurofunctional bases of language organization in bilinguals are intriguing, particularly those which suggest that the two languages might be localized differently. There is also preliminary evidence for considerable right-hemisphere involvement in the early stages of second-language acquisition.

6. Social processes. Conversations among bilinguals typically involve CODE-SWITCHING, and a useful distinction can be drawn between situational and conversational varieties. SITUATIONAL SWITCHING refers to differential use of the languages depending on the situation, whereas CONVERSATIONAL SWITCHING is the change of languages within conversational episodes, often intrasententially. Bilinguals use code-switching for various expressive functions, including emphasis and the marking of group identity. Researchers emphasize that code-switching is the result neither of inadequate competence in the two languages, nor of confusion between them; rather, the languages are situation-bound.

Language as a marker of ethnic identity is important

in marking in-group and out-group membership. Elaborate social psychological models have been developed, taking account of sociological factors such as the dominance relations between the in-group and out-group, to predict convergence or divergence of linguistic markers in intergroup contact. Empirical support for such models is still sketchy, but promising.

7. Bilingualism and education. Issues surrounding bilingual education programs for language majority students need to be distinguished from those surrounding programs for language minority students. In programs for majority students, the goal is additive bilingualism: the L2 is an enrichment, and there is no threat to the status of the L1. In minority language programs, the primary concern is the development of the majority language, with secondary concern, to varying degrees, for the maintenance of the L1.

Considerable research investment has been made in evaluating IMMERSION education programs for majority students, particularly in Canada. In such programs, the majority students receive instruction exclusively in the L2 from the early elementary grades, with later introduction of language arts in their L1. Immersion programs are more effective than traditional foreign language programs, and students maintain age-appropriate levels of performance in the L1 (Genesee 1987).

Bilingual education programs for minority students vary in their philosophy toward maintaining the students' native language and culture. In some programs, the L1 is used only until students have sufficient control of L2, often within two to five years, to receive instruction exclusively through the majority language. In other programs which attempt maintenance, the goal is to enhance and maintain the L1, even after the majority language has been acquired. Regardless of program orientation, such special programs for immigrant and guest-worker children are in many countries a focal point for public attitudes concerning immigration and demographic change.

8. Politics and demographics. The degree to which bilingualism becomes a political issue is related to the activism and critical mass of the minority language groups. Bilingualism at the societal level is not the root cause of political difficulties, as in Quebec or in Belgium; but the symbolic politics of language can be powerful, and often linguistic unity is equated with political unity and nationalism. In many parts of Western Europe, as well as in North America, linguistic minorities in the schools have increased to the point where minorities are about to become a majority. In the United States, such demographic changes have been accompanied by attempts to legislate language through a constitutional declaration for an official language. Such movements attempt to restrict ethnic language usage among minorities. However, attempts to impose language politically have not been very successful in the past. Language shift, e.g. in the United States, is governed more by linguistic minorities' choice to gain access to the economic and political power held by speakers of the majority language.

KENJI HAKUTA

BIBLIOGRAPHY

BAETENS BEARDSMORE, HUGO. 1986. *Bilingualism: Basic principles.* 2d ed. Clevedon, Avon, England: Multilingual Matters.

FERGUSON, CHARLES A. 1959. Diglossia. *Word* 15.325–340.

FISHMAN, JOSHUA A., ed. 1978. *Advances in the study of societal multilingualism.* The Hague: Mouton.

GENESEE, F. 1987. *Learning through two languages: Studies of immersion and bilingual education.* Rowley, Mass.: Newbury House.

GROSJEAN, FRANÇOIS. 1982. *Life with two languages.* Cambridge, Mass.: Harvard University Press.

HAKUTA, KENJI. 1986. *Mirror of language: The debate on bilingualism.* New York: Basic Books.

HAUGEN, EINAR. 1973. Bilingualism, language contact, and immigrant languages in the United States: A research report, 1956–1970. In *Current trends in linguistics,* edited by Thomas A. Sebeok, vol. 10, *Linguistics in North America,* pp. 505–591. The Hague: Mouton.

LAMBERT, WALLACE E. 1972. *Language, psychology, and culture: Essays.* Stanford, Calif.: Stanford University Press.

LEOPOLD, WERNER F. 1939–49. *Speech development of a bilingual child: A linguist's record.* 4 vols. Evanston, Ill.: Northwestern University Press.

SELINKER, LARRY. 1972. Interlanguage. *International Review of Applied Linguistics* 10.219–231.

WEINREICH, URIEL. 1953. *Languages in contact: Findings and problems.* New York: Linguistic Circle of New York. Reprinted, The Hague: Mouton, 1974.

Bilingual Education

'Bilingual education' usually refers to the use of two languages of instruction at some point in the student's career. In other words, it is defined in terms of the means through which particular educational goals are achieved. Proficiency in two languages is not necessarily a goal of bilingual education in this sense. For example, in some contexts bilingual instruction is employed as a temporary measure to help students from linguistic minority groups make a transition between the language of the home and the language of the school without falling behind in the mastery of subject matter. When it is assumed that students have attained sufficient proficiency in the school language to follow instruction in it, home-language instruction is discontinued. However, the term 'bilingual education' is sometimes defined in terms of goals, to refer to educational programs that are designed to promote bilingual skills among students. When used in this broader sense, 'bilingual education' may entail instruction primarily or exclusively through only one language, e.g. when instruction is delivered through a minority language in order to give students the maximum opportunity to learn that language. Second-language IMMERSION programs of this type are implemented widely in certain countries, e.g. Canada's French immersion programs. (For general reference, see Paulston 1980, Spolsky 1986.)

1. Issues. Within the general area of bilingual education, issues that are of particular relevance to applied linguistics include the following:

(a) The consequences of different forms of bilingual education for language learning and academic achievement, in both first language (L1) and second language (L2)
(b) The impact of bilingual education on attitudes toward and use of languages by students and their parents outside the school
(c) Within the general sphere of LANGUAGE PLANNING, the role of bilingual education in conferring status and power on the ethnolinguistic groups whose languages receive institutional recognition in the public education system. [*See* Applied Linguistics, *article on* Language Planning.]

This last aspect of bilingual education involves both sociological and applied-linguistic concerns; it accounts for the considerable controversy that bilingual education policies have engendered in many countries. In the United States, for example, although bilingual education is designed to promote educational equity for minority students, it has frequently been characterized by media and political commentators as socially divisive and 'un-American'. Critics fear that the institutionalization of minority languages in public education may encourage the continued use of those languages outside the school, and may retard the assimilation of minority populations, particularly the rapidly increasing Hispanic population, into the American mainstream.

2. Classifications of bilingual education. Various typologies of bilingual education have been proposed. The most elaborate is that of Mackey 1972, which distinguishes ninety different potential varieties, depending on the intersection of languages of the home, neighborhood, and country. By contrast, the more limited sociolinguistic typology of Fishman 1976 distinguishes the following four types of bilingual education for minority students, based primarily on program objectives:

(a) TRANSITIONAL BILINGUALISM refers to programs that use the minority language to the extent necessary to help students master subject matter until their skills in the majority language are developed to the point where it alone can be used as the medium of instruction.
(b) MONOLITERATE BILINGUALISM programs are intermediate in orientation between language shift and language maintenance: they encourage the continued development of aural/oral skills in the minority language, but concern themselves with literacy only in the majority language.
(c) PARTIAL BILITERATE BILINGUALISM programs aim at fluency and literacy in both languages, but literacy in the L1 is restricted to certain subject matter, generally that related to the ethnic group and its cultural heritage.
(d) FULL BILITERATE BILINGUALISM programs attempt to develop all skills in both languages in all domains.

Skutnabb-Kangas 1981 has developed a typology that focuses on the relationship of program organization to linguistic and societal goals for both minority and majority students. According to this typology, the medium of instruction can be primarily the majority language, the minority language, or both. The program can be designed for the majority (dominant) group, the minority (subordinate) group, or both together (a 'two-way' or integrated program). Societal goals of bilingual education can include direct assimilation of minority students, segregation and possible repatriation of minority students, or enrichment and/or instrumental benefits (e.g. jobs) for both minority and majority students. Finally, the linguistic aims include producing students who are (i) monolingual or strongly dominant in the majority language, e.g. US transitional bilingual programs; (ii) monolingual or strongly dominant in the minority language, e.g. some primarily L1 programs for guest-worker children in Europe; and (iii) bilinguals.

This typology is useful in considering some of the current controversies about bilingual education, insofar as it captures the direct relationship between inter-ethnic power relations and program organization. The scope of the typology could be broadened by elaborating the 'societal goals' category into educational goals, socio-linguistic goals, and socio-political goals. Educational goals include: (i) EQUITY vis-à-vis academic achievement and (ii) ENRICHMENT—access to two languages and cultures. Sociolinguistic goals refer to promoting access to a language of wider communication, usually a language of economic or political power, versus promoting access to a less used language, usually a 'heritage' language whose survival is threatened. Finally, socio-political goals refer to the status and modes of participation envisaged for students upon graduation into the wider society—for example, total assimilation into the mainstream culture, integration that permits maintenance of some bicultural allegiance, or segregation. Sociolinguistic and socio-political goals can overlap, as when proficiency in a heritage or threatened language is made a condition of employment for certain government occupational categories (e.g. Irish in Ireland, Basque in the Basque country).

3. The outcomes of bilingual education. Although there is considerable variation among types of bilingual education, some general patterns have emerged consistently in the research results. First, for both majority and minority students, instruction through the medium of a minority language appears to entail no long-term delay in the development of academic skills in the majority language. Thus students from English home backgrounds who are instructed largely through the medium of French in Canada perform as well in English academic skills as students instructed entirely through English. By the same token, minority francophone students in Canada who are instructed largely through French perform as well in English as do similar students instructed largely through English. The same pattern emerges in the United States for Hispanic students, and in many other countries. This pattern has been attributed to a 'common underlying proficiency' or interdependence that facilitates transfer of academic or conceptual knowledge across languages (Skutnabb-Kangas 1984, Cummins & Swain 1986).

A second general finding is that, for minority students who are at risk of school failure, strong promotion of the students' L1 in school often results in significantly better academic progress in the majority language than does instruction primarily through the majority language. It has been argued that this pattern depends on a variety of factors that operate together with the medium of instruction—e.g. the extent to which the program validates minority students' cultural identity, and the extent of minority community involvement—as well as general pedagogical and assessment practices (Skutnabb-Kangas 1984, Cummins 1986, Hakuta 1986).

Finally, research consistently shows that use of the target language as a medium of instruction is highly effective in developing students' proficiency in that language. Research data are considerably sparser on the effects of bilingual education on language attitudes and use. Some studies (cf. Ireland 1975) have reported that positive attitudes toward the minority language, and actual use of it, are significantly related to previous participation in bilingual or minority language immersion programs. It appears likely that bilingual education is associated with increased proficiency in and generally positive attitudes toward the target language (Lambert & Tucker 1972); but proficiency and positive attitudes by themselves, although necessary, are not sufficient to guarantee extensive use of the language after leaving school.

In conclusion, the research data on bilingual education are considerably more clear-cut than the public debate might suggest. Results support the view that properly implemented bilingual programs can contribute both to equity for minority students and to the enrichment of educational experience, involving access to two languages and cultures, for both minority and majority students. Implementation of such programs, however, also changes the status quo with respect to the power relations (e.g. employment prospects) between different ethnolinguistic groups. In the public debate, the educational merits of different program options often become obscured by the intensity of competing vested interests.

JIM CUMMINS

BIBLIOGRAPHY

CUMMINS, JIM. 1986. Empowering minority students: A framework for intervention. *Harvard Educational Review* 56.18–36.

CUMMINS, JIM, & MERRILL SWAIN. 1986. *Bilingualism in education: Aspects of theory, research and practice.* London: Longman.

FISHMAN, JOSHUA A. 1976. *Bilingual education: An interna-*

tional sociological perspective. Rowley, Mass.: Newbury House.
HAKUTA, KENJI. 1986. *Mirror of language: The debate on bilingualism.* New York: Basic Books.
IRELAND. 1975. *Report of the Committee on Irish Language Attitudes Research.* Dublin: Minister for the Gaeltacht.
LAMBERT, WALLACE E., & G. RICHARD TUCKER. 1972. *Bilingual education of children: The St. Lambert experiment.* Rowley, Mass.: Newbury House.
MACKEY, WILLIAM F. 1972. A typology of bilingual education. In *Advances in the sociology of language,* vol. 2, *Selected studies and applications,* edited by Joshua A. Fishman, pp. 413–432. The Hague: Mouton.
PAULSTON, CHRISTINA BRATT. 1980. *Bilingual education: Theories and issues.* Rowley, Mass.: Newbury House.
SKUTNABB-KANGAS, TOVE. 1984. *Bilingualism or not: The education of minorities.* (Multilingual matters, 7.) Clevedon, Avon, England: Multilingual Matters.
SPOLSKY, BERNARD, ed. 1986. *Language and education in multilingual settings.* Clevedon, Avon, England: Multilingual Matters.

Language Localization in Bilingualism

To study brain organization for two or more languages, one employs observation of breakdown in APHASIA [*q.v.*], as well as more modern instrumental techniques. Most bilingual or multilingual aphasics lose and recover their languages in similar fashion, and to the extent that they knew them before the aphasia-producing incident. However, for an interesting subset of bilingual aphasic patients, there is an unexpected loss of recovery patterns. Rarely, a different sort of aphasia may be seen in each of two or more languages in a patient with a single lesion of the dominant hemisphere (Albert & Obler 1978). Somewhat more frequently, the severity of the aphasic symptoms is markedly greater in one language than in another. Paradis 1977, 1987 has described eight types of recovery from aphasia in bilinguals or multilinguals: parallel, differential, successive, antagonistic, mixed, selective, and alternating antagonistic. The discrepancies in all but the parallel form suggest that there is at least partially differentiated organization in the brain of the two or more languages. (For general reference, see Vaid 1986.)

Three types of explanation have been proposed for differential recovery. Ribot 1882 argued that the first-learned language was most likely to return first. Pitres 1895 observed that the language most practiced around the time of the aphasia-producing accident would return first. Others have argued that affective factors influence the patient for or against using a particular language. Affect can be used to explain any recovery pattern; however, Pitres's rule holds with an accuracy greater than chance, while that of Ribot does not (Obler & Albert 1977.)

It is possible that representation of the languages themselves is not differentially impaired, but rather that ACCESS to one of them is worse. For example, researchers have posited a 'switch mechanism' that might itself be damaged—resulting in the common pattern of differential recovery, in which one language is nearly impossible to produce, while the other is produced in aphasic fashion. However, efforts to localize the switch have proven fruitless, as damage in the clearest cases ranges throughout the language and non-language areas of the brain, from frontal through parietal to temporal lobes.

Few features of aphasia are exclusive to bilinguals, except for differential recovery. In DEMENTED bilinguals, however, inappropriate choice of language occurs in some patients, and some reseachers argue that normal code-switching constraints may be violated. [*See* Dementia and Language.] Most striking are the changes in language choice: the healthy bilingual virtually never chooses to use a language with an interlocutor who cannot understand it, and is quickly able to self-correct if this is done inadvertently. The cognitive loss in demented patients seems to impair this sophisticated pragmatic mechanism; monolingual interlocutors may be addressed in code-switching style, or simply in a language they do not know.

Studies of lateral dominance for language in bilinguals have suggested greater bilateral organization for both their languages, as compared to that of monolinguals—and greater bilateral organization for the second language, as compared to the first. However, these findings are disputed in other studies that suggest no difference in lateral dominance between bilinguals and monolinguals, or between the languages of bilinguals. Tachistoscopic and dichotic studies provide most of the fuel for this debate, but none serves as a frank replication of another study: they invariably differ in factors presumed to affect brain organization (e.g. age or manner of second-language acquisition). Furthermore, there is often inadequate control for factors pertinent to instrumental laterality studies per se, e.g. measures of relative dominance, or equivalent difficulty between stimulus sets in the two languages. Sodium amytal studies or split-brain studies might be more convincing measures of lateral dominance, but these have yet to be systematically carried out on bilingual subjects. Anecdotal reports from researchers involved with such patients indicate no evidence for differential lateral organization for the two languages. Crossed aphasia originally appeared to have higher incidence among bilinguals, which would suggest greater bilateral organization for language among bilinguals than among monolinguals; but the consensus now is that such cases were simply more likely to be reported for bilingual aphasics.

Cortical stimulation studies of two epileptic bilinguals suggest partial but incomplete overlap of organization of the two languages within the left hemisphere (Ojemann & Whitaker 1978). Unfortunately, cortical stimulation studies of the sort used in this research determine apparent localization for naming abilities, but not for syntactic or other linguistic abilities. Nevertheless, the findings of Ojemann & Whitaker are provocative, and probably can be extended beyond the epileptic patients who are usually tested by this technique.

There is some evidence from normal bilinguals that the critical period at puberty for second-language (L2) acquisition (Lenneberg 1967) affects the lateral organization for language (cf. Vaid 1983). These findings contrast with the 'stage' hypothesis: this proposes that, in the early stages of L2 acquisition, more right-hemisphere skills are required—while by later stages, left-hemisphere dominance is more marked. However, some talented L2 learners manage to escape the constraints of a critical period, and learn a second language with apparent native-like proficiency, perhaps as a result of unusual cortical cellular organization (Novoa et al. 1988).

No one has fully succeeded in teasing out what language-specific effects may influence brain organization for language in bilinguals. Cross-language studies are now beginning to compare both aphasic and normal performance in languages where the burden of syntax is borne more by morphology, as compared to those in which it is borne by function words or word order; such work remains to be carried out on bilinguals.

Certain psycholinguistic mechanisms posited for bilinguals imply neurolinguistic structures yet to be substantiated. For example, the notion of a monitor to direct incoming speech for processing via the appropriate language would suggest interaction of frontal as well as temporal lobe structures. The distinction of COMPOUND vs. COORDINATE implies that cortical representation of the lexica of subgroups of bilinguals is distributed differently, depending on language-learning history and patterns of use. Processes such as transfer and interference among languages permit us to speculate about neuronal interactions during the course of L2 acquisition.

LORAINE K. OBLER

BIBLIOGRAPHY

ALBERT, MARTIN L., & LORAINE K. OBLER. 1978. *The bilingual brain: Neuropsychological and neurolinguistic aspects of bilingualism.* New York: Academic Press.

LENNEBERG, ERIC H. 1967. *Biological foundations of language.* New York: Wiley.

NOVOA, LORIANA, et al. 1988. Talent in foreign languages: A case study. In *The exceptional brain: Neuropsychology of talent and special abilities,* edited by Loraine K. Obler & Deborah Fein, pp. 294–302. New York: Guilford.

OBLER, LORAINE K., & MARTIN L. ALBERT. 1977. Influence of aging on recovery from aphasia in polyglots. *Brain & Language* 4.460–463.

OJEMANN, GEORGE, & HARRY A. WHITAKER. 1978. The bilingual brain. *Archives of Neurology* 35.409–412.

PARADIS, MICHEL. 1977. Bilingualism and aphasia. In *Studies in neurolinguistics,* vol. 3, edited by Haiganoosh Whitaker & Harry A. Whitaker, pp. 65–121. New York: Academic Press.

PARADIS, MICHEL. 1987. *The assessment of bilingual aphasia.* Hillsdale, N.J.: Erlbaum.

PITRES, A. 1895. Étude sur l'aphasie chez les polyglottes. *Revue de Médecine* 15.873–889.

RIBOT, THÉODULE. 1882. *Diseases of memory: An essay in the positive psychology.* London: Paul. New York: Appleton.

VAID, JYOTSNA. 1983. Bilingualism and brain lateralization. In *Language functions and brain organization,* edited by Sidney J. Segalowitz, pp. 315–339. New York: Academic Press.

VAID, JYOTSNA, ed. 1986. *Language processing in bilinguals: Psycholinguistic and neuropsychological perspectives.* Hillsdale, N.J.: Erlbaum.

Multilingualism and Multiculturalism

The terms 'bilingualism' and 'multilingualism' refer to competence in the use of two or more languages by the same person. Traditionally, however, the term 'bilingual' has been used as a cover term for bi- or multilingualism for an individual, or for societal bilingualism covering groups, speech communities, and nations, e.g. multilingual Singapore or India. (For general reference, see Condon & Yousef 1975, Hornby 1977, Albert & Obler 1978, Fishman 1978, Grosjean 1982, and Bennett 1986.)

1. Types of speech communities. Speech communities are essentially of three types: MONOLINGUAL (e.g. Japan, Korea); DIGLOSSIC (Haiti, Greece); or MULTILINGUAL (Belgium, India, Nigeria, Switzerland). In a sense, a 'monolingual' speech community is a misnomer, since monolinguals too switch registers and shift styles. In diglossic communities, two distinct varieties of a language are functionally complementary: a H[IGH] variety is used in formal contexts and for writing, while a L[OW] variety is used for ordinary conversation (e.g. in Arabic-speaking countries). A multilingual speech community officially recognizes more than one language: thus the Indian constitution recognizes fifteen national languages out of an estimated number of 1,652 languages and dialects. The Republic of Singapore recognizes Chinese, English, Malay, and Tamil; Switzerland gives official status to German, French, Italian, and Romansch; and Nigeria recognizes English, Hausa, Igbo, and Yoruba.

The general belief that monolingualism is normal, and multilingualism a linguistic aberration, is incorrect. Actually, most of the two hundred or so countries of the world use more than one language of the estimated five thousand used in the world. Language contact and coexistence of languages are normal linguistic phenomena.

The official recognition or non-recognition of linguistic pluralism is not necessarily a reliable indicator of the actual multilingualism of a country. A country which officially recognizes only one language may have numerous languages used by its population. There are over one hundred minority languages used in the United Kingdom; in the United States, over 7 percent of the population use languages other than English. Zaïre recognizes only five languages (French, Kiswahili, Tshiluba, Kikongo, and Lingala), but 250 languages and dialects are actually spoken in that country.

2. Motivations for multilingualism. The factors which encourage and initiate multilingualism are varied and complex. They include reasons which are internal to a country—its multilingual and multicultural composition. In such a situation, a particular language may be chosen as a LINK LANGUAGE for integration and administration. This function was assigned to Latin and Greek in the days of the Roman Empire, and to English, French, Spanish, and Portuguese in European colonies. An additional language may be used for articulation of national identity (e.g. Hindi in India, Bahasa Indonesia in Indonesia, Russian in the USSR, and Hebrew in Israel), or to express a specific attitude toward a language (e.g. Arabic, Sanskrit, and Pali as used in religious contexts for Islam, Hinduism, and Buddhism, respectively). Large-scale migrations have also motivated multilingualism, as for speakers of Bihari (a variety of Hindi) in Pakistan and of Sindhi in India. Cultural and religious identity was responsible for the spread of Sanskrit among the speakers of the Dravidian languages in the south of India, and of Arabic in non-Arabic speaking countries like Bangladesh and Indonesia. Political domination has also motivated language imposition, e.g. Japanese in Korea, Malaysia, and Singapore during the Japanese occupation. Other reasons are the prestige and elitism associated with a language, e.g. Sanskrit in traditional India, Persian in South Asia during the Moghul rule, and English around the world at present. Language policies in the educational systems of linguistically and culturally pluralistic societies directly contribute to multilingualism and language spread; thus the 'Three Language Formula' in India provides that a regional language, Hindi, and English are an integral part of the curriculum. The maintenance and choice of another language may depend on preference and prestige in particular domains of use, e.g. English for science, technology, navigation, and aviation. There are also cases of social custom which motivate multilingualism: among the Tukano of the northwest Amazon, it is incest if a man has a wife who speaks his language. Multilingual Tukano villages have a language of men, languages of women, and a shared regional 'trade' language.

3. Defining a bilingual. There is no generally accepted definition of who is a bilingual. It has sometimes been asserted that a bilingual should have 'native-like control' of two languages. In another view, the effective use of a language in a particular function is considered enough. Weinreich (1953:1) defines bilingualism as 'the practice of alternately using two languages'; for Haugen (1953:61), a bilingual produces 'complete meaningful utterances in other languages'. Bilingual proficiency is viewed in terms of a continuum ranging from AMBILINGUALISM, i.e. equal competence in two languages in all domains of use without interference from one language to the other, to the use of broken varieties of a language. A large number of bilinguals/multilinguals never attain, or aspire to attain, 'native-like' control of a second language (Baetens Beardsmore 1982:1–36).

4. Types of bilinguals. On the basis of attitude toward languages involved in bilingual contexts, two types have been distinguished: ADDITIVE bilingualism (positive value attributed to the language) and SUBTRACTIVE bilingualism (negative value attributed to the language). An example of additive bilingualism is the attitude toward English and French in former colonies. Subtractive bilingualism is exemplified in the reduction of numbers of minority languages or numbers of speakers of languages, e.g. the decline of Welsh speakers in the United Kingdom, and of Irish speakers in Ireland.

5. Measuring bilingualism. A number of variables have been used for measuring bilingualism (Baetens Beardsmore 1982:69–98). These include proficiency in skills such as speaking, writing, reading, and listening; the contexts in which a language is learned (compound vs. coordinate); the domains of learning; and the age of learning (simultaneous vs. sequential). Bilingual literacy is frequently measured in only one direction; e.g., in the United States, literacy among known bilinguals is assessed in English, but rarely in the other languages.

6. Linguistic effects of bilingualism. In individual or societal bilingualism, when two or more languages come into contact, they undergo various changes. Normally, it is the first language of a person which influences other languages. This influence has been termed INTERFERENCE or TRANSFER. Such interference is manifest at every linguistic level, e.g. vocabulary, phonology, grammar, style, and discourse. One result of such interference is a 'foreign accent' (Haugen 1953, Weinreich 1953). This phenomenon can easily be verified if we compare the same language in two contexts of use, monolingual and multilingual. A good example is the worldwide use of English, and its nativization at various levels (Kachru 1983, 1986).

7. Language convergence (Sprachbund). Extensive language contact results in language CONVERGENCE—i.e. the mixture of languages not only in vocabulary but also in over-all structure. The outcome of such convergence is a linguistic area or SPRACHBUND ('language league'). In such linguistic areas, languages with no genetic relationship come together to form a group distinct from genetically related languages. The Balkans form such a Sprachbund, including four genetically distinct language sub-groups of Indo-European (Bulgarian, Macedonian, Rumanian, and Modern Greek). South Asia also forms a linguistic area, as it includes four language families—Indo-Aryan, Dravidian, Munda, and Tibeto-Burman (Masica 1976). [*See* Areal Linguistics.]

8. Interdisciplinary dimensions of bilingualism. The concerns of research on bilingualism are not purely linguistic or educational (Wald 1974). They cross disciplinary boundaries and involve issues such as the effects of bilingualism on intelligence and cognition, the bilingual's brain, the bilingual's grammar, the bilingual's creativity, and strategies of language alternation.

Concern about the effects of bilingualism on intelligence is pronounced in Western societies. Research on this topic has passed through three major phases: the first viewed the effect of bilingualism as detrimental, the second as neutral, and the third as additive. These research findings leave much to interpretation. However, there is a consensus now that the benefits derived from bilingualism far exceed whatever short-term mental deficit may result from it (Cordasco 1978, Baker 1988:1–20). Research on bilingualism and cognition is concerned with the effect of bilingualism on cognitive development (Ben-Zeev 1977, Baker 1988:22–44). The focus of neuropsychological investigation is to see if the neuropsychological processes of the bilingual's two or more languages are the same as those of monolinguals. Attempts to describe the bilingual's grammar raise important theoretical and methodological questions concerning speech communities which use two, three, or more languages.

9. Multilingual societies and language minorities. The question of minority language communities in a multilingual society is a complex one, and is being faced all over the world. These include communities whose first language is other than the dominant or majority language of a country (Skutnabb-Kangas 1981). In India, for example, out of the estimated 1,652 languages and dialects, only fifteen are recognized as 'national' languages. Most of the national languages are used to various extents as languages of administration and education in their respective states. Thus large populations of minority-language users are excluded from using their mother tongues in important contexts. Internationally, the question of minority languages has ceased to be just an educational or a linguistic issue; it has become a complex political issue. In the United States in the 1980s, a number of court rulings and legislative actions demonstrated awareness of minority language rights. In the United Kingdom, a new dimension has been added to the linguistic profile of the country by the minority-language issues raised by recent Asian and African immigration to Britain. In most Asian and African countries, the question of minority languages has developed into an explosive socio-political issue, particularly since such languages represent ethnic identities. The 'English only' movement in the United States is also considered by some as a threat to minority languages. As a reaction to this linguistic discrimination, there is a movement for a 'Declaration of Individual Linguistic Rights' as part of human rights. [*See also* Sociolinguistics, *article on* Minorities and Sociolinguistics.]

10. The bilingual's creativity. A vast amount of literary creation takes place in adopted (second) languages, or in the 'high' variety of a language. It is only recently that attention is being paid to bilinguals' literary creativity. There are numerous examples: English in regions where it is an additional language (e.g. South Asia, Southeast Asia, West Africa, or the Philippines); French in the francophone countries (e.g. Cameroon, Senegal, Togo, Upper Volta, or Zaïre); or Hindi in South India (cf. Smith 1987).

The verbal strategies used by bilinguals in their interaction with others are interesting for what they reveal about attitudes, identity, and functional preferences and about language change. Two such strategies have received considerable attention in recent years: code-mixing and code-switching. CODE-MIXING entails transfer of linguistic elements of one language into another. It is not restricted to vocabulary items, and involves units at intersentential and intrasentential levels, as in Hindi/English *bhāī, khānā khāo* ('brother, food eat') *and let us go*. In several bilingual speech communities, such code-mixing and code-switching has resulted in restricted (or not-so-restricted) additional codes of communication; these have been given specific names to mark their formal and functional distinctiveness, e.g. 'Hinglish' (Hindi and English) and 'Spanglish' (Spanish and English). Often the label given to a variety marks attitude toward the variety; 'Singlish' in Singapore, 'Japlish' in Japan, or 'Tex-Mex' in Texas. CODE-SWITCHING entails the ability to switch codes with reference to function, situation, and participant. Code-switching is used to mark particular types of identity or exclusiveness and to signal 'in-groupness' or asides (Kachru 1983:193–207).

11. Multiculturalism. Biculturalism or multiculturalism refers to an individual's ability to function effectively in two or more cultures. A bicultural person has the facility to identify himself/herself with more than one set of socio-cultural beliefs, values, and behavioral patterns. A strong position on biculturalism would claim that a truly bicultural person has internalized the beliefs and values of another culture. Such a person has access to socio-cultural identities in more than one culture. However, biculturalism does not necessarily imply ambiculturalism. Like bilingualism, biculturalism is a cline, ranging from ambiculturalism to some cultural sensitivity and 'awareness'. Cultural pluralism may result in various types of conflicts because of expectations of distinctly different behavioral patterns within a specific situation. In such situations, ideally, a bicultural person is aware that the conflict is generally of attitudes and not of truths. It is believed that a monocultural person is not able to transcend the attitudes of his/her own culture.

A bilingual society need not be a bicultural society. Much depends on the attitudes toward language identity and cultural identity. In francophone or anglophone countries of Asia and Africa, though significant segments of the educated population have acquired French and English respectively, they have not necessarily become bicultural. In fact, linguistic pluralism need not result in cultural pluralism.

BRAJ B. KACHRU

BIBLIOGRAPHY

ALBERT, MARTIN L., & LORAINE K. OBLER. 1978. *The bilingual brain: Neuropsychological and neurolinguistic aspects of bilingualism.* New York: Academic Press.

BAETENS BEARDSMORE, H. 1982. *Bilingualism: Basic principles.* Clevedon, Avon, England: Multilingual Matters.

BAKER, COLIN. 1988. *Key issues in bilingualism and bilingual education.* (Multilingual matters, 35.) Clevedon, Avon, England: Multilingual Matters.

BENNETT, CHRISTINE I. 1986. *Comprehensive multicultural education: Theory and practice.* Boston: Allyn & Bacon.

BEN-ZEEV, SANDRA. 1977. The influence of bilingualism on cognitive strategy and cognitive development. *Child Development* 48.1009–1018.

CONDON, JOHN C., & FATHI S. YOUSEF. 1975. *An introduction to intercultural communication.* Indianapolis: Bobbs-Merrill.

CORDASCO, FRANCESCO, ed. 1978. *The bilingual-bicultural child and the question of intelligence.* New York: Arno.

FISHMAN, JOSHUA, ed. 1978. *Advances in the study of societal multilingualism.* (Contributions to the sociology of language, 9.) The Hague: Mouton.

GROSJEAN, FRANÇOIS. 1982. *Life with two languages: An introduction to bilingualism.* Cambridge, Mass.: Harvard University Press.

HAUGEN, EINAR. 1953. *The Norwegian language in America: A study in bilingual behavior.* 2 vols. Philadelphia: University of Pennsylvania Press. Reprinted, Bloomington: Indiana University Press, 1969.

HORNBY, PETER A., ed. 1977. *Bilingualism: Psychological, social and educational implications.* New York: Academic Press.

KACHRU, BRAJ B. 1983. *The Indianization of English: The English language in India.* New Delhi: Oxford University Press.

KACHRU, BRAJ B. 1986. *The alchemy of English: The spread, functions and models of non-native Englishes.* Oxford: Pergamon. (Reprinted, Urbana, Ill.: University of Illinois Press, 1990.)

MASICA, COLIN P. 1976. *Defining a linguistic area: South Asia.* Chicago: University of Chicago Press.

SKUTNABB-KANGAS, TOVE. 1981. *Bilingualism or not: The education of minorities.* (Multilingual matters, 7.) Clevedon, Avon, England: Multilingual Matters.

SMITH, LARRY E., ed. 1987. *Discourse across culture: Strategies in world Englishes.* New York: Prentice-Hall.

WALD, BENJI. 1974. Bilingualism. *Annual Review of Anthropology* 3.301–321.

WEINREICH, URIEL. 1953. *Languages in contact.* New York: Linguistic Circle of New York.

BIMA-SUMBA LANGUAGES are spoken on islands in the Flores and Savu Seas, Nusa Tenggara, Indonesia; they constitute a top-level constituent of Central Malayo-Polynesian [*q.v.*].

LANGUAGE LIST

Anakalangu: 14,000 speakers reported in 1981, on the southwest coast of Sumba Island.

Bima: 500,000 speakers reported in 1989, on eastern Sumbawa Island in the Sunda Islands. Also called Bimanese.

Ende: 170,000 speakers reported in 1981, on central Flores Island.

Kodi: 40,000 speakers reported in 1987, on western Sumba Island. Also called Kudi.

Lamboya: 15,000 speakers reported in 1981, on the southwest coast of Sumba Island.

Lio: 300,000 speakers reported in 1989, around Paga and Dondo on central Flores Island. Also called Aku, Tanah Kunu, or Lionese. It is part of a dialect chain that includes Ende.

Mamboru: 16,000 speakers reported in 1981, around Memboro on the coast of northwest Sumba Island. Also called Memboro.

Manggarai: 500,000 speakers reported in 1989, in the western third of Flores Island. Also called Badjava.

Ndao: 3,500 speakers reported in 1981, on the island of Ndao off the west coast of Roti in the Lesser Sundas; also on Sumba, Roti, and Timor islands. Also called Ndaonese or Ndaundau.

Ngada: 70,000 speakers reported in 1981, on south central Flores Island. Also called Ngad'a or Ngadha. The Soa variety may be a separate language.

Palu'e: around 3,000 speakers reported in 1981 on Palu Island, north of central Flores Island. Part of a dialect chain with Ende and Lio.

Riung: 14,000 speakers reported in 1981, on Flores Island.

Sawu: 100,000 speakers reported in 1989, on the islands of Sawu and Raijua, south of Flores and west of Timor, and including 15,000 to 25,000 on Sumba and Flores, and in the Kupang area of Timor. Also called Hawu, Havunese, Savu, Sabu, Sawunese, or Savunese.

Sumba: 200,000 speakers reported in 1989, on Sumba Island, south of Flores Island. Also called Sumbanese, East Sumbanese, or Kambera. Distinct from Sumbawa, a language of the Bali-Sasak group.

Wanukaka: 10,000 speakers reported in 1981, on the southwest coast of Sumba Island.

Weyewa: 75,000 speakers reported in 1981, on west Sumba Island. Also called Wewewa, Wajewa, Wewjewa, Waidjewa, or West Sumbanese.

BINDING. Nominal expressions may be divided into three basic categories: (i) ANAPHORS, such as reciprocals and reflexives; (ii) PRONOMINALS, e.g. *he, she*; and (iii) R[eferential]-expressions, such as NAMES. [*See* Anaphora; Pronouns.] In the G[overnment-]B[inding] framework outlined in Chomsky 1981, 1982, it is assumed that these nominal expressions may be OVERT, like the examples above, or NON-OVERT. [*See* Government/Binding Theory.] A non-overt anaphor is the empty element coindexed with a N[oun] P[hrase], namely NP-trace. A non-overt pronominal is, for instance, PRO, the phonetically unrealized counterpart of a pronoun. A non-overt R-expression is the empty element coindexed with a WH-element, namely WH-trace or variable. For each type of nominal expression, a BINDING REQUIREMENT specifies the domain in which a nominal expression may or may not have an antecedent. These requirements are referred to as the BINDING PRINCIPLES or the BINDING THEORY.

A crucial distinction relevant to the understanding of the Binding Theory is the one made between A[RGUMENT]-POSITIONS and non-argument positions (A′-positions). Positions that receive grammatical functions (e.g. subject-of . . ., object-of . . .) are A-POSITIONS; those that do not receive such functions are A′-positions. For instance, the SPECIFIER of COMP position is an A′-position. [*See* Complementation, *article on* 'COMP' in Formal Grammar.] The Binding Theory, as formulated by Chomsky 1981, is a theory of A-BINDING: it refers solely to antecedents that are in A-positions. This theory requires anaphors to be A-BOUND, i.e. to have a c-commanding antecedent in an A-position, in a certain domain [*see* C-command]. It requires pronominals to be A-FREE (not to have a c-commanding A-antecedent) in a certain domain; and finally, it requires R-expressions to be A-free everywhere. The domains in which the anaphor must be bound, and the pronominal free, are referred to by the term GOVERNING CATEGORY in Chomsky 1981, or COMPLETE FUNCTIONAL COMPLEX in Chomsky 1986. Thus, in ex. 1a, the anaphoric reciprocal must be A-bound in the embedded clause; the antecedent of this reciprocal is *the students*. In ex. 1b, the pronominal element must be A-free in the embedded clause; it has to be disjoint in reference from *Peter*. In ex. 1c, the name *Mary* must be free throughout:

(1a) *The teachers think the students help each other.*

(1b) *Paul expects Peter to criticize him.*

(1c) *She believes the girl caught Mary.*

An extension of the model presented in the above paragraphs considers that the Binding Theory should be generalized from a theory of A-binding to a theory of A- and A′-binding. According to this approach, known as GENERALIZED BINDING, the theory constrains A′-relations (the relation between an element and an antecedent in an A′-position) as well as A-relations (the relation between an element and an antecedent in an A-position). The Generalized Binding principles constraining anaphors and pronominals are as follows:

(2) A-binding principles:
a. An anaphor must be A-bound in a certain domain.
b. A pronominal must be A-free in a certain domain.

(3) A′-binding principles:
a. An anaphor must be A′-bound in a certain domain.
b. A pronominal must be A′-free in a certain domain.

The domains in which anaphors have to be bound, and pronominals free, are not necessarily identical. The application of the generalized binding principles can be illustrated by briefly considering the pronominal system of Mandarin Chinese (cf. Aoun & Hornstein 1990, Aoun & Li 1990). In contrast to English, where Referential Pronouns have very similar distribution to Bound Pronouns—i.e. those linked to a quantificational NP—the parallelism between these two types of pronouns breaks down for some speakers of Mandarin Chinese:

(4a) *Zhāng*$_i$ *shuō tā*$_i$ *dé le jiǎng.*
Z. say he get ASP prize
'Zhang said he got the prize.'

(4b) **Měigerén*$_i$ *dōu shuō tā*$_i$ *dé le jiǎng.*
everyone all say he get ASP prize
'Everyone said he got the prize.'

For these speakers, pronouns essentially must be A-free in the minimal clause or NP in which they occur (see 2b), and A′-free in the minimal clause or NP containing a subject (see 3b). In GB, it is assumed that quantifiers, after the application of a raising rule which applies in the L[ogical] F[orm] component, end in an A′-position (see May 1985). In 4a, the pronoun is free in the relevant domains. In 4b, however, the pronoun is A-free in the embedded clause. However, at LF, it is not A′-free in the matrix clause, which is the minimal clause containing a subject (distinct from this pronoun). As expected, the pronoun can be bound by the quantifier in 5, since it is A-free in the most deeply embedded clause, and A′-free in the intermediate clause:

(5) *Měigerén*$_i$ *dōu yǐwéi nǐ shuō tā*$_i$ *dé le jiǎng.*
everyone all think you say he get ASP prize
'Everyone thinks that you said that he got the prize.'

A generalized binding account of the switch reference phenomena that occur in various natural languages may be found in Finer 1985. An analysis of resumptive pronouns in Modern Hebrew, assuming the generalized binding principles, is given by Borer 1984.

As mentioned earlier, nominal expressions may be overt or not. A generalized binding treatment of non-overt operators and phenomena of CONTROL [*q.v.*] is to be found in Clark 1989. As for WH-traces or variables, Chomsky 1981 treats them as the non-overt counterpart of names (R-expressions). While the assimilation of variables to names is maintained in generalized binding, these elements are also analyzed as A′-anaphors, which as such are subject to 3a. The assumption that a variable is an A′-anaphor, as well as a name-like expression, means that it must have an antecedent, and that the antecedent must occur within the domain determined by the binding principles. This characterization provides an articulated theory of variable types based on their referential properties. It also explains various asymmetries that occur in natural languages between subjects and objects, between arguments and adjuncts, and between referential and non-referential adjuncts. A full treatment of the theory of variable types may be found in Aoun 1985, 1986, and Hornstein 1984. In Aoun et al. 1987, it is argued that the Empty Category Principle [*see* Government], originally suggested by Chomsky 1981, may be subsumed under two separate types of locality requirements: the (generalized) binding principles which operate in the LF component, and a principle of lexical government applying in the Phonetic Form component. The interplay between the two types of locality requirements illuminates various discrepancies between overt extraction, applying in syntax, and non-overt extraction, applying at LF.

The thread common to the accounts mentioned so far is the assumption that A′-relations are regulated by the binding principles. This model has helped uncover notions (e.g. A′-disjointness) which were not previously recognized in grammatical theory; these notions appear to have a wide empirical coverage. They allow linguists to bring a variety of phenomena (switch reference effects, distribution of bound and resumptive pronouns etc.) into the realm of generative analyses. This may well prove to be the main contribution of the generalized binding model.

JOSEPH AOUN

BIBLIOGRAPHY

AOUN, JOSEPH. 1985. *A grammar of anaphora.* (Linguistic Inquiry monographs, 11.) Cambridge, Mass.: MIT Press.

AOUN, JOSEPH. 1986. *Generalized Binding: The syntax and Logical Form interpretation of* WH-*interrogatives.* (Studies in generative grammar, 26.) Dordrecht: Foris.

AOUN, JOSEPH, & NORBERT HORNSTEIN. 1990. Bound and referential pronouns. In *Logical form,* edited by Robert May & James Huang, to appear. Dordrecht: Reidel.

AOUN, JOSEPH; NORBERT HORNSTEIN; DAVID LIGHTFOOT; & AMY WEINBERG. 1987. Two types of locality. *Linguistic Inquiry* 18.537–577.

AOUN, JOSEPH, & YEN-HUI AUDREY LI. 1990. Minimal disjointness. *Journal of Linguistics,* to appear.

BORER, HAGIT. 1984. Restrictive relatives in Modern Hebrew. *Natural Language & Linguistic Theory* 2.219–260.

CHOMSKY, NOAM. 1981. *Lectures on government and binding.* (Studies in generative grammar, 9.) Dordrecht: Foris.

CHOMSKY, NOAM. 1982. *Some concepts and consequences of the theory of government and binding.* (Linguistic Inquiry monographs, 6.) Cambridge, Mass.: MIT Press.

CHOMSKY, NOAM. 1986. *Knowledge of language: Its nature, origins, and use.* New York: Praeger.

CLARK, ROBIN. 1989. *Thematic theory in syntax and interpretation.* New York: Routledge.

FINER, DANIEL L. 1985. The syntax of switch-reference. *Linguistic Inquiry* 16.35–55.

HORNSTEIN, NORBERT. 1984. *Logic as grammar.* Cambridge, Mass.: MIT Press.

MAY, ROBERT. 1985. *Logical Form: Its structure and derivation.* (Linguistic Inquiry monographs, 12.) Cambridge, Mass.: MIT Press.

BIU-MANDARA LANGUAGES are spoken in northeastern Nigeria and northern Cameroon, with some overspill into Chad. These languages form a top-level constituent of the Chadic [*q.v.*] branch of Afro-Asiatic, in the classification shown in Figure 1, which is based on that of Paul Newman.

LANGUAGE LIST

Bachama: 20,000 speakers reported in 1963, in Bachama and Batta Districts, Numan Division, Gongola State, Nigeria. Also called Bacama, Bashamma, Abacama, Besema, Bwareba, or Gboare. A member of the Bata dialect cluster.

Baldamu: spoken in Diamare Division, Far North Province, Cameroon. Also called Mbazia.

Bana: 43,000 speakers reported in 1987, including 30,000 in Mubi District, Mubi Division, Gongola State, Nigeria, and

FIGURE 1. *Subgrouping of Biu-Mandara Languages*

Subgroup A
- **Family A.1**
  - Ga'anda, Hwana, Jara, Tera
- **Family A.2**
  - Bura, Chibak, Kilba, Margi, Nggwahyi, Putai
- **Family A.3**
  - Bana, Higi, Hya, Kapsiki
- **Family A.4**
  - Dghwede, Glavda, Guduf, Gvoko, Lamang, Mabas, Mandara, Ngweshe, Podoko, Xedi
- **Family A.5**
  - Baldamu, Chuvok, Dugwor, Gaduwa, Gemzek, Giziga, Mada, Mafa, Matal, Mbuku, Mefele, Merey, Mofu, Moloko, Muyang, Ndreme, Ouldeme, Zulgo
- **Family A.6**
  - Sukur
- **Family A.7**
  - Buwal, Daba, Gawar, Hina, Mbedam
- **Family A.8**
  - Bachama-Bata, Gude, Gudu, Jimi, Njanyi, Tsuvan, Vimtim, Ziziliveken

Subgroup B
- **Family B.1**
  - Buduma, Jina, Kotoko, Logone, Maslam, Midah
- **Family B.2**
  - Musgu

Subgroup C
- Gidar

13,000 in Cameroon. Also called Fali. Bana is the name used in Cameroon, Fali in Nigeria.

Bata: 39,000 speakers reported in 1971, including 26,400 reported in 1952 in Gongola State, Nigeria, and at least 2,500 along the Benoue River in the vicinity of Garoua, Cameroon, near the Nigerian border. Also called Gbwata, Batta, Demsa Bata, Gboati, Gbwate, Bete, Birsa, or Dunu.

Buduma: 20,000 to 25,000 speakers reported in 1987, on islands in Lake Chad and on the northern shore of the lake, primarily in Chad; also in Borno Division and State, Nigeria, and in Logone and Cari Division, Far North Province, Cameroon. Also called Boudouma, Yedima, Yedina, or Yidana. The majority of the speakers are bilingual in Arabic.

Bura: 250,000 speakers reported in 1989, in the Babur, West and East Bura, and Askira Districts, Biu Division, Borno State, Nigeria. Also called Burra, Babir, Babur, Barburr, Pabir, or Kwojeffa.

Buwal: spoken in Gadala, south of Mokolo in the Mayo-Tsanaga Division, Far North Province, Cameroon. Also called Ma Buwal, Bual, or Gadala. May be mutually intelligible with Gawar.

Chibak: 20,000 speakers reported in 1973, in Margi District, Borno Division, Borno State, Nigeria. Also called Chibuk, Cibak, Kibbaku, Kikuk, or Kyibaku.

Chuvok: spoken in and around Tchouvok, near Zamay, southeast of Mokolo, in Mokolo Subdivision, Mayo-Tsanaga Division, Far North Province, Cameroon.

Daba: 35,700 speakers reported in 1982, northwest of Guider in Mayo-Oulo and Guider Subdivisions, Mayo-Louti Division, North Province, Cameroon, and in the southwestern corner of Diamare and Mayo-Tsanaga Divisions, Far North Province. Also called Dabba.

Dghwede: 30,000 speakers reported in 1980, in East Gwoza District, Borno State, Nigeria. Also called Hude, Johode, Traude, Dehoxde, Tghuade, Toghwede, Wa'a, Azaghvana, or Zaghvana.

Dugwor: spoken west of Tchere Canton between Maroua and Meri, Meri Subdivision, Diamare Division, Far North Province, Cameroon. Also called Dougour.

Ga'anda: 10,000 speakers reported in 1973, in Ga'anda District, Adamawa Division, Gongola State, Nigeria. Also called Ganda, Kaanda, or Mokar.

Gaduwa: spoken in the southwest corner of Mayo-Sava Division, Far North Province, Cameroon.

Gawar: 17,400 speakers reported in 1982, around Gawar, North Province, Cameroon. Also called Gavar, Gouwar, Gauar, Rtchi, or Kortchi.

Gemzek: 4,000 speakers reported in 1982, on the eastern edge of the Mandara Mountains north of Meri, Mayo-Sava Division, Far North Province, Cameroon. Also called Gemjek or Guemshek. Speakers are bilingual in Zulgo.

Gidar: 65,600 speakers reported in 1982, in Guider and Figuil Subdivisions, Mayo-Louti Division, North Province, Cameroon, and in a small section of Diamare Division, Far North Province. Also in Chad. Also called Guider, Guidar, Gidder, Kada, or Baynawa.

Giziga, North: 20,000 speakers reported in 1982, north and west of Maroua, in the Tchere and Mogazang massifs and neighboring Dogba plains, Meri Subdivision, Diamare Division, Far North Province, Cameroon. Also called Guiziga, Gisika, Tchere, Mi Marva, Giziga de Maroua, or Dogba.

Giziga, South: 60,000 speakers reported in 1989, southwest of Maroua in the Diamare plains, Diamare and Kaele Divisions, Far North Province, Cameroon. Also called Guiziga or Gisika.

Glavda: 22,800 speakers reported in 1963, including 20,000 in East Gwoza District, Bornu State, Nigeria, and 2,800 south of Ashigashia in Far North Province, Cameroon, on the Nigerian border. Also called Galavda, Gelebda, Glanda, Guelebda, Vale, or Galvaxdaxa. Different from Vale of Chad and the Central African Republic, which is Nilo-Saharan.

Gude: 57,700 speakers reported in 1982, including 40,000 in Mubi District, Mubi Division, Gongola State, Nigeria, and in Uba District, Borno State; plus 17,700 in Cameroon. Also called Cheke, Tchade, Shede, Mubi, Mapodi, or Mapuda.

Gudu: 1,200 speakers reported in 1971, in Song District, Adamawa Division, Gongola State, Nigeria. Also called Gudo or Gutu.

Guduf: 21,300 speakers reported in 1963, in East Gwoza District, Borno State, Nigeria, and north of Rourou in Far North Province, Cameroon, on the Nigerian border. Also called Gudupe, Afkabiye, Yaghwatadaxa, or Yawotataxa.

Gvoko: 2,500 or more speakers reported in 1963 from Nigeria. Also spoken in Cameroon. Also called Gevoko, Ghboko, or Kuvoko.

Higi: 180,000 speakers reported in 1973, in Gongola State, Nigeria. Also called Hiji, Kamwe, or Vacamwe.

Hina: 8,800 speakers reported in 1982, south of Mokolo, Hina District, Mayo-Tsanaga Division, Far North Province, Cameroon. Also called Besleri. Many speakers are bilingual in Fulfulde.

Hwana: 20,000 speakers reported in 1973, in Ga'anda District, Adamawa Division, Gongola State, Nigeria. Also called Hwona, Hona, Huna, or Whana. Tuftera is what the speakers call their language.

Hya: spoken in Amsa on the Nigerian border, Mokolo Subdivision, Mayo-Tsanaga Division, Far North Province, Cameroon. Also called Ghye or Za.

Jara: 40,000 speakers reported in Tera District, Biu Division,

Borno State, Nigeria, and in Yamaltu District, Gombe Division, Bauchi State. Also called Jera. Different from Jera, which is Benue-Congo.

Jimi: 3,500 speakers reported in 1982, in and around Bourrha, Mayo-Tsanaga Division, Far North Province, Cameroon, on the Nigerian border. Also in Nigeria. Also called Djimi, Jimjimen, or 'Um Falin. Distinct from Jimi of Nigeria in Bauchi State.

Jina: spoken around Zina and east of Waza near the south of Logone-Birni Subdivision, Logone and Chari Division, Far North Province, Cameroon.

Kapsiki: 40,500 speakers reported in 1982, in the southwestern part of Mokolo Subdivision, Mayo-Tsanaga Division, Far North Province, Cameroon. Some in Nigeria. Also called Psikye, Kamsiki, or Ptsake.

Kilba: 100,000 speakers reported in 1980, in Kilba District, Adamawa Division, Gongola State, Nigeria. Also called Huba, Chobba, Xibba, Ndirma, Wuding, or Pella.

Kotoko: 38,000 speakers reported in 1977, north of Kousseri along the Chari River and near Lake Chad, in Logone and Chari Division, Far North Province, Cameroon. Also in Chad. Also called Makari, Mpade, Malgbe, Mser, Malgwe, Gulfe, Goulfei, Sanbalbe, Malbe, or Ngwalkwe.

Lamang: 50,000 speakers reported in 1982, in West Gwoza District, Borno State, and Madagali District, Mubi Division, Gongola State, Nigeria. Part of a dialect continuum with Xedi in Cameroon.

Logone: 38,500 speakers reported in 1982, north of Waza National Park in Logone-Birni Subdivision, from the bank of the Logone River, Logone and Chari Division, Far North Province, Cameroon, across to the Nigerian border. Also spoken north of Bongor in southwest Chad, and perhaps in Nigeria. Also called Kotoko-Logone or Lagwan. The Msowe, Kalo, and Logone-Birni varieties may be separate languages.

Mabas: spoken in the village of Mabas northwest of Mokolo, Mayo-Tsanaga Division, Far North Province, Cameroon, on the Nigerian border; also in Nigeria. People may be bilingual in Mafa. Some speak Xedi. Distinct from Maba of Chad. Maya may be an alternate name.

Mada: 17,000 speakers reported in 1982, in the Mada massif at the edge of the Mandara Mountains and the neighboring plain, Tokombere Subdivision, Mayo-Sava Division, Far North Province, Cameroon. Distinct from Mada of Nigeria, a Benue-Congo language.

Mafa: 138,000 speakers reported in 1982, including 136,000 northward from Mokolo in Mayo-Tsanaga Division, Far North Province, Cameroon, and 2,000 in Borno State, Nigeria. Also called Matakam, Mofa, or Natakan. The name 'Matakam' has a pejorative connotation in Cameroon. Muktele may be a separate language.

Mandara: 42,800 speakers reported in 1982, including 23,500 in a belt starting east of Mora, around it to the north in a semicircle, and northwest to the Nigerian border, in Mayo-Sava Division, Far North Province, Cameroon; also 19,300 in Gwoza District, Borno and Dikwa Divisions, Borno State, Nigeria. Also called Wandala, Ndara, or Mandara Montagnard.

Margi, Central: 200,000 speakers reported for both Margi languages in 1989, in Uba District, Borno State, Nigeria, and in Madagali and Michika districts, Mubi Division, Gongola State. Also called Marghi.

Margi, South: spoken in Magadali, Mubi, and Mbani Districts, Mubi Division, Gongola State, Nigeria, and in Uba District, Borno State.

Maslam: spoken in Maltam and Saho northwest of Kousseri, in Makari Subdivision, Logone and Chari Division, Far North Province, Cameroon.

Matal: 18,000 speakers reported in 1982, on the eastern edge of the Mandara Mountains, southwest of Mora, Mora Subdivision, Mayo-Sava Division, Far North Province, Cameroon. Also called Mouktele, Muktile, or Balda.

Mbedam: spoken northeast of Hina, in Mokolo Subdivision, Mayo-Tsanaga Division, Far North Province, Cameroon.

Mbuku: 6,700 speakers reported in 1982, in the Mbuko massif and the neighboring Mayo-Raneo plain, Meri Subdivision, Diamare Division, Far North Province, Cameroon. Also called Mboku or Mbokou.

Mefele: spoken south and east of Mokolo, in Mayo-Tsanaga Division, Far North Province, Cameroon. Also called Bula, Bulahai, or Boulahay.

Merey: 10,000 speakers reported in 1982, west of Meri on the Meri massif, Diamare Division, Far North Province, Cameroon. Also called Meri, Mere, or Mofu de Meri.

Midah: spoken around Majera in the extreme southern Logone-Birni Subdivision, Logone and Chari Division, Far North Province, Cameroon. Also called Majera, Mida'a, or Da'a.

Mofu, North: 27,500 speakers reported in 1982, in the massifs south of Meri, in Diamare Division, Far North Province, Cameroon. Also in Chad. Also called Mofu-Nord or Mofu-Douvangar.

Mofu, South: 30,000 speakers reported in 1987, in the massifs south of the Tsanaga River in Mokolo Subdivision, Mayo-Tsanaga Division, and extending into Diamare Division, Far North Province, Cameroon. Also called Mofou, Mofu-Mokong, Mofou de Goudour, Mofu-Sud, Mokong, Zidim, or Njeleng.

Moloko: 8,300 speakers reported in 1982, between the Mayo-Mangafe and Mayo-Raneo rivers, east of Meri, in Tokombere Subdivision, Mayo-Sava Division, Far North Province, Cameroon. Also called Melokwo, Mokyo, Molkoa, Molkwo, Molko, or Mikiri. A high percentage of the speakers have some bilingual proficiency in Fulani.

Musgu: 75,000 speakers reported in 1982, including 61,500 in the entire Maga Subdivision, Mayo-Danay Division, Far

North Province, Cameroon; and 13,500 in Chad. Also called Musgum, Musuk, Muzuk, or Munjuk. Speakers call themselves Mulwi.

Muyang: 15,000 speakers reported in 1982, in the Muyang, Mougouba, Gouadagouada, and Palbarar massifs northeast of Tokombere, Mayo-Sava Division, Far North Province, Cameroon. Also called Myau, Myenge, Muyenge, or Mouyengue.

Ndreme: 7,500 speakers reported in 1982, in the southern Mora massif south of Mora, in Mora and Tokombere Subdivisions, Mayo-Sava Division, Far North Province, Cameroon. Also called Mbreme, Pelasla, Vame-Mora, or Vame-Mbreme. Sigila may be an alternate name.

Nggwahyi: spoken in Askira District, Biu Division, Borno State, Nigeria. Also called Ngwaxi or Ngwohi. Possibly a variety of Margi.

Ngweshe: 4,300 speakers reported in 1973, in Central Gwoza District, Borno State, Nigeria, and in Madagali District, Mubi Division, Gongola State. Also called Ngoshe Sama, Ngweshe-Ndaghan, or Ngoshe-Ndhang. Probably close to Gvoko.

Njanyi: 25,000 speakers reported in 1982, including 16,000 in Maiha, Sorau, and Belel Districts, Mubi Division, and in Zummo District, Adamawa Division, Gongola State, Nigeria; and 9,000 west of Dourbeye, Cameroon, near the Nigerian border. Also called Holma, Nzanyi, Nzangi, Njai, Njeny, Zani, Zany, Jeng, Jenge, Njei, Njeing, Kobotshi, or Paka.

Ouldeme: 10,500 speakers reported in 1982, in the Wuzlam massif south of Mora, Tokombere Subdivision, Mayo-Sava Division, Far North Province, Cameroon. Also called Wuzlam, Uzam, Uzlam, or Mizlime.

Podoko: 20,000 speakers reported in 1987, west and southwest of Mora, Mora Subdivision, Mayo-Sava Division, Far North Province, Cameroon. Also called Paduko, Podokwo, Padogo, Padokwa, Pawdawkwa, Gwadi Parekwa, or Kudala. Speakers refer to themselves as Parekwa.

Putai: a few speakers reported in Margi District, Borno Division, Borno State, Nigeria. Also called Margi West. The language is dying out in favor of Kanuri, but the ethnic population is large.

Sukur: 10,000 speakers reported in 1973, in Madagali District, Mubi Division, Gongola State, Nigeria. Possibly spoken in Cameroon as well. Also called Sugur, Adikimmu Sukur, or Gemasakun.

Tera: 46,000 speakers reported in Gombe Division, Bauchi State, Nigeria, and in Biu Division, Borno State. Also called Nyimatli or Yamaltu.

Tsuvan: spoken northeast of Dourbeye in the village of Teleki, southeastern Bourrah Subdivision, Mayo-Tsanaga Division, Far North Province, Cameroon, and by some people in Mayo-Louti Division, North Province. Also called Terki, Teleki, or Tchede.

Vimtim: spoken in Mubi District, Mubi Division, Gongola State, Nigeria. Also called Yimtim, Fali of Mubi, or Fali of Muchella. Distinct from Bana (also called Fali); also distinct from North and South Fali, Niger-Congo languages of Cameroon.

Xedi: 10,000 speakers reported in 1982, in the village of Tourou northwest of Mokolo, Mokolo Subdivision, Mayo-Tsanaga Division, Far North Province, Cameroon, on the Nigerian border. Also called Turu-Hide, Hide, Ftour, Tourou, or South Laamang. Part of a dialect continuum with Lamang in Nigeria.

Ziziliveken: spoken in Bourrah Subdivision, Mayo-Tsanaga Division, Far North Province, Cameroon, near the Nigerian border.

Zulgo: 18,000 speakers reported in 1982, on the eastern edge of the Mandara Mountains northwest of Meri, in the Mayo-Sava and Mayo-Tsanaga Divisions, Far North Province, Cameroon. Also called Zulgwa, Zelgwa, Mineo, or Minew.

BLOOMFIELD, LEONARD, was born in Chicago on 1 April 1887, and died at New Haven, Connecticut, on 13 April 1949. He received the A.B. at Harvard in 1906, and the Ph.D. at Chicago in 1909. Bloomfield taught at Cincinnnati (1909–10), Illinois (1910–21), Ohio State (1921–27), Chicago (1927–40) and, as Sterling Professor of Linguistics, at Yale (1940–49). His main fields of endeavor were Germanic, Malayo-Polynesian (Tagalog), American Indian languages (especially comparative Algonkian), and general linguistics. Bloomfield's influence was strongest in the last area, through his relatively neglected *Introduction to the study of language* (1914) and the widely read *Language* (1933).

Bloomfield and his contemporary Edward Sapir [*q.v.*] were the first influential American linguists to emphasize the importance of a descriptive approach to language, both in its own right and as a necessary preliminary to historical and comparative linguistics. Bloomfield's work on Tagalog and Menomini led him in the 1920s and 1930s to a type of structural analysis, especially in phonemics, parallel to but largely independent of that of the Prague School. [*See* History of Linguistics, *article on* The Prague School.] In comparative linguistics, Bloomfield was a strong defender of the principle of REGULARITY in phonemic change; he found confirmation of it in a certain word of Swampy Cree, an Algonkian language, which justified the postulation of a special Proto-Algonkian cluster */çk/.

In Bloomfield 1933, younger scholars found both a thorough theoretical orientation and a manual of analytical procedure for all levels of linguistic structure, including syntax. Bloomfield fully recognized the importance of semantics in linguistic analysis, but he was skeptical of its amenability to scientific treatment. He was not convinced that one could ever obtain absolutely complete information either on the state of the referent(s) of a linguistic phenomenon, or on that of the speakers and hearers involved.

With regard to meaning, as well as other aspects of language usually considered to fall in the province of psychology, Bloomfield's position in 1933 was radically different from that in his 1914 *Introduction*. In the earlier work, he had followed the then dominant 'Völkerpsychologie' of Wilhelm Wundt, with the basic assumption of a dualism between the physical world and a non-physical 'mind'. In the 1920s, under the influence of the psychologist Albert P. Weiss, Bloomfield argued that it was unnecessary to postulate a non-physical 'mind', or to follow any given school of psychology in order to describe and analyze language. He concluded further that societies are actual 'organisms' held together by the use of language, as individual bodies are coordinated by the brain and central nervous system.

Since some of Bloomfield's conclusions about language were contrary to widely held opinions concerning phonemic change, the nature of meaning, and the importance of 'mind', his 1933 *Language* aroused some opposition even during his lifetime. Some of his followers exaggerated his positions, causing stronger rejection of 'Bloomfieldian' views in the 1960s and 1970s, and leading to gross misunderstandings and misinterpretations; however, a more balanced view came gradually to prevail in the 1980s. (See Hockett 1970, Hall 1987, 1990.) [*See also* History of Linguistics, *article on* American Structuralism.]

ROBERT A. HALL, JR.

BIBLIOGRAPHY

BLOOMFIELD, LEONARD. 1914. *An introduction to the study of language*. New York: Holt. Reprinted, with a foreword by Joseph F. Kess (Amsterdam: Benjamins, 1983).

BLOOMFIELD, LEONARD. 1933. *Language*. New York: Holt. Reprinted, with a foreword by Charles F. Hockett (Chicago: University of Chicago Press, 1984).

HALL, ROBERT A., JR., ed. 1987. *Leonard Bloomfield: Essays on his life and work*. (Historiographia linguistica, 14:1–2.) Amsterdam: Benjamins.

HALL, ROBERT A., JR. 1990. *A life for language: A biographical memoir of Leonard Bloomfield*. Amsterdam: Benjamins.

HOCKETT, CHARLES F., ed. 1970. *A Leonard Bloomfield anthology*. Bloomington: Indiana University Press.

FIGURE 1. *Subgrouping of Bodic Languages*

Bodish
Eastern Himalayan
  Kiranti, Newari
Dhimal

BODIC LANGUAGES are spoken in Tibet, Nepal, and adjacent Himalayan areas. They constitute a subdivision of the Tibeto-Burman branch of the Sino-Tibetan languages [*qq.v.*]. Bodic languages may be subgrouped as shown in Figure 1. [*For data on languages of the Bodish and Kiranti groups, see the corresponding articles. Data on the language isolates Newari and Dhimal are given in the Language List below.*]

LANGUAGE LIST

Dhimal: around 8,200 speakers reported in 1961, in Jhapa, Biratnagar, and the eastern Terai, Nepal. Some speakers are partially bilingual in Nepali or Hindi. The Toto variety may be a separate language.

Newari: 500,000 or more speakers reported in 1985, in Kathmandu, Nepal, and scattered locations in the midlands. Also spoken in Bettiah, Bihar, India. The Dolkhali dialect of Dolakha and Pahri of Sindhupalchok may be separate languages.

BODISH LANGUAGES are spoken in Tibet and some adjacent parts of China, in Bhutan, and in parts of Nepal, northwestern India, and northern Pakistan; the group includes Tibetan [*q.v.*]. The Bodish languages are united with the East Himalayan languages (the Kiranti languages and Newari), and perhaps also with Dhimal, in a higher-level unit called Bodic within the Tibeto-Burman branch [*q.v.*] of the Sino-Tibetan family [*q.v.*]. The internal classification of the Bodish languages is as shown in Figure 1 (though the inclusion of the Gurung and Gyarung groups is less certain).

LANGUAGE LIST

Adap: spoken in south central Bhutan. Has 77 percent lexical similarity with Dzongkha, 62 percent to 65 percent with Kebumtamp, and 41 percent with Sharchagpakha.

Atuence: spoken by around 520,000 people on the Yunnan-Tibet border, China. Also called Anshuenkuan Nyarong or Nganshuenkuan. Probably included officially under Tibetan nationality.

Balti: 400,000 speakers reported in 1986, mainly in northeastern Pakistan; 40,100 in Jammu and Kashmir, in Uttar Pradesh, India, and possibly in Tibet. Also called Sbalti, Baltistani, or Bhotia of Baltistan.

FIGURE 1. *Subgrouping of Bodish Languages*

Gurung
- Baragaunle, Ghale, Eastern Gurung, Western Gurung, Manangba, Panchgaunle, Eastern Tamang, Northwestern Tamang, Southwestern Tamang, Thakali

Gyarung (Jiarong)

Himalayish
- **Almora**
  - Byangsi, Chaudangsi, Darmiya, Rangkas
- **Eastern Himalayish**
  - Baraamu, Thami
- Janggali
- **Kanauri**
  - Bunan, Kanashi, Kanauri (proper), Chamba Lahuli, Tinan Lahuli

Kaike

Kusanda

Monpa (Sagtengpa)

Tibetan
- **Central Tibetan**
  - Atuence, Helambu Sherpa, Humla Bhotia, Kagate, Kham, Lhomi, Mugali, Panang, Sotatipo, Tibetan, Tseku
- **Northern Tibetan**
  - Choni, Golog
- **Southern Tibetan**
  - Adap, Dzongkha, Groma, Jirel, Sherpa, Sikkimese
- **Western Tibetan**
  - **Ladakhi**
    - Changthang, Ladakhi (proper)
  - **Unclassified Western Tibetan**
    - Balti, Purik, Zangskari
- **Unclassified Tibetan**
  - Dolpo, Kutang Bhotia, Kyerung, Lopa, Naapa, Olangchung Gola, Sherdukpen, Thudam Bhote, Tichurong

Tsangla
- Kebumtamp, Sharchagpakha, Tsangla (proper)

Unclassified Bodish
- Chantel

Baraamu: spoken near Kumhali, in north Gorkha District, Nepal. Also called Barhamu, Brahmu, or Bhramu.

Baragaunle: spoken in Mustang, northern Nepal. The two dialects may be distinct languages.

Bunan: 2,000 speakers reported in 1972, in Himachal Pradesh, India, and western Tibet. Also called Gahri or Lahuli of Bunan.

Byangsi: 2,000 speakers reported in 1973 in Mahakali Zone, far western Nepal.

Changthang: spoken in Jammu and Kashmir, India, near the Tibetan border. Also called Byanskat, Rong, Rupshu, or Stotpa. May be mutually intelligible with Ladakhi. Some multilingualism in Urdu, Kashmiri, Hindi, or English.

Chantel: 3,000 to 5,000 speakers reported in 1985, in the Kali Gandaki River valley, Nepal. Also called Chentel Magar.

Chaudangsi: 1,500 speakers reported in 1977, in Mahakali Zone, far western Nepal, and in India; possibly all speakers are in India. Also called Tsaudangsi.

Choni: spoken on the Yunnan-Tibet border, China. Also called Chona or Chone. Possibly the same as Zhongdian (Chongtien).

Darmiya: 1,750 speakers reported in 1977, in Mahakali Zone, far western Nepal, and in India; possibly all speakers are now in India. Also called Darimiya.

Dolpo: 5,000 speakers reported in 1985, in Dolpa, northern Karnali Zone, Nepal. Also called Phoke Dolpa or Dolpa Tibetan.

Dzongkha: 5,100 to 8,500 speakers reported in 1977, in Ha, Paru, and Punakha, Bhutan. Also in Nepal. Also called Drukke, Drukha, Bhutanese, Jonkha, Lhoke, Lhoskad, Hloka, Lhoka, Dukpa, Bhotia of Bhutan, Bhotia of Dukpa, Zongkhar, or Zonkar. Has 48 percent lexical similarity with Sharchagpakha, 47 percent to 52 percent with Kebumtamp, 77 percent with Adap.

Ghale: 10,000 speakers reported in 1961, in the western hills of Gorkha District, Nepal. Also called Galle Gurung.

Golog: 80,000 to 90,000 speakers reported in 1982, in Qinghai, China. Also called Ngolok or Mgolog.

Groma: spoken in Sikkim, India. Also in China. Also called Tromowa.

Gurung, Eastern: 60,000 or more speakers reported in 1985, in Lamjung and Gorkha Districts, Nepal. Also called Daduwa, Lanjung, or Lamjung.

Gurung, Western: 90,000 speakers reported in 1985 in Kaski and Syangja Districts, Nepal, and a few in India. May also be spoken in Burma. Also called Gurung.

Helambu Sherpa: 5,000 to 15,000 speakers reported in 1985, in Nuwakot and Sindhupalchok Districts, Bagmati Zone, down to Kathmandu, Nepal. Bilingualism in Nepali is limited.

Humla Bhotia: in Bajura District, Seti Zone, and Humla District, Karnali Zone, Nepal. Also called Dangali or Phoke.

Janggali: 9,140 speakers reported in 1961, in Mahakali Zone, far western Nepal. There may also be speakers in Himachal Pradesh, India. Also called Jhangal, Jhangar, or Dzanggali.

Jiarong: 100,000 speakers reported in 1990, in Sichuan, China. Also called Jyarung, Gyarong, or Rgyarong.

Jirel: 5,000 speakers reported in 1985, in the Jiri Valley, Dolakha District, Janakpur Zone, eastern Nepal. Also called Ziral or Jiri. Some bilingualism in Nepali.

Kagate: 800 to 1,000 speakers reported in 1985, in Ramechhap District, Nepal. Also called Shuba, Shyuba, Syuba, or Kagate Bhote.

Kaike: spoken in Dhawalagiri Zone, and in Dolpa District, Karnali Zone, Nepal. Also called Tarali Kham.

Kanashi: 1,000 speakers reported in 1977, in Himachal Pradesh, India.

Kanauri: around 28,500 speakers reported in 1961, in Uttar Pradesh, Punjab, Kashmir, and Himachal Pradesh, India; also possibly in Tibet. Also called Kanawari or Tibas Skad.

Kebumtamp: 400,000 speakers reported in 1973, in central Bhutan. Has 47 percent to 52 percent lexical similarity with Dzongkha, 62 percent to 65 percent with Adap, and 40 percent to 50 percent with Sharchagpakha.

Kham: 11,400 speakers reported in 1977, in Ü Province, eastern Tibet. Also called Khams, Khams-Yal, Khams Bhotia, or Kam. Distinct from Takale, Nisi, Sheshi, and Gamale Kham of Nepal. Probably included officially under Tibetan.

Kusanda: now extinct, formerly spoken near Kumhali in Tanahun, western Nepal. Also called Kusunda. The last speaker died in the 1980s.

Kutang Bhotia: 2,000 speakers reported in 1985, along the Buri Gandalei River in north Gorkha District, Nepal. Also called Larkye. Some bilingualism in Nepali. 'Bhotia' or 'Bhote' refers to any people of Tibetan origin, and in some contexts is derogatory.

Kyerung: spoken in Rasuwa District, Bagmati Zone, Nepal, and in Tibet.

Ladakhi: around 57,000 speakers reported in 1971, in Ladakh, Jammu and Kashmir, and Punjab, India. Also possibly in Tibet. Also called Ladaphi, Ladhakhi, Ladak, or Ladwags. Many speakers in urban areas have some bilingualism in Urdu, Hindi, or English, but rural speakers are mainly monolingual in Ladakhi.

Lahuli, Chamba: around 3,020 speakers reported in 1982, in Chamba District, Himachal Pradesh, India. Also called Manchati, Manchad, Patni, or Chamba. Distinct from Lahuli of Lahul and Spiti.

Lahuli, Tinan: around 11,400 speakers reported in 1982, mainly in Lahul and Spiti Subdivisions, Himachal Pradesh, India, and including 450 to 1,600 in China. Also called Lahauli, Lahouli, Rangloi, or Gondla. Distinct from Lahuli of Chamba (Manchati).

Lhomi: 6,000 speakers reported in 1985, with 4,000 near the Arun River in eastern Nepal, 1,000 in China, and 1,000 in India. Also called Lhoket or Shing Saapa.

Lopa: 20,000 speakers reported in 1985, in Dawalagiri Zone, Dolpa and Mustang Districts, north central Nepal. Also called Loyu, Loba, or Mustang. Distinct from Lhoba in China and India, a Mirish language.

Manangba: 4,000 speakers reported in 1977, in Manang District, Gandaki Zone, northern Nepal. Also called Manang, Manangi, or Northern Gurung.

Mugali: 35,000 speakers reported in 1985, in Mugu, Karnali, Nepal.

Naapa: 500 speakers reported in 1985, in Sankhuwasawa District, Koshi Zone, Nepal. Naapa-speaking villages are interspersed among the Lhomi. Also called Nawa Sherpa, Naba, or Naapaa. Some bilingualism in Lhomi.

Olangchung Gola: spoken in Sankhuwasawa District, Koshi Zone, Nepal. Most speakers are in one community in Kathmandu, where younger speakers are losing the language.

Panang: spoken in Tibet. Also called Panags or Panakha. Probably included officially under Tibetan.

Panchgaunle: spoken in Mustang District, Nepal. May be a dialect of Thakali.

Purik: 135,000 to 148,000 speakers reported in 1977, in northern Kashmir, India, and elsewhere in the western Himalayas and western Tibet. Also called Purigskad, Burig, Purig, Purki, Purik Bhotia, Burig, or Burigskat. Low degree of bilingual proficiency in Urdu.

Rangkas: 600 speakers reported in 1977, in Mahakali Zone, far western Nepal, and in India; possibly all speakers are in India.

Sagtengpa: spoken in the Sakteng Valley, Bhutan. Also called Mira Sagtengpa, Dakpa, Brokpa, or Dap. May be a dialect of Sharchagpakha or Dzongkha. The speakers are called Dakpa.

Sharchagpakha: 400,000 speakers reported in 1973, in eastern and southeastern Bhutan. Also called Sarchapkkha, Sharchup, or Sharchop Kha. A speaker is called Schachop. Has 40 percent to 50 percent lexical similarity with Kebumtamp, 48 percent with Dzongkha, and 41 percent with Adap.

Sherdukpen: around 1,140 speakers reported in 1982, in Assam and Arunachal Pradesh, India.

Sherpa: 25,000 or more speakers reported in 1973, with 14,100 in the Solu Khumbu District of northern Nepal, 10,100 in Sikkim, India, and 400 in China. Also called Sharpa, Sharpa Bhotia, Xiaerba, or Serwa.

Sikkimese: around 37,000 speakers reported in 1961, in the higher mountains in the northern half of Sikkim, India. Possibly also in Tibet. Also called Sikkim Bhotia, Danjongka, Denjonke, Denjonka, or Sikami. Partial mutual intelligibility with Dzongkha of Bhutan.

Sotatipo: spoken in Tibet. Probably officially included under Tibetan.

Tamang, Eastern: around 336,000 speakers reported in 1989, in Kathmandu, Nepal, and to the east as far as Sikkim and Darjeeling, India.

Tamang, Northwestern: 100,000 speakers reported in 1989, in Nuwakot District, Nepal, and some in the Terai. Also called Murmi.

Tamang, Southwestern: 100,000 speakers reported in 1989, in the central mountainous strip of Nuwakot District, Nepal, and into the Terai.

Thakali: around 4,130 speakers reported in 1961, in Mustang District, Nepal. Some are fairly bilingual in Nepali.

Thami: 20,000 or more speakers reported in 1985, in Dolakha, Nepal, and some in China.

Thudam Bhote: spoken in Mechi Zone, northern Nepal.

Tibetan: 4,040,000 or more speakers reported in 1982, with 3,870,000 in Tibet, Sichuan, and Qinghai, China, 100,000 in India, 60,000 in Nepal, and others in five other countries. Also called Lhasa, Zang, Bhotia, Phoke, Dbus, or Xifan. One of the main official nationalities in China, called Zang; the term also includes Atuence, Choni, Groma, Golog, Niarong, Lhomi, Panang, Sherpa, Sotatipo, Tseku, Thami, Purik, and Tinan Lahuli.

Tichurong: 1,500 speakers reported in 1980, in Dolpa District, Karnali Zone, Nepal. Also called Ticherong.

Tsangla: 87,000 speakers reported in 1967, with around 80,000 in southeast Bhutan and 7,000 in China. Also called Sangla. Not the same as Tsanglo (Angami Naga) of Assam, India.

Tseku: spoken in Tibet, and also in Bhutan and possibly Nepal. Probably officially included under Tibetan in China.

Zangskari: 8,000 to 10,000 speakers reported in 1984, between the Himalayas and the Indus River, in Kashmir, India, and possibly in Tibet. Also called Zanskari or Zaskari. Some bilingualism in the Leh dialect of Ladakhi.

BODO-GARO LANGUAGES constitute a group spoken in Assam and adjacent parts of India, and in Bangladesh. These languages form a subgroup of Baric within Tibeto-Burman, a branch of Sino-Tibetan [*qq.v.*]. Within Tibeto-Burman, they are grouped together with the Konyak languages [*q.v.*] as an intermediate-level unit. The internal classification of the Bodo-Garo languages is shown in Figure 1.

LANGUAGE LIST

Bodo: 1,000,000 speakers reported in 1989, including 600,000 in Assam and West Bengal, India, and others in Nepal. Also called Boro, Bodi, Bara, Boroni, Mechi, Meche, Mech, or Meci.

Deori: around 14,900 speakers reported in 1971, in Assam and Nagaland, India. Also called Chutiya, Deuri, or Drori.

Dimasa: 70,000 speakers reported in 1987, in North Cachar District and the Cachar Hills of Assam, and in Nagaland, India.

FIGURE 1. *Subgrouping of Bodo-Garo Languages*

Bodo
- Bodo (proper)
- **Tripura**
  - Kok Borok, Riang
- **Unclassified Bodo**
  - Dimasa, Kachari, Lalung

Eastern Bodo-Garo
- Deori

Garo
- Garo (proper), Koch, Megam, Rabha

Garo: 504,000 speakers reported in 1989, with 411,000 in the Garo Hills of western Assam, and in Nagaland, Tripura, and West Bengal, India, and 92,800 in Bangladesh. Also called Garrow or Mande.

Kachari: 45,000 speakers reported in 1987, in north Cachar District and the Cachar Hills, Assam, and in Nagaland, India. Also called Dimasa Kachari.

Koch: 35,000 speakers reported in 1971, with 13,800 in Assam and Tripura, India, and the rest in Bangladesh. Also called Koc, Kocch, Koce, Kochboli, or Konch. Distinct from Koch in West Bengal, of the Eastern Indo-Aryan group.

Kok Borok: around 320,000 speakers reported in 1971, with 269,000 in Assam and eastern Tripura, India, and 50,000 in Bangladesh. Also called Tripuri, Tipura, Usipi, or Mrung.

Lalung: around 10,700 speakers reported in 1971, in Assam, India.

Megam: spoken in northeastern Bangladesh. Also called Migam. Called a dialect of Garo, but may be a separate language.

Rabha: 200,000 speakers reported in 1989, in western Assam and Nagaland, India. Also called Rava.

Riang: 101,000 speakers reported in 1989, with 100,000 in Assam and central Tripura, India, and 1,000 in Bangladesh. Also called Reang or Kau Bru. Possible mutual intelligibility with Kok Borok. Different from Riang-Lang of Burma, a Mon-Khmer language.

BOPP, FRANZ, was born 14 September 1791 in Mainz, Germany, and died 23 October 1867 in Berlin. He was one of the founders of I[ndo]-E[uropean] comparative linguistics, and author of the first IE comparative grammar.

When Bopp was still a boy, his family moved from Mainz to Aschaffenburg, following the Elector's court in the aftermath of the French occupation. There he attended the Gymnasium, and, inspired by K. Windischmann, developed an interest in Oriental languages and literatures. To pursue this, it was necessary for him to leave Germany; from 1812 to 1817, he studied Sanskrit in Paris. He then visited London in order to study Sanskrit manuscripts; during his stay, he made the acquaintance of Wilhelm von Humboldt, to whom he gave instruction in Sanskrit, and who became a firm friend. In 1820, Bopp returned to Germany, taking up residence in Göttingen. In 1821, largely because of the influence of Wilhelm and Alexander Von Humboldt, Bopp was appointed Professor of Oriental Literature and General Philology in Berlin, where he remained until his death.

Bopp has often been hailed as the founder of comparative linguistics, and many consider that the publication of his *Conjugationssystem* (1816, English translation 1820) marks the beginning of the discipline. That Sanskrit was related to Latin, Greek, and other languages of Europe was by this time well known; in 1808, Friedrich von Schlegel (in his influential *Über die Sprache und Weisheit der Indier*) had suggested that a 'comparative grammar' would 'lead to new conclusions about the genealogy of languages'. Bopp, however, was the first to carry out a systematic and detailed comparison of morphological forms. His investigations culminated in the first IE comparative grammar, his *Vergleichende Grammatik* (1833–52). Further contributions to IE linguistics include works on Celtic, Albanian, Old Prussian, and comparative accentuation. Bopp also developed an interest in Malayo-Polynesian and Caucasian languages, and attempted to show that these too were related to Sanskrit. (For reference, see Martineau 1867, Leskien 1876, Guigniaut 1877, Lefman 1891, Verburg 1950, and Morpurgo Davies 1987.)

Today, Bopp is a somewhat controversial figure. On the one hand, he was influenced by exponents of Romanticism, in particular by Schlegel. On the other hand, his concern to discover the 'physical and mechanical laws' of languages makes him seem more of a rationalist. His methodology involved the *Zergliederung* 'dissection' and comparison of forms, on the basis of which he was able to attribute particular roots and inflections to the parent language; these could then be further analysed and explained. One of his central ideas was that endings arose by agglutination of meaningful elements; thus he considered that the personal endings of the verb arose by agglutination of forms of the verb 'to be' and personal pronouns.

Bopp is also remembered for his contribution to the teaching of Sanskrit. His grammars, written along European rather than Indian lines, together with his publication of relatively easy texts with translations, made the language more accessible to European students. In this way too, his work was of importance in the development of IE studies. [*See also* History of Linguistics, *article on* Comparative-Historical Linguistics.]

KATRINA M. HAYWARD

BIBLIOGRAPHY

BOPP, FRANZ. 1816. *Über das Conjugationssystem der Sanskritsprache in Vergleichung mit jenem der griechischen, lateinischen, persischen und germanischen Sprache.* Frankfurt am Main: Andreä. Excerpts translated in *A reader in nineteenth century Indo-European historical linguistics,* edited by Winfred P. Lehmann (Bloomington: Indiana University Press, 1967), pp. 38–45.

BOPP, FRANZ. 1820. Analytical comparison of the Sanskrit, Greek, Latin and Teutonic languages, shewing the original identity of their grammatical structure. *Annals of Oriental Literature* (London) 1:1.1–64. New edition, edited by E. F. K. Koerner, Amsterdam: Benjamins, 1974.

BOPP, FRANZ. 1833–52. *Vergleichende Grammatik des Sanskrit, Zend, Griechischen, Lateinischen, Lithauischen, Gothischen und Deutschen.* 2 vols. Berlin: Dümmler. 2d ed., 1857–61; 3rd posthumous ed., 1868–71. Translation, London: Madden & Malcolm, 1845–53.

GUIGNIAUT, JOSEPH D. 1877. Notice historique sur la vie et les travaux de M. François Bopp. *Mémoires de l'Académie des Inscriptions et Belles-Lettres* 29:1.201–224. Reprinted in Bopp [1820] 1974, pp. xv–xxxviii.

LEFMAN, SALOMON. 1891. *Franz Bopp, sein Leben und seine Wissenschaft.* 2 vols. Berlin: Reimer.

LESKIEN, AUGUST. 1876. Bopp. *Allgemeine Deutsche Biographie* 3.140–149. Reprinted in Sebeok 1966, vol. 1, pp. 207–221.

MARTINEAU, RUSSELL. 1867. Obituary of Franz Bopp. *Transactions of the Philological Society* 1867:305–312. Reprinted in Sebeok 1966, vol. 1, pp. 200–206.

MORPURGO DAVIES, ANNA. 1987. 'Organic' and 'organism' in Franz Bopp. In *Biological metaphor and cladistic classification,* edited by Henry M. Hoenigswald & L. F. Wiener, pp. 81–107. London: Pinter.

SEBEOK, THOMAS A., ed. 1966. *Portraits of linguists.* 2 vols. Bloomington: Indiana University Press.

VERBURG, P. A. 1950. The background to the linguistic conceptions of Franz Bopp. *Lingua* 2.438–468. Reprinted in Sebeok 1966, vol. 1, pp. 221–250.

BORNEO LANGUAGES constitute a division of the West Malayo-Polynesian branch of the Austronesian languages [*qq.v.*]. The subgroups are Apo Duat, Barito, Ida'an, Kayan-Kenyah, Land Dayak, Northeast Borneo, and Rejang-Baram. [*For data on individual languages within these subgroups, see the corresponding articles—except for the language isolate Ida'an, which is covered in the Language List below.*]

LANGUAGE LIST

Ida'an: 6,000 speakers reported in 1987, on the eastern coast in Lahad Datu, Kinabatangan, and Sandakan Districts, Sabah, Malaysia. Also called Eraans, Bulud Upi, Idahan, Idan, or Idayan.

BORROWING. [*This entry is concerned with the transfer of features from one language into another language. It comprises two articles:*

An Overview

Loanword Phonology

For related topics, see Bilingualism; *and* Pidgins and Creoles.]

An Overview

'Borrowing' is a general and traditional word used to describe the adoption into a language of a linguistic feature previously used in another. The metaphor implied can be misleading, since 'borrowing' usually refers to temporary possession and repayment. Linguistic loans are usually permanent, and of course do not imply a quid pro quo. The term was a byproduct of the discovery of the regularity of PHONOLOGICAL CHANGE [*q.v.*] in the early 19th century. Sound change could be summed up in neat formulas that were assumed to account for most of the development of a language. Borrowing was essentially that which remained unaccounted for by the sound laws, and could be explained by outside influence. Loans were mostly lexical items, which came to be known as LOANWORDS. This term did not enter the English language, according to the *OED,* until 1874, when A. H. Sayce used it in his *Principles of comparative philology* (Sayce 1874:200 fn.). The term itself was a loanword, obviously modeled on the German *Lehnwort.*

While the concept of the loanword was soon accepted, the extension of borrowing to other linguistic features was still hotly debated. Borrowing of features other than words was considered evidence of 'language mixture'. In the 1860s, the English-German Max Müller, a popularizer of linguistics, flatly denied 'the possibility of a mixed language'; the Neogrammarians had determined that grammar was 'the ground of classification in all languages' (Müller 1864:76–79). The American Sanskritist W. D. Whitney expressed the same view: 'Such a thing as a language with a mixed grammatical apparatus has never come under the cognizance of linguistic students; it would be to them a monstrosity, it seems an impossibility' (Whitney 1867:199; cf. Whitney 1882). However, the Romance scholar Hugo Schuchardt, a German who was a professor at Graz in Austria, disputed this view hotly. Schuchardt had written his thesis on the origins of Vulgar Latin, no doubt a troubling problem for strict Neogrammarians. He was led into the study of creole languages in West Africa, India, and the Philippines, where he had abundant chance to see the results of borrowing on a large scale. In Austria he turned his attention to the jargons of the Austro-Hungarian Empire, especially the German and Italian spoken by Slavic speakers. Contrary to Müller, he maintained that there was no fully unmixed language. He asserted that the genealogical trees developed by the Neogrammarians on the basis of their sound laws 'needed to be joined by twigs in the form of horizontal lines' (Schuchardt 1884:6). He found the wave theory advocated by Johannes Schmidt (1872) to be more congenial, since it introduced a geographical dimension into the discussion. The dispute over 'mixed' languages has long since been laid to rest, with the realization that linguistic change involves both internal and external influences. [*See* Pidgins and Creoles.]

In more recent studies various advances have been made. Thus Betz 1949 devised an elaborate scheme for classifying early loans in O[ld] H[igh] G[erman]. He compared the OHG translation of the Benedictine Rule with its Latin original, and found it useful to create a new vocabulary for this purpose. He contrasted the *Lehnwort* with what he called *Lehnbildungen* 'loan formations', terms and constructions resulting from foreign influence. The loan formations were classified into loan-translations, -transfers, -creations, -expressions, -meanings, and -syntax, depending on the relation of the German rendition to the Latin original (Betz 1949:28–31). Although Betz did not refer to Schuchardt, his views on the importance of borrowing as a leading factor in the cultural unity of Western Europe were in full agreement with Schuchardt's.

Betz worked exclusively with medieval sources; but like all who had worked on borrowing, he pointed to the need for assuming a certain degree of bilingualism among the many immigrants of the 19th century. One of the first to exploit this field was Einar Haugen, who began field work among Norwegian immigrants in 1936. He studied under George T. Flom, an Old Norse scholar who had also done pioneer work on immigrant language around the turn of the century (Flom 1900–01; see bibliography in Haugen 1942:40–41). Haugen was also stimulated by the work of Hans Kurath (1939) on the New England Dialect Atlas, and used its questionnaire as the model for his own. He interviewed speakers in the Middle West until 1942, assisted by Magne Oftedal in 1947–48. His conclusions appeared in Haugen 1950 and 1953. He distinguished only three kinds of loans: LOANWORDS, LOANBLENDS, and LOANSHIFTS, according to the relation between morphemic importation and the substitution of native equivalents. Loanshifts included loan translations and semantic borrowings.

Independently, Uriel Weinreich had started work on his own Yiddish-American speech at Columbia University; but under the direction of the French linguist André Martinet, he went to Switzerland to study Romansh. That language was not then recognized as one of Switzerland's official languages, and its speakers were under heavy pressure from Swiss Germans to become bilingual. The results of Weinreich's work appeared in the monograph *Languages in contact* (1953), in which he adopted much of the terminology of the Prague School, with which Martinet was associated (see Martinet 1955). Weinreich brought new terms to the field, including CONTACT for the meeting in one population of two or more languages, and INTERFERENCE for the borrowing that resulted. Following the tenets of Prague School structuralism, he did not see loans as mere additions, but as reorganizations of the system. He classified interference as either phonic, grammatical, or lexical; and he chose examples not only from his studies in Switzerland, but also from his own Yiddish background and other bilingual situations. He also had chapters on the problems of the bilingual individual and the socio-cultural setting of the language contact.

Haugen's and Weinreich's studies laid a solid basis for further study of borrowing and related topics. A leading contributor was the Australian Michael Clyne, who in 1967 proposed the term TRANSFERENCE for their 'borrowing' and 'interference' (Clyne 1967). His data were based on German immigrants to Australia (see below).

Meanwhile, attention turned to the social parameters of BILINGUALISM [*q.v.*], which was recognized as a field of its own. It became a special interest of the newly established Center for Applied Linguistics in Washington, D.C., in 1958, headed by Charles A. Ferguson. Ferguson presented one important aspect of bilingualism in an article on 'Diglossia' (1959). This term identified the existence in some nations of a Low (or Informal) and a High (or Formal) variety of the same language; his examples were drawn from Arabic, Greek, Swiss German, and Haitian French/Creole. Such work contributed immediately to the identification of a branch of linguistics to be named SOCIOLINGUISTICS [*q.v.*]. Ferguson directed a seminal conference on the topic at the Linguistic Society of America summer session of 1964 at Indiana University in Bloomington, following a conference at the University of California, Los Angeles, which resulted in a volume edited by William Bright (1966).

Meanwhile, research on borrowing continued, with contributions by a number of scholars for various immigrant languages in the United States; fairly complete surveys are available in Haugen 1956 and 1973 for the preceding periods. A special aspect of borrowing that has recently aroused interest among linguists is connected with language-switching, which is very common among bilinguals, as had been pointed out by Haugen (1953:64–65) and Weinreich (1953:73–74). In this procedure, the speaker does not just adopt a new item into his/her repertoire—but actually, more or less briefly, changes into the other language. This process has come to be called CODE-SWITCHING, and there has been considerable discussion about conditions and constraints that govern it. Clyne 1987 defines it as 'the alternative use of the two languages either within a sentence or between sentences'. He refers to a number of articles that have attempted to address the theoretical aspects of code switching. Unfortunately, the authors, some of whom work in the generative tradition, attempt to arrive at 'universal' principles without having adequate data. Clyne presents examples from a large study of Dutch and German, as spoken in Australia, that appear to contradict these principles. It is obvious that there is much confusion on how to delimit and describe the respective fields of borrowing and switching. The problem is addressed in an exchange of views between Shana Poplack, who has studied bilinguals in various parts of the world, including French Canada (Poplack 1988), and Carol Myers Scotton, who has done field work among Swahili speakers in Kenya (Scotton 1988).

In general, borrowing appears to be a universal feature of language, as maintained by Schuchardt. No language community is or remains so isolated as to avoid some contact with the speakers of other languages or dialects; we may see the bilinguals as the vehicles of borrowing. One problem in delimiting dialects in the contact area is: What is in fact a 'different' dialect? Loans are passed from speaker to speaker, and are probably not normally identified as such by unlettered speakers.

Linguists find it interesting and significant that loanwords are adapted to the phonological, morphological, and syntactic patterns of a different language—as when

Latin *vīnum* became Old English *wīn*, which changed with the English language into modern *wine* [wain]. In bilingual studies, it is now common to speak of the 'donating' language as the SOURCE language, and the one 'receiving' as the MATRIX (or recipient) language. Once adapted, loanwords become an integral part of the matrix language. In practice, it is often found that the adaptation is not complete, and therefore actually increases the repertoire of the matrix language not just with new lexemes, but also with new structures—as when English added the sound *j* [dž] in words like *just* from Latin *iūstus* (through French), or [ž] in American *garage* from French.

The most obvious reason for borrowing is the need of a term in the matrix language for some previously unknown phenomenon. But this is far from being the only reason. Words are often borrowed because they are felt to be prestigious or just novel. This is especially true if the speakers feel inferior to the speakers of the other language, as did the English when they were ruled by the Norman French. The loanword may cause native words to seem inadequate, and gradually to fall into disuse—hence the many loanwords from Anglo-Norman French in English and from Low German in Scandinavian. In studying loans it is therefore important to know about the social relations of the two communities; and loans may actually be a key to understanding such relations.

Uncompounded words offer few obstacles to borrowing; but compounds, if understood as such, may be adapted to native compounds, as when English *skyscraper* was reproduced in German as *Wolkenkratzer*, literally 'cloud-scratcher'. If the result is composed of native and foreign elements, it may be called a LOANBLEND. This may also be applied to words that add prefixes or suffixes by analogy with previously borrowed loans, e.g. Eng. *wondrous* from OE *wundor* plus the suffix of words like Latin-French *amorous*. In some words the result can be classified as a LOANSHIFT, also called a CALQUE—as when Latin *spiritus sanctus* is reproduced as *Holy Ghost*, where both elements are native. An example of a CODESHIFT might be the pronunciation by some of *empire* as [āpír] in reference to an architectural style; on a humbler level, one could hear American Norwegians utter *weather report* with American *w, th,* and *r*, but otherwise in Norwegian. In countries where loans are deliberately resisted, original loans may be replaced by native creations, as when German *Telephon* was replaced by *Fernsprecher*, lit. 'far-speaker'. Icelandic is especially characterized by such tendencies: 'television' has become *sjónvarp* 'sight-cast'.

EINAR HAUGEN

BIBLIOGRAPHY

BETZ, WERNER. 1949. *Deutsch und Lateinisch: Die Lehnbildungen der althochdeutschen Benediktinerregel.* Bonn: Bouvier.

BRIGHT, WILLIAM, ed. 1966. *Sociolinguistics.* (Janua linguarum, Series maior, 20.) The Hague: Mouton.

CLYNE, MICHAEL. 1967. *Transference and triggering: Observations on the language assimilation of postwar German-speaking migrants in Australia.* The Hague: Nijhoff.

CLYNE, MICHAEL. 1987. Constraints on code-switching: How universal are they? *Linguistics* 25.739–764.

FERGUSON, CHARLES A. 1959. Diglossia. *Word* 15.325–340.

FLOM, GEORGE T. 1900–1901. English elements in Norse dialects in Utica, Wisconsin. *Dialect Notes* 2.257–268.

HAUGEN, EINAR. 1942. Problems of linguistic research among Scandinavian immigrants in America. *Bulletin of the American Council of Learned Societies* 34.35–57.

HAUGEN, EINAR. 1950. The analysis of linguistic borrowing. *Language* 26.210–231. Reprinted in Einar Haugen, *The ecology of language* (Stanford, Calif.: Stanford University Press, 1972), pp. 79–109.

HAUGEN, EINAR. 1953. *The Norwegian language in America: A study in bilingual behavior.* 2 vols. Philadelphia: University of Pennsylvania Press. Reprinted, Bloomington: Indiana University Press, 1969.

HAUGEN, EINAR. 1956. *Bilingualism in the Americas: A bibliography and research guide.* (American Dialect Society, publication 26.) University, Ala.: University of Alabama Press.

HAUGEN, EINAR. 1973. Bilingualism, language contact, and immigrant languages in the United States: A research report, 1956–1970. In *Current trends in linguistics,* vol. 10, *Linguistics in North America,* edited by Thomas A. Sebeok, pp. 505–591. The Hague: Mouton.

KURATH, HANS. 1939. *Handbook of the linguistic geography of New England.* Providence, R.I.: Brown University.

MARTINET, ANDRÉ. 1955. *Économie des changements phonétiques.* Bern: Francke.

MÜLLER, MAX. 1861–1864. *Lectures on the science of language.* 2 vols. London: Longman, Green.

POPLACK, SHANA. 1988. Language status and language accommodation along a linguistic border. In *Language spread and language policy* (Georgetown University Round Table on Languages and Linguistics, 1987), edited by Peter H. Lowenberg, pp. 90–118. Washington, D.C.: Georgetown University Press.

SAYCE, A. H. 1874. *The principles of comparative philology.* London: Trübner.

SCHMIDT, JOHANNES. 1872. *Die Verwandtschaftsverhältnisse der indogermanischen Sprachen.* Weimar: Böhlau.

SCHUCHARDT, HUGO. 1884. *Slawo-deutsches und Slawo-italienisches.* (Slawisches Propyläen, 66.) Graz: Leuschner & Lubensky. Reprinted, Munich: Fink, 1971.

SCOTTON, CAROL MYERS. 1988. Differentiating borrowing and codeswitching. *Linguistic change and variation: Proceedings of the Sixteenth Annual Conference on New Ways of Analyzing Variation,* edited by Kathleen Ferrara et al., pp. 318–325. Austin: Department of Linguistics, University of Texas.

WEINREICH, URIEL. 1953. *Languages in contact: Findings and problems.* New York: Linguistic Circle of New York.

WHITNEY, WILLIAM DWIGHT. 1867. *Language and the study of language.* New York: Scribner.

WHITNEY, WILLIAM DWIGHT. 1882. On mixture in language. *Transactions of the American Philological Association* 12.5–26. Reprinted in *Whitney on language,* edited by Michael Silverstein (Cambridge, Mass.: MIT Press, 1971), pp. 170–191.

Loanword Phonology

Words borrowed from one language into another are typically altered to conform to the phonological canons of the borrowing language, in ways that range from changes in individual segments to more global deformations of structure. Loan phonology is often quite revealing of the grammatical constraints and processes of the borrowing language. Complete systematicity is not to be expected, however, since loanwords may enter a language either through orthography or through pronunciation; they may be borrowed at different points in the history of a language; and they may be affected by such factors as the degree of BILINGUALISM [*q.v.*] in the borrowing community, or the similarity of the loanword to taboo words in the recipient language. (For general reference, see Haugen 1950, Weinreich 1953, Byarushengo 1976, Holden 1976, and Broselow 1987.)

Perhaps the most obvious alteration in loanwords is the replacement of single segments, often called PHONEME SUBSTITUTION. This process subjects the loanword to the borrowing language's restrictions on possible phonemes and their distribution; thus, in English, the replacement of the velar fricative by *h* or *k* (as in *Chanukah* and *Bach* respectively) is subject to the restriction that *h* may not occur syllable-finally in English. The allophonic restrictions of the recipient language are also generally obeyed; Spanish *estufa* 'stove' becomes Yaqui *ehtupa,* where non-occurring *f* is replaced by *p,* but *s,* which does occur in Yaqui, is realized as *h,* the appropriate positional variant before *t* (Haugen 1950). The choice of a replacement phoneme is often assumed to be determined by phonetic similarity, though it is not clear which aspect of a given sound will be perceived as most salient by speakers of a particular language. For example, among languages which employ both *s* and *t* as phonemes, some typically replace English *θ* by *s* and some by *t,* for no obvious phonetic reason (Hyman 1970a).

Loanwords commonly conform to constraints on prosodic organization as well as on segmental structure. Constraints on syllable structure are typically maintained by the insertion of vowels, as in Samoan *sipuni* 'spoon', which obeys the Samoan requirement that syllables consist maximally of one consonant followed by one vowel. Another strategy used to maintain constraints on syllable structure is the deletion of a consonant (e.g. loss of *p* in *pneumonia*); even reordering of segments is attested, as in the common rendering by American news reporters of *Ghotbzadeh* (the name of a former Iranian official) as *Gotsbade,* substituting for the consonant cluster *tbz* one which is divisible into possible English syllables. In addition to constraints on syllable structure, borrowing languages commonly enforce restrictions on possible word structure; in Arabic, for example, monosyllabic nouns and verbs must consist of a syllable which is either closed by two consonants, or which contains a long vowel followed by a consonant, so that borrowed *bus* becomes either [ba:s] or [bass]. Borrowing languages also tend to translate the prosodic structure of the loanword into native prosodic configurations; in Japanese borrowings from English, the pitch accent of the borrowed word is generally determined by the position of stress in the English pronunciation (Lovins 1975).

The recasting of loanwords into forms consistent with the phonology of the borrowing language has the consequence that loan phonology may serve as a useful testing ground for hypotheses about the grammar of the borrowing language. For example, the alterations of metrical structure discussed above provide a diagnostic for the recipient language's constraints on syllable and word structure. Another sort of example involves Nupe, a Nigerian language, in which consonants occurring before non-low front vowels *i e* are palatalized, while consonants occurring before back vowels *u o* are not.

However, both palatalized and non-palatalized consonants occur before the back vowel *a*. Hyman 1970b argues that, in the optimal grammar of Nupe, palatalized consonants derive from a rule which palatalizes a consonant before a front vowel; surface *a* following a palatalized consonant is derived from underlying front ε by an absolute neutralization rule that transforms ε to *a* after palatalization has taken place. This sort of analysis is controversial, but it is supported by the Nupe rendering of Yoruba loans like *kɛkɛ* 'bicycle' as *kyakya,* where both posited rules appear to have applied. Thus loan phonology may provide evidence for the productivity of grammatical processes or constraints that are based on distributional facts, but that are not supported by alternations in the native vocabulary.

ELLEN BROSELOW

BIBLIOGRAPHY

BROSELOW, ELLEN. 1987. Non-obvious transfer: On predicting epenthesis errors. In *Interlanguage phonology,* edited by Georgette Ioup & Steven Weinberger, pp. 292–304. Cambridge, Mass.: Newbury House.

BYARUSHENGO, ERNEST R. 1976. Strategies in loan phonology. *Berkeley Linguistics Society* 2.78–88.

HAUGEN, EINAR. 1950. The analysis of linguistic borrowing. *Language* 26.210–231.

HOLDEN, KYRIL. 1976. Assimilation rates of borrowings and phonological productivity. *Language* 52.131–147.

HYMAN, LARRY M. 1970a. The role of borrowing in the justification of phonological grammars. *Studies in African Linguistics* 1.1–48.

HYMAN, LARRY M. 1970b. How concrete is phonology? *Language* 46.58–76.

LOVINS, JULIE B. 1975. *Loanwords and the phonological structure of Japanese.* Bloomington: Indiana University Linguistics Club.

WEINREICH, URIEL. 1953. *Languages in contact.* New York: Linguistic Circle of New York. Reprinted, The Hague: Mouton, 1974.

BOUGAINVILLE LANGUAGES constitute a group spoken in Papua New Guinea, on Bougainville Island and the Shortland Islands (to the east of the island of New Guinea). They form a top-level component of Oceanic [*q.v.*]. (This family is not to be confused with the East Papuan subgroup of the same name.) The subgrouping of the Bougainville languages given in Figure 1 is based on Merritt Ruhlen, *A guide to the world's languages,* vol. 1, *Classification* (Stanford, Calif.: Stanford University Press, 1987).

FIGURE 1. *Subgrouping of Bougainville Languages*

- **North and East Bougainville**
  - **East Bougainville**
    - Torau, Uruava
  - **North Bougainville-Nehan**
    - Nehan (Nissan)
    - **North Bougainville**
      - **Buka**
        - **Halia**
          - Hakö, Halia (proper)
        - **Unclassified Buka**
          - Petats, Selau, Solos
      - **Saposa-Tinputz**
        - Hahon, Saposa, Teop, Tinputz
    - Papapana
- **West Bougainville**
  - Banoni, Minigir, Mono, Nagarige

LANGUAGE LIST

Banoni: 1,000 speakers reported in 1977, on southwestern Bougainville Island, North Solomons Province. Also called Tsonari.

Hahon: 1,300 speakers reported in 1977, on Bougainville Island, North Solomons Province Also called Hanon.

Hakö: spoken on northeastern Buka Island, Buka Passage Subprovince, North Solomons Province. Also called Haku.

Halia: 14,000 speakers reported in 1986, on northeastern Buka Island, Buka Passage Subprovince, North Solomons Province. Also called Hanahan, Tulon, or Tasi.

Minigir: spoken in Lungalunga village on the Gazelle Peninsula, East New Britain Province. Also called Lungalunga.

Mono: 1,700 speakers reported in 1981, on Treasury Island, Shortland Island, and Fauro Island, Solomon Islands. Also called Alu or Mono-Alu.

Nagarige: 550 speakers reported in 1977, along the Piva River on Bougainville Island, North Solomons Province. Also called Piva.

Nehan: 15,000 speakers reported in 1975, on Nissan Island, between New Ireland and North Solomons Provinces. Also called Nissan or Nihan.

Papapana: 150 speakers reported in 1977, on the east coast of Bougainville Island, North Solomons Province.

Petats: 2,000 speakers reported in 1975, on Petats, Pororan, and Hitau islands off the west coast of Buka Island, Buka Passage Subprovince, North Solomons Province. Including second-language speakers, the number of users is 10,000.

Saposa: 1,000 speakers reported in 1981, on small islands opposite the Hahon area, and on Saposa Island south of

Buka Island, off the northwest coast of Bougainville, North Solomons Province.

Selau: spoken on northeastern Buka Island, Buka Passage Subprovince, North Solomons Province.

Solos: 3,200 speakers reported in 1977, on central and southwest Buka Island, North Solomons Province.

Teop: 4,600 speakers reported in 1977, on Bougainville Island, North Solomons Province.

Tinputz: 2,300 speakers reported in 1977, in Buka Passage Subprovince, North Solomons Province. Also called Timputs or Wasoi. The speakers' name for themselves is Vasuii.

Torau: 605 speakers reported in 1963, north of Kieta, on the southeast coast of Bougainville Island, North Solomons Province. Also called Rorovana.

Uruava: 5 or fewer elderly male speakers reported in 1977, at Arawa on the southeastern coast of Bougainville Island, North Solomons Province.

BOUNDARY. *See* Juncture and Boundary.

BULGARIAN is the official language of the Bulgarian People's Republic, where it has about eight million speakers. A South Slavic language, it forms a dialect continuum with Macedonian and Eastern Serbo-Croatian dialects. Bulgarian is also a member of the Balkan language area [*q.v.; see also* Slavic Languages].

Among works published in English, De Bray 1980 and Scatton 1984 are general grammars, covering all aspects of the language. Aronson 1968 is a structuralist analysis of inflectional morphophonology. Hubenova et al. 1983 is a thorough textbook treatment of the grammar, presupposing no prior knowledge of Bulgarian or other Slavic languages. Atanassova et al. 1983 and Mincoff 1966 are comprehensive bilingual dictionaries. Scatton 1975 gives a generative analysis of Bulgarian phonology; Aronson 1967 presents a structuralist analysis of the grammatical categories of the Bulgarian verb; Rudin 1986 is an analysis combining Revised Extended Standard Theory with Government/Binding; and Fielder 1985 deals with aspect selection from a structuralist viewpoint.

1. Phonology. Literary Bulgarian has a six-vowel system, with binary distinctions of front/back, rounded/unrounded, and higher/lower. The phonemes are *i e ə a u o*. Stress is distinctive; unstressed position is characterized by greater or lesser degrees of neutralization of the opposition high/low, in the direction of high.

Among the consonants, the major contrasts are voiced/voiceless and palatalized/non-palatalized. The latter is syntagmatically weakly implemented: palatalization is distinctive only before back vowels—in native words, most commonly before *a*, and before *ə* at morpheme boundaries. The consonantal phonemes are shown in Table 1.

Bulgarian is written in the Cyrillic alphabet in a form close to that used for Russian [*q.v.*]. The letter щ is pronounced *št*; the symbol ъ represents the vowel *ə*.

2. Morphophonology (see Aronson 1968). Bulgarian has regressive assimilation of voicing; e.g.,

(1) /gradové/ 'cities' /grát/ 'city'
/lovéc/ 'hunter' /lofcí/ 'hunters'
/otparíš/ 'from Paris' /odbəlgárija/ 'from Bulgaria'

Morphologically-conditioned alternations in the nominal system include the following.

(a) Vowel/zero alternation:

TABLE 1. *Bulgarian Consonant Phonemes*

	Labial	Dental	Palatal	Velar
Stops				
Voiceless				
Plain	p	t		k
Palatalized	p'	t'		k'
Voiced				
Plain	b	d		g
Palatalized	b'	d'		g'
Affricates				
Voiceless				
Plain		c	č	
Palatalized		c'		
Voiced (Plain)			ǰ	
Fricatives				
Voiceless				
Plain	f	s	š	x
Palatalized	f'	s'		
Voiced				
Plain	v	z	ž	
Palatalized	v'	z'		
Nasals				
Plain	m	n		
Palatalized	m'	n'		
Vibrants				
Plain		r		
Palatalized		r'		
Laterals				
Plain		l		
Palatalized		l'		
Glide			j	

(2) *dvoréc* 'palace', def. *dvorécət*, but pl. *dvorcí*

(3) *knižóven* 'literary (masc.)', but fem. *knižóvna*, neu. *knižóvno*

(b) The alternations *k~c, g~z, x~s* in the plurals of masculine nouns:

(4) *vojník* 'soldier' pl. *vojníci*
antropológ 'anthropologist' pl. *antropolózi*
monáx 'monk' pl. *monási*

(c) Stress alternations from the stem to the singular definite article (masc., fem.) and to the plural desinence (masc., neu.), and from the desinence to the stem in the vocative (fem.)

Alternations in the verbal system include the following:

(d) Alternation of *k~č, g~ž* before *e*:

(5) *peká* 'I bake', but 2sg. *pečéš*, 3sg. *pečé*

(6) *móga* 'I can', but 2sg. *móžeš*, 3sg. *móže*

(e) Stress alternations from the stem to the desinence in the imperative, from the ending to the stem in the aorist, and optionally from the stem to the desinence in some aorists.

Peculiar to Bulgarian is the so-called *jat*-umlaut, where some occurrences of *á* after soft consonants alternate with *e* under the following circumstances:

(i) When the vowel loses stress:

(7) *mjásto* 'place', pl. *mestá*

(ii) When the vowel is followed by a syllable which begins with a palatal(ized) consonant or contains a front vowel:

(8) *vljáza* 'I enter', *vlézeš* 'you enter'

(9) *mljáko* 'milk', adj. *mléčen*

(10) *djásna* 'right' (fem.), *djásno* (neu.), but masc. *désen*, pl. *désni*

3. Noun morphology. Bulgarian has a contrast of three genders —masculine, feminine, and neuter—marked by the adjective:

(11) masc. *tózi nóv véstnik* 'this new newspaper'
fem. *tázi nóva kníga* 'this new book'
neu. *tová nóvo spisánie* 'this new magazine'

In the plural, there are no gender oppositions: *tézi nóvi véstnici, knígi, spisánija* 'these new newspapers, books, magazines'.

As in Macedonian (but not the other Slavic literary languages), Bulgarian substantives and adjectives lack case. However, a definite article is postposed to the first substantive or adjective in the noun phrase:

(12a) *véstnik* 'newspaper', *véstnikət* 'the newspaper'
véstnici 'newspapers', *véstnicite* 'the newspapers'

(12b) *kníga(ta)* '(the) book,' *knígi(te)* '(the) books'

(12c) *spisánie(to)* '(the) magazine', *spisanija(ta)* '(the) magazines'

(12d) *nóv(ijat) véstnik* '(the) new newspaper', *nóvi(te) véstnici* '(the) new newspapers'

The masculine article *-ət* has, in the normative language, an 'accusative' form in *-a, -ja*:

(13) *Lékarjat vížda véstnika.*
'The doctor sees the newspaper.'

The substantive (and masc. adjective) also has a vocative form:

(14) *drág prijátel* 'dear friend', voc. *drági prijátelju*

Most masc. substantives distinguish two plural forms: the 'quantified plural' is used after numerals and other quantifiers, and the other is used in all other environments:

(15) *tézi pét véstnika* 'these five newspapers'
tézi stári véstnici 'these old newspapers'

Personal nouns tend not to take the quantified plural.

Comparison of adjectives and adverbs is by means of the stressed prefixes *pó-* 'more', *náj-* 'most':

(16) *mlád* 'young', *pó-mlád* 'younger', *náj-mlád(ijat)* '(the) youngest'

(17) *dobré* 'well', *pó-dobré* 'better', *náj-dobré* 'best'

Numerals show an opposition of virile (masc. personal) vs. non-virile:

(18) *tríma məžé* 'three men'
tri žení 'three women'
tri véstnika 'three newspapers'

4. Pronominal morphology. The stressed forms of personal pronouns oppose the cases NOM and OBL[ique] (= DAT-ACC); clitic forms have either one OBL, or separate DAT and ACC. The forms are shown in Table 2.

The DAT clitic forms are used to mark possession:

(19) *knígata mu* 'his book'
véstnikət ni 'our newspaper'

In addition, there are stressed possessive adjectives.

5. Verbal morphology. Bulgarian possesses one of the most complex verbal systems in Slavic. In addition to the superordinated, grammatical opposition of perfective/derived imperfective, Bulgarian has the 'screeves' shown below; these are paradigmatic tense/aspect sets varying only in person and number, or in person, number, and gender. Table 3 gives examples of the 1sg. form of the (perfective) verb *opíša* 'describe', derived

TABLE 2. *Bulgarian Pronoun Forms*

	Stressed		Unstressed	
	Nom	Obl	Dat	Acc
1sg.	*áz*	*méne*	*mi*	*me*
2sg.	*tí*	*tébe*	*ti*	*te*
1pl.	*níe*	*nás*	*ni*	
2pl.	*víe*	*vás*	*vi*	
3sg.masc.	*tój*	*négo*	*mu*	*go*
3sg.neu.	*tó*	*négo*	*mu*	*go*
3sg.fem.	*tjá*	*néja*	*ì*	*ja*
3pl.	*té*	*tjáx*	*im*	*gi*
Reflexive	—	*sébe (si)*	*si*	*se*

TABLE 3. *First Person Singular Verb Forms of Bulgarian*

	Perfective	Derived Imperfective
Simplex forms		
Non-past	*opíša*	*opísvam*
Imperfect	*opíšex*	*opísvax*
Aorist	*opísax*	*opísvax*
Pluperfect$_1$	*bjáx opísal*	*bjáx opísval*
Forms with the future particle *šte*		
Future	*šte opíša*	*šte opísvam*
Future preterit	*štjáx da opíša*	*štjáx da opísvam*
Perfect forms (with the auxiliary *səm* 'be')		
Present perfect	*opísal səm*	*opísval səm*
Pluperfect$_2$	*bíl səm opísal*	*bíl səm opísval*
Future perfect	*šte səm opísal*	*šte səm opísval*
Conditional	*bíx opísal*	*bíx opísval*

imperfective *opísvam*. Other forms, which do not have complete paradigms, are shown in Table 4.

Within the past tense, the aorist and imperfect are opposed to each other in aspect: the imperfect denotes an event that occupies more than one moment in the past.

Central to the Bulgarian verbal system is the category of STATUS, which indicates how the speaker vouches for the reality of the event described. The aorist and imperfect are CONFIRMATIVE forms, generally used to mark witnessed events. The perfect forms are basically NON-CONFIRMATIVE; they are widely used to mark non-witnessed events, either reported or inferred. With the meaning 'reported', the 3rd person auxiliaries *e, sa* 'be' are often dropped.

6. Syntax. Like other Balkan languages, Bulgarian replaces the infinitive constructions of Western European and most other Slavic languages with an analytic conjunctive; this consists of the particle *da* followed by a finite form of the verb, e.g.:

(20) *Ískam da govórja s lékarja.*
I.want that I.speak with the.doctor
'I want to speak with the doctor.'

Possession is normally indicated with the preposition *na*, or by clitic dative pronouns:

(21a) *knígata na lékarja*
the.book of the.doctor
(21b) *knígata mu*
book.the to-him = 'his book'

The preposition *na* and the DAT clitics also serve to mark the indirect object:

(22a) *Dádox knígata na lékarja.*
'I gave the book to the doctor.'
(22b) *Dádox mu knígata.*
'I gave him the book.'

TABLE 4. *Other Verb Forms of Bulgarian*

	Perfective	Derived Imperfective
Imperative	*opiší, opišéte*	*opísvaj, opísvajte*
Pres. act. participle	——	*opísvašt*
Past act. participle	*opísal*	——
Past pass. participle	*opísan*	*opísvan*
Gerund	——	*opísvajki*
Verbal noun		*opísvane*

Subject/direct object relations are expressed primarily through word order—normally Subject Verb Object—and by concord in person, number, and gender between the subject and the verb. Object reduplication, through the clitic DAT and ACC pronouns in the verb phrase, can serve to mark subject/object relations:

(23) *Maríja ja vidjá včéra.*
Mary her-ACC s/he.saw yesterday
'S/he saw Mary yesterday.'

HOWARD I. ARONSON

BIBLIOGRAPHY

ARONSON, HOWARD I. 1967. The grammatical categories of the indicative in the contemporary Bulgarian literary language. In *To honor Roman Jakobson: Essays on the occasion of his seventieth birthday* (Janua linguarum, Series maior, 31), vol. 1, pp. 82–98. The Hague: Mouton.

ARONSON, HOWARD I. 1968. *Bulgarian inflectional morphophonology.* (Slavistic printings and reprintings, 70.) The Hague: Mouton.

ATANASSOVA, TEODORA, et al. 1983. *Bulgarian-English dictionary.* Sofia: Nauka i Izkustvo.

DE BRAY, REGINALD G. A. 1980. Bulgarian. In his *Guide to the South Slavonic languages,* pp. 78–136. Columbus, Ohio: Slavica.

FIELDER, GRACE E. 1985. Aspect and modality in Bulgarian subordinate clauses. In *The scope of Slavic aspect,* edited by Michael S. Flier & Alan Timberlake, pp. 181–193. Columbus, Ohio: Slavica.

HUBENOVA, MILKA, et al. 1983. *A course in modern Bulgarian.* 2 vols. Columbus, Ohio: Slavica.

MINCOFF, MARKO, ed. 1966. *Anglijsko-bəlgarski rečnik.* 2 vols. Sofia: Bulgarian Academy of Sciences.

RUDIN, CATHERINE. 1986. *Aspects of Bulgarian syntax: Complementizers and* WH *constructions.* Columbus, Ohio: Slavica.

SCATTON, ERNEST A. 1975. *Bulgarian phonology.* Cambridge, Mass.: Slavica.

SCATTON, ERNEST A. 1984. *A reference grammar of modern Bulgarian.* Columbus, Ohio: Slavica.

BUNABAN LANGUAGES are spoken in northern Western Australia, forming a top-level component in the primarily lexicostatistical classification of Australian languages by Stephen A. Wurm and Shirô Hattori, eds., *Language atlas of the Pacific area* (Canberra: Australian Academy of the Humanities, 1981).

LANGUAGE LIST

Bunaba: 150 speakers reported in 1981, in the Fitzroy Crossing area, Western Australia. Also called Punapa. Most people are bilingual in another aboriginal language, such as Walmatjari.

Gunian: 50 speakers reported in 1981, in Gogo, Fossil Downs, Louisa, and Margaret River stations, Western Australia. Also called Kuniyan, Guniyn, Kunan, Koneyandi, or Gooniyandi. The people generally speak Kriol.

BUNGKU-MORI LANGUAGES constitute a subgroup within the West-Central division of the Central Sulawesi languages [*q.v.*], a constituent of the Sulawesi branch of West Malayo-Polynesian. The internal divisions of Bungku-Mori, spoken in Sulawesi, Indonesia, are shown in Figure 1.

LANGUAGE LIST

Bungku: 35,000 speakers reported in 1979, in 93 villages in central Sulawesi and in the northern part of southeast Sulawesi. Also called Nahine. The To Rete variety spoken around Kendari is reported to be virtually extinct.

Kodeoha: 300 speakers reported in 1989, in southeast Sulawesi.

Kulisusu: 18,000 speakers reported in 1989, in southeast Sulawesi. Also called Kalisusu or Kolinsusu.

Mekongga: 25,000 speakers reported in 1982, near Soroako, southeast Sulawesi. Also called Mekongka. May be a Tolaki dialect.

Mori: 18,000 speakers reported in 1979, at the neck of the southeastern peninsula, in central Sulawesi. Also called Aikoa.

Moronene: 67,000 speakers reported in 1979, in the Rumbia and Poleang Districts, southeast Sulawesi. Also called Maronene. Moronene-Kabaena and Wowonii may be separate languages.

Padoe: 7,000 to 10,000 speakers reported in 1987, in south Sulawesi. Also called South Mori, Soroako, Padoë, Padoé, Tambe'e, Ajo, Karongsi, Sinongko, Nahina, or Alalao. Vigorous language use.

Rahambuu: 500 speakers reported in 1989, in southeast Sulawesi.

Taloki: spoken in southeast Sulawesi. Also called Taluki. May be a Bungku dialect.

Tolaki: 125,000 speakers reported in 1989, in southeast Sulawesi. Also called To'olaki, Lolaki, Lalaki, Laki, or Kolaka. The pejorative names Noie, Noihe, Nehina, No-

FIGURE 1. *Subgrouping of Bungku-Mori Languages*

Bungku
Bungku (proper), Kulisusu, Moronene, Tulambatu
Mori
Mekongga, Mori (proper), Padoe, Tolaki
Unclassified Bungku-Mori
Kodeoha, Rahambuu, Taloki, Waru

hina, Nahina, and Akido are no longer in use. The ethnic name To Wiaoe may designate the Labea'u variety.

Tulambatu: 4,000 speakers reported in 1979, in southeast Sulawesi. May be a dialect of Bungku.

Waru: 500 speakers reported in 1989, in southeast Sulawesi.

BURARRAN LANGUAGES are spoken in Arnhem Land, Northern Territory, Australia; they form a top-level component of the primarily lexicostatistical classification of Australian languages [*q.v.*] by Stephen A. Wurm and Shirô Hattori, eds., *Language atlas of the Pacific area* (Canberra: Australian Academy of the Humanities, 1981).

LANGUAGE LIST

Burarra: 600 speakers reported in 1983, in Maningrida, Arnhem Land, Northern Territory. Also called Bureda, Gujingalia, Gujalabiya, Gun-Guragone, Bawera, or Jikai.

Djeebbana: 100 speakers reported in 1983, in Arnhem Land, on the north coast around Maningrida. Also called Ndjebbana or Gunavidji. Different from Gunawitji, an alternative name for Gunwinggu.

Guragone: 25 speakers reported in 1983, south of Maningrida, along the Mann River, northwest of the Rembarunga language, east of the Gunwinggu language, in Arnhem Land. Also called Gun-Guragone, Gungorogone, or Gutjertabia.

Nakara: 75 to 100 speakers reported in 1983, in Maningrida, Arnhem Land, Northern Territory, on Goulburn Island. Also called Kokori, Nagara, or Nakkara.

BURMESE is the first language of the majority of the approximately thirty-seven million inhabitants of Burma (Myanmar), and a lingua franca for many of the ethnic minorities that make up about a third of that number. The language of the Irrawaddy valley is considered the national standard; other dialects are spoken in peripheral regions, e.g. Arakan and Tenasserim. The dialects differ mostly in pronunciation and lexical choice rather than in grammatical structure. Structural differences added to lexical then distinguish Burmese dialects from closely related 'Burmish' languages such as Atsi (Tsaiwa) and Maru (Lawng). At greater depth, the Burmish group belongs to the Lolo-Burmese (Burmese-Yipho) branch of the T[ibeto-]B[urman] family. (For general reference, see Minn 1966, Okell 1969, Roop 1972.) [*See also* Sino-Tibetan Languages.]

Written records date from the late 11th century. One of the earliest of these, known as the Myazedi Inscription, records an offering in four languages: Pali, Mon, Pyu, and Burmese. Burmese speakers are thought to have settled in Upper Burma several centuries before that time. They borrowed many cultural features from the Mon, including their writing system and the practice of Theravada Buddhism. The Mon language has contributed some specialized vocabulary, and possibly some phonetic features. Other sources of loanwords include Shan and its important relative Thai.

The large body of stone inscriptions dating from the 11th to the 15th century is usually referred to as 'Inscriptional Burmese'. The orthography ('Written Burmese') can be regarded as the partial reflection of a later Middle Burmese period. By the late 18th century, the language was close to its modern form.

The major source of learned words was, and continues to be, Pali [*q.v.*], the language of the Theravada scriptures. Many terms must have come directly from Pali texts, but sometimes the spelling shows evidence of transmission through Mon.

British rule over Burma, beginning in the 19th century, resulted in the use of a large number of English loanwords; however, many of these were abandoned after the resumption of independence. Nowadays, English mostly provides technical vocabulary, e.g. names of car parts, and slang.

1. Phonology. While Indic loans form a prominent layer of polysyllabic vocabulary, native morphemes are almost always monosyllabic or 'sesquisyllabic'. The latter contain an unstressed 'minor' syllable followed by a stressed 'major' one—a pattern more typical of Mon-Khmer languages [*q.v.*] than of TB. The bulk of sesquisyllabic words in Burmese contain derivational prefixes; others represent the reduction of first syllables in compounds. Some words contain two minor syllables followed by a major; these derive from compounds in which the first constituent is itself sesquisyllabic (e.g. *htəmìn* 'rice', *htəmənɛ̀* 'a sticky rice pudding'.)

Major syllables have five possible elements: initial, post-initial, and final consonants, vowel, and tone. Of these, initial (including ˀ-), vowel, and tone are always present. The only post-initial consonants found in the modern standard are *-y-* (after labials) and *-w-*; the only final consonants are -ˀ and *-n* (often just nasalization).

The phonetic realization of phonological units in these positions is partly determined by the nature of the syllable boundary: 'open juncture' between syllables is characterized by a minimal degree of assimilation; 'close juncture', by a maximal degree. Close juncture is common in disyllabic nouns (but not verbs), as well as in certain grammatical environments, e.g. noun + adjectival modifier. Juncture differences are reflected most noticeably by morphophonemic alternation at the initial (typically, voiceless stops become voiced), and by allophonic variation at the final.

The consonant phonemes of Burmese are shown in Table 1; the transcription is based in part on morphological considerations. The series with prescript *h-* alternates with the series without it in about one hundred pairs of verbs, in which the *h-* members are generally transitive and the non-*h* intransitive: *cuˀ, hcuˀ* 'to come off', 'to take off'; *nwè, hnwè* 'to be warm', 'to heat'. This process is no longer productive; it reflects an earlier sibilant 'transitivizing' prefix. This prefix is more directly attested by the 'irregular' pair *ˀeˀ, θeˀ* 'to sleep', 'to put to sleep', in which a favorable phonetic environment allowed the prefix to pre-empt the glottal initial (and later to join in the regular shift to interdental).

The distribution of the voiced stops *b d j g* is defective: in absolute initial position (i.e. excluding those that result from close juncture), they appear almost exclusively in nouns. Some of these items are loan words; others suggest the effect of derivational processes such as prefixation. The distribution reflects the fact that, with few exceptions, neither borrowing nor prefixation gives rise to verbs.

Vowel contrasts vary according to syllable type, as indicated in Table 2. In the modern languages, the [ɔ] of open syllables is in complementary distribution with both [ai] and [au] of closed syllables. The orthography identifies [ɔ] with [au]; here we follow established usage, and write all three. The neutralization of vocalic contrasts in minor syllables is realized as a mid central vowel *ə*.

Burmese can be called a 'pitch-register' language. The 'low' tone, left unmarked in the transcription, and the 'high' tone, marked here with the grave accent, are distinguished primarily by pitch (though high is also more intense and sometimes slightly breathy). The 'creaky' tone, marked here with an acute accent, and the 'checked' tone, with final ˀ, are distinguished from the others mainly by their glottality—and from each other by the presence of creaky (or tense) voicing in the first vs. clear voicing with abrupt glottal closure in the second.

TABLE 2. *Burmese Vowel Phonemes.* The vowel ε occurs only in syllables of form CV, CVˀ; ɔ occurs only in CV; *ai au* occur only in CVN, CVˀ.

	Front	Mid	Back
High	i		u
Higher mid	e		o
Lower mid	ε		ɔ
Low		a	
Diphthongs	ai		au

TABLE 1. *Burmese Consonant Phonemes.* Parentheses enclose rare or restricted phonemes: *r* occurs in loanwords, and *hw* is used mostly in onomatopoeia. The contrast of *f* and *ð* is barely functional.

	Labial	Interdental	Alveolar	Palatal	Velar	Glottal
Occlusives						
Aspirated	hp		ht	hc	hk	ˀ
Plain	p		t	c	k	
Voiced	b		d	j	g	
Fricatives						
Aspirated			hs			
Plain		*θ*	s			h
Voiced		(ð)	z			
Nasals						
Voiceless	hm		hn	hɲ	hŋ	
Voiced	m		n	ɲ	ŋ	
Lateral						
Voiceless			hl			
Voiced			l			
Approximants						
Voiceless	(hw)			hy [š]		
Voiced	w		(r)	y		

2. Writing system. Most of the Burmese script was adapted from Mon, which itself has South Indian antecedents. It retains typical features of Indian 'alphasyllabic' systems, including consonant signs that contain an inherent *a*-vowel. Certain features of the Mon alphabet have been adapted to Burmese conditions, e.g. the use of the Indic long vs. short vowel signs to indicate tonal distinctions in certain syllables. Other signs, such as those for the Indic retroflex and voiced aspirate consonant series, have been retained mostly for Indic loans.

Originally, the script must have represented the Burmese of the day fairly directly. Sound changes occurring since then have multiplied the values of written signs, most notably the vowels; e.g. written ⟨i⟩ is read as *i* in (written) open syllables, *e* in (written) closed; and written ⟨u⟩ is *u* or *o*. Other changes, such as the shift of *s* to *θ*, are revealed only by comparing modern pronunciation with the Indic or Mon values of the letters.

The writing system is illustrated in Tables 3a–b. The usual transliteration (cf. Okell 1971) goes beyond the internal evidence of the script and assigns Indian (Pali) values to the letters. The spelling of Burmese shows complete sets of final oral and nasal stops, including palatal ⟨c⟩ and ⟨ñ⟩, which are found only with the ⟨a⟩ vowel. Each set is reduced to a single contrast in the spoken language, symbolized -ʔ and -*n*; in isolation, -*n* is realized only as nasalization on the vowel.

3. Morphology. Burmese morphology is mainly derivational in function. An exception is the use of creaky tone with pronouns and nouns of personal reference to indicate certain grammatical roles, such as possession (reflecting an original creaky-toned possessive particle) and object.

Derivation involves mainly prefixation or reduplication. Thus nouns are frequently derived from verbs by the addition of the prefix ʔə-; adverbials may be derived by verbal reduplication, or by prefixation of ʔə-.

Compounding is much utilized to create new lexical material, and is preferred over the adaptation of foreign words. As a result, technical vocabulary is often beautifully transparent; 'iron-follow' for 'magnet', 'hand-press-machine' for 'typewriter'.

Word building may also serve aesthetic functions. Many verbs have pleonastic alternates formed by adding (usually afterwards) a synonym, or a semantically empty riming or chiming (alliterative) syllable. In nouns or adverbials, such processes give rise to rhythmically and euphonically balanced four-syllable expressions of a type well known in Southeast Asian languages [*q.v.*]. Similar processes probably account for the proliferation of variants ('word families') that are so common to the region.

4. Major word classes. Nouns and verbs are clearly demarcated; very few words function as both. The class of 'verb' includes adjectival verbs. Nouns are counted by means of CLASSIFIERS which often reflect some physical feature of their referents. In combination with numerals, classifiers may serve pronominal functions of reference. The small set of true pronouns is supplemented by certain nouns which index social information while signaling reference.

Few words are specialized for the adverbial function;

TABLE 3a. *Traditional Order of Burmese Consonants.* Voiceless aspirates are here given in the conventional transliteration as *kh*, etc., corresponding to the alternative transcription with *hk*, etc. Symbols for voiced aspirates, used only in Pali words, are pronounced in Burmese as simple voiced stops. Palatal occlusives are pronounced as alveolar sibilants in Burmese. Retroflex consonants in Pali words are pronounced as dentals.

	Occlusives				Nasals
	Voiceless		Voiced		
	Unaspirated	Aspirated	Unaspirated	Aspirated	
Velar	က k	ခ k	ဂ g	ဃ gh	င ŋ
Palatal	စ c (=/s/)	ဆ ch (=/hs/)	ဇ j (=/z/)	ဈ jh (=/z/)	ည ɲ
Retroflex	ဋ ṭ	ဌ ṭh	ဍ ḍ	ဎ ḍh	ဏ ṇ
Dental	တ t	ထ th	ဒ d	ဓ dh	န n
Labial	ပ p	ဖ ph	ဗ b	ဘ bh	မ m
Resonants:	ယ y	ရ r (=/y)	လ l	ဝ w	
Others:	သ θ	ဟ h	ဠ ḷ (=/l/)	အ ʔ	

TABLE 3b. *Traditional Order of Burmese Vowels.* The initial consonant အ /ʔ/ is used for illustration. Note that some tones are associated with choice of vowel symbol. Also note that tones not 'built into' a vowel (or combination of vowel + final consonant) are indicated by a subscript dot for the 'creaky' tone, and by a following double dot for the 'high' tone, e.g. အေ့ ʔé, အေး ʔè.

Symbol	Transcription	Symbol	Transcription
အ	ʔá	အေ	ʔe
အာ	ʔa	အဲ	ʔɛ
အိ	ʔí	အော	ʔɔ
အီ	ʔi	အို	ʔo
အု	ʔú		
အူ	ʔu		

most adverbials are derived from verbs by productive processes. The work of indicating grammatical relationships and functions is performed by a class of words usually called 'particles'.

5. Syntax. The following sentence illustrates some of the syntactic features discussed in this section. The particle *-dɛ́* is 'realis', with creaky tone signaling subordination; postnominal *-bɛ̀* is emphatic or restrictive:

(1) *ʔɛ̀di hpòndɔjì hɔ̀-dɛ́ gahta hye hniʔ*
this monk preach-PCPL verse long two

poʔ-ko-lɛ̀-bɛ̀ θwà
stanza-OBJ-also-PTCL go

yè-pè-laiʔ-pa.
write-(give)-(follow)-(include)

'And please just go and write down (for me) the two long verses that the monk recited.'

Apart from a subset of 'nominal clauses'—which, in positive form, usually appear without a copular verb—clauses end with a verbal phrase. Minimally, this may consist of only a verb followed by one of a small set of 'clause particles'. (The lack of such a particle, as in the example, signals 'positive imperative'.) In negative sentences, these mark only the distinction of declarative vs. imperative mood; but in positive declarative sentences, additional aspectual distinctions between realis, irrealis, and punctative are possible. Punctative sentences relate a change of state expressed by the verb in relation to a particular time, usually the time of speaking: *tɔ* 'to be sufficient', *tɔ-bi* 'That's enough'; *sà* 'to eat', *sà-bi* 'We've started eating.'

The verb phrase usually consists of a string of morphemes whose grammatical properties lie hidden beneath a uniform syntax of juxtaposition. In historical terms, many such morphemes can be related to verbs; but synchronically, the verbal connection may be difficult to perceive. In ex. 1, the meanings in parentheses are those of the putative verbal prototypes; however, when subordinated to a verb, *pè* indicates that the verbal action benefits someone else ('for'); *laiʔ*, that it requires little effort ('just'); and *pa* shows consideration on the part of the speaker toward the addressee ('please').

Generally, when a morpheme seems closely connected to an independent verb, it appears relatively leftward in the verbal phrase. Such semantic judgments are supported by certain syntactic and phonological features; e.g., the further to the left, the more likely a morpheme is to be directly negatable (in our example, *yè* and *pè* may be negated, but not *laiʔ*), or explicitly conjoined (*θwà* and *yè* only.) A categorial distinction between verb and particle is useful; however, the various criteria for distinguishing the two classes do not completely coincide, so at some point the division is arbitrary.

Within the noun phrase, the order is generally modifier before modified: demonstratives, genitive phrases, nominal attributes, and relative clauses all precede the head noun. Classifier phrases, consisting of numeral + classifier, FOLLOW their head nouns, but the relationship is appositional. The chief exception to the modifier + modified ordering involves adjectival modifiers (e.g. *hye* above), which generally follow their heads. Particles come last in the phrase; those that mark case roles (*-ko* above) precede those that perform quantificational functions (*-lɛ́, -bɛ́*).

Burmese allows core constituents of clause structure to be omitted in contexts where they are recoverable; thus the minimal declarative clause may consist of only a verb and a clause particle. There is no fixed order for preverbal elements, though certain arrangements are more common than others: manner adverbials and WH-question words almost always appear directly before the verb, and objects frequently do so. Subjects, as well as temporal and locative phrases, are likely to be topical. Object Subject Verb order can be found, but is not common.

The semantic roles of clause constituents are indicated by postpositional particles. Adjuncts are almost always marked, but subject and object need not be.

Clause subordination is illustrated by the following sentence, which contains a clausal subject marked by the realis nominalizer *-da,* and a causal subordinate clause, marked by *-ló*:

(2) *Luwuˀ-nɛ́ ne-yá-da mə-pyɔ-ló hpònjì*
layman-with stay-must-NOM not-happy-because monk

pyan wuˀ-θwà-dɛ.
return wear-go-REAL

'Because he was not happy as a layman, he donned (the robes of) monkhood again.'

6. Literary Burmese. Like the orthography, Burmese writing conserves many features of earlier stages of the language. Nowadays, the most prominent differences between written and spoken styles involve substitution of particles and some other grammatical words: e.g. spoken *-hma,* but written ⟨nhuik⟩ (read *-hnaiˀ*) 'at'; spoken *-hpó,* but written ⟨ran⟩ (*-yan*) 'purpose'. Writing based entirely on spoken forms is becoming more common, but it lacks the impersonal, timeless qualities associated with the literary forms, and is still felt inappropriate for serious genres.

JULIAN K. WHEATLEY

BIBLIOGRAPHY

MINN, LATT. 1966. *Modernization of Burmese.* Prague: Academia.

OKELL, JOHN. 1969. *A reference grammar of Colloquial Burmese.* 2 vols. (London Oriental series, 11.) London: Oxford University Press.

OKELL, JOHN. 1971. *A guide to the Romanization of Burmese.* London: Luzac.

ROOP, D. HAIGH. 1972. *An introduction to the Burmese writing system.* New Haven: Yale University Press.

BURMESE-LOLO LANGUAGES, also called Lolo-Burmese, are spoken in Burma and in parts of Thailand, Laos, China (primarily Yunnan Province), and Vietnam. These languages may constitute a top-level component of Tibeto-Burman within Sino-Tibetan [*qq.v.*]. Burmese-Lolo consists of two well-defined branches, Burmish (including Burmese [*q.v.*]) and Lolo; the more detailed subclassification is shown in Figure 1.

FIGURE 1. *Subgrouping of Burmese-Lolo Languages*

- **Burmish**
  - **Northern Burmish**
    - Achang, Atsi, Hpon, Lashi, Maru
  - **Southern Burmish**
    - Arakanese, Burmese, Intha, Taungyo, Tavoyan, Yangbye
  - **Unclassified Burmish**
    - Chaungtha
- **Lolo**
  - Minchia (Bai)
  - **Northern Lolo**
    - **Lisu**
      - Lisu (proper), Taku Lisu
    - **Unclassified Northern Lolo**
      - Kaduo, Naxi, Samei, Yi
  - **Southern Lolo**
    - **Akha**
      - Biyo
      - Honi
      - **Lahu**
        - Kutsung, Lahu (proper)
      - **Unclassified Akha**
        - Akha (proper), Hani, Mahei, Menghua, Phana', Sansu
    - **Phunoi**
      - Bisu, Mpi, Phunoi (proper), Pyen
    - **Unclassified Southern Lolo**
      - Sila
  - **Residual Lolo**
    - Hsifan, Ugong
  - **Unclassified Lolo**
    - Laopang, Lopi, Nusu, Tujia, Zauzou

LANGUAGE LIST

Achang: 22,100 speakers reported in 1982, with some 20,400 in western Yunnan, China, and 1,700 or more across the border in Burma. Also called Achung, Atsang, Acang, Ahchan, or Mönghsa. Spoken Chinese and Dai are in common use. An official nationality in China.

Akha: 260,000 speakers reported in 1990, with 130,000 in southwest Yunnan and Kengtung, China, 100,000 in Burma, 25,000 in Thailand, 5,000 in Laos, and a few in Vietnam. Also called Aka, Ko, Ekaw, Kaw, Ahka, Khako, Kha Ko, Aini, Ekwa, Ikho, or Ikor. Speakers call themselves Akha. Officially called Aini in China and included under the Hani nationality.

Arakanese: 650,000 speakers reported in 1983, with 517,000 in southwest Burma, 123,000 in Bangladesh, and possibly 12,400 in India. There may be speakers in China. Also called Maghi, Morma, Yakan, Yakhaing, Rakhain, Mogh, Magh, Marma, Mash, or Rakhine. One of the better known varieties of non-standard Burmese.

Atsi: 83,200 speakers reported in 1990, with 70,000 in the Tehung Autonomous Choi, Yunnan, China, and 13,200 in Burma. Also called Zaiwa, Tsaiwa, Szi, Atshi, Aci, Azi, or Atsi-Maru. Officially part of the Jingpo nationality in China. Distinct from the Ahi subgroup of Yi.

Bai: 900,000 speakers reported in 1990 out of an ethnic population of 1,130,000, between the Lancang (Mekong) and Jinsha Rivers on the Dali Plain, northwest Yunnan, China. Also called Minchia or Minkia. An official nationality.

Bisu: 1,000 or fewer speakers reported in 1987, in southwestern Chiangrai and northern Lampang, Thailand. Also called Mbisu.

Biyo: 100,000 speakers reported in 1990 in Yunnan, China. Also called Bio. A distinct language from Akha and Kado. Officially included under the Hani nationality.

Burmese: 22,000,000 first language speakers reported in 1986, nearly all in south and central Burma. There are also 100,000 speakers reported in Bangladesh, and 1,600 in the United States. An additional 3,000,000 use Burmese as a second languge. Also called Bama, Bamachaka, or Myen (the Rawang name). Speakers of Burmese seldom speak a second indigenous language; if they have a second language, it is usually English.

Chaungtha: around 122,000 speakers estimated in 1983, in Burma. Possibly a Burmese dialect.

Hani: 520,000 or more speakers reported in 1990, mainly in the Yuanjiang and Lancang (Mekong) River basins and the Ailao Mountains of southern Yunnan, China; includes 20,000 in Vietnam, and others in Burma. There are unconfirmed reports of speakers in Laos. Also called Hanhi or Haw. As an official nationality in China, may include Mengua.

Honi: 100,000 speakers reported in 1990, in Yunnan, China, near the Hani. There may be speakers in Vietnam. Also called Woni, Ouni, Uni, or Ho. Officially part of the Hani nationality, but a distinct language.

Hpon: 1,700 speakers reported in 1983, in Burma. Also called Hpön, Phun, Phön, Phon, Megyaw, or Samong.

Hsifan: spoken in Burma.

Intha: 141,000 speakers reported in 1983, near Inle Lake in southern Shan State, Burma. Also spelled Inntha. One of the better known varieties of non-standard Burmese.

Kaduo: 5,000 speakers reported in 1981, north of Mong Ou Tay, north central Laos, on the China border. Distinct from Kado, a Luish language (Tibeto-Burman) and Katu, a Mon-Khmer language.

Kutsung: 14,500 total speakers reported in 1983, with some 9,500 in Kentung District, Burma, and 5,000 in China, plus a few in Thailand and the United States, and possibly some in Laos. Also called Kucong, Yellow Lahu, Shi, Kui, or Kwi.

Lahu: 580,000 speakers reported in 1982, with 304,000 in the Lanaong Lahu, Gengma, and Menglian areas of southwestern Yunnan, China; 67,400 to 90,000 in Burma; 23,000 in Thailand; and 2,000 to 2,500 in Laos. Also called Lohei, Lahuna, Laku, Kaixien, Namen, Mussuh, Muhso, Musso, Moso, or Mussar. An official nationality in China.

Laopang: spoken in Burma and China. Also called Laopa. Possibly the same as Laba, a Lahu group near the Laos-Thailand border.

Lashi: 55,500 speakers reported in 1983, in Htawgaw Subdivision, Kachin State, Burma. Also in China. Also called Lasi, Letsi, Lechi, Leqi, Lashi-Maru, Chashan, Lachikwaw, or Ac'ye.

Lisu: 635,000 speakers reported in 1982, with 481,000 on the upper reaches of the Lu (Salween) and Lancang (Mekong) Rivers, western Yunnan, and in Sichuan, China; also 126,000 in Burma and 13,000 in Thailand. Also called Lisaw, Li-Shaw, Li-Hsaw, Lu-Tzu, Lesuo, Li, Lishu, Leisu, Leshuoopa, Loisu, Southern Lisu, Yao Yen, Yaw Yin, Yeh-Jen, Chung, Cheli, Chedi, Lipa, Lusu, Khae, or Lipo. An official nationality that also includes Taku Lisu.

Lisu, Taku: spoken around Taku in highland areas of eastern Yunnan, China. Also called Eastern Lisu, He Lisu, Black Lisu, or Taku. Not mutually intelligible with Lisu proper. Officially included under Lisu.

Lopi: spoken in Burma, and possibly also in China.

Mahei: spoken in Burma and China. Also called Mahe or Mabe.

Maru: 98,700 speakers reported in 1983, in the eastern border area of Kachin State, Burma, and across the border in China. Also called Lawng, Laungwaw, Lansu, Lang, Mulu, Diso, Malu, Matu, or Zi.

Menghua: spoken south of Dali in Yunnan, China. Also called Mehua or Mengwa. Probably included officially under Hani.

Mpi: 2,000 speakers reported in 1981, in the villages of Phrae and Phayao, Thailand. Also called Mpi-Mi.

Naxi: around 245,000 speakers reported in 1982, with 225,000 in northwest Yunnan and 20,000 near the Tibet border in Sichuan, China. Possibly also spoken in Burma. Also called Nahsi, Nasi, Nakhi, Lomi, Moso, or Mosso. Speakers resent the term 'Moso', which probably comes from Chinese 'hunter'. An official nationality in China. Written Chinese is in common use.

Nusu: 8,000 speakers reported in 1990, in Yunnan, China. Also called Noutzu, Nutzu. A separate language that is officially part of the Nu nationality.

Phana': 5,000 speakers reported in 1981, in northern Laos near the Yunnan border. Also called Pana' or Bana'. Adults speak some Lahu.

Phunoi: 32,000 speakers reported in 1981, around Phong Saly in north central Laos, plus some in Thailand. Also called Punoi or Côông. 'Kha Punoi' is a derogatory name.

Pyen: 800 speakers reported in 1981, around the Kha River near the Laos border in east central Burma.

Samei: a few speakers reported in Yunnan, China. Children do not speak Mandarin. May be officially part of Yi.

Sansu: spoken in Burma and China. A Hani group; may not be a distinct language.

Sila: 15,000 speakers reported in 1981, north of Muong Hai in north central Laos .

Taunggyo: 443,000 speakers estimated in 1983, from Taunggyi in Shan State southward to Tavoy in Tenasserim State, Burma. Also called Taru, Tavoya, Tavoyan, Dawe, Dawai, Tawe-Tavoy, or Toru.

Tavoyan: spoken in southeast Burma. One of the better known varieties of non-standard Burmese.

Tujia: 200,000 speakers reported in 1982 out of an official nationality of 2,830,000, in northwest Hunan and Hubei, China. Spoken and written Chinese is in use.

Ugong: 1,000 speakers reported in 1983, in Kanchanaburi, Uthai Thani, and Suphanaburi Provinces, Thailand. Also called Lawa. All speakers are bilingual in some variety of Thai. Distinct from Lawa in the Palaung-Wa branch of Mon-Khmer.

Yangbye: around 810,000 speakers reported in 1983, in Burma. Also called Yanbe, Yangye, or Yanbye.

Yi, Central: 200,000 speakers reported in 1990, in China. A separate language within the Yi official nationality of 5,450,000.

Yi, Guizhou: spoken in Guizhou and Guangxi, China. Also called Eastern Yi or Southeastern Yi. Distinct from Yunnan Yi and Sichuan Yi.

Yi, Sichuan: 1,800,000 speakers reported in 1982 out of an official nationality of 5,450,000, in the Greater and Lesser Liangshan Mountains of Sichuan and in southeastern Xizang (Tibet), China. Also called Northern Yi, I, Lolo (derogatory), Ichia, Manchia, Mantzu, Northern Lolo, Sen Nosu, Gni, or Nyi. The terms Black Lolo (Hei-I, Hei Kutou) and White Lolo (Pei-I) are ethnic names that do not refer to linguistic distinctions.

Yi, Western: 750,000 speakers reported in 1990, in China. A separate language within the Yi official nationality.

Yi, Yunnan: spoken in Yunnan, China. Also called Southern Yi, Southern Nosu, Shui Nosu, Nosu, Nasu, Nasö, Nyi, Gni, I, or Southeastern Yi. Derogatory names found in the literature include Lolo, Minchia, Ichia, Keikutou, and Peikutou.

Zauzou: 1,500 speakers reported in 1990, in Yunnan, China. A separate language that is officially part of the Nu nationality along with Nung, Nusu, and Drung.

C

CADDOAN LANGUAGES constitute a family of the Great Plains in the United States. The subgrouping adopted in Figure 1 is based on Wallace Chafe, 'Caddoan', in *The languages of native America: Historical and comparative assessment,* edited by Lyle Campbell and Marianne Mithun (Austin: University of Texas Press, 1979), pp. 213–214. Campbell & Mithun (p. 41) consider the evidence for proposals linking Caddoan genetically with Siouan and Iroquoian to be 'suggestive, though not yet compelling.'

LANGUAGE LIST

Arikara: 200 speakers reported in 1977 from a population of 1,000, in North Dakota. Most speakers are middle-aged or older.

Caddo: 300 speakers reported in 1977 from a population of 1,800, in western Oklahoma. Also spelled Kado. Most speakers are middle-aged or older.

Kitsai: now extinct, formerly spoken in west central Oklahoma, among the Caddo. Also called Kichai.

Pawnee: 200 speakers reported in 1977 from a population of 2,000, in north central Oklahoma. Most speakers are middle-aged or older.

Wichita: 50 speakers reported in 1977 from a population of 750, in west central Oklahoma. Most speakers are middle-aged or older.

FIGURE 1. *Subgrouping of Caddoan Languages*

Northern
- **Pawnee-Kitsai**
  - Kitsai
  - **Pawnee**
    - Arikara, Pawnee (proper)
- Wichita

Southern
- Caddo

CAHUAPANAN LANGUAGES constitute a family of northern Peru; see Čestmír Loukotka, *Classification of South American Indian languages* (Los Angeles: Latin American Center, University of California, Los Angeles, 1968), p. 153.

LANGUAGE LIST

Chayahuita: around 6,000 speakers reported in 1981, on the Paranapura, Cahuapanas, Sillay, and Shanusi rivers, Peru. Also called Chawi, Tshaahui, Chayhuita, Chayabita, Shayabit, Balsapuertino, Paranapura, or Cahuapa. Population includes 80 percent nearly monolingual, 16 percent with routine ability, and 4 percent with nearly native ability in Spanish.

Jebero: 2,300 to 3,000 speakers reported in 1976, in Jeberos District, Peru. Also called Xebero, Chebero, or Xihuila. Widespread use of Spanish.

CAMBODIAN. *See* Khmer.

CARIBAN LANGUAGES constitute one of the large linguistic families of South America. [*See* South American Languages.] The comparative study of this family is two centuries old, and has amassed a wealth of data; its grammatical studies have contributed significantly to linguistic typology.

The Cariban family is named after one of its members, the language of the Caribs. These Indians live near the northern coast of the continent, in an area extending from northeast Brazil through the coastal plains of French Guiana, Surinam, and Guyana to Venezuela. Most of their linguistic relatives live in southern Venezuela, Guyana, and Surinam, and in the adjacent parts of Brazil; as shown in Map 1. The languages in this area include the following: in southeastern Venezuela, Panare, Ya-

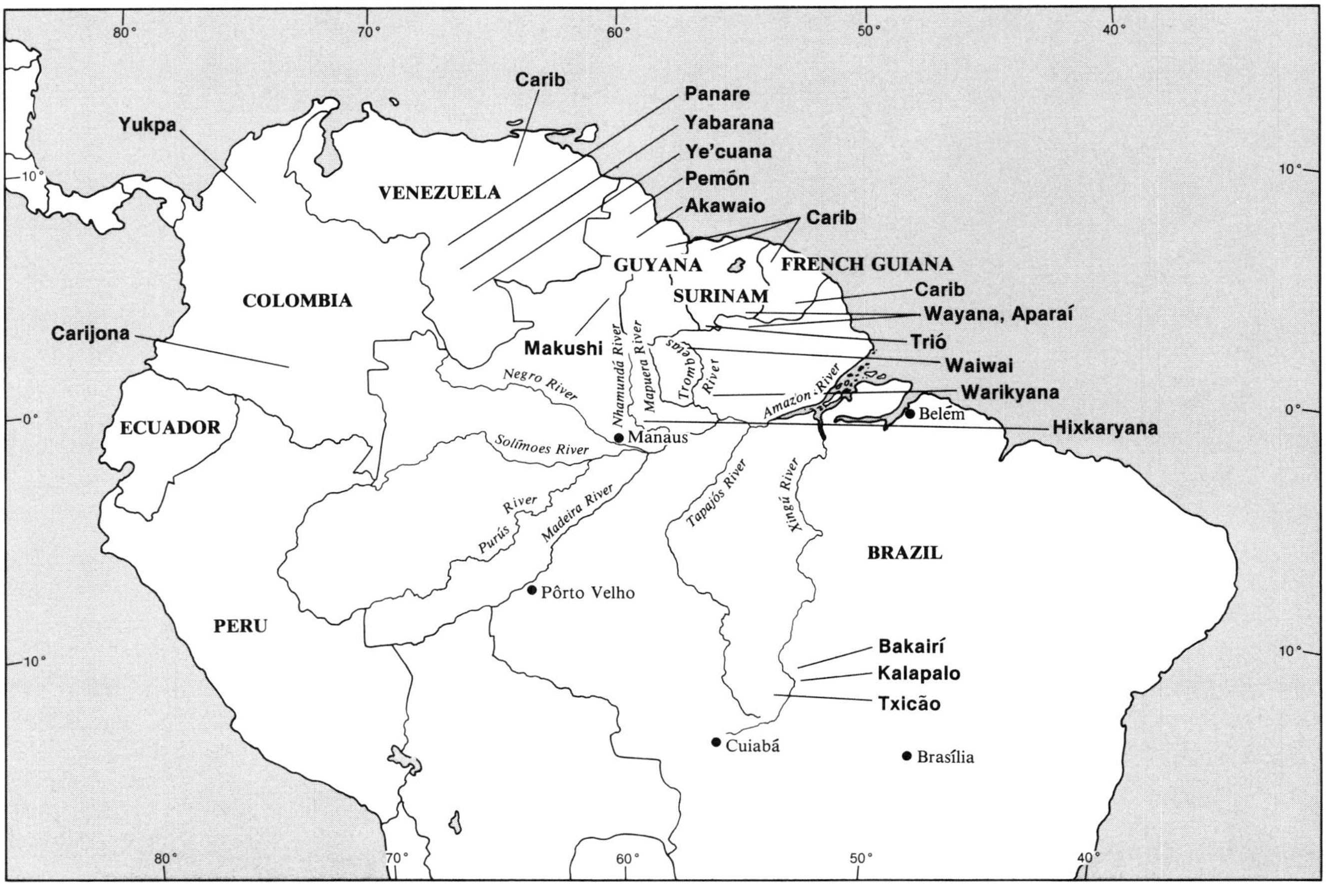

MAP 1. *Distribution of Cariban Languages*

barana, and Ye'cuana; in the Venezuelan/Guyanese/Brazilian border area, Pemón, Makushi, and Akawaio; somewhat farther south, in Brazil, Waiwai, Hixkaryâna, and Warikyana; in Surinam and in adjacent parts of Brazil and French Guiana, Trió, Wayana, and Aparai. A few Cariban tribes have strayed far from this central area: Yukpa in northwestern Venezuela; Carijona in Ecuador and Colombia; and Bakairí, Txicão, and Kalapalo/Kuikuro at the headwaters of the Xingu River in southern Brazil.

This list of eighteen languages accounts for the main extant Cariban-speaking tribes. If smaller groups and finer linguistic distinctions were considered, it would be twice as long. In addition, written data have been salvaged for twenty extinct languages. Comparative Cariban linguistics deals, in all, with some sixty individual languages and dialects. [*For detailed data, see the Language List at the end of this article.*]

Finally, mention should be made of a language which is also called 'Carib' or 'Island Carib', and which used to be spoken on a number of Caribbean islands. The original name of this language was Iñeri; it belongs to the Arawakan family [*q.v.*]. It came to be called 'Carib' after the conquest of the islands by Carib settlers from the mainland, who imposed their nationality and name—which eventually inspired the modern geographical name of the area; however, they failed to displace the native Iñeri language (cf. Taylor & Hoff 1980). A descendant of Island Carib is still spoken in Central America (Belize and Honduras) under the name of 'Black Carib' or 'Garífuna'.

1. Comparative studies in Cariban made a very early start with the work of Filippo Salvadore Gilij in 1782; the contributions of missionaries, explorers, and professional linguists have accumulated ever since. Published work on the subclassification of the family tends to give little actual language data as evidence; subgroupings are proposed and reshuffled with summary discussion, or none at all. However, in terms of bibliographical exploration alone, a tremendous amount of work has been done by a small number of people: the sources have at least been discovered and saved, and a great many cognate pairs have been recognized. A project for the systematic collection of data—the South American Indian Languages Documentation Project, directed by Brent Berlin of the University of California, Berkeley—will, when completed, give new impetus to the internal classification of the family.

The external relationships of Cariban became a research goal after the World War II. In the classification of Greenberg 1987, Cariban is grouped most closely with Andoke, Bora, Kukura, Uitoto, and Yagua; and then with Macro-Gê and Macro-Panoan. However, Rodrigues 1985 has demonstrated a relationship to Tupian.

Recent book-length grammars are available for Carib (Hoff 1968) and Hixkaryâna (Derbyshire 1985). Other important references are Basso 1977, Fock 1963, Koelewijn 1987, and Payne 1990.

2. Phonology. Carib, as spoken in western Surinam, has the following phonemes: /a e o i u ï au ai ei oi ui ïi/ (for long vowels see below), /p t k/, marginal /b d g/, /m n/, /w y/, /r/ (flap), and /s/. A second fricative, /x/, has a distinct status distributionally and historically (see below). Sequences of vowels and of some consonants are permitted, but a regular alternation of V and C predominates. No consonants except nasals occur in word-final position. The Hixkaryâna system is similar but somewhat richer, containing palatal consonants, /ɸ/, and /h/.

In Carib and many of its relatives, word-medial syllables of the proto-language have been lost. This process has left different residues in different languages and dialects. In the Carib dialect of the Saramacca River, Surinam, the residue is breathiness of the preceding vowel; e.g., **wapoto* 'fire' became *wa:ʰto*. Abundant instances are provided by synchronic morphophonemics: *pe:kï* 'to sink it' + imperative *-ko* gives *i-pe:ʰ-ko* 'sink it!' This breathiness corresponds, in other dialects of Carib, to a clear vowel followed by a velar fricative: *waxto, i-pex-ko*.

Carib vowel length is largely prosodic: either the second and the fourth vowel of a word, or the first and the third, are long, provided that they are present, non-final, and not followed by two consonants, e.g. *asa:pará:pi* 'species of fish', *ka:rawá:si* 'species of tree'. Similar rules have been reported for Makushi and Hixkaryâna. Word stress is on the second heavy syllable (containing a long vowel, diphthong, or VC), counted from the left; if there is none, stress is final.

3. Grammar. Many Cariban languages have rich morphologies. In Carib, six word classes have characteristic morphological properties: verbs, nouns, postpositions, adjectives/adverbs, numerals, and demonstratives. Modal particles (e.g. *painare* 'perhaps') and non-modal particles (*era:pa* 'too') constitute separate word classes: syntactically, these have nothing in common with the adverbs, and little with each other. There are no conjunctions, relative pronouns, or complementizers. Dependent clauses contain a non-finite verb, and relate directly to a head in the main clause.

In Carib, Hixkaryâna, and other languages, each transitive finite verb form contains a prefix which identifies both agent and patient (*s-e:ne-i* 'I have seen him', *y-e:ne-i* 'he has seen me'). Such verbs frequently occur as complete utterances, but may of course be complemented by separate nominals.

At a time when typologists still doubted the occurrence of O[bject] V[erb] S[ubject] as an unmarked, 'basic' constituent order, Derbyshire 1977 demonstrated that Hixkaryana constitutes an instance of precisely this. In the following decade, the ensuing discussion provided the starting points for promising further research in three directions:

(a) OVS order was sought and found in other languages of the area, both Cariban and non-Cariban.
(b) Attempts were initiated to relate the rise of OVS in these languages, and the preservation of SOV in others, to other grammatical properties of the languages concerned, such as ergativity.
(c) Interest was stimulated in discourse factors and information structure, as relevant to patterns of constituent order and their change.

BEREND J. HOFF

BIBLIOGRAPHY

BASSO, ELLEN B., ed. 1977. *Carib-speaking Indians: Culture, society, and language*. Tucson: University of Arizona Press.

DERBYSHIRE, DESMOND C. 1977. Word order universals and the existence of OVS languages. *Linguistic Inquiry* 8.590–599.

DERBYSHIRE, DESMOND C. 1985. *Hixkaryana and linguistic typology*. (Summer Institute of Linguistics publications in linguistics, 76.) Dallas: Summer Institute of Linguistics.

FOCK, NIELS. 1963. *Waiwai: Religion and society of an Amazonian tribe*. (Etnografisk række, 8.) Copenhagen: National Museum.

GREENBERG, JOSEPH H. 1987. *Language in the Americas*. Stanford, Calif.: Stanford University Press.

HOFF, BEREND J. 1968. *The Carib language: Phonology, morphonology, morphology, texts and word index.* (Verhandelingen van het Koninklijk Instituut voor Taal-, Land-, en Volkenkunde, 55.) The Hague: Nijhoff.

KOELEWIJN, CEES. 1987. *Oral literature of the Trio Indians of Surinam.* (Verhandelingen van het Koninklijk Instituut voor Taal-, Land-, en Volkenkunde, Caribbean series, 6.) Dordrecht: Foris.

PAYNE, DORIS LANDER, ed. 1990. *Amazonian linguistics: Studies in lowland South American languages.* Austin: University of Texas Press.

RODRIGUES, ARYON DALL'IGNA. 1985. Evidence for Tupi-Carib relationships. In *South American Indian languages: Retrospect and prospect,* edited by Harriet E. Manelis Klein and Louisa R. Stark, pp. 371–404. Austin: University of Texas Press.

TAYLOR, DOUGLAS R., & BEREND J. HOFF. 1980. The linguistic repertory of the Island-Carib in the seventeenth century: The men's language—a Carib pidgin? *International Journal of American Linguistics* 46.301–312.

LANGUAGE LIST

Akawaio: 3,500 to 4,500 speakers reported in 1982, with 3,000 to 4,000 in Guyana, 500 in Brazil, and a few in Venezuela. Also called Acewaio or Akawai. They and the Patamona call themselves Kapon.

Akurio: 40 to 50 speakers reported in 1977, in the southeastern jungle, Surinam. Also called Akuri, Akuliyo, Wama, Wayaricuri, Oyaricoulet, Triometesem, or Triometesen. Not mutually intelligible with Trió, but nearly all are living with the Trió and becoming bilingual in Trió.

Aparaí: 350 speakers reported in 1987, in twenty villages in Pará State, Brazil; also spoken in Surinam. Also called Apalai.

Arára of Pará: 83 speakers reported in 1988, in three villages in Pará State, Brazil. Also called Ajujure. Not to be confused with Arára of Rondônia (a Tupian language).

Atruahí: 350 to 600 speakers reported in 1986, on the border between Amazonas and Roraima States, Brazil. Also called Atroarí or Ki'nya.

Bakairí: 450 speakers reported in 1986 in Mato Grosso State, Brazil. Also called Kura. Speakers are somewhat bilingual in Portuguese.

Carib: around 20,000 speakers reported in 1976, with 10,000 in Venezuela near the mouth of the Orinoco River, 2,500 in Surinam, 1,200 in French Guiana, 900 in Brazil, and 475 or more in Guyana. Also called Cariña, Kalinya, Galibi, or Caribe. None are monolingual except the very old and the very young. Note that 'Island Carib' and 'Black Carib' are Arawakan, not Cariban languages.

Carijona: 110 speakers reported in 1976, on the upper Vaupés, Yarí, and lower Caquetá rivers, Colombia. Also called Carihona, Omagua, Umawa, or Hianacoto-Umaua. (Hianacoto-Umaua may be a separate language.) Some speakers are bilingual in Spanish.

Coyaima: now extinct, formerly spoken in the Tolima region, Colombia. The tribe still exists as an entity, but has spoken Spanish for several generations.

Hixkaryâna: 350 speakers reported in 1987 in Amazonas State, Brazil. Also called Parukoto-Charuma, Parucutu, Chawiyana, Kumiyana, Sokaka, Wabui, Faruaru, Xerewyana, or Xereu. Population includes 95 percent nearly monolingual, and 5 percent with routine ability in Portuguese.

Japrería: 80 speakers reported in 1975, in northern Zulia, Venezuela.

Kalapalo: 70 to 190 speakers reported in 1986 in the Xingú Park, Mato Grosso State, Brazil. Also called Apalakiri. May be a Nahukua dialect; possible mutual intelligibility or bilingualism with Kuikúro.

Kuikúro: 40 to 221 speakers reported in 1986 in the Xingú Park, Mato Grosso State, Brazil. Also called Kuikuru, Guicurú, Kurkuro, or Cuicutl. Kalapalo and Matipuhy may be mutually intelligible with Kuikúro.

Makushi: spoken by around 5,700 people, with 3,000 in northeast Roraima and Rio Branco States, Brazil, 1,300 in west central Guyana, and 600 in south Venezuela. Also called Makuxí, Macusi, Teweya, or Teueia. Bilingualism in Portuguese is increasing. Not mutually intelligible with the Patamona spoken in that area.

Mapoyo: 2 speakers from an ethnic population of 120 reported in 1977, on the Suapure River, Amazonas State, Venezuela. Also called Mapayo, Mapoye, Mopoi, Nepoye, or Wanai.

Matipuhy: 115 to 160 speakers reported in 1986 in the Xingú Park, Mato Grosso State, Brazil. Also called Matipu or Mariape-Nahuqua. Kalapalo may be a dialect. Matipuhy may also be mutually intelligible with Kuikúro.

Panare: 1,200 speakers in jungle and highland communities of Bolivar State, Venezuela. Also called Panari, Abira, or Eye. Nearly all speakers are monolingual.

Patamona: 3,000 to 4,000 speakers reported in 1982, in west central Guyana. Also called Ingariko or Eremagok. Ingariko is the Macushi term for 'bush people'.

Pemón: 5,930 speakers reported in 1977, with 4,850 in the Gran Sábana area of Bolívar State, Venezuela, 400 to 500 of the Arecuna dialect in Guyana, 220 Taulipang and 460 Ingarikó in Brazil. Also called Pemong. Marginal mutual intelligibility with Akawaio and Patamona. A large majority of speakers are monolingual.

Salumá: in northwest Pará State, Brazil, along the Surinam border. Distinct from Salumã in Mato Grosso State.

Sikiana: 33 or more speakers reported in 1986 in northwest Pará State, Brazil, near the Surinam border. Possibly in Venezuela. Also called Shikiana, Chiquiana, or Chikena.

Trió: around 1,130 speakers reported in 1977, with 800 in south central Surinam, and 330 in Brazil. Also called Tirió.

Txikão: 350 speakers reported in 1986 in the Xingú Park, Mato Grosso State, Brazil. Also called Txikân, Chicao, Tunuli, or Tonore.

Waiwai: 885 to 1,060 speakers reported in 1986 in Amazonas and Pará States, Brazil, and in Guyana. Also called Uaieue or Ouayeone. Katawian has been treated as a separate language, but this is doubtful.

Warikyana: 435 speakers reported in 1986 in northwestern Pará State, Brazil. A few live with the Hixkaryâna, but most with the Trió. Also called Kachuana, Kaxúyana, or Kaxuiâna. There is a fair amount of bilingualism between Trió and Warikyana.

Wayana: 950 speakers reported in 1977, with 600 in south-eastern Surinam, 200 in French Guiana, and 150 in Brazil. Also called Oayana, Oyana, Alukuyana, Upurui, or Roucouyenne.

Yabarana: 64 speakers reported in 1975, including some mixed with the Piaroa and Macu, in Amazonas State, Venezuela. Also called Yauarana. Distinct from Yabaana of Brazil.

Yarumá: spoken in the Xingú Park, Mato Grosso State, Brazil. May be extinct.

Ye'cuana: 5,240 total speakers reported in 1975, with 4,970 in Venezuela and 270 in Brazil. Also called Maiongong, Maquiritare, Yekuana, De'cuana, Maquiritai, Soto, Cunuana, or Pawana.

Yukpa: 3,000 speakers reported in 1976, with 2,500 in Colombia on the Colombia-Venezuela border near Agustín Codazzi, and 500 in Venezuela. Also called Yuko, Yupa, or Northern Motilón. Unrelated to Chibchan Motilón (Bari). Language use is vigorous.

CASE is a notoriously ambiguous notion. The traditional notion of MORPHOLOGICAL CASE refers to an inflectional category; however, particular case markers are also referred to with the term 'case'. (For references, see Lyons 1968.) Case markers normally appear on nouns, but they may also occur with N[oun] P[hrase]s. In NPs, two different case categories can sometimes be distinguished: one case is directly governed by the syntactically superordinate unit, while the other appears as a mark of agreement. In adjectives, case is often a mark of agreement. The number of case-markers varies from language to language. Thus there are two cases in Old French, three in Hindi and Rumanian, five in Ancient Greek, seven in Latin, ten in Russian, eighteen in Hungarian, twenty-six in Andi and Archi, and forty-six in Tabassarian (Mel'čuk 1986). However, it is not always clear what should be considered a case-marker; consequently, scholars may differ as to the number of them in a given language.

Morphological cases can be classified in various ways. Each nominal case marks a dependent syntactic role of the noun, and sometimes the meaning of the case is confined to this syntactic role (grammatical case). Typical cases marking syntactic roles in accusative-type languages, such as those of the Indo-European family, are as follows:

(a) Nominative: grammatical subject
(b) Accusative: direct object
(c) Dative: indirect object
(d) Instrumental: instrument or means
(e) Genitive: adnominal attribute

Overlap between these functions is not rare. In Russian and Sanskrit, the instrumental also marks the agent; in Hungarian and Latin, instrumental function merges with the comitative ('along with X'). This merging of functions is called CASE SYNCRETISM. Among the adverbial cases, the local cases (locational and directional), which express localization with respect to the object denoted by the noun, form a particularly rich system. Typical localizations expressed by means of cases are within an object, on/over its upper surface, on/under its lower surface, on its side, behind it, in front of it, near it, or between two objects. In addition, localization can be specified with respect to movement: being at a place, traveling to it, traveling out of or from it, traveling through it, or traveling toward it. The combination of eight localizations with five types of movements produces forty local cases. Actually, more distinctions are made in some languages. For example, a local case may also express the spatial relation of the object to the speaker and/or hearer. Other types of cases may not form such neat systems (Mel'čuk 1986).

The term 'case' is sometimes used to denote DEEP CASE, the semantic relations between a predicate and its arguments (Fillmore 1968). The system of deep case has become one of the modules of generative Government/Binding theory, under the name of THETA THEORY, or the theory of THEMATIC ROLES (Chomsky 1981). Thematic roles include AGENT, PATIENT (or THEME), and GOAL. There is no general agreement as to how many thematic roles are required for the description of predicate/argument structure. A thematic role may correlate in surface structure with various phenomena: syntactic position, adpositions, inflectional suffixes, etc.

CASE THEORY is a theory about abstract cases: it requires phonetically non-empty NPs to be governed by a unique case-assigner. For example, in English, the subject of a tensed clause receives the nominative case from the tensed VP; the possessive NP in a NP receives genitive case from the noun; and the object of a preposition receives accusative case from the preposition. Abstract case need not be morphologically marked; in fact, a language may neutralize all case distinctions. SYNTACTIC CASE is associated with a particular syntactic configuration; in contrast, LEXICAL CASE is assigned to a NP on the basis of lexical information associated with the predicate. Lexical case must be realized morphologically or syntactically in surface structure (cf. Riemsdijk & Williams 1986).

FERENC KIEFER

BIBLIOGRAPHY

CHOMSKY, NOAM. 1981. *Lectures on government and binding.* (Studies in generative grammar, 9.) Dordrecht: Foris.

FILLMORE, CHARLES J. 1968. The case for case. In *Universals in linguistic theory,* edited by Emmon Bach and Robert T. Harms, pp. 1–88. New York: Holt, Rinehart & Winston.

LYONS, JOHN. 1968. *Introduction to theoretical linguistics.* London: Cambridge University Press.

MEL'ČUK, IGOR A. 1986. Toward a definition of case. In *Case in Slavic: Studies dedicated to the memory of Roman O. Jakobson,* edited by Richard D. Brecht and James S. Levine, pp. 35–85. Columbus, Ohio: Slavica.

RIEMSDIJK, HENK C. VAN, & EDWIN WILLIAMS. 1986. *Introduction to the theory of grammar.* (Current studies in linguistics series, 12.) Cambridge, Mass.: MIT Press.

CATEGORIAL GRAMMAR is a framework for grammatical analysis whose historical roots lie in philosophical and logical investigations of compositional relations between syntactic structure and semantic interpretation. Characteristically, a categorial system **C** consists of a vocabulary *V,* a type structure *T,* and a categorial calculus *C*. Each vocabulary element *v* is associated with one or more types in *T*. The combinatorial properties of each pair $\langle v,t\rangle$ are determined by the structure of *t* and the type calculus *C*. Moreover, if **C** is interpreted, the interpretation of $\langle v,t\rangle$ must meet constraints imposed by the choice of *t*. Thus the type structure plays a central role in grammatical composition. [*See also* Mathematical Linguistics.]

The TYPE STRUCTURE *T* is based on a set of primitive types (such as S[entence], N[oun] P[hrase], and N[oun]) and a set of TYPE-FORMING OPERATORS (such as the binary operators '/' and '\'). We can form new types by combining already given types with the type-forming operators, yielding types NP\S, N/N, (NP\S)/NP, etc. Informally, we may think of the type-forming operators '/' and '\' in a number of ways; for example, we may think of an expression e_1 of type α/β or $\beta\backslash\alpha$ as something which combines with an expression e_2 of type β to its right or left, respectively, to form an expression e_1e_2 or e_2e_1, respectively, of type α. Alternatively, when e is assigned to the type α/β or $\beta\backslash\alpha$, we may identify e_1 with a function which maps any element e_2 of type β to the element e_1e_2 or e_2e_1, respectively, of type α. (Relative to these conventions, if *the* is of type NP/N and *sensible world* is of type N, the expression *the sensible world* is of type NP.) The formal characterization of the type-forming operators is given by the calculus *C,* which defines a set of valid ARROWS, typically of the form $\alpha_1, \ldots, \alpha_k \rightarrow \beta$. Given a valid arrow of this form, any sequence $e_1, \ldots, e_k$ of k expressions associated with types $\alpha_1, \ldots, \alpha_k$, respectively, is assigned to the type β.

For example, the categorial system **AB** (based on Ajdukiewicz 1935, and proved equivalent in weak generative capacity to context-free grammars by Bar-Hillel 1964) has a type structure based on the operators '/' and '\', and a type calculus which defines the class of valid arrows by the axioms

(1) $\alpha \rightarrow \alpha$

(2) $\alpha/\beta, \beta \rightarrow \alpha$

(3) $\beta, \beta\backslash\alpha \rightarrow \alpha$

with the rule of substitution: if 4a-b are valid, then 5 is valid (where Δ, Φ, and Ψ represent sequences of types, Δ non-empty):

(4a) $\Delta \rightarrow \alpha$

(4b) $\Phi, \alpha, \Psi \rightarrow \beta$

(5) $\Phi, \Delta, \Psi \rightarrow \beta$

In this system, NP, (NP\S)/NP, NP → S is a valid arrow: apply the substitution rule to the two valid premises

(6) (NP\S)/NP, NP → NP\S

(7) NP, NP\S → S

Thus, if *nature, inspires,* and *wonder* are elements of V assigned to NP, (NP\S)/NP, and NP, respectively, then *Nature inspires wonder* $\rightarrow$ S in **AB.**

This simple example illustrates one characteristic of categorial grammar: subcategorization information can be encoded directly into the structure of syntactic types. A second characteristic is the possibility of higher-order types: a type such as VP/(VP/NP) can be assigned to an element which combines with a VP lacking an NP, to form a VP (such as the accusative clitics in the Romance languages or, with modifications, adjectives like *tough* in *English is tough to learn*). A third syntactic characteristic is the possibility of flexible type-assignment: the validity of the arrow (NP\S)/NP $\rightarrow$ NP\(S/NP) would allow a transitive verb to combine with two flanking NP arguments in two different ways.

An elegant way to interpret the system **AB** defined over primitive types S, NP, and N involves a model structure $\mathcal{M}$ which contains a distinguished substructure t' for every type in T, in a way compatible with the arrows valid in **AB.** Let A be a set of individuals and 2 be the set of truth values {*true, false*}. Let $\mathcal{M}$ be the smallest set which contains A and 2—and which, when it contains α and β, contains the set α^β of functions from β to α. We associate each type t in T with a substructure t' in $\mathcal{M}$ as follows, where simple types are handled by clauses 8–10 and complex types by clause 11:

(8) $S' = 2$

(9) $NP' = A$

(10) $N' = 2^{bA}$

(11) $(\alpha/\beta)' = (\beta\backslash\alpha)' = \alpha'^{\beta'}$

Finally, we may augment the arrows of **AB** so that they define a calculus of pairs $\alpha : a \in \alpha'$ consisting of a syntactic type and a semantic object admissibly associated with it:

(12) $\alpha : a \in \alpha' \rightarrow \alpha : a \in \alpha'$

(13) $\alpha/\beta : f \in \alpha'^{\beta'}\ \beta : b \in \beta' \rightarrow \alpha : f(b) \in \alpha'$

(14) $\beta : b \in \beta',\ \beta\backslash\alpha : f \in \alpha'^{\beta'} \rightarrow \alpha : f(b) \in \alpha'$

(15) If $\Delta : \Delta' \rightarrow \alpha : a \in \alpha'$ and $\Phi : \Phi', \alpha : a \in \alpha', \Psi : \Psi' \rightarrow \beta : b \in \beta'$ are valid, then $\Phi : \Phi', \Delta : a \in \alpha', \Psi : \Psi' \rightarrow \beta : b \in \beta'$ is valid.

It follows that, if every element of a vocabulary V is paired with a type t and associated with a semantic object in t', then any sequence $v_1, \ldots, v_k$ assigned to type t is associated with a semantic object in t'. Although this example is rudimentary, especially in view of the sophisticated elaborations of it by Montague 1974, it is worth noticing that the interpreted calculus arises from coupling a syntactic categorial calculus with a semantic categorial calculus—namely the calculus over the structure $\mathcal{M}$ which recognizes as valid all arrows of the two general forms:

(16) $\alpha'^{\beta'}, \beta' \rightarrow \alpha'$

(17) $\beta', \alpha'^{\beta'} \rightarrow \alpha'$

Each of these instantiates a general convention for representing the application of a function of the type $\alpha'^{\beta'}$ to an appropriate argument of type β. This perspective opens the way to more organized investigations of compositional relations among systems of syntactic and semantic types (Benthem 1986). [*See also* Montague Grammar.]

There are many extensions of the simple example discussed here, deriving both from abstract considerations and from empirical problems. The arrows $\alpha/\beta,\beta \rightarrow \alpha$ and $\beta,\beta\backslash\alpha \rightarrow \alpha$ have analogs in the logical principle 'Modus ponens' (in the tautological form $(p \wedge (p \Rightarrow q)) \Rightarrow q$), and in the application of a function $f : \beta \rightarrow \alpha$ to an argument of type β to yield a value of type α. This leads to the construction and investigation of categorial calculi with broader classes of valid arrows, often corresponding to other tautologies or general operations on functions: $\gamma\backslash\beta,\beta\backslash\alpha \rightarrow \gamma\backslash\alpha$ (invalid in **AB**) is related to the tautology $((p \Rightarrow q) \wedge (q \Rightarrow r)) \Rightarrow (p \Rightarrow r)$, on the one hand, and to functional composition on the other hand. Notable examples of such calculi include the Associative Syntactic Calculus **L** of Lambek 1958, the Lambda-Categorial Languages of Cresswell 1973, and the Combinatory Grammars of Steedman 1988. Buszkowski 1989 surveys the formal properties of various categorial systems and their relations to logic and formal language theory; connections between decidability and parsing are discussed by Moortgat 1989.

While these 'extended' categorial grammars have direct application to linguistic phenomena such as morphological bracketing 'paradoxes' (Hoeksema 1984), empirical problems have provided the impetus for theoretical innovations—a theme especially noteworthy in the work of Emmon Bach. This has led to the introduction of different systems of basic types (Steele 1988); to unification-based categorial systems in which the basic categories are themselves structured objects (Haddock et al. 1987, Klein & Benthem 1987); and to new kinds of type-forming operators (Moortgat 1989).

One result of these innovations is the increasingly sophisticated adaptation of categorial grammars to the syntactic and semantic properties of natural languages. Another is the realization that the perspective developed within categorial grammar—i.e. the study of syntactic and semantic composition as an integrated system—is applicable more generally to the class of problems involving the interaction of properties from different linguistic dimensions. Examples of such problems of 'generalized compositionality' are well known; they include the interaction of syntactic, semantic, and phonological properties in morphology, the interaction of syntax and phonology in sandhi rules, and the syntactic and interpretive constraints on intonational phrasing. Current interest in issues seemingly so remote from its philosophical and logical roots is a sign of categorial grammar's coming of age.

RICHARD T. OEHRLE

BIBLIOGRAPHY

AJDUKIEWICZ, KAZIMIERZ. 1935. Die syntaktische Konnexität. *Studia Philosophica* 1.1–27. Translated in *Polish logic*, edited by Storrs McCall (Oxford & New York: Oxford University Press, 1967), pp. 207–231.

BAR-HILLEL, YEHOSHUA. 1964. *Language and information.* Reading, Mass.: Addison-Wesley.

BENTHEM, JOHAN VAN. 1986. *Essays in logical semantics.* (Studies in linguistics and philosophy, 29.) Dordrecht: Reidel.

BUSZKOWSKI, WOJCIECH. 1989. *Logiczne podstawy gramatyk kategorialnych Ajdukiewicza-Lambeka.* Warsaw: PWN.

BUSZKOWSKI, WOJCIECH, et al., eds. 1988. *Categorial Grammar.* (Linguistic and literary studies in Eastern Europe, 25.) Amsterdam: Benjamins.

CRESSWELL, MAXWELL J. 1973. *Logics and languages.* London: Methuen.

HADDOCK, NICHOLAS, et al., eds. 1987. *Categorial Grammar, Unification Grammar, and parsing.* (Edinburgh working papers in cognitive science, 1.) Edinburgh: Centre for Cognitive Science, University of Edinburgh.

HOEKSEMA, JACK. 1984. *Categorial morphology.* University of Groningen dissertation. Published, New York: Garland, 1985.

KLEIN, EWAN, & JOHAN VAN BENTHEM, eds. 1987. *Categories, polymorphism, and unification.* Edinburgh: Centre for Cognitive Science, University of Edinburgh.

LAMBEK, JOACHIM. 1958. The mathematics of sentence structure. *American Mathematical Monthly* 65.154–170. Reprinted in Buszkowski et al. 1988, pp. 153–172.

MONTAGUE, RICHARD. 1974. *Formal philosophy: Selected papers.* Edited by Richmond Thomason. New Haven: Yale University Press.

MOORTGAT, MICHAEL. 1989. *Categorial investigations.* Dordrecht: Foris.

OEHRLE, RICHARD, et al., eds. 1988. *Categorial Grammars and natural language structures.* (Studies in linguistics and philosophy, 32.) Dordrecht: Reidel.

STEEDMAN, MARK. 1988. Combinators and grammars. In Oehrle et al. 1988, pp. 417–442.

STEELE, SUSAN. 1988. A typology of functors and categories. In Oehrle et al. 1988, pp. 443–466.

CAUCASIAN LANGUAGES. The thirty-eight indigenous languages of the Caucasus can be grouped into four families, which take their names from the geographical regions in which their members are spoken: N[orth] W[est] C[aucasian], N[orth] C[entral] C[aucasian], N[orth] E[ast] C[aucasian], and S[outh] C[aucasian]. (See Map 1.) The three northern families may be genetically related in a North Caucasian group (especially NCC and NEC); however, all attempts to establish such a relationship between SC and any other language or family must be judged unconvincing. NWC Ubykh, spoken only in Turkey since the migration of the entire population in 1864, is virtually extinct, and the future of several other languages is precarious; Hinukh was reported in 1967 as having only two hundred speakers.

Typical areal features, though not necessarily characteristic of all languages and dialects, include ejective consonants, predominantly vigesimal counting systems, agglutination, ergativity (cf. Boeder 1979, Catford 1976), triple deixis, an inferential mood, and use of speech particles to mark direct speech. Except in SC, subordinating conjunctions are absent, and non-finite verb forms are used in subordinate 'clauses'.

Within the USSR, the following are literary languages: Georgian, Abkhaz, Abaza, Adyghe, Kabardian, Chechen, Ingush, Lak, Dargwa, Avar, Lezgi, and Tabassaran. General references are Catford 1977, Greppin 1989, and Hewitt 1981.

1. South Caucasian (also called Kartvelian) consists of Georgian, Svan, Mingrelian, and Laz; the last two are sometimes known jointly as Zan. (See Map 2.) Laz is spoken in Turkey, and the Ingilo dialect of Georgian in Azerbaijan; otherwise, the family is spoken in Soviet Georgia. Georgian [*q.v.*] is the best known and most

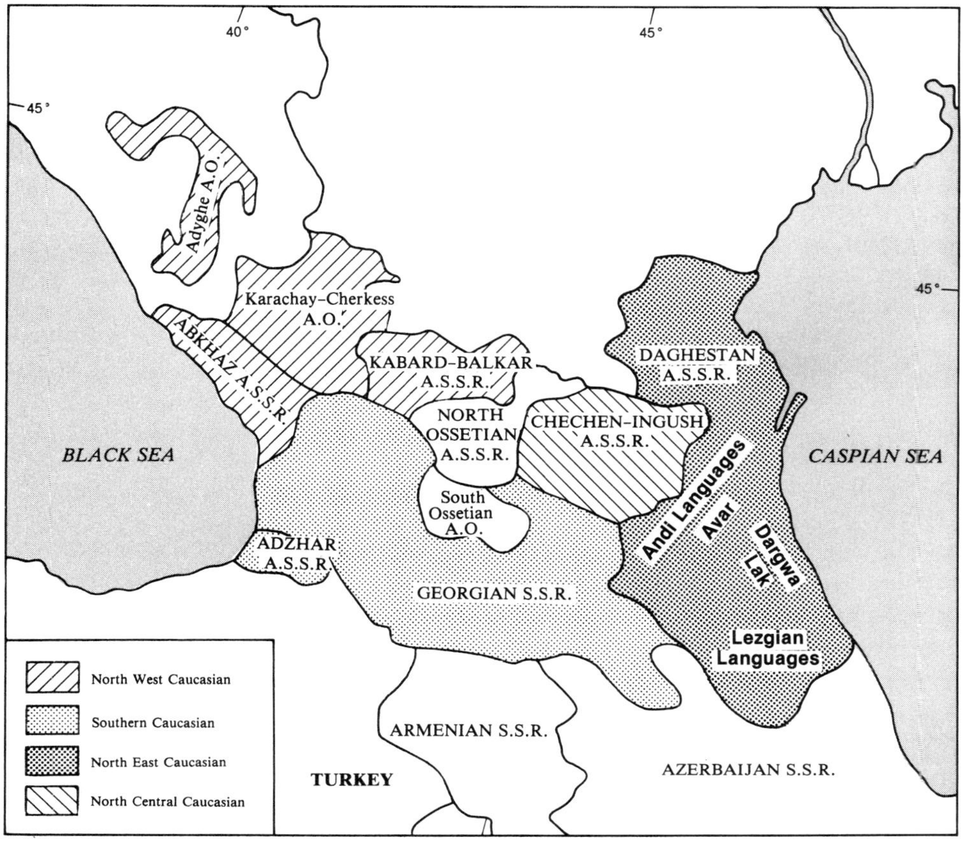

MAP 1. *Politico-Linguistic Divisions in the Caucasus*

MAP 2. *Distribution of South Caucasian Languages*

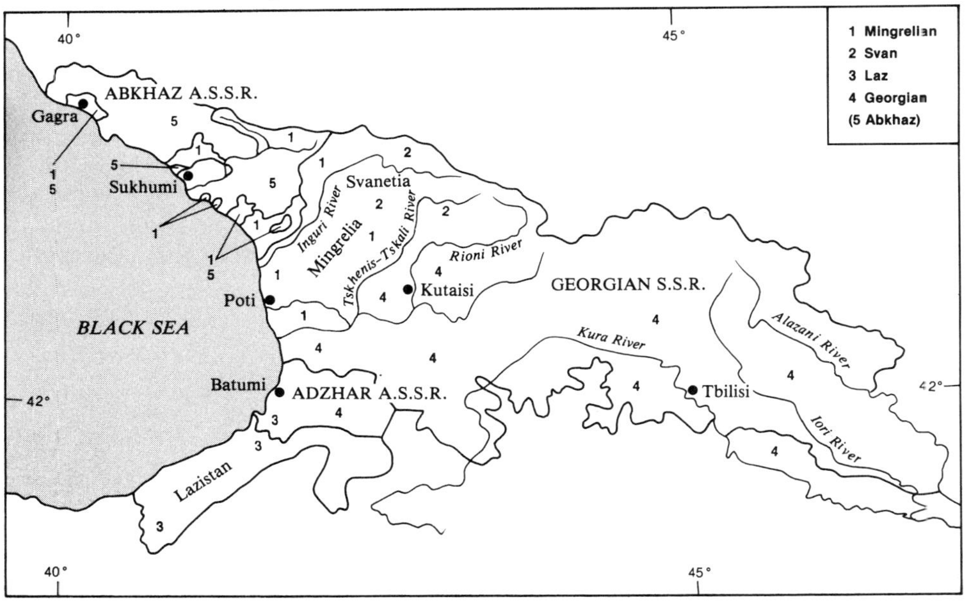

widely spoken of all Caucasian languages, with a literary tradition of fifteen centuries in its own alphabet. The most archaic is Svan, in northwestern Georgia. Mingrelian is spoken in lowland western Georgia. [*For further information, see* South Caucasian Languages.]

1.1. ***Phonology.*** To the phoneme inventory of Georgian, Mingrelian adds ə and ʔ, while Svan adds a variety of long and umlauted vowels. The singularity of Kartvelian lies in its great tolerance of consonant clusters. Disregarding sequences which incorporate a morpheme boundary, Georgian has 740 initial clusters; of these, 233 have two elements, 334 three elements, 148 four elements, 21 five elements, and 4 have six elements. Out of 244 final clusters, 148 are biphonemic, 82 triphonemic, and 14 quadriphonemic (Vogt 1958).

1.2. ***Morphology.*** [*For a fuller discussion of terminology, see* Georgian.] Case systems are roughly comparable throughout the family, though Laz lacks the Adverbial. A distinct Ergative morph seems to have developed independently in each language, since Georgian *-m(a(n))* and Zan *-k* cannot reflect a single protoform. Among a variety of Ergative exponents in Svan, a clue to the proto-SC system may be seen in the pattern which uses *-d* jointly in Ergative/Adverbial function; cf. Adverbial *-(a)d, -o(t)* in Georgian and Mingrelian respectively. The precise number of 'screeves' (i.e. tense/aspect/modal paradigms) differs from language to language. Mingrelian is particularly rich in Inferentials, and distinguishes simple from potential intransitives, as in 1a-b vs. 2a-b:

(1a) Absolute
i-č'ar-u 'it is being written'
(1b) Relative
Ø-a-č'ar-u 'it is being written to/for/on X'
(2a) Absolute
i-č'ar-e 'it can be written'
(2b) Relative
Ø-a-č'ar-e 'X can write it' (Ø = I[ndirect] O[bject])

Verbs can agree with S[ubject]s, D[irect] O[bject]s, and IOs by means of two sets of personal affixes (designated sets A and B); however, there can be no more than two such morphological exponents in a single verb, regardless of that verb's syntactic valency; minimally, a verb requires a Set A affix. Preverbs indicate direction with motion verbs, and perfective aspect elsewhere.

Zan has an extremely rich preverbal system. That of Svan is more simple; but like Old Georgian, it allows 'tmesis', i.e. the separation of the preverb from the rest of the verbal complex. Complexes may also incorporate a causative suffix and a VER[SION] prefix; version vowels indicate a variety of relationships between verbal arguments, such as location, possession, and benefaction (Deeters 1930:70 ff.). A certain number of suppletive verb roots exist, determined by such factors as the screeve, singularity vs. plurality, or animacy vs. inanimacy of the intransitive S or DO; e.g., in Svan:

(3a) *x-uγv-a*
3-VER-have-3.INAN
's/he has it'
(3b) *x-a-q'-a*
3-VER-have-3.AN
's/he has him/her'

In the Present subseries, 'to convey' is realized by the addition of the appropriate directional PREV[ERB] to the basic expression for 'to have'; e.g., in the Lent'ex dialect of Svan:

(4a) *a-x-u-γv-a*
PREV-3-have-3.INAN
's/he brings it'
(4b) *a-x-a-q'-a*
PREV-3-VER-have-3.AN
's/he brings him/her'

1.3. ***Syntax*** (see Harris 1985). Word order patterns include A[djective] + N[oun], G[enitive] + N (Old Georgian had NA, NG), N[oun] P[hrase] + Postposition, and S[ubject] O[bject] V[erb] (fluctuating with SVO). Case-marking for the central arguments of the verb varies according to which screeve series is employed. Svan essentially mirrors Georgian, while Zan has enlarged the role of its Ergative (in *-k*) in two directions:

(a) Laz uses the ergative for transitive Ss in all series, with new non-inverted forms to rival the older inverted ones in Series III (Čikobava 1936:103).
(b) Mingrelian uses the Ergative for all forms in Series II, to give the following ACCUSATIVE configuration:

(5) *k'oč-(i)-k c'eril-i do-Ø-č'ar-u.*
man-NOM letter-ACC PREV-it-write-he.AOR
'The man wrote the letter.'

(6) *c'eril(i)-k d-i-č'ar-u.*
letter-NOM PREV-PASS-write-it.AOR
'The letter was written.'

Note also the Series II pattern for Indirect verbs (i.e. those with Dative S in all series; see Hewitt 1987:336):

(7) *k'o(č(i))-s k-Ø-e-ˀorop(-u)*
man-DAT PREV-he-VER-fall.in.love.with-her.AOR

osur-k.
woman-NOM

'The man fell in love with the woman.'

Transitive verbal nouns display nominal governance by taking objective Genitives—though Old Georgian had an infinitive with verbal governance, whose object stood in either of the language's DO cases (Dative and Nominative). SC subordinate clauses tend to behave like their Indo-European counterparts, as in this Mingrelian relative:

(8) *b-jir-i jgab-i, namu-t i-bir-d-ə.*
I-see-AOR girl who-REL VER-sing-IMPF-she
'I saw the girl who was singing.'

But several alternatives also exist to complicate this picture:

(9) *b-jir-i jgab-i, namu-t i-bir-d-ə-ni* (with subordinator *-ni*)

(10) *i-bir-d-ə(-ni) (peri) jγab-i b-jir-i* (with *peri* 'like')

In Laz, case endings or postpositions are attached to finite clauses, with or without the general subordinator, to produce a range of adverbial clauses:

(11) [*sum c'an-er-i b-or-t'-i*]*-ši*
three year-DER-ADJ I-be-IMPF-INDIC-GEN
'when I was three, . . .'

(12) [*bere k'itx-er-i-na t'-u*]*-šeni*
child read-PPL-ADJ-SUB be.IMPF-it-for
'Since the child was educated, . . .'

2. North West Caucasian (see Map 3) is divided as follows:

(a) Abkhaz, in the Abkhaz ASSR, and Abaza, in the Karachay-Cherkess Autonomous Oblast
(b) West Circassian or Adyghe, in the Adyghe Autonomous Oblast; and East Circassian (Kabardian, Kabardo-Cherkess), in the Kabardo-Balkar ASSR and the Karachay-Cherkess Autonomous Oblast

MAP 3. *North West Caucasian Tribes circa 1880*

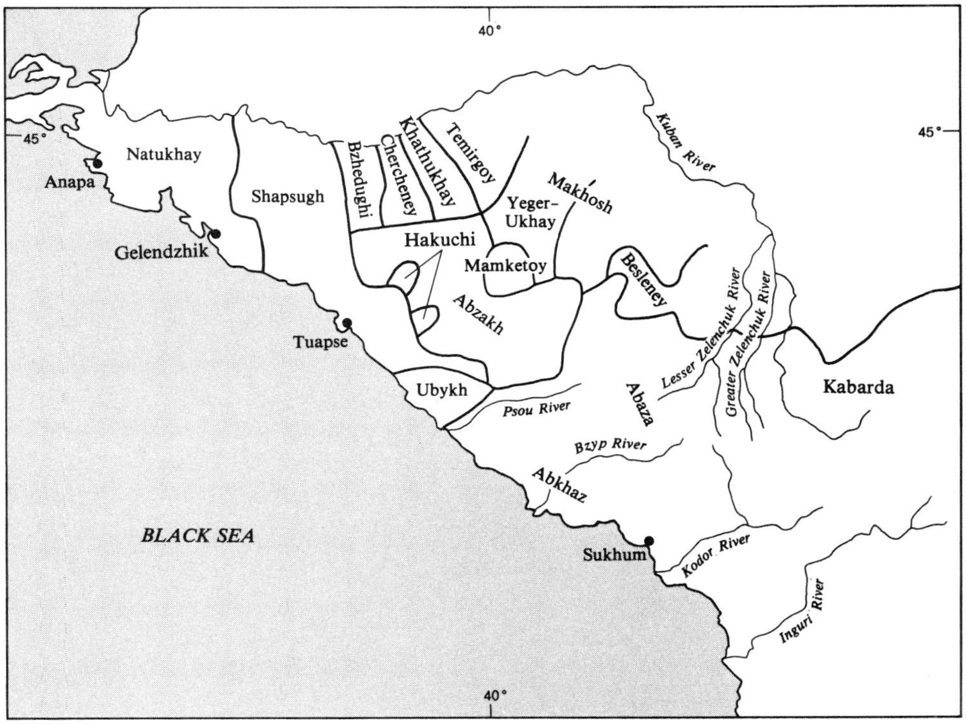

(c) Ubykh (extinct; formerly spoken on the eastern coast of the Black Sea)

Well over half a million ethnic NW Caucasians are found throughout the Near East, predominantly in Turkey (Smeets 1984:51). [*For further information, see* North Caucasian Languages.]

2.1. *Phonology.* Large consonant inventories combine with minimal ('vertical') vowel-systems. Despite the attempt of Kuipers 1960 to prove that there is no phonemic opposition between vowels and consonants in Kabardian, most commentators accept at least *ə* and *a* for these languages. Consonant phonemes range from forty-five (Literary Kabardian) to eighty-three (Ubykh), if one includes three phonemes attested only in loans. The Bzyp dialect of Abkhaz demonstrates NWC's use of secondary features, as shown in Table 1.

2.2. *Morphology.* Case systems are impoverished: Abkhaz formally marks only its adverbial case. The oppositions indefinite vs. definite (generic, for Abkhaz) and singular vs. plural are observed. Possession is always marked on the possessed noun by a personal prefix correlating with the possessor (Adyghe distinguishes alienable vs. inalienable possession); this is paralleled

TABLE 1. *Abkhaz Consonants*

	Labial	Alveolar	Retroflex	Alveo-palatal	Palatal	Velar	Uvular	Pharyngeal
Stops								
Voiced								
Plain	b	d				g		
Labialized		d^{o}				g^{o}		
Palatalized						g′		
Voiceless								
Plain	p	t				k		
Labialized		t^{o}				k^{o}		
Palatalized						k′		
Glottalized								
Plain	p’	t’				k’	q’	
Labialized		t’^{o}				k’^{o}	q’^{o}	
Palatalized						k’′	q’′	
Affricates								
Voiceless								
Plain		c	ç̣	tɕ	č			
Labialized				tɕ^{o}				
Voiced								
Plain		ʒ	ʒ̣	dʑ	ǰ			
Labialized				dʑ^{o}				
Glottalized								
Plain		c’	ç̣’	tɕ’	č’			
Labialized				tɕ’^{o}				
Fricatives								
Voiceless								
Plain	f	s	ṣ	ɕ	š	x	X	ħ
Labialized				ɕ^{o}	š^{o}	x^{o}	X^{o}	ħ^{o}
Palatalized						x′		
Voiced								
Plain	v	z	ẓ	ʑ	ž	γ		
Labialized				ʑ^{o}	ž^{o}	γ^{o}		
Palatalized						γ′		
Nasals	m	n						
Vibrant		r						
Lateral		l						
Semivowels								
Plain	w				y			
Labialized					y^{o}			

by the NP-postposition relationship. Verbs differentiate 'dynamic' from 'stative' categories, and (especially in Abkhaz-Abaza) 'finite' from 'non-finite'. The exponents which build the polysynthetic verb complexes of NWC, discounting tense/mood/aspect formants, include three sets of pronominal prefixes; these are differentiated, if not always formally, by their positions in the complex. Abkhaz-Abaza has human/non-human, masculine/feminine oppositions in part of the pronominal system. There is also a bewildering array of locational preverbs; relative, relational, reflexive, reciprocal, and causative prefixes; potential, orientational, and adverbial affixes; subordinating and interrogative particles; emphatics; and negatives.

2.3. *Syntax.* Word order patterns include SOV, NP + Postposition, GN, and NA (but a few easily characterizable adjectives stand first, e.g. ethnonyms). Relatives are preposed, though Circassian and Ubykh allow the notional head NP to be placed in the adverbial case, and then to stand within the clause. These examples are from Adyghe, both meaning 'The man who killed the woman is coming':

(13) *ɕ°əzə-r* *Ø-zə-wəč'ə-γe* *ƛ'ə-r*
woman-the.ABS her-who-kill-PAST.NONFIN man-the.ABS

Ø-qe-k'°e.
he-PREV-come.PRES

(14) *ƛ'-ew* *ɕ°əzə-r* *Ø-zə-wə́č'ə-γe-r*
man-ADVL woman-ABS her-who-kill-PAST.NONFIN-the.ABS

Ø-qe-k'°e.
he-PREV-come.PRES

Affixal agreement—Set A for intransitive Ss and DOs, B for IOs, and C for transitive Ss—is supported by case-marking, where that exists. It shows ergative patterning, e.g. in Ubykh:

(15) *wa-tət* *(a-)k''a-n.*
that-man.ABS he(A)-go-PRES
'That man is going.'

(16) *yə-tətə-n* *yə-məzə-n* *za-m̄a*
this-man-OBL this-child-OBL an-apple.ABS

Ø-(ə-)n-t°ə-n.
it(A)-to.him(B)-he(C)-give-PRES

'This man gives an apple to this child.'

A few Circassian roots permit two constructions: (unmarked) S-OBL + O-ABS + V vs. (marked, 'anti-passive') S-ABS + O-OBL + V. Many more 'labile' roots may be either transitive or intransitive, depending on deletion of S or DO. Questions are formed by particles. Subordination is by non-finite verb plus subordinating particle. Both these constructions are illustrated below for Abkhaz:

(17) *s-y°ə̀za* *y-ạn*
my-friend his-mother

d-anə̀-tɕ°a-Ø, *warà*
she(A)-when-fall.asleep-AOR.NONFIN you.MASC

wə-cà-Ø-ma *nàsg'ə*
you(A)-go-AOR.NONFIN-Q and

yə-wə̀-c-ca-Ø-da.
who-you-with-go-AOR.NONFIN-who?

'When my friend's mother fell asleep, did you go and who went with you?'

3. North Central and North East Caucasian. NCC, also known as Nakh or Veinakh, consists of Chechen and Ingush (in the Chechen-Ingush ASSR), and Bats or Tsova-Tush (in the Georgian village of Zemo Alvani).

NEC has three divisions:

(a) Avar-Andi-Dido consists of Avar itself; eight Andi languages (Andi proper, Botlikh, Ghodoberi, Karata, Chamalal, Tindi, Bagvalal, and Akhvakh); and five Dido (Tsez) languages (Dido proper, Hinukh, Khvarshi, Bezhta, and Hunzib).
(b) The Lak-Dargwa division contains only Lak and Dargwa, in southern Daghestan; Kubachi is sometimes treated as a separate language.
(c) The Lezgian languages include Lezgi, Tabassaran, Aghul, Tsakhur, and Rutul as well as Udi, Budukh, Khinalugh, Kryts, and Archi. Their range is centered on the Daghestan ASSR, with extensions into Azerbaijan, Georgia, and the Chechen-Ingush A.S.S.R. [*See also* North Caucasian Languages.]

3.1. *Phonology.* Vowel systems can be complicated by diphthongs, length, umlaut, nasalization, and pharyngealization. Strong or geminate consonants are general, and laterals abound in the Avar-Andi-Dido group. The Botlikh consonant system is shown in Table 2.

Tonal accent has been noted for a number of NEC

TABLE 2. *Botlikh Consonants*

	Labial	Alveolar	Palato-Alveolar	Palatal	Lateral	Velar	Uvular	Pharyngeal	Laryngeal
Stops									
Voiced	b	d				g			
Voiceless									
Plain	p	t				k	q		ʔ
Long						k:			
Glottalized									
Plain		t’				k’	q’		
Long						k’:			
Affricates									
Voiced			ǰ						
Voiceless									
Plain		c	č						
Long		c:	č:		kł:				
Glottalized									
Plain		c’	č’						
Long		c’:	č’:		kł:’				
Fricatives									
Voiced		z	ž		l				
Voiceless									
Plain		s	š	x′	ł		X		h
Long		s:	š:		ł:		X:	ħ:	
Nasals	m	n							
Vibrant		r							
Semivowels	w			y					

languages (Kibrik et al. 1978). Four tones are the maximum observed. Four accentual patterns can occur:

(a) The prosodic scheme of the word is defined as a sequence of tonal characteristics of its constituent syllables, as in the Gigatl dialect of Chamalal.
(b) The tone of one syllable predetermines that of another, as in Bezhta.
(c) Tone and stress combine, as in Rutul.
(d) Dynamic stress occurs, as in Lezgi.

3.2. *Morphology.* Relatively simple verb structures are offset by rich case systems, whose complexity arises from their variety of locatives. The system in Andi has been described as follows: for each of seven series, there are essive, allative, and elative forms. The series signify ‘on’ (horizontal), ‘on’ (vertical), comitative, ‘in’ (spatial, sg. objects), ‘beneath’, ‘in’ (masses), and ‘in’ (spatial, pl. objects).

Noun classes, essentially covert, range from zero (Udi) to two (N. Tabassaran), three (Avar), four (Lak), five (Chamalal), six (Chechen), and eight (Bats). In some languages, verbs do not agree with any NP (Aghul, Lezgi); in others, there is personal agreement (Udi); in still others, agreement of person and class (Bats, Lak, Dargwa, Tabassaran); finally, in some there is class-agreement only. Subordination is achieved by the use of non-finite verbs. Five-way deixis is not unknown. Bats idiosyncratically extends its vigesimal numeral system beyond the usual ‘99’, so that ‘10,321’ = ‘$(25 \times 20 \times 20) + (16 \times 20) + 1$’.

3.3. *Syntax.* Patterns of word-order are SOV, GN, AN, NP + postposition, and relative + head. Variety in case-marking patterns for the central arguments of the verb depends on whether the verb is intransitive, transitive, affective, of perception, or of possession, as in Avar:

(18) *yas yekerula.*
girl.ABS run.PRES
‘The girl runs away.’

(19) *ins:uc:a vas vecula.*
father.ERG son.ABS praise.PRES
‘The father praises (his) son.’

(20) *ins:uye vasul rokł:'ula.*
father.DAT sons.ABS love.PRES
'The father loves (his) sons.'

(21) *ins:uda ču bix'ula.*
father.LOC horse.ABS see.PRES
'The father sees (a) horse.'

(22) *ins:ul yas yigo.*
father.GEN daughter.ABS be
'The father has a daughter.'

The basic ergative pattern is sometimes subject to variation; thus antipassives occur, as in Dargwa:

(23) *nu-ni žuz b-uč'ul-ra.*
I-ERG book.ABS it-read-I
'I read the book.'

(24) *nu žuz-li Ø-uč'ul-ra.*
I.ABS book-ERG I-read-I
'I am reading the book.'

The 'double absolutive' configuration is widespread, though apparently limited to analytic verb-forms (Kibrik 1979), where a choice of constructions is sometimes possible, as in Chechen:

(25) *so bolx b-eš v-u.*
I.ABS work.ABS it-doing I-be
'I habitually work.'

(26) *bolx as b-eš b-u.*
work.ABS I.ERG it-doing it-be
'I am engaged in (some specific) work.'

(27) *as bolx b-o.*
I.ERG work.ABS it-do
'I work.'

Bats has adapted its basic ergative configuration in certain interesting contexts (Holisky 1984:184–187):

(a) A few intransitives (e.g. 'run', 'pray', 'fight') require 1st/2nd person subjects to be ergative; some other intransitives permit ergative or absolutive subjects, with the latter marked for non-agentivity.
(b) Among dative-S affective verbs, three ('hate', 'forget', and 'like') allow 1st/2nd person DOs to be either absolutive or ergative; the latter stresses the DO's desire to induce the relevant feeling.
(c) Among dative-S perception verbs, two ('see' and 'know') take ergative subjects in perfective aspectual forms, when some effort is involved on the subject's part.

B. G. HEWITT

BIBLIOGRAPHY

BOEDER, WINFRIED. 1979. Ergative syntax and morphology in language change: The South Caucasian languages. In Plank 1979, pp. 435–480.

CATFORD, JOHN C. 1976. Ergativity in Caucasian languages. *North Eastern Linguistic Society* 6.37–48.

CATFORD, JOHN C. 1977. Mountain of tongues: The languages of the Caucasus. *Annual Review of Anthropology* 6.283–314.

ČIKOBAVA, ARNOLD S. 1936. *Č'anuris gramat'ik'uli analizi* [The grammatical analysis of Laz]. Tbilisi: Academy Press.

DEETERS, GERHARD. 1930. *Das kharthwelische Verbum.* Leipzig: Markert & Petters.

GREPPIN, JOHN A. C., ed. 1989. *The indigenous languages of the Caucasus,* vol. 1, *South Caucasian* (edited by Alice C. Harris); vol. 2, *North West Caucasian* (edited by B. G. Hewitt); vol. 3, *North Central and North East Caucasian* (edited by Rieks Smeets and D. M. Job). New York: Caravan Books.

HARRIS, ALICE C. 1985. *Diachronic syntax: The Kartvelian case.* (Syntax and semantics, 18.) New York: Academic Press.

HEWITT, B. G. 1981. Caucasian languages. In *Languages of the Soviet Union,* edited by Bernard Comrie et al., pp. 196–237. Cambridge & New York: Cambridge University Press.

HEWITT, B. G. 1987. Georgian: Ergative or active? *Lingua* 71.319–340.

HOLISKY, DEE ANN. 1984. Anomalies in the use of the ergative case in Tsova-Tush (Batsbi). *Folia Slavica* 7.181–194.

KIBRIK, ALEKSANDR E. 1979. Canonical ergativity and Daghestani languages. In Plank 1979, pp. 61–77.

KIBRIK, ALEKSANDR E., et al. 1978. O prosodičeskoj strukture slov v dagestanskix jazykax. [On the prosodic structure of words in Daghestanian languages]. *Institut Russkogo Jazyka AN SSSR, Predvaritel'nye publikacii,* vypusk 115, I.5–26.

KUIPERS, AERT H. 1960. *Phoneme and morpheme in Kabardian (Eastern Adyghe).* (Janua linguarum, Series minor, 8.) The Hague: Mouton.

PLANK, FRANS, ed. 1979. *Ergativity: Towards a theory of grammatical relations.* London: Academic Press.

SMEETS, HENRICUS J. 1984. *Studies in West Circassian phonology and morphology.* Leiden: Hakuchi.

Vogt, Hans. 1958. *Structure phonémique du géorgien.* (Norsk Tidsskrift for Sprogvidenskap, 18.) Oslo: Universitetsforlaget.

CAUSATION IN LANGUAGE CHANGE. The oldest view of linguistic change, prevalent even today among non-linguists, is that it is a type of DECAY. The view was accepted also by early 19th-century linguists, who considered it supported by developments like the following: Proto-Indo-European had eight nominal cases, of which Latin preserved six; Old French reduced the number to two, and Modern French to one. One vehicle for such decay was thought to be 'false analogy': the reshaping of words on the ANALOGY [*q.v.*] of other words, motivated by improper understanding of their 'true' structure. False analogy therefore was considered characteristic of late, decaying languages. However, an alternative interpretation views linguistic change as leading to economy, efficiency, simplification, or melioration; cf. especially early generativists such as Kiparsky 1968, 1978.

In contrast, the Neogrammarians argued that reconstructed languages and their early offshoots are no more or less 'perfect' than their descendants. [*See* Phonological Change.] Thus Osthoff & Brugmann (1878:iii-xx) claimed that, for a child learning ancient Greek, the language was no more difficult or perfect than, say, Byzantine Greek for a child learning the language in later times. Mutatis mutandis, this argument is applicable against the claim that change leads to greater simplicity. In fact, it has been argued that linguistic change may lead to grammar complication (cf. Hock 1986, chap. 11.) Further, the Neogrammarians argued that all linguistic phenomena observable in history are possible also for prehistoric stages (the 'uniformitarian principle'). Consequently, analogy could be invoked for the parent language, and did not need to be labeled deviant or 'false' (Osthoff & Brugmann 1878).

1. Regular sound change. The Neogrammarians became better known for their claim that, with specifiable exceptions (see below), sound change differs from all other types of change in the following ways:

(a) It is regular, i.e. it affects all qualifying lexical items simultaneously.
(b) It is 'mechanical', i.e. only phonetically conditioned.
(c) It is unobservable.
(d) It evolves in gradual, imperceptible steps.

The property of regularity was considered to be supported by the fact that it had been possible to explain apparent exceptions to such changes as those described by Grimm's Law; the last important difficulties were accounted for by Verner's Law. [*See* Germanic Languages.]

All other changes were considered (i) to be irregular—affecting only some qualifying lexical items, and those not simultaneously; (ii) to proceed according to 'psychological' principles (the mental association of related forms); (iii) to be observable in terms of competing forms; and (iv) to take place in abrupt leaps. These other changes included not only analogy, syntactic change, and borrowing, but also a specified, notoriously irregular subset of phonetic changes, mainly metathesis, dissimilation, and haplology.

2. Causes of sound change. Since other changes were believed to be caused and explained by the psychological factors which motivated them, interest in causation centered on sound change. Besides the notion of 'decay', earlier linguists had proposed such factors as 'love of freedom' among the Germanic peoples, attempts to speak more distinctively, poetic considerations, heavier aspiration in mountainous areas, change in fashion, or yet other non-linguistic factors (cf. Schuchardt 1885:14–15). Except for 'fashion' (i.e. social motivation, cf. below), none of these was tenable, since similar changes may be observed in very different settings.

The Neogrammarians, instead, offered three major linguistic claims on the causes of sound change (see especially Paul 1920):

(a) As observed by contemporary phoneticians, speech is characterized by minor phonetic deviations from the idealized norm. Instead of canceling each other out, some deviations may become cumulative, and lead to a new norm.
(b) Children may misperceive their elders' norms and develop different norms.
(c) Regular sound change originates in an idiolect, and then spreads to other speakers for reasons of prestige.

In regard to the first two hypotheses, it must be asked why deviations should sometimes be cumulative, rather than continuing to cancel each other out. Some changes—assimilation, weakening, and loss—may perhaps be considered to have 'built-in' directionality; but others cannot, even though they exhibit the same regularity (Hock

1986:20). Moreover, even changes like assimilation can proceed in many different directions: witness the treatment of *-tm-* in Korean *pan-mada* 'every field', Aeolian Greek *kámmoros* 'ill-fated', Swiss German *ōpmə* 'to breathe' (< *ātmən*), late Ancient Greek *Pátnos* (a place-name), Middle Indic dial. *atpan-, attan-, appan-* 'self' (< *ātman-*). As for the second claim, it is difficult to conceive how children would agree on selecting from their parents' speech just those deviations that go into, say, Grimm's Law. Furthermore, recent publications (e.g. Bybee & Slobin 1982) have shown that some deviations are frequent in early child language but have virtually no historical counterparts, and vice versa.

As regards hypothesis (c), it may be supported by the widespread European change of alveolar [r] to uvular [ʀ], said to have originated in the French idiolect of Louis XIV. But Jakob Böhme observed it around 1600, and it has been argued that the change can be motivated dialect-internally. In any event, the postulated scenario is tantamount to borrowing—a development notorious for its irregularity, even when motivated by prestige. Studies of the dialectal spread of sound change show a clear tendency toward decrease in regularity (cf. Hock 1986, chap. 15). It is dubious to attribute regular sound change to this irregular process. (A related claim is that sound change results from language contact; cf. Schuchardt 1885:14–15. But many changes attributed to contact are of very uncertain interpretation; cf. Hock 1986, chap. 16.1.4.) Under these circumstances, some linguists have concluded that it is impossible to state with certainty the cause or causes of sound change.

3. Function and change. In a more recent, 'functionalist' view of change, whole-system changes like Grimm's Law, which are especially difficult to explain in the above scenarios, result from CHAIN SHIFTS motivated by the notions of 'structure' and 'function' (cf. especially Martinet 1964). However, like the Neogrammarian scenarios, chain shifts ultimately cannot predict the directionality of change. Thus, in Swedish, fronting of old [u] occasioned a 'drag-chain' raising of [o] toward the position vacated by [u], and of [ɔ] toward old [o]. Similar developments are known from early French and Ancient Greek. But in Central Illinois, the fronting of [uw] has led to a 'solidarity chain', in which the other back vowels are fronted. This is not to say that functional considerations are irrelevant; however, they are not sufficient to predict the direction of change (see Hock 1986, chaps. 8 and 20).

The situation is no better for non-regular change. Here too, the apparent motivations are not sufficiently specific to predict specific outcomes. Rather, notions such as 'analogy' cover a large variety of possible and natural changes. (For a summary, see Hock 1986.) As in the case of assimilation, it is impossible to predict which of these a language may 'choose' at a given time.

4. Regularity and irregularity. Another difficulty for the Neogrammarian position is that dissimilation and metathesis, though usually sporadic and irregular, sometimes behave exactly like regular sound change (cf. the discussion and references in Hock 1986:111–116, 641). Moreover, some analogical developments like the 'rule re-ordering' of generative grammar (cf. Kiparsky 1968, 1978; Hock 1986, chap. 11) take place with about the same regularity as regular sound change. The Neogrammarians' strict distinction between regular sound change and irregular other change therefore appears oversimplified.

In fact, from its inception, this distinction ran into strong opposition. Frequently, that opposition merely consisted in the reiteration of earlier beliefs: though sound change may be highly regular, one should not expect complete regularity. The Neogrammarians' insistence on a strict distinction between sound change and analogy is also dubious: analogical considerations can block sound change ('preventive analogy'). Furthermore, a detailed study of spoken dialects shows little regularity; rather, 'Each word has its own history' (cf. the recent discussion in Anttila 1972.) Objections like these could be dismissed by the Neogrammarians for failing to provide criteria for deciding whether a regularist or irregularist analysis was preferable. Moreover, the standard cases for preventive analogy turn out to be quite weak (cf. Hock 1986, chaps. 3.5 and 20.8, with references).

5. Sound change versus analogy. A more formidable attack lay in Schuchardt's (1885) claim that the distinction between sound change and analogy was spurious—in that both types of change originate in one or two words, and spread to other lexical items through analogical extension. Unfortunately, Schuchardt offered no supporting evidence; nor did he explain why analogy is overwhelmingly regular in some cases ('sound change'), but not in others (traditional 'analogy'). Moreover, his claim was hidden among the usual anti-Neogrammarian arguments, and like them was generally dismissed.

Later arguments of this type improved on Schuchardt's views. Sturtevant 1917 claimed that the 'spread of a sound change from word to word closely resembles analogical change; the chief difference is that in analogical change the association groups are based upon meaning, while in this case the groups are based upon [phonetic] form.' Sturtevant supported his claim with evidence like the English change of [ū] to [ŭ]: some lexical items show new [ŭ] exclusively (e.g. *good, took*), others preserve [ū] *(food, shoot)*, and a third set varies between [ū] and [ŭ] *(room, roof)*. Such variations, as well as the coexistence of the old pronunciation in some words and the new in others, are features normally associated with analogical change. Like other early studies, however, such arguments were generally ignored.

6. Sociolinguistic approaches. The situation changed only as a result of the work on change in progress initiated by Labov (1965), and since then taken up by other linguists. In addition to providing a strong empirical foundation and an explicit theoretical framework, this work differs from earlier studies in the observation that the starting point and motivation for sound change are not purely linguistic, but social. [*See* Sociolinguistics.] The most persuasive works in this regard include Labov's 1963 study of Martha's Vineyard. In other cases, the social conditioning may be less strong—an issue to be taken up below.

The theory that emanated from Labov's early work (cf. Weinreich, Labov & Herzog 1968) can be summarized as follows:

(a) The basis for change lies in the pervasive low-level variability of speech noted by the Neogrammarians and by 19th-century phoneticians.
(b) One of the low-level variables is selected as a socially significant marker of group identity. The selection appears to depend only on social factors; it is linguistically arbitrary.
(c) Once selected, the variable becomes grammatically significant: over- or under-use becomes noticeable, like a speech error or a foreign accent. The variable must therefore be accounted for by a variable rule of grammar, conditioned by both linguistic and social parameters.
(d) These sociolinguistic parameters may motivate extension of the rule to new environments, word classes, segments, or segment classes. Extension to other segments allows for the possibility of chain shifts. (Such extensions probably are likewise 'propelled' by social factors.)
(e) Because social groups overlap, the process may be extended to other groups. Unless generalization is blocked by other social factors, the process may come to affect the whole lexicon and the whole speech community.
(f) Since change normally takes place through variable RULES, the most common outcome is virtually complete regularity.
(g) In conformity with the 'uniformitarian principle', we can extrapolate from observable history, and postulate this sociolinguistic scenario as a model for all changes.

Labov's framework is a theory not just of sound change, but of linguistic change in general. Thus his data include the variable presence of 'postvocalic [r]' in New York—a phenomenon involving dialect reaffiliation, rather than primary sound change. Structured variability has also been noted in analogical and syntactic change (cf. Hock 1986:660–661, with references).

Moreover, by postulating a social factor as the foundation for linguistic change, the theory provides an explanation in principle for the fact, repeatedly noted above, that the causes and directions of change are not predictable through purely linguistic scenarios. (In practice, of course, the social motivations for past changes are usually impossible to unearth.) And by operating with variable rules, the approach solves the puzzle in GENERATIVE PHONOLOGY [*q.v.*] as to how sound change can be conceptualized as change in the grammar (cf. Hock 1986, chaps. 11 and 20).

7. Lexical diffusion. The notion of sociolinguistically 'variable rules' has been questioned in the work of W. S-Y. Wang and his followers, who instead propose that sound change takes place in terms of individual lexical items, via 'lexical diffusion'; cf. especially Wang 1977. The theoretical claims of this view, and many of the studies supporting it, have been considered questionable (cf. Hock 1986:649–652, with references). But the fact remains that certain changes, including English [ū] > [ŭ], are much less sweeping than originally envisaged by Labov.

The reasons for this slower, 'diffusional' spread of certain changes are still a matter of dispute. Labov 1981 has argued that change is fairly sweeping if it affects relatively superficial aspects of pronunciation, but diffusional if it affects the lexical or underlying representations of phonological forms. Recent publications, however, have cast doubt on this hypothesis. The slow-moving changes examined by Labov differ from the fast-moving ones in that the former are associated with a very low degree of social significance, and he took this to be a secondary phenomenon. However, low social significance characterizes other slow changes, such as Eng. [ū] > [ŭ]. In Labov's original theory, social marking is responsible both for the initiation of change and for its further extension; thus it is possible that the low social significance of diffusional changes, rather than being secondary, is the primary reason for their being slow, in that it provides less motivation for generalization.

HANS HENRICH HOCK

BIBLIOGRAPHY

ANTTILA, RAIMO. 1972. *An introduction to historical and comparative linguistics.* New York: Macmillan.

BYBEE, JOAN L., & DAN I. SLOBIN. 1982. Why small children cannot change language on their own: Suggestions from the English past tense. In *Papers from the Fifth International Conference on Historical Linguistics* (Current issues in linguistic theory, 21), edited by Anders Ahlqvist, pp. 29–37. Amsterdam: Benjamins.

HOCK, HANS HENRICH. 1986. *Principles of historical linguistics.* (Trends in linguistics: Studies and monographs, 34.) Berlin: Mouton de Gruyter.

KIPARSKY, PAUL. 1968. Linguistic universals and linguistic change. In *Universals in linguistic theory,* edited by Emmon Bach & Robert T. Harms, pp. 171–204. New York: Holt, Rinehart & Winston.

KIPARSKY, PAUL. 1978. Historical linguistics. In *A survey of linguistic science,* edited by William O. Dingwall, 2d ed., pp. 33–61. College Park: University of Maryland Linguistics Program.

LABOV, WILLIAM. 1963. The social motivation of a sound change. *Word* 19.273–309.

LABOV, WILLIAM. 1981. Resolving the Neogrammarian controversy. *Language* 57.267–308.

MARTINET, ANDRÉ. 1964. *Économie des changements phonétiques.* 2d ed. Bern: Francke.

OSTHOFF, HERMANN, & KARL BRUGMANN. 1878. *Morphologische Untersuchungen auf dem Gebiete der indogermanischen Sprachen,* vol. 1. Leipzig: Hirzel.

PAUL, HERMANN. 1920. *Principien der Sprachgeschichte.* 5th ed. Halle: Niemeyer. 2nd ed. translated as *Principles of language history* (New York: Macmillan, 1889).

SCHUCHARDT, HUGO. 1885. *Über die Lautgesetze: Gegen die Junggrammatiker.* Berlin: Oppenheim. Translated in *Schuchardt, the Neogrammarians, and the transformational theory of sound change,* edited by Theo Vennemann & Terence H. Wilbur (Frankfurt: Athenäum, 1972), pp. 39–72.

STURTEVANT, EDGAR H. 1917. *Linguistic change.* Chicago: University of Chicago Press.

WANG, WILLIAM S-Y., ed. 1977. *The lexicon in phonological change.* The Hague: Mouton.

WEINREICH, URIEL; WILLIAM LABOV; & MARVIN I. HERZOG. 1968. Empirical foundations for a theory of language change. In *Directions for historical linguistics,* edited by Winfred P. Lehmann & Yakov Malkiel, pp. 95–188. Austin: University of Texas Press.

CAUSATIVE. While the term 'causative construction' could in principle refer to any grammatical device that encodes causation, in practice the term has come to be used to express the kind of construction found in Turkish ex. 2, where the verb expresses the notion of causation:

(1) *Hasan öl-dü.*
H. die-PAST
'Hasan died.'

(2) *Ali Hasan-ı öl-dür-dü.*
A. H.-ACC die-CAUS-PAST
'Ali caused Hasan to die, killed Hasan.'

In 2, causation is expressed by means of a productive suffix; this is called a MORPHOLOGICAL causative. Causation can also be expressed periphrastically, as in the so-called ANALYTIC causative of English:

(3) *Ned made his dog run.*

In Japanese, causation is sometimes expressed by a completely different lexical item, referred to as a LEXICAL causative:

(4) *Taroo ga sin-da.*
T. NOM die-PAST
'Taro died.'

(5) *Ziroo ga Taroo o korosi-ta.*
J. NOM T. ACC kill-PAST
'Jiro killed Taro.'

In addition to these clearly defined types, there are intermediate varieties. Thus the French construction with *faire* 'to make' is formally analytic; however, it has many syntactic properties of a morphological causative, in that the sequence *faire* plus infinitive behaves like a single verb:

(6) *Paul a fait venir les enfants.*
Paul has made come-INF the children
'Paul has made the children come.'

Here *les enfants* must follow the whole sequence *faire* plus infinitive (as if object of the whole sequence), rather than occurring between *faire* and the infinitive (as if it were the object of *faire* or the subject of the infinitive).

In Japanese, the productive causative suffix *-(s)ase* produces morphological causatives; however, non-productive derivational patterns give rise to lexical causatives, e.g. *tome-* 'stop (tr.)' as lexical causative of *tomar-* 'stop (intr.)':

(7) *Taroo ga Ziroo o zibun no uti no mae de*
T. NOM J. ACC self GEN house GEN front at
tomar-ase-ta.
stop-CAUS-PAST
'Taro caused Jiro to stop in front of his (Taro's/Jiro's) house.'

(8) *Taroo ga Ziroo o zibun no uti no mae de*
T. NOM J. ACC self GEN house GEN front at
tome-ta.
stop-PAST
'Taro stopped Jiro in front of his (Taro's/Jiro's) house.'

(In Japanese, the reflexive pronoun can refer back to the subject of the corresponding non-causative of a morphological causative, but not of a lexical causative.) The scale 'lexical, morphological, analytic' corresponds to a semantic scale of cohesion between causing and caused events; e.g., English *kill* implies a closer relation between cause and effect than does *cause to die*.

Cross-linguistically, causative constructions, in particular of the morphological type, show surprisingly similar syntactic and semantic patterns. Syntactically, if we assume a hierarchy of grammatical relations 'subject, direct object, indirect object, other', then the grammatical relation assumed by the causee (i.e. the subject of the corresponding non-causative) tends to occupy the highest position on the hierarchy that is not otherwise occupied (Comrie 1975). This can be seen by comparing Turkish ex. 2 above with the following additional sentences:

(9) *Dişçi mektub-u müdür-e imzala-t-tı.*
dentist letter-ACC director-DAT sign-CAUS-PAST
'The dentist got the director to sign the letter.'

(10) *Dişçi Hasan-a mektub-u müdür tarafından*
dentist H.-DAT letter-ACC director by
göster-t-ti.
show-CAUS-PAST
'The dentist got the director to show the letter to Hasan.'

The pattern illustrated by Turkish is by far the most widespread single pattern across the world's languages. However, exceptions to it are found in various languages, in which a causee of the types in 2 or 9 receives a lower ranking—as in Finnish, where the causee appears in a locative case:

(11) *Minä rakennut-i-n talo-n muurare-i-lla.*
I build.CAUS-PAST-1.SG house-ACC bricklayer-PL-on
'I got the bricklayers to build the house.'

In Sanskrit, two accusative noun phrases may occur:

(12) *Rāma-ḥ bhṛtya-ṃ kaṭa-ṃ kār-aya-ti.*
Rama-NOM servant-ACC mat-ACC prepare-CAUS-3.SG.
'Rama got the servant to prepare the mat.'

Some languages allow alternative grammatical expressions of the causee in certain cases, and these often correlate with semantic distinctions (Cole 1983). In Kannaḍa, for instance, the causative of a transitive construction may have its causee either in the dative, in accordance with the above pattern, or in the instrumental. Use of the dative implies that the causee has less control over whether the situation comes about, while use of the instrumental implies greater control:

(13) *Avanu nana-ge bisket-annu tinn-is-id-anu.*
he I-DAT biscuit-ACC eat-CAUS-PAST-3.SG.
'He fed me the biscuit.'

(14) *Avanu nann-inda bisket-annu tinn-is-id-anu.*
he I-INSTR biscuit-ACC eat-CAUS-PAST-3.SG.
'He got me to eat the biscuit.'

A similar opposition is expressed in Japanese by the alternation of accusative and dative case markers:

(15) *Taroo ga Ziroo o ik-ase-ta.*
T. NOM J. ACC go-CAUS-PAST
'Taro made Jiro go.'

(16) *Taroo ga Ziroo ni ik-ase-ta.*
T. NOM J. DAT GO-CAUS-PAST
'Taro got Jiro to go.'

A range of articles treating theoretical and descriptive aspects of causative constructions is found in Shibatani 1976.

BERNARD COMRIE

BIBLIOGRAPHY

COLE, PETER. 1983. The grammatical role of the causee in universal grammar. *International Journal of American Linguistics* 49.115–133.

COMRIE, BERNARD. 1975. Causatives and universal grammar. *Transactions of the Philological Society* 1974:1–32.

SHIBATANI, MASAYOSHI, ed. 1976. *The grammar of causative constructions.* (Syntax and semantics, 6.) New York: Academic Press.

C-COMMAND. Certain relations and dependencies between phrases in a S[entence] are sensitive to the hierarchical organization of constituents of the sentence, e.g. the following:

(a) The relation between a pronoun used as a bound variable and its antecedent: the condition on pronominal binding is that a pronoun must be C-COMMANDED by its antecedent.
(b) The relation between a WH-phrase and the position it binds: the condition on proper binding is that the trace of a WH-phrase must be c-commanded by the WH-phrase.
(c) The relation between a reflexive or a reciprocal anaphor and its antecedent: Principle A of the Binding theory is that an anaphor must be c-commanded by its antecedent in a local domain. [*See* Anaphora; Binding.]
(d) The relation between a name and a coreferential pronoun: Principle C of the Binding theory is that a name cannot be c-commanded by a pronoun coreferential with it.
(e) Scope relations in general, the scope of negation in particular, and the distribution of negative polarity items (which must be c-commanded by the negative element).

Naturally, there is considerable discussion as to the appropriate characterization of the c-command relation—and as to whether the same notion is at work in all of the above cases, and any other relevant ones. C-command is a member of a family of COMMAND RELATIONS which share the following general idea: Node A commands node B in a tree representation if there is a constituent C which meets property P and contains both A and B. It is usually stipulated that command relations are not reflexive; i.e., a node does not command itself.

The various definitions found in the literature differ on how they state property P. For c-command—introduced under the name 'in construction with' by Klima 1964, to treat relations as in (e) above—P reads: C is the first constituent containing A and some other material (i.e., C is the first branching node over A). Langacker 1969 takes P to be: C is the first S node containing A. Lasnik 1976 modifies this to: C is the first cyclic node containing A. Langacker and Lasnik are concerned mostly with relations of type (d) above.

C-command was rediscovered in a slightly different form by Reinhart 1983, who is also responsible for the name; she deals mostly with relations as in (d) above. She states P as: C is the first branching node over A, or the node immediately above it if both nodes are of the same syntactic category.

M-command is introduced by Aoun & Sportiche 1982 (with a review of several other notions), in the context of a discussion of the GOVERNMENT relation [*q.v.*]. They state P as: C is the first maximal projection containing A. I-command is also sometimes argued for in the literature, and states P as: C is the first node containing A.

Naturally, the correct formulation of the relation depends on a fine analysis of constituent structure. Beyond the most central cases, much debate remains in this area.

HILDA KOOPMAN

BIBLIOGRAPHY

AOUN, JOSEPH, & DOMINIQUE SPORTICHE. 1982. On the formal theory of government. *Linguistic Review* 2.211–236.

KLIMA, EDWARD S. 1964. Negation in English. In *The structure of language,* edited by Jerry A. Fodor and Jerrold J. Katz, pp. 246–323. Englewood Cliffs, N.J.: Prentice-Hall.

LANGACKER, RONALD. 1969. On pronominalization and the chain of command. In *Modern studies in English: Readings in transformational grammar*, edited by David A. Reibel & Sanford A. Schane, pp. 160–186. Englewood Cliffs, N.J.: Prentice-Hall.

LASNIK, HOWARD. 1976. Remarks on coreference. *Linguistic Analysis* 2.1–22.

REINHART, TANYA. 1983. *Anaphora and semantic interpre-*

tation. London: Croom Helm. Chicago: University of Chicago Press.

CELTIC LANGUAGES. The earliest Celts are associated with two major Central European Iron Age cultures—Halstatt, dated to the 7th century BCE, and La Tène, dated to the 5th century BCE. From this central location, the Celts spread throughout Europe in different migrations: southeast through the Balkans and into Asia Minor; south into Italy (they captured Rome in 390 BCE); west into the Iberian peninsula; and north to the Atlantic coast and across into Britain and Ireland, where they were dominant by the 3rd century BCE. Today, the surviving Celtic-speaking communities are located in the peripheries of states with other majority languages: Brittany, Wales, and Ireland each claim around half a million speakers, and about eighty thousand speakers remain in northwest Scotland. Many emigrant Celts are dispersed among other majority populations, especially in the New World. Ethnic communities were established in America, notably by Scottish Gaels in Nova Scotia, from the late 18th century, and by Welsh settlers in Argentine Patagonia in 1865. A few native speakers of Patagonian Welsh and Cape Breton Gaelic still remain.

1. Continental Celtic (see Evans 1981). The first direct mentions of the Celts are to be found in the writings of Greek and Roman ethnographers and historians, who identified them as a separate people speaking a distinctive tongue. This language, Continental or Common Celtic, has been partially reconstructed from place names, inscriptions, and references in Latin texts, and has long been established as a member of the I[ndo-]E[uropean] family [*q.v.*]. It is distinguished by, e.g., its loss of IE *p*: cf. Latin *pater*, Gaelic *athair* 'father'. There seems to have been a range of Celtic dialects even in the earliest period; these are reflected in the remains of Gaulish, Celtiberian, and Lepontic (northern Italy), though the evidence is limited, and some of it is strongly in dispute. No direct evidence of Galatian (Asia Minor) remains, though it survived until the 5th century CE. (On comparative Celtic, see Lewis & Pedersen 1937.)

2. Insular Celtic. Apart from possible enclaves, Celtic speech appears to have died out on the European continent by 500 CE. In Britain, however, Celtic languages survived the Roman occupation (Jackson 1953). Scotland north of the Forth-Clyde line (the domain of the Picts) had avoided Romanization, and Ireland had not undergone Roman occupation at all. The modern Celtic languages derive from Insular Celtic. There are two branches: BRYTHONIC or BRITISH (rarely called 'Gallo-Britonnic', since Britain is regarded as on a continuum with Gaul), and GOEDELIC or GAELIC. These are differentiated by, e.g., their treatments of IE k^w, which became *p* in British (and Gaulish), but remained unchanged in Gaelic. In the ancient Ogam script, which was based on the Latin alphabet, the symbol for this labiovelar is transliterated by scholars as *q*; thus Old Welsh *map* 'son' is in Ogam Irish *maqq-*.

The two branches are usually referred to as P-CELTIC and Q-CELTIC. To P-Celtic belong Welsh (Northern British), Pictish (as far as the evidence shows), and Cornish, which died out in the 18th century. (On Welsh, see Jones & Thomas 1977.) The ancestors of the Bretons emigrated from southwestern Britain in the 5th century. They may have amalgamated with surviving Celtic speakers in northwestern Gaul; the evidence is disputed. (On Breton, see Press 1987.) Q-Celtic is divided into two groups: Western Gaelic, represented by Irish (Ó Murchú 1985); and Eastern Gaelic, including Scottish Gaelic (cf. Ternes 1973) and Manx (the last speaker of which died in 1974; see Broderick 1984). Celtiberian appears to exhibit some Q-Celtic features. Each of the extant languages has a range of dialects.

3. Typological affinities and distinctive features. Typologically, Celtic languages show affinities with the Western European languages with which they have long had contact. In constructions and vocabulary, they show evidence of scholarly influence from Latin; Welsh also reflects its ancient contact with that language as well as the modern influence of English. The Gaelic languages contain many English calques and borrowings; Breton shows strong influences from French in the same areas—with additional phonological relationships, such as comparable loss of final nasals.

Modern Celtic languages also have features which distinguish them from their neighbors. Their basic word order is Verb + Subject + Object (or Complement)—though this was not the case in Continental Celtic, as far as we can judge. For example, 'Tom is in the house' has the following shapes:

(1) Scottish: *Tha Tom anns an taigh.*
Irish: *Tá Tom san tigh.*
Welsh: *Mae Tom yn y tŷ.*
Breton: *Emañ Tom en ti.*

The order of elements above is Verb + Subject + complement (Prepositional Phrase). Items may be highlighted by placing them at the front of the sentence. This was originally accomplished by means of a preceding verbal element and a following main verb in the relative form, as in Scottish:

(2) *(Se) Tom a leughas an leabhar.*
'(It is) Tom who reads the book.'

But such a construction has come to be the neutral word order in Breton:

(3) *Tom a lenn al levr.*
T. REL read the book
'Tom is reading the book.'

Celtic languages have no verb 'have'. Possession is expressed by the verb 'to be' + Possessed[SUBJ] + Possessor[LOC], as in Irish:

(4) *Tá an leabhar ag Tom.*
is the book at T.
'Tom has the book.'

Some modern dialects construct their progressive, perfective, and prospective aspects by means of prepositional phrases with verbal nouns as heads:

(5a) Scottish: *Tha Tom a' leughadh an leabhair.*
(5b) Welsh: *Mae Tom yn darllen y llyfr.*
is T. at/in reading the book.GEN
'Tom is reading the book.'

When the object is pronominal, it precedes the verbal noun, as in Welsh:

(6) *Mae Tom yn ei ddarllen.*
is T. in its.MASC reading
'Tom is reading it.'

However, Breton, and optionally Irish, construct the perfective by using 'have' (i.e. 'be' with a locative possessor) with a past participle.

One notable feature of Celtic languages is the extensive use of initial consonant MUTATION to carry morphological distinctions. We can illustrate some aspects of this complex phenomenon by looking at noun phrases consisting of possessive pronoun + 'dog', shown in Table 1.

TABLE 1. *Celtic Mutation*

	'dog'	'his dog'	'her dog'
Scottish	*cù* /ku:/	*a chù* /ə xu /	*a cù* /ə ku:/
Irish	*cù* /ku:/	*a chù* /ə xu:/	*a cù* /ə ku:/
Welsh	*ci* /ki:/	*ei gi* /i gi:/	*ei chi* /i xi:/
Breton	*ki* /ki:/	*e gi* /e gi:/	*e c'hi* /e xi:/

The change stop → nasal is the third type of change affecting stops; it occurs after the Welsh 1st person possessive (*fy nghi* /və ŋhi:/ 'my dog'), and after the 3pl. possessive in some Gaelic dialects (*an cù* /ə ŋku:/ 'their dog'). In Breton, nasal mutation affects only initial *d*: *an nor* (<*dor*) /ə nɔ:r/ 'the door'. The mutations function differently in the different languages.

DONALD MACAULAY

BIBLIOGRAPHY

BRODERICK, GEORGE. 1984. *A handbook of late spoken Manx.* 3 vols. Tübingen: Niemeyer.

EVANS, ELLIS D. 1981. *The labyrinth of Continental Celtic.* (Sir John Rhŷs Memorial Lecture, 1977.) London: British Academy.

JACKSON, KENNETH H. 1953. *Language and history in Early Britain.* Edinburgh: Edinburgh University Press.

JONES, MORRIS, & ALAN R. THOMAS. 1977. *The Welsh language: Studies in its syntax and semantics.* Cardiff: University of Wales Press.

LEWIS, HENRY, & HOLGER PEDERSEN. 1937. *A concise comparative Celtic grammar.* Göttingen: Vandenhoeck & Ruprecht.

Ó MURCHÚ, MAIRTIN. 1985. *The Irish language.* (Gnéithe dár nDúchas, 10.) Dublin: Department of Foreign Affairs.

PRESS, IAN. 1987. *A grammar of modern Breton.* (Mouton grammar library, 2.) Berlin: Mouton de Gruyter.

TERNES, ELMAR. 1973. *The phonemic analysis of Scottish Gaelic.* (Forum phoneticum, 1.) Hamburg: Buske.

LANGUAGE LIST

Breton: around 500,000 speakers reported in 1989 for whom Breton is the daily language, in western Brittany, France, but also dispersed in Eastern Brittany. Some claim to be monolingual in Breton. Some 1,200,000 others know Breton but do not use it regularly, including 32,700 in the United States. Sometimes called Brezhoneg.

Brythonic: an ancient language of the British Isles, documented as Old Welsh. Pictish may have been a variant. Its modern descendants are Welsh, Cornish, and Breton.

Continental Celtic: an extinct language, spoken on the European continent in classical times. Regional variants included Gaulish, Celtiberian, Lepontic (northern Italy), and Galatian (Asia Minor).

Cornish: extinct since before 1800 as a first language; formerly spoken in Cornwall, southwest England. Currently being revived for cultural purposes; all speakers have English as their first language.

Gaelic, Irish: around 120,000 speakers reported in 1976 as using Irish for everyday purposes, out of 789,000 speakers including bilinguals. Also spoken in Northern Ireland. Sometimes called Erse.

Gaelic, Scottish: 94,000 speakers reported in 1971, with 88,900 in the north and central counties of Scotland and the islands of the Hebrides and Skye, including 477 monolinguals, and 5,000 in Nova Scotia and Prince Edward Island, Canada. In some communities it is primarily used in the home, in church, and for social purposes. Speakers are bilingual in English. Distinct from Scots, a language variety closely related to English.

Goidelic: an ancient language of the British Isles, documented as Old Irish. Its modern descendants are Irish Gaelic, Scottish Gaelic, and Manx.

Manx: extinct as a first language during the 20th century; formerly spoken on the Isle of Man, United Kingdom. It is a second language for 200 to 300 who have learned it as adults. Used for some public functions.

Welsh: 580,000 speakers reported in 1971, with 575,000 in northern and western Wales, including 32,700 monolinguals, and 3,160 in Canada. Also called Cymraeg.

CENTRAL AMERICAN LANGUAGES. Within the geographical area extending from Guatemala to Panama, the northern segment is characterized by Mayan languages [*q.v.*] and falls into the Meso-American language area [*q.v.*]. To the south, we find languages of the Misumalpan and Subtiaba-Tlapanec families [*qq.v.*]. Still farther south, we find Chibchan languages [*q.v.*], whose affiliations are with South American languages [*q.v.*]. Apart from the above, only a few languages have survived to modern times; see the Language List below.

LANGUAGE LIST

Lenca: only a few speakers remaining from an ethnic population of 50,000, in Honduras and El Salvador.

Tol: 250 to 300 speakers reported in 1982, in northwest Honduras. Also called Tolpan, Torrupan, Jicaque, Xicaque, or Hicaque. All ages continue to use the language. There are varying degrees of bilingualism in Spanish; adult male leaders are more fluent, but women and children very limited.

Xinca: now extinct, formerly spoken in southeastern Guatemala. All members of the ethnic group speak Spanish.

CENTRAL AND SOUTH NEW GUINEAN LANGUAGES constitute a group which forms a broad horizontal strip from western Irian Jaya, Indonesia, into western Papua New Guinea. It comprises the language families indicated in the subgrouping given in Figure 1 (apart from some terminological changes). According to Stephen A. Wurm, *Papuan languages of Oceania* (Tübingen: Narr, 1982), pp. 129–140, the Central and South New Guinean group forms, with the Kutubuan languages, a Central and South New Guinea–Kutubuan superstock, itself a highest-level component of the Cen-

FIGURE 1. *Subgrouping of Central and South New Guinean Languages*

Asmat-Kamoro
- Asienara, Casuarina Coast Asmat, Central Asmat, Yaosakor Asmat, Citak, Tamnim Citak, Iria, Kamoro, Sempan

Awin-Pare
- Awin, Kamula, Pare

Awyu-Dumut
- **Awyu**
  - **Aghu**
    - Aghu (proper), Kotogüt
  - Awyu (proper)
  - Pisa
  - Siagha-Yenimu
  - Yair
- **Dumut**
  - Kaeti, Kombai, Wambon, Wanggom
- Sawi
- **Unclassified Awyu-Dumut**
  - Korowai

Bosavi
- Aimele, Bainapi, Beami, Bosavi (proper), Etoro, Kasua, Kware, Onabasulu, Sonia, Tomu

Duna-Bogaya
- Bogaya, Duna

East Strickland
- Agala, Kalamo, Konai, Samo-Kubo

Mombum
- Mombum (proper), Koneraw

Momuna

Ok
- **Lowland Ok**
  - Iwur, Kati, Ninggerum, Yonggom
- **Mountain Ok**
  - Bimin, Faiwol, Kauwol, Mianmin, Ngalum, Setaman, Suganga, Telefol, Tifal, Urapmin

tral and Western part of the main section of his controversial Trans–New Guinea phylum [*q.v.*].

LANGUAGE LIST

Agala: 300 speakers reported in 1981, on the Upper Strickland River, Western Province, Papua New Guinea. Also called Sinale. The Bogaya language divides the Agala into two sections.

Aghu: 3,000 speakers reported in 1987, in the south coast area along the Digul River, Irian Jaya. Also called Dyair or Djair. Distinct from Aghu of Australia.

Aimele: 500 speakers reported in 1981, around Mt. Bosavi in the southwest corner of Southern Highlands Province, Papua New Guinea, and around Lake Campbell, Western Province. Most speakers have moved to the Wawoi Falls area of Western Province. Kware may be the same language.

Asienara: 700 speakers reported in 1978, on the south Bomberai Peninsula, Irian Jaya. Also called Asianara, Buruwai, Karufa, or Madidwana.

Asmat, Casuarina Coast: 8,000 speakers reported in 1988, on the Casuarina coast, Irian Jaya.

Asmat, Central: 50,000 speakers reported in 1987, on the south coast of Irian Jaya. Also called Manowee, Jas, or Yas. Many speakers are becoming bilingual in Indonesian, and some in neighboring languages.

Asmat, Yaosakor: spoken on the south coast of Irian Jaya, Indonesia. Also called Yaosakor.

Awin: 8,000 speakers reported in 1987, in the Kiunga area, Western Province, Papua New Guinea. Also called Aiwin, Akium, Aekyom, or West Awin.

Awyu: 18,000 speakers reported in 1987, on the south coast of Irian Jaya. Also called Auyu, Awya, Awju, Ajau, or Avio. Many speakers are becoming bilingual in Indonesian.

Bainapi: 400 speakers reported in 1981, in the villages of Makapa, Pikiwa, and Bamustu, via Balimo, Western Province, Papua New Guinea. Also called Pikiwa, Dibiasu, or Turumasa.

Beami: 4,200 speakers reported in 1981, east of Nomad, Western Province, Papua New Guinea, extending into Southern Highlands Province. Also called Bedamini, Bedamuni, or Mougulu.

Bimin: 1,100 speakers reported in 1981, in Telefomin District, West Sepik Province, Papua New Guinea, and a few in Western Province.

Bogaya: 300 speakers reported in 1981, in Western Province, Papua New Guinea, and some in the base of the northern neck of Southern Highlands Province. Also called Pogaya or Bogaia.

Bosavi: 2,000 speakers reported in 1987, in Southern Highlands Province, Papua New Guinea. Also called Kaluli. Different from Kasua.

Citak: 8,000 speakers reported in 1985, on the south coast of Irian Jaya. Also called Cicak, Tjitak, Tjitjak, or Kaunak. Language use is vigorous.

Citak, Tamnim: spoken near Senggo, Irian Jaya. Also called Tamnim. Language use is vigorous. Speakers want to be called Citak, not Asmat, though they may be linguistically closer to Asmat.

Duna: around 5,660 speakers reported in 1981, in Lake Kopiago Subprovince, Western Highlands Province, Papua New Guinea, and in Koroba Subprovince, Southern Highlands Province. Also called Yuna.

Etoro: 1,000 speakers reported in 1988, southwest of Mt. Sisa, in Southern Highlands Province, Papua New Guinea. Has 38 percent lexical similarity with Beami.

Faiwol: 4,500 speakers reported in 1987, at the headwaters of the Fly and Palmer rivers, Kiunga Subprovince, Western Province, Papua New Guinea. Also called Faiwolmin, Fegolmin, or Unkia.

Iria: 850 speakers reported in 1978, on the southeast Bomberai Peninsula, Irian Jaya. Also called Kamrau or Kamberau.

Iwur: 1,000 speakers reported in 1987, in the border area of the valley of the Iwur River, Irian Jaya.

Kaeti: 10,000 speakers reported in 1987, in the border area near the Fly River, Irian Jaya. Also spoken in Papua New Guinea. Also called Nub, Dumut, Mandobo, or Mandobbo.

Kalamo: 100 speakers reported from the south bank of the middle Rentoul River past the middle Tomu River, Western Province, Papua New Guinea. Most speakers are now at Wawoi Falls. Also called Nomad.

Kamoro: 8,000 speakers reported in 1987, on the south coast from Etna Bay to the Mukamuga River, Irian Jaya. Also called Kamora, Mimika, Lakahia, Nagramadu, Umari, Mukamuga, Neferipi, Nefarpi, Nafarpi, or Kaokonau. Many speakers are becoming bilingual in Indonesian.

Kamula: 400 speakers reported in 1982, in the villages of Wasapea, Aramia River area, and Keseki and Sokolonepi, Wawoi Falls area, Western Province, Papua New Guinea. Also called Kamura or Wawol.

Kasua: 1,200 speakers reported in 1971, east and south of Mt. Bosavi, Southern Highlands Province, Papua New Guinea.

Kati, Northern: 8,000 speakers reported in 1987, in the south coast area east and west of the Muyu River, Irian Jaya. Also called Northern Muju, Niinati, Kati-Ninanti, Ninatie, or North Muyu.

Kati, Southern: 4,000 speakers reported in 1987, in the south coast area, Irian Jaya. Also called Southern Muju, Metomka, Muyu, South Muyu, Kati-Metomka, or Digul. Kowan may be a dialect.

Kauwol: 500 speakers reported in 1971, in upper Kauwol Valley, Western Province, Papua New Guinea, and across the border in Irian Jaya. Also called Kawol or Kavwol.

Kombai: 10,000 speakers reported in 1987 in the south coast area around Bona, Irian Jaya. Also called Komboy.

Konai: 400 speakers reported in 1982, on the west side of the upper Strickland River, Western Province, Papua New Guinea. Also called Mirapmin.

Koneraw: 300 speakers reported in 1978, on Frederik Hendrik Island, Irian Jaya.

Korowai: 2,000 speakers reported in 1987, in the south coast area, Irian Jaya.

Kotogüt: 1,000 speakers reported in 1978, on the upper Digul River, south coast area, Irian Jaya. Also called Tsokwambo.

Kware: around 400 speakers reported in 1981, around Simo, Western Province and Southern Highlands Province, Papua New Guinea. May be the same as Aimele.

Mianmin: 2,200 speakers reported in 1981, in the north part of the Fak and Aki river valleys, at the headwaters of the August and upper May rivers, Telefomin District, West Sepik Province, Papua New Guinea.

Mombum: 250 speakers reported on an island off the southeast coast of Frederik Hendrik Island, Irian Jaya. Also called Kemelom.

Momuna: 2,700 speakers reported in 1987, in lowlands just south of the Jayawijaya Mountains, Irian Jaya. Also called Somahai, Somage, or Sumohai. No bilinguals.

Ngalum, 18,000 speakers reported in 1987, in valleys on both sides of the border between Irian Jaya and Papua New Guinea, in the main mountain range; 10,000 of them are in Indonesia.

Ninggerum: 4,000 speakers reported in 1975, including 3,000 between the Ok Birim and Ok Tedi rivers, Western Province, Papua New Guinea. Also 1,000 in Irian Jaya. Also called Ninggrum, Ninggirum, Ningerum, Kativa, Kasiwa, Obgwo, Tedi, or Tidi.

Onabasulu: 435 speakers reported in 1981, midway between Mt. Sisa and Mt. Bosavi, Southern Highlands Province, Papua New Guinea. Also called Onobasulu.

Pare: 2,000 speakers reported in 1987, in Western Province, Papua New Guinea. Also called Pa or Akium-Pare.

Pisa: 3,500 speakers reported in 1987, in the south coast area inland from Pirimapun, Irian Jaya.

Samo-Kubo: 2,900 speakers reported in 1981, east of the Strickland River, north and south of Nomad, Western Province, Papua New Guinea. Also called Supai or Daba.

Sawi: 2,500 speakers reported in 1985, in the south coastal lowland near Merauke, Irian Jaya. Also called Sawuy or Aejauroh. Nearly monolingual.

Sempan: 1,000 speakers reported in 1987, on the south coast between Kokonao and Agats, Irian Jaya. Also called Nararapi.

Setaman: 200 speakers reported in 1981, in West Sepik Province, Papua New Guinea.

Siagha-Yenimu: 3,000 speakers reported in 1987, north of the lower Digul River, Irian Jaya. Also called Siagha, Syiagha, Sijagha, Oser, or Yenimu.

Sonia: 410 speakers reported in 1981, ten to twenty miles west and southwest of Bosavi, Western Province and Southern Highlands Province, Papua New Guinea.

Suganga: 700 speakers reported in 1981, in Amanab Subprovince, West Sepik Province, Papua New Guinea. Also called Wagarabai or North Mianmin.

Telefol: 4,800 speakers reported in 1987, in Telefomin District, West Sepik Province, Papua New Guinea. Also called Telefomin or Telefolmin.

Tifal: 3,000 speakers reported in 1985, in Telefomin District, West Sepik Province, Papua New Guinea. Also called Tifalmin.

Tomu: 300 speakers reported in 1981, along the Tomu River, in Western Province (and some in Southern Highlands Province), Papua New Guinea. Also called Tomu River.

Urapmin: 395 speakers reported in 1979, in Telefomin District, West Sepik Province, Papua New Guinea.

Wambon: 3,000 speakers reported in 1987, in the south coast area, Irian Jaya.

Wanggom: 1,000 speakers reported in 1978, in the south border area on the Digul River, Irian Jaya. Also called Wanggo or Wangom.

Yair: 1,500 speakers reported in 1987, on the west side of the Digul River, Irian Jaya. Also called Awyu.

Yonggom: around 17,000 speakers reported in 1987, including 15,000 along the Fly and Tedi rivers and toward the Murray River, Western Province, Papua New Guinea, and 2,000 in Irian Jaya. Also called Yongom or Yongkom.

CENTRAL GUR LANGUAGES form the core of the Gur branch [*q.v.*] of the Niger-Congo family [*q.v.*]; they are spoken in several nations of West Africa. The internal subgrouping given in Figure 1 is based on Tony Naden, 'Gur', in *The Niger-Congo languages,* edited by John Bendor-Samuel (Lanham, Md.: University Press of America, 1989), pp. 141–168.

LANGUAGE LIST

Akaselem: around 26,300 speakers reported in 1981, near Kotokoli in Tchamba, central Togo. Also called Akasele, Kasele, Kamba, Chamba, or Cemba. The men are more bilingual in Tem than the women.

Bago: 5,000 speakers reported in 1983, in the main centers of Bagou and Koussountou, Togo. Also called Koussountou.

Bariba: 250,000 speakers reported in 1989, with 195,000 in Borgou Province, central and north Benin, and 55,000 in Borgu Division, Kwara State, Nigeria. Also called Bargu, Burgu, Batonnum, Berba, Barba, Bogung, or Batombu. Distinct from Biali (Berba).

Biali: 49,400 speakers reported in 1980, including 48,000 in

FIGURE 1. *Subgrouping of Central Gur Languages*

Northern Central Gur
- Bariba
- **Bwamu**
  - Boomu, Bwamu (proper)
- Kurumfe (Kurumba)
- **Oti Volta**
  - **Buli-Koma**
    - Buli, Konni
  - **Eastern branch**
    - Biali, Ditammari, Mbelime, Tamberma, Waama
  - **Gourma**
    - **Moba**
      - Bimoba, Moba (proper)
    - **Ntcham**
      - Akaselem, Ntcham (proper)
    - **Unclassified Gourma languages**
      - Gourma (proper), Konkomba, Nateni, Ngangam, Sola
  - **Western branch**
    - Nootre (Bulba)
    - **Northwest branch**
      - **Dagaari-Birifor**
      - **Unclassified**
        - Mooré, Safaliba, Wali
    - **Southeast branch**
      - Kusaal
      - **Unclassified**
        - Dagbani, Gurenne, Hanga, Mampruli
  - **Yom-Nawdm**
    - Nawdm, Pila

Southern Central Gur
- **Dogoso-Khe**
- Dyan
- **Gan-Dogose**
  - Doghosié, Gbadogo, Kaanse, Komono
- **Grusi**
  - **Eastern Grusi**
    - Bago, Chala, Delo, Kabiyé, Lama, Lokpa, Tem
  - **Northern Grusi**
    - Kasem, Lyele, Nouni, Pana
  - **Western Grusi**
    - Chakali, Deg, Ko, Pasaala, Puguli, Sisaala, Sissala, Tampulma, Vagla
- **Kirma-Tyurama**
  - Cerma, Lobi, Turka

Atakora Province, Benin, and 1,400 in Tapoa and Gourma Provinces, Burkina Faso. Also called Bieri, Bjeri, Bjerb, or Berba. Different from Bariba (Berba).

Bimoba: 70,000 speakers reported in 1988, south of the Kusaal language, north of the Konkomba language, in Gambaga District, northeast Ghana. Also called Bmoba or Moar. Not inherently mutually intelligible with Moba of Togo.

Birifor, Ghana: 60,000 speakers reported in 1988, in the northwest corner of Ghana. Also called Birifo.

Birifor, Malba: 90,000 speakers reported in 1983, in Poni Province, southwestern Burkina Faso. Also called Birifo or Malba-Birifor. Distinct from Dagaari, Wali, and Birifor of Ghana. There are many monolinguals.

Boomu: 300,000 speakers reported in 1982, with 270,000 in Mali, and 30,000 in Djibasso Subprefecture, Burkina Faso. Also called Bore or Western Bobo Wule. May be more than a single language.

Bulba: spoken in Tanguieta, Atakora Province, Benin. Also called Boulba or Nootre.

Buli: 156,600 speakers reported in 1978, including 96,600 in Sandema District, Ghana, and 60,000 in Burkina Faso. Also called Buile, Kanjaga, or Guresha. The people are called Bulsa or Builsa.

Bwamu: 150,000 speakers reported in 1982, including 110,000 in Kossi Province, Volta Noire and Haut-Bassin Prefectures, Dedougou District, Burkina Faso; and 40,000 at San, Tominian, and Mawo in Mali. Also called Eastern Bobo Wule, Red Bobo, Pwe, Bobo, Bwa, Bwaba, Oule, or Bouamou. Speakers call themselves Bwa and their language Bwamu.

Cerma: 50,000 speakers reported in 1982, from just north of Ouangolodougou, Ivory Coast, along the main road to Banfora in Comoé Province, Burkina Faso; population includes 1,140 in Ivory Coast. Also called Gouin, Gwe, Gwen, Kirma, or Cerman. The people are called Gouin or Ciraamba. Distinct from Turka.

Chakali: 4,000 speakers reported in 1988, 40 miles southeast of Wa in northwestern Ghana. The closest lexical similarity is with Tampulma. The speakers are bilingual in Wali, but Chakali is used in the home.

Chala: 2,000 speakers reported in 1988, in the villages of Nkwanta, Odomi, and Ago, Ghana. Speakers are under the Gichode paramount chief. Some are bilingual in Gichode, with higher proficiency than in Twi, which is spoken with outsiders.

Dagaari, Dioula: spoken near Diébougou in the region of Ouéssa-Hamale, Burkina Faso. Perhaps some speakers in Ghana. Also called Jari or Wala. Speakers may be Dagaaba who have become Islamicized.

Dagaari, Northern: 190,000 speakers reported in 1980, in Poni, Bougouriba, Sissili, and Mouhoun Provinces, southwest Burkina Faso. Also called Northern Dagari, Dagara, Degati, Dagati, or Dogaari. The people are called Dagaaba. Distinct from Southern Dagaari in Ghana.

Dagaari, Southern: 311,000 speakers reported in 1978, in the northwest corner of Ghana. Also called Southern Dagara, Degati, Dagati, or Dogaari. The people are called Dagaaba. The language is spoken by all ages. Dagaari and Birifor are in part mutually intelligible; Dagaari is more prominent politically and socially. It is an official literary language. It is distinct from Northern Dagaari in Burkina Faso.

Dagbani: 400,000 speakers reported in 1980, from Tamale to Yendi in northeast Ghana, as well as in Togo. Also called Dagbane, Dagomba, or Dagbamba. The people are called Dagbamba or Dagomba. An official literary language.

Deg: 14,800 speakers reported in 1982, including 14,000 west of Volta Lake, west central Ghana, and 800 in Ivory Coast. Also called Degha, Aculo, Janela, Mo, Buru, or Mmfo. Deg is what the speakers call themselves; Mo is used by outsiders. Has 78 percent lexical similarity with Vagla. Twi is widely spoken as a second language.

Delo: 7,600 speakers reported in 1978, including 4,600 in east central Ghana, and 3,000 across the border in Togo. The people are called Ntrubo, Ntribu, or Ntribou.

Ditammari: 120,000 speakers reported in 1989, from the Togo border toward Natitingou in Atakora Province, Benin. Also called Tamari or Somba. Has 65 percent mutual intelligibility with Tamberma of Togo. Somba is an ethnic name applied to several related dialect groups, and mainly to the Ditamari.

Doghosié: 12,000 speakers reported in 1983, primarily in Sidéradougou Subdistrict, Comoé Province, southwest Burkina Faso. Also called Dorhosye, Dokhobe, Dokhosie, Dorobé, or Dogosé. Distinct from Dogoso.

Dogoso: 4,000 speakers reported in 1983, near the Kaanse and Khe languages in Burkina Faso. Speakers are somewhat bilingual in Jula. Distinct from Doghosié.

Dyan: 11,800 speakers reported in 1983, near Diébougou, Bougouriba Province, Burkina Faso. Also called Dya, Dyane, Dyanu, or Dan. Zanga may be a dialect of Dyan. Distinct from Dan, a Mande language. Speakers have limited bilingual proficiency in Jula.

Gbadogo: 600 speakers reported in 1983, in Bougouriba Province, Tiankoura Subdistrict, Burkina Faso. Also called Padoro, Padogho, Padorho, or Bodoro. The Gbadogo are separated politically from the Kambe. Speakers are highly bilingual in Jula and Kaanse.

Gourma: 393,000 or more speakers reported in 1983, including 300,000 in Gourma and Tapoa Provinces, just south of scrub land that blends into the Sahara in east and southeast Burkina Faso. Also 92,300 around Bidjanga, Dapaon, and Korbongou in Togo, and in Benin and Niger. Also called Gourmantche, Gurma, Migulimancema, or Goulmancema. The people are called Bigulimanceba or Gourmancés.

Gurenne: 525,000 speakers reported in 1988, including 500,000 around Bolgatanga and Navrongo, northeast Ghana, and 25,000 in Burkina Faso. Also called Frafra. Nabt and Talni are varieties intermediate between Gurenne and Mampruli.

Hanga: 5,000 speakers reported in 1977, southeast of the Mole game reserve in Damongo District, north central Ghana. Also called Anga. Politically, speakers form a subgroup of the Gonja. The language has 84 percent lexical similarity with Gurenne. The Kimara variety may be a separate language.

Kaanse: 5,200 speakers reported in 1975, in Gaoua Subdistrict, Poni Province, Burkina Faso. Also called Gan, Gã, or Gane. The people are called Kambe (singular Kan).

Kabiyé: 400,000 first-language speakers reported in 1981, including 375,000 in the Kara region, Togo, centered around Kozah and Binah Prefectures. Also spoken in Atakora Province, northern Benin, and in Ghana. Another 800,000 speak it as a second language. Also called Kabre, Cabrai, Kabure, or Kabye.

Kasem: 85,000 speakers reported in 1978, including 57,100 in Navrongo District, north central Ghana, and 28,000 across the border in Burkina Faso, around Po and Leo. The people are called Kassena or Kasene. An official literary language.

Khe: 1,300 speakers reported in 1983, near the Kaanse and Dogoso languages, Burkina Faso. Speakers are somewhat bilingual in Jula.

Ko: 13,000 speakers reported in 1983, in Boromo Subdistrict around Boromo, Mouhoun Province, Burkina Faso. Also called Kols, Kolsi, or Winye. The speakers are almost entirely monolingual.

Komono: 2,500 speakers reported in 1983, halfway between Kampti and Banfora, Comoé Province, southwest Burkina Faso, near the Ivory Coast border. Also called Kumwenu. Speakers are quite bilingual in Jula.

Konkomba: around 340,000 speakers reported in 1985, including 300,000 in Yendi District, in the northeast border area of Ghana, and 40,000 in central Togo. Also called Likpakpaln, Kpankpam, or Kom Komba. Speakers refer to themselves as Bikpakpaln.

Konni: 2,400 speakers reported in 1987, in a remote area of north central Ghana. Also called Koni or Komung; the people are called Koma. Has 60 percent lexical similarity with Buli. Speakers also use several nearby languages.

Kurumba: 95,000 speakers reported in 1972, mainly in Titao Subdistrict, Yatenga Province, and in Djibi-Aribinda Subdistrict, Soum and Oudalan provinces, Burkina Faso; plus a few at Bandiagara, Mali. Also called Fulse, Foulsé, Tellem, Kurumfe, Nyonyosi, Deforo, or Lilse. Speakers have limited bilingual proficiency in Mooré. Nyonyosi may be a separate dialect or ethnic group.

Kusaal, Eastern: 188,000 speakers reported in 1978, in Bawku District in the northeast corner of Ghana. Also called Kusale or Kusasi. Distinct from Western Kusaal of Burkina Faso. Kusasi are the people, Kusaal is the language.

Kusaal, Western: 10,000 speakers reported in 1983, in Nahouiri and Boulgou Provinces, and in some villages south of Zabré, south central Burkina Faso. Also called Kusale, Kusasi, or Koussassé. Distinct from Eastern Kusaal in Ghana. Many speakers claim to understand the related languages Mooré, Dagbani, Mampruli, and Gurenne.

Lama: 140,000 or more speakers reported in 1987, including 90,000 in the region of Kande and Lama, Togo, and 50,000 in Benin. Also called Lamba, Namba, or Losso. Speakers call themselves and their language Lama.

Lobi: some 215,000 speakers reported in 1972, including 180,000 in the border area of Poni Province around Gaoua, Burkina Faso. Also 40,000 in the northern part of Eastern Department, Ivory Coast, and a few villages in northwest Ghana along the Volta River. Also called Lobiri or Miwa.

Lokpa: 35,000 speakers reported in 1989, in west Djougou and border areas of Atakora Province, Benin, and in Togo. Also called Dompago, Logba, Legba, or Lugba. Distinct from Logba of Ghana.

Lyele: 61,000 speakers reported in 1971, around Koudougou and Tenado, Réo, Didyr, and Tenado Subdistricts, Sanguie Province, Burkina Faso. Also called Lela, Lelese, Lere, L'ele, or Gurunsi Lele.

Mampruli: around 167,000 speakers reported in 1978, east and west of Gambaga, northeast Ghana, and some in Togo. Also called Mamprule, Manpelle, or Ngmamperli. The people are called Mamprusi. Speakers use Gurenne, Bimoba, or Bissa as second languages.

Mbelime: 20,000 speakers reported in 1980, in Atakora Province, Benin. Also called Niendi or Niende.

Moba: some 147,000 speakers reported in 1981, including 145,100 in northwest Togo, with main centers at Dapaong and Bombouaka, plus 1,680 in Burkina Faso. Also called Moab, Moare, or Moa. Natchaba may be a dialect.

Mooré: 4,000,000 speakers reported in 1987, in the central Ouagadougou area of Burkina Faso and throughout the country, plus 15,000 in the northwest corner of Togo. Some have gone into Ghana, Togo, Benin, and Ivory Coast to work. Also called Mossi, Moré, Mole, or Moshi. The dominant African language of Burkina Faso. Mossi is the name of the people, Mooré of the language.

Nateni: 35,000 speakers reported in 1980, in Atakora Province, Benin. Also called Tayari, Tayaku, Natemba, or Natimba. Nateni is the language name; Natemba and Natimba are names for the people; Tayaku is a village.

Nawdm: some 112,000 speakers reported in 1981, around Niamtougou, Doufelgou Prefecture, Togo. Many speakers have settled in Sotouboua, Ogou, and Haho Prefectures. Important minorities live in Lomé and in Ghana. Also called Nawdam, Naoudem, Losso, or Losu. Losso is the name they use for themselves when talking to outsiders.

Ngangam: some 25,700 speakers reported in 1981, around Mogou, Gando, and Namoni, in Togo. Also called Dye, Nbangam, Gangan, Gangum, or Ngangan. Ngangam is the official name. Some people speak Anufo well enough to discuss abstract concepts.

Nouni: 45,000 speakers reported in 1982, around Leo and to the north in Po Subdistrict, Sissili Province, Burkina Faso. Also called Nunuma, Nuna, Nune, Nibulu, or Nuruma.

Ntcham: some 47,800 speakers reported in 1981, in Bassar, Kabou, Kalanga, and adjacent areas, west central Togo. Many speakers in Ghana. Also called Basare, Bassari, Bassar, or Tobote.

Pana: 6,000 or more speakers reported in 1983, around Oué in the valley of the Sourou River where it enters from Mali, on the border due north of Dédougou, Kassoum Subdistrict, Sourou Province, Burkina Faso. Also spoken south of Bandiagara in Mali. Speakers have low bilingual proficiency in Jula.

Pasaala: 50,000 speakers reported in 1988, in north central Ghana. Also called Pasali, Paasale, or Southern Sisaala.

Pila: 50,000 speakers reported in 1989, in the Djougou area, Atakora Province, northwest Benin. Also called Pilapila, Kpilakpila, or Yom.

Puguli: 11,000 speakers reported in 1983, in Dano Subdistrict, Bougouriba Province, Burkina Faso, and in a few villages north of Dana, which is north of Diébougou. Also called Buguli, Pwa, Pwo, or Buguri. Some villages are mixed with Dagaari speakers, but Puguli speakers have low comprehension of Dagaari. Jula bilingualism varies from village to village.

Safaliba: 4,000 speakers reported in 1988, north of Banda, west central Ghana. Also called Safalba, Safazo, or Safalaba. May be mutually intelligible with Wali. Has 79 percent lexical similarity with Dagaari.

Sisaala, Tumulung: 91,400 speakers reported in 1978, in Tumu District, north central Ghana. Also called Sisai, Issala, Hissala, Sisala Tumu, or Isaalung.

Sisaala, Western: 20,000 speakers reported in 1988, in Lambusie and surrounding towns, north central Ghana. Also called Busillu Sisala, Sisai, Issala, or Hissala. Close to Sissala of Burkina Faso, but distinct.

Sissala: 5,000 speakers reported in 1987, between Léo and Ouessa, Sissili Province, south central Burkina Faso. Also called Sisai, Issala, or Hissala. Distinct from the Sisaala languages in Ghana.

Sola: 8,000 speakers reported in 1987, northeast of Kpagouda in Togo, bordering Benin; also around Kouyoria and Sola and in Atakore Province, Benin. Also called Soruba, Bijobe, Biyobe, Uyobe, Miyobe, Kayobe, Kuyobe, Solamba, or Solla. Sola is the official name, Bijobe the ethnic name, and Solla the popular name. Has 47 percent lexical similarity with Ngangam, the most closely related variety. Most people also speak Kabiyé well enough to discuss everyday topics.

Tamberma: some 15,200 speakers reported in 1981, east of Kante, Togo. Also called Tamari, Soma, or Some. Somba is a derogatory name. Tamberma, Bataba, and Batammaraba are names for the people. Has 65 percent mutual intelligibility with Ditammari of Benin. Few people are bilingual.

Tampulma: 8,000 speakers reported in 1977, Damongo District, north central Ghana. Also called Tampole, Tampolem, Tampolense, Tamplima, or Tampele. The people are called Tamprusi. Lexical similarity with Chakali.

Tem: 300,000 speakers reported in 1981, including 156,000 around Bafilo and Sokode, with the main centers in Tchaoudjo, Nyala, and Sotouboua, Togo; plus 75,000 in Benin, and the rest in Accra, Ghana. Also called Kotokoli, Tim, Timu, or Temba.

Turka: 31,000 speakers reported in 1975, north and west of Banfora, Comoé Province, Burkina Faso. Also called Turuka, Curama, or Tyurama. Distinct from Cerma.

Vagla: 7,000 speakers reported in 1984, near Sawla, Damongo District, Northern Province, west central Ghana, and in one village of Ivory Coast. Also called Vagala, Siti, Sitigo, Kira, Konosarola, or Paxala. Has 68 percent lexical similarity with Chakali.

Waama: 40,000 speakers reported in 1989, in Atakora Province, Benin. Also called Yoabou.

Wali: 72,800 speakers reported in 1978, in the northwest corner of Ghana. Also called Waali, Wala, or Ala. A separate language from Birifor and Dagaari.

CENTRAL INDO-ARYAN LANGUAGES constitute a subgroup of the Indo-Aryan languages [*q.v.*]. They are spoken predominantly in western and central India, extending into Nepal and Pakistan; they also include the Romani (Gypsy) languages, spoken westward into Europe and the New World. The best-known languages of the group are Gujarati, Hindi, Punjabi, and Urdu [*qq.v.*]. The internal classification of the Central Indo-Aryan languages is shown in Figure 1.

FIGURE 1. *Subgrouping of Central Indo-Aryan Languages*

Bhil
  Bareli, Bhilala, Bhili, Bhilori, Chodri, Dhanka, Dhodia, Dubla, Gamit, Adiwasi Girasia, Rajput Girasia, Mawchi, Pardhi, Patelia, Pauri, Wagdi
Dom (Domari)
Gujarati
  Gujarati (proper), Kachi Koli, Saurashtri, Vasavi
Khandesi
  Dangi, Khandesi (proper)
Punjabi
  Bhateali, Kahluri, Majhi, Eastern Punjabi
Rajasthani
  Ajmeri
  Bagri
  Bhoyari
  Gade Lohar
  Gujuri
  Harauti
  Lamani
  Malvi
  Marwari
    Dhatki, Marwari (proper), Marwari Bhil, Northern and Southern Marwari
  Nimadi
  Sondwari
Romani
  Balkan Romani
  Northern Romani
    Baltic Romani, Carpathian Romani, Kalo Finnish Romani, Sinte Romani, Welsh Romani
  Vlach Romani
Western Hindi
  Bangaru
  Braj Basha
  Bundeli
    Bundeli (proper), Lodhi
  Chamari
  Gowli
  Hindi
  Kanauji
  Urdu
Unclassified Central Indo-Aryan
  Dang Tharu, Keer, Parya, Saharia, Sansi, Sonha

LANGUAGE LIST

Ajmeri: 580 speakers reported in 1961, in Rajasthan, India.

Bagri: around 1,170,000 speakers reported in 1971, with 1,060,000 in the Punjab and Rajasthan, India, and others in the Sind, Pakistan. Also called Bagari, Bagria, Bagris, Baorias, or Bahgri. Speakers use some Sindhi and understand some Urdu. Has 76 percent lexical similarity with Marwari Bhil of Jodhpur.

Bangaru: 4,000,000 speakers reported in 1977, in Punjab, India. Also called Banger, Bangri, Bangru, Hariani, Desari, or Chamarwa.

Bareli: around 230,000 speakers reported in 1971, in Madhya Pradesh and Maharashtra, India. Also called Barel or Bareli Pauri. Bilingualism in Marathi is limited.

Bhateali: around 5,910 speakers reported in 1971, in Himachal Pradesh, India. Also called Bhatiali, Bhattiyali, Pahari, Bhatiyali.

Bhilala: around 247,000 speakers reported in 1971, in Gujarat, Madhya Pradesh, Maharashtra, Karnataka, and Rajasthan, India. Also called Bhilali.

Bhili: 1,600,000 speakers reported in 1986, in mountainous areas of central India. Also called Bhilbari, Bhilboli, Bhilla, Bhil, or Vil.

Bhilori: spoken in Maharashtra, India. Also called Bhilodi. Limited bilingual proficiency in Marathi.

Bhoyari: around 5,390 speakers reported in Maharashtra, India. Also called Bhomiyari, Bhoyaroo, Bhuiyar, Bhuria, Bohoyeri. 'Bhoyari' may be a cover term for various languages and dialects, not necessarily all in the Rajasthani group.

Braj Bhasha: 11,500,000 speakers reported in 1977, in Uttar Pradesh and adjacent areas, India. Also called Braj, Braj Bhakha, Brij Bhasha, Antarbedi, Antarvedi, Bijbhasha, Bri, Briju, or Bruj.

Bundeli: 8,000,000 speakers reported in 1977, in Uttar Pradesh, Madhya Pradesh, and Maharashtra, India. Also called Bundel Khandi.

Chamari: around 5,320 speakers reported in 1971, in Madhya Pradesh, Uttar Pradesh, Maharashtra, India. Also called Chamar, Chambhar Boli, or Chambhari.

Chodri: 150,000 speakers reported in 1986, mainly in Gujarat, India. Also called Chaudri, Chodhari, Chaudhari, Choudhara.

Dang Tharu: 50,000 speakers reported in 1985, west of Bhairawa-Butwal and north of the India border in Nepal. Also called Dangali, Dangura, or Dangha.

Dangi: around 80,500 speakers reported in 1971, in Gujarat, India. Also called Dangri, Kakachhu-Ki Boli, or Dangs Bhil. May not have mother-tongue speakers.

Dhanka: around 10,200 speakers reported in 1971, in Gujarat, Maharashtra, Karnataka, and Rajasthan, India. Also called Dhanki, Tadavi, or Tadvi Bhils.

Dhatki: 200,000 speakers reported in lower Sind, Pakistan. Also called Dhataki or Dhati. Speakers use some Sindhi and Urdu.

Dhodia: around 75,700 speakers reported in 1971, in central India. Also called Dhobi, Dhore, Dhowari, or Doria.

Domari: a Gypsy language with 500,000 speakers estimated in 1980, with 80,000 in Iran (a 1929 figure), 50,000 in Iraq, possibly 20,000 in Turkey, and 10,000 in Syria. Also spoken in Libya, Egypt, Israel, Afghanistan, and India. Also called Middle Eastern Romani, Tsigene, or Gypsy.

Dubla: around 202,000 speakers reported in 1978, in central India. Also called Dubala, Dubli, Rathod, or Talavia.

Gade Lohar: spoken in Rajasthan, Gujarat, Madhya Pradesh, Maharashtra, Uttar Pradesh, and Punjab, India. Also called Gaduliya Lohar, Lohpitta Rajput Lohar, Bagri Lohar, Bhubaliya Lohar, or Lohari.

Gamit: around 136,000 speakers reported in 1971, in Gujarat, India. Also called Gamati, Gamti, Gamta, Gavit, or Gamith.

Girasia, Adiwasi: 100,000 speakers reported in 1988, in northern Gujarat, India. Also called Adiwasi Gujarati or Garasia. Not mutually intelligible with Rajput Girasia.

Girasia, Rajput: around 60,000 speakers reported in 1984, in Gujarat and Rajasthan, India. Also called Rajput Garasia, Grasia, Dungri Grasia, Dhungri Girasia, Dungari Girasia, or Dhungri Bhili. Not mutually intelligible with Adiwasi Girasia.

Gowli: spoken in Maharashtra, India. Surrounded by Korku, a Munda language.

Gujarati: 33,000,000 speakers reported in 1989, mainly in Gujarat and Maharashtra, India; also in Bangladesh, South Africa, Kenya, Singapore, Pakistan, and nine other countries. Also called Gujrathi or Gujerati. The state language of Gujarat.

Gujuri: 388,000 or more speakers reported in 1971, with 355,000 in Himachal Pradesh, Madhya Pradesh, Uttar Pradesh, Jammu and Kashmir, and Rajasthan, India, plus 23,000 or more in Pakistan and 10,000 in Afghanistan. Also called Gujer, Gujar, Gujjari, Gurjar, Gojri, Gogri, Kashmir Gujuri, Rajasthani Gujuri, or Gojari.

Harauti: around 334,000 speakers reported in 1971, in Rajasthan, India. Also called Hadauti or Hadoti.

Hindi: 182,000,000 or more first-language speakers reported in 1989, with 180,000,000 in Uttar Pradesh, Rajasthan, Punjab, Madhya Pradesh, and Bihar, India; another 120,000,000 people speak it as a second language. There are also 890,000 speakers in South Africa, 685,000 in Mauritius, 233,000 in Yemen, and populations in eight other countries. Also called Khari Boli. On the colloquial level, Hindi is mutually intelligible with Urdu; but Hindi uses the Devanagari writing system, and formal vocabulary borrowed from Sanskrit. The language has official status throughout India, along with English and regional languages.

Kachi Koli: 50,000 speakers reported in 1980, in lower Sind, Pakistan. Also called Kuchikoli, Kachchi, Katchi, Kachi, Kohli, Kholi, Kolhi, Kori, Vaghri, Vagari, or Wagaria.

Kahluri: around 66,200 speakers reported in 1971, mainly in Himachal Pradesh, India. Also called Bilaspuri, Bilaspuri Pahari, Pacchmi, or Kehloori Pahari.

Kanauji: 6,000,000 speakers reported in 1977, in Uttar Pradesh, India. Also called Bhakha, Braj Kanauji, or Braj.

Keer: around 2,890 speakers reported in Madhya Pradesh, India. Also called Kir.

Khandesi: around 147,000 speakers reported in 1971, in Maharashtra and Gujarat, India. Also called Khandeshi, Khandish, or Dhed Gujari.

Lamani: 1,500,000 mostly migrant speakers reported in 1961, scattered over India, but mainly in Maharashtra, Karnataka, and Andhra Pradesh. Also called Lambadi, Banjara, Bangala, Banjori, Banjuri, Gohar-Herkeri, Goola, Gurmarti, Kora, Labhani Muka, Lambara, Lavani, Lemadi, Lumadale, Sugali, Tanda, Vanjari, Wanji, Gormati, or Singali. Gormati is the name speakers use for themselves.

Lodhi: around 44,100 speakers reported in 1971, in Bihar, Madhya Pradesh, Maharashtra, Orissa, and West Bengal, India. Also called Lodha, Lodi, Lohi, or Lozi.

Majhi: spoken in Punjab, India, and in Pakistan. Distinct from the Majhi spoken in Bihar, India, and in Nepal.

Malvi: around 644,000 speakers reported in 1971, in northwest Madhya Pradesh, Maharashtra, and Rajasthan, India. Also called Malwada, Mallow, Ujjaini, Malwi, or Malavi.

Marwari: around 6,810,000 speakers reported in 1971, in Gujarat, Rajasthan, and Madhya Pradesh, India. Also called Rajasthani, Merwari, Marvari, or Mewari. Distinct from Marwari of Pakistan.

Marwari Bhil: 150,000 speakers reported in 1987, in Sind, Pakistan.

Marwari, Northern: 100,000 speakers reported in 1987, in southern Punjab, Pakistan. Also called Merwari, Rajasthani, Meghwar, Jaiselmer, or Marawar. Speakers are moderately bilingual in Sindhi: some are trilingual in Urdu.

Marwari, Southern: spoken in Sind, Pakistan. Also called Merwari, Rajasthani, Meghwar, Jaiselmer, or Marawar. Speakers are moderately bilingual in Sindhi; some are trilingual in Urdu.

Mawchi: around 44,200 speakers reported in 1971, in southwest Gujarat and in Maharashtra, India. Also called Mauchi, Mavchi, or Mawachi.

Nimadi: around 794,000 speakers reported in 1971, in Madhya Pradesh and Maharashtra, India. Also called Nemadi or Nimari.

Pardhi: around 11,000 speakers reported in 1971, scattered over central India. Also called Bahelia, Chita Pardhi, Lango Pardhi, Paidia, Paradi, Paria, Phans Pardhi, Takankar, or Takia. Probably more than one language.

Parya: 1,000 or more speakers reported in 1960, in the Hissar Valley, Tajik SSR, USSR, and some in the Uzbek SSR. Also some in Afghanistan. Also called Afghana-Yi Nasfurush, Afghana-Yi Siyarui, Laghmani, or Paharya. Tajiki is the second language; Parya remains the exclusive language within the home. Speakers refer to themselves as Changgars.

Patelia: around 23,200 speakers reported in 1941, in Gujarat and Maharashtra, India. Also called Pateliya or Pateliya Bhil.

Pauri: 50,000 speakers reported in 1989, in Maharashtra and Madhya Pradesh, India. Also called Pawri, Pawari, or Paura. The language is called Pauri, the people Paura. Bilingual proficiency in Marathi is limited.

Punjabi, Eastern: 20,000,000 speakers reported in 1965, in Punjab, Haryana, Rajasthan, and Jammu and Kashmir, India; 58,000 speakers estimated in Pakistan. Also spoken in the United Arab Emirates, Singapore, and Fiji. Also called Panjabi. Eastern dialects enter into a chain with western varieties of Hindi. Western dialects are related to Western Punjabi, classified as a Northwestern Indo-Aryan language. The religious language of the Sikhs, who write Punjabi in Gurmukhi script.

Romani, Balkan: 1,000,000 speakers reported in 1980, with 120,000 in Yugoslavia, others in Bulgaria, Greece, Turkey, France, West Germany, Italy, Rumania, Hungary, and Iran. Also called Gypsy.

Romani, Baltic: 24,000 speakers reported in the Baltic region of the USSR, and some in Poland.

Romani, Carpathian: 235,000 or more speakers reported in 1980, with 220,000 in Czechoslavakia, 12,000 in the United States, 3,000 in Hungary, and others in Poland, Rumania, and the USSR. Also called Gypsy.

Romani, Kalo Finnish: 5,000 to 8,000 speakers reported in 1980, with 4,000 to 6,000 from an ethnic population of 8,000 in western and southern Finland, and 1,000 to 2,000 and Sweden. Also called Kalo Finnish, Fíntika Rómma or Gypsy.

Romani, Sinte: around 200,000 speakers reported in 1980, with 41,000 in Yugoslavia, 30,000 or more in Germany, 14,000 in Italy, 10,000 to 30,000 in France, and others in Austria, the Netherlands, Switzerland, the USSR, Poland, and Czechoslovakia. Also called Rommanes, Sinte, Sinti, Manuche, Manouche, or Gypsy.

Romani, Vlach: 1,500,000 speakers reported in 1986: 200,000 to 250,000 first-language speakers in Rumania, along with another 250,000 to 300,000 second-language speakers, 100,000 to 210,000 in Latin America, and others in Europe, plus 650,000 in North America. Also called Gypsy, Tsigene, Romanese, Vlach, Vlax, Wallach, Wallachian, or Danubian.

Romani, Welsh: spoken in England and Wales. Not inherently mutually intelligible with Anglo-Romani, which is related to English.

Saharia: around 174,000 speakers reported in Madhya Pradesh, India. Also called Sehri, Sor, or Sosia.

Sansi: spoken in the northwestern Sind, Pakistan. The second language of Sansi speakers is Sindhi, followed by Urdu and Panjabi. Has 71 percent lexical similarity with Urdu, the most closely related variety.

Saurashtri: spoken in Tamil Nadu, India. Also called Sourashtra or Patnuli.

Sondwari: around 31,500 speakers reported in 1971, in Madhya Pradesh and Rajasthan, India. Also called Soudhwari. May be mutually intelligible with Malvi.

Sonha: 10,000 speakers reported in 1985, along the Karnali and Mahakali Rivers in western Nepal. Also called Sonahaa.

Urdu: around 41,300,000 or more speakers reported in 1987, with 33,000,000 in India, and 8,000,000 mother-tongue speakers in Pakistan, where it is the national language and has many more second-language speakers. Also spoken in Afghanistan, South Africa, Mauritius, the United Arab Emirates, and seven other countries. On the colloquial level, Urdu is mutually intelligible with Hindi, but Urdu uses an adaptation of the Arab/Persian writing system, and formal vocabulary borrowed from Arabic and Persian. Urdu is the national language of Pakistan, used alongside English for official purposes.

Vasavi: 300,000 or more speakers reported in 1985, in Maharashtra and Gujarat, India. Also called Vasave or Vasava. Vasavi is the name of the language, Vasava of the people. Bilingual proficiency in Marathi is limited.

Wagdi: around 757,000 speakers reported in 1961, in Rajasthan and Gujarat, India. Also called Wagadi, Vagdi, Vagadi, Vagari, Vageri, Vaged, Vagi, Waghari, Wagholi, or Mina Bhil. The second language is Hindi.

CENTRAL MALAYO-POLYNESIAN LANGUAGES, spoken in Indonesia, form one of the two top-level subdivisions of Central-Eastern Malayo-Polynesian within the Austronesian family [*q.v.*]. The internal subgrouping of Central Malayo-Polynesian consists of the following, based on Merritt Ruhlen, *A guide to the world's languages,* vol. 1, *Classification* (Stanford, Calif.: Stanford University Press, 1987).

Bima-Sumba
Central Maluku
Southeast Maluku
Timor-Flores
Waima'a

[*For Language Lists, see the articles on the individual groups—except the small Waima'a group, which is covered in the Language List below, along with Salas Gunung, a language which remains unclassified within Central Malayo-Polynesian.*]

LANGUAGE LIST

Habu: a Waima'a language with around 1,000 speakers reported in 1981, northeast of Laclubar on east Timor Island, Nusa Tenggara, Indonesia.

Kairui-Midiki: a Waima'a language with around 2,000 speakers reported in 1981, in a small mountainous area of Timor Island, Nusa Tenggara, Indonesia.

Salas Gunung: 100 speakers reported in 1987, on Seram Island, central Maluku, Indonesia.

Waima'a: around 3,000 speakers reported in 1981, on Timor Island, Nusa Tenggara, Indonesia. Also called Waimaha or Waimoa.

CENTRAL MALUKU LANGUAGES constitute a group spoken mainly on Seram and Buru Islands and in the Sula Islands, Maluku, Indonesia; they constitute a top-level component of Central Malayo-Polynesian [*q.v.*]. The internal subgrouping of Central Maluku languages given in Figure 1 is based on Merritt Ruhlen, *A guide to the world's languages,* vol. 1, *Classification* (Stanford, Calif.: Stanford University Press, 1987).

LANGUAGE LIST

Alune: 13,000 to 15,000 speakers reported in 1987, in Seram Barat, Kairatu, and Taniwel Districts, western Seram Island. Has 62 percent lexical similarity with Hulung.

Amahai: 50 speakers reported in 1987, on southwest Seram Island. Also called Amahei. Forms a language chain with Iha and Kaibobo. Has 65 percent lexical similarity with Saparua.

Ambelau: 5,700 speakers reported in 1989, on Ambelau Island off Buru Island, plus a few on the southeast tip of Buru. Also called Amblau.

Asilulu: around 8,750 speakers reported in 1987, on northwestern Ambon Island. Also spoken as a second language on the islands between Ambon and western Seram Islands. Forms a language chain with Hila-Kaitetu (80 percent lexical similarity) and Larike-Wakasihu (67 to 74 percent).

Atamanu: 300 speakers reported in 1987, on western Seram Island. Also called Yalahatan or Jahalatane.

Banda: 3,000 speakers reported in 1987, on Kei Besar Island. Speakers use Kei as a second language.

Bati: spoken on the eastern end of Seram Island.

Benggoi: 600 speakers reported in 1987, on the north coast of eastern Seram Island. Also called Bengoi or Kobi-Benggoi. May be mutually intelligible with Seti.

Boano: 3,240 speakers reported in 1982, on Boano Island west of Seram Island. Also called Buano. Language use is vigorous, but the language may be extinct in southern Boano. Has 61 percent lexical similarity with Luhu and Lisabata-Nuniali, the most closely related varieties.

Boti: spoken on eastern Seram Island. May be the same as Hoti, or extinct.

Buru: around 35,000 speakers reported in 1989, on southern and southeastern Buru Island, including 2,000 living in Ambon, Jakarta, or the Netherlands. Also called Masarete. Population includes 35 percent nearly monolingual, 60 percent with routine ability, and 5 percent with nearly native ability in Ambonese Malay. Some bilingualism in Indonesian. Has 68 percent lexical similarity with Lisela, the most closely related variety.

Elpaputih: spoken on western Seram Island. Also spelled Elpaputi.

Geser: 30,000 to 40,000 speakers reported in 1987, on eastern Seram Island and the Seram Laut Islands. Also called Gesa, Goram, or Gorong.

Haruku: 13,000 speakers reported in 1987, on Haruku Island and the Lease Islands.

Hatue: spoken on eastern Seram Island. May be an alternate name for another language.

FIGURE 1. *Subgrouping of Central Maluku Languages*

- **East Central Maluku**
  - **Banda**
    - Banda (proper)
    - **Seran Laut**
      - Bati, Geser, Watubela
  - **Seram**
    - **East Seram**
      - Benggoi, Boti, Hatue, Hoti, Isal, Kelimuri, Liambata, Masiwang, Sepa, Uhei Kaclakin, Werinama
    - **Nunusaku**
      - **Patakai-Manusela**
        - Huaulu, Manusela, North Nuaulu, South Nuaulu, Saleman
      - **Piru Bay**
        - **East Piru Bay**
          - **Seram Straits**
            - **Ambon**
              - Hila-Kaitetu, Hitu, Laha, Tulehu
            - Kaibobo
            - Solehua (Paulohi)
            - **Uliase**
              - **Hatuhaha**
                - **Elpaputih**
                  - Amahai, Elpaputih (proper), Nusa Laut
                - **Saparua**
                  - Haruku, Latu, Saparua (proper)
              - Kamarian
          - Teluti
      - **Piru Bay** (continued)
        - **West Piru Bay**
          - Asilulu
          - **Hoamoal**
            - **East Hoamoal**
              - Boano, Hoamoal (proper), Larike-Wakasihu
            - **West Hoamoal**
              - Luhu, Manipa
      - Seti
      - **Three Rivers**
        - **Amalumute**
          - Atamanu
          - **Northwest Seram**
            - Alune, Hulung, Iha, Lisabata-Nuniali, Loun, Naka'ela
            - **Unclassified Northwest Seram**
              - Horuru, Kaibobo, Piru
        - Wemale
  - **Unclassified East Central Maluku**
    - Sapolewa, Soow Huhelia, Waelulu
- **West Central Maluku**
  - **Buru-Ambelau**
    - Ambelau, Buru, Hukumina, Kayeli, Liliali, Lisela, Moksela, Palumata
  - **Sula-Taliabo**
    - **Sanana**
      - Mangole, Sula
    - **Taliabo**
      - Kadai, Mangei, Taliabu
  - **Unclassified West Central Maluku**
    - Lumaete

Hila-Kaitetu: around 10,200 speakers reported in 1987, on the north coast of Ambon Island. Also called Seit-Kaitetu. It is part of a language chain with Tulehu (67 percent to 80 percent lexical similarity) and Asilulu (80 percent).

Hitu: around 16,000 speakers reported in 1987, on the Hitu Peninsula of Ambon Island, Maluku, Indonesia. Part of a dialect chain between Hila-Kaitetu (67 percent to 80 percent lexical similarity) and Tulehu (74 to 80 percent).

Hoamoal: spoken on Boano and Kelang islands and the Hoamoal Peninsula of Seram Island. Also called Hoamol. It may be an alternate name for another language, or a cover term for the Hoamoal group.

Horuru: spoken on Seram Island.

Hoti: possibly 10 elderly speakers reported in 1987, on eastern Seram Island.

Huaulu: 300 speakers reported in 1987, northwest of Manusela, eastern Seram Island.

Hukumina: 1 speaker 80 years old reported in 1989, on northwestern Buru Island. Also called Bambaa.

Hulung: 10 or fewer speakers reported in 1985, on western Seram Island. Has 64 percent lexical similarity with North Wemale, the most closely related variety.

Iha: around 4,520 speakers reported in 1982, on western Seram Island. The speakers are originally from Iha village on Saparua Island. Language use is vigorous. Part of a language chain with Amahai and Kaibobo.

Isal: spoken on eastern Seram Island. This may be an alternate name for another language.

Kadai: 300 to 500 speakers reported in 1982, in the interior mountains of Taliabu Island and possibly in the mountains of Mangole Island, in the Sula Islands. May be mutually intelligible with Taliabu.

Kaibobo: 500 speakers reported in 1983, in Kairatu District, Piru Bay, western Seram Island. Also called Kaibubu. The language is nearly extinct in some villages. Part of a dialect chain with Kamarian.

Kamarian: 10 or fewer speakers reported in 1987, on western Seram Island. Also called Kamariang or Seruawan.

Kayeli: 4 speakers over 60 years old reported in 1989 from an ethnic population of 5,000, on Namlea Bay, Buru Island. Also called Cajeli, Caeli, or Gaeli. Most in the ethnic group now speak Ambonese Malay or Lisela as a first language.

Kelimuri: spoken on eastern Seram Island. May be mutually intelligible with Geser.

Laha: around 3,900 speakers reported in 1987, on south central Ambon Island. Also called Central Ambon. Has 67 percent lexical similarity with Asilulu, Hila-Kaitetu, and Tulehu, the most closely related varieties. Parents encourage their children to speak Laha.

Larike-Wakasihu: around 12,500 speakers reported in 1987, on the southwestern Hitu Peninsula, Ambon Island, and in western Seram Island. Has 74 percent lexical similarity with Asilulu, the most closely related variety, at the western end of the Ambon dialect chain. Language use is vigorous in Larike and Wakasihu, weaker in Allang.

Latu: spoken on Elpaputih Bay, southwestern Seram Island. Has 82 percent lexical similarity with Iha, the most closely related variety.

Liambata: spoken on Seram Island. Also called Lenkaitahe.

Liliali: now extinct, formerly spoken on northeastern Buru Island. Also called Leliali. The last speaker died in March 1989.

Lisabata-Nuniali: 1,830 or more speakers reported in 1982, spread across the north coast of Seram Island. Also called Lisabata, Nuniali, or Noniali. Language use is vigorous except in Kawa.

Lisela: around 12,000 speakers reported in 1989, on northern and eastern Buru Island, together with some in Ambon. Also called North Buru, Buru, Li Enyorot, Liet Enjorot, or Wayapo. Language use is not vigorous; a shift to North Maluku Malay is taking place.

Loun: spoken on north central Seram Island. May be nearly extinct.

Luhu: 6,500 speakers reported in 1983, on the Hoamoal Peninsula, western Seram Island, and on Boano and Kelang Islands. Language use is vigorous, but the Batu Merah dialect, also spoken on Ambon Island, is nearly extinct.

Lumaete: recently extinct, formerly spoken around Kayeli on southern Namlea Bay, eastern Buru Island. Also called Lumaiti, Mumaite, or Lumara.

Mangei: 500 to 1,500 speakers reported in 1982, in the interior mountains of Taliabu in the Sula Islands. Also called Mange'e or Mange. May be mutually intelligible with Taliabu.

Mangole: 4,000 to 7,000 speakers reported in 1983, on the southern coast of Mangole and the northern tip of Sulabesi in the Sula Islands. Also called Mangoli or Sula Mangoli.

Manipa: 1,500 speakers reported in 1983, on Manipa Island west of Seram Island.

Manusela: 3,500 speakers reported in 1986, in 30 villages in east central Seram Island. Also called Wahai. Language use is vigorous.

Masiwang: 800 speakers reported in 1987, on Seram Island. Also called Bonfia.

Moksela: now extinct, spoken until 1974 near Kayeli on eastern Buru Island. Also called Maksela or Opselan.

Naka'ela: 5 speakers reported in 1985, on northwestern Seram Island.

Nuaulu, North: spoken along the north coast of central Seram Island and into the interior.

Nuaulu, South: 1,500 speakers reported in 1983, on the south coast of Seram Island. Also called Patakai.

Nusa Laut: possibly 10 speakers reported in 1987, on Nusa Laut and the Lease Islands.

Palumata: now extinct, formerly spoken on northwest Buru Island. Also called Palamata or Balamata.

Paulohi: possibly 50 speakers reported in 1982, on the western shore of Elpaputih Bay, south central Seram Island.

Piru: 10 or fewer speakers reported in 1985, on western Seram Island.

Saleman: 3,000 speakers reported in 1983, on north central Seram Island. Language use is vigorous except in Wahai.

Saparua: 8,000 speakers reported in 1987, on Saparua and Seram Islands and the Lease Islands. Also spoken by several hundred Latu people in Kairatu village.

Sapolewa: spoken on Seram Island. May be an alternate name for another language.

Sepa: 4,000 speakers reported in 1987, on Seram Island. Also called Tamilouw. May be mutually intelligible with Teluti.

Seti: 5,000 speakers reported in 1983, in Seram, Bula, Werinama, and Tehoru Districts in the interior of Seram Island. Language use is vigorous.

Soow Huhelia: spoken on Manipa Island west of Seram Island. May be an alternate name for another language.

Sula: 20,000 speakers reported in 1983, in the Sula Islands, north Maluku, Indonesia, and on Sulabesi Island, and scattered on the north coast of Mangole Island and the northeast coast of Buru Island. Also called Sanana. Vigorous language use.

Taliabu: 2,000 to 4,000 speakers reported in 1984, on Taliabu Island and northwestern Mangole Island in the Sula Islands. Also called Taliabo.

Teluti: 10,000 or more speakers reported in 1987, on Seram Island. Also called Taluti, Tihoru, Tehoru, or Silen.

Tulehu: around 18,800 speakers reported in 1987, on the coast of northeast Ambon Island. Also called Northeast Ambon. The eastern end of the Ambon dialect chain. Language use is vigorous.

Uhei Kaclakin: spoken on Seram Island. May be an alternate name for another language.

Waelulu: spoken on Seram Island. May be an alternate name for another language.

Watubela: 3,000 speakers reported in 1987, on Watubela

Island, north of Kur Island. Also called Snabi Watubela, Kasiui, Wesi, or Esiriun.

Wemale, North: around 4,930 speakers reported in 1982, spread along the north coast of Taniwel District, eastern Seram Island. Language use is vigorous.

Wemale, South: around 3,730 speakers reported in 1987, in fifteen villages on western Seram Island. Also called Tala or Honitetu. Language use is vigorous.

Werinama: 5,000 speakers reported in 1987, on eastern Seram Island. Also called Bobot or Ntau.

CENTRAL PHILIPPINE LANGUAGES constitute a group spoken in the central Philippines, and forming one of the top-level constituents of the Meso-Philippine subgroup of West Malayo-Polynesian [*q.v.*]. The internal subgrouping of the Central Philippine languages given in Figure 1 is based on Merritt Ruhlen, *A guide to the world's languages,* vol. 1, *Classification* (Stanford, Calif.: Stanford University Press, 1987).

FIGURE 1. *Subgrouping of Central Philippine Languages*

Bikol
  Coastal Bikol
    Naga
      Isarog Agta, Mt. Iraya Agta, Central Bicolano
    Virac (Southern Catanduanes Bicolano)
  Inland Bikol
    Mt. Iriga Agta, Buhi-Daraga (Albay Bicolano), Iriga Bicolano
  Pandan (Northern Catanduanes Bicolano)
Bisayan
  Bantoanon
  Cebuano
  Central Bisayan
    Peripheral Central Bisayan
      Ati, Capiznon, Hiligaynon, Masbatenyo, Porohanon
    Romblomanon
    Warayan
      Gubat (Waray Sorsogon), Samar-Waray, (Waray-Waray), Unclassified Warayan (Masbate Sorsogon)
  South Bisayan
    Butuan-Tausug
    Surigaonon
  West Bisayan
    Aklan
      Aklanon, Malaynon
    Kinaray-A
    Kuyan
      Cuyonon, Ratagnon
    North Central West Bisayan
      Loocnon
    Unclassified West Bisayan
      Caluyanun
Mamanwa
Mansakan
  Davaweño
  Eastern Mansakan
    Caraga (Karaga Mandaya)
    Mandayan
      Cataelano Mandaya, Sangab Mandaya, Mansaka
  North Mansakan
    Kamayo
  Western Mansakan
    Kalagan, Kagan Kalagan, Tagakaulu Kalagan
Tagalog
Unclassified Central Philippine
  Ata, Sorsogon Ayta, Tayabas Ayta, Karolanos, Magahat, Sulod

LANGUAGE LIST

Agta, Isarog: a few speakers reported in 1984 from an ethnic population of 1,000, on Mt. Isarog, Bicol Province, Luzon.

Agta, Mt. Iraya: 200 speakers reported in 1979, east of Lake Buhi, Bicol Province, Luzon. Also called Inagta of Mt. Iraya, Rugnot of Lake Buhi East, Lake Buhi East, or Itbeg Rugnot. Some use of Tagalog.

Agta, Mt. Iriga: 1,500 speakers reported in 1979, west of Lake Buhi, Bicol Province, Luzon. Also called San Ramon Inagta, Lake Buhi West, or Mt. Iriga Negrito.

Aklanon: 350,000 speakers reported in 1982, in Aklan Province, northern Panay. Also called Aklan, Aklano, or Panay.

Ata: a few families of speakers reported in 1973, in Negros Oriental Province. Probable high bilingualism in Cebuano; Ata may now be extinct.

Ati: 1,500 speakers reported in 1980, mainly on Panay Island. Also called Inati. Population includes 84 percent with nearly native ability in Hiligaynon, and 61 percent at that level in Kinaray-A. Hiligaynon is used for school, contact with outsiders, outside culture topics, jobs, and religion. Ati is used in the home and with close friends.

Ayta, Sorsogon: 40 speakers reported in 1984, in Sorsogon Province.

Ayta, Tayabas: now extinct, formerly spoken in Quezon Province, Luzon. Completely assimilated to Tagalog.

Bantoanon: 65,000 speakers reported in 1985, in and around Banton, Romblon Province. Also called Banton, Bantuanon, Asiq, Simaranhon, or Calatravanhon. Bilingual in Tagalog, yet over 95 percent of Bantoanon speakers use the vernacular with family, friends, at work, and with Bantuanon officials and teachers. Tagalog is used for some politics and education, and with non-Bantoanon speakers.

Bicolano, Albay: 480,000 speakers reported in 1975, in western Albay and Camarines Sur Provinces, Luzon. Speakers are somewhat bilingual in Central Bicolano.

Bicolano, Central: 2,500,000 speakers reported in southern Catanduanes Province, northern Sorsogon Province, Albay

Province, and in Camarines Norte and Sur Provinces, Luzon. Also called Bikol.

Bicolano, Iriga: 180,000 speakers reported in 1975, around Iriga City in Camarines Sur Province, Luzon. Also called Rinconada Bicolano. Speakers are bilingual in Central Bicolano and Tagalog.

Bicolano, Northern Catanduanes: 65,000 speakers reported in 1975, in northern Catanduanes Province, Luzon. Also called Pandan. Some bilingualism in Central Bicolano.

Bicolano, Southern Catanduanes: 85,000 speakers reported in 1981, in southern Catanduanes Province, Luzon. Also called Virac. Speakers are bilingual in Central Bicolano.

Butuanon: spoken in Butuan City, Mindanao. Speakers are fairly bilingual in Cebuano.

Caluyanun: 20,000 speakers reported in 1981, in the Caluya Islands, Antique Province. Also called Caluyanen or Caluyanhon.

Capiznon: around 446,000 speakers reported in 1975, on northeastern Panay Island. Also called Capisano or Capiseño. Speakers are bilingual in Hiligaynon or Tagalog.

Cebuano: 12,000,000 speakers reported in 1989, in Negros, Cebu, Bohol, Visayas, and parts of Mindanao. Also spoken in the United States. Also called Sugbuhanon, Sugbuanon, Bisayan, or Binisaya. The Boholano variety is sometimes considered a separate language.

Cuyonon: 93,000 speakers reported in 1983, on the Palawan coast and in the Cuyo Islands. Also called Cuyono, Cuyunon, or Cuyo.

Davaweño: around 125,000 speakers reported in 1975, in Davao Oriental and Davao del Sur Provinces, Mindanao. Also called Matino, Davaoeño, or Davawenyo. Distinct from the Spanish-based Creole Davaweño, which is a dialect of Chavacano. Lowland Davaweño speakers are highly bilingual in Cebuano, highland Davaweño much less so.

Hiligaynon: 4,500,000 speakers reported in 1984, in Iloilo and Capiz Provinces, in Panay, Negros Occidental, and the Visayas. Also spoken in the United States. Also called Ilonggo or Hiligainon.

Kalagan: 60,000 speakers reported in 1987, along the shores of Davao Gulf in Davao del Sur and Davao Oriental Provinces.

Kalagan, Kagan: 6,000 speakers reported in 1981, in Davao City, Mindanao. Also called Kaagan or Kagan Kalagan.

Kalagan, Tagakaulu: around 37,800 speakers reported in 1975, in South Cotabato Province, southern Mindanao. Also called Tagakaolo.

Kamayo: spoken in Surigao del Sur Province, Mindanao. Speakers are fairly bilingual in Cebuano.

Karolanos: spoken on mid-central Negros Island.

Kinaray-A: 288,000 speakers reported in 1981, in Iloilo and Antique Provinces, western Panay. Also called Hinaray-A, Kiniray-A, Karay-A, Antiqueño, Hamtiknon, Sulud, Ati, or Panayano. Speakers also use Tagalog or Hiligaynon.

Loocnon: 30,000 to 40,000 speakers reported in 1984, on southern Tablas Island. Also called Looknon or Unhan. Speakers are fairly bilingual in Hiligaynon.

Magahat: spoken in the area of Mt. Arniyo, southwestern Negros Island. Also called Bukidnon or Ata-Man. Speakers may be bilingual in Cebuano or Hiligaynon.

Malaynon: 8,500 speakers reported in 1973, in the lowlands of northwest Aklan Province, Panay. Vigorous language use.

Mamanwa: 1,500 speakers reported in 1981, in Agusan del Norte and Surigao Provinces, Mindanao. Also called Mamanwa Negrito or Minamanwa.

Mandaya, Cataelano: 19,000 speakers reported in 1980, in Davao Oriental Province, Mindanao. Also called Cateelenyo. Speakers are fairly bilingual in Mansaka.

Mandaya, Karaga: 3,000 speakers reported in 1982, in the Lamiyawan area, Davao Oriental Province, Mindanao. Also called Carraga Mandaya, Manay Mandayan, or Mangaragan Mandaya. Speakers are fairly bilingual in Mansaka.

Mandaya, Sangab: spoken at the head of the Carraga River in the highlands of Davao del Norte Province, Mindanao. Limited bilingualism in Cebuano.

Mansaka: 30,000 to 35,000 speakers reported in 1975, in Davao Oriental Province, Mindanao. Also called Mandaya Mansaka.

Masbatenyo: around 333,000 first-language speakers reported in 1986, along with 150,000 to 200,000 second-language speakers, in Masbate Province. Also called Minasbate or Masbateño. Masbatenyo is used in the home, market, at work, and on the street.

Porohanon: 23,000 speakers reported in 1987, in the Camotes Islands. Also called Camotes. Population includes 54 percent with routine ability and 46 percent with near-native ability in Cebuano.

Ratagnon: a few speakers reported in 1981, on the southern tip of western Mindoro. Also called Datagnon, Latagnun, Latan, Lactan, or Aradigi. Rapidly assimilating to Tagalog.

Romblomanon: 200,000 speakers reported in 1987, on Romblon and Sibuyan Islands, and parts of eastern Tablas Island. Also called Romblon.

Sorsogon, Masbate: 85,000 speakers reported in 1975, in Sorsogon Province, Luzon. Also called Northern Sorsogon or Sorsogon Bicolano. Speakers are fairly bilingual in Tagalog, with some bilingualism in Central Bicolano and Masbatenyo.

Sorsogon, Waray: 185,000 speakers reported in 1975, in southern Sorsogon Province. Also called Southern Sorsogon, Bikol Sorsogon, or Gubat. Speakers are bilingual in Tagalog, Central Bicolano, or Masbatenyo.

Sulod: 14,000 speakers reported in 1980, in Capiz, Iloilo, and Antique Provinces, on Panay. Also called Bukidnon or Mondo. Some bilingualism in Hiligaynon and Kinaray-A.

Surigaonon: spoken in Surigao Province. Speakers are reported to be highly bilingual in Cebuano.

Tagalog: 10,500,000 first-language speakers reported in 1975, with 10,000,000 around Manila and on most of Luzon and Mindoro. Also spoken by 377,000 in the United States, and by populations in Saudi Arabia, the United Arab Emirates, the United Kingdom, Canada, and Guam. Another 4,500,000 use it as a second language. The national language, Pilipino, is based on Tagalog.

Tausug: 492,000 speakers reported in 1975, with 330,000 in Jolo, Sulu Archipelago, Philippines; 110,000 in Sabah, Malaysia; and 12,000 in Kalimantan, Indonesia. Another 500,000 in the Philippines speak Tausug as a second language. Also called Taw Sug, Sulu, Suluk, Tausog, or Moro Joloano.

Waray-Waray: 2,180,000 speakers reported in 1984, on Samar and Leyte Islands. Also called Samareño, Samaran, Samar-Leyte, Waray, or Binisaya.

CENTRAL SUDANIC LANGUAGES constitute a group spoken primarily in two geographically separate areas. The western area comprises parts of Sudan, Zaïre, Chad, and the Central African Republic; the eastern comprises parts of Zaïre and adjacent parts of Sudan and Uganda. Central Sudanic forms a subgroup of Nilo-Saharan [*q.v.*], probably a top-level constituent. Joseph H. Greenberg, *The languages of Africa* (Bloomington: Indiana University, 1963) assigned Central Sudanic as a subgroup of Chari-Nile within Nilo-Saharan; however, the unity of Chari-Nile has been questioned in later work. The division of Central Sudanic into East and West subgroups is not universally accepted, but the lower-level groupings as shown in Figure 1 are in general uncontroversial.

FIGURE 1. *Subgrouping of Central Sudanic Languages*

- **East Central Sudanic**
  - **Lendu (Balendru)**
    - Bendi, Lendu, Ngiti
  - **Mangbetu (Mangbetu-Asua)**
    - Asua, Lombi, Mangbele, Mangbetu (proper)
  - **Mangbutu-Efe**
    - Lese, Mamvu-Efe, Mangbutu, Mvu'ba, Ndo
  - **Moru-Madi**
    - **Central Moru-Madi**
      - Avokaya, Kaliko, Logo, High Lugbara, Low Lugbara
    - Northern Moru-Madi (Moru)
    - **Southern Moru-Madi**
      - Luluba, Madi
- **West Central Sudanic**
  - **Bongo-Bagirmi**
    - **Bongo-Baka**
      - Baka
      - Bongo
      - **Morokodo-Beli**
        - Beli
        - Jur Modo
        - Mittu
        - **Morokodo-Mo'da**
          - Mo'da, Morokodo, Nyamusa-Molo
    - **Kara**
      - Furu, Kara, Yulu
    - **Sara-Bagirmi**
      - **Bagirmi**
        - Babalia, Bagirmi (proper), Bilala, Goulai, Gula, Kenga, Kuka, Medogo
      - **Sara**
        - **Sara (proper)**
          - **Kaba**
            - Kaba (proper), Kaba Demi, Kaba Dunjo, Kaba Kurumi, Kaba Na
          - **Unclassified Sara Proper**
            - Dendje, Laka, Mbai, Bediondo Mbai, Ngam, Ngambai, Sar
        - **Vale**
          - Nduka, Tana, Vale (proper)
    - Sinyar
  - Kresh
- **Unclassified Central Sudanic**
  - Horo

LANGUAGE LIST

Asua: spoken in Ituri Forest, Haut-Zaïre Region, Zaïre. Also called Aka, Asuati, or Asuae.

Avokaya: 40,000 speakers reported in 1989, including 15,000 in the basins of the Utua and Dungu rivers and farther east, Western Equatoria Province, southern Sudan. Also spoken by 25,000 in Faradje Zone, Haut-Zaïre Region, Zaïre, close to the Sudan border. Also called Abukeia or Avukaya. Speakers are bilingual in Zande.

Babalia: spoken near Massaguet, in the west central Guera area northeast of Ft. Lamy, Chad. Also called Bubalia. Most speakers are bilingual in Arabic.

Bagirmi: 30,000 to 40,000 speakers reported in 1977, southwest of Guera, below Lake Chad, in Chad, and near Maiduguri, North East State, Nigeria. Also called Baghirmi, Baguirme, Tar Barma, Barma, Tar Bagrimma, Lis, or Lisi. Most speakers are bilingual in Arabic.

Baka: 24,300 speakers reported in 1978, including 23,000 south and west of Maridi and northwest of Yei, Western Equatoria Province, southern Sudan, and 1,300 between Garamba National Park and the Sudan border, Haut-Zaïre Region, Zaïre. Also called Tara Baaka or Mbaka. Distinct from, and unrelated to, Baka of Cameroon. Speakers learn Zande in school. They also intermarry with speakers of Avukaya and Mundu, and are bilingual in their languages.

Beli: 6,600 speakers reported in 1982, in southern Sudan. One group is southwest of Rumbek, at Wulu, westward and south toward the southern border of Lakes Province. In some areas they are heavily intermingled with the Dinka. Another group lives east of Mvolo and has no links with the first group. Also called Behli, Beili, Jur Beli, or 'Beli. Has 46 percent lexical similarity with Jur Modo and 45 percent with Bongo, the most closely related varieties.

Bendi: spoken midway between Bunia and Djalasiga, Djugu Zone, Haut-Zaïre Region, Zaïre. Also called Mabendi. Different from Ngiti (Bindi).

Bilala: 42,000 speakers reported in 1967, north of Lake Fitri, Guera Region, Chad. Also called Boulala, Mage, or Ma.

Bongo: 5,000 to 10,000 speakers reported in 1987, in a large sparsely populated area south of Tonj and Wau, Sudan. Also called Bungu or Dor. Most adults understand Zande, and men understand Dinka Rek.

Dendje: spoken in Chad. Also called Dinje.

Furu: 12,000 speakers reported in 1984, east of Bosobolo in Bosobolo and Mobaye Zones, Nord Ubangi Subregion, Équateur Region, Zaïre. Most speakers are bilingual in Lingala, Sango, Mono, or Gbanziri; but Lingala comprehension is limited.

Goulai: 80,000 speakers reported in 1989, from Sahr to Lai and between Lai and Kourma, southern Chad. Also called Goulei, Gulai, or Goulaye. The people speak Sar as a lingua franca.

Gula: spoken in southeast Chad and in the southeastern Central African Republic. Different from Gula of Chad, which is Adamawa.

Horo: spoken in the the Central African Republic. Possibly in the Sara group.

Jur Modo: 15,400 speakers reported in 1982, in the vicinity of Mvolo and on the Naam (Era) River, southern Sudan.

Kaba: 11,000 speakers reported in 1971, in the Central African Republic primarily, and in Chad, at the eastern end of the northern belt of the Sara-Bagirmi group. Also called Kabba, Sara Kaba, or Sara. Different from Kaba of Ethiopia, which is Cushitic.

Kaba Demi: spoken in Chad. Also called Kaba Dem.

Kaba Dunjo: 17,000 speakers reported in 1971, in the Central African Republic. Also called Sara.

Kaba Kurumi: spoken in Chad. May be mutually intelligible with other Kaba languages. Speakers are bilingual in Sar.

Kaba Na: spoken in Chad. Also called Kaba Nar.

Kaliko: 18,000 speakers reported in 1971, including 10,000 or more south of the Nzoro River, Aru Zone, Haut-Zaïre Region, Zaïre, and 7,000 in the southern part of Yei District, southern Sudan. Also called Keliko or Maditi.

Kara: 800 speakers reported in 1987, at Kafia Kingi in extreme western Bahr el Ghazal Province, and at Kata, in southern Sudan; also spoken near the Sudan border at Kafia Kingi, Central African Republic. Also called Yamegi. Different from Karo of Ethiopia which is Omotic; from Kara of Ethiopia and Israel, which is Cushitic; and from Kare or Kari of Chad, a Niger-Congo language. Many speakers are bilingual in Kresh or Arabic.

Kenga: 20,000 to 25,000 speakers reported in 1971, west of Biltine, Chad. Also called Kenge, Kenya, Cenge, or Bokiyo. Most men are bilingual in Arabic.

Kresh: 16,000 speakers reported in 1987, in Western Bahr el Ghazal Province, southern Sudan. The second language of 4,000 speakers of other languages. Also called Kparla, Kpala, Kpara, Kreish, Kredj, or Kreich. Men and those who have been to school speak Sudanese Arabic as a second language for most everyday topics.

Kuka: 38,000 speakers reported in 1967, around Ati and Lake Fitri, Chad. The people are somewhat bilingual in Arabic.

Laka: 40,000 speakers reported in 1971, from Paoua to the Baibokoum area, southwest Chad. Also in the Central African Republic. Also called Kabba Laka. Different from Laka (Lakka) of Cameroon, which is Adamawa-Ubangi.

Lendu: 490,000 speakers reported in 1989, west and northwest of Lake Mobutu (Lake Albert), Djugu Zone, Ituri Subregion, Haut-Zaïre Region, Zaïre. Also called Bbadha, Bbaledha, Kilendu, Baletha, Batha, Balendru, Bale, Hema-Nord, or Kihema-Nord.

Lese: 35,000 speakers reported in 1972, in Irumu and Mambasa Zones, Haut-Zaïre Region, Zaïre. Also called Lesa, Lesse, Lissi, Walisi, Walese, Balese, or Mbuti. Zaïre Swahili (Kingwana) is the lingua franca; but its use is somewhat limited, especially north of Mambasa, among pygmies and among women.

Logo: 210,000 or more speakers reported in 1989, Faradje Zone and north of Watsa in Watsa Zone, Haut-Zaïre Region, Zaïre, and a few in Yei District, southern Sudan. Also called Logo Kuli or Logoti.

Lombi: 8,100 speakers reported in 1977, in the southern part of Bafwasende Zone, Haut-Zaïre Region, Zaïre. Also called Lumbi, Rombi, Rumli, or Odyalombito. Different from the Lombi dialect of Basa in Cameroon.

Lugbara, High: 320,000 speakers reported in 1986 in northwestern Uganda, plus others in Aru Zone, Haut-Zaïre Region, Zaïre. Also called Terego Lugbara. Used in primary education. Has 68 percent lexical similarity with Low Lugbara.

Lugbara, Low: 600,000 speakers reported in 1988, north of Lake Albert in the northwestern corner of Uganda. Also called Andre-Lebati or Aringa Lugbara. Has 68 percent lexical similarity with High Lugbara.

Luluba: 15,000 speakers reported in 1985, about thirty miles east of the Nile River, eastern Equatoria Province, southern Sudan. Also spoken in Uganda. Also called Olubogo, Oluboti, or Olu'bo. Many speakers are bilingual in Bari.

Madi: around 233,000 speakers reported in 1976, with 215,000 near Nimule, West Nile District, Madi Province, Uganda, and 18,000 in Opari and West Nile Districts, Equatoria Province, Sudan. Also called Ma'adi, Ma'diti, or Ma'di.

Mamvu-Efe: 40,000 speakers reported in 1971, west and southwest of Watsa, Haut-Zaïre Region, Zaïre. There may be some speakers in Uganda. Mamvu and Efe may not be one language.

Mangbele: spoken in Rungu Zone, Haut-Zaïre Region, Zaïre. Also called Majuu.

Mangbetu: 650,000 speakers reported in 1985, in Rungu, Niangara, and Poko Zones, and the northeast corner of Banalia Zone, Haut-Zaïre Region, Zaïre; also on the border north of Lake Albert, Uganda. Also called Nemangbetu, Mangbettu, Mambetto, Amangbetu, or Kingbetu. Perhaps 50 percent of speakers know Bangala well, and another 10 percent know a limited amount.

Mangbutu: 8,000 speakers reported in 1971, south of Watsa, Haut-Zaïre Region, Zaïre. Also called Mombuttu or Wambutu.

Mbai: 100,000 speakers reported in 1981, in the Moissala area, southern Chad. Also in the Central African Republic, with a few speakers in Cameroon and Nigeria. Also called Sara Mbai or Moissala Mbai.

Mbai, Bediondo: spoken in Chad. Mbai Doba and Gor may be mutually intelligible with this.

Medogo: spoken in Chad. Also called Mud. Most speakers are bilingual in Arabic.

Mittu: now extinct, formerly spoken in southern Sudan.

Mo'da: 600 speakers reported in 1977, northwest of Mvolo, on both sides of the border of Lakes and Western Equatoria Provinces, southern Sudan. Also called Gberi, Gweri, Gbara, or Muda. Has 64 percent lexical similarity with Morokodo, 58 percent with Jur Modo, 41 percent with Beli, 49 percent with Bongo, and 38 percent with Baka.

Morokodo: 3,400 or more speakers reported in 1977, between Amadi and Maridi, southern Sudan. Also called Ma'di. Has 63 percent lexical similarity with Jur Modo, the most closely related variety. Speakers are bilingual in Moru.

Moru: 70,000 speakers reported in 1982, in Mundri District, Equatoria Province, southern Sudan. Also called Kala Moru.

Mvu'ba: 5,000 speakers reported in 1981, around Oicha, in Beni Zone, Nord Kivu Subregion, Kivu Region, Zaïre; also in Uganda. Also called Mbuba, Mvuba, Bambuba, Bamvuba, Mvuba-A, or Obiye.

Ndo: 13,000 speakers reported in 1971, primarily west and northwest of Djalasiga, in Mahagi and Aru Zones, Haut-Zaïre Region, Zaïre. Also around Mahigi in northwestern Uganda. Also called Ke'bu, Oke'bu, or Kebutu. In some areas, Bangala is the lingua franca; in others, Zaïre Swahili.

Nduka: spoken in the Central African Republic. May be a dialect of Vale.

Ngam: spoken south of Sarh, Maro Subprefecture, Moyen-Chari District, southern Chad; also spoken in Kabo Subprefecture in the northern Central African Republic. Also called Ngama or Sarngam. Sar is the local lingua franca. Distinct from Gam of Chad, a Chadic language.

Ngambai: 600,000 speakers reported in 1989, around Moundou in Logone District, southwest Chad. A few speakers in Cameroon and Nigeria. Also called Sara, Sara Ngambai, Gamba, Gambaye, or Gamblai.

Ngiti: spoken south of Bunia, Haut-Zaïre Region, Zaïre. Also called KiNgiti, Ngeti, KiNgeti, Lendu-Sud, Druna, or Bindi. Distinct from Bendi.

Nyamusa-Molo: 1,200 speakers reported in 1977, southeast of Beli and northeast of Morokodo, western Equatoria Province, southern Sudan. There is 84 percent lexical similarity between Nyamusa and Molo, and 70 to 75 percent between these and Jur Modo.

Sar: 50,000 speakers reported in 1989, south of Sarh, south central Chad; also spoken in the Central African Republic. Also called Madjingaye, Madja Ngai, Sara Madjingay, or Majingai-Ngama. It is the principal language of Sarh and the area west of Kabe.

Sinyar: 5,000 to 10,000 speakers reported in 1983, at Mogororo, Chad, on the border with Sudan. Also called Sinya or Shemya.

Tana: spoken by some 35,000 people in Chad and the Central African Republic. Also called Tane or Tele. May be mutually intelligible with Vale.

Vale: spoken by around 1,400 people in the Central African Republic and Chad. Also called Louto. May be mutually intelligible with Nduka and/or Tana.

Yulu: 3,000 or more speakers reported in 1987, at Khor Buga west of Raga in western Bahr el Ghazal Province, southern Sudan; also in Habbaniya District, Dar Fur Province, and at Menangba, west of Raga; also spoken in Zaïre and the Central African Republic. Many speakers are bilingual in Kresh or Arabic.

CENTRAL SULAWESI LANGUAGES constitute a top-level constituent of the Sulawesi family within West Malayo-Polynesian [*qq.v.*]. Merritt Ruhlen, *A guide to the world's languages,* vol. 1, *Classification* (Stanford, Calif.: Stanford University Press, 1987), divides the Central Sulawesi languages into the following subgroups: Bungku-Mori, East Central Sulawesi, Kaili-Pamona, and Tomini [*qq.v.*], plus the isolated Banggai and Balaesan languages. For data on these last, see the Language List below.

LANGUAGE LIST

Balaesan: 4,000 speakers reported in 1979, in central Sulawesi, Indonesia. Also called Balaesang, Balaisang, or Pajo.

Banggai: 100,000 to 115,000 speakers reported in 1987, in central Sulawesi. Also called Aki.

CHADIC LANGUAGES. The Chadic family includes some 140 languages spoken in the sub-Saharan region of Africa to the west, south, and east of Lake Chad, from which the family gets its name. Excluding Hausa [*q.v.*], the best known and most populous Chadic language, the family occupies an area which is a rough rectangle, extending from 9° to 13° N. and from 9° to 19° E. (See Map 1). The other languages, many of which have never been described beyond short word lists, are spoken by as many as a half million to as few as fifty people. Most Chadic languages are still unwritten, apart from occasional scriptural texts prepared by Christian missionaries.

Chadic is a constituent of the A[fro-]A[siatic] phylum [*q.v.*] (Newman 1980). Resemblances between individual Chadic languages and other AA families had been noted since the mid 19th century, but the relationship was not generally accepted until a century later, following the publication of Greenberg 1963. The now standard internal classification of Chadic is that of Newman 1977, building on the work of Greenberg and of Lukas 1936. A comprehensive list of languages in the family is shown in Figure 1.

FIGURE 1. *Subgrouping of Chadic Languages*

West Branch
- **Subgroup A**
  - A.1. Gwandara, Hausa
  - A.2. Bele, Bole, Deno, Galambu, Gera, Geruma, Kanakuru, Karekare, Kirfi, Kubi, Kupto, Kwami, Maha, Ngamo, Pero, Piya, Tangale
  - A.3. Angas, Chip, Gerka, Goemai, Jorto, Koenoem, Kofyar, Mapun, Montol, Pyapun, Sura, Tal
  - A.4. Fyer, Karfa, Kulere, Mundat, Ron, Sha, Shagawu
- **Subgroup B**
  - B.1. Bade, Duwai, Ngizim
  - B.2. Diri, Jimbin, Kariya, Mburku, Miya, Pa'a, Siri, Tsagu, Warji
  - B.3. Barawa, Boghom, Dass, Geji, Guruntum, Ju, Mangas, Polci, Saya, Zangwal, Zari, Zeem

Biu-Mandara Branch
- **Subgroup A**
  - A.1. Ga'anda, Hwana, Jara, Tera
  - A.2. Bura, Chibak, Kilba, Margi, Nggwahi, Putai
  - A.3. Bana, Higi, Kapsiki
  - A.4. Dghwede, Glavda, Guduf, Gvoko, Lamang, Mabas, Mandara, Podoko, Xedi
  - A.5. Baldamu, Chuvok, Dugwor, Gaduwa, Gemzek, Giziga, Mada, Mafa, Matal, Mbuku, Mefele, Merey, Mofu, Moloko, Muyang, Ndreme, Ouldeme, Zulgo
  - A.6. Sukur
  - A.7. Buwal, Daba, Gawar, Hina, Mbedam
  - A.8. Bachama-Bata, Gude, Gudu, Jimi, Njanyi, Tsuvan, Vimtim, Ziziliveken
- **Subgroup B**
  - B.1. Buduma, Jina, Kotoko, Logone, Maslam, Midah
  - B.2. Musgu
- **Subgroup C**
  - Gidar

East Branch
- **Subgroup A**
  - A.1. Gadang, Miltu, Mod, Ndam, Sarwa, Somrai, Tumak
  - A.2. Gabri, Kabalai, Lele, Nancere, Tobanga
  - A.3. Kera, Kwang
- **Subgroup B**
  - B.1. Bidiya, Birgit, Dangaleat, Jegu, Kujarke, Mawa, Mesmedje, Migama, Mogum, Mubi, Toram
  - B.2. Mukulu
  - B.3. Barain, Saba, Sokoro

Masa Branch
- Marba, Masa, Mesme, Musey, Zime-Lame, Zumaya

Chadic languages typically have many consonants and few vowels. A common pattern is characterized by a set of glottalized (implosive and/or ejective) consonants alongside the voiced and voiceless ones. However, the glottal stop is not a standard Chadic phoneme. Many languages also have full sets of prenasalized phonemes. Another typical feature is the presence of voiceless, voiced, and (much less often) glottalized lateral fricatives /ɬ ɮ ɬ'/. Margi and closely related languages are unusual in having simultaneously articulated labial-dental and labial-palatal consonants, e.g. /ɓɗ bz pč/.

Typical vowel systems range from two vowels, as in Mandara, to nine (with vowel harmony), as in Tangale; the most common patterns are /i (e) a ə (o) u/ and /i e a o u/. Distinctive vowel length is widespread in the family, but is often limited to word-medial position. Contrary to the common AA pattern, Chadic languages generally allow vowel-initial words. All Chadic languages are tonal; but the function of tone in many cases is primarily grammatical, rather than lexical.

Grammatical gender is commonplace, although not omnipresent in Chadic. There are always two genders, masculine and feminine, with no distinction in the plural. Pronouns distinguish gender in both 2nd and 3rd persons. Verbs are not conjugated for person, but there are scattered instances of number agreement with the subject. Chadic languages exhibit a multiplicity of noun plural formations—involving suffixes (e.g. *-*aki*, *-V*n*, *-*i*),

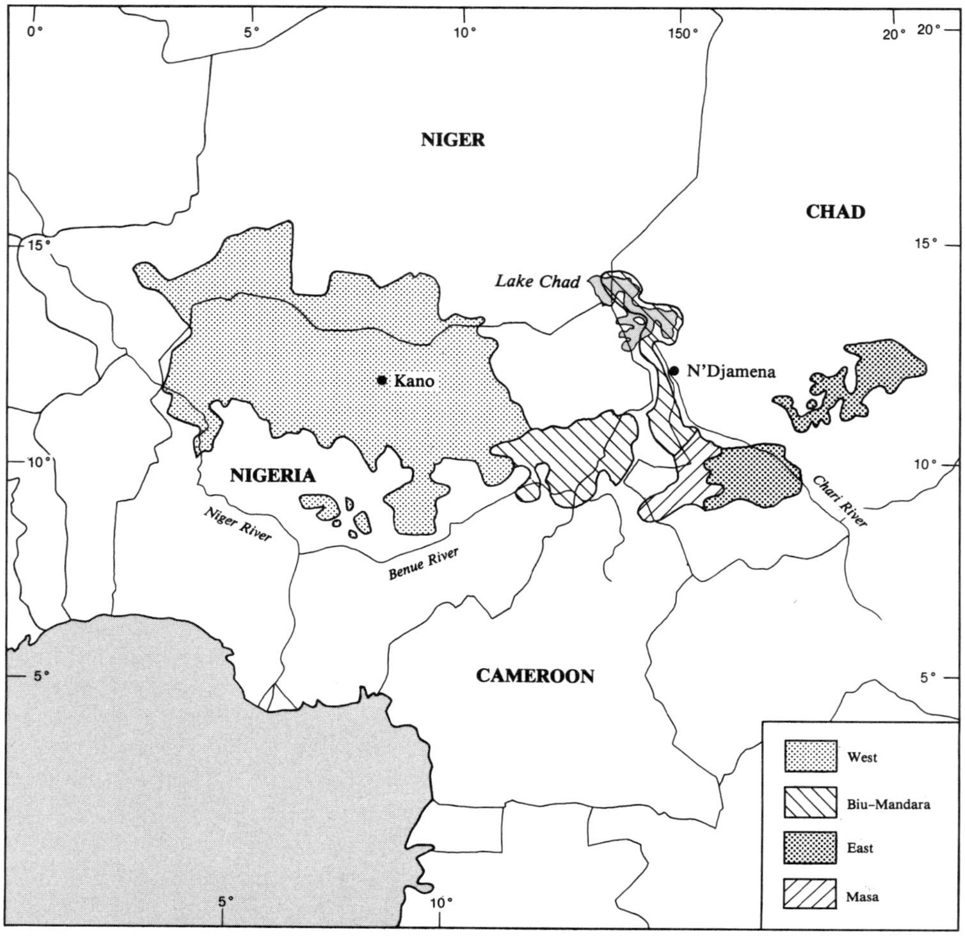

MAP 1. *Distribution of Major Groups of Chadic Languages*

internal vowel changes, and reduplication. Many languages also have 'pluractional' verbs, which indicate an action done many times or involving a number of subjects or objects; these commonly use some of the same processes as noun plurals.

Verbs typically allow one or more suffixal extensions which express action in, towards, down, or away—as well as partially, completely, or well done. Sometimes the extensions are more grammatical in nature, indicating benefactive, perfective, causative, or transitive constructions.

The most common word order is S[ubject] V[erb] O[bject]. A small number of languages in one branch (Biu-Mandara) are VSO; this may be an archaism, reflecting original Proto-Chadic order. All Chadic languages are prepositional. Within the noun phrase, the noun is generally followed by numeral, adjective, or demonstrative; possessed precedes possessor. [*For data on individual Chadic languages, see the Language Lists after the following articles:* Biu-Mandara Languages, East Chadic Languages, Masa Languages, *and* West Chadic Languages.]

PAUL NEWMAN

BIBLIOGRAPHY

GREENBERG, JOSEPH H. 1963. *The languages of Africa.* (Indiana University Research Center in Anthropology, Folklore, and Linguistics, publication 25; International Journal of American Linguistics, 29:1, part 2.) Bloomington: Indiana University.

LUKAS, JOHANNES. 1936. The linguistic situation in the Lake Chad area in Central Africa. *Africa* 9.332–349.

NEWMAN, PAUL. 1977. *Chadic classification and reconstructions.* (Afroasiatic linguistics, 5:1.) Malibu: Undena.

NEWMAN, PAUL. 1980. *The classification of Chadic within Afroasiatic.* Leiden: Universitaire Pers.

FIGURE 1. *Subgrouping of Chapacura Languages*

Guapore
 Itene, Kabixí
Madeira
 Pakaás-novos, Torá, Urupá

CHAPACURA LANGUAGES constitute a group spoken in northeastern Bolivia and adjacent parts of Brazil; the family may be related to Arawakan [*q.v.*]. The subgrouping is shown in Figure 1.

LANGUAGE LIST

Itene: spoken at the junction of the Mamoré and Itenez rivers, Bolivia. Also called Iteneo, Itenez, or More. In 1955, children were not speaking Itene, and only some older people were actively using it.

Kabixí: 100 speakers reported in 1986 on the slopes of the Planalto dos Parecís, Mato Grosso State, Brazil. The name is also used for Parecís or Nambikuara.

Pakaás-novos: 990 to 1,150 speakers reported in 1986 in Rondônia State, Brazil. Also called Jaru, Uomo, Pacahanovo, or Oro Wari.

Torá: 17 speakers reported in 1986, on the lower Rio Marmelos, Amazonas State, Brazil. Also called Toraz.

Urupá: 150 to 250 speakers reported in 1986 in Rondônia State, Brazil. Also called Txapakura.

CHIBCHAN LANGUAGES constitute a family of southern Central America and northernmost South America. The precise extent of the family is controversial, although there is a core group of languages which are generally agreed to be genetically related. The concept of Chibchan adopted here (see Figure 1) corresponds essentially to the Nuclear Chibchan of Joseph H. Greenberg, *Language in the Americas* (Stanford, Calif.: Stanford University Press, 1987), p. 382—but with the exclusion of Misumalpan [*q.v.*], and with the inclusion of Cofan (which Greenberg assigns to Jivaroan [*q.v.*]) and of Paya, which Greenberg assigns to Chibchan but not to Nuclear Chibchan. On the Chibchan affiliation of Paya, see Lyle Campbell, 'Middle American languages', pp. 941–944, in Lyle Campbell and Marianne Mithun, eds., *The languages of native America* (Austin: University of Texas Press, 1979), pp. 902–1000.

FIGURE 1. *Subgrouping of Chibchan Languages*

Antioquia (extinct)
Aruak
 Chimila, Cogui, Ica, Malayo
Chibchan Proper
 Chibcha, Tunebo
Cofán
Guaymí
 Buglere, Guaymí (proper)
Kuna
Motilón
Paya
Rama
 Maléku Jaíka, Rama (proper)
Talamanca
 Boruca, Bribri, Cabécar, Teribe

LANGUAGE LIST

Boruca: 5 women speakers reported in 1986, on the southern coast of Costa Rica. Also called Borunca, Burunca, or Brunca. Other members of the ethnic group speak only Spanish.

Bribri: around 4,000 speakers reported in 1982, in Costa Rica. Also called Talamanca. Spoken in the home.

Buglere: around 2,500 speakers reported in 1986, in western Panama. Also called Bogota, Bofota, Bobota, Bocota, Bukueta, Nortenyo, Murire, or Veraguas Sabanero.

Cabécar: around 3,000 speakers reported in 1986, in the Turrialba region of Costa Rica. Also called Chirripó. Population includes 80 percent nearly monolingual, and 20 percent with nearly native ability in Spanish.

Chibcha: now extinct, formerly spoken in the central highlands of Colombia. Also called Muisca or Mosca.

Chimila: spoken by 300 people in the lowlands near the Sierra Nevada de Santa Marta, Colombia. Also called Caca Weranos, San Jorge, or Shimizya. Language use is vigorous, with limited Spanish. There are two major groups, who live apart from each other as enemies.

Cofán: spoken by 700 people on both sides of the Colombia-Ecuador border. Also called Kofán, Kofane, or A'i. Population includes 34 percent nearly monolingual, 53 percent with routine ability, and 13 percent with nearly native ability in Spanish.

Cogui: around 3,000 to 5,000 speakers reported in 1982, on the northern and western slopes of the Sierra Nevada de Santa Marta, Colombia. Also called Coghui, Kagaba, or Kaggaba. Population includes 99 percent nearly monolingual, and 1 percent with routine ability in Spanish.

Guaymí: around 45,000 speakers reported in 1980, from northeastern Panama, with a few in Costa Rica. Also called Valiente, Chiriqui, Ngobere, or Ngäbere. Population includes 70 percent nearly monolingual, 25 percent with routine ability, and 4 percent with nearly native ability in Spanish. Ngäbere is the name preferred by speakers.

Ica: around 2,000 to 3,000 speakers reported in 1977, in the southern slopes of the Sierra Nevada de Santa Marta,

Colombia. Also called Aruaco, Arhuaco, Bintuk, Bintukua, Ijca, or Ike. The people use the name Ica for themselves.

Kuna, Paya-Pucuro: 650 to 850 speakers reported in 1982, with 400 to 600 in Colombia and 250 in Panama, on the Caribbean coast into the Panama isthmus. Also called Colombia Cuna, Caiman Nuevo, or Cuna.

Kuna, San Blas: around 35,000 speakers reported in 1980, on the San Blas Islands and adjoining mainland, Panama. Population includes 80 percent nearly monolingual, 14 percent with routine ability, and 6 percent with nearly native ability in Spanish or English.

Malayo: spoken by around 1,000 people on the southern and eastern slopes of the Sierra Nevada de Santa Marta, Colombia. Also called Marocasero, Maracasero, Sanja, Sanka, or Arosario.

Maléku Jaíka: 365 speakers reported in 1985, in northern Costa Rica. Also called Guatuso. Population includes 62 percent with routine ability, and 38 percent with nearly native ability in Spanish.

Motilón: 1,500 to 2,000 speakers reported in 1980, with 650 to 1,150 in Colombia, and 850 in Venezuela, in the Oro and Catatumbo River region. Also called Bari or Motilone.

Paya: 200 to 300 speakers from an ethnic population of 600 to 800 reported in 1990, on the north central coast of Honduras. Also called Taya, Tawka, or Seco.

Rama: 15 to 20 speakers reported in 1981 from an ethnic population of 649, in Nicaragua. Most people now speak Rama Cay Creole, a form of Bluefields Creole English.

Teribe: 1,000 speakers reported in 1982 in Panama, along with 5 in Costa Rica. Also called Terraba, Tiribi, Tirribi, Nortenyo, Quequexque, or Naso. Naso is the name preferred by speakers.

Tunebo, Angosturas: spoken in Colombia. Some bilingualism in Spanish. Has 71 percent mutual intelligibility with Barro Negro Tunebo.

Tunebo, Barro Negro: 300 or more speakers reported in 1981, in the Andes foothills south of Tame, Colombia. Also called Eastern Tunebo. Partial bilingualism in Spanish. Tunebo is used exclusively in the home. Has 62 percent mutual intelligibility with Central Tunebo.

Tunebo, Central: 1,500 or more speakers reported in 1982, on the north slopes of the Sierra Nevada de Cocuy and in the Boyacá and Arauca regions of Colombia, with some in Venezuela. Also called Cobaría Tunebo. Population includes 85 percent nearly monolingual, and 14 percent with routine ability in Spanish.

Tunebo, Western: spoken in Santander del Sur, Colombia. Also called Aguas Blancas.

CHILD LANGUAGE. *See* Acquisition of Language; *see also* Discourse, *article on* Acquisition of Competence.

CHIMAKUAN LANGUAGES constitute a language family of northwestern Washington, United States, comprising two languages. Possibilities for external genetic relationships, the most plausible being with Wakashan, are surveyed by William H. Jacobsen, 'Chimakuan comparative studies', in *The languages of native America,* edited by Lyle Campbell and Marianne Mithun (Austin: University of Texas Press, 1979), pp. 792–802.

LANGUAGE LIST

Chimakum: an extinct language formerly spoken on the Puget Sound side of the Olympic Peninsula, Washington.

Quileute: possibly 10 speakers reported in 1977 from a population of 300, on the Pacific side of the Olympic Peninsula, Washington.

CHINANTECAN LANGUAGES, spoken in Oaxaca State, Mexico, constitute a branch of Otomanguean [*q.v.*]. The fourteen languages of this family are listed below.

LANGUAGE LIST

Chinanteco, Chiltepec: around 2,000 to 3,000 speakers reported in 1977. Some bilingualism in Spanish. Tlacoatzintepec, the most closely related variety, is 76 percent intelligible.

Chinanteco, Comaltepec: around 1,400 speakers reported in 1982, in northern Oaxaca. Population includes 55 percent near-monolinguals, 43 percent with routine ability, and 2 percent with near-native ability in Spanish. Quiotepec, the most closely related variety, is 69 percent intelligible.

Chinanteco, Lalana: around 10,000 speakers reported in 1982, on the Oaxaca-Veracruz border, Mexico. Population includes 79 percent near-monolinguals, 20 percent with routine ability, and 1 percent with near-native ability in Spanish. Tepinapa, the most closely related variety, is 87 percent intelligible.

Chinanteco, Lealao: 800 to 900 speakers reported in 1982, in northern Oaxaca. Also called Latani Chinanteco. Population includes 50 percent near-monolinguals; 50 percent have routine ability in Spanish.

Chinanteco, Ojitlán: spoken by around 10,000 people in northern Oaxaca. Sochiapan, the most closely related variety, is 49 percent intelligible.

Chinanteco, Ozumacín: around 2,000 speakers reported in 1977, in northern Oaxaca. Also called Ayotzintepec. Palantla, the most closely related variety, is 63 percent intelligible.

Chinanteco, Palantla: around 10,600 speakers reported in 1982, in Oaxaca. Population includes 35 percent near-monolinguals, 60 percent with routine ability, and 5 percent with near-native ability in Spanish. Tepetotutla, the most closely related variety, is 78 percent intelligible.

Chinanteco, Quiotepec: around 5,000 speakers reported in 1982, in northwestern Oaxaca. Also called Highland Chinanteco. Population includes 55 percent near-monolinguals, 30 percent with routine ability, and 15 percent with near-native ability in Spanish. Comaltepec, the most closely related variety, is 87 percent intelligible.

Chinanteco, Sochiapan: around 2,500 to 3,000 speakers reported in 1982, in northern Oaxaca. Population includes 60 percent near-monolinguals, 33 percent with routine ability, and 7 percent with near-native ability in Spanish. Tlacoatzintepec, the most closely related variety, is 66 percent intelligible.

Chinanteco, Tepetotutla: around 1,000 speakers reported in 1977, in northern Oaxaca. Quiotepec, the most closely related variety, is 60 percent intelligible.

Chinanteco, Tepinapa: spoken by 2,000 to 3,000 people in Oaxaca. Comaltepec, the most closely related variety, is 79 percent intelligible.

Chinanteco, Tlacoatzintepec: around 1,000 speakers reported in 1983, in Oaxaca. Population includes 90 percent near-monolinguals, 10 percent with routine ability in Spanish. Chiltepec, the most closely related variety, is 85 percent intelligible.

Chinanteco, Usila: around 10,000 speakers reported in 1985, in Oaxaca. Population includes 80 percent near-monolinguals, 17 percent with routine ability, and 3 percent with near-native ability in Spanish. Tlacoatzintepec, the most closely related variety, is 48 percent intelligible.

Chinanteco, Valle Nacional: spoken by 3,000 to 5,000 people in northern Oaxaca. High bilingualism in Spanish. Chiltepec, the most closely related variety, is 71 percent intelligible.

CHINESE.

As a language name, 'Chinese' is highly ambiguous. It is used to designate any of the following spoken languages: the official spoken language of the People's Republic of China, where the language is called Pǔtōnghuà; the official spoken language of Taiwan *(Guóyǔ)*; one of the official languages of Singapore *(Huáyǔ)*; or any of the hundreds of regional variants ('dialects') spoken in China. It may also refer to various versions of the written language of an enormous body of literature. Some of this literature represents the vernacular language of different historical periods, and some represents highly stylized written languages used exclusively in certain literary genres. (For reference, see Wáng 1947, 1957–58, Forrest 1948, Karlgren 1949, Chao 1968, Li & Thompson 1978, 1981, DeFrancis 1984, Ramsey 1987, and Norman 1988.)

There is, however, a significant degree of commonality behind the diverse reality of the Chinese language. This commonality is manifested in these facts:

(a) The vast majority of the people of China speak one of the Mandarin dialects.
(b) The Mandarin dialects are by and large mutually intelligible.
(c) The official spoken languages of China, Taiwan, and Singapore are all based on the Běijīng dialect of the Mandarin group.
(d) The contemporary written language used by the Chinese people is primarily based on the Běijīng dialect.

1. Genetic classification and dialects. The various forms of spoken Chinese, which will be designated as 'dialects' in this article, constitute an independent branch of the Sino-Tibetan language family [*q.v.*]. Parallel to Chinese, but distantly related to it, is the Tibeto-Burman subfamily, with the Karen languages sometimes considered a third subfamily rather than a branch of Tibeto-Burman. Within the Chinese branch are hundreds of dialects, many of them mutually unintelligible. These dialects are classified into seven groups, primarily on the basis of phonological evidence, as listed below (see Map 1). [*For further data on individual dialect groups, see the Language List at the end of this article.*]

1.1. ***Mandarin*** dialects are spoken natively by about two-thirds of the one billion people in China. The geographical range of Mandarin includes all of north China, west China, part of central China, and the Sìchuān basin, as well as Guìzhōu and Yúnnán provinces in the South. This large dialect group is often divided into four subgroups, according to their phonological and lexical affinities and their geographical range: (i) Northern Mandarin, (ii) Northwestern Mandarin, (iii) Southwestern Mandarin, and (iv) Eastern or Lower Yángzě River Mandarin. The common characteristics of the Mandarin dialects are: the absence of voiced stops [b d g]; the absence of syllable-final consonants [p t k m]; and a relatively simple system of tones (usually four), with fewer tone sandhi rules. (In the standard Pīnyīn transcription of Mandarin, the symbols *b d g* represent voiceless unaspirated stops, while *p t k* are aspirated.)

1.2. ***Wú*** dialects are spoken around the coastal area of the lower Yángzě River and its tributaries, in the provinces of Jiāngsū, Zhèjiāng, and Ānhuī. Speakers of Wú occupy an area roughly the size of the state of Illinois. The most important feature of Wú dialects is the three-way phonemic distinction between voiced stops, voiceless unaspirated stops, and voiceless aspirated stops in syllable-initial position: [b d g] vs. [p t k] vs. [pʻ tʻ kʻ]. This three-way contrast of stops is attested in M[iddle] C[hinese] (7th c. BCE).

1.3. ***Gàn*** dialects are spoken primarily in Jiāngxī province, to the southwest of the Wú area. The region and its dialect group are named after the Gàn River, which traverses the province from north to south. Some linguists consider Gàn a subgroup of Mandarin. The major difference between Mandarin and Gàn lies in the historical development of the MC voiced stops [b d g]. In Gàn, these have become voiceless aspirated stops [pʻ tʻ kʻ]. (In Mandarin, the historical development of the voiced stops is more varied.)

1.4. ***Xiāng*** dialects are spoken in Húnán province, to the immediate west of the Gàn dialect area. The name Xiāng refers to a river which runs from north to south

MAP 1. *Distribution of Dialects of Chinese*

in Húnán province, as a tributary of the Yángzĕ. There are two dialect groups, 'Old' and 'New'. Old Xiāng, like Wú, preserves the MC voiced stops [b d g]. But unlike the Northern Wú dialects—which typically associate these voiced stops with some sort of laryngeal activity, described as 'murmuring'—the voiced stops in Old Xiāng do not have any unusual phonetic property. New Xiāng, like Mandarin, has lost the series of voiced stops. (In fact, there is no systematic distinction between New Xiāng and Mandarin, which have a greater degree of mutual intelligibility than Old Xiāng and New Xiāng.) Old Xiāng is spoken primarily in rural communities, and New Xiāng in northwest Húnán, as well as in urban areas all over the province. It is likely that New Xiāng has become more and more distant from Old Xiāng because of contact with Mandarin.

1.5. ***Mǐn*** is spoken in the southern coastal province of Fújiàn and the island of Taiwan, as well as the northern coast, the Léizhōu peninsula, and Hăinán island of Guăngdōng province. Mǐn dialects are numerous, and often mutually unintelligible: in Fújiàn province alone, nine mutually unintelligible subgroups of dialects have been reported. In addition, the dialects of northern coastal Guăngdōng and of Hăinán island (Mǐn Nán or Southern Min) are significantly different from the Mǐn dialects of other areas. The definitive characteristic of Mǐn is the contrast between the voiceless aspirated dental stop [t'] and voiceless unaspirated [t] in a particular set of words meaning, e.g., 'tree', 'know', 'hail', and 'insect'.

1.6. ***Yuè*** dialects occupy most of Guăngdōng and Guăngxī provinces. The standard dialect is the speech of the city of Guăngzhōu, known as Cantonese; this is also the language of Hong Kong, and of many overseas Chinese settlements in North America, Europe, and Southeast Asia. Yuè dialects preserve all the MC syllable-final consonants [p t k m n ŋ]. (See O. Y. Hashimoto 1971.)

1.7. ***Kèjiā or Hakka*** dialects are distributed throughout southeastern China, in small agricultural communities in Yuè and Mǐn dialect areas. Historically, they were northerners who moved south during several waves of migration. The name Hakka is a word of Cantonese origin, meaning 'guests'; *Kèjiā* is the pronunciation of *Hakka* in Beijing Mandarin. The Kèjiā dialects share with the Gàn dialects the feature that MC voiced stops have developed into corresponding voiceless aspirated stops [p' t' k']. But differences in other phonological features, as well as in lexicon, keep the two groups separate. It has been assumed that the Kèjiā dialects are relatively homogeneous; however, as new information emerges, this assumption may prove wrong. (See M. J. Hashimoto 1973.)

Although Chinese dialects are numerous and their geographical spread enormous, they share a number of grammatical features; those described below are salient (see Yuán et al. 1960).

2. Tone. In Chinese, every syllable which is not destressed has a contrastive pitch pattern, called its TONE. This pattern is significant because it distinguishes the meanings of words with the same segmental composition, as in the following example from Běijīng Mandarin (the numbers indicate pitch levels, with 5 representing the highest pitch and 1 the lowest):

	Word	Tone	Gloss
(1)	*tōng*	high level (55)	'to open up'
	tóng	high rising (35)	'copper'
	tǒng	low falling-rising (214)	'tub'
	tòng	high falling (51)	'to ache'

Tonal variation accounts for the most common differences among the dialects. With four tones, Běijīng Mandarin has one of the simplest tone systems. In general, the dialects of Wú, Yuè, Mǐn, and Kèjiā tend to have more complex tone systems than Mandarin, Gàn, or Xiāng (see Ballard 1988).

The complexity of the tone system of a Chinese dialect is indicated not only by the number of tones, but also by the phenomenon of 'tone sandhi', i.e. a change of tones when two or more syllables are chained in speech. The most complicated tone sandhi phenomena are found in the Wú and Mǐn dialects. For example, in Cháozhōu, a southern Mǐn dialect, there are eight tones for syllables in isolation. When a syllable is followed by another syllable in Cháozhōu, its 'isolation tone' is changed to a different 'combination' tone. The following table illustrates the Cháozhōu isolation tones and their corresponding combination tones (the numbers represent pitch levels as before):

(2)	Isolation:	5	2	33	11	35	53	213	55
	Combination:	3	5	33	11	31	35	53	13

It should be noted that the presence of tones in Chinese does not imply the absence of intonation and stress. In fact, the Chinese dialects include stress-timed languages, in which stresses typically recur at regular time intervals during speech, as well as syllable-timed languages. Thus Mandarin dialects are stress-timed, whereas Yuè dialects are syllable-timed.

3. Chinese as an isolating language. Most Chinese words have one immutable form which does not change according to number, gender, tense, mood, case, or any other inflectional category (although there is a morphological category of verbal aspect). These categories are either indicated by lexical choice, or are inferred from the discourse context. Concomitant with the absence of inflectional morphology are three other characteristics:

3.1. ***Grammatical relations*** such as subject, direct object, and indirect object play no significant role. Word order may be used to distinguish agent from patient, as shown in exx. 3–4 from Běijīng Mandarin. However, sentences like 5 are perfectly natural and commonplace.

(3) *Wǒ mà tā le.*
1.SG scold 3.SG PERF
'I scolded him.'

(4) *Tā mà wǒ le.*
3.SG scold 1.SG PERF
'He scolded me.'

(5) *Yú chī le.*
fish eat PERF
'(Someone) ate the fish; The fish has eaten.'

As the two readings of 5 indicate, the noun *yú* 'fish', preceding the verb, may be understood as either agent or patient. This type of sentence is called the TOPIC-COMMENT construction. Its common occurrence in Chinese discourse is correlated with the de-emphasis of grammatical relations in the structure of the language.

3.2. There are no overt markers signaling subordination, parataxis, or coordination in 'serial verb constructions'. The serial verb construction in Chinese contains two or more predicates, juxtaposed without any morphological marker to indicate either the relationship between the nouns and the predicates, or that between the predicates. Sentences which in other languages might have subject complementation, object complementation, purposive clauses, conjoined clauses, or other complex structures, are rendered into serial verb constructions in Chinese. The following examples are from Běijīng Mandarin.

Subject complementation:

(6) *Tā bù lái shàngbān shì hěn qíguài.*
3.SG NEG come work be very strange
'It is strange that he does not come to work.'

Object complementation:

(7) *Wǒ zhīdào tā bù zài jiā.*
1.SG know 3.SG NEG be.at home
'I know that he is not home.'

Purposive clause:

(8) *Tā zuò-shēnyi zhuànqián.*
3.SG do-business make money
'He is engaged in business in order to make money.'

'Pivotal' construction:

(9) *Wǒ qǐng tā chī-fàn.*
1.SG invite 3.SG eat-meal
'I invited him to have a meal.'

'Descriptive' clauses:

(10) *Wǒ mǎi-le yījiàn yīfu tài dà.*
1.SG buy-PERF one outfit too big
'I bought an outfit that was too big.'

'Circumstantial Adjunct':

(11) *Tā tǎng zài chuáng-shàng kàn shū*
3.SG lie at bed-on read book
'He lay in bed reading a book.'

Conjoined predicates:

(12) *Tā tiāntiān chōuyēn hējiǔ.*
3.SG daily smoke drink
'He drinks and smokes daily.'

3.3. Chinese discourse, whether written or oral, is characterized by an abundance of zero pronouns, i.e. ones that are understood and have no overt realization (Li & Thompson 1979.). They should be considered the norm in Chinese discourse: it is the occurrence, rather than the absence, of a pronoun that calls for an explanation. The interpretation of the referent for the unrealized pronoun is inferred from discourse principles and from pragmatic knowledge, rather than from the grammatical structure of individual sentences:

I. Two friends, A and B, meet on the street:

A: *Hǎojiǔ bù jiàn! zěme-yàng? Hái hǎo ma?*
long.time NEG see how rather well Q
'I haven't seen you for a long time. How is it? Are you well?

B: *Ài . . . máng de yàomìng! xiànzài lián háizi*
Well busy ADV extreme now even child

dǒu méi kòng chàogù.
all not.have free.time look.after

'Well, I have been extremely busy! These days I don't even have time to look after my children.'

II. Two colleagues, X and Y, are discussing how Mr. Wang is irresponsible and uncooperative:

X: *Zhèyang de rén, nǐ shuō zěme bàn?*
this.kind of person 2.SG say how do
'A person of this sort! What do you think (we) can do?'

Y: *Shì a, yòu bù gōngzuò, yòu méi*
be PCLE not.only NEG work but.also not.have

wénhuà. Chèzhí ba!
civilization dismiss PCLE

'Indeed, not only does he not work, but he is also uncivilized. Let (us) fire (him)!'

4. The written language. A fully developed Chinese writing system first appeared in the late Shang Dynasty (14th–11th c. BCE), as inscriptions on oracle bones and bronze vessels. Each symbol of the Chinese writing system is called a CHARACTER or LOGOGRAPH. It is always pronounced in one syllable, and it usually represents a single morpheme, either synchronically or diachronically. The forms of the characters have undergone several stages of development during the past three millennia. The most recent change took place in the 1950s, when the government of the People's Republic of China began to introduce simplified characters to replace characters which are too complex. Currently the list of simplified characters contains some 2,238 entries. During the same period, the government also authorized an alphabetical writing system, called *Pīnyīn,* which is used for the Mandarin examples in this article.

Historically, there are five processes by which characters were created:

4.1. ***Pictographs*** originated as the pictorial representation of objects. An example is the character 日 *rì,* meaning 'sun': its original form, several millennia ago, was ⊙, which is clearly a picture of the sun.

4.2. ***Ideographs*** are characters derived from diagrams symbolizing ideas or abstract notions. For example, the diagrams 丄 and 丅 were created to symbolize the notions 'above' and 'below'; they have become formalized into the characters 上 *shàng* 'above' and 下 *xià* 'below', respectively.

4.3. ***Compound ideographs*** are characters whose meaning is in some way represented by the combination of the meanings of their parts. Thus the character 明 *míng* 'bright' is a compound of the characters 日 *rì* 'sun' and 月 *yuè* 'moon'.

4.4. ***Loan characters*** result from borrowing a character for a morpheme which is homophonous with another morpheme already represented by that character. For example, in an earlier stage of the Chinese language, the character 易 *yì* 'scorpion' was borrowed to represent the morpheme meaning 'easy', because 'easy' and 'scorpion' were homophonous. In modern Chinese, a new character stands for 'scorpion', obscuring the historical origin of the character 易 'easy'.

4.5. ***Phonetic compounds*** are combinations of two characters—one representing a semantic feature of the morpheme, and the other representing its pronunciation. For example, the character 鈾 *yóu* 'uranium' is composed of the two characters 金 *jīn* and 由 *yóu.* The first means 'metal'; the second has a pronunciation which approximates the first syllable of the English word *uranium.*

5. Contact with minority languages. China is often erroneously perceived and portrayed as a nation composed of a monolithic ethnic group speaking a monolithic language. In fact, not only does Chinese have hundreds of different dialects, but China also has more than fifty-five minority nationalities—speaking scores of different languages belonging to such families as Altaic, Tibeto-Burman, Tai, and Hmong-Mien. Historically, the minority nationalities were the sole inhabitants of more than 60 percent of the territory of China; many of them were once more than equal to the Chinese in terms of military and political dominance in East Asia. Thus the complex ethnic and socio-political situation in China over the past three millennia fostered contact between Chinese and the minority languages. A good part of the differences between northern Chinese (Mandarin) and southern dialects (Yuè, Mǐn and Kèjiā) is the result of contact; see Hashimoto 1976. For example, Altaic probably influenced such northern features as the simpler tone systems, the simplified classifier systems, the exclusive/inclusive distinction in the 1pl. pronoun, and the presence of certain sentential constructions favoring the verb-final word order. In the South, the dialects tend to have more complex tone systems, richer classifier systems, syllable-timed prosody, and word orders that are more strictly verb-medial, with some cases of modifiers following the modified. All these features may be in part the result of influence from Tai and Hmong-Mien languages. One notable feature of Chinese contact with minority languages is that loan words from the latter are relatively rare; this is one reason why the influence of minority languages on Chinese did not receive much scholarly attention until recent years.

CHARLES N. LI

BIBLIOGRAPHY

BALLARD, WILLIAM L. 1988. *The history and development of tonal systems and tone alternations in South China.* (Study of languages and cultures of Asia and Africa monograph series, 22.) Tokyo: Institute for the Study of Languages and Cultures of Asia and Africa, University of Foreign Studies.

CHAO, YUEN REN. 1968. *A grammar of spoken Chinese.* Berkeley: University of California Press.

DEFRANCIS, JOHN. 1984. *The Chinese language: Fact and fantasy.* Honolulu: University of Hawaii Press.

FORREST, ROBERT A. D. 1948. *The Chinese language.* London: Faber & Faber.

HASHIMOTO, MANTARO J. 1973. *The Hakka dialect: a linguistic study of its phonology, syntax, and lexicon.* (Princeton-Cambridge studies in Chinese linguistics, 5.) Cambridge: Cambridge University Press.

HASHIMOTO, MANTARO J. 1976. Language diffusion on the Asian continent. *Computational analyses of Asian and African Languages* 3.49–66.

HASHIMOTO, OI-KAN YUE. 1971. *Phonology of Cantonese,* vol. 1, *Studies in Yue dialects.* (Princeton-Cambridge studies in Chinese linguistics, 3.) Cambridge: Cambridge University Press.

KARLGREN, BERNHARD. 1949. *The Chinese language.* New York: Ronald Press.

LI, CHARLES N., & SANDRA A. THOMPSON. 1978. An exploration of Mandarin Chinese. In *Syntactic typology,* edited by Winfred Lehmann, pp. 223–266. Austin: University of Texas Press.

LI, CHARLES N., & SANDRA A. THOMPSON. 1979. Third-person pronouns and zero-anaphora in Chinese discourse. In *Discourse and syntax* (Syntax and semantics, 12), edited by Talmy Givón, pp. 311–335. New York: Academic Press.

LI, CHARLES N., & SANDRA A. THOMPSON. 1981. *Mandarin Chinese: A functional reference grammar.* Berkeley: University of California Press.

NORMAN, JERRY. 1988. *Chinese.* Cambridge & New York: Cambridge University Press.

RAMSEY, S. ROBERT. 1987. *The languages of China.* Princeton, N.J.: Princeton University Press.

WÁNG, LÌ. 1947. *Zhōngguó xiàndài yǔfǎ* [The grammar of modern Chinese]. Shanghai: Zhōnghuá Shūjú.

WÁNG, LÌ. 1957–58. *Hànyǔshǐgǎo* [A draft history of the Chinese language]. 2 vols. Beijing: Zhōnghuá Shūjú.

YUÁN, JIĀHUÁ et al. 1960. *Hànyǔ fāngyán gàiyào* [An outline of the Chinese dialects]. Beijing: Wénzì Gǎigé Chūbǎn-shè.

LANGUAGE LIST

Dungan: 49,400 mother-tongue speakers reported in 1979 from an ethnic population of 52,000, in the Kirghiz SSR and the Kazakh SSR, USSR, plus a few in the Uzbek SSR. Also called Dzhunyan or Tungan. Speakers call themselves Hui-Zu 'Chinese Muslims'. The language has literary status, based on the Gansu dialect.

Gàn: 20,600,000 speakers reported in 1984, in Jiāngxī and the southeastern corner of Húběi, China. Marginal mutual intelligibility with Mandarin and Wú. Speakers are bilingual in Mandarin.

Kèjiā: 27,365,000 speakers reported in 1984, with some 25,700,000 in China, in eastern and northeastern Guǎngdōng, and in many other areas south of the Yellow River (side by side with other forms of Chinese). Also spoken in Hongkong, Taiwan, Hawaii, Brunei, Malaysia and other southeast Asian countries, Surinam, and Panama. Also called Hakka, Hokka, Kechia, or Ke.

Mandarin: around 731,000,000 speakers reported in 1984, of whom 720,000,000 live in China north of the Changjiang River and southwestward to Yúnnán. Also spoken in Taiwan, Singapore, and twelve other countries. Also called Pei, Northern Chinese, Guóyǔ, Pǔtōnghuà, Potinhua, or Beijinghua. The official language of China. Also the language of the Huí official nationality of 7,220,000, Muslim Chinese who are known as Khoton in Mongolia; see also Dungan.

Mǐn Běi: around 10,500,000 speakers reported in 1984, with 10,300,000 in northeastern Fújiàn, China, on both sides of the Mǐn River, plus others in Brunei, Malaysia, Indonesia, Singapore, Thailand, and elsewhere in southeast Asia. Also called Northern Min, Hinghua Min, or Xinghua Min.

Mǐn Nán: around 45,800,000 speakers reported in 1984, with 25,700,000 along the coast from southern Zhèjiāng to south Hǎinán Island, China, plus 14,200,000 in Taiwan, 1,950,000 in Malaysia, 1,170,000 in Singapore, 1,080,000 in Thailand, 700,000 in Indonesia, 540,000 in Hongkong, 494,000 in the Philippines, and 10,000 in Brunei. Also called Southern Min or Hokkien.

Wú: around 77,200,000 speakers reported in 1984, in Jiāngsū mainly south of the Chángjiāng (Yángzě) River, and in Zhèjiāng, China. Mandarin is used for news and official broadcasts.

Xiāng: around 36,000,000 speakers reported in 1984, in Húnán, China. Also known as Hunanese.

Yuè: around 53,900,000 speakers reported in 1984, with

46,300,000 in much of Guǎngdōng and on Hǎinán Island, and in southern Guǎngxī, China, plus 5,290,000 in Hongkong, 748,000 in Malaysia, 500,000 in Vietnam, 314,000 in Singapore, and populations in nine other countries. Also called Cantonese or Yueh.

CHOISEUL LANGUAGES are spoken on Choiseul Island in the Solomon Islands; they constitute a top-level constituent of Oceanic [*q.v.*]. The subgrouping given in Figure 1 is based on Merritt Ruhlen, *A guide to the world's languages,* vol. 1, *Classification* (Stanford, Calif.: Stanford University Press, 1987).

LANGUAGE LIST

Babatana: 5,000 first-language speakers reported in 1981, with an additional 1,000 second-language speakers, on east Choiseul Island. Also called Mbambatana.
Ririo: 200 speakers reported in 1977, on Choiseul Island.
Tavula: 1,000 speakers reported in 1981, in Tavula, Choiseul Island. Also called Tavola, Vagua, or Vaghua.
Varese: around 3,030 speakers reported in 1976, on northeast Choiseul Island. Also called Varisi.

CHOMSKY, NOAM. *See* Formal Grammar.

CHOMSKY HIERARCHY is the term given to a series of increasingly comprehensive classes of formal languages containing the following principal members: FINITE STATE (also called 'right-linear' or 'Type 3'); CONTEXT-FREE (Type 2); CONTEXT-SENSITIVE (Type 1); RECURSIVE; and R[ECURSIVELY] E[NUMERABLE] (r.e., TYPE 0). Types 1 and 2 were proposed by Chomsky 1963, on the basis of his investigations into the formal properties of phrase-structure systems of syntactic description. The r.e., recursive, and finite-state languages were known from AUTOMATA THEORY [*q.v.*] and recursive function theory; but Chomsky's name has become attached to the hierarchy, since he and his associates first defined the languages in terms of the properties of the formal grammars generating them, and carried out early investigations into the mathematical properties of these and similar systems. (For general reference, see Hopcroft & Ullman 1979, Partee et al, 1990, Savitch et al. 1987.)

FIGURE 1. *Subgrouping of Choiseul Languages*

Northwest Choiseul
Ririo, Tavula, Varese
Central-Eastern Choiseul
Babatana

Briefly, a formal grammar consists of:

(a) A TERMINAL vocabulary, out of which strings in the languages are formed
(b) A NONTERMINAL vocabulary, whose symbols may occur in intermediate strings in derivations
(c) A designated derivation-initial nonterminal symbol
(d) A finite set of rules of the form $\phi \rightarrow \psi$, allowing replacement of an occurrence of the substring ϕ by the string ψ

With no further restrictions (except that $\phi \neq$ the empty string e), such grammars generate the Type 0 languages. With the additional constraint that ψ be no shorter than ϕ, the Type 1 languages are generated. Equivalently, in each rule a single non-terminal symbol may be rewritten as a non-empty string in a specified context χ ___ ω; hence the name 'context-sensitive' for this class. In Type 2 grammars, this context is null; i.e., a nonterminal can be rewritten (perhaps as e) wherever it occurs—hence 'context-free'. Finally, if the rules are further limited to the form $A \rightarrow xB$ or $A \rightarrow x$ (A and B are nonterminals, and x is a string of terminals), the Type 3 languages are generated. Here all derivations are 'right-linear', in that a single non-terminal occurs at the right end of each string except the last. The corresponding 'left-linear' grammars generate the same languages.

A proper subset of a class of grammars does not necessarily generate a 'smaller' class of languages. However, the restrictions just outlined do produce grammars with ever smaller generative capacities. A language is said to be of Type n if there is some Type n grammar that generates it. Thus, although every Type $n+1$ language is also a Type n language (a Type $n+1$ grammar being perforce also a Type n grammar), there are languages of Type n which are not also of Type $n+1$. For example, $\{a^n b^n \mid n \geq 1\}$, i.e. $\{ab, aabb, aaabbb, \ldots\}$, can be generated by a context-free grammar, but by no right-linear grammar. Similarly, $\{a^n b^n c^n \mid n \geq 1\}$ is a Type 1 language, but not Type 2 (or Type 3, of course). The hierarchical relationship is not quite exact—since, technically, no Type 1 language may contain e; but with suitable adjustments made for this detail, and letting L^n be the class of all languages of Type n, we have:

$$L_3 \supset L_2 \supset L_1 \supset L_0$$

The recursive languages correspond to no easily definable grammatical type, but they are known to fall properly between classes L_1 and L_0. It is also known that there exist languages—in fact, uncountably many—which lie outside the r.e. languages (and therefore have no grammars).

The Type 3 languages are exactly those recognized by finite-state automata. Other correspondences with automata are: Type 2, non-deterministic pushdown automata; Type 1, non-deterministic linear bounded automata; Type 0, Turing machines. Thus, corresponding to the Chomsky hierarchy of languages and grammars, there exists a hierarchy of automata of increasing computational power, as measured by the ability to recognize languages. The interconnections among formal languages, grammars, and automata have proven very fruitful mathematically.

The Chomsky hierarchy is often appealed to as a scale of the relative 'complexity' of languages and language-generating devices; and much attention has been given to the question of where natural languages fall on this scale—despite the fact that to regard natural languages merely as sets of strings, with no internal constituent structure, is a rather severe, and perhaps disqualifying, limitation. Considerations of PARSING and LEARNABILITY [*qq.v.*] had led to the supposition that natural languages must be at least recursive (cf. Peters & Ritchie 1973, which showed that the so-called standard theory of generative transformational grammar was excessively powerful in producing ALL of L_0). After some controversy, it has now been firmly established (Shieber 1985) that at least one natural language, namely Swiss German, falls outside L_2, although it lies in some sense 'close' to the L_2-L_1 boundary. This 'mildly context-sensitive' region has been the subject of many recent investigations.

ROBERT WALL

BIBLIOGRAPHY

CHOMSKY, NOAM. 1963. Formal properties of grammars. In *Handbook of mathematical psychology,* edited by R. Duncan Luce et al., vol. 2, pp. 328–428. New York: Wiley.

HOPCROFT, JOHN E., & JEFFREY D. ULLMAN. 1979. *Introduction to automata theory, languages, and computation.* Reading, Mass.: Addison-Wesley.

PARTEE, BARBARA; ALICE TER MEULEN; & ROBERT WALL. 1990. *Mathematical methods in linguistics.* Dordrecht: Reidel.

PETERS, P. STANLEY, JR., & ROBERT W. RITCHIE. 1973. On the generative power of transformational grammars. *Information & Control* 6.49–83.

SAVITCH, WALTER J., et al., eds. 1987. *The formal complexity of natural language.* (Studies in linguistics & philosophy, 33.) Dordrecht: Reidel.

SHIEBER, STUART M. 1985. Evidence against the context-freeness of natural language. *Linguistics & Philosophy* 8.333–343.

CHON LANGUAGES

CHON LANGUAGES, also called Patagon, constitute a language family of southern Argentina and adjacent parts of Chile; see Čestmír Loukotka, *Classification of South American Indian languages* (Los Angeles: Latin American Center, University of California, Los Angeles, 1968), pp. 45–46.

LANGUAGE LIST

Ona: now extinct, formerly spoken in Tierra del Fuego, Argentina, and in Chile. Also called Aona or Selknam.

Tehuelche: spoken by 24 people in Patagonia, Argentina. Also called Aoniken, Gunua-Kena, Gununa-Kena, or Inaquen.

CHRONOLOGY OF LANGUAGE CHANGE

CHRONOLOGY OF LANGUAGE CHANGE. *See* Historical Linguistics, *article on* Mathematical Concepts; *see also* Relative Chronology.

CHUKOTKO-KAMCHATKAN LANGUAGES

CHUKOTKO-KAMCHATKAN LANGUAGES constitute a family of the Chukotka and Kamchatka peninsulas of northeastern Siberia, USSR. [*See* Siberian Languages.] They comprise the subgroups shown in Figure 1.

LANGUAGE LIST

Alutor: 2,000 speakers reported in 1975, in the Koryak National Okrug, Kamchatka Peninsula. Also called Alyutor, Aliutor, or Olyutor. Considered a dialect of Koryak until recently.

Chukchi: 10,900 first-language speakers reported in 1979 from an ethnic population of 14,000, on the Chukotka Peninsula. Also called Chukcha, Chukchee, Chukot, or Luoravetlan. Has literary status.

FIGURE 1. *Subgrouping of Chukotko-Kamchatkan Languages*

- **Northern**
  - Chukchi
  - **Koryak-Alutor**
    - Alutor, Kerek, Koryak
- **Southern**
  - Itelmen

Itelmen: around 340 speakers reported in 1979 from an ethnic population of 1,400, on the southern Kamchatka Peninsula. Also called Itelymem, Kamchadal, or Kamchatka. All speakers are bilingual in Russian.

Kerek: 400 speakers reported in 1975, on Cape Navarin, USSR. Previously considered a dialect of Chukchi.

Koryak: around 5,450 mother-tongue speakers reported in 1979 from an ethnic population of 7,900, in the Koryak National Okrug, on the northern half of Kamchatka Peninsula and the adjacent continent. Also called Nymylan. Has status as a literary language. The Chavchuven, Palan, and Kamen dialects seem not to be mutually intelligible.

CLASSIFIERS. *See* Gender and Noun Classification.

CLASSROOM-ORIENTED RESEARCH—also called 'classroom-centered research', 'classroom process research', or simply 'classroom research'—is educational research that takes the classroom as the starting point, either as the prime source of pedagogic data, or as the essential context for the investigation, or as both. (For general reference, see Ochsner 1979, Long 1980, Allwright 1983, 1987, Gaies 1983, Seliger & Long 1983, Mitchell 1985, Chaudron 1988, and Van Lier 1988.)

Such research in language classrooms arose from a concern in the late 1960s that global methodological comparison studies, the research mainstream, were investigating external variables, i.e. INPUT and OUTPUT, but were neglecting what was actually happening in language classrooms. This was important because such projects were ostensibly investigating the relative value in terms of achievement (the output) of language teaching methods derived from competing theories of language learning (the input); yet their results were largely uninterpretable, because of the impossibility of recovering in sufficient detail what had actually happened in the classroom. Some researchers sought to overcome these problems by dealing with isolated, and therefore more easily specifiable, language teaching techniques rather than complete methods. The whole paradigm could still be seen, however, as essentially behaviorist, with pedagogical prescriptions as the stimulus, achievement as the response, and a corresponding neglect for the organism in the middle—the language learner in the classroom.

Other researchers noted both the difficulty such projects met in yielding decisive results, and the development in cognitive psychology of a focus on 'the organism in the middle'; that trend was reflected in the second language field in the contemporaneous move away from CONTRASTIVE ANALYSIS [*q.v.*] toward error analysis [*see* Interlanguage], with its central concern for the active mental involvement of the learner in language performance. These researchers began to distrust the entire paradigm which relied on the practically problematic notion of the 'controlled experiment', and which aimed ultimately at justifying the prescription of one method or technique over others. They were more impressed by the argument that behavioral phenomena needed very careful observation and description to be understood. To them, understanding was logically prior to prescription; for some of them, understanding was sufficient in itself. This constituted a decisive break with the Skinnerian aims of prediction and control, echoing the earlier break with behaviorism in linguistics, and the general anti-prescriptivist (i.e. anti-authoritarian) tendencies in Western society at that time.

A research interest in observation and description was also able to find support, and considerable experience, in language teacher training. Since the late 1960s, some practitioners, largely following the general educational work of Flanders 1960, had turned to 'non-judgmental' observation and description, using systematic SCHEDULES (category lists of teacher and learner behaviors) as a feedback tool for their trainees, and as a research tool for themselves.

These two key concepts, OBSERVATION and DESCRIPTION, kept classroom-oriented research rooted in the empirical tradition. Researchers might no longer be seeking to establish causal relationships; but they dealt only with observable behavior, and dealt with it both objectively and quantifiably. They developed the schedules used by teacher trainers, or devised new systems, to meet the special needs of language class description. They then produced detailed descriptions of actual language lessons. The laboriousness of such work led classroom researchers, like their contemporaries in discourse analysis, to handle relatively little data—several hours, rather than the one or two years of the global methodological comparisons—and then they moved on, rather than replicating their study. Thus the early emphasis on describing the treatment of language errors soon gave way to a more general concern for documenting learner participation. A parallel and influential move occurred in S[ECOND] L[ANGUAGE] A[CQUISITION] research [*see* Acquisition of Language], from error analysis toward a more holistic look at learner performance—another example of growing concern for the 'organism in the middle'.

At this stage, classroom research techniques were being used principally to seek direct insight into the events of language classrooms. The most striking discovery, however, was the extremely high level of complexity to be found. Indeed, revealing this complexity became almost an end in itself, as a powerful antidote to the apparent oversimplifications of earlier research. Quantifying complexity, however, was a way of showing how far we were from reaching understanding, rather than how near. The more complexity was revealed, the less likely it seemed that classrooms would ever be properly understood through an exclusive reliance on observable behavior. There was at the same time a straightforward demand for empirical work that would simply document current language teaching practices (see Mitchell et al. 1981). There was also an important and developing connection between classroom research and the more 'theory-driven' studies in SLA—a connection which has generated a continuing demand for the description and quantification of classroom behavior.

Not all classroom language-learning researchers accepted the empiricist aims of objectivity and quantifiability. Some saw more promise in a subjective and qualitative approach, going beyond the externally observable to look inside the head of the learner, as it were, and bring in the learner's perspective. DIARY STUDIES were begun, and a whole range of INTROSPECTIVE data collection techniques were developed (see Cohen & Hosenfeld 1981). Controversy immediately began over whether such techniques could offer valid findings (see Seliger 1983), or whether their value would lie only in isolating issues for later investigation by some more standard empirical means. This called into question the ultimate status and aims of pedagogical research. Was it necessary to look for causal relationships? Or was it legitimate to hope for more direct insight, given that the complexities of causality in human affairs might never be reducible to practically useful prescriptions?

There was also a third possibility to be considered: ACTION RESEARCH, which added the teacher's perspective to that of the learner, and which offered a use for the techniques of classroom research that sought neither causal explanations nor direct insights, but practical solutions to immediate problems. It is arguable that the main contribution of classroom research techniques is ultimately not in the findings generated, nor in their support or refutation of any particular theoretical position, but in the techniques themselves and their potential value to teachers and learners who wish to adopt an exploratory approach as a natural extension, perhaps, of 'communicative' language pedagogy.

Thus we reach the current position, in which 'classroom research' has become the name for a wide range of procedures used for many distinct purposes. They deserve a common name only because of their underlying assumption that exploring classroom language learning, for whatever purpose, means putting the processes of the classroom firmly in the center.

DICK ALLWRIGHT

BIBLIOGRAPHY

ALLWRIGHT, DICK. 1983. Classroom-centered research on language teaching and learning: A brief historical overview. *TESOL Quarterly* 17.191–204.

ALLWRIGHT, DICK. 1987. *Observation in the language classroom.* London: Longman.

CHAUDRON, CRAIG. 1988. *Second language classrooms: Research on teaching and learning.* Cambridge & New York: Cambridge University Press.

COHEN, ANDREW, & CAROL HOSENFELD. 1981. Some uses of mentalistic data in second language research. *Language Learning* 31.285–313.

FLANDERS, NED A. 1960. *Interaction analysis in the classroom: A manual for observers.* Ann Arbor: University of Michigan Press.

GAIES, STEPHEN J. 1983. The investigation of language classroom processes. *TESOL Quarterly* 17.205–217.

LONG, MICHAEL H. 1980. Inside the 'black box': Methodological issues in classroom research on language learning. *Language Learning* 30.1–42.

MITCHELL, ROSAMOND. 1985. Process research in second language classrooms. *Language Teaching* 18.330–352.

MITCHELL, ROSAMOND, et al. 1981. *The foreign language classroom: An observational study.* (Stirling Educational Monographs, 9.) Stirling, Scotland: Department of Education, University of Stirling.

OCHSNER, ROBERT. 1979. A poetics of second language acquisition. *Language Learning* 29.53–80.

SELIGER, HERBERT W. 1983. The language learner as linguist: Of metaphors and realities. *Applied Linguistics* 4:3.179–191.

SELIGER, HERBERT W., & MICHAEL H. LONG, eds. 1983. *Classroom-oriented research in second language acquisition.* Rowley, Mass.: Newbury House.

VAN LIER, LEO. 1988. *The classroom and the language learner: Ethnography and second language classroom research.* London: Longman.

CLAUSE-COMBINING CONSTRUCTIONS. In any sort of discourse, individual clauses are combined into larger structures. Different languages afford their speakers various grammatical means to indicate that a clause is closely associated with, but not a part of, another clause or other clauses within a larger unit, which may be thought of as a sentence. [*See* Complementation; Relativization.] The different types of complex constructions which are associated with that kind of clause-combining are of general interest, for they raise questions related to such areas of research as clause structure, coreference across clause boundaries, and the relationship among syntax, semantics, and pragmatics. These constructions have received special attention from those who approach linguistics from functional and typological perspectives: functionalists have generally looked at language in actual use, where wide ranges of clause combinations occur; typologists have generally looked at ways in which languages may vary, and languages vary greatly in the ways in which they combine clauses (Haiman & Thompson 1988).

Morphological and/or phonological (often intonational) cues may indicate that a clause is part of a larger structure. The clauses within that structure may bear any of a large number of semantic or pragmatic relationships to one another: e.g., the actions or states described in the clauses may occur or exist sequentially, simultaneously, or in alternation; one clause may present a cause, a result, or a purpose of another; one clause may give a condition for another, or describe the manner in which some action is done. Grammatical particles or specific construction types may indicate the relationship that holds between the clauses, or may limit the range of possible relationships between the clauses; but there may be no overt sign of precisely how the clauses are to be interpreted. Particular interpretations of strings of clauses, then, will often depend upon context (Stump 1985).

In some languages, like English and other familiar Indo-European languages, a distinction may be made between COORDINATE combinations, in which both clauses are relatively independent of each other, and SUBORDINATE combinations—in which one is more or less dependent, semantically or grammatically, on the other, independent clause. In other languages, including Hua (Haiman 1980) and other languages of New Guinea (Longacre 1972), a more revealing description of clause combination is in terms of CLAUSE-CHAINING constructions. In still other languages, such as Mandarin (Li & Thompson 1981), West African languages, and creole languages (Sebba 1987), there is not always a clear distinction between subordinate and coordinate clauses; instead, SERIAL VERB constructions are used.

1. Coordination and subordination. In those languages which may clearly be analyzed as distinguishing subordinate from coordinate constructions, coordinate constructions will include clauses which may stand alone, by some criteria, and which are either juxtaposed or connected by a conjunction. Ex. 1 is composed of two coordinate clauses, connected with the conjunction *or*:

(1) *She'll give you a call or I'll send you a message.*

Subordinate clauses may be distinguished from independent clauses by special subordinating morphemes, by special word order, by special verb forms (often called participles), or by a restricted distribution of the categories of tense, aspect, or mood (Thompson & Longacre 1985). One class of subordinate clauses is often referred to as ADVERBIAL because some of them function in ways similar to adverbs—e.g. giving information about the time of, manner of, or reason for an action or state described in another clause. Ex. 2 contains a main clause followed by a subordinate clause which gives information about the time of the action expressed in the first clause; the subordinate clause is introduced by *while*:

(2) *I did a lot of sightseeing while I was in the States.*

Subordinate clauses vary in the extent to which they are bound to the clauses on which they depend. They perform a range of functions: they may serve as topics or otherwise provide a framework for the information contained in the main clause; and they often present information which is unfamiliar in its context (Haiman 1978, Chafe 1984).

2. Clause chaining. In a typical string of clauses in a typical clause-chaining language, every clause except the last is marked for SWITCH-REFERENCE (Jacobsen 1967); i.e., it indicates whether its subject is the same as the subject of the following clause, using S[ame] S[ubject] marking, or different from it, using D[ifferent] S[ubject] marking. The last verb of the chain is called the 'final' verb; non-final verbs are called 'medial' verbs. Exx. 3–4 are from Koita, a Papuan language (Dutton 1975, cited by Lynch 1983:210). In each example, the first verb appears with a suffix which indicates switch-reference—SS in 3, and DS in 4:

(3) *daka oro-γo-i era-γa-nu.*
I come-SG-SS see-SG-PAST
'I came and saw him.'

(4) *daka oro-γo-nuge auki da era-γa-nu.*
I come-SG-DS he me see-SG-PAST
'I came and he saw me.'

The clauses in a chain may be semantically related to one another in ways that are characterized by both coordinating and subordinating constructions in other languages (Longacre 1985).

Switch-reference systems are not limited to clause-chaining languages. Switch-reference is a typically verbal category which serves to keep track of the referents in a discourse. On a very general discourse level, SS markers may be seen as marking a kind of referent continuity, and DS markers as marking a kind of discontinuity. Traditionally, switch-reference marking is considered sensitive to the identity of syntactic subjects; a clause will be marked for switch reference with respect to a clause which is on its own syntactic level or on a higher syntactic level. Whether switch-reference should be regarded as syntactic or pragmatic is a matter of controversy (see Finer 1984, Roberts 1988). Many historical sources for switch-reference markers have been proposed; such markers are themselves prone to reanalysis. (See Haiman & Munro 1983 for further discussion.)

3. Serial verbs. In serial verb constructions, two clauses, or two verb phrases—or two finite, relatively independent verbs, which may share arguments—are juxtaposed, with the precise relationship between them generally left unmarked. Exx. 5–6 are from Twi, a Kwa language of West Africa (Sebba 1987:175); they each show two finite verbs which share an agentive argument. No conjunction separates the verbs:

(5) *Kofi de pono no baae.*
K. take.PAST table the come.PAST
'Kofi brought the table.'

(6) *ɔyɛɛ adwuma mã ne nua.*
he.do work give his brother
'He works for his brother.'

In 7, from Mandarin (Li & Thompson 1981:595), the two juxtaposed verb phrases *mǎi piào* and *jìn-qu* may be understood to be related in two different ways:

(7) *wǒ mǎi piào jìn-qu.*
I buy ticket enter-go
'I bought a ticket and went in'; 'I bought a ticket to go in.'

Several different types of serial verb constructions may be found in a given language. Two verbs may have the status of a single lexical item; one verb (often meaning 'give' or 'take') may serve to increase the valence of another; one verb may be analyzed as an auxiliary verb; or two verbs may express relations that are expressed by subordinate and coordinate constructions in other languages. Verb serialization in a wide range of languages is discussed by Foley & Olson 1985 and by Sebba 1987.

The evolution of serial verb constructions has been widely discussed; serial verbs have been suggested as the sources of prepositions (Lord 1973, Givón 1975, Li & Thompson 1974) and of classifiers (Seiler 1986) in various languages.

JANINE SCANCARELLI

BIBLIOGRAPHY

CHAFE, WALLACE L. 1984. How people use adverbial clauses. *Berkeley Linguistics Society* 10.437–449.

DUTTON, TOM E. 1975. A Koita grammar sketch and vocabulary. In *Studies in languages of central and south-east Papua* (Pacific Linguistics, C-29), edited by T. E. Dutton, pp. 281–412. Canberra: School of Pacific Studies, Australian National University.

FINER, DANIEL. 1984. *The formal grammar of switch-reference.* MIT dissertation. Published, New York: Garland, 1985.

FOLEY, WILLIAM A., & MIKE OLSON. 1985. Clausehood and verb serialization. In *Grammar inside and outside the clause: Some approaches to theory from the field,* edited by Johanna Nichols and Anthony C. Woodbury, pp. 17–60. Cambridge & New York: Cambridge University Press.

GIVÓN, TALMY. 1975. Serial verbs and syntactic change: Niger-Congo. In *Word order and word order change,* edited by Charles N. Li, pp. 47–112. Austin: University of Texas Press.

HAIMAN, JOHN. 1978. Conditionals are topics. *Language* 54.564–589.

HAIMAN, JOHN. 1980. *Hua: A Papuan language of the eastern highlands of New Guinea.* (Studies in language, Companion series, 5.) Amsterdam: Benjamins.

HAIMAN, JOHN, & PAMELA MUNRO, eds. 1983. *Switch-reference and universal grammar.* (Typological studies in language, 2.) Amsterdam: Benjamins.

Haiman, John, & Sandra A. Thompson, eds. 1988. *Clause combining in grammar and discourse.* (Typological studies in language, 18.) Amsterdam: Benjamins.

Jacobsen, William, Jr. 1967. Switch-reference in Hokan-Coahuiltecan. In *Studies in Southwestern Ethnolinguistics,* edited by Dell Hymes, pp. 238–263. The Hague: Mouton.

Li, Charles N., & Sandra A. Thompson. 1974. Co-verbs in Mandarin Chinese: Verbs or prepositions? *Journal of Chinese Linguistics* 2.257–278.

Li, Charles N., & Sandra A. Thompson. 1981. *Mandarin Chinese: A functional reference grammar.* Berkeley: University of California Press.

Longacre, Robert E. 1972. *Hierarchy and universality of discourse constituents in New Guinea languages: Discussion.* 2 vols. Washington, D.C.: Georgetown University Press.

Longacre, Robert E. 1985. Sentences as combinations of clauses. In Shopen 1985, pp. 235–286.

Lord, Carol. 1973. Serial verbs in transition. *Studies in African Linguistics* 4.269–296.

Lynch, John. 1983. Switch-reference in Lenakel. In Haiman & Munro 1983, pp. 209–221.

Roberts, John R. 1988. Amele switch-reference and the theory of grammar. *Linguistic Inquiry* 19.45–63.

Sebba, Mark. 1987. *The syntax of serial verbs: An investigation into serialisation in Sranan and other languages.* (Creole language library, 2.) Amsterdam: Benjamins.

Seiler, W. 1986. Noun-classificatory verbal prefixes as reanalysed serial verbs. *Lingua* 68.189–207.

Shopen, Timothy, ed. 1985. *Language typology and syntactic description,* vol. 2, *Complex constructions.* Cambridge & New York: Cambridge University Press.

Stump, Gregory T. 1985. *The semantic variability of absolute constructions.* (Synthese language library, 25.) Dordrecht: Reidel.

Thompson, Sandra A., & Robert E. Longacre. 1985. Adverbial clauses. In Shopen 1985, pp. 171–234.

CLINICAL LINGUISTICS. *See* Pathology of Language.

CLITICS. [*This entry is concerned with proclitics and enclitics, bound elements which, in their phonological behavior, resemble inflectional affixes, but in their grammatical function resemble independent words. It comprises two articles:*

An Overview
Pronominal Clitics

For related topics, see Morphology, *article on* Morphology and Syntax; *see also* Affixation; Inflection; *and* Words.]

An Overview

'Clitic' is a term commonly applied to elements with some properties of inflectional morphology and some of independent words. For references, see Zwicky & Pullum 1983, Kaisse 1985, Klavans 1985, and Zwicky 1985, 1987.

We may consider nine criteria which distinguish inflections (determined, bound, reduced) from words (undetermined, free, full):

(a) The typical word, but not the typical inflection, has an independent accent.

(b) The phonological shape of a word must be listed in the lexicon, but the phonology of an inflection is described in general by saying how the shape of some stem is altered (so that inflections can have 'process', as well as affix, realizations).

(c) Separate, language-specific restrictions can govern the possible phonological shapes of words vs. inflections. In particular, inflections, but not words, are often non-syllabic.

(d) Syntactically, words belong to (lexical) categories, i.e. word classes; but the assignment of inflections to such categories is problematic. [*See* Parts of Speech.]

(e) Syntactic rules introduce word classes as co-constituents with other syntactic categories; but an inflection is syntactically dependent, described by rules which locate it by reference to syntactic constituents (e.g. on the head of VP, in the first word of S, at the right edge of NP).

(f) For each inflectional affix, morphological rules specify the class of words with which it can occur, and the properties of the resultant combination; but the syntactic rules distributing words typically make reference to phrasal categories rather than to word classes. From this, it follows that inflections are typically very selective in the word classes with which they occur, but words are unconstrained with respect to the word classes that happen to occur adjacent to them.

(g) Syntactic rules cannot alter morphological structure. In particular, syntactic rules cannot allow a word to interrupt a stem + affix combination; a word attached to such a combination must have edge position.

(h) Syntactic rules which introduce a lexical category are blind to the internal morphology and phonology of its co-constituents, but rules which introduce an inflection can be contingent on such properties of its stem. From this it follows that there can be arbitrary gaps and morphophonological idiosyncrasies, including SUPPLETION [*q.v.*], in the set of stem + affix combinations, but not in the set of word + word combinations.

(i) Alternative orders of words within a constituent are common, but the ordering of an inflectional affix—with respect to its stem, and to other such affixes—is fixed.

Various mixtures of these properties are possible. Syntactically dependent words, or quasi-clitics, are words by all but criterion (e)—e.g. accented Latin adverbs that are located in 'second position' in the sentence. Prosodically dependent words, or 'leaners', are words by all but criterion (a)—e.g. the English infinitive marker *to*. Phrasal affixes are inflections by all but criteria (f) and (g), e.g. the possessive markers in English and Finnish. Quasi-clitics, leaners, and phrasal affixes are sometimes referred to as clitics; but the term is most often used for items that are words at least by criteria (a) and (c)—items characterizable as BOUND WORDS.

A number of types of bound words can be distinguished, though the analytic status of the distinctions is not clear. Optionally bound words, like the English auxiliary clitics, are in stylistic alternation with independent words in the language, and so behave like words on criterion (e); other bound words behave like inflections in this respect. Permutable bound words, like Tagalog particle clitics, have some ordering freedom with respect to one another, and so behave like words on criterion (i); other bound words then behave like inflections. Head-bound words, like the object pronoun clitics in most Romance languages, attach to words from a single class (verbs), and so behave like inflections on criterion (f); other bound words here behave like words. The Finnish particle clitics belong to none of these subtypes: they are words on criteria (b) and (d)-(g), but inflections on criteria (a), (c), (e), and (i)—and they can be taken as unmarked representatives of the set of bound words.

Clitics in general, and bound words in particular, are of interest not only because of their ubiquity, but also because of the challenges they present to theorizing about the relationships among syntax, morphology, phonology, and semantics. With respect to syntax and morphology, quasi-clitics and leaners might be treated syntactically (as special types of words) and as phrasal affixes morphologically (as special types of inflections); but bound words exhibit such a balance between word and inflectional properties that some sort of dual analysis seems called for. [*See* Morphology, *article on* Morphology and Syntax.]

The phonological interest of clitics lies in at least three areas: (i) phonological relationships between bound words and full words (Eng. *'d* vs. *would* or *had,* French *me* vs. *moi*); (ii) phonological alternations specifically affecting clitics (Fr. *me* vs. *m'*); (iii) a delicate distinction between morphologized forms (clitics) and purely phonological variants occurring in fast speech.

The semantic interest of clitics arises from the fact that a syntactically dependent item (like *'s* in *the man with the hat's problems* or *The man with the hat's going*) is semantically interpreted with respect to the whole constituent on which it is dependent, not the word to which it happens to be attached.

ARNOLD M. ZWICKY

BIBLIOGRAPHY

KAISSE, ELLEN M. 1985. *Connected speech: The interaction of syntax and phonology.* Orlando, Fla.: Academic Press.

KLAVANS, JUDITH L. 1985. The independence of syntax and phonology in cliticization. *Language* 61.95–120.

ZWICKY, ARNOLD M. 1985. Clitics and particles. *Language* 61.283–305.

ZWICKY, ARNOLD M. 1987. Suppressing the Zs. *Journal of Linguistics* 23.133–148.

ZWICKY, ARNOLD M., & GEOFFREY K. PULLUM. 1983. Cliticization vs. inflection: English *n't*. *Language* 59.502–513.

Pronominal Clitics

The term 'clitics' is commonly used to denote elements which serve as syntactic constituents, but which are not phonologically independent words. A primary example of such elements are P[RONOMINAL] C[LITIC]S, as they are found e.g. in the Romance, Slavic, and Semitic languages. (For general reference, see Borer 1986.)

The study of PCs has always enjoyed an important status in the construction of syntactic theories. Since PCs enter both the syntactic and the morphological component, they offer an important insight into the nature of syntactic and lexical phenomena, and the interaction between the two.

Arguably, many of the morphophonological properties of PCs are best captured if we assume that, as with affixes, they are attached to their host by a morphological rule, the output being a word. If this is true, then, according to some syntactic models (notably those assuming the correctness of the Lexical Integrity Hypothesis), cliticization can only be characterized as a lexical phenomenon. This direction has been pursued by, e.g., Andrews 1982 and Grimshaw 1982, within the framework of Lexical-Functional Grammar [*q.v.*].

However, alongside the morphophonological properties of PCs, they also have many syntactic properties. Chiefly, PCs satisfy subcategorization requirements of PREDICATES [*See* Predication]; they normally occur in complementary distribution with the syntactic category which their host predicate selects [*see* Subcategorization and Selection]. Subcategorization requirements are traditionally stated in terms of phrasal categories; but any attempt to accommodate PCs within such phrasal statements requires another mechanism.

Grammatical models which assume movement and empty categories have typically utilized movement to state the relations between PCs and the subcategorized positions (originating with Kayne 1975). The output of such a movement of the French object clitic *les* is depicted in Figure 1.

Alternatively (cf. Jaeggli 1982), it has been suggested that, in a structure like Fig. 1, a base-generated PC can be linked to an empty category in the subcategorized position. Various structural constraints have been discovered to apply to the relations between the clitic and its corresponding empty category. Kayne 1975 argues that the relationship is constrained by the Specified Subject Condition. Borer 1984 argues that it is constrained by GOVERNMENT [*q.v.*], while Aoun 1985 argues for an A′-binding relation [*see* Binding]. Identification relations have also been proposed, on the assumption that the clitic identifies a null pronominal PRO in the empty subject or object position. [*See* Pronouns, *article on* Pronominals.]

FIGURE 1. *Clitic Movement in French*

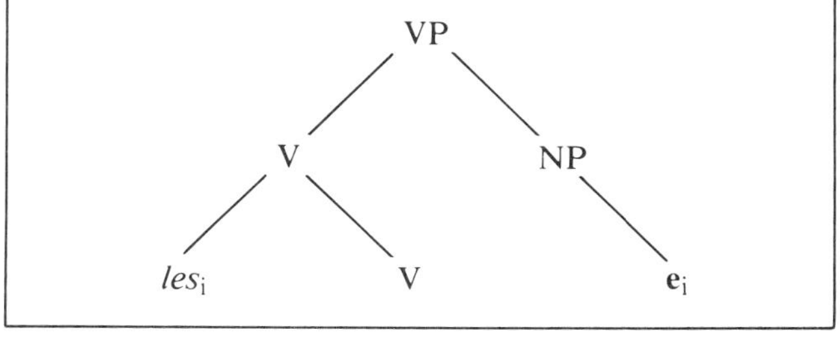

Research on PCs typically addresses questions concerning their interaction with argument structure and their relations with their hosts. As of the late 1970s, it was commonly assumed that PCs may absorb assignment features such as abstract Case and theta-role (cf. Jaeggli 1982, Borer 1984, Aoun 1985). Such absorption results in the unavailability of an overt complement for the predicate in question, explaining the complementary distribution between clitics and, e.g., subcategorized arguments. However, at least with abstract Case, if an independent Case assigner is available, its co-occurrence with a clitic may result in the surfacing of the missing argument. This leads to the phenomenon of CLITIC DOUBLING, exemplified here from Rumanian (OM = Object Marker):

(1)	*L_i-am*	*vazut*	*pe*	*$Popescu_i$.*
	him_i-I.have	seen	OM	$Popescu_i$
	'I have seen Popescu.'			

Subsequent absorption proposals were made, e.g. by Belletti 1982 with respect to Italian *si*; and, with a different set of assumptions, by Grimshaw 1982, who proposes that French *se* may or may not fulfill an argument function in different contexts. The reader should also consult works by Safir 1985, Rizzi 1986, and Burzio 1986, relating to the interaction of PCs with null subjects and syntactic movement.

HAGIT BORER

BIBLIOGRAPHY

ANDREWS, AVERY D. 1982. The representation of case in Modern Icelandic. In Bresnan 1982, pp. 427–503.

AOUN, JOSEPH. 1985. *A grammar of anaphora.* (Linguistic Inquiry monographs, 11.) Cambridge, Mass.: MIT Press.

BELLETTI, ADRIANA. 1982. On the anaphoric status of the reciprocal construction in Italian. *Linguistic Review* 2.101–137.

BORER, HAGIT. 1984. *Parametric syntax: Case studies in Semitic and Romance languages.* (Studies in generative grammar, 13.) Dordrecht: Foris.

BORER, HAGIT, ed. 1986. *The syntax of pronominal clitics.* (Syntax and semantics, 19.) Orlando, Fla.: Academic Press.

BRESNAN, JOAN, ed. 1982. *The mental representation of grammatical relations.* Cambridge, Mass.: MIT Press.

BURZIO, LUIGI. 1986. *Italian syntax: A government-binding approach*. Dordrecht: Reidel.

GRIMSHAW, JANE. 1982. On the lexical representation of Romance reflexive clitics. In Bresnan 1982, pp. 87–148.

JAEGGLI, OSVALDO. 1982. *Topics in Romance syntax*. (Studies in generative grammar, 12.) Dordrecht: Foris.

KAYNE, RICHARD S. 1975. *French syntax: The transformational cycle*. (Current studies in linguistics series, 6.) Cambridge, Mass.: MIT Press.

RIZZI, LUIGI. 1986. On chain formation. In Borer 1986, pp. 65–95.

SAFIR, KENNETH J. 1985. *Syntactic chains*. (Cambridge studies in linguistics, 40.) Cambridge & New York: Cambridge University Press.

COAHUILTECAN LANGUAGES. The term Coahuiltecan has been applied to several languages, all now extinct, which were formerly spoken in southern Texas and northwestern Mexico. Data are scanty on all but Tonkawa. See Ives Goddard, 'The languages of South Texas and the Lower Rio Grande,' in *The languages of Native America,* edited by Lyle Campbell and Marianne Mithun (Austin: University of Texas Press, 1979), pp. 355–389.

LANGUAGE LIST

Coahuilteco: an extinct language documented in southern Texas in the 18th century.

Comecrudo: an extinct language documented from Reynosa, Tamaulipas, Mexico, in the 19th century.

Cotoname: an extinct language documented in the 19th century.

Karankawa: an extinct language documented in the 17th-19th centuries.

Tonkawa: most recently spoken in north central Oklahoma. Probably extinct; in 1977 no fluent speakers were left from a population of 90.

COARTICULATION AND TIMING. 'Coarticulation' refers to the overlap of articulatory gestures associated with separate speech segments, and by extension to its acoustic effects. As a result of coarticulation, segments vary according to their contexts. Thus the /t/ in *tea* may be produced with spread lips, and the /t/ in *two* with more rounded lips, anticipating the rounding of the following vowel. Similarly, the /u/ in *choose* may have a more fronted tongue position, because of the surrounding consonants, than does the /u/ in *poof*; the vowel in *man* may be nasalized, unlike that in *bad*. The term 'coarticulation' was originated in the 1930s by P. Menzerath, who (like others before him, especially E. W. Scripture), argued against the view that successive speech sounds consist of discrete steady states and transitions. Hardcastle 1981 provides a history of early work on coarticulation. [*See* Articulatory Phonetics.]

Coarticulation refers primarily to the timing of articulations; however, it can also involve contextual effects on the spatial extent of articulations, such as reductions in articulatory gestures at faster rates of speech. Such effects eliminate extreme articulatory movements; thus coarticulation has been linked to ease of articulation.

The term 'coarticulation' is sometimes used interchangeably with 'assimilation'. However, Menzerath apparently meant to call attention to the physiological basis of assimilation: coarticulation is the cause, and assimilation the effect. Nonetheless, there are many types of assimilation, not all of them articulatory; and today there are many different opinions on the relation between coarticulation and assimilation.

Many models of coarticulation have been proposed. One (by Menzerath, but also independently influential later) is that articulations begin as early as possible; another is that vowel articulations begin during consonants, and vice versa. Alternatively, certain articulations begin at a fixed amount of time before others. It has also been proposed that higher levels of structure, such as syllables, words, or phrases, may be involved in coarticulation.

Other studies of coarticulation, dating back to the earliest work, have been concerned with possible differences across languages—and more recently, with general principles that would account for such differences. A related question concerns the acquisition of coarticulation: if languages differ, then speakers must learn language-specific patterns.

The study of timing in speech can also involve the measurement of durations of particular events or units, in either physiological or acoustic records (Lehiste 1970). Because of coarticulation, measurements of segment durations are necessarily arbitrary, but have been shown to vary across contexts. The study of segment durations has not been well integrated with the study of coarticulation, although both are concerned with speech timing. However, Fowler 1980 has proposed to unify the two, claiming that measured durations of segments reflect the extent to which they overlap. While this proposal remains controversial, the effort is an important one.

Most work on coarticulation has been published in the major phonetics and speech science journals; the *Journal of Phonetics* has published several review and debate papers since 1977.

Patricia A. Keating

BIBLIOGRAPHY

Fowler, Carol A. 1980. Coarticulation and theories of extrinsic timing. *Journal of Phonetics* 8.113–133.

Hardcastle, William J. 1981. Experimental studies in lingual coarticulation. In *Towards a history of phonetics*, edited by Ronald E. Asher & Eugenie J. A. Henderson, pp. 50–66. Edinburgh: Edinburgh University Press.

Lehiste, Ilse. 1970. *Suprasegmentals*. Cambridge, Mass.: MIT Press.

COMMAND. *See* C-Command.

COMMUNICATIVE COMPETENCE. The term 'communicative competence' was coined by Dell Hymes in 1966, in a proposal to broaden the scope of knowledge and skills embodied in Noam Chomsky's definition of 'linguistic competence' (Chomsky 1965). Hymes argued that speakers who were able to produce all the grammatical sentences of a language would be institutionalized if they went about trying to do so without consideration of appropriate contexts of use, and of the socially and culturally determined norms for production and interpretation. Hymes's proposal was quickly adopted both by sociolinguists and by applied linguists in the field of foreign/second language instruction (although the latter diverge from his original definition). For reference, see Gumperz 1984, Saville-Troike 1989.

From a sociolinguistic perspective, communicative competence includes the following:

(a) Linguistic knowledge: verbal and nonverbal codes, and the range of possible variants
(b) Interaction skills: sociolinguistic rules for appropriate use, discourse organization and processes, and strategies for achieving goals
(c) Cultural knowledge: social structure, values and beliefs, and cognitive maps or schemata for the content domains

This broad scope thus takes into account not only the language code and its referential meaning, but also what may be said to whom; how discourse is to be constructed and interpreted in different contexts; and how what is said (or not said) relates to speakers' role-relationships within the society, and to their structures of belief and knowledge.

From this perspective, the locus of communicative knowledge and skills is in the speech community—although these abilities, like all aspects of culture, are realized variably in its individual members. There is no expectation that a speech community will be linguistically homogeneous; as a whole, it will include a range of language varieties and often different languages, the use of which is patterned in relation to group norms. Speakers' communicative competence includes knowledge of rules (i) for the appropriate choice of variety or language, given a particular social context and communicative intent; (ii) for switching between varieties or languages; or (iii) for maintaining silence when that is the most appropriate mode. Central to the concept is the notion that, in the process of communication, both referential and social/cultural meaning is being conveyed.

Among the most productive areas for application of this perspective has been the study of child language development, where it includes 'discovery of how cultures themselves shape acquisition' (Hymes 1987:224; cf. Heath 1983, Ochs & Schieffelin 1983) [*see* Discourse, *article on* Acquisition of Competence], and the study of classroom interaction in relation to community patterns of communication (Boggs 1972, Philips 1983). Scholars in the field of foreign/second-language teaching generally use the term 'communicative competence' in a narrower sense, to mean the ability to use language appropriately in communicative interaction (cf. Paulston 1974, Savignon 1983). The concept has been applied to the development of 'communicative approaches' to language teaching and testing; these have been widely accepted in most parts of the world. [*See* Assessment.] While the development clearly represents a broadening of scope from the earlier pedagogical emphasis—which was exclusively on the linguistic code (grammar, pronunciation, and vocabulary)—it does not include the breadth of social and cultural knowledge which sociolinguists accept, nor the original concept of communicative competence as being defined by community norms (see Milroy 1987). Attempts to reach agreement on the scope of 'communicative competence' have not been successful, although use of the term has become widespread across disciplines.

Muriel Saville-Troike

BIBLIOGRAPHY

Boggs, Stephen T. 1972. The meaning of questions and narratives to Hawaiian children. In *Functions of language in the classroom*, edited by Courtney B. Cazden et al., pp. 299–327. New York: Teachers College Press.

CHOMSKY, NOAM. 1965. *Aspects of the theory of syntax.* Cambridge, Mass.: MIT Press.

GUMPERZ, JOHN J. 1984. Communicative competence revisited. In *Meaning, form, and use in context: Linguistic applications* (Georgetown University Round Table on Languages and Linguistics, 1984), edited by Deborah Schiffrin, pp. 278–289. Washington, D.C.: Georgetown University Press.

HEATH, SHIRLEY BRICE. 1983. *Ways with words: Language, life, and work in communities and classrooms.* Cambridge & New York: Cambridge University Press.

HYMES, DELL. 1987. Communicative competence. In *Sociolinguistics: An international handbook of the science of language and society,* edited by Ulrich Ammon et al., pp. 219–229. Berlin: de Gruyter.

MILROY, LESLEY. 1987. *Observing and analysing natural language: A critical account of sociolinguistic method.* (Language in society, 12.) Oxford: Blackwell.

OCHS, ELINOR, & BAMBI B. SCHIEFFELIN, eds. 1983. *Acquiring conversational competence.* London: Routledge & Kegan Paul.

PAULSTON, CHRISTINA BRATT. 1974. Linguistic and communicative competence. *TESOL Quarterly* 8.347–362.

PHILIPS, SUSAN U. 1983. *The invisible culture: Communication in classroom and community on the Warm Springs Indian Reservation.* New York: Longman.

SAVIGNON, SANDRA. 1983. *Communicative competence: Theory and classroom practice.* Reading, Mass.: Addison-Wesley.

SAVILLE-TROIKE, MURIEL. 1989. *The ethnography of communication.* 2d ed. (Language in society, 3.) Oxford: Blackwell.

COMPARATIVE METHOD examines items (e.g. phonemes, morphemes, or syntactic constructions) from two or more languages to establish genetic relationship and reconstruct ancestral forms. Unlike typological comparison, which ignores genetic affiliation, the comparative method assumes that the languages compared are (or may be) cognate languages: the descendants of a common ancestor. The ancestor, or PROTO-LANGUAGE, may be unattested (e.g. Proto-Germanic, the ancestor of the Germanic languages), or attested in some of its varieties (e.g. Classical Latin, the literary variety of the language from which the Romance languages are descended). The present discussion will concentrate on phonology and morphology, the two areas that depend on regular sound correspondences; however, the comparative method has been used with considerable success in reconstructing syntax and semantics. (For general reference, see Meillet 1925, Bloomfield 1933:297–320, Allen 1953, Hoenigswald 1950, 1960:119–143, Bynon 1977:45–57, Hock 1986.) [*See also* Semantic Reconstruction; Stylistic Reconstruction.]

The comparative method makes three assumptions:

(a) The relationship between sound and meaning is arbitrary; therefore, widespread similarity in form and meaning between two languages cannot be accidental.
(b) Corresponding features of cognate languages continue features inherited from an ancestral stage or proto-language.
(c) Completed sound changes are exceptionless.

1. Similarity and genetic relationship. The first step in the method is to compile a list of potential cognates. A list of words from several modern Germanic languages, for example, yields many striking similarities of form and meaning (Table 1).

Similarities among these languages are not confined to the words on this list; indeed, the list could be extended greatly. The languages also show many grammatical similarities; e.g., each has some verbs with preterits and past participles formed by adding a suffix containing a dental or alveolar (as in Eng. *work, worked*), and other verbs with preterits and past participles formed by changing the stem vowel (e.g. Eng. *sing, sang, sung*). Grammatical similarities even extend to irregular and suppletive forms. For example, all the languages make a regular comparative by adding a suffix containing *r* to the positive stem, and a regular superlative by adding a suffix with *-st* (e.g. Eng. *sweet, sweeter, sweetest*); but in each a small set of very common

TABLE 1. *Cognates from Modern Germanic Languages*

English	Dutch	German	Icelandic
blood	*bloed*	*Blut*	*blóð*
glass	*glas*	*Glas*	*glas*
(to) hold	*houden*	*halten*	*halda*
foot	*voet*	*Fuss*	*fótur*
side	*zijde*	*Seite*	*síða*
warm	*warm*	*warm*	*varmur*
work	*werk*	*Werk*	*verk*
cold	*koud*	*kalt*	*kaldur*
calf	*kalf*	*Kalb*	*kálfur*
under	*onder*	*unter*	*undir*

adjectives has suppletive comparatives (e.g. Eng. *good, better, best,* Ger. *gut, besser, am besten*). Similarities so pervasive, extending to so much basic vocabulary and to so many detailed points of grammar, have only one explanation: the languages must be genetically related—the descendants of a common ancestor, Proto-Germanic. [*See also* Germanic Languages.]

However, languages can resemble each other for other reasons. Onomatopoetic words, 'baby-talk', and words showing sound symbolism are excluded from consideration: in these, the relationship between sound and meaning is not entirely arbitrary. Similarity can result from borrowing and other effects of language contact, or even from sheer chance—factors which must be eliminated in a list of potential cognates.

Sometimes knowledge of the external history of a language allows us to exclude borrowing as a cause of similarity. For example, we know that many English words resemble French words because English has borrowed extensively from French since the 11th century. Where language contact is less well documented or prehistoric, similarity resulting from borrowing can be excluded with reasonable certainty by selecting items unlikely to have been borrowed. For instance, words referring to technology or material culture, which are often borrowed along with cultural or technological innovations, may make poor candidates for comparison. By contrast, basic vocabulary—kinship terms, numerals, pronouns, pre- and postpositions, and common verbs, adverbs, adjectives, and nouns—are less likely under most circumstances to be borrowed, and are usually more helpful to the comparativist.

Since the relation between sound and meaning is arbitrary, and the phonological inventory of a language is finite, while the number of potential meanings is in principle infinite, we expect a few chance resemblances between any two unrelated languages. For example, *wiro* 'man' in the extinct Timuqua language of Florida looks something like Latin *vir* 'man' (Swadesh 1954:309); but the similarity, while striking, is not evidence for genetic relationship. This is probably one of a handful of cases, at most, where a Latin word looks something like a Timuqua word of similar meaning. By contrast, resemblances among the Germanic languages embrace most of the basic vocabulary. The difference is important: sheer number of resemblances allows us to exclude chance with virtual certainty—because chance, as Thieme (1964:587) observes, 'does not repeat itself indefinitely.'

Length and complexity of sequences is also important. Similarities between whole morphemes or words are far more probative in establishing genetic relationship than are similarities between short sequences of sounds, since the latter are more likely to be accidental. Shared irregularities are very important, especially in morphology or syntax, because languages in intimate contact may come to resemble each other in morphology or surface syntax [*see* Areal Linguistics], and resemblance in syntax sometimes reflects typological universals. [*See* Historical Linguistics, *article on* Typology and Universals.] Irregularity, however, is usually not transmitted in contact situations; and it is language-specific, not universal. Comparisons of words or morphemes that are not members of productive paradigms are especially useful, since the sound correspondences in these are unlikely to have been disrupted by ANALOGY [*q.v.*].

2. Sound correspondences and methodology. To confirm genetic relationship and reconstruct proto-languages, the comparative method uses regular sound correspondences. This makes the comparative method a precise historical tool, rather than a mere cataloging of similarities; and it permits reconstruction of proto-languages even when resemblances among cognate languages are less obvious than those within Germanic.

From the list of Germanic cognates, we can extract the sound correspondences in Table 2 (among others). More data would show that each correspondence recurs.

The correspondence of Eng. *-l-*, Dutch *-l-*, Ger. *-l-*, and Ic. *-l-* only allows us to reconstruct Gmc. **-l-*; but correspondences that differ (e.g. Eng. *-l-*, Dutch *-u-*, Ger. *-l-*, Ic. *-l-*) imply PHONOLOGICAL CHANGE [*q.v.*] in one or more languages. The choice of what to reconstruct depends on the distribution of correspondences, and therefore on the distribution of sounds in each language. In these data, Du. *-u-* occurs only in the sequence *oud* (cf. Eng. *old,* Ger. *alt,* Ic. *ald*), but the distribution of *-l-* is not so restricted: it is apparent that Du. *u* originated as a vocalized allophone of *l* (other data confirm that the preceding vowel was *o,* and show that *l* was also

TABLE 2. *Sound Correspondences from Modern Germanic Languages*

English	Dutch	German	Icelandic
s-	z-	s- /z-/	s-
-l-	-l-	-l-	-l-
-l-	-u-	-l-	-l-
-d(-)	-d(-)	-t(-)	-d(-)

vocalized before *t*). We can reconstruct the following change:

(1) *l > u / o ___ {t, d}

Since correspondences and reconstructions are statements about historical events, they are independent of notation (Hoenigswald 1973:56). Thus the correspondence of Eng. *-l-*, Du. *-u-*, Ger. *-l-*, Ic. *-l-* could be represented by distinctive feature matrices. This approach might have the advantage of showing clearly that the Dutch sound change involved vocalization ([−vocalic] > [+vocalic]), but it would not change the facts.

To the extent that completed sound change is regular, correspondences should also be regular. The REGULARITY PRINCIPLE gives the comparative method a great deal of practical and predictive power. It allows, for example, the prediction of cognates, and it permits the exclusion of similarities resulting from borrowing. For instance, regular correspondences between Eng. /š/ and Ic. /sk/ (e.g. Eng. *ship*, Ic. *skip*) reflect a late Old English sound change /sk/ > /š/. Other words, however, show a correspondence Eng. /sk/ : Ic. /sk/ (e.g. Eng. *skin*, Ic. *skinn*), which betrays them as medieval borrowings from Scandinavian dialects closely related to Icelandic.

Unlike INTERNAL RECONSTRUCTION [*q.v.*], the other major method in historical linguistics, the comparative method recovers both conditioned and unconditioned merger (Hoenigswald 1973:56), as shown in Table 3. Correspondences for the vowels of the words in A and B show two sounds in O[ld] E[nglish] and O[ld] H[igh] G[erman] that correspond to a single long vowel in Gothic: Go. *ē*, OE *ǣ*, *ē*, OHG *ā*, *ia*. But a contrast in one or more descendants of a proto-language should continue, in some form, a contrast in the proto-language. Therefore, the OE contrast of *ǣ* and *ē* (note *swǣr* vs. *hēr*), and of OHG *ā* and *ia* (note *swārs* vs. *hiar*) reveals a Common Germanic contrast between two front vowel phonemes which have merged in Gothic, and which we will provisionally transcribe as *$\bar{e}_1$ (= OE *æ*, OHG *ā*) and *$\bar{e}_2$ (= OE *ē*, OHG *ia*). Since phonemes do not undergo random, unconditioned split, we can exclude the possibility that Gothic reflects the original situation, and that a single phoneme has split into two in Old English and Old High German; i.e., to posit *ē > OE *ǣ/ē* in *swǣr/hēr* and *ē > OHG *ā/ia* in *swārs/hiar* would violate the regularity principle.

The correspondence of Go. *ō*, OE *ō*, and OHG *uo* in section C continues Gmc. **ō* (the earliest OHG documents also have *ō*); but Go. *ē*, OHG *ā* in section D should point to Gmc. *$\bar{e}_1$ as it does in section B. OE *ǣ* and *ō* do not contrast before nasals, but they do contrast elsewhere (e.g. *blōd* 'blood' vs. *dǣd* 'deed'). We would therefore reconstruct *$\bar{e}_1$ for the words in C, positing merger of Gmc. *$\bar{e}_1$ and **ō* before nasals in Old English:

(2) {*$\bar{e}_1$, *ō} > ō / ___ [+nasal]

TABLE 3. *Conditioned and Unconditioned Merger*

	Gothic	Old English (West Saxon)	Old High German (9th c. Frankish)	
A.	*hēr*	*hēr*	*hiar*	'here'
	Krēks	*Crēcas*	*Kriahha*	'Greeks'
B.	*gadēþs*	*dǣd*	*tāt*	'deed'
	swērs	*swǣr*	*swārs*	'honored, heavy'
	swēs	*swǣs*	*swās*	'one's own'
C.	*fōtus*	*fōt*	*fuoz*	'foot'
	blōþ	*blōd*	*bluot*	'blood'
D.	*mēna*	*mōna*	*māno*	'moon'
	nēmun	*nōmon*	*nāmun*	'they took'

TABLE 4. *Phonological Split*

Gothic	Old English	Old High German	
dōmjan	*dēman*	*tuomen*	'to judge'
fōdjan	*dēdan*	*fuoten*	'to feed'
dōmida	*dēmde*	*tuomit*	'(s)he judged'

A major advantage of the comparative method is that it recovers phonological split, even when the conditioning for such split has been lost through further sound change; cf. Table 4.

The correspondence of Go. *ō*, OHG *uo* should reflect Gmc. **ō* as in Table 3, section C; but OE cognates have *ē*, not *ō*. Apparently Gmc. **ō* suffered conditioned split in Old English; but Gothic, not Old English, reveals the conditioning. Wherever the correspondence Go. *ō*, OE *ē*, OHG *uo* occurs, Gothic has *i* or *j* ([i̯]) in the next syllable; but wherever Go. *ō*, OE *ō*, OHG *uo* occurs, the Gothic word lacks *i/j*. Therefore, the split must have involved fronting of Gmc. **ō* to *ē* (through an intermediate stage *ǿ̄*, attested in some early documents) when the next syllable contained **i/j*:

(3) **dōm(i)jan* > **dǿ̄mjan*
**dōmidē* > **dǿ̄midē*

But the **i/j* was later lost through conditioned sound change:

(4) **dǿ̄mjan* > *dēman*
**dǿ̄midē* > **dēmde*

Knowing that the correspondence OE *ē*, Go. *ō*, OHG *uo* points to Gmc. **ō* followed by a syllable containing **i/j* even allows us to reconstruct Gmc. **ō* when **i/j* has also been lost in Gothic. For example, Go. *ō*, OE *ē* in Go. *brōþr* 'brother' (dat. sg.), OE *brēþer* (id.) points to a Gmc. **brōþri* in which **i* conditioned OE fronting (OE *-er-* points to an intermediate stage **brǿ̄þr̥* with **r̥* > *er*).

'Reconstructing forward'—starting with a known feature of the proto-language, and reconstructing the changes that produced the attested features of its daughters—can be a valuable technique when the phonology or morphology of the proto-language is well understood, but the details of development in its daughters are obscure (see Watkins 1969:1–8 for its application in morphology). This is an especially useful technique in Anatolian—where, because of the limitations of the syllabaries used for Hittite, Cuneiform Luvian, and Hieroglyphic Luvian, the phonology of Proto-Anatolian is sometimes better known than the phonology of its daughters. It is, for example, unclear whether Hittite, Cuneiform Luvian, and Hieroglyphic Luvian preserved the I[ndo-]E[uropean] distinction (reconstructed on the basis of sound correspondences among the other IE languages) between initial voiced and voiceless stops. (Lycian, written in an alphabet, has only voiceless stops word-initially.) We do know, however, that Proto-Anatolian retained the voicing distinction, because the languages of the Luvian branch have distinct reflexes for initial *k^w and *g^w (Table 5).

Contrast in daughter languages implies contrast in the proto-language; the contrasting reflexes imply a voicing contrast in Proto-Anatolian and Proto-Luvian: IE *k^w > PAn. *k^w > PLu. *k^w (> Lyc. *t*); IE *g^w > PAn. *g^w > PLu. **w* (> Lyc. *w*).

3. Reconstructing morphology. Reconstruction of morphology depends upon phonological reconstruction,

TABLE 5. *Anatolian Reflexes of IE Labio-velars*

Indo-European	Cuneiform Luvian	Hieroglyphic Luvian	Lycian
*k^w	k^w	k^w (*ku*)	*t-*
*k^w*i/o-*	k^w*is*	*kumana*	*ti*
interrog. pronoun	rel./interrog. pron.	'when, while'	rel. pron.
*g^w	*w*	*w*	*w*
g^w*ou-*		*wawa-*	*wawa-*
'cow, ox'			
*g^w*en-eh*$_2$-	*wana-(tti-)*		
'woman'			

although analogic creation and leveling must often be taken into consideration. Ideally, the regularity principle provides a check on reconstruction, helping to separate phonologically regular descendants of morphemes from those with analogical changes. Neuter *s*-stems in several IE languages illustrate both possibilities (Table 6). Once we establish the segmentation of stem, suffix, and ending in each language, we can set up correspondences among morphemes (Table 7).

Morphological correspondences consist of phonological ones. In the suffix of the oblique stem, regular sound change is implied by the correspondences Skt. *a*, Gk. *e*, La. *e*, Go. *i*, Hitt. *i* (IE **e*), and Skt. *s*, Gk. Ø, La. *r*, Go. *z*, Hitt. *s* (IE **s*). This allows us to reconstruct a suffix **-es-*.

The sound changes implied by these correspondences also permit the reconstruction of additional details of the IE paradigm. In Hittite, IE **e* splits, becoming *ē* when

TABLE 6. *Neuter S-stems in Several IE Languages*

	Sanskrit	Greek	Latin	Gothic	Hittite
Nom./Acc.	*nábh-as* 'cloud'	*néph*^{h}*-os* 'cloud'	*gen-us* 'race'	*riq-is* 'darkness'	*nēb-is* 'heaven'
Oblique Stem	*nábh-as-*	*néph*^{h}*-e-*	*gen-er-*	*riq-iz-*	*nēb-is-*

TABLE 7. *Correspondences among Morphemes*

	Sanskrit	Greek	Latin	Gothic	Hittite
Nom./Acc.	*-as*	*-os*	*-us*	*-is*	*-is*
Oblique	*-as-*	*-e-*	*-er-*	*-iz-*	*-is-*

accented and *i* when unaccented. Go. *z* results from the Germanic sound change known as Verner's Law, by which IE **s* became Gmc. **z* when not immediately preceded by the accent. Hittite and Gothic, then, confirm the root accent of Sanskrit and Greek as an inheritance from IE. Accordingly, we can reconstruct an IE oblique stem, *Root(accented)-*es*- (e.g. **nébh-es*-).

The nominative/accusative in each language is simply the root plus suffix. For the suffix, all the languages agree in showing final -*s*, and we reconstruct IE **s* (actually, Go. -*s* is the reflex of Gmc. *-*z* via devoicing). Correspondences for the vowel preceding the *-*s* are not regular, however. Greek and Latin agree in showing IE **o* (for Gk. *o*, La. *u* in final syllables, cf. Gk. *zdugón* 'yoke', La. *jugum* < IE **yugom*). However, Gothic and Hittite have reflexes of unaccented **e*. (Skt. -*as* is ambiguous, since IE **e* and **o* merge in closed syllables in Sanskrit.) Here we must invoke analogy to explain the divergences. Go. -*is* and Hitt. -*is* can easily result from independent generalizations of the suffix of the oblique stem, but Gk. -*os* and La. -*us* cannot be explained as analogical; therefore, we reconstruct an IE nominative/accusative *Root(accented)-*os* (e.g. **nébh-os*).

4. Limitations. The comparative method has limitations, some of which are inherent in the assumptions it makes. It does not recognize similarities resulting from contact, or from convergent but independent development after a proto-language breaks up. The method is most accurate, therefore, when a speech community breaks up suddenly—e.g. after a group has migrated out of the original community—and the resulting groups have little subsequent contact. The method works well with completed sound changes that have attained a high degree of regularity; but it cannot accurately handle changes that spread unevenly via geographic or sociolinguistic diffusion. [*See* Causation in Language Change.]

The time depth of reconstructions is not great. The earliest texts in IE languages, for example, date from the second millennium BCE, and reconstructed Indo-European reflects a language spoken in about the fourth millennium. In language families without written records before the 19th or 20th centuries (e.g. most languages of Africa and the Americas), the absolute time depth of reconstructions may be much shallower, although the relative gap between the proto-language and the attestation of its daughters could well be comparable (Haas 1969:27–30).

Other limitations lie not in the method, but in the data with which it works. Because changes accumulate with time, the longer cognate languages have been separated, the less they tend to resemble each other. The comparative method has had its greatest successes in cases where the separation between languages is recent. The break-up of the IE speech community in the 4th millennium BCE is a 'recent' event in human history, but accumulated phonological and morphological changes make resemblances less clear, and genetic relationship less easy to demonstrate, when the gap between separation and attestation is greater or the relationship more distant.

The plausibility of reconstructions depends on the quality of data. Sometimes gaps in the data hinder reconstruction. Often we can reconstruct the phonology of a proto-language, but not phonetic details. For example, as we saw above, contrast between OE *ǣ* and *ē* and between OHG *ā* and *ia* requires us to reconstruct two Proto-Germanic vowels. However, as long as we choose distinct symbols to represent the phonemic distinction, any reconstruction of the phonetic details of the two phonemes is essentially an educated guess. We might, for example, reconstruct open */ɛ̄/ for $*\bar{e}_1$ (= Go. *ē*, OE *ǣ*, OHG *ā*) vs. close */ē/ for $*\bar{e}_2$ (= Go. *ē*, OE *ē*, OHG *ia*)—a typologically common opposition that easily explains the sound changes in each language. However, nothing in the comparative method gives us any reason to prefer */ɛ̄/ and */ē/ over, say, */ǣ/ vs. */ē/, or any other typologically possible pair. In fact, early Proto-Germanic probably had no single entity $*\bar{e}_2$. Instead, several minor sound changes may have produced a long vowel distinct from $*\bar{e}_1$ in North and West Germanic (Nielsen 1985).

5. Conclusion. While the comparative method is one of the supreme intellectual achievements of the 19th century, it is by no means an object of mere antiquarian interest; it remains the surest method for demonstrating genetic relationship and for reconstructing the prehistory of languages. Its usefulness is certainly not confined to Indo-European or other language families with long written traditions (see especially Haas 1969). Even within Indo-European, it is the surest guide we have through the mostly uncharted waters of Anatolian phonology (cf. Melchert 1987). Because it permits reconstruction of unrecorded ancestral stages, it can be used, often with great precision, to recover details of vernacular varieties of languages attested only in literary form. This is a property well known to Romance philologists, and one exploited with considerable success by Harris 1987, in his use of data from Atlantic Creoles to reconstruct front-raising of Early Modern English /a/.

Sara E. Kimball

BIBLIOGRAPHY

Allen, William S. 1953. Relationship in comparative linguistics. *Transactions of the Philological Society* 1953.52–112.

Bloomfield, Leonard. 1933. *Language.* New York: Holt.

Bynon, Theodora. 1977. *Historical linguistics.* Cambridge & New York: Cambridge University Press.

Haas, Mary R. 1969. *The prehistory of languages.* (Janua linguarum, Series minor, 57.) The Hague: Mouton.

Harris, John. 1987. On doing comparative reconstruction with genetically unrelated languages. In *Papers from the Seventh International Conference on Historical Linguistics,* edited by Anna G. Ramat et al., pp. 267–282. Amsterdam: Benjamins.

Hoenigswald, Henry M. 1950. The principal step in comparative grammar. *Language* 26.357–364.

Hoenigswald, Henry M. 1960. *Language change and linguistic reconstruction.* Chicago: University of Chicago Press.

Hoenigswald, Henry M. 1973. The comparative method. In *Current trends in linguistics,* vol. 11, *Diachronic, areal, and typological linguistics,* edited by Thomas A. Sebeok, pp. 51–62. The Hague: Mouton.

Hock, Hans Henrich. 1986. *Principles of historical linguistics.* (Trends in linguistics, Studies and monographs, 34.) Berlin: Mouton de Gruyter.

Meillet, Antoine. 1925. *La méthode comparative en linguistique historique.* Oslo: Aschehoug. Reprinted, Paris: Champion, 1966.

Melchert, H. Craig. 1987. Proto-Indo-European velars in Luvian. In *Studies in memory of Warren Cowgill (1929–1985): Papers from the Fourth East Coast Indo-European Conference, Cornell University, 1985,* edited by Calvert Watkins, pp. 182–204. Berlin: de Gruyter.

Nielsen, Hans F. 1985. *English and the continental Germanic languages: A survey of morphological and phonological interrelations.* 2d ed. (Innsbrucker Beiträge zur Sprachwissenschaft, 33.) Innsbruck: Institut für Sprachwissenschaft.

Swadesh, Morris. 1954. Perspectives and problems of Amerindian comparative linguistics. *Word* 10.306–332.

Thieme, Paul. 1964. The comparative method for reconstruction. In *Language in culture and society: A reader in linguistics and anthropology,* edited by Dell Hymes, pp. 585–598. New York: Harper & Row.

Watkins, Calvert. 1969. *Indo-European origins of the Celtic verb.* Dublin: Institute for Advanced Studies.

COMPARISON OF ADJECTIVES. *See* Gradation.

COMPENSATORY LENGTHENING (CL) is the lengthening of a vowel concomitant with the loss of a nearby, usually syllable-final segment; the length apparently functions to restore the syllable to its original weight. CL is attested with loss of both obstruents and sonorants. Affected consonants (except laryngeals) are generally voiced, either underlyingly or by assimilation. (For reference, see De Chene & Anderson 1979, Ingria 1980, Hock 1986a,b, Wetzels & Sezer 1986, Hayes 1989.)

Thus syllable-final uvular stops have been lost with CL in Quechua dialects (perhaps via weakening: **q* > **x* > **h*):

(1) Proto-Quechua **suqta* > Chongos Bajo, Huancayo *sūta* 'six'

The stop *k* (or its allophone *γ*) was lost before *l, m,* and *n* in some Muskogean languages:

(2) Proto-Muskogean **lakna* > Alabama, Koasati *lāna* 'yellow'

The sibilant *s* was lost before voiced consonants in Latin:

(3) **dislegō* > *dīligō* 'I pick out, I like'

Nasals were lost before fricatives in stressed syllables in English:

(4) Proto-West Germanic **γans* > Old English *gōs* 'goose'

The laryngeal *h* was lost before sonorant consonants in Seneca:

(5) **ęhníʔtaʔ* > *ę̄níʔtaʔ* 'month'

Synchronically, underlying syllable-final *g* alternates with length in Latin:

(6) /nigwis/ > *nīvis* 'snow' (gen.)

The same is true of *l* in Zyrian:

(7) /pil/ > *pī* 'cloud'

And of *n* in Cayuga:

(8) /akhrenʔ/ > *akhrēʔ* 'I cut it'

And of ʔ in phrase non-final position in Chitimacha:

(9) *hus šaʔ* 'his mouth,' *hus šāki* 'in his mouth'

The situation in which length originates from loss of a preceding consonant (*CCV > CV·) is less commonly documented. It is not clear that this represents CL, since the effect of such lengthening is not preservation of syllable weight. Rather, a short-vowel syllable becomes a long-vowel syllable; cf. *C*r*V > CV· in the Greek dialect of Samothraki (*kráta* > [kā́ta] 'hold!'), or the contraction of glide plus vowel after certain consonants in Munsee (**wə* > *ō*).

As a diachronic phenomenon, it has been claimed that CL is the result of two independent changes:

(a) Weakening of a postvocalic consonant to a glide
(b) Monophthongization of the vowel plus glide into a long vowel, if the language has a pre-existing contrast in vowel length or syllable weight

In theories that represent timing separately from segmental features, CL is characterized as delinking of a segment from its timing element, with retention of the timing element plus spreading of a neighboring segment to the resulting free element. [*See* Autosegmental Phonology.] Investigations of CL within such theories have focused on length which is occasioned by processes other than loss of a postvocalic consonant; these do not fall under the traditional classification of CL, but the structure of the timing elements is also preserved in them. For example, in LuGanda, prevocalic high vowels lose their syllabicity when they combine with a preceding consonant, and the following vowel lengthens:

(10) *liato* > [l^yato] > [l^yāto] 'boat'

In LuGanda, a vowel also lengthens when a following nasal combines with a stop to produce a prenasalized stop:

(11) *muntu* > [mu^ntu] > [$mū^n$tu] 'person'

In Hindi, degemination produced long vowels:

(12) **satt* > *sāt* 'seven'

In Hungarian and Serbo-Croatian, loss of word-final vowels induced length in the preceding syllable:

(13) Hung. **kezü* > *kēz* 'hand'
(14) S-C. **mostŭ* > *môst* 'bridge'

Lengthening of penultimate vowels in some Micronesian languages (Rehg 1984) and in Iroquoian may compensate for the deletion or devoicing of word-final or prepausal vowels:

(15) Oneida utterance-medial [ohkwalí]; utterance-final [ohkwāli̥] 'bear'

Historically, however, stress may be the conditioning factor. In Attic and Ionic Greek, 'quantitative metathesis' suggests CL of a vowel upon shortening of the immediately preceding vowel:

(16) **basilē̂os* > *basiléōs* 'of a king'

Also in Greek, outside of Lesbian and Thessalian, *VC*s* and *VC*j* > V̄C under certain conditions:

(17) **ékrinsa* > *ékrīna* 'I judged'
(18) **klínjō* > *klī́nō* 'I tend'

In some dialects, *VC*w* > V̄C:

(19) **kalwós* > Ionic *kālós* 'beautiful'

Various intermediate representations are posited in the literature.

Total assimilation (cf. Japanese /kawta/ > [katta] 'bought'; Finnish /tulekpas/ > [tuleppas] 'do come!'; Hausa /batuktukaa/ > [batuttukaa] 'matter' (plural); Seri **tCaX* > [ttaX] 'be hard' (neutral)) is viewed as compensatory, in that it also is analyzed as delinking of a segment plus linking of an adjacent segment to the resulting empty timing slot (e.g. Japanese *kawta* > [kaØta] > [katta].

KARIN MICHELSON

BIBLIOGRAPHY

DE CHENE, BRENT, & STEPHEN ANDERSON. 1979. Compensatory lengthening. *Language* 55.505–535.

HAYES, BRUCE. 1989. Compensatory lengthening in moraic phonology. *Linguistic Inquiry* 20.253–306.

HOCK, HANS HENRICH. 1986a. *Principles of historical linguistics.* (Trends in linguistics, Studies and monographs, 34.) Berlin: Mouton de Gruyter.

HOCK, HANS HENRICH. 1986b. Compensatory lengthening: In

defense of the concept 'mora'. *Folia Linguistica* 20.431–460.

INGRIA, ROBERT. 1980. Compensatory lengthening as a metrical phenomenon. *Linguistic Inquiry* 11.465–495.

REHG, KENNETH. 1984. The origins of 'compensatory lengthening' rules in Micronesian languages. In *Studies in Micronesian linguistics* (Pacific linguistics, C-80), edited by Byron W. Bender, pp. 53–59. Canberra: Australian National University.

WETZELS, LEO, & ENGIN SEZER, eds. 1986. *Studies in compensatory lengthening*. (Publications in language sciences, 23.) Dordrecht: Foris.

COMPETENCE. *See* Communicative Competence; *see also* Discourse, *article on* Acquisition of Competence.

COMPLEMENTATION. [*This entry is concerned with the syntactic process whereby a subordinate predication functions as subject or object of a superordinate expression. It comprises two articles:*

An Overview
'COMP' in Formal Grammar

For related topics, see Clause-Combining Constructions.]

An Overview

In approaches to linguistics within, or influenced by, the generative tradition, the term 'complementation' has come to refer to the syntactic state of affairs where a notional sentence or predication functions as an argument of a predicate, i.e. as a subject or object. The complements are in small capitals below:

(1) THAT ROY FELL OFF HIS HORSE *surprised Dale.*
(2) ROY'S FALLING OFF HIS HORSE *surprised Dale.*
(3) FOR ROY TO FALL OFF HIS HORSE *would surprise Dale.*

Relative clauses, absolutes, and clauses of purpose, manner, time, or place are not considered complements because they are not arguments.

Even within a single language, complements can take a variety of syntactic shapes, referred to as 'complement types'. Examples 1–3 illustrate three different complement types for English—a sentence-like complement (ex. 1), a nominalization such as a GERUND (2), and an INFINITIVE (3). All languages seem to have at least two complement types; the maximum seems to be about five. (For reference, see Givón 1980, Noonan 1985, and Ransom 1986.)

1. Complement types are identified by the following:

(a) The morphology of the predicate, i.e. its part of speech or, if it is a verb, its grammatical mood
(b) The sorts of syntactic relations the predicate has with its arguments, e.g. whether the agent has a subject relation to the predicate, as in ex. 1, or a genitive relation to it, as in 2
(c) The external syntactic relations of the complement as a whole, e.g. whether the complement has a subordinate or coordinate relation to the main (or matrix) clause

Some complement types are regularly accompanied by a COMPLEMENTIZER—a word, clitic, or affix whose function is to identify the construction as a complement. Ex. 1 contains the complementizer *that*. Ex. 2 has no complementizer: neither derivational morphology (the gerund suffix *-ing*) nor inflectional morphology (the genitive *-'s*) are properly complementizers. Ex. 3 has the complementizer *to*.

Complement types may be either S[entence]-like or non-S-like. Complementizers aside, S-like complement types have roughly the same syntactic form as a main clause, but non-S-like complement types may differ considerably from main clauses in their syntax. Further, non-S-like complement types, regardless of the part of speech of their predicates, are typically reduced or DESENTENTIALIZED, in that they may not have the full range of grammatical and inflectional possibilities available to main clauses and S-like complements. For example, neither the infinitive nor the gerund in English can be inflected for primary tense—though secondary tenses, e.g. the perfect, are available to these forms. All languages seem to have at least one S-like complement type.

One way in which complement types can be reduced is that there may be limitations on the sorts of grammatical relations that can hold between predicates and their arguments. The most common limitations affect the relation between a predicate and its notional subject: with infinitives, notional subjects are either RAISED, (4), EQUI-DELETED (5), or made into objects of adpositions (6):

(4) *We wanted* ZEKE TO EAT LEEKS.
(5) *We wanted* Ø TO EAT LEEKS.
(6) FOR ZEKE TO EAT LEEKS *would please Zelda.*

'Raising' refers to the situation where the notional subject of the complement is treated syntactically as the direct object of the matrix clause: in 4, if *Zeke* is replaced by a pronoun, it is replaced by the objective case *him* and not the subjective *he*. In 5, the notional subject of the complement is *we*, coreferential with the subject of the matrix clause; it is said to be 'equi-deleted' under identity with the matrix subject.

2. Features of complement types. Some of the more important features of the most common complement types are summarized below.

(a) INDICATIVE: Predicate is a verb. The syntactic relation of subject to predicate is the same as in the main clause. The range of inflectional categories is the same as for the main clause. The S-like form is (nearly) identical to a declarative main clause.
(b) SUBJUNCTIVE: Predicate is a verb. The syntactic relation of subject to predicate is the same as in the main clause. The range of inflectional categories is typically reduced. The S-like form differs from a declarative main clause; when it is itself a main clause, it is often used in hortative or imperative sentences.
(c) PARATACTIC: Predicate is a verb; it may agree with the subject, but does not form a constituent with it. The range of inflectional categories is the same as for the indicative. The construction is interpreted as a separate assertion; syntactically, it is not a subordinate clause, and cannot take a complementizer.
(d) INFINITIVE: Predicate is a verb, but cannot form a constituent with the subject. The range of inflectional categories is reduced, with no subject/verb agreement. Relations with the object are the same as in the indicative.
(e) NOMINALIZATION: Predicate is a noun; there is an associative relation between the subject and predicate. Inflectional categories are reduced, but as a noun, the predicate may be marked for nominal categories such as case and number. The construction may have the internal structure of a noun phrase; there is often gradation between nominalizations and infinitives.
(f) PARTICIPLE: Predicate is an adjective. The subject is the head, while the rest of the predication is syntactically a modifier. Inflectional categories are reduced; the construction may take adjectival inflections when it agrees with the subject. Syntactically, it may conform to principles governing adjectives.

3. Choice of complement type, in any given situation, is determined by the meaning of the complement type in that language, together with the meaning of the predicate in the matrix clause. For example, in English, gerunds are used to express complement predications treated as facts, whereas infinitives are used to express complement predications treated as potential, projected events. *Remember* is compatible with both, since one can remember both a fact and a projected event:

(7) *Alvin remembered* WASHING THE DOG. (gerund)
(8) *Alvin remembered* TO WASH THE DOG. (infinitive)

Want, however, is compatible only with projected events; what one wants cannot have occurred prior to wanting it. Therefore, *want* is compatible with the infinitive, but not with the gerund:

(9) **Alvin wanted* WASHING THE DOG. (gerund)
(10) *Alvin wanted* TO WASH THE DOG. (infinitive)

Few grammatical principles, if any, are specific to complementation; and though complementation can be given a workable definition, the definition is semantic rather than grammatical. For example, all the complement types have functions both inside and outside the complement system, and their properties cannot be characterized solely by reference to complementation. Complementation can be understood as one mode of CLAUSE-COMBINING [*q.v.*].

MICHAEL NOONAN

BIBLIOGRAPHY

GIVÓN, TALMY. 1980. The binding hierarchy and the typology of complements. *Studies in Language* 4.333–377.
NOONAN, MICHAEL. 1985. Complementation. In *Language typology and syntactic description,* edited by Timothy Shopen, vol. 2, *Complex constructions,* pp. 42–140. Cambridge & New York: Cambridge University Press.
RANSOM, EVELYN N. 1986. *Complementation: Its meanings and forms.* (Typological studies in language, 10.) Amsterdam: Benjamins.

'COMP' in Formal Grammar

The term COMPLEMENTIZER was used in Rosenbaum 1967 to designate the initial elements of embedded clauses, e.g. *that, for*, etc. The syntactic category COMP was first proposed by Bresnan 1970, 1972. She argued for a base-generated category (introduced by the rule

S′ → COMP S) which served two functions: (i) as the sentence-initial category dominating the lexical complementizers; and (ii) as the 'landing site' for WH-movement.

It is in this latter capacity, as a position for preposed WH-phrases, that COMP has played a central role in subsequent developments within generative grammar. Incorporating the analysis of questions outlined in Baker 1970, in particular the Q-morpheme, Bresnan argued that COMP could be instantiated as either [−WH], e.g. *that,* or [+WH], forming part of the structural description of transformations which prepose WH-phrases:

(1) *John believes* $[_{S'}$ $[_{COMP}$ *that* $[_S$ *Bill likes Mary*]]].

(2) *John wonders* $[_{S'}$ $[_{COMP}$ *who* $[_S$ *Bill likes*]]].

Chomsky 1973 adopted Bresnan's proposal and exploited the presence of a clause-initial COMP node to allow certain types of long-distance movement, while unifying a number of Ross's island constraints (1967) under Subjacency [*q.v.*]. Thus long-distance WH-movement is possible when there is an available COMP position to permit successive local movements, as shown in 3. But if COMP is unavailable—as in 4, where it has been filled by a previous instance of movement—then a WH-island is created, and movement is impossible (but see Bresnan 1976 for an alternative analysis).

(3) $[_{S'}$ $[_{COMP}$ *What*$_1$ $[_S$ *did John think* $[_{S'}$ $[_{COMP}$ $\mathbf{t}_1$ $[_S$ *Bob saw* $\mathbf{t}_1$]]]]]]?

(4) $[_{S'}$ $[_{COMP}$ *What*$_2$ $[_S$ *did John wonder* $[_{S'}$ $[_{COMP}$ *who*$_1$ $[_S$ $\mathbf{t}_1$ *saw* $\mathbf{t}_2$]]]]]]*?*

Within the framework of Chomsky's 1981 GOVERNMENT/BINDING THEORY [*q.v.*], much of the work of restricting the power of transformations has shifted from the structural descriptions of individual rules to general principles constraining the class of allowable representations resulting from rule application. In the case of WH-movement, these principles often involve COMP.

The initial formulation of many of these principles was made primarily by Aoun et al. 1980 (henceforth AHS). For example, the observation that WH-movement is obligatory in English is captured by the following FILTER [*see* Filters]:

(5) * $\text{COMP}_{[+WH]}$ unless it contains a [+WH] element.

In English, this filter applies at S-STRUCTURE [*q.v.*]; but Huang 1982 argues that in Chinese, a language which lacks syntactic WH-movement, it applies at L[ogical] F[orm].

AHS also discuss cases of 'WH in situ', where a WH-phrase still occupies its D-STRUCTURE position [*q.v.*] at S-structure, in terms of operations involving COMP. Chomsky 1973 had noted the contrast of 6–7, and formulated a 'superiority condition' to account for the ungrammaticality of 7:

(6) $[_{S'}$ $[_{COMP}$ *Who*$_1$ $[\mathbf{t}_1$ *saw what*]]]*?*

(7) $[_{S'}$ $[_{COMP}$ *What*$_1$ [*did who see* $\mathbf{t}_1$]]]*?*

AHS subsume superiority effects under the Empty Category Principle (Chomsky 1981) [*see* Government]. To do this, they first posit the COMP Indexing Rule of 8; this yields 9 as the LF representation for 7:

(8) $[_{COMP} \ldots X_i \ldots] \rightarrow [_{COMP} \ldots X_i \ldots]_i$
if COMP dominates only i-indexed elements

(9) $[_{S'}$ $[_{COMP}$ *Who*$_2$ *what*$_1$]$_1$ [*did* $\mathbf{t}_2$ *see* $\mathbf{t}_1$]]*?*

In 9, the empty category $\mathbf{t}_2$ is not properly governed; i.e., it is neither lexically governed (e.g. by a verb) nor antecedent-governed, because rule 8 insures that COMP bears the index of the object, which moved at S-structure. Huang 1982 points out that this result also holds for adjuncts:

(10) $[_{S'}$ $[_{COMP}$ *Why*$_2$ *what*$_1$]$_1$ [*did Bill see* $\mathbf{t}_1$ $\mathbf{t}_2$]]*?*

The task of extending the work of AHS has been taken up by many researchers. For example, Lasnik & Saito 1984 argue that COMP, like other phrasal categories, has a head position. Given this, they derive the effect of 8 from the fact that COMP will receive the index of its head.

Chomsky 1986 considers COMP from the perspective of X-bar theory [*see* Phrase Structure], and reformulates the traditional nodes S′ and S as COMP″ and INFL″ respectively. This allows a uniform treatment of phrasal categories as projections of their heads, as well as a restriction of movement of phrasal categories to specifier positions.

PAUL GORRELL

BIBLIOGRAPHY

AOUN, JOSEPH; NORBERT HORNSTEIN; & DOMINIQUE SPORTICHE. 1980. Some aspects of wide scope quantification. *Journal of Linguistic Research* 1:3.69–95.

BAKER, CARL LEE. 1970. Notes on the description of English questions: The role of an abstract question morpheme. *Foundations of Language* 6.197–219.

BRESNAN, JOAN. 1970. On complementizers: Toward a syntactic theory of complement types. *Foundations of Language* 6.297–321.

BRESNAN, JOAN. 1972. *Theory of complementation in English syntax*. MIT dissertation. Published, New York: Garland, 1979.

BRESNAN, JOAN. 1976. Evidence for a theory of unbounded transformations. *Linguistic Analysis* 2.353–393.

CHOMSKY, NOAM. 1973. Conditions on transformations. In *A Festschrift for Morris Halle,* edited by Stephen R. Anderson & Paul Kiparsky, pp. 232–286. New York: Holt, Rinehart & Winston.

CHOMSKY, NOAM. 1981. *Lectures on government and binding*. (Studies in generative grammar, 9.) Dordrecht: Foris.

CHOMSKY, NOAM. 1986. *Barriers*. (Linguistic Inquiry monographs, 13.) Cambridge, Mass.: MIT Press.

HUANG, C.-T. JAMES. 1982. Move WH in a language without WH movement. *Linguistic Review* 1.369–416.

LASNIK, HOWARD, & MAMORU SAITO. 1984. On the nature of proper government. *Linguistic Inquiry* 15.235–289.

ROSENBAUM, PETER S. 1967. *The grammar of English predicate complement constructions*. Cambridge, Mass.: MIT Press.

ROSS, JOHN ROBERT. 1967. *Constraints on variables in syntax*. MIT dissertation. Published as *Infinite syntax* (Norwood, N.J.: Ablex, 1986).

COMPONENTIAL ANALYSIS has its roots in two structuralist traditions: that of the European post-Saussureans (e.g. Hjelmslev 1943), and that of the American anthropological linguists (e.g. Lounsbury 1956). Both groups wanted to show the semantic relationships of words which have no phonological similarity, much as one decomposes the phone [p] into features [voiceless], [stop], and [bilabial]. They also wished to define sets of related words in terms of small numbers of semantic primitives—also called SEMES, semantic markers, or semantic primes. Consider the set of words in Table 1 (from Hjelmslev 1943):

TABLE 1. *Domestic Animals in English*

sheep	ram	ewe	lamb
horse	stallion	mare	colt
chicken	rooster	hen	chick

C[OMPONENTIAL] A[NALYSIS] would define the words in terms of semantic primes: a species term (e.g. OVINE), MALE or FEMALE, and YOUNG.

In addition, linguists and anthropologists often need to define words of other languages, but the nearest translation equivalent may be quite inexact; a kin term might apply to ego's father, paternal grandfather, and fathers' brothers. Therefore, it was necessary to create a metalanguage that was free of translation problems. Presumably all kin terms in all languages can be defined in terms of components such as PARENT OF, SIBLING OF, CHILD OF, CONSANGUINEAL, AFFINAL, MALE, FEMALE, and a few others, together with rules for combination and recursion.

Although many linguists and anthropologists have used semantic components, theories of CA have been worked out in most detail by Katz 1972, 1977, 1981 and Wierzbicka 1972, 1981, 1985. In Katz's theory, intended to be the semantic counterpart of Chomsky's (1965) syntactic theory, each word is to be decomposed into semantic markers, many of which have considerable internal structure. Some aspects of the meaning of sentences, e.g. AGENT, can be interpreted from the syntactic tree. Katz has devised machinery for combining compatible components, filtering out incompatible components, handling presupposition, and predicting judgments of semantic acceptability.

Wierzbicka's analysis into components is the most radical, since she attempts to reduce vocabularies to about a dozen primitives, such as WANT, FEEL, THINK OF, IMAGINE, SAY, BECOME, BE A PART OF, SOMEONE, SOMETHING, I, YOU, WORLD, and THIS. Natural language syntax is assumed and used without discussion. Wierzbicka, however, has a generative principle for defining vocabulary. Thus *cat* is defined as 'an animal thinking of which one would say *cat*' (1972:22). Wierzbicka uses this principle to define natural kinds and physical objects, which then serve as exemplars for defining other things, e.g. *white* 'the color thought of as the color of milk' (1981:42). Recently she has elaborated her definitions so that the one for *dog,* for instance, takes two pages. While Wierzbicka strives for completeness, the earlier CA analysts sought definitions as succinct as possible, stressing lexical contrasts in a language. [*See* Semantics, *article on* Semantic Primitives.]

CA is appealing for several reasons. First, it provides

the potential for a universal metalanguage that could be used to define all vocabulary in all languages. Second, it provides a basis for a theory of translation. It would be possible to show explicitly that some translation equivalents are exact, while others differ. If word A in Language 1 has the features [+a, +b, +c, +d] whereas the nearest equivalent in Language 2 has [+a, +b, +c, −d], then they are shown to differ with respect to feature [d]. Third, CA is a useful descriptive device for comparative lexicology. Semantic fields in different languages can be compared by using a well chosen set of features. Finally, CA can be used to show explicitly the patterns and symmetries of lexical structure.

There are, however, several serious objections to CA. The first is that the ontological status of components is not clear. Are they theoretical constructs, or psychological entities in a language of thought? A second problem is that semantic components may not be universal. Certainly 'functional' categories, such as PET, FURNITURE, WEED, TOOL, and RELATIVE, will be influenced by cultural and even personal factors. People with lawns consider dandelions to be weeds, while those who cultivate dandelions for salads consider them to be vegetables. Even supposedly universal features like ANIMATE, HUMAN, FEMALE, and LIVING may be interpreted differently by different people. The core of such a concept may be the same for all speakers, but differences in the periphery could be overlooked, resulting in the suggestion of more conceptual equivalence across languages than actually exists. Although lack of universality does not invalidate using CA for individual languages, it reduces its appeal for comparative lexicology.

A third objection is that CA is not suitable for all parts of the vocabulary. It is especially deficient in dealing with scalar terms and antonyms (Lehrer 1974, Lehrer & Lehrer 1982). The words *freezing, cold, cool, tepid, warm, hot, burning* share the component TEMPERATURE, but how are the words to be distinguished from one another? Traditionally, features such as INTENSE and EXTREME are introduced, possibly with intermediate degrees. But these features can only be understood with respect to a scale of some sort. Words which function as sentence operators are not well handled by CA. In the sentence *Bill falsely believes that Sue lives in Paris*, the word *falsely* shows that the embedded complement of *believe* is false. Simply assigning NOT TRUE to *falsely* will not provide the necessary semantic machinery. Hence a MEANING POSTULATE will be necessary. [*See* Meaning, *article on* Properties and Relationships.]

Of course, many items in the lexicon are neither scalar nor operators, so perhaps CA would be suitable for them. However, there is a general prejudice against mixed theories, in which part of the lexicon is analyzed into components and the rest handled by other devices.

Any metalanguage needs an interpretation, and as Allan (1986:1.265 ff.) points out, for most purposes the metalanguage must be interpreted in terms of some natural language(s) in order to be used and understood. Even if we were to use semantic components, some components would have to be defined either in terms of words corresponding to themselves, or else in circular terms. Thus the word *human* could be defined by the component HUMAN, or by PERSON; but then *person* would have to be defined either by PERSON or by HUMAN. Most natural language terms are ambiguous, however, so that in adapting natural language expressions as a metalanguage, those expressions must themselves be defined, indexed, or restricted. Whether such a set of universal components can be devised even for parts of vocabularies remains an open question. [*See also* Lexicon.]

ADRIENNE LEHRER

BIBLIOGRAPHY

ALLAN, KEITH. 1986. *Linguistic meaning*. 2 vols. London: Routledge & Kegan Paul.

CHOMSKY, NOAM. 1965. *Aspects of the theory of syntax*. Cambridge, Mass.: MIT Press.

HJELMSLEV, LOUIS. 1943. *Omkring sprogteoriens grundlæggelse*. Copenhagen: Lunos. Translated as *Prolegomena to a theory of language* (Madison: University of Wisconsin Press, 1961).

KATZ, JERROLD J. 1972. *Semantic theory*. New York: Harper & Row.

KATZ, JERROLD J. 1977. *Propositional structure and illocutionary force: A study of the contribution of sentence meaning to speech acts*. New York: Crowell.

KATZ, JERROLD J. 1981. *Language and other abstract objects*. Totowa, N.J.: Rowman & Littlefield.

LEHRER, ADRIENNE. 1974. *Semantic fields and lexical structure*. Amsterdam: North-Holland.

LEHRER, ADRIENNE, & KEITH LEHRER. 1982. Antonymy. *Linguistics & Philosophy* 5.483–501.

LOUNSBURY, FLOYD. 1956. A semantic analysis of the Pawnee kinship usage. *Language* 37.158–194.

WIERZBICKA, ANNA. 1972. *Semantic primitives*. Frankfurt: Athenäum.

WIERZBICKA, ANNA. 1981. *Lingua mentalis: The semantics of natural language*. Sydney & New York: Academic Press.

WIERZBICKA, ANNA. 1985. *Lexicography and conceptual analysis.* Ann Arbor: Karoma.

COMPOUNDING. A prototypical compound is a morphologically complex word containing at least two elements which can otherwise occur as free forms, i.e. as independent words—Eng. *steamboat, delivery van, headhunter, snow-white, Polish-German.* Thus compounding essentially represents a grammatical device by which complex words can be formed from smaller elements which, under normal circumstances, have word status. Compounding differs from affixation in that the latter involves morphemes which cannot have word status. Affixal morphemes are basically of two types, derivational as in *read-er,* and inflectional as in *(he) read-s*; neither type can be freely distributed as independent words. [*See* Derivational Morphology; Inflection.]

1. Word properties. An important indication that a string of elements constitutes a compound is its word-like behavior. Thus parts of compounds cannot be rearranged without a change in meaning (*flower garden* vs. *garden flower*), although rearrangement of constituents might otherwise be possible in a given language. Furthermore, compounds are like words in that their constituents cannot generally be separated by intervening material. Compounds also typically receive stress like that of words, not of syntactic phrases. Thus the German compound *Starkbier* 'strong-beer' has initial stress, which is common in words; but the phrase *starkes Bier* 'strong beer' has phrasal stress, with prosodic prominence on *Bier.* In many languages, compounds are characterized by the occurrence of special morphological elements between the parts of a compound, e.g. *-o-* in Czech *vod-o-pád* 'water-fall' and in Russian *čern-o-zem* 'black-soil'. The Slavic linking morpheme (or interfix) *-o-* is typical of compounds; it appears neither in words derived by affixation nor in syntactic phrases. German linking morphemes, such as *-s-* in *Beobachtung-s-turm* 'observation-tower', can be traced historically to case inflection; however, their distribution and meaning in compounds radically differ from those of contemporary case morphemes. Thus one must again speak of a trait characteristic of compounding.

2. Relations between parts. Two basic relations between parts of compounds are generally recognized: DETERMINATION and COORDINATION. In the first case, there is a MODIFIER (determinans) and a MODIFIED ELEMENT (determinatum); this is characteristic of so-called determinative compounds like *steamboat.* In the second case, represented by COORDINATIVE (copulative) compounds such as *Polish-German,* no part is subordinate to another. This classification is based on the semantic intuition that the modified part of a determinative compound names a set of denotata, while the modifier restricts it to a subset. Thus *boat* in *steamboat* names a set of denotata called 'boats'; *steam* restricts it to a subset, namely 'boats driven by steam'. A coordinative compound, by contrast, typically names a conjunction of sets of denotata named by the subparts of the compound. Thus, in *mother-child relationship,* the hyphenated part is a coordinative compound denoting a conjunction of sets of denotata. The entire phrase, however, is a determinative compound, in which the coordinative subpart functions as a modifier of relationship.

3. Headedness. Since the early 1980s, scholars have stressed the importance of the notion of HEADS [*q.v.*] in word formation, including compounding (Williams 1981). The head of a word, or more generally of a syntactic construction, is that part which determines the morphosyntactic properties of the entire word. Recourse to this notion is useful because 'head' is a category in general theories of phrase structure (such as X-bar theory), and thus is independent of word-formation. However, the definition of head employed in theories of word-structure is not quite the same as in theories of syntactic structure. In particular, it is suggested that the head in word-formation is defined in terms of the positional notions 'right' and 'left'—rather than in terms of the level of projection, as is common in syntactic phrases. In languages like German or English, words are generally right-headed; thus, in *steamboat,* the noun *boat* is termed the head of the entire compound.

In certain subtypes of compounds, the notion of 'head' is not applicable without problems. Thus, in Eng. *pick-pocket,* it is not clear to what degree *pocket* should be viewed as determining the category of the entire compound. As far as semantics is concerned, the compound certainly denotes neither a type of pocket nor a type of picking. Compounds such as these have traditionally been called exocentric in contrast to endocentric; an example of the latter is regular determinative compounds. Another type of compound traditionally described as exocentric is represented by Eng. *redskin* and Ger. *Blauhemd* 'blue-shirt', i.e. a soldier wearing a blue uniform. However, although *redskin* does not denote a type of skin, nor *Blauhemd* a type of shirt, a purely morphosyntactic definition of head requires us to regard them as endocentric, despite traditional classification. This is best illustrated by data from German, where the right-hand element determines the gender of the entire compound: thus *Blauhemd* is neuter, like *Hemd*.

4. Internal structure. Compounds, like syntactic phrases, may have a complex internal structure. This is so because each constituent of a compound can be in itself internally complex. In particular, nominal compounds in languages like German can develop a complex internal structure; e.g.,

[[[[[*Ober*][*schul*]][*lehrer*]][*witwen*]][*verein*]] 'high-school-teacher-widow-union'.

In this sense, compounding rules have a certain recursive property. Complex internal structure is also found in compounds which accommodate material with phrasal properties: *an area-by-area directory, a once-in-a-lifetime opportunity, a what-I-don't-know-won't-hurt-me attitude*.

5. Categories involved in compounding. Depending on the syntactic category of lexical morphemes involved, a variety of combinations, and hence a variety of compounds, can be obtained—including noun + noun compounds *(steamboat),* verb + noun compounds *(hoverboat),* adjective + noun compounds *(snow-white),* etc. Typically, these combinations differ in productivity. Whereas noun + noun compounding is fairly productive in English, compounds of noun + verb *(to baby-sit)* or verb + verb *(to hop-skip)* are not productive. Patterns with minor lexical categories such as prepositions *(onto, undergarment)* are also of rather limited productivity.

6. Semantic relations between parts. Much attention has been paid to the classification of compounds on the basis of the semantic roles which may be satisfied by their subparts. One type of semantic role includes agent, theme, experiencer, and location, which are typically involved in compounds containing verbs and adjectives. In particular, compounds which incorporate verbs, either as pure roots or as nominalizations, have been classified in accordance with these relations. Thus, in German *Putzfrau* 'cleaning lady', the nominal constituent may be interpreted as filling the agent role of *putzen* 'to clean', and in *Trinkwasser* 'drinking water' as filling the role of theme of the verb *trinken* 'to drink'. For compounds without overt predicates, such as noun + noun compounds, scholars have proposed a variety of semantic relations holding between the subparts, in addition to the above semantic roles—including relations such as class-inclusion *(pathway)* and similarity *(blood orange).*

Rather than classifying compounds on the basis of semantic relations, generative studies (Selkirk 1982, Lieber 1983, Boase-Beier et al. 1986) have focused on principles which regulate the distribution of semantic roles in compounds, and have attempted to relate these principles to the so-called theory of thematic roles (θ-theory).

7. Cross-linguistic variation. Both similarity and variation can be detected in compounding in various languages, as is the case with word-formation in general (cf. Anderson 1985). A major distinction concerns the position of the head of the compound. For instance, in Germanic, Slavic, and Finno-Ugric languages, the head typically follows the modifier. Romance languages, on the other hand, display patterns in which the head precedes the modifier; thus Italian *caffellatte* (i.e. *caffè + latte* 'coffee-milk') denotes a type of coffee, not a type of milk. Variation in the position of the head is also found when types of phrases other than compounds are compared.

Another major distinction concerns the productivity of compounding in different languages. Germanic languages utilize compounding extensively, Slavic and Romance languages to a much lesser degree. Typically, even languages which exploit compounding only to a limited degree still have several highly productive compounding patterns. Thus, in Czech, an adjective + noun compound can be formed from any proper name of the form adjective + noun; cf. *Staré Zámky* (lit. 'Old Castles'), *starozámecký* 'pertaining to Staré Zámky'. But other compounding patterns, such as noun + noun or verb + noun, are uncommon. It has been assumed that the presence of compounding in the grammar of a language, or of particular patterns, should be contingent on other properties of the language; but this point has not yet been satisfactorily explicated.

8. History of research. Ancient Indian grammarians, including Pāṇini (5th c. BCE) and Patañjali (2nd c. BCE), are the first linguists known to have dealt with compounding. They studied Sanskrit compounds and presented a classification based on semantic criteria (Mahavir 1978). Some of their terminology—dvandva compounds for coordinative compounds, bahuvrihi compounds for a type of exocentric compounds—is still used. In the European tradition, J. G. Schottelius (1612–76) noted the distinction between the modifying and the modified element in German compounds.

In the 20th century a rich descriptive tradition as well as a variety of theoretical approaches developed. One example of a descriptive approach is that of Marchand 1969. Other approaches include generative grammar (Selkirk 1982, Lieber 1983, Toman 1983, Di Sciullo & Williams 1987), categorial grammar (Hoeksema 1984), and natural morphology (Dressler 1987). Compounds have also been studied from specialized points of view, including their use in situational contexts (Downing 1977), in poetic language (Boase-Beier 1987), and many others.

JINDŘICH TOMAN

BIBLIOGRAPHY

ANDERSON, STEPHEN R. 1985. Typological distinctions in word formation. In *Language typology and syntactic description,* vol. 3, *Grammatical categories and the lexicon,* edited by Timothy Shopen, pp. 3–56. Cambridge & New York: Cambridge University Press.

BOASE-BEIER, JEAN. 1987. *Poetic compounds: The principles of poetic language in modern English poetry.* (Linguistische Arbeiten, 179.) Tübingen: Niemeyer.

BOASE-BEIER, JEAN, & JINDŘICH TOMAN. 1986. On θ-role assignment in German compounds. *Folia Linguistica* 20.319–340.

DI SCIULLO, ANNE-MARIE, & EDWIN WILLIAMS. 1987. *On the definition of word.* (Linguistic Inquiry monographs, 14.) Cambridge, Mass.: MIT Press.

DOWNING, PAMELA. 1977. On the creation and use of English compound nouns. *Language* 53.810–842.

DRESSLER, WOLFGANG U. 1987. Word formation as part of Natural Morphology. In *Leitmotifs in Natural Morphology* (Studies in language, Companion series, 10), edited by Wolfgang U. Dressler et al., pp. 99–126. Amsterdam: Benjamins.

HOEKSEMA, JACK. 1984. *Categorial morphology.* University of Groningen dissertation. Published, New York: Garland, 1985.

LIEBER, ROCHELLE. 1983. Argument linking and compounds in English. *Linguistic Inquiry* 14.251–285.

MAHAVIR. 1978. *Pāṇini as a grammarian, with special reference to compound formations.* Delhi: Bharatiya Vidya Prakashan.

MARCHAND, HANS. 1969. *The categories and types of present-day English word-formation: A synchronic-diachronic approach.* 2d ed. Munich: Beck.

SELKIRK, ELISABETH O. 1982. *The syntax of words.* (Linguistic Inquiry monographs, 7.) Cambridge, Mass.: MIT Press.

TOMAN, JINDŘICH. 1983. *Wortsyntax: Eine Diskussion ausgewählter Probleme deutscher Wortbildung.* (Linguistische Arbeiten, 137.) Tübingen: Niemeyer.

WILLIAMS, EDWIN. 1981. Argument structure and morphology. *Linguistic Review* 1.81–114.

COMPREHENSION. What does it mean to comprehend language? Relevant issues include the importance of CONTEXT for understanding, the structure of DISCOURSE and its relationship to characteristics of the human information-processing system, and the form of the REPRESENTATION in which understanding takes place.

At one level of understanding, a language user first recognizes each of the words in a sentence, and then combines the word meanings appropriately. The result of these processes is a basic MESSAGE-LEVEL understanding of the sentence—i.e. an understanding of who did what to whom. However, the message-level representation is only part of what it means to comprehend a sentence. Consider the following example, adapted from Johnson-Laird 1983:

(1) *The old man often wandered through the streets.*

Without additional knowledge about the man or the city he was wandering through, one cannot really know the significance of the sentence. One would interpret the same sentence in one way if it occurred in the context of a story about Albert Einstein's last years at Princeton, but quite differently in a story about the effects of releasing previously institutionalized persons with mental disabilities. Again, consider this example:

(2) *The car was towed because the man didn't have any change.*

To make sense of this sentence, the reader needs to infer that the man left his car in a metered spot without paying. Or consider sentences such as these:

(3) *Careful or you'll put your foot in it.*

(4) *It's cold in this room.*

Ex. 3 can be interpreted either literally, or metaphorically, as a warning to be careful about pursuing a sensitive line of conversation. Ex. 4 can be interpreted either as a simple comment on the temperature, or as a request (e.g. to shut a window or turn down the air-conditioning), when spoken by a person in a position of authority to a subordinate.

These examples illustrate that comprehension takes place in CONTEXT. A number of factors contribute to context: general knowledge of the world, more specific knowledge that is shared between participants in a conversation, information that was introduced earlier in the discourse, and the specific circumstances in which a discourse or conversation takes place (Clark & Carlson 1981).

Comprehension is a cognitive process that makes use of the human information-processing system. One of the best established facts about human memory and information-processing is that only a limited amount of information can be attended to at a given time. This information is immediately available in what is referred to as 'working memory'. Information not in working memory must be retrieved when it is needed; but retrieval often takes considerable time, and consumes limited processing resources. This implies that connected discourse should be structured so as to help comprehenders manage their resources by keeping relevant information in working memory, in order to avoid extensive memory searches. Numerous observations about the structure of discourse suggest that this is the case. For instance, speakers and listeners seem to follow a GIVEN-NEW CONTRACT, in which sentences are structured so that some of the information in a sentence (typically, the first part of the sentence) is old or given information, and the remainder is new information (Haviland & Clark 1974). The given information specifies how the new information is to be added to that already in memory.

Discourse also has an intricate FOCUS structure: focused information is maintained in immediate memory, and other information is 'backgrounded'. A number of linguistic devices signal the comprehender about what to keep in focus. Consider a short discourse such as this:

(5) *John saw Bill as he was walking down the street. He greeted him warmly.*

Both *John* and *Bill* are possible antecedents for the pronoun *he*. However, readers or listeners typically assume that *he* refers to *John,* who is the subject of the first sentence, and is established as the local focus or 'discourse center'. The discourse would become less natural if the second sentence were *John greeted Bill.* Use of *John* here would signal that the local center was shifting from *John* to *Bill*; however, if this were the case, then the sentence should have continued with *him,* rather than *Bill.* The discourse becomes worse still if the second sentence is *He greeted John.* Readers initially assume that *he* refers to *John*—but find out that they have been led down the garden path when it turns out that *he,* in fact, referred to *Bill.* These examples show that discourse has a rich local structure; that the choice of a pronoun or full noun phrase provides the reader with information about the discourse structure.

The notion of a limited working memory, coupled with that of a highly structured local discourse, helps to explain the ubiquity of ANAPHORA [*q.v.*] in discourse. Anaphors are referring expressions such as pronouns, definite noun phrases, and elliptical phrases, like *her, he,* and *did* in the second sentence below:

(6) *Mary didn't think that John would pass the exam. But much to her surprise, he did (pass the exam).*

One might think that anaphora would be avoided, because it creates a great deal of ambiguity or indeterminacy. In fact, some use of anaphora is necessary simply to avoid tedious repetition—a discourse without anaphors would be a bit like an unedited movie—but much of the function of anaphora seems to be to guide the comprehension process.

One clear function of anaphora is to help maintain discourse COHERENCE through referential continuity. Without such continuity, a discourse becomes difficult to comprehend; e.g.,

(7) *John had always wanted a pet alligator. The alligator was his favorite birthday present this year.*

The definite noun phrase *the alligator* signals readers that they should know about a specific alligator; however, there is no 'real' alligator to which the definite noun phrase can be linked, although the word *alligator* has been previously mentioned. This example raises the issue of the type of REPRESENTATION that is developed during comprehension. Clearly, the representation must contain more than just the propositional content of the discourse. The comprehender must build a MENTAL MODEL in which the discourse can be interpreted. The model includes the events and participants that are introduced in the discourse, integrated in a form that allows the comprehender to establish referential and causal coherence, to make inferences, and to reason about information in the model (Johnson-Laird 1983). Evidence for such a model is necessarily indirect; however, at least three phenomena suggest that something like it is correct:

(a) Research on memory for text suggests that information in a text is combined with real-world knowledge in the resulting memory representation.

(b) Memory representations often do not distinguish between semantically distinct phrases that refer to the same person or object in the particular situation being described.
(c) Discourses that cannot be represented in terms of a coherent situation are extremely difficult, if not impossible, to comprehend—even when each sentence is well formed, and referential cohesion is maintained.

An informative example of how comprehenders seek to interpret discourse within the context of a coherent model comes from ambiguous stories, in which events become increasingly incongruent with one of the possible situations. For example, a story might begin by describing a man getting up at five in the morning, and moving quietly so as not to disturb others who are sleeping. The initial part of the story is consistent with the man going on a fishing trip, although the reader is never told this explicitly. The protagonist eventually turns out to be an escaped convict. Readers continue to try to interpret the story as being about a fishing trip, even when grossly inconsistent episodes are presented (e.g., the man is being chased by tracking dogs and a group of men with rifles).

Thus far, discussion has focused on how the comprehender develops a representation of the information in the discourse. An equally important part of comprehension, especially in regard to understanding conversational language, is knowing how to interpret the intent of the speaker. This was illustrated earlier in examples 3–4. Austin 1962 and Searle 1969 have developed a framework in which sentences can be understood as a series of SPEECH ACTS [*q.v.*]. A performative sentence, such as *I promise you I will come tomorrow,* performs the act of promising. However, the question of how the comprehender identifies a speech act is far from straightforward. In recent years, substantial progress has been made toward understanding speech acts by treating speech-act recognition, as well as the understanding of discourse more generally, as an example of PLAN RECOGNITION. Successful comprehension—and participation in a conversation—requires the comprehender to understand the plan that the speaker is trying to accomplish (Allen & Perrault 1986). The plan recognition approach offers a framework in which work on understanding (at least within limited domains) can be explored within the formal structure of a computer model that contains a parser, a knowledge base, and a reasoning system. Work within this framework highlights the degree to which questions about language comprehension are difficult to separate from more general questions about how knowledge is represented and accessed—and from questions about how people reason and draw inferences given the knowledge base and information provided from the discourse (Allen 1988).

In summary, there are a number of components in the comprehension of language. Successful understanding requires the comprehender to extract the message of the linguistic input, to interpret the message within the appropriate context, and to develop a model of the discourse. Part of understanding, especially of conversations, includes identifying the speaker's plans.

The study of language comprehension is an increasingly interdisciplinary effort. The ideas and examples in this essay have been drawn from researchers in cognitive psychology, linguistics, philosophy, and the emerging discipline of computational linguistics—which links techniques from artificial intelligence with the rigorous analysis of natural language. The techniques used to study comprehension are also diverse. They include (i) building computer models that act as if they understand language in restricted domains, (ii) linguistic analysis of the structure of discourse, (iii) analysis of the structure of conversations, and (iv) detailed experimental studies designed to explore understanding as it takes place in real time. [*See also* Processing, *article on* Comprehension and Production.]

MICHAEL K. TANENHAUS

BIBLIOGRAPHY

ALLEN, JAMES F. 1988. *Natural language understanding.* Reading, Mass.: Addison-Wesley.

ALLEN, JAMES F., & C. RAYMOND PERRAULT. 1986. Analyzing intention in utterances. In *Readings in natural language processing,* ed. by Barbara Grosz et al., pp. 441–458. Los Altos, Calif.: Kaufman.

AUSTIN, JOHN L. 1962. *How to do things with words.* Oxford: Clarendon Press. 2d ed., Cambridge, Mass.: Harvard University Press, 1975.

CLARK, HERBERT H., & T. B. CARLSON. 1981. Context for comprehension. In *Attention and performance,* vol. 9, edited by John Long & Alan Baddeley, pp. 313–330. Hillsdale, N.J.: Erlbaum.

HAVILAND, SUSAN E., & HERBERT H. CLARK. 1974. What's new? Acquiring new information as a process in comprehension. *Journal of Verbal Learning and Verbal Behavior* 13.512–521.

JOHNSON-LAIRD, PHILIP N. 1983. *Mental models: Towards a*

cognitive science of language. Cambridge, Mass.: Harvard University Press.

SEARLE, JOHN R. 1969. *Speech acts: An essay in the philosophy of language*. Cambridge & New York: Cambridge University Press.

COMPUTATIONAL LINGUISTICS. *See* Corpus Processing; Literary and Linguistic Computing; Natural Language Processing.

COMPUTATIONAL MORPHOLOGY creates and implements models of word formation, i.e. inflection, derivation and compounding. Typical applications are systems for word-form recognition and generation. RECOGNITION involves finding the underlying lexemes and grammatical forms of actual inflected (or compounded, or derived) word forms. WORD-FORM GENERATION goes in the opposite direction, producing desired grammatical forms of given lexemes. [*See also* Morphology.]

The primary goal of computational morphology is linguistic—acquiring better and more explicit understanding of morphology. However, many applications are used in practical tasks, e.g. in processing and indexing large corpora of texts, spelling checking, and information retrieval. Computational morphology interfaces with syntactic analysis (and sentence generation) on one hand, and with speech recognition and synthesis on the other.

Some languages, e.g. English, have hardly any inflection. In practical N[ATURAL] L[ANGUAGE] P[ROCESSING] systems, inflection is often ignored by listing all forms of words in the lexicon as such. Other languages (e.g. Greek, Sanskrit, Arabic, or Russian) have more extensive inflection, and the full listing approach is less feasible. In Finnish, for example, each noun has some two thousand distinct inflectional forms, and each verb more than twelve thousand, because of the several layers of endings: nominalization, comparison, number, case, possessive suffixes, and clitic particles. Regular word derivation and compounding increase these figures by several magnitudes.

1. Overview. Word form recognition (or generation) consists of several tasks:

(a) Coping with phonological and morphophonological processes which cause variation in surface phonemes (or letters, in written language). This corresponds to the domain of phonology.

(b) Identification of underlying morphemes of stems and various affixes (prefixes, infixes, suffixes or other inflectional or derivational elements).

(c) Description of possible morphotactic structures of word forms—possible sequences and combinations of morphemes—i.e., how word roots, prefixes, suffixes etc. may be combined to form full words.

(d) Identifying morphosyntactic features and semantic descriptions of full word forms from descriptions for component morphemes (e.g. roots and affixes).

(e) Describing lexicalization, where certain configurations of morphemes have properties that cannot be deduced from the corresponding properties of the individual components.

Figure 1 sketches the domain of morphological analysis and generation by dividing it into four representations, and three modules relating them. Particular models may ignore some of these representations and merge the

FIGURE 1. *Framework for Computational Morphology*

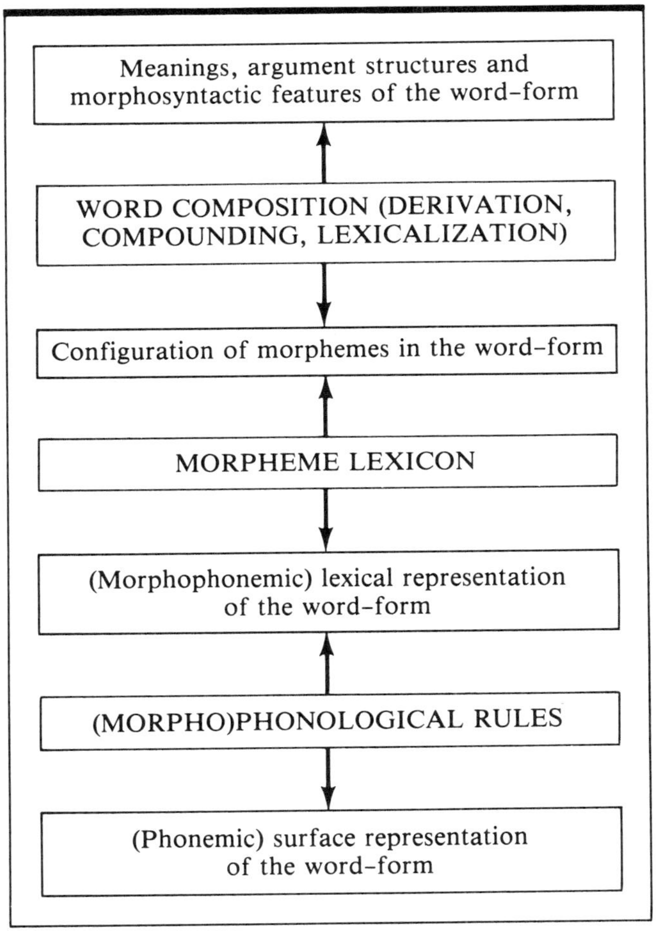

corresponding modules. The topmost module is often assigned to the syntactic component. Word-form recognition corresponds to the upward direction, while generation goes the opposite way.

2. Finite-state phonology. Phonological rules define the relation between the underlying form and the surface form of the word. Douglas Johnson noted in 1972 that phonological rules correspond closely to FINITE-STATE TRANSDUCERS. In 1981, an unpublished paper by Ronald Kaplan and Martin Kay noted that rules of generative phonology can be compiled into a CASCADE of transducers, where the output tape of one transducer is the input tape of the next (Figure 2). These transducers are bidirectional; i.e., they operate in the directions of both recognition and generation. Implementing cascaded transducers depends on the possibility of composing a chain of transducers into a single larger one. For languages with complex phonology, this has proven problematic because of the size of the result.

The two-level model of Koskenniemi 1983 differs from rewriting systems and from the cascaded design by describing the relation between lexical and surface forms directly, without any intermediate stages. All rules are thus parallel and independent of one another.

TWO-LEVEL RULES describe what kinds of alternations occur in the surface forms of morphemes as they occur in different contexts. Thus the Finnish nouns *koira* 'dog' and *risti* 'cross' have the plural inessive (*-I-ssA*) forms *koir+i+ssa* 'in dogs' and *riste+i+ssä* 'in crosses'. Stem alternations correspond roughly to rules *a*:∅ ⇔ ___ *I*: and *i*:*e* ⇔ ___ *I*: where, e.g., the latter reads as 'A lexical *i* corresponds to a surface *e* if and only if it is followed by a plural *I*.' The plural *I* itself corresponds usually to surface *i*; but if it is surrounded by vowels on the surface, it will correspond to *j*, i.e. *I*:*j* ⇔ :*Vowel* ___ :*Vowel*.

FIGURE 2. *Finite-State Transducer*

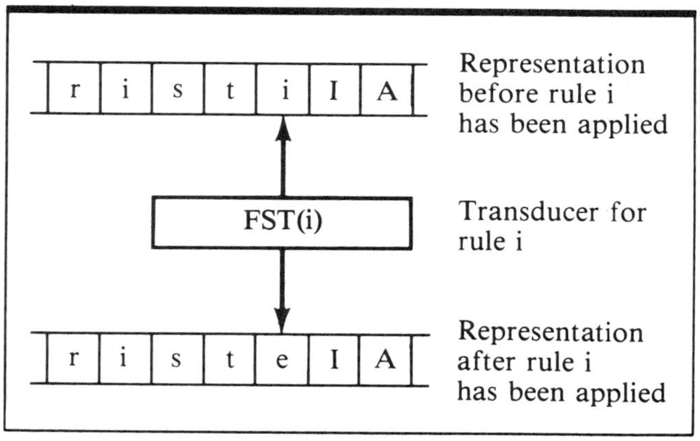

Two-level rules are logical statements defining acceptable correspondences between the two representations; they may be implemented in various ways. Methods for compiling two-level rules into finite-state transducers, which can be used in actual recognition and production programs, have been developed by Koskenniemi 1984 and by Karttunen et al. 1987. This is probably the most efficient implementation.

Bear 1986 has shown that two-level rules can also be interpreted in Prolog as logical statements permitting or forcing correspondences. Furthermore, Russell et al. 1986 have developed an alternative way of interpreting two-level rules which are only partially compiled.

Finite-state automata and transducers are extremely simple and rather well understood formal devices. Finite-state morphology often relies on non-deterministic processes which drive the automata; this entails a source of possible computational complexity. In principle, the formalisms alone do not exclude the possibility of exponentially complex processing. Natural languages, however, seem to have certain characteristics that exclude such behavior. (Most alternations are triggered by strictly local contexts; only a few alternations, i.e. from zero to two, depend on long-range contexts, e.g. vowel harmony.)

Not all alternations need be described in the rule component. For instance, complex endings in fusional languages like Latin may be treated as portmanteau morphs if there is no transparent way to segment them into further components.

3. Alternative models. Many word-form recognition systems have been developed with the idea of procedurally undoing phonological alternations while stripping endings from inflected forms. This often leads to unidirectional and language-specific models.

Even in many heavily inflected languages, there is no technical need to incorporate a phonological component in a recognition system. One may list possible allomorphs of each morpheme, and describe combinatory restrictions in some way. It is not clear whether any computational efficiency can be gained in this way.

Several language-specific systems have been developed for heuristic segmentation of inflectional endings on words in running text. Many programs also assign part-of-speech tags to words. Most models operate without a dictionary and are stochastic in nature.

Programs have also been developed for deducing word

entries out of sorted word-frequency lists of large text corpora. The occurrence of a set of consistent inflectional forms in a list is used as a basis for proposing base forms, part-of-speech codes, and inflectional classes for underlying word entries.

4. Structure of the lexicon and structure of complex words. The lexicon is often considered to be a list of entries. In practical recognition systems, it usually has the form of a LETTER TREE to permit fast incremental look-up.

The MORPHEME LEXICON relates configurations of morphemes to lexical representations. The set of all feasible lexical representations is defined through it. Grammatically correct sequences of morphemes may be partly defined by the lexicon through its division into sublexicons of different classes of morphemes, and by markings of possible continuations to further sublexicons. In addition to this, or instead of it, the morphotactic structure may be controlled, e.g. by Context-Free or Categorial Unification-Based Grammar (see Shieber 1986).

Trees or sets of linked trees are special cases of FINITE-STATE TRANSITION NETWORKS. Word roots in Semitic languages usually consist of three consonants, and inflectional elements of vowels and consonants intercalate with the root elements. Such phenomena may be described as intersections of root and inflection lexicons, represented as transition networks. Kay 1987 has described the morphology of Arabic in the spirit of autosegmental phonology, using a four-tape transducer.

Attribute-value descriptions and unification, which are widely used in NLP grammar formalisms, seem to be suitable for defining feature structures of complex word-forms. [*See* Natural Language Processing, *article on* Grammar Formalisms.] In addition, such feature calculi may be used for defining which combinations of morphemes are grammatical and which are not, especially when the lexicon itself has no continuation facility according to morpheme classes (Russell et al. 1986).

KIMMO KOSKENNIEMI

BIBLIOGRAPHY

BEAR, JOHN. 1986. A morphological recognizer with syntactic and phonological rules. *Proceedings of COLING 86,* pp. 272–276. Morristown, N.J.: Association for Computational Linguistics.

KARTTUNEN, LAURI; KIMMO KOSKENNIEMI; & RONALD KAPLAN. 1987. A compiler for two-level phonological rules. In *Tools for morphological analysis* (Report no. CSLI-87–108, Center for the Study of Language and Information), edited by Mary Dalrymple et al. Stanford, Calif.: Stanford University.

KAY, MARTIN. 1987. Non-concatenative finite-state morphology. In *Third Conference of the European Chapter of the Association for Computational Linguistics: Proceedings,* pp. 2–10. Morristown, N.J.: Association for Computational Linguistics.

KOSKENNIEMI, KIMMO. 1983. *Two-level morphology: A general computational module for word-form recognition and production.* (Department of Linguistics, Publications, 11.) Helsinki: University of Helsinki.

KOSKENNIEMI, KIMMO. 1984. A general computational model for word-form recognition and production. In *Tenth International Conference on Computational Linguistics: Proceedings of COLING 84,* pp. 178–181. Morristown, N.J.: Association for Computational Linguistics.

RUSSELL, GRAHAM J., et al. 1986. A dictionary and morphological analyser for English. In *Proceedings of COLING 86,* pp. 277–279. Morristown, N.J.: Association for Computational Linguistics.

SHIEBER, STUART M. 1986. *An introduction to unification-based approaches to grammar.* (CSLI lecture notes, 4.) Stanford, Calif.: Center for the Study of Language and Information.

COMPUTER-ASSISTED INSTRUCTION.

COMPUTER-ASSISTED INSTRUCTION. Computers have been used for language learning since the early 1960s. In those days, computers were large, but by today's standards relatively primitive. They could be programmed only by computer scientists. Education was influenced by behaviorist views of stimulus-response learning, and by structuralism in linguistics. The language laboratory, with its emphasis on habit-formation, was firmly established as the model for language learning technology; the computer tended to be seen largely as a superior language lab. Not surprisingly, these early applications resulted in a pedagogy characterized by objective, multiple-choice, drill-and-practice materials. The mode was tutorial; the computer replaced the teacher, and the student worked in isolation in a self-access environment. The term C[OMPUTER] A[SSISTED] I[NSTRUCTION], emphasizing the computer as instructor, was appropriate.

From the late 1970s, microcomputers became widely available. This development, as well as the advent of relatively easy-to-use authoring systems, brought educational programming within the grasp of the language teacher. The educational context had also changed. The communicative approach to language teaching had gained acceptance [*see* Pedagogical Linguistics], and there was a shift from a teacher-centered to a learner-centered classroom. This resulted in teacher creativity in small-scale, non-tutorial, game-like programs. These were designed as stimuli to generate interesting language-learning activities, and assumed that students would be working in groups. They were adjuncts to the teacher rather than replacements, and emphasized the student's role. The term C[OMPUTER] A[SSISTED] L[ANGUAGE] L[EARNING], focusing on the learner, became common. More recently, powerful language-learning activities have been developed around computer applications such as word processors, desktop publishing packages, database management systems, viewdata simulations, and electronic conferencing programs. (For general reference, see Higgins & Johns 1983, Underwood 1984, Wyatt 1984, Higgins 1986, Leech & Candlin 1986, Jones & Fortescue 1987, Phillips 1987, Hardisty & Windeatt 1989.)

A number of factors have led to the computer's becoming established in language pedagogy. First, CALL is interactive; learning materials can now adapt to the student, rather than vice versa. Second, it allows learning environments to be created in which all modes of language use can be practiced. Finally, CALL frees teachers to exploit their roles more creatively.

The most recent developments suggest that CALL may even lead to innovations in methodology. Facilities hitherto restricted to large research applications, such as concordancers, are becoming available on microcomputers. Students will be able to analyze the target language for themselves. Such developments could lead to a more critical, observational, and purely descriptive approach to language learning. This development could make an important contribution to methodology.

One potentially significant application is in language testing. Hitherto, the computer has been limited to scoring objective tests, statistical analysis, and record-keeping. Currently, however, there is a considerable research effort dealing with innovative approaches to computer-based language testing. With the speed and power of contemporary computers, it is possible to transcend the traditional multiple-choice format. Tests are being developed which are more 'communicative' in content, and which adapt more flexibly to the individual student's level of proficiency.

The future undoubtedly holds further exciting developments, including the application of findings from artificial intelligence research. There are dangers here: as computers become more 'intelligent', they may be allowed to usurp rightfully human roles. The language-learning expert system of the future could make the authoritarianism of early CAI look benign. If, however, teachers and CALL specialists are alert to this danger, then these applications could help realize the computer's potential to offer a powerful learning environment for students to explore, and a tool in support of their language learning goals.

MARTIN PHILLIPS

BIBLIOGRAPHY

HARDISTY, DAVID, & SCOTT WINDEATT. 1989. *CALL.* Oxford & New York: Oxford University Press.

HIGGINS, JOHN, ed. 1986. *Computer-assisted language learning: A European view.* (SYSTEM, 14:2.) Oxford: Pergamon.

HIGGINS, JOHN, & TIM JOHNS. 1983. *Computers in language learning.* London: Collins. Reprinted, Reading, Mass.: Addison-Wesley, 1984.

JONES, C., & S. FORTESCUE. 1987. *Using computers in the language classroom.* London: Longman.

LEECH, GEOFFREY N., & CHRISTOPHER N. CANDLIN. 1986. *Computers in English language teaching and research.* London: Longman.

PHILLIPS, MARTIN. 1987. *Communicative language learning and the micro-computer.* London: British Council.

UNDERWOOD, JOHN H. 1984. *Linguistics, computers and the language teacher.* Rowley, Mass.: Newbury House.

WYATT, DAVID H. 1984. *Computer assisted language instruction.* Oxford: Pergamon.

CONNECTIONISM is a computational framework for cognitive modeling, based on numerical computation rather than on symbol manipulation. Inspired by mathematical models of neural processes and by associationist psychology, variations of the connectionist approach over several decades have been termed CYBERNETICS, PERCEPTRONS, NEURAL NETWORKS, and P[ARALLEL] D[ISTRIBUTED] P[ROCESSING]. Connectionism developed rapidly in the later 1980s (Rumelhart, McClelland et al. 1986, Anderson & Rosenfeld 1988, Grossberg 1988, McClelland & Rumelhart 1988, Smolensky 1988, 1990, Aleksander 1989, Barnden & Pollack 1990, Reilly & Sharkey 1991). It promises a unified framework within which to address disparate aspects of linguistics, though this goal will require overcoming a number of serious problems (Pinker & Mehler 1988).

A typical connectionist computational system is a

network of simple numerical processing UNITS—NODES or NEURONS; each has an ACTIVATION VALUE which it computes, according to some simple numerical formula, from the activation values of the other units to which it is connected; see Figure 1. A connection from unit 1 to unit 2 has a positive or negative numerical STRENGTH or WEIGHT which governs whether activity at unit 1 will increase or decrease activity at unit 2—i.e., whether it will EXCITE or INHIBIT it—and to what degree. All the processing units compute at once, in parallel. The pattern of activity of all the units in the network represents the DATA currently being operated upon by the network; the connection strengths constitute the PROGRAM (or knowledge) which governs the processing of these data. A pattern of activity encoding an input is presented on the input units, and activity flows through the network (typically through intermediate HIDDEN units) until a pattern of activity encoding the output develops on the output units. Connectionist networks often program themselves: during TRAINING, they are shown examples of the desired input/output pairs; and on the basis of numerical LEARNING ALGORITHMS, they iteratively modify their connections to more closely approximate the desired computation. Connection strengths change slowly enough that they are essentially constant during the computation of output activity patterns from input activity patterns.

1. Representations used in connectionist cognitive models are typically presumed to lie at a level higher than that corresponding to actual neurons in the human brain. The representations which encode inputs and outputs are explicitly designed by the modeler; by contrast, the meaning of the activity of a hidden unit—the situations in which it is active, and the consequences of its activity—is determined by its connections.

Network units often correspond to identifiable hypotheses about the data being processed; the activity of such a unit encodes the current degree to which the network accepts the hypothesis. For interpreting acoustic speech input, two such hypotheses about an utterance might be: (a) that the first segment is voiced; and (b) that there is a vowel preceded by a dental. These two hypotheses illustrate a general approach to the representation of structured information—a particularly important problem for connectionist models of language. Structures can be represented with units denoting the conjunction of a property of a constituent with a property

FIGURE 1. *A Connectionist Network.* Here activity flows from the four input units to the six hidden units, among which it circulates through the lateral connections. From the hidden units, activity flows to the two output units. If a series of inputs is presented over time on the input units, the recurrent activity in the hidden units allows the output at any given time to be sensitive not just to the current input, but also to the previous inputs.

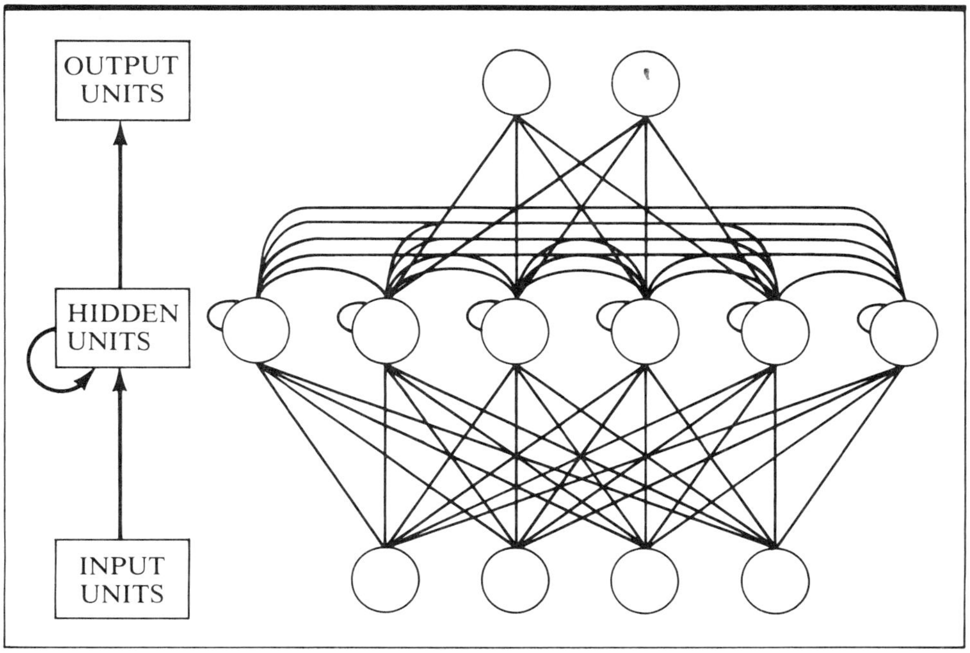

of the role it plays; for the structure of a sequence of phonetic segments, the two hypotheses above illustrate such conjunctions: (i) voiced segment and initial position, and (ii) vocalic segment and post-dental position.

Representation poses central challenges for connectionist models of language. Particularly important is the adequate representation of embedded structure. A second, more general problem is that in most representations of the 1980s, after learning (if any) is completed, the meaning of each unit is fixed during computations of outputs from inputs. Networks must be extremely large, so they can be set up in advance to accommodate any possible piece of data in a large space. This obstacle might be overcome through networks in which the connections to a unit effectively change during activation computation; in such networks, the meaning of hidden units can effectively be determined dynamically during the processing of an input.

Network-defined representations that arise in hidden units through learning are typically difficult to interpret; except in isolated (but often quite interesting) cases, the connection pattern of a hidden unit rarely supports a simple interpretation. In many cases, it is not the activity of an individual unit, but rather the activity pattern over a set of units, that supports a given interpretation: this is DISTRIBUTED REPRESENTATION. Insights into such representations can be extracted using statistical techniques such as hierarchical clustering and factor analysis, and linear algebra techniques such as matrix decomposition. Elman 1990 has demonstrated a network which learned, solely from the distribution of unanalyzed words in sentences, an internal representation of those words in which hidden-unit activities clustered hierarchically into such classes as nouns, verbs, animate nouns, etc.; the network invented this classification itself. (Fig. 1 shows the structure of this network.)

2. Activation computation. The flow of activation in connectionist networks may contain closed loops ('feedback', as in Fig. 1), or no such loops ('feed-forward'). A great variety of equations are used for computing activation values. The equations may be designed to implement statistical inference or plausible reasoning; thus the activation value of a unit represents the probability or plausibility of a hypothesis, given the evidence provided by other units' activities. Each connection in such a framework constitutes a SOFT CONSTRAINT: e.g., a negative connection from unit 1 to unit 2 asserts that, if hypothesis 1 is accepted, hypothesis 2 should be rejected. This constraint can be overruled by those embodied in the other connections to unit 2. The activation equations may involve random decisions. Such models (e.g. Boltzmann machines) often have a 'computational temperature' parameter that controls the degree of randomness; this decreases during the computation of an output ('simulated annealing'). In many models, a HARMONY or 'energy' value corresponds to each activity pattern of a network; states of greatest harmony (lowest energy) represent maximally self-consistent values for the units' hypotheses, and activation equations drive the network toward such states. Goldsmith 1990 has proposed incorporating this principle into phonology: phonological rules apply when the resulting structure exhibits greater harmony, as defined by a combination of universal and language-specific well-formedness conditions. A related harmony-based approach to syntax/semantics has been developed and applied to unaccusativity phenomena by Legendre et al. 1990.

3. Learning. Algorithms for learning are typically designed to minimize the total error made by the network on its training examples. These algorithms perform a complex kind of statistical induction from the observed training set to unseen inputs; we are only now beginning to understand this induction. Training consists in the presentation of example inputs, together with: (i) the corresponding desired output ('supervised learning', e.g. the back-propagation algorithm); or (ii) a global positive/negative reinforcement signal ('reinforcement learning'); or (iii) no additional information ('unsupervised learning'). Some of these learning algorithms can be applied to training from positive examples only; such algorithms can allow a network to judge a novel example as either positive or negative, even though the training set includes no negative examples.

Inputs and outputs may be either static or extended over time. Jordan 1986 has shown that, when connectionist networks learn to control idealized vocal articulators, they naturally exhibit coarticulation effects.

4. Connectionism and associationism. Contemporary connectionism distinguishes itself from its simpler associationist precursors in several ways. There is a major emphasis on internal representation, and considerable interest in how these representations relate to the theoretical abstractions of linguistics and other areas of cognitive science. Distributed representations have constituent structure, unlike the simplest associationist representations, which are atomic (Smolensky 1990). Distributed representations, and the techniques of statistical inference embodied in connectionist computation and learning, lie in new mathematical territory whose power and limits are only beginning to be explored.

5. Connectionism and linguistics. In the late 1980s, connectionism was just beginning to influence linguistics. Much work is under way, addressing such problems as the following:

(a) Linguistic regularities that have not succumbed to discrete, rule-based descriptions, including the statistical characteristics of language and its use
(b) Psychologically real accounts of linguistic representation and real-time processing, especially issues of parallel and serial processes
(c) Neurolinguistics
(d) The innate and empirical components of language acquisition
(e) New rule-based linguistic accounts motivated by connectionist lower-level mechanisms, e.g. Goldsmith's principle of harmonic rule application
(f) Linguistic descriptions based on non-classical categories and analogical mechanisms

If success results from current attempts to show how, under the proper conditions, the functional equivalent of symbol manipulation can emerge as a higher-level description of connectionist computation, then connectionism will be positioned to provide a unified computational framework in which to address not only the preceding issues, but also the integration of activation- and rule-based accounts of psycholinguistic processes, as well as the neural realization of symbolic rules and representations.

PAUL SMOLENSKY

BIBLIOGRAPHY

ALEKSANDER, IGOR. 1989. *Neural computing architectures.* Cambridge, Mass.: MIT Press.

ANDERSON, JAMES A., & EDWARD ROSENFELD, eds. 1988. *Neurocomputing: Foundations of research.* Cambridge, Mass: MIT Press.

BARNDEN, JOHN, & JORDAN POLLACK, eds. 1990. *Advances in connectionist and neural computation theory,* vol. 1: *High level connectionist models.* Norwood, N.J.: Ablex.

ELMAN, J. L. 1990. Finding structure in time. *Cognitive Science* 14.179–211.

GOLDSMITH, JOHN A. 1990. *Autosegmental and metrical phonology.* Oxford: Blackwell.

GROSSBERG, STEPHEN. 1988. *Neural networks and natural intelligence.* Cambridge, Mass.: MIT Press.

JORDAN, MICHAEL I. 1986. Attractor dynamics and parallelism in a connectionist sequential machine. In *Proceedings of the Eighth Annual Meeting of the Cognitive Science Society,* pp. 531–546. Amherst, Mass.

LEGENDRE, GERALDINE; YOSHIRO MIYATA; & PAUL SMOLENSKY. 1990. Can connectionism contribute to syntax? *Chicago Linguistic Society* 26, to appear.

MCCLELLAND, JAMES L., & DAVID E. RUMELHART. 1988. *Explorations in Parallel Distributed Processing: A handbook of models, programs, and exercises.* Cambridge, Mass.: MIT Press.

PINKER, STEVEN, & JACQUES MEHLER, eds. 1988. *Connections and symbols.* Cambridge, Mass.: MIT Press.

RUMELHART, DAVID E.; JAMES L. MCCLELLAND; et al. 1986. *Parallel Distributed Processing: Explorations in the microstructure of cognition,* vol. 1, *Foundations*; vol. 2, *Psychological and biological models.* Cambridge, Mass.: MIT Press.

SMOLENSKY, PAUL. 1988. On the proper treatment of connectionism. *Behavioral and Brain Sciences* 11.1–74.

SMOLENSKY, PAUL. 1990. Connectionism, constituency, and the language of thought. In *Fodor and his critics,* edited by Barry Loewer & Georges Rey, in press. Oxford: Blackwell.

CONNOTATION. The term 'connotation' is employed in semantics as part of a typology of meaning. Two broad uses may be distinguished. In the first place, it was established as a technical term by John Stuart Mill, opposed to 'denotation': for Mill 1843, an adjective such as *white* denotes the class of white things, but connotes, or implies, the attribute of whiteness which they share. This use, which approximates to the linguistic notion of 'sense', is mainly restricted to philosophical semantics. In linguistics, 'connotation' is usually applied more narrowly, much as in everyday language, to various aspects of the communicative value of linguistic units which are seen as lying outside their core meaning: see Kerbrat-Orecchioni 1977 and Sansome 1986 for useful discussion. In this second use, the range and precision of the term vary widely, and many linguists explicitly avoid it. Among the phenomena commonly grouped under this heading, however, at least the following may be distinguished.

First, the term is used with reference to EXPRESSIVE components of meaning, most obviously in the case of terms which carry 'favorable' or 'unfavorable' connotations. Many lexical units serve to express the attitudes or feelings of the speaker towards what they describe, as in the well known 'paradigm' *I am firm, you are obstinate, he is pig-headed.* Here the adjectives may be said to share a common core of descriptive meaning ('adhering to opinions') but express different value-judgments—favorable in the case of *firm,* unfavorable in the case of *obstinate* and *pig-headed.* Expressive connotations vary in strength: *pig-headed* expresses stronger disapproval than *obstinate.* They also vary in the type of emotive involvement expressed; e.g., diminutive and hypocoristic expressions *(doggie, Katie,* etc.) express affection, and many idioms *(a face like a fiddle,* etc.) express jocularity. The encoding of such connotations is discussed by Stankiewicz 1964.

Connotations may also reflect SOCIAL or SITUATIONAL circumstances of use. Lexical units may function as markers of particular speech varieties, either in terms of the social affiliations of their typical users (such as regional provenance, class, sex, or age) or in terms of features of the situation in which they are typically used—such as the social relationships of participants, social setting, or genre of communication. Several of these factors may overlap: thus the use of vulgarisms is in many languages socially unacceptable in the speech of certain groups (e.g. women) and in certain situations ('polite company'). Expressive terms may also be situationally restricted: thus *pig-headed* is more colloquial than *obstinate,* and *doggie* is characteristic of baby talk. Similarly, technical terms not only serve to delineate a particular subject matter, but also connote the specialist roles of their users.

A third type of connotation derives from general CULTURAL ASSOCIATIONS of what is denoted by the lexical unit. Such associations are often highlighted by cross-linguistic comparisons of translation equivalents. Thus English *octopus* and Japanese *tako* denote the same species of animal, but the cultural associations are quite different: weird, sinister *octopus* vs. endearing, edible *tako.* Features of this kind are sometimes held to pertain purely to referents and thus to lie outside language; however, they frequently have linguistic reflexes. Thus octopuses, and by extension anti-social organizations, are said to have *tentacles,* but *tako* simply have *ashi* 'legs'. Similarly, British Eng. *summer* and Japanese *natsu* both denote the warmest season of the year; but the latter carries connotations of enervating heat reflected in expressions such as *natsuyase* 'summer loss of weight' and *natsubate* 'summer exhaustion'.

Connotations may result from associations of various kinds among lexical units themselves: in these cases, the communicative value of a lexical unit is influenced by other units to which it is in some way related. The clearest examples involve the influence of a taboo homonym: thus *rooster* has replaced *cock* in some varieties of English because of the presence of the taboo homonym meaning 'penis'. Similarly, use of the term *niggardly* is avoided as a result of its partial resemblance to *nigger.* Also relevant here are the vaguer phonesthetic affinities which link *twirl* with *curl* and *whirl* on the one hand and with *twist* and *tweak* on the other; such elements often reinforce expressive connotations (cf. initial *sn-* in unfavorable terms such as *sneer, snigger, sneak,* etc.). [*See* Sound Symbolism.]

While connotations are commonly discussed with reference to the vocabulary, the notion is not limited in application to lexical units. Some grammatical elements and constructions (such as personal pronouns, or inversion of noun + adjective in French) carry expressive or socio-stylistic connotations, and features of pronunciation and spelling may serve to mediate communicative value over and above their basic distinctive function. [*See also* Metaphor.]

A. E. BACKHOUSE

BIBLIOGRAPHY

KERBRAT-ORECCHIONI, CATHERINE. 1977. *La connotation.* Lyon: Presses Universitaires de Lyon.

MILL, JOHN STUART. 1843. *A system of logic, ratiocinative and inductive.* London: Parker.

SANSOME, ROSEMARY. 1986. Connotation and lexical field analysis. *Cahiers de Lexicologie* 49.13–33.

STANKIEWICZ, EDWARD. 1964. Problems of emotive language. In *Approaches to semiotics* (Janua linguarum, Series major, 15), edited by Thomas A. Sebeok et al., pp. 239–264. The Hague: Mouton.

CONSONANT HARMONY. *See* Vowel Harmony and Consonant Harmony.

CONSONANTS. *See* Phonetics.

CONTEXT-FREE LANGUAGES AND GRAMMARS. Context-free languages constitute one of the most important classes of formally defined languages. Linguists are most familiar with the definition of CFLs first given formally by Chomsky 1959 in terms of string-rewriting rule systems: a rewriting system in which all rules have the form $A \rightarrow W$, where A is a single nonterminal and W is a non-null string of nonterminals and/or terminals, is called a C[ontext-]F[ree] G[rammar], and by definition generates a CFL. (This is the '*e*-free' definition, which does not allow sentences of zero length. A slightly different formulation allows '*e*-productions', i.e. rules in which W is null, and thus allows the empty string e to be a sentence in a CFL. But any CFG in the latter form can be converted by an automatic procedure to a form that has no *e*-productions except for the rule $S \rightarrow e$, if the empty string itself belongs to the language.)

There are numerous independent characterizations of CFLs. Peters & Ritchie 1969 observed that any context-sensitive grammar G with rules of the form $A \rightarrow W$ / X ____ Y (meaning 'A is rewritten as W between X and Y') determines a CFL. If we interpret the rules of G as node admissibility conditions (where a rule $A \rightarrow W$ / X ____ Y admits a node labeled A with the daughter sequence W if X appears immediately to the left of A, and Y immediately to the right of A in the tree), then the set of all terminal strings of the trees that are admitted is a CFL. Research by Aravind Joshi and his colleagues has established that extension to a much wider range of tree filters leaves this result intact (see Gazdar 1982).

Even under the rewriting interpretation, context-sensitive grammars generate just the CFLs if the non-CFG-form rules are restricted in certain ways—in particular, if each right-hand side contains a string of terminals longer than any string of terminals appearing between two nonterminals on the left-hand side. This important result, provided by Baker 1974, has many other results as corollaries.

CFLs can be characterized in terms of automata [*see* Automata Theory]. Non-deterministic pushdown stack automata accept all and only the CFLs. Furthermore, the CFLs are identical with the set of all the terminal string languages of tree-sets recognizable by frontier-to-root (bottom-up) finite-state tree automata (Thatcher 1973). The abstract device known as a recursive transition network, used in the design of some NATURAL LANGUAGE PROCESSING systems [*q.v.*] also exactly characterizes the CFLs.

Many useful theorems have been proved about the CFLs. The Pumping Lemma for CFLs (Bar-Hillel et al. 1961) says that, for any CFL L, there is a fixed length n such that all strings in L containing more than n symbols can be analyzed into five substrings *uvwxy* such that v and x are not both null, *vwx* contains n symbols or less, and the v and x portions of the string can be 'pumped' to an arbitrary number of (zero or more) repetitions without changing grammaticality—i.e., L contains not only *uvwxy* but also *uwy*, *uvvwxxy*, *uvvvwxxxy*, etc. Demonstrating the absence of the particular type of structural repetitiveness determined by the Pumping Lemma is one way to prove that a language is not a CFL. (However, the presence of the property in question does NOT prove that a language is a CFL: all CFLs satisfy the Pumping Lemma, but so do some non-CFLs.)

Many other properties of CFLs have been proved. CFLs have a kind of stability, in that they cannot be turned into non-CFLs by applying the operations of union, concatenation, Kleene closure, homomorphism, inverse homomorphism, substitution, or intersection with regular sets. It is algorithmically decidable whether a given CFG generates an empty, finite, or infinite CFL—and, most importantly, it is algorithmically decidable whether an arbitrary string is in the language generated by a given CFG.

The latter procedure is called RECOGNIZING a string. [*See* Recognition.] For CFLs, it can be done quite rapidly; the maximum number of computational steps needed is proportional to the cube of the length of the string times the square of the CFG size. (The former is more crucial; grammar size remains constant, and thus constitutes a smaller and smaller proportion of the total burden as longer strings are considered.)

The theory of recognizing and parsing CFLs is a very important topic in computer science. Indeed, it is absolutely central to such areas as programming language design and compiler construction. There is evidence that some aspects of the syntax of programming languages lie beyond the scope of CFGs, but this has not convinced computer scientists to work with other syntactic models. For example, in a programming language in which variables have to be declared before they are used, a CFG cannot ensure syntactically that all of an unlimited number of variables in the body of a program have been appropriately declared earlier; to do this is tantamount to generating a language like

$$\{w_0 \ldots w_n w'_0 \ldots w'_n \mid w_i, w'_i \in V^*, w_i = w'_i, 0 \leq i \leq n\},$$

which is not a CFL. However, those specifying the syntax of programming languages have generally been content to assign the 'bookkeeping' task of checking variable declarations to the semantics (roughly, to treat programs containing undeclared variables as syntactically well formed, but meaningless).

CFGs are clearly reminiscent of traditional statements about phrase structure: e.g., the rule $A \rightarrow B\ C$ says that a B and a C make a phrase of type A; or the rule $D \rightarrow d$

says that the item *d* belongs to the category *D*. (By a theorem of Chomsky, any CFG can be replaced by an equivalent one whose rules are restricted to the two forms shown above. Such grammars are called CHOMSKY NORMAL FORM grammars; Chomsky first called them 'regular', but this term is now used as a synonym for 'finite state'.) Traditional and structuralist grammarians may be regarded as having tacitly assumed that natural languages were CFLs. During the early 1960s, Chomsky and others gave arguments intended to establish that this was not so. These purported demonstrations of the inadequacy of CFGs for natural language description were invalid because of technical errors (Pullum & Gazdar 1982); but the claim seems to have been correct, since non-context-free natural languages are now known to exist. [*See* Mathematical Linguistics.] Reduplication of items of unbounded length is an example of a construction type that a CFG cannot capture. In general, languages whose strings are all of the form *ww* (where *w* is some arbitrary string) are not CFLs. Thus a language in which nouns are productively reduplicated in some construction will not, in general, be a CFL—unless, implausibly, there is only a finite number of nouns (with no noun-noun compounding), so that their reduplicated forms can be listed.

The standard way to prove that a language with a reduplication construction is not a CFL is to find a homomorphism or intersection with a regular set that isolates the subpart of the language containing only the reduplications. This has been done, so that there are natural languages that are not describable by CFGs; however, much interesting linguistic description is expressible in CFG terms. Many formalisms that linguists have found useful describe only CFLs, such as immediate constituent analysis, TAGMEMICS [*q.v.*], other structuralist models of grammar (cf. Postal 1964), Generalized Phrase-Structure Grammar [*q.v.*] (Gazdar et al. 1985), and parsers of the sort developed by Marcus 1980 (as shown by Nozohoor-Farsi 1987).

GEOFFREY K. PULLUM

BIBLIOGRAPHY

BAKER, BRENDA S. 1974. Non-context-free grammars generating context-free languages. *Information & Control* 24.231–246.

BAR-HILLEL, YEHOSHUA, et al. 1961. On formal properties of simple phrase structure grammars. *Zeitschrift für Phonetik, Sprachwissenschaft und Kommunikationsforschung* 14.143–172.

CHOMSKY, NOAM. 1959. On certain formal properties of grammars. *Information & Control* 2.137–167. Reprinted in *Readings in mathematical psychology,* vol. 2, edited by R. Duncan Luce (Reading, Mass.: Wiley, 1963), pp. 125–155.

GAZDAR, GERALD. 1982. Phrase structure grammar. In *The nature of syntactic representation,* edited by Pauline Jacobson & Geoffrey K. Pullum, pp. 131–186. Dordrecht: Reidel.

GAZDAR, GERALD, et al. 1985. *Generalized Phrase Structure Grammar.* Oxford: Blackwell. Cambridge, Mass.: Harvard University Press.

MARCUS, MITCHELL P. 1980. *A theory of syntactic recognition for natural language.* Cambridge, Mass.: MIT Press.

NOZOHOOR-FARSI, R. 1987. Context-freeness of the language accepted by Marcus' parser. In *Proceedings of the 25th Annual Meeting of the ACL,* pp. 117–122. Morristown, N.J.: Association for Computational Linguistics.

PETERS, P. STANLEY, JR., & ROBERT W. RITCHIE. 1969. Context-sensitive immediate constituent analysis: Context-free languages revisited. In *Conference Record of the ACM Symposium on Theory of Computing,* pp. 1–8. New York: Association for Computing Machinery. Reprinted in *Mathematical Systems Theory* 6.324–333 (1973).

POSTAL, PAUL M. 1964. *Constituent structure: A study of contemporary models of syntactic description.* (Indiana University Research Center in Anthropology, Folklore, and Linguistics, publication 30; International Journal of American Linguistics 30:1, part 3.) Bloomington.

PULLUM, GEOFFREY K., & GERALD GAZDAR. 1982. Natural languages and context-free languages. *Linguistics & Philosophy* 4.471–504.

THATCHER, JAMES W. 1973. Tree automata: An informal survey. In *Currents in the theory of computing,* edited by Alfred V. Aho, pp. 143–172. Englewood Cliffs, N.J.: Prentice-Hall.

CONTRASTIVE ANALYSIS. Just as old habits can interfere with the learning of new skills, so one's N[ative] L[anguage] can affect the learning of a F[oreign] L[anguage]. This INTERFERENCE, or NEGATIVE TRANSFER, operates across the differences between the two languages; these differences lead to learning difficulty and the persistence of errors.

The C[ONTRASTIVE] A[NALYSIS] HYPOTHESIS claims that the potential negative transfers from NL onto FL can be predicted by juxtaposing descriptions of the two language systems in order to identify the dissimilarities ('contrasts') between them. The information that CA yields can be incorporated into pedagogic materials, designed to deactivate the potential NL interference, and so to minimize the incidence of errors arising from this source (Fisiak 1981).

The principles of CA derive from studies of language mixing by American immigrant bilinguals (Weinreich 1953, Haugen 1953), and the procedures for CA were formulated by Lado 1957 within the structuralist taxonomic tradition of linguistics. In this period, contrastive analyses were executed at the descriptive levels of phonology/graphology, grammar, and lexis (Nickel 1971). Major achievements within this tradition were launched during the late 1960s in Stuttgart, Poznań, Zagreb, Lund, Jyväskylä, and Bucarest (James 1980:205). In the United States, the University of Chicago Press published notable CAs of English with Spanish (Stockwell & Bowen 1965, Stockwell et al. 1965), with German (Kufner 1962, Moulton 1962), and with Italian (Agard & Di Pietro 1965a,b).

The heyday was shortlived, however, and soon doubts were expressed about the theoretical validity and practical value of CA (cf. James 1980, chap. 7), especially in the following areas:

(a) Doubt grew about the comparability of linguistic categories across different languages: e.g., are the English perfect and the French passé composé really comparable entities?
(b) The predictive power of CAs was shown to be limited: some items of high interlingual contrastivity prove to be easily learned, and vice versa. Consequently, attempts to identify a scale of learning difficulty on the basis of language difference were unsuccessful. Fewer errors could unequivocally be traced to NL interference than had been supposed; early claims that 30 percent of errors were interlingual ceded to almost negligible claims of 3 percent.
(c) ERROR ANALYSIS of attested errors was proposed as preferable to trying to predict potential errors.
(d) Exclusive attention to NL-induced errors morbidly distracted attention from the often facilitative effects of NL/FL similarities, which ought to be emphasized in teaching. There is, in other words, positive as well as negative transfer.
(e) CA seemed not to help FL teachers much, nor to tell them anything that could not be learned from classroom experience.

A modest revival of confidence in CA began to be felt in the early 1980s, attributable to the following trends.

(i) Work was undertaken in the CA of discourse and textual conventions of different languages, encompassing CONTRASTIVE PRAGMATICS (Thomas 1983), CONTRASTIVE RHETORIC (Purves 1988), and CONTRASTIVE TEXTOLOGY (Hartmann 1980). [*See* Contrastive Rhetoric.]

(ii) Work in Universal Grammar (Chomsky 1981) intensified—particularly with respect to the claim that differences between languages are parameterized in such a way that learners have innate, albeit unconscious, knowledge about the ways in which languages can manifest differences. Another claim concerns the differences of MARKEDNESS (Eckman 1977) between languages; thus NL and FL may possess a feature in common (so there is apparently no contrast), but the deployment of that feature may be more marked in one of the languages than in the other, so that there is contrast after all. [*See* Markedness.]

(iii) Attempts were made to identify, in FL performance, traces of transfer from NL. Thus TRANSFER ANALYSIS (Gass & Selinker 1983, Zobl 1984, Kellerman & Sharwood Smith 1986, Odlin 1989) is the intellectual heir to CA: explanation of NL effects on FL learning, not prediction, has become the modest provisional goal. [*See also* Interlanguage; Pedagogical Linguistics.]

CARL JAMES

BIBLIOGRAPHY

AGARD, FREDERICK B., & ROBERT J. DI PIETRO. 1965a. *The grammatical structures of English and Italian.* Chicago: University of Chicago Press.

AGARD, FREDERICK B., & ROBERT J. DI PIETRO. 1965b. *The sounds of English and Italian.* Chicago: University of Chicago Press.

CHOMSKY, NOAM. 1981. Principles and parameters in syntactic theory. In *Explanation in linguistics: The logical problem of language acquisition* (Longman linguistic library, 25), edited by Norbert Hornstein & David Lightfoot, pp. 32–75. London: Longman.

ECKMAN, FRED R. 1977. Markedness and the contrastive analysis hypothesis. *Language Learning* 27.315–330.

FISIAK, JACEK, ed. 1981. *Contrastive linguistics and the language teacher.* Oxford: Pergamon Press.

GASS, SUSAN, & LARRY SELINKER, eds. 1983. *Language transfer in language learning.* Rowley, Mass.: Newbury House.

HARTMANN, REINHARD R. K. 1980. *Contrastive textology: Comparative discourse analysis in applied linguistics.* (Studies in descriptive linguistics, 5.) Heidelberg: Groos.

HAUGEN, EINAR. 1953. *The Norwegian language in America: A study in bilingual behavior.* Philadelphia: University of

Pennsylvania Press. Reprinted, Bloomington: Indiana University Press, 1969.
JAMES, CARL. 1980. *Contrastive analysis*. London: Longman.
KELLERMAN, ERIC, & MICHAEL SHARWOOD SMITH, eds. 1986. *Cross-linguistic influence in second language acquisition*. Oxford: Pergamon Press.
KUFNER, HERBERT L. 1962. *The grammatical structures of English and German: A contrastive sketch*. Chicago: University of Chicago Press.
LADO, ROBERT. 1957. *Linguistics across cultures: Applied linguistics for language teachers*. Ann Arbor: University of Michigan Press.
MOULTON, WILLIAM G. 1962. *The sounds of English and German*. Chicago: University of Chicago Press.
NICKEL, GERHARD, ed. 1971. *Papers in contrastive linguistics*. Cambridge & New York: Cambridge University Press.
ODLIN, TERENCE. 1989. *Language transfer: Cross-linguistic influence in language learning*. Cambridge & New York: Cambridge University Press.
PURVES, ALAN C., ed. 1988. *Writing across languages and cultures: Issues in contrastive rhetoric*. (Written communication annual, 2.) Beverly Hills, Calif.: Sage.
STOCKWELL, ROBERT P., & J. DONALD BOWEN. 1965. *The sounds of English and Spanish*. Chicago: University of Chicago Press.
STOCKWELL, ROBERT P.; J. DONALD BOWEN; & JOHN W. MARTIN. 1965. *The grammatical structures of English and Spanish*. Chicago: University of Chicago Press.
THOMAS, JENNY. 1983. Cross-cultural pragmatic failure. *Applied Linguistics* 4.91–112.
WEINREICH, URIEL. 1953. *Languages in contact*. New York: Linguistic Circle of New York.
ZOBL, HELMUT. 1984. Cross-language generalizations and the contrastive dimension of the interlanguage hypothesis. In *Interlanguage*, edited by Alan Davies et al., pp. 79–97. Edinburgh: Edinburgh University Press.

CONTRASTIVE RHETORIC is the notion that the organization of written text is substantially different in different languages. It originated in pedagogical necessity, having its inception in the period (ca. 1955–1970) when contrastive studies were generally popular—hence the name. It bears a theoretical relationship to a variety of other concepts, being based in linguistic relativity with connections to rhetorical theory, translation theory, information science, and language-learning theory. The theory of DISCOURSE [*q.v.*], in its present stage of evolution, stands between linguistic relativity and linguistic universals. (For general reference, see Kaplan 1966, 1983, 1988, Grimes 1975, Halliday & Hasan 1976, Kaplan & Shaw 1984, Bereiter & Scardamalia 1987, Connor & Kaplan 1987.)

To study C[ontrastive] R[hetoric], two elements are needed: (i) a clear theory of discourse applicable to written discourse in any language, sensitive to both differences and similarities; and (ii) a method for describing discourse structure in particular languages in such a way that useful comparison may be undertaken. A problem lies in what to study; there is no broad agreement about what discourse forms should be examined and compared. Most formal work in CR has attempted to restrict itself to expository prose; though this is not the only genre available for analysis, the impetus to look only at this genre is well founded. While non-narrative structures have been studied, the structure of narrative is simpler and more universal; all societies tell stories, which tend to be organized on the basis of chronological or spatial sequences of events, or on the basis of the characteristics of an individual or a group, and which tend to be clearly dependent on sensory perceptions. Expository structures, on the other hand, have quite different organizational assumptions, relying more frequently on abstract sequences like cause/consequence, comparison/contrast, definition/classification, and analysis/synthesis.

CR has been limited to studies of written rather than oral text. It operates on the assumption that a significant difference exists between the organization of written text, whether or not such text is subsequently instantiated orally, and that of oral text—a distinction that has been supported by recent research. Unfortunately, the dependence on written text has embroiled CR in the product/process debate, which may be spurious in the sense that every process gives rise to some product (or many products) at various stages in the development of the process—and all these products are, ultimately, in process.

Further, CR operates on the premise that there is variation among cultures as regards what is available to be argued, how the argumentative process is defined, what constitutes evidence, and the order in which evidence may be marshaled. Two kinds of logic are presupposed: the universal logic of mathematics (i.e., physics is physics without reference to the culture in which it is conducted), and a logic which functions in relation to culturally and linguistically defined interpretations of the phenomenological world. The question of the order in which evidence may be presented lies at the heart of any definition of rhetoric. Rhetoric is not a logical system; it is merely the vehicle through which some logical system is made manifest. Thus, if mathematical logic is universal, it is not surprising that the rhetoric of science text approaches universal acceptability. A problem, however, is that the linguistic phenomena which function through the rhetorical system subsume an enormous number of variables. Recent research in contrastive rhetoric has examined such issues as how DISCOURSE TOPIC is marked; what syntactic alternatives are available to express particular INTENTIONS; whether relative responsibility for clarity rests with the writer or the reader; and such phenomena as the operation of the anaphoric system, deixis, definiteness vs. indefiniteness, pronominalization, deletion, and various cohesion devices.

Texts have been compared across languages in many ways. Thus, while there is no shortage of studies, the outcomes of many studies remain incomparable because of differences in scope, in the kinds of writers studied, in the writing situations, and in the types of writing activities. A problem lies in the definition of GENRE—in the question whether particular genres exist in given languages, and whether they serve the same discourse function in different languages. Further, research is confounded by the emic/etic problem: whether the description of a rhetorical system is undertaken from within or without that system. If the description originates from within the system, it is likely to be complete, but by definition it will not be comparable to descriptions of other systems. If the description originates outside the system, it will certainly be comparable to descriptions of other systems; but it is likely to be inappropriate to the object of description, or even seriously in error. Some critics have suggested that the manifestations of rhetoric which have been taken to reflect culture-bound logics are only manifestations of differing educational systems; but this criticism is difficult to credit, as educational systems are themselves manifestations of culture-bound structures.

CR, then, has not striven for predictive adequacy, but has concerned itself with descriptive accuracy. It is marked by four features:

(a) Dependence on the weak version of the SAPIR-WHORF HYPOTHESIS. [*See* World View and Language.]
(b) An intent to describe the macrostructure of formal expository prose in some languages—those studied being constrained by the existence of a written expository genre, and by the ability of researchers to deal with them
(c) An operation which contrasts particular intersentential structures (using a discourse bloc analysis)
(d) A heavily pedagogical emphasis, in the sense that a primary objective is to help second-language learners learn to manipulate the discourse structures which lie at the core of tertiary academic study

An added difficulty stems from the fact that research has involved the teaching of both reading and writing. Further, CR has restricted itself largely to those forms of academic discourse whose function is to transmit technical information—essentially ignoring the forms whose function either does not invoke composition (bureaucratic forms, dictation, etc.), or involves the use of writing for heuristic purposes (e.g. belletristic text).

At present, the CR concept remains neither substantiated nor unsubstantiated. It has enormous potential importance, not only in relation to language pedagogy, but also in relation to translation theory, and ultimately for the conceptualization of how certain types of information are processed in the mind. Because CR has had a primarily pedagogical thrust, it has resulted in the production of quantities of pedagogical materials. Much of that material assumes that, while certain features of language may in fact be acquired, writing has to be taught; it recognizes that the learning of writing presupposes certain kinds of a-priori knowledge—of the underlying syntactic system, of lexical and semantic rules, and of the subject of discourse (including 'world knowledge').

CR remains an area for research; but in order for that research to contribute to general linguistic theory, there is a need for the isolated researchers to communicate with each other, so that the existing published research can be more readily available—and so that a clear paradigm can be developed, within which comparisons of text types and functions across languages can be validated.

ROBERT B. KAPLAN

BIBLIOGRAPHY

BEREITER, CARL, & MARLENE SCARDAMALIA. 1987. *The psychology of written composition.* Hillsdale, N.J.: Erlbaum.

CONNOR, ULLA, & ROBERT B. KAPLAN, eds. 1987. *Writing across languages: Analysis of L2 written text.* Reading, Mass.: Addison-Wesley.

GRIMES, JOSEPH E. 1975. *The thread of discourse.* (Janua linguarum, Series minor, 207.) The Hague: Mouton.

HALLIDAY, MICHAEL A. K., & RUQAIYA HASAN. 1976. *Cohesion in English.* London: Longman.

KAPLAN, ROBERT B. 1966. Cultural thought patterns in intercultural education. *Language Learning* 16.1–20.

KAPLAN, ROBERT B., ed. 1983. *Annual review of applied linguistics, 4.* Rowley, Mass.: Newbury House.

KAPLAN, ROBERT B. 1988. Contrastive rhetoric and second language learning: Notes toward a theory of contrastive rhetoric. In *Contrastive rhetoric* (Written communication annual, 2), edited by Alan C. Purves, pp. 275–304. Beverly Hills, Calif.: Sage.

KAPLAN, ROBERT B., & PETER SHAW. 1984. *Exploring academic discourse.* Rowley, Mass.: Newbury House.

CONTROL. The phenomenon of control is illustrated in the following examples:

(1a) *George persuaded his friends* [*to vote for him*].
(1b) *George hoped* [*to become President*].
(1c) *Paul tried* [*to stop the argument*].
(1d) [*To pass the exam*] *would please me.*

In these structures, a verb takes a non-finite complement that has no apparent subject, e.g. [*to vote for him*] in ex. 1a. Although these complements appear to lack subjects, they are understood as if they did have subjects, the interpretation of which is supplied by some N[oun] P[hrase] which is an argument of the matrix predicate—the object NP *his friends* in 1a, the matrix subject in 1b, and so on.

The relation between such an understood subject and the argument which supplies its interpretation is the relation of CONTROL. One says that the complement subject is CONTROLLED by a matrix argument; that argument is in turn known as the CONTROLLER of the complement subject.

Two important issues have dominated research in this area: (i) How are the formal constraints on the Control relation to be accounted for? and (ii) What principles determine which matrix argument controls an implicit subject?

1. The controlled NP. In English, complements headed by infinitive verbs may have controlled subjects (as seen in ex. 1a-d). Complements whose verb is an *-ing* participial may also have controlled subjects:

(2a) *I accused him* [*of being insincere*].
(2b) *I denied* [*stealing the documents*].
(2c) [*Being poor*] *depressed them.*

But finite complements do not allow control:

(3a) **I wanted* [*should go home*].
(3b) **I hoped* [*would become president*].
(3c) **Failed the exam* [*depressed them*].

This restriction constitutes a central puzzle: why should it be that the control relation can reach only into non-finite complements, and never into finite complements?

Furthermore, only subjects may be controlled; this condition is met in ex. 1–3. In 4, however, non-subjects are controlled:

(4a) **George persuaded his friends (for) them to like.*
(4b) **Paul tried (for) his colleagues to respect.*

Most theoretical work on control, then, has assumed that only subjects of non-finite clauses may be controlled, and has sought to construct an explanation for this observation.

2. Selection of controller. Depending on the matrix predicate, either a subject (as in 5a), a direct object (as in 5b), an indirect object (as in 5c), or an oblique argument (as in 5d) may function as controller:

(5a) GEORGE *promised (his wife)* [*to quit smoking*].
(5b) *George persuaded his* BROTHER [*to quit smoking*].
(5c) *Paul shouted to* GEORGE [*to be quiet*].
(5d) *It is impossible for* PEOPLE *these days* [*to get ahead*].

There are also cases in which the controller argument is itself implicit:

(6a) *It is immoral* [*to question authority*].
(6b) *It's fun* [*to trick people*].

Such examples are instances of so-called ARBITRARY CONTROL, in which the implicit subject of the complement is assigned an interpretation commonly called 'generic' or 'arbitrary'. In most if not all such cases, the matrix predicate has an implicit BENEFACTIVE argument which can be viewed as the controller.

3. Early analyses. The earliest generative analyses of this phenomenon were transformational. In this conception, non-finite complements are derived from full clauses which have fully specified subjects; if identical to, and coreferential with, a matrix NP, those subjects are deleted by a transformation known as Equi-NP-Deletion. [*See* Deletion; Recoverability.] An example like 1c, for instance, would be derived roughly as follows:

(7) *Paul*$_j$ *tried* [$_S$ *Paul*$_j$ *stop the argument*].
⇓
Paul$_j$ *tried* [$_S$ Ø *stop the argument*].

The condition that the deleted element must be the subject of a non-finite clause is stipulated.

This analysis brings with it an elaborate theory of RULE GOVERNANCE, since application of Equi-NP-Deletion depends on the presence of particular predicates in the matrix. The rule is obligatory for some (see 8), optional for others (9), and inapplicable for still others (10):

(8a) *Jim tried [to be good].*
(8b) **Jim$_j$ tried [(for) him(self)$_j$ to be good].*
(8c) **Jim$_j$ tried [(that) he$_j$ be good].*
(8d) **Jim$_j$ tried [(that) the students like him$_j$].*

(9a) *Bill wanted [to have a good marriage].*
(9b) *??Bill$_j$ wanted [himself$_j$ to have a good marriage].*
(9c) *Bill$_j$ wanted [that he$_j$ should have a good marriage].*
(9d) *Bill wanted [that everyone have a good time].*

(10a) **Paul screamed [to open the door].*
(10b) *Paul screamed [for George to open the door].*
(10c) **Paul$_j$ screamed [for him$_j$ to open the door].*

The problem is a complex one. The verb *try,* in this conception, has the property that it must be inserted into a syntactic structure in which Equi-NP-Deletion will apply. The verb *want* may (but is not required to) appear in an environment in which Equi-NP-Deletion can apply. The verb *scream* must be inserted into a syntactic structure of such a kind that Equi-NP-Deletion cannot apply to it.

4. Subcategorization analyses (see Brame 1976, Bresnan 1982, Dowty 1985, Gazdar et al. 1985). Partly because of the complexity of the system of rule governance that the transformational analysis made necessary, a number of theorists proposed in the mid-1970s to eliminate the transformation of Equi-NP-Deletion in favor of an analysis of control phenomena in terms of direct LEXICAL SUBCATEGORIZATION. [*See* Subcategorization and Selection.] The general strategy behind this approach is to maintain that the complement of a control-verb like *try* is a V[erb] P[hrase] at every level of syntactic representation, and that it is simply a lexical property of *try* that it demands a VP complement. Neither the deletion transformation nor the associated apparatus of rule governance is now necessary; 8b-d are ungrammatical because they violate lexical requirements of *try*. It follows directly that only subjects may be controlled.

VP complements are supplied with subjects from the argument structure of the matrix predicate, i.e. are supplied with controllers, either by means of LEXICAL RULES (Bresnan 1982), rules of SEMANTIC COMPOSITION (Gazdar et al. 1985), or by MEANING POSTULATES (Dowty 1985). This general approach to the problem of control is a feature, in one version or another, of Generalized Phrase-Structure Grammar [*q.v.*] (Gazdar et al. 1985), Lexical-Functional Grammar [*q.v.*] (Bresnan 1982), and Categorial Grammar [*q.v.*] (Dowty 1985). It has been criticized on two main grounds. First, it leaves unexplained the fact that only a non-finite VP may be a subcategorized complement. That is, there is no account of the observation that only the subjects of non-finite complements may be controlled. Second, it has been argued that control complements exhibit the syntactic characteristics of full clauses, rather than those of VPs.

5. PRO and the PRO-Theorem (see Chomsky 1981, Manzini 1983.) Accounts of the phenomenon of control within Chomsky's Extended Standard Theory and its successor, Government/Binding Theory [*q.v.*], are also non-transformational. These theories assume, however, that control complements are full clauses at every level of representation. Furthermore, they have syntactic subjects; their subject position is occupied by a phonetically null pronoun with quite particular properties. This element, known as PRO, is anaphorically linked with a matrix antecedent:

(11) *Paul$_j$ tried [$_S$ PRO$_j$ [to [$_{VP}$ stop the argument]]].*

The postulation of the silent syntactic subject is consistent with, and required by, the PROJECTION PRINCIPLE—a consequence of which is that, if a structure has a subject argument for semantic purposes, then it must also have a subject argument at every syntactic level of representation.

The question of why only subjects of non-finite clauses can be controlled becomes the question of why PRO may appear only in this position. This restriction is analyzed as deriving from the anomalous character of PRO with respect to Binding theory [*q.v.*]. The element PRO shows the typical characteristics both of ANAPHORS and of PRONOMINALS (Chomsky 1986:125–131). [*See* Anaphora; Pronouns.] Being an anaphor, it is subject to Condition A of the Binding theory, which requires it to be BOUND in its governing category. Being a pronominal, it is subject to Condition B of the Binding theory, which requires it to be UNBOUND in its governing category.

These conflicting requirements can be resolved if PRO has NO governing category; and this can hold true only if PRO has no governor. Therefore, PRO may appear only in ungoverned positions. All non-subject argument positions are governed by lexical categories; the subject position of a finite clause is governed, and Case is assigned to it by the element INFL, which defines a clause as finite. The only argument position which is systematically ungoverned is the subject position of a non-finite clause. Thus PRO may appear there, but not in other argument positions.

This analysis has been challenged on the grounds that its crucial step, the assignment of the element PRO simultaneously to the categories of Anaphor and Pronominal, is unmotivated—and furthermore, that the distinction between subjects of finite clauses and subjects of non-finite clauses in terms of government is artifactual.

The problem of selecting a controller for PRO in a given structure is assigned to the separate subtheory of Control. At the time of writing, the content of this subtheory remains poorly understood (Chomsky 1986:124–31).

JAMES McCLOSKEY

BIBLIOGRAPHY

BRAME, MICHAEL K. 1976. *Conjectures and refutations in syntax and semantics.* New York: North-Holland.

BRESNAN, JOAN, ed. 1982. *The mental representation of grammatical relations.* Cambridge, Mass.: MIT Press.

CHOMSKY, NOAM. 1981. *Lectures on government and binding.* (Studies in generative grammar, 9.) Dordrecht: Foris.

CHOMSKY, NOAM. 1986. *Knowledge of language: Its nature, origins, and use.* New York: Praeger.

DOWTY, DAVID R. 1985. On recent analyses of the semantics of control. *Linguistics & Philosophy* 8.291–331.

GAZDAR, GERALD; EWAN KLEIN; GEOFFREY K. PULLUM; & IVAN A. SAG. 1985. *Generalized Phrase Structure Grammar.* Oxford: Blackwell. Cambridge, Mass.: Harvard University Press.

MANZINI, MARIA RITA. 1983. On control and control theory. *Linguistic Inquiry* 14.421–446.

ROSENBAUM, PETER S. 1967. *The grammar of English predicate complement constructions.* Cambridge, Mass.: MIT Press.

CONVERSATION ANALYSIS.

In its vernacular usage, the term 'conversation' usually refers to casual, informal talk between two or more people. This definition identifies a pervasive type of speech situation, but unfortunately excludes other types of verbal interchange, e.g. interviews and meetings (an issue considered below). Such commonplace talk is addressed in distinctive ways by different approaches to the study of natural language use.

Sociolinguists, for example, study the influence of variables such as race, class, gender, and other social constraints on speech practices. Students of communication measure the communicative competence of speakers and determine how these skills affect persuasive communication or conversational control. Discourse analysts, continuing the linguistic tradition by devising concepts and methodology for units larger than the clause, address issues of cohesion and coherence between the utterances and underlying actions that constitute spoken discourse; or they study information flow, anaphora, etc. All of these approaches utilize conversational data.

The term C[ONVERSATION] A[NALYSIS], however, almost always implies an ETHNOMETHODOLOGICAL approach (Stubbs 1983:10; cf. Levinson 1983:294–296, Garfinkel 1967, 1987); in this usage it evokes the work of Schegloff and Sacks (1973), Sacks et al. (1974), and Schegloff (1979, 1987). CA is concerned with the discovery and description of the methods or procedures that speakers use to engage in conversation and other forms of social interaction involving spoken language. Such procedures constitute a ubiquitous and fundamental form of social organization. [*See* Social Structure and Language.]

Accordingly, this entry will be concerned with CA not merely as a descriptive term, specifying a commonsensically defined subject matter, but in the more restrictive sense of a subdiscipline within sociology, having a distinctive focus—namely spoken language, and parallel gestural and paralinguistic conduct, as a basic form of social interaction. (For collections of papers on the topic, see Schenkein 1978, Psathas 1979, Atkinson & Heritage 1984, and Button & Lee 1987.)

1. Turn-taking. Fundamental to the focus of CA is the assumption that conversation as an interactional activity displays features which can be analyzed as the specific achievements of speakers and hearers. This finely detailed conduct is produced by participants' use of a finite set of general procedures to manage the local contingencies of actual situations. One such set of procedures—the mechanisms for TURN-TAKING in conversation—provides a useful example of conversation-analytic concerns. [*See also* Production of Language.]

In an important and influential paper, Sacks et al. (1974) proposed that any model of turn-taking must account for several observable facts about conversation, for example:

(a) Turn order, turn size, and turn content are free to vary.
(b) Length of conversation is not predetermined.
(c) The number of participants is free to vary.
(d) The distribution of turns (in multi-party conversation) is not prespecified.

Conversation (what Heritage 1984:238–240 has referred to as 'mundane' conversation) is thus observed to be a system characterized by free variation along these (and other) parameters.

If conversation is an orderly activity, there must be some systematic way in which participants manage actual conversations to achieve the particular distribution of turns, turn-length, turn-order, etc., which characterize any given conversation. Sacks et al. 1974 developed a model which operates by a set of general, trans-situationally stable procedures by which turns are interactionally constructed and allocated. These procedures are employed to manage turn-taking on a LOCAL basis; that is, although they are general, they are adaptable to the specific purposes and identities of the parties present, to their actual social circumstances, and to the particular contingencies of the situation.

Turns are principally constructed of sequentially relevant clausal, phrasal, lexical, or other elements; non-lexical vocal elements and gestures are other possible turn-constructional components. Unit boundaries can be anticipated, and are thereby usable by participants to predict points of possible transition. Turns are allocated by an interactionally constrained, temporally ordered set of options which provide, at or near the possible turn boundary, for (i) the current speaker selecting a next speaker, (ii) a next speaker being self-selected, or (iii) the current speaker continuing in the absence of next-speaker self-selection.

This model is general; it pertains to any conversation, face-to-face or electronically mediated, with variable numbers of participants (see Wilson 1990 for a comparison of turn-taking models). Moreover, it furnishes a formal means of specifying 'conversation' as an object of inquiry. That is, 'conversation' is not identified by virtue of being casual, informal, or inconsequential, but rather by the characteristics of the turn-taking system which permits occasions of talk to be DEVELOPED by conversationalists as casual, informal, etc. By virtue of the situated, local (turn-by-turn), and interactional determination of length, order, and content or type of turns, participants are able to systematically generate novel, spontaneous, mundane conversation.

By the same token, when various parameters of the turn-taking are constrained—either by convention, or by other means of coordinating the orientation of the parties present—the occasion and the talk within it are transformed. By pre-specifying the turn order, the number or social category of participants, and the turn content or type, a different mode of organizing spoken interaction comes into operation—i.e., a different SPEECH EXCHANGE SYSTEM. In interviews, for example, turn types (questions and answers, respectively) are pre-allocated to specified categories of participants (interviewers, interviewees), with observable consequences for the interaction; this limits such factors as the range and selection of topics discussed, the length of turns, the speaker selection procedure used, and the organization of closing. (See Atkinson & Drew 1984 for discussion of other speech exchange systems.)

Various forms of spoken interaction, then, may reflect systematic modifications of the organization of turn-taking found in ordinary conversation. Detailed observations of actual conversations have thus yielded not only a model of turn-taking, but also an empirically based characterization of the primary subject matter (mundane conversation) and a means of systematically identifying and comparing different types of spoken interaction in society.

2. Other mechanisms. Another very general conversational mechanism is ADJACENCY PAIR organization (Schegloff & Sacks 1973; Heritage 1984:245–253; Levinson 1983:303–308). This deals with the relationship of adjacent turns where an initial turn is of a particular type (a question, request, invitation, blaming, etc.). The type of the initial turn constrains some designated party to produce a second, adjacent turn of a type matched to the first (e.g. an answer, a granting or denial, an acceptance or declination, a denial or admission, etc.). Other work has identified procedures for opening conversations and establishing and aligning identities; for the initiation, management and closure of topics; for the organization of REPAIR activities addressed to a broad range of conversational 'troubles'; for PREFERENCE organization—the structural allocation of preferred and dispreferred turn types in response to different activities, such as repairing, inviting, requesting, or complimenting—and for CLOSING, e.g. achieving a coordinated exit from talk. The list could be extended; for reviews of research, see Heritage 1984, 1985.

The work briefly mentioned above highlights some specific research on particular types of conversational organization. The fundamental focus of these studies is the SEQUENTIAL ORGANIZATION of particular aspects of spoken interaction. Such organization encompasses the production and recognition of successive turns, where a subsequent turn stands in some specifiable relationship to the prior beyond mere serial placement. Examples include invitations and their subsequent acceptance or declination; the initiation of repair by another in the next turn when the prior speaker has not self-corrected; a second assessment to a first; and opening or closing sequences. The course of conversational interaction is thus managed on a turn-by-turn basis, with the sequential environment providing the primary context for participants' understanding, appreciation, and use of what is being done and said in the talk (Schegloff & Sacks 1973:234). Turn-taking, of course, furnishes the fundamental framework for sequentially organized activities.

Conversation analysts view these activities in terms of their internal constraints, as specimens of socially organized interaction, rather than as products of external influences—e.g. categories such as race or gender, or institutional and organizational processes. In this respect, CA contrasts with sociolinguistics, which is precisely concerned with the effect of such external factors on language use.

When conversation analysts turn to the study of spoken interaction in institutional settings (courtrooms, physicians' offices, news interviews), they focus on how the features of mundane conversation are modified and adapted to the tasks in the setting—e.g., how turn-taking is modified to achieve a unified focus of attention. The features of these interactions as much constitute the setting as they are occasioned by it (Heritage 1984:231–240). For a variety of views on the study of talk in institutional settings, see Boden & Zimmerman 1990.

Spoken interaction, whether in ordinary conversation or institutional settings, is seen as exhibiting features which are PRODUCED and ORIENTED TO by participants as orderly and informative, and which are relied upon as a basis for further inference and action. Indeed, it is the fact that participants themselves LOCATE these features (e.g. through behaviors subsequently addressed to them) that warrants regarding them as relevant to conversational activity.

3. CA and sociology. The view that spoken interaction, as a domain of social action, exhibits a high measure of orderliness, and that this order is produced and oriented to by speakers and hearers, requires further comment, particularly in relation to the usual interests of sociologists. Sociology seeks its orderly phenomena in group, institutional, or societal patterns emerging out of aggregate behaviors. The identification and analysis of these socially organized patterns is thought to require the respecification of observed, reported, or recorded social activities in terms of analytical categories or variables which permit the investigator to link seemingly disparate concrete events (see Garfinkel 1987 and Garfinkel & Sacks 1970 on 'constructive analytical theorizing').

For example, when sociologists investigate interaction, say in a work group, the features of persons' verbal exchanges may be coded in terms of categories such as 'exercises control' or 'gives support' or 'provides information'. Such analytic moves are thought necessary for the extraction of abstract but orderly patterns out of what is otherwise a confusing array of concrete particulars. Thus the concrete occasions of everyday activities are not a promising site for the study of social order.

However, CA focuses on just such mundane activity, seeking to capture for analysis the diverse particulars of everyday conduct. The purpose for turning to the study of conversation was to reorient sociology as 'a natural observational science' (Sacks 1984:21). In this view, sociological inquiry should strive to observe, analyze, and account for the particulars of everyday behavior as deeply and finely organized social conduct. Accordingly, CA considers these details as matters to be accounted for as the workings of a socially organized 'machinery', operating at the level of the most mundane and singular face-to-face interactions. This view runs counter to the conventional wisdom of social science.

Thus CA holds itself analytically responsible for the particulars of interaction. Its formulations must be capable of recovering these details through close description of the methods by which interactants produce them. Its data are the features of naturally occurring talk (contrived or invented discourse is avoided) in which participants are free to employ the resources of conversational organization to deal with the interactional and situational contingencies of the occasion.

In closing, it is important to recognize that Sacks, in initiating the conversation-analytic approach, did not proceed from an initial interest in language as such. Instead, he sought an orderly domain of activity, the details of which could be readily captured and repeatedly observed by using easily available technology. Conversation analysts view spoken interaction as a socially organized activity, and thus are concerned with units such as turns, sequences, and the organization of tasks indigenous to interaction, rather than with the features of language as such (but see Schegloff 1979). It should also be said that the emphasis of CA on interactional units does not preclude attention to the interrelationship of conversational organization, discourse structure, and grammar. Indeed, exploration of these relationships is already under way (cf. Fox 1987, Schiffrin 1987).

DON H. ZIMMERMAN

BIBLIOGRAPHY

ATKINSON, J. MAXWELL, & PAUL DREW. 1984. *Order in court: The organization of verbal interaction in judicial settings.* London: Macmillan.

ATKINSON, J. MAXWELL, & JOHN C. HERITAGE, eds. 1984. *Structures of social action: Studies in conversational analysis.* Cambridge & New York: Cambridge University Press.

BODEN, DEIRDRE, & DON H. ZIMMERMAN. 1990. *Talk and social structure.* Cambridge: Polity Press.

BUTTON, GRAHAM, & JOHN R. E. LEE, eds. 1987. *Talk and social organization.* Clevedon, Avon, England: Multilingual Matters.

FOX, BARBARA A. 1987. *Discourse structure and anaphora: Written and conversational English.* (Cambridge studies in linguistics, 48.) Cambridge & New York: Cambridge University Press.

GARFINKEL, HAROLD. 1967. *Studies in ethnomethodology.* Englewood Cliffs, N.J.: Prentice-Hall.

GARFINKEL, HAROLD. 1987. A reflection. *Discourse Analysis Research Group Newsletter* 3.5–9.

GARFINKEL, HAROLD, & HARVEY SACKS. 1970. On formal structures of practical actions. In *Theoretical sociology,* edited by John C. McKinney & Edward A. Tiryakian, pp. 337–366. New York: Appleton-Century-Crofts.

HERITAGE, JOHN. 1984. *Garfinkel and ethnomethodology.* Cambridge: Polity Press.

HERITAGE, JOHN. 1985. Recent developments in conversation analysis. *Sociolinguistics Newsletter* 15.1–18.

LEVINSON, STEPHEN C. 1983. *Pragmatics.* Cambridge & New York: Cambridge University Press.

PSATHAS, GEORGE, ed. 1979. *Everyday language: Studies in ethnomethodology.* New York: Irvington.

SACKS, HARVEY. 1984. Notes on methodology. In Atkinson & Heritage 1984, pp. 21–27.

SACKS, HARVEY; EMANUEL A. SCHEGLOFF; & GAIL JEFFERSON. 1974. A simplest systematics for the organization of turn-taking for conversation. *Language* 50.696–735.

SCHEGLOFF, EMANUEL A. 1979. The relevance of repair to syntax-for-conversation. In *Discourse and syntax* (Syntax and semantics, 12), edited by Talmy Givón, pp. 261–286. New York: Academic Press.

SCHEGLOFF, EMANUEL A. 1987. Analyzing single episodes of interaction: An exercise in conversation analysis. *Social Psychology Quarterly* 50.101–114.

SCHEGLOFF, EMANUEL A., & HARVEY SACKS. 1973. Opening up closings. *Semiotica* 8.289–327.

SCHENKEIN, JIM N., ed. 1978. *Studies in the organization of conversational interaction.* New York: Academic Press.

SCHIFFRIN, DEBORAH. 1987. *Discourse markers.* (Studies in interactional sociolinguistics, 5.) Cambridge & New York: Cambridge University Press.

STUBBS, MICHAEL. 1983. *Discourse analysis: The sociolinguistic analysis of natural language.* (Language in society, 4.) Oxford: Blackwell. Chicago: University of Chicago Press.

WILSON, THOMAS P. 1990. Social structure and sequential organization. In Boden & Zimmerman 1990.

CONVERSION, also known as functional shift or zero derivation, is the process whereby a new word is derived by change in part of speech, without adding a derivational affix; e.g. $cheat_V$ > $cheat_N$ 'someone who cheats' (= $sing_V$ > $sing\text{-}er_N$), gas_N > gas_V 'treat with gas' (= $alcohol_N$ > $alcohol\text{-}ize_V$), $clean_{ADJ}$ > $clean_V$ 'make clean' (= $legal_{ADJ}$ > $legalize_V$).

Several theoretical approaches exist. In one approach, no derivational process is assumed: words may have multiple class membership (Nida 1948:434–36); or there are special overlapping classes NV, AV, NAV (Hockett 1958:225–27); or separate lexical entries are related only in the semantic component by a directional or non-directional redundancy rule (Lieber 1981:119–139).

In another approach, a directional derivational relationship is assumed, which can take one of the following forms:

(a) Conversion is treated as a syntactic phenomenon—as a simple change of class, typical of languages (such as English) that lack inflectional word-class characteristics; thus German $laufen_V$ 'to run' > $Lauf_N$ '(a) run', $Salz_N$ 'salt' > $salzen_V$ 'to salt' would not count as conversions (Kruisinga 1932:96–161).

(b) Conversion is treated as parallel to explicit suffixation, with the same semantic properties. The suffix takes the form of zero, i.e. *cheat*-$\emptyset_N$, *clean*-$\emptyset_V$, thus preserving the binary structure of word-formation syntagmas (Marchand 1969:359–389).

(c) Conversion is treated as a special 'headless' morphological rule that does not involve any branching (Williams 1981:247, 250, 257).

(d) Conversion is treated as a special derivational process whose output, a CONTEXTUAL, is semantically vague, and derives its concrete meaning by pragmatic factors from the context (Clark & Clark 1979).

DIETER KASTOVSKY

BIBLIOGRAPHY

CLARK, EVE V., & HERBERT H. CLARK. 1979. When nouns surface as verbs. *Language* 55.767–811.

HOCKETT, CHARLES F. 1958. *A course in modern linguistics.* New York: Macmillan.

KRUISINGA, ETSKO. 1932. *A handbook of present-day English,* part 2, *English accidence and syntax,* vol. 3. Groningen: Noordhoff.

LIEBER, ROCHELLE. 1981. *On the organization of the lexicon.* Bloomington: Indiana University Linguistics Club.

MARCHAND, HANS. 1969. *The categories and types of present-day English word-formation: A synchronic-diachronic approach.* 2d ed. Munich: Beck.

NIDA, EUGENE A. 1948. The identification of morphemes. *Language* 24.414–441.

WILLIAMS, EDWIN S. 1981. On the notions 'lexically related' and 'head of a word'. *Linguistic Inquiry* 12.245–274.

COOPERATIVE PRINCIPLE. Like other social activities, language interchange requires that participants mutually recognize certain conventions. Grice (1975:45) wrote of it: 'Make your conversational contribution such as is required, at the stage at which it occurs, by the accepted purpose or direction of the talk exchange in which you are engaged. One might label this the C[OOPERATIVE] P[RINCIPLE].' The present description develops the original conception of Grice, who characterized CP by four categories of maxims:

QUANTITY: The S[PEAKER] (or writer) should make the strongest claim possible, consistent with his/her perception of the facts, while giving no more and no less information than is required to make the message clear to the H[EARER] (or reader).

QUALITY: S's contribution should be genuine and not spurious. Speakers should state as facts only what they believe to be facts, make offers and promises only if they intend to carry them out, pronounce judgments only if they are in a position to judge, etc.

RELATION: An U[TTERANCE] should not in general be irrelevant to the context in which it is uttered, because that makes it difficult for H to comprehend. Sperber & Wilson 1986 argue that RELEVANCE is the fundamental principle of language interaction.

MANNER: Where possible, S's meaning should be presented in a clear, concise manner that avoids ambiguity and avoids misleading or confusing H through stylistic ineptitude.

Such maxims are not laws to be obeyed, but reference points for language interchange—much as the points of the compass are conventional reference points for giving directions and locations over the surface of the earth.

CP holds whenever S and H mutually recognize S's observance of the COMMUNICATIVE PRESUMPTION, the REASONABLENESS CONDITION, and the normal conventions pertaining to FACE AFFECT (politeness phenomena) of their community; see Allan 1986, chap. 1.2. When H perceives S's utterance to be linguistic, H presumes that S has uttered U with the intention of communicating some message using the conventions of natural language. This communicative presumption presupposes that S is acting reasonably; i.e., S has some reason for uttering U, rather than maintaining silence or uttering something different. (Sperber & Wilson would describe this as S observing the principle of relevance.) Furthermore, S does not randomly choose the forms and style to use in U: normally S has some reason for selecting the particular ones used—a reason that H seeks, not necessarily consciously, when interpreting S's utterance.

Some scholars, who have criticized Grice's statement of the maxims for not being universally applicable, have not perceived that CP is motivated by conventions which pertain to face affect and vary between situations and communities. (Leech 1983 even differentiates a 'Politeness Principle' from CP.) Face has two aspects: POSITIVE face is the desire that one's attributes, achievements, ideas, possessions, goals, etc. should be desirable to others; NEGATIVE face is one's desire not to be imposed on by others (Brown & Levinson 1987). Face can be lost (affronted), gained (enhanced), or just maintained. In virtually every utterance, S needs to take care that what is said will maintain, enhance, or affront H's face in just the way S intends to affect it, while at the same time maintaining or enhancing S's own face. There is a general presumption that S will be polite except when intending to affront H's positive face; and S will not normally impose on H without good reason, lest H's negative face be affronted. The meaningful effects of U which result from the Gricean maxims and other kinds of face affect are CONVERSATIONAL IMPLICATURES (Grice 1975, Levinson 1983). A theory of meaning must take account of normal conventions pertaining to face affect within a language community because utterance meaning is partly determined by reference to them.

CP governs one category of positive face affect—making H feel good—and five categories of negative face affect. One is a non-verbal category governing such matters as eye contact; the rest are verbal categories. In the interests of social harmony, S should normally avoid the following four modes of behavior unless S intends to affront H's negative face:

(a) Attacks on H's positive face.
(b) Impositions on H's person, possessions, time, etc. (e.g. requiring H to do something, asking for the use of H's possessions or ideas).
(c) Wittingly misleading H into erroneous beliefs and assumptions, in violation of the maxim of quality.
(d) Requiring H to expend unreasonable effort in order to understand what S means in uttering U because U is uncomfortably loud, inaudible, incoherent, irrelevant, abstruse, or otherwise unreasonable. The maxims of quantity, relation, and manner govern different aspects of this final IMPOSITIVE category.

Were there no CP—no communicative presumption, reasonableness condition, or conventions pertaining to face affects—systematic communication would be impossible. There would be no ground rules for deciding whether U makes sense or what value should be put on it. Conversely, S would have no ground rules for getting a message across to H. [*See also* Pragmatics, Implicature, and Presupposition.]

KEITH ALLAN

BIBLIOGRAPHY

ALLAN, KEITH. 1986. *Linguistic meaning*. 2 vols. London: Routledge & Kegan Paul.

BROWN, PENELOPE, & STEPHEN C. LEVINSON. 1987. *Politeness: Some universals in language usage*. (Studies in interactional sociolinguistics, 4.) Cambridge & New York: Cambridge University Press.

GRICE, H. PAUL. 1975. Logic and conversation. In *Speech acts* (Syntax and semantics, 3), edited by Peter Cole & Jerry L. Morgan, pp. 41–58. New York: Academic Press.

LEECH, GEOFFREY N. 1983. *Principles of pragmatics*. London: Longman.

LEVINSON, STEPHEN C. 1983. *Pragmatics*. Cambridge & New York: Cambridge University Press.

SPERBER, DAN, & DEIRDRE WILSON. 1986. *Relevance: Communication and cognition*. Oxford: Blackwell.

COORDINATION. Constructions in which two or more parts of the sentence are conjoined by words like *and* or *or*, as in ex. 1, are generally referred to by the term 'coordination':

(1a) *John {and/or} Mary went to the park.*
(1b) *John ate dinner {and/or} read a book.*

There have been two main formal approaches to this area of grammar. The first proceeds from the observation that a sequence such as N[oun] P[hrase] *and* NP may appear wherever a simple NP is permitted. This generalization may be formalized as the following phrase structure rule, where α is any phrasal or lexical category:

(2) $\alpha \rightarrow \alpha$ {*and/or*} α

For ex. 1a, α equals NP; for 1b, it equals V[erb] P[hrase]. Coordinate structures are thus base-generated in this approach, sometimes called PHRASAL CONJUNCTION.

The second approach to coordination develops the idea that sentences like ex. 1a-b are reduced from the following:

(3a) *John went to the park {and/or} Mary went to the park.*
(3b) *John ate dinner {and/or} John read a book.*

In this approach, sometimes called DERIVED or SENTENTIAL CONJUNCTION, only sentences are conjoined in underlying structure; a transformation of CONJUNCTION REDUCTION then applies to produce the observed surface structures. It is of course conceivable that the grammar would contain the phrase structure rule in 2, and also Conjunction Reduction; however, for reasons of parsimony, it is often assumed that only one of these two analyses is correct. (For general reference, see Stockwell et al. 1973.)

One reason that both of these approaches have coexisted for so long is that each is faced with difficult prima-facie problems. With the base-generated approach in 2, for instance, it does not appear to be possible to produce sentences in which the conjoined elements are not constituents. Thus no value for α could yield the following:

(4) *Mary put [the car in the garage] and [the bike in the shop].*

Another problem arises if one assumes the existence of NP Movement, since then one cannot account for these sentences:

(5a) *John insulted Bill and was hit by Mary.*
(5b) *Tom lives in Paris and seems to be happy.*

The object of *hit* in 5a and the subject of *be happy* in 5b should have undergone NP movement; but there is no position into which they could have moved, and they simply remain unexpressed.

The Conjunction Reduction approach also presents some difficulties. Given an underlying structure as in 6a, stipulations are required to prevent derivation of the ungrammatical sentence 6b, in which the conjuncts are of differing syntactic categories:

(6a) *John sang the song and John sang at home.*
(6b) **John sang the song and at home.*

In addition, if one assumes that selectional restrictions [*see* Subcategorization and Selection] are enforced at underlying structure, then a sentence like 7b should be deviant, given that selectional restrictions are not satisfied in its source 7a:

(7a) *The car collided and the truck collided.*
(7b) *The car and the truck collided.*

In fact, however, 7b is perfectly well-formed.

In addition to these specific problems, there is also a range of complex facts associated with coordination that present a descriptive challenge to any approach. One such set of facts involves extraction processes such as WH-movement. Ross 1967 noted that extraction is not permitted out of a coordinate structure (his Coordinate Structure Constraint), as in 8a, unless the extraction affects all the conjuncts, as in 8b:

(8a) **This is the book which John read __ and Mary wrote an article.*
(8b) *This is the book which John read __ and Mary wrote.*

The latter case, known as Across-the-Board extraction, appears to be subject to its own particular constraints. Specifically, if we extract an element from the matrix subject position of one conjunct, we must do the same in all conjuncts; e.g.,

(9a) *This is the book which __ appeared on the shelves last week and ___ costs $20.*
(9b) **This is the book which John read __ and ___ appeared on the shelves last week.*

Aside from this, extraction is not required to apply to parallel positions in each conjunct:

(10) *This is the book which John read __ and Mary hopes ___ will be a best-seller.*

The peculiar patterning of facts in 8b, 9, and 10 is sometimes referred to as an 'asymmetry' in Across-the-Board extraction.

Other areas of investigation within coordination include GAPPING, as in 11, where the verb in the second of two conjoined sentences is omitted; and RIGHT NODE RAISING, as in 12, where the rightmost constituent of two conjoined sentences appears to their right (see Neijt 1979):

(11) *John read the book, and Mary the newspaper.*
(12) *John read, and Mary bought, the new book which appeared last week.*

Each of these constructions is subject to a complex set of constraints.

Since the early 1980s, there has been renewed interest in coordination within the context of general syntactic theory. (For general reference, see Oirsouw 1987.) Gerald Gazdar noted that, if one adopts a rule like 2 together with the slash categories of G[eneralized] P[hrase]-S[tructure] G[rammar]—in which a sentence out of which an NP has been extracted is of a different category type than an 'intact' sentence—then the Coordinate Structure Constraint and the Across-the-Board facts in 8 follow immediately. Other properties of coordination, such as the Across-the-Board asymmetries in 9–10, may also be derived from general principles of GPSG (Gazdar et al. 1985).

Within G[overnment/]B[inding] theory, David Pesetsky has argued that these same facts in 8–10 lend support to his Path Containment Condition—an independently motivated constraint on extraction which makes use of the notion of 'paths' among nodes in the tree. Also within GB theory, Goodall 1987 has developed an approach in which the conjuncts of a coordinate structure are not linearly ordered with respect to each other in their syntactic representation; several of the unusual properties of coordination seem to follow from this configuration.

GRANT GOODALL

BIBLIOGRAPHY

GAZDAR, GERALD; EWAN KLEIN; GEOFFREY K. PULLUM; & IVAN SAG. 1985. *Generalized Phrase Structure Grammar.* Oxford: Blackwell. Cambridge, Mass.: Harvard University Press.

GOODALL, GRANT. 1987. *Parallel structures in syntax: Coordination, causatives, and restructuring.* (Cambridge studies in linguistics, 46.) Cambridge & New York: Cambridge University Press.

NEIJT, ANNEKE. 1979. *Gapping: A contribution to sentence grammar.* (Studies in generative grammar, 7.) Dordrecht: Foris.

OIRSOUW, ROBERT R. VAN. 1987. *The syntax of coordination.* London: Croom Helm.

ROSS, JOHN ROBERT. 1967. *Constraints on variables in syntax.* MIT dissertation. Published as *Infinite syntax* (Norwood, N.J.: Ablex, 1986).

STOCKWELL, ROBERT P., et al. 1973. *The major syntactic structures of English.* New York: Holt, Rinehart & Winston.

CORPUS PROCESSING. A computer corpus is a large body of naturally occurring computer-readable texts or text-extracts used for research, and especially for the development of N[ATURAL] L[ANGUAGE] P]ROCESSING] software.

Historically, it became feasible for computers to store and manipulate such large quantities of natural language text in the early 1960s; the first well-known example was the corpus of modern American written text extracts known as the Brown Corpus, compiled at Brown University (see Francis & Kučera 1964, 1982), consisting of over one million text words ('word tokens'). Since that time many computer corpora have been assembled—representing different languages, or different varieties of the same language (e.g. British, American, and Indian English), or encoding different kinds of information about written and spoken texts.

In size, corpora can vary greatly for practical and technical reasons. To build even a relatively small corpus of spoken discourse in reliably detailed transcription may require thousands of hours of transcription by skilled phoneticians. (See Svartvik et al. 1982 and Knowles & Lawrence 1987 for details on two corpora of this kind.) However, as a result of recent advances in optical character recognition, and the availability of machine-readable text as a by-product of word processing and computer typesetting, it is now technically relatively easy to amass a vast corpus, of the order of 300–500 million words of printed text.

In spite of this massive increase in the availability of machine-readable text over the past twenty-five years, the opportunities for using such resources for research have been little exploited, for three main reasons. First, whereas computer corpora of written language exist in abundance, there is a shortage of corpora of spoken language; yet it is speech technology, e.g. automatic SPEECH RECOGNITION [*q.v.*], that has most to gain from corpus-based research.

Second, the availability of corpora for research in a technical sense does not entail availability in a legal sense. In practice, restrictions of copyright and other proprietary rights impede the average researcher's access to corpus data.

Third, it is argued (e.g. in Aarts & Van den Heuvel 1985 and in Garside et al. 1987:16–29) that the value of computer corpora for research has been recognized belatedly and insufficiently in computational linguistics. This is partly because of an unappealing research style: the work of the corpus linguist is strongly data-oriented and labor-intensive. Another reason relates to the evolving state of the art: up to now, computational linguists have been able to avoid confronting the multitudinous messiness of unrestricted natural language use by concentrating on the development of computer systems (sometimes disparagingly called 'toy systems') designed for artificially selected or domain-restricted data. Only recently has NLP research advanced so far as to need testing of grammars, parsers, etc. against non-preselected data; this is precisely the point at which the computer corpus comes to be seen as a valuable, if not indispensable, tool.

The computer corpus satisfies the need for access to a wide range of actually occurring instances of language use when developing wide-coverage tools of language description, such as a dictionary or a grammar. Dictionaries and grammars may exist in the form of printed books (see Sinclair 1987 on the use of a large corpus in the compilation of a printed dictionary). For the present purpose, however, we may focus on machine-readable 'computer grammars' and 'computer dictionaries' (lexicons) used for NLP.

To be useful, the corpus itself has to undergo various kinds of computer processing or analysis. We will discuss four models of the role of corpus processing:

MODEL A. In the linguistic INFORMATION RETRIEVAL model, the computer's role is subservient to the analysis carried out by the human user. The computer sorts, counts, arranges (e.g. by concordance), and presents linguistic data; the human analyst may then use the output for formulating, checking, or testing rules or generalizations about the language.

MODEL B. In the INDUCTION model, the computer is a means of deriving ('inducing') generalizations automatically from data. The generalizations, in this case, will be stated in terms of frequency or probability, since induction is essentially a statistical process.

MODEL C. The AUTOMATIC CORPUS PROCESSING model increases the value of processing for both Model A and Model B by 'annotating' the corpus with descriptive information over and above that found in the original. One useful kind of information is provided by the grammatical tagging of the corpus: to each text word is attached a label or TAG, indicating its grammatical class. In principle, such tags could be added manually; but in practice, the tagging of any sizeable corpus requires an automatic system which will accomplish the task largely by machine. One such system, achieving between 96 and 97 percent accuracy, is described in Garside et al. (1987:30–41).

Many corpora or partial corpora are now undergoing a further stage of annotation, namely parsing. The resulting parsed corpus, or TREEBANK, is extremely laborious to compile by hand, and so the development of an automatic corpus parser is required (cf. Garside et al. 1987, chaps. 6–7). Because of the unrestricted nature of the text, corpus tagging and parsing systems have special requirements, such as an ability to cope with a large and open-ended vocabulary. They often rely on probabilistic methods, which are approximative but preeminently robust.

MODEL D. The SELF-ORGANIZING model addresses a current major problem of Model C: that corpus processing systems such as probabilistic parsers require a large body of already analyzed text on which to be 'trained'—i.e., to be given adequate frequency statistics for the automatic analysis of further text. Thus a treebank of several million words may be needed to produce frequency data adequate for a probabilistic parser. But compiling such a treebank manually is beyond the bounds of practicality. This problem can be overcome by a self-organizing methodology (Jelinek 1986), using a statistical method which enables the computer to 'learn' by interaction with the text data. The computer system, beginning with crude estimates, is able to train itself by progressive approximation to the frequencies inherent in the text data being analyzed.

It will now be evident that Models A-D are closely interdependent. They add up to an extensive and challenging research program which is of interest to linguists, and which also has applications in areas such as speech synthesis, text checking, MACHINE TRANSLATION [*q.v.*], and above all, speech recognition.

GEOFFREY LEECH

BIBLIOGRAPHY

AARTS, JAN, & THEO VAN DEN HEUVEL. 1985. Computational tools for the syntactic analysis of corpora. *Linguistics* 23.303–335.

FRANCIS, W. NELSON, & HENRY KUČERA. 1964. *Manual of information to accompany a standard sample of present-day edited American English, for use with digital computers.* Providence, R.I.: Department of Linguistics, Brown University. 3d ed., 1979.

FRANCIS, W. NELSON, & HENRY KUČERA. 1982. *Frequency analysis of English usage: Lexicon and grammar.* Boston: Houghton Mifflin.

GARSIDE, ROGER; GEOFFREY LEECH; & GEOFFREY SAMPSON, eds. 1987. *The computational analysis of English: A corpus-based approach.* London: Longman.

JELINEK, FREDERICK. 1986. *Self-organized language modeling for speech recognition.* Yorktown Heights, N.Y.: Continuous Speech Recognition Group, IBM Thomas J. Watson Research Center.

KNOWLES, GERRY, & LITA LAWRENCE. 1987. Automatic intonation assignment. In Garside et al. 1987, pp. 139–148.

SINCLAIR, JOHN M., ed. 1987. *Looking up: An account of the COBUILD project.* London: Collins ELT.

SVARTVIK, JAN, et al. 1982. *Survey of spoken English: Report on research, 1975–81.* (Lund studies in English, 63.) Lund: Gleerup.

CREOLES. *See* Pidgins and Creoles.

CRITICAL LINGUISTICS. The term 'critical linguistics' was first used by a group, mainly of linguists, at the University of East Anglia in the 1970s (Fowler et al. 1979). Their linguistics was 'critical' in the sense that it set out to reveal hidden power relations and ideological processes which were at work in linguistic texts. Following the common practice, this article extends the term to other schools who share these objectives; however, some of them prefer to describe themselves as 'discourse analysts', 'pragmaticists' (Mey 1985), or simply 'sociolinguists'. (For general reference, see Thompson 1984, Fairclough 1989.) [*See also* Power and Language.]

Critical linguists see their work as a departure from 'mainstream' linguistics. They criticize the latter for a preoccupation with form and formalism at the expense of social function, for describing the linguistic practices of a society without attempting to explain them socially, and for taking such practices at face value in ways which obscure their ideological and political investment. Much critical linguistics is critical DISCOURSE ANALYSIS—i.e., analysis of spoken or written texts in relation to the social context of their production and interpretation. [*See* Discourse.] Other work is concerned, for example, with finding socially satisfactory bases for grammar, with studies of language standardization as a facet of social or class struggle, or with more critical approaches to language education. This article will focus on critical discourse analysis.

The emergence of critical linguistics is associated with the prominence given to language in recent social theory, which is sometimes said to have undergone a 'linguistic turn'. Major theorists like Michel Foucault and Jürgen Habermas give language a central place in the production and reproduction of society, and in the constitution of relations of power. Developments in the theory of ideology, associated especially with Antonio Gramsci and Louis Althusser, see ideologies as embedded in social practices and as part of 'common sense'; this view has suggested to others a focus upon language practices as the main locus of ideology. Althusser and Foucault have also contributed to a new view of the social subject as non-unitary, constituted in social practice (including language), and constantly open to reconstitution. Other significant influences on critical linguistics include semiology (notably the work of Roland Barthes), and the rediscovery, mainly via literary theory, of the early Soviet critical work of Mikhail Bakhtin and V. N. Voloshinov. [*See also* Literary Pragmatics; Semiotics.]

Michel Pêcheux and the French school of discourse analysis—working within the structuralist articulation of Marxism, linguistics, and psychoanalysis (specifically that of Lacan) which developed in the 1960s and 1970s in France—have highlighted the linguistic dimensions of ideology and of the constitution of subjects, through conceptualizing 'discourse' as the specifically linguistic material form of ideology. Althusser was the main theoretical influence in the earlier work of this school; more recently, they have drawn increasingly upon the theorization of discourse in the work of Foucault. Pêcheux emphasizes semantics and the variability of word meaning according to ideology, associating different 'discursive formations' with different 'ideological formations'; he deals mainly with written political discourse, but more recent French work addresses other linguistic levels and discourse types (Maingueneau 1987).

Pêcheux's method aims to reconstruct discursive formations from corpora of texts, not to analyze specific texts; in contrast, text analysis is primary for the East Anglia group, who aim to provide a critical resource usable by non-linguists. From Michael A. K. Halliday they have inherited a concern to combine close formal analysis of texts with social analysis. They focus on written mass-media texts, and on the analysis of grammar: choices in transitivity and modality, for example, are treated as ideologically determined. Members of the East Anglia group, in collaboration with semioticians and still under the influence of Halliday, have more recently been involved in developing a 'social semiotics' approach in Australia; this approach investigates nonverbal as well as verbal semiotic codes within a critical framework (Hodge & Kress 1988). The East Anglia and social semiotics groups are more eclectic than the French group in their relation to social theory, and their theoretical positions are less coherently developed.

Critical discourse analysis is coming increasingly to be practiced within disciplines such as social psychology, law, and politics; interdisciplinary research is growing in, e.g., medical, educational, media, and political discourse, involving critical linguists and members of these other disciplines. [*See also* Institutional Linguistics; Law and Language; Medicine and Language.] Interdisciplinary collaboration will perhaps prove the most fruitful route toward the integration to which critical linguists aspire—that of text and discourse analysis with the analysis of social processes, relations, and practices.

NORMAN FAIRCLOUGH

BIBLIOGRAPHY

FAIRCLOUGH, NORMAN. 1989. *Language and power.* London: Longman.

FOWLER, ROGER, et al. 1979. *Language and control.* London: Routledge & Kegan Paul.

HODGE, ROBERT, & GUNTHER KRESS. 1988. *Social semiotics.*

Cambridge: Polity Press. Ithaca, N.Y.: Cornell University Press.

MAINGUENEAU, DOMINIQUE. 1987. *Nouvelles tendances en analyse du discours.* Paris: Hachette.

MEY, JACOB L. 1985. *Whose language? A study in linguistic pragmatics.* Amsterdam: Benjamins.

THOMPSON, JOHN B. 1984. *Studies in the theory of ideology.* Cambridge: Polity Press. Berkeley: University of California Press.

CROSS RIVER LANGUAGES are spoken in southeastern Nigeria, with some overspill into Cameroon; they form a top-level constituent of the Benue-Congo group of the Niger-Congo family [*qq.v.*]. The internal classification of the Cross River languages given in Figure 1 follows Nicholas G. Faraclas, 'Cross River', in John Bendor-Samuel, ed., *The Niger-Congo languages* (Lanham, Md.: University Press of America, 1989), pp. 377–399.

FIGURE 1. *Subgrouping of Cross River Languages*

- **Bendi**
  - Alege, Bekwarra, Bette-Bende, Bokyi, Bumaji, Obanliku, Ubang, Ukpe-Bayobiri, Utugwang
- **Delta Cross**
  - **Central Delta**
    - **Abua-Odual**
    - **Kugbo**
      - Kugbo (proper), Mini, Obulom, Ogbia, Ogbogolo, Ogbronuagum
  - **Lower Cross**
    - **East Lower Cross**
      - Anaang, Efik, Eket, Ibibio
    - **West Lower Cross**
      - Ibino, Obolo, Okobo, Oron
  - **Ogoni**
    - **East Ogoni**
      - Gokana, Kana
    - **West Ogoni** (Eleme)
  - **Upper Cross**
    - **Agoi-Doko-Iyoniyong**
      - Agoi, Bakpinka, Doko-Uyanga
    - Akpet (Akpet-Ehom)
    - **Central Upper Cross**
      - **East-West division**
        - **Ikom (Olulumo-Ikom)**
        - **Loko**
          - Loko (proper), Lubila, Nkukoli
        - **Mbembe-Legbo**
          - Cross River Mbembe
          - **Legbo**
            - Legbo (proper), Lenyima, Leyigha
      - **North-South division**
        - **Koring-Kukele**
          - Koring (Oring)
          - **Kukele**
            - Kukele (proper), Uzekwe
        - **Ubaghara-Kohumono**
          - **Kohumono**
            - Agwagwune, Kohumono (proper), Umon
          - Ubaghara
    - **Kiong-Korop**
      - Kiong, Korop, Odut
    - Tita
  - **Unclassified Delta Cross**
    - Ibami
- **Unclassified Cross River**
  - Akum

LANGUAGE LIST

Abua: 24,000 speakers reported in Abua-Odual and Ahoada Divisions, Rivers State, Nigeria. Also called Abuan. Odual is the most closely related language, with about 70 percent lexical similarity.

Agoi: 3,650 speakers reported in 1953, in Obubra Division, Cross River State, Nigeria. Also called Ro Bambami, Wa Bambani, or Ibami.

Agwagwune: 20,000 speakers reported in Egup-Ipa Development Area, Akamkpa Division, Cross River State, Nigeria. Also called Akunakuna, Agwaguna, Gwune, Akurakura, or Okurikan.

Akpet-Ehom: spoken in Akamkpa Division, Cross River State, Nigeria. Also called Ukpet.

Akum: spoken near the Nigerian border, southwest of Furu-Awa, Menchum Division, North West Province, Cameroon.

Alege: 1,200 speakers reported in 1973, in Obudu Division, Cross River State, Nigeria. Also called Alegi, Uge, or Ugbe.

Anaang: 246,000 speakers reported in 1945, in Abak, Ikot Ekpene, and Opoba Divisions, Cross River State, Nigeria. Also called Annang.

Bakpinka: spoken in Akamkpa Division, Cross River State, Nigeria. Also called Uwet or Iyongiyong. Reported to be dying out.

Bekwarra: 60,000 speakers reported in 1985, in Ogoja Division, Cross River State, Nigeria. Also called Ebekwara, Bekworra, or Yakoro.

Bette-Bende: 36,800 speakers reported in 1963, in Obudu Division, Cross River State, Nigeria. Also called Bette, Bete-Bendi, Mbete, Dama, or Bendi.

Bokyi: 53,700 speakers reported in 1973, including 50,000 in Ikom, Obudu, and Ogoja Divisions, Cross River State, Nigeria, and 3,700 in South West Province, Cameroon. Also called Boki, Nki, Okii, Uki, Nfua, Osikom, Osukam, or Vaaneroki. An important district language.

Bumaji: spoken in Bumaji town, Obudu Division, Cross River State, Nigeria.

Doko-Uyanga: spoken in Akamkpa Division, Cross River State, Nigeria. Also called Uyanga, Dosanga, Basanga, or Iko.

Efik: 36,300 first-language speakers reported in 1950, with 26,300 in Calabar and Akamkpa Divisions, Cross River State, Nigeria, and 10,000 on the coast west of Kumba in South West Province, Cameroon. Used by 3,500,000 people as a second language. Also called Calabar. A literary language used in education up to university level.

Eket: 22,000 speakers reported in 1952, in Eket Division, Cross River State, Nigeria. Also called Ekit.

Eleme: 55,000 speakers reported in 1989, in Tai-Eleme Division, Rivers State, Nigeria.

Gokana: 54,000 speakers reported in 1973, in Bori Division, Rivers State, Nigeria.

Ibami: spoken in Akamkpa Division, Cross River State, Nigeria.

Ibibio: 2,000,000 speakers reported in 1973, in Opobo, Itu, Uyo, Etinan, Oro, Ikot Ekpene, and Eket Divisions, Cross River State, Nigeria. Efik is used as a literary language. Ibibio is the main trade language of Cross River State.

Ibino: spoken in Eket and Oron Divisions, Cross River State, Nigeria. Also called Ibeno or Ibuno.

Kana: 90,000 speakers reported in Khana, Bori, and Tai-Eleme Divisions, Rivers State, Nigeria. Also called Khana or Ogoni. An important district language.

Kiong: spoken in Calabar and Akampka Divisions, Cross River State, Nigeria. Also called Akayon, Akoiyang, Okonyong, or Okoyong. Spoken only by elderly people; the younger generation speaks Efik.

Kohumono: some 11,900 speakers reported in 1952, in Ediba and Obubra Divisions, Cross River State, Nigeria. Also called Bahumono, Hohumono, Ediba, Humono, or Ekumuru.

Korop: 12,500 speakers reported in 1982, in Calabar and Akampka Divisions, Cross River State, Nigeria, and northwest of Mundemba in South West Province, Cameroon. Also called Ododop, Durop, Dyurop, or Erorup.

Kugbo: 2,000 speakers reported in 1973, in Abua-Odual, Ogbia, and Brass Divisions, Rivers State, Nigeria.

Kukele: 40,000 speakers reported in 1980, in Ogoja Division, Cross River State, Nigeria, and in Ishielu Division, Anambra State. Also called Ukele or Bakele.

Legbo: 30,000 speakers reported in 1973, in Afikpo Division, Imo State, Nigeria, and in Obubra Division, Cross River State. Also called Agbo, Gbo, Igbo, Imaban, or Itigidi.

Lenyima: spoken in Obubra Division, Cross River State, Nigeria. Also called Anyima or Inyima.

Leyigha: 3,150 speakers reported in 1953, in Obubra Division, Cross River State, Nigeria. Also called Ayiga, Asiga, or Yigha.

Loko: 100,000 speakers reported in 1973, in Obubra Division, Cross River State, Nigeria. Also called Yakurr, Yako, Ugep, or Loke.

Lubila: spoken at Ojo Nkomba and Ojo Akangba, Akamkpa Division, Cross River State, Nigeria. Also called Lubilo, Kabila, Kabire, or Ojor.

Mbembe, Cross River: 100,000 speakers reported in 1982, in Obubra and Ikom Divisions, Cross River State, Nigeria, and in Izi Division, Anambra State. Also called Okam, Oderiga, Wakande, Ifunubwa, Ekokoma, or Ofunobwam. Different from Tigon Mbembe in the Platoid group of the Benue-Congo family.

Mini: spoken in Brass Division, Rivers State, Nigeria.

Nkukoli: 1,000 speakers reported in 1973, at the juncture of Ikom, Obubra and Akamkpa Divisions, and in the Iko Ekperem Development Area, Cross River State, Nigeria. Also called Lokoli, Lokukoli, Nkokolle, or Ekuri.

Obanliku: 19,800 speakers reported in 1963, in Obudu Division, Cross River State, Nigeria. Also called Abanliku.

Obolo: 90,000 speakers reported in 1983, in Opoba and Eket Divisions, Cross River State, Nigeria, and in Rivers State, on the southeastern coast. Also called Andoni or Andone. Speakers use Ibibio and Ibo as trade languages, and learn English in school.

Obulom: spoken in Abuloma, Okrika Division, Rivers State, Nigeria. Also called Abuloma.

Odual: 15,000 speakers reported in 1980, in Abua-Odual Division, Rivers State, Nigeria. Also called Saka. Most closely related to Abua, with about 70 percent lexical similarity.

Odut: 700 speakers reported in 1940, in Calabar Division, Cross River State, Nigeria. It may be extinct.

Ogbia: 100,000 speakers reported in 1989, in Ogbia and Brass Divisions, Rivers State, Nigeria. Also called Ogbinya.

Ogbogolo: spoken in Abua-Odual Division, Rivers State, Nigeria. Also called Obogolo.

Ogbronuagum: spoken in Bukuma village near Buguma, Kalabari Division, Rivers State, Nigeria. Also called Bukuma.

Okobo: 11,200 speakers reported in 1945, in Oron Division, Cross River State, Nigeria.

Olulumo-Ikom: 9,250 speakers reported in 1953, in Ikom Division, Cross River State, Nigeria, and into Cameroon. Also called Lulumo.

Oring: 25,000 or more speakers reported in 1952, in Utonkon District, Otukpo Division, Benue State, Nigeria, and in Ishielu Division, Anambra State. Also called Orri, Orrin, Orringorrin, or Koring.

Oron: 48,300 speakers reported in 1945, in Oron Division, Cross River State, Nigeria. Also called Oro.

Tita: spoken in Jalingo District, Muri Division, Gongola State, Nigeria. Also called Hoai Petel.

Ubaghara: 30,000 speakers reported in 1985, in Akampka

Division, and in the Ubaghara, Egup-Ita, and Umon Development Areas, Cross River State, Nigeria.

Ubang: spoken in Obudu Division, Cross River State, Nigeria.

Ukpe-Bayobiri: 12,000 speakers reported in 1973, in Obudu and Ikom Divisions, Cross River State, Nigeria.

Umon: spoken in Biase District, Akampka Division, Cross River State, Nigeria. Also called Amon.

Utugwang: 12,000 or more speakers reported in 1973, in Obudu and Ogoja Divisions, Cross River State, Nigeria. Also called Putukwam, Mbe Afal, Mbube Eastern, or Obe. Speakers understand Bekwarra well.

Uzekwe: 5,000 speakers reported in 1973, in Ogoja Division, Cross River State, Nigeria. Also called Ezekwe.

CULTURE HISTORY AND HISTORICAL LINGUISTICS. The methods of historical linguistics provide critically important tools for the culture historian concerned with the reconstruction of ancient ways of life. Reconstruction itself is a fundamentally linguistic operation. The COMPARATIVE METHOD [*q.v.*] leads to the establishment of genetic language FAMILIES—and where fully carried out, can lead to the reconstruction of a PROTO-LANGUAGE, the common ancestor of the languages of a family. A language necessarily implies a society, a speech community, and a culture; a proto-language implies a 'proto-culture'—the culture of the users of the proto-language. [*See also* Semantic Reconstruction.]

The same principles have been applied successfully to reconstructed proto-cultures of both the Old and New World. In what follows, the primary focus will be on the I[ndo-]E[uropean] language family and the culture of the speakers of P[roto-]IE. Among the world's languages, this family is best suited for intensive investigation over space and time; its languages extended from Central Asia to Iceland, are attested over a period of nearly four thousand years, and are linked with a variety of cultures of different levels—some very ancient, with rich literatures amply attested in written records. In particular, three branches of the family, with very different languages and cultures (Hittite, Old Indic, and Greek), are attested in the 2nd millennium BCE, halfway back to the conventional date of the break-up of the IE proto-language (time depth ca. seven thousand years). Such a situation is unique in world history, and is invaluable to linguist and culture historian alike.

Language is linked to culture in a complex fashion; it is at once the expression of culture and a part of it. The lexicon of the language or proto-language affords the most effective way to approach or access the culture of its speakers. Indo-Europeanists saw very early that the agreements in vocabulary among the several ancient languages attested significant features of a common ancestral culture. These included such lexical subsets as the kinship terms and the numerals, words for the physical environment, items of material culture like various plants and animals, and artifacts and techniques of pastoralism and agriculture. The reconstructed lexicon was by no means restricted to items of material culture, but included terms of non-material, symbolic culture as well—from the spheres of sovereignty, religion, law, contract, and obligation. Scholars have continued these very useful collections up to the present day, and will doubtless continue to do so. The classic compendium is Schrader & Nehring 1929; more recent are Thieme 1964, Watkins 1985—and, with an anthropological orientation, Friedrich 1970 and Diebold 1985, which give current views on the much discussed distribution of the birch and beech and of the salmon respectively, and their relevance to the location of the IE homeland. The most ambitious to date is the monumental work of Gamkrelidze & Ivanov 1984, 'a reconstruction and historical typological analysis of a proto-language and a proto-culture', with a wealth of ethnographic as well as linguistic data; their conclusions remain controversial.

Outside the IE world, this technique has been applied very successfully by Siebert 1967 to establish the original homeland of the Algonkians on the basis of the wealth of reconstructible Common Algonkian animal and plant vocabulary—some fifty items, far more than we have available for PIE. For Proto-Austronesian, the work of Blust 1980 is particularly rich. Sapir's (1936) classic paper on the linguistic evidence for the northern origin of the Navajo is an elegant demonstration of the mutual dependence of culture history and etymology.

Reconstructed lexicon is indispensable when archeological evidence is lacking or ambiguous. It can also be confirmatory or at least suggestive when archeological evidence does exist. Gimbutas (1974:293), an archeologist, describes the neolithic Kurgan culture from the trans-Caspian region as showing the following:

> a patriarchal society, class system, the existence of small tribal units ruled by powerful chieftains, a predominantly pastoral economy including horse breeding and plant cultivation, architectural features such as a small subterranean or above-ground rectangular hut of timber uprights, small villages and massive hillforts, crude unpainted pottery decorated with impressions or stabbing, religious elements in-

cluding a Sky/Sun god and Thunder god, horse sacrifices and fire cults.

Every word or phrase in that paragraph can be correlated with a securely reconstructible common IE lexical item. Many scholars accept that the carriers of Kurgan culture spoke an IE language or languages in the 4th-3rd millennia BCE, and perhaps a variety of PIE itself in the 5th millennium BCE.

Lexicon and culture are not, however, coextensive—any more than lexicon and semantics, or lexicon and semiotic systems. Neither is the lexicon merely additive or atomistic. Straight reconstruction, i.e. the simple projection of lexical primes back to the proto-language, is not the only historical linguistic approach. As emphasized by Benveniste 1969, historical linguists (and Indo-Europeanists in particular) pursue their study in two opposite but complementary directions. On the one hand, they proceed from the data of the languages compared and restore a common prototype: the detail of the proto-language. On the other hand, they proceed from established forms in the proto-language to follow their development in the individual languages: the emergent independent structures which result from the transformations of elements of the earlier system. The comparatist moves between these two poles, attempting to distinguish both retentions and innovations, trying to account for both similarities and differences.

On the level of the lexicon, the latter approach, most clearly identified with the name of Benveniste, may be described as historical ETHNOSEMANTICS [*q.v.*]. His object was to 'elucidate the genesis' of the vocabulary of IE institutions. His method was to begin with a word in a given IE language, one 'endowed with pregnant meaning'; to study its form and meaning, its associations and oppositions; and finally to compare its cognates in related languages, in order to recover the culture-historical context in which the word was once a term. As described by Toporov (1981:193–4):

> concentration on the linguistic meaning permits a clear and cohesive presentation; the results of linguistic reconstruction and the range of the process become exactly testable; and since establishing the linguistic meaning presupposes the combination of systemic analysis and diachrony, the chronological perspective, as Benveniste shows, acquires an explanatory function. Such a method, which goes out entirely from language, is the most reasonable and most promising in all those cases where above all the language is known, as well as the structures higher than language (as they are articulated in the semiotic systems of myth, poetry, law etc.), but where testimony of the levels lower than language, in the shape of archeological data, are lacking.

Benveniste investigated a series of terms and their relations in six basic areas of human institutions in the IE world: economy, kinship, society (status), authority (royalty and its privileges), law, and religion. The series is open-ended; other equally basic areas, like 'man', are still unexplored. Benveniste observes significantly that comparative grammar, by its very method, leads to the elimination of particular developments to restore the common fund. This procedure leaves only a few IE words: in the case of religion, no word for religion itself, cult, or priest, or any personal gods. All that can be credited to the account of the community is the very notion of 'god', well attested in the form **dei̯u̯-ó-s*. This is originally an adjective 'luminous, celestial', beside the base **di̯eu̯-/diu̯-*, which often occurs in apposition with the word for 'father' **pH$_2$tér-*, an epithet which becomes the name of the (original) head of the pantheon, Latin *Iuppiter,* Greek *Zeús patḗr,* Vedic *Dyáuṣ pítar,* Hittite *attas* ^{d}*UTU-us,* Old Irish *oll-athar* (epithet of the *Dagda* 'good-god'). The god as 'light, celestial' was opposed to man as 'terrestrial' (the meaning of La. *homo,* Irish *duine*), just as the god as 'undying' **n̥-mr̥to-* (Indo-Iranian *ámr̥ta-,* Gk. *ámbrotos*) was opposed to man as 'mortal' (Iranian *marta-,* Armenian *mard* 'man').

But as Benveniste shows, we can inform ourselves about IE religious vocabulary without looking for whole cognate sets; we can simply study essential terms attested only in one or more languages, where they have an etymology. Benveniste's approach may be illustrated by his discussion of the sacred. His examination of critical contexts and oppositions in the ancient texts leads to the recognition of the articulation of the notion 'sacred, holy' in many traditions as a double expression (sometimes triple), usually distinct in each language: Avestan *spənta-* and *yaoždāta-,* La. *sacer* and *sanctus* (and *profānus*), Gothic *weihs* and *hail(ag)s,* Greek *hierós* and *hágios* (and *hósios*). These express, variously, two aspects of the same notion: what is filled with divine power, and what is forbidden to contact by man. The first may express the immanent sacred outside the realm of mankind (*sacer* is both 'sacred' and 'accursed'); the second, variously the externally imposed sacred (*sanctus* 'protected from violation'), the sacred as integrity (Eng. *holy,* cf. *whole, hale, hail*)—or viewed positively as a third term, the notion of 'freed from tabu' *(profānus,* *hósios)*. The semantics of the institutions of religion and of law come together in Avestan *yaož-dāta* 'purified, made ritually integrated' beside Vedic *yóṣ* 'prosperity, integrity; hail!', La. *iūs* 'law'. As Benveniste shows, the IE etymon **ié̯us* must have meant something like the (semantically non-trivial) 'state of conformity to rule and norm required by ritual rules.'

The value of this approach to both culture history and cultural typology is evident. An equally fine-grained analysis of the textual semantics of, for example, the representatives of Proto-Polynesian **mana* 'supernatural force', **tapu* 'prohibited', and **noa* 'common, worthless (*'free from tabu' as in many daughter languages?; cf. Walsh & Biggs 1966) would be indispensable to the determination of any cognates in Western Austronesian, and the eventual projection of these lexemes back to Proto-Austronesian.

Not only individual words or small sets of oppositions, but whole folk taxonomies can be reconstructed. That of 'wealth', of what ideally constituted human material prosperity, can be displayed as semantic features from the identical configurations determined from the texts in Vedic, Avestan, Homeric Greek, and Hittite (Figure 1). The lexical forms that carry these notions may vary from language to language, but the semantic structure as a whole is remarkably constant: 'wealth' itself was typically expressed, then as now, by a form of 'good.' This is in accord with the semi-nomadic character of the earliest Indic and Iranian society; but the complete absence of reference to land tenure as a form of wealth, despite its documented economic significance in Mycenean Greek and in Hittite times, shows strikingly that the folk taxonomy in these societies is an idealized, inherited tradition, rather than a synchronic economic reality (Watkins 1979).

The preceding cases have all dealt with individual lexical items or sets of these. These are, however, not the only entities amenable to reconstruction. On the basis of similarities, we reconstruct language. But it happens that certain texts in some of these cognate languages are genetically related (Toporov 1981:191); in some senses, these texts are the same. Exploration of what may legitimately be termed the 'genetic intertextuality' of these variants casts much light on the meaning of the ancient texts themselves. The similarities are by and large more numerous in older than in more recent texts; on the basis of the samenesses, we may in privileged cases reconstruct to some extent proto-texts or text fragments. At that point, we are led to assume, i.e. reconstruct, a 'user' (Toporov 1981) of the text in the language—another route to reconstructing features of a real proto-culture.

Thus the use of the present participle of IE **H_1sont-* 'to be, exist' in the final solemn affirmation of guilt in the Hittite confessional formula *eszi-at . . . asān-at* 'it [the sin] exists . . . / it (is) existent' provides the explanation of the Latin words *sōns* 'guilty' and *insōns* 'innocent': the guilty one is the one who says *sōns* 'existent'. Taking this together with the widespread use of a form of the verb 'to know, recognize' as 'to

FIGURE 1. *The Indo-European Folk Taxonomy of 'wealth'*

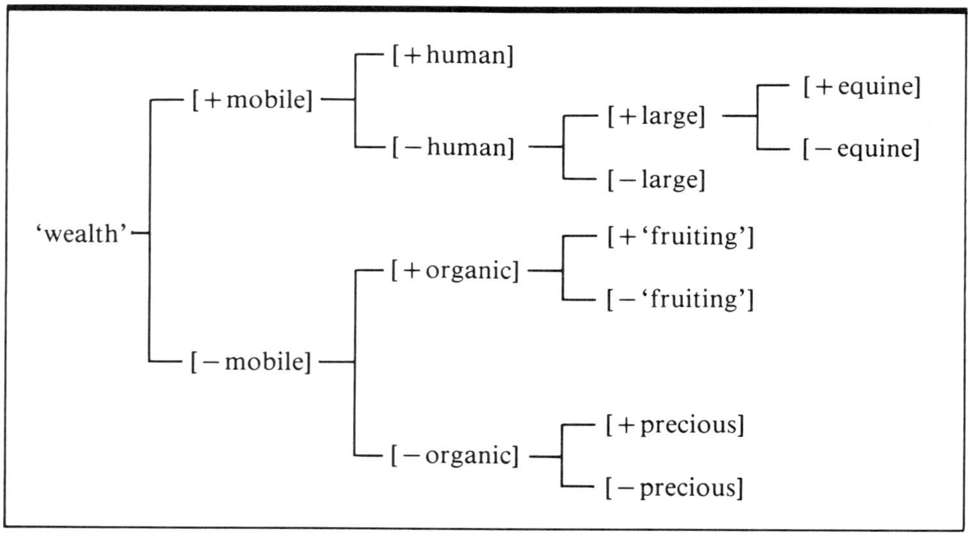

confess', we can assign both the cultural fact of confession and its linguistic form to the proto-language. [*See* Stylistic Reconstruction.]

Particularly useful in connection with proto-texts is the study of inherited formulas: whole noun and verb phrases which are preserved in more than one tradition. [*See* Formulaic Speech.] Since these formulas typically refer to or encode important cultural features, e.g. tabus (Greek *orthòs omeíkhein,* Vedic *mekṣyāmy ūrdhvás* 'urinate upright') or values (Greek *kléos áphthiton,* Vedic *śrávas ákṣitam* 'imperishable fame'), they can offer immediate information about the proto-culture. But they also may encapsulate entire myths and other narratives. The 'signature' formula for the myth of the divine hero who slays the serpent recurs in texts from the Rig Veda (*áhann áhim* 'he slew the serpent') through Old and Middle Iranian holy books, Hittite myth, Greek epic and lyric, Celtic and Germanic epic and saga, down to Armenian oral folk epic of the 19th century. This formula shapes the narration of 'heroic' killing or overcoming of adversaries over the IE world for millennia (Watkins 1987). The formula is the vehicle of the central theme of a proto-text, a central part of the symbolic culture of the speakers of PIE.

Origin legends are a quasi-universal genre the world over. An abundance of such traditions are reported in various IE literatures and texts, some very early. While these must be used with caution, they may contain real historical recollection. It has been plausibly suggested (Witzel 1989) that a late Vedic sūtra text (BŚS 18.44, 397.9), ca. 6th century BCE, may contain a memory of the migration into India proper, perhaps even of the division into Indic (Indo-Aryan) and Iranian: 'Ayu went eastwards. His (people) are the Kuru-Pañcāla and the Kāśi-Videha. This is the Āyava migration. (His other people) stayed at home *(amāvasuḥ).* His people are the Gāndhāri, Parśu, and Arāṭṭa. This is the Amāvasyava ('stay-at-home' group).' Beyond the puns, we may note that Kuru-Pañcāla and Kāśi-Videha are the major Vedic tribes of central and eastern India, while the 'stay-at-home' group, all located west of the Indus, are probably Iranian. The Gāndhāri, known since the Rig Veda and Atharva Veda, can be equated with the province of the Persian empire Ga(n)dara mentioned in inscriptions of Darius the Great (ca. 518 BCE), and the Gandarioi listed by Herodotus (ca. 430 BCE) as an ethnic unity in the Persian army marshaled against the Greeks. The Parśu have been identified with the Persians; the Arāṭṭa are less clear (Arachosia, Iran. *harax^{v}aiti*?)

Such a text approaches history; but origin legend in the realm of myth may be still older. A female of the same name Parśu appears in the Rig Veda as daughter of Manu, the first MAN (the two words are cognate), in a tantalizingly obscure verse: 'the daughter of Manu, Parśu by name, gave birth to twenty at once.' The line recalls the beginning of our one Old Hittite origin legend: 'The queen of Kaneš gave birth to thirty sons at once.' The style of both is that of a folktale. The Hittite tale goes on to relate how the thirty sons are about to marry their thirty sisters, born later of the same queen; at this point the clay tablet breaks off. But the mythological themes of prodigious multiple birth and incest, in a tale of origins, recur exactly in the Greek legend of the fifty daughters of Danaos ('Greek') fleeing an incestuous marriage with their parallel cousins, the fifty sons of Aiguptos ('Egyptian')—the subject of Aeschylus's play *The Suppliants.* Once again we find, in the ancient texts from the three oldest IE traditions, clear thematic reflexes of a single proto-text, this time a common origin legend. The comparative method in historical linguistics can illumine not only ancient ways of life but also ancient modes of thought: we can reconstruct some of the things the Indo-Europeans talked about, and some of the ways they talked about them.

CALVERT WATKINS

BIBLIOGRAPHY

BENVENISTE, ÉMILE. 1969. *Le vocabulaire des institutions indo-européennes.* 2 vols. Paris: Minuit. Translated as *Indo-European language and society* (Coral Gables: University of Miami Press, 1973).

BLUST, ROBERT. 1980. Early Austronesian social organization: The evidence of language. *Current Anthropology* 21.205–247.

DIEBOLD, A. RICHARD. 1985. *The evolution of Indo-European nomenclature for salmonid fish.* (Journal of Indo-European Studies, Monograph series, 5.) Washington, D.C.: Institute for the Study of Man.

FRIEDRICH, PAUL. 1970. *Proto-Indo-European trees: The arboreal system of a prehistoric people.* Chicago: University of Chicago Press.

GAMKRELIDZE, TAMAZ V., & VYAČESLAV V. IVANOV. 1984. *Indoevropejskij jazyk i indoevropejcy.* Tiflis: Izdatel'stvo Tbilisskogo Universiteta. Translation: *Indo-European and the Indo-Europeans.* Berlin: Mouton de Gruyter, 1990.

GIMBUTAS, MARIJA. 1974. An archaeologist's view of PIE in 1975. *Journal of Indo-European Studies* 2.289–307.

SAPIR, EDWARD. 1936. Internal linguistic evidence suggestive of the northern origin of the Navaho. *American Anthropol-*

ogist 38.224–235. Reprinted in Edward Sapir, *Selected writings,* edited by David G. Mandelbaum (Berkeley: University of California Press, 1949), pp. 213–224.

SCHRADER, OTTO, & ALFONS NEHRING. 1917–29. *Reallexikon der indogermanischen Altertumskunde.* 2 vols. Berlin: de Gruyter.

SIEBERT, FRANK T., JR. 1967. The original home of the Proto-Algonquian people. In *Contributions to anthropology: Linguistics I (Algonquian)* (National Museum of Canada, Bulletin 214, Anthropological series, 78), pp. 13–47. Ottawa: Secretary of State.

THIEME, PAUL. 1964. The comparative method for reconstruction in linguistics. In *Language in culture and society: A reader in linguistics and anthropology,* edited by Dell Hymes, pp. 585–598. New York: Harper & Row.

TOPOROV, VLADIMIR N. 1981. Die Ursprünge der indoeuropäischen Poetik. *Poetica* 13.189–251.

WALSH, D. S., & BRUCE BIGGS. 1966. *Proto-Polynesian word list,* vol. 1. Auckland: Linguistic Society of New Zealand.

WATKINS, CALVERT. 1979. NAM.RA GUD UDU in Hittite: Indo-European poetic language and the folk taxonomy of wealth. In *Hethitisch und Indogermanisch* (Innsbrucker Beiträge zur Sprachwissenschaft, 25), edited by Erich Neu & Wolfgang Meid, pp. 269–287. Innsbruck: Institut für Sprachwissenschaft der Universität.

WATKINS, CALVERT. 1985. *The American Heritage dictionary of Indo-European roots.* 2d ed. Boston: Houghton Mifflin.

WATKINS, CALVERT. 1987. How to kill a dragon in Indo-European. In *Studies in memory of Warren Cowgill (1929–1985),* edited by Calvert Watkins, pp. 270–299. Berlin: de Gruyter.

WITZEL, MICHAEL. 1989. Tracing the Vedic dialects. In *Dialectes dans les littératures indo-aryennes,* edited by Colette Caillat, pp. 97–265. Paris: Presses Universitaires de France.

CUNEIFORM, lit. 'wedge-shaped' writing (from Latin *cuneus* 'wedge'), was used in the Near East from ca. 2900 BCE to the 1st century CE; its earliest examples have been found in Uruk (now Warka, ca. 250 km southeast of Baghdad). It was used primarily in Mesopotamia, the area between the Euphrates and Tigris rivers in present-day Iraq. Cuneiform texts have also been found in southwestern Iran at Susa; in Syria at Ugarit, Ebla, and Emar; in Turkey at Boghazköy; in Palestine at Megiddo; and in Egypt at Tell el-Amarna. The great majority of these texts are written in Sumerian, an isolated language, or in Akkadian [*q.v.*] (also known as Assyro-Babylonian), a Semitic language. However, many other languages from various linguistic families used the same system through the centuries, including Eblaite, Elamite [*q.v.*], Hurrian and Urartian [*q.v.*], Ugartian, Ugaritic, Old Persian, Hittite [*q.v.*], Palaic, and Luvian. All these languages use basically the same inventory of signs; only Ugaritic and Old Persian created their own sign systems. [*See also* Babylonian Grammatical Tradition; Writing Systems.]

The normal medium was clay tablets, on which wedge-shaped impressions were made with a stylus. Cuneiform writing could also be carved on stone—or, rarely, painted, e.g. on bricks or ceramics. Documents on perishable materials, such as wood, leather, or papyrus, are known to have existed, but have not survived, except for a few examples on wooden boards covered with wax. As many as 375,000 tablets are now preserved in museums, and more come to light every year in archeological digs. (For general reference, see Civil 1973, Reiner 1973, Diakonoff 1975, Borger 1981, Edzard 1980, 1982, and Walker 1987.)

1. Decipherment. The existence of cuneiform writing was forgotten in the Western scholarly world—in contrast to the more visually appealing Egyptian hieroglyphs, which were never completely forgotten—and was rediscovered by European travelers only in the 17th century. In 1802, G. F. Grotefend succeeded in reading the royal names in a trilingual (Akkadian-Elamite-Persian) inscription. Progress was rapid, and the process of DECIPHERMENT [*q.v.*], which included Akkadian, can be considered completed by 1857. In that year, H. C. Rawlinson, Edward Hincks, W. H. Fox Talbot, and Jules Oppert presented independent and sealed translations of the same text to the Royal Asiatic Society in London; when opened, the four translations were found to be essentially in agreement. In present-day studies, determination of the meanings and phonetic shapes of cuneiform signs is solidly based on native word lists used for scribal training. Lexical collections—mostly Sumero-Akkadian bilinguals with tens of thousands of words, arranged either by sign shapes or thematically—have been reconstructed from school exercises. In their most complete form, the lexical entries include several columns, as shown in the example in Figure 1: (a) the phonological description of the Sumerian word in terms of a set of basic syllabograms; (b) the corresponding logogram, conventionally transcribed in small capitals; and (c) the syllabically written Akkadian translation.

The meanings of the Akkadian words in column (c) are suggested by comparison with closely related languages of the Semitic family, and are confirmed by contextual analysis. The phonological shapes of sylla-

FIGURE 1. *Sumero-Akkadian Lexical Entries*

(a)	(b)		(c)	
mu-še-en		(MUŠEN)	*iṣ-ṣu-ru*	'bird'
gu-up	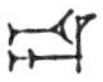	(DU)	*ú-zu-uz-zu*	'to stand up'
pe-eš		(ŠÀxA)	*e-ru-ú*	'to be pregnant'
na-qa		(NAGA)	*uh-hu-lu*	'vegetable ashes'
ši-ni-ik		(ŠINIG)	*bi-i-nu*	'tamarisk tree'

bograms were first established in transliterations of foreign words, and were subsequently refined by comparative Semitic sound correspondences. Frequent alternative spellings, e.g. *ka-al-bu* and *kal-bu* (both representing /kalbu/ 'dog'), provide confirmation. The same syllabograms are used to give the phonemic forms of Sumerian words; however, distortions in the cross-language representation of sounds, and the lack of comparative material, result in a less precise definition of the Sumerian phonemic inventory.

2. The system. Cuneiform signs have three main functions:

(a) As SYLLABOGRAMS, they represent a word, or part of it, on a phonemic level.
(b) As LOGOGRAMS, they represent an entire word on a lexical level.
(c) As CLASSIFICATORS or DETERMINATIVES, they assign the word to a semantic set with no direct phonological connotation.

Some syllabograms ('polyphonic signs') may have more than one pronunciation (polyphonic signs); thus the same syllabogram may be read *ne, dè, bí,* or *bil,* depending on its context. Conversely, different signs can have apparently homophonous readings, which are indicated in transliteration by accents or subscripts. The homophony sometimes is the result of our imprecise knowledge of the phonemic systems, especially the Sumerian. A logogram can have several different meanings, and consequently different phonemic connotations. The system has devices to reduce ambiguity to reasonable levels. In general, a word can be written syllabically or logographically, depending on the language of the text, and on scribal habits and traditions. Examples of syllabically written words are *še-er-ha-an* 'ornament' in Sumerian and *ni-ik-nu-kà-kum-ma* 'we sealed it for you' in Akkadian. A sign used as a logogram, e.g. SINIG in Fig. 1, can be read either as Sumerian /šinik/ or Akkadian /bīnu/, depending on the language of the reader. As a consequence, some texts can be, and in ancient times undoubtedly were, read indifferently in Sumerian or Akkadian.

Uncertainties about readings and meanings are dispelled partly by the context, and partly by the writing system itself, through the use of classificators and 'phonetic indicators'. Thus, when used as a classificator, the sign GIŠ assigns the word following it to the class of trees or wooden objects. About twenty of these signs are in common use, mostly designating physical classes: raw materials, zoological and botanical types, toponyms etc. There is one to indicate human professions or conditions, one for the female gender, and one for divine beings. A 'phonetic indicator' is a syllabogram, used mostly in Sumerian, which is added to a logogram to give its pronunciation, partially or in toto. Such signs are in principle optional, but tradition dictates their use within relatively narrow limits; for instance:

ú + NAGA + *ga* + MUŠEN

(The phonetic complements, the only parts which are 'read', are in lower case). The logogram transliterated NAGA is read /uga/ when it means 'raven'. It will normally be followed by the classificator MUŠEN to show that the word belongs to the lexical set of birds. Traditionally, but not always, it is accompanied by the syllabograms *ú* and *ga* to specify its pronunciation and to prevent ambiguity. With other classificators, the same logogram has different meanings with different readings: /naga/ 'vegetable ashes' with the classificator for vegetables, /teme/ 'a plant, Salsola sp.' with the sign for plants, /ereš/ (a toponym) with the sign for town, and

/nidaba/ (a goddess) with the classificator of divine beings. Phonetic complements are less frequent, and more variable, in Akkadian.

Although the cuneiform signs are the same for Sumerian and Akkadian, they are used in different ways. Sumerian is essentially logographic, using syllabograms to represent proper names, loanwords, and bound morphemes. Examples of Sumerian texts entirely written in syllabograms, perhaps for didactic purposes or because of the scribe's unfamiliarity with the standard system, are secondary and relatively rare. But Akkadian uses predominantly syllabograms, and reserves logograms for convenient abbreviations. In technical or repetitious texts, the number of logograms can be quite high. In a typical letter, for instance, only 3–5 percent of the signs will be logograms; but in long, repetitious lists of omens, the logograms can constitute more than 80 percent of the total number of signs. The other languages (Hurrian, Hittite, etc.) use syllabic cuneiform. In addition, Hittite uses syllabically written Akkadian words as logograms ('Akkadograms').

3. History. In their earliest form, cuneiform signs were pictographic, i.e. representations of physical objects. The curved lines were later replaced by straight stylus impressions, and the shapes were progressively simplified; this culminated in the Neo-Assyrian script, in which only a limited number of wedge shapes are admitted, and every wedge is significant. In earlier, intermediate stages, only the general form of the sign is significant, and there is a certain latitude in the number of strokes of the stylus. To recognize the objects originally depicted, the reader must be aware that, in modern editions, most texts have to be rotated 90 degrees to the right to reposition the signs in their initial orientation. Figure 2 illustrates the historical evolution of cuneiform signs.

FIGURE 2. *Evolution of Cuneiform*

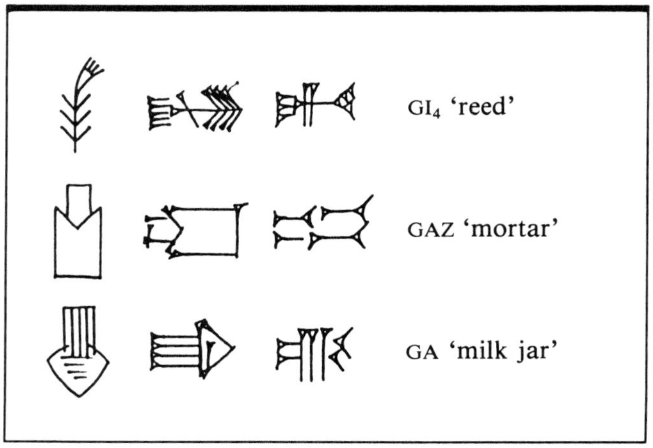

The oldest texts (Early Dynastic Period, 2900–2350 BCE) present two unexpected features. First, texts are divided into 'cases', each of which contains a phrase or clause. The arrangement of signs within a case is free; i.e., the signs do not follow the syntactic sequence, which suggests that scribes represented speech at the sentence level. For instance, the phrase *si gù ba-ni-in-ra* 'he sounded there the horn' can be written:

si gù or as *gù si*
ra ba *ba ra*

or in any other arrangement. This example also illustrates a second feature: sentence elements, mostly bound morphemes, that could be predicted from the context (here the locative infix *-ni-* and the 3rd person agent mark *-n-*) are omitted, to be supplied by the reader. After the 24th century BCE, morphemes are represented in their proper sequence, and very few syllabograms are omitted. Up to the beginning of the Old Babylonian period (19th century BCE), syllabic writings tend to omit final consonants in certain cases, as in *é-ba* 'pair' or *ma-sá* 'a basket' (for later *é-ba-an* and *ma-sá-ab*).

4. Writing and phonology. In older texts, syllabograms tend to represent the consonants in an underdifferentiated way; thus a single sign stands for the voiced and the voiceless homorganic stop (and in Akkadian, also the emphatic plosive)—i.e., the same sign represents /da/, /ta/, and /ṭa/. No conclusions as to the phonemic inventory of a language can be inferred from this purely graphic simplification. The existence of a voicing rule, demonstrably present in the case of Sumerian, seems sufficient to account for this scribal practice. A peculiarity attested so far only in texts from Ebla, ca. 2400 BCE, is the optional omission of the consonant *l*. Alternative writings show that it is a graphic feature of no phonological significance. Similar considerations apply to the occasional use of *l*-signs to represent *r*. In more recent texts, writing seems to render phonological shapes adequately—controllable in the case of Akkadian by comparative etymologies. There are, however, three exceptions:

(a) It is possible that the loss of Semitic laryngeals in Akkadian texts does not properly reflect the linguistic situation; such consonants may simply have been omitted in writing—perhaps because of their

FIGURE 3. *Sumerian Writing (Fable of 17th Century BCE)*

kur-gi$_4$^{mušen}*e* ^{ú}NAGA$^{\text{ga mušen}}$
mu-na-ni-ib-gi$_4$*-gi*$_4$
mušen-dù-e sa ma-ná-e

kurgi-e uga mu-na-ni-b-gi-gi mušendu-e sa ma-na-e
'Crane answered Raven: "The fowler will lay down a net against me." '

absence from the Sumerian phonemic inventory, and the subsequent lack of traditional signs to represent them.

(b) The second exception results from an inherent limitation of a syllabic system: initial and final consonant clusters cannot be directly represented, and the scribe has to add prothetic or epenthetic vowels. Thus a theoretical */pras/ would have to be written *pa-ra-as*. In rare cases, especially in early periods, a cluster C_1C_2 is written C_2, even in medial position.

(c) Finally, in Sumerian and in a few cases in Akkadian, the scribes used morphophonemic representations. For instance, the Sumerian subjunctive/optative verbal prefix is subject to vowel harmony, with the allomorphs *ha-*, *he-*, and *hu-*. In early periods, *ha-* may be written before syllables with *u*, where later texts consistently write *hu-*.

5. Derived systems (Ugaritic, Old Persian). During the 13th–14th centuries BCE, scribes in Ugarit (present Ras Shamra on the Syrian coast) used a system based on the traditional clay and stylus, but radically different in its representation of the language. It consists of thirty purely consonantal signs, with the exception of three which represent the voiceless glottal stop (aleph) followed by the vowels *a*, *u*, or *i*. It thus belongs to the northwestern Semitic tradition, and is functionally similar to Aramaic and Phoenician. In the 6th century BCE, in a different reaction to the complexity of the traditional Sumero-Akkadian system, Old Persian was written with a syllabary of thirty-six new simple signs, completed by half a dozen logograms and auxiliary signs.

6. Writing samples are given in Figures 3–4. Classificators and phonetic complements are written in superscripts; accents and subscripts are used to distinguish homophonous signs. In the Sumerian transcription, hyphens separate morphemes.

MIGUEL CIVIL

BIBLIOGRAPHY

BORGER, RYKLE. 1981. *Assyrisch-babylonische Zeichenliste.* (Alter Orient und Altes Testament, 33/33A.) Neukirchen-Vluyn: Neukirchener Verlag.

FIGURE 4. *Akkadian Writing (Code of Hammurabi, ca. 1775 BCE)*

šum-ma DUMU *a-ba-šu*
im-ta-ha-aṣ
KIŠIB.LÁ-*šu*
i-na-ak-ki-su

šumma mārum abašu imtahaṣ rittašu inakkisu
'If a son strikes his father, they will cut off his hand (lit. "fist").'

CIVIL, MIGUEL. 1973. The Sumerian writing system: Some problems. *Orientalia* n.s. 42.21–34.
DIAKONOFF, IGOR M. 1975. Ancient writing and ancient written language: Pitfalls and peculiarities in the study of Sumerian. In *Sumeriological studies in honor of Thorkild Jacobsen on his seventieth birthday* (Assyriological studies, 20), pp. 99–121. Chicago: University of Chicago Press.
EDZARD, DIETZ O. 1980. Keilschrift. In *Reallexikon der Assyriologie* 5.544–568. Berlin: de Gruyter.
EDZARD, DIETZ O. 1982. Der Aufbau des Syllabars 'Proto-Ea'. In *Societies and languages of the ancient Near East: Studies in honour of I. M. Diakonoff*, edited by M. A. Dandamayev et al., pp. 42–61. Warminster, England: Aris & Phillips.
REINER, ERICA. 1973. How we read cuneiform texts. *Journal of Cuneiform Studies* 25.3–58.
WALKER, CHRISTOPHER B. F. 1987. *Reading the past: Cuneiform*. London: British Museum.

CUSHITIC LANGUAGES is the term applied to a group of some thirty languages which make up one of the sub-families of Afro-Asiatic [*q.v.*]. The territory of Cushitic comprises the northern Sudan from the Egyptian border, the republics of Djibouti and Somalia, a large part of Ethiopia and Kenya, and some isolated areas of northern Tanzania (see Map 1).

The Cushitic language family consists of the subgroup shown in Figure 1, with their territories indicated in parentheses, with names of some individual languages.

FIGURE 1. *Subgroups of the Cushitic Language Family*

Central Cushitic (Agaw)
  Western Agaw (including Kemant and Quara), Awngi, Bilin, Khamtanga
Eastern Cushitic
  Dullay
    Dihina, Dobase, Gaba, Gawwada, Gergere, Gobeze, Gollango, Gorose, Harso, Tsamai
  Highland East Cushitic
    Alaba, Burji, Gedeo, Hadiyya, Kambata, Sidamo
  Konso-Gidole
  Oromo
  Rendille-Boni
  Saho-Afar
  Somali
  Western Omo-Tana
    Arbore, Bayso, Dasenech, Elmolo
  Yaaku
Northern Cushitic
  Beja
Southern Cushitic
  Aasáx, Alagwa, Burunge, Dahalo, Iraqw, Kw'adza

A group of languages considered by some scholars to constitute a West Cushitic branch is regarded by others as constituting a separate Omotic branch [*q.v.*] within Afro-Asiatic. Recently, some scholars have cast doubt on the classification of Northern and Southern Cushitic, suggesting rather that they are independent branches of Afro-Asiatic (Hetzron 1980). [*For data on individual Cushitic languages, see the Language List at the end of this article.*]

Until the 1960s, Cushitic was a neglected area of linguistic research. Since then, however, interest in the investigation of these languages has increased greatly; most of the languages are now documented by modern grammars, or at least by sketches. Some of the minor languages remain undescribed. There is still no general introduction to the study of Cushitic languages; for more limited surveys, see Zaborski 1976, Sasse 1981, 1987; for Central Cushitic, see Hetzron 1976.

Characteristic features of the Cushitic phoneme inventory include glottalized consonants, pharyngeals, rounded velars, and (in a restricted area) vowel harmony. Glottalized consonants appear in many variants: the entire series may be ejective (*p' t' k'* . . .) or implosive (*b' d' g'* . . .); *d'* is sometimes retroflex, and *k'* tends to be uvular. The pharyngeals [ḥ ʕ], very rarely found in languages outside Afro-Asiatic, are fricatives articulated by constricting the pharynx. Vowel harmony occurs in Somali, Boni, and Rendille; these languages possess two varieties of each vowel quality, the distinctive feature being advanced vs. retracted tongue root. All vowels in a word normally belong to the same harmonic category.

In almost all the languages, tonal differentiations play a distinctive role. In contrast to typical tone languages, Cushitic tones are determined primarily by morphosyntax. Generally, two levels are distinguished—high and low—the high tone being the marked member of the opposition. Many grammatical categories (e.g. gender, number, case, mood, focus, and aspect) are marked either by tone alone, or by a combination of a specific tone pattern with a segmental marker. Hyman 1981 has argued that some Cushitic tone systems are so deviant both from the regular 'stress' accent systems and from regular 'pitch' systems found in the tone languages of West Africa and Asia that a third category of 'tone-accent systems' could be justified.

Cushitic morphology is highly synthetic and fusional. Most languages are characterized by extremely complex inflectional systems which use all types of morphemes: prefixes, suffixes, infixes, reduplication, iteration, alter-

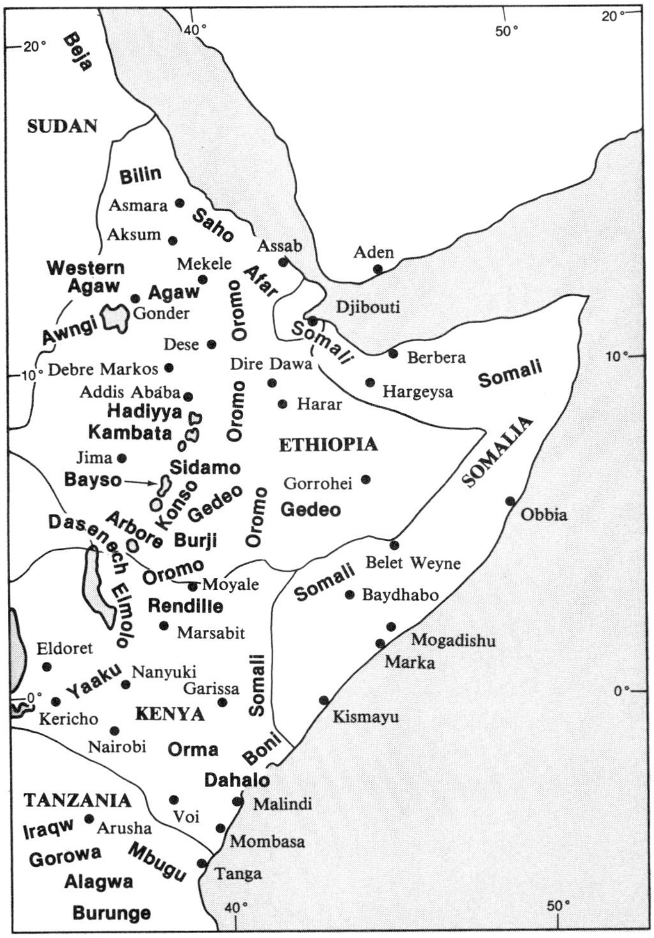

Map 1. *Distribution of Cushitic Languages*

nation of stem consonants and vowels, and suprasegmental changes of tone pattern, glottalization, or quantity. Moreover, a tendency towards morphophonemic complexity results in the formation of inflectional classes ('declensions' and 'conjugations'). The abundance of clitics, and the tendency in some languages to incorporate nominals into the phonological verb word, result in a somewhat polysynthetic character. The complexity of inflection pertains equally to all inflected word classes. Hence the number of morphologically marked grammatical categories is relatively high, and morphological distinctions among word classes are accordingly great: nouns, verbs, and pronouns differ considerably both in their categories and in their inflectional behavior. Word class distinctions are further supported by rich category-changing derivational morphology (nominalization and verbalization). Only the word class of adjectives is comparatively marginal; it is sometimes entirely lacking, or at best constitutes a closed class with a limited number of members.

Nouns generally distinguish gender, number, and case. Gender is twofold, masculine and feminine, but often does not correspond with sex. In some languages, gender is more or less arbitrarily distributed, mostly on the basis of derivational (or stem-building) affixes which have inherent gender; in others, there is a semantic principle according to which masculine is connected with bigness and importance, and feminine with smallness and insignificance. Number categories are singular, plural, collective, and singulative (i.e. a single element of a collective). Number marking is often derivational rather than inflectional; its morphological means are manifold and heterogeneous, including tone, suffixes, and internal changes. Many nouns are number-indifferent, especially in East Cushitic. The morphologically and semantically defined plural category does not always correspond to a plural category defined on the basis of agreement behavior. Many formally plural nouns do not agree with plural verb forms, but with singular forms, mainly of the opposite gender ('polarity'). Hayward (1981:127ff.) was the first to suggest a solution to this problem: plural FORMATION is regarded as part of the derivational system, and plural AGREEMENT as belonging to the grammatical gender system.

The original Proto-Cushitic case system distinguished two basic case forms: an absolutive (the citation form of the noun, predicate, and object case), and a nominative (the subject case). There may also have been a genitive case, as in most modern languages. South Cushitic has totally abandoned case inflection, but many other Cushitic languages have enlarged the case inventory, chiefly by agglutinating postpositions. In Agaw languages, at least seven cases are distinguished (nominative, accusative, comitative, dative, genitive, directive, and ablative). Moreover, the genitive agrees with its head noun in gender, number, and case. Definiteness, deictic categories, and possessive affixes are also part of noun inflection in many languages.

A classical study of Cushitic verb morphology is Zaborski 1976. The basic categories are aspect, tense, and mood; affirmative and negative verb forms are often morphologically distinguished. The original system consisted of four paradigms—imperfective, perfective, subjunctive, and imperative—but this has been enlarged in various ways by different languages. The most conspicuous development has taken place in Agaw, where cliticized conjunctions and auxiliary elements have fused with the personal endings to form a system of fifty or more 'tenses'. The normal Cushitic paradigm consists of seven forms: three persons each for singular and plural, with a gender distinction in the third person singular. Pronominal markers are prefixed in an archaic conjugation type preserved in some languages; otherwise, they are suffixed. The derivational system exhibits a rich array of categories: different types of causatives, a frequentive, a middle voice, a passive, etc.

Cushitic syntax is predominantly discourse-oriented. The discourse categories of topic and focus play a prominent role (for Somali, see Saeed 1984). Grammatical relations such as subject and object are less marked. In many sentences, case distinctions are neutralized; thus, in Somali, the absolutive/nominative distinction is preserved only if the subject is not focused or left-dislocated. In Northern Cushitic languages, there is a tendency towards unmarked S[ubject] O[bject] V[erb] word order, and the NP is head-final. The other languages normally vary their word order according to pragmatic principles, but the verb is generally sentence-final. The only SVO language is Yaaku.

HANS-JÜRGEN SASSE

BIBLIOGRAPHY

HAYWARD, RICHARD J. 1981. Nominal suffixes in Dirayta (Gidole). *Bulletin of the School of Oriental and African Studies,* University of London, 44.126–144.

HETZRON, ROBERT. 1976. *The Agaw languages.* (Afroasiatic linguistics, 3:3.) Malibu, Calif.: Undena.

HETZRON, ROBERT. 1980. The limits of Cushitic. *Sprache und Geschichte in Afrika* 2.7–126.

HYMAN, LARRY M. 1981. Tonal accent in Somali. *Studies in African Linguistics* 12.97–124.

SAEED, JOHN I. 1984. *The syntax of focus and topic in Somali.* (Kuschitische Sprachstudien, 3.) Hamburg: Buske.

SASSE, HANS-JÜRGEN. 1981. Die kuschitischen Sprachen. In *Die Sprachen Afrikas,* edited by Bernd Heine et al., pp. 187–215. Hamburg: Buske.

SASSE, HANS-JÜRGEN. 1987. Kuschitische Sprachen. *Studium Linguistik* 21.78–99.

ZABORSKI, ANDRZEJ. 1976. Cushitic overview. In *The non-Semitic languages of Ethiopia,* edited by Marvin Lionel Bender, pp. 67–84. East Lansing: African Studies Center, Michigan State University.

LANGUAGE LIST

Aasáx: an extinct language of Tanzania.

Afar: 700,000 or more speakers reported in 1987, including 400,000 in southern Eritrea Province and some in Wallo Province, Ethiopia; there are 300,000 in Djibouti and some in Somalia. Sometimes called Adal or Afaraf. The people are called Danakil. Saho is related but distinct. An official literary language.

Alaba: 50,000 speakers reported in 1978, in Ethiopia, separated from the Kambata by a river. Also called Allaaba or Halaba. Has 81 percent lexical similarity with Kambata, 64 percent with Sidamo, 56 percent with Libido, and 54 percent with Hadiyya.

Alagwa: 35,000 speakers estimated in 1987, in Kondoa District, Central Province, Tanzania. Also called Alawa, Wasi, Uwassi, or Asi.

Arbore: 1,000 to 5,000 speakers reported in 1982, around Lake Stefanie, Ethiopia. Also called Arbora, Erbore, or Irbore. Speakers use Konso as a lingua franca.

Awngi: 50,000 speakers reported in 1972, in widely scattered parts of Eritrea Province, Ethiopia. Also called Awiya, Southern Agaw, Awawar, Agau, Awi, Damot, or Agewmidir. Some bilingualism in Amharic and Tigrinya.

Bayso: 500 speakers reported in 1982, in Ethiopia. Also called Baiso. Speakers are bilingual in Wolaytta.

Beja: 980,000 or more speakers reported in 1982, including 951,000 in Sudan; there are 39,000 or more in Eritrea Province, Ethiopia, and some in Egypt. Sometimes called Bedawiye, Bedauye, or Bedja. Beni-Amer is the name of some of the people.

Bilin: 90,000 to 120,000 speakers reported in 1986, in north central Eritrea Province, Ethiopia. Also called Bogo, Bogos, Bilayn, Bilen, Balen, Beleni, Bilein, Bileno, or Bileninya. Some bilingualism in Tigrinya or Tigré.

Boni: 5,000 speakers reported in 1980, in Lamu and Tana River districts, Coast Province, and Garissa District, North-Eastern Province, Kenya; also in Somalia. Also called Aweera, Waata, Sanye, Waboni, Bon, Ogoda, or Wata-Bala. Some bilingualism in Somali, Orma, or Swahili. Different from Sanye (Waat), which is related to Oromo, and from Dahalo (Sanye), which is Southern Cushitic.

Burji: 25,000 to 30,000 speakers reported in 1983, including 15,000 to 20,000 south of Lake Ciamo, Ethiopia, and 10,000 or fewer around Marsabit township in Kenya. Also called Bambala, Bembala, or Burjinya. Has 41 percent lexical similarity with Sidamo, the most closely related variety.

Burunge: 31,000 speakers reported in 1987, in Kondoa District, Central Province, Tanzania. Also called Bulunge, Mbulugwe, or Burungi.

Bussa: 1,000 speakers reported in 1982, in Ethiopia. Has 51 percent lexical similarity with Konso. There is a dialect chain from Konso to Gidole to Bussa.

Dahalo: 3,000 speakers reported in 1987, near the mouth of the Tana River, in Lamu and Tana River districts, Coast

Province, Kenya. Also called Sanye or Guo Garimani. Different from Sanye (Waata). Speakers are bilingual in Swahili. The name 'Dahalo' is pejorative.

Dasenech: 30,000 speakers reported in 1983, with 27,500 in the Lower Omo River region in Ethiopia, along Lake Turkana, and including 2,500 on Lake Turkana in Marsabit District, Eastern Province, Kenya. Also called Daasenech, Dathanaik, Dathanik, Gheleba, Geleb, Gelebinya, Gallab, Gelubba, Dama, Marille, Merile, Morille, Reshiat, Russia, or Shangilla.

Dembiya: spoken in Ethiopia.

Dihina: spoken in Ethiopia. Part of the Dullay dialect continuum.

Dobase: spoken in Ethiopia. Part of the Dullay dialect continuum. Close to Gobeze.

Elmolo: 8 speakers, all over 50 years old, reported in 1976 from an ethnic population of 200, on the southeastern shore of Elmolo Bay, Lake Turkana, Marsabit District, Eastern Province, Kenya. Also called Fura-Pawa, Ldes, or Dehes. Most of the ethnic group now speak Samburu.

Gaba: spoken in Ethiopia. Part of the Dullay dialect continuum.

Gawwada: 50,000 speakers reported in 1982, in Ethiopia. Also called Gauwada or Gawata. Part of the Dullay dialect continuum. Has 78 percent lexical similarity with Gobeze.

Gedeo: 500,000 speakers reported in 1982, in the central highland area of Ethiopia. Also called Derasa, Derasanya, or Darassa. Has 60 percent lexical similarity with Sidamo, the most closely related variety. An official literary language.

Gergere: spoken in Ethiopia. Part of the Dullay dialect continuum.

Gidole: 5,000 speakers reported in 1982, in the hills near Lake Ciamo, Ethiopia. Also called Gardulla, Gidolinya, Dirasha, or Dirayta. Has 55 percent lexical similarity with Konso. Forms part of a dialect chain with Konso and Bussa. Many speakers are bilingual in Oromo or Konso.

Gobeze: 22,000 speakers reported in 1972, in Ethiopia. Also called Gowase, Goraze, Orase, Mashile, or Michile. Part of the Dullay dialect continuum. Has 78 percent lexical similarity with Gawwada.

Gollango: spoken in Ethiopia. Part of the Dullay dialect continuum.

Gorose: spoken in Ethiopia. Part of the Dullay dialect continuum.

Gorowa: 30,000 speakers reported in 1987, in Mbulu and Kondoa districts, Central Province, Tanzania. Also called Fiome.

Hadiyya: 2,000,000 speakers reported in 1987, in southern Shoa Province, between the Omo and Billate rivers, Ethiopia. Also called Adiye, Hadya, Adea, Hadia, or Gudeilla; the last is a derogatory name. Has 82 percent lexical similarity with Libido, 56 percent with Kambata, 54 percent with Alaba, 53 percent with Sidamo. An official literary language.

Harso: spoken in Ethiopia. Part of the Dullay dialect continuum.

Iraqw: 338,000 speakers reported in 1987, in the highlands southwest of Arusha, Mbulu District, Tanzania. Also called Mbulu, Erokh, or Iraku.

Kambata: 1,000,000 or more speakers reported in 1987, in Shoa Province, southern Ethiopia. Also called Kembata, Kembatinya, or Kemata. Has 81 percent lexical similarity with Alaba, 62 percent with Sidamo, 57 percent with Libido, and 56 percent with Hadiyya. An official literary language.

Kemant: 17,000 speakers reported in 1972, north of Lake Tana in Central Gandar Province, northwest Ethiopia. Also called Qimant, Kimantinya, Chemant, Kamant, or Qemant. All speakers may be bilingual in Amharic.

Khamir: 5,000 speakers (counting Khamta and Khamtange) reported in 1977, in Avergele District and the Lasta and Waag regions, Ethiopia, surrounded by Amharic and Tigré speakers. Also called Xamir or Khamit. Separate from Khamta and Khamtanga.

Khamta: spoken in Avergele District and the Lasta and Waag regions, Ethiopia, surrounded by Amharic and Tigré speakers. Also called Xamta. Has 45 percent lexical similarity with Bilin. Separate from Khamir and Khamtanga.

Khamtanga: spoken in Avergele District and the Lasta and Waag regions, Ethiopia, surrounded by Amharic and Tigré speakers. Separate from Khamta and Khamir.

Konso: 150,000 speakers reported in 1987, south of Lake Ciamo in the bend of the Sagan River, Ethiopia, with a few migrants in Kenya. Also called Konsinya, Conso, Gato, Af-Kareti, or Karate. An official literary language.

Kunfal: spoken in Ethiopia. Also called Kumfel.

Kw'adza: spoken in Tanzania.

Libido: spoken in west central Ethiopia in Arusi Province. Also called Maraqo. Has 82 percent lexical similarity with Hadiyya, 53 percent to 57 percent with Kambata, Alaba, and Sidamo.

Mbugu: 32,000 speakers reported in 1987, in Usambara, Eastern Province, Tanzania. Also called Ma'a or Wa Maathi. The people call themselves Va-Ma'a. Said to be a hybrid language, with Bantu prefix and concord system, but non-Bantu vocabulary.

Oromo, Borana-Arusi-Guji: 4,840,000 speakers reported in 1979 and 1980, with 4,730,000 in south central Ethiopia, and 106,000 in the Marsabit and Isiolo Districts, Eastern Province, Kenya. Sometimes called Gallinya or Afan Oromo. The name 'Galla' is pejorative.

Oromo, Garreh-Ajuran: around 72,000 or more speakers reported in 1983 in Mandera and Wajir districts, North-

Eastern Province, Kenya, and in Ethiopia and Somalia. Also called Gurreh, Garre, or Gari. Has 85 percent lexical similarity with the Borana variety of Oromo. Garreh and Ajuran may have limited mutual intelligibility.

Oromo, Orma: around 32,100 speakers reported in 1980, in Garissa and Tana River Districts, Northeastern and Coast Provinces, Kenya. Also called Warday or Wardei. Distinct from the Borana variety of Oromo.

Oromo, Wellega-Central: 5,750,000 speakers reported in 1987, in Ethiopia, and a few in Egypt. Sometimes called Western Oromo, Central Oromo, or Galla. An official literary language.

Qebena: spoken in Shewa Province, west of Kambata and Hadiyya, near the city of Welqite, Ethiopia. Also called Kebena or K'abena. Many speakers are bilingual in Gurage, Amharic, Kambata, or Oromo.

Quara: 28,000 speakers reported in 1989, including 21,000 in Eritrea Province, Gondar Province, north of Lake Tana, and in communities near Addis Ababa, Ethiopia, plus 7,000 in Israel. Also called Kwara, Koura, Kara, Quarasa, Quarina, Qwera, Falasha, Felasha, or Yihudi. The people are called Falashi and are Jewish, but they use Gi'iz as liturgical language.

Rendille: around 21,800 speakers reported in 1979, between Lake Turkana and Marsabit Mountain, in Marsabit District, Eastern Province, Kenya. Also called Randile. The Ariaal Rendille people speak Samburu.

Saho: 120,000 speakers reported in 1982, in southern Eritrea Province, Ethiopia. Also called Sao, Shoho, or Shiho.

Sanye: 5,000 speakers reported in 1980, in the lower parts of the Tana River, Lamu District, Coast Province, Kenya. Also called Sanya, Wasanye, Ariangulu, Langulo, Waata, or Waat. Distinct from Dahalo or Boni.

Sidamo: 1,400,000 speakers reported in 1987, northeast of Lake Abaya and Lake Awasa in south central Ethiopia. Also called Sidaminya. Has 64 percent lexical similarity with Alaba. An official literary language.

Somali: 5,620,000 speakers reported in 1986, including 4,020,000 in Somalia, 888,000 in south Ogaden Province, Ethiopia, 278,000 in Kenya, 181,000 in Djibouti, 169,000 in South Yemen, 60,000 in Yemen, and 25,000 in the United Arab Emirates. Also called Somalinya or Af-Soomaali. Official language of Somalia.

Tsamai: 7,000 speakers reported in 1971, in Ethiopia. Also called Tamaha, Kuile, Kule, or Tsamako. Self-designation is Ṣaamakko. Difficult mutual intelligibility with Gawwada. Part of the Dullay dialect continuum. Speakers use Konso as a lingua franca.

Yaaku: 50 speakers over 40 years old reported in 1983 from an ethnic population of 250, in Mukogodo Forest, Laikipia District, Mukogodo Division, Kenya. Also called Mukogodo, Mogogodo, Mukoquodo, Siegu, or Ndorobo.

CYCLE. The CYCLE has been proposed as a universal property of the way in which linguistic processes (rules) apply; it relates the application of these processes to constituent structure. (For general reference, see Chomsky 1973, Mascaró 1976, Kiparsky 1982, and Rubach 1984.)

Grammatical representations consist, in many components, of a linear sequence which is organized in constituent structure, as shown in Figure 1.

According to cyclic application, grammatical rules apply first to the innermost constituents, i.e. (α), (β), (γ), then to those that immediately dominate only those constituents (α β) and so on, up to the whole domain (α β γ). Thus, in *((condens)ation),* stress is assigned to the innermost constituent to give *(condéns),* and then to larger domains, resulting in *((còndèns)átion).*

The cycle was first proposed for phonology in 1956, to deal with stress in compounds like *(((bláck)(board)) (eràser)).* The stress rule maintains primary stress on the leftmost stressed constituent, and weakens others. Since it applies first to the constituents *((bláck)(boàrd))* and *(eráser),* and then to the whole structure, *(((bláck)(board)) (eràser)),* the stress of *(board)* is weakened twice.

In syntax, the elimination of generalized transformations and the generation of embedded sentences by base rules led to cyclic application. Later, the application of cyclic transformations was limited by the S[TRICT] C[YCLE] C[ONDITION], or 'strict cyclicity'; this states that no rule can apply to a constituent *J* in such a way as to affect solely a sub-constituent *K* of *J*. In fact, the SCC is a return to the effects that were obtained by the distinction between singulary and generalized transformations. This modified version of the cycle was applied, and further elaborated, for phonology.

In its phonological version, (strict) cyclic application can be defined formally as follows:

FIGURE 1. *Grammatical Representation*

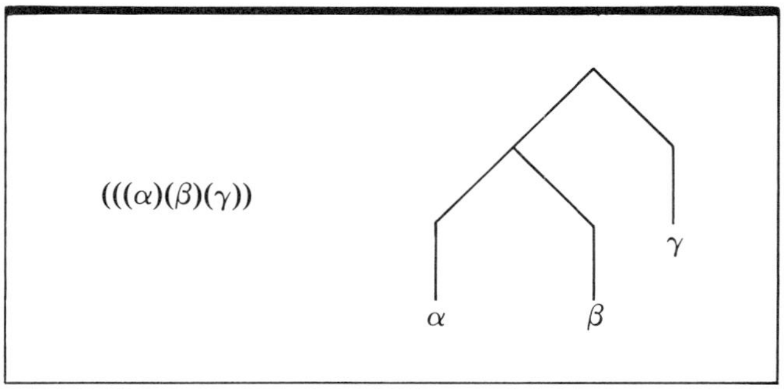

(1) A cyclic rule applies to the domain [$_J$ . . .] only after having applied to the domain [$_K$ . . .] (where *J* dominates *K*).

(2) A cyclic rule applies only to the cyclic domain *J* if its structural description refers to information introduced by virtue of *J*.

There are two cases under which cycle *J* can introduce this information: Given [$_J$ [. . .B] A. . .] or [$_J$. . .A [B. . .]], cycle *J* introduces *A* as new information; or given [$_J$ [. . .A][B. . .]], cycle *J* makes the sequence *AB* adjacent. The structure is then said to be 'morphologically (or syntactically) derived'. The second possibility is that a previous rule introduces the information, in which case we get a 'phonologically derived' structure. Given [$_J$. . .C. . .], a rule with the effect *C* → *A* applying at *J* will introduce *A*. Thus, in Polish, *s* is palatalized to *ś* before the front vowel *e*; in *serwisie* /servis+e/ 'service', however, only the SECOND *s* is palatalized [servíśe]. The cyclic structure is [[servis]e]; palatalization applies only to the morphologically derived sequence [ś]*e*. In Catalan, unstressed *e* goes to [ə] by vowel reduction. However, in the place name *Quebec* [keβέk], the first, lexically unstressed *e* does not undergo the rule. When a stressed suffix is added, as in the derived adjective *quebequès,* it triggers a rule that destresses all the preceding syllables; it creates a rule-derived environment, and thus reduces both *e*'s—[keβέk], [[keβέk]έs] → [[kəβək]έs])—even though they both are within the domain of a previous cycle.

We can distinguish the particular versions of (strict) cyclicity, or other principles that relate to it, from the class of empirical consequences that derive from them, i.e. CYCLIC EFFECTS. There are three main types of cyclic effect. First, rules can apply more than once to the same representation, as in rules of stress or syllabification, or WH-movement in syntax. Second, rules apply 'from bottom to top', i.e. first to most embedded constituents, then to less embedded ones. Third, rules apply only to 'derived' environments: they cannot return to earlier cyclic domains.

Work in the late 1970s and in the 1980s has resulted in the derivation of many (though not all) cyclic effects from principles other than the SCC. Metrical Phonology, Prosodic Phonology, and Lexical Phonology [*qq.v.*] incorporate some of the cyclic effects.

JOAN MASCARÓ

BIBLIOGRAPHY

CHOMSKY, NOAM. 1973. Conditions on transformations. In *A Festschrift for Morris Halle,* edited by Stephen R. Anderson & Paul Kiparsky, pp. 232–286. New York: Holt, Rinehart & Winston.

KIPARSKY, PAUL. 1982. From cyclic phonology to lexical phonology. In *The structure of phonological representations,* edited by Harry van der Hulst & Norval Smith, pp. 131–175. Dordrecht: Foris.

MASCARÓ, JOAN. 1976. *Catalan phonology and the phonological cycle.* Bloomington: Indiana University Linguistics Club.

RUBACH, JERZY. 1984. *Cyclic and lexical phonology: The structure of Polish.* (Studies in generative grammar, 17.) Dordrecht: Foris.

CZECH AND SLOVAK are members of the West Slavonic sub-family of languages, along with Polish, Upper and Lower Sorbian, and extinct Polabian. [*See* Slavic Languages.] They are spoken predominantly in Bohemia/Moravia and Slovakia, respectively, but are equal official languages throughout Czechoslovakia. Czech is spoken by about ten million people, and Slovak by about five million, with several hundred thousand more speakers in enclaves elsewhere in eastern and southeastern Europe, and in more or less cohesive 19th- and 20th-century migrant communities, especially in German-speaking Europe and the Americas.

The two languages are, potentially, mutually intelligible; but parallel texts can be created, based on not entirely peripheral vocabulary, where the coincidence would be far lower than the 90 percent average traditionally quoted.

For pedagogical grammars with reference sections on Czech, see Čermák et al. 1984–86 and Naughton 1987; on Slovak, Baláž et al. 1976 and Oravec & Prokop 1986. Many more sources are listed by Nováková 1985. Outline grammars are given by Mistrík 1983, Short 1987, and Kavka 1988. The historical grammar of Czech is covered by Mann 1957. The most recent comprehensive grammar of Czech is the three-volume *Mluvnice češtiny* (1986–87).

1. Dialects and history. Both languages show considerable dialect variation. Bohemia has only minor distinctive dialects at the fringes; Moravia has greater variation, chiefly through different degrees of phonological conservatism. The most striking dialects are in southern Silesia, and are transitional to Polish. Slovak's three main divisions—Eastern, Central, and Western—are further fragmented by the many mountain ranges and rivers. Western Slovak shares some features with Moravian Czech, and Eastern Slovak with Polish—but also with Western Slovak, supporting the theory that Central Slovakia was colonized later, splitting East from West.

Modern Standard Czech emerged during the national revival of the early 19th century, largely through the work of Josef Dobrovský and Josef Jungmann. In many respects, it is an archaic formation, largely modeled on the 'ideal' of 16th-century Humanist Czech. While this standard is observed in the media, in education, and in other appropriate circumstances, it coexists with 'Common Czech'—a version of the language which has evolved since the 16th century, with some phonological and syntactic differences from the standard, and considerable morphological and lexical differences. Rooted in Central Bohemia, it has spread elsewhere, interacting with other regional (especially urban) dialects; some features are assertive enough even to penetrate colloquial registers of the standard language.

Standard Slovak is also a semi-artificial creation, codified by L'udovít Štúr in the 1840s, with later refinements. However, it is at least based on a modern form (Central Slovak, with some West Slovak features), and thus is in a sense less conservative than Czech. An earlier attempt by Anton Bernolák to codify Slovak, using a West Slovak dialect as the basis, failed to win general acceptance. An unhappy attempt at the beginning of this century to create an additional language based on Eastern Slovak, and called 'Slovjak', was short-lived.

The lexicon has a common core, shared with the other Slavonic languages, but with critical cases of 'false friendship' (e.g. Cz. *statek* 'farm', pl. 'property', Slo. *statok* 'cattle'). Lexical divergence is greatest among loan words: Slovak has long been influenced by Hungarian; there is also a strong element from Rumanian, chiefly connected with upland sheep-farming. Both languages have borrowed heavily from German, but the standing of German loans differs—owing, in particular, to recurrent bouts of purism among the Czechs. Terminologies coincide only partially, and even recent items may differ, e.g. Cz. *dálnice* 'motorway', a native neologism analogous to *silnice* 'main road', Slo. *autostráda,* a loan-word. However, the 1970s and 1980s have shown an increasing tendency toward convergence and/or interference; hence *autostráda* may yet yield to *dial'nica,* the phonological counterpart to *dálnice.* Generally, codifiers and users of Slovak resist obvious Bohemicisms; the pressure of Slovak on Czech is weaker, but perhaps more insidious.

2. Phonology (cf. Kučera 1961). The main distinctive consonantal features of Czech and Slovak—voiced *h* < *g* and (Czech only) *ř* < *r'*—had already developed before the start of the long Czech written tradition, which goes back to the 13th century; other details of the modern consonantism were established by the 16th century. Important to both systems, though operating in different ways, are the voiced/voiceless and palatal/non-palatal oppositions. For the consonant phonemes, see Table 1. Note that the palatal lateral occurs only in Slovak, as do the voiced affricates (in Czech, mere allophones of /ts tʃ). Phonemic /ce ci ca co cu c/ are spelled *tě ti t'a t'o t'u t',* and similarly for /ɟ/, /ɲ/, and Slo. /ʎ/.

In the vocalism, the main phonological developments of Cz. are the 14th-century umlauts of /a/ > /ę/, /a:/ > /ie/ (later > /i:/), /u/ > /i/, /u:/ > /i:/, plus the more restricted /o/ > /ę/ and /o:/ > /ie/ (later > /i:/), in certain well-defined environments. These changes, eventually followed by the merger of /ę/ with /e/, underlie many of the morphological differences between the two languages. Slo. is conspicuous for its diphthongs, which are involved in oppositions over and above the general long/short opposition. Slo. also has a 'law of rhythmical shortening': in a sequence of two (historically) long syllables, the second loses its length, hence Slo. *krásny* 'beautiful' but Cz. *krásný.* The modern vowel phonemes are shown in Table 2. Note that the vowel /æ/ occurs in Slovak only. Long vowels are written with acute accents

TABLE 1. *Czech and Slovak Consonant Phonemes.* Orthographic equivalents are in italics.

	Labial	Apical	Palatal	Velar	Laryngeal
Occlusives					
Voiceless	p	t	c ⟨*t'*⟩	k	
Voiced	b	d	ɟ ⟨*d'*⟩	g	
Affricates					
Voiceless		ts ⟨*c*⟩	tʃ ⟨*č*⟩		
Voiced		dz	dʒ ⟨*dž*⟩		
Fricatives					
Voiceless	f	s	ʃ ⟨*š*⟩	x ⟨*ch*⟩	
Voiced	v	z	ʒ ⟨*ž*⟩		h
Nasals	m	n	ɲ ⟨*ň*⟩		
Lateral		l	ʎ ⟨*l'*⟩		
Vibrants					
Plain		r			
Fricative		ř			
Semivowel			j		

TABLE 2. *Czech and Slovak Vowels*

	Front	Mid	Back
High	i ⟨*i/y*⟩		u
Mid	e		o
Low	æ ⟨*ä*⟩	a	

(and Cz. /ú/ is also written as *ů*). Diphthongs include, in Cz., *ou*; in Slo., *ia ie ô* (= /uo/) and *iu*. Long /o:/ and diphthongs *au eu* occur only in loans. Slo. also has syllabic *l* and *r*, short and long.

3. Morphology. Cz. and Slo. are inflecting languages with complex morphology to express seven cases—nominative, vocative (absent from Slovak), accusative, genitive, dative, locative or prepositional, and instrumental. (For Czech, see Čermák et al. 1984–86 and Kavka 1988; for Slovak, Baláž et al. 1976 and Mistrík 1983.) There are singular and plural numbers; some conservative remnants in Czech of the dual are now treated as anomalous plurals. The genders are masculine, feminine, and neuter. Masculine is subdivided into animate and inanimate, but the scope of the distinction differs between the two languages. In the singular, any masculine noun denoting a living creature is 'animate' in both languages (expressed by having acc. = gen., and by distinctive dat./loc. forms). In the plural, the same range of nouns is covered in Czech, which has a distinctive nom. for animates; in Slo., animacy is confined to nouns denoting male humans, which are morphologically marked in both nom. and acc. (= gen. as in sg.). The patterns are shown in Table 3.

The effect of the 14th-century Czech umlauts, by which the 'soft' declensions moved further away from their 'hard' counterparts, is shown in Table 4. The Czech suffixes should be compared with the equivalent forms of *žena* in Table 3, and with the parallel Slovak, in which no umlaut occurred. Tables 3–4 give some indication of how history has produced varying degrees of case homonymy and syncretism in the many paradigms. This is most marked in the singular of Cz. *paní* 'lady, Mrs.', Slo. *pani* 'Mrs.', which evince no distinct case forms at all.

Adjectival declension is in origin a compound form,

TABLE 3. *'Hard' Noun Declensions in Czech and Slovak*

	Czech		Slovak	
	Singular	Plural	Singular	Plural
'Hard' masculine animate: *pán* 'gentleman'				
Nom.	*pán*	*pánové/páni*	*pán*	*páni*
Voc.	*pane*	*pánové/páni*	—	—
Acc.	*pána*	*pány*	*pána*	*pánov*
Gen.	*pána*	*pánů*	*pána*	*pánov*
Dat.	*pánu/pánovi*	*pánům*	*pánovi*	*pánom*
Loc.	*pánu/pánovi*	*pánech*	*pánovi*	*pánoch*
Instr.	*pánem*	*pány*	*pánom*	*pánmi*
'Hard' feminine: *žena* 'woman'				
Nom.	*žena*	*ženy*	*žena*	*ženy*
Voc.	*ženo*	*ženy*	—	—
Acc.	*ženu*	*ženy*	*ženu*	*ženy*
Gen.	*ženy*	*žen*	*ženy*	*žien*
Dat.	*ženě*	*ženám*	*žene*	*ženám*
Loc.	*ženě*	*ženách*	*žene*	*ženách*
Instr.	*ženou*	*ženami*	*ženou*	*ženami*
'Hard' neuter: *slovo* 'word'				
Nom.	*slovo*	*slova*	*slovo*	*slová*
Voc.	*slovo*	*slova*	—	—
Acc.	*slovo*	*slova*	*slovo*	*slová*
Gen.	*slova*	*slov*	*slova*	*slov*
Dat.	*slovu*	*slovům*	*slovu*	*slovám*
Loc.	*slově*	*slovech*	*slove*	*slovách*
Instr.	*slovem*	*slovy*	*slovom*	*slovami*

TABLE 4. *'Soft' Noun Declension in Czech and Slovak:* duše/duša *'soul' (feminine)*

	Czech		Slovak	
	Singular	Plural	Singular	Plural
Nom.	*duše*	*duše*	*duša*	*duše*
Voc.	*duše*	*duše*	—	—
Acc.	*duši*	*duše*	*dušu*	*duše*
Gen.	*duše*	*duší*	*duše*	*dúš*
Dat.	*duši*	*duším*	*duši*	*dušiam*
Loc.	*duši*	*duších*	*duši*	*dušiach*
Instr.	*duší*	*dušemi*	*dušou*	*dušami*

TABLE 5. *Present Tense Verb Forms of Czech and Slovak.* The Czech alternative 1sg. and 3pl. forms are newer variants, used in more colloquial registers.

		Czech		Slovak	
Infinitive		*psát*	*dát*	*písať*	*dať*
		'write'	'give, put'		
Singular	1	*píši/-u*	*dám*	*píšem*	*dám*
	2	*píšeš*	*dáš*	*píšeš*	*dáš*
	3	*píše*	*dá*	*píše*	*dá*
Plural	1	*píšeme*	*dáme*	*píšeme*	*dáme*
	2	*píšete*	*dáte*	*píšete*	*dáte*
	3	*píší/-ou*	*dají*	*píšu*	*dajú*
Infinitive		*myslet*	*pracovat*	*myslieť*	*pracovať*
		'think'	'work'		
Singular	1	*myslím*	*pracuji/-u*	*myslím*	*pracujem*
	2	*myslíš*	*pracuješ*	*myslíš*	*pracuješ*
	3	*myslí*	*pracuje*	*myslí*	*pracuje*
Plural	1	*myslíme*	*pracujeme*	*myslíme*	*pracujeme*
	2	*myslíte*	*pracujete*	*myslíte*	*pracujete*
	3	*myslí*	*pracují/-ou*	*myslia*	*pracujú*

and differs completely from nominal types; pronominal declensions vary greatly.

There are three main verb conjugations, in *-e-, -á-,* and *-í-*; these have several subtypes (notably a productive class in *-uje-*) and phonologically conditioned variants. Samples are given in Table 5.

The past tense in both languages is formed by means of an earlier participle in *-l,* with added gender/number markers, and with the present tense of *být/byť* 'be' as auxiliary. The conditional is formed analogously, but using a former aorist of *být/byť* as auxiliary. Sample forms are shown in Table 6. Note that singular endings are masc. *-l,* fem. *-la*, neu. *-lo*. Plural endings are Czech masc. anim. *-li,* masc. inan. or fem. *-ly,* neut. *-la.* (Slovak does not discriminate gender in the plural). The written Czech distinction of *-li* vs. *-ly* is not reflected in pronunciation.

The paucity of tenses is compensated for, in both languages, by aspect. The present tense form of an 'imperfective' verb expresses present meaning; that of a 'perfective' verb, a future meaning. Future imperfective is expressed by the imperfective infinitive plus the future of *být/byť* as auxiliary. Verbs, except those of state and some others, must be learned in pairs, which differ either by a perfectivizing prefix (Cz. *psát* > *napsat,* Slo. *písať* > *napísať*'), or by a secondary imperfectivizing suffix (Cz. *přepisovat* < *přepsat,* Slovak *prepisovať* < *prepísať* 're-write'), often with concomitant stem and conjugation changes.

4. Syntax. Czech and Slovak are fundamentally S[ubject] V[erb] O[bject] languages, but the exigencies of enclitic-placing rules and of functional sentence perspective create considerable variation in word order. The main enclitics are the past and conditional auxiliaries and unstressed object pronouns. Relative freedom of order accounts for the low incidence of the periphrastic passive, since 'Peter was killed by Paul' becomes 'Peter(ACC) killed Paul(NOM).' Expression of the passive, especially the impersonal type, is generally by means of reflexive verb phrases containing the pronominal particle Cz. *se,* Slo. *sa*; the reflexive verb phrase expresses numerous shades of meaning, and thus is of high frequency. Czech and Slovak differ from western European languages in having no rule of 'sequence of tenses'; thus 'She said she was ill' is expressed as Cz. *Řekla, že je*

TABLE 6. *Past and Conditional Verb Forms of Czech and Slovak* dát/dať *'to give'*

Czech		Slovak	
Past	Conditional	Past	Conditional
dal/-a jsem	*dal/-a bych*	*dal/-a som*	*dal/-a by som*
dal/-a jsi	*dal/-a bys*	*dal/-a si*	*dal/-a by si*
dal/-a/-o	*dal/-a/-o by*	*dal/-a/-o*	*dal/-a/-o by*
dali/-y jsme	*dali/-y bychom*	*dali sme*	*dali by sme*
dali/-y jste	*dali/-y byste*	*dali ste*	*dali by ste*
dali/-y/-a	*dali/-y/-a by*	*dali*	*dali by*

nemocná, Slo. *Povedala, že je chorá* 'She said she is ill.' Hence, in subordinate clauses after verbs of speaking or perceiving, the present, past, and future express simultaneity, anteriority, or posteriority of the action vis-à-vis that of the governing clause, whatever the tense of the latter.

DAVID SHORT

BIBLIOGRAPHY

BALÁŽ, PETER, et al. 1976. *Slovak for Slavicists.* Bratislava: Slovenské Pedagogické Nakladatel'stvo.

ČERMÁK, FRANTIŠEK, et al. 1984–86. *A course of Czech language.* 5 vols. Prague: Univerzita Karlova.

KAVKA, STANISLAV. 1988. *An outline of Modern Czech grammar.* Uppsala: Slaviska Institutionen, Uppsala Universitet.

KUČERA, HENRY. 1961. *The phonology of Czech.* The Hague: Mouton.

MANN, STUART E. 1957. *Czech historical grammar.* London: Athlone. Revised ed., Hamburg: Buske, 1977.

MISTRÍK, JOZEF. 1983. *A grammar of contemporary Slovak.* Bratislava: Slovenské Pedagogické Nakladatel'stvo. 2d ed., 1987.

NAUGHTON, JAMES D. 1987. *Colloquial Czech.* 2d ed. London: Routledge & Kegan Paul.

NOVÁKOVÁ, LUDMILA. 1985. *Čeština jako cizí jazyk* [*Czech as a foreign language*], vol. 2, *Výběrová bibliografie příruček češtiny jako cizího jazyka.* Prague: Státní Pedagogické Nakladatelství.

ORAVEC, JÁN, & JOZEF PROKOP. 1986. *Slovenčina pre krajanov hovoriacich po anglicky: A Slovak textbook for English-speaking countrymen.* Martin, Czechoslovakia: Matica Slovenská.

SHORT, DAVID. 1987. Czech and Slovak. In *The world's major languages,* edited by Bernard Comrie, pp. 367–390. London: Croom Helm. New York: Oxford University Press.

D

DALY LANGUAGES constitute a family of the Daly River area, in the northern part of the Northern Territory, Australia. They form a top-level component in the primarily lexicostatistical classification of Australian languages by Stephen A. Wurm and Shirô Hattori, eds., *Language atlas of the Pacific area* (Canberra: Australian Academy of the Humanities, 1981), on which source the subgrouping in Figure 1 is based.

LANGUAGE LIST

Ami: 40 speakers reported in 1981, on the coast along Anson Bay, southwest of Darwin. Also called Ame or Amijangal.

Giyug: 2 speakers reported in 1981, in the Peron Islands in Anson Bay, southwest of Darwin.

Kamu: 2 speakers reported in 1981, south of Darwin, east of Daly River. Also called Gamor.

Kuwama: 2 speakers reported in 1981, near the mouth of the Muldiva River, southwest of Darwin. Also called Pungupungu.

Madngele: 20 speakers reported in 1981, south of Darwin and the Daly River, on the west bank of the Muldiva River. Also called Matngala, Warat, Maangella, Mandella, or Muttangulla.

Magadige: 30 speakers reported in 1983, inland from Anson Bay, south of Maridjabin, southwest of Darwin.

Manda: 25 speakers reported in 1983, on the coast southwest of Anson Bay and Darwin.

Maranunggu: 15 to 20 speakers reported in 1983, southwest of Darwin, inland from Anson Bay, east of Manda.

Maridan: 20 speakers reported in 1981, southwest of Darwin, north of Moyle River, east of Magadige. Also called Meradan.

Maridjabin: 50 speakers reported in 1981, inland from Anson Bay, south of Mariyedi and Manda, southwest of Darwin. Also called Maretyabin or Maredyerbin.

Marimanindji: 15 speakers reported in 1983, south of Darwin and the Daly River, west of the Muldiva River near its headwaters. Also called Maramarandji, Maramanandji, Marimanindu, or Murinmanindji.

Maringarr: 50 speakers reported in 1981, south of Moyle River, southwest of Darwin. Also called Marenggar, Marranunga, or Maramanunggu.

Marithiel: 235 speakers reported in 1983, south of the Daly River and on the central Daly River. Also called Maridhiyel, Brinken, or Berringen. The people generally speak Kriol.

Mariyedi: 20 speakers reported in 1981, inland from Anson Bay, south of Manda, southwest of Darwin.

Mullukmulluk: 20 speakers reported in 1983, on the northern bank of the Daly River. Also called Malak-Malak, Malagmalag, Ngolak-Wonga, or Nguluwongga. The people generally speak Kriol.

Murrinh-Patha: 800 speakers reported in 1982, in Port Keats area, Wadeye, Northern Territory. Also called Murinbada or Garama.

Nangikurrunggurr: 100 or more speakers reported in 1983, at the confluence of the Flora and Daly rivers, Daly River Mission, Tipperary Station. Also called Ngenkikurrunggur. The people generally speak English and Kriol.

FIGURE 1. *Subgrouping of Daly Languages*

Bringen-Wagaydy
- **Bringen**
  - Magadige, Maridjabin, Marithiel, Mariyedi
- **Wagaydy**
  - Ami, Giyug, Kuwama, Manda, Maranunggu, Maridan, Marimanindji, Maringarr, Wadjiginy

Malagmalag
- **Daly Proper**
  - Kamu, Madngele
- **Malagmalag Proper**
  - Mullukmulluk, Tyaraity

Moil
- Nangikurrunggurr, Ngenkiwumerri

Murrinh-Patha

Ngenkiwumerri: 50 speakers reported in 1981, south of Darwin, east of Katherine. Also called Nangiomeri.

Tyaraity: 5 possible speakers reported in 1981, in Delissaville. Also called Dyeraidy, Daktjerat, or Wogadj. All or most speakers are bilingual in English.

Wadjiginy: 50 speakers reported in 1953, southwest of Darwin along the coast and inland along the Finniss River. Also called Wogaity or Wagaydy.

DANI-KWERBA LANGUAGES are a group spoken on the island of New Guinea, in north-central Irian Jaya, Indonesia. Stephen A. Wurm, *Papuan languages of Oceania* (Tübingen: Narr, 1982), pp. 149–151, proposes the subgrouping given in Figure 1 (apart from some terminological differences). He assigns the Dani-Kwerba stock to the Central and Western part of the main section of his controversial Trans-New Guinea phylum [*q.v.*].

LANGUAGE LIST

Airoran: 354 speakers reported in 1975, near the north coast of Irian Jaya. Also called Aeroran, Adora, or Iriemkena.

Bagusa: 300 speakers reported in 1987, south of Lake Rombebai.

Dani, Lower Grand Valley: around 100,000 speakers reported in 1987, from the central highlands of Irian Jaya.

Dani, Mid Grand Valley: around 50,000 speakers reported in 1989, in Baliem Valley. Also called Tulem.

Dani, Western: 150,000 speakers reported in 1985, in the central highlands of Irian Jaya. Also called Dani Barat, Ilaga Western Dani, Lani, Laany, Oeringoep, or Timorini.

Hupla: 3,000 or more speakers reported in 1982, in the central highlands of Irian Jaya. Also called Soba.

Isirawa: 1,500 to 2,000 speakers reported in 1987, in Jayapura and Sarmi, on the north coast. Also called Saweri, Saberi, Okwasar. Population includes 30 percent near-monolinguals, and 70 percent with routine ability in Indonesian.

Kauwerawec: 400 or more speakers reported in 1987, east of the middle Mamberamo River.

Kwerba: 1,500 speakers reported in 1987, in the upper Tor River area. Also called Airmati, Kamboi-Ramboi, Koassa, Nogukwabai, Naibedj, or Tekutameso.

Nduga: 10,000 speakers reported in 1985, in Jayawijaya and Tiom, in the central highlands, south of the high ranges. Also called Ndugwa, Ndauwa, Dauwa, Dawa, Pesechem, Pesecham, or Pesegem. Population includes 70 percent nearly monolingual, 20 percent with routine ability, and 10 percent with nearly native ability in a variety of Dani. Some speak Damal, Moni, or Indonesian.

Nggem: spoken along the middle Haflifoeri River. Has 50 percent lexical similarity with Western Dani.

Nopuk: 150 or more speakers reported in 1987, in the mountains east of the Mamberamo River. Also called Nobuk.

Samarokena: 400 speakers reported in 1982, near the north coast, east of the Apawar River. Also called Samarkena, Karfasia, or Tamaya. Speakers are bilingual in Airoran and Isirawa, and some in Kwerba.

Sasawa: 189 speakers reported in 1975, near the north coast in the Jayapura area.

Silimo: 5,000 speakers reported in 1987, in the central highlands west of the Baliem River. Also called South Ngalik or Paiyage.

Walak: spoken in Ilugwa, Wodo, and other villages. Also called Lower Pyramid or Wodo.

Wano: 3,000 to 3,500 speakers reported in 1987, on the upper Rouffaer River in the central highlands.

Yali, Angguruk: 15,000 speakers reported in 1989, in the central highlands area. Also called Angguruk or Yalimo. Distinct from Yali of Ninia and Yali of Pass Valley (Nipsan).

Yali, Ninia: 35,000 speakers reported in 1978, in the central highlands area. Also called Ninia, North Ngalik, Yaly, or Holowon. Distinct from Yali of Pass Valley (Nipsan) and Yali of Angguruk.

FIGURE 1. *Subgrouping of Dani-Kwerba Languages*

Northern Dani-Kwerba
- **Isirawa**
- **Kwerba**
  - Airoran, Bagusa, Kauwerawec, Kwerba (proper), Nopuk, Sasawa
- Samarokena

Southern Dani-Kwerba
- **Dani**
  - Lower Grand Valley Dani, Mid Grand Valley Dani, Western Dani, Hupla, Nggem, Walak
- **Ngalik-Nduga**
  - Nduga, Silimo, Angguruk Yali, Ninia Yali
- Wano

DECIPHERMENT. In a technical linguistic sense, 'decipherment' refers to the decoding of a writing system which is no longer in use and no longer comprehensible. It is usual to distinguish decipherment from cryptoanalysis or cryptology; the latter aims at understanding special writing codes or ciphers devised to disguise the meaning of a message. We also distinguish decipherment from interpretation: a text written in an obscure language but in a known script (e.g. the Latin alphabet) requires interpretation, not decipherment.

Some of these definitions and distinctions are less sharp than we would hope. First, the concept of decipherment is tied to the concept of writing, but it is not always obvious what counts as writing. Second, cryptoanalysis and decipherment often overlap in their techniques. Third, the interpretation of texts is the only test of decipherment: if the language is known, no problems arise—but if it is not, interpretation is necessary for decipherment. Fourth, we often hesitate between the use of 'decipherment' and 'interpretation'. Lycian was an Anatolian language of the 1st millennium BCE, written in an alphabet borrowed from Greek; yet the phonetic values of some of its signs differ from those of Greek, and there are additional signs not found in Greek. If we succeed in understanding these texts, is it decipherment or interpretation? (For general reference on scripts and decipherment, see Gelb 1952, Cohen 1958, Voegelin & Voegelin 1963, Friedrich 1966a,b, and Trager 1974.) [*See also* Writing Systems.]

1. History of decipherment. Decipherment is normally required for scripts which fell out of use, either because they were employed for languages which also became extinct (e.g. Akkadian Cuneiform), or because literacy disappeared (Linear B), or because they were replaced by other forms of writing (Syllabic Cypriot). Modern scholarship has been immensely successful in deciphering all such types; but there are still many scripts (or supposed scripts) for which no full and generally accepted decipherment is available. They include the Indus Valley script of the 3d millennium BCE, Cretan Hieroglyphic of the 2nd millennium BCE, the Mayan glyphs of America, the Easter Island script of the 19th century, and a number of others (see Gelb 1973:266, RAS 1975, Leclant 1975).

1.1. *Early steps.* Interest in ancient scripts goes back to the Renaissance and earlier (Pope 1975). Evidence for languages and scripts was extensively collected in the 16th and 17th centuries, when languages like Coptic (a form of Neo-Egyptian) were rescued. In the 17th century, the interest in universal languages also led to discussions about universal writing, which helped to establish a typology of writing. However, the first serious decipherments belong to the 18th century. In 1754, two scholars—J. Swinton and the abbé Barthélemy—independently deciphered the Aramaic script used in the Palmyra inscriptions of the 3rd century CE; in 1787, Sylvestre de Sacy deciphered Sassanian, the script used in Persia to write the Middle Iranian language of the Sassanid dynasty. In both instances, the script was a form of the Aramaic alphabet, closely related to the Syriac writing which was already known. Both decipherments were based on bilingual texts that included Greek versions. The first methodological principles were also established in the 18th century. As early as 1714, Leibniz had advocated the use of personal names to establish the necessary links between the known and undeciphered parts of a bilingual text. Personal names were important in the decipherment of Palmyrene and Sassanian, and played an essential role in later decipherments.

In the 19th century, the prerequisites for decipherment—extensive knowledge of scripts, adequate editions of texts, philological skills, and ability to reconstruct linguistic forms from limited evidence—became more widely available. Two great decipherments opened the way to further successes: that of the Egyptian Hieroglyphs, and that of the Old Persian Cuneiform.

1.2. *Egyptian hieroglyphs.* For a long time, mystery had surrounded the hieroglyphic script attested in Egypt from the 3rd millennium BCE to the 4th century CE. Later it was assumed that each pictographic sign represented a word or a notion. The decipherment was made possible by the discovery of an Egyptian stele, the Rosetta Stone, dated from 196 BCE, which contained three versions of a decree in honor of King Ptolemy V. One version was in Greek; the other two were written in hieroglyphic and in demotic (a very cursive version of the Egyptian script, often mistaken for alphabetic by early decipherers). Sequences of signs equivalent to the personal names of the Greek version were identified in the demotic, and in one instance (the name *Ptolemaios*) in the hieroglyphic part. The most impressive contributions came from a young Frenchman, Jean-François Champollion (1790–1832), who had prepared himself for the task almost from childhood, through a series of philological studies of the Egyptian evidence (including Coptic). He succeeded in showing that a number of names were written with signs which had phonetic values. This was announced in 1822; in his later work, through a simple count of the number of signs in the hieroglyphic part of the Rosetta Stone and of the number of words in the Greek part, Champollion discredited the old view that, except for personal names, each 'hieroglyph' corresponded to a word. Some of the hieroglyphs indeed had logographic functions, but others had a phonetic value; a word could be indicated by both logographic and phonetic signs. Thus the phonetic values puzzled out on the basis of personal names could also be exploited elsewhere; further, some morphemes seemed to be related to the corresponding Coptic forms. What emerged from the work which followed Champollion's results was a complicated writing system which included logographic signs, determinatives, and phonetic signs corresponding to one or more consonants (cf. Friedrich 1966a:4–25, Pope 1975:43–84). [*See also* Egyptian.]

1.3. *Cuneiform writing* was unknown to the West until the 17th century [*see* Cuneiform]. The first reliable copies of the Persepolis cuneiform inscriptions were published in the second half of the 18th century; some (connected with the Achaemenid kings of Persia, who reigned in the 5th century BCE) were multilingual, with three versions of the same text in different cuneiform scripts used for different languages. At the beginning of the 19th century, a German schoolteacher interested in cryptoanalysis, G. F. Grotefend (1775–1853), recognized (as others had before him) the sign that divided words; he concluded from the number of the signs and the length of the words that the script was alphabetic or semi-alphabetic; he guessed from the pattern of repeated sequences that the text included the formula found in later Sassanian inscriptions ('X, great king, king of kings, son of Y, Achaemenid . . .'); and finally, he recognized the names of the king Darius and his son Xerxes. The first phonetic values could then be assigned, but Grotefend was prevented from going much further by his insufficient linguistic knowledge. In 1826, the great comparativist Rasmus Rask identified the ending of the genitive plural in the phrase 'king of kings', and compared it with the genitive plural of Sanskrit. It then became clear that Old Persian was closely related to Sanskrit and to Avestan; this led to further identification of sign values, and allowed scholars to determine through comparison the meanings of a number of words. An Englishman, Henry Rawlinson (1810–95), succeeded in reading the great Behistun inscription of Darius; on the basis of that evidence, he produced a new decipherment of the Old Persian texts, which partly overlapped with that of Grotefend, but went much further.

The decipherment of Old Persian was crucial: first, it was achieved without the help of a version in a known language; second, it opened the way to the even more important decipherment of Akkadian (Assyro-Babylonian) cuneiform (also started by Rawlinson). The script and language were used in one of the versions of the Persian texts—but also in innumerable clay tablets which formed the archives, recently discovered, of the main Near Eastern centers during the 3d to 1st millennia BCE. The Old Persian version gave no help with the sign values, but it provided the necessary bilingual material and the personal names likely to be found in both versions. The language was found to be Semitic, and comparative Semitic evidence was invaluable in defining the meaning of a number of roots. Like the Egyptian hieroglyphic script, the writing system included logograms, determinatives, and phonetic signs; the last were all syllabic, and indicated a V[owel], C[onsonant] + V, V + C, or (more rarely) C + V + C. The knowledge of the new writing system led to the understanding of a number of ancient Near Eastern languages whose existence had been barely suspected: most important was Sumerian, the non-Indo-European and non-Semitic language attested in Mesopotamia from the late 4th millennium BCE, for which the first forms of cuneiform writing were probably devised. Also important was Hittite, which was written in Anatolia during the 2nd millennium BCE. Most of the texts were written in a form of cuneiform similar to Akkadian; they were easy to read, but they remained incomprehensible until it was discovered that the language was Indo-European (indeed the oldest attested Indo-European language), and until a combination of contextual and etymological work led to the understanding of both grammar and vocabulary (Friedrich 1966a:27–71, Pope 1975:85–122).

1.4. *Linear B*. The most celebrated decipherment of this century was that of Linear B, a script written on clay tablets in Crete and in mainland Greece in the latter part of the 2d millennium BCE. The decipherment, announced in 1952, was the work of a young architect, Michael Ventris, who in the last stages of his work had the help of the linguist John Chadwick. It built on earlier discoveries: given the number of signs, the script was likely to be syllabic, possibly with V or CV signs like the obviously related Syllabic Cypriot; and the language was inflected, since the final parts of words showed regular types of alternations. On the basis of these alternations, Ventris established a grid of signs which had either the same vowel or the same consonant (though their values remained unknown). He then guessed the values of some signs on the basis of various criteria: identification of Cretan place names in the Cretan tablets; graphic similarity between the Linear B signs and the signs of the Cypriot syllabary; and the assumption that the sign most frequently found in word-initial position represented the [a] vowel. The grid was used to test these suggestions and to define the values of other signs. From his first tentative readings, Ventris was unwillingly led to the correct conclusion that most of the words and most of the patterns of word-formation had to be Greek. The script was shown to be syllabic, with approximately eighty phonetic signs of the type V or CV, and with logograms used separately from the phonetic signs (cf. Chadwick 1973).

2. Methods. The work just exemplified led to two immediate results: first, the typology of writing was better understood than previously; second, a rudimentary methodology for decipherment was developed. Yet it is doubtful that there ever was a logical decipherment in which guesswork did not play a considerable part; even now, there is no known recipe for decipherment. What we have is a series of heuristic devices, some of which are mentioned below (cf. Aalto 1945, Friedrich 1966a:134–39, Gelb 1973, 1974).

The importance of preparatory work has been underlined. The decipherer needs to know as much as possible about the linguistic and historical data relevant to the period and area to which the texts belong. Accurate drawings, photographs, or 'squeezes' of the texts are also necessary—as well as a first-hand acquaintance with the monuments, if possible, and an understanding of their relative chronology. The direction of writing, and as many external features of the script as possible, must be identified. Above all, are there word-dividers or any other features which can distinguish words? The next task (only feasible if there are sufficient texts) is to separate the functionally distinct signs (graphemes) from the individual or distributional variants: e.g., in English, the graphic distinction between *a* and *o* is significant, but *z* and *ʒ* are merely graphic variants of the same letter. The total number of graphemes then helps to determine the nature of the writing system. A system with fewer than thirty signs is likely to be alphabetic, while one with fifty to one hundred signs is probably syllabic. Some two hundred to four hundred signs normally point to a system with both logographic and phonetic signs.

It is essential to study the frequency and distribution of the signs (Koskenniemi et al. 1970). It is also necessary to compare similar sequences of signs in the hope of recognizing grammatical features such as prefixation or affixation. Computers may be invaluable for this type of work (Packard 1971). In a simple syllabic system, the decipherer may be able to establish a grid of the type set up by Ventris for Linear B.

The crucial step is identification of the language, and the attribution of meanings and/or phonetic values to the signs or sequences of signs. When there is a bilingual document, those elements which are likely to recur in comparable phonetic forms in both texts (personal names, place names, etc.) must be identified. It may then become possible to recognize other forms; and it may become clear whether the script conceals a known language. If the language is not known, interpretation is still possible if there are sufficient texts, and if the bilingual evidence is adequate. It is also possible that the language, though unknown, is related to known languages; if so, a judicious use of the combinatory method (a contextual approach) and of the etymological method can lead to satisfactory results. A pure etymological approach is in general dangerous and ought to be avoided.

In the absence of a bilingual document, information about the content of the text can be provided by the typology of the texts themselves—funerary monuments, dedications, royal statements, etc.—and by their historical background. Some logographic elements may be immediately interpretable (e.g. numbers, or logograms for men and women); some formulae may be expected. Comparison of the signs with formally similar signs of other scripts must be done with extreme caution, but it may sometimes be useful. Yet even if some of the signs can be assigned phonetic values, there is no guarantee of interpretation if the language is not known.

A decipherment must be tested not on the basis of the method used to achieve it, but on its results. If correct, it must permit an interpretation of the text which does not contradict expectations based on external or internal factors: typology of the monument, historical considerations, arrangement of the text, pictograms numerals, etc. The text should be linguistically coherent. A decipherment of chronologically and geographically coherent texts which yields a mixture of early and late forms, or of geographically incompatible features, is suspect.

In general, the decipherment of a script used for a known language is possible if the body of evidence is not too small; alphabets and simple syllabic systems are easier to decipher than logographic-syllabic systems. It is far more difficult (and sometimes impossible) to decipher a script used for an unknown language. In favorable circumstances, a decipherment may be possible, but it is not always the case that all signs can be assigned a value, and that all texts can be fully interpreted. Contrary to usual belief, most decipherments do not result from the sudden cracking of codes by isolated geniuses who rely exclusively on the sheer power of their intelligence and erudition. In a number of instances, the process of decipherment is extremely slow, and advances are made through the cumulative efforts of a number of experts. Thus the study of the so-called Hieroglyphic Hittite (now Luwian), a logographic-syllabic script used to write an Indo-European language in Anatolia and Syria of the 2nd to 1st millennia BCE, started in the 1910s, obtained considerable results in the 1930s, and had most of these confirmed by the discovery of a bilingual text in the 1940s. This led to the first glossary and full list of signs in the 1960s. The work gained new impetus in the 1970s and 1980s with the attribution of new values to some very frequent signs, and with a number of new editions of texts. Decipherment of the script of the 1st millennium is now almost complete, barring unexpected developments (Friedrich 1966a:72–84, Pope 1975:136–145, Hawkins et al. 1974). Hieroglyphic Luwian is not unique; a similar account could be given for numerous other decipherments.

ANNA MORPURGO DAVIES

BIBLIOGRAPHY

AALTO, PENTTI. 1945. *Notes on methods of decipherment of unknown writings and languages.* (Studia orientalia, 11:4.) Helsinki: Societas Linguistica Fennica.

CHADWICK, JOHN. 1973. Linear B. In *Current trends in linguistics,* vol. 11, *Diachronic, areal, and typological linguistics,* edited by Thomas A. Sebeok, pp. 537–568. The Hague: Mouton.

COHEN, MARCEL. 1958. *La grande invention de l'écriture et son évolution.* 3 vols. Paris: Klincksieck.

FRIEDRICH, JOHANNES. 1966a. *Entzifferung verschollener Schriften und Sprachen.* 2d ed. Berlin: Springer. Translated as *Extinct languages* (New York: Philosophical Library; London: P. Owen, 1957).

FRIEDRICH, JOHANNES. 1966b. *Geschichte der Schrift.* Heidelberg: Winter.

GELB, IGNACE J. 1952. *A study of writing: The foundations of grammatology.* Chicago: University of Chicago Press. Revised ed., 1963.

GELB, IGNACE J. 1973. Written records and decipherment. In *Current trends in linguistics,* vol. 11, *Diachronic, areal, and typological linguistics,* edited by Thomas A. Sebeok, pp. 253–284. The Hague: Mouton.

GELB, IGNACE J. 1974. Records, writing, and decipherment. *Visible Language* 8.293–318.

HAWKINS, J. D.; ANNA MORPURGO DAVIES; & GÜNTER NEUMANN. 1974. *Hittite hieroglyphs and Luwian: New evidence for the connection.* (Nachrichten der Akademie der Wissenschaften in Göttingen, Philosophisch-historische Klasse, 1973:6.) Göttingen: Vandenhoeck & Ruprecht.

KOSKENNIEMI, SEPPO, et al. 1970. A method to classify characters of unknown ancient scripts. *Linguistics* 61.65–91.

LECLANT, JEAN, ed. 1975. *Le déchiffrement des écritures et des langues: Colloque du XXIX Congrès des Orientalistes, Paris, juillet 1973.* Paris: L'Asiathèque.

PACKARD, DAVID W. 1971. Computer techniques in the study of the Minoan Linear script A. *Kadmos* 10.52–59.

POPE, MAURICE. 1975. *The story of decipherment: From Egyptian hieroglyphic to Linear B.* London: Thames & Hudson. New York: Scribner.

RAS. 1975. *Proceedings of the Symposium on the Undeciphered Languages, held in London 25–27 July 1973.* (Journal of the Royal Asiatic Society, 1975:2.) London: Royal Asiatic Society.

TRAGER, GEORGE L. 1974. Writing and writing systems. In *Current trends in linguistics,* vol. 12, *Linguistics and adjacent arts and sciences,* edited by Thomas A. Sebeok, pp. 373–496. The Hague: Mouton.

VOEGELIN, C. F., & F. M. VOEGELIN. 1963. Patterns of discovery in the decipherment of different types of alphabets. *American Anthropologist* 65.1231–1253.

DEFOID LANGUAGES

DEFOID LANGUAGES constitute a group, also called Yoruboid-Akokoid languages, spoken in Benin, in Togo, and in southwestern Nigeria. They form a subgroup of the Benue-Congo branch of the Niger-Còngo family [*qq.v.*]. The best-known language of the group is Yoruba [*q.v.*]. The subclassification of the Defoid languages given in Figure 1 follows Hounkpati B. C. Capo, 'Defoid', in *The Niger-Congo languages,* ed. by John Bendor-Samuel (Lanham, Md.: University Press of America, 1989), pp. 275–290.

LANGUAGE LIST

Aguna: spoken in Zou Province, Benin. Also called Awuna or Agunaco. Speakers are bilingual in Fon-gbe.

Akoko, North: spoken in Akoko Division, Ondo State, Nigeria, and in Ijumu District, Kabba Division, Kwara State.

Cabe: spoken in Borgou and Zou Provinces, Benin. Also called Caabe or Ede Cabe.

Ica: spoken in Zou Province, Benin. Also called Ede Ica.

Idaca: spoken in Zou Province, Benin. Also called Idaaca or Ede Idaca. Many loanwords from Fon-gbe.

Ife: 100,000 speakers reported in 1987, including 68,100

FIGURE 1. *Subgrouping of Defoid Languages*

Akokoid (North Akoko)
Yoruboid
  Edekiri (Yoruba-Itsekiri)
    Aguna, Cabe, Ica, Idaca, Ife, Ije, Isekiri, Mokole, Nago, Ulukwumi, Yoruba
  Igala

around Atakpamé, Gli, and Datcha in southeast central Togo; and 32,000 in Zou Province, Benin. Also called Baate or Ana-Ife. Ana is the official name in Togo.

Igala: 800,000 speakers reported in 1989, in Ankpa, Idah, and Dekina Divisions, Benue State, Nigeria; and in Ishan and Anoicha Divisions, Bendel State, and Anambra Division, Anambra State. Also called Igara. Used in initial primary education.

Ije: spoken in Zou Province, Benin. Also called Holi or Ede Ije.

Isekiri: 500,000 speakers reported in 1989, in Warri and West Benin Divisions, Bendel State, Nigeria. Also called Itsekiri, Ishekiri, Shekiri, Jekri, Chekiri, Iwere, Irhobo, Warri, Iselema-Otu, or Selemo. Used in initial primary education.

Mokole: 10,000 speakers reported in 1989, in Borgou Province, Benin. Also called Mokwale, Monkole, or Féri.

Nago: spoken in Weme and Atakora Provinces, Benin. Also called Nagots, Nagot, or Ede Nago. Some speakers are bilingual in Yoruba.

Ulukwumi: spoken in Aniocha Division, Bendel State, Nigeria.

Yoruba: around 20,000,000 speakers reported in 1987, including 16,000,000 in Oyo, Ogun, Ondo, and Lagos States, and in parts of Kwara State, Nigeria, with 393,000 in Zou and Ouéme Provinces, Benin, and some in Togo. Also called Yooba or Yariba. The official language of southwestern Nigeria.

DEIXIS. Expressions whose reference or extension is systematically determined by aspects of the speech situation (words like *I, you, now, this* and *here*) are called DEICTIC or INDEXICAL terms. Sometimes they denote aspects of the speech situation itself (as with *I*), but sometimes what they denote is only partially determined by reference to the speech situation (as in *local pub, long ago, next year, distant planet, the late president*).

Linguists tend to think of deixis as a unitary field, anchored around the speech event, embracing PERSON DEIXIS (lst and 2nd person pronouns and forms of address); SPATIAL DEIXIS (demonstratives, locative adverbs like *here,* relational positionals like *in front of*); TEMPORAL DEIXIS (tense, adverbials like *today, now,* and *next week*); as well as SOCIAL DEIXIS (e.g. honorifics) and DISCOURSE DEIXIS (like *the latter, the aforesaid*). Typically, the unmarked 'anchor' or deictic center is the current spatio-temporal locus of the speaker. Thus in many languages a demonstrative like *that* can be glossed as distal from the speaker, but in some languages the addressee (or other participants) may play a subsidiary role; thus Japanese *sore* 'that' must be glossed as proximal to the addressee. Hence, as speakers alternate in conversation, the reference of the same deictic expressions tends to change, making acquisition of these terms difficult for children (Tanz 1980; Wales 1986).

Confusingly, philosophers sometimes oppose the terms 'indexical' and 'deictic', so that indexical expressions denote aspects of the speech event as above, while 3rd person pronouns (not deictic in the linguistic sense) are termed deictic wherever they are not anaphoric. One should note too a divergent conception of indexicality in the work of Charles S. Peirce. Philosophers also tend to think of demonstratives as distinct from spatial indexicals, while linguists tend to merge the two classes.

Deixis has a fundamental importance for theories of meaning, because it relativizes the content of utterances to the situation of the utterance; in short, deixis makes it necessary to talk about the interpretation of utterances, not of sentences in the abstract (*I am thirty-three* will be true only if said by certain speakers at certain times). This context-relativity of interpretation proves pervasive; thus, in the familiar European languages (but not in Chinese) virtually all sentences, even if they lack indexical words, have tense and are thus interpreted relative to the time of speaking. Other languages force other kinds of obligatory deictic relativity; e.g., Kwakiutl requires all N[oun] P[hrase]s to be marked for visibility/invisibility from the speaker's locus, while Javanese forces encoding of the social rank of speaker relative to addressee in most sentences. In general, there is a great deal of cross-linguistic variability in deictic categories. Taking systems of demonstratives and locative adverbs as an example: Malagasy encodes seven degrees of extension away from the speaker; Samal appears to encode proximity to speaker vs. addressee vs. non-addressed participant vs. non-participant; and Dyirbal encodes 'above', 'below', 'level with speaker', and 'upriver' vs. 'downriver from speaker' (see Anderson & Keenan 1985, Fillmore 1975).

It is becoming increasingly clear that theorists have underestimated both the complexity and the extent of deixis (for the range of problems, see Fillmore 1975, Jarvella & Klein 1982, and Levinson 1983, 1988). Thus *behind* looks like a two-place relation *(The cat is behind the car),* but it has a covert third deictic argument ('The cat is behind the car from the speaker's locus or the car's intrinsic front'). More generally, NPs may always have deictic elements: definite NPs presuppose contextual uniqueness; quantified NPs presuppose a contextually given domain of discourse; many NPs may have implicit temporal reference *(the president of the United States)*; and even proper names rarely refer uniquely without implicit reference to speakers' connections to entities around them. Another problem is that many deictic anchorings can be shifted from the speech situation to narrative reference points *(John realized that now that he was here in the countryside the local pubs were far away)*. All this means that the treatments of deixis in formal semantic theories like that of Montague are hopelessly inadequate. [*See* Semantics, *article on* Truth-Conditional and Model-Theoretic Semantics.] This has led to new theories, especially Situation Semantics (Barwise & Perry 1983), where a more serious attempt is made to capture the contextual relativity of semantic interpretation. [*See also* Pragmatics, Implicature, and Presupposition.]

STEPHEN C. LEVINSON

BIBLIOGRAPHY

ANDERSON, STEPHEN R., & EDWARD L. KEENAN. 1985. Deixis. In *Language typology and syntactic description,* vol. 3, *Grammatical categories and the lexicon,* edited by Timothy Shopen, pp. 259–308. Cambridge & New York: Cambridge University Press.

BARWISE, JON, & JOHN PERRY. 1983. *Situations and attitudes.* Cambridge, Mass.: MIT Press.

FILLMORE, CHARLES J. 1975. *Santa Cruz lectures on deixis, 1971.* Bloomington: Indiana University Linguistics Club.

JARVELLA, ROBERT J., & WOLFGANG KLEIN, eds. 1982. *Speech, place and action: Studies of deixis and related topics.* New York: Wiley.

LEVINSON, STEPHEN C. 1983. *Pragmatics.* Cambridge & New York: Cambridge University Press.

LEVINSON, STEPHEN C. 1988. Putting linguistics on a proper footing. In *Erving Goffman,* edited by P. Drew & A. Wootton, pp. 161–227. Cambridge: Polity Press.

LYONS, JOHN. 1977. *Semantics.* 2 vols. Cambridge & New York: Cambridge University Press.

TANZ, CHRISTINE. 1980. *Studies in the acquisition of deictic terms.* (Cambridge studies in linguistics, 26.) Cambridge & New York: Cambridge University Press.

WALES, ROGER. 1986. Deixis. In *Language acquisition,* 2d ed., edited by Paul Fletcher & Michael Garman, pp. 401–428. Cambridge & New York: Cambridge University Press.

DELETION. Throughout the history of generative grammar (Chomsky 1957 onward), various phenomena have been argued to involve deletion transformations. Deletion rules were invoked to account for the disparity between deep structures and their syntactically 'reduced' surface strings. For example, Katz & Postal 1964 accounted for the properties of English imperatives by proposing deletion of an underlying *you will*; and Ross 1967 proposed a set of rules (including VP Deletion and Sluicing) to delete constituents under identity with an antecedent. [*See* Coordination; Ellipsis; Recoverability.] Ross also proposed a 'pruning' mechanism whereby empty nodes could be deleted prior to the surface level. In addition, Rosenbaum 1967 accounted for the interpretation of coreferential complement subjects by positing that they were derived from full N[oun] P[hrase]s deleted by Equi NP-Deletion [*see* Control]. Postal 1970, 1972 provided a similar account of the interpretation of pronouns, arguing that they derived from deep-structure full NPs which were subsequently deleted.

Debates concerning the descriptive adequacy of deletion rules centered on the interpretation of deleted constituents. Thus Jackendoff 1972 noted certain problems in using deletion to account for the interpretation of pronouns and complement subjects; he proposed an alternative analysis where both pronouns and empty complement subject NPs could be base-generated, and coindexed with an appropriate antecedent for interpretation. Wasow 1972 observed analogous problems with a deletion account of ellipted VPs; he argued for a similar 'interpretive' approach where empty VPs, like empty complement subjects, could be base-generated and coindexed with an antecedent (cf. Williams 1977; and see Sag 1976, Hankamer & Sag 1976 for an alternative analysis).

In the late 1970s, the notion that constituents could be generated empty and coindexed with an antecedent was extended to account for the relation of categories derived by movement, i.e. TRACES [*q.v.*], to their antecedents. Moreover, Chomsky 1977 observed that certain constraints, applying to the distribution of base-generated empty categories, also constrain the distribution of trace—and that certain deletion operations can even be argued to be derived by movement. Chomsky argued (contra Bresnan 1973, 1975) that sentences like *John is taller than Ron is* involve movement rather than deletion. He also discarded unconstrained pruning mechanisms in favor of a number of specific deletions typically involving COMP—S′ Deletion and Complementizer Deletion—which are required for particular grammars (see also Chomsky 1981). [*See* Complementation, *article on* 'COMP' in Formal Grammar.] Work of the late 1980s continues to reflect the idea of parallel constraints on base-generated empty categories and traces; thus Zagona 1988 argues that ellipted VPs, like traces, are subject to Chomsky's 1981 Empty Category Principle—a proposal extended by Lobeck 1987 to constrain ellipsis across categories in general. [*See* Government; Ellipsis.]

ANNE LOBECK

BIBLIOGRAPHY

BRESNAN, JOAN. 1973. Syntax of the comparative clause construction in English. *Linguistic Inquiry* 4.275–343.

BRESNAN, JOAN. 1975. Comparative deletion and constraints on transformation. *Linguistic Analysis* 1.25–74.

CHOMSKY, NOAM. 1957. *Syntactic structures.* (Janua linguarum, Series minor, 4.) The Hague: Mouton.

CHOMSKY, NOAM. 1977. On WH-movement. In *Formal syntax,* edited by Peter Culicover et al., pp. 71–132. New York: Academic Press.

CHOMSKY, NOAM. 1981. *Lectures on government and binding.* (Studies in generative grammar, 9.) Dordrecht: Foris.

HANKAMER, JORGE, & IVAN A. SAG. 1976. Deep and surface anaphora. *Linguistic Inquiry* 7.391–428.

JACKENDOFF, RAY. 1972. *Semantic interpretation in generative grammar.* (Studies in linguistics series, 2.) Cambridge, Mass.: MIT Press.

KATZ, JERROLD J., & PAUL M. POSTAL. 1964. *An integrated theory of linguistic descriptions.* Cambridge, Mass.: MIT Press.

LOBECK, ANNE C. 1987. *Syntactic constraints on VP ellipsis.* Bloomington: Indiana University Linguistics Club.

POSTAL, PAUL M. 1970. On coreferential complement subject deletion. *Linguistic Inquiry* 1.439–500.

POSTAL, PAUL M. 1972. Some further limitations of interpretive theories of anaphora. *Linguistic Inquiry* 3.349–371.

ROSENBAUM, PETER S. 1967. *The grammar of English predicate complement constructions.* Cambridge, Mass.: MIT Press.

ROSS, JOHN R. 1967. *Constraints on variables in syntax.* MIT dissertation. Published as *Infinite syntax* (Norwood, N.J.: Ablex, 1986).

SAG, IVAN A. 1976. *Deletion and Logical Form.* MIT dissertation. Published, New York: Garland, 1979.

WASOW, THOMAS. 1972. *Anaphoric relations in English.* MIT dissertation. Revised as *Anaphora in generative grammar* (Ghent: Story-Scientia, 1979).

WILLIAMS, EDWIN S. 1977. Discourse and Logical Form. *Linguistic Inquiry* 8.103–139.

ZAGONA, KAREN. 1988. Proper government of antecedentless VP in English and Spanish. *Natural Language & Linguistic Theory* 6.95–128.

DEMENTIA AND LANGUAGE. 'Dementia' currently refers to cognitive loss resulting from certain diseases, e.g. Alzheimer's disease, or from other biological states, e.g. malnutrition or depression. Changes in language use are characteristic of the syndromes of dementia, as are memory decline, behavioral changes, and difficulty in manipulating acquired knowledge.

The linguistic performance traditionally associated with dementia includes naming disturbance, empty speech, press of speech (logorrhea), repetitions (echolalia and palilalia), and muteness. For most of the past hundred years, demented behavior was considered a psychiatric disorder, and attempts were made to classify its linguistic manifestations in relation to those of other psychiatric disturbances (e.g. Séglas 1892).

In the 1970s and 1980s, increasing Western medical study has resulted in clearer understanding of the neurological bases of dementia. Some of these involve primarily CORTICAL damage, e.g. A[lzheimer's] D[ementia] and multi-infarct dementia; others involve primarily SUBCORTICAL damage, e.g. the dementia seen in one-third of patients with Parkinson's disease. In the subcortical dementias, motor performance is primarily affected—e.g. in dysarthria, acceleration (festination) of speech, or illegible handwriting; in the cortical dementias, language performance is affected. (For reference, see Irigaray 1973, Bayles & Kaszniak 1987, Au et al. 1988.)

During the progressive decline involved in AD, scores on naming tests decrease, and responses become semantically farther from the target; comprehension of oral and written materials deteriorates, especially for longer and/or more complex materials; and discourse becomes increasingly devoid of content. However, phonological and syntactic production are spared, as is the ability to read aloud. Automatic speech tasks—e.g. reciting known series, such as the alphabet or the days of the week—soon show omissions or additions. Certain pragmatic abilities are spared until late in the course of dementia, e.g. use of social formulas; others decline early, e.g. appreciating inference. Metalinguistic abilities decline; indeed, it is hard to engage patients in the tasks.

A stage model of progressive decline has proven useful in projecting the language changes of the cortical dementias, especially AD. In the early stages, patients resemble anomic aphasics; by the middle stages, they closely resemble those with Wernicke's aphasia or transcortical sensory aphasia (most strikingly with regard to empty speech, logorrhea, and poor comprehension). By the later stages, we find echolalia, then palilalia, then muteness; and other non-language behavioral deficits render confusion with aphasia unlikely.

Distinguishing the linguistic performance of early- and mid-stage AD from that of certain aphasic syndromes is difficult; thus the question arises as to whether the linguistic disturbance results from damage to brain areas associated with language, or whether language similar to that in aphasia can result from damage to areas responsible for non-language cognitive abilities, such as ideation, memory, attention, and self-monitoring.

Bayles & Kaszniak 1987 argue that disturbance of semantic memory accounts for the breakdown of language and communication in AD; others (e.g. Obler & Albert 1984, 1985) maintain that the predilection for cellular damage to frontal and temporal areas of the brain in AD makes the language areas particularly vulnerable to deficit, especially in conjunction with the decline in the other non-language cognitive mechanisms listed above.

The lexicon is the linguistic level which has received the most experimental study in the dementias. Evidence exists to show primary breakdown in lexical access, with secondary breakdown in lexical representation, and perhaps also in visual perception of the objects to be named. The evidence for breakdown at the stage of lexical access or recall comes from naming studies which find that demented patients make errors related semantically to the target—or use circumlocutions to explain what the object to be named does, instead of naming it. Such responses suggest that knowledge of what the item is remains intact. Evidence from free-association paradigms indicates that demented patients make many fewer paradigmatic (but not syntagmatic) responses than do normal controls. This finding argues for some semantic or conceptual breakdown as well, perhaps resulting from loss of the semantic markers for specific lexical features.

The relation of age at the onset of dementia to the degree and pace (but not the type) of linguistic impairment, remains controversial. Presenile AD, with onset prior to age sixty-five, appears to show earlier and more severe linguistic disturbance than does senile AD. In the rare cases of strong familial AD, with onset in the thirties and forties, language/communication disturbance appears strikingly early in the course of decline.

Lay belief assumes that the behavioral changes of dementia simply represent normal or accelerated aging ('senility'); however, certain admittedly infrequent behaviors—e.g. 'klang'-association, i.e. compulsive phonologically motivated response to phonological cues on a naming task—are seen only in the language of demented patients. More frequent among bilingual demented patients is inappropriate choice of language, or code-switching with a monolingual interlocutor; this phenomenon is virtually never seen among bilingual normals or aphasics. [*See* Bilingualism; Neural Structures.]

LORAINE K. OBLER

BIBLIOGRAPHY

AU, RHODA, et al. 1988. The relation of aphasia to dementia. *Aphasiology* 2.161–173.

BAYLES, KATHRYN A., & ALFRED W. KASZNIAK. 1987. *Communication and cognition in normal aging and dementia.* Boston: Little Brown.

IRIGARAY, LUCE. 1973. *Le langage de déments.* (Approaches to semiotics, 24.) The Hague: Mouton.

OBLER, LORAINE K., & MARTIN L. ALBERT. 1984. Language in aging. In *Neurology of aging,* edited by Martin L. Albert, pp. 245–253. Oxford & New York: Oxford University Press.

OBLER, LORAINE K., & MARTIN L. ALBERT. 1985. Language skills across adulthood. In *Handbook on the psychology of aging,* 2d ed., edited by James E. Birren & K. Warner Schaie, pp. 463–473. New York: Van Nostrand Reinhold.

SÉGLAS, JULES. 1892. *Des troubles du langage chez les aliénés.* Paris: Rueff.

DENOTATION. *See* Sense, Denotation, and Reference.

DEPENDENCY PHONOLOGY. *See* Particle Phonology and Dependency Phonology.

DERIVATIONAL MORPHOLOGY is empirically based on D[ERIVATIONAL] affixes, i.e. morphemes which are bound and placed before I[NFLECTIONAL] AFFIXES, in cases where the lexical category requires inflection. (For general reference, see Motsch 1988.)

1. Definitions. Derivational morphology rests on the following abstract system of definitions:

(a) A WORD FORM is a word plus one or more I-affixes.
(b) A WORD is (i) a root, (ii) a root plus a D-affix, (iii) a root plus a root, (iv) a word plus a D-affix, or (v) a word plus a word. In addition, a root or a word which is a co-constituent of a D-affix is called a BASE. [*See* Stem and Root; Words.]

In this definition, I-affix, D-affix, and root are primitive terms, empirically motivated by restrictions on ordering (I-affixes vs. words) or occurrence (affixes vs. roots). If we assume that I-affixes, D-affixes, and roots are separate categories of word structure, then I-morphology, D-morphology, and compounding may be considered as different branches of morphology, dealing respectively with three separate types of systematic relations between words and I-affixes, between bases and D-affixes, and between words within a word. However, there are several problems with this distinction. For instance, it has been argued that both I-morphology and D-morphology require the same sort of formal processes (cf. Lieber 1980).

A category-based distinction between root and D-affix, and consequently a fundamental difference between D-morphology and compounding, is argued explicitly by Selkirk 1982, but has been denied by Höhle 1982. However, there is a widely shared view that the distinction between prefix and suffix is not a categorial one; prefixation and suffixation are assumed to be governed by the same types of rules. [*See* Affixation.]

The restriction of D-morphology to D-affixes presupposes an essential difference between affixation and other techniques involved in morphological processes, such as CONVERSION [*q.v.*], ABLAUT, and REDUPLICATION [*q.v.*]. These techniques, however, differ only in the way in which semantic processes of the same kind are realized linguistically (see Dressler 1977).

2. Rules and productivity. From a grammatical point of view, derivatives are essentially considered to be the products of rules. This is in keeping with the general assumption that complex linguistic forms of a language may be reduced to units and rules of some type. W[ORD]-F[ORMATION] R[ULE]S, then, are rules that combine word structure units to form new complex words. Complex words typically serve to enrich the permanent vocabulary of a language. Other functions are recategorization (e.g. pure nominalization in languages like English, German, or Russian), and stylistic variation (such as diminutives).

As a result of the first function, the vocabulary of a language includes many derived words from earlier periods of the language, which are related to rules only in a rather limited way. Such limited regularities are covered by the concept of R[EDUNDANCY] RULES. R-rules of the kind proposed by Jackendoff 1975 allow for explicit description of the dependent information, i.e. of (sub)regularities, in the representation of the lexical entries which are part of the permanent lexicon of a language. Such rules account for all types of restrictions which run counter to full regularity. As a borderline case, these rules may be identical to those which form new derivatives, i.e. to WFRs which involve affixes.

The study of WFRs is concerned only with that part of the lexicon which is covered by R-rules which correspond to WFRs, and ad-hoc formations in texts which are presumably the products of WFRs. On one hand, the analysis of lexicalized complex words presupposes the study of the general grammatical properties of WFRs; on the other, it goes beyond the types of regularities relevant to the grammar.

Characteristic of many D-processes are the greater or lesser restrictions on the class of base words which belong to a given process (cf. Aronoff 1976). Often it is not possible to restrict the class using only syntactic and morphological categories. In some cases, it is scarcely possible even to find a proper non-ad-hoc semantic description. There is another peculiarity, labeled the PRODUCTIVITY of a certain type of D-process; some new words predicted by a tentative WFR, abstracted from lexical entries with the same kind of dependent information, come up against acceptability restrictions. Different proposals have been made to account for productivity (Aronoff 1976, Górska 1982, Dressler et al. 1987:87 ff., 112 ff.).

Productivity is frequently considered to be a mere performance phenomenon, to be ignored in grammatical analysis. Some approaches claim a correspondence between productivity and the restrictedness of a class of bases (cf. Aronoff 1976). One promising way to account for these phenomena might be to elaborate on Hermann Paul's reflections on analogy in morphological processes. A suitable program could be sketched as follows: productivity and acceptability are phenomena which depend on different degrees of transparency of dependent information in lexicalized derivatives. The highest degree of transparency is achieved in R-rules corresponding to productive WFRs, and the lowest in the analysis of a simple lexical entry like German *einsam* 'lonely', which is semantically opaque (similar to Eng. *on+ly*). Nevertheless, *zweisam* 'two alone' has been coined by analogy with *einsam*. The main task is to discover what kinds of deviations from properties of productive rules affect the transparency of dependent information to a greater or lesser extent. The explanatory basis of this description is probably to be found in the psychological mechanisms of analogy.

3. Derivational processes. In general, it is claimed that the study of the rules which underlie D-processes in a particular language has to account for all general and particular language-specific properties of such rules, as well as for universal constraints on the form of derivational rules. The formal description of D-processes has to provide the following sorts of information: (i) phonological form of the affix, (ii) syntactic category and subcategory frame of the derivative, (iii) restrictions defining the class of bases available to the affix, (iv) diacritical features of the derivative, and (v) semantic form of the derivative.

Since (ii) and (v) show significant relations to the same sort of information in the representation of the corresponding base, it is necessary to analyze in detail the systematic aspects of 'argument inheritance', or the rebuilding of argument structure in derived words, as well as types of semantic amalgamation. [*See* Inheritance.]

Traditional linguistic approaches to D-morphology postulated a separate component dealing with word formation. In earlier versions of generative grammar, D-processes as well as compounding were treated as syntactic transformations. According to this concept, word formation is only a special case of the construction of syntactic phrases. The transformationalist position, however, has been criticized as inadequate on empirical and theoretical grounds. The general requirement on the study of D-processes since the end of the 1970s has been to find a few simple principles which will enable the linguist to explain the complex phenomena which can be observed in word structures. Besides grammatical principles, semantic and pragmatic ones must be taken into account. A favorite topic is the question of whether there are separate principles which govern word structure.

In all mainstream approaches [*see* Generative Morphology], special rules defining the grammatical properties of derivatives have been elaborated. However, views differ both on the form of WFRs and on their underlying grammatical principles. The most prominent positions are the following.

3.1. WFRs include all aspects of D-processes: the internal morphological structure, the external properties, and the semantic structure of the derived word. Examples are the WFRs and R-rules proposed by Aronoff 1976 and Jackendoff 1975, respectively. Aronoff takes the view that WFRs are constrained by general principles of word structure, such as the Word-Based Hypothesis, the Unitary Base Hypothesis, and the Binary Branching Hypothesis (cf. Scalise 1984).

3.2. WFRs determine the syntax of words; and this in turn is the basis of semantic interpretation (cf. Lieber 1980, Selkirk 1982, Toman 1987). Within this general framework, however, there are different views concerning the principles that govern word syntax. Some linguists argue that syntactic principles (such as X-bar Theory or the θ-criterion) also apply to word structure. Another line of argument stresses the difference between phrase structure and word structure, although similarities are admitted (cf. Selkirk 1982).

3.3. Possible words are defined by general principles of semantic interpretation. The interesting properties of word structure, like argument inheritance and categorial restrictions, can be explained on the basis of these principles. The remaining syntactic properties are very trivial (cf. Fanselow 1988).

3.4. In a further approach, Beard 1986 proposes a strict separation of lexeme and morpheme, as units belonging to entirely different subsystems of the grammar. According to Beard, the structure of lexemes is determined by rules operating on semantic and syntactic properties of lexical entries. By contrast, the properties of morphemes (e.g. suffixes) are governed by entirely separate principles.

4. Semantic properties. Until now, semantic properties of D-processes have been analyzed more or less on an observational level. In the traditional study of word formation, for example, the meaning of affixes has been described more or less intuitively. The same is true of semantically based classifications like nomina agentis, nomina actionis, resultatives, diminutives, collectives, etc. Semantic considerations also include the distinction between modification and transposition, which has been adopted in many works by Soviet linguists on word formation. DIMINUTIVES [*q.v.*] are a typical example of modification; here the concept denoted by the base is semantically modified by the concept denoted by the affix. Transposition encompasses all other types of semantic processes involved in D-rules.

A more precise and theoretically elaborated analysis of D-processes is an important desideratum. Unresolved problems include:

(a) The design of a proper semantic representation of the meaning of derivatives, especially of D-affixes.
(b) The analysis of different kinds of amalgamation, including semantic aspects of argument inheritance and the creation of argument structures conveyed by affixes.
(c) The analysis of operations which will give explicit statements of encyclopedic knowledge, as part of the processes of semantic interpretation.

(d) The search for semantic peculiarities of D-affixes as opposed to other types of linguistic expressions, such as I-affixes, function words, or roots. Aspects of this problem are discussed by Bybee 1985.

WOLFGANG MOTSCH

BIBLIOGRAPHY

ARONOFF, MARK. 1976. *Word formation in generative grammar.* (Linguistic Inquiry monographs, 1.) Cambridge, Mass.: MIT Press.

BEARD, ROBERT. 1986. *On the separation of derivation from morphology.* Bloomington: Indiana University Linguistics Club.

BYBEE, JOAN L. 1985. *Morphology: A study of the relation between meaning and form.* (Typological studies in language, 9.) Amsterdam: Benjamins.

DRESSLER, WOLFGANG U. 1977. *Grundfragen der Morphonologie.* Vienna: Verlag der Österreichischen Akademie der Wissenschaften.

DRESSLER, WOLFGANG U., et al. 1987. *Leitmotifs in Natural Morphology.* (Studies in Language, Companion series, 10.) Amsterdam: Benjamins.

FANSELOW, GISBERT. 1988. Word formation and the human conceptual system. In Motsch 1988, pp. 31–52.

GÓRSKA, ELŻBIETA. 1982. Formal and functional restrictions on the productivity of word formation rules. *Folia Linguistica* 16.149–162.

HÖHLE, TILMAN N. 1982. Über Komposition und Derivation: Zur Konstituentenstruktur von Wortbildungsprodukten im Deutschen. *Zeitschrift für Sprachwissenschaft* 1.76–112.

JACKENDOFF, RAY. 1975. Morphological and semantic regularities in the lexicon. *Language* 51.639–671.

LIEBER, ROCHELLE. 1980. *On the organization of the lexicon.* MIT dissertation. Published, Bloomington: Indiana University Linguistics Club, 1981.

MOTSCH, WOLFGANG U., ed. 1988. *The contribution of word structure theories to the study of word formation.* (Linguistische Studien, Reihe A, 179.) Berlin: Zentralinstitut für Sprachwissenschaften, Akademie der Wissenschaften der DDR.

SCALISE, SERGIO. 1984. *Generative morphology.* (Studies in generative grammar, 18.) Dordrecht: Foris.

SELKIRK, ELISABETH O. 1982. *The syntax of words.* (Linguistic Inquiry monographs, 7.) Cambridge, Mass.: MIT Press.

TOMAN, JINDŘICH. 1987. *Wortsyntax: Eine Diskussion ausgewählter Probleme deutscher Wortbildung.* 2d ed. (Linguistische Arbeiten, 137.) Tübingen: Niemeyer.

DEVELOPMENTAL DISORDERS. *See* Dyslexia; Dysphasia.

DEVELOPMENT OF LANGUAGE. *See* Acquisition of Language.

DIALECTOLOGY is the branch of linguistics which deals with the nature and distribution of variation in language. It has not been easy to define 'dialect' or to distinguish it from 'language'. One of the more successful definitions is that of Ammon (1983:64):

> A dialect is a language such that (i) there is at least one other language with which it has a high degree of similarity; (ii) there is no language which is regionally included within it as a proper part; and (iii) neither its writing system nor its pronunciation nor its lexicon nor its syntax is officially normalized.

(For general reference, see Kurath 1972, Chambers & Trudgill 1980, Francis 1983, Trudgill 1983, Kirk et al. 1985.)

1. History. Although dialectology did not become a formal discipline until the middle of the 19th century, knowledge and illustration of dialect differences go far back in linguistic and literary history. In Classical Greek, certain dialects were recognized as the appropriate media for certain types of literature: Ionic for epic, dating from Homer; Doric for odes, as in Pindar; Aeolic for lyric poetry; and Attic for drama—not to mention the use of her native dialect by Sappho of Lesbos. In English, Chaucer made comic use of Northern English in his 'Reeve's Tale', and Shakespeare identified the Welshman Fluellen by his curious phonology. But it was not until the latter part of the 19th century that serious study of dialect began. Notable were Ellis's extensive survey (1889) of the contemporary phonology of English dialects, and Winteler's study (1876) of the Kerenzen dialect of Switzerland; the latter strongly influenced the Neogrammarians Osthof and Brugmann.

The hypothesis of the Neogrammarians that sound change was exceptionless [*see* History of Linguistics, *article on* Comparative-Historical Linguistics] inspired one of the most ambitious dialect surveys ever undertaken—Georg Wenker's *Deutscher Sprachatlas,* begun in 1876, and in a sense still continuing. Starting as a modest attempt to study the boundary between High and Low German, this was ultimately extended to cover all Germany and Austria. Wenker used the method of translation: he sent out his list of forty model sentences to nearly fifty thousand schoolmasters, asking them to translate the sentences into local dialects with the help of native-speaking pupils. One unexpected result was the discovery of the so-called Rhenish Fan, a spreading pattern of ISOGLOSSES, which seems to refute the hypothesis that sound changes are without exception.

Twenty years after Wenker began his work, another great pioneering linguistic survey was begun: the *Atlas linguistique de la France,* conducted by the Swiss dialectologist Jules Gilliéron and his indefatigable fieldworker Edmond Edmont. It established what has come to be the favored method of dialect collection, in face-to-face interviews with native speakers by a trained phonetician, eliciting items from a set questionnaire. In only four years, Edmont visited more than six hundred localities throughout France, eliciting nearly two thousand items from each. The results were published as maps in thirteen large volumes (Gilliéron & Edmont 1902–1913). This work has been a primary influence on subsequent dialectological surveys the world over. There are now dialect atlases on this model from most countries of Europe, including Italy, Switzerland, Spain, Rumania, the Scandinavian countries, and even tiny Andorra.

2. Methodology. There are basically two types of dialect survey. The first and older type, often called 'traditional', is based on regional distribution, in the manner of Wenker and Gilliéron; this is often called DIALECT GEOGRAPHY. The more recent type emphasizes variation in speech according to social level, often concentrating on a few selected features; it is called SOCIOLINGUISTIC dialectology. [*See* Social Dialects.] Labov 1966, a study of sociolinguistic variation in New York City, is often cited as the first work of this type, although some of the methods had been used earlier. It has largely superseded the traditional type; however, important regional surveys are still being conducted.

Both methods require a large body of language—a CORPUS—as a basis for description and analysis. The corpus to be used consists of a sample of the particular feature or features of the dialect which are to be studied. These may include phonology or pronunciation, morphology, lexicon or vocabulary, and syntax or grammar. Sociolinguistic surveys in particular may also be concerned with informants' attitudes toward their dialect and that of others, and in the cultural interests and values which dialect reveals. The corpus must be gathered with care, to assure that it is representative of the population chosen for investigation.

3. Geographical dialectology. There are two different methods of collecting the data. As in Wenker's survey, questionnaires may be sent to various localities, to be filled in by a responsible person such as the local schoolteacher or clergyman—who may not, in fact, be a speaker of the local dialect. Or, as with the French atlas, the collection may be done in person by a fieldworker, who records data either in writing or on a tape-recorder. The advantage of the former, 'postal' method, which has been used less often in modern surveys, is that it can reach a larger number of sources, and thus can produce a large corpus at relatively low expense. The disadvantage is that it relies on amateurs who may not be actual speakers of the dialect, and who may have no training in phonetic transcription or other phases of language study. The advantage of the interview method is that the interviewer can make sure that the consultants are true speakers of the dialect, that they understand what is being asked, and that their answers are relevant and authentic. Its principal disadvantage is that it is both expensive and time-consuming, and thus results in a more restricted corpus.

Traditional dialect surveys have usually attempted to collect a corpus of the indigenous local dialect of ordinary speakers, who are familiar with it from childhood, and who use it regularly (at least in informal conversation among themselves). Such a dialect is sometimes called a BASILECT. It is not difficult to find and elicit, as long as one is dealing with a stable community, e.g. a small village whose inhabitants are not highly educated or well traveled, and who pursue occupations that do not bring them into frequent contact with speakers of a standard or cultivated variety of the language. Such communities were quite common in Europe at the time of Wenker and Gilliéron. But in modern times, with greater mobility and communication—and with the growth of urban centers which draw population from throughout a country, and even from beyond its borders—the situation is much altered. This has led to objections that traditional surveys are not representative of the actual language of the majority of the population. However, the method has been defended, chiefly on historical grounds; thus it is felt that the *patois* of French villages, now rapidly disappearing, is a sort of endangered species which, if it cannot be preserved, can at least be recorded for the benefit of future historians of the language. The traditional dialectologist is thus a kind of antiquary, collecting and recording the speech of the past.

Once the corpus of the basilect has been assembled, the question arises of how it is to be made public. The two common methods are lists and maps; more recently, tape-recordings of the original interviews have been made available. A list gives the responses from all localities, usually in geographic order. For example, Figure 1 (from Orton & Halliday 1963) lists the responses from five northern counties of England for the word *boots*. Only two lexical items appear: *boots* and *shoes*; the phrase *strong shoes,* reported from some localities, contrasts with *slender shoes* for ordinary footwear. Of particular interest is the variety of pronunciations of the vowel or diphthong in *boots*.

Lists have the obvious advantage of being easy and cheap to produce. Their principal shortcoming is that only the person intimately familiar with the geography can picture the regional distribution of the forms. Others will have to mark the variants on an outline map.

Maps, gathered into atlases, perform this function for the student. Map 1 shows, by means of symbols, the distribution of diphthongs in *boots* in the north of England (from Kolb 1966). The northeastern section has diphthongs that begin with a front vowel or glide, while the southwestern section has diphthongs that begin with a high back round vowel.

A refinement in the making of distributional maps uses isoglosses. An ISOGLOSS is a line that marks the extent of the area in which a particular feature appears, or an approximate boundary between two variants of the same

MAP 1. *Diphthongs in Northern England.* (From Kolb 1966:199.)

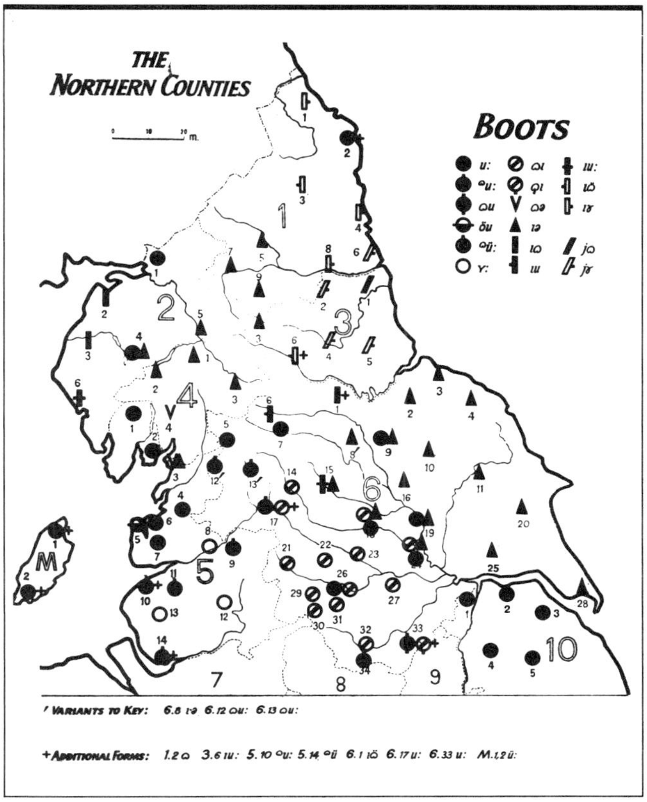

FIGURE 1. *List of Responses.* (From Orton & Halliday 1963:726.)

BOOTS*

Q. What do you call those things that you are wearing?

Rr. (STRONG) BOOTS/SHOES, HIGH BOOTS/TIES

Note 1—Sometimes the f.ws. had to press for the wanted word, and sometimes they omitted to rec. it.

Note 2—Forms of BOOT also occur at VI.14.25 and IX.8.6.

1 Nb 1 bɩɤts 2 bu:ts 3 bɩö̜ts 4 △bɩɤt 5 bɩəts 6 bjɤts 7 bɩəts 8 bɩøts 9 bɩəts

2 Cu 1 ʃɒɷz 2 st̯ɹaŋ bɩɷts 3 bɩɷts 4 bu:ts 5 bɩəts 6 p. bɩu:ts [not used]

3 Du 1 bjɷts, ○~¹ 2 bjɤts 3 bɩəts 4–5 bjɤts 6 bɩö̜ts, ○bɩu:ts²

4 We 1 st̯raŋ bɩəts 2 straŋ ʃᵒu:z, p. bɩəts [rare] 3 bɩəts 4 bɷəts

5 La 1 ʃu:z, bu:ts 2 bu:ts 3 bɷəts 4 bu:ts 5 böuts 6 ɛɩ bu:ts [lastɩksaɩdɩd bu:ts *elastic-sided boots*] 7 stɹəŋ ʃu:n 8 ʃᵚu:n, bʏ:ts ["modern"] 9 ʃɷn: ["older"], bᵒu:ts ["newer"] 10 ʃᵚü:n [old word], p. bᵚü:ts 11 bᵚu:ts 12 bʏ:ts 13 stɹɷŋ ʃʏ:z, p.p bʏ:ts [not used] 14 bᵚü:ts

feature. Map 2 is an isogloss map of England with a line that separates southern *child* from northern *bairn* (from Upton et al. 1987). Both are Old English words; but it is clear that, in the northern area of Scandinavian settlement, *bairn* has been reinforced by Old Norse *barn* (still Norwegian for 'child'). This map is of historical interest, since the isogloss runs parallel to (but a bit north of) the line established under King Alfred in the 9th century to mark the southern limit of the Danelaw, or area of Danish dominance.

Isogloss maps are rarely so simple; often the isoglosses are elaborately convoluted, as in Map 3, which shows two variant terms for 'molars' (from Orton & Wright 1974). Areas marked '1' have some form of *axle-teeth*; those marked '2' have *grinders*; and unmarked areas have either standard *molars,* or some other term like *double-teeth.* To fill in the unmarked areas, one would have to resort to lists like that in Fig. 1. Maps 2–3 are from a type of publication called a WORD GEOGRAPHY, which presents lexical variation but disregards phonetic detail.

4. Social dialectology. Sociolinguistic dialect surveys differ from traditional ones primarily in their purpose.

MAP 2. *'Child' versus 'Bairn' in England.* (From Upton et al. 1987:50.)

While the latter are preoccupied with a basilect, which may be used by only a minority of the population, the former is concerned with the language of all population groups in its chosen locality. This leads to important differences in method—in the sampling of languages and speakers, in the manner of elicitation, and in the presentation of results.

4.1. Instead of attempting to deal with a large sample of the lexicon and the total phonology, the sociolinguistic survey concentrates on features which preliminary research has suggested will show significant variation.

4.2. The variation in these features is correlated with two variables: the social status of the speaker, and the circumstances and types of discourse in which the forms occurred. Variants that prove to be correlated with the former are called SOCIAL MARKERS; those associated with discourse context are called markers of STYLE or REGISTER. [*See* Register and Style.]

4.3. To elicit social variables, consultants are chosen from the total population of native speakers of the language. To avoid bias in the choice, they are normally chosen by a random process which ensures that speakers from all social levels will be included.

4.4. The members of the sample thus selected are classified socially by various criteria independent of language, such as occupation, place of residence, income, age, sex, or level of education.

4.5. To be sure of obtaining language at various levels of style or register, elicitation must be more complicated than a straightforward questionnaire. It may range from reading a list of words to telling an emotionally charged personal anecdote, and from the more formal conversational style used with strangers to intimate exchanges within a family. The material cannot be written down during the interview, but must be recorded for later transcription. Recording is sometimes done surreptitiously, but American practice forbids this as unethical. Hence the interviewer has a great burden of responsibility to reassure informants and to encourage them to speak in a natural manner.

4.6. In presenting the material, linguistic variables are correlated with variations in social status and style. Figure 2 (from Labov 1966) shows class and style variation in two features of New York City speech: the pronunciation or omission of /r/ before consonants or at the ends of words (e.g. *part, car*), and the pronunciation of *th* (as in *thin*) as [t] rather than [θ]. Both features vary with both social class and style. Lower and working-class speakers almost never pronounce *r* in casual

MAP 3. *Terms for 'Molars' in England.* (From Orton & Wright 1974:179.)

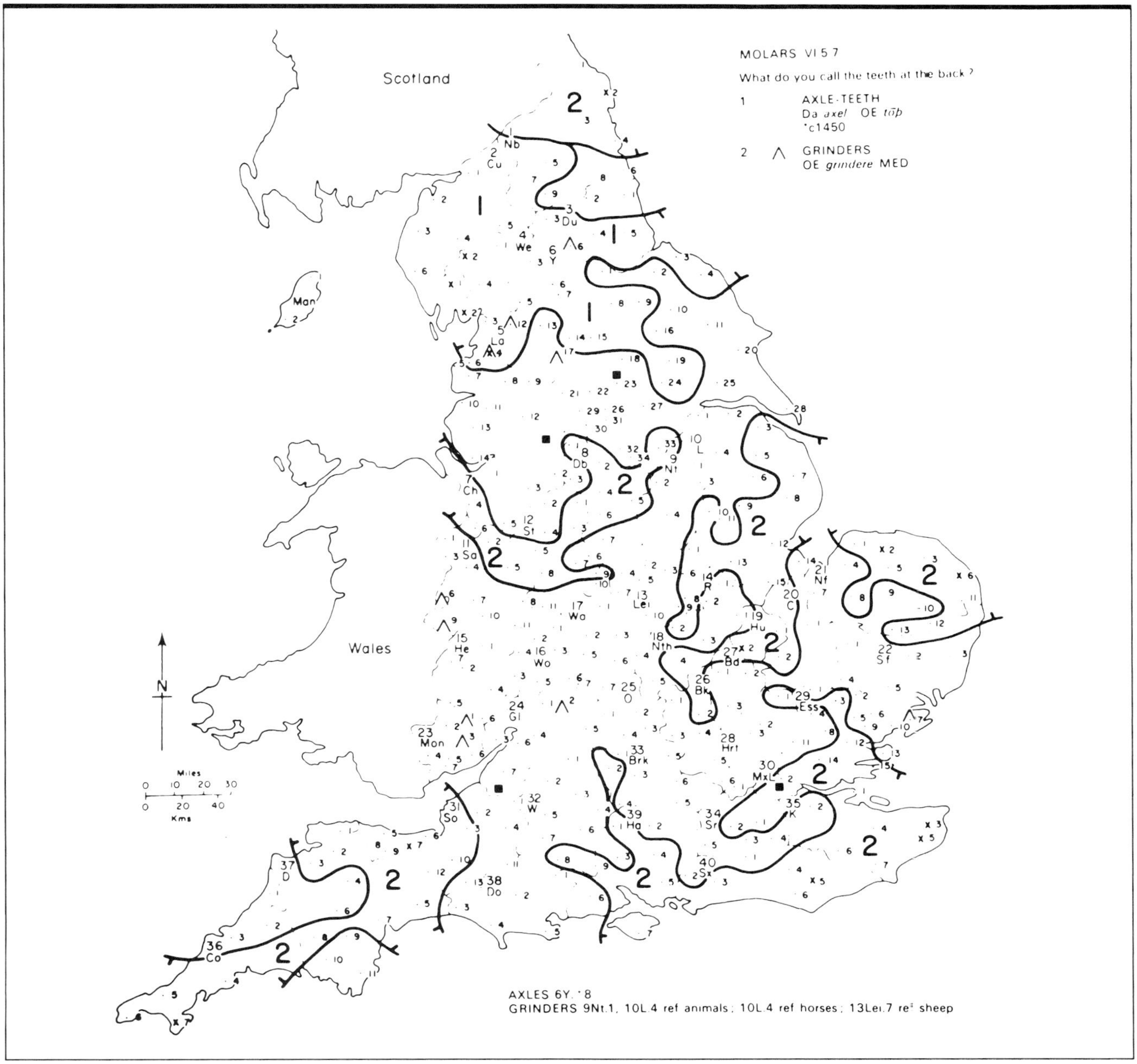

speech; but when they read from lists of words, their use of *r* approaches 50 percent. Similarly, lower-class speakers pronounce *th* as [t] 80 percent of the time in casual style, but only 40 percent of the time when reading aloud from a text.

4.7. Labov relied on simple averages in arriving at these conclusions. More recent sociolinguistic studies use more complicated statistical procedures done with computers. Thus, in the Tyneside Linguistic Survey in England, both social stratification and multiple linguistic features were subjected to CLUSTER ANALYSIS (Jones-Sargent 1983). The application of statistics to dialect study is described by Davis (1983:69–84).

5. Dialectometry. A statistical method of dialect analysis developed during the 1970s and 1980s was called DIALECTOMETRY by its originator, French dialectologist Jean Séguy (e.g. 1973). It has been further developed in Austria by Hans Goebl, and in Germany

FIGURE 2. *Sociolinguistic Variation in New York City.* Context: A = casual speech, B = careful speech, C = reading style, D = word lists. Class: 0–2 = lower class, 3–5 = working class, 6–9 = middle class. (From Labov 1966:222.)

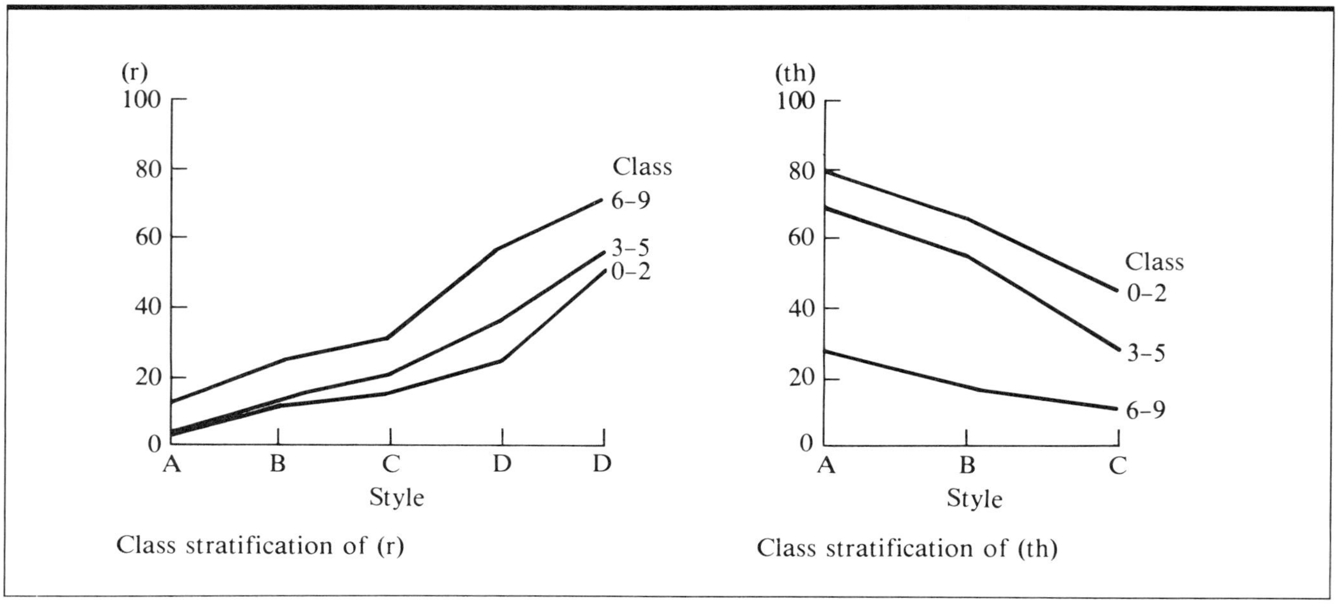

by Wolfgang Viereck. The method is directed at measuring the 'linguistic distance' between individual localities in a dialect region, by counting the number of contrasts in a large sample of linguistic features. Although Séguy's dialect atlas of Gascony was prepared manually, the large number of comparisons involved makes the use of a computer a virtual necessity. This method gives promise of identifying dialect areas by methods more objective than those of traditional linguistic geography.

6. Conclusions. It remains to inquire what use is to be made of the products of dialectological research, whether traditional or sociolinguistic. Obviously, they have added greatly to our knowledge of language—both as a system in itself, and as a major element of human culture and psychology. Traditional dialectology has also established precise scientific methods for identifying and describing the variability which is recognized as an essential attribute of language. It has contributed to historical linguistics by showing that inherent variability is a major source of language change (Weinreich et al. 1968).

Sociolinguistic dialectology has helped to integrate language, perhaps the most characteristic feature of humanity, into the over-all pattern of human culture; and it has contributed to a growing understanding of the diversity of culture. By establishing that dialects are language systems in their own right—rather than degenerate forms of a literate standard, to be eradicated by schooling or even by fiat—it has given them dignity and importance. Dialectology, once the hobby of amateur collectors of odd words, has taken a major position within linguistics; this makes it an important field of study not only for linguists, but for all educated persons.

W. NELSON FRANCIS

BIBLIOGRAPHY

AMMON, ULRICH. 1983. Vorbereitung einer Explizit-Definition von 'Dialekt' und benachbarten Begriffen mit Mitteln der formalen Logik. In *Aspekte der Dialekttheorie,* edited by Klaus J. Mattheier, pp. 27–68. Tübingen: Niemeyer.

CHAMBERS, J. K., & PETER TRUDGILL. 1980. *Dialectology.* Cambridge & New York: Cambridge University Press.

DAVIS, LAWRENCE. 1983. *English dialectology: An introduction.* University, Ala.: University of Alabama Press.

ELLIS, ALEXANDER J. 1889. *The existing phonology of English dialects.* London: Trübner.

FRANCIS, W. NELSON. 1983. *Dialectology: An introduction.* London: Longman.

GILLIÉRON, JULES, & EDMOND EDMONT. 1902–13. *Atlas linguistique de la France.* 13 vols. Paris: Champion.

JONES-SARGENT, VAL. 1983. *Tyne bytes: A computerised sociolinguistic study of Tyneside.* Frankfurt: Lang.

KIRK, JOHN M., et al. 1985. *Studies in linguistic geography: The dialects of Britain and Ireland.* London: Croom Helm.

KOLB, EDUARD. 1966. *Linguistic atlas of England: Phonological atlas of the northern region.* Bern: Francke.

KURATH, HANS. 1972. *Studies in area linguistics.* Bloomington: Indiana University Press.

LABOV, WILLIAM. 1966. *The social stratification of English in New York City.* Washington, D.C.: Center for Applied Linguistics.

ORTON, HAROLD, & WILFRID J. HALLIDAY. 1963. *Survey of English dialects,* vol. 1, *The six northern counties and the Isle of Man.* Leeds: Arnold.

ORTON, HAROLD, & NATHALIA WRIGHT. 1974. *A word geography of England.* London: Seminar Press.

SÉGUY, JEAN. 1973. La dialectométrie dans l'Atlas linguistique de la Gascogne. *Revue de Linguistique Romane* 35.335–357.

TRUDGILL, PETER. 1983. *On dialect: Social and historical perspectives.* Oxford: Blackwell.

UPTON, CLIVE, et al. 1987. *Word maps: A dialect atlas of England.* London: Croom Helm.

WEINREICH, URIEL; WILLIAM LABOV; & MARVIN I. HERZOG. 1968. Empirical foundations for a theory of linguistic change. In *Directions for historical linguistics,* edited by Winfred P. Lehmann & Yakov Malkiel, pp. 97–195. Austin: University of Texas Press.

WENKER, GEORG, et al. 1876–1956. *Deutscher Sprachatlas.* Marburg: Elwert.

WINTELER, JOST. 1876. *Die Kerenzer Mundart des Kantons Glarus.* Leipzig: Winter.

DICTIONARIES. *See* Lexicography; Lexicon.

DIMINUTIVES. This category of derivational morphology is characterized by a basic denotative meaning of smallness, and potentially by a variety of connotative meanings—e.g. endearment, as in Eng. *dogg-ie,* or depreciation, as in Italian *attric-etta* 'starlet'. (For general reference, see Hasselrot 1957, Craddock 1965, Gooch 1970, Wierzbicka 1984, Volek 1987.)

Diminutives are mostly effected by suffixation, with an iconic tendency towards palatal phonemes (Mayerthaler 1981:99, 102, 105): e.g. Eng. *-ie, -ette*; German *-chen, -lein*; French *-et(te), -on*; Spanish *-ito, -ico, -illo*; Italian *-ino, -etto, -ello*; Russian *-ak, -(č)ik*, etc. (Hasselrot 1957:283 ff.). In some cases, suffixes are applied recursively, e.g. Spanish *-it-iqui-it-ico.*

Diminutive formation preferentially applies to noun bases, and more rarely to adjectives, adverbs, and verbs—e.g. It. *magr-ino* (or, with interfix *-ol, magr-ol-ino*) 'rather thin'; French *touss-et-er* 'to cough lightly and repeatedly'). It normally does not change the class of the base, and so is often referred to as 'modification' (Ettinger 1974:112), or even excluded from derivational morphology (Scalise 1984).

Some languages, such as Russian and Italian, use different suffixes to distinguish connotative nuances, e.g. It. pejorative/depreciative *donn-etta* 'woman of mean spirit' vs. *donn-ina* 'dear little woman'. Alternatively, with polysemous suffixes, meaning may have to be pragmatically determined. Thus Polish *śnieżek* 'little snow' is used only by children, or by adults addressing children, and this favors a connotation of familiarity and reassurance (Wierzbicka 1984).

Related derivatives, but with the opposite denotation of bigness and with mostly pejorative connotations, are AUGMENTATIVES, e.g. It. *donn-ona* 'big, unattractive woman'.

LAVINIA MERLINI BARBARESI

BIBLIOGRAPHY

CRADDOCK, JERRY. R. 1965. A critique of recent studies in Romance diminutives. *Romance Philology* 19.286–325.

ETTINGER, STEFAN. 1974. *Form und Funktion in der Wortbildung.* (Beiträge zur Linguistik, 47.) Tübingen: Narr.

GOOCH, ANTHONY. 1970. *Diminutive, augmentative, and pejorative suffixes in modern Spanish.* 2d ed. Oxford: Pergamon.

HASSELROT, BENGT. 1957. *Études sur la formation diminutive dans les langues romanes.* Uppsala: Almqvist & Wiksell.

MAYERTHALER, WILLI. 1981. *Morphologische Natürlichkeit.* (Linguistische Forschungen, 28.) Wiesbaden: Athenäum.

SCALISE, SERGIO. 1984. *Generative morphology.* (Studies in generative grammar, 18.) Dordrecht: Foris.

VOLEK, BRONISLAWA. 1987. *Emotive signs in languages and semantic functioning of derived nouns in Russian.* Amsterdam: Benjamins.

WIERZBICKA, ANNA. 1984. Diminutives and depreciatives: Semantic representation for derivational categories. *Quaderni di Semantica* 5.123–130.

DISCOURSE. [*This entry is concerned with the use of language in stretches longer than the sentence, e.g. conversations or narratives. It comprises five articles:*

An Overview
Acquisition of Competence
Discourse Markers
Emergence of Grammar
Transcription of Discourse

For related topics, see Conversation Analysis; Ethnography of Speaking; Ethnopoetics; Formulaic Speech;

Humor and Language; Information Flow; Law and Language; Medicine and Language; Metaphor; Narrative; Pragmatics, Implicature, and Presupposition; Psychotherapy and Language; Ritual Language; Semantics, *article on* Informational and Rhetorical Structure; Semiotics; Sex and Language; Sociolinguistics, *article on* Interactional Sociolinguistics; Text Understanding; *and* Verbal Play.]

An Overview

The term 'discourse' is used in somewhat different ways by different scholars, but underlying the differences is a common concern for language beyond the boundaries of isolated sentences. The term TEXT is used in similar ways. Both terms may refer to a unit of language larger than the sentence: one may speak of 'a discourse' or 'a text'. 'Discourse' may also refer to the study of such a unit, a branch of linguistics coordinate with morphology or syntax. One may speak of a linguist who specializes in discourse, for example. Often the terms DISCOURSE (or TEXT) ANALYSIS, or DISCOURSE (or TEXT) LINGUISTICS, are used in this way.

The study of discourse has emerged as a distinct and established branch of linguistics only since the 1970s. Within the period between 1977 and 1983, there appeared two major journals, *Discourse Processes* (1978) and *Text* (1981), and at least five major textbooks (Beaugrande & Dressler 1981, Brown & Yule 1983, Coulthard 1977, Edmondson 1981, Stubbs 1983). Published shortly afterward was the four-volume *Handbook of discourse analysis* (van Dijk 1985).

Journal articles, textbooks, and contributions to anthologies on discourse show a great heterogeneity of approaches. The data investigated, the theoretical positions taken, and the overlap with other disciplines are diverse enough to suggest that discourse constitutes more than one distinct subfield of linguistics. Nevertheless, most approaches that look beyond the boundaries of sentences have shared certain research experiences; these have led to some agreement on the general kinds of data that are of interest, appropriate methodologies for handling and interpreting those data, the kinds of explanation that are regarded as significant, and even the kinds of questions that are worth asking.

With respect to data, while sentence-based studies of language have most commonly focused on invented sentences and intuitive judgments of their grammaticality or acceptability, the same procedure is more questionable when applied to discourse. A procedure of inventing whole texts and judging their acceptability has not found widespread application. There is, therefore, a strong tendency for discourse analysts to rely more heavily on observations of naturally occurring language. Conversely, scholars who wish to theorize on the basis of naturally occurring language have inevitably been led beyond the boundaries of sentences, since natural language rarely occurs in isolated sentence form. In pursuing natural language data, discourse analysts have also become more conscious of differences among diverse styles, genres, and modes of language use. Considerable attention has been paid, for example, to possible differences between spoken and written language. Although many discourse studies have focused exclusively on one or the other of these two modes, there has been increasing interest in comparisons between the two. [*See* Written Language, *article on* Writing versus Speech.]

With respect to methodology, research on spoken discourse has benefited immeasurably from the availability of the tape recorder, which allows easy storage and retrieval of discourse samples. The processing of tape-recorded data raises interesting questions regarding the conversion of sound into writing for research purposes. [*See article on* Transcription of Discourse *below*.] Because discourse research deals with large bodies of diverse data, it lends itself to quantitative methods, drawing especially on techniques developed in psychology, sociology, and statistical studies of texts. At the same time, textual studies profit from more humanistically oriented techniques of interpretation—for example, of the type that have been labeled HERMENEUTICS. The breadth and depth of discourse phenomena militate against exclusive commitment to any single mode of analysis.

With respect to explanation, discourse studies have in general focused less on abstract formalisms, and more on some variety of functional explanation. If there is a principle whereby increasingly larger units of language are decreasingly constrained by factors purely internal to language, on a scale from phonology to morphology to syntax to discourse, then discourse constitutes the area of language most subject to influence from psychological and social factors. This realization that discourse cannot be understood apart from its psychological and social contexts can contribute substantially to the more thoroughly studied aspects of language, such as morphology and syntax. It would appear, for example, that discourse considerations are essential to a fuller understanding of such familiar topics as anaphora and word order. [*See article on* Emergence of Grammar *below*.]

Finally, with respect to questions that are seen to be worth asking, discourse analysts tend to be driven to understand how naturally occurring language is determined by, and in turn determines, the ways in which knowledge is acquired, stored, and used by the human mind—as well as how language shapes and is shaped by the ways in which people interact with one another within their social and cultural contexts.

While it is difficult to deal with isolated sentences except in terms of grammar and lexicon, discourse can be studied in terms as varied as are the forces and functions responsible for language itself. In line with the interests sketched above, major areas of research have included the extension of grammar beyond the boundaries of the sentence; the use of discourse to illuminate psychological structures and processes; and the study of discourse as a way of gaining insights into social interaction.

Earlier interests in more restricted areas of grammatical structure have been extended by some linguists into the area of discourse. Early work of this kind included that of Harris 1952, and the ambitious project of Pike 1967. [*See* Tagmemics.] Besides Pike, other researchers associated with the Summer Institute of Linguistics have continued to make important contributions to discourse studies. Especially noteworthy have been the studies of Grimes 1975 and Longacre 1983. Other influential grammarians who have extended their work to discourse are represented by Fillmore 1985, Givón 1983, and Halliday 1985.

The British psychologist Bartlett (1932) used textual material to demonstrate the relevance of knowledge patterns or SCHEMATA to memory. The revival of his findings within cognitive psychology has resulted in an extension of the phrase structure model of sentence structure to larger schemata identified as STORY GRAMMARS. Constructs of this kind have been exploited in psychological research where, as models of knowledge representation, they have been interpreted as shedding light on the nature of memory and language development (see Mandler & Johnson 1977).

The relevance of discourse to cognitive structures and processes has also emerged in studies of INFORMATION FLOW [*q.v.*]—changes in the cognitive status of knowledge as language is produced and comprehended through time. For example, changes in the newness or givenness of information or the identifiability of referents may determine such basic grammatical phenomena as pronominalization, intonation, word order, and the use of definite and indefinite articles. Tracking such elements in discourse can in turn provide insights into ongoing mental processing.

A different and very active branch of discourse study has directed its attention to language as a vehicle of social interaction. Much of this work comes out of, or is relevant to sociological concerns; in fact, most of sociolinguistics can be seen as a branch of discourse analysis. Here belong, for example, the detailed analyses of recorded conversations that have been conducted in the styles of two rather different traditions: CONVERSATION ANALYSIS [*q.v.*], an outgrowth of ethnomethodology, and what is here called INTERACTIONAL SOCIOLINGUISTICS, in the tradition of Gumperz 1982. [*See* Sociolinguistics.] Here belongs also the work of William Labov on the negotiation of social meaning through the use of evaluative devices. [*See* Narrative, *article on* Conversational Narrative.] The analysis of conversations has shed new light on grammatical elements of the type identified as DISCOURSE MARKERS [*see article on* Discourse Markers *below*], and has highlighted the import role of FORMULAIC SPEECH [*q.v.*] in everyday language. Of particular social relevance has been the study of gender asymmetries in language use. [*See* Sex and Language.] Other studies have investigated the development of discourse competence in children. [*See article on* Acquisition of Competence *below*.]

Many anthropologically oriented studies of discourse have been pursued under the heading ETHNOGRAPHY OF SPEAKING [*q.v.*], where speaking is seen as one of the principal elements of culturally determined behavior. [*For specific manifestations, see* Verbal Play; Humor and Language; Ritual Language.] More humanistically oriented approaches are represented in the work of Becker 1979, Friedrich 1986, and Tedlock 1983.

Finally, because discourse studies aim at an understanding of language in its great variety of natural settings, a number of discourse studies have looked at language use during interactions between clients and the practitioners of various professions. [*See* Law and Language; Medicine and Language; Psychotherapy and Language.] Discourse analysts also concern themselves with language in such domains as education, politics, and advertising.

The diversity of discourse linguistics reflects the richness of its subject matter. Increased understanding of language in actual use calls for the examination of a maximally wide range of data, as well as free access to an unrestricted arsenal of methods and theoretical approaches (Chafe 1986). Discourse provides a focus and meeting ground for all investigations of language as it really is. Its diversity, reflecting as it does the diversity of language and the human mind, offers a liberating challenge to a linguistics freed of the bonds of parochial concerns.

WALLACE CHAFE

BIBLIOGRAPHY

BARTLETT, FREDERIC C. 1932. *Remembering: A study in experimental and social psychology.* Cambridge: Cambridge University Press.

BEAUGRANDE, ROBERT-ALAIN DE, & WOLFGANG U. DRESSLER. 1981. *Introduction to text linguistics.* (Longman linguistics library, 26.) London: Longman.

BECKER, ALTON L. 1979. Text-building, epistemology, and aesthetics in Javanese shadow theatre. In *The imagination of reality: Essays in Southeast Asian coherence systems,* edited by Alton L. Becker & Aram A. Yengoyan, pp. 211–243. Norwood, N.J.: Ablex.

BROWN, GILLIAN, & GEORGE YULE. 1983. *Discourse analysis.* Cambridge & New York: Cambridge University Press.

CHAFE, WALLACE L. 1986. How we know things about language: A plea for catholicism. In *Languages and linguistics: The interdependence of theory, data, and application* (36th Georgetown University Round Table, 1985), edited by Deborah Tannen & James E. Alatis, pp. 214–225. Washington, D.C.: Georgetown University Press.

COULTHARD, MALCOLM. 1977. *An introduction to discourse analysis.* London: Longman. 2d ed., 1985.

EDMONDSON, WILLIS. 1981. *Spoken discourse: A model for analysis.* (Longman linguistics library, 27.) London: Longman.

FILLMORE, CHARLES J. 1985. Linguistics as a tool for discourse analysis. In van Dijk 1985, vol. 1, pp. 11–39.

FRIEDRICH, PAUL. 1986. *The language parallax: Linguistic relativism and poetic indeterminacy.* Austin: University of Texas Press.

GIVÓN, TALMY, ed. 1983. *Topic continuity in discourse: A quantitative cross-language study.* (Typological studies in language, 3.) Amsterdam: Benjamins.

GRIMES, JOSEPH E. 1975. *The thread of discourse.* (Janua linguarum, Series minor, 207.) The Hague: Mouton.

GUMPERZ, JOHN J. 1982. *Discourse strategies.* (Studies in interactional sociolinguistics, 1.) Cambridge & New York: Cambridge University Press.

HALLIDAY, MICHAEL A. K. 1985. Dimensions of discourse analysis: Grammar. In van Dijk 1985, vol. 2, pp. 29–56.

HARRIS, ZELLIG S. 1952. Discourse analysis. *Language* 28.1–30.

LONGACRE, ROBERT E. 1983. *The grammar of discourse.* New York: Plenum.

MANDLER, JEAN M., & NANCY S. JOHNSON. 1977. Remembrance of things parsed: Story structure and recall. *Cognitive Psychology* 9.111–151.

PIKE, KENNETH L. 1967. *Language in relation to a unified theory of the structure of human behavior.* 2d ed. (Janua linguarum, Series maior, 24.) The Hague: Mouton.

STUBBS, MICHAEL. 1983. *Discourse analysis: The sociolinguistic analysis of natural language.* (Language in society, 4.) Oxford: Blackwell. Chicago: University of Chicago Press.

TEDLOCK, DENNIS. 1983. *The spoken word and the work of interpretation.* Philadelphia: University of Pennsylvania Press.

VAN DIJK, TEUN A., ed. 1985. *Handbook of discourse analysis.* 4 vols. London & Orlando: Academic Press.

Acquisition of Competence

'Discourse' refers to the set of norms, preferences, and expectations relating language to context, which language users draw on and modify in producing and making sense out of language in context. Discourse knowledge allows language users to produce and interpret discourse structures such as verbal acts (e.g. requests and offers), conversational sequences (such as questions and answers), activities (such as story-telling and arguing), and communicative styles (such as women's speech). Competent language users know the formal characteristics of these structures, the alternative ways of forming particular structures, and the contexts in which particular discourse structures are preferred and expected. For example, competent communicators know the range of linguistic structures which one can use to ask for things, and they know which particular structures are preferred in particular social circumstances. (For general reference, see Ervin-Tripp & Mitchell-Kernan 1977, Shatz 1978, Bullowa 1979, Ochs & Schieffelin 1979, Umiker-Sebeok 1979, Garvey 1984, Romaine 1984, McTear 1985, and Hickman 1987.)

Discourse knowledge relates language to psychological as well as social contexts. Competent language users vary their language according to their perception of the cognitive states of interlocutors. Every language has structures used to elicit others' attention, to heighten attention to something expressed, and to distinguish old from new information. Terms of ADDRESS, emphatic particles, pitch, voice quality, and repetition are attention-getting devices. Similarly, certain determiners, pronouns, and word order mark old and new information.

Psychological context includes perceived emotion. Languages throughout the world have linguistic resources for conveying emotion. In Thai and Japanese, for example, passive voice indicates negative affect towards a proposition. In other languages, affixes, particles, quantifiers, tense-aspect marking, word order, and intonation carry emotional meaning. Competent language users know which structures convey affective meaning, and they know the norms, preferences, and expectations surrounding their use.

1. Acquisition by children. In the course of experiencing language in context, children come to know how language sometimes reflects context, and sometimes creates it. They learn how to use language as a tool to elicit attention, to establish relationships and identities, to perform social actions, and to express certain stances. All this is part of being a speaker of a language. Acquiring a second language entails discourse knowledge for use of that language. In many cases, second-language acquirers are grammatically competent, but their discourse competence may lag, as they map norms, preferences, and expectations from their first language onto second-language situations. Second-language acquirers may have different norms from native speakers for greeting, asking, essay-writing, interviewing, story-telling, instructing, or arguing, and for displaying interest, fear, concern, pleasure, or emotional intensity. Discrepancies between non-native and native discourse competence have both personal and economic consequences when interlocutors misunderstand the contextual meanings of one another's language behavior.

Children are born with a predisposition to be social; they begin communicating long before they can speak. They shout, cry, point, and tug at others for communicative purposes in the first year of life. These behaviors establish joint attention, a prerequisite of communication. In this period, infants monitor and respond appropriately to expressions of emotion and to greetings, directives, and certain other speech acts. In all societies, care-givers encourage the sociability of infants, although cultural conceptions differ as to appropriate communicative behavior for infants. Further, societies differ in the discourse practices expected of care-givers. In some societies, care-givers are expected to converse with infants from birth on. In much of middle-class Europe and the United States, mothers engage infants in greeting exchanges as early as twenty-four hours after birth. Long before infants can utter words, mothers impute communicative import to infants' nonverbal behavior and vocalizations, and they speak for the infant as well as for themselves. In other societies, care-givers do not presume that infants are necessarily intending to communicate when they vocalize and gesture; they wait until infants are somewhat older before engaging them as conversational partners. Through such differing discourse practices, care-givers socialize infants into the local culture.

When infants around the world begin to speak, how do they use words to accomplish social acts and activities, to express affect, and to constitute social identities and relationships? In other words, how does discourse competence develop? Let us examine some specific domains.

2. Social acts. All children come to know that language is a tool not only for representing the world but also for constituting and changing that world. Children use linguistic structures as resources to carry out a range of tasks, such as asking questions and making requests, offers, or promises. They also develop understandings of what others are trying to accomplish with their words, and they adjust their subsequent linguistic acts accordingly—e.g. accepting/rejecting offers, assessing announcements, agreeing/disagreeing with assertions, satisfying/refusing requests, and answering questions.

Let us consider how children acquire competence in one of these acts: the request for goods and services. In the first year of life, infants vocalize and gesture to request desired objects. At the single-word stage, English-speaking children incorporate single words such as *more* and *want* into these schemata for requesting. In many speech communities, young children also use affect-laden constructions to get what they want, e.g. sympathy-marked pronouns, affixes, and particles. English-speaking as well as Italian children use imperatives *(Gimme bear!)* and declaratives expressing 'want/need' *(I want/need bear)* before they use interrogative forms *(Can you give me bear?, Will you give me bear?)* and declarative hints *(I sure miss bear)*. These latter forms appear in children's speech around two and a half to three years of age, but not frequently. While young children use indirect request forms, they may not distinguish the various indirect forms of request used by others. They may respond appropriately to formally variant requests, either because they attend primarily to action predicates embedded in them, or because of contextual clues as to what action is desired by the speaker. By age four, however, children are able to comprehend a wide range of indirect request types.

3. Affect. The term 'affect' refers to expressed emotion, including displays of moods, attitudes, dispositions, and feelings. Early in their development, children display affect and interpret the affective displays of others. Before using words, children vary intonational contours and voice quality to indicate affect. At the single-word stage, children perform a variety of affect-loaded SPEECH ACTS [*q.v.*], such as greeting, begging, teasing, cursing, and refusing. In certain speech communities, they use affect-marked pronouns and affixes, morphological particles, and respect vocabulary. They switch from one phonological register to another to intensify or deintensify affect, and to display sympathy, anger, deference, or other feelings. Research to date indicates that very young children use language rhetorically, and draw on affect-marked language to achieve rhetorical ends.

4. Activity. A set of coordinated practices is called an 'activity' when it realizes some motive. Telling a story, arguing, reviewing homework, and giving a lecture are all activities in which language plays an important role. Activities are socially constructed, even where participants do not speak. Eye gaze, facial expressions, and other demeanors of those present affect the direction that an activity takes, along with more explicit verbal contributions. In this sense, activities are joint accomplishments of at least two persons. In all societies, members guide the participation of novices in culturally relevant activities. However, societies differ in what is expected of novice and member. Some, such as middle-class European and American societies, frequently plan language activities in which young children are given roles that place high cognitive, social, and linguistic demands on them, requiring skills they do not yet fully command. To accomplish the activity, members then provide considerable assistance—speaking for the children, and prompting or expanding their verbal contributions. In other societies, young children are given actions to perform as part of larger language activities, but close assistance by members is rarely elicited or provided.

Activities entail complex discourse structures. Narrating and arguing, for example, have internal components; they are constrained by norms, preferences, and expectations concerning their order and form. These constraints vary across speech communities; what counts as a narrative for Anglo-Americans, for example, does not match what counts as a narrative for Athabaskan Indians. To succeed in mainstream educational institutions, children growing up in culturally distinct, non-mainstream communities often have to acquire narrative competence in mainstream terms as well as their own. Most research on the acquisition of narrative skills has focused on white middle-class English-speaking children, and on the narrative structures preferred in their communities.

While scholarly definitions of narrative vary, most agree that a narrative contains a sequence of clauses with at least one temporal juncture. Narratives may depict events in the future (e.g. plans) and in the present (e.g. radio broadcasts), but research on the acquisition of narrative structures focuses on past-time narratives. The development of such narratives is rooted in children's early attempts to refer to non-present objects and to past events, observed as early as fifteen months of age. Children talk about the past long before acquiring past tense morphology (around twenty-seven months). In white middle-class households, children are encouraged to remember experiences already known to mothers. The mother elicits and helps to structure such narratives, in addition to providing tokens of appreciation and support. By contrast, in speech communities such as the Kaluli of Papua New Guinea, young children are not asked to recast shared past experiences in narrative form; care-givers do not scaffold children's narratives through prompting, questioning, or expanding the child's talk about the shared past.

Narratives of past experience may include an introduction, abstract, orientation (to person, time, place, etc.), complicating actions (e.g. initiating event, attempts), evaluation, result, and coda. [*See* Narrative, *article on* Conversational Narrative.] Up to age three, children rarely include all these components in their narratives. Three-year-old middle-class English-speaking children frequently omit the abstract, orientation, and results. Five-year-old children more consistently provide all narrative components. In relating one clause to another within a narrative, younger children tend not to use connectives that specify consequence and causality, but rather leave such meanings implicit.

Three-year-olds routinely engage in narrative activities with peers and adults at home and at school. Four-year-old children not only initiate stories, but actively acknowledge and comment on stories that their peers initiate. Indeed, the stories of three- and four-year-old children are often motivated by a story just related. In this sense, children are actively constructing stories early in the pre-school years.

5. Social identities and relationships. A critical domain of discourse competence is the ability to create and maintain social identities and relationships through language. In every social group, children acquire the ways of speaking expected of children, adults, peers, males, females, people of lower and higher status, intimates, strangers, and members of other social categories. Linguistic forms associated with social acts, stances, and activities are also associated with specific speaker/writer identities and specific social relationships. Indeed, these identity/relationship contexts are part of the 'social meaning' of these forms. Very young children are sensitive to such variation and modify their speech accordingly. For example, two-year-old English-speaking children adjust their request forms to the age and rank of addressees—using imperatives to peers, while directing desire statements, questions, and requests for permission to adults and older children. Similarly, Samoan-speaking children of this age switch phonological registers to create or reflect intimacy vs. distance, and they modify the form of their requests with the ranking of speaker and addressee. By four years of age, children everywhere display considerable competence in altering communicative styles to establish particular identities and relationships.

Discourse competence involves the ability to build contexts through linguistic structures. Children and other acquirers come to understand that a single structure or a set of structures may, in the same moment of use, build a multitude of contexts—e.g. a type of affect, a social act, and a social identity. Acquirers also come to understand that contexts are built sequentially; they develop the competence to create and interpret language activities through ordered acts and expressed stances.

ELINOR OCHS

BIBLIOGRAPHY

BULLOWA, MARGARET, ed. 1979. *Before speech: The beginning of interpersonal communication.* Cambridge & New York: Cambridge University Press.

ERVIN-TRIPP, SUSAN, & CLAUDIA MITCHELL-KERNAN, eds. 1977. *Child discourse.* New York: Academic Press.

GARVEY, CATHERINE. 1984. *Children's talk.* Cambridge, Mass.: Harvard University Press.

HICKMANN, MAYA, ed. 1987. *Social and functional approaches to language and thought.* Orlando, Fla.: Academic Press.

MCTEAR, MICHAEL. 1985. *Children's conversation.* Oxford: Blackwell.

OCHS, ELINOR, & BAMBI B. SCHIEFFELIN. 1979. *Developmental pragmatics.* New York: Academic Press.

ROMAINE, SUZANNE. 1984. *The language of children and adolescents: The acquisition of communicative competence.* (Language in society, 7.) Oxford: Blackwell.

SCHIEFFELIN, BAMBI B., & ELINOR OCHS, eds. 1986. *Language socialization across cultures.* (Studies in the social and cultural foundations of language, 3.) Cambridge & New York: Cambridge University Press.

SHATZ, MARILYN. 1978. Children's comprehension of their mothers' question-directives. *Journal of Child Language* 5.39–46.

UMIKER-SEBEOK, D. JEAN. 1979. Preschool children's intraconversational narratives. *Journal of Child Language* 6.91–109.

Discourse Markers

The production and interpretation of coherent discourse is an interactive process that requires speakers and hearers to draw upon several different types of knowledge. One type of competence is SOCIAL and expressive—the ability to use language to display personal and social identities, to perform actions, and to negotiate relationships between self and other. Still other types of competence are COGNITIVE, e.g. the ability to organize conceptual information and to represent it through language, and TEXTUAL, e.g. the ability to create and understand messages within units of language longer than a single sentence.

One set of linguistic items that function in the cognitive, social, expressive, and textual domains is commonly referred to as D[iscourse] M[arker]s: sequentially dependent elements which bracket units of talk (Schiffrin 1987a:31). Examples are connectives *(and, but, or),* particles *(oh, well),* adverbs *(now, then),* and lexicalized phrases *(y'know, I mean).* DMs typically characterize units of talk which can be defined only through their role in discourse. Sometimes the unit being marked is a sentence; at other times, the unit is defined as an action, an idea unit, or the like (Schiffrin 1987a:31–36). The functions of the markers are always relative to the form and content of both prior and upcoming discourse. The particular aspect of discourse to which they pertain, however, varies for different markers; e.g., *oh* pertains most to the distribution and management of information, while *I mean* and *y'know* pertain most to the organization of participation and involvement (Schiffrin 1987a, chap. 10).

DMs have recently become the focus of attention of linguists concentrating on developing functionalist models of language. [*See* Functional Grammar.] The application of different perspectives to the study of DMs means the influence of different theoretical assumptions and frameworks, and the use of different methods of analysis. Not surprisingly, some studies result in different substantive findings (cf. Carlson 1984 and Schiffrin 1987a, chap. 5), and different conclusions about their specific role in theories of language and communication.

Despite differences in individual studies, we can draw some general conclusions about the relationship of DMs to language structure and use. Research reveals that such markers both reflect and create the interpretive and interactive contexts in which discourse is constructed. In fact, the use of DMs is not only a part of what makes a way of speaking seem natural and appropriate to its context, but also a part of what makes language seem distinctly human—in the terms of Wierzbicka (1986:519), what 'distinguishes human language from the language of robots'. These interdependencies mean that the study of DMs is quite central to our understanding of COMMUNICATIVE COMPETENCE [*q.v.*]—how our cognitive, social, expressive, and textual knowledge allows us to use language in culturally appropriate ways.

The analysis of DMs contributes in still other ways to our understanding of language structure and use. DMs whose function is based on their meaning (e.g. *and, or*) often figure critically in ideational aspects of discourse coherence—in the indication of semantic relationships between different propositions. Such DMs, as well as others whose meaning is not propositionally based, also help to segment discourse into smaller chunks, e.g. idea units, which are cognitively differentiated from one another as separate foci of attention (Chafe 1980, 1987); or into smaller chunks which are structurally and/or functionally different from one another, but nevertheless interrelated (Hymes 1981, Sherzer 1982). Thus many DMs bracket small chunks of discourse that are cognitively and textually organized in speakers' competence.

Other DMs bracket units of talk that function in more social and expressive domains. Thus the markers *I mean, y'know,* and *now* are important means of displaying speaker attitude and subjective orientation toward what is being said and to whom (Östman 1981, Schourup 1982). Markers such as *so, then,* and *well* have a role in solving both mechanical problems (e.g. turn-taking, topic transition) and interpersonal problems of conversational management (e.g. face-saving; Svartvik 1980). Still other DMs work in both cognitive and social domains; thus *oh* as a marker of information receipt displays a transfer of information during clarification sequences in conversation (Heritage 1984; Schiffrin 1987a, chap. 4). That DMs have these functions means that their study is important not only for our understanding of communicative competence, but also for our understanding of meaning (as conveyed through situated utterances) and of conversational organization.

Most DMs frequently have several simultaneous functions. Thus *well* may convey the fulfillment of a conversational obligation, e.g. an answer to a question, at the same time that it conveys speaker attitude, e.g. distance from a proposition; and it may signal the continuation of an action, e.g. a continued response to a question, at the same time that it segments topics in a text, e.g. items in a list (Schiffrin 1987a, chap. 5–6). This multiple function is important for our understanding of form/function relationships, and for the development of functionalist models of language. It also has a very general theoretical consequence. It suggests that the processes through which coherent discourse is constructed are essentially INTEGRATIVE: processes in which meanings, actions, and structures must be synthesized with one another in the service of sense-making and message formation.

The discussion thus far has assumed that DMs can be considered a set of some kind, despite the fact that the linguistic items serving as markers are members of word classes as various as conjunctions, interjections, and adverbs. What criteria allow us to include these different terms in a single class of items? This is an important question not only for definitional purposes, but also because studies of intonational patterns in discourse suggest that we may have to broaden even further the criteria by which we define DMs, to include prosodic and other non-segmental phonological processes.

One criterion that has thus far been a unifying source of definition for DMs is structural: they are forms whose distribution defies analysis on the local clausal level, but can be explained by reference to the more global structures of discourse. Another criterion is pragmatic: DMs are terms whose meaning defies analysis on a level of sentence meaning, but can be explained by reference to speaker attitude and orientation. Note that both these approaches begin by defining markers as items that resist analysis in more familiar linguistic terms. Both approaches also highlight functional similarities among markers: functions that concern either the organization of discourse, or pragmatic meaning.

If the above structural and pragmatic criteria are applied more broadly, many terms other than those discussed above may also be seen as DMs. Various scholars have analyzed sentence-internal (in addition to sentence-initial) devices as DMs, simply because their function is text-dependent—e.g., their role is to define a given stretch of sentences as a bounded segment in a text—or because analysis of their distribution requires reference to textual structure. Thus Stein 1985 views the historical present tense in narrative as a DM, since shifts of tense in narrative separate one section from another (cf. Wolfson 1982). Other scholars (e.g. Wierzbicka 1986) broaden their view in another way: they include DMs, interjections, and adverbials (including words like *just, only, even*) in a larger class of PARTICLES, simply because they display speaker attitude instead of truth-functional meaning. (Note that connectives with logical meaning, e.g. *and,* would be excluded from this definition because of their semantic character.)

The potential openness in the category of DMs might suggest that our definitions are inadequate. However, this openness actually reflects a duality in the definition of discourse itself. That is, discourse is defined both as structural—a unit of language larger than a sentence—and as pragmatic, i.e. language in use. Thus it is not surprising that DMs, as terms that define units of discourse, can also be identified as both text- and speaker-based.

At another level, the potential openness of the class of DMs may reflect on-going semantic transitions from propositional meanings grounded in relatively objective situations, to textual meanings grounded in text, to expressive meanings grounded in speakers' attitudes to what is said (Traugott 1989). Thus the discourse marker *then* may be seen as a synchronic reflection of a change from a word with basically propositional meaning (referring to the time of events), to one marking discourse connections between temporally successive textual units, to one functioning in an expressive (perhaps epistemic) domain to indicate a recently warranted inference. Such changes figure in GRAMMATICALIZATION [*q.v.*], the historical process whereby lexical items acquire a new status as grammatical, morphosyntactic forms. Studies of grammaticalization have done a great deal to challenge more conventionally held views of grammar as a static, closed system with discretely bound categories (Hopper 1988). If DMs do reflect, or participate in, processes of grammaticalization, then their analysis can be relevant not only to functionalist models of language and communication, but also to formalist models of language and grammar.

DMs have been characterized as 'linguistic Cinderellas: familiar, drab, hard-worked, and lacking in morphological, phonological, and etymological glamour' (Enkvist 1972:95). Research on their function, however, reveals not only that they are important for the construction of coherent discourse and the organization of communicative competence, but also that their analysis may be relevant to debates about the structure of grammar.

Finally, the analysis of DMs can also contribute to the development of sociolinguistic theory. Schiffrin (1987a, chap. 10) suggests that, despite the individual functions served by different markers, a very general shared function is INDEXICAL: markers point to the 'contextual coordinates', both textual and pragmatic, in which utterances are produced and in which speakers intend them to be interpreted. DMs share their indexical function with two key sociolinguistic constructs—contextualization cues and sociolinguistic variables—which point not to discourse, but to utterance interpretation and social meaning respectively (Schiffrin 1987b). Contextualization cues are verbal and non-verbal elements of behavior which point to the culturally schematized frameworks in which utterances are understood as messages. Sociolinguistic variables are alternative realizations of linguistic form which point to the circumstances in which an utterance is produced, e.g. speaker identity or definition of the situation. The shared indexical functions of DMs, contextualization cues, and sociolinguistic variables provide a valuable link among different levels of sociolinguistic inquiry whose relationships have not often been apparent: discourse, utterance interpretation, and social meaning. Establishing such links can be one step in developing a sociolinguistic theory to explain how utterances (their structure and their use) are socially constituted.

DEBORAH SCHIFFRIN

BIBLIOGRAPHY

CARLSON, LAURI. 1984. *'Well' in dialogue games: A discourse analysis of the interjection 'well' in idealized conversation.* (Pragmatics & beyond, 6.) Amsterdam: Benjamins.

CHAFE, WALLACE L. 1980. The deployment of consciousness in the production of a narrative. In *The Pear Stories: Cognitive, cultural and linguistic aspects of narrative production* (Advances in discourse processes, 3), edited by Wallace Chafe, pp. 9–50. Norwood, N.J.: Ablex.

CHAFE, WALLACE. 1987. Cognitive constraints on information

flow. In *Coherence and grounding in discourse* (Typological studies in language, 11), edited by Russell S. Tomlin, pp. 21-51. Amsterdam: Benjamins.

ENKVIST, NILS ERIK. 1972. Old English adverbial *þā*—an action marker? *Neuphilologische Mitteilungen* 73.90–96.

HERITAGE, JOHN. 1984. A change-of-state token and aspects of its sequential placement. In *Structures of social action: Studies in conversation analysis,* edited by J. Maxwell Atkinson & John Heritage, pp. 299–345. Cambridge & New York: Cambridge University Press.

HOPPER, PAUL. 1988. Emergent grammar and the A Priori Grammar Postulate. In *Linguistics in context: Connecting observation and understanding* (Advances in discourse processes, 29), edited by Deborah Tannen, pp. 117–134. Norwood, N.J.: Ablex.

HYMES, DELL. 1981. *'In vain I tried to tell you': Studies in Native American ethnopoetics.* Philadelphia: University of Pennsylvania Press.

ÖSTMAN, J. 1981. *'You know': A discourse-functional approach.* Amsterdam: Benjamins.

SCHIFFRIN, DEBORAH. 1987a. *Discourse markers.* Cambridge & New York: Cambridge University Press.

SCHIFFRIN, DEBORAH. 1987b. Discovering the context of an utterance. *Linguistics* 25.11–32.

SCHOUROP, LAWRENCE C. 1982. *Common discourse particles in English conversation.* Ohio State University dissertation. Published, New York: Garland, 1985.

SHERZER, JOEL. 1982. Poetic structuring of Kuna discourse: The line. *Language in Society* 11.371–390.

STEIN, DIETER. 1985. Discourse markers in Early Modern English. In *Papers from the Fourth International Conference on Historical Linguistics* (Current issues in linguistic theory, 41), edited by Roger Eaton et al., pp. 283–302. Amsterdam: Benjamins.

SVARTVIK, JAN. 1980. 'Well' in conversation. In *Studies in English linguistics for Randolph Quirk,* edited by Sidney Greenbaum et al., pp. 167–177. London: Longman.

TRAUGOTT, ELIZABETH C. 1989. On the rise of epistemic meanings in English: A case study in the regularity of semantic change. *Language* 65.31–55.

WIERZBICKA, ANNA. 1986. Introduction to special issue on 'particles'. *Journal of Pragmatics* 10.519–534.

WOLFSON, NESSA. 1982. *CHP: The conversational historical present in American English narratives.* (Topics in sociolinguistics, 1.) Dordrecht: Foris.

Emergence of Grammar

Functionalism in linguistics is usually taken to encompass approaches in which grammatical structure is related to discourse-pragmatic distinctions such as new and old information, or cognitive domains such as attention and memory. Consequently, much functionalist research takes as given the existence of grammatical structure, and searches texts for examples of specific grammatical constructions, which are then shown to occur in particular discourse environments. For example, Prince's study (1978) of cleft sentences subsumes two structurally similar but functionally distinct constructions, the WH-cleft *(What Bill wanted was credit for the discovery)* and the *it*-cleft *(It was this discovery which made him famous)*; she gives extensive examples of their uses in actual texts, showing the clear relationships between these constructions and the distribution of new and given (presupposed) information in the discourse. Studies of this kind, far from questioning the principles of formal linguistics, may be said to reinforce them by foregrounding the idea of autonomous grammar, and then calibrating selected aspects of this grammar against presumed discourse functions. Such work, important as it has been, has two major limitations. It focuses on precisely those aspects of grammar which are most prominent at the sentence level, such as cleft sentences; and by taking as its starting point a structurally similar family of constructions, it often fails to see each construction as part of a functional network whose other members may be structurally quite diverse.

During the late 1970s and the 1980s, a number of linguists experimented with approaches which would, to a greater or lesser degree, see grammatical structure as being much more closely integrated with discourse functions, and perhaps even inseparable from them. Common to these approaches is an understanding, implicit or explicit, that discourse in a broad sense provides the only motivation for grammar; and that the standard strategy of exhaustively describing the grammar of a language in abstract terms, and only then studying its implementation in discourse, should be replaced by one in which the two areas of study were continually juxtaposed and seen as mutually interacting. Although adumbrated in a variety of scholarly contexts in the 20th century (e.g. Prague School syntax, Malinowski 1922, J. R. Firth, Voloshinov 1973), the idea that external facts about the use of language—e.g. textual and cultural context, speaker intentions, and memory—cannot be separated from grammatical structure was stressed with increasing urgency by Bolinger (e.g. 1977). Also highly influential in the 1970s was the work of Li & Thompson 1974, 1975 on Chinese, which showed that semantic features of Chinese like DEFINITENESS, or the categorial distinction of verb vs. preposition, are not intrinsic, but are secondary to the organization of information in discourse. A similar conclusion was reached by Hopper 1977 in regard to aspect: this category appeared elusive when approached in terms of purely sentence-level distinctions, but was shown to have universal discourse motivations when studied textually.

The landmark study of Givón 1979 combined Bolinger's extreme functionalism with a universalistic stance toward characteristic features of human communication and cognition, and was foundational for many linguists in the 1970s and 1980s who thought of themselves as 'pragmaticists'. One theme of this work is that of a typological progression of linguistic modes from loosely organized speech to tighter, more structured modes. This progression is manifested in such polarities as child vs. adult, pidgin-creole vs. standard, spoken vs. written, informal vs. formal, and unplanned vs. planned. The looser pole is 'pragmatic', and achieves its goals more by means of pragmatic inference in conjunction with less structured areas like word order and lexicon; the tighter pole is 'syntactic', and relies to a greater extent on constructions and morphology in explicit, grammaticalized structural relationships. Grammar is then to be understood as the fixing or systematization of the looser pragmatic relationships, in which meanings were expressed basically by lexical items in a simple linear arrangement. Strongly influenced by Givón's ideas, Hopper & Thompson undertook studies of two broad areas of grammar from the point of view of discourse: transitivity (1980) and lexical categories (1984). Their goal was the same in each case: to show that the notions of TRANSITIVE CLAUSE and of NOUN VS. VERB were derivative from discourse needs. The results of the work on transitivity were to show that a number of parameters universally govern the degree to which a clause is coded as transitive in the world's languages. These parameters included:

(a) Features of the situation, e.g. effectiveness and punctuality
(b) Features of the agent, e.g. volitional involvement
(c) Features of the object: its presence (which defines the traditional use of the term 'transitive'), and its individuation, i.e. its distinctness from the action of the verb

Transitivity now became definable as the presence of one or more of these features in contrast to its absence. Inseparable from this morphosyntactic characterization of transitivity was the insistence that discourse alone provided the motivation for each of the features. Basing their argument on the notion of foregrounding (Hopper 1977), Hopper & Thompson suggested that the Transitivity features were nothing less than the typical semantic/pragmatic properties of foregrounded parts of the discourse—those parts which reported participants interacting in completed effective actions.

The study of lexical categories (Hopper & Thompson 1984) was likewise an attempt to show that the traditional categories of noun and verb were nothing other than prototypical instantiations of the basic discourse functions of identifying participants, especially those new in the discourse, and reporting events. It further contended that the cross-linguistic morphosyntactic peculiarities of nouns and verbs were directly attributable to these functions. Thus, cross-linguistically, forms were given characteristically noun-like attributes—such as case-markers, classifiers, etc.—to the degree that they functioned to identify actual participants; but they would lose these attributes when no identification was involved, e.g. *drove in the bus* vs. *went there by* (Ø) *bus*.

Givón's idea (1983) of TOPIC CONTINUITY adopted a somewhat different explanatory approach. It aimed to motivate not only various strategies for identifying participants (such as lexical nouns, pronouns, and verb indexes), but also focusing mechanisms such as voice and word order, transitivity-related phenomena such as ergativity, and verbal aspect. Topic continuity is based essentially on two textual parameters: (i) REFERENTIAL DISTANCE or 'look-back'—the number of clauses which intervene between a current and a previous reference to a participant; and (ii) PERSISTENCE or 'decay'—the number of subsequent clauses in which the participant continues, without interruption, to be mentioned.

Givón and his coworkers found a variety of grammatical phenomena to be significantly sensitive, in a statistical sense, to topic continuity calculated with these parameters. The cognitive explanation which relates topic continuity to grammatical phenomena is to be sought, Givón suggests, in relative processing difficulty. Shifts in topic and the introduction of new topics, or the reactivation of relatively old ones after a long gap, demand special coding mechanisms to facilitate cognitive tracking of the discourse. These mechanisms may attach themselves to the verb, to the noun phrase, or to various syntactic constructions, including word order.

Highly influential also has been an organized research project directed by Wallace Chafe at Berkeley, in which a narrative film (the 'Pear Film') was shown to speakers of a wide variety of languages, whose re-narrations of the film formed the basis of numerous studies of oral language (Chafe 1980). One of the more important results of this research has been an increasing recognition of the formulaic nature of spoken language—a tendency to see freely produced utterances as being modeled in a concrete way on previous utterances. Thus Lambrecht 1984 was led to see speech as existing on a cline linking idiomaticity to newly created syntactic forms, and eventually (1987) to emphasize the use of what he called P[referred] C[lause] U[nits] in the construction of discourses—following the idea of P[referred] A[rgument] S[tructure] as presented by Du Bois 1987. These are short, commonly occurring clauses consisting of a verb and any clitic pronouns associated with it—plus, optionally, a single lexical noun. In the PCU, this noun would be an object or part of a prepositional phrase, but would not be a subject. On this basis, Lambrecht was able to show that much of the emergent grammar of spoken French is invested in strategies for ensuring that 'new' referents appear in object or adverbial positions in the clause. E.g., in *J'ai pas mon père qui fait les poubelles* 'My father doesn't do dustbins' (Lambrecht 1987:229), the verb form *j'ai (pas)* 'I have (not)' has no function other than to provide for an object slot into which the new lexical noun phrase *mon père* can be fitted.

Du Bois 1987 concerned himself especially with the phenomenon of ergativity, a case-marking system in which intransitive subjects are classified grammatically with transitive objects (the so-called absolutive case), and receive a zero case marker, while transitive agents are set aside with a special case marker known as the ergative. [*See* Transitivity and Argument Coding.] In such systems, it is quite often found that ergative case-marking is restricted to lexical nouns; pronouns and verbal clitics receive some other set of case markers. Studying texts in an ergative language of the Mayan family, Sacapultec, Du Bois showed that the vast majority of clauses have one or no lexical nouns, and that lexical nouns tend to show up in the more salient object or oblique object position, or as the new ('presented') subjects of intransitive verbs like 'appear'. Clearly this distribution, the PAS, is identical with the distribution of elements in the absolutive slot in the clause. Conversely, agents, being highly topical elements, are almost never new lexical nouns, but tend to be old or 'given' (the 'Given A Constraint'); when, counter to this constraint, they are new, they have to trigger ergative case morphology (marked here, as in other languages of this family, on the verb rather than on the noun phrase itself). Somewhat counteracting this ergative tendency in discourse, Du Bois proposed, is another tendency to place agents and topics of all kinds, transitive or intransitive, in a consistent position with respect to the verb. This tendency brings about a grammatical alignment of subjects, transitive and intransitive, vs. objects of all kinds. Such 'competing motivations' (Du Bois 1985) result in the two most widespread case-marking systems observed, the ergative/absolutive and the nominative/accusative.

Many linguists who studied discourse and grammar in the 1980s moved towards an increasing sense of the inextricability of grammar from language use. This notion was thematized in Hopper 1987, 1988 with an explicit distinction between two conceptions of grammar underlying linguistic methodology: one saw grammar as basic with respect to discourse; the other saw grammar as secondary to and emergent from discourse. These two conceptions corresponded in a wider sense to the debate in critical circles between structuralism and 'post-structuralism', with the latter's 'deconstruction' of the notion of fixed pre-contextual meanings. A concomitant of this idea has been a growing emphasis on GRAMMATICALIZATION [*q.v.*], a field of study whose domain is the co-opting of lexical elements by languages into their grammars. A standard example of this would be the use of the lexical verb *to do,* e.g. in *He did his homework,* as a grammatical auxiliary having no other function than to carry tense affixes in constructions like negatives *(did not speak)* and questions *(Did they pay?).*

Grammaticalization as such is not necessarily incompatible with the idea of an a-priori grammar, since lexical elements might be seen as entering the core grammar from the periphery. However, the concept of grammar as emergent suspends provision for fixed structure, and sees all structure as in a continual process of becoming, as epiphenomenal, and as secondary to the central fact of discourse. Grammar is then to be seen as the codification of a socially and historically situated set of such regularities, endorsed and hence fixed through institutions like education and writing. Viewed from this perspective, the central project of linguistics would be the study not of 'grammar', but of 'grammaticalization'—the ways in which some of the collectively possessed inventory of forms available for the construction of discourse become 'sedimented' through repeated use, and eventually are recognized as being to a greater or lesser degree 'grammatical'.

PAUL J. HOPPER

BIBLIOGRAPHY

BOLINGER, DWIGHT. 1977. *Meaning and form.* (English language series, 11.) London: Longman.

CHAFE, WALLACE L., ed. 1980. *The Pear Stories: Cognitive, cultural, and linguistic aspects of narrative production.* (Advances in discourse processes, 3.) Norwood, N.J.: Ablex.

DU BOIS, JOHN W. 1985. Competing motivations. In *Iconicity in syntax,* edited by John Haiman, pp. 343–365. Amsterdam: Benjamins.

DU BOIS, JOHN W. 1987. The discourse sources of ergativity. *Language* 63.805–855.

GIVÓN, TALMY. 1979. *On understanding grammar.* New York: Academic Press.

GIVÓN, TALMY, ed. 1983. *Topic continuity in discourse: A quantitative cross-linguistic study.* (Typological studies in language, 3.) Amsterdam: Benjamins.

HOPPER, PAUL J. 1977. Some observations on the typology of focus and aspect in narrative language. *NUSA: Miscellaneous studies in Indonesian and languages in Indonesia,* edited by Soepomo Poedjosoedarmo, pp. 14–25. Jakarta: Badan Penyelenggara Seri NUSA. Reprinted in *Studies in Language* 3.37–64 (1979).

HOPPER, PAUL J. 1987. Emergent grammar. *Berkeley Linguistic Society* 13.139–157.

HOPPER, PAUL J. 1988. Emergent grammar and the a-priori grammar postulate. In *Linguistics in context: Connecting observation and understanding* (Advances in discourse processes, 29), edited by Deborah Tannen, pp. 117–136. Norwood, N.J.: Ablex.

HOPPER, PAUL J., & SANDRA A. THOMPSON. 1980. Transitivity in grammar and discourse. *Language* 56.251–299.

HOPPER, PAUL J., & SANDRA A. THOMPSON. 1984. The discourse basis for lexical categories in universal grammar. *Language* 60.703–752.

LAMBRECHT, KNUD. 1984. Formulaicity, frame semantics, and pragmatics in German binomial expressions. *Language* 60.753–796.

LAMBRECHT, KNUD. 1987. On the status of SVO sentences in French discourse. In *Coherence and grounding in discourse* (Typological studies in language, 11), edited by Russell Tomlin, pp. 217–261. Amsterdam: Benjamins.

LI, CHARLES N., & SANDRA A. THOMPSON. 1974. A linguistic discussion of the 'co-verb' in Chinese grammar. *Journal of the Chinese Language Teachers Association* 9.109–119.

LI, CHARLES N., & SANDRA A. THOMPSON. 1975. The semantic function of word order: A case study in Mandarin. In *Word order and word order change,* edited by Charles N. Li, pp. 163–195. Austin: University of Texas Press.

MALINOWSKI, BRONISLAW. 1922. *Argonauts of the Western Pacific.* London: Routledge.

PRINCE, ELLEN. 1978. A comparison of WH-clefts and *it*-clefts in discourse. *Language* 54.883–906.

VOLOSHINOV, V. N. [= M. M. Bakhtin]. 1973. *Marxism and the philosophy of language.* New York: Seminar Press. (Translation of 1929 publication.)

Transcription of Discourse

For linguists who work with data from ordinary conversation, transcription has become such a commonplace tool that it is easy to forget that it is an artifact. The transcript is necessarily selective and interpretive, rather than exhaustive and objective. It is not a direct mirror of reality; it is a translation of a selected set of spatio-temporally organized oral and gestural events into a written medium with properties of its own. Communicative gestalts are analyzed into components, such as gestures, words, or prosodics; continua are divided into discrete categories, e.g. pitch or stress levels, pause lengths, and intonation contours; and logical and temporal interrelationships among these parts are signaled by a handful of visually processed cues—spatial positioning and proximity, relative visual prominence (font size, upper vs. lower case, parentheses), and explicit labeling with alphabetic and non-alphabetic characters.

When complementary to discourse type, research topic, and theoretical perspective, transcription is a tremendously effective research tool; it can freeze in time a relevant subset of normally transient events, expressed in the researcher's own categories, and free of extraneous detail. When this is not the case, the transcript may give rise to irrelevant or misleading perceptions, and may actually hinder the detection of interesting regularities. For example, Ochs 1979 noted that, when turns at talk are printed one beneath the other, the eye is biased to perceive the speakers' turns as mutually contingent. To capture the much more asymmetrical structuring of early child/adult discourse, which is child-centered and child-controlled, Ochs advocated isolating the utterances of adult and child in separate columns, with the child's column to the left to enhance its perceived dominance in the interaction (considering the left-right bias of reading).

For other discourse types, or other research purposes,

different conventions may be preferable. Discourse theory provides little guidance in these matters, partly because some of the biases arise from competing influences at the written/spatial level. Transcription methods must therefore be devised inductively, subject to change with subsequent screenings of the recorded data—which are primary. Crucial for minimizing bias is an awareness of the alternatives, and of what each implies interpretively. The following discussion surveys alternatives concerning words and larger units of the discourse, pauses, prosodics, non-verbal phenomena, contextual notes, and suitability for computer-assisted analysis.

1. The words. The syllables and words spoken in an interaction are usually transcribed in standard orthography, sometimes supplemented by phonetic transcription (IPA) when finer distinctions are necessary. However, conversation analysts trained in sociology use a third method, an impressionistic extension of English spelling known as EYE-DIALECT:

(1) It's rilly intresti:ng:: (0.2) I showed Tom how tuh pro- (.) how doo uh: program a: hhh the computer doo: make a ra:ndom number CHA:RT EHHEH! ·HH! (Davidson 1984:122)

Critics claim that eye-dialect is inadequate for scientific purposes for reasons of uninformativeness, inconsistency, ambiguity, faulty phonetics, and poor readability, especially for non-native English speakers. Table 1 contains examples from published work (mostly from Atkinson & Heritage 1984), which demonstrate these faults.

TABLE 1. *Shortcomings of Eye-Dialect*

	Eye-Dialect	Standard English Spelling
Inconsistency	*of, uv*	*of*
	cuz, excuz	*'cause, excuse*
Ambiguity	*go::d*	*God* (rather than *goad* or *goed*)
Uninformativeness	*wuz, uv*	*was, of*
False Phonetics	*brou:ght*	*brought* (with lengthened vowel)
	askedche	*asked you* (rather than *asktche*)
	dz, wz, w'z, sm	*does, was, some*
	difference:	(entire last syllable lengthened)
Poor Readability	*tih, ahhndh, iht*	*to, and, it* (extra aspiration)
	bighta lunch, doo	*bite of lunch, to*

Since the distorted spellings do not enter into the analyses, eye-dialect seems intended to give the general flavor of the dialect without being precise. Contextual notes are preferable for this purpose, since they avoid the false impression of precision. Where precision is needed, it is preferable to use IPA-related conventions like those of Labov 1973—not only for scientific reasons, but also because they avoid the cartoon-like stereotypes reinforced by eye-dialect, which makes non-standard dialects appear substandard, and their speakers lower-class or unintelligent (Preston 1985).

2. Larger units. The literary model of the dramatic play is sometimes adopted in preserving conversation data:

(2) Woody Allen: *I finished my first film,* Take the Money and Run, *in 1968 or something, and the day that I was through that—put it out in movie theaters, I never, ever looked at it again, nor have I looked at any of them again.*
Safer: *Really?* (official transcript of CBS, 60 Minutes, December 13, 1987)

However, this is inadequate for discourse analysis, because it is biased toward the written rather than the spoken language. Its units are syntactically rather than intonationally defined, and its punctuation captures only partially the prosodic contours of spoken discourse (Chafe 1987, Tedlock 1983).

Preferable for discourse analysis are systems which are organized around intonation or tone units:

(3) *And he comes down,*
.. from the ladder,
[1.1] *and he's wearing an apron,*
that holds the pears,
in deep pockets.
And he dumps them [.45] *into some baskets .. that he has.* (Chafe 1980:34)

Here punctuation marks unit-final prosodic contours, such as falling, rising, continuing (actually non-falling/non-rising), extra-low falling, and disrupted intonation. These decisions may rest on acoustic similarity to a set of contours that are believed to be socio-culturally relevant to the speaker. The alternative is to examine larger stretches of speech by the speaker, attempting to infer from the context of use which contour serves which function for the speaker. Neither method is strictly objective. Since the prosodic contours for different discourse functions (question, statement, etc.) vary across cultures and languages, Du Bois et al. 1990 mark both the contours and the functions. These authors have also prepared an audio-cassette, of examples from actual discourse, which is highly useful for training transcribers to make prosodic distinctions reliably.

For narrative discourse, the EPISODE is a useful unit; but it may have fuzzy boundaries because of anaphoric ties to earlier parts of the discourse. The TURN is a useful unit where multiple speakers are involved; but it is not objectively delimitable where there is much overlapping talk. [*See* Conversation Analysis.] When overlap involves entire utterances by different speakers, the decision of whose utterance is leftmost or topmost is arbitrary; but it has implications for perceived priority, because of the direction-of-reading bias. When an overlap ends because one speaker seems to drop out in mid-utterance, some researchers mark it 'interrupted'. This is useful for locating points of difficulty in an interaction, but it involves interpretive leaps with respect to (i) judged incompletion and (ii) attribution of cause or even blame.

3. Pauses. What is considered a 'short' pause is found to vary interestingly with research purposes. It tends to be 0.5 seconds or less for sociolinguists, but 0.2 seconds or less for those investigating more intra-individual processes, such as the packaging of information in narratives.

A particular pause is known to seem longer or shorter depending on its position in the discourse (mid-utterance vs. between-turns) as well as on the influence of other acoustic features such as syllable lengthening and deceleration (O'Connell & Kowal 1983). With socio-culturally similar speakers, where intonational fine-tuning may carry much communicative weight, more context-sensitive categories seem preferable, assuming that the researcher's categories are the right ones. For cross-linguistic research, objective measurement may be preferable, since it highlights the specific acoustic cues which are interpreted differently by various cultural groups.

An inter-turn pause may be placed in any of three locations: at the end of the pre-pause utterance, at the beginning of the post-pause utterance, or on a line in between. The third implies most clearly the shared responsibility of interactants for the length of such pauses. Where a speaker resumes a turn after an exceptionally long pause, that pause may be perceived as an intra-turn pause. Transcribing such a pause instead as a 'silent turn' by the other speaker (Labov & Fanshel 1977) may be an effective method for indicating speaker reticence; but it is clearly an interpretive judgment, as Tannen 1981 observes.

4. Prosodics. Some systems mark distinctions in intonation and tempo more finely. In the following example, capital letters indicate the nucleus of the tone unit; hollow arrows signal the relative pitch register; line arrows signal rising, falling, and level tone; double and single quotes signal stress; and dashes and dots signal pauses (London/Lund Corpus S.1.10, Svartvik & Quirk 1979:256).

(4) **A** [364] ▮[↘m]▮ - - - [365] ▮but [ə:m] · you ▮know it's △very ▷↘INTERESTING [ə:m]■ · [366] [ə:] a ▮great ˈgreat ˝flap and ge△fuffle ˈwent ↗ON [əm]■ [367] when ˝▮S↘ESAME ˈStreet {▮came to Ausˈtralian △T↘ELEVISION■} ■ ·
b [368] [m]
A [369] ▮everyone ▷→SAID■ [370] ▪▮H↘EAVENS you KN↗OW■ [371] ▮what a DR↗EADFUL TH↘ING■ [372] our ▮children will ˈnow talk A△M↘ERICAN■

The decisions involved in such a transcription take time, and are not needed for all research questions.

Many of these conventions involve subdividing dimensions into discrete categories. In the 1950s, American 'levels' theorists marked four distinct pitch levels and four distinct stress levels in an attempt at precise description. British 'configurationalists', concerned with effective foreign-language training, criticized the approach as overly atomistic; they noted that it overlooked the fact that many non-identical contours (e.g. /4 1/ and /3 1/) function equivalently in discourse, i.e. as falling contours (Ladd 1980). This controversy has subsided in recent years. Both sides now emphasize pragmatic distinctiveness, and the marking of pitch has become restricted to the structurally important 'anchor points' of tone units, with intervening syllables considered more the result of local laws and as less communicatively significant (Ladd 1983).

5. Nonverbal phenomena. Coughs, laughs, and yawns are often noted within brackets, directly on the utterance line. This preserves the temporal ordering of verbal and nonverbal events, while implying the subordination of nonverbal to verbal. More detailed descriptions of nonverbal events are generally placed on a separate line, co-indexed at the relevant point on the verbal line. Transcription methods and typologies for gaze, gesture, and posture are found in the intra-individually oriented approach of Ekman & Friesen 1969, and in the more discourse-oriented approaches of Erickson & Shultz 1982 and Heath 1986.

6. Contextual notes. For some analyses, the transcript is useless without adequate ethnographic information concerning the participants, their relationships, and the context of data-gathering. Although such information is of far less relevance to Conversation Analysis than it is to sociolinguistics, it is expedient to include it, especially in an era of increasing collaboration and data-sharing among researchers with different theoretical perspectives.

7. Transcription for computer search. The following are necessary for efficient and exhaustive computer-assisted search of patterns (words, phrases, or codes) in the data:

(a) Systematic differentiation of speakers
(b) Systematic differentiation of speech from non-speech events (e.g. comments or contextual notes)
(c) Associating a standard version with each nonstandard (IPA or eye-dialect) variant in the corpus ('normalization')

The first two requirements are satisfied in practically all systems; but the third is violated with alarming frequency, even in highly respected corpora which are explicitly intended for computer search (e.g. the computerized version of the London/Lund Corpus, cited above). Diacritics can be suppressed en masse as special characters, but no such filtering is possible for nonstandard spellings and IPA variants. Unless the researcher is able to anticipate all nonstandard variants in the data (which is highly unrealistic), the danger exists that the retrieved instances constitute a partial and potentially biased sample, and that conclusions based on them cannot be generalized. For example, to locate all instances of *the* in the London/Lund corpora, the researcher would need to think of looking also for any and all other nonstandard spellings or IPA variants of *the* (e.g. [dhi]) which might also be present in the data—only about half of which are normalized. This flaw is shared by many other corpora, no doubt because of the newness of the computerized methodology. There are various ways of tying a nonstandard item to its normalization. Regardless of the method chosen, it is best to normalize during initial data entry, before the human eye becomes habituated to interpretively inconsequential surface differences which the computer will take quite literally.

Choices among such alternatives as those surveyed here may facilitate the perception of some types of structure in the data, but may hinder the perception of others. Thus a transcript simultaneously embodies and influences the analyst's perspectives on the data. To minimize misleading biases in a transcript, it is important to choose carefully among alternatives, with awareness of what each of them implies; and to view each stage of the transcript as provisional and derived—subject to change with subsequent screenings of the recorded data, which are primary.

Jane Anne Edwards

BIBLIOGRAPHY

Atkinson, J. Maxwell, & John Heritage, eds. 1984. *Structures of social action: Studies in conversation analysis.* Cambridge & New York: Cambridge University Press.

Chafe, Wallace L., ed. 1980. *The pear stories: Cognitive, cultural, and linguistic aspects of narrative production.* (Advances in discourse processes, 3.) Norwood, N.J.: Ablex.

Chafe, Wallace L. 1987. Cognitive constraints on information flow. In *Coherence and grounding in discourse* (Typological studies in language, 11), edited by Russell S. Tomlin, pp. 21–51. Amsterdam: Benjamins.

Davidson, Judy. 1984. Subsequent versions of invitations, offers, requests, and proposals dealing with potential or actual rejection. In Atkinson & Heritage 1984, pp. 102–128.

Du Bois, John W., et al. 1990. Outline of discourse transcription. In *Transcription and coding methods for language research,* edited by Jane A. Edwards & Martin D. Lampert, to appear. Hillsdale, N.J.: Erlbaum.

Ekman, Paul, & Wallace V. Friesen. 1969. The repertoire of nonverbal behavior: Categories, origins, usage, and coding. *Semiotica* 1.49–98.

Erickson, Frederick, & Jeffrey J. Shultz. 1982. *The counselor as gatekeeper: Social interaction in interviews.* New York: Academic Press.

Heath, Christian. 1986. *Body movement and speech in medical interaction.* Cambridge & New York: Cambridge University Press.

Labov, William. 1973. *Language in the inner city: Studies in the Black English vernacular.* Philadelphia: University of Pennsylvania Press.

Labov, William, & David Fanshel. 1977. *Therapeutic discourse: Psychotherapy as conversation.* New York: Academic Press.

Ladd, D. Robert, Jr. 1980. *The structure of intonational meaning: Evidence from English.* Bloomington: Indiana University Press.

LADD, D. ROBERT, JR. 1983. Levels vs. configurations, revisited. In *Essays in honor of Charles F. Hockett* (Cornell linguistic contributions, 4), edited by Frederick B. Agard et al., pp. 50–59. Leiden: Brill.
OCHS, ELINOR. 1979. Transcription as theory. In *Developmental pragmatics,* edited by Elinor Ochs & Bambi B. Schieffelin, pp. 43–72. New York: Academic Press.
O'CONNELL, DANIEL C., & SABINE KOWAL. 1983. Pausology. In *Computers in language research,* vol. 2, *Notating the language of music, and the (pause) rhythms of speech* (Trends in linguistics, Studies & monographs, 19), edited by Walter A. Sedelow Jr. & Sally Y. Sedelow, pp. 221–301. Berlin: Mouton.
PRESTON, DENNIS R. 1985. The Li'l Abner Syndrome: Written representations of speech. *American Speech* 60.328–336.
SVARTVIK, JAN, & RANDOLPH QUIRK, eds. 1979. *A corpus of English conversation.* (Lund studies in English, 56.) Lund: Gleerup.
TANNEN, DEBORAH. 1981. Review of Labov & Fanshel 1977. *Language* 57.481–486.
TEDLOCK, DENNIS. 1983. *The spoken word and the work of interpretation.* Philadelphia: University of Pennsylvania Press.

DISTINCTIVE FEATURES. *See* Phonological Features.

DJAMINDJUNGAN LANGUAGES constitute a family of the northwestern part of the Northern Territory, Australia. They form a top-level component of the primarily lexicostatistical classification of Australian languages [*q.v.*] by Stephen A. Wurm and Shirô Hattori, eds., *Language atlas of the Pacific area* (Canberra: Australian Academy of the Humanities, 1981).

LANGUAGE LIST

Djamindjung: 100 speakers reported in 1983, on the Victoria River. Reports indicate that Djamindjung and Ngaliwuru are so close as to be a single language; only some elderly people can distinguish the difference. The people are bilingual in Ngarinman and in Kriol.

Nungali: 2 speakers reported in 1981, in the upper Daly River area.

DJERAGAN LANGUAGES constitute a family of the northern part of Western Australia and the Northern Territory. They form a top-level component of the primarily lexicostatistical classification of Australian languages by Stephen A. Wurm and Shirô Hattori, eds., *Language atlas of the Pacific area* (Canberra: Australian Academy of the Humanities, 1981), on which source the subgrouping of Figure 1 is based.

FIGURE 1. *Subgrouping of Djeragan Languages*

Kitja
Miriwungic
Gadjerawang, Miriwung

LANGUAGE LIST

Gadjerawang: 3 speakers reported in 1981; their territory is on the north coast of Australia from Wyndham to the mouth of the Victoria River and inland. Also called Gadjerong.

Kitja: 100 or more speakers reported in 1983, near Hall's Creek, Western Australia. Also called Gidja or Kidja.

Miriwung: 20 speakers reported in 1983, in Kununurra and Hall's Creek, Western Australia. Also called Mirung, Merong, or Miriwun. Some older people still speak Miriwung, but most of the people speak Kriol, and young people use only Kriol.

DOWNSTEP AND DOWNDRIFT. The terms 'downstep' and 'downdrift' refer to a lowering of the realization pitch for phonological tones at certain points in an utterance or phrase. [*See* Tone.] This lowering is called 'DOWNDRIFT' when its conditioning is overtly phonological, as in the following example from Akan, where the pitch is lowered automatically between L and H (´ = high tone; ` = low tone; '!' = downstep/downdrift):

(1) *kò!fí bì!sá sì!ká nó.*

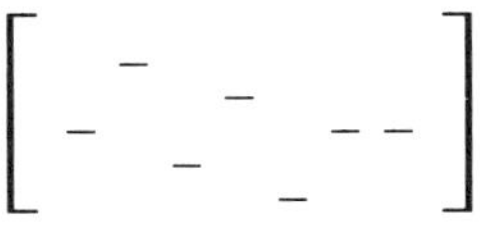

'Kofi asks for the money.'

By contrast, DOWNSTEP appears to be phonologically unconditioned. For example, there is a downstep between the two high tones of the Akan proper name *Á!má*. Kikuyu exhibits both L!L and H!H sequences, which contrast with non-downstepped LL and HH:

(2a) *ŋɔ̀mbɛ̀ hɔ̀:rɛ̀:rì ! ndìtò*

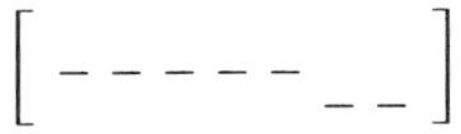

cattle heavy gentle
'heavy, gentle cattle'

(2b) *kàriòkí* ꜝ *né moɛ̀γá.*

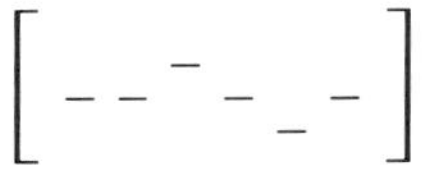

'Kariũki is good.' Cf. 2c:

(2c) *ìrìá né reɛ̀γá.*

'Milk is good.'

Downstep and downdrift are referred to collectively as REGISTER LOWERING or KEY LOWERING. Register lowering affects all tones to the right of the register-lowering point. In 'partial' register-lowering systems, such as that of Akan, a lowered high tone is lower than a preceding high, but higher than a preceding low. In 'total' register-lowering systems (such as Kikuyu), a high tone is lowered all the way to the preceding low. Liberman & Pierrehumbert 1984 have shown that, at least in English, register-lowering (which they refer to as 'downstep') lowers the high pitch register by a constant proportion each time; that is,

(3) $X_{i+1} - r = s \cdot (X_i - r)$

Here X_i and X_{i+1} = the height of the high pitch register, in Hertz, before and after register-lowering; s = the register-lowering constant; and r = the reference line from which the high pitch register is measured.

The nature of the phonological environment for downstep has been the subject of much controversy. Early theorists such as Schachter & Fromkin 1968 assumed that register lowering takes place only between L and H; a downstep between high tones was attributed to an L-deletion rule which took place after phonetic pitch assignment. Later theorists, uncomfortable with this mixing of the phonetic and phonological components, noted that downstep often occurs between low tones (as in 2a), and between high tones where there is no evidence for an underlying low (as in Akan *Á*ꜝ*má*). Thus they have generally adopted one of the following approaches, or some combination of them:

(a) The DOWNSTEP-ENTITY approach: downstep is treated as the phonetic reflex of an otherwise unrealized phonological entity—either an abstract downstep 'operator' (Stewart 1971, Clements 1979), or a floating tone (Clements & Ford 1979).

(b) The DOWNSTEP-FEATURE approach: downstep is represented by a PHONOLOGICAL FEATURE on an overt tone—either a diacritic feature such as [echo] (Carrell 1970), or a tonal feature or feature-combination which is otherwise unused in the language. [*See* Phonological Features.] For example, Goldsmith 1976 treats the downstepped high tone of Igbo as a mid tone, with a register-lowering rule which applies between [+hi] (= H or M) and [+lo] (= L or M).

(c) The REGISTER-TIER approach: downstep and downdrift are represented on a 'register tier' which is superimposed on the tonal tier. This tier may take the form of a metrical tree, as in Figure 1 (Clements 1983). Or it may be linear, as in Figure 2 (from the analysis of Bamileke-Dschang by Hyman 1985).

(d) The IDENTICAL-TONE approach, which has been argued for by Odden 1982 and Clark 1990, exploits the contrast which the autosegmental theory permits, in principle, between shared features and sequences of identical features (Figure 3). In this

FIGURE 1. *Metrical Tree Analysis*

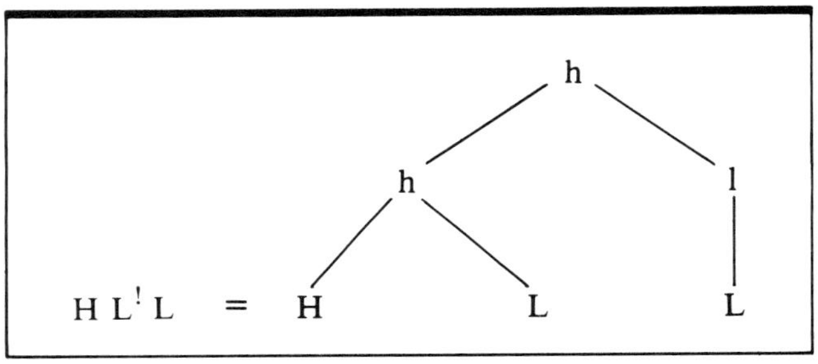

FIGURE 2. *Linear Analysis*

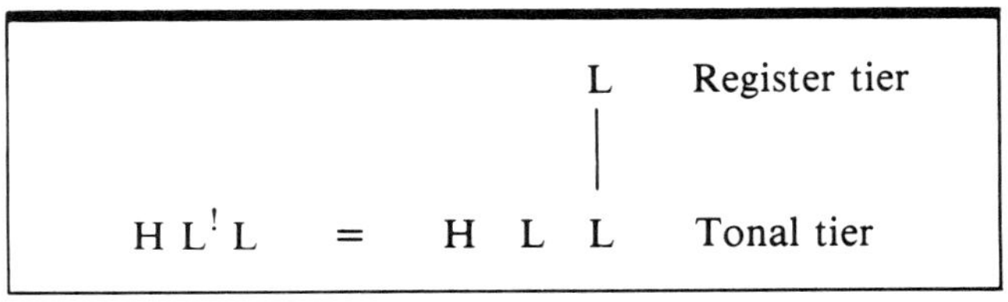

FIGURE 3. *Identical-Tone Analysis*

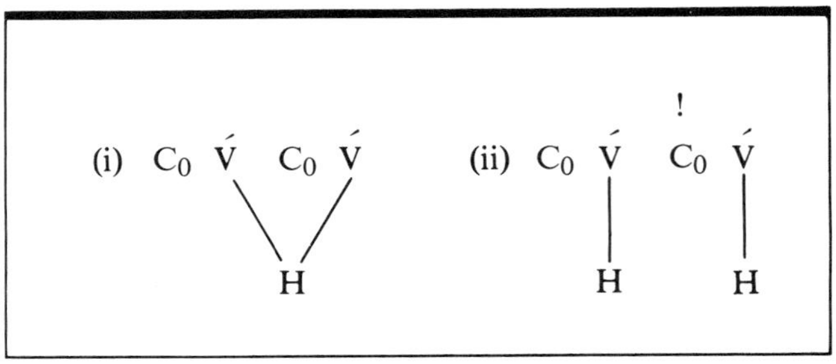

analysis, downstep is the phonetic reflex of a sequence of identical tones, as in (b).

MARY M. CLARK

BIBLIOGRAPHY

CARRELL, PATRICIA L. 1970. *A transformational grammar of Igbo*. London: Cambridge University Press.

CLARK, MARY M. 1990. *The tonal system of Igbo*. Dordrecht: Foris.

CLEMENTS, GEORGE N. 1979. The description of terraced-level tone languages. *Language* 55.536–558.

CLEMENTS, GEORGE N. 1983. The hierarchical representation of tone features. In *Current approaches to African linguistics*, vol. 1, edited by Ivan R. Dihoff, pp. 145–176. Dordrecht: Foris.

CLEMENTS, GEORGE N., & KEVIN C. FORD. 1979. Kikuyu tone shift and its synchronic consequences. *Linguistic Inquiry* 10.179–210.

GOLDSMITH, JOHN. 1976. *Autosegmental phonology*. MIT dissertation. Published, New York: Garland, 1979.

HYMAN, LARRY M. 1985. Word domains and downstep in Bamileke-Dschang. *Phonology Yearbook* 2.47–83.

LIBERMAN, MARK, & JANET PIERREHUMBERT. 1984. Intonational invariance under changes in pitch range and length. In *Language sound structure: Studies in phonology presented to Morris Halle*, edited by Mark Aronoff & Richard Oehrle, pp. 157–233. Cambridge, Mass.: MIT Press.

ODDEN, DAVID. 1982. Tonal phenomena in KiShambaa. *Studies in African Linguistics* 13.177–208.

SCHACHTER, PAUL, & VICTORIA A. FROMKIN. 1968. *A phonology of Akan: Akuapem, Asante, Fante*. (Working papers in phonetics, 9.) Los Angeles: Department of Linguistics, University of California.

STEWART, JOHN M. 1971. Niger-Congo, Kwa. In *Current trends in linguistics*, edited by Thomas A. Sebeok, vol. 7, *Linguistics in Sub-Saharan Africa*, pp. 179–212. The Hague: Mouton.

DRAVIDIAN LANGUAGES.

More than twenty-five languages of the Dravidian family are spoken in India, Pakistan, and Sri Lanka (see Map 1); they are divided into four geographic/genetic groups, as shown in Figure 1. Of the above, Tamil, Malayalam, Kannada, and Telugu [*qq.v.*] are literary languages; the rest have oral traditions. [*For data on individual languages, see the Language List at the end of this article. Note that genetic classification is not established for all languages in the list.*]

1. Historical relationships. Various scholars have proposed a major subgrouping including South-Central and Central Dravidian (Krishnamurti 1961). However, there is now better evidence to group South and South-Central into a major subgroup vis-à-vis Central and North. The main isoglosses supporting the present subgrouping are given below. (Citations of *DEDR* refer to Burrow & Emeneau 1984.)

FIGURE 1. *Subgrouping of Dravidian Languages*

Central Dravidian
Gadaba, Kolami, Naiki, Ollari, Parji
Northern Dravidian
Brahui, Kurux, Malto
South-Central Dravidian
Gondi (including Koya), Konda, Kui, Kuvi, Manda, Pengo, Telugu
Southern Dravidian
Irula, Kannada, Kodagu, Kota, Malayalam, Tamil, Toda, Tulo

(a) **i u* > **e o* / (C)__C*a*
(b) The back-formation of **ñān* 'I' (*DEDR* 5160) from **ñām* 'we (inclusive)' (*DEDR* 3647) beside PDr. **yān* 'I' (*DEDR* 5160)
(c) The change **c* > *s* > *h* > Ø in South and South-Central

South Dravidian is distinguished by the innovation of **awaḷ* 'she (far)' **iwaḷ* 'she (near)' (*DEDR* 1, 410) representing feminine gender, and the loss of the final syllable in **awanṯu* (*DEDR* 1), **iwanṯu* 'he' (*DEDR* 410). Changes such as **ṯ* > *d, ḍ* / V__(V), and the innovation of derived numerals in the female category (e.g. **īr-aḷ* 'two women', *DEDR* 474, **mū-aḷ* 'three women' *DEDR* 5052) distinguish the Central subgroup from the others. The sound change **k* > *x* / #__V (V = all but *i ī*) characterizes North Dravidian.

Contact between Old Indo-Aryan-speaking peoples and native Dravidians dates to the middle of the 2nd millennium BCE. Bilingualism through the ages has led not only to extensive lexical borrowing between Dravidian and Indo-Aryan, but also to convergence in several phonological, morphological, and syntactic features (Emeneau 1980). Diffusion from Dravidian into Indo-Aryan is thought to be responsible for the progressive increase in the incidence of retroflex consonants in later Indo-Aryan; the increased use of echo-words and onomatopoetic expressions; compound verbs; dative subject constructions; and changes in noun declension. [*See also* South Asian Languages.]

Attempts have been made to discover distant relationships of Dravidian with Uralic (Ural-Altaic), Proto-Elamite—or, more recently, Japanese; however, none

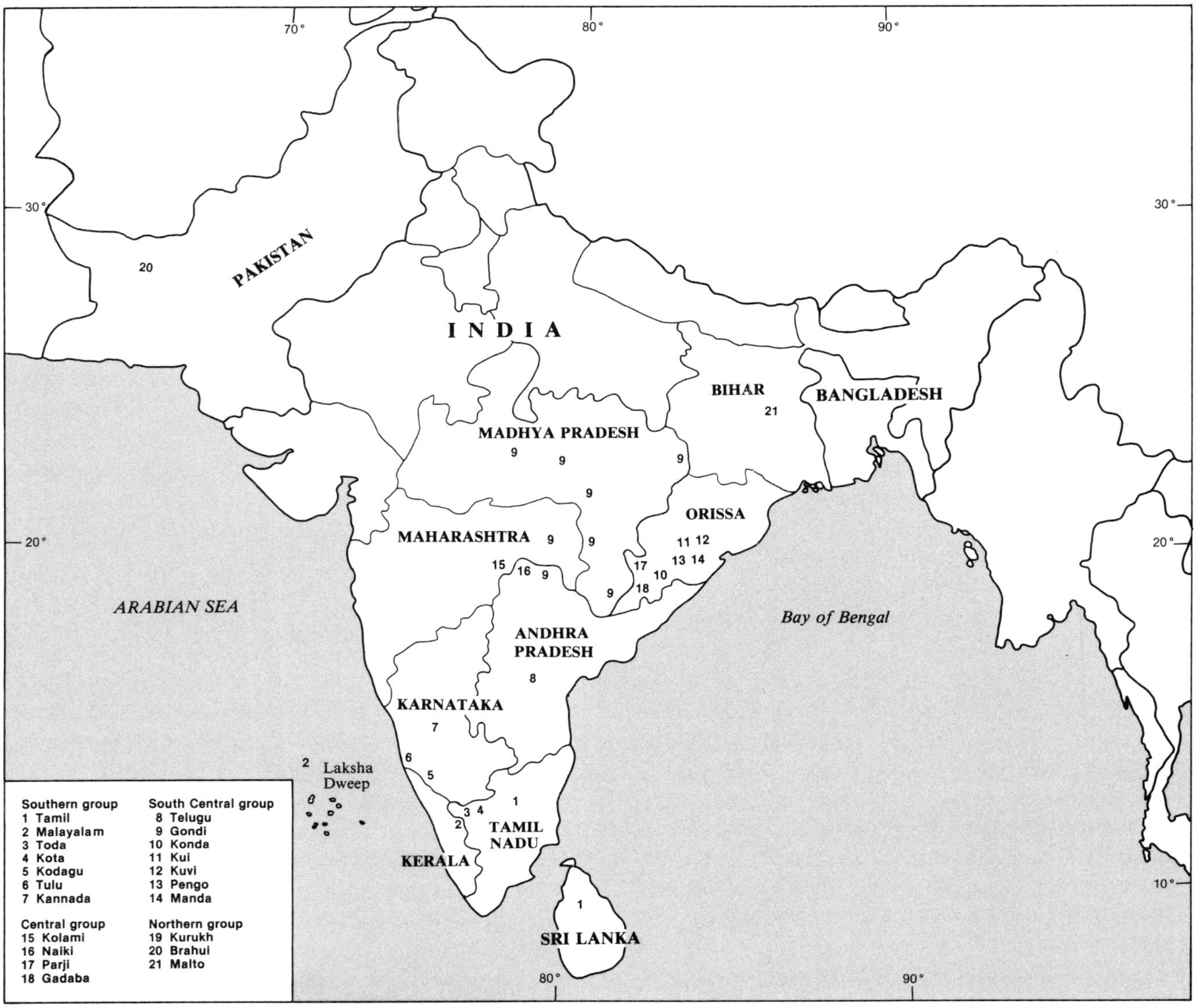

MAP 1. *Distribution of Languages in South Asia*

of these has been established beyond reasonable doubt (Krishnamurti 1969, 1985).

2. Phonology. P[roto-]D[ravidian] had ten vowels, *i e a o u* plus their long counterparts, and sixteen consonants, as shown in Table 1. In addition, a laryngeal **H* figures in some reconstructions.

PD roots have the shape (C)V_1(C) = V_1, CV_1, V_1C, CV_1C (V_1 = long or short). There are no prefixes. Alveolar and retroflex consonants do not begin a root or word. All consonants except *r* and *ẓ* can be geminated postvocalically. The vowel-ending roots may take formative suffixes of the shape C, CV, CCV, CCCV. Roots ending in C take formative suffixes of the above types preceded by V_2 = *a, i, u*. A base-final stop is followed by *u*. There are no consonant clusters word-initially. Postvocalic clusters are either geminates or sequences of nasal + stop (+ stop).

TABLE 1. *Proto-Dravidian Consonants*

	Labial	Dental	Alveolar	Retroflex	Palatal	Velar
Obstruents	p	t	ṯ	ṭ	c	k
Nasals	m	n		ṇ	ñ	
Laterals			l	ḷ		
Vibrant			r			
Glides	w			ẓ	y	

The obstruents, when intervocalic, had lenis allophones [w d ṟ ḍ s g]; after a nasal, they were voiced stops, and geminates were always voiceless. The descendant languages have maintained this pattern, but have also developed word-initial voicing and aspiration through sound changes and borrowing from Indo-Aryan.

3. Grammar. The following are the shared native syntactic and morphological features of the Dravidian languages. (For reference, see Caldwell 1856, Shanmugam 1971, Subrahmanyam 1971, and Zvelebil 1978). [*For examples, see articles on* Tamil, Malayalam, Kannada, and Telugu.]

Dravidian languages are verb-final (SOV); adverbs precede verbs, and adjectives precede nouns; auxiliaries follow the main verb.

A sentence may have a VP or NP predicate, i.e. S → NP + PRED; and PRED → {VP, NP}. The finite verb, inflected for tense, carries agreement with the subject in G[ender/]N[umber]/P[erson] in the 3rd person, but only in number and person in the 1st and 2nd persons. A predicate NP also carries subject agreement in many cases.

The main clause ends in a finite verb with the internal structure stem + tense/mode + GNP; subordinate clauses end in non-finite verbs, such as perfective, durative, conditional, and concessive. A NP + NP clause becomes subordinate when a non-finite form of the verb **ā* 'to be' (*DEDR* 333) or **yan* 'to say' (*DEDR* 868) is added to it. Quotatives carry the perfective participle **yan* 'having said' as a complementizer. Sometimes two main verbs are fused as the predicate in a simple sentence (Steever 1988).

Interrogative sentences are formed either by the use of question words, or by adding (in the yes-no type) a question particle **ā* to the phrase or clause questioned.

Relative clauses are formed by changing the finite verb to a participle (stem + tense + adjectival suffix), and shifting the head noun to the position following the participle.

In verbal predications, negation can be a part of verb inflection; in nominal predications, use is made of a negative inflected form of **ā, *man* 'to be' (*DEDR* 333, 4778), or of a negative verb **cil* 'to be not' (*DEDR* 2559).

The major grammatical categories are nouns (including pronouns and numerals) and verbs. Most adjectives are nouns in the genitive. There are some basic adjectives which often occur in compounds, e.g. **kem* 'red' (*DEDR* 1931), **weḷ* 'white' (*DEDR* 5496a), **kiṯu* 'small' (*DEDR* 1594). The deictic bases **a̤/*aH* 'that' (*DEDR* 1), **ī/*iH* 'this' (*DEDR* 140), **ū/*uH* 'yonder' (*DEDR* 557a), and **yā/*yaH* 'which' (*DEDR* 5151) are used only as modifiers. Demonstrative pronouns denoting person, time, place, quantity, etc. are derived from these roots; e.g. PD **awanṯu* 'that man', **atu* 'that woman, thing', **ap-pōẓ(u)* 'then' (*DEDR* 1); **iwanṯu* 'this man', **itu* 'this woman, thing', **ippōẓ(u)* 'now' (*DEDR* 410).

Nouns carry gender and number; in the Southern group, a three-way distinction of gender occurs in the singular, e.g. **awan* 'he', **awaḷ* 'she', **atu* 'it'; in plural **awar* 'they (human)' and **away* 'they (non-human)' are distinguished. South-Central and Central Dravidian show a two-way distinction in the singular and plural: **awanṯu* 'he', **atu* 'she, it'; **awar* 'they (men, or men and women)'; **away* 'they (non-human, or women)'. Telugu and North Dravidian deviate from the above in the plural, i.e. **awar* 'they (men and/or women)', **away* 'they (non-human)'. It is assumed that South Dravidian innovated **awaḷ* in the singular, whereas North Dravidian and Telugu independently added an exclusive semantic category of 'women' under **awar*. North Dravidian (Kurux and Malto) also introduced gender in the 1st and 2nd persons through contact with Indo-Aryan. There are two numbers, singular (unmarked) and plural: human **-(V)r* vs. non-human **-k*(V), **-nk*(V), **-nkk*(V); **-ḷ*; *-V(*n*)*kaḷ* (the last is a sequence of two underlying plural morphemes).

Non-nominative cases are added to the oblique stem (formed with one or more of the suffixes **tt, *n, *i, *a*), which also functions as the genitive. The cases reconstructible for PD are nominative (unmarked), accusative, dative, and possibly instrumental/locative. Sociative and ablative cases also exist, but are not clearly reconstructible to Proto-Dravidian. A number of postpositions denoting cause, purpose, direction, etc., with the status of independent words, are also used in different languages.

The numerals 1 to 5 and 8 to 10 consist of a root + a fused neuter morpheme **t, *tt, *k,* e.g. **on-ṯu* 'one' (*DEDR* 990), **ir-aṇṭu* 'two' (*DEDR* 474), **mū-nṯu* 'three' (*DEDR* 5052), **nāl-(k)ku* 'four' (*DEDR* 3655), **caym-tu* 'five' (*DEDR* 2826), **eṇ-ṭṭu* 'eight' (*DEDR* 784), **paH-tu* 'ten' (*DEDR* 3918); the forms **cāṯu* 'six' (*DEDR* 2485) and **ēẓ* 'seven' (*DEDR* 910) are also used with neuter (non-human) agreement; a human suffix **-war* is added to the numeral roots when they qualify human nouns, e.g. **mūwar* 'three persons', **mūnṯu* 'three (non-human)'.

An inflected finite verb consists of a verb stem (simple or complex) + (modal auxiliary) + tense + GNP. An extended verb stem may contain transitive/causative marker + reflexive. There are at least two tenses reconstructible to PD: past and non-past. The NPs which are the constituents of a VP carry case morphemes denoting object, instrument, source, location, etc. generally interpreted in terms of the semantic structure of the verb.

There are many clitics, of which two are reconstructible: *-ā interrogative and *-ē emphatic. Each language and subgroup has evolved many others, mostly representing contraction of finite verbs.

Adverbs of time and place are inflected for case like noun stems, but do not carry number and gender. Adverbs are also formed from descriptive adjectives by adding an inflected verb 'to be'. Onomatopoetic words and echo words generally function as adverbs.

BH. KRISHNAMURTI

BIBLIOGRAPHY

BURROW, THOMAS, & MURRAY B. EMENEAU. 1984. *A Dravidian etymological dictionary*. 2d ed. Oxford: Clarendon Press.

CALDWELL, ROBERT. 1856. *A comparative grammar of the Dravidian or South-Indian family of languages*. London: Harrison. 3d ed., London: Routledge & Kegan Paul, 1913. Reprinted, Madras: University of Madras, 1956.

EMENEAU, MURRAY B. 1980. *Language and linguistic area*. Stanford, Calif.: Stanford University Press.

KRISHNAMURTI, BH. 1961. *Telugu verbal bases: A comparative and descriptive study*. (University of California publications in linguistics, 24.) Berkeley: University of California Press.

KRISHNAMURTI, BH. 1969. Comparative Dravidian studies. In *Current trends in linguistics*, vol. 5, *Linguistics in South Asia*, edited by Thomas A. Sebeok, pp. 309–333. The Hague: Mouton.

KRISHNAMURTI, BH. 1985. An overview of comparative Dravidian studies since *Current trends 5* (1969). In *For Gordon H. Fairbanks* (Oceanic Linguistics, Special publication no. 20), edited by Veneeta Z. Acson and Richard L. Leed, pp. 212–231. Honolulu: University of Hawaii Press.

SHANMUGAM, S. V. 1971. *Dravidian nouns: A comparative study*. Annamalainagar: Annamalai University.

STEEVER, SANFORD B. 1988. *The serial verb formation in the Dravidian languages*. (Motilal Banarsi Dass series in linguistics, 4.) Delhi: Motilal Banarsi Dass.

SUBRAHMANYAM, P. S. 1971. *Dravidian verb morphology: A comparative study*. Annamalainagar: Annamalai University.

ZVELEBIL, KAMIL. 1978. *A sketch of comparative Dravidian morphology*, vol. 1. (Janua linguarum, Series practica, 180.) The Hague: Mouton.

LANGUAGE LIST

Abujmaria: 16,000 speakers reported in 1981, in Bastar District, Madhya Pradesh, India. Also called Abujhmadia, Abujhmaria, or Hill Maria. Gatte Maria is an ethnic group that seems not to be distinct linguistically from Abujhmaria.

Adiyan: 2,500 to 5,700 speakers reported in Cannanore District of Kerala, Tamil Nadu, and Karnataka, India. Also called Eravas. Speakers constitute a scheduled tribe.

Allar: spoken by 350 people in Palghat District, Kerala, India. Also called Chatans.

Alu: 2,000 speakers reported in 1987, in the Nilgiri District of Tamil Nadu, India. Also called Alu Kurumba.

Aranadan: spoken by 600 people in Tamil Nadu, Karnataka, and Calicut and Palghat Districts of Kerala, India. Also called Eranadan. A scheduled tribe.

Badaga: around 105,000 speakers reported in 1971, in Tamil Nadu, India. Also called Badag, Badagu, Badugu, or Vadagu.

Bharia: around 5,400 speakers reported in 1971, in Bilaspur, Chhatarpur, Chhindwara, Datia, Durg, Jabalpur, Mandla, Panna, Rewa, Sidhi, Surguja, and Tikamgarh Districts of Madhya Pradesh, India. Also called Bhar, Bharat, Bhumia, Bhumiya, or Paliha. A scheduled tribe.

Brahui: 1,710,000 speakers reported in 1981, with 1,500,000 in south central Pakistan around Quetta and Kalat and in east Baluchistan and Sind, plus 200,000 in Afghanistan and 10,000 in Iran. Also called Brahuidi, Birahui, or Kur Galli. Some bilingualism exists in Baluchi.

Dandami Maria: spoken in Madhya Pradesh, Maharashtra, and Orissa, India. Also called Bison Horn Maria, Maria Gond, Madiya, or Dhuru.

Dorli: around 24,500 speakers reported in 1971, in Andhra Pradesh, Madhya Pradesh, Maharashtra, and Orissa, India. Also called Dorla.

Duruwa: 90,000 speakers reported in 1986 from an ethnic population of 100,000, in Bastar District of Madhya Pradesh and Koraput District of Orissa, India. Also called Dhurwa, Dhruva, Durva, Parji, Parjhi, Parja, Paraja, Parajhi, Thakara, Tagara, or Tugara. The name of the people is Dhurwa, that of the language Parji. Parji is spoken as mother tongue by 90 percent of the ethnic group. Halbi (Indo-Aryan) is the principal second language. There are monolinguals, including children. Hindi is the official language, but is not well known except by the educated. Parji is also spoken by the Madiya for communicating with the Dhurwa people.

Gadaba: 8,800 speakers reported in 1981, in Koraput District, Orissa, India. Also called Kondekor Gadaba. Distinct from Gadaba in Munda family, spoken in the same district.

Gondi: around 1,950,000 speakers reported in 1981, in Madhya Pradesh, Andhra Pradesh, Maharashtra, and Orissa, India. Also called Gaudi, Gondiva, Gondwadi, Goondile, Goudwal, Ghond, Godi, Gondu, Goudi, or Koitor. Gatte Maria is quite distinct. North Gondi and Central Gondi have only 68 percent mutual intelligibility.

Holiya: around 3,100 speakers reported in 1961, in Madhya Pradesh and Maharashtra, India. Also called Holar, Holari, Hole, Holian, Holu, or Golari-Kannada.

Irula: 48,000 speakers reported in 1985, in the Nilgiri Hills of Tamil Nadu, India. Also called Eravallan, Erukala, Irava, Irular, Irular Mozhi, Iruliga, Iruligar, Korava, or Kad Chensu.

Kadar: 800 speakers reported in 1981, in Kerala, Andhra Pradesh, and Tamil Nadu, India. Also called Kada. A scheduled tribe.

Kaikadi: around 12,000 speakers reported in 1971, in Maharashtra and Karnataka, India. Also called Kokadi, Kaikai, or Kaikadia.

Kamar: around 10,100 speakers reported in 1971, in the Raipur and Rewa districts of Madhya Pradesh, India. A scheduled tribe.

Kanikkaran: 10,000 speakers reported in Calicut, Ernakulam, Quilon, and Trivandrum Districts of Kerala, and in Tirunelveli District of Tamil Nadu, India. Also called Kanikkar, Kannikan, Kannikaran, or Kannikharan. A scheduled tribe. It may be identical with Malaryan.

Kannada: 26,890,000 speakers reported in 1989, in Karnataka, Andhra Pradesh, Tamil Nadu, and Maharashtra, India. Also called Kanarese. The state language of Karnataka.

Kannada, Southern: 10,000 or more speakers reported in 1987, in Coimbatore and Charmapuri districts of Tamil Nadu and adjacent sections of Karnataka and Andhra Pradesh, India. Also called Southern Nonstandard Kannada. Limited bilingualism in Tamil and Standard Kannada.

Khirwar: spoken by around 34,300 people in Madhya Pradesh, India. Also called Khirwara.

Kodagu: around 93,000 speakers reported in 1981, in Coorg, Karnataka, India. Also called Coorg, Kadagi, Khurgi, Kotagu, Kurja, or Kurug.

Kolami, Northwestern: 78,500 speakers reported in 1989 from an ethnic population of 66,900, in Andhra Pradesh, Madhya Pradesh, and Maharashtra, India. Also called Kolamboli, Kulme, Kolam, or Kolmi. The speakers are called Kolavar or Kolam. Nearly all adults are somewhat bilingual in Marathi, Telugu, or Gondi. Proficiency is limited in Marathi (a non-standard regional variety).

Kolami, Southeastern: 10,000 speakers reported in 1989, in Andhra Pradesh and Maharashtra, India. The speakers in Maharashtra are not functionally bilingual in either Telugu or Marathi.

Konda-Dora: around 15,700 speakers reported in 1971, in Visakhapatnam District of Andhra Pradesh, and in Koraput District of Orissa, India. Also called Kubi or Porja. Bilingualism in Telugu is very limited. Many speakers along the roads through Araku are competent in Adiwasi Oriya.

Koraga, Korra: spoken by around 1,500 people in Kerala, India. Also called Koragar, Koragara, Korangi, or Korra.

Koraga, Mudu: spoken in Kerala, India. Also called Mudu.

Kota: 900 speakers reported in 1961, in the Nilgiri Hills of Tamil Nadu, India. Also called Kotta.

Koya: 242,000 or more speakers reported in 1981, along the Godavari River in Andhra Pradesh, and in Maharashtra, Madhya Pradesh, and Orissa, India. Also called Koi, Koi Gondi, Kavor, Koa, Koitar, Koyato, Kaya, Koyi, or Raj Koya. May be considered a variety of Gondi. Telugu is the second language used, but bilingual proficiency is low.

Kudiya: spoken by 100 people in Cannanore District of Kerala, in Coorg and South Kanara Districts of Karnataka, and in Tamil Nadu, India. A scheduled tribe.

Kui: around 508,000 speakers reported in 1981, in the Udayagiri area of Orissa, Andhra Pradesh, Madhya Pradesh, and Tamil Nadu, India. Also called Kandh, Khondi, Khond, Khondo, Kanda, Kodu, Kodulu, Kuinga, or Kuy.

Kurichiya: spoken by around 12,000 people in Cannanore District of Kerala and in Tamil Nadu, India.

Kurumba: 700,000 speakers reported in 1987, in Andhra Pradesh, Kerala, Tamil Nadu, and Karnataka, India. Also called Korambar, Kuramwari, Kurumar, Kurumbar, Kuruba, Kurumban, or Kurumvari. May be more than one language.

Kurumba, Betta: 2,000 to 5,000 speakers reported in 1987, on the north side of the Nilgiri Hills in Tamil Nadu and in Mysore District, Karnataka, India. Also called Betta Kurumba Nonstandard Tamil. May or may not be the same as Betta Kuruba in Coorg District.

Kurumba, Jenu: spoken on the north side of the Nilgiri Hills on the border between Tamil Nadu and Karnataka, India. Also called Jennu Kurumba, Nonstandard Kannada, or Jen Kurumba. May or may not be the same as Jenu Kuruba, a variety of Kannada.

Kurux: 1,264,000 speakers reported in 1981, in Bihar, Madhya Pradesh, West Bengal, and Orissa, India, and the rest in Bangladesh. Also called Uraon, Kurukh, Kunrukh, Kadukali, Kurka, Oraon, or Urang. Distinct from Nepali Kurux.

Kurux, Nepali: spoken around Danusa in the eastern Terai, Nepal. Also called Dhangar, Jhanger, Janghard, Jangad, Uraon, Orau, or Oraon. Distinct from Kurux of India and Bangladesh.

Kuvi: 300,000 speakers reported in 1989, in Orissa and Andhra Pradesh, India. Includes the Jatapu variety. Also called Kuwi, Kuvinga, Kuvi Kond, Kond, or Khondi.

Malankuravan: spoken by around 5,000 people in Kerala, India. Also called Male Kuravan.

Malapandaram: spoken by 500 people in Kerala, India. Also called Malapantaram, Malepantaram, or Hill Pantaram. A scheduled tribe.

Malaryan: spoken by around 5,000 people in Ernakulam, Kottayam, and Trichur Districts of Kerala, and in Tamil Nadu, India. Also called Maleyarayan, Male Arayan, Malayarayan, Arayans, Karingal, or Vazhiyammar. Possibly the same as Kanikkaran.

Malavedan: spoken by around 2,000 people in Ernakulam, Kottayam, Quilon, and Trivandrum Districts of Kerala, and in Tirunelveli District of Tamil Nadu, India. Also called Malavetan, Towetan, or Vedan.

Malayalam: around 26,000,000 speakers reported in 1981, with 21,900,000 in Kerala and the Laccadive Islands, India, 300,000 in the United Arab Emirates, and 300 in Fiji. Also called Alealum, Malayalani, Malayali, Malean, Maliyad, or Mallealle. The state language of Kerala.

Malto: around 95,000 speakers reported in 1981, in northeast Bihar and West Bengal, India. Also called Malti, Maltu, Malpaharia, or Rajmahalia.

Manda: spoken in Kalahandi District of Orissa, India.

Manna-Dora: spoken by around 8,500 people in East Godavari, Srikakulam, and Visakhapatnam Districts of Andhra Pradesh, and in Tamil Nadu, India. A scheduled tribe.

Mannan: around 5,000 speakers reported in 1961, in Kerala and Andhra Pradesh, India. Also called Manne or Mannyod.

Maria: around 78,500 speakers reported in 1971, in Andhra Pradesh, Gujarat, Madhya Pradesh, and Maharashtra, India. Also called Madi, Madiya, Madia, Modh, or Modi.

Muka-Dora: 9,970 speakers reported in Andhra Pradesh and Tamil Nadu, India. Also called Reddi-Dora, Conta-Reddi, Reddi, or Riddi. May be a dialect of Telugu.

Mulia: a few speakers reported in Andhra Pradesh, near the Adiwasi Oriya, India. May be the same as Muria.

Muria: around 13,000 speakers reported in 1971, in Andhra Pradesh and Madhya Pradesh, India. Also called Jhoria or Mudia. May be the same as Mulia.

Muthuvan: spoken by around 7,000 people in Andhra Pradesh and Kerala, India. Also called Mudavan, Muduvar, Mudugar, Mutuvar, or Muduvan. A scheduled tribe.

Nagarchal: around 7,100 speakers reported in 1971, in Madhya Pradesh and Maharashtra, India. Also called Nagar or Nagarchi.

Ollari: 800 speakers reported in 1931, in Koraput District, Orissa, India. Also called Hallari, Allar, Ollaro, Hollar Gadbas, or Kondkor.

Paliyan: 600 speakers reported in 1941, in Kerala and Tamil Nadu, India. Also called Palaya, Seramar, or Palayan.

Paniyan: around 6,330 speakers reported in 1971, in Kerala and Tamil Nadu, India. Also called Pania, Paniya, or Panyah.

Pardhan: 500 speakers reported in 1961, in Andhra Pradesh, Madhya Pradesh, and Maharashtra, India. Also called Pradhan or Pradhani. Probably more than one language.

Pengo: around 1,300 speakers reported in 1961, in Koraput District, Orissa, India. Also called Pengu.

Tamil: 50,000,000 or more speakers reported in 1986, with 45,000,000 in Tamil Nadu, India; 3,346,000 in Sri Lanka; 1,000,000 in Vietnam; and others in South Africa, Malaysia, Fiji, Singapore, Mauritius, and the United Arab Emirates. Also called Tamizh, Tamalsan, Tambul, Tamili, Tamal, or Damulian. The state language of Tamil Nadu.

Telugu: around 54,000,000 speakers reported in 1981, with 44,700,000 in Andhra Pradesh, India; 2,000 in Fiji; and others in the United Arab Emirates and Singapore. Also called Telegu, Andhra, Gentoo, Tailangi, Telangire, Telgi, Tengu, Terangi, or Tolangan. The state language of Andhra Pradesh.

Toda: 800 speakers reported in 1961, in the Nilgiri and Kunda Hills of Tamil Nadu, India. Also called Todi or Tuda.

Tulu: around 1,157,000 speakers reported in 1971, in South Kanara District, Karnataka, India, and in adjacent areas. Also called Tal, Thalu, Tilu, Tuluva Bhasa, Tullu, or Thulu. Bellari may be a separate language.

Ullatan: spoken by around 1,500 people in Kerala, India. Also called Katan, Kattalan, or Kochuvelan.

Urali: around 1,100 speakers reported in 1961, in Kerala and Tamil Nadu, India. Also called Oorazhi, Uraly, or Urli.

Vishavan: 150 speakers reported in Ernakulam, Kottayam, and Trichur Districts of Kerala, India. Also called Malarkuti.

Waddar: around 36,000 speakers reported in 1971, in Andhra Pradesh and Karnataka, India. Also called Vadari or Werders.

Yanadi: spoken by around 206,000 people in Andhra Pradesh, Tamil Nadu, and Orissa, India. Also called Yadi, Yandis, or Yenadi.

Yerava: around 11,000 speakers reported in 1971, in Coorg, Karnataka, India. Also called Yoruba.

Yerukala: around 68,000 speakers reported in 1971, in East Godavari District, Andhra Pradesh, India. Also called Yarukula, Yerkula, Yerukla, Erukala, Korava, or Yerukala-Korava. May be considered a variety of Tamil.

D-STRUCTURE has been one of the most characteristic elements of transformational-generative grammar since its inception. As a replacement of the older notion 'deep structure', it was introduced in Chomsky 1980 as a technical term, in order to avoid the unintended connotations of the older term. Its primary function is the representation of those structural aspects of sentences in which thematic (theta) roles, such as 'agent' and 'goal', are directly assigned. D-structures are defined by the categorial component of grammar (so-called X-bar theory) and the lexicon. [*See* Lexicon; Phrase Structure.] D-structures are transformed into S-STRUCTURES [*q.v.*] by a possibly multiple application of a single mapping, 'Move alpha'. [*See* Transformations.] In S-structures, the theta-roles are not necessarily directly assigned to categories; instead, they may bind TRACES [*q.v.*] in the positions from which they are moved. The structures defined by X-bar theory and the lexicon are also referred to as BASE STRUCTURES. Only those base structures that correspond to well-formed S-structures qualify as D-structures. (For general reference, see Chomsky 1965, 1981, 1986, and Koster 1987.)

As an illustration, consider a simple declarative sentence like *Mary visited Cambridge*. In the structure underlying this sentence, the theta role 'goal' is directly assigned to the N[oun] P[hrase] *Cambridge,* which is in the position subcategorized by the verb *visit*. [*See* Subcategorization.] The structure in question can be transformed into the corresponding passive structure *Cambridge*$_i$ *was visited* **t**$_i$ *by Mary*. In this S-structure, *Cambridge* is no longer in a position in which the theta role 'goal' is directly assigned. Instead, the theta role is assigned to the trace (in the original position of *Cambridge*), which forms a CHAIN together with *Cambridge* in the new position. Unlike S-structure, D-structure is always 'trace-free', and therefore has its NPs in direct theta positions.

Common confusions about D-structure concern its role in semantics and in Universal Grammar. Outside of linguistics, it is sometimes thought that deep structure (or D-structure) is the level of meaning representation. This is an error since, according to modern linguistics, both D-structure and S-structure contribute to meaning. The contribution of D-structure lies mainly in lexical information such as the assignment of theta roles. 'Move alpha' may change the linear order of elements, which can have certain semantic effects.

Another common confusion identifies deep structure with Universal Grammar. The notion of Universal Grammar concerns not only D-structure but the whole organization of grammar—including the organization of S-structure, and the nature of the mappings between levels of representation. [*See* Formal Grammar.] The confusion stems from the so-called UNIVERSAL BASE HYPOTHESIS that was considered in earlier stages of generative grammar. According to that hypothesis, all languages have a common deep structure. The hypothesis was never generally accepted; it also obscured the fact that deep structure (or D-structure) is only a technical term for the initial PHRASE MARKER of a set that leads to S-structure by the mapping 'Move alpha.' D-structures can differ from language to language, because certain parameters (e.g. those concerning word order) are set in different ways.

JAN KOSTER

BIBLIOGRAPHY

CHOMSKY, NOAM. 1965. *Aspects of the theory of syntax.* Cambridge, Mass.: MIT Press.

CHOMSKY, NOAM. 1980. *Rules and representations.* (Woodbridge lectures, 11.) New York: Columbia University Press.

CHOMSKY, NOAM. 1981. *Lectures on government and binding.* (Studies in generative grammar, 9.) Dordrecht: Foris.

CHOMSKY, NOAM. 1986. *Knowledge of language: Its nature, origins, and use.* New York: Praeger.

KOSTER, JAN. 1987. *Domains and dynasties: The radical autonomy of syntax.* (Studies in generative grammar, 30.) Dordrecht: Foris.

DUTCH. Modern Standard Dutch is the official language of the Netherlands, and one of the official languages of Belgium—where it is often called FLEMISH, and competes with French. AFRIKAANS, spoken in South Africa, is a direct descendant of Dutch. The number of native speakers in Holland and Belgium together was approximately twenty million in 1988. Dutch is also spoken to some extent in Surinam (formerly Dutch Guyana) and in the Netherlands Antilles. It had some influence on the creole languages in those areas; it also influenced the standardized form of Malay that is now the official language of Indonesia.

In the Netherlands, the usage of standard Dutch is widespread. There still exists a remarkable variety of dialects, but active dialect speakers are declining in numbers. (The same is true of Frisian, the only other language spoken in the Netherlands.) Politically as well as linguistically, the situation in Belgium is more complex. The present-day language is the outcome of two major developments: the rise of Amsterdam as the political center of the Dutch Republic, and the mass immigrations of speakers of southern dialects after the fall of Antwerp in 1585.

Historically (cf. van Loey 1970), Dutch belongs to the so-called Low German dialects, and contrasts with the varieties of High German that formed the standard language of Germany; cf. Dutch *appel,* English *apple,* but German *Apfel* with [pf]. With German, however, Dutch shares the devoicing of word-final consonants: Dutch *rond* 'round' (adjective) and Ger. *rund* with final [t], but Eng. *round* with final [d]. A peculiar development is the change of Germanic [g] to the velar fricative [x]: Dutch *goed* 'good' [xut], but Ger. *gut* [gut] and Eng. *good* [gud]. Dutch retained many Germanic words that have disappeared from English, but the number of words of Romance origin in its vocabulary is also considerable. Sometimes a Germanic and a Romance word co-exist: *verhouding* and *relatie* 'relation'. [*See also* Germanic Languages.]

In its morphology, Dutch is similar to English in the loss of inflectional endings and case endings. In the syntax of words, phrases, and clauses, it is similar to German [*q.v.*] in all fundamental respects.

A comprehensive survey of Dutch grammar is Geerts et al. 1984. A useful practical reference is Donaldson 1981.

1. Phonology. The vowels and consonants of Dutch are shown in Tables 1 and 2, respectively.

The consonant system is comparatively simple. Word-final devoicing leads to morphophonemic alternations in the nominal and verbal paradigms; the feature [voice] also plays an important role in rules for assimilation in compound words and across word boundaries.

The difference between long and short vowels is contrastive with mid and low vowels: *boom* 'tree' vs. *bom* 'bomb'; *baas* 'boss' vs. *bas* 'bass'; *beek* 'brook' vs. *bek* 'beak'. The diphthongs are rising: [ɛi] is the counterpart of Eng. and Ger. [ai], as in *rijden* 'ride', Ger. *reiten.*

2. Morphology. Nominal as well as verbal paradigms have been drastically simplified since the period of Middle Dutch. Case endings are absent, except for the occasional use of the genitive *'s,* and gender distinctions have been reduced to two. The majority of nouns select the determiner *de,* but original neuters select the determiner *het.* The distinction between strong and weak inflection is preserved to some extent; adjectives take the strong (non-suffixed) form only in noun phrases with the indefinite determiner *een* when the noun is of the neuter category. Compare:

(1a)	*het grote paard*	*de grote koe*
	'the big horse'	'the big cow'
(1b)	*een groot paard*	*een grote koe*
	'a big horse'	'a big cow'
(1c)	*de grote paarden*	*de grote koeien*
	'the big horses'	'the big cows'

The plural of nouns is formed by adding *-en* to the stem; it is usually pronounced without the final *-n.* Nouns that form their plural in *-s* are a minority. Dutch orthography preserves the distinction between word-final plosives that are underlyingly voiced, and those that are voiceless throughout.

The paradigm of the present and past tenses of the regular (or weak) verb *spelen* 'to play' is given in Table 3.

After stems ending in a voiceless consonant, the ending of the past tense is *-te,* and that of the past participle is *-t*: thus *ik gokte* 'I gambled', *ik heb gegokt* 'I have gambled'. As in other Germanic languages, so-called strong verbs form their past tense by vowel change—e.g. *geven, gaf, gegeven,* corresponding to Eng. *give, gave, given.*

Word formation is of a mixed type. Inflection and derivation are predominantly suffixal, but many deriva-

TABLE 1. *Consonant Phonemes of Dutch.* Common orthographic equivalents are given in brackets.

	Labial	Alveolar	Palatal	Velar	Uvular	Glottal
Stops						
Voiceless	p	t		k		
Voiced	b	d				
Fricatives						
Voiceless	f	s		x ⟨*ch*⟩		h
Voiced	v	z		γ ⟨*g*⟩		
Nasal	m	n		ŋ ⟨*ng*⟩		
Liquid		l			ʀ ⟨*r*⟩	
Glide	ʋ ⟨*w*⟩		j			

TABLE 2. *Vowel Phonemes of Dutch*

	Front		Central		Back	
	Unrounded	Rounded	Unrounded	Rounded	Unrounded	Rounded
High	i	ü				u
Higher mid	ɪ	ö				o
Lower mid	e		ə	œ		ɔ
Low	ɛ		a		ɑ	
Diphthongs	ɛi			ʌü		ɑu

TABLE 3. *Present Tense and Past Tense in Dutch*

	Present	Past
Singular		
ik	*speel*	*speelde*
jij/u	*speelt*	*speelde*
hij/zij/het	*speelt*	*speelde*
Plural		
wij	*spelen*	*speelden*
jullie	*spelen*	*speelden*
zij	*spelen*	*speelden*
Participle		
	spelend	*gespeeld*

tions are lexicalized and non-productive. One of the most productive suffixal derivations is the formation of diminutives, e.g. *paard+je* 'small horse'. Prefixation is more transparent, and occurs frequently in the formation of verbs. The following verbs are all derived from the intransitive verb *werk+en* 'to work': *be+werken* 'to work (the land), to adapt (a text)'; *ver+werken* 'to process, to digest'; *door+werken* 'to work one's way through'; *tegen+werken* 'to obstruct'. Nominal compounding is frequent and productive, e.g. *huis* 'house', *huis+dier* 'domestic animal, pet'.

3. Syntax. In the structure of its sentences, Dutch is a typical continental Germanic language. In declarative sentences, the finite verb (which agrees in number with the subject) is in second position in the main clause, and is typically separated by adverbials from its immediate complements. This 'Verb Second' phenomenon also occurs in Scandinavian languages, but is more conspicuous in Dutch and German.

(2a) *Jan wast de auto.*
'John washes the car.'

(2b) *Jan wast morgen de auto.*
'John will wash the car tomorrow.'

(2c) *Jan heeft de auto gewassen.*
'John has washed the car.'

The structure of these sentences becomes transparent under the assumption that the clause is basically verb-final—which is the ordering that actually occurs in the dependent clause:

(3a) *omdat Jan de auto wast*
'because John washes the car'

(3b) *omdat Jan morgen de auto wast*
'because John will wash the car tomorrow'

(3c) *omdat Jan de auto heeft gewassen*
'because John has washed the car'

In dependent clauses, constituents are ordered from right to left, with the main verb as the focal point; in the independent clause, that ordering is broken up by moving the finite verb. Thus compare:

(4a) *Jan gaat morgen met de auto naar*
John goes tomorrow with the car to
Amsterdam.
A.

(4b) *als Jan morgen met de auto naar*
when John tomorrow with the car to
Amsterdam gaat
A. goes

In complex sentences, verbs from different clauses are strung together—a phenomenon known as Clause Union or Verb Raising. This is obligatory with some verbs, and optional with others. Thus either 5b or 5c are acceptable:

(5a) *Jan probeerde [de auto te besturen].*
John tried the car to steer
'John tried to drive the car.'

(5b) *Jan heeft geprobeerd [de auto te besturen].*
John has tried the car to steer

(5c) *Jan heeft de auto [proberen te besturen].*
John has the car try to steer

Ex. 5c also shows another particularity: when verbs are strung together, the infinitive replaces the past participle in the perfect tense.

In declarative main clauses, the sentence-initial position can be occupied either by the grammatical subject or by other constituents. Under appropriate contextual conditions, the following sentences are equally acceptable in the meaning 'I have given that book to John':

(6a) *Ik heb aan Jan dat boek gegeven.*

(6b) *Dat boek heb ik aan Jan gegeven.*

(6c) *Aan Jan heb ik dat boek gegeven.*

The finite verb stays in second position; otherwise, word order is quite free, and is subject to much stylistic variation. Prepositional phrases can also move to a position after the main verb, but noun phrase complements cannot. Compare these sentences meaning 'I have bought that book for John':

(7a) *Ik heb voor Jan dat boek gekocht.*

(7b) *Ik heb dat boek gekocht voor Jan.*

(7c) **Ik heb voor Jan gekocht dat boek.*

JAN G. KOOIJ

BIBLIOGRAPHY

DONALDSON, BRUCE C. 1981. *Dutch reference grammar.* The Hague: Nijhoff.

GEERTS, GUIDO, et al., eds. 1984. *Algemene Nederlandse spraakkunst.* Groningen & Leuven: Wolters-Noordhoff.

VAN LOEY, ADOLPHE. 1970. *Schönfelds historische grammatica van het Nederlands.* 8th ed. Zutphen: Thieme.

DYSLEXIA refers to a continuum of severe impairments in the acquisition and development of written language. These childhood disabilities result in reading and spelling performance from one and a half to two years or more below levels appropriate to age.

Definitions of dyslexia vary; many, intentionally exclusionary, further define the syndrome as having no instructional, environmental, intellectual, emotional, or gross neurological basis for the impairments. The incidence of dyslexia in the population is estimated at between 5 and 10 percent, depending on the definition used. The sex ratio is heavily biased toward males; estimates range between 3:1 and 10:1. Common characteristics include specific speech and language problems (e.g. in speech segmentation, word-finding, or phonology); delayed speech development; a familial history of dyslexia; short-term memory problems (e.g. in following verbal commands, or in remembering spelling patterns); directional confusions; and neurological softsigns, such as abnormal reflexes and coordination problems (see Thomson 1984).

The typical dyslexic child would be a male of average to superior intelligence, who has great difficulty in learning to read, to spell, and often to write, despite adequate instruction and opportunities. The discrepancy between general intellectual potential and specific written-language impairment is critical: this distinguishes dyslexic children from poor readers whose impaired reading is either commensurate with their intellectual abilities, or is the product of their instructional environment.

To avoid excluding cases of complex disability, some researchers advocate definitions of dyslexia which include any profound, age-inappropriate reading deficit. They question the arbitrariness involved in determining adequate instruction, and in distinguishing major from minor neurological deficits.

1. History of research. The history of research on dyslexia contains numerous contradictions, as well as multiple names and definitions for the syndrome. Confusion stems from two flawed assumptions: (i) that reading is primarily visual in nature; and (ii) that dyslexia is a unitary syndrome, with a single cause and a homogenous group of dysfunctional readers (see Ellis 1984). For most of its history, dyslexia was considered a visual problem, as reflected in its first name, 'word-blindness'. Later researchers, when confronted by severely impaired readers with different characteristics than found in previous studies, renamed and redefined the syndrome accordingly.

Adolf Kussmaul, a 19th-century neurologist, first used the term 'word-blindness' to describe impaired adults with discrete brain lesions. Other 19th-century neurologists, including Rudolf Berlin and J. J. Déjerine, used the terms 'dyslexia' (< Greek 'bad' + 'word') and 'alexia' ('not' + 'word') to describe ACQUIRED reading loss. [*See* Alexia.] Childhood cases were discovered in the late 19th century by the British physicians James Kerr and Pringle Morgan; these were thought to be the developmental analog of acquired reading disorders in adults. The Scottish ophthalmologist James Hinshelwood summarized such cases in 1917, and renamed the syndrome 'congenital word-blindness'. Hinshelwood was the first to emphasize the presence of dyslexia in children of normal or above-average intelligence, and its high incidence in boys. A precursor to modern neurological and cognitive theorists, he attributed the cause of dyslexia to failure of the angular gyrus to function properly in the visual memory of letters and words.

In the 1930s, Samuel T. Orton renamed the syndrome 'strephosymbolia' (< Gk. 'twisted' + 'symbol'), based on the following hypotheses:

(a) The cerebral hemispheres contain mirror images of the same information (e.g. *bud* vs. *dub*).
(b) In dyslexia, cerebral dominance is incomplete [*see* Reading and Lateralization].
(c) Images and symbols are reversed for dyslexics, because information competes between hemispheres.

Although Orton's view of the brain was incorrect, his extensive work contributed both to a major method of remediation, and to later neuropsychological theories of reading failure. Orton's emphasis on reversals was problematic. Many still regard the developmentally NORMAL letter-reversals made by young children as primary dyslexic symptoms, which they are not (see Vellutino 1979).

Since Orton, hundreds of dyslexia studies have been conducted on perceptual and cognitive variables (e.g. eye movements, intra- and inter-sensory processing, sequencing, and memory) to determine the underlying differences between average and severely impaired readers. Dyslexic readers differ significantly on most tested variables. This has exacerbated disagreement about the explanation of dyslexia, and has caused some scholars to deny specificity to the syndrome. Rutter et al. 1970 used an inclusionary definition of dyslexia in their classic Isle of Wight study, where they demonstrated SPECIFIC READING IMPAIRMENTS distinct from GENERAL READING RETARDATION. Children with specific reading problems, compared to generally poor readers, had average to high IQs, specific speech and language problems, a higher proportion of males, persistence of impairment over time, and poor response to conventional reading instruction.

During the 1970s, there was exponential increase in theoretical knowledge about the cognitive structure of reading, its development, and its breakdown. New directions in dyslexia research arose from each area. First, reading came to be depicted as a complex, interacting continuum of perceptual, cognitive, and linguistic subprocesses: each requires rapid (or automatic) rates of processing, attention, and memory (see overviews in Ellis 1984, Just & Carpenter 1987, Perfetti 1985). Focus on the centrality of language sub-processes (Shankweiler & Liberman 1972), and on the rate and allocation of attention, represented major changes in understanding the reading process.

Second, Chall 1983, Frith 1985, and others emphasized developmental changes in reading skills and processes over time: basic phonological processes are emphasized in early acquisition; but semantic and comprehension processes dominate as reading proficiency increases.

Similar changes marked dyslexia research. Vellutino 1979 exemplified the move from a 'perceptual deficit' view of dyslexia to one giving centrality to linguistic deficits. Multi-componential views of reading resulted in emphases on multiple causes, and on heterogeneity among impaired readers. Important to diagnosis and remediation, attempts to classify the major subtypes of dyslexia proliferated. Most classifications included: (i) a small subgroup with visual/spatial deficit; (ii) a large group with primarily linguistic deficits—phonological, auditory, and naming problems; and (iii) a mixed group. Other classifications were based on a breakdown of reading, spelling, and writing skills. Despite their importance, efforts at classification have had inconclusive results because of inconsistencies in tests, populations, and methods (see overviews by Doehring et al. 1981 and Ellis 1984).

Better models of reading and reading development have helped to clarify earlier contradictions and persistent questions about specificity in dyslexia. Stanovich 1986 uses a cognitive developmental framework to argue that many cognitive differences in dyslexia are prominent only in early stages; others are caused by reading problems (e.g. by eye movements); and still others have relationships of RECIPROCAL CAUSATION with reading. For example, most younger dyslexic readers do not have vocabulary problems; but, because of their reading deficit, they develop them, which further impedes reading. Through this framework, Stanovich was able to eliminate or reinterpret many cognitive differences—and also to highlight critical, SPECIFIC deficits underlying dyslexia, such as phonological problems.

The third major direction in dyslexia research emerged from advances in the neurosciences on reading pathology. The neurologists Norman Geschwind, Albert Galaburda, and Thomas Kemper demonstrated anatomical differences in dyslexic brains, originating during fetal development. Architectonic studies indicated aberrant neuronal organization in particular language areas (e.g.

area Tpt, in the left planum temporale, part of Wernicke's area), with cell migration into inappropriate neuronal layers, and cortical thinning in others (Geschwind & Galaburda 1984).

More speculative research by Geschwind concerned possible connections between aberrant neuronal migratory patterns and the symptom cluster of left-handedness, auto-immune diseases, migraine, and severe learning disorders. Geschwind hypothesized that abnormal testosterone levels in the fetus may delay development of the left hemisphere and thymus, and may underlie a co-occurrence of these symptoms. This work to date involves a small number of cases and can not be generalized.

Other work in the neurosciences involves the use of various technologies, such as Evoked Potential, Magnetic Resonance Imaging, C[omputerized] A[xial] T[omography] and P[ositron] E[mission] T[omography] scans, and B[rain] E[lectrical] A[ctivity] M[apping]. Computerized images of the brain are used to detect possible differences in brain structure and metabolism; Evoked Potential and BEAM research can compare differences between average and dyslexic readers during performance on cognitive and behavioral tasks. The latter studies are redirecting attention to dyslexic differences in the rate of processing tasks, particularly those which are linguistic in nature.

2. Remediation. Bridging theory and educational practice is difficult in the dyslexias, because of technological advances and several other basic factors:

(a) The biological, genetic component in dyslexia causes many researchers to assume mistakenly that remediation is useless.
(b) Written-language deficits in dyslexia persist over time and, in large part, appear resistant to CONVENTIONAL instruction.
(c) Underlying deficits take on new forms in later development (e.g. problems in the organization of writing, or in comprehension of complex reading material), despite earlier remedial successes.
(d) Although significant convergence across disciplines has advanced diagnosis, more convergence in remediation is needed (cf. Chall 1983, Stanovich 1986, Lovett et al. 1988).

Thomson 1984 has summarized the literature on remediation; he emphasizes that the genetic propensity in dyslexia was 'multi-factorial', and highly influenced by instruction. Thomson and other educators stress four components in remedial efforts:

(i) Programs should be systematically, sequentially organized around the structure of the written language system.
(ii) Instruction should be gradual and phonically based, providing a phonological route in reading.
(iii) Intrinsic problems in memory and self-esteem require overlearning techniques and novelty.
(iv) Strengths of the individual child should be continually emphasized, along with work on specific areas of deficit.

A central message in remediation is that developmentally dyslexic readers are neither lacking in intelligence nor lazy; they benefit from an individualized, life-span approach to the varied problems that can emerge.

MARYANNE WOLF

BIBLIOGRAPHY

CHALL, JEANNE S. 1983. *Stages of reading development.* New York: McGraw-Hill.

DOEHRING, DONALD, et al. 1981. *Reading disabilities: The interaction of reading, language, and neuropsychological deficits.* New York: Academic Press.

ELLIS, ANDREW W. 1984. *Reading, writing, and dyslexia: A cognitive analysis.* London & Hillsdale, N.J.: Erlbaum.

FRITH, UTA. 1985. Beneath the surface of developmental dyslexia. In *Surface dyslexia: Neuropsychological and cognitive studies of phonological reading,* edited by Karalyn E. Patterson et al., pp. 301–330. London: Erlbaum.

GESCHWIND, NORMAN, & ALBERT M. GALABURDA, eds. 1984. *Cerebral dominance.* Cambridge, Mass.: Harvard University Press.

JUST, MARCEL A., & PATRICIA CARPENTER. 1987. *The psychology of reading and language comprehension.* Boston: Allyn & Bacon.

LOVETT, MAUREEN W., et al. 1988. Treatment, subtype, and word-type effects in dyslexic children's response to remediation. *Brain & Language* 34.328–349.

PERFETTI, CHARLES A. 1985. *Reading ability.* Oxford & New York: Oxford University Press.

RUTTER, MICHAEL, et al. 1970. *Education, health, and behaviour: Psychological and medical study of childhood development.* London: Longman. New York: Wiley.

SHANKWEILER, DONALD, & ISABELLE Y. LIBERMAN. 1972. Misreading: A search for causes. In *Language by ear and by eye: The relationships between speech and reading,* edited by James F. Kavanagh & Ignatius G. Mattingly, pp. 293–317. Cambridge, Mass.: MIT Press.

STANOVICH, KEITH E. 1986. Matthew effects in reading: Some consequences of individual differences in the acquisition of literacy. *Reading Research Quarterly* 21.360–407.

THOMSON, MICHAEL E. 1984. *Developmental dyslexia: Its assessment and remediation.* London: Arnold.

VELLUTINO, FRANK R. 1979. *Dyslexia: Theory and research.* Cambridge, Mass.: MIT Press.

DYSPHASIA. Between 8 and 15 percent of all preschool children have D[evelopmental] D[ysphasia] (Silva 1980). Such children—also referred to as 'congenitally aphasic, 'language-impaired', 'language-delayed', and 'language-disordered'—are typically defined by exclusionary criteria, i.e. by what they are not, rather than by inclusionary criteria. They are children for whom language development is delayed, problematic, and protracted; but their language learning problems cannot be attributed to more primary disorders, such as mental retardation, autism, hearing impairment, emotional disturbance, or frank neurological dysfunction. (For reference, see Tallal 1987, Johnston 1988.)

The first to suggest a distinct clinical syndrome that meets this definition was Benton 1964. He also noted that the syndrome was manifested in two basic ways: as an impairment primarily in language production, or as an impairment in both comprehension and production. The most recent definition by the American Psychiatric Association (DSM-III, 1981) remains essentially the same as Benton's, identifying two basic types: EXPRESSIVE dysphasia, characterized by serious problems in the 'vocal expression' of language, despite relatively intact language comprehension; and RECEPTIVE dysphasia, characterized by serious problems in both comprehension and production. A third type, characterized primarily by problems in comprehension, is considerably rarer than the other two, but has been reported by many clinicians and researchers. (Developmental articulation disorder is recognized as a separate category of impairment by both Benton and DSM-III.)

No underlying etiology for DD has yet been agreed upon. Many researchers have noted that, despite normal nonverbal intelligence scores, developmentally dysphasic children demonstrate difficulties with many aspects of nonverbal cognition: means/ends knowledge, interpreting and drawing inferences from visually depicted events, classification, figurative thought, rule and hypothesis formulation, and short-term memory processes. Some researchers have hypothesized that language-impaired children do not have a selective language deficit, but have a more general representational deficit which underlies both their linguistic and non-linguistic difficulties (cf. Morehead 1972). Other researchers have noted specific perceptual deficits in this population—notably, an impairment in processing rapidly changing acoustic information (Tallal & Piercy 1973, Tallal 1976); they hypothesize that this impairment in processing fundamental aspects of the speech signal underlies the language learning problems of this population. However, evidence in the late 1980s does not indicate conclusively whether the non-linguistic and linguistic deficits of DD children arise from a single source.

Describing patterns of language acquisition in DD children has been a major focus of research. In phonology, numerous studies have examined the phonetic realization of segments and syllables in the speech of DD children; these studies consistently conclude that such children demonstrate, on the whole, phonological processes nearly identical to those found in the grammars of younger, normal children (e.g. syllable and segment simplification and assimilation). Other studies, examining the kinds of phonological rules and representations constructed by DD children, also conclude that these children are similar to normal younger children in their surface and underlying lexical phonologies. While there is some evidence that DD children may have difficulty in acquiring particular language-specific rules, there is no evidence to suggest that they construct impossible phonological rules, i.e. rules not allowed by known human grammars.

Similar findings hold for the patterns of acquisition displayed by DD children with respect to other aspects of the grammar: morphology, syntax, and lexicon. The order in which grammatical morphemes are acquired is similar to that found in normally developing children; the relationship between the production of these morphemes and other aspects of their grammatical development may be atypical, but there is no evidence that DD children violate either word-formation rules, or the syntactic classification of roots and inflectional morphemes. Investigations of the syntax of DD children have been largely taxonomic; however, they suggest that DD children use syntactic structures similar in type and frequency to those of normal younger children. To the extent that it is possible to ascertain, it seems that DD children construct grammars that embody both universal and language-specific syntactic principles—e.g. construction of all constituent types, consistent head-complement order within constituents, and grammatically constrained constituent movement. Studies of lexical and relational semantic development in DD children also suggest that largely normal mechanisms of acquisition are at work. They appear to express the same meaning relations, and to acquire lexical items in the same manner (and perhaps at the same rate) as do normal children.

An important question is whether DD children are delayed in their acquisition of language because of a maturational lag, or some other cause, and yet show normal patterns of acquisition—or whether they are deviant as well as delayed. Most of the data on their language development, as of the late 1980s, reveal delayed but normal acquisition patterns. However, some evidence suggests that acquisition in this population may be deviant in certain respects. In phonology, it has been reported that early acquired forms persist, or coexist in free variation with later acquired forms, over protracted periods of time. Since the acquisition of new phonological forms presumably reflects changes in the grammar that should rule out the old forms, the coexistence of distinct and competing phonological representations may mark the phonological development of DD children as deviant. It suggests that DD children may be constructing grammars which tolerate a variance in representations that would be disallowed in the normal course of acquisition.

There is also evidence of deviance with respect to developments across components of the grammar. For example, the order in which the grammatical morphemes of English are acquired may be normal; but they are reported to appear earlier, and to be mastered later, by comparison with concomitant acquisitions in other areas of the grammar. Similarly, DD children construct many ungrammatical utterances that appear to result from using semantically appropriate lexical items, the syntactic requirements for which lie outside their competence. Along the same lines, a normal rate of lexical acquisition, coupled with lexical impairments of other sorts, may give rise to some of the production abnormalities noted—e.g., where more advanced or fully specified lexical entries coexist, and are used alongside less fully specified entries to express the same meaning. This again raises the possibility of deviance in the grammar; again, it calls for more research.

As of the late 1980s, research has not shown clinical subtypes to be characterizable along grammatical lines. That is, it has not been shown that expressive dysphasia embodies a specific set of grammatical impairments, and receptive dysphasia a different set. Rather, each subtype is characterized by difficulties in performing particular kinds of linguistic activities, and thus each has task-specific impairments. This suggests that DD may involve linguistic (and perhaps non-linguistic) processing impairments, rather than problems at the level of linguistic representation or knowledge.

SUSAN CURTISS

BIBLIOGRAPHY

BENTON, ARTHUR L. 1964. Developmental aphasia and brain damage. *Cortex* 1.40–52.

JOHNSTON, JUDITH. 1988. Specific language disorders in the child. In *Handbook of speech-language pathology and audiology,* edited by Norman Lass et al., pp. 685–715. Philadelphia: Decker.

MOREHEAD, DONALD. 1972. *Early grammatical and semantic relations: Some implications for a general representational deficit in linguistically deviant children.* (Papers and reports in child language development, 4.) Stanford, Calif.: Department of Linguistics, Stanford University.

SILVA, P. A. 1980. The prevalence, stability, and significance of developmental language delay in preschool children. *Developmental Medicine and Child Neurology* 22.768–777.

TALLAL, PAULA. 1976. Rapid auditory processing in normal and disordered development. *Journal of Speech and Hearing Research* 19.561–571.

TALLAL, PAULA. 1987. *Report to the U.S. Congress: Developmental language disorders.* Washington, D.C.: Interagency Committee on Learning Disabilities.

TALLAL, PAULA, & MALCOLM PIERCY. 1973. Defects of non-verbal auditory perception in children with developmental aphasia. *Nature* 241.468–469.

E

EAST BIRD'S HEAD LANGUAGES

EAST BIRD'S HEAD LANGUAGES constitute a proposed language family spoken on the Vogelkop (Bird's Head) Peninsula of the island of New Guinea, in western Irian Jaya, Indonesia. Stephen A. Wurm, *Papuan languages of Oceania* (Tübingen: Narr, 1982), pp. 248–249, does not assign East Bird's Head to any higher-level genetic unit. The subgrouping is shown in Figure 1.

FIGURE 1. *Subgrouping of East Bird's Head Languages*

Mantion
Meax
Meah, Moskona

LANGUAGE LIST

Mantion: around 12,000 speakers reported in 1987, south of Manokwari, in East Bird's Head. Also called Manikion, Sougb, or Sogh.

Meah: 10,000 speakers reported in 1985, west of Manokwari, in East Bird's Head. Also called Meax, Meyach, Meyah, Mejah, Mejach, Arfak, or Mansibaber. Many speakers are becoming bilingual in Indonesian; some are bilingual in Mantion.

Moskona: spoken west of Meah, in East Bird's Head.

EAST CENTRAL INDO-ARYAN LANGUAGES

EAST CENTRAL INDO-ARYAN LANGUAGES constitute a subgroup of the Indo-Aryan family [*q.v.*], spoken in the east central part of northern India; they are also known collectively as Eastern Hindi. The individual languages are listed below.

LANGUAGE LIST

Awadhi: 20,300,000 or more speakers reported in 1951, with 20,000,000 in northeastern India and others in Nepal. Also called Abadi, Abohi, Ambodhi, Avadhi, Baiswari, Kojali, Kosali. Caribbean Hindi is related to Awadhi.

Bagheli: around 231,000 speakers reported in 1971, in Madhya Pradesh, Maharashtra, and Uttar Pradesh, India. Also spoken in Nepal. Also called Bagelkhandi, Bhugelkhud, Mannadi, Riwai, Ganggai, Mandal, Kewot, Kewat, Kawathi, Kenat, Kevat Boli, Kevati, Kewani, Kewati, or Nagpuri Marathi.

Baiga: around 11,100 speakers reported in 1971, in Bihar, Maharashtra, Madhya Pradesh, Orissa, and West Bengal, India. Also called Baigani, Bega, or Bhumia.

Binjhwari: spoken by some 48,800 people in Bihar, Madhya Pradesh, Maharashtra, and West Bengal, India. Also called Binjhal, Binjhawar, Binjhawari, or Binjhwar.

Chattisgarhi: around 6,690,000 speakers reported in 1971, in Bihar, Madhya Pradesh, Maharashtra, and Orissa, India. Also called Lariaor Khatahi.

Dhanwar: around 21,100 speakers reported in 1961, in Madhya Pradesh and Maharashtra, India. Also called Dhanvar or Danuwar. A distinct language from Danuwar Rai in Nepal.

Ojhi: around 1,070 speakers reported in 1961, in Madhya Pradesh and Maharashtra, India. Also called Ojaboli, Ojha, Ojhe, Oza, or Ozha.

EAST CENTRAL SULAWESI LANGUAGES

EAST CENTRAL SULAWESI LANGUAGES constitute a group spoken in the eastern part of the Sulawesi region (Celebes), Indonesia; they form a top-level constituent of the Central Sulawesi subgroup of West Malayo-Polynesian [*qq.v.*].

LANGUAGE LIST

Andio: 1,600 speakers reported in 1979, in Lamala Subdistrict, Central Sulawesi. Also called Bobongko, Andio'o, Imbao'o, or Masama. The name Bobongko is derogatory; Masama is preferred.

Balantak: 30,000 speakers reported in 1982, in Luwuk, Balantak, Tinangkung, and Lamola Subdistricts, east central Sulawesi. Also called Kosian.

Saluan, Coastal: 74,000 speakers reported in 1979, in 136 villages of east central Sulawesi. Also called Loinang, Loindang, or Madi. The name Saluan is preferred by the speakers.

Saluan, Kahumamahon: spoken in east central Sulawesi. Also called Interior Saluan.

EAST CHADIC LANGUAGES

EAST CHADIC LANGUAGES constitute a group spoken in south central Chad and in adjacent parts of Cameroon and the Central African Republic. This group forms a top-level constituent of the Chadic branch of Afro-Asiatic [*qq.v.*], in the classification of Paul Newman. [*For subgrouping, see* Chadic Languages.]

LANGUAGE LIST

Barain: spoken south of Mongo and east of Melfi, south central Chad. Also called Barein. Speakers use Arabic as a second language.

Bidiya: spoken west of Abu Telfan, Chad. Also called Bidyo or Bidiyo. Most men are bilingual in Arabic.

Birgit: spoken west of Abu Telfan, south central Chad.

Dangaleat: 20,000 speakers reported in 1967, around Mongo, north of Jebel Geira, Chad. Also called Dangla. Most men are probably bilingual in Arabic.

Gabri: 40,000 speakers reported in 1978, in southwest Chad. Also called Gaberi, Gabere, or Tobanga. Erroneously called Sara.

Gadang: spoken near Boussou, south central Chad.

Jegu: spoken west of Abu Telfan, south central Chad.

Kabalai: spoken in Chad. May be mutually intelligible with Gabri. Speakers are bilingual in Nancere or Lele. Also called Gablai.

Kera: 14,000 to 20,000 speakers reported in 1987, from near Datcheka in Mayo-Danay Division, Far North Province, Cameroon, and southward into Chad to the region south of Lake Tikem. Also called Keri.

Kujarke: spoken by 1,000 people in southeast Chad near Je[illegible]irra. Also called Kujarge or Kujur.

Kwang: spoken northeast of Bongor, Chad.

Lele: 30,000 or more speakers reported in 1989, in the Logone District, Kelo area, southwest Chad. Different from Lele (Kasena) of Ghana and Burkina Faso.

Mawa: spoken in the Abu Telfan area, south central Chad.

Mesmedje: 11,000 speakers reported in 1967, east of Ati, Chad. Also called Masmaje. May be mutually intelligible with Mubi.

Migama: 15,000 to 16,000 speakers reported in 1971, south of Mongo in the Abou-Telfan and Jebel Geira areas, in central Chad. Also called Jongor, Djonkor or Dionkor.

Miltu: spoken around Miltou, Bousso District, south central Chad.

Mod: spoken east of Goundi, southwest Chad.

Mogum: 6,000 speakers reported in the Melfi-Abu Deia area, south central Chad.

Mubi: 36,000 speakers reported in 1971, east of Mongo in south central Chad. Also called Monjul. Different from Mubi (Gude) of Cameroon and Chad. Most speakers are bilingual in Arabic.

Mukulu: spoken in south central Chad. Most men are bilingual in Arabic. Also called Jonkor of Guera.

Nancere: 50,000 speakers reported in 1987, around Lai in Logone District, southwest Chad. Also called Nanjeri, Nantcere, or Nangjere.

Ndam: spoken in southwest Chad near Goundi. Also called Dam or Ndamm.

Saba: spoken in south central Chad east of Melfi. Arabic is the second language.

Sarwa: 400 speakers reported in 1971, near Miltou in south central Chad. Also spoken in southern Bourrah Subdivision, Mayo-Tsanaga Division, Far North Province, Cameroon, with a few speakers in North Province. Also called Sharwa, Sarua, or Saroua. May be mutually intelligible with Miltu.

Sokoro: 8,000 speakers reported in 1971, northeast of Melfi, Chad. Also called Bedanga or Tunjur. Most men are bilingual in Arabic.

Somrai: 5,000 or fewer speakers reported in 1968, southeast of Bongor in southwest Chad. Also called Soumray, Sounrai, Somrei, or Sibine. Erroneously called Sara.

Tobanga: 14,000 speakers reported in 1968, in southwest Chad. Also called Gabri-North.

Toram: spoken south of the Birgit language in south central Chad.

Tumak: 10,000 speakers reported in 1968, near Goundi in southwest Chad. Also called Tummok or Dije. Erroneously called Sara Toumak.

EAST INDO-ARYAN LANGUAGES

EAST INDO-ARYAN LANGUAGES, also called Magadhan languages, constitute a subgroup of the Indo-Aryan [*q.v.*] group of languages; they are spoken in northeastern India and Bangladesh, with some overspill into Nepal. The best-known language of the group is Bengali [*q.v.*]. Their internal classification is given in Figure 1.

LANGUAGE LIST

Anga: around 424,000 speakers reported in 1971, in Bihar, India. Also called Angika or Angikar.

Assamese: 20,000,000 speakers reported in 1987, with 10,000,000 in Assam, India, and 10,000,000 in Bangla-

FIGURE 1. *Subgrouping of East Indo-Aryan Languages*

Bengali-Assamese
Assamese, Bengali, Chakma, Hajong, Halbi, Kawari, Kayort, Kharia Thar, Kishanganjia, Koch, Marpaharia, Nahari, Rajbangsi, Sylhetti, Tangchangya
Bihari
Anga, Bhojpuri, Caribbean Hindi, Gawari, Magahi, Maithili, Dehati Maithili, Majhi, Musasa, Oraon Sadri, Sadani, Tamaria
Oriya
Bagata, Bhatri, Bhuiya, Bhunjia, Jagannathi, Jharia, Kupia, Mali, Oriya (proper), Adiwasi Oriya
Unclassified East Indo-Aryan
Bote-Majhi, Degaru, Chitwan Tharu, Deokri Tharu, Mahotari Tharu, Rana Thakur Tharu, Saptari Tharu

desh. Also possibly spoken in Bhutan. Also called Asambe or Asami. The official language of Assam State.

Bagata: spoken by some 55,200 people in Andhra Pradesh, Madras, and Orissa, India. Also called Bagat, Bakta, Bhakta, or Bagbot.

Bengali: around 162,000,000 speakers reported in 1989, with 110,000,000 in Bangladesh, 52,000,000 in India, 70,000 in the United Arab Emirates, and 600 in Singapore. Also called Banga-Bhasa, Bangala, or Bangla. The official language of West Bengal State, India, and of Bangladesh.

Bhatri: around 104,000 speakers reported in 1971, in Andhra Pradesh, Madhya Pradesh, Maharashtra, and Orissa, India. Also called Bhattri, Bhattra, or Bhatra.

Bhojpuri: 41,000,000 speakers reported in 1977, in Bihar, Assam, Madhya Pradesh, and Uttar Pradesh, India, including 1,330,000 in Nepal. Also called Bhojapuri, Bhozpuri, Bajpuri, or Bihari. The extent of variation between India and Nepal is not yet determined.

Bhuiya: around 4,430 speakers reported in 1961, in Bihar, Madhya Pradesh, Maharashtra, Orissa, Uttar Pradesh, and West Bengal, India. Also called Bhuinhar, Bhuinya, Bhuiyali, Bhumia, Bhungiyas, or Bhuyan Oriya.

Bhunjia: around 5,240 speakers reported in Madhya Pradesh, Maharashtra, and Orissa, India. Also called Bunjia, Bhumjiya, or Bhunjiya. Possibly a divergent dialect of Halbi.

Bote-Majhi: 6,000 speakers reported in 1971, mainly in Chitawan District, Nepal. Also called Kushar.

Caribbean Hindi: 150,000 speakers reported in 1986 from Surinam, with 45,000 in Trinidad and Tobago, plus other speakers in Guyana and French Guyana. Also called Sarnami Hindi or Aili Gaili. Related to Bhojpuri, with links also to Awadhi (East Central Indo-Aryan).

Chakma: 513,000 speakers reported in 1987, with 300,000 speakers in Assam, Tripura, and West Bengal, India, and 213,000 speakers in Bangladesh. Also called Takam.

Degaru: spoken in Bihar and West Bengal, India. Also called Dhekaru.

Gawari: around 21,100 speakers reported in 1971, in Andhra Pradesh, Madhya Pradesh, Bihar, and Maharashtra, India. Also called Gamari, Gauuari, or Goari.

Hajong: around 24,000 speakers reported in 1971, in Assam and West Bengal, India. Also spoken in Bangladesh. Also called Haijong.

Halbi: 600,000 speakers reported in 1989, in Madhya Pradesh, Maharashtra, and Orissa, India. Also called Bastari, Halba, Halvas, Halabi, Halvi, Mahari, or Mehari.

Jagannathi: around 1,310 speakers reported in 1961, in Andhra Pradesh, Maharashtra, and Karnataka, India. Also called Jaga Aad, Jaganathi, Jagannatha Bhasha, or Surya Jagannathi. May be a dialect of Oriya.

Jharia: around 2,060 speakers reported in 1961, in Orissa, India. Also called Jhaliya.

Kawari: around 33,800 speakers reported in Madhya Pradesh, Maharashtra, and Orissa, India. Also called Kavar, Kamari, or Kawar. Possibly a divergent dialect of Halbi. Distinct from Kamar, a Dravidian language of Madhya Pradesh.

Kayort: spoken in Koshi Zone, Morang District, Nepal.

Kharia Thar: spoken in Bihar, India.

Kishanganjia: around 56,900 speakers reported in 1971, in Bihar, India. Also called Kishangangia, Shreepuri, or Siripuria.

Koch: spoken in West Bengal, India. Distinct from Tibeto-Burman Koch in Assam, Tripura, and Bangladesh.

Kupia: 4,000 speakers reported in Andhra Pradesh, India. Also called Valmiki.

Magahi: 10,000,000 speakers reported in 1977, in Bihar and West Bengal, India. Also called Magadhi, Magaya, Maghaya, Maghori, Magi, or Magodhi.

Maithili: around 23,800,000 speakers reported in 1981, with 22,000,000 in Bihar, Madhya Pradesh, Maharashtra, and West Bengal, India, and the rest in Nepal. Also called Maitli, Maitili, Methli, Mithil, or Tirahutia.

Maithili, Dehati: spoken in Bihar, India, and adjacent districts of southern Nepal. Also called Dehati, Dahati, or Deshiya.

Majhi: around 5,900 speakers reported in 1961, in eastern Nepal and in India. Also called Manjhi. Distinct from Majhi in Central Indo-Aryan, and from Bote-Majhi.

Mali: 970 speakers reported in 1961, in Andhra Pradesh and Maharashtra, India.

Marpaharia: around 9,080 speakers reported in 1961, in Assam, Bihar, and West Bengal, India. Part of the Malto ethnic group.

Musasa: spoken in Sindhuli Garhi, Morang, and Dolakha Districts, Nepal. Also called Musahar.

Nahari: spoken in Madhya Pradesh and Orissa, India. A divergent variety of Halbi.

Oraon Sadri: 39,000 speakers reported in 1988, in Rajshahi Division, Bangladesh. Speakers originally used Kurukh

(Oraon), a Dravidian language; some shifted to an Indo-European variety resembling Sadani (Sadri). Oraon Sadri has 57 to 66 percent lexical similarity with Bengali. Speakers' bilingual proficiency in Bengali is limited; vernacular language use is vigorous.

Oriya: 23,000,000 speakers reported in 1971, with 19,900,000 in Orissa, Bihar, West Bengal, Assam, and Andhra Pradesh, India, and others in Bangladesh. Also called Uriya, Utkali, Odri, Odrum, Oliya, Orissa, Vadiya, or Yudhia. The official language of Orissa State.

Oriya, Adiwasi: 200,000 or more mother-tongue speakers and 200,000 second-language users reported in 1987, in Andhra Pradesh and Orissa, India. Also called Tribal Oriya, Desia, Kotiya, Kotia Oriya, or Adivasi Oriya. The language is called Adiwasi (Tribal) Oriya, the people Kotia.

Rajbangsi: around 55,000 speakers reported in 1971, in Jhapa and Morang, Nepal. Also spoken in Bangladesh and India. Also called Rajbansi or Tajpuri.

Sadani: 807,000 or more speakers reported in 1971, in Assam, Bihar, Madhya Pradesh, and West Bengal, India. Also called Nagpuria, Nagpuri, Sadana, Sadati, Sadari, Sadhan, Sadna, Sadrik, Santri, Siddri, Sradri, Chota Nagpuri, Sadri, or Dikku Kaji. May be mutually intelligible with Bhojpuri.

Sylhetti: 5,000,000 speakers reported in 1987, about 100 miles north of Dacca, Bangladesh; also 100,000 in the United Kingdom, and possibly some in India. Also called Sylhetti Bangla. Has 70 percent lexical similarity with Bengali.

Tamaria: spoken by some 5,050 people in Bihar, India. Also called Tair, Tamara, Temoral, or Tumariya.

Tangchangya: around 17,700 speakers reported in 1981, in Bangladesh. Also called Tanchangya.

Tharu, Chitwan: 30,000 speakers reported in 1985, in the low country of the Rapti Valley, Chitwan District, Nepal. Also called Chituan Tharu or Chitawan Tharu. Tharu of Dang and Tharu of Jhapa are varieties of different Indo-Aryan languages.

Tharu, Deokri: spoken on the eastern border of Nepal with India. Also called Deokhar. Distinct from Chitwan Tharu and Dang Tharu, and may be distinct from Don Tharu spoken south of Bhairawa in India.

Tharu, Mahotari: spoken in Mahottari District, Nepal. Also called Mahottari.

Tharu, Rana Thakur: 500 speakers reported in 1985, on the eastern border of Nepal and India. Also called Rana Thakur.

Tharu, Saptari: 500,000 speakers reported in 1985, in Saptari District, Sagarmatha Zone, Nepal. Also called Saptari.

EAST MALAYO-POLYNESIAN LANGUAGES

constitute part of the Central-Eastern branch of the Malayo-Polynesian family, itself a division of the Austronesian languages [*q.v.*]. East Malayo-Polynesian is itself divided into the South Halmahera–West New Guinea languages, on one hand, and the Oceanic languages on the other. [*For further subdivisions, and for data on individual languages, see the articles on those groups.*]

EAST MON-KHMER LANGUAGES

are spoken in Cambodia, Laos, Vietnam, and adjacent areas; they form a top-level constituent of the Mon-Khmer group within Austro-Asiatic [*qq.v.*]. The internal subgrouping of East Mon-Khmer is shown in Figure 1.

LANGUAGE LIST

Alak 1: 3,000 speakers reported in 1981, mainly in Saravane Province, southern Laos. Also called Hrlak 1. A Bahnaric language, distinct from Alak 2, which is Katuic.

Alak 2: spoken near Ngeq, southern Laos. Also called Hrlak 2.

Bahnar: 85,000 speakers reported in 1973, in southeastern Gia Lai-Cong Tum Province, Vietnam; some speakers in the United States.

Brao: 18,000 speakers reported in 1984, on both sides of the Laos-Cambodia border; a few speakers live in France and the United States. Also called Braou, Proue, Love, Lave, or Laveh.

Bru, Eastern: 50,000 speakers reported in 1984, in Thien Province, Vietnam. Also called Brü, Kalo, Galler, Van Kieu, or Quang Tri. The name Bru means 'minority people'; the So of Laos also call themselves Bru. Chali and Kaleu may be alternate names or separate languages.

Bru, Western: 70,000 or more speakers reported in 1984, with 50,000 in Savannakhet Province, Laos, 20,000 or more in Thailand, plus some in the United States. Also called Galler or Vankieu. Partial mutual intelligibility with Eastern Bru of Vietnam.

Chong: 8,000 speakers reported in 1981, on both sides of the Thailand-Cambodia border, with 5,000 in Cambodia. Also called Chawng, Shong, or Xong.

Chrau: 20,000 speakers reported in 1981, mainly in Dong Nai Province, Vietnam, and others in Tayninh and Binhlong Provinces. Also called Jro, Ro, or Tamun. The name Chrau means 'mountain dweller'.

Cua: 10,000 to 15,000 speakers reported in 1973, in Gia Lai-Cong Tum Province, Vietnam. Also called Kor, Traw, or Bong Miew.

Halang: 12,000 or more speakers reported in 1973, with 10,000 in Gia Lai-Cong Tum Province, Vietnam, and 2,000 to 4,000 in Laos. Also called Koyong.

Halang Doan: 2,000 speakers reported in 1981, with 1,000 in northeastern Dac Lac Province, Vietnam, and 1,000 in Laos. Also called Halang Duan, Duan, or Doan.

Hrê: 100,000 speakers reported in 1981, in Gia Lai-Cong

FIGURE 1. *Subgrouping of East Mon-Khmer Languages*

- **Bahnaric**
  - **Central Bahnaric**
    - Alak 1, Bahnar, Lamam, Tampuan
  - **North Bahnaric**
    - **Eastern division**
      - Cua-Kayong, Takua
    - **Western division**
      - **Duan** (Halang Doan)
      - Jeh-Halang
      - Rengao
      - **Sedang-Todrah**
        - **Sedang**
          - Hrê, Sedang (proper)
        - Todrah-Monom
      - **Unclassified Western division**
        - Talieng, Trieng
    - **Unclassified North Bahnaric**
      - Katua
  - **South Bahnaric**
    - **Sre-Mnong**
      - Mnong, Sre (Koho)
    - Stieng-Chrau
  - **West Bahnaric**
    - **Brao-Kravet**
      - Brao, Kravet, Krung 2, Sou
    - Laven
    - Nyaheun
    - **Oi-The**
      - Jeng, Oy, Sapuan, Sok, The
- **Katuic**
  - **East Katuic**
    - Kaseng
    - Katang
    - **Katu-Thap**
      - Kantu, Katu
    - **Ngeq-Nkriang**
      - Alak 2, Klor, Ngeq
    - Pacoh-Phuong
    - **Ta-Oy-Tong**
      - Ong, Lower Ta-oih, Upper Ta-oih, Yir
    - Tariang
  - **West Katuic**
    - **Kuy-Souei**
      - Kuy, Nyeu
    - **Sô-Bru**
      - Eastern Bru, Western Bru, Khua, Leun, Mangkong, Sapoin, Sô, So Tri
- **Khmeric**
  - Central Khmer, Northern Khmer
- **Pearic**
  - **Eastern Pearic** (Pear)
  - **Western Pearic**
    - **Chong**
      - Chong (proper), Sa-och
    - **Samrê**
      - Samrê (proper), Somray
    - Suoy

Tum Province, Vietnam. Also called Davak or Davach.

Jeh: 10,000 or more speakers reported in 1973, in Quang Nam-Da Nang and Gia Lai-Cong Tum Provinces, Vietnam; also spoken in Laos. Also called Die, Yeh, or Gie.

Jeng: 5,400 speakers reported in 1981, north of Attopeu, Laos. Also called Cheng.

Kantu: reported in 1981 as spoken in east central Laos, near the Vietnam border. Also called High Katu. Closely related to Katu, and lumped with it in the 1981 population figure of 80,000, but distinct.

Kaseng: 6,000 speakers reported in 1981, in southern Laos near the Vietnam border, and on the Boloven Plateau. Also called Koseng or Kasseng.

Katang: 10,000 speakers reported in 1981, around Muong Nong, southern Laos. Also called Kataang.

Katu: 30,000 speakers reported in 1989, in Quang Nam-Da Nang Province, Vietnam. Also spoken in Laos. Also called Attouat, Ataouat, Kado, Cao, Thap, Teu, Khat, or Ta River Van Kieu.

Katua: 3,000 speakers reported in 1981, around Mang Bu, southern Vietnam.

Kayong: 2,000 speakers reported in 1981, in the more remote mountains of Gia Lai-Cong Tum Province, Vietnam. Also called Kagiuong, Ca Giong, or Katang.

Khmer, Central: 7,030,000 or more speakers reported in 1984, with 6,120,000 in Cambodia, 700,000 in Vietnam, 50,000 or more in France, 50,000 in the United States, and 10,400 in Laos. Also called Cambodian.

Khmer, Northern: 1,010,000 speakers reported in 1989, in northeastern Thailand, mainly in Surin, Sisaket, Buriram, and Korat Provinces, and in Khmer refugee camps.

Khua: 5,000 speakers reported in 1981, southeast of Giap Tam, west central Vietnam. Also spoken in Laos. Distinct from Cua.

Klor: 10,000 speakers reported in 1981 (counted together with Ngeh), in Saravane Province, Laos, south of Yir and Ong. Also called Khlor or Lor.

Koho: 100,000 speakers reported in 1973, in Lam Dong, Dong Nai, and Thuan Hai Provinces, Vietnam, and in the United States.

Kravet: reported in 1981 as spoken in northeastern Cambodia. Also called Kowet or Khvek.

Krung 2: reported in 1981 to be spoken in northeastern Cambodia. Distinct from Krung 1, a dialect of Rade spoken in Vietnam.

Kuy: 650,000 speakers reported in 1981, in northeastern

Cambodia. Also spoken in Thailand and Laos. Also called Kuoy, Suai, Suoi, Soai, Suei, Khamen-Boran, Old Khmer, or Kui. Na Nhyang may be a dialect or a separate language.

Lamam: 1,000 speakers reported in 1981, near the northeast corner of Cambodia on the Vietnam border. Also called Lmam.

Laven: 25,000 speakers reported in 1981, on the Boloven Plateau in southwestern Laos; some speakers in the United States. Also called Loven, Love, Boloven, Laweenjru, or Jaru.

Leun: spoken in Saravane Province, Laos. Also called Leung, Leu, Muong Leung, Luun, or Ruul.

Mangkong: 2,000 or more speakers reported in 1989, in east central Laos, from northeast of Kouang to the Vietnam border. Also called Mang-Koong, Makong, So Makon, or Mankoong.

Mnong, Central: 90,000 speakers reported in 1981, mainly in Song Be Province and western Dac Lac, Vietnam, and into Cambodia. Also called Pnong or Budong. The Biat variety may be a separate language.

Mnong, Eastern: 48,000 speakers reported in 1981, in Darlac Province, Vietnam, and into Tuyonduc; also spoken in the United States.

Mnong, Southern: 48,000 speakers reported in 1981, mostly in Quang Duc Province, Vietnam.

Monom: 5,000 speakers reported in 1973, in eastern Gia Lai-Cong Tum Province, Vietnam. Also called Bonom, Menam, or Monam.

Ngeq: 4,000 speakers reported in 1981, in southern Laos. Also called Ngeh, Nge', Kriang, or Nkriang. Population includes 70 percent monolingual. 'Kha Koh' is a derogatory name that means 'mountain people'; speakers call themselves Nkriang.

Nyaheun: 4,000 speakers reported in 1981, on the Boloven Plateau, Laos. Also called Nha Heun, Nyah Heuny, Hoen, Nia Hoen, Hun, Hin, Niahon, or Nyahön.

Nyeu: a few speakers reported in 1983 in Sisaket, Thailand. Also called Yeu. Closely related to Kuy.

Ong: spoken in Saravane Province, Laos.

Oy: 10,600 speakers reported in 1981, at the foot of the Boloven Plateau in southern Laos. Also called Huei or Oi. Population includes 80 percent monolingual.

Pacoh: 15,000 speakers reported in 1973, in Thien Province, Vietnam, and in Laos. Also called Bo, River Van Kieu, or Pokoh.

Pear: 1,000 speakers reported in 1981, in southwestern Cambodia. Also called Por or Kompong Thom.

Phuong: 5,000 speakers reported in 1973, southeast of the Pacoh language, Vietnam. Also called Phuang.

Rengao: 15,000 speakers reported in 1973, in Gia Lai-Cong Tum Province, Vietnam. May be mutually intelligible with Halang Doan.

Sa-och: 500 speakers reported in 1981, in southwest Cambodia. Also called Sauch or Saotch.

Samrê: 200 speakers reported in 1981, just north of Siemreap, Cambodia.

Sapoin: spoken in Saravane Province, Laos. Also called Hapool. Distinct from Sapuan.

Sapuan: 2,400 speakers reported in 1981, on the banks of the Se Kong and Se Kamane rivers, Attopeu Province, southern Laos. Distinct from Sapoin.

Sedang: 40,000 speakers reported in 1973, in Gia Lai-Cong Tum Province, Vietnam. Also called Roteang, Hadang, Hoteang, Rotea, or Hotea.

Sô: 130,000 speakers reported in 1987, with 80,000 on both sides of the Mekong River in Laos, and 50,000 in Thailand. Also called Kah So. Because of contact with the Laotian Tai, speakers also use Tai dialects.

Sok: 1,600 speakers reported in 1981, in Attopeu Province, southern Laos. Also called Sork.

Somray: 2,000 speakers reported in 1981, around Phum Tasanh, western Cambodia, and on the Tanyong River around Phum Pra Moi.

So Tri: 10,000 speakers reported in 1981, half in Laos and half in Thailand. Also called Tri or So Trii.

Sou: 1,000 speakers reported in 1962, in Attopeu Province, southern Laos. Also called Suq, Souk, or Su.

Stieng: 70,000 speakers reported in 1973, with 48,000 in Song Be Province, Vietnam, and the rest in Cambodia.

Suoy: 200 speakers reported in 1981, northwest of Phnom Penh in central Cambodia.

Ta-oih, Lower: spoken in Laos. Also called Tong. Not mutually intelligible with Upper Ta'oih, although some speakers are bilingual in it.

Ta-oih, Upper: 30,000 speakers reported in 1981, in Saravane Province, Laos, plus some in Vietnam and the United States. Also called Ta-Oy, Ta-Oi, Tau Oi, Ta Hoi, or Kantua. Not easily mutually intelligible with Lower Ta'oih. Population includes 70 percent monolinguals.

Takua: 5,000 to 10,000 speakers reported in 1973, in Quang Nam-Da Nang Province, Vietnam. Also called Quang Tin Katu or Langya.

Talieng: spoken in the Muong Phine-Bung Sai area of Savannakhet Province, Laos. Also called Taliang. Apparently distinct from Tariang, which is East Katuic.

Tampuan: spoken in the northeast border area of Cambodia. Also called Campuon, Tampuen, Tampuon, Kha Tampuon, Proon, or Proons.

Tariang: 5,000 speakers reported in 1981, east of Kayong in Laos, just west of the Vietnam border. Also called Tareng. Apparently distinct from Talieng, which is North Bahnaric.

The: 1,500 speakers reported in 1962, in Attopeu Province, southern Laos. Also called Thae. May be mutually intelligible with Oy.

Todrah: 5,000 speakers reported in 1973, northeast of Kontum, Vietnam. Also called Didrah, Didra, Podra, Modra, Kodra, or Sedang Todra. Didra may be a separate language.

Trieng: 30,000 speakers reported in 1973, northwest of Dak

Rotah, western Quang Tin Province, Vietnam, and in Laos. Also called Strieng. Possibly a dialect of Jeh or Talieng in Laos.

Yir: 10,000 speakers reported in 1981, in Saravane Province, Laos. Also called In or Ir.

EAST NEW GUINEA HIGHLANDS LANGUAGES are a group spoken in the eastern part of the Highlands of Papua New Guinea; they comprise the families and subfamilies indicated in Figure 1. Stephen A. Wurm, *Papuan languages of Oceania* (Tübingen: Narr, 1982), pp. 116–128, regards the East New Guinea Highlands stock as a top-level member of the Central and Western part of the main section of his controversial Trans-New Guinea phylum [*q.v.*]. This subgrouping differs from that given by Wurm, other than terminologically, in that the Waibuk family is excluded, following Wurm's suggestion that it may belong rather to the Sepik-Ramu phylum.

FIGURE 1. *Subgrouping of East New Guinea Highlands Languages*

- **Central Division**
  - **Chimbu**
    - Chuave, Dom, Golin, Kuman, Nagane, Nomane, Salt-Yui, Sinasina, Sua
  - **Hagen**
    - **Kaugel**
      - Imbo-Ungu, Mbo-Ung, Umbu-Ungu
    - Medlpa
  - **Jimi**
    - Kandawo, Maring, Narak
  - **Wahgi**
    - Kumai, Nembi, Nii, Wahgi (proper)
- **East-Central Division**
  - **Fore**
    - Fore (proper), Gimi
  - **Gahuku-Benabena**
    - Alekano, Upper Asaro, Benabena, Tokano
  - Gende
  - **Kamano-Yagaria**
    - Inoke-Yate, Kamano, Kanite, Keyagana, Yagaria
  - **Siane**
    - Hakoa, Siane (proper), Yaweyuha
- **Eastern Division**
  - **Gadsup-Auyana-Awa**
    - Agarabi, Awa, Awiyaana, Gadsup, Kosena, Usarufa
  - Owenia
  - **Tairora**
    - Binumarien, Tairora (proper), Waffa
  - **Unclassified Eastern Division**
    - Kambaira
- **Kalam**
  - Gants
  - **Kalam-Kobon**
    - Kalam (proper), Kobon
  - **Unclassified Kalam**
    - Tai
- Kenati
- **West-Central Division**
  - **Angal-Kewa**
    - East Angal, South Angal Heneng, West Angal Heneng, East Kewa, South Kewa, West Kewa, Samberigi
  - **Enga**
    - Bisorio, Enga (proper), Ipili, Katinja, Kyaka, Lembena, Nete
  - Huli
- Wiru

LANGUAGE LIST

Agarabi: around 13,400 speakers reported in 1981, in Kainantu Subprovince, Eastern Highlands Province. Also called Agarabe.

Alekano: around 16,100 speakers reported in 1981, in Goroka Subprovince, Eastern Highlands Province. Also called Gahuku or Gafuku.

Angal, East: 10,000 speakers reported in 1971, in the Mendi area, north into Mendi Valley, west into the east side of Lai Valley, Southern Highlands Province. Also called Mendi.

Angal Heneng, South: around 17,100 speakers reported in 1981, from Nembi Plateau on the west through the southern half of Nembi Valley, east through the southern half of Lai Valley, Southern Highlands Province. Also called South Mendi.

Angal Heneng, West: 25,000 speakers reported in 1971, centered in Nembi Valley, from Wage Valley on the west to the western half of Lai Valley on the east, Southern Highlands Province. Also called Augu or West Mendi.

Asaro, Upper: 30,000 speakers reported in 1987, in Goroka Subprovince, Eastern Highlands Province.

Awa: around 1,790 speakers reported in 1981, in Okapa and Obura Subprovinces, Eastern Highlands Province. Also called Mobuta.

Awiyaana: 6,500 speakers reported in 1975, in Kainantu and Okapa Subprovinces, Eastern Highlands Province. Also called Auyana.

Benabena: around 20,300 speakers reported in 1981, in Goroka Subprovince, Eastern Highlands Province. Also called Bena.

Binumarien: 265 speakers reported in 1984, in Kainantu Subprovince, Eastern Highlands Province. Also called Binumaria or Binamarir.

Bisorio: 230 to 280 speakers reported in 1983, at the headwaters of the Karawari, Wagupmeri, and Korosameri rivers in East Sepik Province. Also called Inyai-Gadio-Bisorio or Iniai. Has 70 percent lexical similarity with Nete.

Chuave: around 23,100 speakers reported in 1981, in Chuave Subprovince, Chimbu Province. Also called Tjuave. May be mutually intelligible with Sua.

Dom: around 9,830 speakers reported in 1981, mainly south of the Wahgi River from Kundiawa west of the Sinasina area, Chimbu Province.

Enga: around 165,000 speakers reported in 1981, in Enga Province. Also called Caga, Tsaga, Tchaga, or Mae.

Fore: around 16,700 speakers reported in 1981, in Okapa Subprovince, Eastern Highlands Province.

Gadsup: around 11,900 speakers reported in 1981, in Kainantu Subprovince, Eastern Highlands Province.

Gants: around 1,890 speakers reported in 1981, in Madang Province. Also called Gaj.

Gende: 8,000 speakers reported in 1987, near Bundi, Madang Province. Also called Bundi or Gene.

Gimi: around 22,500 speakers reported in 1981, in Labogai District, Okapa Subprovince, Eastern Highlands Province, near the Papua border.

Golin: around 51,100 speakers reported in 1981, in Gumine Subprovince, Chimbu Province. Also called Gollum or Gumine.

Hakoa: around 6,870 speakers reported in Chimbu Province.

Huli: 70,000 speakers reported in 1987, around Tari on the southern fringe of Southern Highlands Province and Enga Province. Also called Huli-Hulidana or Huri.

Imbo Ungu: 16,000 speakers reported in 1985, in Ialibu District, Southern Highlands Province. Also called Imbongu, Ibo Ugu, Imbonggo, or Awa.

Inoke-Yate: 8,000 speakers reported in 1987, in Okapa and Henganofi Subprovinces, Eastern Highlands Province. Also called Inoke or Yate.

Ipili: around 7,770 speakers reported in 1981, around Porgera patrol post, Enga Province. Also called Ipili-Paiela or Ipili-Payala.

Kalam: 14,000 speakers reported in 1987, in Ramu Subprovince, Madang Province. Also along the north side of the Jimi River into Kaironk Valley, Hagen Subprovince, Western Highlands Province. Also called Aforo or Karam.

Kamano: 50,000 speakers reported in 1975, in Kainantu and Henganofi Subprovinces, Eastern Highlands Province. Also called Kamano-Kafe.

Kambaira: 135 speakers reported in 1971, in Kainantu Subprovince, Eastern Highlands Province. Speakers also use Binumarien and Gadsup.

Kandawo: 4,000 speakers reported in 1987, in the upper Jimi headwaters, Hagen Subprovince, Western Highlands Province. Also called Ganja.

Kanite: 5,000 speakers reported in 1987, in Okapa and Henganofi Subprovinces, Eastern Highlands Province.

Katinja: spoken beyond Kandep on the middle southern edge of Enga Province.

Kenati: 640 speakers reported in 1982, in villages close to Womenara, Womenara Subprovince, Eastern Highlands Province. Also called Kenathi, Ganati, or Aziana.

Kewa, East: 25,000 speakers reported in 1982, in Ialibu and Kagua Subprovinces, Southern Highlands Province.

Kewa, South: 6,000 speakers reported in 1987, in Southern Highlands Province. Also called Pole.

Kewa, West: 25,000 speakers reported in 1982, in Kagua and Mendi Subprovinces, Southern Highlands Province. Also called Pasuma.

Keyagana: around 12,300 speakers reported in 1981, in Okapa and Henganofi Subprovinces, Eastern Highlands Province. Also called Keigana, Keiagana, or Ke'yagana.

Kobon: around 4,670 speakers reported in 1981, on the Kaironk River in the lower Jimi River area north of Mt. Hagen, Ramu Subprovince, Madang Province, and in Western Highlands Province.

Kosena: 2,000 speakers reported in 1987, in Kainantu and Okapa Subprovinces, Eastern Highlands Province.

Kumai: around 3,940 speakers reported in Chimbu Province. Also called Mid Wahgi.

Kuman: around 71,700 speakers reported in 1981, in Kundiawa Subprovince, Chimbu Province, overlapping into Minj Subprovince of Western Highlands Province. Also called Chimbu. A major language of the area.

Kyaka: around 15,400 speakers reported in 1981, in Enga Province. Also called Baiyer or Enga-Kyaka.

Lembena: 600 to 4,000 speakers estimated in 1990, in the northeast corner of Enga Province, and in Erem village, East Sepik Province. Speakers have poor bilingual proficiency in Enga, the local church and prestige language.

Maring: 8,000 speakers reported in 1987, in Hagen Subprovince, Western Highlands Province, with a small number over the Bismarck Range in Madang Province. Also called Mareng or Yoadabe-Watoare.

Mbo-Ung: 23,000 speakers reported in 1985, in Hagen Subprovince, Western Highlands Province, extending into Papua. Also called Miyemu, Tembogia, or Tetalo. Some speakers are bilingual in Medlpa.

Medlpa: around 68,300 speakers reported in 1981, in Hagen Subprovince, Western Highlands Province. Also called Melpa or Hagen.

Nagane: 1,000 speakers reported in 1981, in Chimbu Province. Also called Genagane or Genogani. All speakers understand Kuman.

Narak: 4,000 speakers reported in 1987, at the Jimi headwaters in Hagen Subprovince, Western Highlands Province.

Nembi: 20,000 speakers reported in 1987, in Western Highlands Province.

Nete: 1,000 speakers reported in 1982, in Enga Province and East Sepik Province, adjoining the Hewa area. Also called Iniai. Has 70 percent lexical similarity with Bisorio of East Sepik.

Nii: 9,300 speakers reported in 1975, in Minj Subprovince, Western Highlands Province. Also called Ek Nii.

Nomane: around 4,650 speakers reported in 1981, in Chimbu Province.

Owenia: 350 speakers reported in 1981, in Obura Subprovince, Eastern Highlands Province. Also called Owena, Owenda, Waijara, or Waisara.

Salt-Yui: 6,500 speakers reported in 1981, in Chimbu Province. Also called Salt, Salt-Iui, Yui, or Iui.

Samberigi: around 3,130 speakers reported in 1981, east of Erave, Lake Kutubu Subprovince, Southern Highlands Province. Also called Sau or Sanaberigi.

Siane: 18,000 speakers reported in 1975, in Goroka Subprovince, Eastern Highlands Province, and some in Simbu Province. Also called Siani.

Sinasina: around 50,100 speakers reported in 1981, in Chimbu Province.

Sua: 4,290 speakers reported in 1962, in Chimbu Province.

Tai: spoken in Dundrom village, southwest Madang Province.

Tairora: around 13,300 speakers reported in 1981, in Kainantu and Obura Subprovinces, Eastern Highlands Province.

Tokano: around 6,000 speakers reported in 1982, in Goroka Subprovince, Eastern Highlands Province. Also called Zuhuzuho.

Umbu-Ungu: 23,000 speakers reported in 1985, in Hagen Subprovince, Western Highlands Province, extending into Papua. Also called Ubu Ugu, Kaugel, Kauil, Gawigl, Gawil, or Kakoli. Some speakers understand Medlpa.

Usarufa: 1,500 speakers reported in 1982, in Okapa Subprovince, Eastern Highlands Province. Also called Usurufa or Uturupa.

Waffa: 1,000 speakers reported in 1978, at the headwaters of the Waffa River in Kaiapit Subprovince, Morobe Province.

Wahgi: 45,000 speakers reported in 1975, in Minj Subprovince, Western Highlands Province, overlapping into Chimbu Province.

Wiru: around 15,300 speakers reported in 1981, in Ialibu Subprovince, Southern Highlands Province. Also called Witu.

Yagaria: around 21,100 speakers reported in 1982, in Goroka Subprovince, Eastern Highlands Province. Also called Kami.

Yaweyuha: around 1,900 speakers reported in 1981, in Goroka Subprovince, Eastern Highlands Province. Also called Yabiyufa or Yawiyuha.

EAST PAPUAN LANGUAGES

EAST PAPUAN LANGUAGES constitute one of the major phyla into which the Papuan languages [*see* New Guinea Languages] are divided by Stephen A. Wurm, *Papuan languages of Oceania* (Tübingen: Narr, 1982), pp. 231–244. These languages are spoken in the eastern islands of Papua New Guinea and in the Solomon Islands. Wurm subgroups them as shown in Figure 1 (note that Bougainville is not to be confused with the Austronesian family of the same name).

FIGURE 1. *Subgrouping of East Papuan Languages*

- **Bougainville**
  - **East Bougainville**
    - **Buin**
      - Buin (proper), Siwai, Uisai
    - **Nasioi**
      - Koromira, Nagovisi, Nasioi (proper)
  - **West Bougainville**
    - Keriaka
    - Kunua
    - **Rotokas**
      - Eivo, Rotokas (proper)
- **Reef Islands–Santa Cruz**
  - Ayiwo, Nanggu, Santa Cruz
- **Yele–Solomons–New Britain**
  - **New Britain**
    - Anem
    - **Baining-Taulil**
      - Kairak, Makolkol, Mali, Qaqet, Simbali, Taulil-Butam, Uramat
    - Kol
    - Kuot
    - Pele-Ata
    - Sulka
  - **Yele-Solomons**
    - **Central Solomons**
      - Baniata, Bilua, Lavukaleve, Savo
    - **Kazukuru**
      - Dororo, Guliguli, Kazukuru (proper)
    - Yele

LANGUAGE LIST

Anem: 435 speakers reported in 1982, in on the northwest coast and inland, West New Britain Province, Papua New Guinea. Also called Karaiai.

Ayiwo: around 3,960 speakers reported in 1976, in the Santa Cruz Islands, eastern Solomon Islands. Also called Aïwo, Gnivo, Nivo, Nifilole, Lomlom, Reef Islands, or Reefs.

Baniata: 900 speakers reported in 1981, on south Rendova Island, Western Province, Solomon Islands. Also called Mbaniata or Lokuru. The speakers are becoming less bilingual in Roviana.

Bilua: around 4,470 speakers reported in 1976, on Vella Lavella Island, Western Province, Solomon Islands. Also called Mbilua or Vella Lavella.

Buin: 17,000 speakers reported in 1987, in Buin Subprovince, southern North Solomons Province, Papua New Guinea. Also called Telei, Rugara, or Terei.

Dororo: now extinct, formerly spoken in New Georgia, Solomon Islands. Also called Doriri.

Eivo: 1,200 speakers reported in 1981, in the mountains of south central North Solomons Province, Papua New Guinea.

Guliguli: now extinct, formerly spoken in New Georgia, Solomon Islands. Also called Gulili. Possibly was a Kazukuru dialect.

Kairak: 750 speakers reported in 1988, on the Gazelle Peninsula, East New Britain Province, Papua New Guinea. Some speakers know some Mali or Uramet.

Kazukuru: now extinct, formerly spoken in New Georgia, Solomon Islands.

Keriaka: 1,000 speakers reported in 1981, on the coast of North Solomons Province, Papua New Guinea.

Kol: 3,600 speakers reported in 1987, from Open Bay to the waterfall, East New Britain Province, Papua New Guinea. Also called Kole or Kola.

Koromira: spoken in the central mountains and southeast coast, Kieta Subprovince, North Solomons Province, Papua New Guinea.

Kunua: 1,500 speakers reported in 1981, in inland villages, northwestern North Solomons Province, Papua New Guinea. Also called Konua. Tok Pisin is used in the schools.

Kuot: 1,000 speakers reported in 1985, on the northwest coast, New Ireland Province, Papua New Guinea. Also called Panaras.

Lavukaleve: 700 speakers reported in 1981, in the Russell Islands, northwest of Guadalcanal, central Solomon Islands. Also called Laube, Laumbe, or Russell Island.

Makolkol: 7 or fewer speakers reported in 1988, on the Gazelle Peninsula, East New Britain Province, Papua New Guinea.

Mali: 2,200 speakers reported in 1988, on the eastern Gazelle Peninsula, East New Britain Province, Papua New Guinea. Also called Gaktai or Mar.

Nagovisi: 5,000 speakers reported in 1975, in Buin Subprovince, North Solomons Province, Papua New Guinea. Also called Sibbe or Nagovis.

Nanggu: 240 speakers reported in 1976, on Santa Cruz Island, Solomon Islands. Most speakers are bilingual in the Santa Cruz language.

Nasioi: 17,000 speakers reported in 1986, in the central mountains and southeast coast, Kieta Subprovince, North Solomons Province, Papua New Guinea. Also called Naasioi or Kieta.

Pele-Ata: 1,320 speakers reported in 1982, inland from Bongula Bay, West New Britain Province, Papua New Guinea. Also called Wasi, Uase, Uasi, Uasilau, or Peleata.

Qaqet: 6,350 speakers reported in 1988, on the Gazelle Peninsula, East New Britain Province, Papua New Guinea. Also called Baining, Xaxet, Chachet, Makaket, Makakat, or Kakat.

Rotokas: 4,320 speakers reported in 1981, in the central mountains, Kieta Subprovince, North Solomons Province, Papua New Guinea.

Santa Cruz: 3,230 speakers reported in 1977, in the Santa Cruz Islands, eastern Solomon Islands. Also called Natügu, Nendö, Nambakaengö, or Mbanua.

Savo: around 1,150 speakers reported in 1976, north of Guadalcanal, Savo Island, central Solomon Islands. Also called Savo Island or Savosavo. Use of Savo is reported to be declining among the younger generation.

Simbali: 350 speakers reported in 1988, on the Gazelle Peninsula, East New Britain Province, Papua New Guinea. Also called Asimbali. Some speakers use some Mali or Uramet.

Siwai: 6,600 speakers reported in southeastern North Solomons Province, Papua New Guinea. Also called Motuna.

Sulka: 1,900 speakers reported in 1982, on the Wide Bay coast, East New Britain Province, Papua New Guinea. A dialect chain.

Taulil-Butam: 825 speakers reported in 1982, on the Gazelle Peninsula, East New Britain Province, Papua New Guinea. Speakers are bilingual in Tolai.

Uisai: 1,060 speakers reported in 1975, in Buin Subprovince, North Solomons Province, Papua New Guinea.

Uramat: 1,450 speakers reported in 1988, on the Gazelle Peninsula, East New Britain Province, Papua New Guinea. Also called Uramot, Uramit, Uramet, or Auramot.

Yele: 3,300 speakers reported in 1988, on Rossel Island at the eastern end of the Calvados chain, Misima Subprovince, Milne Bay Province, Papua New Guinea. Also called Yelejong, Rossel, Yela, or Yeletnye. Speakers who have been to school know some English.

EAST SUDANIC LANGUAGES are spoken in a continuous area (with some outliers) from central Tanzania north to central Ethiopia and southern Sudan, with other outliers as far north as Eritrea, northern Sudan, and Egypt. East Sudanic is widely considered a top-level constituent of Nilo-Saharan [*q.v.*]. Joseph H. Greenberg, *The languages of Africa* (Bloomington: Indiana University Press, 1963) assigned East Sudanic as a subgroup of Chari-Nile within Nilo-Saharan, but the unity of Chari-Nile has been questioned in later work.

The East Sudanic languages have been divided into four groups: an Eastern division, a Western division, Kuliak, and Nilotic. [*For information on the last two groups, see the articles with those titles.*] The subgrouping of the Eastern and Western divisions is given in Figure 1, and a Language List for those divisions follows.

LANGUAGE LIST

Abou Charib: 25,000 speakers reported in 1967, south of Biltine, east central Chad. Also called Abu Sharib. Sometimes considered a dialect of Mararit.

FIGURE 1. *Subgrouping of East Sudanic Languages*

- **Eastern Division**
  - **Eastern Jebel**
    - **Aka-Kelo-Molo**
    - Gaam
  - Nera
  - **Nubian**
    - **Central Nubian**
      - Birked
      - Nile Nubian (Dongolawi)
      - **Hill Nubian**
        - **Kadaru-Ghulfan**
          - Debri, Ghulfan, Kadaru
        - **Unclassified Hill Nubian**
          - Dair, Dilling, El Hugeirat, Karko, Wali
    - **Northern Nubian**
      - Nobiin
    - **Western Nubian**
      - Midob
  - **Surma**
    - Bale
    - **Kwegu**
      - Kwegu (proper)
      - **Suri**
        - Mursi, Suri (proper), Tirma
      - Me'en
    - Majang-Shabo
    - **Murle**
      - Didinga, Longarim, Murle (proper), Tenet
    - Zilmamu
- **Western Division**
  - **Daju**
    - **Eastern Daju**
      - Liguri, Shatt
    - **Western Daju**
      - Bego, Dar Dadju Daju, Darfur Daju, Lagowa, Nyalgulgule, Sila
  - **Nyimang**
    - Afitti, Nyima
  - **Tama**
    - Kibet
    - **Merarit**
      - Abou Charib, Merarit (proper)
    - **Tama-Sungor**
  - **Temein**
    - Jirru, Temein (proper)

Afitti: 4,500 speakers reported in 1984, around Sidra, on eastern Jebel ed Dair, Nuba Hills, northern Sudan. Close to Nyima. Also called Dinik, Ditti or Unietti.

Aka: spoken in northern Sudan, Sillok Hills, west of the main Berta-speaking people. Also called Sillok or Jebels Sillok. Speakers call themselves Fa-c-aka.

Bale: 2,000 to 3,000 speakers reported in 1982, on the Boma Plateau, Ethiopia. Also called Balethi or Baletha. Some speakers are bilingual in Suri.

Bego: now extinct, formerly spoken in the hills east of Kube (Kubbi), Jebel Beygo, Southern Darfur Province, northern Sudan. Also called Baigo, Baygo, Beko, Beigo, or Beygo. Close to Daju of Darfur. The ethnic group do not use the name 'Daju'.

Birked: now extinct, formerly spoken in northern Darfur Province, northern Sudan, and by a few in north Kordofan Province south of El Obeid. Also called Birguid, Birkit, Birqed, Murgi, or Kajjara. Has 60 percent lexical similarity with Kadaru, 51 percent with Midob.

Dair: 1,000 speakers reported in 1978, in the western and southern parts of Jebel Dair, Kordofan Province, northern Sudan. Also called Daier or Thaminyi.

Daju, Dar Dadju: 27,000 speakers reported in 1971, in the Ouaddai Region, southeast Chad. Also called Dadjo, Dajou, or Saaronge. The majority of speakers are bilingual in Arabic.

Daju, Darfur: 70,000 to 90,000 speakers reported in 1983, in the Daju Hills, Darfur Province, Sudan; also in Dar Masalit, Geneina District, and in western Kordofan Province. Also called Nyala-Lagowa, Nyala, Fininga, Dagu, Daju Ferne, or Beke.

Debri: spoken in the Nuba Mountains, Kordofan Province, Sudan. Also called Wei. Has 87 percent lexical similarity with Kadaru, the most closely related variety.

Didinga: 58,000 speakers reported in 1978, in the Didinga Hills and north of Nagishot, southern Sudan. Also called 'Di'dinga, Xaroxa, Toi, or Lango. Has 83 percent lexical similarity with Longarim, the most closely related variety. Different from the Nilotic language Lango.

Dilling: some 5,290 speakers reported in 1984, in the town of Dilling and on the surrounding hills including Kudr, Kordofan Province, northern Sudan. Also called Delen, Warki, or Warkimbe.

Dongolawi: 750,000 to 1,000,000 speakers reported in 1971, south of Aswan, Egypt, and 170,000 south and north of Dongola, Northern Province, Sudan. Also called Kenuz, Kunuzi, Kenzi, Kenuzi-Dongola, Metoki, Nile Nubian, or Ratana. Has 67 percent lexical similarity with Nobiin.

El Hugeirat: 1,000 speakers reported in 1978, in the El Hugeirat Hills, West Kordofan Province, northern Sudan.

Gaam: 10,000 speakers reported in 1972, in and around Jebel Tabi, and on Tabi Massif and outlying hills, northern Sudan. Some speakers also live in Ethiopia. Also called Ingassana, Ingessana, Tabi, Metabi, Muntabi, Mamedja, Mamidza, or Kamanidi.

Ghulfan: 16,000 speakers reported in 1984, on two hill ranges south of Dilling, Kordofan Province, northern Sudan. Also called Gulfan, Wunci, or Wuncimbe.

Jirru: 1,400 speakers reported in 1971, at Keiga Jirru west of Debri and northeast of Kadugli, Nuba Hills, northern

Sudan. Also called Teis-Umm-Danab or Keiga Jirru. Has 67 percent lexical similarity with Temein.

Kadaru: 7,000 speakers reported in 1978, in the north and east parts of the Kadaru Hills between Dilling and Delami, in the Nuba Mountains, Kordofan Province, Sudan. Also called Kadaro, Kaderu, Kodoro, Kodhin, or Kodhinniai.

Karko: around 2,120 speakers reported in 1977, in the Karko Hills twenty miles west of Dilling, including Dulman, Kordofan Province, Sudan. Also called Garko or Kithonirishe.

Kelo: now extinct, formerly spoken in the Tornasi Hills at Jebels Tornasi and Beni Sheko, northern Sudan, west of the Berta-speaking people. Also called Tornasi, Kelo-Beni Sheko, or Ndu-Faa-Keelo.

Kibet: 16,000 to 22,000 speakers reported in 1977, in Chad. Also called Kibet-Mourro-Dogel. Most speakers are bilingual in Arabic. Has also been associated with the Maban family.

Kwegu: 300 speakers reported in 1982, north of the Kara and south of the Mursi, on the Omo River bank among the Me'en and Bodi, Ethiopia. Has 36 percent lexical similarity with Mursi.

Lagowa: spoken near Kabira, Nyukri, and Tamanyik, in the Kordofan region of Sudan. Related to Daju of Darfur.

Liguri: 2,000 speakers reported in 1971, on Jebel Liguri and other hills northeast of Kadugli, central Nuba Mountains, northern Sudan. Speakers use local names for their language varieties, rather than language names like 'Liguri' or 'Daju'.

Longarim: 6,000 speakers reported in 1982, in the Boya Hills, southern Sudan, north of the Didinga. Also called Narim, Lariminit, or Boya.

Majang: 28,000 speakers reported in 1975, in Ethiopia. Also called Mesengo, Masongo, Majanjiro, Tama, Ojanjur, or Ajo.

Me'en: around 40,000 speakers reported in 1982, in the Kafa Region, Ethiopia. Also called Mieken, Meqan, Men, or Shuro.

Merarit: 42,000 speakers reported in 1971, east of Abeche, east central Chad, and in Darfur and Dar Masalit in northern Sudan. Also called Mararet, Mararit, Abiyi, Abiri, or Ebiri. Most speakers are bilingual in Arabic.

Midob: 1,800 speakers reported in 1977, at Jebel Midob, Darfur Province, Sudan. Also called Meidob, Midobi, or Tidda.

Molo: 100 speakers reported in 1988, at Jebel Malkan, Sudan, south of the Blue Nile near the Ethiopian border, near the Berta language. Also called Malkan. Speakers call themselves Tvra-Ka-Molo.

Murle: 66,000 speakers reported in 1982, including 60,000 in Pibor District, south of the Akobo River, Upper Nile Province, Sudan; and 6,000 in Ethiopia south of the Akobo River. Also called Murelei, Merule, Mourle, Beir, Ajibba, Agiba, or Adkibba.

Mursi: 5,000 speakers reported in 1982, near the Amar, in Ethiopia. Also called Murzi, Murzu, Merdu, or Meritu.

Nera: 25,000 speakers reported in 1975, in and north of Barentu, western Eritrea, Ethiopia, adjoining Kunama territory to the south. Also called Nara, Barea, or Baria. Baria is a derogatory name. Speakers use Tigré to communicate with the Tigré people.

Nobiin: spoken in northern Sudan, on the Nile between Dongola and the Egyptian border. Also spoken in the upper Nile Valley, Egypt. Also called Fiadidja-Mahas or Mahas-Fiyadikkya.

Nyalgulgule: 900 speakers reported in 1977, on the Sopo River just above its confluence with the Boro, in southern Sudan, west of the Dinka language area. Also called Nyolge, Nyoolne, Ngulgule, Njalgulgule, Njangulgule, Begi, Bege, or Beko. The speakers are bilingual in Arabic.

Nyima: 70,000 speakers reported in 1982, northwest of Dilling on the range of hills of which Jebel Nyimang is a part, in northern Sudan, and in the Mandal range of the Nuba Hills in Kordofan Province. Also called Inyimang, Nyimang, Ama, or Nyiman. Speakers learn Arabic in school.

Shabo: 400 to 1,000 speakers reported in 1986, in Illubabor Province, Ethiopia, living among the Majang and Mocha. Also called Shako or Mikeyir. Distinct from Shako (Sheko), an Omotic language. Speakers are bilingual in Majang or Mocha.

Shatt: 15,000 speakers reported in 1984, in the Shatt Hills southwest of Kadugli, and in parts of Abu Hashim and Abu Sinam, northern Sudan. Different from Shatt (Thuri) in the Lwo group, or the Shatt dialect of Mundu.

Sila: 33,000 speakers reported in 1971, in northern Sudan. Nearly all speakers have migrated into Darfur Province in recent times. Also spoken in the Ouaddai region of southeastern Chad. Also called Dar Sila Daju, Sula, Mongo-Sila, Bokor, Bokoruge, or Bokorike. Different from Daju of Darfur (Nyala).

Sungor: 60,000 speakers reported in 1983, including 45,000 northeast of Abeche between Abeche and Adre, mainly at Gereda, Chad, and 15,000 in Darfur and Dar Masalit, northern Sudan. Also called Azanguri, Asong, Assangori, Asungore, Erenga, Madungore, or Shaale. The majority of speakers are bilingual in Arabic.

Suri: 15,000 speakers reported in 1983, including 10,000 in Kafa Province, Ethiopia, in the Maji area with center at Koma, extending toward Sudan, with some groups west of Mizan; and 5,000 speakers on the Boma Plateau in southern Sudan, near the Ethiopian border among the Murle. Also called Churi, Dhuri, Surma, or Kichepo.

Tama: around 105,000 speakers reported in 1982, including 45,000 in east central Wadai, in Dar Tama and Goz Beida

Districts, Chad, and 60,000 in Darfur Province, northern Sudan. The majority of speakers are bilingual in Arabic.

Temein: 10,000 speakers reported in 1984, in the Temein Hills southwest of Dilling, between Jebel Ghulfan Morung and Jebel Julud, in the Nuba Hills of northern Sudan. Also called Temainian, Rone, or Ronge.

Tenet: 3,000 speakers reported in 1987, in the Lafit Hills north of Torit, Equatoria Province, southern Sudan. The people's second language is Murle.

Tirma: 1,000 or more speakers reported in 1983, on the Boma Plateau among the Suri, southern Sudan, near the Ethiopian border. Also spoken in Ethiopia. Also called Tirima, Terema, Terna, Dirma, or Cirma.

Wali: 490 speakers reported in 1977, in the Wali Hills, south of the Karko Hills, northern Sudan. Also called Walari or Walarishe.

Zilmamu: 2,000 to 3,000 speakers reported in 1975, in Ethiopia on the Ethiopia-Sudan border. Also called Zilmamo, Zelmamu, Zulmamu, or Tsilmano. Has 40 percent lexical similarity with Murle.

EAST TRANS–NEW GUINEA LANGUAGES

EAST TRANS–NEW GUINEA LANGUAGES are spoken in southeastern Papua New Guinea. Stephen A. Wurm, *Papuan languages of Oceania* (Tübingen: Narr, 1982), pp. 156–165, considers these languages to form the Eastern part of the main section of his controversial Trans–New Guinea phylum [*q.v.*]. The subgrouping into families shown in Figure 1 is based on his system (with some terminological changes).

FIGURE 1. *Subgrouping of East Trans–New Guinea Languages*

Binanderean
- **Binanderean Proper**
  - Aeka, Ambasi, Baruga, Binandere, Dogoro, Ewage-Notu, Gaina, Hunjara, Korafe, Mawae, Orokaiva, Suena, Yega, Yekora, Zia
- Guhu-Samane

Central and Southeastern Trans–New Guinea
- **Dagan**
  - Daga, Ginuman, Jimajima, Kanasi, Maiwa, Mapena, Onjab, Turaka, Umanakaina
- **Goilalan**
  - Fuyuge
  - **Kunimaipa**
    - Biangai, Kunimaipa (proper), Weri
  - Tauade
- **Koiarian**
  - **Baraic**
    - Barai, Managalasi, Ömie
  - **Koiaric**
    - Mountain Koiali, Grass Koiari, Koita
- **Kwalean**
  - Humene, Kwale, Mulaha
- **Mailuan**
  - Bauwaki, Binahari, Domu, Laua, Mailu, Morawa
- **Manubaran**
  - Doromu, Maria
- **Yareban**
  - Aneme Wake, Bariji, Moikodi, Nawaru, Yareba

LANGUAGE LIST

Aeka: 2,000 speakers reported in 1981, around Kikinonda village, Oro Province. Also called Aiga. Has 60 percent lexical similarity with Orokaiva, the most closely related variety.

Ambasi: around 1,200 speakers reported in 1981, between Ioma Binandere, Aeka and Ewage, and in a few villages on the coast, Oro Province. Also called Tain-Daware, Davari, or Dawari. Has 67 percent lexical similarity with Binandere, the most closely related variety.

Aneme Wake: 580 speakers reported in 1973, on both sides of the Owen Stanley Range, Central Province, and north from Ianu along Foasi and Domara creeks, Oro Province. Also called Abie or Abia. Has 65 to 73 percent lexical similarity with Moikodi, the most closely related variety. Speakers are bilingual in Motu or Yareba.

Barai: 3,000 speakers reported in 1975, in Popondetta Subprovince, inland Oro Province, to the middle of Central Province. Barai on the southern slopes of the Owen Stanley Mountains in Central Province may be a separate language.

Bariji: 260 speakers reported in 1973, on the south bank of the Bariji River, Oro Province. Also called Aga Bereho. Speakers are bilingual in Hiri Motu. Has 49 percent lexical similarity with Moikodi.

Baruga: around 1,050 speakers reported in 1971, east of the Managalasi, Oro Province, between the Gaina and the Korafe. Some speakers are bilingual in Tok Pisin or Hiri Motu.

Bauwaki: 380 speakers reported in 1971, most of them at Amau, Central Province, extending into Oro Province. Also called Bawaki. Has 66 percent lexical similarity with Domu, the most closely related variety. Population includes 85 percent to 100 percent bilingual in Magi, Suau, Motu, or English.

Biangai: around 1,260 speakers reported in 1981, at the headwaters of Bulolo River, Wau Subprovince, Morobe Province.

Binahari: 770 speakers reported in 1971, on both sides of a range of hills inland from Cloudy Bay, Central Province. Has 70 percent lexical similarity with Morawa, the most closely related variety. Population includes 80 percent to 100 percent bilingual in Magi, Suau, Hiri Motu, or English.

Binandere: 3,300 speakers reported in 1981, along the Eia, Ope, Mambere, and Kumusi rivers, between Zia and Ambasi, Oro Province, plus a few in Morobe Province. Also called Ioma Binandere. Has 50 percent to 54 percent lexical similarity with Suena and Zia, 67 percent with Ambasi. The people who live near the coast are more bilingual.

Daga: 5,500 speakers reported in 1977, in Rabaraba Subprovince and Abau Subprovince, Milne Bay Province. Also called Dimuga or Nawp.

Dogoro: 120 speakers reported in 1981, in Bendoroda and Sebaga villages, Dyke Ackland Bay, Oro Province. Baruga is the most closely related variety.

Domu: 480 speakers reported in 1975, on the coast east of Cape Rodney and inland, Central Province. Also called Dom. Population includes 85 percent to 100 percent bilingual in Mailu, Suau, Hiri Motu, or English. Has 66 percent lexical similarity with Bauwaki, the most closely related variety.

Doromu: 840 speakers reported in 1966, south of Mt. Obree, west of Mt. Brown, Central Province. Also called Doram. Has 63 percent lexical similarity with Maria, the most closely related variety.

Ewage-Notu: 12,000 speakers reported in 1988, on the coast between Bakumbari and Pongani, Popondetta Subprovince, Oro Province. Also called Notu or Ewage.

Fuyuge: around 9,620 speakers reported in 1981, in southeastern Goilala Subprovince, Central Province. Extends into the Chirima River valley, Oro Province. Also called Fujuge, Fuyughe, or Mafufu. Has 28 percent lexical similarity with Kunimaipa, the most closely related variety.

Gaina: 1,130 speakers reported in a sago swamp area next to Baruga, and in the villages around Iwuji, Oro Province. Has 61 percent lexical similarity with Dogoro, the most closely related variety.

Ginuman: 775 speakers reported in 1971, from Mt. Simpson to the coast at Naraka, Milne Bay Province. Also called Dime. Has 42 percent lexical similarity with Kanasi.

Guhu-Samane: around 6,290 speakers reported in 1978, Lae Subprovince, Morobe Province, and a few from Kanoma and Sidema villages northward, Oro Province. Also called Paiawa, Tahari, Muri, Bia, or Mid-Waria. Suena and Zia are the most closely related varieties.

Humene: 440 speakers reported in 1966, on the lower edge of the Sogeri Plateau and the adjacent plain between Gaire and Kapakapa villages, Central Province. Has 65 percent to 74 percent lexical similarity with Kwale, the most closely related variety. Some speakers know Hiri Motu and Motu, some English.

Hunjara: 4,300 speakers reported in 1973, in villages from Koroda to Waseda, Oro Province. Also called Huntjara or Koko.

Jimajima: 545 speakers reported in 1971, along the coast east of Moi Bay, almost to Posa Posa Harbour, and along the Ruaba River, Milne Bay Province. Also called Dima. Has 41 percent lexical similarity with Daga, the most closely related variety.

Kanasi: 2,000 speakers reported in 1987, on both sides of the main range river valleys from Mt. Thomson, Milne Bay Province. Also called Dima or Sona. Has 42 percent lexical similarity with Ginuman, the most closely related variety.

Koiali, Mountain: 1,700 speakers reported in 1975, in Port Moresby Subprovince, Central Province, north of the Koita, Koiari, and Barai. Also called Mountain Koiari. Has 50 percent to 57 percent lexical similarity with Grass Koiari, the most closely related variety.

Koiari, Grass: 1,800 speakers reported in 1973, east of Port Moresby and to the coast, Central Province. Also called Koiari. Has 60 percent to 65 percent lexical similarity with Koita, the most closely related variety.

Koita: 3,000 speakers reported in 1990, around Port Moresby, Central Province. Also called Koitabu. Population includes 43 percent near-monolinguals, 40 percent with routine ability, and 17 percent with nearly native ability in Hiri Motu. Some speakers are bilingual in Motu, Tok Pisin, or English. Has 60 percent to 65 percent lexical similarity with Grass Koiari, the most closely related variety.

Korafe: 4,200 speakers reported in 1973, near the Baruga and Tufi Subprovince headquarters, Oro Province. Also called Korape, Korafi, or Kwarafe. Has 44 percent lexical similarity with Baruga, the most closely related variety.

Kunimaipa: 10,000 speakers reported in 1975, in northern Goilala Subprovince, Central Province, and in Wau Subprovince, Morobe Province.

Kwale: 720 speakers reported in 1973, on the coast south of Port Moresby, at Kemp Welsh River, Central Province. Has 65 percent to 74 percent lexical similarity with Humene, the most closely related variety.

Laua: 1 speaker reported in 1987, northwest of Laua, Central Province. Also called Labu. Different from Austronesian Labu in Morobe Province.

Mailu: 6,000 speakers reported in 1980, from Gadaisu to Baramata, Table Bay and Toulon Island, on the south coast of Central Province. Also called Magi.

Maiwa: 1,400 speakers reported in 1985, on the northern slopes and foothills of the Meneao Range, Milne Bay Province, extending into Oro Province. Has 41 percent lexical similarity with Mapena, the most closely related variety. Wedau is used as church language.

Managalasi: 5,000 speakers reported in 1982, in Popondetta Subprovince, Oro Province, southeast of the Omie. Also called Managulasi.

Mapena: 275 speakers reported in 1973, around Mt. Gwoira, Milne Bay Province. Has 51 percent lexical similarity with Daga, the most closely related variety.

Maria: around 2,110 speakers reported in 1973, from Marshall Lagoon to Mt. Brown, Central Province. Also called Manubara. Has 63 percent lexical similarity with Doromu, the most closely related variety.

Mawae: 945 speakers reported in 1978, in Morobe and Oro Provinces.

Moikodi: 570 speakers reported in 1981, on the north slopes of the Owen Stanley Range around Mt. Brown, Oro Province, and down to Komi west of Foasi Creek. Also called Doriri. Speakers are bilingual in Hiri Motu. Has 65 percent to 73 percent lexical similarity with Aneme Wake, the most closely related variety.

Morawa: 755 speakers reported in 1973, on the south coast around Cloudy Bay, Central Province. Has 70 percent lexical similarity with Binahari, the most closely related variety. Population includes 85 percent to 100 percent bilingual in Magi, Suau, Hiri Motu, or English.

Mulaha: now extinct, formerly spoken just southeast of Gaile on the coast, Oro Province.

Nawaru: 190 speakers reported in 1990, around the upper Musa River valley, Oro Province. Also called Sirio. Speakers are bilingual in Hiri Motu or Yareba.

Ömie: 1,100 speakers reported in 1987, in Kokoda Subprovince, Oro Province, northwest of the Managalasi, in the Mamama and upper Kumusi river valleys. Also called Aomie or Upper Managalasi.

Onjab: 160 speakers reported in 1981, in Koreat and Naukwate villages, Oro Province. Also called Onjob. Has 30 percent lexical similarity with Maiwa, the most closely related variety.

Orokaiva: 27,000 speakers reported in 1989, in Popondetta Subprovince, Oro Province, between the Hunjara, Notu, Binandere and Managalasi. Also called Orakaiva.

Suena: around 2,280 speakers reported in 1978, north of Yekora in Lae District, Morobe Province. Also called Yema: Yarawe, or Yarawi.

Tauade: around 8,620 speakers reported in 1981, Goilala Subprovince toward the northeast, Central Province. Also called Tauata. Has 44 percent lexical similarity with Kunimaipa, the most closely related variety.

Turaka: 35 speakers reported in 1981, five miles southwest of Radarada and Ruaba, Milne Bay Province.

Umanakaina: 2,400 speakers reported in 1987, on the coast of Goodenough Bay, inland between Mt. Gwoira and Mt. Simpson, Milne Bay Province. Also called Gwedena, Gweda, Gwede, or Gvede. Ginuman is the most closely related variety. Some speak English.

Weri: around 4,170 speakers reported in 1978, at the headwaters of the Biaru, Waria, and Ono rivers, Wau Subprovince, Morobe Province. Also called Weli or Wele.

Yareba: 750 speakers reported in 1981, in Popondetta Subprovince, Oro Province. Also called Middle Musa. Speakers are highly bilingual in Hiri Motu.

Yega: 900 speakers reported in 1981, between Notu and Bareji, Oro Province. Also called Gona.

Yekora: 675 speakers reported in 1978, north of Zia, Morobe Province. Most speakers are bilingual in Suena or Zia.

Zia: around 2,800 speakers reported in 1978, near the mouth of the Waria River, Morobe District, Morobe Province. Also called Tsia, Lower Waria, or Ziya. Has 68 percent lexical similarity with Yekora, the most closely related variety.

EDOID LANGUAGES are a group spoken in central southern Nigeria; they form a subgroup of the Benue-Congo branch of the Niger-Congo family [*qq.v.*]. An earlier classification, whereby the Edoid languages would form part of the Kwa branch [*q.v.*] of Niger-Congo, is not followed here. The classification of the Edoid languages given in Figure 1 follows Ben Ohi Elugbe, 'Edoid', in *The Niger-Congo languages,* ed. by John Bendor-Samuel (Lanham, Md.: University Press of America, 1989), pp. 291–304.

LANGUAGE LIST

Degema: 10,000 speakers reported in Kalabari Division, Rivers State. Also called Atala or Udekama.

Edo: 1,000,000 speakers reported in 1989, in East and West Benin Divisions, Bendel State. Also called Bini, Benin, Addo, Oviedo, or Ovioba. Used in adult and primary education.

Emai-Iuleha-Ora: 48,000 speakers reported in 1952, in the divisions of Owan, Akoko-Edo, Ishan, and West and East Benin, Bendel State. Also called Kunibum or Ivbiosakon. Ora is used in initial primary education.

FIGURE 1. *Subgrouping of Edoid Languages*

Delta Edoid
Degema, Engenni, Epie
North-Central Edoid
Edo-Esan-Ora
Edo, Emai-Iuleha-Ora, Esan
Ghotuo-Uneme-Yekhee
Etsako, Ghotuo, Uneme
Unclassified North-Central Edoid
Ikpeshe, North Ivbie-Okpela-Atte, Ososo, Sasaru-Enwan Igwe
Northwestern Edoid Igwe
Osse
Uhami-Iyayu, Ukue-Ehuen
Southern Northwestern Edoid
Okpe-Idesa-Oloma-Akuku, Okpamheri
Southwestern Edoid
Eruwa, Isoko, Okpe, Urhobo, Uvbie

Engenni: 20,000 speakers reported in 1980, in Ahoada and Yenagoa Divisions, Rivers State. Also called Ngene or Egene.

Epie: 12,000 speakers reported in 1973, in Yenagoa Division, Rivers State. Also called Epie-Atissa. Most speakers are bilingual in Ijo.

Eruwa: spoken in Isoko Division, Bendel State. Also called Erohwa, Erakwa, or Arokwa. Most speakers are bilingual in Central Isoko, which is replacing Eruwa. Not mutually intelligible with any Isoko dialect.

Esan: 200,000 speakers reported in 1973, in the divisions of Ishan, East Benin, Agbor, and Aniocha, Bendel State. Also called Ishan, Isa, Esa, or Anwain. A regionally important language, used in initial primary education and television. Nigerian Pidgin English is spoken or understood by 99 percent of the population.

Etsako: 150,000 speakers reported in 1989, in Etsako and Ishan Divisions, Bendel State. Also called Yekhee, Afenmai, Iyekhee, or Etsakor. The name 'Kukuruku' is derogatory.

Ghotuo: 9,000 speakers reported in 1952, in Owan and Akoko-Edo Divisions, Bendel State. Also called Otwa or Otuo.

Ikpeshe: spoken in Etsako Division, Bendel State. Also called Ekpeshe or Ikpeshi.

Isoko: 300,000 speakers reported in 1980, in the east part of Urhobo and Isoko Divisions, Bendel State. Also called Igabo, Sobo, or Biotu; Sobo and Igabo are offensive names. A regionally important language. Used in initial primary education.

Ivbie North-Okpela-Atte: 20,000 speakers reported in 1973, in Atsako and Akoko-Edo Divisions, Bendel State.

Okpamheri: 30,000 speakers reported in 1973, in Akoko-Edo Division, Bendel State. Also called Opameri.

Okpe: spoken in Western Urhobo Division, Bendel State. Distinct from Okpe-Idesa-Oloma-Akuku of Akoko-Edo Division, which is Northwestern Edoid.

Okpe-Idesa-Oloma-Akuku: spoken in Akoko-Edo Division, Bendel State. Different from Okpe of Western Urhobo Division, which is Southwestern Edoid.

Ososo: spoken in Ososo, Akoko-Edo Division, Bendel State.

Sasaru-Enwan Igwe: some 3,780 speakers reported in 1952, in Akoko-Edo Division, Bendel State. Also called Sasaru.

Uhami-Iyayu: spoken in Idoani, Owo Division, Ondo State. Also called Ishua.

Ukue-Ehuen: spoken in Ukpe and Ekpenmi, Akoko Division, Ondo State. Also called Ekpenmi, Ekpenmen, or Epinmi.

Uneme: spoken in Etsako, Ishan, and Akoko-Edo Divisions, Bendel State. Also called Uleme, Ileme, or Ineme.

Urhobo: 340,000 speakers reported in 1973, in East and West Urhobo Divisions, Bendel State. Also called Biotu or Sobo. Used in initial primary education.

Uvbie: 6,000 speakers reported in 1952, in Western Urhobo Division, Bendel State. Also called Evhro, Uvhria, Uvwie, Evrie, or Effurun; the name Evhro is offensive.

EGYPTIAN represents an independent branch of the Afro-Asiatic family [*q.v.*], showing the closest relations to Semitic and Berber. With its more than four millennia of productive history—from 3000 BCE to 1300 CE—it provides an ideal field for both diachronic and typological investigation.

Gardiner 1957 is the most widely used handbook for the study of hieroglyphs. Callender 1975 gives a generative/transformational approach to the grammar of the classical language. Edel 1955–64 is a philological reference work on the language of the Old Kingdom. Černý & Groll 1984 presents a structural analysis of Late Egyptian. Erman & Grapow 1926–53 is still the standard dictionary of Egyptian; for Coptic, Crum 1929–39 offers a philologically much more detailed compendium; and Westendorf 1965–67 is the important instrument for etymological reconstruction. Polotsky 1971, 1976 present the modern standard theory of Egyptian grammar, from which most contemporary linguistic research in Egyptology begins. On verbal and nominal systems, see Loprieno 1986 and Osing 1976, respectively.

1. History. The history of Egyptian can be divided into two main stages, each of which is further subdivided into different phases, which affect mainly the writing system.

OLDER EGYPTIAN refers to the written language from 3000 to 1300 BCE, surviving in religious texts until the 2nd century CE. It is characterized by its preference for synthetic grammatical structures (no definite article, V[erb] S[ubject] O[bject] order, etc.). Its main phases are:

(a) Old Egyptian, the language of the Old Kingdom and the First Intermediate Period (3000–2000 BCE).
(b) Middle Egyptian, from the Middle Kingdom to the end of the XVIII Dynasty (2000–1300 BCE). This is the classical literary language; it differs from Old Egyptian mainly in having a regularized orthography.
(c) Late Middle Egyptian, the language of more formal texts from 1300 BCE onward.

In the Greek and Roman period (Ptolemaic Egyptian, 3rd c. BCE to 2nd c. CE), the language shows a considerable elaboration of the set of hieroglyphic signs (see below.)

LATER EGYPTIAN refers to the language of literature and administration from the XIX Dynasty to the Christian era (1300 BCE to 1300 CE), with the following phases:

(a) Late Egyptian (1300–700 BCE)
(b) Demotic (7th c. BCE to 5th c. CE), differing from Late Egyptian basically in its graphic system
(c) Coptic (4th–14th c. CE), the alphabetically written language of Christian Egypt

As a spoken (and progressively also written) language, Coptic was superseded by Arabic beginning with the 9th century, but it survives to the present in the liturgy of the Coptic Church. Later Egyptian exhibits a tendency toward the development of analytic features—e.g. a definite article, and SVO periphrastic patterns.

Because of the centralizing nature of the political and cultural models that underlay the evolution of Ancient Egyptian society, there is hardly any evidence of dialect differences in pre-Coptic Egyptian; however, the origins of Older Egyptian are probably to be placed in Lower Egypt (Memphis), and those of Later Egyptian in Upper Egypt (Thebes). Coptic displays a variety of dialects.

2. Writing system. The basic graphic system of Ancient Egyptian is the HIEROGLYPHIC writing. It consists of a set of signs representing realia—about one thousand such symbols in the Old Kingdom, and approximately 760 in the classical language, dramatically increasing to many thousands in Ptolemaic Egyptian. The system combines phonological and ideographic principles. A word begins with a sequence of monoconsonantal, biconsonantal, or triconsonantal signs, called PHONOGRAMS, which convey its phonological structure; vocalic (and often also semivocalic) phonemes remain unexpressed in writing. The sequence of phonograms is usually followed by one of a group of SEMAGRAMS, called 'determinatives', which indicate iconically the semantic sphere of the word (especially in later stages, there may be more than one semagram in a word). Some words of common usage—pronouns, prepositions, and a few lexical items like *ḏd* 'to say'—are written only phonologically. But many items of basic vocabulary are expressed by semagrams which represent, symbolize, or evoke (through rebuses) their semantic reference; these are called LOGOGRAMS or IDEOGRAMS. Egyptian writing displays a set of twenty-four alphabetic (i.e. monoconsonantal) signs, which correspond to the consonantal and semiconsonantal phoneme inventory of the language; yet it never developed into a genuine alphabetic system until the Coptic period. The increasing consciousness of the symbolic potential inherent to the relation between signifiant and signifié, within this writing system, led to the use of cryptographic solutions in Ptolemaic Egyptian.

The hieroglyphic system, which was used mainly for monumental purposes, has two cursive varieties: HIERATIC (2600 BCE to 3rd c. CE), which simply represents a cursive rendering (with ligatures and diacritic signs) of a sequence of hieroglyphic signs; and DEMOTIC (7th c. BCE to 5th c. CE), which radically modifies the writing conventions by introducing a shorthand-like simplification of hieratic sign-groups. The basic orientation of the Egyptian writing system—and the only one adopted in the cursive varieties—is from right to left; epigraphic hieroglyphs can invert this order for reasons of symmetry.

The hieroglyphic-based system was superseded in Coptic by an alphabet derived from that of Greek, with the addition of seven Demotic signs for the indication of phonemes extraneous to Greek; it was written from left to right.

3. Phonology. The reconstruction of the Egyptian phoneme inventory is bound to be highly hypothetical. Vocalism and prosody can only be reconstructed by combining the contemporary, but not always unequivocal, Akkadian transcriptions with the much later Coptic evidence. Furthermore, the value of many consonantal oppositions is still open to debate. The consonants are shown in Table 1.

Note the following details:

(a) The Egyptian phonological system does not display the 'emphatic' phonemes common to most Afro-Asiatic languages. The most frequent etymological counterparts of Semitic emphatic fricatives seem to be the affricates; and of Semitic emphatic stops, the corresponding voiced phonemes.
(b) In mode of articulation, the voiced/voiceless opposition tends to a progressive neutralization into the voiceless, possibly aspirated, variant (3rd–2nd millennia BCE).
(c) The existence of a phoneme /l/ seems to be established; however, it exhibits no autonomous graphic rendering, being expressed in different lexemes by *3*, *n*, or *r*.
(d) The point of articulation of stops tends to be pro-

TABLE 1. *Egyptian Consonants*

	Labial	Apical	Alveo-palatal	Palatal	Velar	Uvular	Pharyngeal	Glottal
Stops								
Voiceless	p	t			k	q		3,j /ʔ/
Voiced	b	d			g			
Affricates								
Voiceless				ṯ				
Voiced				ḏ				
Fricatives								
Voiceless	f	s	š	ẖ /ç/	ḫ /x/		ḥ /ħ/	h
Voiced		z					ʿ /ʕ/	
Nasals	m	n						
Lateral		3,n,r /l/						
Vibrant		r						
Glides	w			j				

gressively moved to the front: (velars, postpalatals) > palatals > dentals (2nd millennium BCE).

(e) Oppositions between fricatives in the palatal region (/š ç x/) tend to be neutralized (2nd millennium BCE).

(f) The opposition between /ʕ/ and /ʔ/ tends to be neutralized, and the phonemes disappear altogether in Coptic.

(g) Initial /j/ tends to become /ʔ/ from the very beginning.

(h) Final /r/ and /t/ tend to become /ʔ/, then to disappear (2nd millennium BCE).

The vowels are front /i i:/, mid /a a:/, and back /u u:/. Some historical changes include:

(i) /a/, /a:/ > /o/, /o:/ (about 1000 BCE)

(ii) /i/, /u/ > /e/; /u:/ > /e:/ (2nd millennium BCE)

(iii) In particular phonetic surroundings, /e:/ > /i:/, /i:/ > /e:/

4. Morphology. As in other Afro-Asiatic languages, the basic Egyptian morphological unit is the root (biliteral or triliteral, with very few exceptions); this is modified by suffixes, or less frequently by prefixes. The gender and number markers are shown in Table 2, and the personal pronouns in Table 3. (Suffixes, as opposed to words, are marked by periods preceding them.)

TABLE 2. *Egyptian Gender and Number Markers*

	Masculine	Feminine
Singular	.Ø, *.w*	*.t*
Dual	*.wj*	*.tj*
Plural	.Ø, *.w*, *.ww*	*.t*, *.jt*, *.wt*

Of the series shown in the table, the independent pronouns are used as focus of a cleft sentence, usually a marked N[ominal] P[hrase]:

(1) *Ntf mrr sj.*
'He is the one who loves her.'

Less frequently, a marked V[erbal] P[hrase] occurs:

(2) *Ntf sḏm.f sj.*
'He is the one who will hear her.'

Dependent pronouns are used (i) as object of a VP (*Sḏm.f sj* 'He will hear her'); (ii) as subject of an unmarked NP (mostly an ADJ[ectival] P[hrase]: *Nfr sw* 'He is good'); and (iii) as subject of an ADV[erbial] P[hrase], in the 1st and 2nd persons only after initial particle:

TABLE 3. *Egyptian Personal Pronouns*

		Independent	Dependent	Suffixed
Sing.	1 c.	*jnk*	*wj*	*.j*
	2 m.	*ṯwt, ntk*	*kw, ṯw*	*.k*
	2 f.	*ṯmt, ntṯ*	*ṯm, ṯn*	*.ṯ*
	3 m.	*swt, ntf*	*sw*	*.f*
	3 f.	*stt, nts*	*sj, st*	*.s*
Dual	1 c.		*nj*	*.nj*
	2 c.	*ntṯnj*	*ṯnj*	*.ṯnj*
	3 c.	*ntsnj*	*snj*	*.snj*
Plur.	1 c.	*jnn*	*n*	*.n*
	2 c.	*ntṯn*	*ṯn*	*.ṯn*
	3 c.	*ntsn*	*sn*	*.sn*

(3) *(Mk) sw m jjj.t.*
'(Behold,) he (is) in coming' > 'He is coming.'

(4) *Mk wj m pr.w.*
'I am in the house.'

Suffixed pronouns are used (i) as subject of a VP (*Mrr.f sj r-wr* 'He loves her greatly'); (ii) as possessive pronoun (*pr.w.j* 'my house'); and (iii) as object of preposition (*J3.w n.k* 'Praise to you').

Demonstratives follow the noun to which they refer, and include masc. *pn pf pw*, and fem. *tn tf tw*—thus *rmṯ pf* 'that man', *ḥjm.t tn* 'this woman'. The corresponding plurals *nn, nf, nn* are also used as pronouns in partitive constructions: *nn nj srjw.w* 'these officials'.

The most frequent prepositions are *m* 'in, with', *n* 'to, for', *r* 'toward', and *ḥr* 'on.'

Finite forms of verbs are built by attaching a suffix pronoun to the root, either directly (*mrr.f* 'that he loves', *mrj.k* 'while you love'), or after the insertion of a morpheme indicating tense, aspect, or voice features:

(5) *Mrj.n.f sj r-wr.*
'He loved her greatly.'

(6) *Mrj.w.k wj.*
'May you love me.'

The most important verbal indicators are *n* (past tense), *t* (perfective, sometimes prospective aspect), *w* (prospective aspect and passive voice), and *tw* (passive voice). Some classes of verbal roots show a reduplication of the second radical in a form originally indicating imperfective aspect—but, in the classical language, a VP with nominal function: *mrr.f* '(the fact) that he loves'. The imperative has no suffix pronoun: *ḏd* 'say!' A verbal form carrying the feature of perfectivity (variously called Old Perfective, Pseudo-participle, or Stative), displays a set of suffix pronouns, which are etymologically linked to the Semitic suffix conjugation, thus *prj.kw* 'I have come forth; see Table 4.

There are two types of non-finite forms: the Nomina Agentis (participles) exhibit nominal suffixes (masc. *.Ø*, *.w*, and fem. *.t*, etc.); and the Nomina Actionis (infinitives) show a suffix *.Ø* in the regular verbs (*sḏm* 'to hear'), and *.t* in the weak classes (*mrj.t* 'to love'). A special Nomen Actionis with a suffix *.w* is used after verbs of negative predication:

(7) *tm* 'not to do something'
tm.f mrj.w 'that he does not love'

It is a matter of dispute whether the radical element of finite forms is originally a Nomen Agentis (*mrj.f* *'a-loving-one-is-he' > 'he loves') or a Nomen Actionis (*mrj.f* *'loving-by-him' > 'he loves'). Verbal predications can also be analytically expressed by prepositional constructions; these characterize the evolution of the verbal system in Later Egyptian:

(8) *Sw ḥr sḏm.*
'He is on hearing > 'He is hearing.'

(9) *Sw r mrj.t.*
'He is toward loving' > 'He is going to love.'

TABLE 4. *Egyptian Suffixal Pronouns*

	Singular	Dual	Plural
1	*.kj > .kw*		*.wjn*
2	*.tj*	*.tjwnj*	*.tjwnj*
3 m.	*.w*	*.wj*	*.w*
3 f.	*.tj*	*.tj*	*.tj*

5. Syntax. Egyptian shows three types of sentences, classified according to their PRED[ICATE]; the SUBJ[ECT] is always a NP.

(a) Nominal, with substantival or adjectival PRED; the unmarked order is PRED + SUBJ:

(10) *Rmṯ pw.*
'He is a man.'
Nfr sj.
'She is beautiful.'

This is inverted into SUBJ + PRED by focalization of SUBJ:

(11) *Ntk jtj n nmḥ.w.*
'Only you can be a father for the poor one.'

If SUBJ is topicalized, it is extraposed and resumed by a coreferential pronoun:

(12) *Jr sf, wsjr pw.*
'As for yesterday, it is Osiris.'

(b) Adverbial, with adverbial or prepositional predicate; the order is SUBJ + PRED:

(13) *Sw ṯnj.*
'Where is he?'

(14) *Zẖ3.w m pr.w.*
'The scribe is in the house.'

(c) Verbal, with verbal predicate; the order is PRED + SUBJ (+ obj):

(15) *Ḫ^c^j.w.k.*
'You will appear.'
Jrj.w.j st.
'I shall do it.'

Except in the prospective aspect, verbal sentences are much less frequent than in cognate languages: VPs tend to be embedded as SUBJ and/or PRED, within a SUBJ + PRED (or Topic + Comment) sequence. In Egyptological literature, this phenomenon is called 'transposition'; the Topic + Comment sequence is called a 'complex adverbial sentence'. Examples are:

(16) *M33.f wj m pr.w.*
'That-he-sees me (is) in the house' > 'He sees me in the house.'

(17) *Zj pn mrj.f sj.*
'This man (is) in-that-he-loves her' > 'This man loves her.'

The generalization of the use of this syntactic pattern eventually leads to the progressive disappearance of the VSO order in Later Egyptian. Whether 'transposed' VPs of Older Egyptian still maintain their predicative force—or whether they fully transform themselves into NPs and AdvPs, respectively—was a topic of considerable Egyptological debate in the 1980s.

ANTONIO LOPRIENO

BIBLIOGRAPHY

CALLENDER, JOHN B. 1975. *Middle Egyptian.* (Afroasiatic dialects, 2.) Malibu, Calif.: Undena.

ČERNÝ, JAROSLAV, & SARAH I. GROLL. 1984. *A Late Egyptian grammar.* 3d ed. (Studia Pohl, Series maior, 4.) Rome: Biblical Institute Press.

CRUM, WALTER E. 1929–39. *A Coptic dictionary.* 2 vols. Oxford: Clarendon Press.

EDEL, ELMAR. 1955–64. *Altägyptische Grammatik.* 2 vols. (Analecta Orientalia, 34–39.) Rome: Biblical Institute Press.

ERMAN, ADOLF, & HERMANN GRAPOW. 1926–53. *Wörterbuch der ägyptischen Sprache.* 6 vols. & supplements. Leipzig: Hinrichs. Berlin: Akademie-Verlag.

GARDINER, ALAN H. 1957. *Egyptian grammar, being an introduction to the study of hieroglyphs.* 3d ed. Oxford: Griffith Institute, Ashmolean Museum.

LOPRIENO, ANTONIO. 1986. *Das Verbalsystem im Ägyptischen und im Semitischen: Zur Grundlegung einer Aspekttheorie.* (Göttinger Orientforschungen, 4:17.) Wiesbaden: Harrassowitz.

OSING, JÜRGEN. 1976. *Die Nominalbildung des Ägyptischen.* 2 vols. Mainz: Philipp von Zabern.

POLOTSKY, HANS-JAKOB. 1971. *Collected papers.* Jerusalem: Magnes Press, Hebrew University.

POLOTSKY, HANS-JAKOB. 1976. Les transpositions du verbe en Égyptien classique. *Israel Oriental Studies* 6.1–50.

WESTENDORF, WOLFHART. 1965–67. *Koptisches Handwörterbuch.* Bearbeitet auf Grund des Koptischen Handwörterbuchs von Wilhelm Spiegelberg. 2 vols. Heidelberg: Winter.

EIGHTEENTH-CENTURY LINGUISTICS. *See* History of Linguistics, *article on* Seventeenth- and Eighteenth-Century Europe.

EKOID LANGUAGES are spoken in southeastern Nigeria and adjacent parts of Cameroon; they form a top-level constituent of the South Bantoid branch of the Niger-Congo languages [*qq.v.*].

LANGUAGE LIST

Abanyom: 3,850 speakers reported in 1953, in Ikom Division, Cross River State, Nigeria. Also called Abanyum or Befun.

Efutop: 10,000 speakers reported in 1973, in Ikom Division, Cross River State, Nigeria. Also called Ofutop or Agbaragba.

Ejagham: 80,000 speakers reported in 1982, including 45,000 in Akampka, Ikom, and Calabar Divisions, Cross River State, Nigeria, and 35,000 in Cameroon west of Mamfe. Also called Ekoi.

Ekajuk: 15,000 speakers reported in 1976, in Ogoja Division, Cross River State, Nigeria. Also called Akajo or Akajuk.

Nde-Nsele-Nta: 10,000 speakers reported in 1973, in Ikom and Obubra Divisions, Cross River State, Nigeria.

Ndoe: 3,000 speakers reported in 1953, in Ikom Division, Cross River State, Nigeria. Also called Anep or Anyep.

Nkem-Nkum: 16,700 speakers reported in 1953, in Ogoja Division, Cross River State, Nigeria.

Nnam: 1,230 speakers reported in 1953, in Ikom and Ogoja Divisions, Cross River State, Nigeria. Also called Ndem.

ELAMITE, the second language of the trilingual inscriptions of the Achaemenid kings of ancient Persia, was deciphered in the 1840s, after G. F. Grotefend in 1802 had read and identified the first, simplest script as Old Persian. The inventory of the cuneiform syllabary used to write Elamite was much smaller than that of the third language, Babylonian, which was deciphered soon after the first; but the interpretation of Elamite lacked the help of cognates that the Semitic languages could provide for Babylonian, and is still hampered by lack of comparative material. [*See* Cuneiform.]

1. The corpus. Elamite was spoken in the lowlands of southwestern Iran and in the highlands of Fars, from the 3rd millennium BCE probably to the 1st millennium CE. It was written with cuneiform syllabic signs from ca. 2200 BCE to 400 BCE. Another script—as yet undeciphered, but presumably also recording the Elamite language—is attested from ca. 3200 onward, first in pictographs (Meriggi 1971–74) and later in linear form (for an attempt to decipher the latter, see Hinz 1962, 1975).

Texts from the O[ld] E[lamite] period are rare. Even the longest, the so-called 'Treaty of Narām-Sin', ca. 23rd c. BCE, is poorly understood; and only a few texts survive from the 18th century BCE. The corpus of the M[iddle] E[lamite] period, ca. 1300–1100 BCE, consists of two types of documents: royal inscriptions, mostly on bricks decorating temples whose dedication they record (König 1965); and administrative documents, which come mainly from Malyān in Fars (Stolper 1984). N[eo-] E[lamite] is represented by 8th–7th century dedicatory inscriptions, some on bricks and some monumental; by administrative documents, legal texts, and letters on clay tablets from the 7th–6th century BCE; by a bronze plaque; and even by an astrological omen text. Best attested is A[chaemenid] E[lamite], which comprises inscriptions of Darius and his successors in one, two, or three languages, plus several thousand administrative texts found at Persepolis (Cameron 1948, Hallock 1969).

The structure of Elamite was sketched by Labat 1951; Royal Achaemenid Elamite was analyzed in descriptive terms by Paper 1955. Elamite of all periods—with special emphasis on ME, since AE morphology was somewhat simplified and the syntax influenced by Old Persian—is discussed by Reiner 1969, McAlpin 1981, and Grillot-Susini 1987. Details on grammatical features continue to be contributed by French Elamitologists and by others working in related fields (Diakonoff 1973, Wilhelm 1978, 1982; see the bibliography in Grillot-Susini 1987). In the dictionary of Hinz & Koch 1987, the many unknown words (and sometimes desperate guesses at meaning) emphasize that the major problem in Elamite studies is our inadequate knowledge of the lexicon.

2. Writing and phonology. The cuneiform syllabary was adapted in a manner somewhat simplified, both as to forms and selection of signs, from that of neighboring Babylonia; it consists of V, CV, VC, and (more rarely) CVC signs, plus a limited number of logograms, i.e. Sumerian words also used in the Assyro-Babylonian syllabary. The latter are identified in Elamite texts, as are also some Akkadian loanwords, by the Sumerogram MEŠ 'plural', which is usually transliterated as 'lg.' (for 'logogram'). This system can express only four vowels: *a, i, u* and (in combination with a limited number of syllabograms only) *e*. It cannot express initial or final consonant clusters, or medial clusters of more than two consonants; and it neutralizes voice in syllable-final position. Hence certain elements of Elamite phonology must be inferred from spelling variations. Thus nasal vowels are inferred from spellings with or without a following nasal consonant (*Hu-ban* and *Hu-um-ban,* a proper name; *te-em-ti* and *te-ep-ti* 'lord', presumably /tẽpt/). Two sets of stops (and possibly also of sibilants) are inferred from the fact that some words are always spelled with intervocalic geminated consonants, and others never (*hu-ud-da* or *hu-ut-ta* 'make', but *ku-tu-* 'prosper'?; *ik-ki* 'to' but *i-gi* 'brother')—a practice which, in Hittite orthography, distinguishes voice or lenition (Mayrhofer 1973). The existence of at least final clusters is inferred from variation between word-final *i* and *u* after two consonants, and from such variant spellings as -VC-CV-CV and -VC-VC-CV, e.g. *ku-ši-ih-ši-ta* and *ku-ši-ih-iš-ta* (presumably /kušihšta/ 'they have built').

3. Morphology and syntax. The most conspicuous feature of the syntax is a type of labeled bracketing (aptly called 'Elamite brackets' by Bork 1934). In the sentence, which is of the Subject-Object-Verb type, only one verb may occur; all other elements show nominal inflection. Accordingly, the grammar distinguishes two inflectional categories:

(a) Finite verb conjugation with inflection for 1st, 2nd, and 3rd person, and for singular and plural number, but not for gender or tense.
(b) Nominal inflection for the categories of speaker (ending *-k*), person addressed (*-t*), and person or thing spoken of. These 'genders' are called LOCUTIVE, ALLOCUTIVE, and DELOCUTIVE by Reiner 1969, and 'object-class', 'person-class', and 'I-class' by Diakonoff 1973.

The delocutive distinguishes inanimate (ending *-me,*

in OE perhaps also *-t* and *-n*) vs. animate (singular ending *-r*, plural *-p*; proper names and kinship terms have zero ending). These endings operate the concord which brackets elements that belong to the same clause. Nominals which participate in this inflection (the 'appellatives' of McAlpin 1981) comprise substantives, numerals, demonstratives, the negative particle, and nominal forms derived from the verb stem by the suffixes Ø (infinitive or gerund), *-n* (active participle), and *-k* (passive participle).

Subject and object are distinguished by the object case-ending *-n* in personal pronouns only, as shown in Table 1. Directional relations are expressed by postpositions, for example *ukku* 'upon', *ikku* 'toward', and *pat* 'under'.

A verb stem, normally of the shape CV(CV), may be reduplicated as C_iVC_iCV (*peli* 'place?', *pepli*; *hutta* 'make', *huhta*); or it may enter as the second element into a compound with a substantive (*mur* + *ta* 'earth-place' = 'to erect') or an adverb (*teppa* + *ta* 'before-place' = 'to set up in front').

The personal suffixes are *-h, -t, -š* for 1, 2, and 3 sg., and *-hu, -ht, -hš* for 1, 2, and 3 pl.; the final clusters *ht hš* are followed in the writing by a vowel, which either is purely graphic, or denotes some such category as aspect. The first of two conjoined verbs may lack the personal ending (*pepši kuši-h* 'restore built-I' = 'I rebuilt'). The clitics *ta* and *a* express, respectively, tense (pluperfect?) or aspect (completive?), and coordination or subordination. Between the verb stem and personal endings, the elements *-ma-* and (more rarely) *-nu-* function somewhat as modal auxiliaries. Inflected verbs may also take a gender suffix when embedded, as in a relative clause.

For arguments as to whether Elamite is an ergative language, see Diakonoff (1973:14–15) and Wilhelm 1978, 1982. Its relation to Dravidian [*q.v.*] is as yet undecided; it is argued by McAlpin 1981. It certainly is so related typologically, even if not genetically. Features including the following are strikingly similar in both languages: the restriction that only one finite verb may appear in the sentence; inflection of nouns for person (Medieval Tamil); grammatical case for personal pronouns only; and case relationships expressed by postpositions.

TABLE 1. *Elamite Personal Pronouns*

	Nominative	Accusative
1sg.	*u*	*un*
2sg.	*nu*	*nun*
1pl.	*nuku*	*nukun*
2pl.	*num/nun*	*numun*
3pl.	*ap*	*apun*

ERICA REINER

BIBLIOGRAPHY

BORK, FERDINAND. 1934. Die elamische Klammer. *Archiv für Orientforschung* 9.292–300.

CAMERON, GEORGE G. 1948. *Persepolis Treasury Tablets.* (Oriental Institute publications, 65.) Chicago: University of Chicago Press.

DIAKONOFF, IGOR M. 1973. Bemerkungen zu einer neuen Darstellung altkleinasiatischer Sprachen. *Orientalistische Literaturzeitung* 68.14–16. [Review of Reiner 1969.]

GRILLOT-SUSINI, FRANÇOISE. 1987. *Éléments de grammaire élamite.* (Synthèse, 29.) Paris: Éditions Recherche sur les Civilisations.

HALLOCK, RICHARD T. 1969. *Persepolis Fortification Tablets.* (Oriental Institute publications, 92.) Chicago: University of Chicago Press.

HINZ, WALTHER. 1962. Zur Entzifferung der elamischen Strichschrift. *Iranica Antiqua* 2.1–21.

HINZ, WALTHER. 1975. Problems of Linear Elamite. *Journal of the Royal Asiatic Society* 1975:106–115.

HINZ, WALTHER, & HEIDEMARIE KOCH. 1987. *Elamisches Wörterbuch.* 2 vols. (Archäologische Mitteilungen aus Iran, Ergänzungsband 17.) Berlin: Reimer.

KÖNIG, FRIEDRICH W. 1965. *Die elamischen Königsinschriften.* (Archiv für Orientforschung, Beiheft 16.) Graz: Weidner.

LABAT, RENÉ. 1951. Structure de la langue élamite. *Conférences de l'Institut de Linguistique de l'Université de Paris* 10.23–42.

MCALPIN, DAVID W. 1981. *Proto-Elamo-Dravidian: The evidence and its implications.* (Transactions of the American Philosophical Society, 71:3.) Philadelphia.

MAYRHOFER, MANFRED. 1973. Der Reiner-Test. In *Festschrift Heinrich Otten,* edited by Erich Neu & Christel Rüster, pp. 191–197. Wiesbaden: Harrassowitz.

MERIGGI, PIERO. 1971–74. *La scrittura proto-elamica.* 3 vols. Rome: Accademia Nazionale dei Lincei.

PAPER, HERBERT H. 1955. *The phonology and morphology of Royal Achaemenid Elamite.* Ann Arbor: University of Michigan Press.

REINER, ERICA. 1969. The Elamite language. In *Altkleinasiatische Sprachen* (Handbuch der Orientalistik, I.2/1–2, Lieferung 2), edited by Bertold Spuler, pp. 54–118. Leiden: Brill.

STOLPER, MATTHEW W. 1984. *Texts from Tall-i Malyan*, vol. 1, *Elamite administrative texts (1972–1974)*. (Occasional publications of the Babylonian Fund, 6.) Philadelphia: Museum of the University of Pennsylvania.

WILHELM, GERNOT. 1978. Ist das Elamische eine Ergativsprache? *Archäologische Mitteilungen aus Iran* 11.7–12.

WILHELM, GERNOT. 1982. Noch einmal zur behaupteten Ergativität des Elamischen. *Archäologische Mitteilungen aus Iran* 15.7–8. (With a note by Igor M. Diakonoff, p. 8.)

ELEMAN LANGUAGES are spoken in southern Papua New Guinea. Stephen A. Wurm, *Papuan languages of Oceania* (Tübingen: Narr, 1982), pp. 177–179, who gives the subgrouping into families given in Figure 1, considers the Eleman stock to be a top-level component of his controversial Trans–New Guinea phylum [*q.v.*].

LANGUAGE LIST

Keuru: around 4,520 speakers reported in 1981, from the mouth of the Purari River east to the Bairu River, Gulf Province. Also called Keuro, Belepa, Haura, or Haura Haela.

Opao: spoken near Orokolo and Keuru, Gulf Province.

Orokolo: 13,000 speakers reported in 1977, from the mouth of the Purari River east to the Bairu River, around Kerema, Gulf Province. Also called West Elema, Kairu-Kaura, Haira, Kaipi, Vailala, Bailala, Muru, or Muro.

Purari: 7,000 speakers reported in 1987, between Kapaina Inlet and the Orokolo language area, along the Purari River, Gulf Province. Also called Koriki, Evorra, Namau, Iai, or Maipua.

Tate: 270 speakers reported in 1977, in Uriri, Lovera, and Lou villages, Gulf Province. Also called Raepa Tati, Tati, Lorabada, or Lou. Speakers are bilingual in Toaripi. Distinct from Torricelli (Lou) in East Sepik Province and from Lou in Manus Province, an Admiralty Islands language.

Toaripi: 23,000 speakers reported in 1977, from Cape Possession to Cape Cupola, around Kerema, Gulf Province. Also called Motumotu or East Elema.

Uaripi: spoken in Uaripi town near Toaripi, Gulf Province. Also called Tairuma.

FIGURE 1. *Subgrouping of Eleman Languages*

Eleman Proper
  Eastern Eleman Proper
    Toaripi, Uaripi
  Western Eleman Proper
    Keuru, Opao, Orokolo
Purari
Tate

ELLIPSIS structures are sentences containing gaps which are interpreted under identity to some other constituent, not necessarily in the same sentence. There are two general types of ellipsis. In the first, the gap corresponds to a constituent of S[URFACE-]STRUCTURE [*q.v.*], e.g. V[erb] P[hrase] or S[entence] (the full range of possible elliptic constituents is discussed in Lobeck 1986):

(1a) *Everyone yawned when Lucie did* **e.** (VP ELLIPSIS)

(1b) *I'm supposed to meet someone, but I can't remember who* **e.** (SLUICING)

The second type includes various kinds of GAPPING. Here the missing nodes—such as *rode*, or *in the zoo* in 2, below—do not usually form a syntactic constituent:

(2) *Lucie rode an elephant in the zoo, and Zelig a camel.* (GAPPING)

Although only cases like 2 have been traditionally labeled 'gapping', this type also includes cases where only one argument is left in the ellipsis clause:

(3) *Lucie liked the camel, but not the elephant.* (STRIPPING)

The two types have different distribution. Most notably, gapping can occur only in coordinate structures, but constituent ellipsis can be embedded, as in ex. 1a.

Research on ellipsis has focused on its derivation and interpretation. The early assumption (e.g. Ross 1967, Neijt 1979) was that it is obtained by deletion transformations applying at the mapping from D[eep-]Structure to S-structure [*see* Deletion]. However, Sag 1976 and Williams 1977 showed that the level at which the ellipsis rules apply must be L[ogical] F[orm]. [*See* Grammatical Meaning.] It has been argued that neither the sense of IDENTITY relevant for the ellipsis rules, nor the restrictions on the possible interpretations of the missing constituent, can be fully captured at D-structure or S-structure. Thus, if 4a is derived by a deletion operation on 4b, the deleted constituent is not identical syntactically with its antecedent:

(4a) *Lili said that everyone*$_1$ [*walked his*$_1$ *dog*] *after Lucie did* [**e**].

(4b) *Lili said that everyone*$_1$ [*walked his*$_1$ *dog*] *after Lucie* [*walked her dog*].

(4c) *Everyone* [λx(x *walks* x's *dog*].

There is also no way to explain why *her* in 4b can refer to either *Lucie* or *Lili,* but in the missing predicate of 4a it can denote only *Lucie.* In LF, however, the first VP of 4a is analyzed along the lines of 4c, which denotes the property of 'walking one's own dog'; and copying this predicate yields the correct interpretation (known as 'sloppy identity').

In the case of gapping, LF provides the level at which the missing material forms a constituent—if we assume, following Sag 1976, that a rule similar to Quantifier Raising applies to the antecedent clause. For 3, this yields the LF [$_S$ *the camel* [$_S$ *Lucie liked* **e**]]. The predicate corresponding to the internal S (λx(*Lucie liked* x)) can then take the second conjunct as argument. Since this rule obeys SUBJACENCY [*q.v.*], the island restrictions on gapping (reported in Neijt 1979) are explained. For other reference, see Ross 1969, Rooth 1981.

TANYA REINHART

BIBLIOGRAPHY

LOBECK, ANNE C. 1986. *Syntactic constraints on VP ellipsis.* Dissertation, University of Washington. Published, Bloomington: Indiana University Linguistics Club, 1987.

NEIJT, ANNEKE. 1979. *Gapping: A contribution to sentence grammar.* (Studies in generative grammar, 7.) Dordrecht: Foris.

ROOTH, MATS. 1981. A comparison of three theories of VP deletion. *University of Massachusetts Occasional Papers in Linguistics* 7.212–244.

ROSS, JOHN ROBERT. 1967. *Constraints on variables in syntax.* MIT dissertation. Published as *Infinite syntax* (Norwood, N.J.: Ablex, 1986).

ROSS, JOHN ROBERT. 1969. Guess who? *Chicago Linguistic Society* 5.252–286.

SAG, IVAN A. 1976. *Deletion and Logical Form.* MIT dissertation. Published, New York: Garland, 1979.

WILLIAMS, EDWIN. 1977. Discourse and Logical Form. *Linguistic Inquiry* 8.103–139.

ENCLITICS. *See* Clitics.

ENGLISH. Among the world's languages, English has the widest dispersion, and only Chinese has a larger number of native speakers. As a second language, English today serves as the lingua franca of diplomacy, government, science, commerce, and scholarship. It is the sole official language of some two dozen nations, and shares official status in around twenty others; it is one of six official languages of the United Nations.

English belongs to the West Germanic subgroup of the Germanic branch of the I[ndo-]E[uropean] language family, along with German, Dutch, and Frisian. [*See* Germanic Languages; Indo-European Languages.] It began its history as a distinct tongue about 449 CE, when (according to Bede) Angles, Saxons, and Jutes speaking Germanic dialects arrived in Celtic-speaking Britain. Bands from these tribes sailed to Britain to aid the Romanized Britons, who were weakened after the withdrawal of Roman protection in 410 and besieged by invading Picts and Scots.

The history of English is divided into three periods: O[ld] E[nglish] (Anglo-Saxon) from about 700 to 1100 CE; M[iddle] E[nglish] from 1100 to 1500; and Modern English (abbreviated NE, i.e. 'New English') from 1500 to the present (cf. Hogg 1991–).

1. Germanic characteristics. English naturally shares some linguistic features with other IE languages; however, its lexicon, morphology, and phonology display distinct Germanic characteristics. Among words not found in IE outside the Germanic branch are *drink, drive, leap, bone, fowl, meat, king, sea, ship,* and *wife.* The IE system of indicating tenses by vowel alternation remains in certain English verbs (*sing/sang/sung*); but the productive past tense inflection with [d]/[t], as in *judged, kissed,* is Germanic. The effects of Grimm's Law can be seen in the initial consonants of Eng. *father, three, horn,* reflexes of IE [p], [t], and [k] (compare Latin *pater, trēs, cornus*). Also characteristically Germanic is the system of fixed primary stress on the first syllable of the root (*bróther, brótherhood, unbrótherly*); this pattern is now obscured by wholesale borrowing, where the characteristic shifting stress of IE often prevails (*promíscuous, promiscúity*).

2. Old English (see Pyles & Algeo 1982, Mitchell & Robinson 1986). OE was a highly inflected language, with suffixes on nouns, verbs, adjectives, and demonstratives, and with an elaborate system of personal, interrogative, and relative pronouns. Written records date from the late 7th century. Four dialects are recognized in the OE period: Kentish in the southeast, West Saxon in the south and southwest, Mercian in the Midlands, and Northumbrian above the Humber River. Most extant materials are written in West Saxon, which achieved status as a written standard in the reign of Alfred the Great (871–899).

2.1. *Orthography and phonology.* The few Old English graphs that differ from those of NE occur frequently in texts; among them are *þ* (thorn) from the runic alphabet, and *ð* (eth) and *æ* (ash) adapted from the Roman. The sequence *sc* (*Englisc, scip*) represents NE *sh* [š]. The graphs *k* and *q* were not used (*folc* 'folk', *cwēn* 'queen'); *c* represented both [k], as in *nacod* 'naked', and [č], as in *cild* 'child'. The letter *g* represented a glide [j] initially before certain front vowels, and finally after them (*geard* 'yard', *halig* 'holy'), but [g] or [γ] elsewhere.

OE permitted certain consonant clusters which are now prohibited, as in *hlūd* 'loud', *hring* 'ring', and *cniht* 'boy' (the latter survives orthographically in *knight*, cf. *knee, know*). Three pairs of sounds whose members are now distinct phonemes were then allophones of single phonemes: [f] and [v]; [θ] and [ð]; and [s] and [z] (compare *wīf* [wi:f] 'woman' and *wīfes* [wi:vɛs] 'women').

OE had systematic long and short vowels, plus diphthongs. Short vowels have remained relatively stable over the centuries, and many words containing them are pronounced today essentially as in OE: *him, horn, fisc* 'fish', *glæs* 'glass', *ecg* 'edge'. But long vowels have undergone dramatic shifting, as described in section 4.1 below.

2.2. *Morphology.* OE nouns carried one of three grammatical genders, and N[oun] P[hrase]s were inflected for five cases; however, nominative and accusative forms were often identical, as were dative and instrumental. Table 1 gives sample paradigms for nouns.

From the *fox* declension come the only productive NE noun inflections, with plurals and possessive singular in *-s*. The *dēor* paradigm survives in uninflected plurals like *deer* and *sheep*; the *fōt* declension has yielded *foot/feet, goose/geese, tooth/teeth, louse/lice, mouse/mice, man/men*. Modern English phrases like *a ten-foot pole*, containing an apparently singular form, derive from the OE genitive plural ('a pole of ten feet'), where *foot* < *fōta*. Demonstratives were inflected for five cases and three genders in the singular, and for three cases without gender distinction in the plural, as shown in Table 2. An instrumental case was used (sometimes with a preposition) to indicate accompaniment or instrument.

Like other Germanic languages, OE had two adjectival declensions. In a NP containing a (highly inflected) possessive pronoun or demonstrative, adjectives exhibited the 'weak' declension, as in *sē gōda mann* 'the good man'. When markers of case were few or nonexistent, as with predicative function, the more varied forms of the 'strong' declension were required, as in *Hē is gōd* 'He is good.' Adjectives were inflected for gender, number, and case, in agreement with their heads.

OE personal pronouns have retained more of their morphological variation in NE than has any other form class, as can be inferred from the paradigms in Table 3.

OE also had dual forms in the 1st and 2nd person pronouns. These eventually disappeared, along with distinct number and case forms in the 2nd person, and distinct case forms for the neuter nominative/accusative and the dative/instrumental 3rd person singular (*hit* and *him*).

In its verbs, OE exhibits two types: 'weak', with a [d]

TABLE 1. *Old English Noun Forms*

Singular				
Nom.	*fox* 'fox'	*dēor* 'animal'	*lār* 'lore'	*fōt* 'foot'
Acc.	*fox*	*dēor*	*lār*	*fōt*
Gen.	*foxes*	*dēores*	*lāre*	*fōtes*
Dat./Inst.	*foxe*	*dēore*	*lāre*	*fēt*
Plural				
Nom./Acc.	*foxas*	*dēor*	*lāra*	*fēt*
Gen.	*foxa*	*dēora*	*lāra*	*fōta*
Dat./Inst.	*foxum*	*dēorum*	*lārum*	*fōtum*

TABLE 2. *Old English Demonstratives*

	Singular			Plural
	Masculine	Feminine	Neuter	M/F/N
Nom.	*sē*	*sēo*	*þæt*	*þā*
Acc.	*þone*	*þa*	*þæt*	*þā*
Gen.	*þæs*	*þǣre*	*þæs*	*þāra*
Dat.	*þǣm*	*þǣre*	*þǣm*	*þǣm*
Inst.	*þȳ*	*þǣre*	*þȳ*	*þǣm*

TABLE 3. *Old English Pronouns*

	1st Person	2nd Person	3rd Person		
			M	F	N
Singular					
Nom.	*ic*	*þū*	*hē*	*hēo*	*hit*
Acc.	*mē*	*þē*	*hine*	*hie*	*hit*
Gen.	*mīn*	*þīn*	*his*	*hiere*	*his*
Dat./Inst.	*mē*	*þē*	*him*	*hiere*	*him*
Plural					
Nom.	*wē*	*gē*		*hīe*	
Acc.	*ūs*	*ēow*		*hīe*	
Gen.	*ūre*	*ēower*		*hiera*	
Dat./Inst.	*ūs*	*ēow*		*him*	

or [t] past-tense suffix, as in *love/loved*; and 'strong', with vowel gradation (ablaut), as in *ring/rang/rung*. The principal parts of the seven strong verb classes are shown in Table 4.

Verbs were inflected for present and past tenses and for indicative and subjunctive moods, in three persons and two numbers. The twelve distinct forms of an OE weak verb, *dēman* 'judge', are shown in Table 5; compare today's typical verb with only four forms (*judge, judges, judged, judging*), and no distinct subjunctive.

2.3. *Syntax.* OE relied on inflections to mark grammatical relations, and word order was thus more flexible than in NE. OE does exhibit a preference for S[ubject] V[erb] O[bject] order in main clauses, and SOV in subordinate clauses; however, all orders occurred. Following the frequent introductory adverb *þā* 'then', the verb occupied second position. In context, grammatical subjects were not obligatory.

The order of elements in NPs was usually determiner + adjective + noun (*sē gōda mann* 'that good man'); genitives usually preceded nouns (*þæs landes folc* 'that land's people'); and prepositions preceded nouns, but often followed pronouns (*him tō* 'to him'). As in NE, adjectives usually preceded head nouns (*æt sumum sǣle* 'at a certain time'). Relative clauses followed nouns, and were introduced by invariant *þe* (often compounded with a form of the demonstrative *sē* or a personal pronoun); demonstratives also occurred alone as relatives.

TABLE 4. *Old English Verb Classes*

	Infinitive		Past Sg.	Past Pl.	Past Participle
1.	*rīdan*	'ride'	*rād*	*ridon*	*geriden*
2.	*sēoðan*	'boil'	*sēað*	*sudon*	*gesoden*
3.	*bindan*	'bind'	*band*	*bundon*	*gebunden*
4.	*beran*	'bear'	*bær*	*bǣron*	*geboren*
5.	*cweðan*	'say'	*cwæþ*	*cwǣdon*	*gecweden*
6.	*standan*	'stand'	*stōd*	*stōdon*	*gestanden*
7.	*feallan*	'fall'	*fēoll*	*fēollon*	*gefeallen*

TABLE 5. *Old English Verb Conjugation*

	Indicative	Subjunctive
Present		
Singular		
1	*dēme*	
2	*dēmst* (or *dēmest*)	*dēme*
3	*dēmþ* (or *dēmeþ*)	
Plural	*dēmaþ*	*dēmen*
Past		
Singular		
1	*dēmde*	
2	*dēmdest*	*dēmde*
3	*dēmde*	
Plural	*dēmdon*	*dēmden*
Gerund	*to dēmenne* (or *dēmanne*)	
Present Participle	*dēmende*	
Past Participle	*dēmed*	

Although the verb *dōn* 'do, put, make' could be used as a substitute, or 'pro', verb, it was not available as an auxiliary. Interrogatives generally inverted subject and finite verb. Negatives usually showed the negative particle *ne* before the verb. Multiple marking of negation within a clause, now non-standard, was common: *Nis nū cwicra nān* . . . '(There) isn't now alive no one . . .'

A striking characteristic of OE writing is the strong preference for linking sentences with *and* 'and' or *þā* 'then'. The frequent use of subordinators (*because, since, until*) to make explicit the relations between clauses was a later development.

2.4. *Lexicon.* During the Viking age (about 750–1050), Britain suffered a second Teutonic invasion, principally of Danes, who settled in central and southeastern England. By 1000, although corners of Britain remained Celtic-speaking, most inhabitants of the island, including the assimilated Danes, spoke OE. Hardly a trace of Celtic influence survives, except in a few toponyms, e.g. *Kent, Devon, Thames,* and possibly *London.* Likewise, Latin influence through the Celts is negligible, except in place names, notably the element *-chester* (< La. *castra* 'camp'), as in *Dorchester, Winchester, Worcester.* With the Christianizing of Britain at the end of the 6th century, there was an influx of Latin words, mostly of a religious nature (*monk, abbot, monastery, bishop, cloister, candle, chalice, mass*). The Danish assimilation contributed wholesale to the word stock of English, including about two thousand place names or elements thereof, e.g. the *-by* in *Derby* and *Whitby*—as well as many everyday verbs (*take, give, get*) and nouns (*sky, skirt, skin, skill*). Even so common a phrase as *they are* is Scandinavian, suggesting a remarkable intermingling of Danish and English. Despite such openness to foreign importations, the most characteristic way of expanding the OE word stock was by combining native elements in prefixing, suffixing, and compounding.

3. Middle English. ME is a telling name for the period of transition between Old and Modern English. After the Norman conquest in 1066, English was relieved of many duties in the affairs of the court, government, and learning, as these activities were carried out by French-speaking (and often Latin-writing) Normans. Gradually, members of the middle classes became bilingual, speaking English to those below and French to those above. Only in 1204, when King John lost Normandy, did Britain's future as an English-speaking nation begin to look up. Partly as a consequence of the social and linguistic upheaval wrought by the conquest, ME reveals dramatic variation and evolution over its four centuries (Mossé 1952).

3.1. *Phonology.* OE long vowels were generally maintained in ME, except that /a:/ (*bān, stān, bāt*) became /ɔ:/ (NE /o/, as in *bone, stone, boat*). Many diphthongs were simplified in late OE and early ME. Short vowels in unstressed syllables, which had remained distinct at least in early West Saxon, merged in *e* [ə].

The initial consonant clusters *hl- hn- hr- kn-* lost their initials, as in *hlāf* 'loaf', *hnecca* 'neck', *hrōf* 'roof', *cniht* 'knight'. Of considerable consequence was the merging of word-final *m* into *n* in unstressed syllables; by the end of ME, even this *n* had dropped.

3.2. *Morphology.* Because of the loss of final *m n*, and the weakening of unstressed *a o u e* to [ə], many OE inflections became indistinguishable in early ME, and dropped in late ME. The frequency of subject and object NP forms established the nominative/accusative plural form (and the *-es* inflection for nouns in general) throughout the plural, and the nominative/accusative singular (sometimes with analogical *-e* from the dative) throughout the singular—except that the genitive in *-s* was maintained. Thus the ME paradigm for a noun like *fox* came to be essentially what it is in NE: sg. *fox*, possessive *foxes* (now *fox's*), and plural *foxes*.

In other paradigms, the reduction of inflectional distinctions was even greater. The *dēor* class was reduced to three forms (*deer, deeres, deere*), while *lār* was reduced to two (*loor, loore*); these distinctions were further leveled when final inflected *-e* vanished, by about 1500. Adjectival inflections were greatly simplified at the beginning of ME, and completely lost by the end.

ME has more or less the same verb inflections as NE, except that the 3sg. present tense ends in *-(e)th* (*lyketh, hath*), and plural present tense in *-n* or *-en* (apparently borrowed from the OE subjunctive): *gon, eten, bryngen*. The reduction of the verbal inflectional system brought about a marked increase of periphrastic constructions in the future and perfect; modals replaced the OE subjunctive. Thus the establishment of an auxiliary system, including perfective *have* and *be*, is in large part compensation for inflectional reductions. The historical present is a late development of ME.

3.3. *Syntax.* Such morphological leveling inevitably influenced the syntax; as flection grew less able to signal grammatical relations and semantic roles, word order and the deployment of prepositions came to bear those communicative tasks less redundantly. Gradually, the freer word order of OE yielded to relatively fixed orders, which were capable of signaling grammatical relations. Whereas Old English used both SVO and SOV orders, and did not require a grammatical subject, ME is distinctly SVO, with obligatory subject. Also lost were impersonal constructions like *Euery man taketh what part that him lyketh*—lit. 'that to him (it) likes', i.e. 'that (it) pleases him'; here, since OE times, the verb had required not a nominative but an oblique case. Also during the ME period, interrogative pronouns came to serve as relatives.

Given the Norman invasion and the social distribution of bilingualism in the early ME period, there is every reason to believe that English writing and speaking were relatively close in form. Thus the parataxis characteristic of earlier prose and of typical speech continues for much of the period, and a vigorous use of hypotaxis arises only later.

3.4. *Lexicon.* By the beginning of the 14th century, as English came again to be known by all inhabitants of England, its lexicon had been enhanced by thousands of Norman French borrowings. Approximately ten thousand found their way into ME, and most survive today. Especially abundant are words in the semantic fields of religion, government, law, and the military; but the Normans also exerted great influence in food, fashion, and education. The following exemplify words borrowed in the ecclesiastical arena: *abbey, baptism, cardinal, chaplain, clergy, communion, confession, convent, creator, dean, faith, miracle, passion, penance, parson, pastor, pray* and *prayer, prelate, religion, sacrament, saint, sanctuary, salvation, sermon, theology*.

4. Modern English. Standard written NE derives not from the West Saxon dialect of Old English, but from the East Midlands dialect of medieval London—the variety used by Chaucer and the Chancery, and disseminated when Caxton established his printing press at Westminster in 1476 (cf. Barber 1976). In the spoken varieties, considerable diversity has always existed, particularly in pronunciation.

4.1. ***Phonology.*** Between Chaucer's death in 1400 and Shakespeare's birth in 1564, all long vowels were systematically raised, and the highest were diphthongized, as shown in Figure 1.

Subsequently, in the early 18th century, /e:/ was further raised to /i:/ in just those words where ME had /ɛ:/. Thus words like *meet* (< OE /e:/) and *meat* (< OE /ɛ:/) were merged.

4.2. ***Morphology.*** The early NE period witnessed the disintegration of the distinction in pronouns of the 2nd person singular (*thou, thee*) vs. plural (*ye, you*). Probably under French influence, speakers of English began using the plural forms to signal deference. Among the upper social classes, the plural forms came to indicate mutual respect, even in informal conversation between equals. In time, the singular forms all but disappeared, as did the distinction between the subject and object forms *ye* and *you*. From the six-fold distinction of OE and much of ME, only the two-fold distinction of *you* vs. *your(s)* survives.

By early ME, *þe* had become the invariant definite article in the north, replacing the varied forms of the earlier demonstrative, and its use soon spread to all dialects: Chaucer used only *the*. Although OE did not exploit indefinite articles, *a(n),* from OE *ān* 'one', developed in the ME period to become the fifth most common word in written English today.

Of the 333 OE strong verbs, fewer than half survive today, and only sixty-eight are inflected as strong (Baugh & Cable 1978). Among those that have become weak are *burn, brew, climb, flow, help,* and *walk.* (In the course of history, about a dozen OE weak verbs have become strong, including *wear, spit,* and *dig*). With few exceptions ME verbal inflections were like those of NE; and in early NE, even these exceptions faded. Whereas Chaucer consistently used *-(e)th* in the 3sg. present, Shakespeare used both *-s* and *-(e)th,* favoring *-s* except in *doth* and *hath.*

FIGURE 1. *The English Vowel Shift*

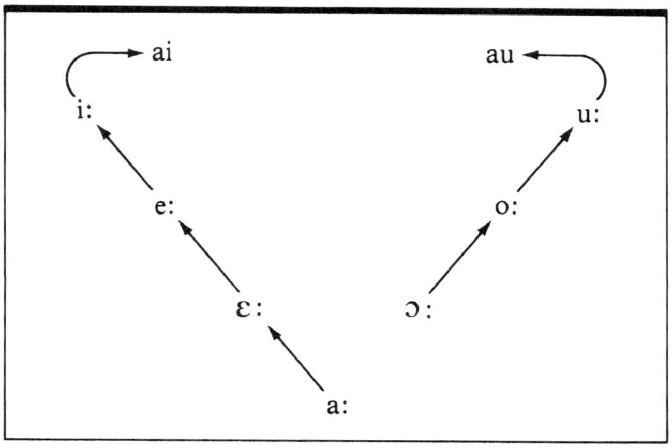

4.3. ***Syntax.*** Deprived of its rich inflectional system, English has become an analytical language, with a great increase in prepositional phrases and in periphrastic verb constructions (Quirk et al. 1985). Although *do* as an empty auxiliary is attested from the ME period, it is not until the 17th century that its characteristic NE distribution is reached in questions and negatives, as well as for emphasis. Similarly, the progressive, attested only rarely in early ME, becomes robust during the early NE period. The progressive passive—*whose upper grinder is being torn out*—is a development of the late 18th century.

4.4. ***Lexicon.*** During the later medieval period, English had been written principally for personal and for popular literary functions. Consequently, during the Renaissance revival of learning—when English displaced Latin in philosophy, science, and other learned arenas—it was lexically deficient. Typical words borrowed to fill the gap are the nouns *allusion, anachronism, antipathy, antithesis, appendix, atmosphere, autograph,* and *axis* (from Latin, or from Greek via Latin); the adjectives *abject, agile, appropriate, audible*; and the verbs *adapt, alienate, assassinate* (from Latin, sometimes via French); and *acme, anonymous, criterion, idiosyncrasy, lexicon, ostracize,* and *tonic* (from Greek). Despite some strident criticism of such 'inkhorn' terms, more than ten thousand words from fifty languages were borrowed in the first 150 years of NE (see Baugh & Cable 1978).

English shows a renewed openness to foreign words in the present century, borrowing from more than seventy-five languages. Now, as nearly always, the principal donor is French; but other languages have made valuable contributions, including Japanese, Spanish, Italian, Latin, Greek, German, Yiddish, Russian, Chinese, and Arabic—in roughly that order (cf. Cannon 1987). Despite such international trafficking in words, the preferred OE practices of affixing and compounding have displaced borrowing as the favored method of enlarging the English word stock today. As a combined result of borrowing and the creation of new words from existing elements, today's lexicon has been reliably estimated to contain 170,000 lemmas (exclusive of proper nouns and highly specialized and technical terms).

4.5. ***Dialect variation.*** Spoken dialects, while strikingly diverse from place to place, are customarily divided into two principal branches: BRITISH, in England, Ireland, Wales, Scotland, Australia, New Zealand, and

South Africa; and NORTH AMERICAN, in Canada and the United States. Various other regions intermingle patterns to such an extent that one hears increasingly of 'Englishes' rather than of English. English is also the basis for a number of pidgins and creoles worldwide. [*See* Pidgins and Creoles.] Given such spoken diversity, it is notable that written English has maintained a relatively uniform standard around the globe.

Linguistic variation across social groups within a single community reveals strikingly similar patterns from community to community. Thus in Norwich, England, and in New York City, the pronunciation of several phonological variables correlates with socio-economic status in similar ways (Labov 1972, Trudgill 1974). In both cities, to cite a single example, alternation between final [-n] and [-ŋ] in the suffix *-ing* (*swimming, walking*) follows parallel patterns, with each socio-economic status group pronouncing more [-ŋ] than the next lower group. Similar linguistic variation also reflects gender and ethnic affiliation.

4.6. *Register variation.* As regards variation across situations of use, all social groups tend toward increased realization of specific forms in situations of increasing formality; and these are the forms generally preferred by the upper socio-economic groups. Thus there is virtually universal movement to increased [-ŋ] in more formal situations.

In the course of its history, English has developed marked language differences across a wide range of registers. While some are qualitative differences, with distinct lexical or syntactic features—characteristic of registers such as slang, legalese, telephone conversation, or science fiction—recent computational work with standardized corpora indicates that quantitative variations in lexical and syntactic co-occurrence patterns are especially significant. (See Francis & Kučera 1982 on the Brown University Corpus of Present-Day Edited American English; Johansson & Hofland 1989 on the Lancaster-Oslo/Bergen Corpus of British English; and Svartvik & Quirk 1980 on the London-Lund Corpus of Spoken English; cf. also Biber 1988.) In this respect, register differences and differences across social groups within a community are similar to one another, and distinct from the traditional interpretation of regional differences, which have been viewed as primarily qualitative.

EDWARD FINEGAN

BIBLIOGRAPHY

BARBER, CHARLES. 1976. *Early Modern English.* London: Deutsch.

BAUGH, ALBERT C., & THOMAS CABLE. 1978. *A history of the English language.* 3d ed. Englewood Cliffs, N.J.: Prentice-Hall.

BIBER, DOUGLAS. 1988. *Variation across speech and writing.* Cambridge & New York: Cambridge University Press.

CANNON, GARLAND. 1987. *Historical change and English word-formation: Recent vocabulary.* New York: Peter Lang.

FRANCIS, W. NELSON, & HENRY KUČERA. 1982. *Frequency analysis of English usage: Lexicon and grammar.* Boston: Houghton Mifflin.

HOGG, RICHARD M., ed. 1991–. *Cambridge history of the English language.* 6 vols. Cambridge & New York: Cambridge University Press.

JOHANSSON, STIG, & KNUT HOFLAND. 1989. *Frequency analysis of English vocabulary and grammar.* Oxford: Clarendon Press.

LABOV, WILLIAM. 1972. *Sociolinguistic patterns.* Philadelphia: University of Pennsylvania Press.

MITCHELL, BRUCE, & FRED C. ROBINSON. 1986. *A guide to Old English.* 4th ed. Oxford: Blackwell.

MOSSÉ, FERNAND. 1952. *A handbook of Middle English.* Baltimore: Johns Hopkins Press.

PYLES, THOMAS, & JOHN ALGEO. 1982. *The origins and development of the English language.* 3d ed. New York: Harcourt Brace Jovanovich.

QUIRK, RANDOLPH, et al. 1985. *A comprehensive grammar of the English language.* London: Longman.

SVARTVIK, JAN, & RANDOLPH QUIRK, eds. 1980. *A corpus of English conversation.* (Lund studies in English, 56.) Lund: Gleerup.

TRUDGILL, PETER. 1974. *The social differentiation of English in Norwich.* (Cambridge studies in linguistics, 13.) Cambridge: Cambridge University Press.

ESKIMO-ALEUT LANGUAGES. This language family comprises the Eskimo and Aleut branches, which are believed to have diverged no more than 4,000 years ago. Useful general references are Bergsland 1986, Krauss 1973, and Woodbury 1984.

1. Geography. As shown on Map 1, the ALEUT branch contains a single language, Aleut, spoken in the Aleutian and Pribilof Islands of Alaska and the Commander Islands of the USSR. The ESKIMO branch has two divisions. One is Inuit, a dialect continuum spoken from Norton Sound in Alaska northward and eastward across the Alaskan and Canadian Arctic, to Greenland. Inuit displays a great deal of dialectal variation, but the gradual change from one dialect to another makes it difficult to identify separate languages. Inuit is referred to by a number of different names, of which the principal ones are Inupiaq in Alaska, Inuktitut in Eastern

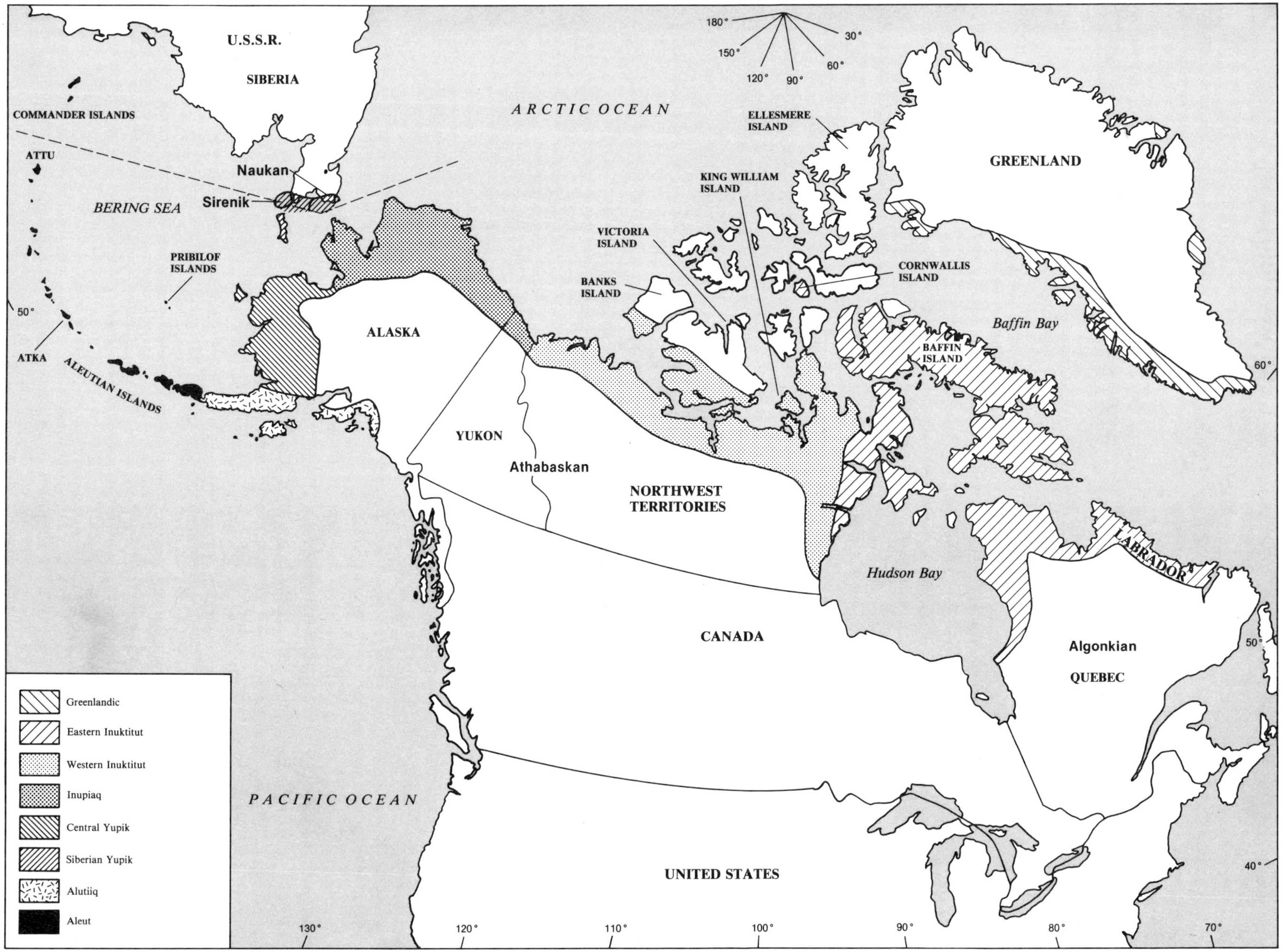
U.S.S.R.
SIBERIA
COMMANDER ISLANDS
ATTU
Naukan
Sirenik
BERING SEA
PRIBILOF ISLANDS
ATKA
ALEUTIAN ISLANDS
ALASKA
YUKON
Athabaskan
NORTHWEST TERRITORIES
ARCTIC OCEAN
ELLESMERE ISLAND
KING WILLIAM ISLAND
VICTORIA ISLAND
BANKS ISLAND
CORNWALLIS ISLAND
GREENLAND
Baffin Bay
BAFFIN ISLAND
Hudson Bay
LABRADOR
Algonkian
QUEBEC
CANADA
UNITED STATES
PACIFIC OCEAN
180°
150°
120°
90°
60°
30°
50°
60°
40°
130°
120°
110°
100°
90°
80°
70°
Greenlandic
Eastern Inuktitut
Western Inuktitut
Inupiaq
Central Yupik
Siberian Yupik
Alutiiq
Aleut

MAP 1. *Divisions of the Eskimo-Aleut Language Family*

Canada, and Kalaallisut (or Greenlandic) in Greenland.

The other Eskimo branch, Yupik, includes at least three separate languages. Central Siberian Yupik is spoken on St. Lawrence Island, Alaska, and on the facing coast of the Chukchi Peninsula in the USSR. Central Alaskan Yupik is spoken in Southwest Alaska, from Norton Sound south to Bristol Bay. Alutiiq (also called Suk, Sugpiaq, or Pacific Yupik), is located in Alaska on the Alaska Peninsula, Kodiak Island, the southern Kenai Peninsula, and the shores of Prince William Sound. The divergent and nearly extinct language of Sirenik on the Chukchi Peninsula appears, from its conservative phonology, to be either another branch of Yupik, or a third division of Eskimo. Naukan Siberian Yupik appears in some respects to be intermediate between Central Siberian and Central Alaskan Yupik and may be considered a separate language. There is a degree of mutual intelligibility among the Yupik languages, especially Alutiiq and Central Yupik, but virtually none between Yupik and Inuit.

Many now prefer the name 'Inuit' to 'Eskimo' (which some consider derogatory). However, specialists feel that 'Inuit' cannot properly include the Yupik languages or peoples, and thus they continue to use 'Eskimo' as a cover term. The name 'Inupik', for the Inuit language, is out of date; its usage is discouraged, since it combines an Inuit stem (*inuk* 'person') with a Yupik suffix (*-pik* 'real').

There are about 105,000 Eskimos and Aleuts, of whom about 80,000 speak an E[skimo-]A[leut] language. Half of this number are in Greenland—where, as in much of eastern Canada, the Inuit language remains fully viable. In Alaska and western Canada, Inuit is not spoken by younger generations, and is threatened with extinction. Aleut and Alutiiq are similarly endangered. Of the Yupik languages, only Siberian and Central Yupik have significant numbers of younger speakers. [*For details on individual languages, see the Language List at the end of this article.*]

Several distant relationships have been proposed for EA, although none has been proved. Among these are Indo-European, Chukotko-Kamchatkan, and Uralic; the last enjoys the greatest current support.

2. Phonology (cf. Krauss 1985). Eskimo languages show variation primarily in their phonology and lexicon, rather than in syntax. Aleut phonology is quite unremarkable, compared to the interesting phenomena exhibited by most varieties of Eskimo.

Proto-Eskimo had four vowels, */i a u ə/, but few or none of the long vowels or diphthongs found in the modern languages. Nearly all dialects of Inuit have lost *ə (shwa), which has merged with *i* and sometimes *a*; however, its traces remain in processes of vowel alternation, which affect only reflexes of shwa, and in consonant assibilation and palatalization, which are conditioned only by reflexes of **i*. The Proto-Eskimo voiced continuants have been largely lost between single vowels in the daughter languages (except in Sirenik), yielding contrastively long vowels and diphthongs. Inuit has undergone further consonant lenition and deletion: stops become continuants, and original continuants become glides, or disappear entirely. Related synchronic processes in Inuit are found both in East Greenlandic and in Bering Strait dialects; in the latter, these are related areally to syllable-adjustment rules in nearby Yupik languages. Assimilation in consonant clusters increases from west to east, severely limiting possible clusters in some dialects. Some Inuit geminate consonants may be historical; but others are morphologically conditioned, alternating with single consonants. Consonant metathesis appears sporadically throughout Inuit, and is systematic in some eastern and far western dialects. In many dialects, diphthongs tend to lose their distinctness, and to merge with other diphthongs or long vowels.

The Yupik languages are characterized phonologically by retention of Proto-Eskimo shwa, and by prosodically-based processes of vowel lengthening (e.g. in the second of two open syllables), or of consonant gemination—typically before an underlying long vowel or diphthong. Siberian Yupik lacks gemination, but lengthens initial syllables to preserve stem stress (/ku:vuq/ 'it spilled'); in the same words, Central Yupik may contain a geminate C (/kuv:uq/). Siberian Yupik maintains many velars which are deleted in other languages: SY /pani:ga/, CY /pan:ia/ 'his daughter'. Yupik languages permit more varied clusters than Inuit, namely clusters of fricative plus stop. No Eskimo language permits consonant clusters initially or finally in the word.

Alutiiq consonants may be fortis or lenis, depending on complex rules of syllable adjustment, which may also shorten long syllables. Voiced fricatives have tense and lax allophones in Alutiiq; the former may be devoiced, and the latter may be deleted.

3. Grammar (cf. Bergsland 1981, 1989, Fortescue 1983, 1984, Reed et al. 1977). EA languages are polysynthetic; their remarkably long words are often equivalent to entire sentences in more analytic languages. A typical word consists of a nominal or verbal stem which is expanded by a number of derivational suffixes, with an inflectional ending. There is only one known prefix, **taž-*, which is used with demonstratives for specificity or anaphora. All nouns and verbs are marked for singular, dual, or plural number. Gender plays no role in the grammar, and is not reflected even in pronouns.

Eskimo languages have an ergative case system with two primary syntactic cases, absolutive and relative (ergative); the latter also acts as a genitive, marking possessor nouns. The possessum is inflected for number, as well as for the person and number of the possessor. Eskimo languages have six oblique cases: instrumental, ablative, locative, allative, aequalis (comparison), and vialis or prosecutive (means of transport or route taken). The Yupik languages have no separate ablative; this function is covered by the instrumental. Aleut has a different ergative system and is somewhat more analytic than Eskimo: it has auxiliary verbs, and spatial or temporal relations are expressed by possessed nouns rather than by cases.

Verbs are either transitive or intransitive; the former are inflected for person and number of both subject and object, and the latter for subject only. Eskimo also permits an intransitive construction, the antipassive, in which a noun in the instrumental case acts semantically, but not syntactically, like an object. Third person forms distinguish reflexive from non-reflexive, marking both possessed nouns and subordinate verbs as referring (or not) to the subject. Complex anaphoric processes in Aleut distinguish it from Eskimo. All EA languages have an elaborate system of demonstratives.

4. Vocabulary. Lexically, Aleut and the Yupik languages contain significant borrowings, for the most part recent: Aleut, Alutiiq, and Central Yupik have borrowed from Russian, and Siberian Yupik from Chukchi. Inuit has much less borrowing, and influence on EA from the adjacent Athabaskan languages has been very slight.

LAWRENCE D. KAPLAN

BIBLIOGRAPHY

BERGSLAND, KNUT. 1981. *Atkan Aleut school grammar.* With Moses Dirks. Anchorage: National Bilingual Materials Development Center, University of Alaska.

BERGSLAND, KNUT. 1986. Comparative Eskimo-Aleut phonology and lexicon. *Journal de la Société Finno-Ougrienne* 80.63–137.

BERGSLAND, KNUT. 1989. Comparative aspects of Aleut syntax. *Journal de la Société Finno-Ougrienne* 82.7–74.

FORTESCUE, MICHAEL. 1983. *A comparative manual of affixes for the Inuit dialects of Greenland, Canada, and Alaska.* (Man and society, 4.) Copenhagen: Commission for Scientific Research in Greenland.

FORTESCUE, MICHAEL. 1984. *West Greenlandic.* London: Croom Helm.

KRAUSS, MICHAEL E. 1973. Eskimo-Aleut. In *Current trends in linguistics,* vol. 10, *Linguistics in North America,* edited by Thomas A. Sebeok, pp. 796–902. The Hague: Mouton.

KRAUSS, MICHAEL E., ed. 1985. *Yupik Eskimo prosodic systems: Descriptive and comparative studies.* (Research papers, 7.) Fairbanks: Alaska Native Language Center, University of Alaska.

REED, IRENE, et al. 1977. *Yup'ik Eskimo grammar.* Fairbanks: Alaska Native Language Center, University of Alaska.

WOODBURY, ANTHONY C. 1984. Eskimo and Aleut languages. In *Handbook of North American Indians,* vol. 5, *Arctic,* edited by David Damas, pp. 49–63. Washington, D.C.: Smithsonian Institution.

LANGUAGE LIST

Aleut: around 500 speakers, almost all in the Aleutian and Pribilof Islands, USA, from a total population of 2,000; Western Aleut has speakers under 20 years old, while speakers of the Eastern dialect are over 50. In the Commander Islands, USSR, about 10 older speakers are reported from a population of 500.

Inuit, Western Canadian: around 4,000 speakers reported in 1981 from a total population of 7,500, in the Central Canadian Arctic and west to the Mackenzie Delta and coastal area. Includes varieties called Caribou Eskimo, Netsilik, Copper Eskimo, and Siglit. Language use is vigorous only in the Eastern part of this area (Caribou and Netsilik).

Inuit, Eastern Canadian: around 14,000 speakers from a population of 17,500 west of Hudson Bay, Canada, and east through Baffin Island, Quebec, and Labrador. Also called Eastern Arctic Eskimo or Inuktitut. Vigorous language use, except in Labrador, where less than half the Inuit are speakers.

Inuit, Greenlandic: around 40,000 speakers reported in Greenland, with another 7,000 in Denmark. Also called Greenlandic Eskimo, Greenlandic, or Kalaallisut. Language use in Greenland is vigorous.

Inuit, North Alaskan: around 3,500 speakers from a population of 8,000, extending from Norton Sound, Alaska, USA to the Mackenzie Delta region in Canada. Also called North Alaskan Eskimo, Inupiat Eskimo, or Inupiaq. Most speakers are over 30, and younger speakers often prefer English. Includes varieties called North Slope and Malimiut or Kobuk/Kotzebue Sound.

Inuit, Seward Peninsula: around 700 speakers from an ethnic population of 4,000 on the Seward Peninsula and adjacent islands in Northwest Alaska, USA and originally on Big

Diomede Island, USSR, although speakers have been relocated. Includes varieties called Bering Strait and Qawiaraq. Most speakers are over 40.

Yupik, Naukan: around 75 speakers from an ethnic population of 350, formerly spoken in Naukan village and the region surrounding East Cape, Chukchi Peninsula, Siberia, USSR. Population has been relocated. May be considered a separate language intermediate between Central Siberian Yupik and Central Alaskan Yupik. Also called Naukanski.

Yupik, Pacific: around 600 speakers from a population of 3,000 on the Alaska Peninsula, Kodiak Island, and the Alaskan coast from Cook Inlet to Prince William Sound, Alaska, USA. Also called Suk, Sugpiaq Eskimo, South Alaskan Eskimo, Sugcestun, or (locally) Aleut; the currently preferred term is Alutiiq. Most speakers are middle-aged or older.

Yupik, Central Siberian: around 1,400 speakers from a population of 1,900 with 1,000 on St. Lawrence Island, Alaska, USA (nearly the total population) and 400 on the eastern tip of the Chukchi Peninsula, Siberia, USSR, from a population of 900. Also called St. Lawrence Island Eskimo. Language use is vigorous in Alaska; younger people in the USSR do not speak the language.

Yupik, Sirenik: formerly spoken on the Chukchi Peninsula, Siberia, USSR; nearly extinct, with two elderly fluent speakers. Other Eskimo residents of Sirenik village now speak Central Siberian Yupik. Also called Sirenikski and Old Sirenik.

ETHNOGRAPHY OF SPEAKING is an approach to the relationship among language, culture, and society. Involving both theoretical and methodological perspectives, it describes in cultural terms the patterned uses of language and speech in a particular group, institution, community, or society. It includes native theories and practices of speaking, both as overtly articulated by individuals and as enacted by them in a range of situations.

More specifically, the ethnography of speaking is concerned with the following:

(a) The sociolinguistic resources available in particular communities. Such resources include not merely grammar in the conventional sense, but also a complex of linguistic potentials for social use and social meaning—variables, styles, terms of reference and address, and words and their relations.

(b) The use and exploitation of these resources in discourse (speech acts, events, and situations), and in social interaction: agreeing, disagreeing, showing deference and respect, greeting, and cajoling.

(c) The patterned interrelationships and organizations of the various types of discourse and social interaction in the community.

(d) The relationship of these patterns of speaking to other aspects and domains of the culture of the community, such as social organization, religion, economics, and politics.

A complete ethnography of speaking would deal with each of these topics; however, most research and publications tend to focus on particular ones—e.g. the description of linguistic resources organized as styles or ways of speaking (men's/women's speech, baby talk); the analysis of particular speech events (greetings, drinking encounters); or the role of speaking in a particular segment of social life (politics, religion).

The ethnography of speaking began in the early 1960s with a series of papers by Dell Hymes, who called for an approach to language and speech which dealt with the aspects of language use that fall between, or otherwise escape, such established disciplines as anthropology, linguistics, and sociology (see Hymes 1974). Essentially, his argument was that language and speech have a patterning of their own, like social organization, politics, religion, and economics; therefore, they merit attention by anthropologists. This patterning is not identical with the grammar of the language, in the traditional sense; yet it is linguistic as well as cultural in organization, and thus merits attention by linguists.

Hymes introduced the notion of the SPEECH EVENT as central to the ethnography of speaking. He argued that analysis of speech events requires study of the interrelationships of many components or factors; these may include setting, participants, purposes, verbal or textual organization in terms of constituent acts, KEY or manner of delivery, the linguistic varieties used, norms of interaction, and genres. The careful study of these components of speaking in their own terms—with regard to their terminology, patterned organization, and function—leads to a description that captures each society's unique cultural organization of language and speech.

Collections of papers published in the mid and late 1960s and early 1970s helped to develop this field (Gumperz & Hymes 1964, 1972, Bauman & Sherzer 1974). These articles describe aspects of language and speech that had often been overlooked or treated as marginal by anthropologists, sociologists, and linguists. Some titles indicate their focus: 'Baby talk in six languages'; 'How to ask for a drink in Subanun'; ' ''Rhetoric,'' ''Logic,'' and ''Poetics'' in Burundi: Culture patterning of speech behavior'; 'Sequencing in conversational openings'; 'Signifying and marking: Two Afro-American speech acts'; 'Social meaning in linguistic structures: Code-switching in Norway'.

In the 1970s, a new group of researchers focused on particular societies, with the specific goal of studying the ethnography of speaking. This research has led to a number of dissertations, articles, and books. Once again, titles are usefully illustrative; in the bibliography below, note Gossen 1974, Scollon & Scollon 1979, K. Basso 1979, Feld 1982, Abrahams 1983, Bauman 1983, Heath 1983, Philips 1983, Sherzer 1983, E. Basso 1985, and Blakely 1986.

While research in the ethnography of speaking continues to be based on its original assumptions and goals, certain specialized foci have emerged: inter-cultural and inter-ethnic communication and miscommunication (Gumperz 1982); the traditional verbal art of non-literate peoples (Sherzer & Urban 1986, Sherzer & Woodbury 1987); the relationship between oral and written discourse (Heath 1983, Scollon & Scollon 1979); the acquisition of communicative competence (Ervin-Tripp & Mitchell-Kernan 1977, Schieffelin & Ochs 1986); and language use within modern complex societies, especially in such institutional settings as education (Heath 1983, Philips 1983).

The research methods of the ethnography of speaking integrate those of SOCIOLINGUISTICS [*q.v.*] with those of social and cultural anthropology, in a unique constellation. From sociolinguistics is borrowed the assumption of a heterogeneous speech community, and the concern with collecting and analyzing a selection of representative forms of speech within it. From social and cultural anthropology is adopted the assumption of cultural relativity, and the concern with an 'emic' or native insider's view, as well as the necessity of eliciting and analyzing native terms and concepts for ways of speaking, in the context of participant-observation. Also anthropological is the ethnographic method of constant interpretation—relating ways of speaking to one another, and situating them in the contexts from which they derive meaning, and to which they contribute meaning.

One special feature of the ethnography of speaking is that it has been discourse-centered since its inception. It studies the speech acts, events, and situations—everyday and informal, in addition to formal and ritual—that constitute the social, cultural, and especially verbal life of particular societies. This involves attention to the relationship between text and context, as well as among transcription, translation, analysis, and theory. Discourse is considered to be the focus of the relationship among language, culture, society, and individual—the place where culture is conceived and transmitted, created and recreated.

The basic theoretical contribution of the ethnography of speaking is the demonstration that there are coherent and meaningful patterns in language use and speaking practices in societies around the world, and that there are significant differences in these patterns across cultures. The role of language in society cannot be taken for granted; nor can it be intuited on the basis of one's own experience, or projected from a single language, culture, or society onto another.

JOEL SHERZER

BIBLIOGRAPHY

ABRAHAMS, ROGER D. 1983. *The man-of-words in the West Indies: Performance and the emergence of creole culture.* Baltimore, Md.: Johns Hopkins University Press.

BASSO, ELLEN B. 1985. *A musical view of the universe: Kalapalo myth and ritual performances.* Philadelphia: University of Pennsylvania Press.

BASSO, KEITH H. 1979. *Portraits of 'The Whiteman': Linguistic play and cultural symbols among the Western Apache.* Cambridge & New York: Cambridge University Press.

BAUMAN, RICHARD. 1983. *Let your words be few: Symbolism of speaking and silence among seventeenth-century Quakers.* Cambridge & New York: Cambridge University Press.

BAUMAN, RICHARD, & JOEL SHERZER, eds. 1974. *Explorations in the ethnography of speaking.* Cambridge & New York: Cambridge University Press.

BLAKELEY, THOMAS D. 1986. *Hemba visual communication and space.* Lanham, Md.: University Press of America.

ERVIN-TRIPP, SUSAN, & CLAUDIA MITCHELL-KERNAN, eds. 1977. *Child discourse.* New York: Academic Press.

FELD, STEVEN. 1982. *Sound and sentiment: Birds, weeping, poetics, and song in Kaluli expression.* Philadelphia: University of Pennsylvania Press.

GOSSEN, GARY H. 1974. *Chamulas in the world of the sun: Time and space in a Maya oral tradition.* Cambridge, Mass.: Harvard University Press.

GUMPERZ, JOHN J. 1982. *Discourse strategies.* Cambridge & New York: Cambridge University Press.

GUMPERZ, JOHN J., & DELL HYMES, eds. 1964. *The ethnography of communication.* (American Anthropologist 66:6, part 2.) Menasha, Wis.: American Anthropological Association.

GUMPERZ, JOHN J., & DELL HYMES, eds. 1972. *Directions in sociolinguistics: The ethnography of communication.* New York: Holt, Rinehart & Winston.

HEATH, SHIRLEY BRICE. 1983. *Ways with words: Language,*

life, and work in communities and classrooms. Cambridge & New York: Cambridge University Press.

HYMES, DELL. 1974. *Foundations in sociolinguistics: An ethnographic approach.* Philadelphia: University of Pennsylvania Press.

PHILIPS, SUSAN U. 1983. *The invisible culture: Communication in classroom and community on the Warm Springs Indian reservation.* New York: Longman.

SCHIEFFELIN, BAMBI B., & ELINOR OCHS, eds. 1986. *Language socialization across cultures.* Cambridge & New York: Cambridge University Press.

SCOLLON, RONALD, & SUZANNE B. K. SCOLLON. 1979. *Linguistic convergence: An ethnography of speaking at Fort Chipewyan, Alberta.* New York: Academic Press.

SHERZER, JOEL. 1983. *Kuna ways of speaking: An ethnographic perspective.* Austin: University of Texas Press.

SHERZER, JOEL, & GREG URBAN, eds. 1986. *Native South American discourse.* Berlin: Mouton de Gruyter.

SHERZER, JOEL, & ANTHONY C. WOODBURY, eds. 1987. *Native American discourse: Poetics and rhetoric.* Cambridge & New York: Cambridge University Press.

ETHNOPOETICS. The term 'ethnopoetics' was introduced with the journal *Alcheringa* (1970–78). Such a term suggests an intersection between a general subject (in this case, verbal art) and something anthropological. Ideally, ethnopoetics is an intersection of all fields concerned to discover local knowledge and practice of verbal art, and to represent and interpret them (Sherzer & Woodbury 1987:2).

ORAL LITERATURE and VERBAL ART are older, established terms; and RHETORIC and POETICS may be used without the modifier 'ethno-'. 'Ethnopoetics' especially identifies work in which there is close attention to linguistic detail and verbal form, and experimentation with ways of reflecting on the page something of an oral original—both as regards expressive uses of the voice (as in Tedlock 1972) and as regards the cohesion and shape of a performance or text as a whole (Hymes 1981). [*See also* Narrative.]

A central premise is the universality of the LINE. Until recently, only song texts and such highly marked genres as the couplets of Middle America and Indonesia were taken to be poetry, consisting of sets of lines. Narratives were assumed to be prose, and were published in often arbitrary paragraphs. Even the dramatic significance of turns at talk has often been obscured, jumbled together within a block of print. Now it is widely recognized that oral discourse commonly consists of lines. Where a narrative can be heard, attentive listening for intonation units (or tone groups), whether on recordings or in daily life, makes lines clear. For narratives known only in writing, other relationships may indicate the presence of lines. The general principle was stated by Jakobson 1960: the recurrence of any feature of language may mark segments as equivalent for the purposes of poetic form. We are familiar with recurrences, within lines, of features such as stress, initial consonants, vowel length, and tone—and, between lines, with rhyme and grammatical parallelism. Syntactic particles are common markers of the start of lines in oral narrative. A turn at talk is regularly a distinct unit. [*See* Conversation Analysis.]

Lines of oral narrative often do not have an internal scheme or metric. Rather, they usually enter into an external scheme, a measure that relates them to one another. Here are lines (in English) from 'Coyote steals fire', told by Julia Starritt in Karok (Bright 1979):

'And so then he arranged them,
the people,
he arranged all the swiftest people.
'And he told them:
'You sit a little ways upriver,
and you other one, sit like that a little farther upstream' —
eventually they reached [all the way] upriver,
they reached the northern people's country.
And to the first one, Frog, he said:
'Sit on the river bank.'
And up on the mountain top, he said:
'Turtle, sit here.'

Whenever *And* introduces an action or a turn at talk, it marks the beginning of a verse. The four verses constitute a stanza, and a scene, within the whole. (Within the stanza, the first pair has to do with people in general, while the second singles out actors crucial to the outcome.) The narrative is a set of overlapping arcs of lines, verses, stanzas, scenes, and acts.

More and more oral traditions are being found to have such architecture. There seem to be just a few alternative principles: pairs and fours (as in the example), with a 'this, then that' rhythm; threes and fives, with a 'this, then this, then that' rhythm; and combinations, such as one in which pairs come in sets of three. Where pairing is normal, a set of three may mark intensification; where three and five are normal, pairing may mark intensification. These relationships of onset and outcome are usually out of awareness. Nonetheless, they are not fixed grids, but options that narrators use to give point, proportion, and shape. The general principle was stated by Burke 1925: a work of verbal art is shaped by the arousal and satisfying of expectation.

Most published work on ethnopoetics has been concerned with indigenous languages of the Americas; however, the same principles have been found to hold for materials in a variety of languages from the Old World, Africa, and Asia, as well as in English (cf. Hymes & Hymes 1991).

Ethnopoetics contributes to the teaching and interpretation of indigenous literatures (cf. Swann & Krupat 1987). The display of lines and sets of lines, and the visual highlighting of quoted speech, may make intelligible—and, often enough, exciting—material whose point, pacing, and proportion were previously unclear. It is a starting-point for poets who find stimulation in 'primitive' material, and who seek to retranslate or rework it (cf. Tedlock 1983; Hymes 1981, Chap. 1). It can be an integral part of understanding another way of life (Basso 1985, Briggs 1988). To linguistics, it contributes a dimension of cohesion, and illuminates the discourse function of grammatical elements; it gives evidence of cognitive activity (planning, remembering) and of language as interactional accomplishment (Tedlock 1983, Sherzer & Urban 1986). It may point toward a general conception of grammar. Oral performance calls on two interdependent spheres of elements and relationships, one PROPOSITIONAL (grammar as usually pursued), one PRESENTATIONAL (cf. Woodbury 1987).

Organization in lines and sets of lines is likely to prove universal. That universality, along with the apparent limitation of principles of organization to just a few alternatives, suggests an innate basis and the kind of modularity internal to language. Yet the display of such competence is highly sensitive to situation. The opportunity to acquire and develop it beyond its rudiments was once perhaps universal in human communities, but is vulnerable to social change. Ethnopoetics brings together the biological and cultural starting points for the study of language.

DELL HYMES

BIBLIOGRAPHY

BASSO, ELLEN B. 1985. *A musical view of the universe: Kalapalo myth and ritual performances.* Philadelphia: University of Pennsylvania Press.

BRIGGS, CHARLES. 1988. *Competence in performance: The creativity of tradition in Mexicano verbal art.* Philadelphia: University of Pennsylvania Press.

BRIGHT, WILLIAM. 1979. A Karok myth in 'measured verse': The translation of a performance. *Journal of California and Great Basin Anthropology* 1.117–123. Reprinted in William Bright, *American Indian linguistics and literature* (The Hague: Mouton, 1984), pp. 91–100.

BURKE, KENNETH. 1925. Psychology and form. *The Dial* 79:1.34–45. Reprinted in Kenneth Burke, *Counterstatement* (New York: Harcourt Brace, 1931), pp. 38–56.

HYMES, DELL. 1981. *'In vain I tried to tell you': Essays in Native American ethnopoetics.* Philadelphia: University of Pennsylvania Press.

HYMES, DELL, & VIRGINIA HYMES. 1991. *Verse analysis so far.* Berlin: Mouton de Gruyter.

JAKOBSON, ROMAN. 1960. Linguistics and poetics. In *Style in language,* edited by Thomas A. Sebeok, pp. 350–377. Cambridge, Mass.: MIT Press.

SHERZER, JOEL, & GREG URBAN, eds. 1986. *Native South American discourse.* Berlin: Mouton de Gruyter.

SHERZER, JOEL, & ANTHONY C. WOODBURY, eds. 1987. *Native American discourse: Poetics and rhetoric.* Cambridge & New York: Cambridge University Press.

SWANN, BRIAN, & ARNOLD KRUPAT, eds. 1987. *Recovering the word: Essays on Native American literature.* Berkeley: University of California Press.

TEDLOCK, DENNIS. 1972. *Finding the center: Narrative poetry of the Zuni Indians.* New York: Dial. 2d ed., Lincoln: University of Nebraska Press, 1978.

TEDLOCK, DENNIS. 1983. *The spoken word and the work of interpretation.* Philadelphia: University of Pennsylvania Press.

WOODBURY, ANTHONY C. 1987. Rhetorical structure in a Central Alaskan Yupik Eskimo traditional narrative. In Sherzer & Woodbury 1987, pp. 176–239.

ETHNOSEMANTICS comprises the referential meanings of linguistic expressions, the analysis of the roles of those meanings in particular cultures, and the formulation of universal cognitive principles that govern particular ethnosemantic phenomena. [*See also* Semantics.]

'Ethnosemantics' is synonymous with ETHNOGRAPHIC SEMANTICS. These terms were introduced in the late 1960s by anthropologists working in the tradition of ETHNOSCIENCE, the anthropological expression of the cognitive science 'revolution'. Ethnoscientists promoted an ethnography based on explicit and replicable methodology and mathematically precise theory, but responsive to the complexity of particular cultural systems. Ethnoscientists—or cognitive anthropologists, as their intellectual descendants are now known (see Tyler 1969)—construe a culture, to paraphrase Ward Goodenough, as 'what one needs to know to act appropriately' as a member of that culture. Cultures as bodies of knowledge are most readily accessible through the native languages of the culture bearers. The vocabulary of a language is a cultural inventory, while texts reveal cultural presuppositions and modes of inference. Ethnosemantics looks to linguistics, to cognitive psychology—and, since the mid-1970s, to artificial intelligence—for useful conceptual and methodological insights.

Ethnosemantics first addressed referential kinship terminologies, borrowing the strategy of COMPONENTIAL ANALYSIS from structural linguistics. A set of kin terms was analyzed as a semantic space structured by intersecting semantic dimensions (e.g. sex of referent, generation), each of which was composed of a set of contrasting semantic features (e.g. male, female; +1, +2). The goal was to define each kin term as a logical conjunction (set intersection) of features. However, the componential paradigm proved inadequate for this task—and entirely inappropriate for analyzing other domains, such as color, biology, illness, emotion, and personality.

In the 1970s, the initial emphasis on componential analysis gave way to a search for varied models appropriate to the substantive referential content of specific domains, and more sensitive to the complexities of terminological usage in natural speech contexts. Kinship terminologies may now be analyzed elegantly using Atkins's (1974) General Relational Algebra For Investigating Kinship (GRAFIK), which synthesizes features of componential analysis with an algebra of relations akin to that pioneered by Floyd Lounsbury. Folk-biological nomenclature has been analyzed primarily in taxonomic terms. In the restricted ethnobiological sense defined by Paul Kay, a TAXONOMY is a hierarchy of sets of organisms related by set inclusion with associated names. In Brent Berlin's analysis of 'general principles of folk biological classification and nomenclature', folk biological classifications are hierarchic structures like the Linnaean taxonomy of Western biological science. Folk biological taxonomies, in Berlin's scheme, are built upon a set of basic, 'natural' categories (e.g. *oak, cobra*), plus derivative superordinate life-forms *(tree, snake)* and folk specifics *(live oak, king cobra)*. Whether this hierarchic scheme is universal is the subject of debate; however, the close correspondence of basic folk taxa with scientific species suggests that the cultural recognition of biological species is constrained by discontinuities in nature (cf. Hunn 1982).

Berlin & Kay 1969, an analysis of universals and 'evolutionary' patterns in COLOR nomenclature, proves that ethnosemantic research is not essentially particularistic. Berlin & Kay used the Munsell Color Chart as an etic grid to systematically compare color classifications in a large number of languages. Basic color terms (e.g. *red*, but not *scarlet, reddish,* or *bay*) were first elicited; then their foci and ranges were mapped by native speakers. The number of basic terms has been shown to vary systematically among languages; however, the foci or best examples of each category are virtually invariant across languages, suggesting a neurophysiological constraint. Wierzbicka's (1985) analysis of universals in the classification of emotions uses an etic grid based on a set of 'simple' concepts presumed to be universal. [*See* Semantics, *article on* Semantic Primitives.]

Color categories become vaguer toward their boundaries, a fact manifested in the use of linguistic hedges such as *very red* or *reddish*. Classical set theory—in which something can be only 'red' or 'not red'—proved an inadequate formalism. Kay & McDaniel 1978 apply a more general mathematical scheme—that of FUZZY SET THEORY, in which set membership is a matter of degree—to capture this aspect of the ethnosemantics of color. However, it is clear that category membership varies not only in degree, but also qualitatively. Ethnosemantic analyses of lexemes must account not only for the structure of semantic fields (composed of relations among concepts), but also for structure within the concepts named. Thus Coleman & Kay 1981 have dissected the English word *lie* 'falsehood', isolating three semantic criteria that contribute to a native speaker's judgment that a situation involves a 'lie'. The prototypical lie exhibits all three. Situations lacking one or two of these criteria are either 'sort of a lie' or 'like a lie'. [*See* Prototype Semantics.] Ethnosemantic analyses of METAPHOR [*q.v.*] require that semantic features be differentiated by role, i.e. criterial vs. statistically normative features, and linguistic usage by function, i.e. semantic vs. pragmatic. Lakoff & Johnson's (1980) ethnosemantic analysis of metaphor shows how conceptual links among prototypes in diverse domains aid inference and memory. Thus more sophisticated analysis of the internal semantic structure of lexemes supports improved understanding of whole cultures as semantic systems.

Artificial intelligence, especially in the work of Schank & Abelson 1977, has inspired a new brand of ethnosemantic analysis in the 1980s. This work focuses on events, scripts, plans, goals, and themes as fundamental units of cultural understanding, rather than on lexemes and semantic domains. [*See* Natural Language Processing, *article on* Semantics and Knowledge Representation.] EVENTS and PLANS are not structured by intersecting semantic dimensions; instead, the component units of events and plans are analogous to the functional components of sentences—actions or states, actors in various roles, time and space relations, instruments, etc. Emphasis falls on what knowledge must be presupposed in order to make sense of a narrative, or of the events it describes—and on the networks of logical inference that link events into meaningful sequences of action. Notable examples of this research direction include Hutchins's (1980) demonstration of the inferential consistency of Trobriand legal discourse; Naomi Quinn's abstraction of American cultural themes from extended texts on marriage (see Holland & Quinn 1987); and analyses of concepts of illness and of personality in several cultures.

EUGENE HUNN

BIBLIOGRAPHY

ATKINS, JOHN R. 1974. GRAFIK: A multipurpose kinship metalanguage. In *Genealogical mathematics*, edited by Paul A. Ballonoff, pp. 27–51. The Hague: Mouton.

BERLIN, BRENT, & PAUL KAY. 1969. *Basic color terms: Their universality and evolution*. Berkeley: University of California Press.

COLEMAN, LINDA, & PAUL KAY. 1981. Prototype semantics: The English word *lie*. *Language* 57.26–43.

HOLLAND, DOROTHY, & NAOMI QUINN, eds. 1987. *Cultural models in language and thought*. Cambridge & New York: Cambridge University Press.

HUNN, EUGENE. 1982. The utilitarian factor in folk biological classification. *American Anthropologist* 84.830–847.

HUTCHINS, EDWIN. 1980. *Culture and inference: A Trobriand case study*. (Cognitive science series, 2.) Cambridge, Mass.: Harvard University Press.

KAY, PAUL, & CHAD MCDANIEL. 1978. The linguistic significance of the meanings of basic color terms. *Language* 54.610–646.

LAKOFF, GEORGE, & MARK JOHNSON. 1980. *Metaphors we live by*. Chicago: University of Chicago Press.

SCHANK, ROGER C., & ROBERT P. ABELSON. 1977. *Scripts, plans, goals, and understanding: An inquiry into human knowledge structures*. Hillsdale, N.J.: Erlbaum.

TYLER, STEPHEN A., ed. 1969. *Cognitive anthropology*. New York: Holt, Rinehart & Winston.

WIERZBICKA, ANNA. 1985. *Lexicography and conceptual analysis*. Ann Arbor: Karoma.

ETYMOLOGY—as an aspect of linguistics, a scholarly activity, or a specimen of such activity—is widely recognized, but is not a proper field in itself. Taken most strictly as a relationship, an etymology is the history and prehistory of a locution; it is sometimes presented as a recitation of evidential sets containing the locution in question, which exemplify systematic correspondences through cognates that validate a genetic familial relation among languages. [*See* Historical Linguistics, *article on* Ancestry and Descent.] A modern etymology and its study presuppose an adequate grasp of the nature of phonological, morphological, syntactic, and semantic change; of ANALOGY [*q.v.*], borrowing, reconstruction, and INTERNAL RECONSTRUCTION [*q.v.*]—in fact, an older acceptance of 'etymology' centered on the synchronic derivational relation between words—and of AREAL LINGUISTICS [*q.v.*].

Among introductions to etymology, the only modern work is Bammesberger 1984. For the early background of the topic, see Thurneysen 1905. More recent discussions include the flawed but well intended book of Ross 1958, the intelligent and informed work of Pisani 1967, and the richly annotated bibliographies of Malkiel 1976, 1989; see also Keller 1958, Schmitt 1977, Pfister 1980, and Seebold 1981.

1. History of etymology. The attempt to find or explain the source(s) of a word, especially a name, is as ancient as anything we know in human documents. In the *Rig Veda* (5.2.12), the name of the fire god *Agni* (really < I[ndo-]E[uropean] **ŋ̥g-ni*) is derived from *ajāti* 'may he drive/capture (as spoil)' (really < IE **H_aeĝ-*), as if *j* were here the palatalization of *g*. It was the duty of an ancient Irish court poet to know (or invent) and recite his lord's genealogy and the origin of local place names—whence history for them, and much early literature for us. Plato's *Cratylus* is seriously occupied with the (fantastic) derivation of names from ordinary predications; it contains truth *in nuce*, but vitiated by lack of principled constraints. The fallacy in such ancient attempts, and in untutored modern ones, lies in urging synchronic combinations of phonetic segments, arbitrarily chosen and perhaps discontinuous, with grammatically uncontrolled phrases and vague semantics.

The Greek term *etumología* 'account or derivation of the true' (for Cicero, *verbum ex verbō vēriloquium*) seems to have arisen with the Stoics. Varro termed it the part of grammar which explained 'why and whence words are', and he characterizes it as *disciplīna verbōrum orīginis* (*Lingua Latina* 6.1). So too, Quintilian (1.6.29) equates it with *orīginātiō*. In speaking of etymology and rhetoric, Cicero uses the term *notātiō*. Varro recognized that earlier intervocalic *s* had become *r* in Latin; but he did not apply this knowledge, doubtless not aided by the total loss of the same *s* in Greek. Failure to perceive regularity in phonetic development, and ethnocentric provinciality with foreign languages, persisted through the Renaissance: in 1554, Périon tried to derive French *feu* from Greek *pûr*. (Fr. *f*, from La[tin] *focus* 'hearth', bears no relation at all to Gk. *p*.) The fact that Varro could guess that *medius* 'mid' underlay La. *merīdiēs* 'midday' does not attest to a systematic method or penetrating theory. Isidore of Seville, an important theorizer in the transmission of this branch of study, in his *Origines* (also known as *Etymologiae*) seems to equate *etymologia* with *orīgō* and *(ad)notātiō*, and to base his linkage of *cognitiō* and *interpretātiō* on Quintilian's relation of *verba* 'words' to *rēs* 'things'.

The development of etymology in the West has in fact been neither linear nor cumulative. The Greeks failed to look seriously outside Greek; the Romans, in their adulation of Greek learning and models, neglected their neighboring Italic laboratory; and Romance scholars looked piously to Latin, with deviations taken simply as vagaries. Edward Lhuyd (*Archaeologia Britannica*, 1707) marked a distinct advance in theoretical principle, perceiving that the 'comparative etymology' of languages was based on 'their correspondence to one another', through 'shewing by the collection of examples methodized, that etymology is not . . . a speculation merely groundless or conjectural'. Perhaps his insight was fostered by his multilingual background in framing this statement of an embryonic Comparative Method [*q.v.*].

We might expect that the virtues or shortcomings of an etymology, in explicating the diachrony of a locution, would reflect the views of its epoch on the transmission and genesis of human languages. In 1853, the great Romance comparativist Friedrich Diez considered that the aim of the etymology of a word was the citation of an earlier or source word, i.e. in Latin (or in Latin borrowed from Greek, or in Arabic, or in more removed sources), yet no justification for the transmission was attempted. Thus *street* might be credited to La. *strāta*, i.e. *via strāta* 'paved way', but without mentioning the role of Roman road-building. With the coming of a true comparative method, Romance derivations from Latin could also point to whole source words, since Latin is known directly; but IE derivations produce pure reconstructions, and have tended to recover simple roots, or bases. Furthermore, reconstructions of the Romance type have been offered for Polynesian, Chinese, Bantu, and Algonkian, because of their intrinsic structures, or their high morphological comparability; while IE-type reconstructions are found for Semitic, Uralic, Oto-Manguean, and the poorly understood Hokan family. Clearly we are here prisoners of our material as well as our Zeitgeist. In the early 19th century, Franz Bopp and August Friedrich Pott [*qq.v.*] aimed to inventory the IE elements that could be recovered by SEGMENTATION into roots, affixes, etc.—a method obviously borrowed from Hindu grammar.

Antoine Meillet (d. 1936) claimed that it is not enough simply to show correspondences, i.e. to indicate roots; we must also strive to recover the structure and function of IE locutions. We must not just perform a dissection, but rather write a history. A good etymology, said Meillet, clarifies both form and use, and must be exhaustive. For over a century, the requirement of total accountability has been generally assumed for the sounds in an etymon; but all too often it has not been applied strictly to morphology and semantics. Thus otherwise serious etymologies frequently neglect morphophonemic alternations (i.e. of vowels or 'ablaut'), or semantic shifts which misleadingly appear to be slight. A correct etymology must account for every feature at every stage. Thus if La. *truncus* 'tree trunk' is to be derived from **dru-n* 'tree, wood' + *-iko-s*, a suffix of appurtenance, it is important to show evidence of its early use as an adjective. Ever since the era of Jules Gilliéron (1854–1926), the explanatory value of geographic dialect sources (e.g. Eng. *vat, vixen, cuss*) has been appreciated; but Meillet touched an under-appreciated aspect by insisting on the proto-dialectological area of COMPARANDA for an etymon. At all stages, we must observe (or allow for) the social use, distribution, and stratification of a form; much of our early IE vocabulary is attested in poetic, probably 'aristocratic' texts, while nearly all we know of Dacian, the ancient language of Rumania, consists of plant names. Meillet called for the full use of all the tools of historical linguistics, while acknowledging that our account of loans in their social context, and of contaminations between contemporaneous alternatives, depends on the degree of our information. In the case of a language with an attested history, we must heed not only geographic and social variation, but also textual style and the role of foreigners in the society.

2. A formal definition. We may now attempt a more formal definition of a modern etymology, while keeping Meillet's stipulations in mind. For the past century, laymen as well as linguists/philologists have expected an etymology of a word (less usually of a phrase or clause) to respect, but not to explicate, its synchronic grammatical constitution, and primarily to trace its FORM and MEANING back in time or forward from a stated point, as far as responsible scholarship can manage. Such 'tracing' should be expressed in explicit formulations for every discriminable chronological stage in the known life of the expression. 'Form' refers to the nexus of phonological features with morphological elements and strings; 'meaning' refers to the association of morpheme groups with cultural or propositional semantic entities.

More technically, an etymology is an excerpt, over a selected bundle of morphonological and semantic features, from the known historical grammar(s) of a set of culturally connected language stages. To every extent possible, the dating of all stages and attested forms must be specified, either through RELATIVE CHRONOLOGY [*q.v.*] or through external evidence or documentation. As an excerpt, a good etymology will mention as many ancestor and related forms and stages as are relevant, and permitted by constraints of space and format. If the total reconstruction cannot be shown, sufficient forms should be supplied to outline and substantiate the argument.

3. Types of descent. An etymology may trace various kinds of descent, such as inherited, i.e. totally internal to the language, or borrowed, i.e. external. Descent may also be mixed, with the following types of borrowed elements.

(a) Base: *duke-dom, be-muse* (cf. *to muse, amuse*).
(b) Affix: *laugh-able, re-make.*
(c) Semantics: American Eng. *corn* 'maize', or Greek and Albanian 'oak' < IE phonological shape for 'beech'.
(d) Syntax: Eng. *That goes without saying* < French *Ça va sans dire.*
(e) Morphology: Rumanian *douăzeci* 'twenty' (lit. 'two tens', with 'ten' in fem.pl.), instead of La. *vīgintī.*
(f) Morphology and semantics: La. *accentus* 'accent' = *ad + cantus* < Gk. *pros + ōid-ía,* as Quintilian tells us.
(g) Syntax and semantics: Eng. 'expanded' *I am drinking* < Welsh (or late British) *yð wyf yn yfed.*
(h) Morphophonemics, as where the idiosyncratic syllabic syncope in Mandrítsa Albanian numerals precisely matches those of the surrounding Bulgarian.

Etymology may also have to take account of foreign phonology, as with the clicks of Nguni Bantu or the front rounded vowels of (now extinct) Greek dialects in central Turkey—or of foreign phonetics, as in affective particles used in endogamous Albanian enclaves in Calabria.

4. Inherited descent may involve the following patterns:

(a) A single morpheme: La. *-que* = Gk. *te* = Old Irish *-ch* 'and' < IE **-k^we.*
(b) A possible complex: Italian *e(d)* < La. *et* < IE **eti* 'beyond', with mild change in sense; or Slavic *i* 'and' < **(j)ĭ* < IE **i* (locative with zero ending) '(t)here(on), at it', with greater semantic change.
(c) A clear original complex: Armenian *ew* 'and' < '(there)upon' = Gk. *epi* 'upon' < IE **ʔepi*; or Eng. *and* = La. *ante* 'before' = Gk. *antí* 'opposite' (Hittite *ḫant-* 'front' < IE **ʕent-i* loc. 'in front'); or Eng. possessive *'s* < Old Eng. gen.sg. *-es* < Germanic *-esa* (~ *-asa*) ← **-asa-* < IE thematic **-o* + gen. **-(o)s* + empty NP enclitic **-o.*
(d) A lineal complex: Old Lithuanian *ēsti* 'is' < IE **ʔes-t-i* 'be-3SG.-now'; Gk. *patér-es* 'father-s' (nom.) < IE **pH$_a$tér-es*; or Gk. *árotron* 'plow' < IE **herʕ^w-tr-o-m* 'plow-INSTR-INAN-NEUT'.
(e) A paradigm of complexes, such as the declined forms of the Sanskrit nouns *svásar-* 'sister' and *tráyas* masc., *tisrás* fem. 'three'; or the conjugated forms of the Greek verb *dídōmi* 'give', when we trace these paradigms back to IE.
(f) A compound: Eng. *hussy* < *hussive, hussyf-* < Old Eng. **hūs + wīf* 'house-wife'.
(g) A phrase: Eng. *daisy* < Old Eng. *dæges ēage* 'day's eye'.
(h) A clause or sentence: La. *volup est* 'it's pleasant, okay' < IE **uél-əp-ʔesti* (with enclitic copula) 'it is desire-reaching'.
(i) A suppletive paradigm: Albanian *jam* 'I am' < IE **ʔes-m-i,* but past tense *kle, qe* (employing different roots).
(j) A defective or skewed paradigm: Albanian *jep,* OIr. *do·beir* 'gives', but Alb. *dha,* OIr. *do·r-a-d* (< **to + pro-ad-dʕ^w-*) 'gave', matching Gk. *é-do-men* (< **dʕ^w-me*) 'we gave' which also in IE was aoristic and formed a derived present.
(k) A structured system of lexical terms interlocking with other aspects of culture or social structure, such as the IE or Algonkian kin terms for the nuclear family and avuncular relations.

Most inherited descents are not so lineal as those just illustrated, and require appeal to near-cognates and to formational and syntactic rules and shifts. Thus Germanic **fiskaz* 'fish' and Albanian *peshk* < **piḱsko-* is an *o*-stem; La. *piscis* < **pik̑ski-* is an *i*-stem; Old Irish *iasc* < **peik̑sk-o-* is a thematic derivative; and the Russian placename *Pskov* is perhaps an adjective of appurtenance. Syntactic reassignment results in such descents as *all ready* > *already,* analogous to the lexical split of *shade* and *shadow,* founded on inflectional misassignment. Shifts over time in morphology can be seen in Eng. *above* < Old Eng. *abufan,* a petrified phrase with *on-*; the balance matches Dutch *boven* with *b(e)-* (Eng. *by*), and then German *oben,* Old Frisian *uva,* an archaic stem alternant in *-n-* corresponding to *over* = Skt. *upári,* Gk. *hupér* 'above, over'. Non-lineal inherited descents of this kind are closely akin to the type of internal descent involving what is termed ANALOGY [*q.v.*], and there is no sharp line between the varieties. A descent involving paradigms or inflections which come to function in alternations—or become stranded and are left to atrophy, as when *(for)lorn* is displaced by *lost*—may yield opaque chains which resist or alter segmentation: *grist/grind, rust/red, seam/sew, tithe/ten, water/wash, yolk/yellow.* They may invite a new independent descent: La. *com-esse* → *com-edere* > Spanish *com-e-r* 'eat' → *com-i-d-a* 'meal'). Portions of formations get replaced by synonyms: IE **suH-n-ú-s* (**suH-* 'bear, give birth') > Lithuanian *sūnùs,* Eng. *son*; but it is replaced by **b(h)er-u-s* in Albanian *i bir* 'son'. Thus the replacement of a suppletive paradigm is merely an elaborate root analogy: IE pres. **ei-,* aor. **g^{w}em-/g^{w}eH$_a$-* 'go' (> Eng. *come*) was leveled in Latin to *eō, īre, iī, itum*; but it was redistributed to Old Eng. *gān,* past *ēode* (> later dialect forms *yVd(e)*) > Eng. *go, went.*

The descent of collocations leads to seemingly abrupt replacements: La. *iecur* 'liver' was replaced in Romance by the adjective *fĭcātum,* referring to the gourmet liver in animals fattened with *fīcī* 'figs'. The Germanic tribes had no figs, but knew that the result was 'fatty' (cf. Gk. *liparós*), hence Eng. *liver,* Ger. *Leber.* La. *cauda* 'tail' may be the stranded participle modifier **cau-ed-a* from *caveō* 'ward off', with the deletion of the noun for the object that wards off flies in a farm setting.

5. Borrowing. The step from such replacements to outright BORROWING [*q.v.*] is nearly imperceptible; in fact, borrowings enter the language much as the above inherited alternants move about. Thus Albanian has *vjen* 'comes' < La. *venit,* and so on throughout the presential system; but the past is *erdh-,* non-finite *ardhur,* both inherited. La. *altus* 'high' was contaminated by a Germanic (Frankish) counterpart in *h-* to give French *haut* 'high'. Borrowings can intrude intimately: Rumanian *leurdă* 'garlic' results from misdivision of **(ista) (a)lli(u)-hurda(-illa),* a blend of La. *ālium, allium* and the autochthonous word seen in Albanian *hudhrë.* On George Eastman's testimony, *Kodak* favored *k* because that was the initial of his mother's name. Nothing comes from nothing. Phonesthemes, as in *flip, flop/flap* [*see* Sound Symbolism], seem to develop from internal convergence, then to become fresh sources of derivation.

6. Associated processes. Borrowings and inherited material alike betray cultural correlates (as in 'Wörter und Sachen' research): Eng. *spoon* (Ger. *Span* 'chip', Gk. *sphēn* 'wedge') points to ancient wooden chips; Eng. *sooth,* the participle to *is,* attests a conceptual equivalence of truth and reality. The gender of Algonkian 'stone' which we call 'animate' tallies with modern Crees' attribution of internal 'power' to stones. With sufficient ethnographic reconstruction, we can understand potential conundrums: later Welsh *go-ganu* (< 'sing in aid', from *canu* 'to sing') can mean both 'revile' and 'praise' because an early bard's duty was to praise his lord and satirize the court's enemies. Borrowings, like the names of most cultigens, can label new concepts *(sputnik, boutique),* but not always. Conjunctions, e.g. *pero* 'but' from Spanish in most Mayan languages, get borrowed by bilinguals at points of discourse shift.

Accidental merger leads to homonyms (Eng. *let* 'hinder', 'allow')—and to the conflation known as 'étymologie croisée', when two source formations with similar semantics become blended. A semantic component can be extracted and copied into a separate morpheme, yielding HYPERCHARACTERIZATION. A bleached or empty morpheme may be exploited to disambiguate: Italian *frate* > 'monk' → *fratello* 'brother'; Old Irish *arcu* 'I ask' → **to·com-airc* 'woos'. FOLK ETYMOLOGY endows opaque strings with parsing, either appropriate (La. *terrae mōtus* > Italian *terremoto* 'earthquake' → *tremuoto* on the basis of *tremare* 'tremble') or nonsensical (Old Eng. *brȳd-guma* 'bride's man' → 16th-century *brydegrome* → *bridegroom*).

7. Etymological dictionaries. The bracketed etymological inclusions in general-purpose dictionaries are of varying quality; however, English readers may consult Flexner 1987.

A chronological sampling of innovative and notable etymological dictionaries may begin with the work on Indo-European by Fick 1868 (revised, 1890–1909); this is the first and last adequate dictionary of comparative IE which gives principled attention to the separate branches. From the same period is the etymological dictionary of German by Kluge 1883 (20th ed., 1967); this work provides a model updated tool for the general public. The Armenian etymological dictionary of Hübschmann 1897 subdivides and analyzes the lexicon of the classical language in terms of inherited words vs. borrowings from various sources.

In the 20th century, the Romance etymological dictionary of Meyer-Lübke 1911 (3d ed., 1930–35) served as a model for later works. The Balto-Slavic dictionary of Trautmann 1923 continued the tradition of Fick in a family of disputed status. The monumental etymological dictionary of French by Wartburg (1922–), arranged by etyma in some 20 volumes, was based on an enormous dialectal corpus; revised portions are still being published. Bloch & Wartburg 1932 (3rd ed., 1960) deals with French in more reduced scope, for the general public. The etymological dictionary of Latin by Ernout & Meillet 1932 (4th ed., 1959–60) is the most prudent and sophisticated such work in existence; the authors divide their task between the internal history of Latin and its IE prehistory.

The comparative Gothic dictionary of Feist 1939 (a greatly revised 3rd ed. of a 1909 work), dealing with a closed corpus, was exhaustive for its time. The etymological dictionary of Latin by Walde & Hoffmann 1939–65 (5th ed., 1982) focuses on Indo-European, with full segregated citation of rejected hypotheses. The dictionary of IE synonyms by Buck 1949, arranged semantically by English glosses, provides knowledge essentially as of 1930; it omits Armenian and Albanian. The Sanskrit etymological dictionary of Mayrhofer 1956–80 represents a gigantic task never before completed; it improved in quality and detail during the years of publication, profiting from reviews (a new and much enlarged revision has now also begun to appear).

The etymological dictionary of ancient Greek by Frisk 1960–72 is a monument of precision, richly documented in the handling of a well researched language. The Dravidian etymological dictionary of Burrow & Emeneau 1961 (2d ed., 1984) is a fine example of work on a non-IE family; few such families have been so amply studied. The Indo-Aryan comparative dictionary of Turner 1962–69 is a pioneering work, built on Turner's own Nepali dictionary of 1931, and modeled on Meyer-Lübke 1911. The etymological dictionary of Rumanian dialects by Papahagi 1963 (2d ed., 1974) is a remarkable achievement for a set of enclave dialects with complex multilingual contacts. The comparative dictionary of Germanic strong verbs by Seebold 1970 is a detailed and careful inventory of the paradigms in a complex form class. The Serbo-Croatian etymological dictionary by Skok 1971–74 is a model of attention to historical sources and multilingual borrowings. The Proto-Slavic dictionary by Sławski et al. (1974–), arranged alphabetically by reconstructed etyma, puts strong emphasis on systematic word formation.

Most recently, the etymological dictionary of Hittite by Puhvel (1984–) summarizes a body of scholarship, with fresh philological interpretation and many independent judgments.

Eric P. Hamp

BIBLIOGRAPHY

Bammesberger, Alfred. 1984. *English etymology.* Heidelberg: Winter.

Bloch, Oscar, & Walther von Wartburg. 1932. *Dictionnaire étymologique de la langue française.* Paris: Presses Universitaires de France. 3d ed., 1960.

Buck, Carl Darling. 1949. *A dictionary of selected synonyms in the principal Indo-European languages: A contribution to the history of ideas.* Chicago: University of Chicago Press. Reprinted, 1988.

Burrow, Thomas, & Murray B. Emeneau. 1961. *A Dravidian etymological dictionary.* Oxford: Clarendon. 2d ed., 1984.

Ernout, Alfred, & Antoine Meillet. 1932. *Dictionnaire étymologique de la langue latine: Histoire des mots.* Paris: Klincksieck. 4th ed., 1959–60.

Feist, Sigmund. 1939. *Vergleichendes Wörterbuch der gotischen Sprache, mit Einschluss des Krimgotischen und sonstiger zerstreuter Überreste des Gotischen.* Leiden: Brill. 1st ed., 1909.

Fick, August. 1868. *Vergleichendes Wörterbuch der indogermanischen Sprachen: Ein sprachgeschichtlicher Versuch.* Göttingen: Vandenhoeck. 4th ed., Göttingen: Vandenhoek & Ruprecht, 1890–1909.

Flexner, Stuart Berg. 1987. *The Random House dictionary of the English language.* 2d ed. New York: Random House.

Frisk, Hjalmar. 1960–72. *Griechisches etymologisches Wörterbuch.* Heidelberg: Winter.

Hübschmann, Heinrich. 1897. *Armenische Grammatik,* vol. 1, *Armenische Etymologie.* Leipzig: Breitkopf & Härtel.

Keller, Hans-Erich, ed. 1958. *Etymologica: Festschrift Walther von Wartburg zum siebzigsten Geburtstag.* Tübingen: Niemeyer.

Kluge, Friedrich. 1883. *Etymologisches Wörterbuch der deutschen Sprache.* Strassburg: Trübner. 20th ed., Berlin: de Gruyter, 1967.

Malkiel, Yakov. 1976. *Etymological dictionaries: A tentative typology.* Chicago: University of Chicago Press.

MALKIEL, YAKOV. 1989. *A tentative autobibliography.* (Romance Philology, special issue.) Berkeley: University of California Press.

MAYRHOFER, MANFRED. 1956–80. *Kurzgefasstes etymologisches Wörterbuch des Altindischen / A concise etymological Sanskrit dictionary.* Heidelberg: Winter.

MEYER-LÜBKE, WILHELM. 1911. *Romanisches etymologisches Wörterbuch.* Heidelberg: Winter. 3d ed., 1930–35.

PAPAHAGI, TACHE. 1963. *Dicţionarul dialectului aromân, general şi etimologic / Dictionnaire aroumain (macédo-roumain).* Bucharest: Editura Academiei Republicii Socialiste România. 2d ed., 1974.

PFISTER, MAX. 1980. *Einführung in die romanische Etymologie.* Darmstadt: Wissenschaftliche Buchgesellschaft.

PISANI, VITTORE. 1967. *L'etimologia: Storia, questioni, metodo.* 2d ed. Brescia: Paideia.

PUHVEL, JAAN. 1984–. *Hittite etymological dictionary.* Berlin: Mouton.

ROSS, ALAN S. C. 1958. *Etymology, with especial reference to English.* Oxford: Oxford University Press. Fair Lawn, N.J.: Essential Books.

SCHMITT, RÜDIGER, ed. 1977. *Etymologie.* Darmstadt: Wissenschaftliche Buchgesellschaft.

SEEBOLD, ELMAR. 1970. *Vergleichendes und etymologisches Wörterbuch der germanischen starken Verben.* The Hague: Mouton.

SEEBOLD, ELMAR. 1981. *Etymologie: Eine Einführung am Beispiel der deutschen Sprache.* Munich: Beck.

SKOK, PETAR. 1971–74. *Etimologijski rječnik hrvatskoga ili srpskoga jezika.* 4 vols. Zagreb: Jugoslavenska Akademija Znanosti i Umjetnosti.

SŁAWSKI, FRANCISZEK, et al. 1974–. *Słownik prasłowiański.* Wrocław: Wydawnictwo Polskiej Akademii Nauk.

THURNEYSEN, RUDOLF. 1905. *Die Etymologie: Eine akademische Rede.* Freiburg in Breisgau: Speyer & Kärner.

TRAUTMANN, REINHOLD. 1923. *Baltisch-slawisches Wörterbuch.* Göttingen: Vandenhoek & Ruprecht.

TURNER, SIR RALPH L. 1962–69. *A comparative dictionary of the Indo-Aryan languages.* London & New York: Oxford University Press.

WALDE, ALOIS, & JOHANN B. HOFFMANN. 1939–65. *Lateinisches etymologisches Wörterbuch.* 3d ed. Heidelberg: Winter. [1st ed., by Walde, 1906.]

WARTBURG, WALTHER VON. 1922–. *Französisches etymologisches Wörterbuch: Eine Darstellung des galloromanischen Wortschatzes.* Bonn: Klopp. Basel: Helbing & Lichtenhahn.